JEAN COCTEAU

JEAN COCTEAU

A Life

Claude Arnaud
Translated by Lauren Elkin
and Charlotte Mandell

Yale

UNIVERSITY

PRESS

New Haven and London

#958084208

This book has been published with the help of a generous donation from Philippe Camu.

This book has been published with the help of a generous donation from Béatrice Corrêa do Lago.

An anonymous donor provided generous support for this publication.

Cet ouvrage, publié dans le cadre d'un programme d'aide à la publication, bénéficie du soutien de la Mission Culturelle et Universitaire Française aux Etats Unis, service de l'ambassade de France aux EU. (This work, published as part of a program of aid for publication, received support from the Mission Culturelle et Universitaire Française aux Etats Unis, a department of the French Embassy in the United States.)

Yale University Press books may be purchased in quantity for educational, business, or promotional use. For information, please e-mail sales.press@yale.edu (U.S. office) or sales@yaleup.co.uk (U.K. office).

Set in Postscript Electra type by IDS Infotech, Ltd.
Printed in the United States of America.

ISBN 978-0-300- 17057-3 (hardcover : alk. paper)

Library of Congress Control Number: 2016930231

A catalogue record for this book is available from the British Library.

This paper meets the requirements of ANSI/NISO Z39.48–1992 (Permanence of Paper).

10 9 8 7 6 5 4 3 2 1

Photographs courtesy of the Comité Jean Cocteau: Jean Cocteau as a boy; Cocteau's mother, Eugénie, with her two elder children, Marthe and Paul; Cocteau with Marie Laure; Jean Cocteau, or Fame at the Age of Eighteen; Édouard Dermit, leaving the mines of Lorraine.

COMITÉ
Jean Cocteau

for Edmund White

CONTENTS

INTRODUCTION

I tremble, I die, I begin again every morning.
—*Jean Cocteau to Max Jacob, March 1926*

A writer doesn't dance, or play drums in a bar. He creates his works in solitude and abandons them only to devote himself to the great problems of his time. We like thinking of creative geniuses as preoccupied more by world events than by the sets of his new play. But Jean Cocteau, though sensitive to the dramas of other individuals, was less concerned with the collective fate of men. Contrary to his suffering nature, his "good education" meant that he always tried to put himself forward as happy and detached. This internal conflict, along with the more dramatic events he experienced over his lifetime, as death haunted him more and more, led him to grow ever more attentive to his close relationships rather than current events. Cocteau also didn't play the commonly imagined role of the artist in another sense: whereas other artists of his generation typically tried to pass themselves off as rebels or nonconformists, he accepted all prizes, like a child conscious of his parents' need for diplomas.

Abroad, Cocteau was fêted as the embodiment of early twentieth-century France. F. T. Marinetti and Ezra Pound, Rainer Maria Rilke and Thomas Mann—many celebrated this prodigy who evoked this uniquely French spirit of intelligence and irony. Novelists like Alejo Carpentier and Ernest Hemingway encouraged their ex-pat friends, condemned to observe Paris from across the Atlantic, to read him; he embodied "the Parisian" for the Cuban Picabia, and "the delight of Europe" for the American Glenway Wescott. From Tokyo to Havana, Cocteau was the symbol of 1920s France, echoing the innovation and liveliness of the decade. (Charles Péguy, the well-known patriotic writer, said of his compatriots: "The peoples of the earth find you light [léger] because you are a quick people.") Young American and Russian film directors cited *Le sang d'un poète* or *La belle et la bête* among the works that had the greatest influence on them, thirty years before campus rebels and rock fans identified with *Les enfants terribles*, *Thomas l'imposteur*, or *Opium*.

But Cocteau's fame in France dwindled. The reputation of the writer whom Mayakovsky had visited during his first trip to Paris became increasingly undermined by his protean activity, his rivalry with André Breton, and the "art pompier" style that weighed over his last period and influenced his ceramic Orpheuses. Unevenly respected, easily hated, almost always suspected of being inferior to his reputation, Cocteau is often reduced to the "coq-à-l'âne" that his name unfortunately evokes.[1] "A *will o' the wisp*, a vapid emanation of swamp gas," sneered the Christian writer Paul Claudel, who thought him "profoundly superficial," perhaps not knowing that Nietzsche praised the Greeks precisely for having been "superficial—out of profundity."[2]

Throughout his lifetime, Jean Cocteau's brilliant forays into theater, drawing, or sculpture—all of which were imbued with the old Wagnerian dream of total art—were viewed poorly. Since good seats in posterity's waiting room are precious, his originality was challenged; people who had not a single one of his talents accused him of fraud, ascribing some of his poems to Max Jacob, the avant-garde poet of *Le cornet à dés*, and some of his drawings to Picasso: Picasso, whose powerful charisma always made him seem a genius, even though the painter pillaged from his neighbors.

Thanks to Cocteau's homosexuality, his all too obviously bourgeois origins, and his intensive social life during his lonely formative years, rejection of his work has persisted like a class or racial prejudice. Instead of taking the trouble to read, watch, or experience his entire body of work, as a way of plunging into his abundant imagination, people fall back on well-worn labels like "acrobat" and "Jack-of-all-trades." Worse than a "poète maudit"—an artist damned or doomed—Cocteau is little read and poorly thought of, victim of an intellectual laziness by an audience that, despite professing otherwise, reduces him to his fancied nature. Apparently Einstein was right: it is harder to break a prejudice than an atom.

No major critic has ever taken the time to analyze Cocteau's work. Universities take little interest in him, this dunce who failed his *bac* twice.[3] There still exists no definitive collection of his correspondence—not even of his letters to Picasso, Stravinsky, or Proust. He is not a member of the club, even though the club sometimes lets him in on the sly. But this rejection remains local. It lessens as soon as one reaches the United States, Japan, or Germany, where people understood early on the profundity of a work whose themes form a unique constellation. This is especially true across the Atlantic, where the Surrealists' invective never had an impact, and where Cocteau, that icon of the counter-culture, is recognized as the innovator who, along with Buñuel, introduced dream in cinema.

Widely underestimated, like poetry itself for half a century, Cocteau the poet, finally published in a Pléiade edition, deserves a premier spot, from *Plain-chant* to *Léone*. The autobiographical essayist as well is remarkably lucid and astute, in works from *La difficulté d'être* to *Journal d'un inconnu*, as is the memoirist of *Portraits-souvenir*. Although his works are rare and short, the novelist Cocteau remains excellent, too, as books from *Le grand écart* to *Le livre blanc* attest—while the choreographer Cocteau is often surprising, and the artist is occasionally brilliant. Though the film director and man of the theater veered at times from excellence to catastrophe, even Cocteau's failures in these areas remain surprisingly personal.

Cocteau's oeuvre certainly lacks those heavyweight novels that establish a man, or the challenging theoretical material that makes a dramaturge—but one could say the same of Tennessee Williams. Scattered among dozens of publishers and genres, hard to read exhaustively, Cocteau's work is less a continent than a vast, unstable archipelago where many languages are spoken. No doubt the sheer variety of his output contributes to his discredit by exposing him too much and emphasizing his about-faces, but he was incapable of premeditation. Writing came to him only at unforeseeable moments, and almost never when he was seated at a desk. He would scribble on a pack of cigarettes and then move on to all available surfaces before ending up drawing, without thinking about it much. He didn't know if what he did was excellent or insipid: he just did, the way blacksmiths forge or bees gather pollen.

He signed too many occasional pieces at the end of his life. The organism in charge of transcribing messages from his unconscious was no longer capable of enchantment; it was not the divine Orpheus but his old secretary at work: an evil twin who sometimes makes us, his admirers, wish we could have stood behind him to help know when he was in the thrall of his obsession with adding titles for posterity. Time, however, will decide. The bad films, the series of ceramics, the grandiloquent frescoes will fall into oblivion, while the poems, fiction, autobiographical essays, splendid drawings, strange films, will all remain—along with his surprising, explosive personality.

Cocteau's off-the-cuff talks condensed a lifetime of experience—or, to paraphrase Whistler, who was reproached for having demanded a fortune for a portrait executed in ten minutes: "Ten minutes and ten years." And if his deft

conversation, rich in paradoxes and interpolated clauses, left many perplexed—
"One must withdraw and meditate in order to understand," said Abbé Mugnier,
a witty memorialist—this precipitation of thought was also, along with sleep,
drugs, and divination, a way for him to access the unconscious, as well as the
most hidden dimensions of life.

Cocteau's frivolity? There has scarcely been a writer, past his twenties, who
more surely evoked tragedy. His dilettantism? He was one of the most single-
minded workers of the century, methodically preparing for that second life—
longer, more ample, and radiant—when his poetry and theater, his films and
stories would finally be welcomed. His lies? It is true that he readily told tales
and attracted other mystifiers like Jean Genet, the writer-thief, and Maurice
Sachs, the young receptionist who looked up to him like the Messiah—to say
nothing of the madmen who assailed him at the end of his life. But this absurd
reproach can only be understood as a compliment. For there were many who
defined art, with Proust, as the mark of transformation that the artist makes
reality undergo: to create meant to amplify, to distort, to make mythical, if
possible. From Céline to Hemingway, or even filmmaker Orson Welles, there
were many who reinvented their lives, whether to don the horns of the devil or
the feathers of the peacock.

With the help of the cult of transparency, today we no longer trust only the
"established" truth or the suffering confession. The secret desire to take the existential anomaly of a writer's life and reduce it to a series of facts comprehensible
to "people like us" often leads the biographer to a purely moral judgment, which
almost always mirrors the conformism of the times. The ultimate example was
created thirty years ago by a biographer who devoted four hundred pages to
reproaching Cocteau for his lies, without even perceiving the uniting organic
link (in the author of *Thomas l'imposteur*, as in any novelist worthy of the name)
between lie and fiction, creation and self-creation. Francis Steegmuller came to
doubt the reality of Cocteau's love affairs—as if he couldn't believe he had
sincere feelings, or that a man could truly and completely love another man.

If I deliver a biography here, it is not, then, out of a detective's desire for
exactitude, but because Cocteau's life seemed to me an oeuvre in itself, half-
novelistic, half-poetic, and also because Cocteau's inability to live reality—like
his need to surround himself with a magical halo—made him imagine everything in a semi-fictive way. "Truth made him uneasy as lies," he said of Thomas
the Impostor; he himself lived a long dream, colorful and then nightmarish,
that gave a muffled, cloudy feel to his awareness. Some sleepwalkers walk while
improvising verses on a roof; he was one of the rare somnambulists who
remember all things when they wake.

Everything in him was strange. His hair grew sideways, his teeth were poorly set, his face verged on the asymmetrical. Afflicted with dental abscesses, recurrent insomnia, and countless allergies, he was the hostage of uncontrollable forces. Some of his works are so contrary, like *Parade* and *Renaud et Armide*, that one would fear a short-circuit if they were placed face to face. Lightning always seemed on the point of striking this inspired person whose reactions were so unpredictable and disconcerting that his apparition on earth, among the blossoming of species, could pass for a sport of nature.

Cocteau never managed to unify his desires, or even to impose a line around himself. Divided between the fundamental anarchy of his components and his physical need for serenity, he harbored a constant conflict of tendencies that only opium appeased. Not only did he continually need to change activities, but like the inspired and religious he always needed to let his soul migrate; his texts themselves metamorphosed as he was writing them, encasing narratives like so many Russian dolls. Unable to stand still, he could climb over walls to leave the room where he was smoking to enter all of a sudden the room where Proust lay dying.

Cocteau's antennae twitched with the slightest variations in the fashions of the times. He would lock himself in, immerse himself, or take drugs in order to emerge as another after a few weeks. His aesthetics would change, his writing would become more tense or imagistic; he no longer believed in planes, but in God—no longer in skyscrapers, but in roses. Light had finally dawned, the "good" cycle was beginning since he had discovered the values that suited him. His old skin was already falling away; a new animal was expressing itself, impatient to make its voice heard by the world: "All roses lose their petals / on the rug how many masks," he writes in "Locutions."[4]

This perpetual becoming would permit Cocteau no respite for half a century. Always running after a version of himself, he enjoyed in one lifetime that existential proliferation that the Buddha promises his disciples via past or future incarnations. That was his karma: born on the wheel of reincarnations, he died endlessly, like a Hindu transmigrated into a Christian universe. Didn't, after all, the American photographer Halsman give him six hands and six arms?

Many creators have their "periods"; not so many benefit from such a capacity for self-engenderment that they produce enough people to fill ten biographies—this book could have been titled *Cocteaus*. "He doesn't have one lifeline; he has several," notes the palmist reading the hand of Thomas the Impostor. Cocteau's variability, rooted as it was in childhood, that life-before-life where all self-images are possible, could make people ill at ease; he himself was the first to feel like a "case," and when this was mentioned by someone else it would jolt him awake. Something, though, prevented him from taking on, or staying with, just one creative form. The only art missing from his incredible roster was, significantly, architecture. Kot Jelenski, a Polish essayist, said that Witold Gombrowicz sought to fix his own softness in bronze; composed of waves and nerves, Cocteau could produce only fluctuating forms.

In short, this creature of air was a fragile genius—a combination almost impossible in art, where force is as necessary as in politics. He was, however, the first to employ his animal capacity to shed his skin and bring to life the personalities swarming within him, even if molting left him skinned alive. This suppleness logically led him to want to become that tougher other—less lively but more stable—to which he was drawn his whole life. Every "genius" he approached, from Chaplin to Stravinsky, perceived this strange desire—Picasso first of all. Always Cocteau insisted that they too absorb him and integrate him somehow into them. Secretly desirous of ingesting their strength and cannibalizing their "mana," he got ever closer: everything that happened to them seemed so full, so real. Did he sense how his own multiplicity, while enriching him, rendered him fragile as well? Nietzsche, who was always his major philosophical reference, would not have found him wrong, haunted as he himself was by the cases of Goethe and Wagner.

Though Cocteau needed to immerse himself in the other, it was his own universe that he served. He produced Verlaine-like poems, a film that could be described as Surrealist, a Sartrean play, yet he can always be recognized in the least of his phrases or poems: flitting from branch to branch, chirping here and dancing there, but always in the same tree, he would say. "The snake changes only its skin," asserts an Albanian proverb. Yes, a core of Cocteau does exist—an original, passionate form, soon recognizable to the ear, but always able, like a musical tone, to take advantage of a fugue in order to reshape itself elsewhere.

The discredit that assailed him could also have stemmed from a vision of the world in which, socially and psychically, everyone had a place—only one—and where the self itself was forced to respond to the dominant desire for uniqueness and stability. The personalities of the classic and bourgeois eras had to be constant and loyal; they had to work for their whole lives like blacksmiths or artisans toward the same goal. A heroic subject underwent ordeals with courage and brio. And the writer, even if he flattered himself on recognizing neither homeland nor religion, was still supposed to have a territory and a law, and to reside in the center of an intangible system of values. Human archetypes get accepted by the majority; Molière's miser was fascinating because he was the literal incarnation of his defect, Balzac's Père Goriot because he was only an inexhaustible progenitor. Yet those incapable of any role but serving their masters—the Sganarelles, the Sancho Panzas, and other Harlequins—were hissed off the stage.

Still monotheistic, even in its laicized decay, our culture engendered, at the end of the nineteenth century, a literary religion that is today in decline. The author was supposed to be a saint, a cause, or a monster, so that the purity of his work would shine: Mallarmé or Whitman on one hand, Dostoyevsky and Wilde on the other. This marvel not only had to have an aesthetic and an ideology; but also was required to produce poetic summas and defend a vision worthy of mystics; to dominate the heaven of ideas, like the One who rules over the sun and commands the lightning; and to be callous as a prisoner and luminous as a prophet. The priests of this religion could denounce Cocteau as a mind without roots or beliefs, lively and volatile as the weather. Faced with a yeoman like Paul Claudel or an engineer like Paul Valéry, he seemed like a gardener of atmospheres, everywhere at ease but nowhere at home. Despite Nietzsche's assertion of the all-importance of betrayal and the cycles of eternal return, Cocteau was taken for a mere opportunist.

A principle of uncertainty set in, however, around the years 1910–1915. Determined until then by blood and heritage, environment and faith, the individual became a variable form, one moved more by obscure forces than by one's own will. The regular world of Euclid found itself at the same time destabilized by the emergence of quantum physics, for which bodies change nature according to the wave that carries them: an object or a being no longer existed in itself and for itself, but by and in the sinusoidal curve that its movement completed. With the discovery of the unconscious, the self lost its stable aspect as the "house of the soul" and resembled more a flow of magma or a colloidal precipitate whose gelatinous suppleness Robert Musil could analyze. People began to doubt the ultimate existence of immanent psychic terrains, then came to favor adaptation, even hybridization and self-contradiction. The modern era was beginning, with its apology for flexibility and even opportunism—and it is not over yet.

Heir to the old culture, and also a pure product of these influences that led him to molt around 1913, Cocteau always pointed to aesthetic mobility as the source of his productivity. To weigh him book by book, like an accountant, to reduce him to narrow sequences of time and style by pausing at each step, as in a museum, would be to miss the essential thing: Cocteau's work, marked by his symbolist origins, is not wholly modern, but his personality is resolutely so.

André Breton could well have been the key agent in Cocteau's bad reputation; the Surrealist was one of those who denied any integrity to Cocteau's personality, and any weight to his work. A great deal of personal jealousy and intellectual rivalry was at work here, but also homophobia—a prejudice from which Cocteau often suffered, especially under the Occupation. Genius was recognized only when it was characterized by tough arrogance of the kinds championed by Claudel or Breton. Were literature measured according to hormones, the most narrow-minded could claim that Cocteau did not exist: that the impostor passing himself off as the famous Jean Cocteau was the literary equivalent of the Grand Duchess Anastasia, supposed daughter of the last tsar, a poor unfortunate condemned to subsist through imitation—a characteristic ostensibly unique to homosexuals, Jews, and women.

There did indeed exist a part of Cocteau—exceptional in such a gifted creator—that borrowed from others. This tendency stemmed not only from an exacerbated awareness of the styles of the times, but also from an openness to others that was as remarkable as his attention to himself. "He immediately put himself in the place of his interlocutor, suffering from his weaknesses, his lacks, his ugliness," said the dwarf Pieral in his memoirs.[5] According to the composer Henri Sauguet: "Cocteau partook so much in others' lives that he became the young bride at a wedding, the baptized baby in a christening, the dead man in the funeral of a friend."[6] Although he was aware of this capacity for alteration, Cocteau was also cognizant that he was scarcely as changeable as Stravinsky—that melodic sponge who began by copying Rimsky-Korsakov, excelled at ironic imitation of Tchaikovsky, Pergolesi, and Handel, and ended up joining forces with the twelve-tone composers. Nor was he as protean as Picasso, whose aesthetic about-faces were so sudden that he managed to exhaust his pursuers, and were so haunted by clowns, Pierrots, monkeys, and Harlequins that his works often inspired re-readings of great predecessors. But no one now would dare call Picasso or Stravinsky chameleons.

There is actually a Cocteau within every creator, an embryo of availability urging him to become another, to emerge from himself in order to return to himself to engender unreal figures. This faculty can haunt him, however, and even threaten his integrity—Breton himself confessed as much to Trotsky.[7] For rigid people and those set in their ways, Cocteau's flaunted fragility made him the ideal scapegoat. To call him a trickster was to reject the share of imposture that every identity bears; to attack that "Fregoli," that quick-change artist, was to wash one's hands of all other influences; to condemn that sexual Jew was to clear oneself of all mimicry and to assert oneself as an authentic artist. Cocteau ended up internalizing these attacks and setting himself up as his own judge. Although he never doubted his literary originality, he could accuse himself of lacking existence and roots. His feeling of strangeness turned, around the middle of his life, into a persecution complex; after having lived like a young god, at the end of his adolescence, he ended up seeing himself as a famous pariah, a corrupt old celebrity.

His epileptic intelligence and his mercurial vivacity helped him hold firm. His tragedy was almost to be too resilient, too prolix: four novels, six films, seven plays, seven collections of poetry, four autobiographical works, thousands of drawings, and a few sculptures, all in fifty-five years of activity—the sheer scale of his output would prove the exceptional character of the poet, the graphic artist, the filmmaker, the man of the theater, the costume designer, and the decorator who, unfortunately for him, were all named Cocteau.

Things could change. In the neighboring art that is the cinema, contradiction and variety are more welcome. The intense heterogeneity of a Pasolini is applauded, as is the wide-ranging work of a Fassbinder, who preferred to accomplish many things instead of great things. The philosophical contribution of Gilles Deleuze contributed to this, by privileging those consciousnesses that grow less by taking root, like oaks, than by proliferating in every direction, like rhizomes. Already over a century ago Bergson thought that the real stuff of our ego, "la durée," or experienced time, made us into a continuous creation—a thesis that served as a loom for Proust's *Recherche,* which swarms with lives in progress throughout the ages, lives as different from themselves as from the lives of others. Literary criticism, however, has not yet accomplished its quantum revolution. It continues to demand straightforward, heavy, canonic works, and to ignore that ability to alter oneself—unique to creators and madmen—that made other selves spring from Cocteau. It has not yet drawn all the lessons from the work of Cocteau's Portuguese cousin Fernando Pessoa, who created sixteen fully-fledged poets and who was no one, since, by a fabulous chance, that was the meaning of his patronymic, with "pessoa" stemming from the Latin term "persona," referring to the mask of actors, and "personne," meaning "no one."

More exhibitionistic than the uneasy Portuguese writer, Cocteau tried to unite these Cocteaus that divided him, to crown this private anarchy with a single name. If Pessoa masterfully exploited the possibilities of his own literary democracy, Cocteau clung to a more classic idea of the "auteur," even though he also refused, with his tendency to welcome everyone, to choose between his variants, and instead encouraged the multiple personalities that he harbored. This multiplicity is now part of our cultural horizon, especially in the United States, where redefining oneself over one's lifetime is considered not just legitimate, but even a sign of vitality. Cocteau indeed seemed to be ahead of his time. His lack of snobbishness about what was considered "high" and "low" art anticipated the 1980s, when postmodernism was in full flight, in France at least; Warhol had set the mood as early as the 1960s in the United States. During the

1980s, pioneers in the so-called minor arts—photography, fashion, animation—all celebrated and laid claim to the influence of that "Paganini of the 'violon d'Ingres' [hobby]" (the phrase is his) who had given proof in all the arts of his strangeness by anticipating our era with his never-sectarian brilliance. Leaving his signature tattooed on every mirror, Cocteau thus proclaimed the Warhol era better than anyone in France, except perhaps for his exact counterpart Marcel Duchamp, that master of silence, sarcasm, retreat—and of stealthy, fatal chess moves.

The allergic reactions that Cocteau provoked for so long, though, did serve him in the end by keeping him alive even today. The literary corpses of the major Surrealists and Dadaists Breton, Éluard, or Tzara are consulted scarcely more than those of Mauriac or Montherlant, who were much more traditional writers. Nicknamed "Le contemporain capital," André Gide was petrified as soon as he breathed his last breath, for having had everything while he was alive. But Cocteau and Aragon are still discussed—Louis Aragon, that other chameleon who managed to make himself a heavyweight by submitting himself to a domestic dragon and an ideological apparatus to the point of identifying himself with Love and the Communist Party, values with a formidable capacity for self-absolution.

Le livre blanc is still read, and not only as a precocious defense of homosexuality; *Le sang d'un poète* continues to be projected in every cinema. Cocteau's plays, like Sartre's, are no longer widely performed, but his *Voix humaine*, which Rossellini brought to movie theaters and that Almodóvar's films never fail to cite, remains one of the most sought-after monologues. Cocteau is one of those rare writers whose mere name provokes categorical judgments, even among people who have only turned the pages of *Thomas l'imposteur*. "So magnetic is his fascination that hostile critics have devoted years of their lives to proving that he has no artistic existence," Francis Steegmuller justly observed.[8] But while the world remains unchanged by the death of most of us, Cocteau has imagined phrases and shaped images that will forever define his legacy. A cultural history that began at his birth and ended at his burial would have no deeper meaning; nevertheless his life traversed an entire culture, even an entire century.

The biographies published in the United States are already forty years old and they privilege Cocteau the character too much, to the detriment of the creator. A thousand documents have been made public over those same forty years, documents that have allowed me to reevaluate the influence that Cocteau had on literature of the 1920s, avant-garde cinema, wartime poetry and poetry of the New Wave, and our modern sensibility in general. And then there was the matter of reconstructing the innumerable experiences of a man who has for too long been reduced to a reputation as simply a brilliant Jack-of-all-trades. I sifted through hundreds of letters and memoirs, pored through police and court archives, and read about American boxing and the unconscious in the cinema. Cocteau was wildly prolific. On some days he might write as many as two hundred letters, "pneus" (messages sent by pneumatic tube), or telegrams. He himself kept the least note and smallest photo in his boxes and, although thefts or gifts have mutilated this treasure, it would still be enough to fill volumes. Every day we find an unpublished poem, an unknown letter, an outline for an article or play; in the basement of his house in Milly, now a museum dedicated to his work, a manuscript has been exhumed that includes an essay about Jünger's *Auf den Marmorklippen*, as well as the correspondence related to it.

Cocteau's drawings, counterfeit or real, and variations of his manuscripts have invaded auction houses; the ubiquity he evinced all his life is accentuated in death. Indeed, there is not a book devoted to the literature, cinema, ballet, theater, or music of the twentieth century in which his name doesn't figure frequently. Too many minor encounters and false friendships trumpeted abroad cannot make us forget that he knew everyone, and that everyone spoke about him. His notebooks make one dizzy: the cream of the twentieth century had his phone number. The hundreds of painters and photographers whom he sought out at each stage of his metamorphoses all caught his enigma on paper or film. And no one left more portraits, written or drawn, of the figures who marked him.

We might groan from the density of famous names that accompanied Cocteau as he followed his destiny, but this proliferation was vital to him—well-known people constituted a kind of race apart for him, a kind of people who made him feel better and whom he ended up mirroring, unable to make himself the center. He would fall in love with a stranger whom he would then hurry to introduce into this knot of chosen people; he would meet an exceptional personality and immediately feel the need to immerse himself in his life or introduce himself into his work. Yet although this whirlwind has now blown over, there remains the best of an era whose riches have not yet been entirely explored.

Early on, it became clear that any attempt at exhaustiveness in creating this biography would condemn me to pinning down sterile minutiae, to being like that Borgesian cartographer who dreamed of drawing a map as big as the territory it depicted. Instead, in order to capture and convey the man and his work, I had to evaluate his works, strip bare the life—in other words, make a book that "decoctified" Cocteau. I was a child when Cocteau died, but this lack of an overlap had its advantages. I relied on books, along with interviews with the few survivors I was able to meet. Inheriting no obligation, whether aesthetic, moral, or personal, I treated him as a writer; I was careful not to call him "Jean," as so often happens in France, including in certain conferences, as if he were the Evangelist—can you imagine academics calling the founder of Surrealism "André"? "A stranger, who judges our character according to our works, judges us better than our entourage, who judge our works according to us," wrote Cocteau.[9] I would like to prove him right.

Many people are dead, but do not know it. Jean Cocteau, by contrast, was alive, but he doubted this so much that he seemed often to be dreaming with his eyes wide open. I hope to recreate here this strange feeling that grounds both the genius poet and the extraordinary man.

The Child Prodigy

We know that inside us many people breathe
Who come from far away and are one within our brows.
—*Apollinaire, Sanglots, banalités*

IN THE FAIRY KINGDOM

Jean Cocteau loved his childhood. More than a time or a state of being, it was a country of its own, without customs inspectors or police, with its own secret rituals and magic spells. Since his parents rarely entered his bedroom, he reigned over this still boundless place where he would spend hours lying back, playing or reading, until time and space blurred. His heightened emotionality not only made him sensitive to all the elements of this kingdom, but also plunged him into a sort of ecstasy.

It was hard for the young Cocteau to rise from this solitary hypnosis at mealtimes. As soon as his soup was finished, he would go curl up on his German nanny's lap. He writes:

> What a delight it was to follow this dinner beneath the tablecloth, in the half-sleep of childhood. The noise of jaws and stomachs, the crumbs falling, the soul-searing sighs that housekeepers emit who are overwhelmed by their responsibilities, all the drama of a servants' dinner accompanied by eyes lifted to heaven and pinkies raised would reach me, cushioned by cloth.[1]

This Atlantis, bounded in the summer by the big family house in Maisons-Laffitte, with its park adorned with fountains and fireworks, and in the winter by the townhouse on rue La Bruyère in the 19th arrondissement, would remain for him the equivalent of that primal paradise where we are supposed to have lived before we were born, and which, according to Plato, we miss all our lives.

Jean's sister, Marthe, was twelve and his older brother, Paul, eight when Jean saw the light of day at dawn on July 5, 1889, a few hours before the inauguration of the Eiffel Tower, the star attraction of the World's Fair celebrating the first centenary of the French Revolution. His mother, whose maiden name was Eugénie Lecomte, was the daughter of a stockbroker from Champagne; his paternal grandfather was a lawyer in Le Havre. Originally Catholics from the provinces, both families had produced diplomats and admirals, and had maintained their position in Parisian society. The Cocteau household raised the three children, surrounded by servants, within this dynamic social milieu.

Marthe was serious; Paul was "a model of moderation, reserve, and equilibrium"; and little Jean was restless. "A funny little boy, very frail. Most of the time, his mother kept him in bed and bustled about him. He liked to dress as a girl," said his cousin Marianne, who was something of a tomboy.[2] As soon as he was taken away from his wet nurse's arms, he was entrusted to a redheaded, unpleasant German woman, Joséphine Ebel, who at first did not make a good impression. It was only by reading fairytales and singing German nursery rhymes to him that the woman he called Jéphine came to be accepted, since these rhymes had the gift of calming his fears and fevers. The haunted castles, enchanted sleep, and giant's footprints in *Puss in Boots*, *Sleeping Beauty*, and *Hansel and Gretel* would have a lasting influence on him; by imposing themselves as convincing representations of the external world, these stories would give rise in his imagination to an intense expectation of wonders: the less credible a story seemed, the more he wanted to believe it, even as an adult, in the hope of reviving the dazzling atmosphere of childhood. "It's incredible," his characters in *Les parents terribles* say over and over again: Cocteau, however, was always the first to believe.

As for the real external world, from which his nanny and mother were protecting him, the young Cocteau caught glimpses of it at the dance classes he attended in the hope of curing his scoliosis. But the strangers in top hats he met disconcerted him so much that he suspected them of talking nonsense or even of only pretending to speak—the only possible language being in his eyes the one he heard among his family members. Right away, this universe populated by enigmatic, cold, sad strangers seemed to him to betray the fairytale promises that Jéphine read. Entitled "Mensonge," the first poem in his first collection denounced the real forest as a fraud devoid of the elves and fauns that fill it in myths. Indeed, nothing could better reveal the annoyance he felt with this world deprived of imagination than his fantasy in verse that appears in the same collection—a poem in which Puss in Boots, Sleeping Beauty, the Ogre, and Prince Charming, after emerging from a bound volume of Perrault's *Fairytales*, are terrified to see how much more stifling reality is than the book in which they had been living.[3]

Far from setting obstacles in the way of his tendencies, his family implicitly encouraged them. Against the triumphant positivism conveyed by the engineers at the extremely selective educational establishment of the École Polytechnique, against the republican worship of steel, of secular teaching, and of progress in general, the Cocteau-Lecomtes wielded the rites of an already bohemian bourgeoisie. Like thousands of people of private means flourishing because of the stability of the franc, they had no particular complaints about the established order, living as they were in the heart of a universally envied city. In reply to the exclamation of the chemist Marcellin Berthelot in 1897, "From now on the world is without mystery!," they welcomed orchestras into their home, purchased paintings, or tried their hand at photography in order to come ever so slightly closer to the enigma of life. One day the father of the young Cocteau would set up an easel in the Maisons-Laffitte park and his elder sister would make watercolor paintings of poppies while reciting monologues from *Cyrano de Bergerac*. On another day, the Spanish composer and violinist Pablo de Sarasate would come to play his new composition to them, contributing to the active idleness of amateurs who, far from the rude realism of Maupassant or the hallucinations of Van Gogh, perpetuated a post-Romantic climate tinged with fantasy, light erudition, and melancholy.

In a France overcome with melomania, music occupied a central place in the life of the Lecomtes. Every Sunday, a concert was arranged at Maisons-Laffitte around a quartet of virtuosi—including Cocteau's maternal grandfather, who held the cello "as if he were carving leg of lamb," and a minuscule violinist who plucked his strings as if he were poking strawberries with a toothpick. This weekly musicale was a ritual for the Lecomtes, who had lived in the same house that Rossini had lived in and had preserved one of the wigs of the composer. (Rossini, who had lost his hair at an early age, had stored his wigs in order of length, and wore them one after the other "until the fictional visit of the hairdresser."[4]) This heirloom was probably inherited from Émilie Lecomte, Cocteau's maternal grandmother, whom Cocteau always said had been an opera singer.

With its farm and its cows, its lilacs and its swings, its gillyflowers and its frogs, its stables and its greenhouse, the Mansart-built summer home at Maisons-Laffitte, located halfway between the Forest of Saint-Germain-en-Laye and the stud farms, evoked those wisteria-covered dachas where Chekhov's Saint Petersburg natives would spend the summer months, divided between the euphoria of the moment and the anguish of a happiness doomed to become part of the past. Detesting solitude, little Cocteau was always the first to protest against the deserters who left this house, and the first to greet a storm, the "gentle bowling of April thunder" that would gather his relatives and friends around him.[5] Since his brother and sister were too old, he played with his first cousins, Pierre and Marianne Lecomte. The billiard room (in which his grandfather stored his two Stradivariuses) was their special retreat, with its marble Venus on her pedestal that turned from the gaze of a plaster mask of Antinous with formidable enamel eyes; but they also loved his mysterious bedroom, with its silver, swan-necked bathtub. Stuffed with shoes and books, the tub made a terrible gong noise when the children ran into it. In the kitchen garden, they would find the gardener's children and wander around the stable-boys' cottages, then the stalls where the horses munched carrots soaked in warm burgundy. Their complicity broke out in cruel giggles at a broken mechanical swimmer that had only one spring left, baptized Moscovi when its penis-like spring was stretched out, Moscova when not. These were the beginnings of an initiation that the mischievous Marianne would complete by hustling her cousin into the family horse-drawn omnibus that carried them to Mass on Sundays in order to confide in him, her heart beating: "Listen, I know everything. There are big people who go to bed in the middle of the day. The men are called 'jackrabbits,' the women, 'tarts' [cocottes]. Uncle André is a jackrabbit. If you repeat this, I'll kill you with a spade."[6] This was enough to arouse the sense of the absurd peculiar to childhood. (In another example of the peculiar understanding of the world that children have, the young Cocteau would later tell a little girl with whom he fell in love, two years his senior, that he would wait to marry her until he was two years older than she.)

Cocteau was not a boy eager to prove his strength. Rather, his appearance and personality were more evocative of Alice in Wonderland: lively, strange, naïve. He was capable of staring for hours at a dead frog he came upon near the Maisons-Laffitte ornamental pond, one hand on its heart, "posed like a tenor." Wandering through his parents' immense domains, he would explore the farthest reaches of their Parisian house where, far, very far, from his bedroom, "in an unreal, fabulous zone," was his grandfather's room, made incredibly exotic by its overflow of blue curios and lacquered wood: in *Le Potomak*, Cocteau would write that until he was seven years old, he thought he lived in China.[7]

The sense of mystery deepened during the day devoted to the Lord. The family rooms were as silent as a mausoleum: the parents digested, the streets emptied out, the weather grew cold. Infected by a naïve metaphysics, Cocteau as a child saw his own emptiness overcome the world and reduce everything to inertia; the last adults to pace through the deserted city were themselves changed into bizarre figurines that Time, the Devil, or Nothingness slid across an immense chessboard. When boredom threatened to fix everything in place, the child would open his wardrobe and put on the first outfit he found, and become a troll coming from the kingdom of the snows; already he could make out through the window the silent progression of a painted wooden sled; the boots he heard crunching were those of a Father Christmas bundled in a leather coat. Frightening whistles reached his ears; fortunately he had the equipment—pistol, felt hat, whip—to magically vanquish the Cheyennes who were shooting arrows at him from a nearby window. Claiming a power over his life in inverse proportion to his everyday powerlessness, he emptied his closet and reappeared as a new character every time. And whereas ten minutes earlier he had been a nobody, he was suddenly anybody, everyone, with a heady feeling of being able to conquer any sort of adversity.

This childlike Sunday syndrome would animate Cocteau until his last breath. Likening his childhood to "a theater in which you played every role, in unequalled possession of the world," he took special pleasure in playing by himself. Overcome by a frenzy of self-creation, mimicking the look and rituals of the person he wanted to become, he fabricated selves until he was dizzy with avatars. Many Pygmalions are anxious to see their creation come to life, but Cocteau was a much rarer kind of self-Pygmalion: he took on personas that he would abandon as soon as he had outgrown them, only too happy to exercise that fairy power that—at an age when so many others already know they will be a pharmacist, an engineer, or a mechanic—let him picture himself in every human role.

The surprising stability of the French franc, in that golden age of the French bourgeoisie, allowed his father to give up his job as a lawyer. Lacking the temperament of an investor, the gentle, melancholy man proceeded to live as an artistic person of private means and spent the remainder of his life painting, emptying teapots, playing billiards with his father-in-law—taking on a bit part in an existence directed by others. Was it difficult for this Sunday painter to believe in himself, under the potent sway of the Ingres drawings, Delacroix canvases, and Félix Ziem landscapes owned by his father-in-law? Neither the eclecticism practiced by the Lecomtes nor their native brio would help this self-effacing father, living apparently at half-speed, to emerge from the shadows and from the clutter of a townhouse whose second floor was given over to him.

Hemmed in by the personalities of his three brothers-in-law, Georges Cocteau felt so little at home on their property that Jean, author of *Les parents terribles*, would at the end of his life still make this Freudian slip: "My family lived . . . the Lecomtes lived . . ."[8] The task of this humble prince consort was in fact reduced to attending a wife who was sufficiently lively and certain of her elegance to pose for the camera of Nadar *fils* and for the easel of Jacques-Émile Blanche, and to be taken out to the theater, concerts, and the Opéra. It was she, not the bland man of private means, whom Cocteau would always remember, assisted by her kneeling maid, adjusting her long dress and donning endless gloves: a Madonna "strangled by diamonds, bedecked with a nocturnal aigrette, a sparkling sea urchin bristling with rays of light" as she prepared to leave for the Opéra. These Proustian departures laid the foundation for his art, by suggesting to his childlike imagination a beyond as mysterious as that in fairytales. Cocteau would never stop describing "the adorable final rite that consisted of buttoning onto her wrist . . . the little keyhole opening of the glove where I would kiss her naked palm."[9] With this act the little servant knight was honoring his first queen, on the threshold of her departure for a nebulous theatrical event that would always seem more real to him than reality.

The young Cocteau would mentally recreate these theatrical spectacles that he had missed, using the programs that his mother, returning at night, would place in silence on his quilt. If by chance he was confined to bed because of scarlet fever or measles, the truant schoolboy would "stage" the repertoire of his choice in a feverish state, taking turns at being the director, the actors, and the audience, dreaming of that "total art" wherein drama, music, poetry, and chore-ography would cross-fertilize each other according to the demiurgic ambition of the Wagnerian era. As Cocteau wrote in *Portraits-souvenir*, "The child wants a bedroom, to gather together his belongings and loves there. He hates things that disperse. He likes illnesses, which bring people together and leave him in seclusion." Some parents like to induce illnesses in their children, in order to increase their dependence: in Cocteau's case it was more a matter of deliberate self-dependence, with the fever having the power to levitate the little boy to a place between dream and reality, while gathering around his bed, in an excess of love, his mother (in the astrakhan jacket in which he loved to bury his face), his German governess, and the maid.

Scarcely had his fever broken than the child would lay flat on his stomach, chin resting in his hands, to devour a picture book or babble out one of Jéphine's stories. It was this precocious literary intoxication, more than the collective disciplines of school, that contributed to his cultural upbringing, his unfitness for any form of normal life, and the guiding spirit that would push him, via dream or drugs, toward the marvelous.

His father, whom he would watch painting for hours, initiated Cocteau early into drawing, and made several portraits of him in red chalk, graphite, and charcoal, one of which shows him wearing a sailor's outfit. Guided by this depressive father who medicated himself by drawing, Cocteau soon learned to sketch his family, their friends, and the house musicians. If he got tired of playing, Jéphine would send him to a matinee of *Around the World in Eighty Days* at the Châtelet, or to that other planet over which soared the acrobats of the Médrano Circus, amid a strong smell of manure. There he could see the august Footit inflict sonorous slaps on Chocolat, a clown stupid enough to have let his cooked calf's head fall in the water, which they would then magically make reappear by waving oil and vinegar above it. Only Jéphine's grip, as they emerged together into the silent anticlimax of the street, could rouse the child from his hypnosis.

The young Cocteau earned pocket money by selling his first drawings to his grandfather, then spent it skating at Loop-the-Loop or the Palais de Glace on the Champs-Élysées, where Liane de Pougy and Liane de Lancy glided on their steel feet, winding around their teacher, the comedian Polaire, and Colette, as thin as a "little fox in a cycling outfit." These cocottes, armed with braided belts, corsets, and tights, and bristling with "tulle, light rays and eyelashes," were still the terror of families.[10] But their allure intrigued Cocteau enough for his cousin to hear him say, as she was obediently leaving at five o'clock: "I am a man, and I'm staying."[11] He also saw these "pleasure troops" at Châtelet matinées.[12] There they imposed strange negotiations on the regulars in evening dress; their striptease was a long, costly enterprise whose price had to be "fixed in advance."[13] At some point his parents made him flee their approach, warning him urgently as if he were going to contract syphilis just by observing them, but their brusque call to order came too late: working like a diaphragm on a lens, his eye had already registered thousands of pictures that he would develop a few years later.

Did the young Cocteau know that he belonged to that fragile species that survives only by lying? Or that, from the age of eighteen, he would live by borrowing his personality from "the great"? Born a child, as others are born adults, he found in the universal heritage of that age the impressions and energy that would feed the enormous artistic effort he would maintain for half a century. When asked what he wanted to be later on, he would reply: "Ingenious." In order to emphasize his strength, he swore that he had killed with his air rifle the rabbit that he had just found dead in a field: making stories up was so easy for him that he supported his invented stories with much more conviction than the ones he experienced. "It's more beautiful than if it were authentic," he exclaimed in front of a fake Greco—all lies seeming a priori more interesting to him than the reality they mask. He would come to wonder in *Opium* how one can write the life of poets, since they themselves would be incapable of it—"too much mystery, too many true lies, too many tangled branches."[14]

On Sunday he went to Mass; twice a week he attended the matinees at the Français; and every weekend he could be found at the Conservatory concerts, with a passion that contributed to making him a dunce at school. Already regarded as the most gifted, the most vulnerable, and the most difficult of all the Cocteau children, he annoyed his grandfather with his instability, but was always absolved by a family that was compelled by artistic dreams.

OEDIPUS'S CHILDHOOD

While he was still a child, an active, domineering, spiritual, hardworking painter came into his mother's life: Joseph Wencker, a student of Jean-Léon Gérôme, leader of the *art pompier* movement. Ready to do anything to succeed, Wencker embodied the impatience of the Alsatians, who were eager to assert their artistic superiority over German painters while awaiting a greater redress— the return to France of their province, occupied since the defeat of 1870. Did the arrival of this self-confident, cheerful, highly rated painter aggravate the internal exile of Georges Cocteau, six years his senior?

On April 5, 1898, at 9:30 in the morning, Georges Cocteau, only forty-nine years of age, was found dead in his bed of a gunshot wound. The little Cocteau was returning from a walk with his favorite cousin when his mother's shouts brought him the news; not understanding what it was about, he went back to playing, unable to believe in the disappearance of a man who only the day before had promised to bring him back a camera being repaired, and who always kept his promises. Having provided a home for Georges while he was alive, the in-laws opened the doors of their vault to him, at the Montmartre Cemetery—although not without arranging things first, since suicide was still punished with excommunication, and the Church refused religious funerals to whomever took a life not his own.

Had Georges Cocteau guessed a liaison between his wife and Joseph Wencker, or even doubted the paternity of little Jean? No matter: people soon stopped talking about that odd visitor.

Cocteau very seldom mentioned the effect that his father's suicide had on him, as if it had been as discreet as the departure of the gentle, naïve king, likened to a "silent ghost," in "Conte simple," a poem he dedicated to his brother.[15] Fifty years later, he would allude in front of his housekeeper to his mother's elopement with a Polish lover.[16] Finally, as his own death approached, Cocteau would speak of the bullet his father had shot upon waking, in the silence of the conjugal bedroom, but elsewhere he referred to how his father's throat had supposedly been cut with his own razor. Marianne Lecomte had heard that Georges Cocteau was found in bed, bathed in his own blood, after shooting himself in the head.

The causes of this suicide are even more enigmatic. Admiral Durand-Viel, a first cousin of the Cocteaus, remembered announcing to them a few days before the tragedy the decline of certain stocks. "We were a family on the edge of ruin, so my father killed himself in circumstances under which no one would kill themselves now," Cocteau asserted.[17] But his mother never lacked money. Another possibility was hinted at by Cocteau himself: under the anonymity of *Le livre blanc*, his homoerotic tale, and assisted by the poetic license of fiction, he had in 1928 suggested that his father's sexual tastes were close to his own. "He probably ignored his downward slope and instead of going down it climbed up another one with difficulty, without knowing what made his life so heavy," he remarked, adding: "In his time people killed themselves for less."[18]

Cocteau's Lecomte grandmother had been very attached to him as a child; when finally she died, he became the heir to the throne, the little prince whom his mother still coddled. Authoritarian and flirtatious, possessive and melancholic, anxious and worldly, the very pretty widow shaped her son in her image, passing on to him her anxieties and her narcissism—he already bore the masculine version of her name as his middle name. Never had a mother complained so much of being neglected; never had a son shared his news so assiduously: a letter a day during vacation, sometimes redoubled by a postcard showing her, with crosses or dotted lines, the hotel at which he was staying, the room where he slept, his view upon waking, his path to the beach, the inn where he dined. Telling her everything that was sayable, he linked her virtually to all his actions, then—predicting her obsessions—he came to observe the world through her eyes, and almost to live his life according to her criteria.

Having made up her mind to remain a widow, Mme Cocteau shifted all her affection to her last-born, who in turn learned to impose himself as her little husband. The son's fervor was coupled with a lover-like attention: "I adore you," the teenager whispered to her, though he had only distant feelings for his brother and sister. "I adored my mother," he confirmed, "not because she was my mother, but because she was a surprising woman."[19] A good pianist—she had inherited Rossini's piano—Mme Cocteau adored the theater and opera. She was "a bit sarcastic, without bitterness," Maurice Sachs once said.[20] Always Cocteau's surest confidant and his steadiest friend, it would never occur to her to attack a republican institution in front of the boy who already introduced himself as her "old Jean," her "big chatterbox." But she knew society enough to laugh at its actors and had enough imagination to perpetuate, in the eyes of her adored son, the blessed time of his childhood. In turn, he would always try to live in the refuge of a "credulous enchantment as if in the maternal womb."[21]

The physical resemblance between mother and son was troubling—the same sharp nose, the same angular, ferret-like face; with longer hair the son could almost have replaced his mother in ordinary society. His dark complexion, black hair, and slanted eyes, however, gave him an Arabic-Hindu aspect that would encourage him, in a decade marked by the *Thousand and One Nights* translated by J. C. Mardrus, Sergei Diaghilev's *Scheherazade,* and Paul Poiret's Persian dances, to imagine that he came from elsewhere. Could a genius like his have been born in a simple family of stockbrokers? Georges Cocteau, as his cousin Marianne said, loved him as a father. His authority was so weak and his physical traits so French, however, that the young Jean imagined himself as instead the forgotten child of some oriental diplomat linked to his maternal Uncle Raymond, the embassy councilor.[22] When musing about his origins, he would talk not only about a socialite archeologist leading a dig in Persia, but also about a prince of that country—putting the finishing touches on his transformation in the aura of the Orient.[23] Might a stork from the land of Scheherazade or Harun Al-Rashid have deposited him in the privet hedges of Maisons-Lafitte?

Cocteau's tendency toward mythomania flourished. The creative mechanism that pushed him later to reinvent the figures of his life encouraged him to make himself into an uncommon being, temporarily realized in the body of a Parisian but capable of taking on a thousand different aspects. He found it difficult to draw borders between the world and himself, instead oscillating between the intoxicating idols he took for himself—pinning them to his teenage bedroom walls—and the image that he made of his own being. Fascinated by the brutal casualness of Dargelos, a student from Condorcet whose knees were always scraped under his velour breeches, he clung to him in his imagination, as if to absorb his *mana* and mythologize him in a process Cocteau likened to one undertaken by a "larva greedy for love." Flying from one hero to the other, trembling here and attaching himself there, like a string capable of undoing its outline, he came to lose all center and all consistency—until the yo-yo felt the need to snap back to its anchorage. "There is nothing but my love for you that ties me to anything real," he would say to his mother. "Everything else seems like a bad dream to me."[24]

At the end of the string was his mother, the ultimate reality of that *luftmensch* who dreamed of someday becoming a creature of the clouds—even though his mother feared she hadn't entirely finished him. When financial dependence was added to the emotional bond, the couple took on a truly conjugal air. When he confided his sadness to his mother, she became sad; to spare her, he learned to keep silent and became even more melancholic, though ultimately unable to prevent himself from talking to her about it; and this continued to such an extent, and so eloquently, that they would sink into an emotive spiral from which they would emerge only by an excess of shared love, with the disturbing conviction of having become one being with two heads. Is there a "household gentler or more cruel, prouder of itself, than that couple of a son and a young mother?" Cocteau would ask in *La machine infernale*; scarcely was there one so complicit, or so stifling.[25]

Not a word, not a regret, not even an allusion would recall—throughout their entire, abundant correspondence—the memory of the suicide. Did mother and son secretly take advantage of the father's disappearance? Never cited, Georges Cocteau seems more like a man vanished *ad vitam aeternam* than like a dead man—an absence perpetuated in the beyond. To judge from the omnipresence of the figure of Oedipus in his oeuvre and the recurrence of paternal ghosts in his theater, Cocteau seems to have paid for this oblivion by a secret guilt: as if he secretly held himself responsible for a disappearance that had opened up the favors of his mother exclusively to him.

Cocteau hated school and (most of all) punishment. At school he was a dunce except for gym, German, and drawing—with drawing being the subject that catered to his "almost magical sense for imitation."[26] School officials in 1903 reported about the young Cocteau: "He has a liveliness of mind; some ability to develop his ideas, some taste; but much irregularity, fantasy, and sometimes nervousness in work."[27] He charmed his teachers by his insolence, but intimidated them as well by his impromptu alexandrines. Some students read his verses aloud or proudly exhibited his caricatures. Others had little patience for his behavior as a lazy young genius, always impatient to get back to the skating rink, which he cut with figure-eights and where—his head thrown backward—he spun until he no longer felt his weight and instead mingled, intoxicated, with the stars.

His talent for drawing was so great that he could already copy the style of Sem and Cappiello, the two caricaturists of the Belle Époque, when he sketched, on the spot, guests at Maisons-Laffitte. Ten years later, Jacques-Émile Blanche would watch him outline a canvas with an almost oppressive ease; and in the 1930s, Jean Hugo watched him spend hours distorting turn-of-the-century illustrations copied from journals. If he devoted himself to drawing, the gift for the piano that his mother had imparted to him was just as striking, even if he was already looking for other forms able to express his monstrously expansive artistic sensibility. The flame that burned inside him and kept him from

sleeping also made his temples throb if he had to appear in public and gave him
the impression of slipping into freefall when he failed to please.

Cocteau's best friend, René Rocher, dreamed of directing a theater. Together,
they gathered a jumble of papers, paste, tin sheets, metal cans, rags, and ink in
the courtyard on the rue La Bruyère or at Rocher's house on rue Taitbout. The
sets were created in part from boxes emblazoned with Old England, where
Cocteau's clothes had been bought; from bits of boards were born miniature
pieces of furniture that they assembled and nailed together; and Joséphine
sewed costumes from patterns that Cocteau had sketched and then cut from
leftover rags. On this puppet theater that included a prompter's box and footlights made of candles, the schoolboys produced not only "pretentious" texts
outlined by Cocteau—little "grandiloquent" dramas—but also boulevard
plays.[28] Starting at the age of five, he wrote these plays in verse, featuring Nero
and Alexander as the tragic heroes.[29]

The painter his father dreamed of being, the musicians his grandfather
Lecomte hosted, the prima donnas whom the family applauded in the evenings,
the writers—friends of his mother's—whose books he devoured: Cocteau had
to become all of those things to take his place next to that joyful widow. And
within a family that excluded no artistic discipline whatever, perhaps it was not
too difficult to believe he could become anything. By turning his hand to the
cinema thirty years later to create a masterpiece at his first try, Cocteau would
prove that he didn't need to see a director holding a movie camera to film on his
own. His mimetic gifts were no doubt unique, but they were borne by an equal
ability to invent.

At the age of twelve, Cocteau was already dying of pride and suffering from
a need for recognition that he himself would call unhealthy.[30] His pianist's
fingers, often lashed by the red pencil of the mean, thin woman who made him
practice his scales; his long, girlish eyelashes; and his delicious poetic babbling
made his mother's friends swoon. All of them would have liked to have a similarly gifted child. But already merely to please others was not enough; he wanted
to confound and enchant, and sometimes dreamed that a lily was growing in his
mouth, symbolizing all his singularity. His gifts seemed truly limitless: at the
age of fifteen, he learned in a week the role of the Vicomte in *Tripleplatte*, a
play by Tristan Bernard, and was applauded onstage by the residents of the
Hôtel de Caux in Switzerland; at sixteen, he completed his first full-length play;
and at eighteen, overcome by a devouring desire to write, he planned a tragedy
on King Midas, who changed everything he touched into gold (though in this
case the subject was so grandiose that it paralyzed him), and was already able to
list his comedies like a seasoned author. Surrounded by his models and his

dress patterns, the young demiurge, an explorer unconstrained by borders, invented beings and drew landscapes, remade the world, and surveyed the universe.

A text conveys this universal hunger in a troubling way. In 1908, while staying in Italy with his mother, Cocteau, suffering a night of insomnia in a stifling hotel, opened the blinds looking out on the Grand Canal in Venice, and felt the

> anguish of peopled solitude, melancholy of never feeling native to the places one likes, revolt of not being many, and of living captive in our narrow strip of space, weariness of going through the normal phases of a tenderness for which we desire immediate reciprocity . . . I remained there, inert, leaning over that motionless river overflowing with lanterns, and mourning the fact that I was not the self-satisfied soloist, the author of the music, and that I was not all the couples on all the gondolas.[31]

Cocteau's entire being was contained in this irrepressible desire to play every role, to be in some way the sensitive soul of the world. He vibrated in such unison with the entire world around him that at the theater he felt responsible for the ridicule of an actor, and even reproached himself for it, as if the very intensity of his projection had been the cause for the disturbance. The almost Proustian amplitude of his empathy made him reachable by everyone, but, by its insane extent, made him also foreign, and ended up plunging him into a world where "no real person exists."[32] Once these cosmic bursts of energy had dissipated, he awoke, having only his solitude to share.

Every gathering inflamed Cocteau's desire to be recognized, applauded, and loved. He sought in every lake of eyes—that same lake where Narcissus, seeking his enigma, ended up drowning—evidence of his incredible vivacity. Did his arrival in Saint Mark's Piazza cause the pigeons to take flight? Was the thunder of applause that he heard meant for him? Just as he could confuse himself with the universe by being too sensitive, he expected in return the earth to conceive a passion for his verses, or his Arab-Hindu features. The excessiveness of his narcissism also ensured its fragility. A single look was enough to instill doubt and to form, in dotted lines, a question mark around his presence. Suddenly fearing he had done too much, he would look for the source of this fear, and instead of defending himself, rush to judge himself. He would then be seized by a desire to go straight up to the most hostile person and say: "Understand me, I harbor nothing of what you think I do. I have only the joy of living and the treasures of affection. I am so naïve that all arrows reach me!"[33]

These oscillations never stopped. While his lack of modesty pulled him up to unbreathable heights, judgment could drag him down to a depression usually concluded by an imaginary trial in which he sought to convince his prosecutors of his universal sensibility and the purity of his intentions. If these prosecutors, struck by the sincerity of his defense, did not become his best friends upon emerging from the courthouse, fear would overtake him again. For Cocteau, who lived to please, only the gaze of the other could give an earthly measure to whatever divine quality he possessed. For him to truly become *Cocteau*, he had to be recognized as such. Sartrean before the term was invented, the young Cocteau was a being-for-others who sought, in others' approbation, existential legitimacy. There would be neither rebellion nor rupture at the origin of his trajectory. Like a rising star, he would first ask the earth to give him flesh, if not to make him authentically "human." His own family was moreover too artistic for him to rebel against it, or even to perceive the limits of it. The only milieu he could dream of was the one where he was born.

As Virginia Woolf's father once said, "We inherit thoughts as we inherit wealth."[34] Cocteau, being so brilliant, was hardly tempted to throw away this mental furniture. The Lecomte-Cocteaus, who pushed back against the Victorian Puritanism that the Bloomsbury circle justly fought, left him a precious legacy: that of a joyful, eclectic, and never-intimidating culture, experienced from within by prominent interpreters who remained his natural audience to the end.

THE MIRROR STAGE

Cocteau "was a very handsome teenager," said Félix Fénéon, the art critic.[35] Women stared at him, but his delicacy also moved men; all sorts of sexual futures could be envisaged for him. "The eye is the lamp of the body," said Matthew the Evangelist, and nothing illumined as much as the gaze of this young, thin, febrile man endlessly looking for the approval of the other. Neither Cocteau's physique nor his nature satisfied him, however. "His own beauty displeased him," he would say of Jacques Forestier, the hero of *Le grand écart*, in an opinion that seemed to sum up his feelings about himself. "He found it ugly." Unlike Butades, who outlined the profile of his daughter's fiancé that the sun projected on a wall, thus inventing painting, Cocteau's foundational act would be to correct his own profile as it appeared to others. In all mirrors he sought to retouch his features; he urged all photographers to improve his face, and thus his idea of himself. Lenses and screens would end up forming a visual echo chamber around Cocteau's otherwise shapeless self, which was so prompt to reflect whatever struck it. Since mirrors were content to "reflect" him, instead of thinking about him, he found that by viewing himself he was thrown back to this mysterious *I*—which their mirroring surfaces reproduced ad infinitum—until his flesh, eyelashes, and bones trembled like water.

Anxious to solve his enigma, Cocteau held it out to those close to him. Their gazes on him formed a gallery that he tried, by moving in every direction, to view in a 360-degree panorama, though only the eyes of a fly could embrace it all at once; there always remained that blind spot that limits and protects every personality. It would become impossible for Cocteau to forget himself or leave himself: he heard himself speak and breathe, watched himself draw, run, or love, all with an unsettling precision—his erotic drawings prove it—as if he could create an alter ego that would observe himself clearly.

Did Cocteau's idea of himself stem from the unfathomable sum of all the Cocteaus that he sensed existed within himself? To find out, he again questioned the first person who came along, in the hope of capturing that initial gaze, usually so correct. If that other person was handsome, Cocteau was immediately galvanized as if struck by lightning. Gender didn't matter, at the beginning—as with Wilde's "supernatural sex of beauty," the only thing that made a difference was aesthetic power, which established the one who was being viewed as a model and thus as an object of desire. It was almost the same thing for Cocteau; the beauty of the other made Cocteau strong, thus stable; the mirrors in which he, the other, contemplated himself were petrified perfections, not agitated seas; he simply *was*, in an intransitive sense. Cocteau recognized that already as a child, "at that age when sex doesn't yet influence the decisions of the flesh," his most ardent desire was less to embrace than to *become* the chosen person. "I imitated her tic," he said of the little Marthe, by "shifting a lock of hair from right to left and shrugging my shoulders."[36] Did he secretly hope, by slipping into that envied body, that he could start over with a happier life? When these tics ended up taking him over, a doctor advised his mother to give him cold showers.[37]

Cocteau would go on to multiply his identification-loves. Trying to better himself through co-option, he tried to project himself onto the other, to love him and raise him in esteem, by deciding that the other was handsomer, stronger, or more virile than he. "This Narcissus is unable to love himself," wrote Jacques Brosse. "He needs the other, who is his image in the mirror, but a magnified image, the image of what he would like to be but is aware he is not."[38] By encompassing and cannibalizing the other, Cocteau, starving, would pillage in order to shine. He would always worry about himself, always confuse being and having, in his impatience to *become*. Some writers like Hugo or Tolstoy could infiltrate another's soul and gain power by making themselves into a farmer or a drunkard; the nature of the young Cocteau instead pushed him to besiege uncommon personalities in order to devour their nectar and ensure his own growth.

Expelled from the Lycée Condorcet around Easter 1904 because of repeated absences, Cocteau finished the school year by means of private lessons given at home. As soon as the fine weather arrived, though, he spent his time looking out for the emergence of the mule-driven hansom cab of the great Réjane from the Théâtre du Vaudeville on the boulevard des Italiens, or running after the carriages of the idols from the Théâtre Français. When he couldn't get a free spot in the top balcony during dress rehearsals, he would go to the Eldorado, a hall on the boulevard de Strasbourg, where he'd take an upper box with his friends René Rocher and Carlito Boulant (who pretended he was the actor Coquelin, reeling off monologues from *Cyrano*). They had access to the box because the son of the world-famous actress and singer Mistinguett was their classmate at Condorcet. In her performances, "fist on her hip, sombrero cocked, a Spanish shawl draped around her skirt," Mistinguett would intoxicate the students with her cheeky humor.[39] Cocteau was the first to praise this master-piece of effrontery as she sat on the prompter's box, spreading her thighs with the assurance of a harlot to crudely express her passion for pleasure, before leaving in a cascade of laughter toward a stairway of swooning boys.

Cocteau, Rocher, and Boulant regularly drew lots for who would stand up to the Cerberus guarding the wings, in order to slip past and shower the singer with violets. As much as the brazen street singer, for whom Arletty would be the ultimate epitome, Cocteau approved of this muse of a city—for Mistinguett would be given many nicknames, from "Lady Paname" to "Pantruche," all of which described her incarnation of a distinctly Parisian myth that New York had not yet supplanted. Indeed, Cocteau once confessed that the voice of Mistinguett could exalt his Parisian patriotism to the point of tears.

"La Miss" would usually end up receiving the boys in a wrapped, flowered peignoir, then would do them the honor of giving them "bicycles," a makeup design that consisted of "drawing the blue spokes of a wheel, as if they were the shadows cast by eyelashes."[40] "I don't know if my singing—*Je suis la femme-torpille, pille* . . . —seduced them," Mistinguett wrote in her *Memoirs*, "but they were very nice. At night, I'd find myself with them . . . at the Eldo café . . . We were happy to be together and we didn't imagine ourselves the center of the world."[41]

Did La Miss, at the age of thirty-five, want to grow young again by frater-nizing with her very young fans, or does this "we" convey an intimacy that Cocteau preferred, unusually, to conceal? The singer, who took good care of her legend, would always boast that she stole his virginity, and Steegmuller adds: "She caused him undisguised pleasure every time she repeated this story, which he never confirmed."[42] The Parisian diva with the legendary appetite, who to the very end loved to surround herself with gigolos and "boys," might have wanted to devour the Adonis who ironically saw her grow younger with time. But did Cocteau have the fortitude to meet her painted mouth and her "silken legs"? Whatever the case, Mistinguett was the first star whose audacity, energy, and huge ego Cocteau venerated. Proust knew what he was talking about when he denounced, in *La Bible d'Amiens*, the idolatry that leads one to aestheticize real life by enriching it with successive layers of artistic references: Cocteau did not hesitate to elevate this laughing chorus girl to the status of a superstar, that is, into an untouchable, self-sufficient entity in the heart of that Parisian heaven where he already dreamed of appearing.

Cocteau's precocious passion for the singer would have consequences, however. The top-billed performer on the Eldorado program where La Miss sang, Jeanne Reynette, impressed him with her sex appeal, her natural style, and the humor with which she sang her wrong notes, or presented herself as the dunce of the scene. "She carried a slim cane, wore a billowing short skirt, socks, and her knees were less noble than, but just as battered as, those of Dargelos," he said. The dazzled schoolboy would wait for her at the artists' exit, take her to the Taverne Pschorr, and write to her constantly. Older than the teenager, the music-hall actress tried to reason with him but, seeing him falling in love, ended up offering herself to him. "If you only knew how much I love you and how happy I was yesterday in your arms to feel you there, in me. I had been yearning for that moment for so long," she wrote to him.[43] The liaison would make him fail his *bac*.

Cocteau had his first sexual experience, however, neither with Mistinguett nor with Jeanne Reynette, but with Albert Botten, a jockey from Maisons-Laffitte whom he met in the paddock while disguised as a stable boy, bucket and sponge in hand—or at least so he would assert later. This tryst with the famous jockey, in honor of whom Cocteau would write one more text not long before he died (on the occasion of the gala for the races at Deauville), even elicited a warning from Mme Cocteau about preserving the social honor of her family, though she seems not to have known about the exact nature of their relationship.[44]

Cocteau remained discreet about this episode for a long time, as he did about so many others implicating his homosexuality, but he seems to have been happy with his sexual preferences throughout his growing-up years. Already as a young man he flaunted himself in the sulfurous entourage of De Max, an actor whom he met through his friend Rocher, who at the time was studying comic routines with De Max. Mannered and declamatory on stage, made-up and bejeweled around town—invariably in pearl gray, from the powder on his cheeks to the tips of his polished boots—De Max was known for his legendary performances and his brilliant wordplay, his genius for improvisation and his inimitable Romanian accent. This colossus whose telluric ego flourished in the role of Oedipus and who was carried on an illuminated curule seat in Aeschylus's *The Persians*, straightaway dedicated one of his photographs to his precocious admirer—"To your sixteen years in bloom, my forty years in gloom"—linking their extreme narcissisms, then and forever.

The young Cocteau began to read his verses to the actor, whose taste for poetry was well-known, in De Max's apartment on the rue Caumartin. De Max was dazzled by Cocteau's quatrains, which evoked, in a disturbing coincidence, pomp worthy of the excess in which he himself received visitors: lying on his grand bed, a ring on each finger, he would keep his arm plunged into a saucer of gold pieces that he would then distribute to initiates with the royal abundance of a decadent Roman. A "fat Siamese cat curled up in the half-light amongst dirty cushions," De Max was soon convinced that Cocteau was a budding genius, and even the precious and delicate heir of Edmond Rostand, the idol of a triumphant Third Republic.[45] Not content with keeping his door open for Cocteau at all hours, De Max lauded his poems everywhere, until his praise became a kind of vocal refrain in the halls of the Odéon, between his performances as the Buddha or Timon of Athens. Other mothers would have fretted to see their sons rushing to that "diva" whom they had seen running around on all fours as a sacred bull in *Nebuchadnezzar* and to whom a procession of ephebes continually came to pay homage. Confident of the "propriety" of her son, however—or too naïve to imagine him as a sexual being yet, since at seventeen he had declared that he thought only of "returning to the cradle" during vacations—Mme Cocteau allowed him the freedom to share his verses with this strange protector.

De Max enjoyed an enviable position, it is true. Phenomenal in Paris, where every night he went out in his pearl-gray car (which he called his "electric") to show off his persona to the crowd in the Bois de Boulogne, his popularity turned into idolatry in the provinces, where ignorance meant that homosexuality was less of a problem—many people thought it simply didn't exist. The imposing pomp with which he moved about was so impressive, like the zealous applause that greeted each of his monologues, that he could strut about in platform shoes or have his hair plucked from ears to ankles by a barber from Béziers (in order the better to present the role of Prometheus, semi-nude, in the heart of ancient arenas), without provoking any sanction other than an increase in requests for his autograph. Used to the excesses of Sarah Bernhardt, the public even came to snatch up De Max's hairs when the barber put them on sale after that imperial exfoliation.

Electrified by his popularity, the young Cocteau would often return to honor this idol capable of wearing on stage gold tiaras weighing six kilos and laden with steeples and minarets—tiaras that he removed in private so that he could bend nonchalantly over his opium apparatus while keeping one ear free for Cocteau's compliments. Dressed as Elagabalus, eyelashes darkened with mascara, the novice would flaunt himself in the perfumed wake of the actor, who himself would be helmeted with an eagle and veiled like a geisha at a Théâtre des Arts ball. The audience in the hall would burst out laughing when it saw Cocteau appear on a litter carried by Maurice Rostand, André Germain (the son of Le Credit Lyonnais's founder), and two black wrestlers, then stand up to wave his toe-rings and his painted nails like a Thai dancer beneath a tiara overflowing with red curls and followed by a pearl-embroidered train.[46] "If I were your mother, I would pack you off to bed," Sarah Bernhardt once said to him through her attendant, but no one must have had the courage to warn Mme Cocteau, since no punishment ensued.[47] No doubt that bearded eunuch was no threat whatsoever to the unusual complicity uniting her to her son. He could even be useful, since there was more than a gap, in her eyes, between the sensitive, smooth-faced, amateur painter capable of "doing anything" artistically, as her husband was, and a member of the Académie Française. That is, Mme Cocteau still doubted her son's talents, as well as his ability to showcase them.

Fate willed it that the press, during that same year of 1906, brutally brought to light the habits of Mme Cocteau's brother Raymond, the then leader of the Lecomte family. First secretary in the French Embassy in Berlin, where he had risen in the ranks due to his charm and his paradoxical, ironic wit, Raymond was publicly accused of having had licentious relationships with Prince Eulenburg, the favorite of Wilhelm II, emperor of Germany. Both had formed, with the heirs of the upper aristocracy of across the Rhine, a kind of Byzantine coterie with unnatural habits, a secret, sodomite knighthood—their own Round Table of men drunk on music, spiritualism, and "socialite mysticism."

Since the prince passed for a Francophile and a pacifist, and his supposed lover, Helmuth von Moltke, was the governor of Berlin, the nationalist German press accused Mme Cocteau's brother of having transmitted state secrets to France, which was known to be anxious to recover Alsace and Lorraine. Raymond Lecomte avoided a humiliating appearance before the German courts but not his recall from office. It was a time when a hunt for homosexuals was inflaming the Empire, and when forced "outings" were commonplace, including of the founder of one of the first homosexual associations, Magnus

Hirschfeld. The first hints of the Dreyfus Affair emerged during Oscar Wilde's trial; the ensuing drama was followed with passion, by Proust first of all, and led to the fall of the prince, a cascade of resignations for supposed homosexuality, a redoubled hostility toward male homosexuality in Germany, and Gaulish jokes at the expense of the "Eulenbuggers." It also resulted in the gradual reversal of Prussian foreign policy, which was already taking shape after the crisis of Tangier, a shift that would culminate in the First World War.

Assigned to Egypt and then to Persia, but destroyed by the scandal and his secret, Raymond Lecomte killed himself fifteen years later, in the home of his sister and of his nephew Jean Cocteau. About the whole affair, Cocteau remembered only "the hidden newspapers and the conversations that stopped as soon as I entered the room"; the subject was as explosive as his father's suicide. This repression may well have provoked in Cocteau, a born storyteller, a Germanic and pederastic fantasy that bloomed, not long before the Second World War, in a play entitled, with a certain logic, *Les chevaliers de la table ronde*. "After his death, my mother found some sealed packets that were thrown into the fire on her orders. On my uncle's side, nothing remains, alas!, that can shed light on the enigma of a tragedy from which Freud and many other profound things might have arisen," he wrote, without any other explanation.[48] To bury compromising secrets—that was the practice of a tribe that Cocteau would never go against, he who had indirectly chosen that uncle as father-substitute but spoke of him only to display his snobbery when Paul Morand, the writer-diplomat, described him as "one of the old aunties at the Quai d'Orsay."[49]

THE CALL OF THE DUNCE

With Marthe married and Paul, the new head of the family, having left to set himself up as a stockbroker, Mme Cocteau had only her son Jean left on the rue La Bruyère. Having once again failed at the summer exam for the *bac*, Jean was sent to Val-André, a Breton seaside resort, to the home of M. Dietz, a teacher at the Lycée Buffon who gave remedial courses to students who had failed so they could retake the exam in October. He "surprised us by the contrast between his Protestantism and his odalisque poses," wrote Cocteau. "He would stretch himself out, slither about, knot himself up and unknot himself, sending an arm here, a leg there."[50] This odd pedagogue, who had enthralled André Gide at the École Alsacienne twenty years earlier, did not succeed at awakening the spirit of competition in Cocteau the student, who was less concerned with reviewing his classics than with playing tennis, paddling about in the sea, working on his first poems, or sketching out his theatrical work.

Frustrated by having to deal with those around him, the dunce complained to his mother in writing; bombarded his Parisian friends with letters and verses, demanding responses; and even learned to form some connections with students whom he didn't find very interesting. His family feared the effects of his weakness; he was already struggling against the image that people had of him. "Never fear, there is beneath my seeming frivolity something great and profound, which I have wanted to mask," he wrote to his mother the next year, before insisting, as he would so often have to do: "People are very mistaken about me. How do they think I'm cheerfulness personified when I'm a filthy mill of darkness? I am constantly thinking—and observing even more."[51] Unable to bear any more, the little prodigy ended up asking his mother, "as a friend," not to talk about the *bac* anymore, a subject that obsessed him as well but did not interest him.

For the time being, every day he would set himself up next to a bottle of cider, sketch Prof. Hermann Dietz as a crow, and learn the basics of palmistry— his first step toward other occult practices—at least when he wasn't being pelted with pebbles by a teacher enraged by his caricatures. On December 30, 1906, the students performed his *Sisowath en balade*, a farce showing the King of Cambodia fleeing the Bastille Day festivities and the élysée of President Fallières in order to mix with the riff-raff on the Rive Gauche: this would be not only Cocteau's first text performed, but also the first role for Pierre Laudenbach, Hermann Dietz's own grandson, whom films (such as *Grand Illusion*) he would make famous under the name of Pierre Fresnay. On this occasion, Cocteau became a human-object "embodiment" onstage, first by placing a lantern on his belly, then by portraying one of the metal caissons that had just been used in digging the Metro tunnel beneath the Seine, and finally by representing the Les Halles-Porte d'Ivry tram. In doing so, he showed his taste for cliché and burlesque metamorphosis, a favorite theme that would reappear later in his avant-garde self-transformations.

These festivities led to another failure at the *bac*, followed by a deferment from military service because of fragile health. Unsuited to any discipline, the hypersensitive trifler decided to abandon studies for which his intelligence seemed to harm him more than anything else. Instinctively he rejected the divided life endured by wage-earners, the submission demanded in working for others, the cult of utility commanded by the market. Endowed with a nature that could only, like clay, take the forms his hand gave it, he knew he was destined to be, not to make or to have. No doubt he would financially have been able to defer his entrance into "adult" life, but he also sensed the dangers of the dilettantism practiced by his family; already he was showing himself to be anxious to overcome his privileges.

His mother, who willingly read his first writings, thought them encouraging. But she also knew, having observed it in her husband, that talent is far from being enough to succeed. By the end of his vague studies, Cocteau had absorbed only Baudelaire and Verlaine, and read only Victor Hugo and Maurice Rollinat—author of *Les névroses* and a Satanic, macabre, Baudelairean poet who was very influential in the symbolist-decadent sphere. Despite his obvious lack of preparation, Cocteau had made up his mind to devote himself entirely to writing.

His calling seemed obvious. He felt such a joy in polishing his rhymes, those mirroring pools of ink where his slightest, most intimate ripples were reflected— his brain seemed to follow his hand, and his hand, his pen. He saw in these writings the best way to discover himself, even to perpetuate the child that elves and satyrs evoked. "Recently again I hesitated about the way to follow," he wrote at the age of eighteen to his mother, "but the peremptory decision of talent and genius has pushed me once and for all toward the ideal that I am forging for myself."[52] The Mallarméan phrase expresses his steadfast determination to write, even if a doubt about the exact nature of his inspiration persists.

His first verses bear witness to an anguished brio, turning quickly to melancholy, and to an appetite for happiness spoiled by constant pangs of the heart. Already at this age he revealed a tendency to idealize the past, his strong fear of death, and the sadness that he fought by working too much. The son of a man who never found his place on earth, or even any reason to live with his wife and son, Cocteau elaborated a system of reminiscences where "every destroyed memory" is a "little death," and where everything is thus potentially able to be saved in an opus that served as a poetic double of life.[53]

Nevertheless, Cocteau's so obviously literary nature threw him into a panic. Clumsy with gravity yet annoyed by his lack of gravitas, he evokes one of those *Luftphantoms* of which Goethe writes. Light as air, undulant as water, deprived of roots and soil, he knew he was made to fly or clear the way, more than to return to earth. The connections he had to the practical world were distant, if not fantastic: he could neither hammer a nail nor make an omelette, never learned how to drive a car or fill out a tax form. This ignorance was encouraged by his privilege surely, but also by a secret desire to escape the laws of everyday life and even the laws of earthly gravity, like Kant's dove that, tired of flying, dreamed of the atmosphere being abolished.

His creative desire, however, was not born of a hope to retreat from the world, or even from the need to find a hidden meaning in the world, but rather from the wish to subjugate it. Preternaturally receptive to signs, colors, and waves, the young Cocteau wrote in order to discharge his energy; he reacted to invasion by expulsion, and responded to visitors with each one's own message, filtered by experience, in the hope of doubly pleasing them. Anxious to build himself an ideal world of which he would be the spinning center, he filled reality with fantastic figures, like the forests of the Middle Ages, in order to dazzle or intoxicate. He believed in table-turning, in the power of the spirits, as well as in forces capable of stopping the waves halfway up the shore; he feared comets, meteors, and the peopled worlds that flourished on the outskirts of our own. Born into an intellectual climate that was still fin-de-siècle, he clung to any kind of irrational explanation, poetry not the least of them.

In 1907, at the age of fifty-two, Mme Cocteau settled near the Trocadéro, on the avenue Raymond-Poincaré—then the avenue Malakoff—with her son and Cyprien, a valet with an emperor's profile who still worked as a gardener at the Maisons-Laffitte. On Wednesdays—that was her "day"—she received with her last-born the Daudets, the Princesse Murat, or the Paleologues, those trendsetters for society and literary Paris. And she was still accompanied by her son when, ornamented with aigrettes and mousseline, she answered invitations by the Barronne de Pierrebourg, a maker of academicians on the avenue du Bois, where Cocteau, leaning on the mantelpiece, read his poems, or those of the Duchesse de Rohan, whose verses made Proust laugh so.

Lucien Daudet would be the first to recognize Cocteau's talent. Eleven years older than Cocteau, Daudet, the son of the author of *Letters from My Windmill*, was himself a good enough poet to sway the opinion of a scene whose workings he had mastered perfectly. A "handsome boy, curled, laundered, pomaded, painted and powdered" (in the words of Jules Renard, the marvelous diarist who also mentions his "little waistcoat-pocket voice"), Lucien Daudet cultivated the exquisite and the precious in his language, which was nourished by "perishing" boredom and people "to damn yourself for."[54] Proust passionately sought out Daudet's physical delicacy, his large brown eyes and his long eyelashes, and always cherished his sense of the absurd and his gifts as a mimic of society—not to mention that exaggerated but critical snobbery that caused them countless nighttime fits of laughter, as reckless and exhausting as the passion they replaced. This heir who flatters himself to love physically working-class boys, and whose handsome Adonis mask would so strike Paul Morand ten years later, did not think himself worthy of writing, however.[55] Without artistic ambition or vanity, despite a sensibility worthy of his new protégé's, Daudet the younger was content with a place as dilettante in the shadow of his father's lasting fame. Trained in the studio of Whistler, master of the London fog, he preferred to paint for himself—a wonderful portrait of Count Robert de Montesquiou testifies to this—and for the rest scattered his gifts with a princely hand.

No doubt Daudet felt stifled by the fame of his late father, as well as by the volcanic temperament of his elder brother, Léon, the famous polemicist of *L'action française,* who was cordially detested. But his dilettantism was also the neurotic fruit of pretensions to a title that would have led him to give away his father's entire opus in order to be called the Prince d'Audet. Eaten away by a formidable "irreality" principle, as well as by an "added taste for earthly owner-ship," which Proust in his usual affectionate perversity would speak of after having loved him in vain, Lucien Daudet was content to hold the flattering parasol of the Empress Eugénie, then eighty-six years old—a delicious, superan-nuated dream mother whose slightest gestures he described to his real mother. Greedy for affairs whose characters were for the most part titled, like Proust's characters, he embellished the life of Napoleon III's widow so well, by the gossip he spread between her English castle and her estate in Cap-Martin, that Eugénie and he came to believe they were the heroes of an imaginary empire of which Lucien would have been at once the great chamberlain and the histo-rian, the page boy and the historiographer, a quarter of a century after the fall of the real empire, in 1870—with the empress herself readily believing herself a reincarnation of Marie-Antoinette, with whom she sometimes entered into contact during séances.

Lucien Daudet, this sterile double, was generous enough to give Cocteau the self-confidence that he personally lacked. The salon that his mother held on rue de Bellechasse, in the heart of the new faubourg Saint-Germain, where family portraits signed by Pierre-August Renoir, Eugène Carrière, or Albert Besnard were gathering dust after the great man's death, was frozen in its sickly sweet smell of lavender. But the name of Daudet, the shimmer of Alphonse Daudet's *Tartarin of Tarascon* and of *Little Good-for-Nothing,* still attracted the cream of the literary establishment, from whom the young Cocteau won almost immediate recognition. Impatient to become a character as much as a writer— it was almost the same thing, with the help of the salons—Cocteau walked in the footsteps of his friend Lucien, taking on his post-Balzacian dandyish airs and his habit of punctuating his phrases by holding up his index finger, like Da Vinci's Saint John the Baptist—a gesture that Lucien Daudet himself had copied from Montesquiou.

The closeness of the two men, which was soon obvious, worried Mme Cocteau no more than it did Mme Daudet, whose liberalism seemed to have been unfailing—society connections obviously carrying the day over fear of gossip. Cocteau, welcomed as a chosen brother by Lucien, who could never bear seeing him laugh at the jokes of his evil brother Léon, found an extra family on rue de Bellechasse. The long list of salons to which Lucien introduced him would be too tedious to compile, and the names of their hostesses too many to remember: since the end of the ancien régime, that paradise of conversationalists, Paris had never known so many "committees of wit," from the mansion in the Parc Monceau where the Proustian Mme Lemaire attracted the Bohemian upper crust, to the fine home where Marie Scheikevitch gathered together fine cultivated souls, including the literary pests that Mme Le Chevrel was mad about. They adored carnival disguises and chamber concerts, parlor games, charades, and word games, which Cocteau would make into the springboards for his fantasies—like his story about children who expect the girl "flitting about" in a palace to actually fly away. No one more than Cocteau could better captivate these regulars whose intelligence "had not emerged beyond the niceties of conversation," as Proust would say of Charlus, the unforgettable character of *La recherche*, partly inspired by Montesquiou.

Lucien would also introduce Cocteau to Reynaldo Hahn, the musician and pianist whom Proust had passionately loved before him.[56] Hahn, a Venezuelan, had begun his slow career by singing in the salons of Princesse Mathilde, Napoleon III's cousin, starting at the age of six. His exquisite voice made the dark cruelty of his face that much more surprising.[57] Supple, sinuous, and nostalgic, his phrases on the piano snaked around verses by Leconte de Lisle or François Coppée. When Hahn sang, from lines by Verlaine,

> You believe in coffee grounds
> In omens
> In the Major Arcana
> I believe only in your big eyes.
> You believe in fairytales
> In dies nefasti
> In dreams
> I believe only in your lies

the ladies would pine—in vain—for him, and the men would soften at the inflections of this light baritone voice brimming over with delicacy. Anyone who wants to glimpse, beyond the obstacle of time, the nuances felt by the young Cocteau, has only to listen to these melodies with their diaphanous, almost chlorotic, vibrato that wavers between *lied* and canticle. The velvety voice of this disciple of Massenet evoked the whiff of a memory, and so perpetuated the declining dreams of symbolism, the literary trend extinguished around 1895 that, after Baudelaire's *L'art romantique*, claimed for itself "an irritated melancholy, a representation of nerves, of a nature exiled in the imperfect that wants to take hold immediately, on this very earth, of a paradise revealed."[58]

Having set its mark on the generation before Cocteau's, symbolism expressed a form of inner dissidence confronting the narrow-minded materialism and utilitarian obsession of the industrial revolution, and hence a reaction to triumphant naturalism, in literature at least. Nourished by medieval, Renaissance, and Romantic art, symbolism, probably the last great backward-looking movement hatched in the West, had given rise to a desire to explore the secrets of the world and the confines of the soul. Beyond its androgynous Mercuries, its pale Narcissuses, and its Orpheuses borne by rosaries of angels, it gave rise to a whole misty alchemy wherein some found their way into esotericism and even into the religious, since the Universe was only the symbol of another world into which entrance was gained not only through poetry, spiritualism, dreams, and the Ideal, but also via the play of analogies and the study of ciphers. These 1890 values were still permeating the Proust-Hahn-Daudet trio. Unlike the scientific bourgeoisie, who were so proud of having pierced all the mysteries, these three had leaped headlong into the occult, according to which a sacred breath animated every being, every tree, every stamen—and ancient myths remained news of the day: Proust could thus recognize masked divinities in the duchesses on the Faubourg; echoes of the muse Euterpe in Mme Straus's pianists; and remote heirs of the superb Hercules in the strong workers whom he passed at dawn in the markets of Les Halles.

The music of Hahn, that "midnight Sun," suited so well the nocturnal tempo of Proust's destiny that the writer became infatuated with him, excessively so as always. When the voice of the musician, a Judeo-Catholic like Proust, murmured softly, making his piano into a harp, Proust, his heart melting, wrote: "Your soul is a lake of love whose swans are my desires." Hahn's successes had become larger than Proust's own; Hahn was the creator whom Proust could not become, the exquisite expression of a cast that Proust had not yet pounded in his own mortar. Reynaldo Hahn's art pales today in the shadow of Proust's mountain; back then, though, this height of melodic delicacy was the star that guided Proust, the god he had made the kingpin in *Jean Santeuil*—that unfortunate sketch for *À la recherche du temps perdu*. If Hahn had not been the first to awaken the untiring energy that Proust could pour into unhappy passions, at least he was his greatest love.

After years of sad passion, Proust ended up shifting his overabundant feelings onto Lucien Daudet, a beauty just as haughty who also answered to the definition given by the legendary Sâr Péladan to visitors of the sixth Rosicrucian salon of 1897: "The men you see here are heroes, hierophants, demi-gods, the women are fairies, princesses, saints . . . They do nothing servilely or lowly."[59] Daudet too had soon fled that love of Proust's, which verged first on veneration and then on asphyxia, but he remained attached enough to those values to see in the young Cocteau their late-arrived heir. Along with Hahn, Daudet decided to support Cocteau's ambitious efforts to dominate the social scene, which he was already pursuing with a surprising level of confidence.

THE FEMINA MATINÉE

On April 4, 1908, De Max organized and financed a matinee in honor of Jean Cocteau, that still minor poet. Aided by the savoir-faire of Lucien Daudet and Reynaldo Hahn, the phenomenal popularity of the actor led to a full house at the Théâtre Femina, on the Champs-Élysées. Combing his gray hair before screwing in a glass eye beneath his monocle, the symbolist poet Laurent Tailhade walked onto the stage to read a flattering lecture that demolished most living poets and left standing only that sober, elegant, precise, eurythmic young prodigy who was, "in a word, French"—and whom he compared to that hero in the *Thousand and One Nights* who discovers heaps of fairy jewelry, then turns back only to find the cave's entrance blocked by a stone. Cocteau, just eighteen, heard himself praised for his bitter conceits and the teenage pessimism that made him, in the eyes of the old determined anarchist, a new Rimbaud.[60] The most famous tragedians from the Comédie-Française and two of the greatest voices from the Opéra then took over to read poems that the prodigy, a year later, would print in *La lampe d'Aladin*. De Max himself appeared on stage to support his young protégé who was witnessing, transfixed, his own consecration and who, when pushed onto the platform, was copiously applauded. As Roger Martin du Gard would later write about his novelistic double, who inspired *Devenir*, Cocteau felt "carried away on the wings of glory . . . so young, so slender, so touching, with his eyes shining with tears."[61]

A virtual crown had just been placed on the head of the new prince of official poetry, and the ecstasy Cocteau felt next came from two sources. First his readers were demonstrating their enthusiasm—a rare experience for a writer— just nine months after his second failure at the *bac*. And second, his family eased up on him. Indeed the family's relief was immense; Mme Cocteau stopped fearing she had produced a son as weak and apathetic as the amateur painter who had willfully disappeared from her life.[62] The Cocteau-Lecomte family, so full of dilettantes with irons in many fires, "judged people by their success," he said later, acknowledging that this was also the case with him: that is, if prominent actresses read his verses and connoisseurs acclaimed him as a diva at La Scala, he knew he had a future.[63] In Cocteau's family, origins mattered as a criterion for excellence: one was born a musician as one was born a duke. At the Théâtre Femina, Jean Cocteau had just proven that he had been born a poet.

Invited to take part in the Salon des Poètes, published in *Je sais tout*, the debutant saw doors opening by the dozens, by doddering academicians to Freemasons. The Duchesse de Rohan, at whose house lectures were given on the art of carrying a cane, was already squabbling over him with Mme de Loynes, an ex-mistress of Prince Napoleon who had gone over to the Action Française and whose Royalist campaigns she financed. A prodigious period opened up for Cocteau, who took advantage of it to make a conquest of anyone who had a name in Paris and who offered him a public status worthy of a consecrated academician. All the old glories fascinated him equally, as if their aura would propel him into that Olympus of poets, actresses, painters, and princesses reigning over Paris.

This was his high-society era, the only one really to deserve the name: like a thoroughbred finally unfettered, the young prodigy made the rounds of the great Parisian houses and lived over and over, amplified, that tremendous minute when an entire auditorium had acclaimed him as the reincarnation of the legendary author of the *Illuminations*. The Théâtre Femina, then the little streets of fin-de-siècle *précieuses*, became the first examples of this anti-world, without weight or density, theatrical and aestheticized, that would always offer him an alternative to the real world. While some of his comrades were still playing in the schoolyard of the *lycée*, he had moved immediately from motherly love to the astonished gratitude of society, and was beginning his career to bravos that would leave him with a blindingly bright model of what success could look like.

By allowing Cocteau to magically enter adulthood without having to grow up, fame also had the advantage of ensuring the future of his odd family name, which he had sworn he would keep. Like David Copperfield at the start of Dickens's novel, the surge of applause had revealed to the young Cocteau that he could be the hero of his own destiny—the finest role that had ever been assigned. It was a triumph that, while confirming the hopes that De Max had in him, also showed him a sea of approving gazes that, in the future, only the presence of an enthusiastic crowd could bring back to him. That form of love from the multitude would long echo in his memory, and would make him forever addicted to glory and fame as proof of his precocious excellence.

To reward Cocteau for his triumph at the Théâtre Femina, his mother took him on a trip to Italy by rail, in a sleeping car. They paused at Lake Maggiore, admired Juliet's balcony in Verona, then stayed for a while in Venice, capital of the fin-de-siècle religion of beauty, in the company of Jéphine. Proust too had made a pilgrimage there with his mother, eight years earlier. It was the sort of excursion that the privileged classes in Europe liked to carry out at the end of summer: a little "Grand Tour," during which they abandoned London, Vienna, Paris, or Saint Petersburg in order to perfect, through the spectacle of Palladian architecture or Tintoretto's frescoes, the aesthetic essence of their own idleness.

Like Mme Proust, who was for a long time the only person to see genius in her son, Eugénie Lecomte was a good enough musician and reader to feed her own son's insatiable curiosity. Her tolerance for his "predilections," so long as they remained hidden; her related rejection of prudishness and vulgarity; and the openness of her mind—which placed her, if we are to believe her son, far above "all those snobbish, pedantic women who alas form most of society!"[64]— made her an accomplished example of that bourgeois civilization which, despite its moral blinders and already legendary hypocrisy, played a crucial role in turn-of-the-century Parisian culture.

This woman who could attract the friendship of creators as diverse as Erik Satie, Marcel Proust, and Paul Morand was now aware of having brought forth a wunderkind. But she was also authoritarian enough to make her son understand that he deserved her love only if he always behaved well, morally and socially. She knew that during their stay in Venice—a city already described as "against nature" by Chateaubriand—her son, after having met a nephew of Oscar Wilde, had found a young twenty-two-year-old dilettante, Raymond Laurent, who was staying at the Hôtel Europa with his American friend, Langhorn Whistler. But did he tell her about their stroll through the Giardino Eden, a place well-known for masculine encounters, on the island of Giudecca? Or about the frightening amorous embrace that Raymond Laurent forced on him? So many secrets of that nature had already been buried in their family that he must have hesitated to confide in her that the young Laurent, out of despair of not being loved, had shot himself with a revolver just an hour after Cocteau had left him on the steps leading to the church of Santa Maria della Salute the night of September 24, 1908. This suicide by someone whose name reminded him so much of his uncle's made such a mark on Cocteau that his mother and he quickly left Venice; he later tried to evoke it, to his mother's displeasure, in several poems and in *Le grand écart*, his most autobiographical novel.[65] It was as though the event had made the young writer anticipate the despair of unreciprocated love.

ARIEL

Mirrors would do well to reflect a little more before sending back their images.
—*Jean Cocteau, "Essai de critique indirecte"*

THE PROTECTOR AND THE ACTOR

After coming home from Italy, Cocteau didn't take long to create some distance from his mother. Across the symbolic frontier of the Seine, he rented a bachelor flat in the annex of a Regency mansion called the Hôtel Biron on the rue de Varenne, with gardens full of forget-me-nots, fallow plots, and rabbits. Rodin had made the central portion of this enchanting building into his studio: today it is the Rodin Museum. In a gallery that has since been destroyed, Isadora Duncan gave dance classes "à la grecque," draped in her legendary scarf. At night, Cocteau could see the lighted window of Rodin's young Austrian secretary—"but I was stupid and pretentious," commented Cocteau, "and I didn't even know Rilke's name."[1] Located near the house of the Daudets, Cocteau's apartment allowed him, for the first time, to receive his friends freely. His home's furnishings consisted of a stove, a sofa, some crates covered with goatskin, and a piano on which Reynaldo Hahn, cigarette in mouth and eyes gazing up to heaven, played "languid, troubling" Venetian tunes. "We were two thousand leagues away from Paris, in the midst of the Orient, in the midst of *The Thousand and One Nights*," confides Théophile Gautier, the author of *Captain Fracasse*, in a phrase that Cocteau would place as the epigraph to his *Sonnets de l'Hôtel Biron*.[2]

The den attracted a flood of visitors, from Christiane Mancini, a pupil at the Conservatory, to Abel Bonnard, a "chevalier de la manchette" (homosexual) who would one day become a minister of the Vichy government.[3] "Nom de

Dieu! Nom de Dieu!" cried Catulle Mendès, one of the literary glories of the period, upon discovering this little corner of paradise hidden on the edge of the faubourg Saint-Germain and the fake Persian prince who enchanted it. The shy, unknown high-school student came to submit his manuscripts to Cocteau, and was suddenly welcomed into the redoubt where the prince of French letters was holding forth:

> It was incredible, how much he knew, how much he had read, the freshness of his ideas, the pithiness of his expressions . . . I had the uneasy, uncomfortable sensation of being in the presence of a monster: the extent, the power, and the scintillating variety of his mind, and the clarity of his thinking, contrasted so strongly with his physique—the nervous, slender, body that seemed almost fragile.[4]

Had De Max become infatuated with Cocteau, the debutant he had so brilliantly launched? When he in turn came a few months later to settle in the disused chapel of the Hôtel Biron, the actor noted with pique that, if Cocteau was still courting worthies, the one he sought after most was now Mendès, whom De Max himself had introduced to Cocteau at the same time as his lover Lou Teleguen, also a regular at the Hôtel Biron.[5]

Mendès had literary assets: not only was his first wife, Judith, the daughter of Théophile Gautier, but he had often met Baudelaire and spent long evenings with Victor Hugo. Author of plays that were more like Hugo's than Hugo's own, of poems more Parnassian than Bainville's, the death of his role models had given him, in the words of Frederick Brown, a kind of originality.[6] As an elder statesman, Mendès seemed like the kind of celebrity who could definitively authenticate the crown on the young Cocteau's brow. Having contributed to the Parisian craze of "Wagneromania" at the turn of the century, Mendès was actually an outmoded author, deemed even more ridiculous than the tremendous ham De Max—so ridiculous that Gide's very young *Nouvelle revue française* didn't even bother to laugh at him any more. Having called for the condemnation of Captain Dreyfus, Mendès—a Jew himself—was one of many who proclaimed Jewish artists to be nothing but imitators. But his self-hating anti-Semitism coexisted with a literary facility, a certain amount of talent, and an oceanic complacency that led him to read his poems for entire nights to female admirers (who were occasionally relieved by his young male admirers).

Mendès's eclecticism drew Cocteau like a lark to a mirror; and his intoxicating talk about Nerval, Rimbaud, and Verlaine propelled Cocteau into the mostly closely guarded of pantheons. "A child has prejudices, thus he is just as old as his parents," said Éric Marty.[7] Indeed, the children of that time prized celebrities and old men. The *monstres sacrés* that Cocteau, his mother, and their world admired were often aged: Sarah Bernhardt was still playing the Aiglon in 1912 and was approaching her seventieth year; Mounet-Sully and Coquelin the Elder were even older. To be prestigious was to have a prophet's beard or the wrinkles of a Liszt as photographed by Nadar the younger: as Picasso would say, Cocteau took a long time to be young.

The range of Cocteau's sexual preferences remained wide, however, to judge from his affair with Christiane Mancini, a young female student in the Conservatory of Dramatic Art, his peer in age and position.[8] They would lunch together, go for a car ride, see a show at the Grand-Guignol; he would host picnics in his apartment, with bottles of beer and sandwiches bought on the rue de Bourgogne, to which she wore a black velvet dress with a train. The young woman, in love for the first time, sent Cocteau passionate letters brimming with naturalness and spontaneity. But this sentimental flood frightened the young man, and the poor girl, after waiting for him for entire nights, fell into a deep depression:

> Not a word from you, you have no pity on my suffering, for I love you enough to shout it from the rooftops, to kill myself and I don't have the courage for that, but I am suffering, since yesterday I've lived a century, I called you all night . . . We who were made to be so happy, the two of us, what happened, write to me I'm begging you, I want to see you, you love me, I'm sure of it, we're young, we have to love each other, ah it hurts, my darling . . . I'm all crushed to the ground.[9]

These accounts of suffering aroused only embarrassment and rejection. The student actress had to leave the lodging where they met on the boulevard Pereire and take refuge in Wiesbaden, at the risk of flunking her exams. From the train that carried her to Germany, she wrote to Cocteau:

> My darling, I no longer have the strength to do anything, if you had pity on me you'd see me again as a friend, I won't say it and whenever you like we'll say it, but I need you . . . What did I do wrong, tell me, but no you love me I know it because you'd have sent my photos back, ah no if that's not true don't send them back, leave me in doubt I'm suffering so, whatever, this suffering is precious to me.[10]

Later, when he too came to love tough, distant boys, Cocteau would react with characteristic empathy. But at the time, Mancini's weakness awoke in him a Baudelairean sadism, as betrayed by the harsh lines from his first collection, dedicated to the young Christiane:

Sometimes I want to scratch and bite you
Gouge out your too-black, too-deep, too-slant eyes,
See you convulse with horror at the brutalities of a command,
And steal away from you all the happiness you deserve!

I want to laugh at your burning pain,
Crush with punches the roundness of your breasts,
May my ferocity be implacable and slow . . .
And freeze you with fear beneath my murdering fingers![11]

Thus he made her suffer, without any compunction, just as he himself would suffer whenever he was loved without reciprocation.

Published at the author's expense, with a dedication from the poet to his mother and an insert wishing good luck "to this extraordinary and precocious talent of dandyism," *La lampe d'Aladin* appeared in February 1909. It was bathed in an atmosphere of German *lied* and Nordic fog, and Cocteau wore a butterfly-hunting outfit, with a plant-collecting box over his shoulder, when he took the train to deliver a copy to the famous Jacques Doucet. Sporting Bavarian leather breeches and alpenstock, tartan socks and hobnailed boots, and a plucked edelweiss in the ribbon of his Tyrolean hat, Cocteau in all his folkloric excess amused the passengers in the Swiss station where they met, but Doucet was not amused. Cocteau had counted on meeting Doucet the fashion designer, but Doucet the bibliophile—the modern art collector who in 1912 would sell his collection of eighteenth-century volumes in order to acquire manuscripts by his contemporaries—was the one who received him.

The nephew of Raymond Lecomte was already too sensitive, too profound, to content himself with simply being a beautiful human object. Cocteau's anguish at the shortness of life, his fear of not having enough time to say every-thing, created a panic of being forgotten. Alarmed by his own ephemeral nature, the young *dauphin* viewed himself condemned to the dazzling, suffocating fate of a hothouse flower. The young stag who butted against the pilasters at salons as if against tree trunks in a forest was also hypersensitive and easily wounded: he was unable to take an elevator without his heart leaping to his throat, unable to feel pleasure without remembering that he was doomed to putrefy. Only dreams, and the ideal, helped him escape. Death at times seemed to him so gentle that he sometimes willfully called for it, as his friend Raymond Laurent had done in Venice. But this praise of suicide and this hypersensitivity, sincere as they were, stem wholly from the Symbolist canon, like the Salomés, the satyrs, and all the Bacchuses that animate its menagerie. Happy to read his poetry in ancient salons, Cocteau enthusiastically condemned himself to repetition—"to an old-fashioned air of romance," he himself confessed.[12] Yet even with all his energy it was impossible to resuscitate themes already dealt with and to write, so young, a poetry already so dated.

The *Mercure de France*, the leading literary journal of the time, paid homage to Cocteau's first collection, where it rightly discerned a fierce love of life and the promise of glory.[13] But was the *Mercure de France*, soon to be outshone by the *Nouvelle revue française*, best placed to judge these clever virtuosic exercises? Cocteau would later denounce the "atrocious mess" of his hasty beginnings, but at the time he savored the incredible swiftness with which the great symbolist journal had crowned him.

THE "I" AND THE "WE"

Cocteau would always claim that a chance visit had revealed to his mother the existence of his bachelor apartment tucked away in the Hôtel Biron, leading her to demand his immediate return home. This story, which portrays him as the rebel son he was not, is contradicted by a letter from Mme Cocteau proving that she had come to join him there, no doubt in order the better to chaperone him. In any event he cheerfully followed her when she moved in 1910 to a large apartment on the top floor at 10 rue d'Anjou, behind the Madeleine, where the two would live together and receive visitors for ten years. The creaking elevator, upholstered in red velvet and worked by pull ropes, seemed so unreliable that there were fringed ottomans on every landing for whomever preferred to take the stairs. "An elevator from the time before elevators," Cocteau called it. Apollinaire, who was also fascinated by the huge copper lamp that hung from the ceiling down the entire length of the spiral staircase, lighting each floor by double branched gas globes, described the elevator as "the eighth wonder of the world."[14]

It was here that the young star Cocteau welcomed his friends, his admirers, and his first journalists. With majestic courtesy the valet, Cyprien, would lead visitors solemnly across the vestibule decorated with oriental lamps into Cocteau's little bedroom covered with fetish objects and portraits of writers, with a twin bed facing the balcony that overlooked the rue d'Anjou. Sometimes Cocteau received them in his bathroom, where he would shave and powder himself in the steam from the bath before donning a custom-fitted shirt made at Charvet, on the place Vendôme. It was with his mother that he received his guests, and it was together that they went to the theater, to the Opéra, or were invited to houses in the faubourg Saint-Honoré and the Plaine Monceau. Although he fully assumed his father's role of prince consort, and let himself be advised on which people to see, what flowers to send, or what customs to respect, Cocteau was still the star—a preeminent status that his mother did not contest. She did, however, make clear to him the obligations it entailed.

Madeleine Carlier, an actress from Montmartre who was well known at the Palais de Glace, that northern paradise of Parisian cocottes, would disturb this smoothly run household by rousing Cocteau's sole feminine passion—before Natalie Paley, at least. This voluptuous beauty, who at the age of twenty-eight looked barely twenty, was, as Cocteau remembered shortly before her death, a girl who was "very simple, but very fashionable," and she was always followed by a cohort of ecstatic admirers when she and her sister performed on the ice.[15] Already kept by a rich Greek gentleman, the skater-actress had a little favorite— Carlito Boulant, Cocteau's own high-school comrade. With her nectarine complexion; her round, full cheeks; and her lewd, sulky looks—Cocteau would compare her to Brigitte Bardot, who had torrential hair like hers—the "Carlier kid" soon became the sun that polarized Cocteau's gazes and electrified his gestures, without whose presence his day lost all meaning. But this attraction did not stem from mimicry, which so often took the place of sexuality with him. In a novelistic transposition of this relationship, Cocteau wrote:

> He did not want to be Germaine. He wanted to possess her. For the first time, his desire did not manifest in its form of illness. For the first time, he did not hate his own image. He thought he was cured.[16]

Seven years older, the actress made him feel intimidated almost as much as Christiane Mancini had made him feel cruel. He admired her too much to enjoy fully their sexual effervescence. She inspired him to create erotic drawings, where she is shown taking his sex between her breasts.[17] But she also evoked in him the fear of transgression: "Contemplating that Desdemona on her back, dying on her pillow, frighteningly pale, her teeth exposed, he piled memories of shame onto her face and slipped out of her like a knife," he said of Jacques Forestier, his fictional double in *Le grand écart*.

Cocteau discussed Madeleine Carlier eagerly with his neighbor and friend Sacha Guitry, son of the legendary actor Lucien. Sacha Guitry would hire her eight years later for his play *L'illusionniste*, in which she would have her first real critical success. "Don't leave her right away, and tell her I admire her," Henry Bernstein, the future king of the boulevard, wrote to Cocteau.[18] Cocteau talked about her to everyone, proudly displayed his happiness and his virility, gave the press drawings that he had made of her. Though he would confess being afraid that people might misunderstand his taste for whispered endearments and his exaggerated Platonism as "an excuse for physical impotence," Cocteau—not for the last time—was unaware that his constant flaunting of the relationship would end up harming him.

He spent his mornings hoping for a telegram, a call, the least sign—but the anonymous letters that reached the rue d'Anjou made him doubt the reality of their relationship. How could this young man, so unvirile, rival the wealthy protectors with whom actresses commonly surround themselves? These missives affected him so much that Madeleine Carlier had to console him each time, during the hours she granted him:

> And you would dry my cheek with your curving eyelashes,
> And you would place your hand firmly on my mouth.
> You would say, and I can still hear your voice,
> Your protective, tender voice, and I can see again
> Your sisterly gesture, you would say: "Poor kid!"[19]

He lived like an open parenthesis, a body that took on meaning only when the actress arrived, and grew empty when she left. Endlessly hoping for her arrival, he prowled around her in his thoughts, and, when the appointed hour for their meeting approached, mentally accompanied her progress, breathing with her and melting into her as she finally entered the vestibule on the rue d'Anjou and pressed the elevator button with her finger. When finally the apparatus reached his landing, releasing the real Madeleine Carlier, the gate as it closed tore into his eardrums.

Though Carlier found Cocteau brilliant, lively, and winsome, she didn't love him. Nor did she seem to sense how much he loved her, although she met his frantic declarations with theatrical aplomb. Dedicating a photograph to him, she wrote: "In this one you have chosen, Jean, read in my eyes that I love you. *Made.*"[20] Cocteau's dependence frightened him to the point of illness; his love ate at him like a tapeworm, as if in vengeance for the unhappy Mancini. In a "fictive" letter to a friend, which the journal *Pan* would publish in June 1909, he wrote:

> This woman, you see, is everything to me . . . everything! I am a rag in her hands: my personality, which you already knew was almost dying, is dead under her caresses; I am not free, I am not even happy, I disgust myself! . . . If I ask her for an explanation, oh!, even for the most insignificant things— she brings her eyelashes close, her eyes roll, she plants the cool, soft flesh of her lips on my mouth, and stays there, a long time, a long time . . . until I have forgotten![21]

A lascivious serpent, Carlier stifles him. She is the Eve of the Church fathers, the Pandora of the pagans, the Aïsha Kandisha of the Muslims. "This woman is diabolical, I adore her!" he exclaims, comparing himself to a thirsty desert. The world is encapsulated in her elusive face, in her unavailable body that he dreams to impregnate. Cocteau, who showed, in *La lampe d'Aladin*, his heart pouring itself out "on the intruder plundering it," is dying of silence as one dies of hunger. Discovering to his dismay "the mute horror of unreciprocated love" that had cost Raymond Laurent's life, his heart bursts with each wound she gives him, and his hands are sticky with blood. "Do you know the double staircase in the [Château de] Chambord?" he once asked. "You climb together, but you never meet."[22]

Not content with introducing Madeleine Carlier to his mother as his fiancée, he mentioned their wedding to her and claimed she was pregnant. Giving in to the bourgeois obsessive anxiety about illegitimacy—she herself was born out of wedlock—Mme Cocteau denounced this unequal match: "Poor Jean! With an old woman."[23] A family council ratified the rejection, adducing the thirteen years that separated the lovers. Totally possessive, Mme Cocteau hounded the cocotte who was eating away at her son. In an equally bitter disappointment for Cocteau, the actress in turn took her distance—in order the better to get closer to Carlito Boulant, he would later claim. "Not seeing each other is agony. Vertigo like a rollercoaster. All day long, a soft knife is cutting my heart in two."[24] The actress had carried away with her much of his happiness: with her departure those thighs against which he curled up, that peace he had absorbed, and that fundamental self-contentment that would always cruelly fail him, had left as well.

Madeleine Carlier ended up having an abortion: the coup de grâce. "Jahel has to get used to thinking 'I.' It is hard. 'We' haunts him . . . When he stops thinking about it, he stops thinking," Cocteau would write one year later, in a text in which he gives himself the name Jahel, close to the "Japh" with which he signed his first drawings.[25] He would still remember Carlier enough, twelve years later, to make her into Germaine in *Le grand écart* and into Jeanne in *Le livre blanc*.

> Love came: Madeleine with the pretty squinting eyes.
> Her fingers and mine played with each other in the muff . . .
> She hurt me as much as one can hurt anyone.[26]

Not being indispensable to another would always be a hell for him.

THE LOVE THAT DARE NOT SAY ITS NAME

Mme Cocteau no longer had much occasion to influence her son's heterosexual desires—unless perhaps in the opposite direction: the episode with

Carlier was enough to suspend for a long time any impulse Cocteau might have had toward women. "I took nineteen years to understand my breed," he would write in a poem entitled "The Fall of Angels," which concludes: "And we have slept with the daughters of men / Horrible misdeal."[27] Was this a way of hinting to his mother what he could not say outright—as he would do later on in writing to a young disciple: "Around the age of twenty-two I understood that in order to become a rooster you had to kill hens"?[28] This "detail" must not have escaped Mme Cocteau.

Having seen him flaunt himself with De Max and falling into such raptures over Oscar Wilde that he wrote a play based on *The Picture of Dorian Gray*, Mme Cocteau could only suspect the nature of his friendships for Carlito Boulant, Jacques Renaud, René Rocher, or Lou Teleguen—even if she didn't manage to surprise her son at home in his bachelor apartment, pomaded and made up, his hair gleaming with copious spritzes of Eau Miracle (a rejuvenating lotion whose recipe the Empress Eugénie had revealed to Lucien Daudet) while he clutched a goatskin and enthused, "I love the smell of fur."[29]

In the society of the Belle Époque, such an eccentric masculinity could not escape a mother; nor could the praise he wrote for the "naked god who does not say his name," in *Le prince frivole*, published the same year as that encounter, 1910, in an explicit homage to Wilde and to Lord Alfred Douglas, Wilde's lover.[30] What's more, as early as his first collection, when Cocteau was only eighteen, he portrayed fauns with transparent intentions and an equivocal young man, "his eyes wrinkled through abuse of a clandestine vice"; three years later, *La danse de Sophocle* would clearly pay homage to the "supple attractions" of Saint Sebastian's torso bristling with arrows, as well as to the "sweet cage" of his eyelashes. Mme Cocteau, more indulgent of Lucien Daudet's affectations than Madeleine Carlier's sensuality, obviously tolerated these excesses; her severity toward ridiculous clothing might lead one to suppose that she did not look kindly on the relationship between her son and Lucien Daudet, but no doubt she knew, as any overbearing mother would, that this kind of love threatened her less directly.

Having no clear right to either sex, Cocteau logically enough overinvested in writing: confusing ink, blood, and semen. But there was danger here too, for if his social successes were flattering to his mother, his writing threatened her with its veiled, inopportune revelations: the family secrets were so formidable that she couldn't help but fear their sudden reappearance. For Mme Cocteau, every play, every poem, was potentially a transgression and a danger to their reputation. Despite his later protestations of bisexuality, Jean Cocteau's homosexuality would become, with one or two exceptions, exclusive and systematic from that time on, perfectly in accord with a personality seeking its comple-ment in virility and dependent on the strength of the other. "Any man who places his truth in his Being-for-the-Other finds himself in a situation which I have called prehomosexual," Sartre would say in his *Saint Genet,* using certainly an overgeneralized definition, but one that finds a distinct echo in the eminently dependent personality of Cocteau.[31]

Some people have examined Cocteau's nature through the glass of psycho-analysis, even if doing so means shooting a cannon at a mosquito. But it takes more—or less—than a father's suicide to create a writer, and more—or less—than a mother's passion to make a homosexual; desire and creativity are in the end self-explanatory. "He did not know what original sin was," said a surprised Abbé Mugnier, the priest to whom Cocteau confided his metaphysical preoc-cupations in 1913: "he confused it with the union of the sexes." As if he had deduced from a vague religious education that Adam and Eve were the source of all evil, Cocteau would always tend to regard homosexuality as purer, nobler than heterosexuality—and in this he must have reflected the unconscious view of his moralistic mother.

Cocteau's preference for men, though, remained more acted than lived, and no doubt a certain amount of self-conscious dandyism entered into it: "Jahel lives for the moment . . . enjoys a verse, a flower, a piece of cloth, a cigarette, a sky. He does not hate. Hate is quite a useless exhaustion. He refrains from reading newspapers and passes through life with a smile on his lips."[32] It was as if his way of conceiving life were above all aesthetic, hence less threatened by homosexuality than by a union weighty with consequences. From affectation, he would pass soon to more exaggerated mannerisms when, after Lucien Daudet and Reynaldo Hahn, whose tastes were already no secret, he befriended Maurice Rostand, son of the author of *Cyrano de Bergerac*—a boy so outra-geously perfumed that his appearance gave Proust attacks of asthma.

If Cocteau imagined himself as a Persian prince, Rostand the younger believed himself the reincarnation of Antinous, the favorite of Emperor Hadrian. His extraordinary career had begun under the aegis of Sarah Bernhardt; after having made triumphs of three of his father's plays, she had pointed him out to the audience one night when she was playing *La dame aux camélias.*[33] Though he had only recently published his first poems, at the age of nineteen, Maurice Rostand actually thought he was everything: the most handsome boy in the French Empire, but also a poetic genius who when he was just five years old had been dramatically visited by a redheaded fairy godmother wrapped up in chinchilla: the great Sarah Bernhardt, who came in a carriage drawn by two geldings.

Rostand's mythomania was received enthusiastically by Cocteau. As they walked up and down the Champs-Élysées discussing Oxford, with plucked gardenias in their buttonholes, the two poets took themselves for Byron and Shelley—though Wilde and Beardsley would have been more like it. *Schéhérazade*, the journal founded by Cocteau in which Maurice Rostand published pieces by his father, had already attracted collaborators like the painter Pierre Bonnard, Natalie Barney (to whom Remy de Gourmont dedicated his *Lettres à l'Amazone*), the watercolorist Marie Laurencin, and Paul Iribe, a multitalented artist. Soon Cocteau and Rostand would write collaborative poems, "Les Bucoliques basques," with epigraphs that reveal their incredible elation over being together: "O frenzy of pleasure!" (Walter Pater), "I blushed very quickly and on one side like a peach" (Shelley), "He wore rather short brown pants, white socks and polished shoes" (Baudelaire).

Their major reference, logically, was Wilde, that unrivaled storyteller who, at the height of his fame, had destroyed himself by engaging in a trial he was certain to lose. Cocteau loved Wilde's enchanting ease, as well as his aesthetic of looking at things from a fresh angle and his predilection for paradox. "I treated art as the supreme reality and life as a mere mode of fiction," Wilde once said.[34] Cocteau's everyday unreality would also be the single tangible prime material for his books—Cocteau, after all, had begun to write before he began truly living, and he would remain, until his death, incapable of separating his experience from the literary translation he had made of it. Each of Cocteau's gestures would be conceived with an eye to its effect on paper, since everything in the world was made to end up in a book, according to the adage by Stéphane Mallarmé that Wilde could have countersigned.

Sometimes pressing needs tore the young dandy from his dreams. He would at times throw himself on the first prey to come along, counting on their social timidity. He spent a summer at the Rostand's house in Cambo, in Basque country, "corrupting young boys and organizing *ballets bleus*," until Edmond Rostand was forced to intervene and put an end to the affairs.[35] Cocteau would yield, then wait for the next opportunity to satisfy his imperious sexuality.

Maurice Rostand and Cocteau had become acquainted in 1909, perhaps at the wedding of Rostand's friend Tiarko Richepin, Jean's son.[36] The stylish Richepin, who set his poems to music first, had chosen Cocteau as best man along with Maurice Rostand; he had been the lover of Maurice Rostand and of Rostand's mother at the same time. "I wore a frock coat, a silver tube in my lapel, and a purple carnation," Cocteau wrote, remembering that strange wedding. "The caterers laughed at me as I went by, and my mother, at the window on avenue Malakoff, wept at how ridiculous I looked."[37] The dandyism of the

Cocteau-Rostand pair would only get worse—it took Cocteau five years, according to his own avowal, to free himself from the fascination that *The Picture of Dorian Gray* exercised over him.

The salons applauded the pair's aplomb, their taste for farces and charades, and their ability to imitate the ladies of rival houses by wearing white wigs and the tawdry rags of a "once-elegant pauperess." Capable of imitating an old man like Rodin or a soldier like Lyautey, just as Sem caricaturized them in the press, and to be able to ape the body language of personalities as famous as the pope or De Max, both Cocteau and Rostand the younger had a clear predilection for impersonating women. Received at the Château de la Roche into what he viewed as his second, more literary, family, the Daudets, in the summer of 1911, Cocteau won a triumph for himself by lampooning in turns Sarah Bernhardt, Maurice Rostand's mother, and Mme Mühlfeld, a famous salon hostess.[38] His imitations went so far that the Guitrys, in their house in Honfleur, saw him actually "become" Lucie Delarue-Mardrus, a Sapphic poetess married to the translator of *The Thousand and One Nights*, who in turn was imitated by the younger Guitry, to the point of exceeding her in "reality"—a term that, among American transvestites, designates those who have perfectly impersonated "adored" women. We should not be surprised that families applauded the young men: their role-playing was so trendy that Mme Rostand, Mme Cocteau, and Mme Daudet were the first to rejoice at seeing their sons shine—with Lucien in particular doing a wonderful imitation of Montesquiou, in a performance often rehearsed with Proust.

Nothing exalted Cocteau more than those sessions when he could drop one personality to take on another and make it chat with a third, sometimes for half an hour, until he seemed to be dividing himself ad infinitum. Just as when he was at school, he was already able to imitate De Max parodying Sarah Bernhardt, so now he could counterfeit voices, gestures, ways of drawing and writing— even of the dead, one witness said.

In the spiraling loops of his magical thinking, Maurice Rostand had the firm conviction that he was a replica of his model: the same Sarah Bernhardt who, after creating his father's plays, played in his own until 1922. Not content with declaiming his verses like the diva, the future author of *La femme qui était en lui* would paint himself with eyeliner and rouge and treat his "bleached tigress mop" with a curling iron and hair dye. His primping style would give rise to cascades of laughter when he paraded down the street in high heels, wearing suits with seams ready to burst—but that ridicule was a kind of triumph. His mother approved of him in every way—during the Occupation, on the last métros before curfew, they could be found clinging to each other for warmth. Maurice Rostand ended up living as a star, indirectly confirming, even among the third sex, the influence of the cult of womanhood that defined the era.

The extravagant sissy Rostand impressed Cocteau with his nerve — or his lack of awareness. No one else in Paris had dared go so far — in London the condemnation of Wilde had discouraged the Elect, numerous as they were. Much like De Max, but without any fame other than his father's to protect him, the young Rostand embodied that narcissism encouraged by the fin-de-siècle cult of the self, but also the emergence of a sexuality that, while still doomed to the margins of society, could not stop asserting its right to exist. Cocteau would later describe him, in a letter revealing their complicity, as a fat odalisque moving around his house in sumptuous transparent pajamas, "a curly cowpat balanced on his skull."[39] The need to theatricalize his difference is so great in the Cocteau of that period that we might suspect the pot of calling the kettle black.

Cocteau's homosexuality, however, would always remain less infantile than Rostand's. While still leading Cocteau regularly back to his mother, it would also send him eventually to explore sailors' brothels in Toulon and Parisian opium dens, the arcana of a shady sphere as far from the faubourg Saint-Honoré as Empress Ts'eu-Hi's China was from President Loubet's France. Cocteau's desire to adorn himself with eroticized features, from sailors' pompoms to the cape of the student Dargelos, would eventually give rise to a complex mythology that served as a guide for three generations of homosexuals. Like African ritual masks, these fetishes would allow these men to recognize each other and get together, just as they themselves opened to Cocteau another parallel, secret, even sectarian, existence, one that did a little bit more to abolish the frontier separating his imagination from reality.

But this creature so ready to borrow the gestures and turns of phrase of others no longer needed Maurice Rostand to capture attention. Instead, Cocteau's "fascinating, turbulent intelligence, always changing and in movement," as Rostand described it, referring to their first meeting, took charge of this.[40] No doubt the energy his intelligence drew from the electric shock of opposites made him sometimes act incoherently, but in striking the person or work that attracted it, it illuminated as if with a camera flash. The salons were greedy for this rapid-fire intelligence, which gave events so much intensity and so much pungency that Paul Valéry would one day nickname Cocteau "the salt of the earth."[41] In those overheated rooms, Cocteau felt that he fully existed: whereas the pollen-charged atmosphere of the outdoors assaulted him, the vapors one breathed indoors were stimulating.

One must be careful not to speak of hysteria when examining Cocteau's character, yet his inability to inhabit his body and make it his bulwark, as well as his incapacity to resign himself to old age and thus to death, mean that some doubts linger. Generally feeling like he was lacking something, and so all the more voracious, Cocteau felt assailed by an avalanche of sensations: strange, bizarre, overexcited, he aroused that irritated fascination evoked by the sickly aspect of precocious geniuses. The frivolity he assumed deceived only the most unthinking people; he seemed haunted by a command to do things, a victim to that strange, disturbing principle urging him always to surpass himself and devour his models in order the better to reject them, as Rostand would learn, as had Daudet and De Max. As graceful and feverish as a dragonfly striking against glass, he could pass for an accident of nature were it not for his resemblance to the woman who gave him life.

His physical strangeness was striking. Thin and electric, his body seemed to be content with air and words, compliments and sparring matches. Mastication and copulation seem functions too coarse for that nearly immaterial organism reminiscent of those characters that, in Persian fairytales, emerged from a bottle to fill the room with their whirlwind. Nicknamed "Ariel" by Jules Lemaitre, a literary critic whom Nietzsche, in *Ecce homo*, ranked among the most curious psychologists of the time, Cocteau was a being made not of flesh but of vapor, bewitching but too unstable not to suffer from it—like a cloud traversed by horizontal flashes of lightning.

Cocteau also sought to flee his body, which had been assailed from childhood with recurrent illnesses that made life almost impossible. His yearly bouts of hay fever shook him with the violence of a cyclone, and he suffered allergies and abscesses, rheumatism and diseases of the skin, insomnia and shingles, flu and toothaches. If genius is sometimes the accidental brainwave of a subject desperately looking for a way out of its distress, in this case it was an outlet for that "soul that had met a body by accident, and that was coping with it as best it could," as Chateaubriand reported of the moralist Joseph Joubert.[42]

In short, no one corresponded so well to the picture Max Nordau had drawn of the hysteric: someone driven mad by technical acceleration. Cocteau to be sure was not subject to those crises that had made "good theater" from the sick people whom Professor Charcot had presented at the Pitié-Salpêtrière Hospital twenty years earlier. But Cocteau's extraordinary emotionalism, his receptiveness to suggestions, his tendency to lie, his taste for spiritualism, his "irresistible mania for imitation," and his need "to fascinate his entourage with his person" by means of frantic inventions by which he was the first to be taken in, certainly put him, among the minds of his time, in the family that Nordau had likened to the already more worrisome group, the degenerates.[43]

A YOUNG MAN IN FLOWER

Attracted by his strangeness, a number of painters began to make portraits of the Cocteau phenomenon. Although Lucien Daudet found it difficult to render Cocteau's incredible vivacity, he succeeded in emphasizing the delicacy of his profile in pencil. Romaine Brooks sketched him as a thin, sad young man on a balcony, dominating the Eiffel Tower in the background (to which Cocteau was already comparing himself)—his sparking intuitions making him (in his own eyes) like a living antenna mast, transmitting images and sounds. Paulet Thévenaz, Cocteau's first recorded lover, and Coco de Madrazo, who was part of Reynaldo Hahn's entourage, would soon be joined by hordes of news photographers and newspaper sketch artists through which that volatile ego sought to give itself tangible reality.

In May 1910 Cocteau published *Le prince frivole*, his second collection of poems. While in it he uses all techniques meant to please—including shock—it is also shot through with allusions to the ancien régime and expresses, through deliberate archaisms, his impatience to join the Academie Française and the aristocrats seated near the gods:

> I want a worldly name that will remain immortal!
> To be Prince Charming in a mysterious fairytale.

Well-known even before he was published, the young prodigy who saw himself as the "center of Paris" was already thinking more about his position than about his art, more about his influence than his poetry.

Cocteau's collection was deemed very "artistic," and critics appreciated his tendency to imitate less. But they encouraged him to choose more contemporary subjects, and warned him about his precocity: though he was the youngest poet in France, his verses might have been written in 1890. Were they evoking Baudelaire, who encouraged his peers to look to the street, not the museums, for the unusual and hence modern forms of beauty? Cocteau responded by recalling the nostalgic taste for "remembrances" in the author of *Les fleurs du mal*. Proust would learn at his expense that it was difficult to expect objective judgment and reflection from a prodigy stricken with an acute case of Parisianism.

Cocteau could never recall where he had met the gazelle-like gaze and weary smile of Marcel Proust for the first time: on the red banquettes of the luxurious restaurant Larue, on the place de la Madeleine? At the home of Mme Alphonse Daudet, on the rue de Bellechasse?[44] In the salon of Madeleine Lemaire, where every Tuesday Reynaldo Hahn played the piano—for "the woman who created the most roses after God," as they said about that monomaniac watercolorist—

or, more probably, at the home of Mme Straus, the widow of Georges Bizet? The black moustache was already prominent on Proust's olive-colored face, but whether he then wore his hair cut short or parted down the middle, whether he was bearded or clean-shaven, Cocteau could not recall. Proust had in the meantime become an intrinsic element of the milieu that he was already beginning to describe; looking back, Cocteau introduced him everywhere, like a social trump card.

Probably Cocteau felt as if he had always known Proust, thanks to the stories of his close friends Hahn and Daudet. Both of them equally admired Proust ("Binibuls"), and Lucien Daudet treated the "petit Marcel" with the respect that genius deserved. Most Parisians, however, still knew him only as a society columnist and society's untiring flatterer in *Le Figaro*. Although Hahn's music was already being played beyond the confines of Europe, and Daudet's distinctiveness often led Proust to say he had been influenced by his spoken and written style, it was more likely Daudet who imitated Proust, as he had done before with Montesquiou. And it was they who, to return his devouring politeness, celebrated Proust everywhere, becoming untiring ambassadors of his still unexpressed gifts.

Since Proust had somewhat detached himself from Daudet, it was more likely Reynaldo Hahn who, in early 1910, served as intermediary between Proust and Cocteau. It is difficult to imagine two personalities so compatible as the sons of Jeanne Proust and Eugénie Cocteau. Their keen sense of observation, their taste for gossip, and their gifts of imitation made them instantly recognizable as members of the same species. If their nervousness was insect-like, their strangeness almost made one want to classify them among hothouse orchids (if not a carnivorous plant, in Proust's case). But although Proust had withdrawn from Parisian life two years earlier in order to devote himself to writing, he had been talking so long about the À *la recherche du temps perdu* that Mme Cocteau's circle still doubted the concrete existence of this great work, and saw in it only a pretext for endless conversations, "téléphonages," and other genealogical investigations. Or else they judged Proust (as Daniel Halévy had done when the two were adolescents) as completely lacking talent, and of having an unbearable literary pretension—someone who, obviously, could aspire only to a career as a man-about-town.[45]

So Proust's name still evoked, for the young Cocteau, only prose and verse poems, the pastiches and portraits of *Les plaisirs et les jours* (which he probably hadn't read), and Proust's endless descriptions of the lilac dresses and turquoise parasols that embellished the parties given by the Comte de Montesquiou. Proust must have seemed to Cocteau to belong to that category of wealthy amateurs better suited to comment on others' works than to produce their own—a class to which Cocteau's own family belonged. Though certainly Proust was more perspicacious and profound than most fin-de-siècle aesthetes, he lacked the social authority that alone could confer importance; and though he was the commentator on the literary and society divinities who peopled the Panthéon into which Cocteau wished to make his entrance, was he for all that their equal? It is not out of the question that such a doubt might have prevented Cocteau from admiring Proust as he deserved to be—Proust, a man more sickly even than himself, and one who had waited for the death of his parents, five years earlier, before daring to live on his own.

Surprisingly attentive to newcomers, Proust would be among those curious to know this twenty-year-old Cocteau, whose mercurial vivacity Paris was already praising. He would admire Cocteau's fascinating eyes and envy his striking phrases and his "conversation full of incessant invention."[46] He would also soon be convinced of the scope of Cocteau's gifts and not reduce them, as was sometimes done, to an ability to recreate (an ability that Proust himself would demonstrate in his *À la recherche du temps perdu,* and in life when he imitated Montesquiou's heel taps as he barked out his verses, head thrown back, like a "rearing cobra"). But Proust would guess that the young Cocteau was less at ease in his earthly skin than he seemed. With the same sure instinct that enabled him to sense the approach of a barometric depression from the Azores, Proust sometimes characterized the phenomenon that was Cocteau as being airborne, thanks to his "wonderful ascending power," and sometimes as being immersed in water, "with his fish-beak of a nose."[47] The limits of Cocteau's precocity did not escape him either, whether that precocity emanated from the eloquence that Proust brilliantly analyzed as "a defensive organ" charged with covering the faults of his character, or from a deceptive intelligence beneath which Proust detected a lack of profundity, if not of heart—at least toward him.[48]

Their twin nature further restrained their connection. They had both grown up under the attentive gaze of mothers who expected the world of them, and they both reproduced in every other relationship this internal hope, along with the secondary interactions and associated jealousies that it entailed. Proust did not enjoy that real, substantial "self" that helps one stand up to social life—the self that Proust taught us to distinguish from the self that makes us write—any more than Cocteau did. Proust, too, passionately became the men and women he loved; by forbidding his infinitely labile personality from becoming fixed, recognizable, and hence desirable—including by himself—he could instead admire everything that could in his eyes embody an essence or a myth. Cocteau could already lay claim to deserving such an embodiment, by virtue of his youth and precocity: whether Proust could too was not so certain. Neither Proust nor Cocteau could bear it if people resisted their dual needs to be admired and to please.

Whether he expressed himself through letters, viva voce, or through telephone handsets, Proust had the gift of weaving extraordinary fabrics of language around those bodies he wanted to delight, the better to empty them of their substance. He knew perfectly how to flatter people, while at the same time letting them glimpse, for a brief flash, the absurdity of his compliments; and the pleasure he took in embarrassing them by overwhelming them bordered on vice. He knew how to captivate with those interminable *Scheherazade*-style periodic sentences whose flow was regulated by a complex system of syntactic gateways that Cocteau could control magisterially—just as he had the ability, through letters, to complicate it all with reproaches and reprimands that could raise friendly tension to the level of lovers' jealousy.

Proust began to pay public homage to the author of *Le prince frivole* by calling him, in an article in *L'intransigeant,* a "twenty-year-old Banville destined for higher things."[49] From there to regarding himself as the youngest member of the group of Saturnians surrounding Proust was a step that Cocteau must have taken easily, already familiar as he was with his social circle, from the Bibesco brothers to their cousin Marthe, from Madeleine Lemaire—who was one of the inspirations for Mme Verdurin—to Louis Gautier-Vignal, a child of the Parisian haute-bourgeoisie.

Both Proust and Cocteau were of course aware of the variations in interest of that world, the ultimate reflection of which *À la recherche du temps perdu* would create, much as the Sun King's court was described by Saint-Simon. Together they laughed at the cultural pretensions of Norpois-like personages: Norpois, the pompous Proustian ambassador who, when commenting on a brochure describing the repeating rifle in the Bulgarian army, believed that he was discussing literature. So snobbish were they that they perceived the potential inanity of these exchanges and ascribed them to the void of the ultra-urbane: that realm of signs that refer only to themselves and take the place of real things. Newer to the game, however, Cocteau still continued to hope for the approval of that inane society—a weakness that did not escape the sharp-eyed Proust. Although involved in one of the greatest literary efforts ever undertaken, and busy describing the circles of Parisian hell at its center, the author of *Jean Santeuil* had always shown a passionate interest and a teacher's enthusiasm for his friends, especially when they were young and malleable. He still showed that quasi-maternal concern for Cocteau, expressed so well in this letter, sent after the young poet had pestered him:

Your silent lines spoke to me with the friendly and remote sparkling of a star and filled me with tenderness and dreams. I thank you. I didn't motion to you when I went out so as not to bother you. But I've sometimes thought of you and have formed useless wishes with the vain indiscretion of friends and philosophers; for example that some event will isolate you and sever you from the pleasures of the mind, leaving time in you to be reborn after a fast sufficient for a true hunger for those beautiful books, those beautiful paintings, those beautiful countries, that you leaf through today with the lack of appetite of someone who has made New Year's visits all day long during which he hasn't stopped eating candied chestnuts. That is, according to my prognosis—sometimes clairvoyant for others, but always powerless for myself—the stumbling block to be feared for your wonderful and stifled gifts. But the life I would wish for you would be not very pleasant for you, at least judging from the way your desires seem—from my very different sense—to be taking shape at the moment. So, fortunately, my wishes will be vain, and nothing will be changed . . . For intellectually as well as physiologically, diet is less powerful than temperament, and there are people who walk ten hours a day without ever losing weight.[50]

Cocteau still lacked the maturity to appreciate the wit of these recommendations. Proust's failing health was making him die and so leave the world; Cocteau's own health was propelling him ever higher in the "enchanted" circle that À *la recherche du temps perdu* would define as a "kingdom of nothingness." Caught in his abyssal undertaking of recollection, Proust must have found the sudden newcomer frivolous indeed—at least as observed from the labyrinthine rooms in the palace of Time, made even larger by the insomnia darkening his eyes.

Later on, Proust would pity Cocteau for not knowing how to distinguish art from life, and for confusing the man who writes with the man who lives. In particular, he reproached Cocteau for indiscretions having to do with Mme de Chevigné—indiscretions that concerned Proust, whose constant care to hide his own homosexuality extended even to À *la recherche du temps perdu*. Based on various rumors, and after reading Proust's book, Cocteau suspected Proust of having a sexual life as "depraved" as that of Charlus; Proust, in turn, accused Cocteau of falling for the myth of Life as Art, à la Wilde, when the unfortunate truth was that one had to sacrifice all to the Book—even if it meant slaving in misery for the Beautiful like a Bergotte, an Elstir, or a Vinteuil. Confirming Proust's prediction, Cocteau would follow his besotted socializing to its sickening end, without ever guessing that it was delaying the necessary moment when he himself would transform from a happy, light-hearted shade into a specter with ink for blood. After his fiftieth year, Cocteau would write:

No doubt Proust, unique in disentangling the architecture of a life, knew more than I about that future that everything hid from me, all the more so since I thought my present was top-notch, whereas, later on, I came to regard it as a series of serious mistakes.

The fact is that Proust was just as subject as Cocteau to defects of identity, and the first to doubt the consistency of the other. He thought it was urgently necessary, lacking a stable self, to build a coherent architecture able to resist not only the modifications that Time inflicts, but also the feeling of inanity that Society instills—since in the end the cathedral outlined by the Work is the only tangible reality. This reality, which Proust hadn't encountered either in love or in society, had first been revealed to him through brief reminiscences, when a slice of toast—later a madeleine—dipped in some tea suddenly confronted him with the man he had been twenty years earlier. But this work on the self, at the origin of Proustian theories on the supremacy of involuntary memory, was not yet within Cocteau's reach, caught up as he was in a perpetual becoming that prevented any prolonged retrospection, or even any critical approach to the present.

So Cocteau denied being scattered and society-obsessed, a denial Proust readily allowed—but was Proust in the best position to judge the matter? These adjectives hadn't come by chance to Proust, who knew all too well himself the thousand excuses for not writing—telephoning, chatting, improvising—while still believing oneself a poet at every instant. So Cocteau kept reminding Proust of the time that he, Proust, had wasted, over two decades of socializing, while *À la recherche du temps perdu* was inscribing in marble the very same stratified and inexhaustible Time that he was patiently rediscovering.

By one of those perverse coincidences of which he was the master, Proust continued to question Cocteau during his visits, demanding those little facts dear to Stendhal that give the puppets of his *À la recherche* their humanity. This insistence on detail had gotten "little Marcel" called a halfwit by Maurice Barrès, the great writer of the time, who was used to a haughtier—even theoretical—way of seeing things. Yet Proust's requests for detail encouraged Cocteau in turn to find truly novelistic qualities in those same shadows that Proust had reproached him for visiting.

Proust loved to take the opposite position of his prey, and to inflict on them those redoubled constraints that children use when they flip coins: "Tails I win, heads you lose"—a twisted logic that psychoanalysis would baptize a "double bind." And friendship obsessed Proust almost as much as love; he had to possess the secrets of those close to him in order to invade their privacy, and thereby to install himself as first in their hearts. Aware of their obvious kinship but just as concerned as Cocteau was to be the favorite, he paid court to Cocteau in a strangely sinuous way, the extent of which had been surpassed only by Reynaldo Hahn, and then Lucien Daudet. The exuberant clump of mistletoe that Cocteau received during Christmas celebrations in 1910 reached him with these enigmatic lines weighty with hope and reproach intermingled: "If I love you / If you love me, / If we love each other." Abandoning himself to confidences, for which he would of course blame Cocteau, multiplying avowals in order the better to lose him and parentheses in the hope of bewitching him, Proust also composed for Cocteau these revelatory lines, in response to Cocteau's request for funds for a statue of Verlaine, where for the first time he addressed him with the familiar "tu":

> Silence is leaden, speech silver [*argent*]
> And words profit you . . .
> Receive all these, then, as a meager salary
> For your lively charm which knows so well how to please me.[51]

How deep did the feelings run of this man who wrote five thousand letters we know of but none of them love letters, the ones addressed to Lucien Daudet remaining for the most part unpublished? Maurice Sachs's theft of the hundred or so letters that Cocteau received from Proust, as well as the dispersal of the letters that Cocteau wrote to Proust, prevent us from answering more clearly, but the inclination is obvious: the human and literary promise that Cocteau represented was one of the last to mobilize the humanity remaining to Proust.

The experience did in fact prove to that sentimental man deprived of love that real things only happen to us when we no longer desire them. This radical disillusion, at the origin of the philosophy of À *la recherche*, led him to put his poem away in a drawer and not send it until several months later. His repeated failures in the matter of love had taught him to arrange his exits, to escape the pangs of unreciprocated love. As payback for his imperfect devotion, as so many others were punished—"They tell me you are everywhere, except at my place," Proust was already saying to Jacques-Émile Blanche—Cocteau was again addressed as "vous," a degradation that led him in turn to distance himself a little more from that overly exclusive admirer.

Cocteau's silence, we suspect, led to Proust's jealousy. Proust thought he could guess, from some turns of phrase, that Cocteau was frequently visiting Lucien Daudet, and took umbrage at this. Soon convinced, based on vague rumors, that "the utmost intimacy" joined the two, Proust avenged himself by describing Cocteau as being under the literary thumb of the young Daudet.[52]

This idea had already been suggested by Proust's friendly allusion to *Le prince frivole* in the article he had devoted to Daudet's just-published collection with a strangely similar title: "The Prince of Cravats."[53]

Proust's jealousy actually knew neither limits nor logic: everything that others had lived before him, especially those experiences related to love, made him suffer intensely. The totalitarianism of sensitivity that is the glory of *À la recherche*, that *monstre* without literary parallel, made Proust its first victim. These tortures wounded him so much that he ended up turning from his beloved—then, later, trying to recover that relationship through an excess of generosity. Dissimulating his desire under literary encouragements and maternal reproaches, Proust proceeded to the second phase of his harassing offensive, meant to make him loved not now for what he was—or was not—but for what his protection could procure.

Thus one winter night Cocteau, upon entering the den of 102 boulevard Haussmann and complaining of the cold that was freezing Paris, had the surprise of being offered an emerald with which to buy the fur coat that Cocteau needed so acutely that night. Cocteau flatly refused the exorbitant gift and dismissed the tailor who came two days later to take his measurements, rejections that vexed Proust so much that he sent a very long recriminatory letter. (As Cocteau would write in *Opium*, "flattery joined with reproach formed his method of friendship.") In conclusion, the offended Proust demanded that Cocteau transmit his grievances to one of their shared friends, the Comte de Beaumont. He elaborated them for over twenty pages before clarifying in a postscript of unexpected terseness to the go-between: "In fact, say nothing."[54]

Proust's legendary generosity suffocated as surely as asthma: his horrible compulsion "to lock people up in order to keep them to himself and not let them go anywhere else" weighed on Cocteau.[55] Everything he was, did, or said seemed destined to feed in Proust an "interior dummy" whom he could torture as he liked. How was one to behave toward this man for whom simple friendship procured only mediocre pleasure—indeed a sensation very close, if we are to believe him, to fatigue and boredom—and which incited him to extract secrets he could use to start interminable lawsuits? Proust's pathological sensitivity, his episodic grievances, his hourly demands, and his "exclusive" friendships made the two men's relationship go from glacial to white hot. Proust might almost have been the age of Cocteau's father: was that a reason to reproach Cocteau severely for not looking at him, one night at Larue, when Cocteau simply hadn't noticed him? Cocteau—who elsewhere demonstrated certainty verging on arrogance—ended up taking the blame in that instance, although he was certain he really hadn't seen Proust. Soon he returned as a penitent to that literary Captain Nemo who, greedy for offenses, invented them for the pleasure of being able to reproach the "guilty party."

Deep within himself, Cocteau likely feared the fanciful views that Proust might entertain of him much less than his frightening lucidity. Cocteau could not speak to Proust without feeling that he was being morally x-rayed by someone capable of piercing his best-kept secrets. Perhaps Cocteau did not see the incredible wealth that Proust's obsessions hid, and perhaps he lacked respect for that man who was so quick to admire — but in fact no one could satisfy Proust. "Marcel is nice," Lucien Daudet had warned Cocteau. "But he's an atrocious insect. You'll understand someday."[56]

THE CHEF OF SOPHISTICATED ODORS

But Cocteau already had other literary objectives. Proust had sensed this so well from Cocteau's frequent questions about the legendary Robert de Montesquiou, that he, Proust, offered to give Cocteau the letter he had just received from that "correspondent who was more colorful" than himself.[57] Proust's role as intermediary would only wound more deeply, one imagines, his feelings of amour-propre.

Adorned with new furs as if flaunting weasels he had just killed, his spine curved and his chin jutting up, with a hip that betrayed his inclinations but his pocket swollen by an arrogant fist, the Comte de Montesquiou was a rare poet, a self-proclaimed "chef of sophisticated odors" who had the implicit support of Mallarmé. In an age of decadent symbolism he was a haughty, refined bard whose virtuosity verged on the baroque and whose layered, iridescent sensibility was lauded by Jean de Tinan; Paul Verlaine too saluted, between rounds of absinthe, this "art as delicate as it was clear."[58] Not content with having inspired J. K. Huysmans's character Jean Des Esseintes in À *rebours*, Jean Lorrain's novel *Monsieur de Phocas*, and the peacock in Edmond Rostand's play *Chantecler*, this extravagant radical still reigned over "society" by the violence of his diktats and the outrageousness of his hyperbole. Happy to intimidate snobs and scorn men of letters, Montesquiou displayed everywhere his true worth and his unbearable assurance, until he created both the violent desire to be him and the irrepressible need to strangle him. Proust, after having wanted for a while to act as the Saint-Simon to that superstar of 1900 Paris Montesquiou, whose defects the unforgettable and hilarious Charlus would inherit, confessed that "it was as difficult not to try to imitate him as it was to do so."[59]

No one, in fact, was more often portrayed than that ceaselessly posing personage whose anecdotes, according to Léon Daudet, continually ridiculed "the idols of the moment," the old "ultra-noble, ultra-fossilized" people.[60] As intelligent and conceited as the Sun King, and as convinced that he had no equals but in heaven, the count became Cocteau's new idol in 1911. It is true that Montesquiou had the advantage over Proust (who admired the count sincerely and over whose taste he had a lasting influence) of having written actual books and of growing up in a princely environment—one that included tortoises with gilded shells, flowers plunged in human blood, and shelves spilling over with cravats and pearl stickpins. Was it the "professor of beauty," whose exquisite taste "petit Marcel" praised, whom Cocteau sought to meet? Or was it the demiurge of pride, whom the same Proust compared to a divinity capable of striking the earth with lightning, before pointing out how Montesquiou's poetry was already sinking into oblivion? Cocteau no doubt did not make a distinction: the sophisticated poet Montesquiou, haunted by the "chimeras of princeliness," and the grandiloquent neurasthenic Montesquiou, who sparingly received the upper crust of society at his Versailles estate surrounded by deep-blue hydrangeas that he caressed like "sick infants," formed in Cocteau's eyes a single flattering entity.

Political sense was the one thing that Cocteau never had. Instead of inter-preting actions of crowds or governments as part of a social movement, he would always prefer to transform them into myths; between anecdote and legend, he made no place for any historical dimension. "History is made of truths that become lies, and mythology is made of lies that eventually become truths," he liked to say.

In Cocteau's view, then, societal change occurred not due to the actions of classes or parties, but through the initiative of individuals pregnant with a secret, a work in progress, or a unique aesthetic. The more spectacular this symbolic "pregnancy" was, the more his appetite was whetted. Without being particu-larly monarchist, he placed titled personages at the center of his attention. Their attributes—crowns, coats of arms, "de" or "von" prefixes, double-barreled patronymics—created a halo around their heads. No one was quicker than Montesquiou at spotting this kind of fascination, of which he was both grand-master and first victim. Ignoring the flattering letters of the young commoner and not even cutting the pages of the books he sent, as well as forgetting to invite Cocteau, despite his repeated overtures, to the regal parties he gave at Versailles, this descendant of d'Artagnan turned an implacable cold shoulder to the young supplicant. The poems and dedications that Cocteau wrote praising the infallible steadiness of the count's gaze and the indefatigable weapon of his shrill voice didn't manage to win him over any more than the letters celebrating his "disconcerting verbal precision" or his "cutting courtesy."[61] The man whose brother had had the good idea of dying very early and leaving all the family fortune to him would reject all Cocteau's compliments—just as he refused, like a social faux pas, any attempt at shifting to the more intimate "tu" form of address.

According to a Russian proverb, "A peasant is concerned with making friends, an aristocrat with making enemies." Cocteau made the mistake of being unaware of this maxim, which would have revealed the motivations of a man who pushed snobbery to heights unknown, even in England. Proust had been able to make Montesquiou an ally by lavishing him with those blue hydrangeas and those colorful birds his poems celebrated—but he still got slapped down when the count learned that he and Lucien Daudet were imitating him as soon as his back was turned. For his part, Cocteau couldn't even attend the lunches offered by Montesquiou, which were said to be served by bats—an allusion to the title of one of Montesquiou's most famous collections of poems, *Les chauves souris*. Opening his doors to an aspiring poet would have meant a loss of social authority for this ultimate relic of the ancien régime who claimed to be the "sovereign of transient things." And since Montesquiou treated anyone claiming to be his friend more harshly every year, how could he have resisted the pleasure of humiliating someone thirty-five years his junior? Nothing could have placated the count, especially not the "tardy" remorse of a little arriviste who had the nerve to confess to Montesquiou that, when he was younger, he had been guilty of gravely misjudging Montesquiou's poetry, but like the shores of a river that are formed and unformed, he had never let himself be carried away. This confession, in Montesquiou's mind, only added affront to immodesty.

So Cocteau was reduced to fawning ever more, and soon to imploring Montesquiou, who was related to a whole host of European aristocrats, to receive his admiration. But the lower Cocteau abased himself, the more ruthless Montesquiou became, since satisfying the masochism of others was the sole pleasure that this sadist ever took in interpersonal relationships. Was it really that Montesquiou saw the overexcited and berouged yearling as a "social liability," as one said while pinching one's nose—in other words, as someone who might reveal his own sexual tastes? In public, the count would never stop pretending to mistake Cocteau for Anna Pavlova, the ballerina in the Ballets Russes with whom he knew Cocteau was friendly: "But I know her well!" Montesquiou would bellow, arching his back, when people insisted on introducing Cocteau to him—the "her" designating all that he himself feared seeming: a hybrid creature that fear of ridicule had condemned to quasi-abstinence.

The aristocratic poet refused as well to be lowered to the rank of dandy. Though he was sexually attracted by ambiguity, Montesquiou could absolutely not endure it socially, his father having made the unforgivable mistake of marrying a woman of the Protestant bourgeoisie—a mismatch that, starting in the cradle, he punished his father for by reserving his affection for a servant. Just as Montesquiou demanded clear distinctions of rank (although his ancestor was the first to call for abolishing privileges on the night of August 4, 1789), the count had so thoroughly internalized the rejection of his sexual inclinations that he thought himself unassailable by always being the first to scorn them in others. Montesquiou did have strange audacities, though: "The effeminate one works and thinks, and predominates / Over the mire of the opaque, heavy male," we read in his first poems.[62] This is a crucial confession for that aesthete whose desires excited every rumor and who, immodest and chaste at the same time, ended up fleeing into the company of objects, until he became one of them.[63] But the young bourgeois Cocteau remained in Montesquiou's eyes one who primarily suffered the mistake of being a social climber, and who would, in all probability, betray him soon for more useful poets—a nightmare for the count who, unable to bear the idea of having to begin a career from scratch like anybody else, suffered from never having been really recognized by the world of letters.

Like a well-guarded house, a blueblood so well defended had to harbor a treasure. Excited by so many rejections, Cocteau came to mimic Montesquiou at a distance by absorbing Proust's imitations of him. "Montesquiou's intonations were still echoing through the air and Cocteau, like a radio wave, captured them. Like a network of telegraphic wires, he spread the different currents that converged on Paris," noted Élisabeth de Gramont—though this time it wasn't Cocteau who was comparing himself to the Eiffel Tower.[64] His letters to Montesquiou became more convoluted, whether he was flattering the count or denigrating himself. Since Montesquiou had publicly reproached him for his presence in the same theater and a few rows away from him, Cocteau's letters of excuses became as *précieux* and arched as their recipient; they were so submissive that they didn't so much convey any strategy as communicate a raw psychophysical need. Cocteau, in keeping with his habit of taking on the color of the celebrities he met, even came to mimic the count's style, down to his ivory-knobbed cane, his close-fitting suits, and his satin sleeves, which he would soon turn up, making him "the last and most volatile travesty of that 'generous Proteus.'"[65] But when Montesquiou finally opened his little apartments to Cocteau, who was duly escorted by Lucien Daudet and Maurice Rostand, Cocteau had already lost all interest in the count.

SITUATION OF SODOM

Cocteau absorbed not only the extravagant compliments of which Proust had made himself the perverse champion; he devoted his first years to imitating (like the author of *Les plaisirs et les jours*, who had in turn imitated La Bruyère, La Rochefoucauld, and Baudelaire) masters whose tics he would soon publicly mock. "I am made of rubber," he would say after meeting Gide; "when I come into contact with people I lose my shape, take on their views and their manners; scarcely have they gone away than I resume my own shape, like a ball."[66] Indeed Cocteau would refuse to meet Maurice Barrès out of a fear of being influenced by him. Along with his fear of not resembling others enough, Cocteau felt an irrepressible need to imitate them. And though his originality was garish, so was his homosexuality—with both giving him profound reasons for pride while at the same time reason for anxiety. But was he unique or ridiculous, this late-arriving dandy who delighted in evoking the odor of violets because Alexander the Great's sweat smelled of them? Uncertain, Cocteau preferred to model himself after unanimously respected figures, waiting for a time when he would, in turn, be able to act as a model.

This ability to change himself made him worry. Despite being confident of his genius when writing to his mother, he had to acknowledge that it was first of all his lineage that people applauded in him. He would confess later that at the time, ten years after his father's death, he would have the same dream several times a week—a dream that his father had become a parrot:

> My mother and I were about to sit down at a table at the Pré-Catelan farm, which mingled several farms with the terrace of cockatoos from the hothouse Garden. I knew my mother knew and didn't know I knew, and I guessed she was looking to see which of these birds my father had become, and why he had become it. I would wake up in tears because of his face which was trying to smile.[67]

The dream is apt. Cocteau's father had been condemned to purely imitative talents as a painter, and this dream-parrot surely expresses the fears of a young writer whom his mother's friends were always comparing to the poets of the dwindling Parnassus movement. Didn't he also betray himself when he stated that everyone carries "a parrot on the left shoulder and a monkey on the right shoulder"—one charged with repeating what habit has already consecrated, the other with laughing, through imitation, at that same habit?[68] One day he would set about killing "these filthy animals," but for the time being he stuffed himself with them: he needed to affix his singularity on an acknowledged strangeness.

This mimicry was ascribed to a sexuality that was understood to render him unstable, like women or Jews—"those two virtuosi of adaptation," said Nietzsche. Indeed his native sycophancy, as well as his taste for imitation, marked him in that era as a mixture of those two types. A few years earlier Otto Weininger, a Jew himself—who while acknowledging humans' fundamental bisexuality only valued man freed of his femininity—had written, "The congruity between Jews and women further reveals itself in the extreme adaptability of the Jews, in their great talent for journalism, the mobility of their minds, their lack of deeply-rooted and original ideas, in fact the mode in which, like women, because they are nothing in themselves, they can become everything."[69] The homosexual, however, was indeed man coming as close as possible to woman, that entity without any real self playing different personalities to the point of hysteria, depending on her amorous phases.

These theories, inherited from fin-de-siècle Europe, were not rare at the time—with Wagner going so far as to condemn the Jews for being only imitators in music, and Weininger noting the total absence of female composers.[70] The first calls for women's rights, the assimilation of Jewish minorities, and the increasing visibility of "men-women" like Proust or Cocteau had all encouraged a mass reflection on identity. Psychiatry had progressed; works by Charcot, Magnan, and Féré, not to mention Richard von Krafft-Ebing's *Psychopathia Sexualis* and Max Nordau's *Degeneration,* had provided the public with the ethnic, medical, and genetic keys to interpreting homosexual customs (so often perceived as a contorted and sacrilegious imitation of real love) and to understand their historical context—"the most Jewish and most effeminate of all time," said Weininger. Did these theories encourage the asthmatic Proust to make the connection between his mimicry and his tendency to develop the most contradictory symptoms? "Neurosis is a brilliant imitator; there is no illness it can't counterfeit perfectly," he would have his character Docteur Du Boulbon say—a phrase that Cocteau could have countersigned, since he had very early feigned illness to keep to his bed and knew full well what power this "gift" conferred to him.

Other theories were circulating. Without naming the model of authentic humanity defined in the works of Weininger or of Nordau—a man with a healthy sexuality, a Christian either by birth or by choice (like those two essayists, both converted Jews), and sufficiently master of himself to make his heritage flourish—Gabriel Tarde had written a little earlier, in *The Laws of Imitation:*

The social like the hypnotic state is only a form of dream, a dream of command and a dream of action. Both the somnambulist and the social man are possessed by the illusion that their ideas, all of which have been suggested to them, are spontaneous. . . . *Society is imitation, and imitation is a kind of somnambulism.*[71]

Instead of this mass mimicry, Cocteau practiced a very personal form of imitation destined to perfect him by giving him access to the "genius" of the prestigious figures whom he absorbed, as Chinese calligraphy tends to take the form of the object it designates. Though some of this process certainly escaped his conscious control, he resisted its force only periodically; he was instead delighted at regular intervals in how it reshaped him. Cocteau would seize these opportunities to escape from himself, even if it meant losing all personal specificity, hence all literary authenticity. The very paradoxical Weininger—who saw genius only in the masculine principle—asserted: "The number of different aspects that the face of a man has assumed may be taken almost as a physiognomical measure of his talent."[72]

When Cocteau was twenty-two, his nose began to grow longer until it closely resembled the long, nervous, and decidedly unsensuous nose of his mother. People stopped complimenting him on his looks and instead found nonhuman resemblances in him: the whirring insect sampling every pond, the moth singed at every lamp, or the shrew pointing its snout at the slightest smell. To Proust he would be a seahorse or a mermaid, to Ravel a fawn always getting its feet tangled up.[73] Not content with having created him in a different mold, nature seemed to delight in emphasizing his zoological peculiarities, making him resemble strange species.

Homosexuality, which in that era was perceived as an anomaly, even a curse—Proust's work testifies amply to this—was still regarded as an act against nature. The homosexual's threat to family, nation, and even humanity was due to the fact that he was not created the right way up, which is why he is often called an invert: slimy as a snail, the hermaphrodite animal par excellence, and just as twisted as its shell. A playful, even condescending attitude toward homosexuality is considered appropriate today; the male homosexual passes then for a moral weathervane, ingratiating in public and perfidious in private, both supposedly symptoms of a deeper, more shocking undependability. Widespread in the circles that Cocteau frequented but rarely avowed in public, punishable by no law in France but nonetheless a reason for discrediting someone, homosexuality still produces, through oppressive silences and damaging lies, lives lived nearly exclusively in the closet, relieved only by brief exhibitionist fits of hysteria in the shelter of out-of-the-way places. But if veiled language and awkwardness were customary in the provinces, an old tradition of welcome maintained a close network of associations, bars, and baths in a capital city that pretended to be surprised by nothing, and in fact has been inhabited by extreme figures since the ancien régime, from the *chevalier de la manchette* dancing with the Sun King to the transvestite minister working for Louis XV, from the chevalier d'Éon in the *Incroyables* strutting about under the Directory to the sterile dandy celebrated by Baudelaire, from the decadent dear to Huysmans to the man-woman performed by Rachilde, to name just a few.

The invisibility of virile inverts, who were disgusted by any form of effeminacy and almost never came out of the closet, meant that only the most garish and flamboyant figures appeared as the public images of homosexuality.[74] Mothers, too, were inclined to shadow their mannered sons, shielding them from associations with the love that dared not say its name. These prejudices indirectly encouraged Proust, Cocteau, and Lucien Daudet to maintain these maternal relationships as a way of experiencing the love they could not find elsewhere. Maurice Rostand, for instance, would never leave his mother, and the Ochsé brothers went so far as to set up their mother's coffin in their dining room in Neuilly.[75] This connection with the mother as friend and love is not accidental. Because whereas during this era man was synonymous with power—as the bearded, hatted, potbellied, amplified one with fur coats and opera hats, fur collars and top hats, the one who orders and pays, thinks, and governs—a woman could leave her domestic domain only to become a frivolous fairy, whose undulating undergarments and toxic charm were exalted by the aesthetics of 1900 through seaweed and jellyfish, ghouls and dragonflies, bats and orchids, arabesques and flourishes. Grace and pleasure, fantasy and expense remained her exclusive domain.

Mockery, however, remains a form of tolerance. Since French Republican morality, just as much as Christian morality, frowned on the sterility, narcissism, and supposed anomalies of homosexuals, thousands of men simply refused to shake the hand of a pederast, as if their reputation, or even their virility, could be affected by it. That was the case for Paul Morand's father, to whom it happened without his knowing—and he a subtle, cultivated man, who directed a museum and translated Shakespeare: "The bourgeois, ordinarily, had a horror of 'buggery' . . . from father to son," confirms François Porché.[76] These prejudices were spread even among the literary ranks, where only Octave Mirbeau, Marcel Schwob, and Hugues Rebell rose up against the sentencing of Oscar Wilde to the "reading jail," where he spent two years unknotting tarred ropes after the trial he had brought against the father of his lover, Lord Alfred Douglas. Even someone as unconventional as Pierre Louÿs had chosen to break with the author of the *Picture of Dorian Gray*; Alphonse Daudet, Lucien's father and the friend of Reynaldo Hahn, also slipped away.

But homosexuality was not shameful in France. Consider Jean Lorrain, the writer who took pride in loving hoodlums long before Genet, and who always escaped punishment, despite his exhibitionism and a few duels—one with Proust, whose inclinations he had the misfortune of hinting at, calling him effeminate. In fact a bourgeois homosexuality existed, of which the unsurpassable embodiment was that same Proust. This bourgeois homosexuality had its scriptures and its initiations; its members flattered themselves as being the heirs of Antiquity via Alcibiades, of the Renaissance via Michelangelo, or of Wilde's England. The most radical defended the theory of the ancients, who saw in love a kind of illness, making it a Christian invention. In this kind of homosexuality one tries to appear cultivated, spiritual, and nasty if necessary, and one can exhibit dandyism or decadence without great risk, in the midst of the cult of the self: after all, the Rimbaud-Verlaine couple had accustomed readers to seeing in these loves a licentiousness inherent in poetry.

Cocteau would later have recourse to the marginal circuits of the "other" homosexuality, from Villefranche to Toulon. Like Proust in the beginning, he was at first attracted by the boys in his milieu, in his impatience to be recognized by that milieu. Because he was not an activist either by conviction or by nature, he still knew only the ghetto of his own caste. Homosexuality would become a weapon of literary blackmail with Genet; before Genet's tremendous breakthrough, it stemmed from a subterranean world, sensed everywhere but rarely named, unless by coded allusions. After his initial period of attraction was over, Cocteau always preferred discretion over deliberate exhibition.

UPPER-CRUST EN ROSE AND FAUX NOBILITY

The salons that Cocteau's mother frequented, in the strongholds of Parisian high society like the Plaine Monceau, the faubourg Saint-Honoré, or the avenue de l'Impératrice (now the avenue Foch) were actually where Cocteau felt most at home. Far from being ostracized, he was immediately welcomed for bringing to the group the culture and refinement that husbands (jealous, incurious, or inherently awkward as they were), and bachelors (by nature overly womanizing) sometimes lacked. Even if Cocteau had written nothing, a man with his manners already passed for a kind of basic artist, a sort of missing link between enlightened amateur and demanding creator—"a bachelor of art" (*un célibataire de l'art*), as Proust called those writers without books who appeared so frequently in À *la recherche du temps perdu*.

How could Cocteau not have felt grateful to these elites who treated him so well and always reserved a place for him at the feet of the queens, real or symbolic, who were still at its center? And by what miracle could the "inverts" who aspired to these salons be anything but conservative? One had to wait until the 1920s and 1930s to see another kind of homosexuality appear on the scene, one that frequented bars rather than salons, and one personified by those like René Crevel or Pierre Herbart who became involved in politics despite the growing intolerance of the USSR for any nonconformist desires. Proust had indeed valiantly defended the innocence of Captain Dreyfus at the risk of having important doors closed to him, but that faithful reader of *L'action française* basically desired nothing but to belong to the cream of society.[77] Why would Abel Hermant, a writer famous at the time, or De Max the actor have wanted to revolt—they who dined in the best houses before slipping off to the public urinals on the boulevards? And why would the young provincial who was François Mauriac, who followed Cocteau with dazzled eyes, want to declare his sexuality—he who would later approach the "frivolous prince" by speaking of Barrès, his literary idol? Everyone had understood, from Mauriac's clothing and his turns of phrase, that this shy man who had arrived in Paris in 1909 from Bordeaux was not a great womanizer. As Maurice Rostand exclaimed one day, when the voluminous Paul Claudel, between diplomatic missions, revealed that he was surprised that "creatures" like him weren't social outcasts: "But, Your Excellency! If they were, the salons would be empty!"[78] As a member of a minority that was easy to ridicule, Cocteau was content with the hothouse where he was born, since only there could "sensitives" like Lucien Daudet, Marcel Proust, and him grow and prosper. The bourgeoisie, whose path had been opened by the populace that stormed the Bastille, was triumphing at the turn of the century. Sure of its rights and legitimacy, it was preparing to absorb by osmosis, after a century of domination, what was left of the old nobility. Living partly off private income, like the Lecomte-Cocteaus, and just as convinced of its enlightened role, it laid claim to the heritage of the pre-1889 aristocracy, whose mansions, social habits, and even sometimes titles it had usurped—finding an Oedipal way to celebrate the caste it had contributed to "curtailing," starting with the sale of national property. With the haughty but smiling expression of a sovereign in exile, Mme Cocteau wonderfully embodied this false nobility—elites who, in their impatience to adopt old-fashioned customs in order to orchestrate an imitation of the ancien régime, gave balls at Versailles and suppers in fake straw huts, like Marie-Antoinette at her Hameau de la Reine model farm. Mme Cocteau summed up this usurpation for which Robert de Montesquiou was the active guilty conscience—he who still regarded the absence of "de" in one's name as an infirmity and loved nothing so much as socially tormenting his guests. A prominent member of the upper crust of the

Republic, Mme Cocteau would be aware enough of her privilege to fear, during the First World War, a return in force of the authentic nobility that would again exclude her from the "best" salons. But for now, the aristocracy had such a great need to regild its coats of arms that it couldn't do without the bourgeoisie, which had taken up the aristocracy's former role as protector of the arts, much like the virile and superb Winnaretta—the American heir of the Singer sewing machine fortune who had married the Prince de Polignac and now held literary and musical salons.

A generation younger, Cocteau only now and then shared Marcel Proust's and Lucien Daudet's preference for fallen queens, from the Empress Eugénie to the picturesque Ranavalo (the ex-sovereign of Madagascar, a regular at Madeleine Lemaire's salons). Cocteau's Persian-prince airs, though, hinted at the dreams of grandeur he harbored, just like the allure of Proust's "Rajah dressed in European style" or the emir's silhouette of the younger Daudet, who was sometimes compared to a nonchalant Arabic ruler.[79] All of these influences and experiences led Cocteau to see himself as the cream of that gentlemanly bourgeoisie—especially Cocteau's visit to the ex-empress Eugénie around Easter 1911, which was arranged by Lucien Daudet and the aide-de-camp of Her Imperial Majesty. At the end of a slow stroll through the gardens of the Villa Cyrnos at Cap-Martin, the imperial hands decorated the poet's buttonhole with a flower picked expressly for him. "An interminable minute, a frightening minuet dance step, lost in the night of time," exclaimed the wunderkind as he left this very old celebrity, born during the reign of Charles X; his mother had inherited the empress's first name, but not the ability to ennoble.

There still remained a Comtesse de Chevigné to give the youngster the cold shoulder in the entryway of their building on the rue d'Anjou. With a face of an angry bird of prey and masculine looks, her voice gravelly from chainsmoking caporal cigarettes and "hoarse as if from centuries of commands," this descendant of the Marquis de Sade and the Laure de Noves celebrated by Petrarch offered up a royal brusqueness in opposition to the gushes of the young snob whom fate, so unfair socially, had made her neighbor, and what's more whose apartment was above her own.[80] This woman, whom Morand had claimed was the first woman in the world to say "merde" and who asserted she had learned everything "en baisant," had, during her first encounters with Cocteau, become increasingly ribald. Seeing Cocteau rush to her Pomeranian, named Kiss, to scratch its muzzle, she had cried out, "Watch out, you'll get rice powder on him!," as if the young perfumed man risked making her pet, and by extension she herself, effeminate.[81] The Comtesse de Chevigné's keen sense of independence had made her one of the rare women in Paris to go out without a husband,

and it wasn't easy to sway this libertine dragon who would shout at her old servant, when he dared disturb her, "Now what, Auguste?"[82] Proust himself, who had been pursuing her with a platonic passion since he was a child, had to be content with writing her untiringly flattering letters or dashing out to the countryside where, if he wasn't turned away, he could see the comtesse, an excellent sharpshooter dressed in clothes the color of dead leaves, "inhaling powder through open nostrils" like a real battle horse.[83]

Curly-haired like a pageboy and hard as a country squire, the Comtesse de Chevigné hid beneath her bad mood a real strangeness, almost the beginnings of madness. Apollinaire himself sometimes came to pay solitary tribute to this unhinged member of royalty who every afternoon received mature men of high birth, arranging them like the Knights of the Round Table around the Grail, their top hats carefully placed on their knees. The author of *Alcools* liked the officer's-mess humor and the coarse babbling—with its half-aristocrat, half-coachman elements—of this Diana risen from a hunting party. Did she embody the height of coarseness or the most extreme refinement? That was the question Cocteau asked himself for a long time, while the countess's doors remained doubly closed to him—"My old beasts growl when they smell fresh meat," she pretended to regret.

Proust remained the most fervent follower of the Comtesse de Chevigné, whose inaccessibility only reinforced her charm. His attachment had become so profound and desperate, after twenty years of rejection, that À *la recherche du temps perdu* can be seen as an attempt to embalm the mythological essence of the countess under the somewhat transformed but still recognizable envelope of the Duchesse de Guermantes, in a literary cathedral that would illuminate her for eternity.[84] He was no longer the transfixed lover who cried, at the age of twenty, when he recognized the features of his idol in the face of her young nephew, but he did dream obsessively of seeing, convincing, and captivating the woman who still refused to notice him.

Cocteau too knew how to be patient. Pushed to the point of exaggeration by repeated refusals, he developed a strategy for flattering that was reminiscent—minus the genius, but with a certain extra sobriety—of the literary arabesques of "petit Marcel." While Proust likened the countess to someone "descended from a goddess and a bird," Cocteau learned above all not to offend the touchy virility of the woman whom he nicknamed "Corporal Petrarch," as well as to never oppose her tastes, which had been peremptorily formed from a thousand disgusted reactions inflamed by the slightest familiarity. The friendship of this descendant of the greatest families of France was indeed rewarding, as was her past intimacy with the Comte de Chambord, the last credible pretender to the throne of France, during her exile in Frohsdorf.

Cocteau was no doubt already less fooled than Proust by this game, judging from the portraits he drew of that queen in pants after she had finally accepted him. But his malice never reached the complexities of Proustian cruelty, or the dizzying profundity that Proust, in *À la recherche*, would accord to Oriane de Guermantes, the ostrich-plumed dowagers, the eagle-beaked Jockey-clubbers, and the other caricatures that "petit Marcel" had the patience, and finally the kindness, to change into archetypes, even if it was only the better to capture them. The fact is that Proust had to love the froglike Chevigné in order to inject into her his brilliant venom and puff her up to the point of absurdity, even if only to leave her for dead at the end of a three-thousand-page narrative that did away forever with the formula of the social novel. Too restless to dig so deeply, Cocteau was also too concerned with the reflections of his own social advancement. Of that ancien régime ersatz, Cocteau retained literarily only the old-fashioned charm of her *fêtes galantes*, with their wisteria-covered swings à la Watteau. The parody remained credible enough, with its wigged lackeys and titled lords straight out of the letters of Mme de Sévigné or the anecdotes of Chamfort, for Cocteau to imagine himself the little prince: France had after all almost relapsed into a monarchy, under the rule of Mac Mahon, and the greatest European powers, from England to Austria-Hungary, still bore the crown.

From these salons, Cocteau would in the end retain only a way of gathering his intuitions together into striking phrases, with a skillful dose of drollery and spite. He cultivated the art of the portrait, or rather the silhouette, with the graphic intuition that his writing also sustained: Mallarmé? "A lump of crystal." Francis Jammes? "Primrose that belches." André Germain?[85] "A child who gives strychnine enemas to his doll."[86] No almanac would be big enough to contain all Cocteau's phrases, which he scattered until his last breath, and which floated aloft, took root a little further on, and were later attributed to Proust, Léon Daudet, or Maurice Barrès, whose turns of phrase Cocteau may indeed have adapted. Thus Paris spoke a single language through a hundred mouths trained to say everything quickly.

These social hothouses, no doubt the hottest and most fertile in Europe, made Cocteau an overdeveloped prodigy. "Talking is for me a kind of joy, just as flying must be for Latham [an aviator who fell into the sea] or dancing for Duncan," he wrote at the time to François Mauriac, his elder by four years, whom he had summoned in order to hand him his verdict about Mauriac's *Mains jointes*, a collection of poems to which Barrès had just devoted a laudatory article.[87] Outdoing himself in his natural vivacity, Cocteau spoke so quickly that he came to evoke a kind of dervish, one drunk on his own superiority in the heart of that fleur-de-lis republic. His eye, too, seemed to have been influenced by those overcharged interiors whose inventory had already been sketched by Vuillard, Moreau, and Huysmans. Mauriac, Cocteau's accomplice in society from then on, along with Lucien Daudet, also noticed this neo-oriental bric-à-brac. Remembering the soirées given by the painter Jacques-Émile Blanche at Offranville, Mauriac would recall those old houses where "the bricks, the flint and the sandstone have the color of a turtledove's neck—yellow living room with cloudy mirrors, lacquered cabinet, Chinese paintings, boxes of shells, blue-and-white porcelain from Canton and Delft."[88] To this collection of things were added, at the home of Robert de Montesquiou, the cane of Beau Brummell, a plaster cast of the chin of the Comtesse Greffulhe, and Bonaparte's chamber pot.

Such decorative abundances and verbal orgies would not satisfy Mauriac for long. The intimidated provincial finally declared his desire for the young Parisian, who responded so poorly to Mauriac's burning expectations that the rejected one soon wrote, at the bottom of one of his poems, "I kiss your cracked lips."[89] Mauriac would never forget this disappointment, and later also wrote to Cocteau, with semi-mystical force: "I would have liked to be the person in your life who carries a little bit of real Light."[90] In keeping with the naïve arrogance of his precocity, Cocteau accepted the rejected man's complaints philosophically: after all, Cocteau had called his second collection of poetry *Le prince frivole*, asserting from the outset:

> Disdainful, frivolous and thin,
> Dreaming and childlike,
> I was born to be a prince;
> A little prince in exile.

3

THE LIVING GOD

That is what they do not understand, for they are now undoubtedly
discussing me, saying I escape them, am evasive. They do not understand
that I have to effect different transitions; have to cover the entrances
and exits of several different men who alternately act their parts as Bernard.
—*Virginia Woolf*, The Waves

THE MAN-BIRD

On May 19, 1909, Jean Cocteau and Lucien Daudet, in Cocteau's mother's
box at the Théâtre du Châtelet, attended the dress rehearsal of "The Dance of
the Polovtsian Maidens" from Borodin's opera *Prince Igor*, to be performed by
the Ballets Russes and staged worldwide by Gabriel Astruc, the theater's director.
The auditorium was packed; his mother's box had been newly renovated for the
occasion. And those wonderful barbarians—flying from the splendors of
Versailles to the deserted steppes of Asia—made Cocteau dream with his eyes
open. A unanimous shout had greeted this spectacle from distant Russia, and
part of the audience, including Anna de Noailles, Reynaldo Hahn, Jacques-
Émile Blanche, and Misia, the Polish wife of the press mogul Alfred Edwards,
had rushed onto the stage to get close to these extraterrestrial beings: Nijinsky
and Karsavina, the leading dancers; Fokine, the choreographer; and Bakst and
Benois, the set designers.

From box to box, Cocteau had sung the praises of both the troupe,
which had so expertly brought to life the fashionable oriental universe of Paul
Poiret, as well as *Schéhérazade*, the journal Cocteau had recently launched. By
the collective use of set, music, and costumes, Diaghilev's elaborately maquil-
laged dancers had managed to synthesize all the arts—something that hadn't

happened since the Parisian triumph of Wagnerism—and augment their performance with eroticism. With his sylph-like grace and the endurance of a muzhik, Nijinsky broke immediately into Cocteau's imagination. Half-angel, half-leopard, he embodied in his powerful leaps the incarnate human-bird hybrid so yearned for by Romantic dance throughout the nineteenth century. Members of the audience, disturbed by his animality, likened him to a cat, snake, or even stallion—but given the fragility they sensed in him, even more frequently to a fish thrashing about on the deck of a boat.

Introduced by the Rostands to Misia Edwards, the sponsor of the Ballets Russes, then to Diaghilev, their impresario, Cocteau had hurried to their box (much more strategically placed than his mother's) to watch Nijinsky's super-human leaps—then later was granted access backstage, thanks to Leon Bakst, the set designer. The contrast between the dancer's lethargic indifference before the performances and the intensity of his presence on stage struck Cocteau. Whereas in ordinary dress Nijinsky called to mind "an overdressed stable-boy, or a department store salesman with thinning hair," the athletic dancer had only to put on his costume for the poetry of his unfinished personality to blossom from "tiny monkey" to elf. The stage elongated him extraordinarily; the "jockey . . . with a pale Kalmuck face," with stocky legs and short fingers, "as if cut off at the knuckles," seemed to lengthen at the neck, like a column—as if his body were conceived not for the open air, but for the strict format of theater and opera boxes.[1]

Cocteau would miss none of the dancer's triumphs during the seasons to come. In the gardens of Jacques-Émile Blanche, in Passy, he outlined in graphite the rump of a sphinx leaning in the grass—Nijinsky in the Siamese costume of the *Orientales*—while amusing the irresistible Karsavina with his imperson-ations. He came even closer to representing Nijinsky in motion, though the ambiguity of the dancer stirred him so much that he signed his sketch as "an accidental draftsman"; the image would be used for magnificent posters announcing *Le spectre de la rose*, in which Nijinsky and Karsavina seem to soar from their slippers like two lilies from the bud.

Le spectre de la rose constituted the public apogee of Nijinsky, a prodigy whose ability to turn himself into a rose Cocteau exalted in the magazine *Comoedia*. The dancer seemed to embody the spread of a rose's perfume, and, by his "leap that was so moving, so contrary to all laws of equilibrium," to suggest a rose's scent wafting through an open window. In the orchestra seats, the audi-ence had the impression of endless flight—Jacques Rivière would ever after see in his mind's eye the loop Nijinsky opened by launching himself through space "as if picked up . . . by the indeterminate mass of the possible."[2] Backstage,

Cocteau found a poor creature soaked with sweat and smeared with makeup, clutching his heart with one hand and leaning on the set with the other. The ballet lasted only eight minutes, but each second was pure torture; to make his final leap more spectacular, he knotted himself in the air before falling straight down in the wings, as at the end of a double leap. "He was given a boxer's treatment, with hot towels, roused with slaps and water which his servant Dmitri spat in his face," said Cocteau.[3] Holding his sides, leaning on a support, "almost fainting, showered, massaged, sponged off by his caretakers and by us," the poor athlete still had to catch his breath to return for his bows: more than an idol, it was a hero Cocteau saw smiling under the encores, sometimes fifty in a row.[4]

The agonies that Nijinsky inflicted on himself marked Cocteau for a long time. More effectively than Proust's suggestions or his mother's warnings, the single-minded labor of Nijinsky convinced Cocteau that one deserves artistic recognition only when one devotes oneself radically to the art form. During the Femina matinée, all Cocteau had had to do to earn applause was present himself: in the future, by contrast, he would devote himself until he drew blood. Nijinsky typified everything that Cocteau admired—artistic selflessness, proud timidity, overweening ambition. Whether he was tiptoeing across the stage *en pointe* or leaping up toward the rigging loft, thighs tense as springs, he embodied the height of discipline while magically surpassing it at the same time. On stage, he had the delicacy of a memory, they said; but scarcely was he in the street than his little body melted into the mass of humanity. Did he abolish gravity for fun, or from nostalgia for the heaven that had conceived him? Firmly in touch with the cosmos, this creature who compared himself to an earthquake above all evoked Zarathustra's cry: "A god dances through me." Nietzsche's Dionysian expectations, which Gautier-Vignal had just helped Cocteau discover, were finally being realized.

Nietzsche was in fact a significant influence, the only master with whom Cocteau would unreservedly identify himself. The philosopher, who had recently died but was already influential in France, had revealed to Cocteau his own profound contradictions and inspired him to develop his aesthetic versatility. It was as if this subtle stylist, this powerful thinker, "true as the sun and the sea," had personally appealed to Cocteau to create a kind of mastered excess, in hopes of reintegrating, via strong personalities, the vital force that centuries of civilization had undermined.[5] Nietzsche anticipated Cocteau's intuitions, the poetry of his ideas, the theory of his whims. By proving the fertile use that one could make of malady, he showed all creators the pathway of endurance while suffering for them like a pagan Christ. Before Nietzsche, Cocteau saw himself as a winged, inspired being; after Nietzsche, through contact with Nijinsky, he thought of himself as a superhuman entity charged with spreading the warmth of divine actions over the earth.

"I can only believe in a god that can dance," said Nietzsche, and no one seemed to have understood him as well as Nijinsky, embodiment of that divinity. Indeed Nietzsche, the "philosopher with the hammer," seemed almost to live again in this muzhik's body, which was so desirable to others and yet a source of such suffering to himself. This utter gift that Cocteau would demand from love, often in vain, he now could enjoy every evening, thanks to Diaghilev's creature. A booklet of six Cocteau poems about the dancer, printed on rice paper and illustrated by Paul Iribe, made this love concrete, even if at a distance. The dancer who was controlled with an iron fist by his Pygmalion Diaghilev—Stravinsky said that Nijinsky's spirit was as weak as his muscles were strong—appeared as a Hermes capable of "carrying all hearts on invisible wings," and again as an inspired marionette, like Petrushka:

> Apollo holds the thread from which he hangs,
> Sultan's moor, he soars fleeing away . . .[6]

Thus would it always be with Cocteau: climbing and descending, passing from realism to mythology. No doubt he would have been even more lyrical without the intimidating presence of Apollo-Diaghilev, that "bulldog with a tooth showing at the rim of his smile."[7] Did he ever find elsewhere such a perfect fusion between body, ideal, and will? It was no accident that most of Cocteau's lovers and his "sons," from Radiguet to Desbordes, from Jean Marais to Édouard Dermit, would have a savage, animalistic touch of Nijinsky about them.

MISIA, "CHINCHILLA," AND "LITTLE MARCEL"

Diaghilev was lucky, when he landed in Paris in 1908, to "scatter his Muscovite seed" there: his *Boris Godunov* had made such a strong impression on the sensual, redheaded Misia that she bought up all the seats for the eight performances to come and filled them by the deadline.[8] Misia, a friend of Mallarmé, a guiding light of *La revue blanche*, and a legendary muse who had inspired dozens of canvases by Vuillard, Vallotton, Bonnard, Toulouse-Lautrec, and Renoir, prepared the way for the Parisian triumph of the Ballets Russes and their impresario.

Misia became the royal exception to Diaghilev's famous misogyny, and his beloved "sister." Not only did Misia enjoy the social power of filling auditoriums and granting her chosen ones a kind of "travel pass" that was equivalent to belonging to a club; she also wielded this power with a cruel strength, as a woman without an oeuvre or children of her own who thrived on seeing the progeny of others aborted—Mme de Chevigné seemed like an honest friend in comparison. But Diaghilev was filled with gratitude when Misia set about celebrating him and introducing him to the Parisian social and erotic "morsels" he relished. As a supreme homage, Diaghilev went so far as to swear, between quarrels, that she was the only woman with whom he could have lived. "Terribly naughty, adorably kind, destroying anything that didn't come to her," according to Valentine Hugo—this icon with a baby face usually frightened people. "If she was tormented by some anxiety, the atmosphere became unbreatheable," wrote Cocteau about Misia's novelistic double, the Princesse de Bormes, in *Thomas l'imposteur*: "She carried her atmosphere around her as the earth does, and, like the earth, she had difficulty believing in other inhabited worlds."9 But Cocteau, in his irrepressible thirst for conquest, liked nothing so much as confronting this sort of *monstre*.

Previously married to Thadée Natanson, the founder of *La revue blanche*, but leaving him and then Alfred Edwards for José Maria Sert, "the Michelangelo of the Ritz," Misia received people in her salon on the quai Voltaire opposite the Tuileries, among screens by Bonnard, panels painted by Vuillard (who had long loved her), and those lacquered screens from Coromandel that could later be found at the home of her young protégée, Coco Chanel. Determined to cast a spell on this fairy of the arts, Cocteau turned up at her place with the assurance of a Bonaparte, launching into stories that he would conduct with his arms like a maestro, or discussing his poems with an authority he'd acquired in the Daudet circle. Making people laugh, think, and feel at the same time—the ideal achievement for a salon—this Franco-Persian *djinn* imposed himself on the very woman who had already formed prejudices about his character. "He was irresistible," said Misia, quite content to flee earthly reality without leaving her apartment. The hostess of the quai Voltaire was nothing but instinct, as her shallow memoirs would prove. Unlike those women unbalanced by their virile intelligence in *Thomas l'imposteur*, she remained profoundly feminine in her impatience to dominate, seduce, and influence. Her need for veneration fed Cocteau's tendency to become all the famous people he met, without too much discernment, and soon the pair were seen everywhere, only too happy to contradict gravity together.

Like great Pan, full of atmosphere, will, power, and cruelty, Diaghilev could also have intimidated Cocteau: he had the air of a colonel of some degenerate cavalry, always about to horsewhip his subaltern. But Cocteau was in that state of exaltation in which the stronger the personalities he approached, the more powerful he himself felt—and his taste for *monstres sacrés* redoubled his hidden desire for Nijinsky. "A royal aura floated around Diaghilev," said Maurice Sachs, describing the prime narcotic that Cocteau sought. Cocteau thus approached the impresario with as much ardor as if he were the Shah of Persia or Pope Pius X—impatient as he was to be baptized by Misia's "big brother," a man already known for detecting genius in its embryonic state.

With his crocodile smile and his swindler's cane, his coachman's belly and his procurer's fur coats, Diaghilev did indeed have a royal authority: the big white streak in his black hair evoked the ostrich feather of cocked hats of princes or presidents of the time and earned him the nickname "Chinchilla." "Your Majesty, I am like you, I don't work, but I am indispensable," he would say, when Alfonso XIII was concerned to know what he actually did. Neither dancer, nor composer, nor choreographer, not even a set designer—that is, lacking in both scruples and real talent—this young man from the provinces was content to direct his Ballets Russes with all his Jupiter-like personality. To be able to resist the physical and social agility of Cocteau, ordinarily one would have had to hate his milieu or be afraid of Paris. These tragedies had been spared Diaghilev. Cocteau, however, unlike Misia, would lack the ability to frighten this brute, who must have found the urban refinements of *La lampe d'Aladin* mannered in comparison with his own rough origins. Moreover, Diaghilev shared Montesquiou's prejudices against homosexuals, who were often the first victims of his misogyny. Although Diaghilev himself dyed his hair black, he sniffed at any suggestion of the "Damenimitator," as female impersonators would be baptized in Berlin in the 1920s; in private, he sometimes accused Cocteau of being "female," the way you might throw a glass of cold water on a cat in heat.

The thought that anyone could resist his charm or not recognize his talents was unbearable to Cocteau. Faced with the cold, slimy eye of Diaghilev, Cocteau multiplied his attempts and outdid himself in flattery. One evening he went so far as to walk on the tables at Larue, the famous restaurant on the Madeleine, hand his possum fur to the impresario, then, after seeking Proust's table, rejoin Nijinsky's in a pirouette—all from his wish to show that he too could dance. After this display he left, balancing on the red banquettes, drunk on his own levity.[10] "Obviously, you needed more than that to get Diaghilev to collaborate with you," commented Misia Sert, who, as Proust said, liked to gather her friends so as to better make them fall out with each other.

Yet Cocteau and Diaghilev would soon collaborate, for the author of *À la recherche du temps perdu* was also hovering around the Ballets Russes, to see the deluxe avant-garde company that he had admired early on. Karsavina would remember him, sprightly, polite, and shy as a ghost—(or "a day-old gardenia," according to Jacques Porel, one of his friends)—accompanying her at night back to her apartment. This shared passion brought Proust and Cocteau together. Even though Proust didn't wholly share Cocteau's fascination with Nijinsky, the Dionysian choreography of the Ballets Russes was the ultimate expression of the pair's oriental dreams, peopled as they were with sultans and hetaerae.

Did Proust send Cocteau this poem, when he returned from their evening at Larue?[11]

> To cover me with furs and silks,
> Without spilling the black ink from his great eyes,
> Like a sylph on the ceiling, like skis on the snow
> Jean leaped up on the table beside Nijinsky—
> It was in Larue's crimson dining room
> Whose gold, in doubtful taste, never grew dim . . .[12]

Whoever wrote them, these alexandrines bear witness to the attraction that Diaghilev's ballets already exercised over the informal pléiade uniting Reynaldo Hahn, Lucien Daudet, Marcel Proust, and Jean Cocteau. Proust went so far as to compare the excitement that the ballets aroused to the electricity that surrounded the Dreyfus case. Diaghilev loomed over them all, with his cackles of laughter and his byzantine intrigues, his ogre's physique and his witch's grudges, his excessive personality surpassing in theatricality everything that these already larger-than-life characters knew. He had lived other lives before the Ballets Russes, and the failed baritone as well as the humiliated musician lent their fire to the impresario's terrible fits of rage. Capable of dozing off at a moment's notice like Gulliver, but also able to leap up just as quickly to enforce his sadistic will, he evoked by turns Ivan the Terrible and Catherine the Great, Nero and Lorenzo the Magnificent.

Since derision was at the time inherent in homosexual culture, veneration soon veered off into buffoonery. Proust and Cocteau weren't content to laugh only at fools; they also had to make fun of those whom they admired, as if to erase the memory of their own obsequiousness and snobbism. Although Proust's weakness for dusty dukes was scarcely shared by Cocteau, both liked to ensnare remarkable social samples, whether comic or bizarre, and examine them with that benevolent cruelty peculiar to superior minds. They then revived them through new imitations, even fiercer, in a process that assured them a fanciful control over a society that was at the time all-powerful—and in Proust's case, served as a step in the transformation of these "captives" into butterflies in print.

Cocteau was not only "very remarkably intelligent and talented," as Proust confided to his friend Robert de Billy; he was amusing to the point of inducing uncontrollable fits of laughter (Cocteau describes "petit Marcel" holding back his merriment with his hand, stroking his beard, tittering "as if behind a woman's fan"). These moments of shared hilarity encouraged Proust, in early 1912, to take Cocteau to see Mme Ayen's collection of paintings by Gustave Moreau, then, at the Louvre, Mantegna's *Saint Sebastian*, a subject whose arrow-riddled body had already inspired Wilde and Montesquiou. Fifteen years earlier, Proust had taken the very young Lucien Daudet to the same museum almost every day in order to sharpen his sensibility, if not make his heart catch fire. The pilgrimage with Cocteau was striking enough for Proust to talk, months later, about that "glorious morning when the sun pierced Saint Sebastian with its arrows" as Cocteau recited one of his poems, "La Pallas d'Homère."

As an ultimate sign of this rediscovered closeness, after the "betrayal" of Cocteau's intimacy with Montesquiou, Cocteau was now treated to readings from À *la recherche du temps perdu* when he visited the boulevard Haussmann. A valet led him through rows of furniture, covered with sheets that the movers seemed to have just deposited, to that "bedroom of cork, dust and phials." There he found Proust in bed, gloved, writing and crossing out in the light of a single lightbulb, daylight having become unbearable to him.[13] Soon the smell of mothballs and Legras anti-asthma fumigations that were indispensable to the growth of À *la recherche du temps perdu* enveloped Cocteau, whose shadow came to join the narrator's in the ambient smoke. "Marcel Proust's bedroom, on the boulevard Haussmann, was the first darkroom where I witnessed every day—it would be truer to say every night, since he lived at night—the development of a powerful work," he would say.[14] The comparison with photography is characteristic of Cocteau, to whom the quasi-electric aura emanating from Proust's frail body evoked a camera's flash dazzling in darkness.

Proust, with his frozen hands, who scarcely ate and only rarely went outdoors, kept writing when Cocteau entered his bedroom. Then he would push back the covers and the *boules*—big hot-water bottles warming his stomach—to seize his manuscript folder and submit Cocteau to a test. But Proust's reading would scarcely reach its regular rhythm before the recumbent figure with the waxlike complexion, interrupting the muted voice, would decree his own book "deadly dull" and leave Cocteau hanging in mid-sentence (with Cocteau himself too sensitive to the timbre of Comédie-Française actors not to privately agree with him). Though Cocteau felt he was already dismissed, he would then beg for Proust to agree to let him dip again into the manuscript. Proust would finally consent, but only after complaining about his own disastrous aptitude as a reader. The reading would then resume, but at an episode with no relationship whatsoever to the previous one, to Cocteau's great confusion.[15]

On other occasions, the two men's sensibilities were so profoundly in tune with each other that they seemed to fuse: "Our minds, those twin mirrors," Proust would say, in a dedication to his younger friend.[16] But despite their similar natures, Proust could feel only memories of desire and love, and Cocteau only an amused fascination for his elder. There remained their active mimicry. But Cocteau could not become Proust—he already was Proust, in part. And although Proust seemingly could become Cocteau for a time—he had already been that character, twenty years earlier—he was much further along in his development. (A revealing detail: Cocteau never attempted a literary imitation of Proust, whereas Proust parodied Cocteau's style in a text meant for his *Pastiches et mélanges*, which remained uncompleted and unpublished.[17])

The two artists' modes of expression, to tell the truth, were worlds apart: although the pair resembled each other in terms of what they wanted to show of themselves, an abyss separated their hidden worlds. Proust's consciousness was a huge greenhouse dazzled by the slightest ray of sunlight, where the smallest sound echoed like a shout, like an express train hurtling through a tunnel. A tiny grain of pollen deposited by the wind could threaten the whole organism with asphyxia. And unlike Cocteau's intelligence, which endlessly registered moments as they happened, Proust's hurled away backward in time and space, expanding the past to the point of vertigo. Just as the chosen one always overwhelmed Proust in love, so too would a friend's slightest reserve have the effect of an earthquake on him, so much energy did his book require. From those around him, he asked only that they feed him anecdotes about his contemporaries, which he would mix with Time, that acid destined to dissolve individuality in order the better to resuscitate it as character on paper.

Cocteau's attention was much more nervous, furtive, detail-oriented. Though it registered with the same hyperacuity people's physical presence and body language, it also tended to reduce them to silhouettes without historical depth: as in *Portraits-souvenir*, which features people who inspired Proust's *À la recherche*. "You who, for the highest truths, are content with a flamboyant sign that summarizes them," Proust would say to him at the end of the First World War.[18] The "petit Marcel," who often thought himself devoid of talent, and was long a victim of his oversensitivity and his ponderous style, envied Cocteau's quick intelligence that perceived immediately all it would ever perceive: an ability he had mastered at the age of fifteen. But this quickness also prevented Cocteau from perfecting a massive masterpiece, and condemned him to texts of nearly epileptic brevity.

While Proust was burying himself in his cork-lined mausoleum, with the satisfaction of a jailor inflicting the perfect punishment, Cocteau kept on scattering himself in the false belief that he was enriching himself before he felt the need to gather his talent together into one redeeming whole.

Proust must also have wondered what made Cocteau run about. A heart murmur seemed to prevent the younger writer from staying still, whether to enjoy another's presence or the dawn's silence. He was always driven blindly to become close to new luminaries and marvels, as if in their combined experience lay the ultimate significance of his life. Of all the leading figures in 1900 Paris, Proust was of course the best placed to understand these means of escaping anguish and nothingness: becoming the intimate friend of beings worthy of Athena or the Minotaur, and celebrating those kinds of superwomen and supermen who would complete himself personally. Unlike major religions, most ideologies see in the human species an aim in itself, and it is in humanity's name, and for its fulfillment, that they assign a supreme objective for it—Equality, Wealth, Superiority. If neither Proust nor Cocteau ever adhered to any ideology, it's because they recognized no other goal—and no doubt no other faith—than creative activity.

THE SIBYL AND THE FAUN

When Cocteau asked Proust for a letter of introduction to Anna de Noailles, whom he still hadn't managed to meet after three years of scheming, it confirmed to Proust that he would never be Cocteau's literary hero. This now-extinct star, dead among the dead, a symbol of antiquated poetry, shone brightly then in the heaven of letters. Scarcely thirty-six—Cocteau was twenty-two—Noailles was already taught in schools and regarded not only as the greatest living poet but also as the leading light of European literature, like a Victor Hugo. Proust said he had learned to write in her light, and swore that her personality could arouse nothing but fanaticism; Barrès had coveted in vain her small "Spanish Christ" body and was forever dazzled by her; Rilke admired her so much that he translated her and commented on her works; and Cocteau himself, after a very brief time at school, had been "wracked" by love when he read *Les éblouissements*, her first cult collection. Proust's urgent recommendation finally removed all her doubts about the very young author of *Le prince frivole*. Emerging from her "raptured silence," Anna de Noailles, at the behest of "petit Marcel," sent Cocteau some of her poems, and Cocteau soon came to knock on her door to express his admiration for her. "A cold tone in which out of discretion you told her but a quarter of what you really thought—which might seem the best of taste to M. de Sacy—would not touch her at all," Proust had explained, so Cocteau immediately offered Noailles all the praises she dreamed of hearing.[19]

With a swan's neck and sultry eyes, straight-cut bangs and an aquiline nose, Anna de Noailles was "royal, peremptory, cutting and secretly mournful," in Léon-Paul Fargue's words. Fame had struck this tiny, ivory-skinned woman as soon as her first poems were published ten years earlier; since then she had held court high above humans and nations, in the heart of a literary and political Valhalla peopled by saints and princes, poets and scholars, and a few symbolic victims, like Captain Dreyfus, whose *preux chevalier* (white knight) she became.

So many leaders of state came to this muse that she ended up revering all governments, without any real political commitment. Caught up and exalted by every event, she claimed to be sad not to be able to experience everything that happened, all over the world. Just as her veneration for the Greek gods was mixed with aesthetic homages to the Christian pantheon, her friendship with so many kings stimulated per contra her republican credo: nothing delighted her so much as this alternation of opposites. "She ran after red—Lenin's, a cardinal's, a rose's, the Legion of Honor's," Cocteau would write in *Reines de France* about the poetess, who would applaud the 1917 revolution and later present her salon as the cradle of the League of Nations. "She was the most sensitive point in the universe," Barrès would say, his gaze darkened with frustration, before confiding that even though she was dead, he still desired her. Her exceptional mind was not her only appeal; she dressed in evocative, desire-inducing negligees that none of the chosen had the right to touch—not even her butler who, secretly in love with her, was the inspiration for Sacha Guitry's main character of *Désiré*. What human caresses could this woman need who fed herself solely on tempests and words, electricity and perfumes?

A descendant of the ancient sovereigns of Wallachia, the Bessarabian princes of Brancovan, Anna de Noailles had revived the royal use of the tabouret, from which she was assisted to bed and helped at meals, as at palaces of the sovereigns of the petty courts of central Europe. Pietro Citati called her "queen of daydreams, midwife to fairies, minuscule in her coach as small as a walnut, with its wheels made of spider-legs."[20] But the kingdom commanded by Noailles was made exclusively of words, images, and legends, of pleas for feminism and allusions to mythology, of sovereigns' secrets and theories on the identity of the real Shakespeare. A detail that struck the young Cocteau: Byron had died in the arms of one of her ancestors, while fighting to free Greece from Ottoman oppression.

To speak of a "salon" in this instance is excessive, since Anna de Noailles generally held forth alone in her room on the rue Scheffer, in the heart of Passy. This room was a talking-place, a *gueuloir* where she set forth her ideas and her alexandrines. Just as an actor has his rehearsals and the musician his scales, Noailles had her recitations where, eyes closed and arms stretched out—half Sarah Bernhardt, half Sibyl of Cumae—she declaimed verses that she seemed to have gathered from the gods. Whereas the actors who had served as Cocteau's first role models appeared publicly on stage, Noailles, with infinitely more "lines," preferred to reserve the spectacle of her life for a handful of the chosen. She seated her favorites near the bed where she wrote, ate, telephoned, and spoke without respite. The confessions she would then make to these "happy few" would collide with each other in her mouth; exhibiting with a collector's pride the unknown facets of her person, she came to form, by dint of revelations and phrases, a hodge-podge of "ideas and sensations, a tutti-frutti accompanied with hand gestures," said André Gide. She stunned her audience; many people wondered upon leaving if there was any point in going to visit anyone else; the world, without her, seemed as poor as a silent film without a script.[21]

People listened to Anna de Noailles in silence, sitting nymph-like at her feet, even when she deigned to step down from her throne to go and honor a rival salon. The listener gave in to the hypnosis of her words relayed by her "small open hands, thrown from her as if from a sling, her gestures strewing the floor with veils, scarves, necklaces, Arabic rosaries, muffs," Cocteau would say. Her short-circuits of ideas and dizzying leaps of logic "froze the mind," Léon-Paul Fargue added. A listener's overwhelmed brain ended up addicted to her, replying to her with nothing but flattering echoes—Cocteau would describe turning into a "walking shrine" for her. When finally the hour rang to refuel her tiny doll's body, the poetess would sweep the scene with a tyrannical arm to silence her neighbor just long enough to swallow a mouthful or empty a glass—then the monologue would start up better than ever, as if after the passing of a baton.[22]

As the night advanced, the immaterial Anna would expand beyond the space circumscribed by her drawn curtains. In summer, her oceanic ego would invade the neighboring streets; her words would insinuate themselves into nearby buildings to suspend arguments. It was as if a talkative tightrope walker were walking in the middle of the night above the rooftops; servants and chauffeurs strained their ears, like sailors to the Sirens' song. The "trees, plants, stars" were under her charm; a tornado whirled through the capital, encircling the past and the future, the living and the dead, and all yet uncreated worlds.[23] Cocteau no longer knew if it was eleven at night or seven in the morning—and the poetess was still speaking.

The effect of this genius with a little girl's body was huge. With her intelligent, cheeky humor, the "urchin from Byzantium" stood out, in the eyes of the young *prince frivole,* as the foundation for a kind of eighth art—film, the seventh, was already twenty years old—which would be life itself pushed to its incandescence. Galvanized by this new figure of hysterical chastity, supplanting Montesquiou, Cocteau lost the little modesty he still had and did away with all remaining barriers dividing public and private life, the literary and the emotional. His books would always dexterously weave together these four dimensions of existence; until his death, he would live and work as an open book.

Ordinarily Anna de Noailles would dart a black look at any interrupter, a glare that Colette would describe as saying, "Why aren't you dead?" But Cocteau was not able to enjoy the show without attempting to perform himself. Incapable of keeping quiet, convinced too of being a bearer of divine news, he reminded the countess that he was one of the most sought-after "conversationnists" [*sic*] in Paris, a person able to supply the same pleasure as books do, minus the solitude and plus the laughter. And since no one could silence Cocteau, the two came to discuss things with each other. "Everything turned up in those conversations, from God to Barrès . . ., from the plays of Henry Bataille to the meaning of the universe, passionately sought among the graves, the stars," said Emmanuel Berl, a young heir, witness to the verbal ping-pong matches that rang out from the Louis XVI room on the rue Scheffer.[24] Their shared admiration for Nijinsky and Isadora Duncan led them to comparable raptures; wonders gushed from their mouths, prolonging their jousts deep into the night, breaking all links to the real world and abolishing time and space, as if in the depths of Atlantis. When Henri Frank, Berl's favorite cousin, died in 1912 from tuberculosis, Cocteau succeeded him in the role of the countess's page.

Anna de Noailles's words acted like opium; her spiraling phrases would conquer the listener's mind until it grew deeply intermingled with hers. To the charm of Scheherazade she added the mind of Ronsard—one who combined the genius of song with that of rhyme (as Cocteau said), which placed her higher than Hugo or Racine. Her poetry threw him into that altered state of excited bewilderment that he had experienced after hearing Beethoven's Ninth. A privileged listener to her brainstorms, an indispensable companion at her "occasional dinners" or her theater outings, the page soon addressed his Lady as "Dear Minerva," and swore out loud that she made him forget all men. Constantly threatened by imaginary illnesses, they cured each other; Noailles's self-confidence calmed Cocteau, and so did her certainty of being right about everything—"she wanted to take care of her doctors," he would say. In return,

Cocteau's praises intoxicated a poetess who was "divinely simple and sublimely proud," as Proust had said when introducing her to Cocteau.[25] Cocteau's and Noailles's respective hysterias, when fused, somehow created a semblance of reality.

Cocteau would supplant in Noailles's circle not only Henri Frank but also the memory of Barrès's young nephew, who had killed himself out of love for the poet. Treated as an equal, he also began to regard himself as one of the chosen. Convinced of their genius, but dependent since childhood on the affection of others, they began to evolve in an alternative universe in which she was the star and he the magus. Though Proust denounced passionate admiration as the sole form of literary criticism permitted at the time, it did characterize the cult of mutual admiration to which Anna de Noailles and Jean Cocteau devoted themselves. They filled their letters with nebulous maxims dripping with unbearable affectation, as in this poem by Noailles: "You, live, be vast as your desires, / With shivers and ecstasies."[26] Such were the pompous apostrophes they exchanged from different slopes of Olympus. Sometimes they amused themselves by descending to earth like Juno and Jupiter, as in the summer of 1912, when Anna intoned "La Carmagnole," a song of the French Revolution, in a brasserie near the Bastille and when Cocteau led her in a polka at the big July 14 ball, being careful first to alert the photographer from *Excelsior.*

ANNA, ARIEL, AND CAESARION

For a long time Noailles, the Byzantine Minerva, had held court over Proust's universe. Proust wrote:

> She constantly made people laugh by comic juxtapositions . . .; she discovered something funny in every circumstance of life . . ., since a refined person, whose faculty of sympathy puts her in someone else's place instead of remaining all the time in her own, sees the comic everywhere.[27]

Cocteau added that she always found the most comical angle and the harshest lighting to highlight things, like a sculptor using the world as plaster. Proust, however, hadn't succeeded as well with Noailles; he had finally hidden his disillusionment under a laughable excess of flattery. Cocteau was poaching on his territory; the idyll between the two beings he had joined together wounded him, as in the case of Mme de Chevigné. He was the first to detect all the smugness in the constant gaiety on rue Scheffer; eventually he reproached Cocteau for wasting his time in idle chatter.

Anna de Noailles's passionate friendship undeniably constituted one of the highest rewards that Cocteau ever received. Though the Ballets Russes had produced some of his oriental dreams, the Bessarabian exoticism of the Brancovans, with the name evocative of a sultan's pomp, fulfilled his magical hopes by offering him a flattering transcendence of reality. And when one evening he received a note from his idol declaring "I am rereading you and once again admiring you *sans cesse*," paradise opened up: as a poet, a snob, and a suitor, Cocteau was overwhelmed.[28]

Cocteau's thirst for recognition had left little place for love until then: he had wanted never again to experience the sufferings that Madeleine Carlier had inflicted. But he was so attached to his lady that he thought he was in love. If she was a Romanian princess, then he was a Persian prince. The instinct that causes the orchid to imitate the bee that will pollinate it began to work on Cocteau; soon a thin moustache appeared on his face, which was protected by a straw boater; and a very young version of Barrès returned to haunt Anna, but in a sexually reassuring version, it seemed—though the resemblance ended up *really* disturbing her. Impatient to bring an end to the hold each had over the other, if not to shorten the evenings from which they returned exhausted, Cocteau dreamed, at night, of their physical union. She was both the origin and the goal, the Ovum and the Word; he would be Love that fertilized and the Genius that exalts. Won over by his dynastic ambitions, Noailles began in turn evoking the miraculous children that their genetic union could produce. Would they have the features of Perseus, son of Danae and Zeus, or those of the divine Caesarion, the child of Cleopatra and Caesar? They would have every talent, that was certain.

The countess's phobia of syphilis, however, kept her from leaving her gauzy Olympus for a horsehair mattress. She could have married the sun or the wind, said the Abbé Mugnier; but since no proposition from these elements was forthcoming, and since no Jupiter appeared from heaven to tear her away from humans, she remained to brood over the young poet, using his praise to keep intact her small, delicate body, to which only the Comte de Noailles himself had the right, at least for a little while.

Cocteau became her "child prodigy," even her poetic Siamese twin—"Anna-male," *Anna-mâle*, the Bibescos brothers said, eager to give a name to this mimetic animal. Both victims of the "vertigo of speech," they continued to cross-fertilize each other at a distance in the manner of the Angel of the Annunciation impregnating Mary with a whisper, as they continued their idyll between earth and sky, like Wagnerian demi-gods. Soon Cocteau would no longer know if he loved her or if he *was* Anna de Noailles: an obscure consanguinity seemed to join him to this woman, who was histrionic and sincere at once. Sharing the same morbid fascination with their own ending—Anna was "made to be dead," Cocteau said—they were prey to the same greed for love and fame. They both felt the same jubilatory unfulfillment, "brother" and "sister" communing in a Nietzschean concept of poetry experienced as a "panicked" (Pan-like) celebration of the senses. She became for Cocteau the sacred language meant to return the mystery of being to earth, the esoteric code in charge of reminding us, at all times and in all places, how poorly we understand and how little we know.

Already the younger poet imitated the elder's gestures and way of inclining the head. From the matching fountain pen she offered him, he produced, with the same violet ink, her flowery handwriting. The counterfeit was so precise that Mme Cocteau herself couldn't decipher her son's letters, and had to get help from a friend of Anna de Noailles. Noailles herself burst out laughing when she in turn received a note from her page: "It's the first time I've sent myself a message," she confided to her own son, delighted with this begetting in a mirror. "She turned herself into the figure of Cocteau, and Cocteau turned himself into the writing of Anna," Morand confirmed, in *L'allure de Chanel*. Together they formed a single being, with the same aesthetic demands and the same expectations. He was wherever she went; she experienced everything he told her; their respective sadnesses saddened them; they felt in echo, like great choir soloists. The world belonged to Anna de Noailles, hence also to Jean Cocteau: "You who can do everything," he would say to her, fifteen years later, still dazzled by that whirlwind.

Raised by her into the European stratosphere, Cocteau put the finishing touches on an unprecedented program of literary, social, and aesthetic perfection. He swore to himself that he would become the writer of his generation, even the poet of the brand-new century, an illuminating symbol and a constant source of admiration. His goal? To be everything. To charm people, and to take from them what one normally obtains from one alone—at best. To enchant "the trees, the plants, the stars," like Orpheus, and Anna de Noailles after him. If the nightingale is the tree's mouth, he wanted to be the earth's mouth, like Bulbul in the tales of the *Thousand and One Nights*—the lyre-bird capable of giving speech not only to peacocks and flowers, grandfather clocks and armchairs, but also to the moths fluttering around lamps at night until they burned.[29] Just as much as his mother, De Max, and Proust, Noailles was indeed one of the coauthors of this man without a shadow who would haunt the century under the name of Jean Cocteau.

Cocteau charged his voice with the task of captivating his audience. He worked on its timbre like an actor—tried to curb its surges by holding his breath, so to give it a melodramatic flair. His monologues were punctuated with "what?" and "how so?," meant perhaps to encourage the listener's questions, but more likely to make him seem at a loss for words and lend a hypnotic quality to his sentences. One has only to hear the reading he recorded of *La machine infernale* to discover what summits he reached; the exhilaration his diction still produces does much to renew the power it had while he was alive: the listener would be dazzled or stunned and in any case left breathless, as if Cocteau had gulped up all the air available in the room. Not content with making better drawings than others in his circle—even Sacha Guitry was not as inventive—he strove also to become *the* dancer of his generation. He learned the tango—the first South American dance to appear on the European scene and one tantalizingly censured by Monsignor Amette in 1914—which he practiced on occasion with Nijinsky. The ultimate goal: to be "a marble bust, but with legs to run everywhere."[30]

The book he was drafting at the time logically enough showed the influence of Anna de Noailles—she read its proofs so closely that we might guess that some of the poems in *La danse de Sophocle* were written with four hands—and with Verlaine, Mallarmé, and Albert Samain co-signing the others. This is because Cocteau, who would always enjoy collaborating with his friends, still wrote the books he sought in vain in libraries. But when by chance he found them, he felt relief, as if the text thus exhumed released him from his work. And since all of him, literarily, was not in him, he was also capable of taking hold of his find until he had wholly appropriated it.

Any talent shown by someone else kindled Cocteau's native abilities; any unknown work engaged his sensibility. Finding himself the co-creator of what was published, played, and painted, he didn't hesitate to become, in his exaltation, the sculptor, the singer, the painter—Praxiteles, Chopin, and Manet all at once. No doubt he was initially aware of imitating, even stealing. But precisely because he managed to absent himself in order to welcome the other into him and make the other's procedures his own, he soon forgot the reason for these borrowings, and soon their very existence. This brief escape from himself was enough to erase all trace of burglary. Snug in the fog of his own personality, he was convinced that he had improved everything he borrowed, while also clinging to the originals with that fetishistic sense of property peculiar to thieves. Thus he truly became Anna-male, the man gathering together the maximum of words in a minimum of time; the little Mozart of conversation; the virtuoso capable of interpreting his nature in all its forms, like a role; and the insolent one who could make Anna-female and her friend, the actress Madame Simone, laugh until they wept. Later Mme Simone would say, of that period: "None of us knew what despair was."[31]

Certain of having finished his lessons, Cocteau began receiving guests in his room. Visitors like Proust and Noailles who knocked on his door were led immediately into a room cluttered with bizarre objects—a skull, a crystal ball, ceramics—as well as a gramophone playing Gluck and Cocteau's work table, where Napoleon's death mask lay. "Too much is just barely enough for me," said a phrase written on a slip of paper pinned to the wall. Dressed in a simple robe, Cocteau was already communicating his enthusiasm to his visitor, along with his conviction that, if all the world's a stage, he was one of its main characters. Having a tremendous opinion of himself, Cocteau became more than ever an organ delivering tirades, paradoxes, and epigrams. He nicknamed one balding lady with dyed hair "la 3 cheveux citron" and compared another to "a profile on a medal found in a field of Vaseline"—phrases that Anna was proud of quoting in town, when she wasn't appropriating them, starting up a counter-imitation that exalted her protégé a little more.[32]

> It was not enough for him to be the handsome "Euphorion," the "child genius," the "poet of spring," to draw all gazes to him and attract all hearts; he still saw himself as Merlin the Enchanter, and wanted to transform everything around him with a wave of his magic wand: his creative imagination, wrote a young admirer.[33]

To Marie Scheikévitch, a close friend of Proust and Noailles, Cocteau called to mind what the young Voltaire must have been like in his day. "He walked with the pride of a wild bird fallen by chance into a farmyard," confirmed Princess Bibesco, rarely so enthusiastic.[34] "Jean was not a handsome man. But it was hard to find a prettier boy . . . to have more charm and to join this with a livelier wish to charm . . . In a word, he was irresistible," wrote Jacques Porel, son of the great actress Réjane.[35] "I have known no other young man who so recalled Wordsworth's 'Bliss was it in that dawn to be alive,'" Edith Wharton remarked, then at the center of all the salons.[36] Dazzled by his intelligence, the American novelist regretted, like Proust, that he didn't withdraw to the countryside in order to write the work he had promised to write, the importance of which everyone could guess given the thousands of stories he told. "He seemed like one of those 'princes of youth' that all Athens celebrated so much," remembered Bernard Faÿ: "a precious youth, . . . the ladies looked at him as if he were Lancelot, and more than one man ogled him, just as Zeus, father of the gods, eyed Ganymede."[37] Gabriele D'Annunzio himself, the famous author of *Il fuoco*, marveled at seeing Cocteau proceed by "blazing associations."[38] All were convinced that his name would one day be a byword for youthful prodigy—"He's a real Cocteau"—the way a man with many mistresses is always a Casanova.

THE FABULOUS OPERA

It was this phenomenon, gardenia in his buttonhole, who came to the studio of Jacques-Émile Blanche in Passy one February day in 1912. Recommended by his mother, whose portrait Blanche had painted, the young Cocteau didn't stop talking the entire time he posed. Bemused by his pathological volubility, Blanche immediately perceived him as the ultimate specimen of those camellia-wearing dandies whom he had painted twenty years before, from Beardsley to Wilde to Proust: the same rhetorical preciosities, the same studied poses, the same readiness to damn themselves for a *bon mot*—and that mad desire to want to be everything all at once. At first the painter could only pity "that poor, frail little being, who seems in a hurry to live and sing his poet's song—but in salons, where his lungs are corrupted." Having proven his obedience to the proprieties by marrying against his own desires, Blanche exaggerated the annoyance produced by this overly affected Cocteau ("he should go to a man's tailor," said the ladies Cocteau visited). Blanche also thought Cocteau so proud of his superiority that he was "odious to others." Thus whereas some people attributed every good quality to the prodigy, Blanche would be one of the first to allow him all his defects.

Beneath the frightening aspect of a young consumptive, Blanche sensed a hypersensitive. With his quasi-hereditary gifts for introspection that hampered his painting even as they allowed him to be a good portrait artist (and which had made his father and his grandfather into famous alienists for writers), Blanche saw something morbid in his model's precocity.[39] "The freshness of an eternal adolescent, and the terrible, disastrous experience of an old man," he noted, evoking the social savoir-faire of a debutant and superior amateur who, twenty years after Proust, went off to conquer the same celebrities—while benefiting from Proust's experience as if he had already lived it. Blanche had been able to grasp, deeply from within, writers like Marcel Proust and Henry James, both of whom had achieved artistic transcendence by putting their sexuality and their snobbism to the service of superior aesthetics. After a few sittings, he already knew the frightening price that Cocteau would have to pay to do the same, and worried about what would become of this imaginative child afflicted with migraines, "feverish depressions," and, already, a past.

"Everything fascinates him," Cocteau, for his part, noted of Blanche, adding: "His existence is a kind of slow frenzy." The openness of mind that had allowed him to garner the first homosexual confidences of Mauriac led Blanche, after a few weeks, to suspect Cocteau's very particular nature. A better writer than painter (though he over-wrote, just as he under-painted), and an even better reader (the range of writers he painted, from Mallarmé to Crevel, is remarkable), Blanche yielded to the fragility of his genius. Proust claimed that the painter's venom, which had earned him the nickname "viper without a tail," stemmed from these protective neuroses that nature invents so that talent can flourish. But Blanche became all solicitude and curiosity when it came to Cocteau.

Blanche's admiration increased even more when, upon inviting Cocteau to his country house in Offranville, in Normandy, with Edith Wharton and Proust's close friend Antoine Bibesco, he discovered the young poet's ardor for work. Having no idea of the time, the indefatigable Cocteau was always the last to leave off writing, sometimes until dawn. Blanche, the next day, had to wake him so he could finish poems whose reading brought together the whole household. Together he and the Anglophile Blanche sketched out a comedy, *Albion.* At night, as rain confined them to the salon, it was still Cocteau who tirelessly led the conversation, held his elders breathless with his multilayered stories, then started in with impersonations that made them laugh until they cried. The performances lasted until midnight. "One is afraid in the presence of such a phenomenon," Blanche confessed.[40]

One is struck by the strange acuity that radiates from Cocteau's writings and that nourished his talent for drawing. Half-painter, half-soothsayer, Cocteau "saw." He described to his mother the flanks of a large cow in Offranville "that one might think Blanche has used to sketch a storm quickly."[41] His Argus eyes perceived the tiny pink feet peeping from under the gray bellies of pigeons, and even the inky splashes on the wings of the butterflies flying behind his back; his nostrils dilated at the slightest smell of wisteria, smelled the acrid odor of reproduction in flowering apple trees, isolated the "cool abyss" sculpted in the atmosphere by the heady perfume of lilies. His ears amplified the silence of the sea, nightingales' trills, the cry of trains. Each petal opened to him with "the racket of a small bomb"; he so intensely became what he perceived that just a few words were sometimes enough for him to convey the unbearable quality in the simple fact of being alive, when the dew putrefies the Norman earth until it spreads a macabre smell.

Cocteau saw his face as an "oval mirror" reflecting the world, a magnifying glass amplifying its infinite expansion. In his imagination each cloud transported him to distant kingdoms; he was a bird soaring above an earthly life that was already a dungeon. Sometimes he even pictured himself as a ghost returning to haunt the places where he had lived, brushing against the hollyhocks that flamed up in the Blanches' park; at other times, his exaltation led him to wonder if some unprecedented miracle might allow him to avoid the grave: "People have died before me, but who knows if I'll die?"[42] Already, though, he anticipated the day when youth would detach itself like a dead skin sloughing off him, and when he would glance enviously at the sea, the landscape, and the sky, "sad at their ever-renewing, rivalrous beauty."[43] Center of an earth animated by his own heartbeat, the little animal keen with a "panicked joy" of living feared the oblivion into which he would surely fall in a hundred generations.

So Cocteau wrote to perpetuate his name, but also to affirm himself as a ray of divine light and a piece of the great whole. Thanks to his supple sense of self, his desire to please became truly universal, unlimited by space or time: according to this view the entire universe was nothing but an extension of the principle named Jean Cocteau.

As a teenager, Cocteau had the opportunity to explore the fourth dimension with Henri Poincaré, famous mathematician and inventor of the Fuchsian group. Poincaré had compared our helpless ignorance of the Beyond to that of miners unable to apprehend anything except the sound of pickaxes in a neighboring tunnel—a metaphor that opened an immense field of investigation to a boy who sensed everywhere the existence of another world. Walking on the beach at Varengeville, next to a stupefied Blanche, Cocteau "saw" Nausicaa, the princess who welcomed Ulysses after his shipwreck. The same logic that had revealed Anna de Noailles to him as Minerva enabled him to sense pretty much everywhere the deities that once upon a time had haunted the Mediterranean, and that had been awakened first by Symbolism, and then by Nietzsche. Since reality seemed to exist only very faintly on its own, Cocteau augmented it with mythical figures, then made it magical by rewriting it, until he had raised it to the level of a work of art in which each sound had become a musical note, each action a poem. "I became a fabulous opera," said Rimbaud, after comparable effort.[44] Such an approach made Cocteau afraid of dying from "living too much at once."

Cocteau's metaphysical intuitions were such that the rationalist certainties of the agnostic Blanche began to waver. Cocteau was interested in visionaries, chiromancers, spirits; he believed in managed chances, objective omens, annunciations, even if doing so meant regularly changing his faith. Anyone possessing occult powers fascinated him; Rudolf Steiner's theosophy already inspired his poems. Condemned by Christianity to a dolorous and hidden existence as exiles, the pagan gods were accessible only through occult rites, according to Heinrich Heine: Cocteau, unfazed, sought every occasion to reach these repressed genies, Dionysian or Apollonian, who had made ancient civilization great.

Cocteau was so uncertain of reality at this point that he was willing to believe anything. If a rumor was circulating that a German chemist had succeeded at resuscitating Bismarck, Cocteau would immediately adopt it as a scientifically proven fact. While on vacation at the Daudets he heard Léon, the formidable polemicist, give gloomy speeches on planetary larvae and claim that a reflection gesturing in a mirror opposite to one's own can take on its own life. This revelation would have a profound effect on Cocteau's credulous mind and would receive ample consideration in his films *Le sang d'un poète* and *Orphée*. In the eyes of the young Cocteau, life was only a brief interlude without any reality—a handful of seconds snatched from the eternity preceding our birth and following our death. "Our favorite subject that arises as soon as we are together: death," Blanche noted on August 11, 1913, in his *Carnets*; he felt a paternal affection for this moral orphan twenty-eight years his junior.

In the spring of 1912, Cocteau was preparing his *La danse de Sophocle*, the largest and most concerted of the collections of his youth. Referring to the dance that "the young and divine Sophocles" performed naked in Athens after the naval victory of Salamis, the title expresses not only Cocteau's state of exaltation after his discovery of the art of choreography, but also his ambition. A torch that burns "in front of every temple," a game-cock proud of being young and living in France, "wild" to find the place he deserves, the young Cocteau reminds readers who haven't understood his title: "It's you, Paris, my dear Athens." The breeze that swept Nijinsky to the summits carries Cocteau along with it. Like the dancer able to make himself into a rose, a bird, an African, or a doll, Cocteau expressed his heady certainty of being born gifted. Proud of the "hidden treasure" he had received, he sang of his joy at seeing arise, as soon as he dipped his pen in ink, "verses you'd want to shout out . . . sing, sigh, laugh." Like the child Septentrion who invented dance when he saw the sea rise up, but who died from gamboling too much on the beach, the young Cocteau made himself into a spinning top, only to end up, drunk on his own breath, raising himself above a capital that was already treating him as a hero. Comparing himself by turns to a "divine violin" and to a "radiant insect," he ended up beseeching his book to delight his readers, asking it to attach them to his winged chariot so he could reign forever over those "dazzled captives."[45]

Proust and Reynaldo Hahn were the first to read the new collection: when one pointed out his favorite poem, the other would quote a second that seemed even more beautiful. Rivaling each other through these selections, they reread the entire volume and then amended their own choices, having discovered in the meantime new wonders. Though Proust might fear that "La Pallas d'Homère," the poem Cocteau had recited to him in front of the *Saint Sebastian* in the Louvre but which lost in writing the radiance emitted by Cocteau's voice, was too reminiscent of the intonation of pieces by Anna de Noailles, he also acknowledged that its emphasis was completely different, for the "I" of Cocteau had nothing to do with that of the poetess. And even if in certain places Cocteau reminded one of Musset, it was with "a different kind of amplitude in the imagery and profundity in inspiration."

> I have already written to you all the beautiful things I found in the pieces that appeared in *Le Figaro* and *La revue hebdomadaire*. I die of jealousy when I see your delightful pieces on Paris, since you know how to evoke things I have felt and that I have been able to express only in such a pale way . . .[46] Always you find the detail that drives in the vision. . . .
>
> *Voilà*, dear Jean; it is moving to think that this single flower, so beautiful and so sweet, so innocent and so inclining, as you are, has been able to grow and construct itself, without the stem bending and ceasing to please or losing flexibility, this immense and solid and dense column of thought and perfume. Tenderly and admiringly yours.[47]

Already before he met Anna de Noailles, Cocteau had readily taken for himself the roles of Heine the poet or Aladdin the magician. He believed that it was the diversity of his talents that had helped him to surpass Noailles even before his book was published. What's more, with his abilities he could not only compose verse like hers—though with his particular grace and his themes—but also draw like Sem, master the stage like De Max, or dance in unison with Nijinsky while remembering the sarabandes of King David in front of the Ark in Jerusalem.

This propensity for metaphor would only increase his thirst for metamorphoses. Wasn't he becoming, like Sappho or Alexander, one of those characters that you can be no longer certain is real or mythical, even while it's alive? Did he concentrate within himself the entire human condition, with a few extra skills thrown in? The feeling of being involved in a mission, the enthusiasm that, in the ancient world, marked one overcome by the sacred delirium that would take hold over an interpreter of the gods; the trance that overcame him when he wrote, drew, or danced: he believed that these talents, along with his ability to slip into the most intimate part of another's being, to reproduce that person's language and gestures in ways that helped that person to see herself or himself more clearly, meant that he was a fragment detached from the Creator, an earthly organ by which that evolving Being decided to invent in order to improve his creation. Like the best artists, he was an interpreter between God and the earth. By dint of hearing Anna de Noailles evoke Apollo and Orpheus as if they were close friends, Cocteau believed he was one of the "gods of all cults / With all heroes," from Krishna to Saint John and from Bonaparte to Caesar. Did he share with Krishna the ability to take on a thousand forms, and with Caesar a limitless horizon? He was the total being, like Purusha, the cosmic giant who, in Indian religion, sacrifices himself in order to engender humanity—his mouth giving birth to priests and intellectuals; his arms, to kings and warriors; his thighs, to merchants and farmers.

THE ALGERIA OF SAADI

Cocteau fell in love at that time with a gloomy young poet whose name has not come down to us. The mere mention of the beloved intensified his natural exaltation. "My happiness fastens wax wings and feathers to my shoulders . . ., with all my strength I beat at the fluid, warm air."[48] As with Madeleine Carlier, however, he spent his days in the vestibule on the rue d'Anjou, waiting for the arrival of the elevator. His love obsessed him so much that he lost his ability to reason; solitude was enough to tear him from Purusha's heaven and bring him brutally to earth: he was Saint Sebastian, naked against a tree, his torso offered to the arrows; the chosen one was both archer and savior, executioner and healer. His megalomania was reversed; he had the terrible feeling of living under the gaze of a society that scrutinized his slightest gestures and argued his fate. His suffering was so profound that he found some consolation in it, since it rendered his existence more real to him, more anchored: he would end up almost thanking this beloved who wounded him for stretching out his time and giving his life some constancy.[49]

After the affair he wanted to distance himself, have a change of scene, flee this failure—incomprehensible for a demi-god. Lucien Daudet suggested North Africa, a sensual paradise that Gide had told his friends about, one peopled with shy boys and free odalisques like Mériem, who appears repeatedly in Gide's autobiography *Si le grain ne meurt* and who served as the model for Pierre Louÿs's Bilitis. The trip, made in an immense cabin of white silk with Pompadour curtains, left Cocteau somewhat cold. Unlike the Arab-Persian Orient of the *Thousand and One Nights*, Algiers reminded Cocteau of a sub-prefecture worthy of Angers, with its buildings assembled in a half-circle around the sea. The natives stank, the camels looked fake, the hills of the Atlas were as dull as maps from an atlas at school. Taken aback by this festival "of urine and filth," Cocteau was disgusted by the immensity of the poverty that surrounded Europe. Gradually, however, he overcame his disappointment and opened up to the charms of Algiers: "ladies" who shut themselves in with a Zouave by making the "precarious little theater" of their blue room vanish from sight by one sweep of a curtain; men climbing the dark streets of the Casbah, their little fingers linked together.[50]

The North African sun managed to free Cocteau from his Parisian symptoms—insomnia, anxiety, jealous love. At a fishermen's café, he held breathless an audience made "ecstatic" by his improvisations. Reprising his role of Scheherazade, he took up his pen to write to his mother about his happiness and to ask her to guard his letters closely: he counted on collecting some of the poems into *Les vocalises de Bachir-Selim,* a collection that would remain unpublished but whose orientalism bears witness to the influence of the warmth and work of the great Persian Saadi, who sang the praises of the wine, roses, and young men of Shiraz.[51] Cocteau in his turn sang of the flies that drank in the eyes of boys in Blida; the monkeys leaping in groups into the branches of a rubber tree; the nightingale warbling in the rosebushes of Germany and Persia—the alpha and omega of his imagination; the talents of his little guide, an intimate scholar of the hideaways of Algiers, its girls and boys. When a poet brought him a love note, in the half-light of the Café Malakoff, tambourines jingling in the background, Cocteau advised the suitor to go to the home of the young Zaïnale and there seek out the memory of his lips and smell of his body; one could not be more sexually ambiguous.

While Lucien Daudet, with his emir's profile, fell in love with the son of a great Arab landowner, Cocteau was content to praise in verse the "beautiful Arab advantage," the "beautiful arming for battles of love."[52] He scribbled urgent notes documenting the disorder of the souk and its many images. The sensual happiness that had won him over made his style more sober, though it remained tense, as if his brio had begun to entrance him less.

It is true that, on the advice of the "closet queen" Blanche, Gide's neighbor in Normandy, Cocteau had brought in his luggage Gide's *The Immoralist,* which revealed, in 1902, Gide's pederastic pleasures. The sensitive austerity, pagan eroticism, and literary density of this first novel impressed Cocteau, who was struck as well by the surprising frankness of this Puritan who, under the spell of the Tunisian sun, the gaze of the young Moktir, and Nietzschean morality, went so far as passively to kill his wife. The young Cocteau's writing style became much more nervous: by eliding syntax, leaving out verbs, and writing phrases in spasms, he created a syncopated line that would flourish in the 1920s. Walking in the footsteps of Gide, whose literary influence continued to increase after 1910, Cocteau followed the gorges of Chiffa as far as Biskra, where Matisse himself had come on pilgrimage, to salute the memory of Gide in a poem that tracks Mériem, a "little Kabylian with a star on her forehead."

Always asking for more details, Mme Cocteau told him in return about the "sublimely mean" lectures given by Jules Lemaitre, the literary critic of the moment and the "most enthusiastic barometer" of the success of her son's publications.[53]

For Cocteau was still keeping his weather eye open in the Saharan confines: back from a long, wandering visit through the Algiers Casbah (guided by the picturesque Mahieddine, whom he compared to Gide's Arab companion, Athman), he wrote to Marie de Rothschild, suggested to his mother that she send some candies to Mme de Courcelles, and sought to find Anatole France, who was rumored to be in Algeria. His social attentions during this African stay make one dizzy: at the age of twenty-four, he was already demonstrating the worldly savoir-faire of a man his father's age.

Summoned urgently by Empress Eugénie, Lucien Daudet returned prematurely to the metropolis. Cocteau continued the trip alone, reading the poet Abu Nuwas of Baghdad, whose revealing line he would never tire of quoting: "I love to love." He acclimated so well to Algeria that melancholy overcame him as soon as he left this Araby nourished by Persian authors. The landscape he had at first rejected became so familiar to him that he suffered a thousand deaths at the idea of being separated from it. He wrote:

> When I approach the chosen city [he could just have easily been speaking of the beloved, or of the book yet to come], immediately the ideal thread stretched between it and my heart coils up in my chest. As soon as I move inside it, the ball of thread increases or diminishes, and produces a voluptuous disturbance in me. But when I leave and the ball . . . unfurls with dizzying speed, what a vague, immense suffering, enough to make me scream.[54]

Though his imagination projected him to the four corners of the universe, Cocteau endured the dilemma of a man who would never feel at home anywhere. His excessive sensitivity transformed every pleasure into anxiety: departure frightened him as much as the Parisian agitation that awaited him. "Each instant that I live without too much indifference / Closes around me like my native land," he wrote.[55] Guessing that this "atrocious vertigo of place" would recur during the next journey, he even wondered if it might be better for him to stay, living forever under the African sun, head and arms bare, living on fruit. Every attachment changed into an umbilical cord that he found it hard to cut, as if the earth held him in its arms.

When he returned to Paris, Cocteau wrote his first letter to Gide to convey the admiration of a simple reader who had brought all Gide's books to Algeria with him.

THE BLUE GOD

Diaghilev had an almost abstract passion for Paris: more than the city of pleasures, which he never much enjoyed, it was the chosen city, capital in every respect for whomever wanted, like him, to make his name resound throughout Europe. The Cossack hetman held the upper hand in Diaghilev over the beringed Wildean; he thought of nothing but perfecting his conquest, and despite the triumphs that Paris afforded him, he sometimes complained about the conservative taste of the Parisians, whom he accused of expecting from the ballet the sort of theater the Comédie-Française gave them unless they were countermanded by wiser counsel, the thirty or so arbiters of Parisian taste.

Since Cocteau stood out as one of the favorites of that circle, which joined Anna de Noailles to the Comtesse de Chevigné and to Misia, Diaghilev got into the habit of calling him when he arrived in the capital, to learn about the latest Parisian entanglements. In return, more and more often Cocteau's face appeared in the box he reserved at the Opéra between the already rounder faces of Misia and José Maria Sert. Seeing the friendliness between them, Diaghilev also sometimes used Cocteau to lift Nijinsky's spirits, as he did after the dress rehearsal of *Petrushka*, in June 1911: the writer recited to the dancer then the umpteenth dithyramb he had dedicated to Nijinsky in *Comoedia*.

The relations linking Diaghilev to his protégé were actually beginning to degrade: during *Petrushka*, Nijinsky refused to go onstage until his camera had been redeemed from the pawnshop—which Diaghilev ended up doing, despite his own overwhelming debts.[56] After that time Nijinksy continued to assert himself, raising his voice as needed, as if hoping to escape the fate of the poor puppet whose role he danced every night: a puppet that ended up smashed. Cocteau was no dupe of Diaghilev's intrigues, but he was eager as well to participate on an equal footing in the romantic life of a troupe that celebrated all things together, from work to love, from Karsavina's birthday to the hundredth performance of *Spectre de la rose*—when the package of petals blown by the fan at Larue's had almost knocked over the great Réjane. Borne aloft by the audience's enthusiasm and their impresario's Parisian networks, the Russes, to Cocteau, formed a true chosen family, almost an intimate counterso-ciety—a formula that would remain his emotional ideal. Regularly forced to pawn his jewels, and to flee the Ritz for lack of cash, Diaghilev electrified the daily papers with his temper tantrums, which only fueled his journalistic success.

The attraction exercised by Nijinsky was universal from then on. His painted lips, his mascara-laden eyelashes, his almost feminine grace provoked turmoil during performances; it was whispered that his valet Vassily had been able, by selling the petals the dancer had spread, to buy himself a house dubbed "the castle of the Specter of the Rose." Although he scarcely showed any particular sexuality, or perhaps by that very absence, Nijinsky disturbed even the least suspicious men: at one point Cocteau surprised Rodin in the middle of masturbating, while Nijinsky was posing for him, back turned.[57] The belts set with emeralds and rubies that an Indian prince had given him aroused strange rumors about the caprices to which the dancer had been subjected. The inhabitants of the brothel on rue Chabanais where Cocteau went, with Diaghilev and Bakst, were clearer: "I want the virgin," said one of the girls, pointing to Nijinsky, in order the better to repel her coworker.[58] Might Diaghilev's grasp, twice that of an overprotective mother's, as well as the terrible discipline he inflicted, have dampened the man-bird's fervor? "Nijinsky makes love only to the nymph's scarf," asserted Stravinsky, in a clear allusion to the *Faune*: conversely, all of Paris took pleasure from the spectacle of this androgynous genie, endowed with a sumptuous mouth and Asiatic cheekbones, who danced straddling the animal, vegetable, and human realms.

To escape bankruptcy, and in hopes of attending the coronation of George V, the King of England and Emperor of India, Diaghilev decided to assemble the finest the Ballets Russes had to offer: Nijinsky in the title role, Bakst as set designer, Fokine as choreographer, and, for the music, works by Reynaldo Hahn, whose position in society was considerable; the salons especially appreciated his melancholic restraint. Even in Russia, Diaghilev had tended to choose his dancers from the aristocracy in order to attract patrons and fill the halls. At the prompting of Bakst, the impresario resigned himself to promoting Cocteau from the rank of poet and poster artist to that of librettist, in collaboration with Coco de Madrazo, a wealthy amateur linked to Proust, who was also Hahn's nephew—his lover above all, apparently.[59] Thus the presumed heir of Sophocles came to collaborate with the Venezuelan composer, a privilege that Proust had never enjoyed, in all thirty-eight years of friendship.[60]

Diaghilev asked the librettists for a piece more choreographic than *Firebird*, more oriental than *Scheherazade*—a new creation that could surpass the two great successes of the Ballets Russes, while highlighting the talents of Nijinsky independently of Karsavina (since Diaghilev wanted to see Nijinsky replace a declining Fokine). Cocteau outlined a draft that was joyful, entrancing, even magical, situated in a marvelous country modeled on the India of the rajahs and the Siam of the dancers. Borrowing from the legend of the *Firebird*, which Karsavina had recounted to him extensively, Cocteau added to it a eulogy for pagan life and a condemnation of oppressive Christianity, showing a blue god saving at the last moment a pair of lovers who had been condemned by terrible priests to die by crucifixion.

The others liked the libretto. Beginning to believe in the spectacle, Diaghilev devoted a huge budget to it, which was partially swallowed up by the set. Royally nicknamed "Jeanzhick," halfway between prince and muzhik, Cocteau was even authorized to go backstage in order to help Bakst make the appearance of Nijinsky more splendid. With its princes and gods, its formal debauchery and exalted androgyny, the set designer's visual universe was close to what Cocteau himself had conjured. Won over by the sumptuousness of his sets, Cocteau worked together with Bakst to set colors in motion—with the writer even devoting a brief essay to the subject of this element of set design.[61] Starting with extras, then stagehands, and feeling quite happy with his ease in incorporating the laws of ballet, Cocteau began advising the dancers, despite the presence of Fokine, and then despite his scant experience contributed to the choreography as well. The ballerina Lydia Sokolovska saw him dress the extras with skirts, wigs, and thick white ropes for the ballet of the dervishes—"the dancers spun faster and faster; at the end of the dance, you could see nothing but extraordinary whistling disks," she wrote, struck by this visionary discovery.[62] Propelling the troupe into the whirlwind of his overactivity, Cocteau became its radiant emanation, then its new mascot. This mischievous fox terrier, who made Karsavina laugh with the exuberance of his imitations, even ended up imposing himself as a kind of counter-Diaghilev whom the real one had sometimes to command, with his booming voice, to leave the set, onto which he would soon reemerge to run all over the stage.

Because Nijinsky spoke only poor French and tended to stay silent, Cocteau's exchanges with him remained limited. The dancer was content to follow Cocteau with his eyes as Cocteau emphasized his cheeks with blush and his mouth with red lipstick; and Cocteau's constant good humor, as much as his *djinn*-like leaps, helped keep Nijinsky in good spirits. Not only did Nijinsky follow Cocteau to Maxim's to be admired, or dance tangos with him (as immortalized by a photographer), but the dancer—who barely ate, in order to hold in check thighs that were already deforming his trousers—began to wear makeup in town as well, to the great displeasure of his sister Bronislava, who was openly worried. "It's very Parisian," her younger brother retorted, with that innocence that earned him the nickname "genius idiot" from Misia.

At barely twenty-five, Nijinsky was more than an incredible dancer: capable of conquering gravity, he could also conceive a choreography. Endowed with an excellent musical ear, he played the piano wonderfully, as well as the clarinet and the balalaika. Jotting down in pencil each of his dance moves by means of a transcription method he himself invented, Nijinsky thought carefully about the choreographies in which he would star. The slightest idea found him an attentive listener; the first suggestion, a demanding critic—as Cocteau himself discovered while discussing with the star a ballet that would retrace the dance of King David in front of the Ark of the Covenant.

Cocteau's insistence in hovering around Nijinsky ended up exciting the feudal jealousy of Diaghilev, who detested the influence that the librettist was having over the most precious "soul" in his possession. Cocteau's reputation as thief was the final spark that set the fire. Convinced that Cocteau wanted to take his protégé away from him, the cloaked "puppeteer" got angry; though he had done everything in his power to make Nijinsky disgusted with women, it was certainly not done to interest him in this dolled-up dandy, who was leading him into deplorable habits. It was risky, even in normal times, to contradict that "hippopotamus" Diaghilev who was so viscerally linked to his enterprise, but if the corps of the Ballets Russes was his body, even in its erotic dimension, Nijinsky was his life. From the brutal to the sneaky, reprisals became a feature of every rehearsal, with Diaghilev even whispering to the chauffeur bringing them back from a soirée to drive Cocteau not to Paris but to Versailles, where Reynaldo Hahn lived. Invisible in the darkness of the wings, color pencil in hand, Cocteau took his revenge by drawing the tyrant as a deformed little girl, a rose stuck in her corsage. On one point Diaghilev was right, however: Cocteau, impatient to prove his choreographic gifts, was already thinking about his own ballet for Nijinsky.

Le dieu bleu was a disappointment. Reynaldo Hahn, with his "somber, reticent" nature, was neither energetic nor joyous enough to recreate musically the pagan splendors of the Orient. From its first performance in Saint Petersburg on May 13, 1912, Fokine's first ballet with its Massenet-like score was perceived as salon entertainment depicting a docile, stupid Asia. The brilliance of the sets and costumes, usually such a credit to Diaghilev's troupe, this time seemed excessive: the exorbitant talent of Bakst had crushed the frail melodies of Hahn, that determined supporter of French moderation, beneath its weight of gold and pearls, its orange sugarloaves and rainbow peacocks, its Milky Way and its sacred lotus from which arose, like a little god, a Nijinsky overloaded with gold and sapphires.

The libretto was also considered a factor in the ballet's failure. Pointlessly convoluted, its "forced" orientalism seemed to exploit all the resources of a troupe that had been seeking, ever since *Le spectre de la rose*, to recast its overly Russian image. Nijinsky seemed to be suffocating beneath the thick, blue-green makeup of Bakst and Cocteau, who by further feminizing him had lessened the dancer's erotic power: a fatal handicap for a work intended to revive the spell-binding sensuality and religious terrors of the Far East, and whose baroque, motley quality anticipated the excess of Josef von Sternberg. Brussel, a critic who had fallen in love with Karsavina, was indeed the only one to find the spectacle "perfect"; the rest of the press was as severe as the artistic agents that could have run the show. The choreography of Fokine, who had seen dances in the court of Siam, was deemed far inferior to the debauchery orchestrated by Baskt, with his grimacing monsters and young polychrome rajahs. The golden age of the first Ballets Russes was coming to an end in the waters of an enchanted lake chilled by the Seine, after having led dazzled spectators for four years "from the gates of the Orient to the shores of the Ganges."[63]

Cocteau had contributed too much to Bakst's and Fokine's pomp not to take the general disapproval as a personal insult. Sure of having raised Nijinsky to his own level—that of a young god worthy of Nietzsche's expectations—Cocteau experienced a childish feeling that it was all unfair. He who, in his excess, had believed that he was an integral part of the Ballets Russes, found it difficult to come back down to Parisian earth. Diaghilev was in a foul mood during all the performances. One evening at the Place de la Concorde, when Cocteau persisted in asking him why the ballet had failed, Diaghilev, in front of a glum Nijinsky, issued him this challenge: "Astonish me!" Cocteau had no idea what he meant.

SOPHOCTEAU

The publication of *La danse de Sophocle*, in June of that same year, 1912, would constitute an even more stinging disappointment. The critics reproached Cocteau for an all-too-obvious plagiarism of his guiding star, Anna de Noailles, who herself delivered the most flattering and unsettling commentary: "I prefer at every page" [*sic*].[64] After being assiduously courted, the critic Jules Lemaître freed himself from any obligation with a polite letter comparing Cocteau, among other "talented, bruised" young men, to Byron and Musset. While recognizing his talent, elegance, and ease, Georges Duhamel advised Cocteau, in the July edition of the *Mercure de France*, to rid himself of all the poetic trinkets encumbering him. But even then Cocteau insisted on believing that the critics had misunderstood him or were jealous.

They say that true genius always makes itself known. But this cliché ignores the reality that, in order to be printed, as well as published and then supported—and even better to be launched and listened to, commented on, and, who knows, well received—a writer must also be ambitious and scheming. Cocteau, certain that one flourished more surely in recognition than in failure, learned to overcome the indifference of publishers, to confront the critics, and to push for his own fame, even if it meant disturbing people by his insistence. There are two forms of megalomania for a writer just hired by a newspaper: one makes him say that the sales will double, the other that they will plummet. Naïvely believing in his calling, Cocteau knew only the first type of immodesty. Heir to symbolism's priestly function, he saw himself as an intercessor between occult forces and the world they direct, and he just had to make sure he was heard.

When Gide, his new literary model, kept silent about his latest book, Cocteau wrote to him again to find out if he had found his *Danse de Sophocle* truly bad. Finally in the summer of 1912, he announced to his mother that he had received a reply that was Protestant and affectionate, calling him "prodigiously, dangerously gifted," but also adding, in one of those disturbing asides that Gide himself had once so masterfully concocted: "How can one criticize the dance, when the dancer is so charming?"[65] Wounded by this verdict, as much as by the silence that had preceded it, Cocteau took up his pen to defend his collection. But these criticisms had dampened his enthusiasm, and it was only with difficulty that he returned to a work already becoming remote: "Although puerile influences impregnate it and although such leaps fill me with unease, it represents despite everything an entire phase of my experience, and I possess neither the right, nor the means to deny its disorder."[66] His entire life would confirm the validity of this attitude, uttered through a letter whose signature, "your Nathaniel," revealed that his imitative powers remained strong.[67]

Cocteau still hoped for a positive review in the *Nouvelle revue française*, which had just opened up to Blanche after suspecting him of being too concerned with high society, but its reviewer Henri Ghéon twisted the knife two months after the publication of the *Danse de Sophocle*. Like others before him, Ghéon noted the ballet's lexical boldness and an unsettling ability to be by turns lyrical, epic, and elegiac, but he also reproached Cocteau for being unable to unify his qualities, and for the work's lack of moral wholeness and fortitude. "This madman is too sure of himself; this artist too often loses his head; he has not yet found his equilibrium," noted Ghéon.[68] The worst was yet to come. Belittling this tyro who was already claiming the title of a Parisian divinity by comparing himself to Sophocles—a model of complete glory, with his twenty plays!—Ghéon denounced the extraordinary arrogance of this poet, adored by the Boulevard, who had attained perfection only in brief snatches. Criticizing his mannered elegance, his Parisianism, and his excessive facility, Ghéon expressed regret that Cocteau's social aspect stood between his verses and his readers, as well as surprise that the purveyors of instant fame could proclaim Cocteau's genius everywhere. At the same time, Ghéon afforded himself the luxury in retrospect of putting up with Cocteau's previous collection, *Le prince frivole*, which he deemed characteristic of an author "extremely talented," equal to a Musset, but also suspected of borrowing from others.

Called by turns a ludicrous figure and a paragon, Cocteau suffered from this article, which also wounded Proust by association, and which, sustained by the prestige of the *Nouvelle revue française*, found a real echo in Paris. With the cartoonist Sem depicting Cocteau in the same journal as a chimera—part doe, part ladybug, part chameleon—Cocteau was already resolving never again to read the press, whose frequent reservations depressed him. But didn't he himself suggest the negative labels people applied to him, by comparing himself, in his books, to a Persian magician, then to a white butterfly, "sprinkled with pollen and perfume," which reveals the "petty thefts he perpetrated"? Incapable of understanding the reasons for his failure, the poet whom Montesquiou had jokingly nicknamed "Sophocteau" denounced the public's ignorance and railed against the Académie Française (some members of which he had tried to influence, but which preferred to award its prize for poetry to another author) and for the first time took against those blasé "socialites" about whom he said, during a monologue-driven stroll through the Croissets' garden in Grasse: "In fifty years they will deify me, those imbeciles!"[69]

Already Cocteau was dreaming of more journeys, displaying that muddle-headed ardor that for so long had prevented him from settling down. Taking his vacation in Cambo, the Basque Versailles of the Rostands, he exhausted himself with footraces, country dances, and fandangos until he had stirred up the regulated lives of the Rostands to the point of absurdity. From hearing his *Danse* criticized he had come to question his tendency to watch himself live; he blossomed so well in Cambo that Mme Rostand saw with amazement her husband, naturally melancholic and shy, go from party to party with this young friend of Maurice, her beloved son. And how could the *prince frivole* reinstate himself into the literary scene? All that summer, he was subject to "visitations"—the poetic result of which dazzled the author of *Cyrano*, who thought himself, compared to Cocteau, devoid of talent.[70] Though Cocteau gained in lucidity, it was at first to the detriment of the young Maurice, who continued to believe that he had been blessed by the gods (despite Cocteau's reproaches for his extravagant outfits and his tendency to spoil his talents by exhibitionism). Rather than bring this semi-transvestite to Proust, despite Maurice Rostand's repeated requests, Cocteau used his precocious literary authority to sponsor his first poet, Henri Bouvelet, a seventeen-year-old with "mythological beauty," and his energy to help Proust find a publisher—a task that would end up taking over a year.[71]

The Ballets Russes, however, with whom Cocteau continued to associate, had fallen into a crisis. After the ruinous failure of *Le dieu bleu*, the radical choreography developed by Nijinsky for *L'après-midi d'un faune* dug even deeper into the budget. Dreaming of zinc trees for the set, the dancer had ended up agreeing that Bakst do more to "illustrate" the piece by Debussy, born from the poem by Mallarmé, but Nijinsky was so impatient to seize his independence that he greeted his mentor's pressing questions with aggressive silences and refused to sleep near his pillows blackened by hair dye. Only on the necessity of Europeanizing the Ballets Russes could the two men agree.

Caught up in his platonic passion for Nijinsky, Cocteau had again been witness to the silent rebellion of a dancer dreaming of restoring to dance its dimension of panic, in homage to the deity Pan. "Before the premiere of the *Faune*, at dinner at Larue's, he [Nijinsky] surprised us, on several days, by moving his head as if he had a stiff neck," Cocteau wrote. "Diaghilev and Baskt were worried, questioned him, got no reply. We learned later that he was training himself for the weight of the horns."[72] The tension reached such a point that the dancer, thinking Cocteau was taking Diaghilev's side, went to Cocteau's house, pushed him aside to grab a statue and throw it on the floor, then left without a word.[73] The night before the premiere, seeing Nijinsky immersed in his choreographical notes, Diaghilev tried to cancel everything, but the dancer would not give in. Advancing sideways, in a leotard stained with shoe polish like the warriors on ancient vases discovered at the Louvre, his head thrown back as if in ecstasy—this was the trance movement in Dionysian rites, as Isadora Duncan had revived them a few years before—Nijinsky, on the evening of May 29, 1913, before an astonished audience, presented his slow, succinct sketch, the fruit of silent years of research.[74] Finally asserting his virility but also his modernity, his *Faune* was no longer a graceful prodigy but a summit of proud rigidity who stressed tango steps and proud movements of his chin—an anti-*Spectre de la rose*.

Cocteau had predicted, in the program, that this "episode of panic" would go down in history. And by breaking with the luxurious virtuosity of Russian choreographies and orchestrating a clumsy but studied bestiality, the *Faune* in fact comprised the first anti-ballet of the modern era: no longer the aerial triumph of woman, celebrated since Romanticism, but a slow, earthly demonstration of masculine power, ending up in the jittery bliss of the faun. By depersonalizing the gestures in order the better to sexualize the absence of action, by placing his erratic choreography, far from any psychological motivation, under the auspices of elemental savagery, Nijinsky made the first metaphorical leap into twentieth-century dance. "This is neither audacity nor archeology,"

Cocteau declared. "It's the plastic attempt of a friendly young barbarian, moved by recent strolls through museums, greedy too to be of his time and to reduce dance to the schematic expression of a state of the soul."[75] This was a good definition of the unique contribution of Nijinsky, who went so far as to introduce into his score gestures observed in the psychiatric asylum where his brother was vegetating.

The insidious eroticism of the grape clusters adorning the faun's organ, or of the tulle scarf abandoned by the fleeing nymph against which he pressed himself, alone, aroused stormy reactions. The ornamental debauchery of *Le dieu bleu* had merely bored people: by contrast, this obscene rigidity, and these "clonic" or spasmodic movements, were the gestures of an "exasperated primitive." Humiliated that people couldn't recognize the formal triumph of his genius, Nijinsky ended up hating the spectacular roles in which he had been applauded, and began to perform them, especially his role in *Le spectre de la rose*, only reluctantly. "I'm not a jumper, I am an artist!" he said, more stubborn than ever.

Le dieu bleu was not the only thing to seem dated compared to this *Faune*, through which Nijinsky had confessed his sexual problems. Cocteau himself was thrown off-balance by the revelation. Had he been misled from the beginning? He had run so quickly that he barely had time to grasp what had happened to him. Should he, like Nijinsky, turn his back to the flowery style and profitable formulas? But since the *Faune* was a huge public failure, Cocteau found himself, for the first time, without a model to help him form an answer.

Sixteen months earlier, in January 1912, a sixty-year-old clergyman had made Cocteau's acquaintance at the home of Princesse Bibesco. Taking note of Cocteau's exaggerated sense of phrasing, sometimes obscured by excessive brio, the Abbé Mugnier was at the same time surprised by his sickly aspect, like Blanche's. He was also stunned by what he perceived as Cocteau's desperation, which he noticed after the young writer had provided an avalanche of descriptions upon plucking a rose during a stroll. This confessor to high society compared Cocteau—whom he was convinced would die young—to a kind of insect that, condemned to a brief life, hastens to dazzle before they fall. It was to this priest, still wearing an outdated clerical hat and a threadbare cassock—this priest, who said about life "How interesting!" and dreamed of holding firm for over a century—that Cocteau confided his first reservations about Anna de Noailles. In a strange but familiar cannibalistic impulse, this male Anna, this *Anna-mâle*, had discovered that the verses of Minerva conveyed her verbal genius only imperfectly. Coming as it did on the heels of the disappointing *Faune*, this realization could not leave Cocteau unharmed. Doubt returned to him like a boomerang, and "Sophocteau" began questioning his talents for being everywhere at once, as well as his ability to lay his literary eggs in another's nest. "I'd have liked to live the life of others," confided the indolent, cheerful Abbé Mugnier; but while the *prince frivole* began to want to live his own life exclusively, he also sensed that it could be less comfortable than if he continued as a prodigy sponsored by Anna, the Sibyl of the rue Scheffer.[76]

With the drug of Noailles having less effect every day, Cocteau found himself confronted with his own emptiness. Unable to work, he remained inert for days on end and even confided to Anna de Noailles herself, *"I no longer have any talent*—if I were waiting for God, it would be less serious, but I'm writing stupid things and am beginning to despair."[77]

———•———

THE MOLTING

The man of genius is the man who is capable of everything.
Sometimes a question suddenly arises: Are masterpieces alibis?
—Jean Cocteau, "Essai de critique indirecte"

SWANN AND MME DE CHEVIGNÉ

Throughout 1913, Cocteau had done everything to find a publisher for Proust. Not content with intervening himself at Fasquelle, which had published Zola, he urged Edmond Rostand, who had real influence over that publisher, to push for publication of the complete manuscript, while also putting pressure on the young Maurice Rostand, who desperately wanted to meet Proust. But Fasquelle rejected the manuscript, as did Ollendorff, and since the hostility of the *Nouvelle revue française* had led to rejection by Gaston Gallimard, whose publishing house was only two years old, Proust had to wait until the end of 1913 for Bernard Grasset to agree to publish *Du côté de chez Swann* at the author's expense, and only with cuts. With the book finally sent off to press, Proust determined which critics would report on it: Lucien Daudet for *Le Figaro*, Jacques-Émile Blanche for *L'écho de Paris*, Cocteau for *L'excelsior*, and, through Cocteau, Maurice Rostand for *Comoedia*. All of the critics were gay. A coherent campaign and aggressive distribution would create quite a stir about the great work, largely thanks to the unexpected, if somewhat reserved, reinforcement of the influential Paul Souday in *Le temps*, predecessor to *Le monde*.

Cocteau had already come to Proust's apartment on the boulevard Haussmann to read him the "paper" that had praised his novel and placed it in the company of masterpieces, stressing "the multiplied mirrors of this prodigious open-air labyrinth." The author of À *la recherche du temps perdu* felt moved to write to Cocteau again, nine days after the publication of *Du côté de chez Swann*, when the article appeared in *L'excelsior* praising his "vast miniature, full of mirages, hanging gardens, plays between space and time, and sweeping, fresh gestures à la Manet":

> Your marvel, gone beyond the sonorous manner in which I first experienced it to a graphic, ornamental silence, seemed new to me in this way, and in the silent astonishment of the letters persisting beyond the gazes that read them (Mallarmé would have expressed this in a line of impenetrable simplicity), seemed to me even more delightful, and how proud I was of it, and touched.[1]

No doubt Proust would have rather been the one to launch Cocteau on the literary scene, but the slowness of Proust's maturation, the precocity of the *prince frivole*, and the chances of life led to Cocteau's helping to make famous his elder by twenty years.

In private, Cocteau was just as enthusiastic. To the Abbé Mugnier, he expressed his admiration for a novel in which everything was placed on the same level, from actions to descriptions, as in the marvelous canvases by Uccello: "a book by an insect with tentacular sensitivity," a "cross-section of the brain," he proclaimed.[2] One has only to compare Cocteau's reaction to that of Reynaldo Hahn, who after just the first line of *Swann's Way* asked his friends to get used to the idea that a great genius was at work, or to compare Cocteau's article to Lucien Daudet's, to sense that Cocteau might not have taken the full measure of Proust's genius.[3]

The best of *In Search of Lost Time* still remained to be written, however—its staggered publication wasn't complete until 1927—and Cocteau was, obviously, too concerned with his own growth to devote to that first volume all the attention it deserved. "If you had really read *Swann* . . . ," Proust wrote to him, even six years later.[4] Perhaps too the first draft, with its slow progress, slightly disappointed Cocteau. Proust ruminated so long over his philosophical novel that this opening, which evoked nothing more consequential than his difficulty falling asleep or his taste for the names of towns, may have fallen short of what Cocteau expected. Although Grasset had shortened it by two hundred pages, the book was extraordinarily long—at least according to Cocteau, who would always rather inhale than reread; at times it reminded him of a carriage that keeps being loaded but never gets moving. "After seven hundred and twelve pages of this manuscript (at least seven hundred and twelve, since many pages have numbers with *b, c, d, e* added to them) . . . one has no idea, no idea at all, what it's about. What's the point of all this? What does it all mean?" the reader at Fasquelle had asked.[5]

But perhaps the main defect of this printed *Swann*, for Cocteau, was its failure to convey the atmosphere of Proust's private readings, especially Proust's strange voice, muted by the cork lining his walls, rising thinly from the cloud of the hypochondriac's bedroom fumigations. To any text without voice, gestures, or body, Cocteau would always prefer a flesh-and-blood book. Even if he thought Proust's vocal timber not very dramatic, and, truthfully, unworthy given their shared passion for actors, he must have missed Proust's presence as much as the fussy, and finally comical, ritual that surrounded his readings.

The fact remains, however, that in 1913 not many people were proclaiming Proust's genius. The majority of readers confirmed the verdict of the big publishing houses: Proust's work suffered from a radical lack of action, an abundance of impressions-within-impressions, endless sentences collapsing beneath the weight of parenthetical clauses. As for the more experienced critics, they regarded the countless beginnings and re-beginnings of this pure Right Bank product with much detachment. Like the *Nouvelle revue française* coterie of Schlumberger, Gide, and Ghéon, who were just as much dwellers in Sodom as Proust's coterie, they remained radically allergic to the mincing, perfumed homosexuality of Proust, whom Gide had long regarded as "the most fanatical of snobs"—a reproach that would also for a long time afflict Cocteau. Just as the critics at the *Nouvelle revue française* had been discouraging about the triumph of the Ballets Russes, they persisted in seeing this wealthy salon habitué as the diametric opposite of the aesthetic austerity that was their ideal. Instead of compromising, they preferred to state its party line and choices in each issue. "By concentrating on focusing its opera glasses," said Cocteau, "*La nouvelle revue française* never watches the performance."[6]

Cocteau's insistence on praising *Swann's Way*, however, may well have contributed to rattling the *Nouvelle revue française* team.[7] Early in 1914, Ghéon suddenly let it be known that Proust's "work of leisure," while it stubbornly persisted in constituting "the very opposite of a work of art, that is, an inventory of sensations," had managed to trap, like a net thrown into the ocean of time, all the flora and fauna emerging from his memory.[8] Gide too, whom Cocteau suspected of fearing being dethroned by the author of *Swann* in the halls of Gallimard, was beginning to regret his rejection of the manuscript, which was due mainly to Schlumberger's negative report on this "book full of duchesses." Was Cocteau the key to this reversal, which led Gide to give the most abject apologies? Proust in any case was very grateful to Cocteau for his support, even though it was given without his bothering to reread the book—*À la recherche du temps perdu* never served as a literary model for Cocteau.

Having fallen in love with Agostinelli, an out-of-work chauffeur whom he had just made his secretary, Proust had already complained to Cocteau in June 1913, a time when he had to abridge his work even more, that "Life is so cruel to me, now." In December, after Paul Souday's critical essay drawing attention to the novel, but also noting its weaknesses, naïvety, and improprieties, it was again Cocteau to whom Proust turned as confidante: "I saw my book in it as in a mirror advising suicide," Proust had written, anticipating the highs and lows that Cocteau himself would experience every time he published a book.

Then life brought Proust back to his masterpiece, and Cocteau back to his flight into society, which still had the power for him to suspend all the questions that he would ask himself in literature. Women like Mme de Chevigné, it is true, treated the young effeminate man (whose powder she once so feared) a little better every day, on the staircase on the rue d'Anjou. Since the countess was overflowing with gratitude for anyone capable of amusing her—and Cocteau's electric insolence did wonders in this respect—she had attached him to herself like a devoted escort. At the Opéra, at dinners in town, it was a Cocteau very elegantly dressed by Henry Pool and Charvet who now accompanied her; at the English ambassador's, Cocteau boasted, the messenger in livery would announce them with the flattering title "Count and Countess of Anjou," from the name of the street delimiting their little kingdom—an ennobling that must have doubly satisfied Mme Cocteau, since her son risked nothing but flattery with the comtesse—even when they stuffed their sleeves with silver cutlery so that they could play at being a couple of thieves unmasked by the subjects of Her Majesty. Cocteau could even take the liberty of shutting the countess's dog Kiss behind a glass fire-screen, and setting sugar cubes all around it, without the Countess being offended: appeasing her page's allergies came before the comforts of her Pomeranian.

These remarkable favors soon aroused the jealousy of "petit Marcel," who tirelessly persisted in courting their common friend, with less success every year. His way of doing so was strange, admittedly; while plying Mme de Chevigné with compliments so convoluted and adulatory as to be irreverent, he persisted in demanding details about, say, the straw hat dotted with cornflowers that she wore on such-or-such a day in 1903—insisting that she recall a scene that sometimes went back to the previous century. This zeal only imperfectly flattered the countess, who would end up interrupting his fastidious demand for inventory by proclaiming, in her gendarme's voice: "Only Mother Daudet keeps her old hats!"[9]

Cocteau, however, distracted her and made her feel younger: to Chevigné, he spoke less about her past than about the glories of the day, from Anna de Noailles to Nijinsky and Diaghilev. The little consort of Mme Cocteau soon became, despite himself, the one in whom Mme de Chevigné confided her increasing boredom with Proust. "He bores us to death with those scribbles," exclaimed this woman unscathed by any artistic ambition, and who required of her court only a maximum of entertainment. This rejection obsessed Proust for years on end, and made him renew his campaign obsessively, but the more he insisted, the more Chevigné, completely ignorant of his literary prowess, tended to see him as a social climber who knew nothing about the world he claimed to be describing—as well as an antiquarian of the absurd who sought to coax old memories from her by ridiculous flattery. Swallowing his pride, Proust asked Cocteau to act as his advocate to bring him closer to the countess. But Chevigné, a good walker, didn't like to feel she was being followed, and Cocteau had to invent ever more subtle pretexts not to wound "petit Marcel." Caught between the threads of the wounded spider and the fire of the heraldic dragon, Cocteau no longer knew which saint to swear by. "You are an admirable person, but one has to resolve oneself to face the fact that you are not a true friend," a piqued Proust finally wrote to Cocteau, in July 1913.[10]

Did Cocteau lack respect for Proust, whom he saw one day, through a half-open door on boulevard Haussmann, wolfing down a dish of noodles while standing up, then buttoning a velvet waistcoat over "a poor square torso that seemed to contain his working parts"? Proust would later reproach Cocteau for his "affectation of indifference" toward those who loved him, and accuse him of trying to puff himself up by treating others with contempt ("Cocteau grated on his nerves," confirmed Paul Morand).[11] One wonders what Proust would have said had he known that the Comtesse de Chevigné had stopped opening his interminable letters, which she had no capacity to understand, employing them mainly to "test" the curling irons with which her maid curled the small amount of hair that her hats had left visible.[12]

It is also not out of the question that Proust may have guessed, through a confidence of Lucien Daudet's or a slip of the tongue, the pleasure that Cocteau took in imitating him, after their meetings. Perhaps Proust had forgotten how he and Daudet had amused themselves imitating Montesquiou, fifteen years earlier. Proust instead decided that Cocteau was one of those men "who so long as they are near you understand you, cherish you, grow tender to the point of tears, yet take their revenge a few hours later by making a cruel joke about you, but who come back to you, always more understanding, just as charming, just as temporarily like yourselves"—a group to which Proust knew he was himself condemned to inhabit ever since the death of his mother, and which he described with all the more intelligence since he was part of it.

Perhaps too the way in which Cocteau addressed his letters seemed a little offhand to Proust: imitating Mallarmé, he decorated his letters with comments like "Mailman, carry these words, ridding yourself of them / At the boulevard Haussmann at the home of Marcel Proust, 102," said one. "102, boulevard Haussmann, oust! / Run, mailman, to the home of Marcel Proust," stated another. More likely, Cocteau made the mistake of not always respecting the absurd rituals surrounding Proust's outings; unlike so many others, he was unimpressed by Proust's legendary tardiness and eccentricity about time.[13] When Proust was very late, Cocteau was content to wait for him at Mme de Chevigné's place, two floors down—which only irritated Proust more. One night as Cocteau returned to his apartment from hers, around midnight, he found Proust plunged in the shadows, on the wicker seat he shared with his mother. "Why didn't you at least wait for me in my apartment? You know the door's always open!" Cocteau asked. "Dear Jean," Proust replied, "Napoleon had a man killed who waited for him at his house. Obviously, I'd only have read the Larousse, but there might have been letters lying around."[14] There were other laughable arguments, too, all thick with threats.

These rebuffs, which would have made Proust suffer horribly twenty years earlier, had become a part of his philosophy of love. "He would rather have been scorned than not loved," wrote Pietro Citati; "and if he was loved, he remained overwhelmed by it, almost at a loss."[15] By confirming the impossibility, in friendship and in love, of bridging the radical separation of worlds where even the closest beings lived, Cocteau and Chevigné encouraged him to dissociate feelings and pleasure, to make friends only in complete independence, and to content himself physically with the company of men who were foreign to his milieu, if not to his tastes, like Agostinelli. Proust, it is true, found the knowledge that two people he loved were together very difficult to bear: for Chevigné's refusal to tell him about her hats, out of fear of seeming old, Proust took his revenge in À *la recherche du temps perdu* by equipping Oriane de Guermantes with a lineage going back through the ages like a "yellowing" tower, and with cheeks that were "composite like a nougat," overcome by verdigris.

STRAVINSKY'S *SACRE*

Cocteau left Proust all the more readily to his investigation of the past when, on exactly May 29, 1913, he had the confirmation that a turning point was under way—the premiere of *Le sacre du printemps*, at the brand-new Théâtre des Champs-Élysées. The red herd of girls, the bright green of the hills painted by Nicolai Roerich, the brown mass of human bears performing their primitive dances with feet splayed out: all this acted on Cocteau like a drug. Those popular Russian colors that at the same time Kandinsky was using in his new abstract canvases dazzled Cocteau. During the symphony his ears vibrated to cymbals that gave the beat of the great pagan rites, passed down from the time of the Scythians, and the violent bursting forth of the Russian spring, which made the frozen *zeml* [earth] crack, like a giant ice-breaker, over millions of acres.

Despite the power of mass movement, the most traditional way to evoke the "Russian soul," the audience—decked out in pearls, plumes, and ostrich feathers—had immediately revolted against this sonorous cataclysm. "Couched in Louis XVI garlands, Venice gondolas, soft divans, and cushions of an Orientalism for which the Ballets Russes could be reproached," Cocteau wrote, the audience had stamped its feet upon discovering the cold, new hall; hissed at the first notes by Stravinsky; then laughed aggressively until the sound drowned out the orchestra.[16] They also balked repeatedly at the hieratic poses created by the full-fledged choreographer that Nijinsky had become—not to mention the sacred dance of the Chosen One, the young virgin convulsing until death in order to regenerate the earth by her sacrifice.

Cocteau had seen and felt everything: the frustrated expectations of the audience, which had consecrated Stravinsky in an evening, at the premiere of *Firebird*; then the despair of Nijinsky in the wings who—exhausted by months of rehearsals, tours, and conflicts with Diaghilev, but also with the composer, on whom he had imposed his choreography only through sheer obstinacy—was discovering with horror that he was being taken for a big phoney. After a certain point the deafened dancers could no longer even hear the orchestra, so Nijinsky climbed onto a chair to beat the measure of their movements, shouting out inaudible numbers to them punctuated by "It's weak!" This development obliged Stravinsky to tug on Nijinsky's coat to prevent him from broadcasting his judgment to the audience—a sea of angry ticketholders that Astruc, the director of the theater, was already trying to reassure by shouting, "You can hiss later."

Just like a *poilu* recounting a 1914 war story, Cocteau would narrate this premiere a thousand times. It was capped by the arrival of policemen who, though they threw out the most violent protesters, were unable to restore order. One obnoxious spectator, upon seeing the violent trembling of "The Chosen One" during her sacrificial dance, had cried out: "A doctor! No! A dentist!" The high society that had supported the Ballets Russes from the beginning now rebelled against the savagery of these "Images of Pagan Life," and the ladies cried out against the obscene dances. "Be quiet, you bourgeois bitches!" someone shouted from one of the boxes. "That's the first time in sixty years anyone has dared disrespect me," the old Comtesse de Pourtalès stammered, getting only a "Shut it!" in response. Meantime Diaghilev demanded that the auditorium be plunged into darkness, then brilliantly lit to reestablish a semblance of order, but that only brought new calls for the firemen and the doctor: Ravel was even called a "dirty Jew" for having acclaimed the work as genius.

"They laughed, booed, hissed, imitated bird cries," Cocteau added, at once envious of the response encountered by Stravinsky and fearful given the "martyrdom" that Nijinsky—by far the main target of the protesters—was enduring.[17] The scandal, however, was not entirely spontaneous. Diaghilev, only tepidly liking the musician's score and fearing a complete failure (the Parisian audience had already shown its reservations toward the audacity of *Petrushka*, three years earlier), had been careful to fill the dress circles with aggressive supporters, who applauded just as mechanically as those nostalgic for the original Ballets Russes were protesting. "The incompetent acclamations of some were more unbearable than the sincere hisses of others," Cocteau would say later, though clearly that evening he had rejoiced to see Stravinsky's sonorous expression of the obscure forces that control nature (as well as, perhaps, our minds). The composer's "biological" music expressed both force and delicacy, blind tragedy and naïve cheerfulness; this "prehistoric" monster had just laid an egg so full of living matter that it contained enough to re-make the earth in sheer sound. Modernity would always call for a form of elemental savagery: Stravinsky was one of the few, along with Picasso, Cendrars, and Kandinsky, to possess it instinctually.

No doubt the amplitude of the *Sacre* scandal contributed to Cocteau's enthusiasm: at that time public opinion to him was dogma. But the *Sacre* also mobilized a sensibility vacant in Cocteau since his idyll with Anna de Noailles had begun to wane. His cricket antennae perceived the shapes that watched him, from behind, burrowing into the past. A powerful blow of the gong had just struck a world lulled by the impressive harmonies of Reynaldo Hahn and the fading piano of Debussy, destroying "the peaceful musical landscape of the nineteenth century in a thirty-five minute eruption," as the duo pianist team of Gold and Fizdale wrote.[18] Nationalist critics, fierce about geography, saw in this transformative shift an invasion worthy of the Huns, or even the pretext for a larger Germanic act of vengeance.

After joining the troupe backstage to comfort Nijinsky, Cocteau emerged to dine at Larue's with Proust, Diaghilev, and the composer; Nijinsky, still upset by the shouts he had roused, remained silent. The meal ended at about two in the morning, and Cocteau got into a carriage with the three Russians. As Stravinsky had said, Diaghilev's most keenly developed artistic sense was that of success, and—looking like a sated drug dealer—"Chinchilla" (Diaghilev) began murmuring Pushkin as they left Paris, the coachman's lantern revealing tears on his cheeks.

> It's hard to explain, Stravinsky replied, when Cocteau questioned him on the reasons for this sadness . . . too Russian . . . It's something like "Do you want to visit the islands?" . . . You understand, in our country, you go to the islands the way you go to the Bois de Boulogne, and it's by going to the islands that we imagined *Le sacre du printemps*.[19]

Russia had just taken the place of Persia and India in Cocteau's expanding imagination.[20]

Cocteau would always claim to have met Stravinsky in the spring of 1911, when Nijinsky was dancing *Le spectre de la rose*. According to the composer, it was instead a year earlier, at the end of the rehearsals for *Firebird*, when a stranger had shouted to him, in the street: "Is that you, Igor?" before introducing himself as Jean Cocteau. But their true relationship, which would always be more artistic than human, seems to have grown after this historic premiere, with Cocteau thinking about offering the composer the ballet he hoped to see Nijinsky dance.[21]

This evocation of pagan Slavs from the Stone Age in fact convinced Cocteau that he had started out in the wrong way. A creator could not content himself with perpetuating ancient forms, merely adapting them to his time or his person, but had to effect his own spring, in a way; he had to try to make waves of new sensations arise, and untested, raw emotions be felt, even if it meant displeasing people. Whereas Cocteau could sometimes be lightning-like, Stravinsky was thunder. Cocteau spoke divinely; Stravinsky saved himself wholly for his music. Cocteau dreamed of mythology; Stravinsky made the gods be heard. And though Cocteau wanted to be French, a frivolous prince, Catholic and pagan at once, Stravinsky was an imperial peasant whose music expressed all the Russias, shaman and Orthodox.

The challenge issued by Diaghilev, after the failure of *Le dieu bleu*, was suddenly made clear to Cocteau. By "Astonish me," the impresario obviously meant: "Don't imitate us, stop wanting to please us, become what you are." The gifted student—capable of reproducing any admired style—understood that he had to surpass himself to surprise those who thought they already knew him. Was Cocteau embracing his inner adult or indulging in further immaturity? This desire to throw people off balance became his own formula, and Diaghilev's command grew to be his motto. Until then, Cocteau had understood culture to renew tradition in ways just lively enough to keep elegant company breathless. "I came from a family where no one thought at all about being surprising. They thought art was serene, calm, various—you didn't have to choose." The mega-lomania of Anna de Noailles had indeed expanded this model but without changing its essence, which was both cumulative and backward-looking. Yet Stravinsky's art, at least at first glance, did not rest on knowledge but rather, like Wagner's creations, on unprecedented elemental drives and grand motives; Stravinsky sought not to prolong culture, but to subvert it in order to reach nature. Lifted up by these blocks of pure music that had renounced any kind of "sauce," Cocteau was already thinking, one year after the failure of *Le dieu bleu*, only of recreating, by pen and paper, a vital orgy worthy of the *Sacre*.

By coincidence or dumb luck, Gide, the *Nouvelle revue française*, Cocteau— as well as Proust—were becoming closer. Ghéon's formidable article "saluting" Cocteau's *La danse de Sophocle* had led Cocteau to fire off a tactical mea culpa to the journal and then return to the attack, during all of 1913, to convince Gide and Ghéon of his originality: ventriloquist and cannibal, he agreed, but follower, never. An essential doubt overtook Gide every time this self-proclaimed admirer appeared. Bombarded with a hail of letters, enthusiastic replies, and fervent requests, Gide remained reserved, like a cat watching the flutters of a swallow in disbelief. Gide did contribute to Cocteau's evolution, however, with one of those oblique remarks that he was master of, by encouraging him to disentangle his "J"s—advice that was much more than calligraphic, since Cocteau's verses still imitated those of Anna de Noailles.

At the end of 1913, Gide was planning on publishing two—and then, at Cocteau's urging, seven—poems by Jean Cocteau in an issue of *La nouvelle revue française*, which at the time was in the process of becoming "the only journal," according to Proust. The rest of the editorial committee, however, with the exception of Ghéon, opposed the arrival of this symbol of old salon-style poetry, with Rivière denouncing the incoherence of these poems "that, to excuse themselves, try to pass themselves off as intentional."[22] The Proust affair began again, with an additional aggravating factor: categorized as being in the circle of the *Mercure de France* by the journal's editors, Cocteau risked dragging in his wake figures as scandalously mannered as Maurice Rostand—which would be a tragedy for Gide and Ghéon who, just like Montesquiou or Diaghilev in their way, were partisans of virile love. "There might not exist at the present time in

Paris a personality more representative of all we detest, all we are basically opposed to," wrote Jacques Copeau to Gide, on January 30, 1914. "Cocteau will never be one of us. To say so would be [to provoke] the sorrow, even the shame, of Gaston Gallimard."[23] And Gide gave in to these arguments. No longer receiving his books, Cocteau played the emotional card—"Gide is too sure of Jean Cocteau's heart; he's taking advantage of it"—but with even less success.[24] By deciding to create a youthful style for himself on the shoulders of Rivière and Copeau, Cocteau had instead made them take a moral stance against him.

The memory of the easily obtained praise he had received for five long years suddenly began to fade. "M. Cocteau is talented, but now he has to devote himself to his talent," Ghéon had warned, and the message had finally gotten through, while all Proust's admonishments had done nothing.[25] The republican Walhalla of Anna de Noailles, the ducal nostalgia of Lucien Daudet, the exquisite French moderation of Hahn—all seemed now to Cocteau as if they came from another time. Polytonal and seismic, Stravinsky's music had rendered obsolete the unashamed languor and sickly emotional agitation of the quatrains, rondos, and other nostalgic poetic forms that had been Cocteau's foundational repertoire. The Symbolist imaginary realm abounded with lakes reflecting Narcissuses, palaces haunted by hysterical Salomés, and forests where fauns and fairies pursued each other—classical Antiquity as revised by Baudelaire, Byzantium, Japan. It was time to leave all of that behind and enter into the century of vital energy announced by Nietzsche.

Impatient to rid himself of his reputation as a pet for elderly virtuosi, Cocteau threw into the fire the books of his masters, the sonorous molds into which he had poured his alexandrines, as well as the canvases of Jacques-Émile Blanche, his elder by twenty-eight years who had ended up feeling just as he did. After those years of brilliant dispersion and exalted imitation, a need for sobriety, order, and silence seized Cocteau. "Those massacres of trinkets, those auto-da-fés of pieces of paper, they flagellate feebleness, they give a shower to the soul," he would say three years later.[26] He knew then that he was breaking with the cumulative art and mythological overloads inherited from the reign of Napoleon III. "I always try to find a fresh spot on the pillow," said Stravinsky, to justify his frequent about-faces—a phrase that Cocteau repeated ad nauseam. As Apollinaire had written just a year earlier in "Zone,"

> In the end you are tired of this ancient world
> Shepherd oh Eiffel Tower the herd of bridges is bleating this morning
> You've had enough of living in Greek and Roman antiquity
> Here even the cars look antique.[27]

Soon Cocteau would repudiate *La lampe d'Aladin*, *Le prince frivole*, and *La danse de Sophocle*, going so far as to forbid their reprint even in anthologies, and requesting that all extant copies be burned. The outline of *Le dieu bleu*, likewise, was deleted from his *Oeuvres*; like a Phoenix recreating his youth by throwing himself into the flames, Cocteau dragged into his audo-da-fé the Musset he had dreamed of reviving, along with "poetic" poetry, of which he had become the youngest herald. Against the idiots ("abrutis," as the Surrealist poet Arthur Cravan would call them) who saw beauty only in beautiful things, Cocteau called for "an aesthetic of the minimum," like the simple architect's table he wrote on from then on, and turned to the new and immediate, the rough and unnamed. "Genius is childhood clearly expressed," Baudelaire had said. Cocteau would follow this calling and write a prose "of his age" that would represent this fresh start: "Virginity of tomorrow, what worn-out yesterday can equal you?"[28]

Still hostage to a style that the war would sweep aside, the young Barrès-follower François Mauriac was indignant about Cocteau's about-face, reacting as though he felt rejected a second time. But at the time, this "betrayal" ("He left us without a backward glance") entailed great risk for Cocteau.[29] "I could have written *La Marseillaise* or *Plaisir d'amour* [a popular French love song]," noted the former protégé of De Max, knowing his facility at rhyming. But wasn't it exactly the courage to go against one's own success that Cocteau had admired in Nijinsky? "I placed my entire fortune in escrow; now I don't have a penny," he added.[30] Like Nietzsche overturning all his values by immolating Wagner on the altar of Bizet, Cocteau sacrificed Anna de Noailles on the steps of the brand-new modernity, as if he had lived until then with sick masters and was finally ready to sing of health.

Since Mauriac had also in the meantime learned to be young, Cocteau could later reply to him: "So I didn't turn my jacket inside-out, I turned my skin."[31] Mauriac was unaware at the time that the Parisian Cocteau was obeying the strange cyclical logic of a nature that would always summon him to evolve, sometimes against his own interests. Cocteau would later complain of the cliché comparing him to a born acrobat, but he himself would introduce it, in *Le Potomak*, with a lucidity bordering on self-criticism. It was a vital need, never hindered by major regrets: he had to contradict himself, even repudiate himself, turn himself upside-down so as not to wither in place. "I would have been transformed, if I had looked back, into a statue of sugar," he added, in an indirect allusion to the damnation of Sodom: he had to flee in order to escape the hell of repetition.[32]

His body felt this molting intimately. The epidermis of the old Cocteau was already falling away in tatters and giving way to a new self. Would he evolve into a venomous plant, a multicolored insect, or a formidable mammoth?

Instinctively, he classified himself as among those species given to metamorphoses, like Narcissus, whom death changes into a flower. In *Les vocalises de Bachir-Selim,* Cocteau writes:

> Just as the bud hopes to be a rose,
> The deer's antlers burn the forehead of the fawn,
> The soft butterfly in its stifling sheath
> Before being born longs for metamorphosis . . .

Ignoring his limits, "Sophocteau" was already cavalierly eluding the crucial questions that every creator eventually asks himself: who, if anyone, will be my model? Stravinsky no doubt was the unconscious teacher of this autodidact, who learned from creators more than from books; but Cocteau also knew that he could not simply substitute himself as is for his former self, or, even less, avoid introspection altogether—for it was in the creator alone that his treasure lay. "I understood that in order to rise up one had to descend into oneself; I saw the void and I reacted," he had written to his mother as early as 1906, during his retreat at the home of M. Dietz: the start of his transformation, at the end of 1913, spoke to the same impulse. "I had quickly climbed the ladder of official values," he would say; "I saw how short, narrow, and overloaded with people the ladder was. I learned the ladder of secret values."[33] After dreaming of floating over the world as a demi-god, Cocteau now intended to explore nothing but his own secrets—to penetrate into the explosive firedamp around veins of coal whose atoms, with time, might change into those of diamonds. It had taken him seven years to form his first skin; he would need almost as many to form the new one and to reconcile himself with poetry.

MODERN RELIGION

There is one constant in the fairy world: once its princes are familiar and its illusions disclosed, the yearned-for paradise loses its brilliance. Since magic can't be observed from close up without causing disappointment, the enchanted territory becomes more and more dull as one gets to know it, and one is tempted to gaze instead at the new castle taking shape in the distance. So it was with Cocteau: scarcely had he found a territory as a writer than it began to seem ordinary to him; scarcely had he forged an identity than he began to suffer from its lack of mystery. The aura of Anna de Noailles stemmed from her prestige as someone unattainable, as indeed she had been during the two years Cocteau had vainly tried to approach her; but the better he got to know her, the more the Byzantine imp lost her luster: a woman with whom one takes tea three times a week does not remain divine for long. Cocteau continued to see her, to love and personally admire his "sister" in poetry, but it was no longer with her, even less by embodying her persona and style, that he would write.

A huge construction project thus opened up for the twenty-four-year-old poet. He had to remake, if not a universe, at least an aesthetic—an arduous task for someone so accustomed to navigating with the help of the current. Having made up his mind to enlarge the field of his inquiry, Cocteau began to read Apollinaire, one of the three or four canonical poets for the still scattered troops of the avant-garde, and subscribed to Apollinaire's journal *Les soirées de Paris*, in which Max Jacob and Alfred Jarry rubbed shoulders with Picasso. Having come from a milieu calling for "what is done," Ariel discovered the humble list of works that had the ambition of indicating what has yet to be done. After Cocteau posed for the young painter Juliette Roche that spring, she reported that he was still making fun of the Cubists, yet no sooner had her lover Albert Gleizes appeared in her studio than he and Cocteau, abandoning their reciprocal prejudices, had exchanged friendly remarks, then visiting cards. "A few days later, Cocteau spoke of nothing but Duchamp-Villon, Jacques Villon, Albert Gleizes," the young woman wrote, surprised at seeing Cocteau come round to a trend he knew almost nothing about, a trend that had been born seven years earlier under the aegis of Braque and Picasso, the first to introduce into painting actual pieces of reality—newspapers, playing cards, beer coasters, and so forth. But Cubism didn't get good press at the time, and no one then could have guessed that it would open floodgates that, half a century later, would bring about an end to the predominance of painted canvas.

Cocteau had no doubt been one of the first Frenchmen to see the films of the Lumière brothers in the basements of the Old England store where his mother used to buy his clothes.[34] He returned to the cinema to see Rio Jim in *Pour sauver sa race, Fantômas, Le capitaine Scott*, and *Les mystères de New York*: a whole popular cinema that later on Breton and the Surrealists would discover. But he also watched documentaries that showed boxing matches in slow motion, an enlarged eye of a fly, a rose unfurling in fast motion—images that left a mark on his imagination. While many writers scorned this "fairground art," Cocteau spent hours watching the cone of light filled with actors and horses streaming from the projection booth, only to vanish, once they'd crossed the canvas wall, into electricity and photons. "Cinematography is the revelation of the gaze," Rudyard Kipling would confirm to him.[35] And so film became one of the vectors of Cocteau's metamorphosis. At the same time, he was developing a passion for photography and cut out pictures of soccer players from the papers, snapshots in which he saw biblical poses.

Already Cocteau was publicly mocking Anna de Noailles: her political predictions ("She's playing hopscotch with a stone from the Acropolis," he said), and even her latest dress, which he called "a New Year's candy bag."[36] He began to do imitations of her at Misia's home—a revealing detail, because Misia was regarded as the muse of the new style of the Ballets Russes, one barbaric and refined at once. These imitations would be seen by some as so many dagger thrusts; but by their very perfection, they were more likely the ultimate and logical homage of a poet too talented to grow old in the role of a page.

Spectacular as Cocteau's *volte-face* was, there was nothing unique about it: the whole old aesthetic system was beginning to totter. It was during that same year of 1913 that Kandinsky finished his first great abstract paintings, and Cendrars made his *Transsibérien* run in a prose that conveyed the train's sudden jolts, by an unprecedented technique of simultaneous collage; when Larbaud inaugurated, with *Barnabooth*, a play on language that Joyce would continue the next year, before Valéry decreed that one could no longer read a novel beginning with "The Marquise went out at five o'clock"; when Duchamp presented at the Armory Show in New York his *Nude Descending a Staircase No. 2*, a Cubist-Futurist composition in which no nude was portrayed, and so was all the more shocking; and when Apollinaire did away with punctuation in his *Alcools* before announcing the end of syntax, of the sublime, and even of history, in a manifesto in favor of Italian Futurism.

A year earlier, Jacques-Émile Blanche had asserted: "Everything proves to us that we're headed for a cataclysm; even little Cocteau, with his youth, says he feels it."[37] The most superstitious, like D'Annunzio, started dating their mail "1912+1," from fear of writing a fatal "13"; after the killings of the Great War, Léautaud would wonder what readers *La danse de Sophocle* could still attract, while Cocteau would realize the radical uselessness of installing his portrait bust in a gallery condemned to close. Just as Proust had made up his mind to set off "in search of lost time" just as the first mechanisms were appearing that allowed one to fix each sonorous, visual, and moving detail of life in place forever, Cocteau's molting has begun. The transformation, strangely, took place in the very year when Niels Bohr presented, in a simplified form, an application of Planck's quantum theory to the atom, whereby we learned that it is impossible to determine simultaneously the speed and position of an electron—a discovery that cast doubt on the principle of the sameness of bodies, and even their very reality. This suspicion in turn would win over the entire century, via Nietzsche's philosophical paradoxes and the discovery of the unconscious by Freud, in a process that slowly substituted modern virtuality for what remained of old sacredness, and of nineteenth-century scientism.

This strong personality in search of an identity, as Cocteau was at the time, found itself thus stripped bare, without head or tail, left or right. Half-Ruhmkorff induction coil, half-living-Faraday cage, he was a simple mass of electrons able to assemble in overvoltage according to a thousand changing structures, through extraordinary tactile, visual, or olfactory faculties (as Ernst Mach had just asserted, the self is nothing but a waiting room of sensations). Cocteau was far from afraid: instead the chasm that opened up beneath him encouraged him to make the great leap. His organism was molting: he claimed in advance all the forms it could take, just as a new mother accepts her newborn child, whatever his or her anomalies. By re-engendering himself, did Cocteau want to take away from his mother a little of the abusive power she had over him? From then on, whatever happened, he would be the son only of his own works.

Aware that he was late to the party, Cocteau worked twice as hard. After Stravinsky confided that the sacred dance of the Chosen One had appeared to him in a dream, as he was composing *Le sacre du printemps*, Cocteau lay in wait for the dreams that peopled his daytime and nighttime sleep.[38] When he learned that sugar could help make a person dream, he ate entire boxes and drew the curtains shut twice a day to slip, still clothed, under the sheets, with his ears blocked with wax so that his oneiric episodes would be influenced by only internal sounds. Until then he worked with his eyes wide open, "terribly awake, ambitious, absurd," he said.[39] He abandoned the visions projected by his Aladdin's lamp to descend like a miner, armed with a single torch, to explore the unknown person he had become. No longer the gods, but his unconscious, became his guide; he retreated from the Greco-Christian pantheon as from the night of the elements, and turned toward the cave of the self. "At the age of twenty, I entered poetry as one enters the priesthood," he wrote in the preface to *Requiem*, fifty years later. The former living god was now nothing but a novice being initiated into the sober religion of modernity.[40]

THE SHAPELESS AND THE OMNIVOROUS

Le Potomak was the first book to emerge from this period. Difficult at times because of its density, its mood switches, and its mannerism, this literary UFO bears witness to a radical break with the psychology and symbols of the time.

As is often true of Cocteau's works, an actual experience led to this book. Charged with amusing Blanche's nephew with stories, Cocteau had spun a tale of a sea monster swimming in an aquarium hidden under the Madeleine. When the story met with success, he adorned the monster with large pink ears; supplied it with visitors who fed it olive oil, mandrakes, and hot-air balloons;

and soon gave it a rich, complex, allegorical life reflecting his own. If the child asked to see this marine diplodocus, whose amorphous shape recalled the lungs of a cow or an elephant's brain, Cocteau, careful to guard the mystery, refused to give it a face, other than in a single drawing he took care to leave out of his book.[41] Impatient to signal his conversion to Modernism, whose other pole was American, Cocteau gave this monster the name of the river flowing through Washington, D.C., substituting a *k* for the final *c*. Then—betting on the dream-like potential of drawing, which is traditionally less tied to thinking than writing is—he let himself be guided by his pen like an automaton. Strange sketches took shape in the margins of this huge absent center, with no logical connection between them; inspired by the guests Blanche received in his house in Offranville, two rival species of bourgeoisie came into being. By their steely, paunchy roundness, their Tyrolean folk costume, and their pathological voraciousness, their bloodthirsty goals and their irrational attitudes, the Eugènes—one of Cocteau's four Christian names—soon turned out to be the sworn enemies of the brave Mortimers, provincial petits-bourgeois whose geniality did little to hide a persnickety habit of supervising things, and who would be literally inhaled by the Eugène women, who were insatiable ghouls.

"The Eugènes are setting the world on fire," Cocteau announced to his mother in October 1913. Blanche described their little group as haunted by these Michelin men who signified nothing other than the absurdity of our gregarious behavior, like Jarry's Ubu or like the animated Shadocks on French television in the 1970s. Their success was so great that Cocteau decided to add a text to the drawings, but the task would prove difficult, since the fear of his old habits returning clashed with the fear of exhausting people by an excess of delirium. He dug his tunnels in every direction, hesitated, then started up again, ran out of breath, took fright, and soon confided to his mother: "Being weak, I admire those who carry their plans to completion."[42] Instinctively moved to exaggeration and detail, Cocteau went from evoking his "spring" to creating a mocking tale of his first visit to Catulle Mendès (Pygamon). But he found it difficult to provide a general outline of the story, and feared he'd succeed, at the same time. "By dint . . . of waiting sometimes for hours, alone, standing up, my lamp extinguished, for representatives of the unknown, I became all machine, all antenna, all Morse," he wrote in 1916, in the introduction to *Le Potomak*.[43]

One evening, joining a laughing group of friends, Cocteau asked to see the manuscript that was making them laugh so. He saw, written in the middle of a white page, "Dining is west." The work, *Tender Buttons*, written by the American novelist Gertrude Stein, whose name was unfamiliar to Cocteau, would not be published until the following year. Despite Jarry's previous renown for absurdity, such a statement, in 1913, still seemed the fruit of mental derangement, especially in Blanche's entourage, but Cocteau found in it a new incitement to attempt his own absurd phrasings and sudden changes of subject. To the drawings and themes peculiar to him, Cocteau was already incorporating fragments of an aesthetic manifesto, in tune with an avant-garde fertile in enigmatic works, an avant-garde that also loved manifestos. Drawings surrounded by captions, texts filled with Nietzschean encouragements—"Cultivate whatever the public reproaches you for: that is you"—were augmented by prefaces to his future life and with aphorisms; cartoons turned into wild farces that pursued the pyrotechnic exuberance of Stravinsky's *Sacre,* but also the throbbing allure of Gide's *Paludes.* But can we still call this a "book," this unstable patchwork of poems, fables, and puns where the Eugènes, like the Potomak itself, have only an anecdotal presence?

Molting at the pace of its author, revised as much as Joyce's *Work in Progress* would be, the unidentified object would continue through the long months of its gestation to recycle its various influences until it devoured itself. Entering into his story, Cocteau surrounded himself with companions whose names, chosen from the medicinal plants in the Offranville pharmacy—"with a friend common to Gide and me," he points out, in a clear allusion to Blanche—evoke Gide's *Les nourritures terrestres:* Persicaire, Bourdaine, Argémone.[44] As Cocteau was constructing his book from emptiness, he decanted and clarified this intimate puzzle, like a gardener suddenly hostile to flowers, trying both to betray himself and disguise himself. He crowded his text with proverbs and "flashes," some of which anticipate Dadaism, with one asserting that "a masterpiece of literature is never anything but a disordered dictionary," and another—"Ideas are born from phrases"—evoking the phrase that Tzara would utter in 1921: "La pensée se fait dans la bouche," or "Thought takes shape in the mouth."[45] As Cocteau would say to Stravinsky, his ultimate goal at this moment was to fit an entire book into a telegram.

There were also spelling errors—he would always make many. Denying what he loved, Cocteau let himself be carried away by his associations of ideas. Coming from the most diverse sources—encyclopedias, atlases, railroad guides—words and images would make a place for themselves in this giant stewpot that still simmered three years later. People wanted to see in this Potomak a symbol for a grieving childhood, or the image of a fetus moving, dreamlike, in the womb. Cocteau himself in 1915 spoke of it (to Abbé Mugnier) as a monster representing infinity. Today, this giant coelenterate vegetating beneath the church, where it met its author every day, seems to reflect an imagination fond of metamorphoses, but still bound by the weight of its education.

Blanche had already noted Cocteau's surprising receptivity to the atmosphere of the time: *Le Potomak* followed by only five years Sigmund Freud's "Creative Writers and Day-Dreaming," which wouldn't be translated until 1933 but whose arguments were already reaching France.[46] As vague, shapeless, and omnivorous as the id of the analysts, the Cocteau-ian polyp may well have described the physical intrusion of the unconscious into national literature.

Having disowned his first three collections, Cocteau would always cite *Le Potomak* as his actual first book, the founding act of his journey. Rarely republished because of its solitary esotericism, this strange book is thought to make known the cruelties of war, and even the rising power of the irrational. Yet this discontinuous autobiography, where Cocteau lays claim to the same tabula rasa as the Rimbaud of "Délires II," is remarkable first of all as a lucid graph of Cocteau's transformation. With its extremely modern nonchalance, its way of recounting everything and nothing, it follows the fits and starts that would always be Cocteau's. His life might even be summarized by the series of aesthetics that he sought to devalue after making himself their herald.

Already Cocteau foresaw another book that would recount his journey, with the eloquent title *Le voyageur vers la gauche*. He was unaware of how difficult, long, and chaotic this journey would be. Like this *Potomak*, it would inaugurate a genre of which it remains the sole representative.

THE FAILED SACRE OF *DAVID*

Cocteau's public metamorphosis set tongues wagging on the Right Bank, where no one gave him (or wished him) the slightest chance of success. Anna de Noailles was logically one of the first to deplore Cocteau's betrayal of the Anna-male, with the twin now a spy. "Whoever has seen Nijinsky dance remains forever impoverished by his absence," she would say.[47] Once her anger had passed, she must have thought the same of Cocteau, but though he continued to write to her, he was already making himself scarce. "Why did you introduce Jean to the Cubists?" Misia Sert reproached Juliette Roche, who in the meantime had become Mme Gleizes. "He's a man of the right wing, not a man of the left wing," she added. "He'll get lost in those circles."[48] But the machine was running already. On the rue d'Anjou, Rimbaud and Apollinaire reigned; Cocteau compared Apollinaire's poems to free-rolling dice, all landing in the end on the number six. Nothing and nobody—neither family prejudices nor avant-garde taboos—could prevent Cocteau from taking the Nord-Sud, the metro that connected Montmartre the poor to Montparnasse the cosmopolitan, two villages separated by the Seine, one of which produced Cubism and the other of which spat it out. The Madeleine metro station (near Cocteau's apartment) marks the point exactly halfway between the two.

The conviction that he could become anything that moved him, under the auspices of Anna de Noailles, persuaded Cocteau that he could produce from his rib a modern creator, an authentic Adam of new art, free of all ancient old influences, as gifted in poetry as in drawing, dance, or choreography: a very young Jean Cocteau, for whom the older was already dreaming of an homage worthy of the matinee at the Théâtre Femina.

The impulse that had pulled Cocteau toward Minerva encouraged him to seek out Stravinsky when the composer came to Paris in January 1914. Cocteau wanted to speak to him about *David*, his ballet project that had matured since they had last communicated about it. Sure that their collaboration would be as important to Stravinsky as it was to him, Cocteau could only imagine being met with enthusiasm. But Stravinsky, whose haughty independence is well-known, tried to calm Cocteau's eagerness, not realizing that was the best way to inflame him. Used to coming back in through the window as soon as he was thrown out the door, Cocteau overwhelmed Stravinsky with a shower of letters, addressing him by the familiar "tu" and gently manipulating him until he had forced an agreement from him, though without any dates specified. Cocteau could never tell the difference between his emotion, the talent that had aroused it, and the person who possessed it. Hearing *Le sacre du printemps* was enough for Cocteau to become that brilliant cacophony, and to understand from within the contradictory soul that had conceived it; he had only to approach Stravinsky to participate in his genius on the same level, both elementary and acrobatic, and become his translation in the visible world. Stravinsky the enchanter was one of the forms that Cocteau's self had taken: the only task that remained was to convince Stravinsky of that.

The plot of *David*, which had ripened before that of *Potomak*, was also more traditional. It perpetuated the heroic-mythological vein exalted by Anna de Noailles and repeated Cocteau's assurance, after *La danse de Sophocle*, of being one of those dancing gods invoked by Nietzsche. Cocteau wanted to translate his own belated spring into music, scenery, and choreography—hence his recourse to Stravinsky, with whom he was already claiming the right to lead two aesthetics all by himself.

Convinced he had finally found himself, Cocteau called for a kind of continuity: "Since God created man in His image, the closer one is to oneself, the closer one is to God," he asserted. He put an equals sign between the unconscious and heaven as sources of inspiration, and added: "Tempted by God as others are by the devil, I press against myself with all my strength." In order to nourish his *David* libretto, Cocteau spoke of religion with the Abbé Mugnier, calling the Apocalypse a bad poem, a "gaffe of God."[49] Unfortunately for him, the abbé didn't have a metaphysical fiber in his body: devoted solely to the religion of literature, venerating only the manuscripts of Chateaubriand, the abbé was first of all a gourmand of earthly things who preferred dining in town to saying Mass, and who exercised his priestly vocation only to authorize some devout countess to read d'Annunzio, which had recently been placed in the Vatican's Index of Forbidden Books. The Abbé Mugnier could indeed flatter himself on having brought about the conversion of Huysmans, among other fin-de-siècle writers, but all things considered, he would certainly have rather been converted to writing by the author of *Le Potomak*.

Cocteau also spoke of the Beyond with Charles Péguy in the château of Mme Simone, a famous actress born with the name Simone Benda. He put as much questioning ardor into the conversations as the newly converted author did; after saying he was sure that one would wear into the other life the same clothing as in this one, Péguy suggested that they both go to Chartres on foot.[50] Cocteau's art of knowing "when one goes too far" struck the author of *Jeanne d'Arc*; Cocteau, in turn, was surprised by Péguy's sense of humor, which unleashed uncontrollable contortions of laughter that left him fit to be "pressed out with a hot iron." "No more of him," Péguy said the next day, however (if we are to believe the actress).[51]

To bring to life David's dance around the holy Ark after killing Goliath, when he was intoxicated by having been made King of Israel by Yahweh, Cocteau frequented the theosophists, those disciples of Rudolf Steiner who claimed to be heirs of sacred knowledge, and came to complicate his argument "with esotericism, with the Bible," as he himself acknowledged.[52] While asserting to Stravinsky that the dance didn't *mean* anything, Cocteau could not forget that dance was the action by which, from Greek rites to voodoo ceremonies, man becomes like the gods, through possession or orgiastic rites. He had some reason for remembering this, for at the School for Eurhythmy on the Rue de Vaugirard, which taught the Dalcroze method—a discipline for "Norwegian artists" that joined athletics, vegetarianism, and dance—he had met Paulet Thévenaz, a young man from Geneva who was the most talented student at the school and who, having followed the teaching of Dalcroze, in Hellerau, near Dresden—as Nijinsky had done in 1912—also believed in the body as an instrument in itself, the equal of the violin or the piano, but one that had to be "played" independently of any music.[53]

This principle so interested Cocteau that he confided his projects to the young, receptive dancer. Dazzled by the rhythmic movements that Thévenaz executed, at night, in the garden of Count Étienne de Beaumont's mansion, and charmed by his chamois-like suppleness, Cocteau decided to give him the title role in *David*, which he already knew Nijinsky couldn't take.[54] Later, he conceived three dances inspired by acrobatic and music-hall performances — "fairground gym-circus [*gymnasiarque*] acrobatics" — using for the set nothing but the head of Goliath. Carried along by the sour memory of *Le dieu bleu* and the sweet memory of *Petrushka*, Cocteau was already planning a circus atmosphere, a small, intimate stage, and a refined kind of dance, as a way of counteracting whatever symbolist or pompous aspects might still linger in his biblical subject matter. "It's a parade. It's music-hall. Three acrobat numbers," he said to the formidable Misia Sert, whom he tried to rally to his cause by dedicating the work to her.[55] To others, Cocteau spoke of an acrobat parading in vain in front of a fairground stand, urging the public to come in and see *David*, the spectacle being given inside: this scenario would be the very subject of Cocteau's later ballet, *Parade*.

Having taken refuge in Switzerland, in Leysin, Stravinsky was completing for Diaghilev, whose favorite composer and proclaimed "brother" he had become, *Le rossignol*, a work he had abandoned and resumed twenty times. He immediately recommended complete secrecy to Cocteau, knowing that his producer and distant cousin, always so jealous, would certainly plan on scuppering the project. Cocteau readily agreed. He was well placed to know the cruelty of that impresario Diaghilev, who had clutched Stravinsky as his very own ever since he had introduced him to the world via *Firebird* and *Petrushka*. He was also already in trouble with the Russian tyrant for having encouraged Nijinsky's independence. Only three months after the premiere of *Le sacre du printemps*, that poor *mujik* had taken advantage of a tour in Argentina to let himself be approached by, and then to marry, a young Hungarian named Romola de Pulsky, whose language he didn't even speak and who had become a ballerina out of love for him. Nicknamed "the boa" by Stravinsky and "Monsieur Déloyal" by Cocteau, Diaghilev had no equal (except perhaps Misia herself) in his ability to kill a budding artistic project from a distance.

Cocteau, however, couldn't keep himself from mentioning their project in his letters to Gide and to his friend Jacques Copeau, the director of the brand-new Théâtre du Vieux-Colombier, whose ambition was to purify the dramatic arts from the *boulevardier* abuses of actors like De Max and by the realism of André Antoine, and who wanted to welcome rhythmic gymnastic sessions into his dramatic community.[56] But in his haste to find a venue for a ballet that still had no music — as well as to get closer to *La nouvelle revue française* with Gide and Copeau at its center — the librettist of *David* spoke too much. And everybody in Paris was already following, and sometimes financing, the attempt of Copeau to erect a "living, sincere" stage with which the young Dullin and Jouvet were collaborating.[57] Diaghilev got wind of the collaboration between Cocteau and Stravinsky and immediately bombarded the musician with telegrams that urged him to finish *Le rossignol* right away, and even offered him more money. He knew how greedy Stravinsky was; as expected, the composer quickly asked Cocteau for an equivalent fee for *David*. With an astounding mixture of pathos, offhandedness, and condescension—which was still the tone of Anna de Noailles—Cocteau wrote to Stravinsky in February 1914:

> My dear, *mon cher petit*, all my hope of escaping sadness and bad health was our meeting in Leysin—your letter tortures me . . . I have tears in my eyes. The V. Colombier is the theater of the young and the present movement . . . It was hoping from you and me an old thing to do again, or three very short dances . . . It wasn't a "work" but a few measures and your name at their theater . . . My dear—if I had 6,000 francs, I'd send them to you right away.[58]

A musician who was already famous, and seven years older than Cocteau, the "cher petit" put forward his fear of seeing Diaghilev seize the project to hand it over to Fokine and distort it by taking it to a very large theater. But this was obviously a pretext, and as Cocteau recognized this, he immediately began again to harass Stravinsky; Cocteau was certain Stravinsky was giving in to Diaghilev out of weakness, and soon began to speak of traveling himself to Switzerland.[59]

Again there was an avalanche of threatening telegrams, demands about accommodations, and embarrassing confessions—Cocteau saying he had to flee not just the telephone, but also a strong fever and a woman who was oppressing him, while at the same time announcing that he could not travel alone, and that the Swiss cold was bad for his lungs. After begging him to delay his arrival, Stravinsky finally revealed his impatience, and in March 1914 Cocteau at last joined him at the Grand Hotel in Leysin, accompanied by his now-lover Paulet Thévenaz, whom Cocteau introduced as an "unpolished, simple, fresh intelligence."

The Swiss climate turned out to be ideal. Galvanized by the purity of the air and the brilliance of the snow, drinking in "that dense sorbet of oxygen and hydrogen," Cocteau went from skating rink to bobsled run. Won over by the intoxication of the mountains, he let Stravinsky finish his *Rossignol* on the hotel piano and sketched very Cocteau-ian costumes for Thévenaz, who agreed to be a modest instrument performing acrobatics in front of an empty set. At the same time, Cocteau settled with Thévenaz the dance of the He-Goat, three short jigs around the head of Goliath, and wrote the proclamations meant to be sung by three voices joining together in an inhuman tonality in the pavilion of a huge cubical structure—a chorus designed to recapture the force of ancient tragedy whose disappearance Nietzsche so deplored.

With their blinding whiteness, the mountains inspired Cocteau to simplify his sets even more. The balding spa-goers who, after confusing him with a famous skater, blushed and avoided him, managed to "encourage" Cocteau's metamorphosis anyway by mistaking him next for a Cubist painter. He drank in the scenery, ate like an ogre, and slept like a baby. The near proximity of the "dynamo" Stravinsky electrified him. With his innate understanding of dramatic motivations, the composer, "admirable in his great intelligence and his intelligent greatness," dazzled Cocteau. Mobilized by the health of his wife and daughter, who were being treated in the neighboring sanatorium, Stravinsky had only started outlining the adaptation of a Jewish dance from Poland as the central theme of the ballet, but his enthusiasm was such, when he spoke of their short (about twenty-minute) creation, that Cocteau described it, in letters to his Parisian correspondents, as having become "a drop to poison an elephant," and a slung pebble knocking down the "pompous giants" of official music.

In denial about the irritation he provoked—Cocteau had pleaded his pride when Stravinsky reproached him for his arrogance—Cocteau wanted to read, in Stravinsky's eyes, the amused interest that had led the men to become table companions when Stravinsky was living at the Hôtel Crillon in the spring of 1912. Not aware that the composer still saw Cocteau as a self-important storyteller impatient to make his career, Cocteau extrapolated the remarks he had elicited from Stravinsky describing this work as being of considerable significance, as if he could already hear "their" *David*. Stravinsky was to be not just the dreamed-of witness of his transformation, but also the magical proof of its accomplishment.

Likewise, Cocteau no longer doubted that Copeau—although the most hostile of the *Nouvelle revue française* editors—would end up welcoming *David* at the Vieux-Colombier, with Paulet Thévenaz as the lead, and with a choreography, set, libretto, and costumes by Jean Cocteau. Wasn't Gide becoming close to the Ballets Russes—as well as to Proust, whom the *Nouvelle revue française* would soon publish in extracts? From there could it be long until *Le Potomak* saw the light of day in the brand-new Gallimard stable?

An accomplice to his metamorphosis, nature started its work at the end of that March. "The thaw is magnificent because of a muffled, subterranean rise of sap. The whole mountain can sense the effort and smell the resin," Cocteau wrote to his mother, for whom he drew himself, strangled by a scarf à la Isadora

Duncan, speeding down the trails in a bobsled.[60] Impatient to burn what remained of his old self in the snows of Leysin, Cocteau took part with his whole being in the Stravinsky-like emergence of spring: "My feet made the sound, in the snow and ice, of sugar a horse crunches in its mouth," he would say five years later.[61] Trampling the powdery snow around him, the golden fawn of the salons forgot his minimalist resolutions and gamboled again on the peaks.

David was proceeding so well, by Cocteau's lights, that he celebrated his ballet, in his letters to Gide, as "something extraordinary."[62] Cocteau also decided to dedicate *Le Potomak* to Stravinsky; he was refashioning it at the time, and offered Stravinsky this "old skin" as a trophy. Since their piece, by its modernity, would testify to their common genius, as well as their adherence to the great natural cycles, the musical collaboration was becoming something of a mystic marriage. They were no longer in Leysin but in Tribschen, where Wagner had completed *Siegfried* and *Die Götterdämmerung* while Nietzsche — still a close friend — was for his part working on his *Die Geburt der Tragödie*.

An immensely fertile alliance was taking shape, with Stravinsky playing the role of the beret-wearing composer and Cocteau that of "the philosopher with the hammer" (Nietzsche). It represented a new "inversion of all values," as the clown-barker intimated when delivering the prologue to *David* (before being changed into a box):

> Come in, ladies and gentlemen!
> Come inside and into our place
> On the other side! Inside
> There is no 'our place' — Behind — Inside . . .[63]

"*David* promises to be admirable," gushed the prince of the changeable in his letters to Ghéon, the editor of the *Nouvelle revue française* who was the most on his side — before adding, in a spurt of modesty that deceived no one but him: "I speak for Igor."[64] Stravinsky, for his part, sent an enthusiastic letter to Copeau.[65] At this moment, too, Thévenaz was painting Stravinsky's portrait, in between two other watercolors.[66]

David would never get past this stage. Determined to nip this "ready-to-wear work" in the bud, Diaghilev suddenly increased pressure on his compatriot Stravinsky. Ten weeks had barely gone by between Nijinsky's marriage and his dismissal; the impresario could certainly have done without Stravinsky's services too, if the composer had resisted him more energetically. But Stravinsky put *David* aside. Cocteau became convinced that Stravinsky had a pressing need for money to take care of his wife, so he returned home and reverted to a more prudent tone, writing to his "dear Igor" to remind him that Paris was waiting for

David just as sand waits for water. "He pestered me about *David* and had to be driven away. He was an embarrassing young man at that time, utterly persistent. One soon had enough of his wheedling and his flattery."[67] The impresario's *Nightingale* had sung louder than the poet's canary.

Stravinsky, however, still asked Cocteau to accompany him to London, in case Diaghilev called him there, in order the better to resist his pressure. He then begged Cocteau to continue sending him passages of the libretto, all the while protesting his fidelity, even when they met at the Hotel Édouard-VII in the presence of a hate-filled Diaghilev. It was Cocteau who insisted in the end that the composer stop mentioning their project to him. "*David* is all the same to me—never speak to me of *David*—*David* is already transposed in my head . . . *David* is a moment of ours."[68] Bitter moral: it was easier to meld with Anna de Noailles than to work with a musician whose rigidity was equaled only by his ambiguity. As Debussy remarked about Stravinsky, "He kissed the hands of duchesses while stepping on their toes."[69]

The declaration of war came on August 3, 1914. With general mobilization decreed, Parisians joyfully toasted the departure of soldiers for the front. The printing of the *Potomak*, which the publishing house Mercure de France had ended up accepting without enthusiasm, was suddenly halted. Cocteau's two great projects of the year had just gone up in a puff of smoke. It seemed as though the intense energy required by Cocteau's metamorphosis had been expended for naught; the *Nouvelle revue française* had sent Cocteau back to the boulevard from which he came, while finally admitting Proust, whose attempts to approach it had until then, always been done in conjunction with Cocteau. To cap it all off, Paulet Thévenaz wanted to follow Copeau's troupe to the United States—where he would die a few years later. Cocteau wrote to Gide:

Indifference of an eye that inspects you and that once drank you in.
Weakness of a hand that once sought only yours.
It's excruciating.[70]

Cocteau's entourage tried to console him: "Laugh above all when you think of the incredible gifts the gods have given you," the generous Anna de Noailles wrote to him. But these dithyrambs from the past only increased his melancholy.[71]

The desolate Cocteau sought out the tolerant Abbé Mugnier, explaining not only his sorrow at the death of a young American woman who had tried to forget a previous liaison with him, and with whom he had fallen in love—but also his disappointment that the friend on whom he had counted to support him in his ordeal had let him down. "When the female peacock calls the male peacock," he added, quoting Michelet, "he hurries from the end of the world." This was a revealing use of the feminine gender for someone who complained that people came to him but didn't stay, and who now was fearfully rediscovering the depths of his amorous distress. "Cocteau cannot cry. He drinks his tears," the abbé noted, sending him consoling prayers.[72] "Cocteau, who wants to die because of X," wrote Mauriac, in his *Journal d'un homme de trente ans*.[73]

All doors were closing again for Cocteau. His artistic rebirth had resulted in more frustration and heartache. At the age of twenty-five, he felt the disappointment of a man at the end of his life.

5

THE WAR AS OPÉRA

You can't fake what you don't have.
—*Dr. Lasseigne*

LE COQ TÔT

As September 3, 1914, dawned, the residents of Paris awoke to notices announcing the government's retreat to Bordeaux. German troops were only sixty kilometers away from the Champs-Élysées. Hundreds of thousands of civilians fled the capital, while the cheerful reservists who had lifted Misia Sert onto a cuirassier's white horse just a month earlier donned uniforms. Artists, merchants, and tailors—including the poet Charles Péguy and the novelist Alain-Fournier, two of the first to be killed in the ensuing battles—were ordered to join the front; the studios of Montmartre and the bookstores of Montparnasse emptied out. Animals, cars, and wagons were requisitioned, along with the six hundred taxis that had saved the City of Light *in extremis* by bringing reinforcements to the Marne. Soldiers as improbable as Reynaldo Hahn found themselves in the trenches; Proust himself narrowly avoided being carried off in a mobilization from which Drieu la Rochelle and Blaise Cendrars did not escape.

It was the first time that history had erupted into Cocteau's life. Surprised to have felt a thrill of excitement at the summons of the "blue-white-red flag," he had even gushed about the patriotic enthusiasm that August brought; he who felt Parisian above all else discovered, in responding to the drums of Arcole and the gunfire of Valmy, that he was in fact a Frenchman as well.[1] Exempted from military service in 1909 due to a weak constitution, the "young barometer laden with storms" had presented himself at the barracks, demanded to be enlisted body and soul, then, when denied, shouted in the streets and became dissolved into the crowd.[2] Incapable of not being where things were happening, Cocteau wanted to leave with the others, don a uniform and be another one to stick a flower in his rifle. The cascading closures of theaters, concert halls, and music halls that had made his evenings so thrilling now left him adrift: only "the great ball of France," which had just opened up at the border, interested him, as suggested by the exalted message he had sent on August 1 to Jacques-Émile Blanche: "We will all die. I kiss you from the bottom of my heart. I'm signing up. Jean."[3]

Bidden by the Red Cross to check farms for milk that could be distributed in train stations to departing troops, Cocteau suffered from the comical nature of his "disguise" as a milkman. After the review board confirmed his exemption from service twice, Cocteau had thrown himself into the jubilation of the crowd, much as the legendary salamander threw itself into the fire before being reborn, and just as the ladies of the upper-crust neighborhoods had thrown themselves into the projects of changing the names of the rue Richard-Wagner and of eau de Cologne, which now became eau de Louvain. Thus the unhappy author of *David*, relieved to put off yet another transformation, reinvested all his overflowing energy to become a patriot *extraordinaire*.

Even before she suggested that General Gallieni use Parisian taxis to reinforce the troops holding the Marne, Misia had taken the initiative in August to form a convoy of ambulances to reinforce the Red Cross, using delivery vans lent by the big couture houses. Impatient to "vivre double," Cocteau found himself in an officer's uniform designed by the fashion designer Paul Poiret next to Misia in a tweed suit, José Maria Sert in knickerbockers, and the designer himself in a Mercedes driven by the decorator and cabinetmaker Paul Iribe, whose outfit evoked that of a deep-sea diver.[4] Loaded with shredded linen seized from mansions belonging to Germans, the thirteen improvised ambulances headed for L'Haÿ-les-Roses.

Cocteau eagerly drank in the countryside and the destruction, like a child coveting a pastry. The spectacle veered to butchery as they advanced east; he protected himself from the horror he could make out through the windows of their Mercedes by a flow of exalted words and comic anecdotes about the busy intrigues in their convoy. Although Misia was a little older (Morand would describe her two years later cleaning her teeth with a pair of scissors, "very 1895, very Renoir, with a voluminous blouse, bangs, hair like a helmet"), she too overflowed with bossy vitality.[5] She sent packing the sentinels who stopped them, suspecting them already of being spies in the service of the Central Powers, and gave the order to start up again while barking out the name of

General Gallieni as a challenge. Like Cocteau, she needed extreme situations to feel that she existed, and sought without realizing it the limits of her own unreality. "Fashion was in danger; she would die of calm," the author of *Thomas l'imposteur* wrote about the Princesse de Bormes, Misia's literary double, and Cocteau's own reflection as well.[6]

Arriving at L'Haÿ-les-Roses, these chance ambulance drivers saw animal carcasses hanging from trees, and what they took to be a squad of black men lying on the ground: German soldiers whose faces, riddled with gunshots, already swarmed with maggots. On the way back, too, the convoy had to drive at night with all its lights out, since the authorities didn't want Parisians to see that they were bringing back amputees, victims often delirious with pain. Moreover, the convoy's atrocious discoveries, which flew past them like movies because of their speed, evoked images that Cocteau hoped, under the influence of sugar, to dream about and acquire: more than a field of ruins, war was first of all for him a prodigious image factory. Misia, whom Cocteau had already forgiven for having applauded the cancellation of *David*, helped to distance the group of travelers from the violence of the war: with her ferocious verve—a lioness disguised as lion-tamer—she kept Cocteau in good humor.

Galvanized by everything he had just seen, Cocteau made arrangements to meet with Gide on August 20 in an "English tearoom" on the avenue d'Antin. Gide's extreme kindness couldn't keep him from being shocked by Cocteau's overly brilliant witticisms about war, which he trotted out like luxury items during a famine. As Gide later wrote in his *Journal*:

> He was dressed almost like a soldier, and the stimulus of recent events indeed gives him an improved complexion. . . . He finds amusing epithets, gestures, to describe the butcheries of Mulhouse; he imitates the sound of the bugle, the whistle of shrapnel. Then, changing the subject, since he can see he's not amusing me, he proclaims he is sad; he wants to be just as sad as you, and suddenly espouses your way of thinking, explains it to you, then speaks of Blanche, then mimics Mme Mühlfeld, then speaks of that lady at the Red Cross who shouted in the stairway: "They promised me fifty wounded for this morning; I want my fifty wounded." Yet he crushes a piece of cake on his dish and ingests it in small mouthfuls; his voice speaks in sudden bursts, then checks; he laughs, leans over, bends towards you and touches you. The strange thing is that I think he would make a good soldier.[7]

Annoyed by the mannerisms of this self-proclaimed disciple, Gide was very close to seeing Cocteau as a performing mimic endowed only with the genius of appropriation—"a follower of the avant-garde," repeated his friend Du Bos.[8]

At the same time, he realized that it was when he was with this man who was twenty years his junior that he himself felt "clumsiest, heaviest, most morose." Prone to embarrassment, if not exactly to moralizing, Gide seemed like a principled family man trying to protect himself from the perfumed agitations of a fairy.

The Misia-Cocteau caravan took to the road again in September. After witnessing the battle of Coulommiers through a mist of alcohol, the amateur ambulance drivers helped evacuate the wounded to Champagne. More curious than ever to see death up close, Cocteau discovered Reims as it was being bombed. There he saw a mass of severed limbs strewn across sidewalks, encountered a horse stumbling over its own intestines, and visited the cathedral where the kings of France had been crowned and whose windows were now hanging in tatters: "une femme vitriolée," he would say, using a phrase that Proust would take up a few months later.[9]

This time Cocteau was horrified by the sight of these victims—whose lips, sealed by lockjaw, were sometimes opened with a cutlass by priests in order to administer the last sacraments. He was likewise aghast to see the expression on the face of a *poilu* (infantryman) when he learned that he would have to undergo amputation without chloroform, then remained on his pallet indefinitely as his doctor, who also had been injured by a bomb, died in front of Cocteau's eyes. Three thousand men dead of hunger, wounds, and gangrene: the list is truly Dantesque. Having himself escaped a shell in extremis—he used crutches to support a thigh bone that was dislocated during the blast—Cocteau twice visited the very popular Maurice Barrès, the champion of deep-rootedness in soil and blood, to whom he would dedicate the most lyrical of his war poems, in order to plead the cause of the wounded.[10] Known for his sensitivity to the sufferings of the combatants, Barrès seems to have received Cocteau rather offhandedly, or to have been only incompletely moved by his evocations of the suffering of thousands of victims waiting for relief, since the Red Cross vehicles could only transport twelve or eighteen of them a day. Cocteau would judge Barrès's "indifference" severely in 1920, when in *La noce massacrée* he ridiculed, and probably exaggerated the inattention of that outdated inventor of the "cult of the self."

By finally offering Cocteau a horizon big enough for his destiny, these macabre round trips between Paris and Reims exalted him: impatient to be wherever death prowled, Cocteau forgot to eat and no longer slept. Being entirely mobilized, he found the dispersed parts of his being now gathered together and exalted, more than he could have hoped. He was only one among the crowd, and all the components of that crowd were joined together in him.

Was there ever a remedy better than war for the dull heroism, never rewarded, demanded by everyday life? Far from his mother's salons, far from the over-whelming routine of ordinary days, battle finally introduced Cocteau to the most personal adventure. Hadn't his patronymic announced, in a disturbing kind of predestination, the morning song of the Gallic rooster ("coq"), symbol of the uprising of the masses? "There's only one person like him in a genera-tion," Barrès had said.[11] When their team joined the front at dawn, encouraged by the blows of the morning bugle, "that pure sound unfurling from every hamlet as cock after cock takes up the cry," ended up convincing their partic-ular "coqueteau" that he was the Frenchman par excellence.[12]

Already France could speak of nothing but Roland Garros and his first nonstop solo flight across the Mediterranean: the ace Garros was blessed with both the endurance of Louis Blériot, the first aviator to cross the Channel, and the audacity of a reconnaissance pilot. Cocteau had been introduced to Garros's entourage by Gautier-Vignal, a friend of Proust's, not long before the war; urged on by the example of Cocteau's brother, Paul (also an aviator), Cocteau rushed to Garros's humming aircraft, which took off from the Aérodrome de Buc with Cocteau aboard for his first flight with aerial acrobatics.[13] The freefalls produced extreme sensations in Cocteau; the hypersensitive curled up in a ball to keep from vomiting, then clung to the leather straps as if inside an elevator taking him to the sun, then to the earth, indefinitely. "These planes were made from old handkerchiefs and old pen-holders," said Cocteau, who at the time exagger-ated everything.[14] Having experienced during the flight the loss of all reference points, Cocteau found himself in familiar territory: that between-space where neither left nor right, neither up nor down, exists, and from which landscapes flash by.[15] He would never have the boldness of the war hero D'Annunzio, but with Garros he would carry out reconnaissance flights over enemy lines—after flying with him over the western part of the capital, which Garros was entrusted to defend—they would zoom through the neighborhood of the Madeleine, and whirl around the Eiffel Tower.

As a child, Cocteau imagined himself an oriental prince set down in Paris by a stork; intoxicated by a bottle of Sauternes, he envisioned himself atop the Alps as an angel come from heaven, bathing in the constant morning found at the summits. Relieved of his weight of blood, his body was as ethereal as those of mystics; encompassing everything, he transcended borders and appropriated kingdoms: animals, flowers, shepherds belonged to him without weighing him down. Cocteau once asked Garros the acrobat to land on the side of a moun-tain, where he opened the cabin door, removed his leather helmet, and left to gather a bouquet of anemones.[16]

These acrobatics, as bombs were raining down on France; this drunkenness that made Cocteau one with the sun, constituted more than a baptism with air: they represented an initiation into heroism, if not an introduction to infinity. Won over by this succession of precarious survivals that defines an air ace, Cocteau decided to inscribe his fate under one seal and chose the star as the personal symbol that would always authenticate his letters, like a fragment torn from the Milky Way. Was it really at Cocteau's home, on the rue d'Anjou, that Garros got the idea for a machine gun that would let the pilot himself fire through the whirling propeller of his plane—no longer needing the assistant who aimed at enemy aircraft—when he watched the blades of a fan shred a photo of Verlaine?[17] Whatever the case, Cocteau would become a personal friend of Garros; during his leaves, Cocteau brought him to the homes of the Princesse Bibesco and Misia, who won over the aviator while playing him Chopin, and who would also be treated to a terrifying series of spiraling falls.

But Cocteau was still awaiting his baptism of fire. Assigned in November to the auxiliary service, he volunteered for an army ambulance group that had recently been created by Étienne de Beaumont. More efficient than Misia— more extravagant as well—Beaumont installed radios, showers, and catheters in his vehicles in order to make them into real mobile operating rooms that could bring the severely wounded home from the front. At the same time, like the colonels of the ancien régime regiments, he was careful to dress his ambulance drivers—Cocteau, Paul Iribe, and François Le Grix—in regalia of his own colors, inspired by the uniforms of Russian admirals and Argentine policemen: uniforms he designed with the same care that he used for organizing his grand costume balls.[18]

The group set off at dawn, in the December fog and cold. Since each of the passengers of the ambulance at the head of this convoy had freely adapted the outfit designed by Beaumont, the group evoked, with its frogged cloaks and opera hats, a Bouglione circus on tour more than a delegation of emergency medical personnel. After two hundred kilometers on the road, a few flat tires, and some navigational errors, black ice forced the convoy to pause in a hotel in Saint-Omer, in the Pas-de-Calais, where a monocled General Haig—the supreme commander of the British Expeditionary Corps—was dining with twenty or so officers. The apparition of the head of the army ambulance section and his friend emerging from the bathroom stupefied the English officers: "Beaumont was coming down the staircase in black pajamas, followed by Cocteau in pink pajamas, both of them wearing gold bracelets around their ankles, which clinked," recounts Bernard Faÿ, adding: "Cocteau was scurrying behind him like a nymph surprised in its bath by some fauns."[19] The two must have seemed like recruits from the Ballets Russes fallen straight from a Bakst set onto the front, where the strange ambulance group would spend Christmas.

Beaumont, however, revealed a rare audacity. Holding firm beneath volleys of shots "as if under chandeliers at parties," that amateur dancer, whom Thévenaz had trained in the Dalcroze method, directed the waltz of the wounded and the minuet of corpses.[20] The "theater of operations" was no longer a phrase for that group—they applauded combat as they would a dress rehearsal at Châtelet: "Silence of Bethlehem, smell of a manger, machine gun truce, soldiers standing and serious as Magic," wrote Cocteau, so moved by those "splendid men" that he allowed himself, when it was their turn to come under the shower, a few soothing gestures.[21] Proust said of Saint-Loup that he found a cerebral pleasure "in living out in the open with the Senegalese who were sacrificing their lives at every instant," but Cocteau's pleasure was already taking a more physical turn.[22]

And so the scandalous "No. 2 automobile convoy" lived, until Cocteau's "kindness" toward a Senegalese rifleman aroused the fury, if not the jealousy, of a sergeant of *goumiers*. Caught in the act, threatened with a court-martial, Cocteau placed his fate in the hands of the aristocratic Beaumont, who showered gifts, smiles, and shouts to pull him out of the affair, before imperiously recalling the entire group under the pretext "that we were no longer fighting in Flanders"—a very optimistic interpretation of the facts.

LE MOT, PICASSO, AND COXYDE

Frustrated by the war, Cocteau took revenge, back in Paris, by way of *Le mot*, the illustrated magazine he concocted with Paul Iribe in the fall of 1914.[23] Subject to censorship and dependent on military information, the press at the time had been reduced to semi-servility: deprived of trustworthy news, the Parisians had the impression of an abstract, even unreal, war. *Le mot* managed to give a graphic equivalent of the violence of the conflict thanks to the clarity of its cartoons and its revolutionary use of color. Realizing he was in a state of war, Cocteau turned his old poetic talent, of which he had wearied a year earlier, to the service of the nation. Modernist minimalism was no longer the thing. The hymns to the French generals that Cocteau would sing, in the style of Rostand or Hugo, would suggest a kind of reverse molting, in the man and the poetry, if it hadn't so obviously been artistically imposed by the era of conflict.

Almost as crude as the anarchist weekly *L'assiette au beurre* in its first issues, *Le mot* would cleverly exploit an unambiguous patriotism. Under the influence of Iribe, who would eventually be at the forefront of the right wing, the journal came close to espousing Barrès's theories on rootedness in the land, attacked the "Boches" and their taste for the *kolossal*, "charged" German nannies—at the time quite common in the "good" Parisian families, like the Cocteaus—and created a warmongering reputation for itself, even going so far as to suspect Gide of Germanophilia (thus shocking Proust, who, even so, was an early admirer of *Le mot*). Certain that Gallic anarchy, with its unmethodical inventiveness, would finally gain the upper hand over heavy Teutonic machinery, Cocteau worked at *Le mot* in full harmony with Iribe—the two cosigned some magnificent drawings. While the name of Nietzsche, fashionable in Parisian salons around 1900, was becoming taboo (his work having already been deemed to have inflamed the German aspirations for power), at the same time the "philosopher with the hammer" was recruited for the Gallic side as having so often extolled the soaring foibles of the French, as opposed to the stifling German virtues of labor, discipline, rigidity.[24] The Ballets Russes, by contrast, were indirectly condemned for having performed *Josephslegend*, a ballet created by the German-speaking Strauss and Hofmannsthal. Chauvinistic poems written by Cocteau in *Le Figaro* even made Anna de Noailles regret not being able to write like him—a fitting turnabout.

The editors of *Le mot* attacked the supposed passion of the Germans for the commonplace—Strauss—as well as for the unconventional—Schoenberg. They attacked Wagner too, at the exact moment when Saint-Saëns was campaigning to ban German music from Paris. Cocteau would indeed argue with Saint-Saëns, for whom *Le sacre du printemps* did not qualify as music and whose xenophobia extended even to Shakespeare, but *Le mot* always happily repeated prejudices about *Deutschsein*—the famous "German way of being"— as well as stereotypes about Serbian heroism or Romanian treachery, just as it never hesitated to evoke the congenital barbarism of the Boches or to give credit to the craziest rumors accusing "them" of cutting off the hands of little Belgian children or raping widowed mothers.[25]

Graphically, Cocteau's drawings were somewhat reminiscent of his style in *Le Potomak*. The Kaiser became a super-Eugène, and the zeppelin, whose ponderous mobility Cocteau imitated in society, became a slug just as disturbing as the jellyfish of *Le Potomak*, which seem to have announced the conflict a year ahead of time. The very Gallic roundness of the Mortimers and the helmet-shaped skulls of the Eugènes too seem destined to clash. Yes, these paunchy soldiers whom the painter Gromaire would stylize, these brave, cheerful, rational soldiers, as the French are still supposed to be, reminded Cocteau strongly of his Mortimers—"nature imitates art," Wilde had said. But soon

Cocteau would open *Le mot* to the least radical of the Cubists, provoking the indignation of those more traditionalist circles that had made the magazine successful. A general outcry greeted a drawing by Gleizes as insulting "good French taste" and bordering too much on "Kubisme"—that "Teutonic" invention that had become victim to its own name, which sounded similar to that of Kub bouillon cubes—though there was no well-known German in the Cubist movement. Having become too modern, if not bizarre, for its first readers, *Le mot* stopped appearing; having grown apart from Iribe, Cocteau rediscovered his characteristic changeability by now defending Cubism, which he had been mocking only two years earlier. While Apollinaire, won over by the ambient patriotism, was breaking off all contact with his German friends, painters, and poets, Cocteau was refusing to extend to the poetry of Heine the hatred [*haine*]—the play on words is his—that he aimed at the Kaiser's Crown Prince. Having returned from his patriotic orgy, he would take care never to let it turn into cultural hatred.

In March 1915, finally called back to service, Cocteau was assigned first to a Parisian barracks in the twenty-second section of engineers, which looked like something out of a Courteline satire. While there he served in the supply corps. The actual war came to interest him less than the aesthetic questions it aroused. It seemed to Cocteau that the conflict, by intermingling classes and nations, was in the process of creating a new society, and hence a new sensibility: pens in the future would need to have been dipped in that blood if they hoped to claim any lasting quality. Events of such magnitude would serve as a literary challenge for his generation. Since Cocteau's only great feats of glory had happened during his flights with Garros, he sketched out a poem that he hoped would be anti-Romantic, clean, clear, rousing, and laconic, in keeping with Nietzsche's command over language as well as with the aviator's mastery over atmospheric chaos. Since Garros had caused French aviation to make a giant leap, Cocteau's ambition was to be finished with the old "transports" of poetic poetry, as well as with its whole train of metaphors, to express the vertigo he had felt in the weightlessness of the biplane but with language "stripped bare" of aerial "arabesques." "He speaks my language in his art," Cocteau said about Garros in the spring of 1918.[26] He was careful to add, however: "I speak his language in *my* art."

For Cocteau, there were men of the air and men of the earth. Men of the air were devoted to adventure, summits, the arts; men of the earth set themselves to working hard and raising their families in the same house in which they would die. How could the earthbound men be made to vibrate in tune with the planets, to feel physically these words, so revealing of Cocteau's sensibility: "A strand of sky cuts / a clod of heart in half"? How could he change them into "deep-sea divers" of the air? Since war stems from thunderbolts and fate, Cocteau hurled his readers into Garros's airborne cabin, snatching them from the "despotism of the ground" to make them fly over the earth.[27] The memory of their flights led Cocteau to use a radical typography where, cut up by the aviator's propellers, his notations explode in a rain of words and images. The form Cocteau envisioned, made of line spacings and silences—a thousand miles away from the doggerel he gave to *Le Figaro*—tries to abolish the margins, to reintroduce them rather into the very body of the text in the form of white spaces, so as to convey the air pockets and joyful leaps aroused by aeronautical acrobatics: he sought nothing less than a way of actualizing Mallarmé's *mises en page* and Apollinaire's lyrical *calligrammes*. In 1910 Apollinaire was already singing the praises of "Aviation," which recycled the syncopated power of American advertisements to make poetry fall in step with technology. At the great 1912 exposition of aerial locomotion, too, Marcel Duchamp had declared: "Painting is over, what can do better than this propeller?"

Like the polychromatic circles of Robert Delaunay, which abolished the outline of objects to leave only their color (with Delaunay himself paying homage to Blériot), the propeller would be the means for transforming matter into pure vibratory energy, abolishing the thing itself in favor of its perceptible impact. To convey these aerial wonders that fade away in the sky, barely perceived, Cocteau tried to break his planes down into cylinders and make his "verses" spin to the rhythm of divisionist canvases or war reports. "Mobilizing the immobile and not immobilizing the mobile" was already the word of the day for the Orphists, those painters christened by Apollinaire whose leader was Delaunay: this mantra, too, became Cocteau's way of orchestrating the slow speed of poetic perception.

Providing further proof of his power to self-replicate, Cocteau even envisaged a "revolutionary" and abridged version of *A Midsummer Night's Dream*. Max Reinhardt had staged that play in Berlin just before the war—a production that was a "Boche distortion," in the words of Cocteau, who regarded Shakespeare as an eternal ally. Since mobilization had closed the theaters, Cocteau was already thinking of having the play performed at the Médrano circus, in a production by Firmin Gémier, a future reformer of the Cartel—but with Fratellini clowns as actors, wearing English uniforms and Phrygian caps, and with sets that Gleizes was going to build, that is, until he flew to New York to marry Juliette Roche.[28] Conducted by Edgar Varèse, who was then on his quest for the fourth musical dimension, the orchestration would include Erik Satie's *Cinq grimaces*, along with pieces by Ravel, Stravinsky, Florent Schmitt, and Varèse himself. In other words, it was a project that would probably have broken the eardrums of the readers of *Le mot*, had it come to fruition.

At once chauvinist and Cubist, *pompier* (conventional) and Orphist, Cocteau was assembling aesthetics that were on their face irreconcilable. It was as if the war had opened up a second front within him, one at once plastic and ideo-logical, where weapons would never again fall silent and so cause a hiatus that, while keeping him in ammunition, would forever deprive him of the equilib-rium that on occasion provides a stable line.

Valentine Gross contributed in her way to that mild schizophrenia. Encountered for the first time during a rehearsal of *Josephslegend* in the spring of 1914—she made pastel portraits of most of the dancers in the Ballets Russes who fascinated her—she would later say that she initially looked at Cocteau with the coldness of a candle at a moth's approach. With large doll's eyes and a long bird's neck, Valentine Gross had what one might call a poetic tempera-ment. Marked, like Cocteau, by an all-consuming love of her mother and by the early suicide of her father, the woman whom Cocteau would nickname the "Swan of Boulogne" grew up in a semi-magical universe made more so by the mists of the North: at the age of twelve, she managed to take three steps without touching the ground, on the rue de la Tour-Notre-Dame in Boulogne-sur-Mer; at eighteen, she saw a fabulously elegant English officer fall from the ramparts—an experience that would always make her dream of Prince Charming. As mistress of Edgar Varèse, the young Valentine undeniably was connected and lively enough to interest Cocteau, her junior by two years. Every Wednesday she received in her all-black apartment on the Île Saint-Louis publishers, poets, and painters from Valery Larbaud to Paulet Thévenaz, who painted her portrait, while Ricardo Viñes, the ex-friend of Léon Bloy, played Satie on the piano.

Valentine Gross—later Hugo—would assert after their tiff that she always avoided receiving Cocteau on Wednesdays, so as not to annoy her friends at the *Nouvelle revue française,* Jacques Copeau above all, who thought of Cocteau as a simple arriviste who was already out of fashion. Actually she was arranging not only to introduce him to Edgar Varèse, but also to have him dine with Satie, and finally to integrate him over time into that clearly avant-gardist group.[29] "I was the key, in a way, the heart of what he strove for," she would say half a century later.[30] Varèse offered the unquestionable advantage of being a nerve center. His interest in all the artistic practices had placed him in close contact with Picasso, who in 1908 had introduced "black" forms in *Les demoiselles d'Avignon,* a painting that was long kept private, but which would be exhibited the following year, in 1916.

Picasso was one of the people whom Cocteau most eagerly sought to approach. The young writer immediately began to pester the artist under various pretexts, such as to suggest to Picasso that he do Cocteau's portrait, or to nag him to create the stage set that Gleizes had abandoned in order to get married. Sometimes Cocteau sent Picasso tobacco rations, precious in that time of austerity; sometimes he threatened, through the text of a song, to hate him if he didn't reply. His first visits to Picasso in the summer of 1915 were difficult. Too concerned with being modern, Cocteau did not appreciate either the copy of the Parthenon frieze that graced Picasso's staircase on the rue Schoelcher, or the African masks cluttering the studio, which was vast as a church. But the hundreds of canvases piled up there, amidst a Niagara of cinema tickets, paper cutouts, and tubes of gouache, made speechless that poet who, already in the face of Anna de Noailles, loved the eye "which from the profile looks as if it's seen from the front."

The two men took each other's measure for a long time, to the surprise of Varèse, who acted as intermediary. *"Il n'est pas discours, il est formule.* He gathers and sculpts himself into objects," Cocteau would say of Picasso, who readily confirmed: "I don't say everything, but I paint everything."[31] The painter obviously didn't expect much from that bothersome renegade eight years his junior. Stocky and well built, Picasso was content to take Cocteau's measure with his formidable *mirada fuerte*, that shamanic eye that immediately aroused fear. The century hadn't yet made its Minotaur, but already the list was being compiled of those who had killed themselves around him—as if his mere look possessed the power to kill. Cocteau's paradoxes and drollery would make Picasso emerge from his reserve. His agility at twisting concepts was equal to Picasso's skill at twisting wire; an equality of brio established itself. Cocteau's thinking didn't condense as suddenly as the painter's, but he had a theatrical eloquence and dazzling sense of image that Picasso would always envy. With his ease, Cocteau's passions extended beyond those of the slightly provincial, slightly narrow bohemian group of which the painter was beginning to tire, as well as of their "conventional vices" and programmed intoxications. Bound by puritanism to poverty, the exalted daubers of the Rotonde continued to regard failure as the best guarantee of genius; Cocteau embodied a refreshing alternative mindset.

Lonely after the loss of his companion Eva from tuberculosis in December 1915—and of Braque, his twin in Cubism, who enlisted in the army, Picasso didn't resist the avalanche of affectionate gestures, little gifts left with his concierge, and shameless flattery showered on him by Cocteau, who used his art to fabricate a relationship from nearly nothing. Happy to be called "Prince Pablo de Picasso" and to learn that his genius would be celebrated in articles published in America, the painter sensed in Cocteau a good potential publicity agent. In step with literature—Pierre Caizergues would describe him as an "immobile writer, as if asleep"—Picasso always needed a poet to sing of his exploits but also to serve as a "suggestion box" for him, a role in which Apollinaire, who was now himself busy at the front, had supplanted Max Jacob.[32]

As for Picasso, he seemed right away like one of those virile totems around which Cocteau liked to gravitate, from which to draw strength or reputation. Picasso was a source both of energy and prestige, a guarantee of radicality and of a future. For Cocteau, gaining admittance into Picasso's work, stepping into his life, was already to make an appointment with posterity, intelligence, and, in passing, cruelty. Finally summoned to join the field of battle, Cocteau tried coercion in the fall of 1915: "You must paint my portrait quickly, because I'm going to die," he wrote to Picasso, citing the need to illustrate the posthumous edition of his work.[33] When he signed up again in December, still as an ambulance driver with the marines in Nieuport, an elegant seaside resort in the North not far from the French border, Picasso still had done nothing.

Cocteau returned to see him, however, during his first Paris leave, wearing a Harlequin costume beneath his trench coat—an avowal of one who, since his molting, had spoken of his skin as a "fantasy costume."[34] Gleizes had already painted a portrait of Cocteau in uniform, Cubistly reduced to Harlequin diamonds. It was hard not to see in that too a mirror offered to the changing Picasso who, taking up again with the acrobats whom he had painted ten years earlier, had begun painting informal, Cubist Harlequins again—as if this costumed patchwork were an allegory for their fates: "Your Harlequin already bore / Cubism in his lozenges," Cocteau would write in *Les embarcadères*. Had he fallen into what zoologists studying mimetic species call the "exaggerations of precautions," those parades that often provoke the opposite of the desired effect, with the predator's aggressiveness increasing when faced with the sight of pretenses meant to lure him? It seems so, for despite this intense labor of seduction, Picasso did not paint the portrait of that literary Harlequin, not because Cubism forbade it—he had no use for that kind of *diktat*—but because he hated to have his hand forced.[35]

THE OPERETTA OF DEATH

"Here begins the battle front that ends in Salonica," Cocteau said proudly, settling in December 1915 in Coxyde, postal code 131, in a partially demolished villa where the dunes hid the mouth of the Yser but left the ruins of the town exposed. More than an open-air barracks, the front at night reminded Cocteau of a huge Luna Park illuminated by the glowing flares from the Navy cruisers, which revealed, like a magic lantern, kilt-wearing Scots, Zouaves with caps, Legionnaires in convicts' outfits, and sailors with pompoms. He loved these fierce fireworks, these attractions and involuntary "fancy dress" shows, as well as the spotlights searching the sky.[36] The "great celebration of death"—where roads looked like an opera from the wings, lined with miles of painted canvases—exalted his taste for spectacle. Ultrasensitive to the fictional aspect of reality, despite the stench of gangrene and the mounds of wounded at the front, Cocteau—like those holy fools at the heart of great tragedies—rejoiced at the sight of that grand production that kept all his fears at bay.

Reading the letters he sent to his mother, one would think that he was on the stage of a huge Théâtre Châtelet on which was being played out, instead of *The Adventures of Michel Strogoff*, "The deadly affinities of Wilhelm and Marianne."[37] Misunderstandings in the trenches bordered on vaudeville under his pen; tragedy turned to barrack-room comedy; death itself, although omnipresent, didn't manage to convince the actors of their own mortality—instead its grand gestures looked like nothing worse than the skeletons jiggled alongside ghost trains at carnivals. After the prewar salons, which in hindsight seemed so rational, the front stood out as a fiction relieving him of all tragic weight. "Our sun is Jean," wrote the young officer Pierre de Lacretelle, who met Cocteau during the time of the Ballets Russes, recalling the evenings when, improvising games and songs, Cocteau made the whole barracks laugh until they cried, helping them forget the mud, boredom, and horror of the torrential rain, which were often more trying than the Boche artillery.

The spectacle was even more fairylike at night, as seen from the half-open "window" of Cocteau's regulation tent, from the hammock he sometimes stretched between two pine trees that a shell had just split, or even from the simple stretcher on which he carried "his" wounded and that served as an improvised bed for him, in the corner of a path, when he fell from fatigue or got lost. Once his eyes were closed, the constant rumbling of the cannons acted on him like that opium into which a marine captain would initiate him: it was the forest of Dunsinane on the march, the Norse fairytales that Joséphine used to read to him. Finally the world was attaining a mythical dimension; the everyday was giving birth to a spectacle worthy of those Shakespearean tragedies from which one emerges with cheeks glistening with tears, from laughter as much as from emotion; during those moments Cocteau was the war, as profoundly as he had "been" Anna de Noailles during their exalted nights.

Wandering among a labyrinth of sandbags, wooden planks, and logs, not knowing whether at the end the sea or the Boches awaited him, Cocteau sometimes felt as if he were dreaming with his eyes wide open. As their unit was repairing their ambulance in La Panne, he came face-to-face with Albert I, the prestigious King of Belgium, on a visit to the front; in the bend of a trench, he surprised a German buried in a corridor of snow, devouring a chocolate bar; elsewhere he saw a society lady in hat and furs, come to encourage the soldiers, emerging from a background of shells and fog, and a Boy Scout with his tongue stuck out using nail scissors to cut the buttons off the uniform of a German amputee. At those moments, war, which could re-enchant the world visually, was more pleasurable to Cocteau than reading the best novels.

His gaze still retained only the poetic strangeness of the conflict. Cocteau liked to see moon-blue soldiers moving silently under an invisible rain of stars, only to be suddenly revealed by the glowing flares announcing the offensives and forming a circus of a sky; but he also liked to see the Boches make the same gestures, as if inside a mirror. This amoral confrontation attracted him so much that he regretted, like a good Nietzschean, not being able to relive each action a second time, in order to jot down the tiniest details. He was also like Apollinaire, who was fighting for real in the hope of obtaining his naturalization by arms, and who sang of the horror, the mystery, and the savage beauty of war with as much freshness, even after his trepanning, as a Boris Vian encouraging desertion. Cocteau was able to write to Picasso: "My dear Pablo the war lasts / Blessed war and not harsh / Tender war of gentleness / Where each bomb-shell is a flower."[38] Traumatized by the front, people like Drieu La Rochelle and Céline would come back struck by catastrophism, haunted by European decadence. Of the dozens of writers confronted with atrocities, only Apollinaire and Cocteau would return enthusiastic, if not filled with wonder.

This unawareness, as much as his patriotism, would make Cocteau courageous. More than to the artillerymen, who kept back from the front, he felt close to the bold men who emerged from the trenches denying death—the African riflemen in particular, who saw war as an imitation of ritual, and the gaudy wounds as a kind of makeup. Only their gods were important to them, their gods whom they celebrated with dances where *grigris*, necklaces made from glass trinkets and bracelets made from teeth, clinked in rhythm. The faith they preserved in the power of their *grigris* to deflect bullets, which they changed just in case of wounds; their confusion at the sight of their hands torn apart— "*Grigris* not good for cannons"; their way of dying without understanding, murmuring, "Too cold France," upset Cocteau. Didn't he himself think he was protected by the antique medal that Barrès had given him during one of his visits, and that he wore at his wrist as he carried the wounded on a stretcher or while accompanying the leaders to the front in his ambulance?

Popular among the Zouaves, with whom he played soccer and who offered him prehistoric rings, and adored by the Senegalese, who covered him with amulets and leather *grigris*, which he braided into switches, Cocteau had "Arab spells" written for him on the metal hands of Fatma talismans that he had asked his mother to buy him. He loved the joie de vivre and schoolboy pranks of the Senegalese, their way of talking about the back of beyond as they wrapped round their sashes, the naturalness with which they took advantage of the tragic wealth of the front where, from gasoline to food, everything belonged to everyone. An insomniac, he especially liked and admired their ability, despite the cannon fire or the rain, to abandon themselves to dream. Finding in them his own laughing candor, his own blind generosity, his own naïve altruism, Cocteau already no longer felt any aggressiveness toward the men they were facing: didn't he choose to leave unkilled the German eating chocolate whom he had surprised? The camaraderie of those soldiers from Africa was his balm, and their heroism, worthy of the *sans-culottes* of Valmy, his stimulant, while their inexhaustible kindness was what gave him the courage tirelessly to bring back broken bodies. Their laughter helped him see in this great butchery the earthly projection of his own excess of energy; dancing with them, he managed to remove all reality from the carnage and hoisted himself up to the summit of that universal upheaval.

On Christmas night, loaded down with foie gras and Sauternes, he joined the ranks of the Zouaves, who bestowed on him a fez of honor. To celebrate the Nativity, one of them climbed up on his chair and began imitating the scratchy sound of a gramophone playing Arabic music, then the trills of an Italian tenor. When they learned of the death of a private (whose pockets they would later empty), a man in the troop whistled Gounod's *Ave Maria* in the candlelit banquet hall. The night was so warm when they went out to look at the moon that the troop decided to sneak out to the front line. Donning a Zouave uniform, Cocteau dove deep into the earthen catacombs afraid that his helmet would be visible from above, then advanced from trenches to tunnels with water reaching up to his thighs—wading among fat rats. At around four in the morning, they came to within a hundred meters of the German lines. At this point the trench looked like a vast metro station; dozens of Arab riflemen, wearing sheepskins lined with newspapers, formed a line of men at attention keeping watch through their peepholes on the Germans, prisoners of a similar labyrinth that sometimes met up with the allied network without touching it, like a Möbius strip.

Cocteau was overcome with vertigo at the idea that the alleyways of this "hollow city" snaked from one end of the border to the other, from the Channel to Switzerland, involving enemy troops ad infinitum. When finally he came to within eight meters of the Boches, fingers rested on all lips: the slightest misstep could trigger the deluge. He hugged the ground, held his breath, stared at the void, filled his ears with silence: fear made all his skin prick up in attention, like a squirrel emerging from its hideout.[39] Nothing now separated him from Them except undergrowth and metal: the same men stared at each other after having also celebrated the Christian midnight; the condensation of their breath intermingled in the cold air of that no man's land; for a little while they could have introduced themselves to each other, fraternized, and, why not, go off together. "We heard the voices of the German army," he wrote in *Le Cap de Bonne-Espérance:* "O Tannenbaum / o Tannenbaum / wie grün sind deine Blätter"—a song that Joséphine used to sing to him when he was a child.

From the emotion this a capella singing aroused in him, Cocteau realized that he could just as easily have been born a German: the stork would only have had to stop in the Alsace, at the home of Joseph Wencker, his mother's supposed lover, or in neighboring Baden-Wurtemberg; he no longer felt any fundamental antinomy, just a distance due to chance and the wind, forces as reversible as those that rule the human mind. Returning to camp as if in a dream, Cocteau, feeling like a sleepwalker, agreed to attend Mass: when twelve *poilus* removed their helmets to put on their lace cassocks, the service confirmed for Cocteau the crucial role of uniforms—it was indeed the uniform that changed a priest into a grunt, an Alsatian into a Boche, a Harlequin into a hero.

Cocteau's best friends, then, would be neither officers, who mistrusted his mimicries, nor the workers in uniform, with whom Fernand Léger was finding camaraderie at the time, but the black men. He hid a Kodak in his gas-mask box—officers forbade any photo-taking—but was sensitive to their modesty when, once in the shower, they refused to strip naked and protected their private parts by cupping their hands over them—unlike the Scottish guards who, feigning indifference, let the north wind reveal their virility. Natural, at home in their bodies, and good, they were the opposite of the "black inside and pink outside" white man, and instead were the hidden brothers of Cocteau, who saw himself as "pink inside." He was dazzled by their gums, gleaming and mauve "like coral at night," by the "gold typewriter" of their teeth, by their matte skin that became covered in "oily sweat" when he danced with them, by their "dirty bronze" feet: "the black man, miner of the azure / that rain will never moisten," he observes in one of his poems, which Honegger later set to music.[40]

As everyone was aware, desire entered into Cocteau's attraction for soldiers who would allow him to live his sexuality freely, far from the maternal gaze, actually or in his thoughts. But if the words he devoted to them betrayed remnants of colonial paternalism, they also bear witness to an empathy that was rare for the time. As a child, he had seen at the circus a parade of black men, following the Elk clowns, fold themselves into four and then into six, bring their knees higher than their faces, all while a top hat tilted over one eye. He would never stop admiring the "rubber-like" agility of these powerfully sexual angels. Their way of acting, thinking, or speaking marked him so profoundly that his letters adopted what was then called the Negro style: verbs reduced to the infinitive, elided articles, magnified substantives. "World in new aspect, landscapes of moon and aquarium, canals of Mars, incomprehensible planet, dead, without humans."[41] It's Zuydcoote-in-ruins seen by Cocteau-the-Black, whose syncopations were meant to convey the science-fiction-like atmosphere of the front, where deep-sea divers appeared out of the mist, gas masks like snouts, like in the engravings illustrating H. G. Wells's *The First Men in the Moon* that Cocteau read between explosions. The figurines that Apollinaire had shown Picasso had convinced the painter of the genius of Africa; it was the Senegalese of Coxyde who converted Cocteau, via the photos he took of them.

Cocteau's early love for photography had, as we may remember, kept him from believing in the death of a father who had promised him, the day before his suicide, to bring back his repaired camera. At the age of seventeen, at the Dietz *pension* preparing to retake his *bac*, Cocteau the dunce was already taking "huge" quantities of photos; now, in Coxyde-bains, the Kodak his mother sent him again allowed him to satisfy his unflagging curiosity. Although mirrors had been something of an obsession in Paris; here and now, with no time to worry about the effect he made on others, Cocteau himself transformed into a diaphragm greedily open for snapshots. Even after he'd put his camera away, his fly eyes saw everything without having to turn his head, kept recording what was behind him, or else, as he was leaning over the navy's observation post, recorded the bomb exploding among the German ranks, even before he could hear the sound of the explosion.

THE COUNTERFEITER

When photography was no longer enough, Cocteau began drawing not only his comrades, but also the huge dirigibles crisscrossing the sky and the submarines full of warriors "entering the port of Ostend like fish from Troy." He covered his notebooks with sketches and notes detailing the ranks of the soldiers and the colors of their uniforms, in a darkness dazzled by the bursting of a bomb, always in the heat of action, and in such a hurried way that he was often unable to read these hieroglyphs that seemed to be emerging from before the dawn of time, when he was on leave. What would become of these things seen, worthy of a painter, but even worthier of a filmmaker? The impact of events was too close for him to think of giving it shape yet; after having delayed the publication of *Le Potomak* and severing himself from facile flattery, the conflict encouraged Cocteau to stand back before writing. The style of *Le Potomak* was artistic and elitist; by contrast, the "subject" in this case had such force that it required his hand to reproduce what he saw, without additions or embellishments, before he thought of making it into "art." The ordeal could well have been providence deciding his transformation, by giving a human, or rather inhuman, universality to his new aesthetics. The Italian Futurists and the German Expressionists also thought in this way.

Already shaken by his reading of Gide's *Marshlands*, the style of Cocteau's letters became electrified. The pressure of events forced him to abbreviate; aware of being a reporter for the future, he "futurized" himself by linking contradictory metaphors in order to make the horror dreamlike. Whereas until then his prose had been resolutely egotistic, now it turned to the world and became clearly "extraspective": image-laden, shot through with sparks, his letters became the written equivalent of the shock treatment of the battleground; his legendary sense for phrases veered toward volleys; his body seemed to attract all the violence of the war like a lightning rod. Just as revolutions discourage literature—allowing history, by arousing excessive hopes, to take the place of fiction—so did war's Dionysian dimension stimulate Cocteau. If the medical attendant didn't escape the totalitarian grip of the conflict, the poet was ready, as an eternal onlooker from outside of society, to draw from the bloody, magical ordinary a supra-temporal topicality that, as much as possible, approached myth. He was already working on the "cantata" form—a long poem that would bear witness to his definitive entrance into the century of steel, speed, and industrial massacre. While he was as yet unaware that he would entitle it *Discours du grand sommeil*, after the poem he had dedicated to Roland Garros, he was already thinking of singing in it of families dispersed, gangrene, and the wounded, to make art starting not from art, but from the rags littering the ground of France—to violate poetry in order to make it speak of the horror.

It was during that winter that Cocteau first felt the sting of being unpopular: he was called a "counterfeiter" by his higher-ups, since a newspaper had cited him as a soldier in the 4th Zouave regiment even though he was not a combatant. He was even more poorly received when he was sent to a barracks to take the place of a private who had been dismissed for cheating at cards but had animated the evenings wonderfully well. The "Sidis" in his unit accused Cocteau of having requested the gambler's dismissal, and as revenge, sent him to the front.

Sent on the worst missions, he always came back alive, to the obvious disappointment of some. When his company mounted an offensive on the Somme, it left him to keep watch in front of the latrines—he was photographed in front of the WCs with the caption "Réservé au genie," which means both "Reserved for military engineering" and "Reserved for genius." "It's the first time people hate me, despise me, 'drop' me, a real ordeal for someone who is so generous with his heart and who sobs at not being loved by the seals in the zoo," he wrote, full of sad humor.[42] The trenches, in the end, were much less sexually tolerant than the salons.

The atrocities he witnessed, as well as the vapors of phenol and the "sweet-musk" stench of gangrened limbs, affected Cocteau deeply. After transporting "poor guys in pieces" or seeing some soldier give up the ghost at the feet of a mad horse, he sometimes felt empty, unable to write: from the orchestra of a cheerful Châtelet, he had fallen into the pit of an Opéra orchestrated with saws, constant bombardments, and the explosive din of shells, all of which caused him facial tics. Winter eclipsed the sun of the Zouaves. Cocteau followed the everyday routine of military life, with its endless evenings and its heavy jokes: after the reign of Proust the superfine and Stravinsky the artful, this was the reign of uncouth men, playing poker, holding farting competitions, digging cubicles with their bayonets where the street singers who came to sing for them stripped. It was a time of hard, damp beds; piercing cold; an intellectual void; and those sleepless, insomniac nights maintained by the electric lamps trained on him to check officially if he was sleeping, to see what he was actually doing under the sheets.

Sometimes tears came to him during those nocturnal tunnel-crossings, when, his eyes wide open, his stomach full of Somnol sleeping pills, his nerves felt "at once dilated, exposed, tense and soft." How much he would have liked to be pitied, at those moments! But he received only elbow-nudges and sniggers, since after all, he was the nurse. It was up to him to console, to bandage the wounds "lacquered" with blood, to bury the poor grunts whom he saw laughing "as they prepared their graves"—levels dug always deeper, until they formed an underground city whose crossroads bore the names of the North-South Parisian metro line, from Abbesses to Notre-Dame-des-Champs, with the very front lines nicknamed, wryly, rue de la Paix.[43]

He would adapt, as Gide had predicted. Making use of that ease that allows fragile species to survive in hostile environments, he made himself invisible by transforming himself into a basic soldier. Helmeted, booted, swathed in rubber, he moved through the ranks, armed only with his electric lamp, until he melted into the thirty million soldiers fighting over Europe—an experience that would inspire *Thomas l'imposteur,* his best novel. "Faithful to my system, I coincide," said Cocteau, who escaped at night by working on his poems and reading passionately—Dostoyevsky's *The Brothers Karamazov,* Tolstoy's *War and Peace.* Ten years later, Cocteau would speak of the dried skin he had let float on the Grand Canal, after Raymond Laurent's suicide—"one of those skins that garter snakes leave hanging on wild rose bushes, light as foam, open at the mouth and eyes"—it was another of his epidermises that was peeling off, under his layer of medical attendant condemned to the front.

He ripened from contact with these foreigners and proletarians, who sometimes shared his insouciance but rarely his anxieties. He lost his haughtiness, and the prejudices of his milieu: "And everyone is the same / all men are equal / having mouths noses ears / and a shooter," he would write in *Le Cap de Bonne-Espérance.* Casting off for good his guise as the Duc d'Anjou, he watched beavers and otters building in the water and sand, then adopted a little goat that fed on the marines' Balto cigarettes or hid behind "the sleeping dune with the pink hips"—when it wasn't kicking him in the forehead. Death already haunted him, but here it ended up becoming an element of the living, like that doorless house where he discovered after the battle of Vareddes, around a plush armchair where a peasant woman was "sleeping," a swarm of wasps. The butchery would always remain slightly abstract for the French behind the lines: for Cocteau it was embodied in the wounded whose hands he held, and the thousands of dead whose blood was already soaking into the ground. Plowed by bombs, then *seeded* with fresh corpses, the battlefields became laboratories of a metamorphosis that brought to his mind the "vegetal" reappearance as flowers of men killed at dawn, or their persistence in the bread he ate, once the wheat was cut, or the wine he drank, once the grape harvest was done—a wine so red it evoked the Transubstantiation and encouraged the poet to change all his blood into ink.[44]

The amputees with their blue-green faces who died in front of Cocteau—one trying to describe the polar climate he was sinking into, the other wanting to close all the openings his soul could escape through—inspired Cocteau's "Visite," one of his most beautiful poems in which, dead, he addresses a living person in the name of all those he has accompanied into the beyond.[45]

> I'm speaking to you. I'm touching you. How good it is, relief! I still have the memory of my relief. I was water that had the shape of a bottle and that judged everything according to that shape. Each of us is a bottle that imprints a different shape on the same water. Now, having returned to the lake, I collaborate with its transparency. I am We. You are I.[46]

Neither standing, nor lying down, nor sitting, this dead man, seeing his body "like a costume taken off the day before," experiences the semifluid, semisolid magma that reigns in the beyond. This hinterland where dead and living meet, this mysterious "zone" that his father had preferred to wife and children, would never stop haunting him. Peopled with masculine revenants, with sons but also with women pursued by the shade of a dead man, Cocteau's work could seem entirely magnetized by the black sun of suicide, but it's just as much the poet to whom he would give posthumous life that Cocteau, anticipating his own death, glimpsed in the trenches. "Dying means everything is over, Kierkegaard said, but dying death is to live the dying [*mourir la mort, c'est vivre le mourir*], and to live it for a single instant is to live it forever."[47] Fascinated by this key instant, half-instant half-eternity, Cocteau already saw himself as a shaman charged with interpreting the silence of the dead, as well as the oracles of the gods—a ferryman between the two worlds, coming and going from the unreality of the spirits to earthly reality, from the supernatural where spirits reign to nature where humans move forward, as people condemned to death.

But on the front, could one still speak of reality?

MOTHER AND FRIEND

In her way, Mme Cocteau took part in the war effort. Together with her neighbor and friend, the Comtesse de Chevigné, she tore linen into bandages for the wounded and sent her son packages of cheeses and canned tuna, snow boots and bottles of Miracle Water (the rejuvenating lotion made by the Empress Eugénie), as well as bouquets of flowers that arrived already dead.[48] Cocteau, who had no one in his life, and who since the departure of Paulet Thévenaz described himself as better at making friends than making love, expected from his mother everything that his existence refused him. By telling her everything that happened to him, aside from anything that might shock her, his feverish letters made her feel as if she were in the back of his ambulances being promenaded like a queen along the whole front line; she was at once his friend and confidante, wartime penpal, and faithful collaborator charged with keeping his letters and duplicating his photos, in case they would be useful for later projects. She was his mother, but he could also become hers, in case of illness; never forgetting he was the fruit of her womb, he often regretted being unable to take her in his arms to rock her. She constantly feared for his life, and he already dreamed of ending it with her, "in any flowery spot," where he would write duly reflective books. He prayed that death would take him before her. Didn't they share the same tastes, curiosities, friends? Expecting everything from each other, they gave the impression of living on either side of a glass wall, in a transparency that spared only sexuality.

When daily letters were no longer enough for this couple, who missed each other "terribly," the son sent the mother twigs gathered just eight meters from the Boches, a Virgin rescued from the ruins of a church, cartoons inspired by his regimental comrades—many, many relics that she would place on the altar of their shared life. Fascinated by his power of evocation, Eugénie Lecomte in turn adopted his "Negro" style to help him experience the Parisian scenes that she described to him. When she became him over the course of a letter, it was as if Jean continued to haunt, as a woman, those salons from which he had distanced himself in 1913—to his mother's great regret.

She remained so naïve, however, that she could write to Cocteau things like "How I understand . . . your admiration for the marines who have always had my sympathy," or "I am very happy about the touching charm you tell me you find in the riflemen."[49] This anxious mother, whose elder son risked his life every day flying over the German lines, couldn't imagine that the younger one, on the ground, might at the same time be intimate with a Zouave in his sentry box. Her vigilance elsewhere, however, remained intact, as when he boasted of his "discreet, faithful" new friend Valentine Gross, whom he found on leave in Boulogne, where she was practicing engraving on wood with "an Amazon's strength and a monk's patience." Feeling that Cocteau needed to be called to order, as a child of twenty-six, she worried about the presence of a "failure" like Satie near that young artist, and scolded her own son's natural tendency for dispersion. He then grew indignant at the little trust she placed in him, as he walked that "profound line" from day to day. Ready to acknowledge the "atrocious waste" he had made of his prewar years, he thought that the immense effort of work and calm that he had made since then deserved a better reception. "I am trying to raise myself up for those who follow me, to be worthy of a procession," he confided in her. As if after having squeezed out all of the milieus "down to the skin," he now sought only solitude.

Never had Cocteau put so much effort into seeming studious, noble, humble, and pure to his mother. After all, it was she who made him live, that son who had tried to stand in for her little husband, but who remained a poor poet threatened with oblivion in the torment that was overwhelming Europe.

THE ORDEAL OF BOHEMIA

Poetry gets us nowhere — so long as we remain within it.
— *Pierre Reverdy, Le livre de mon bord*

FROM SECTOR 111 TO MONTPARNASSE

The six million shells that fell on Verdun in February 1916 had practically no effect, except to bury the front more deeply in mud and gore. Eighty thousand men had died, and the troops were beginning to fear the conflict would never end. As Cocteau observed, in a rare "political" comment on a standoff that no longer roused enthusiasm in anyone: "The Boches took forty years preparing for a two-year war, and we spent two years preparing for one that could last, if necessary, forty years." The arch-patriot of 1914 had lost all his ardor. Outraged by the death sentence passed on some riflemen at a listening post who had invited two Germans to their table to play cards, Cocteau hastened to take advantage of his first Parisian leave, at Easter, to see Picasso again. Finally, on May 1, 1916, Picasso made his first drawing of Cocteau, a pencil portrait "in the style of Ingres," he said, marking the first time those two painters would be compared. Immediately Cocteau had it printed and proudly showed it to Proust. Never a minimalist, Proust thought it surpassed, with its "so noble rigidity," the portraits by Carpaccio.

Meanwhile Diaghilev was in search of a spectacle that could relaunch his Ballets Russes, after Nijinsky's catastrophic departure and the cancellation of spectacles because of the war. Cocteau decided to take up his "old" *David* again and approached Erik Satie, Valentine's friend, to rewrite the music for it. Did the musician have doubts about the project's viability — beyond his mistrust of any commission?[1] Or perhaps he felt reticent given the volubility of a writer who, after only two weeks, already called him "Erik"—an unusual familiarity, even between artists? When listening to Cocteau, Satie, a member of the old Montmartre bohemia, twisted his gray beard, or conspicuously straightened his pince-nez, as if he expected something crooked to come of Cocteau's mouth. Yet Cocteau's missives, which were so insistent as to border on harassment, finally convinced the musician with the huge but passive ego. Ever since he had made a name for himself by inflicting a hail of fire on the principal music critics of the time, in the name of a fabulous "Metropolitan Church of Art of Jesus Christ" of which he was the sole member, the half-starved Satie had been in search of money, and more secretly, recognition, with each concert representing an important event for him. Wasn't Cocteau's Parisian position a promise in itself?

Upon departing from the capital after his furlough, Cocteau left Satie with bundles of notes on the three main characters. Back at the front, he then joined a mobile unit that had an x-ray machine, moved with the same convoy to Sector 129, and finally joined the big evacuation hospital of Sector 111. But already he was worried about what the musician had done with his *David*, soon renamed *Parade*. His experience with Diaghilev had taught Cocteau that a manager had to be present at every stage of production. And he was frustrated with the military standoff; this battle without battles exasperated him, just as that life of a "gypsy of the apocalypse" had—now filled up on the sensations of war, he missed the "stench of manure" of Paris, which made such excellent fertilizer for artistic roses. Although he was pampered by the Marines and respected by the authorities, and although Cécile Sorel, the most popular singer of the age, sang "Sambre-et-Meuse" to the men at the front, Cocteau was irritated at not being able to move forward in writing his *Discours du grand sommeil* or his *Le Cap de Bonne-Espérance*, the poem he wanted to dedicate to Roland Garros. After having done everything in his power to enlist, Cocteau was ready to risk court martial to get back to Paris.

To escape, he dreamed. Out of the fog that enveloped the front lines, there appeared the nephew of the famous Général de Castelnau, whom Cocteau had met at the beginning of the conflict in an outfit that was a cross between those worn by a military academy graduate and an ambulance driver.[2] The prestige enjoyed by the nephew was huge, but behind the recruit who was so "modestly" proud of his illustrious lineage Cocteau had soon sniffed a "prince of tall tales," and in May 1915 evoked him in a character in an anonymous piece in *Le mot*. The war lent itself to that sort of subterfuge: Cocteau had previously encountered a young Englishwoman disguised as a Zouave in the trenches of Sector 131, where she was searching for her lover. Cocteau himself, who had been signed up by force—so to speak—and who had tried to pass as a member of the 4th Zouave regiment but who now wanted only to flee the war that he found less real every day, was beginning to think of himself as one of those imposters.

And what if everything he had experienced at the front had been nothing but the product of his imagination? At the end of his life, Cocteau would write this to André Fraigneau:

> I should not have gone to that war of '14. I went there as a fraud, with convoys from the Red Cross. And then I slipped in . . . amongst the marines, where I was forgotten. The marines adopted me, I wore their uniform and I ended up believing I was a marine.[3]

As the years went by, this lie would gather amplitude. Like a climbing plant covering all his memory, it would feature Cocteau becoming the regiment's mascot (when he was actually just a ghost) and then carrying out a series of exploits, until an admiral nominated him for the Military Cross. When the military administration hesitated, according to this version of the tale, two gendarmes came to arrest Cocteau the usurper in Saint-Georges, on the Yser, to bring him back to Coxyde. The fake rifleman asked the gendarmes to wait for him on the road while he got his kit, then went out the back of his hut, running into a car carrying the commander in chief of the sector along with his chief of staff, Colonel Gillet, who was actually an old friend. "Do me a favor," he whispered into the car: "drive me across the camp." Thus the fake rifleman gave his gendarmes the slip, under the gaze of the real ones, who mourned his departure before they were killed the next day in Saint-Georges.[4] Meanwhile Cocteau himself escaped court martial only thanks to the express intervention of Philippe Berthelot, head of the Quai d'Orsay.[5] And so the lie grew for an ambulance driver who had been duly registered in the war effort but who became capable of anything as soon as it was a question of escape.

Actually, it was thanks to the intervention of Philippe Berthelot that Cocteau left the front, at the end of July 1916, unaware that he would never return. He left the battlefield solely because Berthelot appointed him to the propaganda service for the Ministry of Foreign Affairs.[6] Cocteau's life changed completely and abruptly: in the morning of his last day he watched Senegalese die; later that same day Étienne de Beaumont, the head of his ambulance service, received him clad in silk pajamas and sprawled in his chaise lounge in a garden of bright red roses. After six months of war, Cocteau readapted to Parisian life with the ease of a chameleon. He brought out his notebooks to resume adding, to his outlines of *David*, the details of a parade that this time would take place in front of a Parisian fairground theater. He imagined a Chinese magician, a pair of acrobats, and a little American girl executing feats to convince the crowd to come in to see their spectacle. Taking this parade for the spectacle itself, the skeptical spectators end up dispersing. His aim? To cure the public, by amusing it, of its bias against modern artworks, which it tends to judge poorly despite their profound content (consider, for instance, the reaction to Stravinsky's *Le sacre du printemps*). And to show that every innovative spectacle, by offering new rules of the game, also tends to advertise itself—to create its own parade. The means thus become the end, as will always be the case for avant-garde aesthetics.

Things would progress quickly. "Long live Cocteau!" Satie was already proclaiming in his third letter to "the man with ideas," offering a comforting burst of enthusiasm to an artist often received with hostility. By midsummer, the musician was still exclaiming, with an enthusiasm this time tinged with derision, "What a being!" in a letter to Misia.[7] But Cocteau labored to decipher the strange "faun's language" of this eccentric disguised as a civil servant, complete with bowler and umbrella, summer and winter alike. How could he be at his ease with a composer who every night set off on foot—sometimes weaving side to side (from the effects of rum, brandy, or plum wine)—to the shoebox apartment in Arceuil that served as his shelter? An exhibitionist due to his extreme shyness, fastidious and absent-minded at the same time, the musician whom Picabia would nickname "Satierik" had long dreamed of bringing his melodies to the theater, with its costumes and colors.[8] If this *Parade* was therefore an occasion for Satie to apply to the ballet this "stripped-down" form of art that his piano pieces already foretold, he seemed to see at the same time in Cocteau a springboard. Yet his first reflex would be to "sell" to Diaghilev, without Cocteau knowing it, the idea for a ballet taken from La Fontaine's *Fables*. How could Cocteau trust or understand the logic of Satie, a clearly crazy and paranoid man whom Blaise Cendrars discovered one night lying at the foot of the Concorde obelisk during a bombardment from Big Bertha, composing a sonata "for the Pharaoh who is buried underneath"?[9]

The collaboration between Satie and Cocteau would be a meeting between "a faun and a seahorse," as Ornella Volta would say, a coming together of a wounded but proud "old man" and a young man hiding his cleverness beneath his friendliness.[10] Satie was the first composer to introduce emotional distance and derision into the oceanic gravity of music, but in 1917 he was still a semi-unknown who, despite the efforts of Debussy and Ravel, was able to keep from becoming homeless only by giving piano lessons. Never pushy, rather "passive," Satie had been called the "old sleeping oboe" by Cocteau.[11] (He actually continued to be known, by "serious" music critics, as the pianist at the Chat

Noir, a honky-tonk dance hall in Montmartre that had served as headquarters for the *zutiste* movement.[12]) Cocteau obviously knew how to make use of Satie's lack of social fortitude, even if, overwhelmed by his own emotionality, he would be tempted to "take charge of" the musician, like an overbearing mother protecting her old bachelor son.

Until the end Satie remained an enigma for Cocteau, who was usually so clever at reading others. Since Satie's sexuality had never found a palpable outlet—except for thirty years earlier, with Suzanne Valadon, a painter whom he had ended up denouncing for "harassment" to the police after a few weeks of communal life—Cocteau was reduced to guessing. But did the musician, who would declare in a supplement to 391, Picabia's magazine, "I'd like to play with a piano that had a *grosse queue*," even have erotic preferences?[13] Since Satie had told Cocteau he did, the investigation took secondary importance in Cocteau's concerns. Thus the former page to Anna de Noailles and the proto-Dadaist of Scottish ancestry found themselves embarking, without realizing it, on one of the most complex episodes in the history of the Parisian avant-garde.

Money, as well as a definitive go-ahead, still had to be obtained from the formidable Diaghilev. In principle Cocteau could count on the impresario's curiosity, as well as on his desire to renew his ballets, since Bakst's orientalist and princely pomp, already in contradiction with the choreographic modernity of *Prélude à l'après-midi d'un faune*, suddenly seemed old, given the war. But how would "Chinchilla" accept the presence of a librettist whom he had never liked, even and especially when he had used him? Guessing that more was needed to "astonish" the Russian, Cocteau had decided, during his Easter furlough, to offer the set and costumes to Picasso, whose passion for acrobats, Harlequins, and clowns was long established. This was truly a bold plan, since neither Satie nor Picasso had ever worked for the theater or shown any interest in it—and the Châtelet, where the Ballets Russes would perform, had the deepest stage in Paris. What inspired such a move? Was it the Cubist impulse to devalue the arts of spectacle, to hate the picturesque (or, as Cocteau would say, because "To paint a set was a crime")? Was it the ignorance of a painter who knew absolutely nothing about the Ballets Russes, music, or contemporary dance? Picasso was surely aware that, although the war had emptied out Montparnasse, seats would not always be vacant. He delayed his reply.

The wait stimulated Cocteau's imagination. The rehearsals of *Le dieu bleu* in the shadow of Diaghilev, as well as the "writing" of *David* while close to Stravinsky, had convinced him that he could be much more than a literary extra. Naturally gifted at drawing, endowed with a real musical sense since the concerts of his childhood, Cocteau was capable of imagining the spaces occupied by both performance and melody. Instinctively identifying with the actors, he knew wonderfully well the repertory of both the Opéra and the Opéra-Comique— "Offenbach, Lecocq, the melodies of Chabrier and Massenet," as the pianist Jean Wiener said, adding, "Jean sang with a delightful tenor voice."[14] Cocteau was just as good at animating a stage, ever since *Le dieu bleu*, as he was at becoming the stage on which he produced his own existence.

More than a ballet, Cocteau wanted a spectacle that combined painting, dance, and the sculptural and figurative arts—the "total work of art" that everyone had been seeking since the triumph of Wagnerian drama. Taking up one of the propositions of the futurist musician Luigi Russolo, Cocteau considered integrating mechanical noises into the musical score—motorcycle engines, fire sirens, foghorns, gunshots—in order to convey the sound of modern life, "which stifles the nightingale's song under the rumble of the trolley."[15] Not content with dreaming up the music and set for *Parade*, he outlined a choreography that he wanted to be more "popular" than the somewhat rigid blueprints of Nijinsky, but as remote from classical ballet as Picasso's painting is from the academic canvases of James Tissot. Reflecting on the costumes, sets, texts, and subtexts that comment on the actions of characters (none of whom, from the acrobat to the American girl, were alien to him), he would "become" *Parade* for months on end. But he was incapable of sitting down at a desk to work on it. His nervous constitution prevented him from any prolonged motionlessness; he had to throw off all shackles, move around in the open air, scribble notes down on a beer coaster on a café terrace, take the city's pulse, and capture the energy that kept him wound up and that *Parade* was supposed to convey—for at the time, Parisians feared more than ever deadly raids from zeppelins and "Gothas."

On the rue d'Anjou, avenue de Messine, and rue Scheffer, where Cocteau had lived before the war, life still hadn't started up again. Exhausted by its excess of patriotism, old literature had become stuck in the cobwebs of the last active salons; Anna de Noailles herself was sorry to have become a prewar poet. The wealthy, smug, high-living society of 1900, so propitious for asthma and cork-lined rooms, lilies and peacock feathers, was going downhill as the thunder of cannons drowned out the sound of its carriages and the hubbub of their regattas. Already denounced before the conflict by Apollinaire for its fake artists and "bogus" opium smokers, the Montmartre of the poets, like the Bateau-Lavoir of the painters, had suddenly grown old. Because the war had closed down many bookstores and galleries, artistic activity took refuge in the pockets on the Left Bank occupied by bohemia, the foreigners who hadn't been mobilized, or the deserters being hunted by the police on the terrace of La Rotonde—with the bookstore Aux Amis des Livres, opened in 1915 on the rue de l'Odéon by Adrienne

Monnier, gathering the hard core of writers who had escaped service, and soon thereafter, Pound and Joyce. Since the notion of "homeland" was foreign to the modernist movement, which was already holding court around the Vavin intersection, no one—Picasso least of all—was troubled about the war.

Impatient to celebrate the moment, machines, and speed, painters, photographers, and poets concerned themselves with the war only to capitalize on the energy it produced. The values of bohemia, at the same time, were beginning to invade everything: being *maudit* (damned) was cool. What Cocteau had sensed since the explosive premiere of *Sacre* was suddenly taking shape. Since African primitivism had the advantage of seeming, to European eyes that still hadn't had the scales fall from them, like a perpetual present, motionless and mythical, the Western past seemed to have less of a future than the traditional civilizations of Africa from which modernism took its inspiration. Hadn't Stravinsky and Picasso asserted themselves like revolutionaries by illustrating other traditions—Stravinsky by reviving archaic Slavic dances to animate his *Sacre*, and Picasso by reworking "African" aesthetics to underpin his *Demoiselles d'Avignon?*

In the evenings, Cocteau took in panoramic American films or went to the circus to applaud the trained geese marching to a Spanish beat. Following in his footsteps after having met him in Proust's circle, Paul Morand discovered the Médrano Circus with amazement: "Green gas, hypertrophic, chlorophylic clowns, pink bodysuits, acid manure. Jean knows everyone, goes crazy over the hare-chases and the tightrope walkers. He says, 'I like clowns so much more than actors; they're so much more intelligent!'"[16] The evening continued at the Bal Tabarin on Montparnasse, for a skating session among "vile hoodlums, Incas from the outer boulevards, and . . . coke dealers" who exhibited fake military medals to protect themselves from the police. Then Cocteau brought Morand back to the Right Bank to show him the pink pavement of the Grands Boulevards, where candles and acetylene were used for lighting instead of the absent coal: "pale, off-color scoundrels, women dressed as men, aviators as widows, a bizarre world," concluded the stunned embassy attaché, who until then had been strictly limited to outings that his Proustian snobbism would permit.

This time Cocteau approached this Montparnasse he had discovered during his Easter furlough not as an ambulance driver but as a Bonaparte. He knew the people and the rules, and had mastered all the intrigues; once he had acquired the modernist "formula," he had no doubt that the barriers would fall away, like the doors to the salons had opened to him ten years earlier. Having decided to cross the Seine once and for all, he invested in an abandoned basement studio on the rue Huyghens, his gateway to the new bohemian world. There, in April 1916, his friend Valentine Gross had introduced him to the *Morceaux en forme de poire* for the first time, played by Satie himself—while everyone sat huddled around a stove "reclaimed" from the Luxembourg Garden. Musicians, poets, and sculptors from the avant-garde group Lyre et Palette gathered there, as well as Pierre Reverdy, a militant, austere, uncompromising poet, and Max Jacob, whose work would help Cocteau conceive of a more functional literary aesthetics, without heraldry or symbols, even before his reading of Rimbaud had cured him of the custom of introducing his metaphors with "like" and "as."

NEW YORK–ON-SEINE

Cocteau's new neighborhood was inhabited by profoundly different populations than the faubourg Saint-Honoré and the plaine Monceau. Scrawny Ligurians, hairy Byelorussians, black-and-red Catalans, Poles with fiery breath, Jews with no titles of nobility, property, or homes—the Montparnasse hodgepodge was the exact opposite of the vast boudoir where the former Cocteau had gravitated. Every Polish child from the shtetl and every transplant from the Italian countryside, if he was good at drawing and intrigue, landed in this village where grass was still sprouting from the cobblestones, between vegetable peddlers' stalls. This was not the faubourg Saint-Antoine of artisans, the Belleville of Jewish tailors and North African workers, but rather a *petit* New York where budding artists flocked from all over Europe to find "ideas, people, visions of painting for the century to come," as Kisling had heard it spoken of in Krakow.[17]

Cocteau "dabbled" in this bohemia that spoke *parigot* with a Yiddish accent, this source of the international style that would dominate the artistic scene until the next war.[18] He who was such a virtuoso at manipulating the relationships of his caste learned that it was better here to seem a self-destructive alcoholic and braggart than to play the witty card, better to appear with hollowed-out cheeks and fisherman's sweaters than jackets with camellias in their buttonholes, better to play the madman, Van Gogh style, than the Oscar Wilde dandy. He knew "wonderfully well" how to imitate the guests of the Baronne de Pierrebourg; now he had to learn how to behave badly in the studio-turned-canteen of Marie Vassiliev, a painter rumored to have been Trotsky's lover, whose twenty-sous soups, exempted from curfew, saved Modigliani and Soutine from starvation.

As Cocteau would say later, if he had tried in 1913 to conquer Montmartre, headquarters of an austere Cubism, he would have had a much more difficult time. But the prodigy who thought of himself as a prince was still out of place in this new world. His cane, his gloves, and his wing collar annoyed the artists—with the exception of Max Jacob—who saw in these signs of elegance the "symbols of inanity" of a bourgeois still living at the skirts of his mother; in Cocteau's untiring courtesy, they saw a trait of those heirs, whether triumphant or ragged, who will always tolerate the social order. How could this super-selective avant-garde not increase its mistrust, seeing Cocteau so generous with his friends? "I'd like a little to be the friend of everyone, / And wrap my arms around beautiful naked bodies," he wrote in *La danse de Sophocle*.[19] Nothing could repel these purists more, who were already inclined to view homosexuality as a bourgeois vice.

Disappointed by the human limitations of artistic sectarianism, Cocteau defended himself with a decidedly Right Bank humor: "I just appear and disappear despite the welcome of the circle (perhaps I should say the cube)," he wrote to Valentine Gross, his accomplice in this capture of the Arcole Bridge.[20] He who reeled off volleys of ideas and phrases at top speed became impatient with the afternoons these post-Cubists spent on café terraces, remaking the world while nibbling olives. He spread himself wide with gusto; they concentrated with austerity, like objects diffracted by their pitiless geometry—bottles, pipes, ashtrays. The author-to-be of *Jules et Jim*, Henri-Pierre Roché, wrote in his diary, "Overly spiritual conversation tires me."[21] Cocteau replied through Valentine Gross: "We stifle ourselves around saucers."

Cocteau's nomadic life would be ample proof that he was the opposite of a staid property-owner—instead he had become a creature of flight and gauze, inept at taking root anywhere or even at exploiting his own reputation. At the time, however, he still had all the appurtenances of a circle that respected wealth and believed in class, even when he claimed to laugh at both. "Try to be vulgar," he noted in one of the draft notebooks for *Parade*.[22] Even after months of training, however, he would never succeed. "From a bourgeois family, I am a bourgeois monster," he confessed in *Le Potomak*. Unable to go beyond the civility that everyone reproached him for, he would even pass as a millionaire, despite his repeated denials—because in that neighborhood, anyone who had a mother ready to pay off his debts was rich. The misconception was confirmed after he invited to the rue Huyghens some wealthy representatives from the Right Bank curious to hear Pierre Reverdy or Max Jacob read their poems, or eager to buy canvases and musical scores by creators whom they had vilified just a year before. The visitors included Misia, Mme Errazuriz, and the painter José Maria Sert, wrapped "in huge automobile overcoats, felt hats pulled down over their noses," as well as the fashion designers Paul Poiret and Jacques Doucet, who came in limousines, with furs round their necks.[23]

Threatened by this pushy, pure offshoot of the Rostand-Noailles style, the Montparnasse avant-garde reacted with its usual purism. He had the moral backing of the hefty, cloak-wearing bourgeoisie that had been feasting since the Belle Époque, whereas the avant-garde still survived by eating hard-boiled eggs on credit, in bistros smelling of cheap wine, sawdust, and vomit. His jingoistic poems had appeared in *Le mot* just three months earlier, whereas the Montparnasse avant-garde had been publishing typographical fireworks since 1900, sometimes in poorly inked journals that guaranteed its authors nothing but poverty. How could they have given full citizenship to the poet who, in eulogizing a city as hackneyed as Verona, had called it "Virgin of modernism with heavy vandal's hands"?[24] If the hero of the Théâtre Femina matinée wanted to turn over a new leaf, the Montparnos were ready to cut him a new suit. "How many times has Anna de Noailles's influence been held against me," Cocteau would write half a century later. "No one reproaches Rimbaud for the detestable verses he wrote to Banville, or painters' canvases that preceded their self-discovery."[25] He could have said the same of Marinetti, the father of Futurism, who had also lived a first life as a Symbolist poet—ten long years when he had translated and published the very young Cocteau—or later on Tristan Tzara, who had begun as a Romanian disciple of Parnassus before setting the temple on fire. But Cocteau had not yet become Rimbaud, Marinetti, or Tzara.

His reputation as a copycat wouldn't help his cause, in the eyes of an avant-garde that was less concerned with a particular anti-poem or non-painting than with the month it had been shown or published for the very first time. From Max Jacob, who closed his trunk of manuscripts as soon as a visitor took interest in it (especially Reverdy) to the "old" Cubists who turned over their canvases when Juan Gris entered their studio, a real paranoia of plagiarism united the avant-garde. Jacob went so far as to publish only by subscription, so that he could know the name of each of his readers. True, no one threatened people at gunpoint in order to publish a poem, as in the heroic time of the Bateau-Lavoir, but the fight for priority still remained so intense that some artists predated their works to make themselves seem ahead of their time. This anxiety about intellectual property would find an ideal scapegoat in Cocteau, that "show-off" whose genius at capturing the feel of the time was an immediate threat to groups jealous of their radical anteriority. Soon warned against the arrival of this gentleman-burglar prowling around their professional secrets, the radical craftsmen of the neighborhood would still have to come to terms with Cocteau's incredible audacity when he would knock on their doors with the best sponsors.

Blaise Cendrars, a typical Montparno, free-spirited and lively, the perfect embodiment of the rough style the war encouraged, could claim a central place in the literary avant-garde, on equal terms with Apollinaire, Max Jacob, Pierre Reverdy, or André Salmon. This man in the rough, smelling of iodine and grease, this "bruiser" whose mythomania was reinforced by his very real war injury—an arm lost in the ranks of the Foreign Legion—was also an afficionado of typography and syntax: he had the heart of a Russian formalist in the skin of a pirate. At first Cendrars, like the others, looked suspiciously at Cocteau, but that poet who had "come from Catulle Mendès's fly" soon became interested in Cocteau because of Cocteau's receptivity to tales of journeys that Cendrars had never made to Sumatra and Mexico.[26] Galvanized by this limitless credulity, the author of *Bourlinguer* introduced Cocteau to the "other" poetry, including that of Rilke, between two alcoholic rounds and three sonnets scribbled on a piece of blotting paper. When Cocteau read him the first draft of *Le Cap de Bonne-Espérance*, inspired by Garros, Cendrars immediately suggested he publish it at Éditions de la Sirène, of which he was literary director, but only the better to put him in competition with Apollinaire—"the far right and the far left"—and so create an entertaining clash. "He's a snob," Apollinaire would say about Cocteau. "He just has to appear in order to have success. And tell me, frankly, without us, would he be a poet?" Cut to the quick, Cocteau in turn would accuse Apollinaire, quotations in hand, of owing everything to Anna de Noailles—an accusation that still showed great ignorance of Apollinaire's work, and that ended up implicating his own writings. But that drama too amused Cendrars, that dynamiter of sentences and trafficker in gunpowder.

Cocteau soon went from author to collaborator for Éditions de la Sirène. Despite revealing differences about the two men's way of interpreting the name of the publishing house—a factory siren for Cendrars, a mermaid-woman of mythology for Cocteau—the two men would publish some beacons of modernism in it, from poems by Apollinaire to musical scores of the Nouveaux Jeunes, those musicians whom the lazy, unstable, and capricious Cendrars had introduced to Satie, but whom he would leave to Cocteau to patronize, since Cendrars's calling as a buccaneer made him unsuitable for pursuing any collective discipline. That is how Cocteau made his way into the artistic maquis of the Left Bank and became the *éminence grise* of a publisher whose catalogue sums up the great harvest of those years.

Because of his avant-garde legitimacy, Picasso was another weighty ally for Cocteau as he rose to prominence in Montparnasse, but it would still take time for the writer to feel completely at ease among Picasso's friends, especially Max Jacob. Cocteau judged too quickly the radical foreignness of the Jewish Breton poet, funny and sorrowful at the same time, with his excessive taste for paradox and his sexual guilt strengthened by his conversion to Catholicism. In Jacob, who launched "Cubist" poetry and was the first to tint his prose with dream imagery, Cocteau still saw only "a Rousseau of the WCs . . . a 'dancing sacristy rat,' a tender, dirty meddler."[27] But did Cocteau even know that the elder writer—along with Apollinaire, who represented him as the leader of the chorus in his *Mamelles de Tirésias*—had contributed to shaping the "new spirit"? It wasn't until Jacob's *Cornet à dés* appeared in 1917 that Cocteau realized the measure of Jacob's poetic importance.

The reputation of that other plagiarist, Picasso, added to the formidable standoffishness that his new friend Cocteau encountered: the Montparnos would not open their studios to them without double-padlocking their latest creations. "He'll steal my way of painting trees," said one. "He'll take away the siphon I introduced into painting," another declared. The wolves were entering the austere Eden where the lingering disciples of Braque, Gris, and Picasso himself cultivated objects indispensable to their moral survival. During his Easter furlough, though, Cocteau had been welcomed by the amusing Moïse Kisling, the least sectarian but also least interesting of the Montparnos, and a fervent admirer of Picasso.[28] Since the bottle of gin Cocteau had brought, with the idea of composing a ready-to-paint still life, was immediately emptied by Modigliani, Cocteau suggested a portrait in its place. Lacking the reluctance of Picasso, who was watching them in a cowboy shirt, Kisling had set to painting the newcomer, in bowtie and gaiters, hands resting demurely on his lap, as a young mama's boy focused on his poetic future, the dog, Kouski, sleeping at his feet—while at the same time Modigliani sketched his face in pencil, before adding this promise (not kept): "I, the undersigned, author of this drawing, swear never to get plastered again during the entire duration of the war."[29]

Modigliani would also evince that he felt biased against the dandy Cocteau, whom André Salmon describes as entering his studio as a "pretty soldier from the Ballets Russes wearing a dolman and tailored red trousers."[30] Fearing the alcohol-fueled aggressiveness of a painter whom Cocteau would compare to those scornful, haughty Gypsies who read your hand between fits of rage—Modigliani felt kindly toward no one, with the possible exception of Picasso—Cocteau deemed his painting "diabolical." So he left it at Kisling's apartment, with the excuse that he didn't have the money to bring it back in a taxi. The little weasel with pinched lips, daintily posed in a mauve armchair, to which Kisling had reduced him, piqued Cocteau.[31] But it did mean that Cocteau's image had at last joined a "gallery" that already included portraits of Max Jacob, Apollinaire, and Salmon: not so bad for his beginnings in the avant-garde.

There were also late-night jaunts with Kiki de Montparnasse, the legendary model and muse of the Montparnos, who liked to drink her cognac from a tooth glass.[32] Modigliani the drinker always refused to go to bed at the end of these outings. "Kisling caught him by the belt—he was wearing a Zouave sash—and then he unfurled, unfurled, out to where the statue by Rodin is now, and then he re-wound, and did a kind of bear's dance," Cocteau would say, writing about their pranks.[33] Sensing that his own requests for a portrait always made him seem even more like a scion, he changed tactics. His still very French conception of art broadened; now the great national artists were for him a Spaniard, a Russian, and an Italian—Picasso, Stravinsky, and Modigliani—not forgetting the Norman-Scottish Satie, whose derisive allusions to the "Bochie" finally dissolved Cocteau's chauvinism. "We'll get them!" Cocteau shouted, drunkenly and sarcastically, shocking Morand, on New Year's Eve, 1916. He then made the group of friends sick with laughter by imitating "with brilliant irony" an old fogey with the promise of a fine future, General Clapier, a kind of cantankerous Colonel Blimp who reeled off intense patriotic platitudes for two hours right in the middle of the Place de la Concorde.[34]

Who could have stopped that prodigious promotional machine that was Cocteau? His evolution could be seen even in his apartment on the rue d'Anjou. If his mother's salon breathed of bourgeois respectability—family portraits, tapestries, fine porcelain—the room into which Cyprien, Cocteau's elderly valet, introduced her son's friends evoked the cell of a monk surrounded by his own relics. That is where the intangible part of his personality was expressed, on the big notepaper where he drew and jotted down thoughts and addresses, but also on the walls where he pinned the faces of his idols, opposite the portrait that Picasso had just made of him—and it was the model of his soul one seemed to see when, as Morand wrote after being received there in October, he was greeted by a Cocteau "in a bathrobe, amidst plaster masks . . . glass prisms, Cubist drawings, allied flags."[35]

After a few weeks, Cocteau, the former protégé of the Baronne de Pierrebourg, had made his place in the radicalized bohemia of Montparnasse, and already viewed the war as nothing but a big fair (thanks to preparations for his ballet). Probably his first libretto for *Parade* was influenced by Marinetti's already old proposition demanding that the music hall and circus invade the theater in order to renew it. Actually it was Paris, and all of France behind it, that was lagging behind Italy where, for several years already, a bellicose avant-garde had put an end to the desperate overreaching of every generation, ever since Romanticism, to seem more sensitive and more marked by bad temper than the previous ones. Marinetti and the Futurism group had been the first to sing, with an entirely Nietzschean vigor, of the "good incendiaries with carbonized fingers," of energy and ill will, of beautiful ideas that kill and of scorn for women—not to mention steel and speed, cynicism, and war, "the only hygiene in the world." "A roaring motor-car, which seems to run on machine-gun fire, is more beautiful than the Victory of Samothrace," Marinetti declared in 1909, in a manifesto published by *Le Figaro* calling on their country to deliver itself from its gangrenous assemblages of professors, archeologists, and antiquarians.[36] Seven years later, Picasso and Satie were still ill-informed about the work of the Futurist painter-decorators and musician-noisemakers ("bruitistes"), even though, in 1911, Picasso had received Boccioni and Carrà in his studio. Apollinaire, at the vanguard of the "new spirit," had introduced Futurism to France; it was through Apollinaire that Cocteau had heard tell of Marinetti. But the violence espoused by Marinetti, who encouraged his recruits to become visionaries worthy of the age of electricity, caught hold in literature only during the war.[37] Then, unlike the Italian avant-garde, the Parisian avant-garde glorified violence less for its own sake than in order to denounce the good manners of leaders in top hats and white gloves, whom they held responsible for the most barbarous conflict ever known.

It was in the wards of the military hospital in Val-de-Grâce, next to bodies wounded by shrapnel, that André Breton and Louis Aragon bonded; it was when he was back from the front that Céline, another doctor traumatized by the trenches, polished his machine-gun prose with its sputtering volleys. All the new literature had been forged in the mud of the front—while the creators who remained in Paris had contented themselves with formally conveying the violence, or starting journals defending equally Mallarmé and trolley cars, Picasso and factories, Marinetti and the inventors of the telephone, all the "divine killers of habit."[38] In this new aesthetics, metallic and brutal, machines relegated humans to the rank of servant, as seen by the pictorial eye of Fernand Léger, who became fascinated by the breech of a French 75 set on fire by the sun.[39] Becoming one with their helmets, made of pliers and bolts, the *poilus* of Marcel Gromaire shouted in silence that one has to be as inhuman and aggressive as the war itself to defend one's artistic trench. The backward morality that persists even today imposed itself at the time with a conviction that the base actions of some, under the Occupation, would only weaken: from 1916 onward, the tougher ones would a priori be the more righteous.

Already, though, suspicion that members of the avant-garde were collaborating with the enemy—distant or metaphorical—was floating in the air. Attacks against the "patriotic plaything" launched in 1891 by Remy de Gourmont, the indifference shown to the wounded and to mourning widows, incensed all those who identified with the nation, even the ultra-Left, and generated whole sectors of opinion against the artists emerging from "Kubisme," that abstract, sad, dry, and therefore German, heresy that some accused of undermining good French taste and leading citizens away from national morality. But these patriots of the paintbrush were already powerless against the emergence of that violent art that, along with advertising, praised the electric battery, the detonator, the dirigible, the plane, the turbine, the propeller, and the tire, and put forward the Eiffel Tower as the definitive symbol of force—and hence of beauty. Technical inventions like these, which had been accumulating since the end of the previous century, were becoming fully realized, and recognized, in both literary and pictorial forms, as art moved away from the Apollonian demands of clarity and harmony inherited from Greece, via (neo)classicism, and instead shifted toward chaos, asymmetry, ugliness, speed, and madness—all Dionysian virtues. We can define the West as the civilization that sought to bring to light its roots and reinvent its codes, to the point of losing all awareness of the obvious and the "natural"—a civilization that can force us to live from crisis to crisis as we multiply our technical skills and endlessly liberate ourselves only to add some flavor back to things. If we are right, we can think of Cocteau as a late-arriving but sincere modernist.

THE DRUMS OF *PARADE*

A major obstacle soon stood in the way of *Parade:* Misia wanted Diaghilev to produce only projects approved by *her,* and thought that only Satie's early works—in particular, the *Trois morceaux en forme de poire,* which she had introduced to the impresario—deserved to be danced. While Cocteau and Satie tried in vain to make her believe that the idea for *Parade* came from her, she rather cattily warned the irascible Stravinsky that they were trying to have his *David* rewritten by another musician—which forced Cocteau to offer new, more convoluted explanations and made Satie, already furious at having his musical past preferred over his present—"Satie is old, let him stay old," said Misia—a little more jealous of the Russian.[40]

Since Misia's negativity was legendary—Satie called her "the kill-all mother," or sometimes "aunt Brutus"—Cocteau had to maneuver even more when he learned that the "maker of angels" was lavishing care on Apollinaire, who was wounded at the front, and who had also been receiving Picasso at his hospital bedside. Sensing approaching danger, Cocteau ended up obtaining, by dint of follow-up requests, Picasso's participation in *Parade,* on August 12, 1916—a piece of news that a triumphant telegram signed Cocteau-Satie conveyed to Valentine Gross, along with a request to encourage Diaghilev to give a definitive green light to the trio.[41] Picasso's assent was perceived as a betrayal in Montmartre and Montparnasse, in the Cubist "circle" especially, but the painter was already strong enough — and his paintings coveted enough — not to make him hesitate. To justify himself, Cocteau had written to Stravinsky that he wanted to rediscover with *Parade* the emotion unique to circuses, music halls, carrousels, popular dances, factories, ports, and movies, and that was also the painter's objective. "Picasso is molting," he wrote then, proud of having managed this historic transformation — he who was still associated with the old poetry of Anna de Noailles. Some people were already warning him against the risk of having his "idea" stolen, but the extraordinary effect of this double transformation prevented him from lingering over such petty fears.[42] Wasn't the painter he was already calling, without much modesty, "my collaborator," moving to the right just as Cocteau was moving to the left?

When Cocteau finally introduced Satie and Picasso to each other, he was happy to see that they got on well together — every collaboration awakened in Cocteau an almost erotic need for fusion. Returning from their work sessions, through a Paris emptied by curfew, the painter and musician learned to appreciate each other.[43] "Picasso is splendid! He gives me goosebumps," Satie confided, in that indecisive tone with which he made an appointment to meet him in a café, clarifying, "I'll be inside, like the poultry."[44] But already the ideas of Cocteau, who was anxious to give a human *and* allegorical dimension to his characters, no longer fit very well with those of the painter who, hostile to any pathos, wanted to brutalize the plot of their "thing," as Satie called it, in order to reinforce it visually. So when Picasso suggested that they introduce brash businessmen characters and a huge horse into it, so as to reduce the other characters to simple playing-card figures and so animate the stage with the contrast, Cocteau balked: the matter was too close to his heart, ever since the failure of *David*, for him to imagine amending every detail of a spectacle that he had conceived. What right did he have to meddle with my dialogues? Cocteau must have said to himself. What was the point of a librettist, once his libretto was written? Picasso must have thought. The intellectual seduction that had followed their meeting turned into rivalry.

When Cocteau refused to drop the original dialogues and commentaries, Picasso advised Satie to write his score based on Cocteau's outline but rewritten by Satie — that is, stripped of all dialogue, freed from that symbolism from which Picasso had so labored to rid himself. Did the painter conclude, from Cocteau's haste to celebrate Picasso's genius, that he was better at imagining *Parade* than Cocteau? Until then Satie had been following the directives of Cocteau, whom he sometimes called, ironically, "admirable," and sometimes "my son." But Picasso's harsh conviction awoke the fragile megalomania of that autarch who always needed the other to affirm him, since he lacked that Camelot instinct so useful in art. With years of experience under his belt, Satie suddenly wondered why, at the ripe age of fifty-one—Picasso was thirty-six—he had to obey Cocteau, an ex-pillar of the Right Bank impatient at the age of twenty-eight to make an impression on the avant-garde, of which he, Satie, was the pure product (although Satie had returned at the age of thirty-nine to the Schola Cantorum de Paris to study musical composition).

The struggle among these three very strong personalities took a bitter turn. Cocteau found himself at odds with Picasso and Satie, whose alcohol dependence increased his touchiness; Morand even called Satie a "half-failure . . . whom Debussy always put down and who's still suffering from it."[45] And perhaps this transformist ballet might have died a second death if Picasso's determination hadn't finally compelled Cocteau to give way. Forced to adopt the painter's figures of businessmen, the librettist managed to convince himself that they came straight out of his *Potomak* and wrote them dialogues that were meant to be "spat out" by stand-ins hidden in the orchestra pit. Since Picasso persisted in refusing all speech, these three auxiliaries sitting with the orchestra were reduced to shouting loud demands for Kub bouillon cubes during musical pauses, through fairground megaphones and then an amplifier emerging from the loudspeaker conceived of for *David*—in a prelude to a complete retreat of the librettist.

Seeing how well Picasso's intrepidity had paid off, Satie in turn abandoned his seeming humility in order to defy Cocteau. Since the "total work of art" Cocteau wished for placed Satie almost in the position of an underling, Satie asked Cocteau to suppress the words accompanying the American girl's "rag," whose musical motif Satie had borrowed from Irving Berlin.[46] No more desirous than Picasso to use a text, but with his mind more than ever made up to visualize *his* music, Satie again suggested to Cocteau to withdraw the patter that was supposed to burst forth from the wings with every appearance of the businessmen.[47] He then attacked the "noises" that Cocteau wanted to include in his score, where a Chinese melody was already competing with ragtime tunes. When the three men met now, Satie would point to Picasso and exclaim, "You're the one I'm following! You're my master!"[48]

Distressed to see the musician and painter agreeing behind his back to pilot a project that existed only due to his insistence, Cocteau asked Valentine to remind Satie that he, Cocteau, was a part of *Parade* for a reason. "Does he even hear my voice?" he worried about the alcoholic musician, whom he accused of speaking "in Sauternes" rather than in French—before confessing that he would "die" if he had another failure.[49] Though he didn't have the authority he desired, Cocteau still revealed himself to be more tenacious—and on one point more modern—than his collaborators. While agreeing in extremis to eliminate the airplane noises and the Morse code sounds, he stubbornly refused that the other sounds be separated by brief silences, as the musician had demanded. Picasso, always looking out for himself, then abandoned Satie in exchange for the complete suppression of all dialogue. This allowed Cocteau to assert that Picasso and he had agreed to lie to Satie, and to reimpose his "trompe-l'oreille" sounds into the score, including the clacking of a typewriter meant to remind the audience that a writer is behind the ballet.[50] Hence it's very much in spite of himself that Satie passes today for one of the ancestors of *musique concrète*—though in all fairness he did plan, during his first meetings with Cocteau, a curious *bouteillophone* (bottlephone) made of glass tubes.

So it seems that there could have been no "light-hearted happiness" in this undertaking, contrary to what Cocteau told Valentine, without whose "marble kindness" everything might have fallen through. "Every collaboration is a more or less successful misunderstanding," Cocteau added to Gross, who was already well placed to know that the birth of a ballet rarely lends itself to acts of altruism. Although the final production also lacked the poster curtains that Cocteau had envisioned separating each scene like the cards in silent movies, *Parade* remained the fruit of Cocteau's tenacious ambition, greatly strengthened by two failures in this field.

Cocteau's meeting with Diaghilev and Léonide Massine, whom Diaghilev had sent for from Russia to replace Nijinsky, would at least turn out well. Appreciating "the fresh intelligence and behavior" of Diaghilev's new favorite, who had the merit of lacking experience—*Parade* would be his first real chore-ography—Cocteau also felt for once in tune with Diaghilev. The impresario, having learned his lesson from the failure of *Le dieu bleu*, did not overwhelm Cocteau with orders and because he was happy to be in contact with Picasso, he presented Cocteau with a sizeable contract. The monster was also capable of gratitude, Cocteau noted, this time comparing Diaghilev to a pink rhinoc-eros. Satie would not deliver his piano score—"scholarly pop music," as the conductor Ernest Ansermet described it—until January 1917. Faced with Cocteau's victory at his completed contribution, he went everywhere asserting, with his paradoxical humor, "I composed a background for certain noises that the librettist deemed indispensable," before adding, in an excess of ironical submission, "It will be—and it is—the first time (upon my word) that a ballet is actually made by a poet."[51] Satie, however, took poorly the financial arrange-ments made between Diaghilev and Cocteau, who had generously agreed, even while claiming the lion's share of the work, to transfer all his rights to the composer. "Decidedly a brute and a swine," Satie confided to Valentine. "I can't see him anymore—never . . . What a dolt! What a pain in the neck!!"[52]

That's when Diaghilev decided, as he waited for Satie's orchestration, to gather everyone in Italy, where the Ballets Russes were scheduled to perform in the spring: Picasso could build his sets there; Cocteau could enrich the emerging choreography of Massine, who was deemed too fragile to coordinate such diverse talents on his own; and Satie could work there with every possible material comfort. While Picasso would always leave his studio with regret, it was in great spirits this time that he came with Cocteau to announce to Gertrude Stein on the rue de Fleurus that they were leaving "on their honeymoon"—at least that's what Cocteau would affirm.[53] Satie was much less enthusiastic. He had indeed already spent his entire advance on traveling bags and umbrellas, which he was crazy about ("he buys a parasol a day," Cocteau wrote to Valentine, and Cocteau had even seen Satie hide his umbrella under his coat when it rained, to protect it). But the musician hated to travel. "Do you know Rome, Mr. Satie?" asked Berthelot, the head of the Quai d'Orsay. "By name . . . only by name!" replied the musician, who would remain in Arcueil, happy to be able to work quietly with his bottles of rum, which he preferred a thousand times over their sound-alike city.[54] Time had healed some wounds: again Cocteau heard Satie call him "Dear Fat Old Man," as if nothing had happened between them.[55] But "the Cubist code forbade any journey other than the North-South one between the Places des Abbesses and the Boulevard Raspail," Satie wrote, furious at seeing Cocteau take Picasso to the train station on February 17, 1917. A great many Montparnos predicted that after this departure for Italian sensuality, Picasso would never be the same again. Indeed, it was in the phantom capital of the Roman Empire that Picasso would bury Cubism.

The Parade of Peace

Art loves chance and chance loves art.
—*Agathon, fifth century B.C.E.*[1]

THE LATIN PARADISE

Cocteau and Picasso's stay in Rome ended up bringing the two men closer together. They stayed near the Piazza di Spagna, in two adjacent rooms in the Hôtel de Russie, which had a private courtyard garden worthy of a cloister, and from which the two men could simply reach out of their windows to pick oranges. To explore the city, there was Diaghilev's automobile, because he was living in princely style in a palace in the Corso, and to make themselves understood, they had Picasso's Spanish. "We live in an earthly paradise," Cocteau wrote to his mother on February 20, 1917.[1] The enthusiastic welcome by the Futurists of the Caffè Greco would be decisive—Balla, Prampolini, and the others turned out to be real "Impressionists of ideas," as Cocteau said. Excited at working in the same avant-gardist mode of excess, the idealist Depero shared his discoveries with them, then showed them the costumes he had just created for Stravinsky's *The Song of the Nightingale* at the Ballets Russes, which transformed the human body into shapes and machines. Upon seeing this spectacular clothing, Picasso revised and futurized his American and French businessmen characters, who until then had been represented in almost Ingres-like classicism in his studio in Montrouge. In the lineage of Marinetti, who recommended that the "declaimers" electrify their voices and take on the rigid forms of traffic lights or lighthouses in order to dehumanize themselves, Depero's men-sandwiches were twice normal size and covered with three-dimensional constructions—a skyscraper and cardboard tailcoats made by Depero himself.[2]

Feeling inspired and working quickly, the Picasso machine began producing engravings and charcoals, inks and sculptures, collages and prints in the studio that Diaghilev had rented for him on the via Margutta. As he drew and painted the costume of the Chinese magician, then of the American girl, Cocteau stood at the ready, working out in the notebook that Massine had given him the body language of the businessmen that Picasso had insisted on—characters that he still wanted to give an epic dimension—or sketching out choreographical elements. The two men also began drawing the Villa Médicis, which they could see through the studio's window, with Picasso doing three magnificent studies of it, one Ingres-like, the second pointillist, the last semi-abstract, and Cocteau taking charge of the Cubist version. Then the painter did a very "cabaret" cartoon of Cocteau, with his long shrew-like nose, before Cocteau doodled Picasso smoking a pipe, shooting his dark gaze sideways at the viewer.

Cocteau was shocked by the intense work ethic and inventiveness of Picasso, who as a schoolboy had attached ink cartridges to flies so they would draw random patterns in notebooks and skulls. Genius gushed everywhere from him, "like a watering can!" noted Cocteau, who was both intimidated and electrified by this mixture of impassive bullfighter and prancing young bull, a man capable of contemplating him with "tears in his eyes" but also of giving him looks of yawning indifference. Cocteau was a nervous rosebush, almost pathological in his impatience to give but yielding only a few blossoms every year. The writer expected to be visited, ever since he had dropped his attachment to Symbolism, but the wonderful phrases or esoteric messages that emerged from his mouth left him lifeless, like an old rag just barely able to write letters, or scribble drawings.

By contrast, whether it was raining or sunny, whether he was cheerful or gloomy, Picasso constantly produced. His animal-like obstinacy made him look everywhere for the optimal conditions for concentration; he refused almost all invitations to dinner, as well as most commissions. He took root in his studio, absorbed solely by his work, and left it only to study the museums. Picasso was a paragon of discipline, a wonder of productivity, a monster of asperity who was capable too of sudden acts of generosity. His ability to assimilate the ideas of others made him a thing of wonder. Did Cocteau know that after alternating between Montmartre daubs and catastrophic first communion paintings, Picasso also took his inspiration from everyone? Careening from Cézanne's kaleidoscope to Ingres-inspired classicism, from sub-Puvis de Chavannes to para-Gauguin, from Van Dongen lookalikes to proto-Matisse, Picasso surpassed even Cocteau in his predatory gluttony. "What is a painter?" Picasso asked one day, with the cynicism that served as his mask. "It's a collector who forms a collection, by making by himself the paintings he likes at other people's places."[3]

When he "borrowed," Cocteau almost seemed to feel guilty. That crocodile-sized chameleon that was Picasso, however, never felt the need to justify his flights or about-faces, especially not in order to obtain the approbation of the masters he copied. Sure of his right to pillage, he threw material away as soon as he had used it, unless he recycled those forms or materials twenty years later, forgetting their provenance. "You have to take what you like where you find it, except in your own works," said Picasso. After having co-signed for two years paintings that he had created with Braque, who had left their relationship artistically drained, it was clear that this monster was capable of copying most any style in order to serve his own.

One day, while discussing his drive to be among the great painters in history, Picasso argued that, having been unable to reach the top of the ladder, he had broken all the rungs. In Cocteau's eyes, however, Picasso was pursuing less a goal than movement, just as he was less a father than a lover. Picasso's advancements were destined to seed the world, and it mattered little if they dazzled in passing. Picasso had one more idea than everyone else about every subject, but didn't boast about it—"Like all great things, the Picasso event presented itself naturally," Cocteau would say. He had just found in him a subject worthy of his mythology, a creator worthy of the god he once dreamed of being.[4]

Picasso's very nature revealed Cocteau's need for osmosis and (reciprocal) desire for annexation, his generosity and his admiration, his sycophancy and his need for affection. Cocteau liked to lend out his addresses and references, the way some schoolboys lend their marbles, with a momentum that often turned against him—and no one liked to take as much as Picasso. An exalted, fragile, minority genius, subject to mood swings, Cocteau continually sought to legitimize his transformation once and for all. Picasso, a direct, well-equipped genius, sure of himself, standing firmly in place in front of his canvases, became both Cocteau's center and his circle. The painter's bull-like fecundity and his innate spirit of contradiction, his courage to call himself into question with every painting—but also not always to finish, never to want to make an oeuvre, would make him a model of modernism. "He . . . taught us not to pay any attention to the unity of surface, not to be afraid of seeming like a juggler or an acrobat," Cocteau would say forty years later, in appreciation of how this approach helped him proudly assert his own aesthetic inconstancy.[5]

Cocteau had always thought he could surpass, by assimilation, the talented artists whom he admired. De Max and Anna de Noailles were bearers of an aesthetic that was especially easy to burgle, if not parody. But with Picasso, Cocteau came up against a power that was stylistically very difficult to define, and so seemed able to be divided ad infinitum, without seeming to weaken, and always changing shape. "These men never open anything for others. What they open, they close," he said, aware that trying to imitate Picasso was to condemn himself to sterility.[6] Cocteau sought not to be the equal of this superlative self, but to understand it, by writing texts in which he would shower praises that he no longer dared to address to himself. Picasso would become in turn a Hindu god with a hundred arms, then an Orpheus that enchanted people and animals, transforming matter and renaming objects. But the more Cocteau took apart the clockwork of the Picasso machine, the more he noticed his own fragility. Whereas the genius painter outran his critics and left his pursuers out of breath — "the man who runs faster than beauty," Cocteau wrote in the *Ode* he would dedicate to Picasso in 1919 — Cocteau was a writer whose breakdowns and crises would frequently stop his work, giving his detractors the chance to take stock of him.

They had been living together for just a month when Cocteau wrote to his mother, "I admire him and am disgusted by myself."[7] Was he suddenly aware of having inherited a nature that was not divine but human? Did the ease with which Picasso imposed his "businessmen" on his creation and the secret shame he felt at his submission turn his megalomania into insecurity? Two years later, introducing his *Le coq et l'arlequin*, Cocteau would say that he loved Picasso's harlequins, but disapproved of the character who wears an eye mask and multi-colored costume, and who hides "after having denied the rooster's call." Because he would prefer men capable of proudly denying themselves? That would not always be his case, as we will see.

Held in a hall in the basement of the Caffè Faraglia, a famous Belle Époque ballroom on the Piazza Venezia, the dance rehearsals of *Parade* would help Cocteau regain equilibrium. Right from the start Massine showed great understanding of his suggestions and ideas. The dancer admired not only Cocteau's intimate knowledge of dance, but also the taste with which Cocteau advised Diaghilev for the private painting collection that the impresario had chosen for him.[8] In short, he turned out to be much more cooperative than Picasso or Satie: Cocteau and Massine worked together on the choreography for the American girl — whom Cocteau wanted to be halfway between a female Chaplin and the heroines portrayed by Pearl White — as well as on the dance score for the horse, which was played by two men holding each other by the waist in a canvas skin, in the music-hall tradition.[9]

Happy finally to be listened to, when his presence might have seemed superfluous, Cocteau could only congratulate himself on Massine, who agreed, on his advice, to take the role of the Chinese man, in which he would in fact excel, after at first reserving for himself the role of the acrobat. "You'd laugh at seeing me become a dancer," Cocteau wrote to his mother, "for Massine wants me to show him the slightest thing, and I invent roles that he transforms forthwith into a choreography."[10] Massine was a real Stradivarius in Cocteau's hands, a dream for that expansively creative man-orchestra who also, like Pygmalion, loved his creation even if he sometimes reproached the dancer for confusing "originality with complication." "Massine's discoveries in *Parade* and in the following ballets stem directly from Cocteau, with their literary side and their stylization of the circus," Serge Lifar would write in *Serge de Diaghilev*. Massine would confirm this judgment indirectly when he restaged *Parade* fifty-six years later, in 1973, for the Joffrey Ballet in New York, and reported, looking back, that "I was just a greenhorn when I did the first choreography for it."[11] There was no realm in which Diaghilev's new protégé caused Nijinsky to be forgotten, except perhaps in the heart of his mentor.

THE BULL AND THE HARLEQUIN

In the end it would be a very happy stay. Proud of creating close to the painter he so admired, in the midst of splendid ruins, Cocteau was jubilant at finally being at the center of this *Parade*. The arrival in early March of Stravinsky, whom he had scarcely seen since the failure of *David*, brought his excitement to its height. Happy to serve as an intermediary between Picasso and Stravinsky, two men who didn't know each other and knew almost nothing about each other's work, Cocteau's famous wit sparkled during lunches that would be recalled later by the conductor Ernest Ansermet. At these lunches, Cocteau revived his "General Clapier," the old fogey he'd invented on the front who, on his hospital bed, kept making the military salute every minute. "Watch out, you'll end up like that," Picasso remarked, as if he sensed what this jingoistic, rigid military man owed to the admirals in the Lecomte family. Exalted by the smiles of the two confirmed geniuses of this new century, and comforted by the ties that already bound them, Cocteau recognized himself in these creators who learned in the shadow of their fathers to draw and compose "in the old style," respecting perspective and melody, before they threw themselves into the modern frenzy. Cocteau didn't dare call himself their equivalent in literature, but he had the secret conviction of being the third part of a fundamental Trinity: "and none / better than you fugue Igor / none / better than Picasso the anatomy / none better than me the alexandrine / arithmetic," he would write in *Le Cap de Bonne-Espérance*.

While afternoons were reserved for the dancers' rehearsals, evenings were free. Picasso followed Cocteau to the homes of Roman personalities whose addresses he knew, from the San Martino princes to the Marquise Casati, an eccentric straight out of D'Annunzio's belle époque whose faded luxury would have shocked the painters of the Bateau-Lavoir. Their nocturnal outings ended for the painter in Roman brothels, whose prices delighted him. "I go to bed very late, and I know all the ladies in Rome," Picasso wrote to Gertrude Stein, claiming sixty dancers for his list, as if to make her jealous.[12] In fact, Diaghilev's ballerinas were beginning to take an interest in him, and even to offer him Chinese gifts bought in San Francisco. Olga Koklova, one of the twelve little princesses who had danced in *Firebird*, was at first the least attentive. With her oval, full face, long chestnut hair, and aura of a blossoming virgin, this daughter of a colonel in the Imperial Army had been chosen because she resembled a real little girl. "I have a much better dancer for you!" protested Diaghilev, but the pearl was in Chile, and the painter was in a hurry. "No, no, Monsieur Picasso, I won't let you in," cried out Olga Koklova, hearing him knock on the door of her room in the Hotel Minerva; the bull insisted, however, and the descendant of Russian squires gave in.[13]

Already fascinated by Picasso's creative power, Cocteau came to envy the effect the artist had on women, with the two phenomena seeming to stem from the same miraculous fertility. Unlike Picasso, whose gaze was saturated with a sexual energy that drew prey to him effortlessly, Cocteau was condemned to talk in order to subjugate. Yet he had some success in enticing women. Around this time he redis-covered his old desires for music hall stars and approached the seventeen-year-old Russian dancer who had the role of the little American girl. Lively, tiny, and mischievous, Marie Chabelska illustrated wonderfully well the definition he would give his character: "A girl in whom the pleasure of being happy is more important than the sense of her beauty."[14] After guiding her movements in the afternoon—coaching her in how best to, say, leap into a moving train, swim across a river, or fight with a pistol—Cocteau would meet her in the evening at the Hotel Minerva, where Stendhal used to stay a century earlier. Since the ballerina also had the luck of pleasing Picasso, who would draw her silhouette on his stage curtain, the librettist took her away from the group on nocturnal strolls. He showed her the Forum—"it's the disorder of a bedroom after burglars have broken in . . ., the safe open . . . They took away the treasure," he would say, then he'd open the notebook given him by Massine to draw, in the bend of a small street, the childlike face of the dancer, the freshness of her eyelashes and her heart-shaped mouth, or her comic silhouette, drawn much like the very first cartoons and placed side by side with his own, to form a paper couple.

Did Cocteau take advantage of this Roman interlude to play with his sexu-ality, in order to get even closer to the painter? Did he dream in a confused way of completing his transformation by bringing to a close his pederastic period? To be modern was to be direct and brutal; to incorporate the erotic aura of Picasso was magically to give himself the power he lacked, in the eyes of the Montparnos; and to become heterosexual would be once and for all to stop being Proustian and to assert himself forever as contemporary. The "honeymoon" announced to Gertrude Stein became more involved: the two men took up residence in the Hotel Minerva, whose hallways Picasso paced in pajamas. "You would like my little Chabelska," an already very protective Cocteau announced in a letter to Misia. "I'm sleeping with a Russian dancer and Picasso with a lady who thinks he's a 'prompter' in a musical hall," he added proudly to Apollinaire, who must have been somewhat surprised.[15]

Was it in memory of their evenings that Cocteau would evoke, in these unusually erotic terms, in his poetry?

> Oh
> erection
> simply at contact
> with your breasts, my darling
> a branch rises from the body's tree
> an equally virile sign swells
> inside me
> fills your mouth Calliope
> and forces upon you
> the passive silence of servants.[16]

The ballerina, for her part, seems to have accepted as a game this courting of a man more overawed by Picasso's virility than by her embryonic femininity. Hardly taken in by the scene she would describe, fifty years later, recalling the day Cocteau had rumpled the bedsheets in Picasso's studio when Picasso was away, to make him suppose an explosive encounter, she would conclude to Steegmuller: "Picasso laughed with the rest at the tribute being paid him."[17] In the margin of a new portrait of Picasso, Cocteau himself would write in marievaudages, suggesting how much the painter's erotic energy had contributed to the flourishing of their amorous quartet.[18]

Having been unable to obtain an audience for Cocteau with the Pope, who had already been so obliging as to bless his troupe, Diaghilev decided, at the beginning of that March, to take Cocteau, along with Stravinsky, Picasso, and Massine, on vacation to Naples.[19] Cocteau would adore that "Arabic Montmartre" for the same reasons that made the historic cesspool fascinating to Nietzsche. "Antiquity swarms brand-new," Cocteau exclaimed when he saw pagan altars everywhere dedicated to the Virgin and the saints. Twenty centuries after their official dismissal, the gods of Olympus seemed still to haunt that superstitious, dirty, crowded port known for fornication and its joyful cult of death. Vesuvius inspired Cocteau to write streams of letters and poems: all the clouds in the world seemed to flow from this Cyclopean forge, this echo from the underworld where the ancients had placed the Elysian Fields.

There were more delightful days in this sunny premonition of paradise—as Cocteau remarked, "The Pope is in Rome, God is in Naples." The incredible gaiety of the Neapolitan people, as well as their pagan-Christian syncretism, which was colorful, even carnivalesque, and of which Cocteau was so aware, set Picasso and Stravinsky in search of Pulcinella (that cross between Harlequin and Petrushka)—a Punchinello born in Spain, and that could be seen in the rows of laundry decorating the theater of the streets. Cocteau walked up Spaccanapoli, the street that slices through the old city like a sword, then, after Diaghilev fed them pasta with tomato sauce, climbed with Picasso up the alley-ways full of sailors, where the half-open doors of brothels gave glimpses of candelabras, Holy Virgins, and golden gramophones.

The same men, minus Stravinsky, visited Herculaneum and Pompeii, in the company of a Diaghilev exhausted by the heat. Cocteau took photos of Picasso and Massine, in suit and tie and dandy's cane, off-handedly leaning on blocks of broken marble. The painter climbed up on the shafts of columns to survey the ruins in their full extent, before sketching erotica inspired by the marble phalluses that pointed the way to brothels in ancient times. These houses ready to re-open, these cobblestones still nicked by chariot wheels, and on the horizon the waving wheat . . . time seemed to have been abolished in this city suffocated nineteen centuries earlier by the lava of Vesuvius. Like Gradiva, the heroine in the novella by Wilhelm Jensen whose dreamlike qualities fascinated Freud, Cocteau walked with a strange feeling of familiarity, as if he were an escapee from the catastrophe, or the brother of the statues bordering the stone paths. "I was right at home," he wrote to his mother. "I had waited a thousand years, not daring to return to see its poor ruins."[20] This "return" would feed Cocteau aesthetically during all the years to come, as he created masterpieces ranging from *La statue retrouvée* to the film *Le sang d'un poète*. The experience would also influence Picasso's neoclassical period, encouraging his identification with erotic deities like Dionysus or Jupiter.[21]

Stravinsky had returned to Rome in a hurry, to orchestrate the very popular *Volga Boatmen* so that it, not the Imperial anthem, could open the Ballets Russes on April 9, 1917. Nicolas II, czar of all the Russias, had just abdicated—

he would soon be made prisoner—and Kerensky's new government was waiting for an opportunity to offer Diaghilev the position of Minister of Fine Arts. On the same day, after an absence of almost two months, Cocteau returned alone to Paris to resume his functions at the Maison de la Presse, the government agency for war information. Picasso and Stravinsky accompanied Cocteau to the train station, then went back to work on *Pulcinella*, the ballet that Massine would choreograph three years later. Cocteau later described his farewell, for which he carried the new portrait Picasso had made of him two days before, on Easter:

> From the train car I lean out
> Pablo Igor
> Your two hands in mine
> Finally
> The marriage of gold and mercury . . .
> I leave you in Rome
> United in me.[22]

Upon his return, Cocteau dazzled Paris with tales of their trip. At dinner at the home of Princesse Murat, he bombarded those present with his Roman exploits and Picasso's wonderful achievements. Jacques-Émile Blanche grumbled into Morand's ear:

> Cocteau has periods. He is cyclical. Six years ago, I knew the Anna de Noailles phase; Jean spoke to us so much about her that we, who all liked Anna very much, could no longer bear her name! Now it's his Picasso phase.[23]

Marie Chabelska, the "little American" in *Parade*, would continue to keep Cocteau busy for some weeks. "Think of me in the bedroom of Marie, my little beggar girl, and kiss the hand of the daughter of General Koklow," Cocteau wrote to "Pablissimo," who had remained in Rome with Olga.[24] A few daily letters later, he pleads, "Talk to me about Marie, my little mouse. I miss her and dream about her at night."[25] He would complain once again about her unfaithful silence, remember in a poem that she would lay out her cards to read and smoke, and smoke, and then go on to something else. "I loved Marie Chabelska . . ., but she was Russian, and I was not," he would write later on in his *Cahier intime*. To Gide, he had confided, not long before his departure: "I'm going through a 'little death' crisis," adding: "These nymph phenomena are very tiring and make me sad."[26] The chrysalis, obviously, was unable to emerge as a heterosexual butterfly. "In Rome, in 1917 . . . I had eyes only for my collaborator," he would confess.[27] That would still be the case forty years later.

THE SUPPORT OF THE AVANT-GARDE

Exasperated at hearing Cocteau sing Picasso's praises, and still not having forgiven him for having strayed from them in favor of a Russian impresario whom they saw as an entertainer for the wealthy, the avant-garde closed ranks against the intruder who had the gall to continue to visit Anna de Noailles, a woman Proust himself already perceived as a historic monument. Pierre Reverdy, the poet whom Cocteau had met through Modigliani, banned Cocteau from the journal *Nord-Sud*, a temple of the new spirit that had been "erected" in homage to Apollinaire. Reverdy still compared Cocteau to a salon nightingale whose constant twittering sounded like a glass roof pounded by the rain. In short Cocteau, the sandwich-man who changed his posters every era and who, though among the last to join the avant-garde, was already claiming to gather its ideas into a ballet, had to stay on his guard.

Reverdy's gestures always promised slaps, Philippe Soupault would say. And he often kept his promises, as the Mexican muralist Diego Rivera could testify at his own expense. Far from keeping a low profile, however, Cocteau didn't hesitate to slyly apply to him one of the obscure paradoxes scattered through his still-unpublished *Potomak:* "There is no forerunner, there are only latecomers." Hearing himself called a follower, Reverdy attacked Cocteau, who then justified himself by explaining that, for him, genius alone arrived in time. This phrase Reverdy again took poorly, leading to new clashes at the end of which the "boxer" excused himself, crying. This was a habit with Reverdy, whom Aragon would nickname the "offended angel."

Faced with these difficulties, Cocteau had gone to seek Apollinaire's backing, even before his departure for Rome. Apollinaire, anxious about seeing Cocteau poaching on his territory, jealous too of the friendship being shown him by Picasso, jewel of his artistic domain, only reluctantly allowed himself to be approached. Since the theme of *Parade* used some views that Apollinaire had developed in his *Antitradition futuriste, manifeste-synthèse,* the ease with which *Le prince frivole* or *La danse de Sophocle* had been launched reminded him by contrast of the difficulties that had forced him to earn his living in a bank. Apollinaire had even passed for a long time as a Sunday poet, before the publication of *L'enchanteur pourrissant* and *Bestiaire ou cortège d'Orphée* placed him at the heart of the extremist literary scene, and his "discovery" of the Douanier Rousseau as well as *l'art nègre,* Braque, Picasso, and Delaunay, had set him up as the founder of "l'esprit nouveau."

True, Cocteau had discovered Apollinaire belatedly, but the admiration he had for his "poem events," or for his way of mixing invention with tradition, or continuing to focus on the natural world when all his "colleagues" were already singing the praises of machines, was sincere. For didn't this other Symbolist, Apollinaire—one modernized from contact with Cubism, Matisse, and the Italian Futurists—have the courage to confess his own haziness in these lines?

> One day I was waiting for myself
> I said to myself Guillaume it's time for you to come
> So I can finally know the one I am
> I who know others
> I know them by the five senses and a few others
> It's enough for me to see their feet to be able to recreate
> These people by the thousands . . .[28]

One could still read, in the *Calligramme* in the heart of which Apollinaire had written his name: "In this mirror, I am enclosed alive and real as we imagine the angels and as reflections are." Cocteau could have said the same.

Cocteau was hooked. Determined to justify his transformation, humanly if not theoretically, he had bombarded Apollinaire with letters, and had gone so far as to copy out for him an extract from Shakespeare's *Troilus and Cressida* where Calchas reminds the Greeks of all he has abandoned in Troy by joining their camp:

> Appear it to your mind
> That, through the sight I bear in things to love,
> I have abandon'd Troy, left my possession,
> Incurr'd a traitor's name; exposed myself,
> From certain and possess'd conveniences,
> To doubtful fortunes; sequestering from me all
> That time, acquaintance, custom and condition
> Made tame and most familiar to my nature,
> And here, to do you service, am become
> As new into the world, strange, unacquainted . . .[29]

But the more he justified himself, the more Apollinaire doubted him.

Picasso's intervention finally influenced Apollinaire, who, according to Cocteau, saw the painter as the prince of the movement, "the killer of boredom, the wrecker of the weak, the superb disturber of traffic."[30] Picasso began to take care to show great respect for Cocteau in public. Something in Cocteau, too, may even have touched Apollinaire, beyond their shared passion for cinema and *Fantômas*. "He has much more innocent kindness than I thought," Apollinaire had confided after a walk to Picasso, whom they had helped move from the rue

Schoelcher to his new studio on Montrouge.[31] It was Cocteau whom Apollinaire, "prevented by a glorious headache," had asked to read "Tristesse d'un étoile" and other war poems of his during a poetic matinée organized by the group "Lyre et Palette" on November 24, 1916, on the rue Huyghens—where the African sculptures and masks from Paul Guillaume's collection, exhibited for the first time, faced works by Picasso, Matisse, and Modigliani.

The night of November 26, Cocteau found Apollinaire the Enchanter in the same place. There, in front of three hundred people packed in, including the impassive Satie, Cocteau read innocently pre-Dadaist poems written by a five-year-old cousin, but which the audience attributed to him.[32] Fascinated by the confidence shown by his friend in this place that was entirely new to him, Morand had on this occasion discovered the already mythic Apollinaire, in uniform and with his head bandaged, being faithful to his motto: "I fill with wonder [*J'émerveille*]." Again on December 31, Cocteau joined the honor committee of the banquet luncheon where guests paid homage to Apollinaire for the publication of *Le poète assassin*. The avant-garde had reproached Apollinaire for his obvious nationalism, but the Enchanter couldn't care less.

Once in Rome, still in search of a publisher, Cocteau asked Apollinaire to sponsor his *Potomak* and sang to him the praises of the still-in-progress *Parade*. He also contrasted the sober idealism of the Cubists with the contemporary excesses of the Futurists in order to encourage Apollinaire's new reservations about extremes of all kinds. Even better, Cocteau expressed the wish to create a journal with Apollinaire called *Le journal de l'ordre*, a title that enchanted Apollinaire and encouraged him to proclaim a henceforth "indissoluble" friendship, and rejoice in the "wonderful harmony" reigning between their ideas: "For all the pure and the good I feel in your letter, I rejoice at the hole I bear in my side," he had even added in March 1917.[33]

Cocteau spoiled him. Preparing to publish, with Éditions de la Sirène, *Le flâneur des deux rives* and a new edition of *Le bestiaire*, Cocteau had already asked Apollinaire for a novel—probably *La femme assise*—and by his untiring availability conquered Apollinaire's final reservations about completing it. "Apollinaire and Cocteau are getting along swimmingly," noted an annoyed Reverdy.[34] Cocteau also hoped that Apollinaire would write a text to introduce *Parade*, but the writer left him dangling. "If you cite my name, cite it as the name of a thoroughbred that hasn't raced yet," Cocteau asked him, at once anxious and happy, not knowing that his efforts to make the Femina matinée forgotten would be enough to make it unforgettable to him.[35] Some mistrust persisted, however. In twelve years of friendship, Apollinaire never stopped praising Picasso's genius, but none of the projects he had submitted to him had resulted in anything, since the painter always shied away when it came to taking action. So Apollinaire had reason to take umbrage at a collaboration with Cocteau that Picasso had accepted after just a few months of friendship, even though it offered him a truly central place in *Parade*. This wound probably explains the "general explanation" that Apollinaire had demanded from the painter at the end of 1916.

Finally Satie submitted his orchestral score. Cocteau was delighted, since Satie had been able to convey both the parade and the inner spectacle, all the while skillfully incorporating his "noises" in crude rhythmic schemas, making great use of the drums. "A linear, sauceless music," "a SOBER, EASY masterpiece," he had asserted, happy to see that their conflict had left no trace in the ironically light score.[36] Satie had composed more striking pieces, but this was a wonder of expressive harmony and cheerful melancholy given the constraints under which he had been working.

The conductor's baton was entrusted to Ernest Ansermet. But since his musicians deemed Satie's orchestration very poor—more fitting for a café concert— rehearsals, which Apollinaire sometimes attended, turned out to be difficult. "Satierik," who was known for not knowing how to conduct, wanted to get involved but ended up flying into wild rages, which he would conclude by brandishing his umbrella and slamming the door.[37] Cocteau had to fetch the prestigious Ravel: he soothed the musicians by calling the creation of Satie, the man who had so influenced his own music, "a kind of masterpiece."[38] But Ravel, unable to dismiss all their doubts, would make himself just as hated by Satie—"He refuses the Légion d'honneur but all his music accepts it," Satie would say in 1920. And Satie returned to the Châtelet more impenetrable than ever. "Apparently you think I'm an idiot!" a flutist shouted, seeing him resume his place. "No, no, I don't think you're an idiot," the composer replied. "But I may be mistaken."[39]

Finally Picasso returned from Rome, on May 4, 1917. Cocteau went to meet him in the studio near the Buttes-Chaumont where, "making giant figures, fresh as bouquets, gush forth from his brush," Picasso, with the help of the Futurist Carlo Socrate, was completing the opening curtain for *Parade*.[40] The curtain was huge—more than fifty-five by thirty feet, and if the set itself remained Cubist, with its beveled houses and angled kiosque, the painted canvas, marked by "commedia dell'arte," fairground life, and the theater of Italian street scenes, represented a distinct departure from the aesthetic he had imposed during the Braque period. With its sylph perched on a winged horse, its turbaned black man, its sailor, and its priest, all framed by architectural fragments and painted curtains, it marked a spectacular return to those acrobats he had painted during his pink period. Cocteau, who had been hoping for a curtain-poster announcing their names much like at the cinema, was disappointed to see that Picasso had filled this "naïve" curtain with only personal symbols—a guitarist bullfighter, a Harlequin, a monkey, and a Pierrot.

Satie caused more obstruction, this time on the subject of the noises, forcing Cocteau, a month before the premiere, to arrange mechanisms to amplify the sound for the Théâtre du Châtelet. But Apollinaire's text was an even greater disappointment.[41] Content to cite only in passing the name of the librettist who had conceived of *Parade*, Apollinaire reserved the lion's share for "Picasso's discipline," for "the boldest of choreographers," namely Massine, and for "the innovative musician"—Satie. He did, however, contrast the "realism" claimed by Cocteau, in his wish to convey the sonorous and visual climate of large cities, with "a kind of sur-realism"—a term invented for the occasion, in order to describe this attempt at total art, the first in the history of the "new spirit."

Although Cocteau had let Apollinaire know, by letter, that his pride was so strong that it stretched to humility, Apollinaire's text wounded him. Cocteau's mistake was being unaware that Apollinaire, who was determined to remain the central figure of the "new spirit," had reason to fear that *Parade*, coming first, might overshadow his own *Mamelles de Tirésias*. The aesthetics of Apollinaire's creation were similar, and it was going to be performed a month later. (Apollinaire would also describe his own work as "surrealist," this time without a hyphen.) The blow was so harsh that Cocteau was reduced to writing to him: "If even a man like you cannot distinguish my profound depths, then no one will ever do so."[42] In a bitter epilogue, Apollinaire then tried to have Satie set to music his *Mamelles*, already thirteen years old, all while showering praises on Massine in the hope that Diaghilev would eventually draw a ballet from it. Since Apollinaire was also a victim of the moods of the solitary Satie, he would finally have to ask Cocteau to persuade the musician to look kindly on him; with this in mind, Apollinaire commissioned a poem from Cocteau that he would integrate into the program of the *Mamelles*. The poem was eventually titled "Zèbre," which would irritate the Cubist "tribunal" by its play on words.[43]

Already Satie had begun composing a *Vie de Socrate* in the company of a librettist whom he deemed much more accommodating than Cocteau: the late Plato. So much for friendship in the paradise of the arts.

THE "SCANDAL"

Parade didn't look very promising: the Left suspected Cocteau of being an arriviste fraud, while the Right held Satie as a shirker and Picasso as a swindler.

A technical incident on the night of the final rehearsal forced the librettist and Diaghilev, at the last moment, to get rid of the third "businessman," a "black" puppet that kept falling from the canvas horse it was riding, through a scene of magnificent dreamlike languor. Cocteau had made it look startling—the animal's rump leading its own autonomous, joyful life, like the "horse of Fantomas' fiacre" getting rid of its shoes in fits and starts.

So when Cocteau attended the premiere on May 18, it was a performance shorn of his dialogues, his "captions," and his choreographic highlights. Welcomed in the foyer of the Châtelet by Misia (the erstwhile aborter of the project), who was dressed for the occasion like the mother of the bride, Cocteau joined three thousand spectators who invaded the orchestra, boxes, and balconies, with season subscribers and snobs intermingling, from the Princesse de Polignac to the Comtesse de Chevigné. Since *Parade* was the first creation of the Ballets Russes in two years, and the most ambitious since the dismissal of Nijinsky, Diaghilev had taken care, this time, to mobilize a "claque" led by Apollinaire and Pierre Albert-Birot, the publisher of *Nord-Sud*, the avant-garde review. The tension was palpable, since the Ballets Russes had aroused indignation a week earlier by, at the end of a repeat performance of *Firebird*, making a "muzhik" brandish the red flag of the Soviets who were demanding a separate peace with Germany. The failed French Nivelle Offensive had, in just two weeks, led to 140,000 *poilus* being killed or wounded on the Chemin des Dames—a number never previously reached. By placing Paris in danger, the massacre had awakened the patriotic ardor of spectators whose plush seats were just 125 miles from the front.

In his program, Apollinaire spoke of a music so clean and simple that one could "recognize the wonderfully lucid spirit of France." Cocteau had taken care to publish that same morning in *L'excelsior* an article emphasizing the patriotic virtues of the libretto as well as the winning card in such a conflict— laughter—which he described as a truly "homegrown" exercise and a Latin weapon destined to fight "heavy German aestheticism."[44] The manager of the theater had also been careful to announce that the profits would be donated to works for the wounded, with Diaghilev filling the amphitheater with "muzhiks" in uniform, sent from the Russian brigade in Champagne, and with a "ballet corps on duty," in order to make sure that the red flag of the defeatists would be forgotten.[45]

Picasso's immense opening curtain was well received. With its crimson folds and animals, its acrobat and clown, its turbaned black man and its guitar-playing picador, the huge painted canvas evoked the slightly melancholy freshness of fairground spectacles, and so reassured, by its nicely narrative aspect, those who were just discovering the work of the Spaniard. (Picasso's works, absent from the salons, were really only sold abroad, via the German-Jewish dealer Kahnweiler—a sensitive detail at the time.) Yet this curtain, which appeared as old-fashioned as a slipcover—Bakst himself would speak of a curtain that was "backward-looking by design"—perplexed Picasso's "old" supporters by its naturalism, which made it seem much closer to Manet's *Déjeuner sur l'herbe* and Seurat's equestrians than Kandinsky's prodigious abstract symphonies.

The dance of the French "businessman," dressed in knee breeches and stockings, carrying a pipe and an ancien régime cane; the delicate maneuverings of the Chinese magician, worthy of the Royal Khmer ballet; the exuberant movements of the little American girl and the couple of acrobats, were all well received. The handsome Massine charmed the audience, pulling an egg from his braid and finding it at the tip of his sandal after its digestion, and they liked when Marie Chabelska—the American girl in her navy-blue pleated skirt— shot the invisible pickpocket. This actualization of puppet theater and circus, which stressed the pathetic gaiety of fairground crowds and had playful, child-like qualities, was sure to charm.

The arrival of the American "businessman" stuffed into his ten-foot-tall card-board costume annoyed people greatly: brandishing a megaphone and firing gunshots, this caricature in a red shirt and cowboy chaps looked like a stovepipe carrying some skyscrapers on its shoulders. The Cubist stage curtain, with its brutal geometry; the loud volley of the four Underwood typewriters marking the return of Marie Chabelska as an American typist, who was supposed to start up an automobile with an imaginary crank, finally stirred up the vague hostility against "boche" Kubism. Copiously booed, the little Russian dancer ran crying into the wings and returned only under Massine's threats of punishment. A final robotic dance with the national "businessman" was deemed "outrageously" grotesque for French taste, as were the out-of-the-blue sounds—roulette wheel, foghorn, fire siren—that these practical jokers wanted to pass off as music, when they had really just emerged from a contrivance that Cocteau had exhumed from the wings of the Châtelet.[46] "This revolutionary art should be reserved for Red Russia, if it can accommodate itself to it," noted the critic from the *Carnet de la semaine*.[47]

Did the huge bodies of the "businessmen" symbolize the mechanization of modern life, and their superhuman gestures, warlike barbarism? Picasso and Cocteau had agreed to say that *Parade* meant nothing, but the offhanded attitude of this innocence, at a time when thousands of families were mourning a son or a brother, was even more shocking than enemy flags. These puppets

moving about in the void, this "studio farce" that once again claimed to revolutionize art, this dauber's hasty sketch executed to fanfare tunes . . . it was making
fun of the audience. A simple parade, when the country was partly occupied,
with Champagne and then Paris daily threatened with invasion, seemed grossly
out of step. "Is that what French art is?" an indignant woman exclaimed.
"Indeed it is," Apollinaire replied, smiling. This war that Cocteau had already
stopped thinking about continued to haunt the public so much that just a few
months earlier, passengers on a crowded trolley, seeing an "artist" catch up to
them at a run, had reproached his presence and had watched as the ticket
collector shouted, "Get out, draft-dodger!," smacking him with her metal ticket
carrier. The events of that day would be supported by the first general assembly
of the National League against Draft-Dodgers. And what else but draft-dodgers
were these Cocteaus, these Picassos, these Saties, who were composing
gibberish while brave *poilus* were enduring the horror of the trenches for the
third consecutive year?

The actors on the stage began to be ignored in the hall, already informed by
the press of jokes about the war of the Montparnos. Hostility gained ground
when the horse kicking its legs, which Picasso had burdened with an African
mask, entered the stage. Patriotism began to shout out—"Long live France!"
"Cocorico!"—while hisses and applause converged on the "flushed" figure of
Gaston Gallimard, who had been targeted as director of the *Nouvelle revue
française*.[48] "Make him leave, in the name of French art!—In the name of all
art!—Send him to the trenches!" One spectator asked for the rowdies to be
thrown out, but his neighbor reproached him for not having a French accent,
setting off an avalanche of "Boches!," "Deserters!," and "Curtain!" According to
Cocteau, the virulence of the shouts made Diaghilev think that a huge chande-
lier was crashing down.

With time, the librettist of *Parade* would turn the spectacle into myth. As
Cocteau was on his way to join Satie and Picasso in the boxes, a singer cried out,
through the halls of the Châtelet: "There's one." Then, as Cocteau retold the
tale, that "veritable Gorgon" would have thrown her hatpin in his eye "if her
husband hadn't pulled her by the skirt" and if Apollinaire hadn't made his body
into a shield, with his uniform, war medal, and bandaged head.[49] The hall
seemed full of all the problems that Misia, Satie, Picasso, Diaghilev, and
Apollinaire had caused Cocteau; the infernal intrigues that had surrounded the
birth of his ballet, now reintroduced in the form of catcalls, fed the audience's
very real incomprehension. Four decades later, it would be not just an isolated
singer, but rather a pool of furies demanding his death. Since his influence kept
increasing, Cocteau could sustain his grandiloquent version of the facts to the

last witnesses. *Parade* did indeed introduce the violence of the conflict to Parisian theaters, and set off the fury of patriots; but it was excessive to give it more importance than Verdun, or to describe it as "the greatest battle in the war."

From reading certain critics of the time, including Amédée Ozenfant, we can soon discern a mixture of outraged hostility and amused connivance, with some of the audience wanting to see in *Parade* a sophisticated opportunity to laugh, "a music-hall spectacle for distinguished people in the vanguard of the most advanced *bon ton*."[50] "Much applause and a few boos," noted Morand, who—out of natural aloofness?—seemed not really to have witnessed a plot against the ballet.[51] This reaction by some audience members, which is understandable given the joint desire of Picasso and Satie to remove any pretension from the spectacle, as well as Diaghilev's wish, for his first collaboration with the Parisian avant-garde, to stress its humor more than its dogmatic severity, was not without its paternalism. Cocteau did not conceal his desire in *Parade* to display the melancholy of this human-puppet theater "under the thick wrapping of clowns." On this point, he was not at all understood. Didn't he hear a woman cry out, "If I had known it was so stupid, I'd have brought the children!"[52] In the end, *Parade* satisfied absolutely no one. Caught between the traditional grace of the music hall and the subversive radicality of the ateliers, the ballet passed for a compromise among Cubism, carnival poetry, and naturalism. Warning spectators that they would be surprised, "but in the most pleasant way, and charmed," Apollinaire had clearly indicated the limits of the project, which obviously deserved better than the articles denouncing it as a "farce of spiritual daubers" featuring a "scarcely picturesque" ugliness, "simpleminded ravings," and from its librettist, "erotic hysteria."[53] It came as no surprise, then, that these insults led to a total collapse of ticket sales, then to the closing of the production. As Morand wrote only ten days after the final dress rehearsal, "the authors of *Parade* are desperate."

The press didn't merely attack the silliness of the librettist, or the "geometric scribbling" and "picassotises" of the painter, who had been stigmatized for ten years as the demiurge of Cubism.[54] It also, and especially, denounced the "sinister buffoonery" of Satie, that "typewriter and rattle composer," that "inharmonious crank." Called a cacophonist and ranked lower than a player of "the Senegalese tam-tam"—everything he had feared ever since Cocteau had imposed those sounds on him—Satie went into a Homeric rage when he discovered the review by Jean Poueigh, a critic who had dared to congratulate him in person at the premiere but who didn't hesitate, in his paper, to speak of Satie's music as "outrageous" to French taste.[55] A hail of open letters rained down on the critic who had the misfortune of being a composer too: "You are an asshole—if I dare say it, an 'asshole' with no music," Satie insulted him, in clear allusion to the "melodies" of the very popular Pétomane, who made his farts resound throughout the Parisian stages.[56] Then Satie added, "Never again hold out your bastard's hand to me." Although Poueigh had also stigmatized the triviality and remarkable silliness of his libretto, Cocteau managed to reason with Satie, and the missive that the critic received, four days later, already seemed more serene. "You're not as much of an 'asshole' as I thought . . . Despite your stupid looks and low view, you see things from afar," Satie granted, in his inimitable tone of sincerity. Again refusing to reply, Poueigh was named "chief of blockheads and dolts" in a final postcard sent from Fontainebleau: "Evil asshole, I am here, and from here I tell you with all my might to go fuck yourself."[57]

This time the critic was outraged by this note, which his own concierge could read. He brought action for slander and asked for a prison sentence, along with damages.

RETREAT

At the trial, Théry, the journalist's lawyer, presented Satie as an absurd old man, and his client as an honest man who had been permanently wounded. Since Théry was a friend of Apollinaire's, whom he had defended in the affair of the statuettes stolen from the Louvre, in which Picasso had also been involved, Satie thought he could count on Apollinaire.[58] Did the poet with the bandaged head remember then that "Monsieur le Pauvre" had refused to set his *Mamelles* to music? In any case, Apollinaire was content to write to Cocteau and express his surprise at seeing "the critics robbing those they had tried to kill," rather than travel to court to support him.[59] Satie found himself alone facing the judge.

Fined a thousand francs and given eight days in prison, the musician appealed, but only to have his sentence confirmed. Outraged by the "ferocious joy" of Théry's pleading against Cubism, Cocteau accused him of being in the pay of the conservative gallery owners, and spoke of "smashing the face of that c—— in." The lawyer lost his head and Cocteau's barrage became physical: "White with rage under the artificial ochre of his cheeks," Cocteau was already slapping Théry—others saw him raise his cane against him—when a commissioner of police intervened. Unceremoniously taken hold of by the guards, led to the court's police station in the basements of the Conciergerie for questioning, Cocteau owed his salvation only to the intervention of Satie, who had come to plead indulgence for him with all the humility he could muster.

The fact remained, however, that the musician had to sleep at the Santé prison. This fact led to the loss of not only the little reputation that he still had, but also the possibility of being played in a nationally supported theater, and even the ability to travel abroad—not to mention his students in Arcueil from whom he made his living by teaching piano. This time no one was laughing.

Cocteau mobilized his mother, who played on the sympathies of her literary relations, including Misia. The "kill-all mother" launched a petition that obtained a suspension of the sentence, provided the musician showed proof of good conduct for five years. Threatened in turn with a trial by Poueigh, Cocteau hired the famous Maitre Henri-Robert as his lawyer—the lawyer of lost causes, as Morand said—and "another martyr to Cubism," Princesse Soutzo joked, learning that Cocteau risked six months in prison.[60] All the cream of society watched with consternation as its former favorite threw himself into the melee, attacked the stupidity of the public, and compared this fourteen-minute ballet to the "battle" of Hugo's *Hernani*.[61] The avant-garde was condemned to solidarity with this unexpected victim of bourgeois justice, but the Right Bank was openly hostile to this traitor. "Enter, triumphant one!," the pretty Cécile Sorel exclaimed ironically, receiving Cocteau for dinner and seating him next to a journalist who had just called *Parade* "pretentious inanity."

Did Cocteau feed his pride on the insults, as these escapees from the prewar period thought? He seemed rather to have been wounded by them, judging from his cancellation of his subscription to *L'argus*, by which he learned all the press said about him. His mother had made him a wunderkind who could draw, paint, sing, play the piano, write, and dance—and he could not understand that his society could treat him in any other way. But society wanted to see, in the desperate effort of the magicians and acrobats in *Parade* to introduce the audience to the profundity of their art, an allegory for the fate of this turncoat, who had been passionate about the theater since forever but who had once again failed to draw the crowds. Unlike Picasso, who never asked for anything, Cocteau was always concerned to appease his rivals, if not his enemies; this time he had to admit that fame bore its share of obligatory hatred.

While Marie Chabelska also suffered from the hisses—"she made many signs of the cross . . . and cried a lot," Cocteau said—Satie had the sad consolation of seeing his notoriety grow with his trial, and young musicians like Auric and Honegger rally to his cause.[62] The valiant Cocteau was called "dear beloved son," the successoral equal to Valentine, and received this certificate of recognition from Satie, at once sincere and mocking, signed "Crâne-Poli": "Good Black Old Man. You, good heart all white. Me love you."[63] This euphoria was soon tempered by the financial consequences of the public failure of *Parade*, which forced the composer to beg Valentine, a year later, to find him a job, "however small"—even as a factory supervisor if necessary.

Familiar now with Parisian crowds, Picasso by contrast saw his standing take off. Finally exhibited next to Matisse by Paul Guillaume, he became the exemplary painter—for Paris, for Europe, and finally, for the world. Having reached what in the physics of solids is called escape velocity, beyond which a body escapes all form of attraction, he held himself above all criticism: he had just won forever his right to use simultaneously many rival aesthetics, going against a Cubist dogma that would never recover from this, as well as to earn as much money as he wanted, putting an end to the "misérabiliste" attitude of bohemia, as well as to his post-Romanticism as a "maudit." "He's a clever man who uses people, beneath his straightforward air of Montmartre dauber," said Jacques-Émile Blanche. He used Cocteau."[64] Although Cocteau would acknowledge all the spectacle owed to the painter, he would also reproach him for having, with his "fierce, unkempt, vulgar, flashy" "businessmen," taken all the credit from him. He was also angry at Satie for having forced him to get rid of some of his "sounds," if not for being responsible for the breakdown of the compressed air machine, which had made the remaining sounds almost inaudible. "Our *Parade* was so far from what I would have wanted," he would confess in *Le coq et l'arlequin*, "that I never went to see it again in the theater."

Cocteau was never able to stomach these mutilations. Scarcely had Diaghilev mentioned reviving the ballet, three years later, than Cocteau went to work trying to bring back in all his sounds, while Satie worked, with apparently greater composure, to eliminate them once and for all. Since Diaghilev seemed more inclined to satisfy the demands of the librettist, the temperature began to rise again. "The orchestra in *Parade* is a musical background for noises," Cocteau declared, repeating verbatim the ironic statements with which Satie thought he could pacify him in 1917, and going so far as to claim, in front of Massine, that he had dictated, note by note, *his* music to Satie. "He takes us down so much, Picasso and me, that I'm quite done in," the composer confided to his "old" friend Valentine. "With him it's a mania, *Parade* is by him 'alone.' I wouldn't mind that," Satie added, with his special sense of derision: "Cocteau has also written little melodies that I had the nerve to sign."[65] The disagreement remained intact between Satie and Cocteau, whom the composer would call an "adorable maniac"—and it took one to know one. When Gide met Cocteau in the wings, he found him "older, tenser, pained." He also confirmed the violence of his wish for reappropriation: "He is well aware of the fact that Picasso created the sets and costumes, and that Satie created the music, but he suspects he himself may have created Picasso and Satie."[66] One couldn't do a better job of describing the strange identitarian alchemy animating the character named Jean Cocteau.[67]

He wouldn't have to complain about *Parade*, though. Managing finally to "astonish" Diaghilev, as well as earn the heartfelt congratulations of Stravinsky, the ballet avenged the double failure of *Le dieu bleu* and *David*. The sachems of the avant-garde would stop calling him an impostor, and the big shots at the *Nouvelle revue française* would stop scorning him—although their reservations would again make him fire off a few shafts against those bees "making floor wax." The doors of the prestigious journal *Nord-Sud* opened to the "anti-poet" whom Reverdy had battled, so Cocteau could tell his story about the genesis of *his* ballet.[68] Cocteau's poems, along with poems by Apollinaire, Max Jacob, and Blaise Cendrars, were read at a concert given in homage to *Parade*, three weeks after the dress rehearsal, one of those "Lyre et Palette" soirées of which Cocteau became a pillar, to the great displeasure of Jacques-Émile Blanche, who saw in them only "Cubist fetuses" and show-off poseurs from the studios.

Cocteau's transformation seemed finally under way. Adam had pulled from his side a new version of himself, one more modern, more honest, not to say brutal. The operation had been painful, but both men were doing rather well, and showed their pride at having linked their names to those of Apollinaire, Picasso, and Satie—the ultimate achievement for a poet who knew nothing whatever of their work only four years before. Proust was the first, with his deep empathy, to perceive all the importance of this change:

> I cannot convey to you enough my joy at this profound effect your ballet is having. It would be very unworthy of you and your collaborators to speak of "success." And yet as inexplicable as it seems, it also exists, and it is so great! You must not look down on it when it is merely, as in this case, an anticipation, a propitious "aura," emanating from the Future.[69]

A model for all the avant-garde ballets of the 1920s, and even for some American musical comedies, *Parade* would in the end have considerable importance.[70] "Everything that is now current in ballet was invented by Cocteau for *Parade*, each step of which Cocteau had suggested, and which he knew by heart," Lifar wrote in *Serge de Diaghilev*. For the first time, daily reality was danced, and modern life, with its ubiquitous advertisements, was shown on the stage. Ballet sets had until then only been representational and in the background; in the future, choreographers would amuse themselves by moving them around, like costumes, to make them play an active role. If Cocteau was not one of the authentic progenitors of the twentieth century, he certainly triumphed now as one of its obstetricians, by offering the Ballets Russes their first entirely modern and European spectacle.

Suddenly placed back in the saddle, the manager Diaghilev got closer to the painters of the Paris school and now made use of its musicians, when they were not Russian, in the entourage of Cocteau and Satie: he was just as flexible as *Jeanchik* in this way that he managed to keep himself in the avant-garde, which would always be obliged to him for providing a fresh scandal. Rarely staged again, their ballet has since escaped the fate of Satie's most beautiful pieces, which have become musical clichés.[71] Less a masterpiece than a crossroads of works, marked by its promises almost more than by its obvious reality, *Parade* announced to the "great" public the aesthetic death of the interminable nineteenth century. The graybeards had still been able to marginalize the "obscene" work of Rodin and chase from the salons the too "prosaic" canvases of the Impressionists: from now on the avant-garde would give the tone to the century. *Parade* was not as important as Verdun, and its musical score was not the most revolutionary of the century, but the echo it produced was as great as the scandal of *Le sacre du printemps*.

LE CAP DE BONNE-ESPÉRANCE

The war went on forever. Coal, metal, electricity, gas, and paper were all rationed: Paris spent its nights in darkness, with no paper to read or music to listen to. The thousandth day of the conflict had already gone by and the dead numbered in the millions. Pacifism gained more followers, leading to cascading mutinies that rekindled indignation on the home front. Anti-Boche sentiment surged stronger than ever—rumor had it that little Germans were being born without fingernails, for lack of mother's milk. This suicidal conflict seemed like it would never stop when, in June 1917, the first American troops disembarked.

But the tragic war was already no more than a literary topic for Cocteau. *Le Cap de Bonne-Espérance* was going well: decanted, then filtered, Cocteau's experience at the front was transformed into poetic material. His concern for sparseness and directness could not, however, prevent images from returning in force: the arrival in the trenches of tanks was represented by a safe falling from the sixth floor and landing on its hind feet; rails and locomotives clashed to make "metal children." More than a hymn to technology and modernity, or a simple apology for vertigo and speed, *Le Cap* aimed to be the legend of a man seeking to conquer gravity and reach the clouds. The Futurists were singing of the pure force of propellers and engines, the Cubists of the abstract beauty of pipes and guitars: as a modern intercessor between heaven and humans, Roland

Garros, the hero who was still a prisoner of the Germans, looked something like a metal angel. Half a century later, Yuri Gagarin would return from his orbit in space to announce triumphantly that God does not exist; but if Cocteau followed Garros, it was with the secret hope of meeting one of God's envoys.

So it was another web of images of Symbolist origin that Cocteau was weaving, in this poem where all the themes that would shape his work lie in latent form. Here Garros's plane is a bird suffering in flight and once on land, is like an amputee. It's also an apprentice deity that seeks, in leather helmet and insect goggles, to cross the heavenly cape, just as its author dreamed of rounding the one that would make him once and for all a modern figure. Cocteau's first wish had even been to make Garros's flights mythic, to make him into a Jupiter who had come to abduct, in the form of a steel eagle, a kind of modern Ganymede convinced (as Cocteau himself would say in *Le discours du grand sommeil*) that he was not made for the earth. Spokesman of technology, Cocteau was still, partly unaware, floating around the Olympus where Anna de Noailles had held court—he whose dream was to be able to observe people without being seen, with the impervious omnipotence of angels.

These literary contradictions were probably inevitable. After years of Symbolist impregnation, when he had thought himself "divine" in all disciplines, Cocteau could not change overnight into a simple lover of steel, and even less make fun of the haven of art, like a Duchamp exhibiting an authentic new urinal or an ordinary restaurant hat stand. His joy in flying and his voyeur's delights hid a desire to possess all secrets, but also an oceanic thirst to be loved, and no simple airplane cabin would have sufficed.[72] Cocteau's aesthetic ambiguity was coupled with a social balancing act that saw him leaving a lunch at the home of the Princesse Murat for a drink at the home of Modigliani. Now both banks of Paris were indispensable to Cocteau's existence, even though they themselves were determined to remain irreconcilable. "He has a need to please everyone, at the same time—Picasso, Mme de Chevigné, the marines, etc. To waste his finest years pleasing people, instead of trying to displease," Misia Sert grumbled.[73]

It was in fact a feverish campaign that Cocteau was leading, in order to prepare for the Parisian publication of this poem that, in his eyes, marked his actual entrance into poetry. He inaugurated it, when he returned from the front, with a reading at the home of the Beaumonts in the presence of Anna de Noailles and some idols from his youth, including the novelist Paul Adam and the mathematician Paul Painlevé, whom his first collections had impressed. The audience was troubled by his ragged "verses," full of ads for KUB bouillon, BYRRH aperitif, and LE PETIT JOURNAL; they could no longer recognize the author whom they had applauded before the war. Mme Cocteau was the first to be confused, suddenly aware that after "that," her son could never be a member of the Académie.

Far from weakening, Cocteau had gotten it into his head to convert his old supporters to his new cause. "All of Paris is working on the *Cape*," he had declared to Gautier-Vignal, Proust's friend, saying that Mme de Chevigné herself was having textual explanations made for her. Since these study groups were not enough, protests had increased, with Anna de Noailles herself accusing him openly of ingratitude and plagiarism—probably because she was in fact no longer the one he was copying—and Misia pitying him for having to rehabilitate himself constantly, for having denied everyone. "You must coincide or commit suicide," Cocteau was content to reply to them, and that was all too obvious: if he had continued to write as before, he would surely be just as forgotten today as Anna de Noailles, Catulle Mendès, or the late Parnassians who had served as models for him.[74] Proust himself had indirectly noted the healthy aspect of his transformation, pointing out to him, "You have (like people who made automobiles before the war and now make airplanes or bombs) adapted your words."[75]

Crowned by the "success" of *Parade*, Cocteau had in the meantime decided only to read his poem—or "interpret" it rather—in front of listeners open to modern theses. It was in the apartment of Paul Morand, at the Palais-Royal, that he introduced this new series of readings, on June 15, 1917, at ten o'clock at night. Proust, his relations strained with the writer-diplomat Morand, but probably also appalled by the efforts that the Comtesse de Chevigné had made to understand *Le Cap* when she had showed herself to be so intolerant of his own approach, cancelled once again, to the fury of Cocteau, who had pestered him to come.[76]

The heat was stifling—not a breath of air, not a sound—when Cocteau, standing in the gleam of a lamp, opened the notebook covered with his large purple writing. His calm, his bearing, and his gravity struck all those who, not having seen him since the war, knew only the "prince frivole." His new style was disconcerting. Morand wrote:

> We have difficulty following the image [of the] machine-gun; then a beautiful piece on the hangars, another on the Marne, with Garros' final flight, from Fréjus to Tunis. Those last two pieces, the best in the poem, very short, without metaphors, silences that are like holes in the air.[77]

They could sense that Cocteau was trying to talk about himself under the guise of these aerial images, but the ease with which this "self" kept changing was unsettling. The explanations he gave to the skeptics were so eloquent, however, that he gained back some territory. It was "impossible to resist him," noted Jacques Porel, who still couldn't manage to overcome the unease caused by this dry, nervous, corrosive poetry.[78] And Roger Lannes found "lyricism in the ether." But didn't Cocteau want precisely to suggest, through this patchwork, his own internal imbalance?

He was not discouraged. Convinced that he alone could give a superior life to his poem, thanks to the powers his voice possessed, he planned new reading sessions. "More than anyone else, [he] had the sensation of being surrounded by his soul, as Proust said, and he was almost carried away by a constant impetus to surpass it," one witness said.[79] His person was at stake, in *Le Cap*, and it was this person he had to make seen and known. On August 4, still in the same building as the Palais-Royal, where Valentine Gross had just wallpapered the studio she had moved into with wax wrapping paper and American flags, a small group took their places in the gleam of a gas lamp that lit Valentine's doll-face from below. Again they awaited Proust's arrival, but after an hour Cocteau resigned himself to starting without him. Facing the portrait that Thévenaz had made of him, he stood in front of a very learned audience including Gaston Gallimard with the *Nouvelle revue française* to Valery Larbaud, author of *Barnabooth*. Cocteau had never looked so tense or troubled—and with good reason, for in fact the publisher would reject *Le Cap*.

Suddenly, at midnight, Proust finally arrived, with a naturalness bordering on off-handedness. "Get out, Marcel, you're spoiling my reading!" shouted Cocteau, with a virulence unusual for him. Then followed a cycle of letters and protests, reproaches and justifications, at the end of which Proust would accuse Cocteau "of being, beneath all the appearances of a young poet, an old dandy like Montesquiou."[80] That was striking where it hurt. Proust then confided to a friend: "If I had Jean's talent—something I'd like very much—I don't think I'd attach any importance to my work, and even less to its reading."[81] Did admiration have the upper hand over scorn, in this remark? Cocteau might doubt it—he who had devoted so many hours to listening to Proust read to him incomprehensible fragments of the *Recherche*. It is true that other people tended to become unreal in Proust's eyes—his friends especially, who made the mistake of trying to encroach on the time that Proust was devoting to the only reality still existent in his eyes. Proust, who compared friendship "to the error of a madman who thought the furniture was alive and chatted with it," had nothing more to give except to his work: a piece of furniture is what Cocteau had become, in the forever wounded heart and oversaturated brain of "petit Marcel."

There was a fourth session on August 13, on the rue d'Anjou. Never neutral, Mauriac noted the "admirable art" with which, after claiming his poem lost something from being heard, Cocteau set it to voice, in front of socialites shouting, "It's the poem of the era!" and in the presence of a "deadpan Picasso who couldn't care less."[82] Valentine hosted another, fifth, reading, on August 15, but nobody knows if her guests were receptive to the "I have trouble being a man" message that the author of the work confided. Finally, on December 3, Cocteau took out his notebook in front of a group including the actor Pierre Bertin and the painter André Lhote, two friends he could take for granted. This time the reception was good—Cocteau read so well! Misia even revealed herself to be somewhat receptive—out of indifference to poetry, suggested Jean Hugo. Meeting (despite everything) the cold gaze of a young soldier of the medical corps, Cocteau turned confidently to him and ventured, "It's very beautiful, don't you think?" But the aquiline mask of the young medic did not bat an eyelid and Cocteau, realizing what reprobation this silence was pregnant with, thought it good to reply in his place: "But . . . that's no longer what should be done." Cocteau then turned to Jean Hugo, the great-grandson of the author of *Les misérables*, and said, "It's too sublime, too Victor Hugo." Seeing the young soldier's haughty silhouette heading for the exit, Cocteau finally turned pale, not knowing he would find André Breton in his path again, throughout the rest of his life.[83]

Not accepting defeat, the author gathered his strength to give another "performance" in the mansion of the Beaumonts. There

> Jean standing in the middle of the big salon began declaiming, not as an actor coming forward, but as an aviator taking off from the ground . . .: he returned hedge-hopping, his lines crowded together, broke apart, then took flight again . . . and when he landed on earth, exhausted, we were mute.[84]

The response was complete incomprehension. "My little Jean, you are Voltaire," Beaumont ventured, to buck him up—a comparison that was so grotesque it made Cocteau break down in tears.

If there was one place that could grant legitimacy to such a work, it was the prestigious bookstore that Adrienne Monnier ran on rue de l'Odéon, where many actors, often affiliated with the *Nouvelle revue française*, were in the habit of gathering. Monnier, for example, would play a decisive role in the publication in France of Joyce's *Ulysses*. Cocteau managed to make the bookseller think that Gide had recommended his poem, whereas Gide, who had been disappointed in *Le Cap*, was persuaded that "la" Monnier was waiting impatiently for him to come to a reading of this same *Le Cap* in her bookstore. But here again, the most attentive ones ended up breathless from the virtuosity of a poet who, already on earth, ran faster than his reader, and who in the sky unfailingly left him behind. And the less attentive ones? They, like Adrienne Monnier, noted that his poetry was more perceptible in prose.

Cocteau continued to revise *Le Cap* until June 1918, when he submitted the text to its publisher, still the Sirène, which published 510 copies of it. Critics were tepid: some declared that they were incompetent to judge this "Cubist" prose, others placed it halfway to Symbolism, and then there was Marinetti, the leader of "Futurismo," who described Cocteau as a "collector of electro-chemical roses."[85] Sometimes Cocteau's syntactic innovations were compared to pidgin, or even animal cries; sometimes he was congratulated for having known *not* to compare Garros to Icarus—a cliché that still showed that the "man-bird" image was not so far from mind for the reader, given Cocteau's references to Minerva and Saint George. And at least one critic placed Cocteau at the extreme Left of "Cubism."[86]

Although Proust was absent for the third time from these readings, he finally did read *Le Cap*, which he admired even though he felt less enthusiastic about its repetitions and its blustery metaphors aroused reservations. But was Proust in the best position to judge new poetry? Proust preferred Helleu to Cézanne in painting, and Jacques-Émile Blanche over Degas.[87] "They were visions, brief flights, lightning-bolts of simultaneous things," the Abbé Mugnier said of the images in the poem.[88] He knew that Cocteau had long liked to identify with the telegraph, that central emitter of modern times, but the abbé himself understood nothing of this discharge of divorced words. Reverdy, from whom Cocteau had learned the art of using typographical blank spaces, could with some justice suspect him of using Garros's popularity to make his own work seem new and more appealing to the public. Didn't the author of *Le Cap* implicitly recognize his debt, by a very Apollinaire-like "O Tour Eiffel," to the first authors who had, along with Cendrars, tried to describe the new speed of reality in modern times?

The collection probably made the mistake of coming out five years too late, but it was also neither the most personal nor the most polished work by its author. Impatient to join the modern movement, but probably too impatient to accomplish his modernization in a profound way, Cocteau could indeed be content to make mincemeat of his poetic universe, and to "patch up Romanticism with telephone wire," as Jacques Vaché would reproach both him and Apollinaire for, in a letter to André Breton.[89] The failure—as much in form as in essence—probably also came from a lack of resolution. "People have written about the war, but the war hasn't yet written about people," Jacques Porel suggested.[90] That is, this collection evoked a conflict that was still killing people every day and that announced a new poetic style that Cocteau would abandon almost immediately as he continued to develop as a poet. "Once upon a time there was a chameleon. Its master, to keep it warm, placed it on a multicolored Scottish plaid. The chameleon died of fatigue," Cocteau wrote in *Le Potomak*: nothing could better describe the exhaustion that overwhelmed him then, or the anxiety he faced from the pitfalls of having such a variegated nature.

He wondered sometimes if he was too intelligent, or if maybe he was missing a set of those blinkers so useful for containing a creator within certain themes— his own blinkers, like those of Barrès, were obviously made of crystal. He worked relentlessly, but a bit in every direction at once, and without much revision, loving "too many things and people," as the libretto to *David* confessed.[91] Picasso needed no one, and everything worked out perfectly for him. But why did Cocteau, who had proven he could become anything, remain incapable of *being* Picasso? His spirit, the one that made him transform himself in just three years, suddenly seemed to make him turn against himself: "If I were listening to myself, I would burn *Potomak* and *Cape of Good Hope*," he wrote at the time to Apollinaire.[92] Aware at the same time that he could never go backward, he came to blame a nature whose strangeness disturbed everyone—Cocteau himself first of all. "I am doomed to solitude / I feel awkward everywhere," he acknowledged, unable to turn the page.[93] To Jacques-Émile Blanche, he confided the unease that would accompany him all his life: "There is no harbor that suits me. I 'cross.' I walk on."[94] Twentieth-century literature had just found its Wandering Jew.

When the war was over, Cocteau applied himself once again to *Le Cap*, aiming at a republication that would never occur. He even resumed a reading tour—reading aloud in January 1919 at the home of the Beaumonts, in front of Gide, Jacques-Émile Blanche, and the Princesse Soutzo, who had become the companion of Morand, and then, in April, in the gallery of Léonce Rosenberg, the godfather of Cubism. But no new opportunities resulted from his efforts. "The *Cape* has fallen from high up, straight down, and heavily," he wrote in February, still feeling the blow of this announced failure.[95] For the first time, Paris disgusted him. Too much touchiness, ingratitude, lack of enthusiasm, and love, and too many low blows—it was always struggling and never convincing. Discouragement overtook Cocteau at the mere mention of the enthusiasm that just five years earlier had met the slightest of his poems. Abel Bonnard, the salon poet whose early years Cocteau had eclipsed, was already comparing him to a torch that ignites to interest the world, and to "a butterfly that has singed itself on a lamp and that is dying on the tablecloth, while people continue to eat without seeing it."[96] In 1922, taking up his collection once again, Cocteau concluded a final preface with this troubling note: "If I had the courage, I would melt it down and pour it into alexandrines."[97] The circle was closed.

FRANCE'S ARIZONA

Finally rid of any military obligation, Cocteau left in August 1917 for Piquey, a hamlet in the Arcachon Basin known only to a few painters. He went to join André Lhote, a precocious and light Cubist whose *Escales*, lithographs showing sailors at a brothel, he was going to accompany with poems. A steamboat deposited him on a wild strip of land where, completely cut off from the world, a little wooden hotel with flowerbeds of mimosas scraped an existence. His beard grew out, his nails turned clawlike, his brain got fresh air. He rowed, rolled in the sand, walked alone in "American" landscapes, made candlesticks from cork debris, and shot a bird occasionally. Hay fever, which had spoiled all his vacations—Morand compared his sneezes to a railroad catastrophe—eased from contact with the iodine and sea breezes. The ocean, into which he dipped and dipped again—he would never really learn how to swim—turned into a miraculous pool.

Many people advised Cocteau against this stay, exaggerating his need for luxury and distraction. They weren't aware that Cocteau took on everything— society, poverty, solitude, comfort, and marginality—with the same passionate indifference.[98] Roman life had enchanted him during preparations for *Parade*, but the solitary laziness of Piquey agreed with him even more; happy to see swallows landing on his rifle, the town mouse watched himself turn dark from the sun "with a potter's interest," and found he was in sync with nature.[99] The sun, that "opium of healthy people," made him so thoroughly forget the disappointment of *Le Cap* that he came to adore it on all fours, like a premodern man. He slid, naked as Adam, between copses of cacti and rows of canoes, and gave in to the sensual pleasure that Paris had refused him. Piquey was the Arizona of the Westerns by day, the prehistoric planet by night. Water, sun, wind, pleasure . . . wasn't that how life had begun?

In the morning, he drifted on a sailboat in whose bow he abandoned himself to the sun; at noon, he ate under sweet-smelling fig trees; in the evening, he read in the shadow of a hut; and at night, he set out in a flat-bottomed *pinasse* to fish for red mullet in phosphorescent foam. Back at the hotel, he warmed his chapped hands over a fire crackling with driftwood—creating images in his mind from which his poems and letters would draw, even many years later. "Ovation of all things to the light," he wrote in *Le Cap*, invoking the Mediterranean; never had he felt less alone, or so strong, as when he faced the dazzling mass of the Atlantic. He was no longer a blue god or the young Septentrion dancing on the beach, but rather a thin, dry body that was storing its strength for winter, secreting its antidotes against Paris, making inner coal, as

he said, and changing his skin, which had been sensitized by his transformations, into tough leather. He forgot himself, to his great relief—as Nietzsche
claimed, men like nature because it holds no opinions about them. Cocteau
reread Nietzsche's books, which helped him to ignore the mediocrity of the
visitors with whom he was mixing. Some were surprised to see him writing
poems, knowing "you have to be dead to be a poet." His writings helped him
once again feel confident. Because he was far from Paris, his mother and his
friends, who were frequent victims of his emotional blackmail, grew less sensitive to his countless illnesses and thought of him as the sturdiest of them all. He
merged with these "Mexican" landscapes in front of which the future mural-
painter Diego Rivera painted his portrait—a dream setting, where nothing
reveals the era.

A few weeks without letters, however, would be enough to make this handsome exile become more fragile. Cocteau discovered that his friends were all
calmly pursuing their fates and soon got used to his departure, as if his absence
were relieving them of a heavy weight. Valentine, whom Cocteau once
described in a letter with the phrase "Heart of gold, tireless friend," especially
disappointed him by her silence; this lazy creature who never wrote was overwhelmed with his notes outlining wittily not only his existence as a primitive
being, but also his sadness at not being missed by anyone.[100] Unhappy when the
Comte de Beaumont threw in Cocteau's absence a big *nègre* party where
American soldiers played jazz—Cocteau thought he was now black enough to
form part of this band—he went back to work and took notes on Stravinsky,
D'Annunzio, and the Empress Eugénie.[101] Some of these he would include in
his *Portraits-souvenir*, but all awakened a thousand forgotten episodes of his
early days and his subsequent transformation.[102]

The invisible umbilical cord tying Cocteau to Paris began to tug again;
already the mention of the evenings he was missing made him miss the energy
he drew from the city, which was otherwise so polluting: "Take away the dung
heap, the rooster [*coq*] dies."[103] Cocteau, who dreamed of becoming "black,"
returned after two months of his solitary retreat to launch the fashion of the
suntan that, with the help of Coco Chanel, a young stylist whom he had met in
the wings of *Parade*, in the shadow of Misia, would conquer the aristocratic
model of paleness. When he confronted the skeptical faces of the Parisians,
however, he was overcome with disappointment. Caught up in celebrating new
names, the city no longer seemed to take an interest in him. One more month
and, assailed with neuritis, rheumatism, insomnia, toothaches, and dermatitis,
Cocteau gave himself over to Dr. Capmas, a semi-charlatan who, diagnosing
low blood pressure and weakened adrenal glands, prescribed a home cure for

him. "Wounded from cupping and needle pricks," Cocteau confided to his mother: "I feel as if I'm so little alive, except by an effort of will that no one in the world could guess in me, that I accept all his conditions."[104] That was the first confession of a physical weakness that Cocteau would fight with what little strength he had, and of a "difficulty of being" that would follow him to the grave.

His character became darker. Suffering from sluggish awakenings and recurrent eczema, he was also victim to fits of anxiety that he didn't know how to escape. While others criticized his poems, or cast doubts on the sincerity of his conversion to modernism, it was his entire person that he himself came to reject. He who loved happiness so much, who thought of himself as the equal of Sophocles, Alexander, or the Buddha, discovered disgust and self-hatred in the mirrors that surround solitude. Three months weren't even up before he returned to the Midi.

FROM ANGEL TO HERO

After his spectacular escape from Germany, Roland Garros quickly took to the air again, even though Cocteau and others begged him to stay on the ground. Aviation had evolved greatly during the years of his detention, and the ace was shot down on his third flight, on October 5, 1918, above the Ardennes massif. Found in the wreckage, his body was solemnly buried and his name celebrated throughout all of France, where it would bless stadiums and schools. Had he had time to read and annotate the proofs of *Le Cap* that Cocteau had sent to him and that lined his cabin, as Cocteau said, at the time of the accident? It only had to be possible for it to be probable, in Cocteau's eyes, who stayed faithful to the reflex that prevents children from distinguishing an action that could have happened from the one, scarcely more convincing, that actually took place. Wasn't it logical for Cocteau's ode to speed and steel to complete its fusion with the metal bird it exalted?[105]

Garros's death reminded Cocteau of the deadly risk every inventor takes, and every acrobat as well: this *"Cape,"* so poorly named *"of Good Hope,"* had just claimed its second victim. "He had to be consoled and almost reanimated," according to Bernard Faÿ. But then Cocteau received this long letter of condolence from Proust: "My consolation is to think that you will have the sweetness, you who loved him so, of having fixed him in your verses forever in a heaven where there are no more falls and where human names remain like those of the stars."[106] Confessing that he had always avoided approaching the aviator, from fear of being disliked by Cocteau—a trait that was aimed only at his own jealousy—the author of the *Recherche* eventually asked Cocteau if Garros had gotten wind of details about the death of Agostinelli, his chauffeur. Proust had been so much in love with Agostinelli that he had offered him flying lessons, and even promised him his own plane, but the chauffeur had crashed a few weeks before the First World War, in circumstances that Proust was still trying to understand.[107]

On April 26, 1918, it was Jean Le Roy's turn to die, in Belgium, at the age of twenty-three. Cocteau had met him a year earlier through Apollinaire—his verses had been read on the rue Huyghens—and Le Roy had been writing to Cocteau nearly every day since Christmas. He was a delicate boy, enduring a martyrdom in the mud of the trenches, among the frogs and drowned rats—and a promising writer, whom Cocteau was guiding in his studies and encouraging to observe a level of discipline that he himself sometimes found difficult to follow. Was Le Roy Cocteau's disciple or already his lover? From the way Cocteau talked about him to Gide, in whom he would often confide about his loves—"Le Roy whom I adored and for whom I was everything"—we would be inclined to guess that they were intimate, but the letters they left behind undermine that idea.[108]

This second death left Cocteau stunned. "I suffer from him like an amputee," he wrote to his mother, adding to the very young Georges Auric: "I rebel against this living death."[109] When they found in young Le Roy's bunks letters and poems that Apollinaire had sent him, and Cocteau learned that he would have to take them back to their author, he was overcome. He made of him an angel. Did this come from seeing the winged pilots carved on the top of graves in the cemeteries, or was it a way of sublimating his desires in his mother's eyes? Whatever the reason, Le Roy became the prime hero held aloft in Cocteau's poetry. Young, handsome, good, brave, kind, and pure, Le Roy was portrayed as one of those poets who see through life, while life, out of an abundance of caution, rids itself of them early. Often glimpsed at the front, the kingdom of the dead opened up again for Cocteau. Remembering the suicide of his father, Cocteau had often "explored" this strange territory that Orpheus, in ancient times, had had the courage to confront—when he wasn't tempted to make the dead speak, through the many mediums who turned tables at that time, to place survivors in contact with their dead.

Cocteau had already been convinced, before Le Roy's death, that thunderbolts came from the immense invisible world surrounding us, and that we were just a minuscule part of this world; now his stormy perception saw in every lightning bolt a sign charged with omens. He had no trouble seeing, in the shell that had struck the young poet, an allegory for fate, as he had in the bullets that

had killed, the very day after his departure, some of the marines who had
adopted him in Coxyde. These repeated tragedies, and the "miracle" of not
being killed himself, pushed Cocteau to try his hand at the language of the
dead in use in the zone where these soldiers now "lived." This effort of identification led to "Visite," a brief prose poem in which Jean Le Roy leads Cocteau
to the underworld a few centuries after Orpheus, the poet from Thrace, had
traveled to the same kingdom in search of Eurydice.

For some days Cocteau tried to "live" the experience of his young, dead
friend—that is, without substance or heat. Becoming a pure envelope that had
just abandoned its body, he haunted the planet, passing through doors and
walls without letting himself be seen or heard. He felt the strange ease of one
swimming underwater, or letting himself be deformed by funhouse mirrors—
but also the secret guilt of one who is breaking a taboo and knows he is an
impostor among earthlings, an authentic and pitiful swindler of life. The
strength emanating from the dead man transmitted to him at the same time
inhuman messages, which he took under dictation. It was as if an Announcer
had awakened within him to make strings of verses emerge from his mouth.
Thus was born the angel of which Cocteau would make such great poetic
use—a terrible figure warning him that he would give birth "in sadness," and
spurred on by him, because he alone could deliver the printed, but scrambled,
text that preexisted in him.

"Visite" would be one of Cocteau's greatest poems. He was no longer
anxiously craving to be modern, but instead expressed from within his panicked
being a desire to pull down the invisible wall separating him not only from all
those he had lost, but also from living beings who were already turning away
from him: the fall of that wall would always be the final pride of his poetry.
More personal than *Le Cap de Bonne-Espérance*, more embodied too, the
Discours du grand sommeil, which he dedicated to Jean Le Roy and to which
"Visite" was added, harmoniously mingles elements of a war journal and a
chronicle of the self. In it, Cocteau did not describe the horrors of events at the
front, but rather that dreamlike place where the most confident men are
suddenly confronted with the anguish of dying and the urgency of existing—
Cocteau's daily lot. Less the hell of noise than the strange, insouciant silence
that precedes gunfire—the "calm sector." Not an account of the boredom, cold,
or blood, but instead an exploration of that redoubled life produced by the
multiplication of risks. A kind of super-life, without super-men.

Seven years of revision would remove all pathos and all patriotic posturing
from this collection, which would not be published until 1925, in *Poésies*. It
would go from the war of *Le Mot* to that of the soldiers who refused to fight in

1917, and from Marshal Foch's great army to the death factory, where the conquerors themselves were doomed to execration. Less picturesque and more desolate: that was now the moral state of the poet who would assert that he then understood that poetry was "a religion without hope" to which everything must be sacrificed—especially its facility.

THE SEASON OF WEDDINGS

In the spring of 1918, the war suddenly came close again. Three German offensives made Paris fear for itself anew. Shelled for months by the Big Bertha ambushed near Amiens, Parisians felt once again under seige. Sixty-five faithful had been killed in March in the nave of the Église Saint-Gervais, leading to the temporary closing of all churches and the celebration of first communions in the basement of the Bon Marché department store. By early June, the Germans were no more than forty miles away from the capital—exactly as in the summer of 1914.

On July 12, Picasso married Olga Koklova, in a Russian Orthodox ceremony held in the Russian church on the rue Daru. The union of a former Montmartre dauber and the daughter of a White Russian officer had all the trappings of a sacred rite: the dancer "picked up" in Rome and the painter finally in love seemed as if they were performing *Boris Godunov*. Cocteau, a witness for the bride who set a golden crown on her head during the ceremony, rejoiced: as a sponsor for the meeting between Picasso and Olga, via *Parade*, he was now rubbing elbows with Max Jacob and Apollinaire, witnesses for Picasso. Driving off in a coupé, after the banquet given by Misia at the Meurice, the couple spent their honeymoon in the sumptuous villa in Biarritz belonging to Eugenia Errazuriz, a rich Chilean woman whom Cocteau had introduced to them. Then they moved into a duplex on the rue La Boétie, near the rue d'Anjou, just above the gallery of Paul Rosenberg, who had just signed the painter to a contract. Picasso went over to the Right Bank with weapons and luggage: a capture of the Arcole Bridge in reverse, and a crossing that was much more successful than the one made in the other direction by Cocteau two years earlier.

Cocteau was already quite involved in this transfer; it was again he who would introduce Picasso to the balls of the Comte de Beaumont and would contribute, with the help of the bourgeois Olga, to changing the ways that Picasso dressed and socialized with friends. He would make the painter into an urban animal, someone happy to be seen with his wife who was impatient to lead this brilliant life that the Bolsheviks were demolishing in her own country.

Picasso never sent anything but telexes; though at least he sometimes took the initiative, along with Apollinaire, of adding to his few words a portrait of Apollinaire as an artilleryman or a Pope, or a caricature in pen of one of their friends. But it was in vain that Cocteau pursued Picasso with an assiduity in which admiration jostled with love, and identification with desire; in vain did he send him letters, drawings, and gifts, or pick pears for him in front of Cézanne's home, in Sainte-Victoire; answers remained rare. No matter, Olga liked Cocteau and always invited him to the rue La Boétie as part of her impatient efforts to make Picasso less bohemian; Max Jacob, by contrast, she thought too marginal.

Cocteau was convinced that Picasso brought him luck, like a talisman that gave him the strength he otherwise lacked. On one of the many days he felt sick, the painter finally sent him a very small dog cut out of cardboard with a curled-up tail and moving head: immediately he felt better. Like Petit-Cru, Iseult's fairy dog, this canine fetish seemed to symbolize, for Cocteau, Picasso's extraordinary abilities as a creator, as one of those "mother-men" about whom Nietzsche says escape all remorse and all criticism, since their fertility occupies their entire being. Yes, Picasso was a man and a woman at once, the furious bull and the "dancer" who wraps it in red, the sentimental mandolinist and the cold predator. This pairing was probably a quarrelsome one, but the two beings loved each other enough to mingle every night, so that every morning they could give birth to a new Pablo, one ready to demolish everything the old one had made the day before—a real phoenix of beauty.

Cocteau had known strong personalities but none of them, except perhaps Anna de Noailles, had given him the impression of being larger than life, greater than reality, like Picasso. A wild thing in the jungle of the studios, the Spaniard, from dawn to dusk, every day the good Lord made, had only to mark a piece of wood with cigarette burns to raise it to the rank of art: everything he imagined took shape that instant, without leaving the slightest remainder. Cocteau would never stop singing the praises of this tornado "transporting objects, like lightning, from one signification to another, crushing iron, tearing shapes apart, magnificently insulting the human face." Everywhere Cocteau went he celebrated this genius of destruction and rebirth, recovery and renovation, who was so talented at converting what was usually called "ugliness" into "beauty"—and vice versa. No one spoke with so much lyricism about this hand that threw "into the street" objects that were seen as museums' treasures, and that forced elements of the street, such as "posters, signs, graffiti," to enter one day into those same museums.[110] Only Picasso could give Cocteau strength and courage, when he lost his spirit; Picasso alone could be both dark and optimistic at the same time, never complaining, always moving forward. The more that reality stripped away from Cocteau his reasons to love himself, the more he found to admire in this *creator regnans*, this reigning creator whom he was beginning to think was infallible, like the kings of old. It was as if Picasso, in marriage, had placed a golden crown on the forehead of Cocteau.

On August 7, Cocteau was a witness again, with Satie this time, at the wedding of Valentine Gross. Satie, that solitary man from Arceuil who had confided four months earlier to Cocteau "I like salads, shit and fish," drank heavily with the meal, but everything went fine, except perhaps for Mme Cocteau.[111] She had given so many lunches where Valentine, not as fierce as she pretended, had played her role wonderfully, speaking here of her blue blood and there of her salon, that Mme Cocteau had finally imagined uniting Valentine with her own son.[112] She had even told her guests, upon seeing Valentine arrive wearing a long white veil, that she was hosting an engagement dinner.

It was indeed a Jean whom Valentine was marrying, but his last name was Hugo. With a constant suspicion of irony at his lips, with the charm and strangeness of those who are sure of themselves, Hugo, a friendly colossus with the profile of a virile goose—"very tall, very vast"—in Maurice Sachs's words, surprised people by his silences. He had grown up in Guernsey, where his great-grandfather was living out his exile, but as a painter produced only tiny works; his canvases were as small and colorful as the novelistic panoramas of his ancestor were somber and huge. ("The grandfather was fond of castles, the grandson prefers country villas," observed the Abbé Mugnier.) Cocteau right away liked the large, Jupiter-like eyes, "almost monstrous calm," and Eurasian smile of Hugo, who has left us the subtlest memoirs about the postwar period. "One is always sure of his indifference," said a woman whom Sachs would quote. But Jean Hugo was all kindness to Cocteau, who for his part treated Hugo almost like a brother—since Valentine remained in his eyes his chosen sister.

When Cocteau was again invited to a wedding—that of Darius Milhaud, in December—everyone knew there could no longer be a Parisian wedding without Cocteau as witness.

THE ARMISTICE

For two years, the war seemed to Cocteau to be occurring in another country. But in November, when the peace treaty signed by the Bolsheviks in Brest-Litovsk in March 1918 had allowed the Germans to concentrate their efforts on the western front, everything came to a head. On November 9, the abdication of Wilhelm II, the hated Kaiser (Guillaume II in French) was announced, and the Republic in Germany was established. That same day, Guillaume Apollinaire, suffering from an epidemic of Spanish influenza that would claim 300,000 victims in France and 25 million throughout the world—more than the war itself—was dying.

A thousand times Cocteau would describe the atrocious scene: the crowd shouting "A mort Guillaume!" and the poet, cloistered on the top floor of 202 boulevard Saint-Germain, looking on the rue Saint-Guillaume, misunderstanding, in his delirium, that these calls were for his own murder. It was a cruel end, at the young age of thirty-eight, for one who had fought so furiously, and whose skull still housed a German bullet. That morning, Picasso and Max Jacob had come to the rue d'Anjou to ask Cocteau to send to Apollinaire his Dr. Capmas, the doctor in whom Cocteau had such blind faith. But the doctor, whose advice was often harmful, could do nothing to help—both lungs were afflicted. Picasso, too grief-stricken to write the obituary, asked Cocteau to do it; Cocteau did so, giving the obituary to André Salmon before going to the boulevard Saint-Germain at nightfall, where Picasso was already watching over the corpse.

The lamp the painter held revealed features of rare delicacy, with a particularly calm, young expression. "He is as I knew him," murmured Picasso.[113] Cocteau agreed, scarcely able to believe in the death of this vivacious giant, who still received his "seer's" messages through his little leather helmet: "When he laughed, his hand in front of his mouth, like someone yawning, his entire being shook and became somehow disrupted. It took a long time for this little volcanic tremor to return to order, after which he resumed his bishop's mask."[114] But this body, heavy and light at once, "obese and full of luminous breath," stable as a hot-air balloon and fragile as a kite, was now nothing more than a mass of stiff flesh. Twenty times Cocteau would retell the scene, giving it always more brilliance, since the face of the dead man seemed, "by the magic of a candle, of twilight, and of silence," to rise up from its shroud and evoke "the cut-off head of Orpheus," the poet mutilated by the Furies. "The king is dead, long live the king!"

Just six months earlier, a radiant Apollinaire had thanked Cocteau for the stone Egyptian cat he had given Apollinaire in honor of his wedding to the young Jacqueline by writing this poem:

My dear Cocteau come see me
Now it's in the colonies
I'm there morning and evening

Protected by the gods of our Mauritanias

. . .

We'll talk about your plans
About Egypt or else Asia
And about all the gods, those subjects
Of us kings of poetry.[115]

In his impatience, Cocteau had interpreted these lines as a summons to "share the moral direction" of the "new spirit." But Apollinaire had meant only to promise him, for the Éditions de la Sirène, the "Petites merveilles de la guerre" and a collection of pamphlets that never saw the light of day. For lack of a real friendship, they had shared a few projects, two friends (to the point of jealousy) — Picasso and Le Roy — and a certain French lyricism fed by ritornellos, Ronsard's poems, and popular dances that the front had celebrated. "In his [Apollinaire's] war," Cocteau said, at the same time evoking his own war at least just as much, "sky-blue soldiers moved under clusters of stars, to the pretty fireworks of bombs." This time Apollinaire, the "perfect minstrel" who intoned his poems while writing them, the creator of French *lieder* whom Cocteau placed between Heine and Rilke, had ceased enchanting. "I picture him sunk into the void that he leaves," Cocteau said, when he inaugurated, fifty years later, a bust of Picasso paying homage to the man who in the meantime had become one of the most popular poets in the French language.[116]

With Apollinaire buried, Cocteau naturally took on the role of poet laureate that Picasso needed so sorely, and that Max Jacob had held in the beginning of the century, just before Apollinaire. He showered with prefaces, texts, and portraits that ogre who had already fed on the half-admiring, half-loving affection of Max Jacob, without giving him the essential thing. "Braque is the woman who loved me most," Picasso said, exaggerating his (sex) appeal and the feelings of the least suspicious of his friends.[117] By choosing Cocteau, he could ensure himself a passionate admirer. Who knows? Cocteau may also have allowed him to satisfy that abstract form of desire that fills certain women-loving men, when they can only manage to establish respectful, equal relationships with men. As Picasso himself asserted, "I have no real friends, I just have lovers."[118]

8

WITH RADIGUET

May you live during sensational times.
—*Ancient Chinese proverb*

THE WAR TO END ALL WARS AND *LE POTOMAK*

Then there was victory, with crowds dancing to the sound of accordions, children climbing trees, grandmothers waving banners—but also the return en masse of the crippled. Of every ten men of fighting age in 1914, two were dead and four disabled. Since most of the battles had taken place on national soil during those four disastrous years, 2,500 French towns had been destroyed: Reims, Verdun, Soisson, and others were all in ruins, and thousands of acres of land were now nothing but sterile fields harboring bombs, some of which would still be deadly almost a century later. All in all, 1.4 million Frenchmen had been killed. All of Europe was turned upside-down by this butchery. After the revolutionary putsch of October 1917 and the collapse of the Kaiser's troops, all the European empires had fallen, from the Russian to the German and from the Austro-Hungarian to the Ottoman—something that neither the French Revolution nor the Napoleonic Wars had been able to achieve. Only the English and Italian monarchies were still standing, with the republic imposing itself everywhere else in Europe, aside from the Balkans. The Spartacist movement was threatening Germany with another change of regime, the Russias were prey to civil war, and Bela Kun was getting ready to seize power in Hungary. Everywhere Communist parties were forming with the declared objective of bringing an end to the old world.

In France, it was the war itself that upset the social state of affairs. Ruined in large part by the collapse of the stock market, the social world that had been apotheosized by Proust—whose own portfolio had melted like snow in the sun—experienced a revolution. The Republic of dukes and bourgeois with double-barreled names gave way to one of the *nouveaux riches* born from the conflict, like the tank-maker Louis Renault, or the profiteers who knew, like Boussac, how to transform miles of military-surplus airplane canvas into shirts and luggage.[1] The war had already aged the learned assembly of bearded men of private means who controlled the institutions. Caught between the glittering memory of aristocratic debauchery and the radical hope the people were already beginning to feel, the elite of the Right Bank entertained only intermittently. The salons finally lost their prestige and dismissed their footmen—and then Proust relegated them forever to the attic of ridicule, via *Le temps retrouvé*, by peopling them in extremis with moldy grotesques and specters promenading their peroxided hairpieces and their smell of decay. A few months were enough to strip clean the cultural aura of the class that had dominated the century, of which the Lecomte-Cocteaus were a good example; Belle Époque Paris was sinking along with its jewels and its titles, with all the majesty of the *Titanic*.

As Paul Morand explained, "1914 was still 1900, and 1900 was still the Second Empire."[2] The twentieth century was brutally being born, after an endless pregnancy under Art Nouveau ivy. It was the end of the puns of the Almanach Vermot, of vaudeville songs and of frills, as well as prophetic beards, frock coats, and top hats (which were replaced by fedoras).[3] Sons of the aristocracy abandoned, with an emperor's stride, their fur capes, while the women, some of whom had become bomb makers during the conflict, left behind corsets and whalebone once and for all to cut their hair short, flapper-style, like Coco Chanel and Édith de Beaumont (according to Cocteau, their shorn hair, gathered by the paper *La presse*, was sold to benefit the disabled). The French then, just as they did fifty years later, used revolution as an excuse for new fashions.

Hookers gave way to young women free to go out at night, and the National Assembly granted women the right to vote, though this progressive step was immediately rejected by the Senate. Doing away with two millennia of Christian dictates and social prejudices—such as that being suntanned evokes a peasant's life—the youth began to look for sun and sea, to cultivate their bodies and tan their skins like Cocteau had in Piquey. "Surprise parties" became trendy: thirty or forty people would gather; stock up on food, records, and alcohol; and descend on the home of unsuspecting friends—who were sometimes in bed. The group would then stay until dawn, with everyone present encouraged to leave "exposed that part of one's body that one considered the most interesting."[4] Dances would be given everywhere, as at the end of the Terror—the same passion to exist took hold of the young spared by the massacre. "We surprised ourselves thinking like Brissac who, under *La Fronde,* charged a hearse, shouting, 'There's the enemy!'" wrote Morand.[5] The multicolored, motley world that *Parade* had allowed glimpses of was finally taking shape. Too austere, and too simplistic, Cubism itself stopped attracting interest.

With the urge to enjoy life was mingled the desire to get rich, quickly and by any means possible—even by sleeping with the right people. "Apparently morality is going bankrupt, in a war like this," the Abbé Mugnier had written three years earlier, in his exquisite diary. "Every sin seems insignificant to me, compared to this collective crime."[6] This sentiment, stemming from artistic milieus, became the majority opinion in the big cities, where people no longer hid to smoke opium, have group sex, or even be approached by people of their own sex. Since the virtues attributed to the German people—courage, discipline, endurance—had produced more tragedies than idleness would ever create, people rallied around a phrase that summarized the feeling of the time well: "It's bad because it's good, it's good because it's bad." The war? Everyone was convinced that the one they had just survived would be "the war to end all wars," and that an irresistible golden age, made of speed and pleasure, had arrived.

At the end of the war Cocteau had seen Proust approach a concierge at the Ritz to ask him, *mezza voce:* "Could you lend me fifty francs?" before adding, "Keep them, it was for you."[7] This redoubled politeness would in turn collapse: people would become rude, frank, cynical, brutal like Radiguet, and cosmopolitan like Morand. The ultra-elitist thrust of 1913 became democratized in the arts; the beginnings of American influence could be seen in the "sporting" style, whereas the Soviet influence was perceptible only in the formal, academic explorations of the avant-garde. Paris stopped smelling of gas and manure as electricity and cars were introduced everywhere, and planes allowed the wealthiest to reach London via Deauville. Demonstrating a certain concern for hygiene, young industrial leaders had clean, geometric, luminous houses built for themselves. The sun warmed and lit homes during the day, and as evening fell, electricity was immediately converted into pleasure and energy, making somber interiors cluttered with bibelots a thing of the past. Everything that was useful would tend to become beautiful, and what was ornately, richly beautiful to become useless.

Cocteau was right: The society that had nourished, launched, and applauded him was now nothing but a memory. The Daudets, the Comtesse de Chevigné, and the Princesse Murat would continue to receive him, but no longer influenced his opinion. Morand, who had just shed his skin, four years after Cocteau, confirmed, "I lived yesterday in the midst of men from another time; I had even come to see the world only through the Ancestors."[8] Thousands of thirty-somethings were discovering their generation along with him, and the public was calling for fresh skin and mellow voices. Just a few months earlier it had demanded that the seventy-year-old Sarah Bernhardt play Napoleon II—a twenty-year-old character in *l'Aiglon*, Rostand's play—and that the quavering de Max play juvenile leads, but the world had stopped belonging to the old.

Cocteau saw the historic opportunity presented by this immense commotion: with the notable exception of Valéry, Gide, and Claudel, the literary celebrities of the pre-war period were already fading away; Maurice Barrès and then Anatole France would yield to debutants determined to make an argument of their youth. "Everything was empty, gaping, offered," Morand wrote in *Venises*—so he threw himself into the breach at the speed of a racecar. "We have killed the dead a second time," Drieu La Rochelle confirmed, who had returned from the front determined to reject the nostalgia for times gone by. Having already been young, Cocteau realized he had to remain so.

It was the most joyful, the most musical, and the most electric of postwar periods. Having gone directly from prehistory to the age of cathedrals, Europeans would now embrace, with the efforts of D. W. Griffith and others, American cinema: from the Western to Charlie Chaplin and the over-the-top films of Cecil B. De Mille, the Old World got used to a rougher dramatic rhythm.[9] Already happily feeding on, with corned beef and chewing gum, the war-torn children whose parents had sometimes starved or exiled their own ancestors, US soldiers are proud to prove that the United States was a culture with astounding jazz tempos. Served up by black infantry regiments, the "sonorous cataclysm"—for which Cocteau would become the tireless announcer, in among others the "Jazz" section of the newspaper *L'intransigeant*—gave rise to an incredible euphoria.[10] Having emerged from an interminable nineteenth century, the old Gallic nation, republican and royal, still physically cramped, was undergoing the shockwave of these "wild" syncopations.

Cocteau wasn't content just to ask Gleizes to bring back from America every kind of "great Russian-Jewish-American music" he could find.[11] Having seen Pilcer hurl notes from the trumpet "the way you hurl raw meat," he had the "Billy Arnold Band" come from London to the stage of the Agriculteurs—the first jazz to be played in concert outside of dance halls—and introduced it to the furious hisses of an audience expecting the pieces by Bach, Mozart, and Vivaldi announced on the program.[12] Forty-five musicians had inflamed the air with their golden trombones, while those other escapees from the prewar period, the Beaumonts, had given the first *nègre* party in the summer of 1917.

The thundering of the big French cannons had since been everywhere replaced by the beating of drum skins, and the noise of machine-gun fire by volleys of drumsticks. Speed was not just in the process of overtaking the roads and the skies and production methods: the protagonists of peace wanted to experience it speed with the same intensity—and the same risks—as war.

In 1917, Proust, Morand, and the Abbé Mugnier had heard Princesse Soutzo mention at the Ritz the existence "of a Jew, a doctor in Vienna, Freud, who has a special theory: dream, liberation of conflicts, etc."[13] Since then, the happy few had spoken of nothing but that, and Morand, who would marry that same princess, had mentioned "that Freud we're all crazy about" in his *Journal d'un attaché d'ambassade*. The Abbé Mugnier, so liberal, wrote after Verdun: "I think the sexual instinct is the explanation for everything, since everything stems from it."[14] The century would continue to prove him right.

The victims of shell shock had been handed over to Freud by the Austrian authorities. In the Val-de-Grâce, it was now the young André Breton who took care of the madness of soldiers using the method of the great Viennese man who was so intrigued by the "science" of dreams, and whose ideas, translated into French, would reach the public from 1920 onward. Already people were laughing about the atrocious conflict that had just ended. "But these are old newspapers!" protested Cocteau when a man tried to sell him three rags in the restaurant where he was lunching with Picasso. "Yes, monsieur," replied the street peddler, "but in these THERE'S STILL WAR"—exactly what no one wanted to hear about anymore.[15]

Le Potomak, whose publication had been suspended by the hostilities, finally came out in June 1919, six years after its conception. Cocteau would never have written this book, with its prewar outlook, now. After forcing himself not to rewrite it, Cocteau took it on and gave public readings from it—"we are all *encoctoqués*," said Liane de Pougy—making his internal struggles reach their height.[16] "How many different sides of you in six months!" marveled Anna de Noailles, noticing that *Le Cap* had come out in January, and *Le coq et l'arlequin* in February. But if the poetess found in this *Potomak* pages that were "heart-rending with profundity," she also wondered what fly had bitten her former brother. Reproaching Cocteau for having "leaped with one bound over all the steps," Gide in the *Nouvelle revue française* described what many were feeling more generally: that Cocteau was an author who doesn't stay his course.

Cocteau wouldn't stop there. Always ready to take extreme risks like a circus artist—but not yet imagining that people might be hoping for his fall—he was preparing to make other leaps sideways, even if it meant always walking in profile in relation to others, like Nijinsky's Faun.

THE ROOSTER, THE HARLEQUIN, AND LES SIX

Was it the shared ordeal of the war, or the spectacular discovery of the myste-rious, seething unconscious, as revealed by Freud? Never would collaboration between creators be so intense, or artistic bridges so numerous, as during those months right after the war's end, when everyone seemed ready to place his or her talents into a group kitty and shake. This era of collective compositions, manifestos, and groups was a lucky one for Cocteau, who was never so happy as when he mingled his life with that of others.

Parade had brought Cocteau closer to composers who were part of the "Lyre et Palette" group that Cendrars had gathered under the label of the Nouveaux Jeunes. Since its beginning, the group's desire to be sarcastic musically, and to Gallicize melody, had lent appeal to the works of Satie, who had shown the group, along with Debussy and Ravel, how to escape from the metaphysical megalomania of Wagnerism. Satie's modest arrogance, his subversive taste for the absurd, and his self-proclaimed rejection of "satisme," all contributed to making him the ideal anti-master in their eyes. Yet "Monsieur le Pauvre" (Satie) was vexed at seeing Ravel invited to one of their concerts, and Cendrars didn't like the collective life any more than Satie did, which left room for the omni-present Cocteau to supplant them. He who, in February 1915, in *Le mot*, had diagnosed the decline of the "pianistic mists" of Debussy and Ravel, began to use his promotional talent to gather a wide range of musicians into a new group.[17] Drawing in individuals who were sometimes ten years apart in age, and with disparate backgrounds and tastes, Cocteau coolly formed a collective—according to that avant-gardist logic that had succeeded at so many groups of artists, ever since Der Blaue Reiter. This informal collective lacked only a manifesto.

The demand of a public impatient to break away from prewar melodies, as well as the interest aroused by *Parade* abroad, encouraged Cocteau, in January 1918, to gather his ideas on music.[18] Nourished by intense conversations with Georges Auric, the youngest member of the group, but also from reading Nietzsche's *The Case of Wagner*, Cocteau's *Le coq et l'arlequin* would allow its author to rediscover his most consistent passion—nationalism—in order to advocate for the especially French values of lightness, irony, and rapidity, and to encourage loudly the rise of an autonomous national art. Contrasting the clear call of the Gallic Rooster with the motley effects of the Harlequin, Cocteau attacked German and Russian music, which had more or less dominated the French landscape for three decades. Everything is vague and oceanic in Wagner, Cocteau said; but everything should be clear and musically situated, as was the case for the Greeks. Attacking along the way the impressionism of Debussy, who had nonetheless denounced "the ironmongery of the Ring Cycle," Cocteau finally turned against the "intestinal music" of Stravinsky, which he thought stemmed from Debussy's music (even though the Russian had sometimes harsh things to say about Debussy).

These arguments might appear oversimplified to music lovers—or even unfair or preposterous: Ravel and Debussy, for whom music was supposed to "be likeable" and who had integrated into their own music elements of jazz long before Satie or Stravinsky had, were already responding to all these demands. But it was a question of foregrounding Satie, and thus demolishing his rivals and ex-friends, by outlining the framework for the Nouveaux Jeunes (unilaterally renamed the Groupe des Six by a music critic in January 1920). Also, of course, Cocteau, in order to create his own line, needed to suppress the two "leeches" who had musically stunned him: Wagner, the "giant it's suitable to hate," as he wrote to his mother, and Stravinsky, the Russian who had influenced him during the time of David—with no result.[19] As much as Wagner, Stravinsky was in fact the musician to go against, the "sad" Scythian to be drowned under the waves of cheerful, Latin sonorities, the barbarian whom the Groupe des Six (or "Les Six") would have to defeat, guided by the mischievous Satie, with his caustic titles like Véritables preludes flasques pour un chien, Sonatine bureaucratique, and Embryons desséchés. Didn't Nietzsche eventually contrast the tragic truth of Bizet's Carmen with Wagner's theatrical weightiness?

Thus was born, far from German excess and the pagan gigantism of the Russians, in joyful reaction against pompous melodies to listen to with one's head in one's hands, as well as against that other avant-garde led by the "blackboard" composer Schoenberg, the "French music of France," which set out to be as cheerful as its megaphone, as blazing as its witty words, as light and magical as the fairytales it celebrated. Cocteau's approach, however, was not jingoistic. Greedy for sounds from abroad—jazz or ragtime—he continued to admire secretly the operas of Wagner and to call Le sacre du printemps a masterpiece, even though he no longer wanted them to become models here in France, where Wagnerism, he said, too often led to Germanophilia, and where already clouds from Bayreuth were reappearing, "more formidable than [those from] Krupp," he thought.[20]

If others retorted that Satie's mother was Scottish, Cocteau would reply that nothing germinates without cross-pollination. For Cocteau, France was a style, not a region—an idea more than an essence. When Cocteau asked Picasso for two monograms representing a rooster and a harlequin to illustrate the book, along with his portrait in uniform, it was to show his desire to Gallicize this modernity whose founding fathers, from the Montparnos to Kandinsky, were usually foreign. If people reproached Cocteau for being unfair to musical glories that were still fertile, he would reply, "A young man should not buy guaranteed investments," with the knowledge he had lacked in his own youth. It was a tone, more than a homeland, that he wanted to introduce, by digging the grave of prewar music—even if it meant clashing swords with Stravinsky, whom Cocteau knew well had, and continued to have, a crushing influence. Since Cocteau didn't have the constancy or rigidity required to found a real aesthetics, *Le coq* would represent a manifesto without meaning, or a *marteau sans maître*—though its series of aphorisms profoundly express him.[21] An organic link in fact connects music and poetry in Cocteau— in keeping with the conviction of the ancient Greeks, they comprised two stabilizing expressions of his undulating soul, a soul infinitely apt to espouse the ebbs and flows of the world and residing in a person who according to most musicians with whom he worked, was endowed with a prodigious auditory memory.

More than tactical or promotional, Cocteau's collaboration with Les Six would be aesthetic and human, a lever for his constant formal searches as well as a stimulant for his nervous kindness: "He gathered them together, taught them, introduced them, advocated them, raised them to the heavens; he drew them, photographed them, imposed them on his friends: finally he reconciled them, no small task," noted Bernard Faÿ.[22] The group became the soundtrack for the era, due not only to Cocteau's impresario's proselytism, but also to his way of expressing his own moods through a music of cheerfulness, hybridization, syncopation, and incompleteness—a music carried by his aerial presence and his leaping, impish wit. "Auric, Milhaud, Poulenc, Tailleferre, Honegger / I've put your bouquet in the water of the same vase, / And I've carefully twisted you from the base, / All free to choose your way into the air," Cocteau would write in *Plain-chant*, omitting the name of Louis Durey, who had quickly detached from the group. It was a cascade of languorous or lightning-quick tunes, stemming from jazz and Haydn's symphonies, that cited Schubert, Charpentier, street songs and folk tunes, pastorals and serenades, the laments of the slaves and the quadrilles of their masters. There were pieces of music that were more powerful and inventive, but none would testify better to the liveliness of that postwar period, which brought to its height the rerouting of melodic and narrative clichés.

Francis Poulenc, a young, eighteen-year-old musician who was an indirect heir to factories on the Rhone that would later manufacture aspirin, had already sprung onto the scene with his *Rapsodie nègre*, a piece that evoked Asia as

much as Honolulu and was played in a concert at the Vieux-Colombier organized at the end of 1917 by Satie and Cocteau. Born (like Cocteau) in the
neighborhood of the Madeleine, Poulenc, who openly detested Wagner and
Beethoven, had thought for a long time about musical aesthetics. Awakened by
Debussy and Stravinsky, Satie and Bach, he at first enjoyed exploring lesser
paths, as in his *Mouvements perpétuels*, which would soon become famous. He
increased his eclecticism by melodically translating Cocteau's hilarious
Toréador, but also was drawn to the poet's fascination with sleep—"Sleeping / a
twitch of the toe one flies"—which he illuminated in his *Cocardes* (1920), one
of the pieces by Les Six that Cocteau liked best. Some people, including Misia
and Diaghilev, might in secret speak of "charming little droppings"—possibly
referring to the music that Poulenc had made for the *Gendarme incompris*, a
farce by Cocteau and Radiguet—but the same Poulenc showed he was also
capable of major works like *Dialogues des carmélites* or *La voix humaine*, which
also followed texts by Cocteau. In this way Poulenc, who at this point was a
blend of stingy monk and erotomaniac lout, contributed to making known,
even in the depths of America, some of the rare sorts of music stripped of ideological abstraction—music that was playfully modest and never pompous.[23]

It was Milhaud, however, who knew best how to translate the effervescence
of the time—in *Le Boeuf sur le Toit*—as well as Cocteau's witticisms, in the
miraculous *Caramel mou*. Part of an old Jewish family from the Comtat
Venaissin in Provence, Milhaud was the first musician to make deliberate use
of polytonality and, preceding Gershwin, to borrow Latin and black rhythms,
before inventing the *opéra minute*. His prolific talent (there are 450 compositions to his name) may have declined over the years, but his genius was in high
gear during the few months that followed his return from Brazil, where he had
accompanied Paul Claudel as a diplomatic secretary.

Although Germaine Tailleferre gave Cocteau the bracing *Valse des dépêches*,
in *Les Mariés de la tour Eiffel*, it was Georges Auric from which Cocteau would
expect the most. Extremely intelligent, this bear of a man, always unhappy in
love, had at the age of fourteen dazzled Satie with a long article on his music,
and at sixteen impressed Misia Sert with his melodies. Probably Auric was too
delicate and erudite a critic to be a torrential creator: he was slow to produce
works, aside from those commissioned by theatrical producers and filmmakers.
His vast cultural knowledge and remarkable ability to see the overall picture
made him an ideal companion—the perfect sparring partner for a Cocteau
interested in music.

Cocteau was not content just to offer his verses to Les Six: like those children
who, by dint of riding on a rocking horse, *become* the horse, he jumped into

making the music himself. After playing percussion in *Les choéphores*, a cantata by Milhaud sung to a libretto by Paul Claudel, Cocteau celebrated New Year's Eve 1921 in the big hall of the Olympia, playing along in a little improvised jazz band with Milhaud, Auric, and Poulenc. Participating in this way would give him enough credibility not only to advise cuts to one or another of Les Six, but also to make suggestions to Milhaud for the drums, proposing "brass bouquets" and buzzing cicadas for a *Hymn to the Sun* drawn from his poem "Batterie"—in other words, to make himself into a real co-composer.[24]

Published in February 1919 with the Éditions de la Sirène, *Le coq et l'arlequin* raised doubts among many critics: the author's wish to be *le coq tôt* singing French national music could not deceive those who knew him first as a Harlequin. Didn't the history of the word *coq* (on which he always liked to play, convinced he saw in it the sonic expression of his destiny) suggest multiple meanings? We think of the Latin *coctor*, a cook who boils all kinds of fowl in his pots, which would form such French words as *queux* (tails), but also *coquereau* (small boat), *coquet* (flirt), or *caquetant* (cackling)—not to mention the *coq tôt* (the early rooster) and the *cocotte* of his early days?[25] Gide, however, in an open letter he gave to the *Nouvelle revue française*, acknowledged that while some of Cocteau's arguments were sound, "some of them seem to me less in agreement with the person you are, than with the person you would like us to believe you to be. . . . And I'm not claiming your aphorisms are not sincere—no—but that very sincerely you are deceived about yourself and you are deceiving us."[26] Gide would never again stray from this skeptical tone about Cocteau: despite finding him charming, and repeating his affection for him at regular intervals, Gide had only to see Cocteau in person to become exasperated.

Cocteau, furious at again being accused of a lie, had trouble controlling the ensuing controversy. In his impatience to take his position against Gide, the new godfather of French letters—who himself felt anxious about seeing the youth of the time drifting away from him, after the long war—Cocteau wanted to believe that the "harlequin" he had been was being attacked in the pamphlet. More likely, however, Gide had been annoyed at finding his own phrases used in it without his name being cited. His insistence forced Cocteau to add to his pamphlet an insert indicating that some omitted quotation marks had prevented him from attributing to Gide this phrase: "The French language is a piano without pedals." Gide answered, with consummate cruelty, that if Cocteau had signaled each of his borrowings with inserts—*papillons*, or "butterflies" in French—they would have reminded people of those butterflies that Darwin speaks of in his travel journals, "so numerous that they suffice to change the landscape."[27]

Cocteau's reply was deemed too personal to be published in the *Nouvelle revue française*, whose circulation had gone from 1,000 to 5,500 after the war. In it, Cocteau called Gide a shepherd and a bacchante—in private Cocteau called him "Androgyde"—then, with an aggressiveness that was surprising coming from the ex-Anna-male, compared him to a swimmer "who doesn't dare leap into the water and who wets her breasts, emitting little cries." Furious that the *Nouvelle revue française* would not publish his reply, Cocteau threatened to submit it to Gaston Gallimard through a bailiff, with orders to publish it, as authorized by the law of July 29, 1881—but finally, in August 1919, gave it to *Les écrits nouveaux*. The controversy was once again in print, for all of Paris to see.

Never did Gide lose his control. He did, however, reproach Cocteau for undeservedly giving himself the airs of a schoolmaster and inventor, or "not so much following as pretending to precede."[28] He added, in another article: "It is not given to everyone to be original. M. Cocteau has not reached his first imitation." These stings angered their victim, especially when they were accompanied by the humiliating tale of the visit that Cocteau had made to Gide at the Villa Montmorency, during which, at Cocteau's humble request, Gide had condescended to read him his open letter before publication, and Cocteau had tried, by supplications, curses, gestures with his sword-cane, and oaths on the heads of his parents, to get him to soften it.

If Gide did indeed end up tempering his open letter, the most wounded of the two was without a doubt Cocteau. Although Gide confessed he felt like a bear facing a squirrel at each of their encounters—he has so much honey on his paws you can barely make out his claws, Cocteau cracked—Gide's arguments had aimed true, even when they weren't really arguments, and so cemented Cocteau's reputation as a thief. Satie, by contrast, could only congratulate himself on *Le coq et l'arlequin*. The "franco-lunaire" musician Satie, whom *Parade* had made to seem ridiculous in the eyes of the public, was praised in *Le coq* for his cleanness, his detachment, his melodic "whiteness," and treating all genres as equal in stature. By consecrating this anti-master as the head of the new generation, Cocteau contributed significantly to establishing, in a finally positive way, the notoriety of Satie—a genius, but an incomplete composer, as Ravel described him—and to make him into a legendary character, thanks to the international success of the pamphlet.[29]

The debate, however, played well for Cocteau. Part of the younger generation recognized itself in his plea in favor of a modernity that was no longer sectarian or heroic, but supple, mischievous, and vital. Despite or because of its anarchic disorder, its internal contradictions, and its obscurities, *Le coq et l'arlequin* took shape as an aesthetic manifesto and stood out paradoxically for its slogan "We must respond with works, not with manifestos." Cocteau's image as a modernist was strengthened, after the failure of *Le Cap* and *Potomak*, and for the first time he sold more than two thousand copies of a book.[30] Nothing more was needed to make him love this *Coq* that bore his arms: "I don't tire of rereading it, whereas my other books disgust me," he confided to Auric, with a disturbing frankness.[31]

Francis Picabia might joke about "Auric Satie with Cocteau sauce," but he acknowledged the role of Cocteau in the new music.[32] Since Breton was even less interested than Apollinaire in music, and Tzara scarcely more, Cocteau could call himself a godfather of avant-garde music over the next three years. *Paris-midi* offered him a weekly column, "Carte blanche." Cocteau took advantage of his column to introduce to the public at large, in simple and "journalistic" terms, not only Les Six, but also, like Apollinaire before him, many painters, writers, and avant-garde poets, some of whom he published at the Éditions de la Sirène but who were still unknown beyond the first ten arrondissements of Paris. No talent of the time escaped him, from Man Ray, "l'Homme-Rayon," who was still dreaming of using painting as a medium and whom Cocteau was the first writer to hail, in April 1922, to Brancusi, whose prehistoric studio he describes as "Tree trunks, blocks of stone, an oven where the master of the house, primitive man, grills meat on the tip of an iron spear."[33] These columns, gathered into one volume and published under the title *Carte blanche* in June 1920, would convey the poetic essence not only of the performances given by Mistinguett and Chaplin, but also of jazz and American films.

WHEN GIDE LOSES IT . . .

If Cocteau annoyed Gide, Cocteau felt ill at ease in the presence of the Immoralist, since his admiration was tinged with anxiety about facing this elder with the mysterious oriental smile, who seemed to him less a human being than a character polished a hundred times by his books — the lucky charm of his own collection. "He has made himself," Cocteau liked to repeat, "with a method we'll call military, and is confident of obtaining the best from himself, at will . . . Can one be Gide at such an extreme?"[34] The reply to that question, which was certainly "yes," profoundly embarrassed Cocteau, whose desire to please was increased tenfold by any resistance he encountered. Cocteau was the one who looked everywhere for what he was not, and who preferred risk to the most basic of securities. He never stopped trying to conquer his elder and was always in search of the piece that would complete his puzzle, which made him seem to Gide to often want to impose his flaw on the world. Gide not only tended to perceive as thefts Cocteau's literary homages; he was convinced that his very substance was threatened by that born imitator. If in his divine enthusiasm Cocteau had believed he could also become Gide, he soon saw there was room only for one person with that name—unlike his own name and person, which seemed nearly infinitely divisible. Gide didn't tolerate versatility, except in himself. As Gide writes in *Les faux-monnayeurs* about his own fictional representative, Édouard:

> I don't know what I think of him. He is never the same for long together. He is attached to nothing, but nothing is more attractive than his elusiveness. You have known him too little a time to judge him. He is perpetually form-ing, unforming, re-forming himself. One thinks one has grasped him . . . He is Proteus! He takes the shape of what he loves, and one must love him to understand him.[35]

A misunderstanding was soon to complicate the relationship of Gide and Cocteau. Marc Allégret, Gide's twenty-three-year-old "nephew" and protégé, had been being "protected" since 1916 by his "uncle" who, under the pretext of completing his education, had fallen in love with him. (Marc's father, the pastor Élie Allégret, had been Gide's own teacher thirty years before.) This was the first time, and it would be the last, that Gide experienced a violent emotion: he wanted his boy with the spectacular physique and demanding tastes near him. But if Marc gave all the appearances of "liking him well enough," he obvi-ously took more pleasure in going to the circus or to the first Dadaist exhibits with Cocteau than with haunting the slightly dated library of his fifty-year-old relative.[36] This torturing love had already claimed a first victim, Madeleine Gide. Returning from a trip to England with his student-lover a year before, Gide had discovered that his beloved (but never touched) wife had thrown into the fire all of the letters he had written to her in thirty years—a holocaust that almost brought an end to their marriage. And now Marc Allégret was infatuated with Cocteau.

   The student saw in Cocteau a way to give himself airs, if not real importance. Scarcely had his "uncle" left before he would leave to see Cocteau; when Gide returned, he'd go off to attend Cocteau's lectures, or set to work learning by heart *Le Potomak*—a book in which Gide had perceived, not without reason, little more than his own influence. Since the young Allégret took the opposite position on everything that Gide said, the Immoralist was convinced that the friendship with Cocteau, his rival, was harming his own reputation. But he could do nothing; Marc Allégret remained fascinated. Cocteau spoke to Allégret's generation, as *Le coq et l'arlequin* proved yet again. He was exchanging letters with Tristan Tzara, a Romanian poet who was just beginning to be discussed, and had known the pioneers of the Dalcroze method, the rhythmic dance into which the young Allégret was being initiated. Gide, by contrast, was defined much more by the era before the war, and viscerally rejected the avant-garde. Unable to keep Allégret, who would go on to become the director of films such as *Le lac aux dames* and *L'entrée des artistes*, Gide came to hate anything that might have been influenced by Cocteau. Yet something in him also feared like the plague being stored away on the Symbolist shelf by the youth of the day: like all those who were adults during the post-1918 era, Gide was already haunted by the thought of being called old and seen as a nineteenth-century author, with his amorous shepherds outside of time and his North Africa worthy of Vergil.

Cocteau was very openly interested in the brilliant youth Allégret, whom he called, in letters to Gide, sometimes "your wild colt" and sometimes "our Marc."[37] With the success of *Le coq et l'arlequin*, young people impatient to write and compose were knocking on Cocteau's door every day, and already he was envisaging giving Marc Allégret the editorship of a journal that could unify, under Cocteau's authority, various small avant-garde publications, to give more strength to the movement. He then hoped to make Allégret his own personal secretary. Did Cocteau hope to convince Gide that he was not so frivolous, since his young lover was himself an artist? It is possible. And perhaps the *Nouvelle revue française* might look with a kinder eye on Cocteau's productions.

Allégret's enthusiasm for Cocteau finally made the usually calm Gide explode. Roused by a female cousin of the Allégrets, Gide's jealousy convinced him that Cocteau planned to steal Marc from him, and then that Marc was falling in love with Cocteau.[38] At this point, venturing to mention the name of Cocteau—the rival with the disparaging wit, salon-based vivacity, and renegade talents—was like showing red to a bull. Anything Cocteau would write in the future would be odious to Gide. During a revival of *Parade*, Gide wondered aloud what one should admire in it most, "pretentiousness or poverty."[39] And upon hearing Mme Théo Van Rysselbergh, his confidante, say about Cocteau's first real novel, *Le grand écart*, "So much mastery to say so little," he went even further: "Yes, yes, that's right; try to say that again in front of Marc . . ., it's good for him to hear criticisms from others besides me."[40]

For five years, Gide would experience the anguish of seeing his "nephew" abandon himself to the artificial world of Cocteau, the ex-frivolous prince. When Allégret became a film director's assistant, with Man Ray, on Marcel Duchamp's first film, *Cinéma anémique*, or when he was adviser to the Comte de Beaumont for those Soirées de Paris where Cocteau would perform his adaptation of *Romeo and Juliet*, the same terror would seize Gide. In 1926, Gide would confide again to a literary critic:

> My greatest suffering, my need to bash in my head, my life turned com-
> pletely upside-down, stemmed from the moral influence of C . . ., from his
> brio which had dazzled, bewitched a still childlike mind . . . I was like
> Pygmalion finding his statue damaged, his work devastated . . . by another.[41]

One year before his death in 1951, the author of *Paludes* would confess to Cocteau that he had even reached a point, in an "almost feminine" fit of jealousy, of wishing for Cocteau's death, and had thought several times of stran-gling him.[42]

Gide got his revenge in February 1926 through a character in his novel *Les faux-monnayeurs* named Comte Robert de Passavant.[43] As Gide imagined him, de Passavant used young men to launch Dadaist journals—a complaint remi-niscent of Gide's views of the deplorable influence that Cocteau then had over Marc Allégret (called Olivier in the novel), views he had shared with Claude Mauriac.[44] "Nothing is more harmful or more widely applauded than people of his kind, except possibly women . . . without laws, without masters, without scruples," adds Édouard, the fictional representative of Gide, referring to de Passavant, whose never-ending intrigues and literary kleptomania completed Cocteau's portrait, under the rainbow of his "Wilde-like" *mots*: a moral nuanced by the confession of jealousy about de Passavant's skill in keeping controversy raging around his name. No doubt the maxim taken from Édouard's journal— "The one who will soon seem oldest is the one who will have first seemed the most modern"—was first recited to Marc Allégret by Gide.[45]

THE MYOPIC CHILD

Apollinaire's fame, though, was beginning to surge. The obscure avant-gardist who inflicted sleepless nights on typographers was becoming the national poet he had dreamed of being. A seemingly unanimous homage had been made to him on June 8, 1919, during a poetic matinée at a gallery called L'Effort moderne. There some of the people who had known him, from Max Jacob to André Breton, read their works aloud. Cocteau read his poem "Coupe à ta muse les cheveux" [Cut your muse's hair], in an atmosphere that was both meditative and tense, before giving the stand to a child who had never cut his own: Raymond Radiguet.

Wrapped in a long beaver-colored coat in which he looked as if he had spent the night, Radiguet marched through the crowd to read at random, in a muffled voice, poems from *Calligrammes*, without even lifting his eyes from the paper, then left alone, like a sleepwalker into the night. This boy with the fixed stare of an owl was one of the youngest recruits of the brand new Dadaist movement, whom Tzara was trying to implant in Paris from Zurich. Born just fifteen years and eleven months earlier into a large family, this monster of precocity had already published poems, stories, short plays, and articles, then outlined a novel that would become *Le diable au corps*, inspired by his affair with the wife of a *poilu* during the war. He corresponded with André Breton, slept at the home of Juan Gris, the Cubist painter, was friends with Max Jacob, appeared in state in the journal *Dada* with his phonetic poems, but didn't identify with any living master, and so disliked being called a prodigy. He said he was nineteen to surprise others only with his talent.

Cocteau had already met the very young Radiguet in that same gallery three months earlier, during a homage to Reverdy, and again a few weeks before that, during a matinée devoted to Max Jacob. Since Paul Dermée had dared to compare the poetry by Jacob, the author of *Le cornet à dés*, to the writings of "madmen," Cocteau, Radiguet, and the future Surrealists had rallied protectively around the poet who, ten years later, would probably have been flattered by the comparison. "Dermée isn't a madman but an idiot," Cocteau had exclaimed in defense of his friend. During the homage to Apollinaire, however, everyone present seemed only to admire the dead poet.

"Monsieur, there's a child asking for you, a child with a cane," announced the wife of Cyprien, the valet of Mme Cocteau, a few days later, in the vestibule on the rue d'Anjou. Recommended by Max Jacob, the badly dressed Radiguet advanced into the room where Cocteau received people in the morning, usually in a bathrobe. It was a routine visit for the boy, who at the age of fourteen was already knocking on Brancusi's door, and whose portrait Modigliani had already painted, but it was a visit that would be influential for both of them—for Cocteau, because of the quality of the poems he heard, and for Radiguet, because he was welcomed by a poet whom he admired. Cocteau wrote:

> He drew out of his pockets little pieces of schoolboy's notebook paper which he had crumpled up into a ball. He smoothed them out with the flat of his hand and, bothered by one of the cigarettes he rolled himself, tried to read a very short poem. He held it right up against his eyes.[46]

Radiguet was like a disabled person let loose in the city, with a single cane as guide, by parents too absorbed by his seven younger siblings. "His entire fragile, serious, absent person seemed to be swimming clumsily behind that gaze he brought to things. He pretended not to see them and recorded them once and for all," wrote Cocteau.[47] The miracle didn't stop there. With his well-defined lips and coal-black gaze, and his stocky, well-built body, Radiguet was truly desirable and "disturbingly handsome," as Stravinsky said when he met him in a café with Diaghilev, who immediately became jealous of him.[48] In fact, there was something of Nijinsky in this boy with a Kalmuck's eyebrows, who arrived in Cendrars's office, "shy and chubby-cheeked like a girl," but very determined to spread his name.[49] Radiguet had not only the same stubborn silence as Nijinsky, as well as the instinctive intelligence, but also the same embarrassment about facing the public, an experience that he still sought out. He possessed a fragile strength: his right leg, which was shorter than the left, limped; at times streams of red drops dripped from his nose; and he couldn't open his mouth without closing his eyes, and vice versa, "as if his skin were too short."[50]

It would be difficult to imagine two beings who were more unlike each other, this elf in his thirties who was overflowing with ease and this tiny figurine paralyzed by a shyness that could make him furious. The elder man flitted between doors, like the fairytale characters he loved so much; the younger, nearly immobile, preferred the concrete things in life, little truisms, and to read newspapers exhaustively.

Though Radiguet sometimes lost his voice in front of editors of the journals he sought out, he was determined enough always to return. Unkempt and pale—"the radish of the Parc Saint-Maur," said Cocteau—myopic to the point of not recognizing his friends, even two feet away; seemingly unfamiliar with normal life; capable of obliterating idiotic chatter with stinging disdain; and letting bizarre grimaces appear on his face; there was even something slightly monstrous about Radiguet. Cocteau would speak of those children who remain quiet so long as they chew their saliva: there was something of a spitting kid about "this good candidate for cruelty" who, at the age of fourteen, was noticed by the journalists of *L'intransigeant* to whom he brought his caricatures. "His juvenile insolence, by turns spontaneous and calculated," made him hated as much as admired.[51]

Far from keeping him at a distance, this fertile harshness attracted Cocteau, who recognized in it a sign of being chosen, as irrefutable proof that this inspired boy was the champion of his own poetry, like Rimbaud, the Seer conceived in Charleville, had been. Never had Cocteau seen a child so mature, or a blind man so lucid, or a mute person with so much to say—a poet so determined to make his poetry known. And never had a boy so clearly roused his desire, and his tormenting need to shape, encourage, and influence, which Henri Bouvelet and Jean Le Roy, Cocteau's first disciples, had awakened. It was the atmosphere of Cocteau's childhood that he found again through the young Radiguet, the hours spent pushing a duck on the surface of a bath, that oceanic period of time when, suffering from a fever, he would sink into Atlantis on the rue La Bruyère. Radiguet had started out drawing in the shadow of his father, a caricaturist for *L'assiette au beurre*, an anarchist weekly—though without Cocteau's self-motivation the adolescent needed encouragement to write, as well as a hand to tear him away from women and bring him back to himself.

Determined to integrate him into his life, Cocteau introduced Radiguet to the readers at *Paris-midi*, brought him to the masked victory ball given by Paul Poiret on July 14, 1919, and encouraged the other fashion designer, Jacques Doucet, to acquire Radiguet's manuscripts for his collection of holographs, which spanned those of Baudelaire to those of the very young Aragon. Urged to write regularly, Radiguet dedicated a lewd Dadaist story to that "delicious friend" who planned on publishing with Éditions de la Sirène *Devoirs de vacances*, Radiguet's first poems, and wrote a story announcing the ironic content of his next book: a hundred models of letters "for all circumstances" titled *Le secrétaire des poètes*. Radiguet in turn showed Cocteau the Île d'Amour and the shores of the Marne, where he spent so many hours reading, sheltered in his father's dory—as well as the copses of the Parc Saint-Maur, where he brought the least shy of the girls whom he met on trolleys or in bars. This detail did not dampen Cocteau's enthusiasm—quite the contrary: he went about renting a room in a hotel on the rue de Surène, next to the rue d'Anjou, for the evenings when Radiguet couldn't come back to sleep at his parents' house in Saint-Maur. Scarcely had Cocteau arrived in Basque country, where he would spend part of the summer, than he regretted not having seized the young man by the neck and forced him to come with him. The poems that Radiguet sent Cocteau, in reply to Cocteau's, he pinned on the walls of his room, with that feverishness that others evince in pinning up photos of actresses. In Cocteau it was the beginning of a process in which desire, admiration, the need to shape someone else, maternal affection, the desire to be loved, and the absolute requirement to be occupied and to obsess fed each other until they produced an explosive mixture that had to be given the name of love. "When I arrived at his little room, above the clouds where vultures soared, he had been crying for a long time," Jean Hugo would recall.[52]

Already Cocteau, in his role as a trainer, was worried about the places where Radiguet could work on his poems. Cocteau guessed that Radiguet's enemy was lack of discipline, bohemianism, alcohol, and that coquetry that made the lazy young man write too "ornately," or that prevented him from putting on the little round glasses that gave him the airs of a Chinese poet. "All these young people hang out in the streets and don't rest," Cocteau wrote to Irène Lagut, an illustrator and once the mistress of Picasso, who was allowing herself to be courted at a distance by Radiguet. "Actions of another world. I myself lead a proper life, I soap and brush them. I have a father's soul."[53]

To Radiguet, with the help of the good country air, Cocteau described himself more clearly as "Hercules in love," while hinting at ambiguity within his nature. "I have a fat lady on my left thigh and a sailor on my right thigh (heads or tails?)," Cocteau wrote to him, from the train taking him from Biarritz to Aix-en-Provence. Soon convinced that Radiguet knew, and wasn't bothered at all, he tried again to tell him in detail about his love affair with Madeleine Carlier, which the teenager didn't fail to mention to journalists.[54] Obviously this "open" style of life charmed Radiguet, who never inflicted moral judgment on others and welcomed all pleasures with the same curiosity. It seemed as if his awareness of his own ambiguity, his hedonism as a precocious adult, as well as his strange ability to observe everything at a distance, with the objectivity of a taxidermist, spoke in favor of a limitless tolerance. Cocteau usually thought he could control those close to him by having a keen prescience of their reactions; he could guess immediately their inner waverings, penetrate their thoughts, and anticipate their actions until he felt more like them than they did. This time, however, Cocteau came up against someone stingy with words and smiles, a compact form under a fragile envelope. How could he reach the innermost thoughts of a boy who might, as they rested on the banks of the Marne, opposite *his* Île d'Amour, ask him if there was a good inn there, with the same amused calmness of children tearing the wings off of dragonflies?

Moved by Radiguet's silence, Cocteau fell in love. Nothing seemed to be able to upset the strange control the teenager had over himself, or that analytical mind always on the watch that prevented him from losing himself; even when drunk, Radiguet still knew what to hold onto, emotionally and literarily. Unable to guess what Radiguet thought of him, confronted with a gaze that was as opaque as a two-way mirror, Cocteau ended up going to pieces: the one who would become the great love of his life would also be the one whose intimate workings he was least able to grasp. Harshness always tended to arouse in Cocteau tenderness and love. He loved to conquer those who yielded only with difficulty. He was overcome when he managed to make them share his state of mind, even for an instant. "I am seduced by people who have a mysterious prestige . . . that comes probably from a lack of heart," he acknowledged at the end of his life.[55] Did he secretly dream, in loving Radiguet, of acquiring the boy's strength and his insensitivity, and ridding himself of his overwhelming fragility? Guessing that the young prodigy was the part of himself that he had always lacked, he forgot all prudence, and of his opposite made his complement.

LOVE, ALONE

Just a few weeks after their first meeting, Radiguet was already completely occupying Cocteau's thoughts. While the torrent of accounts loosed daily in his letters—some fourteen pages long—hid disturbing confidences, the romantic poems that Cocteau sent Radiguet no longer hid his feelings:

My weak heart
breaks down (*repeat*)
at your sweetness

Your hand so soft
amongst the soap suds.[56]

Radiguet's replies, as rare as Picasso's and often rendered illegible by bad handwriting, didn't do much to satisfy the questions of the elder man so greedy for confidences; sometimes Radiguet even claimed that he hadn't received Cocteau's letters. Unhappy about the youngster's distance, but feeling that he wasn't being encouraged to say more, Cocteau confided to Radiguet that he kissed the muzzles of mules when he felt too alone. He also stifled his frustration with pots of jam or candied fruit, many samples of which he sent to Radiguet, as well as to his countless brothers and sisters.

On September 15, Radiguet received from Aix-en-Provence this other letter that Cocteau had sent him via registered mail, to make sure it reached him:

My dear boy,
I'll be back before next week. I won't tell *anyone in the world* (except in my house) *and will await you at the Hôtel M. at 2:30.* (A telegram will tell you the day.) Promise me you'll be *very* punctual (not 3 o'clock) . . .

Radiguet's father, finding out the reply his son was getting ready to give—which may have been the letter in which he wrote to Cocteau "I'm writing to a delicious friend whom I love" before adding "I adore you," demanded an explanation.[57] The caricaturist had already been warned against his son's excessive friendship with Cocteau by his colleagues at *L'intransigeant* and had sent the supposed corrupter a brief remonstrance. Cocteau protested his innocence, with all the ambiguity he could muster, and confessed an exceptional admiration for Raymond—all the while agreeing that, from a distance, the borders might seem confused:

His literary future counts above all else for me, for he is a kind of prodigy. A scandal would spoil this freshness. You shouldn't believe for a second that I'm not trying to avoid one by all the means in my power.

I am unaware of the letter from Raymond you mention. If he hasn't sent it to me it's probably because it was of an imaginative kind he might have felt uncomfortable sending me.

About the hotel, your son has sometimes spent the night there if he missed his train back, since I was unable to put him up at my house.

The meeting at the Hotel M. was the Hôtel Meurice where I was supposed to stay on my return from Grasse and where I did not stay.[58]

Still thinking it strange that his son would stay at the expense of an adult at the hotel, M. Radiguet wrote a second letter that forced Cocteau to offer a more in-depth explanation. While vouching for his own good influence by citing the money he had already helped the boy earn, via that fashion designer autograph collector ("[I'm] happy to say that his library began with Baudelaire and ended with your son"), Cocteau suggested to the father a joint guardianship:

Look at Raymond. The abnormal development of his brain prevents the normal development of his body. He walks bent over. He is pale, myopic, speaks in a frail voice. Before thinking about a job, we must cure him, get his strength back. My role is to push him towards you; yours to demand he do his exercises, eat, sleep.[59]

A real godfather, seeking to set on the right path the boy who was seemingly so docile, but actually so fractious—a trainer too, furious he couldn't be every instant behind him, leaning over his writings, in order to force him to simplify his style and clarify his ideas. In short, the antithesis of his actual indolent, permissive father, to whom Cocteau would write, a year later: "Act. Force him to stay at the Parc 3 days a week. I am not his father."[60]

But the arrival of this young bohemian at the rue d'Anjou soon began to worry Mme Cocteau as well. That her son was renting a hotel room for him, under the pretext of getting him to work, was also a concern. The homosexuality of her younger son could pass as a temporary disturbance, but he had just turned thirty, and marriage was still not on the horizon. To spare the woman to whom he owed his life, Cocteau had tried until then to keep midway between the sexes, displaying a semi-disinterested purity—no one would so have liked to marry others. But this time, despite Cocteau's idealizing his relationship with Radiguet and describing it as angelic, and even presenting the child as his adoptive son, Mme Cocteau, that reader of Pascal, knew very well that "qui veut faire l'ange fait la bête"—he who wants to be an angel acts like an animal. Cocteau had lied to her so often! He was like those adorable children who, living on two simultaneous levels of reality, but unable as a "perfect" child to ask for money, brazenly pilfer from their parents' wallet. Mme Proust was obviously not taken in when she saw her son use as an excuse, in order to be able to go out at night, a "dinner of *cocottes* [tarts]"; Mme Cocteau was scarcely any more taken in by the theory of seraphs her son surrounded himself with: Wasn't it angels that the inhabitants of Sodom had tried to rape in Lot's house?

Seeing Satie solicit Cocteau for money, Mme Cocteau had come to believe that her son, whom she was still supporting, was living surrounded by "spongers" and was paying for the affections that surrounded him: his "tendencies" didn't just clash with her moral principles, but also with her spirit of order and economy. Publishing such phrases as unambiguous as "I would be sorry if people believed in my disinterestedness," Radiguet would prod her a little further; she began to fear that this little sixteen-year-old devil was becoming the "damned soul" of her son, with whose emotional dependence she was well acquainted.[61] Having already warned Cocteau about Radiguet's nature, she urged him again to remain vigilant against those who wanted to "take his youth." But it was too late, he was in love.

To justify his extraordinary campaign, Cocteau plotted. He spoke of Radiguet's "stone age"—as if he had been the genius of the *Sacre du printemps*—and compared his prodigious talents to those of Rimbaud. Evoking his own beginnings under the tutelage of De Max, he referred his mother to their twin desires for recognition: wasn't it his duty to pass on the good fortune he had had, during the Femina matinée, to this boy who so deserved it? Didn't she see the link between the precocity of the dunce to whom she had given birth and that of a Radiguet who, fleeing a childhood that was "flat as a lawn," had spent a year cutting classes reading a book a day, from Stendhal to Racine? A Radiguet who, having published at the age of fourteen a "paper" on Sade, had, at an age when others tirelessly twirl mustard spoons on the banquettes of bistros, dedicated a poem to Apollinaire that *Sic* had published?[62] True, Apollinaire had accused Radiguet of copying him, but he had added: "Do not despair, Sir: Arthur Rimbaud didn't write his masterpiece until he was seventeen."[63] Cocteau's many arguments ended up easing Mme Cocteau's misgivings; at least she didn't risk seeing her son go to live with Radiguet, as he had with Madeleine Carlier: with Radiguet, he would still need his mother.

So it was with the complicity of all the parents that Radiguet got into the habit of ringing the doorbell on the rue d'Anjou, and then working at Jean's desk, or reading on his little iron bed, while Cocteau waved his visitors back with a final story told with his hands, until he seemed to be making a sculpture in the air, actually meant for the adolescent. Sometimes Radiguet would fall asleep over his notebook, knocked out by fatigue, as happened once among Max Jacob's jars of gouache, and Cocteau would stay to study this perfect union of male and child, perversity and innocence. The more he admired Radiguet's physique, the more pleasure he found in his offered body, and the more in return Radiguet melted into him, became his own substance. "Since childhood," Cocteau would say about the hero of *Le grand écart*, a novel he would describe as autobiographical, "he felt the desire to *be* those he found handsome, not to make himself loved by them."

Radiguet, however, remained unattainable. The silence he surrounded himself with, for entire afternoons sometimes, placed him under a glass dome that was both erotically exciting and dissuasive: when traveling, at the hotel, or visiting their friends, Cocteau and he would always take two separate rooms. True, Morand saw them one day sleeping in the same armchair, and Radiguet took pleasure baring his naked body to the sun at Piquey, but Cocteau always drew him dressed, even when asleep. Radiguet might sometimes let himself go, such as during one of their first nighttime encounters in the hotels on the Madeleine, but Cocteau never felt that the adolescent belonged to him physically.[64] Radiguet had "something of the young bull in him . . ., but without having any special morals," confirmed Stravinsky.[65] Enjoying a real sexual power over men, he actually sought out intimacy only with teenage girls as smart as he or with mature women he didn't have the financial means to attract. His extreme youth and apparent willingness encouraged all kinds of audacities, but the men-loving men soon turned away when they discovered that Radiguet was ready for anything, except with them. "I never refused myself to anyone— no one had the patience—my insensitivity vexed them too much," Radiguet noted, in a brief diary he kept at the end of his life.[66]

Cocteau was too much in love, however, for Radiguet not to be the tacit accomplice of his emotion. Out of a need to succeed or a wish to please, Radiguet let doubt linger, even more than he'd done with his previous protector, Max Jacob, from whom he was distancing himself at the time, and who complained bitterly that Cocteau had "taken" Bébé away from him. A masterpiece of ambiguity, Radiguet's novel *Le bal du comte l'Orgel* would prove the distress that Radiguet felt when he sensed that the man whose wife he coveted was falling in love with him. "Go ask the ball in the cup-and-ball game if it got caught or if it caught hold," the teenage Radiguet would write in his journal, among other phrases with double entendres. Monique Nemer, one of Radiguet's biographers, stresses Radiguet's frequent poetic identification with the Narcissus of mythology.[67] Cocteau, for his part, never denied the rumor that seeing them always together meant they were in bed together, but he made no erotic confession to that effect—even though he was usually loquacious about his other lovers. After the boy's death, however, Cocteau would confirm Radiguet's preferences in a poem bearing his name: "He set a ladder up to women / To gather their red, transparent fruit."[68] Radiguet's opacity increased Cocteau's love tenfold. The more the teenager withdrew into his own enigma, the more that Cocteau's fairy-like imagination made him into an untouchable entity, and hence one worthy of being adored—a solid impossible to penetrate. Half a century later, André Fraigneau would note that Cocteau the medium, capable through mimicry of instantly bringing to life figures like Barrès, Proust, or Satie—not to mention dead men whom he had never even met—found it absolutely impossible to imitate the author of *Le diable au corps*—as if Radiguet was taboo, in the etymological sense of set apart, or forbidden.[69]

There would be much exaggeration, and some Catholic guilt, in the comparison that Max Jacob would make between Cocteau's admiration-love for Radiguet and the feeling that Mary Magdalene had for Christ, or Jacob himself for Picasso.[70] But there was some justice in this comparison. Until his death, Cocteau would call the adolescent "Radiguet"—never Raymond—and would allow himself to use nicknames like Bébé or Radigo only in Radiguet's absence. The two addressed each other formally as "vous" until the end, with a respect indicating the complicity of creators more than the intimacy of lovers. Cocteau had sometimes been loved despite himself, or else suddenly abandoned; here he got used to loving without being loved and to nourishing himself only with sincere and often expressed literary admiration for Radiguet, who began reading him systematically and soon learned his poems by heart. Cocteau resigned himself to living alone with his emotion—"I love you; does that matter to you?" said Goethe—and to hide his love took on the guise of father, mother, pawn, or schoolmaster. Cocteau was able to tolerate this lack of reciprocity all the more easily since his stifled sexuality was never so stimulated as by strangers.

Radiguet, in return, let Cocteau suggest anything he liked, and was happy to be described as "le coq de l'Île d'Amour," in homage to his sexual prowess as well as in memory of the "cock of the high school" (*coq de college*) that was Dargelos, the desirable dunce from the Lycée Condorcet whom Cocteau would go on to mythologize, and who was Radiguet's twin in many respects. Radiguet still wore the triple ring made of white, grey, and yellow gold rings that Cocteau had designed for the two of them, taking his inspiration from a Chinese version supposed to have a beneficial Saturn influence, and which the jeweler Cartier had made: apparently a little tenderness, some signs of gratitude, an evening spent "reading each other" (*s'entrelire*), and you'd get all you could want from Cocteau.

The author of *Le coq* would recast this handicap as a weapon. Lacking sweet words and caresses, he would make "Monsieur Bébé" work, would train him and goad him on like a race horse. His obsession? To make Radiguet avoid the mistakes of his own beginnings and the tragedies that accompany a poorly handled precocity. True, the teenage Radiguet had the remarkable privilege of having begun to read and write after 1913, but his poetry still lacked force, as the publication of *Les joues en feu* would confirm. The reflective Radiguet "willingly erased himself and sought to please himself much more than to succeed," said Jacques de Lacretelle, author of *Silbermann*.[71] Yet won over by the nervous energy of his mentor, Radiguet changed his style, slowly but inexorably, to become more laconic and rhythmic—progress that is visible in the two men's letters, and that would be for Cocteau the most beautiful proofs of love. "There are weaknesses that are more powerful than any kind of strength," he would say one day—a phrase that could be applied to the passionate Pygmalion as much as to his beloved subject.[72]

ALL AGAINST DADA

The men who really believe in themselves are all in lunatic asylums.
— G. K. *Chesterton*, Orthodoxy

THE GRAND SPECTACLE OF DISASTER

Suddenly, in the first months of 1920, there was talk of a trio of Musketeers determined to take up Apollinaire's torch. Paris was used to these kinds of rumors, but these particular conspirators—André Breton, Philippe Soupault, and Louis Aragon—seemed capable of carrying out such an ambitious project, as well as forming the literary generation of the Armistice. The three men had just appeared on the Parisian literary scene and were now preparing to launch a journal. It had been quite a negative encounter, remember, when Breton had met Cocteau for the very first time, at the home of their common friend, Valentine Hugo. Another reading from *Le Cap de Bonne-Espérance*, in Adrienne Monnier's bookstore, hadn't produced better results in February 1919. Breton, then a medical student, and the young Philippe Soupault, who trotted along behind Breton "like a nice little myopic goat," had stood very straight, radiating hostility, during the entire reading.[1] But Cocteau so wanted to have these young men pulling for him that he had still offered them his friendship "with both hands."[2] This time again Breton had taken Cocteau's measure, from the heights of that Olympus whence aesthetic vetoes and moral ukases had begun to fall, and had given his judgment in his nasal, slow, barking voice, which gave a strange authority.

Since their journal in preparation, *Littérature*, vitally needed sponsors, the Musketeers didn't reject Cocteau's offers for long. Cocteau hurried first to introduce them to Gide, who for his part also had his eye on Apollinaire's heritage. In response, Breton proclaimed himself ready to revise his opinion of *Le Cap*, and opened the doors of *Littérature* to Cocteau, who then sent Breton a more than friendly letter, swearing that their friendship would no longer suffer from any disagreements—and wasn't Cocteau the literary adviser for the Éditions de la Sirène, a publishing house that enjoyed great prestige in the field of new literature? The very young Louis Aragon, a student of medicine as well, also approached Cocteau. "The bad things they said about Cocteau seemed to me so disproportionate, that I naturally attributed them to envy. So I found myself in a very good mood," Aragon would say later on.[3]

Ambitious as he was talented, but fragile to the point of crying at the obscene jokes of medics, this natural child of the nice neighborhoods soon submitted some of his poems to Cocteau, and then confided more personal, if not compromising, things, to him—"I love André Breton / who does not love me."[4] An exchange of letters ensued. Their affectations make these messages difficult to read, but how could modesty have found a place between the so-elegant Aragon, whose inaugural manifesto was entitled *Moi*, and the ex-man-god in the midst of his regeneration?

Aragon paused in front of the flattering reflection that Cocteau held out to him. Belonging to that age group so marked by prewar readings—like Breton, who in 1916 swore only by Valéry—this illegitimate son of a prefect of police, raised by a mother he thought was his sister and nurtured on the milk of Barrès, was one of the very last candidates for literary dandyism. But if he had the time to frequent the academic salon of Mme Mühlfeld, being less precocious than Cocteau, who was seven years his elder, Aragon also had the luck, in a way, of publishing nothing before 1914. Sexually more confused than he appeared, Aragon would respond to Cocteau's dance of seven veils by an equivalent propensity to undress himself literarily, in order the better to cover himself with the flowing garments of his phrases.[5]

This beginning of a relationship had allowed Cocteau to see his name, in March 1919, on the masthead of the inaugural issue of *Littérature*, which was still quietly sponsored by Gide and Valéry. Thinking that he was already Aragon's friend, Cocteau no longer hesitated to read his letters in Paris and, getting ahead of himself as he so often did, envisaged himself as Aragon's protector—just as Breton dreamed of being Radiguet's. To manage this, Cocteau tried to drive a wedge between Aragon and Breton, whom he had just called a "Rimbaud gendarme [tough cop]." This elicited such fury in Breton that the idyll ended right there.[6] In fact, the incident permanently ended any possibility of "friendship" between these self-proclaimed disciples of Apollinaire the Enchanter.[7]

But that same year, 1919, a stranger put Cocteau back in the center of the "ultra" scene. Tristan Tzara, who wanted to create a fief in the capital for himself long-distance, but not very aware of how to go about it, had written to Cocteau from Zurich after seeing his name, in the months after *Parade*, on the mastheads of the best avant-garde journals. Of the leading figures on this Parisian scene that the Romanian knew only from afar, Apollinaire had been one of the few to refuse his backing, since Apollinaire had deemed the Dada movement's approach to Germany ambiguous. Cocteau, for his part, soon sent to Tzara three poems that the journal *Dada* hastened to publish, in its number 4–5 issue. This imprimatur, which included the following piece of "Enfants de troupe," turned out to be enough to integrate Cocteau into the informal Dadaist constellation:

Ticla notre âge d'or Pipe Carnot Joffre
J'offre à toute personne ayant des névralgies,
Girafe Noce un bonjour de Gustave
Ave maria de Gounod Rosière.[8]

Actively prepared by Breton and Aragon, Tzara's journal, whose publication Cocteau had happily announced—prematurely—in *Paris-midi*, had reopened the game by intermingling talents that had stopped mixing with each other and by including authors whose publication had been limited to very small journals.[9] Cocteau and Drieu la Rochelle read poems by Jacob and Cendrars at the first *Littérature* "Friday" event, which was organized by Breton and Aragon and held at the Palais des Fêtes on the rue Saint-Martin on January 23, 1920. Lured by André Salmon's theme for the "conference"—"The crisis of change"— neighborhood businessmen quickly booed the canvas that Breton held up: a superimposition of black lines by Picabia marked by the inscription "Bottom" on top, and "Top" on bottom, which was covered with red letters—L.H.O.O.Q.— whose obscene alliteration only added fuel to the fire.[10] "Back to Zurich!" people shouted as they heard the tiny Tzara declaim in a muffled voice, through a concert of bells, a recent speech in the Chambre des Députés by the very nationalistic Léon Daudet, presenting it as his own most recent poem. "Dada has just claimed its first victim," Aragon concluded when he heard about the heart attack that struck Jacques-Émile Blanche as he was on his way to his huge happening. It was the start of a storm during which no one would recognize himself for months on end.

Cocteau was up to the challenge of these early days. Already used to Satie's aggressive eccentricities, he let himself be carried away by this tornado of animal cries, *bruitiste* insults, concerts of vowels, obscene onomatopoeias, and shards of glass. "Gadji beri bimba glandridi lauta lonni cadori gadjama gramma berida bimbala glandri," they heard in the cabarets of Zurich.[11] Cocteau began to live to the frenzied rhythm of Tzara, who would sway his backside like an Eastern dancer between African songs and poems in invented languages. Indeed, Cocteau gave such a warm greeting to the great Dada ball planned in Geneva for March 1920—they would "replace pants and hat with the mechanical doctor writer," said the program—that he came to figure among the 391 "présidents et présidentes" of the movement. Of all the avatars that Cocteau would take on over his lifetime, this Dadaist Cocteau remains one of the least believable, not to say most crazy. But, as always, he was answering not only his vital need to be there, at the most incandescent center of the postwar euphoria, but also an underlying anxiety, unique to any revolution: that of not yet having come to the end of the old man who, before the war, had so gravely compromised himself literarily.

For the first time, a movement was openly attacking sensibility and beauty, reason and progress, psychology and language, tradition as well as dream. The logic, politics, and philosophy bequeathed by the Greeks? Toys to be thrown away. The hilarious, nihilistic wind that Hans Arp and Hugo Ball had been blowing since 1916 into the smoke-filled cabarets of Zurich and Berlin had reached the country of Descartes, through that fire-breather Tzara, who was himself determined to abolish all morality, all ideology, all consecrated artistic expression. "You don't understand what we're doing, isn't that right? Well, dear friends, we understand even less," proclaimed the *Bulletin Dada*, not without logic: for only imbeciles could still want to be reasonable, according to that hyper-nervy imp Tzara, whose immense monocle seemed to belong to some giant friend, as Maurice Sachs said.

Knowing only by hearsay the artistic guerilla warfare that the Futurist declaimer-performers had already been waging for ten years, and to which Dada owed so much, the Parisians stood open-mouthed. The Dadaists, who had been supporters of peace at any price during the time of Verdun, three years later reintroduced a new kind of war in the City of Lights, showing their teeth at every opportunity and banging their fists when necessary. They relaunched the effort to mechanize bodies and brutalize customs that was already under way, leaving an unmistakable taste of ash in the mouth.[12] For creators, there was already only one choice left: to "machinify" oneself or to be forever outdated.

For months, Tzara's shouts tore through the sky of Paris. In his *Dada Manifesto*, which reached Paris in early 1919, this spectacle-animal swore:

> I tell you, there is no beginning and we are not trembling, we are not sentimental. We ... are preparing the great spectacle of disaster, fire,

decomposition . . . DADA DADA DADA, the shout of tense colors, intertwining
of opposites and of all contradictions, of grotesques, of inconsistencies.[13]

It was the end of the artist, of the critic and the patron, and the emergence
of a new type: "a mixture of man, mothballs, sponge, plastic animal, and beefsteak with soap."[14] Like the trumpets of the Last Judgment, Tzara had just
brought down the last aesthetic beliefs, from literary property to dreams of
posterity, in order to bring about a form of higher existence, permanently realized—LIFE—the only art to which no one had ever dared devote himself
completely.

How could one imagine that this devastating gnome, shouting his non-
poems in several languages, had begun as a Symbolist poet in the years from
1912 to 1915?[15] Seeing the epileptic trances he entered into once thrown onto the
stage, and his fury that would be imitated by the nail-studded punks of 1975,
those who saw him thought he seemed like a kind of demon come to wreck any
form of order or connection, reasoning or intelligence. Drunk with dark energy,
this bundle of nerves seemed no more able than the Huns to set a limit to his
destructiveness—if not his own glory—a "self-styled barbarian," said Richard
Huelsenbeck, one of the pioneers of the movement.

Cocteau's transformation left him grappling with a latent confusion. The
inversion of all his values had produced, in his hardly dialectic mind, a doubt
about his beliefs, at least about their precise hierarchy. When members of the
Dada movement proclaimed "I am against systems, the most acceptable system
is on principle to have none," he acknowledged a form of familiar nihilism, and
if the Dadaists added, "Order = disorder; ego = non-ego, affirmation = negation," that obscure part of Cocteau that refused to take on any definitive form,
and even doubted the principle of identity, still approved.[16] Cocteau was not
always at ease when he met Tzara, however. This frenzied man, capable of
remaining motionless for hours on end, like an "exotic, depressed poodle,"
before leaping up at the mere word *Dada!*, sometimes welcomed Cocteau with
open arms, and sometimes stared at him with an expression of cold cruelty.[17]
Intermediaries like Picabia had warned Tzara in March 1919, when he was still
in Zurich, that Cocteau was viewed askance by everyone—with Satie himself
considering him an idiot.

Openly regretting not having had the strength, out of fear of boredom, to
become an "adventurer of great sophistication," adding, with a smile, "One has
an almost hygienic need of complications"—Tzara felt and heard only blows
and shouts: that is, with his metal monocle and his plastic heart, he was at the
opposite end of the spectrum from Cocteau.[18] A collective organ, the leader of

the Dadaists wanted to be a metal gullet, inhuman, sarcastic, and contradictory. Even if he had played with this idea in *David* and then *Parade*, Cocteau was too sensitive to become Tzara's rival in this effort. Their common need for publicity, as well as their similar gift for ubiquity, would soon lead them to appear together: Cocteau seemed specially designed to attract the attention of the press to the movement that Tzara knew so well how to orchestrate. They were seen inaugurating the Jockey, a bar on Montparnasse, together with Ezra Pound, and posing before the camera of Man Ray, entwined in a big cardboard S evoking carnival novelties.[19] After seeing them climb up on the same platforms or appearing in the same concerts—from the music hall of the Alhambra to the Gaya, where Tzara liked to join the Cocteau jazz band—the press assumed a two-headed direction, and Tzara saw nothing inconvenient in that, so long as he remained the inventor.[20] Hadn't Picasso, Satie, and Les Six already taken advantage of this fantastic public relations agent, Cocteau?

The idyll lasted a few months. Cocteau was seen at the home of Picabia, the only artist-artist of the movement, or rather at the home of his companion, Germaine Everling, whose immense apartment in the 16th arrondissement suited Cocteau better than the Certà, a Basque bar behind the Opéra where the undiluted Dadaists had taken up residence under the nascent authority of Breton. Everling would remember her assiduous guest as being like Dresden china.

> He comes in, fine, delicate, a gaudy silk tie knotted around his neck, and, right away, he charms those present. Still standing, he looks as if he were dancing ... He mimes by turns Marinetti, Breton, Tzara, Mme Lara, Crommelynck, Picabia, Mme Rachilde, Cocteau himself ... Who can express the charm of Picabia's smile as he listened to Cocteau?[21]

In this way, the darling of the Rostand era hadn't changed one iota.

With his steep-heeled shoes and his Mafia-like panama hats, Picabia had all the looks of a homosexual as they were imagined at the time in the Dada ranks.[22] Gossipy and scandalmongering, changeable and cruel, eager to fall out with everyone in order to make his capricious voice heard, like a cackling prima donna, this Cuban scion could only live, if he was to be believed, wallowing in perfumed rice powder, with his buttocks strapped in sable. Cocteau and he had in common only their drollness and their taste for the most contradictory existential experiences; as for the rest, Cocteau was a kind of chaste partner-swapper, fleeing his sexuality in passionate friendships and suppressed love affairs—unlike the sybarite Picabia, who loved only women and opium. Since he had first made a name for himself as a post-Impressionist, then Orphic, painter,

Picabia lived happily in that labyrinth of interlinked fictions that would make him betray all his aesthetics with a radical opportunism.

Co-founder in 1917 of the journal 391 with Arthur Cravan, Picabia had soon perceived in the tabula rasa of Tzara a springboard for his own absence of values; it was such a delight, for this arch-society man, to call for the destruction of the old world, from a flowered balcony in fashionable Passy! Picabia, however, found a pretext never to appear at the soirées where the Dadaists, some armed with revolvers, threatened the audience during their sonorous productions. He who feared police like the plague may have feared even more his radical friends, each of whom had good reasons to be mad at him—they would see him with ferocity end up in a kind of sarcastic *pompier* style. The irritation that Cocteau provoked among these dyed-in-the-wool Dadaists would help Picabia establish his right to say out loud whatever he wanted, outside of any logic—an authentically Dada right, but one the movement didn't grant to everyone. Thus he escaped this "censorship" that as a good dandy he himself brandished like a cane, from the heights of that amused indifference that would lead him to have one child with his wife and another with his mistress, six months apart; to buy sixty-three racing cars in twenty years; and to receive with delight visits from this Cocteau, the very one he insulted elsewhere: "He found it more amusing to shoot at the shooting-gallery lady than at the target," Cocteau would say about him.[23]

Sometimes there appeared a tall young man, close-cropped and purebred as his own dogs, long linked with Picabia, who light-heartedly pillaged his inventions—unless it was the other way around.[24] Marcel Duchamp's discreet presence wouldn't lead anyone to guess for an instant that he was about to turn the century upside-down by his anti-oeuvre. The inventor of the ready-made so willingly let his host, Tzara or Cocteau, have the limelight, that he seemed like a secondary character—amused observation of everything was already more important to him than the wish to put himself forward. Actually, however, Duchamp had been at the origin of this desire to overturn art, or at least to have it become integrally realized throughout society.

Carried along by his easiest talent, mimicry, Cocteau had only to open his mouth to catch—and spread—the Dada spirit. If the telephone rang at the home of Germaine Everling, Cocteau's quavering voice would be heard calling itself Picabia's grandfather, and announcing that, since he was now only able to read with his behind, he could not make out, without lowering his pants, the note in which his "grandson" wrote the day on which he was returning. In Cocteau's version of Sarah Bernhardt—that old glory who was still treading the boards—she became a stage machine, visibly deploying her pincers in the wings to choose her accessories—wig, false teeth, wooden leg. If Cocteau passed a child on the footpaths of the Champs-Élysées, he would shout, according to Morand: "Hurry up and play, little dead man from the next war!"[25] The same Morand would remember him, at the home of Daudet's widow, manipulating to her great displeasure a little bud vase that the brothers Goncourt had given her long ago. "Don't be afraid," retorted Cocteau, "if this piece is really old, it won't break when it falls"—and he threw it to the ground.[26] In her journal Liane de Pougy, a former *cocotte* who was accepted into the fold of Prince Ghika, noted in her journal about Cocteau: "He makes fun of everything cruelly, sharply, respects nothing, plays with everything."[27]

At ease in this nihilistic but luxurious bohemia, Cocteau followed each of the group's performances and events, even the most violent ones. Since the mainstream newspapers had made Cocteau the leader of the movement—he was its only figure who was already well-known—he claimed he was the precursor, in one of those mimetic overreachings to which he alone held the secret evidence: didn't *Parade* announce, two years before the arrival of Dada, the approach of a spectacle that would never arrive? "He's never the one who climbs into the breach, but he's always the one who plants the flag there," noted Adrienne Monnier, adding, like a good bookseller: "There has to be someone."[28]

This overreaching claim by Cocteau was like waving a red flag at Breton, who had welcomed Tzara like the Messiah, believing he saw in him a Rimbaud exalted by Marinetti. It also reawakened in Breton the exasperating events of 1917, when all the avant-garde was afraid of being overtaken, during the creation of that same *Parade*, by the ex-protégé of Anna de Noailles. Knives would soon be sharpened.

THE "MOST DETESTABLE BEING OF THIS TIME"

The Dada movement took on an unexpected amplitude, during the year 1920. There was room now only for one-upmanship in the generation emerging from the war, with everyone wanting to contribute his stone to the destruction of the old institutions and the "stupid nineteenth century" that Léon Daudet himself would mock two years later. The more pleasure Tzara took in being exasperating, the more he was assured of an enthusiastic audience, with any reservation expressed in the name of reason arousing outbursts of sniggers. "The public threw itself into the avant-garde with so much vehemence that there was not only no more rear-guards, but no army at all," said Morand, who prudently remained a spectator: "I don't have the talent for delirium," he confided.[29] In April 1920 Gide himself would finally salute Dada in the pages of the austere *Nouvelle revue française*, probably thinking he saw in these supporters of virtual murder heirs of Lafcadio, the character who commits a crime for fun in his *Caves du Vatican*. This approval came too late, though, to dazzle Marc Allégret, and already Breton was impatient to outdo the Dada movement.

Under pressure from Breton, who was exasperated by Cocteau's cuddling up to Aragon, Cocteau's name disappeared from *Littérature*: the second issue, published in April 1919, does not mention him.[30] Aragon, the last of the Musketeers to break with him, had still been able to report on *Le coq et l'arlequin* without citing his name, but six months hadn't gone by before he too was ridiculing Cocteau in his novel *Anicet ou le panorama*, citing him among the claimants to modern beauty under the transparent name Miracle Angel, that "dandy in whom, merely from his sincere accent, you'd recognize the first mask."[31] Soupault had asked Tzara to withdraw from number 4–5 of the journal *Dada* the note on Cocteau's *Le Cap* that Soupault had sent him: in this nephew by marriage of the industrialist Louis Renault, a man "always elegant, properly raised, which weighed on him," in the words of Maurice Martin du Gard, Cocteau had just found a lasting enemy.[32]

The first signs of irritation went back, long before the readings of *Le Cap*, to the time when Apollinaire was alive. In May 1917, one of the "historic" friends of Breton, Théodore Fraenkel, had published in the journal *SIC* some verses apparently signed by Cocteau; the initial letters of the lines in acrostic spelled out "Pauvres Birots," which furtively made fun of the supposed naivety of the editor who had just printed them, Pierre Albert-Birot, and his wife, Germaine, author of the music for Apollinaire's *Mamelles de Tirésias*. Written with the probable support of Breton, this forgery protested against allowing the ex-page of Anna de Noailles entry to a journal that had been hostile to him until *Parade* and that claimed to be on the side of Apollinaire, whose spirit Breton was already claiming exclusively to embody.[33]

The young medical student, Breton, sincerely admired Apollinaire. Awed by Breton's talents, the Enchanter introduced to him another young poet, Philippe Soupault. But Breton became less enamored of Apollinaire when the elder man began to betray his anti-Boche bellicosity, his desire for the Légion d'honneur, his dreams of the Académie française, and his willingness to work as a censor at the Ministry of War. Worse, Apollinaire no longer hid his annoyance with the triumph of modernism, even if he had actively prepared for it, or his desire to return to classical rhythms. "He even, having opened a floodgate, sometimes insulted the flood, under the pretext that he had opened the floodgate as a practical joke," Cocteau added.[34] Apollinaire had died in time, Jacques Vaché said, one of Breton's models. But Apollinaire had always played with aesthetics and ideologies, and history would treat him well. Apollinaire was both the brute and the gentleman, the rapist and the troubadour, Villon and Ronsard. He drew from the writings of the mystics as much as pornography, and sang of the syncope of trolleys as well as the charms of Pope Pius X, whom he called "the most modern European." Breton could only applaud this ambiguity. After the death of the Enchanter, in order the better to establish his own status as his heir, he began courting Marie Laurencin, whom Apollinaire had loved until 1912, and with whom Cocteau was also connected. Laurencin was a "pretty lamb fed on mist," said Morand.[35] "The Milkmaid and pot of milk of Cubism," added Blanche.[36]

Had Breton developed some jealousy when the Enchanter, ill, confided the reading of his poems to Cocteau, and reserved for Breton only the organization of his patriotic lecture on "The New Spirit and the Poets"? The seemingly unanimous homage that both men had paid to Apollinaire, in the presence of Radiguet, had only exacerbated the competition. As the months passed, Cocteau concealed less and less his claim to be the direct heir of Apollinaire, and added more poetic titles to his name, whereas Breton still had published nothing. Cocteau acted in the name of free literary adventure and the experimentation with self that the Enchanter had always lived and advocated, but also in the name of that Pohésie and Phrance that the Dadaists laughed about, but which he refused, after Apollinaire, to discard.

More serious for Breton was that Cocteau was already central to an artistic network of which Les Six, Satie, and Picasso—not to mention Cendrars, Lhote, and the Ballets Russes—were already crown jewels. It was an entourage whose quality rivaled the one that Apollinaire had wanted to lead, and it made Cocteau a very plausible candidate for that central place that Breton was impatient to occupy, even if he still remained in the shadow of Tzara. But ever since Vaché had called Apollinaire a clever versifier, on a par with Cocteau, he was no longer *the* poet to follow. Under the influence of this immobile, ironic, sterile adventurer (Vaché), who had gone so far as to threaten the crowd with a revolver during the dress rehearsal of *Les mamelles de Tirésias* in 1917, Breton retrospectively blocked his ears when hearing Apollinaire demanding "On new thoughts let's make ancient verses," like André Chénier had in 1785. Tzara had in the meantime only gone further than Vaché in undermining Apollinaire: in Tzara's view, one could no longer defend a man who, in his final speech on the "new spirit," had claimed to found it on order and a classical sense of duty, and who said that France held all the secrets to civilization and was mother to all geniuses.[37]

Still Breton secretly admired Apollinaire, who had carried out, in *Onirocritique*, a first attempt at automatic writing. Then too he had written as preface to his *Mamelles:* "When man wanted to imitate walking, he created the wheel that does not resemble a leg. In that way he created surrealism without realizing it." The Enchanter remained the solar face of a poetic constellation of which Vaché and Tzara were moons. With the Dadaist episode over, it was naturally Apollinaire who sat enthroned in the pantheon that the now-baptized Surrealists would construct, amid the strange or magnificent figures from Lautréamont to Raymond Roussel. But there would still remain a hiccup: that word sur-realism. It was first used by Apollinaire to baptize *Parade*, Cocteau's ballet, even though Cocteau himself, in the view of many, did not have the slightest claim on having invented this modern movement.

"Why this nastiness, at once confused and meticulous, of your friends?" Cocteau asked Aragon in February 1919. The future Surrealists would find reasons for this hostility all right, though they seemed somewhat jumbled. Seriously wounded at the front and then hospitalized in Paris, Soupault would say he was revolted to hear "snobs and draft-dodgers" speak with emotion about *Parade*—though that reaction simply matches the most jingoistic public opinion of the day.[38] Breton would assert for his part that Apollinaire had had time to warn him against Cocteau, and to point out to the same Soupault that Cocteau "is a trickster and a chameleon."[39] If we are to believe him, the Enchanter even told him that Paponat the Algerian, the character of the "*fopoâte*"—read *faux poète*, fake poet—in *Le poète assassiné* had been inspired by Cocteau, where he figured clearly as Public Enemy No. 1.[40] But this passage was written when Apollinaire hadn't yet met Cocteau, and even though the two men had an uneven relationship, as we've seen, it was never a hateful one.[41]

Did Breton remember the great disdain that Jacques Vaché had himself shown for the *pohètes*, when Breton had confided to him his desire to become a writer? By Dadafying himself, Breton began to turn Cocteau into his *bête noire*, and to call Apollinaire the "last poet," with all the hauteur of which he was capable. No sooner had Tzara set foot in Paris than Breton was warning him against sending more letters from Zurich to Cocteau: "You don't know him well. My completely disinterested feeling, I swear to you, is that he is the most detestable being of this time. Again, he has done nothing to me, and I assure you that hatred is not my strong suit."[42] Cocteau, a nightingale born in the lap of luxury, had made the mistake of beginning to sing twelve years before Breton: he must not be allowed to be the loudest. "It's the fashion to write bad things about me everywhere," Cocteau had to acknowledge at the end of 1919, after he had become, thanks to a secret pact made among Breton, Soupault, and Aragon, the symbol of the poetry they had sworn to destroy.[43] Breton took some time, though, before he outlined a line of attack that could separate him from Tzara:

he had neither the Romanian's destructive genius nor his madness in handling people, but he did have a capacity for organization that Tzara lacked. In the meantime, he would make himself each day more vigilant against the "traitor" Cocteau, who in his opinion prevented Dada from going as far as it could. He did everything he could to poach Cocteau's friends, regardless of whether they were famous or just promising, by inviting them to write in *Littérature*. In this way he became close to a group ranging from Satie to Morand, and including Georges Auric who, treated during the war for serious depression, had become Breton's and Aragon's friend at the Val-de-Grâce Hospital in Paris.

Radiguet was treated the best. Breton, as he would confess later on, saw himself as a "natural" protector of the young Dadaist, whose poetry Breton liked. He would even claim to have been at the original meeting of Radiguet with Cocteau, either at the matinée of homage to Apollinaire, or on a street in the neighborhood next to the Madeleine, and for having immediately understood that this meeting would have a lasting influence on them both.[44] These intimations were probably contradictory, but they reinforced Breton's desire to integrate the teenager into the team he was gathering every Friday at the Certà. Radiguet soon tired, however, of the authoritarianism of the twenty-four-year-old ex-medic, and four or five meetings with the hardcore members of the movement had been enough to lead him to resume his liberty. Cocteau's tutelage might be stifling, but at least his artistic tolerance was total: Cocteau's unconscious harbored a mother, with whatever potential abuse that might imply, but Breton's hid a policeman—and Radiguet did not like to pass as a recruit; he demanded to be admired for himself.

If defections made Cocteau despair, they made Breton furious—he did everything he could to get Radiguet back, and concentrated his attacks a little more on Radiguet's protector. Aware of his key role, but determined not to serve as a pawn, Radiguet raised the stakes: with that brusqueness usual at the Certà, he demanded that Aragon, who had the gift of prodigiously annoying him— "very nice aside from that"—be excluded from their meetings, then with a rare offhandedness said to Breton, "And say that everyone is accustomed to making you responsible for the words, actions, gestures of that PUPPET."[45] That was the tone that had to be used with the editor of *Littérature*, who would hurry to publish a poem that Radiguet himself didn't like.[46] "I know the limits of your susceptibility," Breton wrote in reply, adding in passing, as if to soften his attempts at annexation: "I have good news from Jean Cocteau." Wanting to avenge the latter, while at the same time asserting his independence, Radiguet twisted the knife in his reply: "I read two fragments from *Les champs magnétiques*.[47] It didn't bore me, I confess I was very much surprised by it. I'll do what

I can to come to the Certà tomorrow, despite my horror of 'aestheticians,' from Montmartre or not."⁴⁸ Where did the sixteen-year-old find the cheek to send another letter, eleven days later? Despite its seeming deference, Breton probably had never before received such an insolent one:

> I can now confess to you that *Les champs magnétiques* disappointed me, because very boring, in my opinion. I might be wrong. The second act is a masterpiece (I don't think you've heard me utter that ridiculous word yet). I'd like to focus on the role that Philippe Soupault's collaboration played (whatever it is, it is, without a doubt, the best thing he did). This reading awakened in me a very great liking for Philippe Soupault. Not for you, of course, since I've liked and admired you for a long time.⁴⁹

Soon Paris would speak only of Cocteau and Radiguet—the "anti-Aragon," in Tzara's words—and the sight of this couple, omnipresent in town, provoked an uncontrollable expansion of Breton's literary jealousy, as did their repeated feats, during the years 1920 and 1921, and the admiration that Radiguet expressed to Cocteau, in words and writing.

Cocteau was far from having Radiguet's strength of character: the "club" that had rejected him had real prestige in his eyes, while the one welcoming him was losing its brilliance after just a few months. Breton's rejection, as we've seen, made Cocteau even more concerned to get closer to him, at first: his thirst for recognition went so far as to make him say later that it was his own decision not to form a part of the Breton group. "Surrealism proceeded by ukases. I am a free man . . . and I will remain so till the end."⁵⁰ But the more obstinately that Cocteau refused to reply to their attacks, the more that Breton picked up on his fear of rejection and silence, and the more the group took pleasure in sawing through the already wobbly chair on which Cocteau was sitting. And Cocteau could see how far he was falling. He who just ten years earlier had treated Proust with the assurance of a literary elder, or Anna de Noailles with the offhandedness of the super-talented, was being provoked relentlessly by "tyros" just as inexperienced as he had been then, but already much more aggressive, since they had immediately perceived in Cocteau a point of vulnerability: the couple he was forming with Radiguet.

Destabilized by these intersecting attacks—Gide's *Nouvelle revue française* was no more tender than *Littérature*—Cocteau would for some months write and distribute manifestos and exhaust himself in self-justifications. "One of the most noble dramatic situations?" he would ask in *Le coq parisien*, six months later, taking up an argument that had already served to convince Apollinaire of the validity of his conversion: "Calchas going over to the Greeks out of love of justice, in *Troilus and Cressida*. The Trojans watch him betray them. The Greeks suspect him of espionage. He is truly alone in the world."[51]

LE BOEUF SUR LE TOIT

During this period, Cocteau's overexcited intelligence did find joy in organizing others, at first with Les Six, who were impatient to submit their projects to him. Darius Milhaud, the cheeriest of them, appointed in 1917 secretary to his friend Paul Claudel, who was at the time posted to Brazil, had returned fascinated by the rhythms he had heard during Carnival. Once back in Paris, Milhaud had mixed popular tunes from Rio with a Portuguese *fado,* and some tangos with some maxixes and sambas, with the idea of setting it all to a movie by Chaplin—a sort of globalized potpourri with themes looping like the Brazilian dancing "machines" did, but also like Satie's *Parade.* When Cocteau discovered a version of Milhaud's composition for two pianos—a ray of sunshine in a genre still dominated by the pale colors of the Impressionists—he suggested to Milhaud that he make it into a quick orchestral farce, for which Cocteau would write the theme.

The marriage was good for Milhaud. With the cricket-like rhythms of the conga drums, the wonderful *Boeuf sur le Toit,* from the name of a famous samba, *O boi no telhado*—the equivalent of Le Chien Qui Fume—did better than convey the Brazilian rainbow, and realize this incisive music that Cocteau had so desired: the twenty-five musicians in the orchestra raised themselves, beyond the sum of their individual talents, to a kind of collective genius.[52] The precocious "jazzmaniac" that was Cocteau stimulated in a wonderful way Milhaud, the "fat Lustucru."[53] Making full use of the ups and downs of Cocteau's nature, Milhaud wreathed an exquisitely melancholic tune around his cheerful rondo, in which crickets, toads, and cockatoos stridulate, with all the sonorous teases that implies. Comparing the freshness and insolence of this *Boeuf sur le Toit* to the ballet that Milhaud would extract from *La création du monde,* an outline by Cendrars created three years later, is enough to let us glimpse the kind of fervent energy that Cocteau could elicit and communicate, for the composer too in this instance would be called a chameleon, a magician, and Proteus.

An American bar under Prohibition serves as the set, with clowns from Médrano that Cocteau was already planning on using in 1916—including the famous Footit and Chocolate he'd admired since childhood—performing the main roles, wearing huge fake heads all with the same expression. The lesson of *Parade* had been learned: neither intentions nor symbols weighed down this farce where the head of a cop, decapitated by the bar's fan, does dance steps in the arms of a redhead in drag—since the piece was played exclusively by men—until the acrobat Albert Fratellini turns, walking on his hands, around his scalp. Relying on only action, rhythm, and joy, Cocteau added no dialogue to his spectacle, and scheduled the rehearsals with the rigorous discipline demanded by any comic mechanism, in film or on stage. Unlike the deluge orchestrated by Milhaud, his choreography set out to evoke the slow motion peculiar to silent films, in order to give the spectator the illusion of living in a dream, or, even better, of moving underwater. To make it seem like an improvisation, he regulated each movement with a vivacity and exactness that would lead Radiguet, who had followed all the rehearsals, to say two years later: "I know nothing more austere, more chaste, than the dressing room of a clown."[54]

Determined to do without Diaghilev, whose imperialism he could no longer bear, Cocteau established himself as his own impresario. But this time he decided *not* to create a scandal, unless it meant shocking in hindsight, in order to get people to hear this "cinema-symphony on South American themes set to a farce by Jean Cocteau," subtitled "The Nothing Doing Bar" [English in original], at the Comédie des Champs-Élysées, on February 21, 1920. The carnivalistic, popular aesthetics that *Le coq et l'arlequin* had called for found its expression in this mixture of Parisian street spirit, Dada insolence, and poetic rigor, which would characterize the idyll created between the librettist-choreographer and Les Six. Cocteau had learned from Diaghilev how to speak about art to the wealthy, how to delicately position the drain into which their gold could pour, in order to create beauty: Étienne de Beaumont was in charge of selling the boxes, and then organizing the word of mouth outreach effort, and soon the little hall was sold out; the last box—with no view—was rented in extremis by the Shah of Persia, who spent a fortune on obtaining these few square meters where he housed his entourage; as for the publicity, the "genius" impresario that Cocteau had become (according to Poulenc) gave the task to Radiguet, who wrote a program promising the presence during intermission of an American bar—which was none other than the spectacle itself.

Conceived by a Parisian who had never set foot in the United States, this Yankee farce was well-received: Proust said he was enchanted; Morand, happily surprised; Léautaud praised a "disjointed, voluptuous fantasy" in his column in *Le Mercure*; and the very young Maurice Sachs would speak of the only spectacle of the season that had seemed superior to a film.[55] The success was helped by the title, and Cocteau was able to prolong its run by having three hundred pneumatic telegrams sent containing "Good for one small box" that provoked mini-riots. "You can't say it's funny, but since it's different, it's funny," said a cap-wearing worker about this spectacle that Mme Rasimi would integrate into her shows of naked women, at the Ba-ta-clan, a big hall near the Bastille.[56] And Mme Alphonse Daudet, who had ended up, like her son, going with this new flow, created a surprise for the authors and for Firouz Mirza, the Minister of Foreign Affairs from Persia: she served them, at the end of a dinner she gave for them, a house made of caramel topped with a sugar bull, which was then sliced to the sound of ukuleles. But already Mme Cocteau was worried about seeing her so-unstable son become an organizer of spectacles: "He suffered with Diaghilev, he will suffer even more, in the incoherence he is undertaking," she had announced to Valentine Hugo.

The production left for London and set itself up in the Coliseum, whose doors announced in gold letters: HUGO RUMBOLD PRESENTS COCTEAU'S GREAT PARISIAN SUCCESS.[57] Disturbed by Radiguet's absence, Cocteau didn't get much enjoyment out of the city, or out of Prince Firouz's white car. "Paris is better. No doubt about it," he wrote to the young dandy with the monocle, whom he renamed his "dear venerable Boby Esq." and to whom he promised a top hat—when he wasn't imagining him playing soccer, wearing the wool cap of English schoolboys. These were letters in which Cocteau was worried about Radiguet's neglect in producing Le coq, the paper they had just launched, but to which Radiguet didn't even reply, despite his regular promises and repeated telephone calls from Mme Cocteau. This neglect made the author of these letters not even bother caring about his Anglo-Saxon consecration: "As soon as I leave Anjou—it's death," concluded Cocteau.[58] For the first time, he sensed the profundity of his dependence and the extent of his fragility. Formerly so sure of himself, faced with the "old men" of his youth, he found himself at the mercy of a mute, elusive teenager who was sometimes subject to forms of social paralysis, and at other times inclined to those sudden emotional rejections inherent to adolescence, which Cocteau was incapable of not taking personally.

Suddenly aware of being alone in his love, and of having to answer the questions he had asked his "Bébé," Cocteau quickly returned to Paris, took Radiguet in hand, and tirelessly, almost maternally, began again to produce enough love for both of them. He rewarded each literary effort of his protégé by a social or Parisian reward, to the extent that the two could be seen at almost all the parties, premieres, and balls that occurred that year, 1920. A ball at the home of a princess? Radiguet would stop by the rue d'Anjou to pick up a tuxedo and the gloves that the designer Jacques Doucet offered him. A dinner at the home of the Daudets? Cocteau would get out his bowties and wing collars to dress the prodigy, who was just a little smaller than he. It was an intense social life, which Radiguet saw as a means to sharpen his sense of observation and his witty repartees. The key event for this practice may have been the premiere of *Pulcinella*, the ballet that Stravinsky, Picasso, and Massine had written during their travels between Rome and Naples. All the leading figures of those years, some of whom would appear in Radiguet's second novel, *Le bal du comte d'Orgel*, went to drink and dance at the soirée on May 15 given by the Persian prince Firouz in a suburb called Robinson, in a faux chateau rented by an ex-convict who had to move constantly to avoid being apprehended by the police. Among the guests were the Beaumonts, Diaghilev, Auric, and Picasso; eventually Stravinsky, drowned in champagne, began throwing pillows, bolsters, and mattresses from an upstairs balcony, in a prelude to a huge pillow fight that lasted until 3:00 a.m. Was this a return to schoolboy shenanigans, or the dawn of a new antiquity? Never had art seemed so joyful and easy.

THE TOUGH CHICK

Since the publication, in June 1919, of *À l'ombre des jeunes filles en fleurs* and *Pastiches et mélanges*, Proust's situation had strengthened considerably. In November, thanks to the ardent campaign led by Léon Daudet, Lucien's brother, he had been awarded the Prix Goncourt. There was still one columnist who wagered that Proust would remain forever unknown, and the young Aragon, in *Littérature*, insulted that "laborious snob." Critics too would persist in insulting Proust during the publication of the first volume of *Du côté de Guermantes*, in the fall of 1920, after one of the copyeditors at Gallimard, André Breton, irritated Proust with his inopportune remarks and carelessness.[59] But these publications also brought Proust some spectacular shows of support.

Despite the immense energy required to correct his proofs, Proust, whom no one dared any more call "le petit Marcel," still found the strength to organize some dinners at the Ritz, go see *Le Boeuf sur le Toit* at Cocteau's invitation, and attend the repeat performance of *Parade*, which he had been unable to see at its premiere. Performed twelve times for a public that had hissed, laughed, or stamped their feet three years earlier, Cocteau, Satie, and Picasso were even given personal standing ovations. When saluted by Radiguet in *Le Gaulois* on December 25, 1920, the spectacle affected Proust even in his "spleen," since he regretted not having enough strength to go to the circus anymore.[60] The man who had condemned himself to the *théâtrophone*, a strange apparatus allowing him to follow dramatic or musical performances from his home, was trying one last time to enjoy life, which meant escaping the antediluvian era that he revived every day in his *Recherche*.

Proust would see these 1920s in part through the prism of Cocteau, who would introduce him to Picasso (whose beauty struck him), and would tell him about the bars that were opening up everywhere, and the dances that were being given—since Proust didn't want to let himself grow distant from the times. But Proust was looking more and more like a revenant, that early-old man whom Cocteau still found sometimes, when he returned to the rue d'Anjou, collapsed on the bench on his landing, having knocked in vain on Cocteau's door but not wanting, he said, either to go back or to go downstairs to find him at his neighbor's, Mme de Chevigné (who for a long time had been a cause for discord between them). Five years earlier, Proust was already suspecting Cocteau of repeating to the countess that Proust replied to all questions asked him about the war: "The war? I haven't yet had time to think about it. At present I'm studying the Caillaux affair."[61] Through this piece of gossip, Cocteau thought he could summarize in a flattering way the density of life "under the bell jar" that Proust was leading. But despite himself, he had degraded Proust's image in the eyes of a woman already convinced that he was much too interested in the past—so much so that Proust again accused Cocteau of not being able to distinguish the man who writes from the one who lives.[62]

This time, Proust once again complained about the silence of the woman to whom he had indeed sent his book late, but who still hadn't replied to his previous three-page letter. This was an embarrassing situation for Cocteau: the Comtesse de Chevigné, brandishing her dedicated copy of *Du côté de Guermantes*, had asked him to annotate only the passages concerning the Duchesse de Guermantes, and he knew how furious the countess had been to recognize herself in this deforming mirror. But Proust still didn't understand. He had made an almost inaccessible sovereign of an obscure lady-in-waiting to the last claimant to the throne of France, and he would have liked her to recognize, if not the supremacy of book over birth and ink over blood, at least the greatness of his memorial. How could the countess who was being celebrated unreservedly, throughout the world, under the guise of that Duchesse de Guermantes, and about whom courses were being given in Sweden and conferences in Holland—not to speak of the eight hundred letters Proust had received about her, without his finding the physical strength to reply to them—how could she scorn his book?[63]

Cocteau knew "Corporal Petrarch" well enough to know that Proust's expectations were destined to remain forever frustrated. "You can't ask a bug to read natural history," he ended up replying to Proust.[64] But that couldn't appease Proust, whose "models" were rebelling, one after the other—although he fiercely rejected being labeled with the vices of some of his characters, he was only too likely to lend them his own. He went on to write yet another, interminable missive, which that descendant of the Marquis de Sade had the pleasure of not opening, just like the others. But Proust insisted, and de Chevigné, exasperated, finally asked Marie Laure, her granddaughter, to destroy "the nonsense [*dindonnades*] of that bore."[65] So hundreds of letters went up in smoke, putting an end to a thirty-year passion, which from the beginning had been governed by the snobbishness of a woman who had rejected the young Marcel, in the Champs-Élysées gardens, as if he were an untouchable in rags, repeating dryly, "Fitz-James is waiting for me!"[66] Of the bird of Paradise whose song Proust had sung, throughout a correspondence forever lost, there remained only a "tough chick [*une poule coriace*]," stupid and mean, whom he would soon change into a blotchy, red vulture.[67]

By bringing an end to Proust's cyclonic jealousy, this quarrel sealed his literary complicity with Cocteau. Since the world in which they had gotten to know each other had pretty much disappeared, Proust no longer had to reproach Cocteau for distracting himself in it. Proust had been one of the rare survivors of the prewar era to have encouraged Cocteau's transformation because he was sure it would purify him and bring him closer to the book he bore within him. True, Proust had noted the contradictions that were scattered throughout *Le coq et l'arlequin*, but he had sincerely admired its aphorisms; Proust himself confessed that he frequently contradicted himself. And he had been so moved to see Cocteau beg him in vain to enrich the already prestigious catalogue of the Éditions de la Sirène with one of his titles that he had sent him this letter, probably the most touching he ever wrote to Cocteau:

> Ever since the last few occasions I saw you, I've suddenly begun to like you much more. You know the feelings I've always had. But there were clouds, I had to make an effort of memory to remember the form of the star they veiled.[68] It would be rather difficult for me to tell you why our recent meetings have been for me like a practical, definitive demonstration of what you actually were. Dear Jean, I won't insist on this, since it's kind to say it but kinder still not to say too much.[69]

Consecrated by *Parade* and *Le Boeuf sur le Toit*, Cocteau's dramatic journey seemed so convincing to Proust that it inspired the character of Octave, a shallow elegant that plays golf and gambles at the casino and that, long suspected of usurping others' talents, ends up surprising everyone (Proust must also have put a little of himself in this character). In a passage from *Albertine disparue*, published in 1925 but written at this time, the Narrator even says of that nephew of the Verdurins that his performances, sets, and costumes had revolutionized contemporary art as much as the Ballets Russes, adding, "The most authoritative judges regarded his works as something capital, almost as works of genius, and I too think like them."[70] This comment captures some of the affection that Proust had for his younger friend at this stage, while still leaving room for the reservations that Cocteau was still confronting.[71]

"LE COQ"

Tzara's troops, after a triumphal entrance into Paris, were now finding it difficult to renew themselves. Since the amazement produced by the appearance of Tzara was dwindling, they thought it a good idea to announce the enthusiastic conversion to their movement of Charlie Chaplin, Georges Clemenceau, and the Prince of Monaco, and then to announce the presence of these men at another festival. The crowd, furious at having been fooled yet again, pelted with coins the innumerable readers of manifestos succeeding each other on stage. Unable to shock anyone, Cocteau himself began to feel much less at ease. The more that Tzara's men ordered artists to go beyond the accumulative-bourgeois-fecal stage to indulge in stupendous feats or public mystifications, the more trouble Cocteau had following them. The cult of light, speed, and steel had probably signed the death warrant of old artistic subjectivity, but Dada wasn't even advocating a new one, and while Crevel could shout in the face of Anna de Noailles, "We don't write verses here anymore, Madame!," such an invective would definitely have seemed suspect coming from Cocteau. Since creators were supposed to have condemned themselves for responding in the past to commands of political, religious, or financial authorities, the most radical now advocated the dissolution of artistic practices in a classless society: ballets would give way to citizens marching in harmony, music would yield to spontaneous popular celebrations, architecture would lead to wonderful improvised houses, and painting would succumb to the splendid immorality of the world.

Cocteau believed too much in literature to proclaim its end, as so many were doing at the time. The era when writers were publishing the message that people should stop writing, and painters were painting their rejection of painting, was beginning, but it was not Cocteau's. The insults thrown at the spectators and Tzara's censorship by sonorous excess; the dissolution of all artistic forms into shouts, sounds, pistol shots, or bugle calls; the piano pieces composed at random; the spurts of ink on singers in tears—all that was no more Cocteau's cup of tea than the sketches orchestrated by radicalized high school students that decried a war they had not waged with a drama that seemed halfway between symbolic murder and hazing, and that "snow colder than death" that they caused to fall on the euphoric post-Armistice crowds.[72] "Art is dead, let's kill it," shouted the Dadaists, but for Cocteau, it was time to put an end to this parody of butchery.

Indeed Cocteau had been wrong, when young, to think of himself as a divine creator, content to interpret well-known tunes as a virtuoso. But from that to acting like those cats they would throw onto a Steinway to record the sonorous footsteps, and to call themselves "engineers" or "editors" in order, above all, not to seem to have anything to do with inspiration? The audiences at the salons had made themselves look ridiculous by blindly applauding the feats of their favorites, but the avant-garde was showing itself to be just as complacent, with its boasts and its self-satisfied shouts. The acrobats in *Parade* had despaired to see the audience flee the performance, whereas Tzara was delighted to show them nothing, after having promised them the moon. Could one consider a pamphlet a "collected works" or regard spitting as a song, and an advertisement as a work of art? Yes the act of living was the supreme art (Wilde had said as much), but why forbid painting, poetry, dance—those so-called stale old things? An artist to the tips of his fingers, Cocteau had to write to live, had to bear witness to what he was in order to exist, since art remained the only medium capable of mooring him to existence: for Cocteau, everything deserved to be safeguarded, printed, reproduced. This is just exactly what all the Dadaists in question would do, Tzara first of all, and what allows us today to discuss their works. The obscenity of the artistic condition never bothered Cocteau: the slightest poem or the first drawing by him that was reproduced was equivalent, in his eyes, to a little vaccine against oblivion. Cocteau had thought it vital to become modern; obviously he lacked that teenage rage that urges us to kill father and mother, to spit on our uncle or on the flag, or to want to "shit in colors," as the Dadaists wanted. Cocteau's place among the poseurs of nothingness suddenly seemed untenable to him. How could he, who feared death so acutely, have encouraged Tzara to play so much with it and to threaten his audience with it nearly constantly? Cocteau had suddenly become indifferent to being modern.

Cocteau had already been reproached for having left a Dada soirée for a reception at the English embassy. Tzara and Picabia indirectly returned the favor by destroying the proofs of poems he had given to 391, after he had invited them to a "feast" at Prunier. It seems that Cocteau was not made to be a follower. At the end of March 1920, he sent a confidential letter to Picabia expressing the intolerable unease that Dadaism caused in him, with its private soirées featuring every kind of sensual pleasure and invention, every sad and atrocious act—and protesting, as a Parisian patriot, against "the first attempt of foreign propaganda at work." Picabia promptly published this letter in *Cannibale*, the journal that succeeded 391, in the midst of some arrows to isolate it from everything else.[73] Cocteau's opposition was not, for him, a question of espousing the arguments of nationalist criticism, which perceived in the furious cries of the Jewish Tzara (his actual name was Samy Rostenstock) and in the horrors of *art nègre* a desire to make France "barbaric" again: he had joined Dada in the first place as a way of rejecting cheap patriotism. Now it was instead a matter of freeing himself of a sterile undertaking and reasserting his absolute artistic freedom, for himself and others.

This new turning point engendered another kind of overreach. Cocteau began by reproaching Tzara for being too timid, too "artistic": "No Dada dares to kill himself, or kill a spectator. One attends plays, one listens to music," people would read in the first issue of *Le coq*, the paper Cocteau created with Radiguet, who also wrote, in the ninth issue of *Littérature*: "Murder, like literature, is not within reach of all souls."[74] Picabia asserted that painting was for dentists, and yet he painted. Dada was still about art, and this art—although often virtual—was in the process of becoming as outmoded and boring as Alphonse Allais's schoolboy jokes, the boulevard de Guitry, or the poetry of Edmond Rostand. Although the Dada collector Walter Arensberg asserted that true works of art shouldn't live more than six hours, he collected them with as much love as Frick collected Watteaus. "The real Dadas are against Dada," Tzara's *Bulletin Dada* was already proclaiming.

With its Dada typography and radical-conservative slogans, its pink paper folded in six (a lucky number) and its aphorisms from Satie—a precursor claimed by Dada—*Le coq* would express, beginning in May 1920, all the complexity of Cocteau's new "line" being worked out on the rue d'Anjou.[75] This paper, coveted today by collectors, focused on nonchalance and cheerfulness, provocation and clarity; a cocktail mixed from interjections by Cendrars and verses by Jacob, declarations by Marie Laurencin, but also phrases from the reversible Picabia—"2+2=22"—in the midst of praise of the French spirit by Morand, a way to make Dadaism lean toward a certain tradition. Declaring himself right away as the "anti-Dadaist type, with a contortionist's aplomb," Cocteau positioned himself, faced with the literary extreme left embodied by Tzara, as a representative of the other pole, in order the better to point out that the two extremes touched: "On the other side of the wall, without raising my voice, I can converse with Tzara and Picabia, my neighbors from the end of the world."[76] One day affirming not to be Dadaist—"still the best way to be"—and the next day calling for a return to order, that is, to "veritable anarchy"; here praising Schoenberg and there printing his paper in blue-white-red, Cocteau leaned toward that turning point where his identity imperceptibly flipped inside out, just as a Möbius strip twists without moving, to the point of arousing vertigo.[77]

Alone Cocteau would have had trouble leaving these extreme circles, and this chair they were constantly half-pulling out from under him. The intense effort his transformation demanded, between 1913 and 1917, and the little result it had produced since (from *Le Cap*), remained too much in his memory for him to be able, two years later, to produce an opposite effort, at the risk of going back to square one—which in the meantime had disappeared. It was Radiguet who would give his elder the courage to break off, Radiguet who was surprised at seeing Cocteau suffer from the attacks coming from the Certà and who was the first to tire of the machine-gun fusillades from Tzara—his poems had always used rhymes more readily than typographical gaps. It was Radiguet too who would urge Cocteau to put into practice the gracious and ironic aesthetics whose arrival Cocteau himself had announced, in *Le coq et l'arlequin*, and on which Radiguet relied. Didn't Radiguet, in December 1919, send to Jacques Doucet, the fashion designer and book collector, a text celebrating Cocteau for having turned his back on New York, with Les Six, by translating the "melancholy of fairground festivals" at a time when slogans were dying out? "Art," wrote this precocious ideologue, "has no homeland, they say. Lie of La Palisse! A homeland of artists, like our own, gains nothing from this fallacious internationalism."[78] And it was Radiguet who called for that spirit of lightness praised by Nietzsche, that French cheerfulness embodied so well by his mentor, and who added, to encourage Cocteau's new transformation: "That is why Jean Cocteau will always be eighteen."

The precocious Dadaist that was Radiguet had no hangups about turning the page: in May 1920, he sent to Breton and to Jacques Doucet a letter indicting "Dada or the Cabaret of Nothingness" after claiming, in February's issue of *Littérature*, "Senility has become fashionable." As radical in his rupture as in his belonging, Radiguet asserted in all candor his return to the clear line, cold irony, and national classicism called for by *Le coq et l'arlequin*—since in his eyes France remained much fresher than America (whose skyscrapers were invading the journals) and hence better placed to lead the modern movement.[79] Was there ever a more fertile Dadaist than François Couperin, with his *Culbutes Jxcxbxnxs*, his *Willful Cuckoos*, his *Vieux galants* sonatas and his *Trésorières surannées*? "Be careful, the Cock has crowed thrice. We are going to deny our masters," claimed their paper, whose title clearly evokes the identification so often suggested by Cocteau between his family name and his country.

THE PARMENTIER OF THE JAZZ BAND

The move back in time made by those two still kept something avant-gardist about it, in Cocteau's mind at least, which would bring him closer to the turning point that Apollinaire outlined during the war or to the anti-modern league that Max Jacob was thinking of founding. Writing regular poems, without rare words or insults, without fake publicity or typographical accidents, seemed to them a first challenge to the now-dominant aesthetics, in the margins at least. By substituting a sensual prose for the belligerent onomatopoeias of Dada, the two writers wagered on making order as subversive as anarchy, and tradition newer than rupture. Both of them were acting in the name of the "ironic conformism" that animated Satie, in his bureaucrat's clothing, but Cocteau was making the break less cleanly. Stating as late as May 1920 that he felt obliged to defend Dada against boors, he protected himself for a while behind this new slogan: "Respect movements, flee schools." He added, for anyone who might not understand, as a dropout who knew only how to cut school: "There is no school, only individuals."[80] He then confided to the Abbé Mugnier: "Schools are the lice and fleas [*les poux, les puces*] of authors."[81] This was sounding the end, not of the collective era, but of his forced ideological affirmation.

The tightrope walker, though, trembled on his wire during all these months. Cocteau's incredibly swift intelligence found it difficult for him to find himself among all the messages produced by his transformations, retro-transformations, and other special phases. In 1919 he decreed, with his tendency to compare everything, that Marinetti the Futurist (thinking about a locomotive in front of the *Victory of Samothrace*) and D'Annunzio the backward-looking (comparing that same sculpture to a locomotive), were obeying the same reflex. Cocteau, so receptive to tendencies and hence to clichés, came to believe that the symbolism where he had shed his first skin had given way to another collection of allegories that were just as picturesque: a eulogy for "roaring" New York supplanting the cult of fin-de-siècle Venice, the electric lamp replacing the orchid, and steel bolts supplanting the onyx of rings. The "Hegelian" credo of the avant-garde, which advocated an infinite surpassing of forms, was abandoned: unlike technology, poetry, that "motionless vibration," was not "dependent on progress." Hence this transhistorical aesthetics that, in fact, would be Cocteau's until his death, but whose longevity no one could have predicted at the time.

Aware that he wasn't the kind to settle down, Cocteau preferred to warn his readers in 1924: "Ever since *Le Potomak*, I have been searching for my way, and I will search for it until my death."[82] Lucid about the serious risks that this new about-face entailed, Cocteau decisively confirmed it would not be his last, writing in issue four of *Le coq*: "We are already seeing a third Cocteau being hatched. Expect even more." The main thing, for him, was not to stay fixed in place.[83] He wanted to exercise his right to write in complete freedom, in hiero-glyphs or Braille if necessary, in a Telex style or in alexandrines, even if it meant waving a red flag at the "preservers of old anarchies."[84] To the journalist at *Les nouvelles littéraires* who was surprised about this, Cocteau explained his thinking: Poetry is light. Regardless of whether it comes from the Right or Left, from the sun or from a spotlight, its sole mission was to illumine. Why worry about the shape of the lamps or their shades?[85] More clear-sighted, Radiguet knew there was no going back. Seeing the Dadaists ready to try anything "so long as the public boos them," he was already becoming interested in creators who were being applauded for good reasons.[86] Having established himself in this anti-modern movement, he was rediscovering whole swaths of classic French culture, and set about celebrating the *real* "maudits"—the successful authors like Dumas, Labiche, or Stendhal. These were writers whom the literary Left had scorned for the supposed transparency of their style, whereas in Radiguet's view, style should be the simplest way to express the most compli-cated things, not the other way round.

Though since his first transformation Cocteau had published only *Le Cap*, he had never stopped writing (and rewriting) poems during his evolution. Some pieces from *Poésies*, which he published that same year, would thus have gone through two stages, one versified and the other "deconstructed." After Radiguet's severe comments about *Le Cap*, Cocteau decided to return to the simplicity of rhymes, subject, melody, and representation, in other words to stop—at least temporarily—listening to jazz in order to listen again to the "music" of Ronsard, Du Bellay, and La Fontaine.[87] One might almost swear that Radiguet was the architect of this new transformation, as Stravinsky had been of the previous one. But in fact he was encouraging Cocteau above all to be himself and he himself had a vital need for discipline in this domain.[88] The teenager was indeed taking on literary authority. Correcting texts by Satie himself, he gave "advice to great poets" from all the height of his seventeen years. In the fourth and last issue of their journal, renamed *Le coq parisien*, he encouraged poets to write like everyone else, and even in an ordinary way, like Cocteau, Max Jacob, and a third poet he did not let himself mention because "it is good to feign everything, even modesty."[89] This time again, Radiguet was relying on a statement from *Le coq et l'arlequin*: "An original artist is not able to copy. So he only has to copy, to be original."

It was Cocteau who was attacked. Picabia made fun of the "Coq-Auric-haut" launched by the writer along with Les Six, and Breton compared Cocteau's

advocacy for all things French to the jingoistic reflexes that labeled Cubism
"Boche" art.[90] Leading the fight against the traitor who had "taken" Radiguet
from him, the young lion Breton mobilized his troops, during another Dada
festival hosted by the very respectable Salle Gaveau, on May 26, 1920, where
"All the Dadaists will have their heads shaved in public," the program promised, and there will be "Sodomist music." Five red balloons inscribed with
shameful names rose up from a magician's trunk, while twenty extras played
Tzara's "Vaseline symphonique." But Soupault in blackface solemnly punc-
tured with his scimitar only the one marked "Cocteau," letting the ones marked
"Clemenceau," "Benoit XV," and "Pétain" float through the smoke-filled auditorium, through volleys of raw meat, bread balls, and rotten eggs. The break
between Cocteau and the Certà habitués was unmistakable. Cocteau replied to
them in writing, in Picabia's 391: "Rimbaud went to Harrar to flee *Littérature*,"
a journal that Varèse would in turn reproach for having had ties with Cocteau —
ties that he too had.[91] This was the beginning of a violent cycle of excommunications among individuals living in an area the size of a pocket handkerchief;
the nickname that was given at the time to Cocteau — the anti-Tzara — proved
again, by its very hyphen, that the bridge was not completely cut between the
other Dadaists and Cocteau.

Picabia, with his expansive perversity, saw a wonderful motive for quarrels in
this terrible imbroglio: he relished, for example, that both Tzara and Cocteau
were invited to an exhibition of his recent canvases, including the famous *Jésus-
Christ rastaquouère*, in a gallery on the rue Bonaparte, in Saint-Germain des
Près, on December 9, 1920. Aware of playing the villain's role, Cocteau appeared
in a capitalist's tuxedo and top hat, armed with drums, cymbals, and castanets,
and followed by his jazz band. As Auric and Poulenc sat down at the piano, he
stood over his drums, augmented with a glass of water and a car horn, and
inflicted on them a rain of drumsticks, with the pianists following with the first
well-known tunes by Les Six, from *Adieu New York* to the tango from *Boeuf*. To
spice things up a bit, Picabia had also invited Breton and Aragon, but there was
no riot, despite the French-Cuban's secret wishes. Breton was content to stare
furiously at this "bartender of noises," and Aragon to wax ironic on the "poet-
orchestra" — both knowing the scorn that Picabia had for Cocteau's labor:
"What I prefer in Cocteau is himself, because he doesn't bother me," the
painter would say.[92]

Cocteau was still playing the kazoo when Tzara began reading his "Manifesto
on Feeble Love and Bitter Love," a text he didn't hesitate to describe as historic,
before confiding to the audience, "How charming, nice and delicious I have
become."[93] Alarmed by this alliance against nature, as well as by this excess of

absurdity—although he had seen quite a few others—Breton now shouted, "Pitiful! Idiot!" at Tzara, and left, slamming the door. Afterward, the audience heard "Mon homme," a fashionable tune, and Tzara revealed to the idiots who still wanted to perfect Poetry the recipe to succeed at a *real* poem: cut a newspaper with scissors, reduce each phrase to its words, then throw said words into a bag.[94] While the minister from Cuba, the impassive Pablo Picasso, the slightly tipsy Erik Satie, the serious Drieu la Rochelle, and the facetious Max Jacob all applauded, Tzara yelled "Scream! Scream! Scream!" two hundred times at the dazzled ground.

Picabia concluded the soirée—a success in the eyes of Tzara, that star of the absurd—by giving Cocteau a new mocking nickname: He was the "parmentier of the jazz band," the discoverer who had "brought back" from America that sonorous potato, the new universal food. But from that day on, Breton stopped admiring Tzara, with his sterile happenings and his beliefs about societal collusions. "Dada is the dictatorship of the spirit," shouted the Romanian at that same opening, and Breton, the editor of *Littérature*, could no longer bear this nihilistic project. Since Tzara himself had announced, six months earlier, "Dada is the chameleon of quick and self-interested change," he was predicting a future for himself à la Cocteau.[95] Three men now had the ambition to take over an avant-garde in the process of falling apart: Tzara, Cocteau, and Breton. Who would inherit the role?

—■◆■—

THE MIRACULOUS YEARS

There are no principles, there are only events; there are no laws, there are only
circumstances: The superior man embraces both events and circumstances.
—*Honoré de Balzac*, Vautrin

THE ROSE

Radiguet's impassive face seemed sometimes to be reproaching Cocteau for
his lack of firmness at their neoclassical turning point. But the elder had known
too, ever since the previous winter, the price of these repeated breaks between
"tradition" and avant-garde—the mental breakdown of Vaslav Nijinsky seemed
proof of the possible dangers. Having abandoned his entire professional and
social life, Nijinsky had reminded the world of his existence by sending letters
to former collaborators or sometimes even to no one. Pinned down by bipolar
schizophrenia, the man-bird and radical choreographer, a man who had broken
with a dance tradition that required angels, not sexual beings, had been
committed to a mental institution at the request of his wife. Nijinsky was
exploring nothing now but his own dark places. The miracle that had made a
subversive intelligence blossom in a docile body had turned to tragedy; the
dancer who, according to his wife, had been "soft wax" in the hands of Diaghilev
was reduced to the schizophrenic grimaces he had used in the *L'après-midi
d'un faune.*

Of the letters that Nijinsky wrote at the time, to say he had always loved only
women—and to swear he was neither Diaghilev, nor a wild animal, nor a bullfighter, nor gold, but at once Dance, Love, and God—the most surprising may
have been the one he sent to Cocteau, the writer who had contributed so much,
ten years earlier, to mythologizing him, through his articles in *Le dieu bleu*. "I

love you, my dear Cocto," the former dancer had written in his notebooks, with his large, little-girl handwriting: "*Coc, coc,* to, not the *coc.* I am *coc* you are a *coc* . . . *Coc iyage* is not a *coc* . . ." and so on for pages that one can't read without dread, full of onomatopoeias echoing the ones that the same Cocteau was publishing at the time in *Le coq,* his homonymous journal-tract.[1]

The puppeteer Diaghilev had only to cut a few strings for Petrushka to break; despite the nymph that hatched him, the Faun had shown himself unable to live on his own, just like Lucien de Rubempré without Vautrin, in Balzac's *Human Comedy.* The dancer's gaze emitted the same crazy gleams as Nietzsche's, as a servant said who had met the philosopher in Sils-Maria before meeting Nijinsky. The prodigy who had lived through an "earthquake" was now nothing but a phantom slowed down by medication. "When I see you . . . burning your future whose light ash is accumulating in you and little by little weighing you down, it seems to me that you are also dancing, in short, with death," Cocteau had written ten years earlier.[2] For one who had reached artistic heaven too soon, and wanted to forge his path on his own, the price to pay was exorbitant.

By a strange back and forth, Cocteau was reviving the theme that had ensured Nijinsky's glory in *Le spectre de la rose.* For the flower that the dancer had ended up hating, for the overfacile success it had brought him, had the advantage of hiding, beneath its ultra-conventional and perennially fashionable appearance, a prodigious vegetal transgendering, from the emergence of its bud, that "young foreskin" uncurled by Love, to its blossoming into a sensuous vaginal calyx. But in order to grasp the gracefulness of this change of sex, one had to renounce all claims to originality and agree to take up old, much-used clichés (yet ones that kept in their heart all their freshness, as Radiguet insisted).

Cocteau was only rediscovering himself, as he did so often. His *Discours du grand sommeil* (1918), a superb rosebush, "virile in buds, soon feminine," blossomed on mass graves. But here it was no longer a question of the dead; just of life. And of that simple, elementary life that could on the face of it surprise no one, but that would make its author stand out even more, in the poems in *La rose de François.* "There is enough novelty in him that he can allow himself to breathe a rose," the young Radiguet had already noted in the first issue of *Le coq,* suggesting that modernity did not reside in objects, but rather in the freshness of a perception always hungry to renew itself.

The symbol would turn out to be beneficial. Cocteau, already an admirer of the Persian Saadi at the time of *Les vocalises,* found in this flower a metaphor for his turning point. "I always seem to be being born at the instant that I die," he would note in *Plain-chant*.³ That was also true for the rose, whose buds follow each other with a wonderful prodigality. Wasn't the poet's sensibility urged to flourish, like the rose's perfume—to spread from the basement to the attic, to penetrate walls or projects? Like Narcissus, changed by his death from self-fascination into the flower that bears his name, Cocteau identified with this delicate bud that, as it blossoms, changes its sex. Rediscovering Ronsard, the nightingale of Renaissance poetry, the poet most remote, by his fertility and sweetness, from the belligerent literature encouraged by Dada, Cocteau wrote rhymed poems now, challenging even more his former companions. The herald of the "beautiful today" [Ronsard's *le bel aujourd'hui*] and of pleasure was like nectar to Cocteau. Wasn't that the real subversion? Rediscovering the metrics whose rules it had internalized with rare precocity, his pen rejoiced. Alexandrine quatrains came to him spontaneously, as if the constraint of versification freed him. For his poetic water, he needed a container, and rhyme acted like a reflective vase—a mirrored vessel in which his verses fed on their own reflected image. Happy to see, again, that his angel's bag was full of spare wings, Cocteau let himself give in to the elegiac.⁴ It was a fresh, abundant spring, cheerful and sensual.

The publisher François Bernouard became Cocteau's accomplice, like he had at the time of *Schéhérazade*. After Radiguet's *Les joues en feu*, he printed this *Rose de François*, a source of seemingly inexhaustible alliterations involving Ronsard, the rose, Bernouard, the bath, and François, France. And so Cocteau and Radiguet threw into the smoke-filled premises of the avant-garde a few rose petals in the form of a bomb. They were now the real anarchists.

THE BALM OF PIQUEY

While a wonderful literary companion and critic, Radiguet scarcely made himself vulnerable to his mentor's amorous possessiveness. Rude, selfish, and indifferent, he would wander from bars to nightclubs and from hotels to inns, using any pretext he could to sleep here or there. Cocteau, who always had to justify himself by his work, suffered from seeing how scattered Radiguet was becoming—as if the younger author's absence of discipline confirmed how little Cocteau was loved. "My heart is more and more a poor sponge," he wrote to Auric, eleven years his junior. "Tears, which I don't shed, swell it up, and I suffocate from morning to night."⁵ Since he was unable to impose himself as a lover, Cocteau decided to assert himself more clearly as a tutor by taking the teenager in the greatest secrecy to Piquey, the village in the Arcachon basin that he had been visiting since the end of the war. Or rather he asked a dozen friends to tell no one that he was leaving with Radiguet, who had just lost one of his little sisters. Mme Cocteau herself would long know nothing about the presence of the young prodigy in the seaside resort.

Radiguet in turn discovered the deserted beach, the sand undulating as far as the eye could see, the pine forest and the oyster beds, the Pyla dune and the horses carrying provisions at low tide for the Grand Hôtel Chantecler — a simple wooden shack perfumed by mimosas. Isolation agreed with them — Cocteau because finally he had the adolescent to himself, and "Monsieur Bébé" because he began to write again. Shaved like a convict by Lipchitz, who was already making a bust of him, cured of his skin ailment and his varicose veins, Radiguet soon exhibited a superb brown complexion. "He is working," Cocteau wrote to Mr. Radiguet. "He surprises and astonishes me every day by his culture and wisdom, which never damage his freshness."[6] Radiguet's mere presence calmed and fulfilled Cocteau; with his enigmatic smile and the thick down joining his eyebrows, the adolescent was the magnet that attracted his iron filings, the totem that gathered his psychic fluids. Cocteau's own nesting-doll personality remained a mystery to himself: one Cocteau enclosed a second, already pregnant with a third who was himself ready to turn upside-down to produce a fourth. With Radiguet, Cocteau felt both analyzed and understood, hence encouraged. The intense mind of the "coq de l'île d'amour" dissipated the vague state of mind where his narcissism had kept him: "Alone, I empty myself," Cocteau would say to André Fraigneau; but the "pair" of them, Radiguet and Cocteau, encouraged a dialectic that forced Cocteau to be more precise, to think, and thus to make him work.

Roasted by the sun of Piquey, rejuvenated spectacularly by his new transformation, Cocteau was radiant. This life of shared pleasures and projects was so rich in intimacy that it was equal, in Cocteau's mind, to a virginal form of sexuality. Love did better than exalt him: it gave him a cohesion, a weight, that "normal life" had refused him. Radiguet's calm quieted Cocteau; his strength made him concentrate. Cocteau, who was affected by the slightest variation in temperature, and who would describe himself as a "Stradivarius of barometers" — Cocteau who underwent a metamorphosis at each new infection, attack of shingles, or rheumatism — felt that the coarse Radiguet was like a panacea. "The smallest of your marks of love makes me so happy," he wrote to his mother.[7] Cocteau thought of Radiguet just as much, charmed just watching him walk on the beach with the clumsiness of adolescents who have sprouted too quickly.

The simple sight of his body, which Radiguet readily showed naked, recharged Cocteau erotically. It was a happiness to possess him with his eyes, when he lay on the beach, or curled up on his little bed. Finally the prodigy had laid down his weapons; his anatomy was losing its rigidity; his lips were parting to take the air. A year later, Cocteau would write:

> Ah! I would like, keeping your profile against my throat,
> From your mouth that sleeps
> To hear from your breasts the delicate forge
> Blow until my death.[8]

The frustrating splendor of his untouchable lover's abandoned body and relaxed face excited Cocteau. By giving in to his gaze, to the pencil that was already drawing him, to the pen that was sketching out a few verses—in short by letting himself be desired without resistance, Radiguet was opening to Cocteau the corridors of his profound self. A kind of superior penetration propelled Cocteau into the heart of the dreams of a boy who claimed he never dreamed. It made him imagine the spaces where Radiguet frolicked, these mental rooms arranged along a hallway, like the abandoned hotel he would film in *Le sang d'un poète*.

But these mental entrances in turn produced other anxieties. Radiguet had haunted "the woods, the currant bushes, the farms" since his childhood, but Cocteau had no place there, and now he (Cocteau) was concerned to chase away the women who might slip in. Barely had he readied himself to grasp his companion's secret than he realized it could evaporate at any moment.

> I kiss your cheek and embrace your limbs,
> But you go out of yourself,
> Without making a sound, as if out of a room,
> You leave by the roof.[9]

Struck by the heat of Radiguet's desires, Cocteau would eventually inhabit this sleeping body, and awake as if they had spent the night together, united by pleasure. Who knows if he didn't possess Radiguet more profoundly by watching him sleep than by sharing his bed? This ability Cocteau had to take his pleasure [*jouir*] from a distance would eventually inspire *Plain-chant*, the most personal, profound, and touching poem he had conceived of to date. For now, he was content to haunt Radiguet's thoughts with his presence, in the hope of making a teenager productive who, without him, would only work occasionally. Like the Angel Gabriel visiting the Virgin, Cocteau dreamed, by thought, of impregnating the undisciplined child with his Word.

The result was not yet up to their hopes. An excellent critic, Radiguet was content to give shape to his iconoclastic ideas. Neither *Paul et Virginie*, the book they adapted, according to the rules of Japanese Noh, from the bucolic eighteenth-century novel by Bernardin de Saint-Pierre, nor *Le gendarme incompris*, a farce that made fun of Mallarmé's jigsaw syntax, made its mark. Neither did *Une soirée mémorable*, a second attempt at melodramatic critique, which was intended to ridicule Rimbaud, another tutelary figure of new poetry.[10] Even their readings remained peripheral: dragged onto the iconoclastic slope, Cocteau judged the novels of the "plebian" Balzac loosely stitched, confirming him in his predilection for Stendhal. Interspersed with evenings in the hotel bar, where two Parisian stage girls sang *La Tosca* and Félix Mayol songs, their life remained one of superior dilettantes, with Cocteau spending his mornings drawing, as he did every time he felt incapable of writing. Suddenly, as the March sky was freely pouring showers, a huge three-act tragedy for the boulevard "fell" upon him, *Le baron Lazare*—Bernstein but better written, he said to his mother—which he was already planning to subtitle, in his strategy of assumed common language, "A Play Like Any Other."[11] This startling new piece, at which Cocteau was the first to be surprised, so worried his mother that he agreed to burn it. After having resigned herself to the idea of an avant-gardist son, his mother feared seeing him undertake a third cycle where no one would recognize him at all anymore.

Radiguet was the first to take a *pinasse* (flat-bottomed boat) to Arcachon and go back to his home in Saint-Maur. Cocteau in turn resigned himself to returning to that city he no longer liked much, but without which he could not live. The vague part-time job Cocteau found there for Radiguet, at the Éditions de la Sirène, didn't stabilize the adolescent. Despite Cocteau's pleas, and also because of them, Radiguet's little salary evaporated in alcohol-fueled evenings that often made him miss the last train from the Bastille station that could take him home to the Parc Saint-Maur. Then Radiguet would go back on foot to his parents' place, along the Vincennes zoo, despite his fear of the wild animals whose shadows slithered behind the bars, or he would stay and sleep at the home of the Hugos, whose "parental" tutelage was lighter than Cocteau's and who would improvise a bed in their Palais-Royal living room. He also was known to sprawl among the gouaches in Juan Gris's studio, in the midst of "blocks of polished metal" by Brancusi.[12] And finally, if he could be found at none of those places, he might be at the top of the rue Lepic, in the heart of a Montmartre in full decline, asleep on the kitchen table of the pretty Thora de Dardel, twenty-two, whom he was beginning to follow like a shadow and who seems to have become his mistress, after he coldly murmured to her, "je t'aime."[13]

Radiguet also made mini-escapes, which Cocteau always ended up finding out about but could not prevent. Thus when Radiguet's father wrote to Cocteau again to complain about his son's repeated absences, this time Cocteau could be indignant in good faith: he could not force the young Raymond to go to the office, catch his train, or be on time for an appointment made with Lipchitz. "The fact that he is not at the Parc this morning proves to me that he is lying to me as well as to you . . . We would never have to leave him alone. My life makes this role impossible for me."[14] Cocteau was not his father, after all.

Cocteau's solitude during this period awakened his oldest anxieties. He certainly knew the harshness of love, "that ineffable disaster" that was already evoked in *Le Potomak*. Not being essential to the other person remained a torture for him, even in friendship: it brought on insomnia, which he fought, unsuccessfully, with Somnol pills. Feelings that Radiguet did not reciprocate made Cocteau once more fear that he was not entirely like other people. Is that when he wrote "Crown of melancholy" on the virgin canvas that Picabia sent around to all his friends, which would soon figure on the walls of the Boeuf sur le Toit, under the name *L'oeil cacodylate?*[15] From the sadness in his face, he looks as if he were in the process of agreeing with Proust's worst suppositions about the utter nonreciprocity of human passions. He had hoped in vain: Radiguet did not respect him, and what they had together could not be called a "relationship." His love was "politeness," Cocteau would say, thinking of Radiguet's heaped-up lies, his frequent meetings with "people from elsewhere," his ability to flee through mirrors—but the teenager wasn't happy either. Weary of his overly alcoholized nights, as well as the reprimands of his Pygmalion, Radiguet decided on his own, in February 1921, to withdraw to a little hotel "with one foot in the water" called the Gilly-et-Jules that the Hugos had just discovered on the French Riviera near Carqueiranne, between Toulon and Hyères.

Radiguet changed overnight. Up at dawn and in bed at eight o'clock in the evening, he took to milk, like those excessives capable of lightning-quick periods of sobriety evoked by Baudelaire.[16] "Unaware of his bohemia . . . virgin in excesses, amoral, ingenuous, attentive to pleasure and full of scorn for the dissolute," according to Maurice Martin du Gard, Radiguet outlined odes to Venus inspired by his first stay on the Mediterranean.[17] Happy to devote himself to writing, but sometimes worried too about not knowing anymore what he was doing, he began after three weeks alone to lose his footing, as if he did in fact need that demanding tutor, whom he had fled through quatrains evoking his erotic adventures on the shores of the Marne:

> But I, thinking of plucking
> Planted in your grassy sex

A mushroom from which you drank
The dew of dawn undone.[18]

Having come to visit him on March 18, 1921, soon after Juan Gris, Cocteau spent his first hours watching him write. The schoolboy who had dropped out of school at the age of fifteen had given way to an impassive writer, leaning over his notebooks till he touched them with his nose, rolled like a cat around his pen. His heavy, obstinate face betrayed the power of concentration of a chess player, but also the wisdom of the "ancient" Chinese. "Radiguet astounds me," Cocteau wrote to Valentine Hugo on March 24. "His poems have peach cheeks. They sprout from him like violets, like wild strawberries . . . The bedroom is a beehive."[19] The erotica that Radiguet composed would in turn inspire sixty-five licentious stanzas by Cocteau, always on the theme of the rose, which Cocteau would work over to obscenity and that eventually appeared in *Vocabulaire*.[20] "We are amusing ourselves putting Venus in every posture," he wrote to Valentine Hugo, happy to have managed to curb Bébé's libido with literary pursuits: Venus, at least, is a woman without danger. At the same time, he had Radiguet read the second opus that the war had breathed into Cocteau—*Le discours du grand sommeil*—which inspired in the younger poet longer and more serious poems. Indeed, formidable angels began to appear in the adolescent's poems, and women began to haunt Cocteau's. Their universes stimulated each other reciprocally—they were like intertwined rose bushes marrying their stalks and thorns, as Cocteau would write: "I gave Bébé a madness for death in poetry, and he gave me a madness for improprieties."[21] Co-creation, for lack of co-penetration.

Was it the elder influencing the younger, by encouraging simplicity in him, or vice versa? "For pity's sake stop writing in ink; / The words fished from it are bitter": these lines were signed by Radiguet.[22] "The copse was better / Where Narcissus plays / Alone on his flute": those were by Cocteau.[23] But the opposite could have been true. Marked by the almost perfect fusion that he had achieved with his mother—to the point of abolishing, like Proust, any notion of alterity— Cocteau had a totalitarian view of love: either he submitted himself completely to the beloved object, or that object had to identify unreservedly with him. Although this particular vampirism lacked actual erotic intimacy, it ended up in a sort of compromise, made of alternate submissions and crossed identifications: Cocteau "radiguéd himself" (*se radiguisa*), while Bébé "cocteau'd himself" (*se coctelisait*).

Every day the couple went for a walk through the palm trees, the eucalyptus and the vines surrounding the hotel, before eating on the terrace in the sun, near a fat bearded man who, after belching, would scrutinize the horizon with his binoculars, in search of the ship that might have made this strange noise. Stuffing themselves with garlic and langoustines *à l'Américaine*—"I'm eating like 4," Cocteau wrote to his mother—Cocteau indulged in orgies of sleep and would awaken only to take the copy from the impassive "Bébé," who for his part would set down his pen only to roll a cigarette.[24]

The sight of the Mediterranean, that same wave unfurling under that same pine since ancient times, would feed the "timeless" aesthetic they had been advocating since they left Dada. Born on these same shores, Venus—but also Pan and Leda—made their reappearances under Cocteau's pen, after seven years of banishment. It was not a question, however, of returning to the old Symbolism, but of perfecting a style that never seemed to be "on purpose" or "out-of-date" in the Nietzschean sense of the word. "We must learn the real world by heart and rebuild it above the clouds, from a blueprint that is poetry," Cocteau wrote in 1919 to the Abbé Mugnier.[25] That heaven, which the Dadaists sought to deflate forever, was being revived by Cocteau and Radiguet. For his previous transformations, the author of *Le Cap* hadn't even thought of justifying himself; instead only the polishing of his new skin interested him—"I change outfits often and do not respect my old rags," Cocteau would write to Gide six months later. Salmon aren't asked to justify the thousands of miles they travel to reproduce; one merely observes their migration to the river where they were born, since only these to-and-fros could stimulate their fertility: Cocteau too needed to coast along and then do battle with the current in which he was born, not only in order to better know himself, but also in order to be himself. *Le sacre du printemps* had thrown him outside of himself; he was returning to his native lands.

Upon discovering compromising rumors in the press, Mme Cocteau urged him to get a grip on himself again. This teenager who dictated his themes; these poems she understood nothing about; this beard he was allowing to grow; these "blacks" with whom he was drumming at night; these Six for whom he expended himself, without their bringing him anything in return; these hyenas who were spreading obscene rumors about him, in the magazines . . . "When will you stop seeing me through the eyes of *Le crapouillot?*" he replied, furious.[26] "Haven't you seen yet that my life is spent letting my instincts go, observing them, sorting them, once they are outside, and taming them so they're to my advantage?"[27] Accusing him of wasting his time, when a single one of his seasons would easily fill ten winters of another person! Reproaching him for his beard, when he felt he was severing so many nerve endings whenever he shaved! "Never again expect me to do anything according to a conventional method. It's over," he concluded.[28]

THE MUTUAL ADMIRATION SOCIETY

The vacation was so beneficial that upon returning Cocteau got into the habit of gathering, every Saturday evening, his amateur musician or writer friends in an inexpensive restaurant. Everyone, rich or poor, ate the special of the day and paid his share. Those attending ranged from the austere Arthur Honegger to the delightful Pierre Bertin, the favorite actor for Dada happenings; from Marie Laurencin, Apollinaire's ex-mistress, to the Hugos (whom Cocteau called "Les Zugo"). Satie and Paul Morand occasionally completed the circle—Morand had just published *Tendres stocks*, with a preface by Proust (*Fancy Goods*, Ezra Pound's translation). Also included were the faithful Auric and Poulenc, two of the composers in Les Six, the pianist Marcelle Meyer, and the singer Alexandre Koubitzky, all personalities who would never otherwise have met and whom "the dazzling prestige of the author of *The Cape*" assembled, as Jean Hugo said.[29] Together they made a kind of chosen family, which also included some heirs, since Jean Hugo was related both to the Lacretelles and to Lucien Daudet.

Cocteau would arrive first, impatient to seat everyone, take command, and orchestrate the interactions: only an excessive number of guests could weaken the "delicious tyranny" that made him hold the center of the conversation. He often talked from morning to evening or onward, but the source never ran dry; others filled it as he spoke of them, "never envious, never precious," Maurice Martin du Gard would say, "playing the comedy with profundity on occasion, as a virtuoso, without confessing anything intimate"—casting into everyone's ears "a fortune in pocket money."[30] Carried along by the warmth of a man in whom the young pianist Arthur Rubinstein found a child's mischievousness ("something feminine as well" with his delicate hands), and by "the unimaginable diversity" of his intelligence, even Satie and Radiguet themselves would finally abandon their silence.[31] "Time passes quickly when Cocteau is there, and one feels so intelligent when he speaks with that high, fascinating rapidity, strewing oracles, puns, birds, angels, caricatures," added Maurice Martin du Gard.[32]

Once the bill was delivered, Cocteau would do the math and collect the money—always paying himself for Radiguet—before leading this informal tribe, whom Morand would nickname the "Mutual Admiration Society," for a drink at the home of Milhaud on rue Gaillard, near the Trinité—an area with no electricity where chickens still gamboled. Morand would make cocktails, Poulenc would play his *Cocardes*, Auric his *Adieu New York*, and Milhaud his *Caramel mou*, a shimmy in which Cocteau suggested:

Take a young woman,
Fill her up with ice and gin
—Don't you think that art is a little . . .—
Shake it all up to make an androgyne
And return her (*three times*) to her family.

Then everyone would go to the Foire du Trône, which had become a sort of cult place since *Petrushka* and *Parade*, or else to the Folies Bergère, the fairground attractions at Luna Park, or drag dancing at the Magic City, a carnival set up at the foot of the Eiffel Tower where hundreds of men danced.

The evening could also turn to a binge when the humorous Poulenc, the only wealthy one in the group, opened his bachelor pad, nestled in the courtyard of a fashionable building on the rue de Monceau. Undressed by the group, the future composer of *Les Carmélites*, then nicknamed Poupoul, would wind up on a bed of empty bottles defending his boxer shorts. A few days later he would reappear in a pink turban and a puce suit, in the hope of seducing Morand. This boarding-school atmosphere could make Valentine Hugo afraid that her maid might appear, one night when "the beautiful Poulenka" was exhibiting himself naked at her home, "as much at ease as if he were wearing a cowl," as Cocteau said. He himself would carry off a series of obscene drawings with a naked Sarah Bernhardt, "lustful grotto adorned with stalactites," in front of winged, mustachioed phalluses drawn by Radiguet.[33]

Music did more than unite the Mutual Admiration Society; it exalted it to the point of making it, for two entire seasons, a free dance band, always ready to improvise, laugh, and sing in any place willing to welcome this happy flurry: for example, the house hidden behind the Porte Maillot of a young dancer, who earlier had taught Dalcroze rhythmic dance, with Coco Chanel as student, in 1912, and who would later become known as Caryathis. Cocteau improvised powerful cocktails with a base of benzoin, Gyraldose, and Champagne, but also gin, eau de Cologne, and antiseptic, which Satie would throw up in the stairway.[34] A secretary of Apollinaire, Baron Mollet, danced there in a morning coat and pink boxers, while Radiguet was dressed as a "melancholic from the *Fleurs du mal.*" Mercury with the winged helmet (Cocteau) might even fly off, during a masked ball, above the "muzzle" of Morand, whose fly let a tail of his shirt show through. "I had the impression that an imaginary character was entering into my life," the dancer would say, recounting her first meeting with Cocteau: it was indeed Ariel, in his 1920s costume, who persisted in Cocteau-the-impresario.[35] It was this Cocteau that Satie asked to do the choreography for *La belle excentrique*, his last "serious fantasy," in which Caryathis would dance.

Working with Cocteau was exciting. Caryathis developed a crush on the poet, who encouraged her to take her inspiration from the flouncy walk of the Demoiselle crane, an African bird in the Jardin des Plantes zoo (despite angry protests from Satie, who wanted her to be Parisian and not a "négresse"). The outspokenness of the woman Cocteau nicknamed "the dancer of Les Six" charmed him, but this first attempt to divert him would be a failure for Caryathis—Cocteau would call her "intelligent as her feet" when he dedicated *Thomas l'imposteur* to her. About the poet she had approached in vain, she would say: "That one, nothing doing . . .," before making a second—successful— attempt with another gay writer Marcel Jouhandeau, who would make her known under the name Élise.[36]

The whirlwind didn't stop for two years. The Madeleine, where Morand moved, became once again the center of Paris; everything happened there, from Picasso's gallery openings to the Opéra ballets, not to mention the cinemas where the Mutual Admiration Society would go watch Chaplin's walk sped up. The highlight remained the fair in Montmartre, on the Boulevard de Clichy, with its enraged acrobats—"Don't swing so high," shouted Cocteau, / The sky is everyone's"—and the Médrano Circus where the Fratellini brothers boxed in an atmosphere of broken drums and fake telephones, sawdust and elephant piss. "Steam-powered merry-go-rounds, mysterious boutiques, the Daughter of Mars, the shooting ranges, the lotteries, the zoos, the racket of mechanical organs and their perforated cylinders which seemed to crank out implacably and simultane- ously all the popular music from music-halls and revues" fascinated all the members of the Mutual Admiration Society, as Milhaud said.[37] Everyone had adopted the rituals of Cocteau, who was the first to recognize himself in the piti- less discipline of tightrope walkers, under their sleepwalker pose.

Born unbalanced, but apt too to balance itself in any circumstance, Cocteau's soul soared with these tumblers who flirted with death every night. He might at times envy earthlings, solid beings—the "sitters," as Rimbaud would have said; but these gypsies given over to vertigo, these "beautiful satin prey killed by the drum," constituted his true family. When they dismantled their tents and set off in their caravan, drawn by a carthorse, with the sad smiles of nomads on their lips, Cocteau would remember bedtime fables told to him as a child, in which gypsies tore him away from his mother to train him on the trapeze, after storks from Persia had deposited him on the chimney. At the Foire du Trône, whose funhouse mirrors accentuated his giddy feeling of shifting identities, Cocteau would take his Society to see the siren in her boat, the lion tamer in his cage, and the wrestlers grabbing each other, semi-naked, while an egg danced perpen- dicularly in the fountain spray. The most beautiful attraction, for one who loved snacking on gingerbread pigs or sugar-coated fennel seeds, was a flying creature in a pink satin corset named Miss Aérogyne. She would go through rows of hoops while showering the crowd with kisses, then remain suspended in the air, against a painted night scene, without moon or stars, to the sound of a piano: "Fly, pigeon, Aérogyne! / She tells lies with her body," Cocteau wrote, dazzled.[38]

Having neither rules nor doctrine, the Society ignored all the theoretical excommunications that were the rage, around Breton at the Certà, as well as the blows already being exchanged by ultra-Dadaists. As Morand wrote in his *Éphémérides*:

> There are certainly ambitious ones amongst us, but they don't stand out, they don't affect the naturalness, the solidarity, or the kindness of the group. A pretentious person, a Left-Bank thinker . . . would not be tolerated here.[39]

Bohemia, its luxurious version, had just reconquered the Right Bank, with the cheerful and rebellious spirit of an era that marked the fusion of "elements of working-class life and aristocratic dilettantism," according to René Crevel: a utopia light as a gauze veil, in which everyone was happy to share time and energy, and that unfettered enthusiasm without which creation is nothing but a product.

Mme Cocteau herself was brought into the act, through restrained lunches to which Radiguet would finally be invited. Rather than Dadaist bohemia, the unkempt ex-teenager now preferred visiting the mansions of the Beaumonts, the flamboyant Misia Sert, or the alcoholic princesse Violette Murat—a monster with no neck who looked more like a truffle than a violet—over conversations with Proust. And it was in a starched shirt and fedora, hands gloved in cashmere from Hilditch & Key, that the young man came to the rue d'Anjou. This new elegance, with his jacket sleeves rolled up and a silk foulard around his neck, owed much to Cocteau; from contact with him, "Monsieur Bébé" would even once and for all abandon glasses—whose fashion had the fault of coming from America—for the aristocratic monocle, which was meant to make idiots with prejudices run away. Were his monocle and cane meant to make him look like a sprouting Dadaist or a Royalist-to-be? It was impossible to tell. But Mme Cocteau got along as well with Radiguet as she had with Satie, and her son felt even more gratitude toward the woman who always ended up accepting his choices.

Morand turned out to be more than a traveling companion—he was a true friend. Born the same year as Cocteau, and coming from the same milieu— with more emphasis on society at the home of the Cocteaus, and more on culture at the Morands'—they shared the same vitality, a keen sense of the times, and the memory of that ironic snobbism, fed on pilgrimages to Venice and teas at ladies' homes, that had made Morand and his future wife, the very wealthy Princesse Soutzo, intimates of Proust. A career diplomat, Morand continued to be perceived as a literary dilettante, since his poems had only been published in journals and the short stories that Cocteau had read had disturbed, wearied, and at the same time delighted him. Struck solely by the "cyanide" cruelty of his *Feuillets de température*, Cocteau had even at first attributed to their author "a tin heart," not seeing that this metallic quality was precisely what made his style so modern.[40] This amateur reputation was finally shed with the collection of stories that Morand entitled *Tendres stocks*, which was published at the end of 1921 with a preface by Proust. At the end of 1922, too, dazzled by "La nuit de Putney," the final story in *Fermé la nuit*, which had just been published in a journal, Cocteau fully recognized the "clear, rapid, sober stylist, rich as Croesus and simple as hello."[41] Morand wrote like Cocteau, thin and muscular, with even more happiness perhaps, since he was not compelled by an excess of nerves but rather by Eros and a keen love of life that had made him gouge his hand with a knife as a child after a fortuneteller searched in vain for his line of luck.

If Cocteau could feel annoyed by Morand's too-neighborly pyrotechnics, the admiration Morand bore for Cocteau was also tinged with reservations at the beginning. But the more Morand asserted himself separately as a modern, the more grateful he was to Cocteau for having led him in his conquest of the Left Bank. "It took me ten years to rid myself of all these clinging vines," Morand would say at the end of his life (alluding to the florid style of the 1900s).[42] On this point, Cocteau had proved to be quicker than Morand, who was impressed by the "second youth" Cocteau had been able to make for himself—even if, after his own literary transformation, the stylist Morand asserted himself as more purely modern. The two men's styles were the written equivalents of the effervescent tablets the pharmacy had just invented, freeing bubbles of sensitive intelligence in a sea of thinking images. But if Cocteau gave constant loud proofs of this, Morand was reduced, by a kind of shyness tinged with indifference, to seem always as if he were listening—and nothing was more captivating than to follow the one-man orchestra that was Cocteau. As early as 1916 Morand wrote:

It is impossible to tell a story by Cocteau, especially for me, who can never manage to make my muffled voice heard and who shortens stories so much, out of boredom with listening to myself, that no one understands. After Cocteau, his eyes spinning, his hands speaking, his mimicry, the gestures of others seem heavy; the next day, you remember nothing.[43]

Morand admired that Cocteau, when he had a thought to express, had at his disposal a panoply of words, and if necessary could invent more, like the day he had mentioned the existence of an unknown species of wasps, the "vrombines," for the pleasure of making Gide, who was present at the time, jealous. Fifty years later, Morand would add in *Venises*:

> From Cocteau-the-Pointed, electricity emerged from every angle. Walking down the Henri III stairway of the building on the rue d'Anjou, where he lived with his mother, you felt idiotic, delayed, aching, clumsy; he alone could sleep while dancing, on the tips of his toes.[44]

The severe judgments made of Cocteau by Giraudoux, Morand's childhood tutor, came to nothing: the author of *Ouvert la nuit* found in the author of *Le Cap* a vector of emancipation, and in the Society the ideal hermetically sealed door to make his Proustian prehistory forgotten and to settle into modernity. This was the beginning of a long friendship between, as Cocteau would call Morand, a "pessimist who wished that everything would succeed," and Cocteau, the optimist who feared that everything would fail, as Pierre Caizergues said. Stripped bare of meanness, the potential rivals decided to travel together through part of the decade, even if doing so meant causing a certain stylistic confusion, since their universes were at opposite ends. That is, by attaching his heart to his brain, and by wanting to be loved for his ideas as well as his about-faces, Cocteau risked rejection, while Morand, content to think with his eyes, as a lover of racecars, could only be admired, or at worst, envied.

Strangely, the Society included another escapee from the Proustian era, a connection that he betrayed with his emir's profile, his refined clothing, and his Montesquiou-like poses.[45] Lucien Daudet had been sincerely shocked by Cocteau's about-face in 1913, but like so many others, moved by a growing terror of aging, he had finally come round to the new style—as long as he could ignore the new aesthetics. An extremely precocious former page to Empress Eugénie, Daudet began receiving at his mother's home a Society that morally made them both grow younger (even if, in his eyes, it could not rival the phantom court of the widow of Napoleon III, where he had figured as a kind of quirky Aiglon, the lost child of the emperor).

Was he suffering from a name that had always been too weighty to him, and that made him belong a little more every year to the previous century? Was he afraid they would discover how fearful he had become about that time that, unlike Proust, he had truly lost? Daudet, who had been unable to translate his strange sensibility into books, unlike his ex-alter ego Cocteau, and even less into paintings, seemed to be angry with this era that had condemned him in advance.

The wounds of this revenant were so palpable, in any case, that the Society always feared seeing him appear, and he himself clammed up as soon as he was approached. "He has a bad cocktail shaker," Morand noted; "he shakes it and mutters between his teeth: 'I'll lose you all!'" Valentine Hugo, taking him for the devil, predicted that he would disappear some Saturday through the trap door.[46] And when people saw him appear as a Specter of the Rose, at a ball given by Caryathis, everyone thought they could smell an odor of mothballs—the ones that protected the costumes of the first Ballets Russes, perhaps? Only Cocteau's fidelity kept on the saddle this old adolescent who seemed secretly to wish for the death of the young people on whom he depended.

THE MEDIUM OF THE ROARING TWENTIES

Whatever they thought of Daudet, everyone could agree that it was no longer the time for making pilgrimages to Farnborough, the residence of the Empress Eugénie, but for going on jaunts to the dubious establishment that René de Amouretti, the former convict who had hosted the after-party for *Pulcinella*, ran on rue Demours—two empty rooms where everyone ate cross-legged on a rug to the sound of Hawaiian guitars. Dinner on the ground, for one who would have given away his rights to *Lettres de mon moulin* to call himself d'Audet![47] Since the place turned out to be a little too expensive for Satie, Cocteau had everyone search for a different regular spot and spoke of organizing a tontine to help out the most penniless among them.[48] That's how Darius Milhaud discovered the existence of the Gaya, a little port-wine bar at 17 rue Duphot, near the Madeleine, where you could still eat for 10 francs, but which was suffering from an unpopular pianist and an overly aged, inconsistent clientele. "Keep your pianist and send your customers away," Cocteau ruled, leading the Society in the rags, fox trots, and Bach extracts that Jean Wiener at the piano and the American black musician Vance Lowry, on the sax or the banjo, started up without warning. The place resembled a little bath house tiled in ceramic; Moysès, the manager, had only to adorn the walls with multicolor posters to the glory of Les Six to make the bathtub overflow and engulf the Saturday diners. "Happiness gushed from all over, ripe, new, centripetal," said Léon-Paul Fargue, who was already seeing heavily made-up, secretly available women venture onto the rue Duphot. The "feeling nègre" of the orchestra of the Pelican Variety Five was so attractive! A frisson came over the room when the powerful Vance Lowry attacked his banjo with his nails, communicating to the audience his aphrodisiac energy. Morand had some ulterior motive, too, when he said to one in charge of this pre-orgy atmosphere, "Vance, night is day for black people, play some more." Actually, the jazz musician who would conquer white people—male and female alike—would help Morand take advantage of this "seething mass of serendipitous finds, sonatas, English sauces, and rapid adulteries."[49]

Cocteau had all the percussions conveyed to the Gaya that Stravinsky had given him (and that Stravinsky had used to orchestrate *Les noces*). Sitting astride drums and cymbals to produce a little "splash" with his fingers, then giving a big kick to the bass drum, he would play with Wiener with incredible confidence, manipulating his drumsticks, his hair standing on end, arms twined around various drums : "With Wiener at the piano and Vance on saxophone, jazz made me more buzzed than alcohol, which I don't hold well," Cocteau would write in *D'un ordre considéré comme une anarchie*, hoping to "jazz up" his books.[50] Around three in the morning, the rhythm would change Cocteau into a Chagall character; he was no longer a drummer but a kind of half-breed angel soaring over the ten cubic smoke-filled meters of the room. "In jazz twenty arms are pushing you; you are a god of sound," Cocteau confided.[51] Borne by the "demon of harmony" that was Vance, Cocteau once again became the multiple being of the Noailles era, with this exception: the medium who was so moved by the notes, the "jazzmaniac" who was still singing in the morning in his bath one final rag that Wiener hurried to transcribe, the Vishnu who set all wood on fire, had the sole ambition of living among humans and working with them—at least the most modern ones: collective genius was replacing individual divinity.

Enumerating the list of the future famous people who passed through the Gaya would be tedious; from Tzara to Picabia and Arthur Rubinstein, who thought Fred Astaire's voice was more moving than that of divas, the first third of the century passed by in this postage-stamp-sized place that was licensed for fifty people but held twice that number. Success was so swift that Morand sometimes had to fetch extra ice in a napkin or collect snow from the window ledges. Rumor had it that Cocteau had finally found his vocation—that of a nightclub manager. The gossip columnist at a Belgian paper even launched a slogan "One cocktail, some Cocteaus," which would identify Cocteau forever with that maelstrom of fiestas and balls for which his aerial body was the live wire.[52]

A wind from Africa was already spreading over some parts of the capital. The beguine bands that were making West Indians in madras dance on rue Blomet; the black rhythms that were raising a racket on rue de Lappe; and the jazz that was invading even the dining rooms in Maxim's, that temple of 1900s style renamed the American Bar—it was an ersatz black magic that Paris was experiencing, just after the arrival of Josephine Baker, a Venus who appeared out of the Atlantic baring her breasts. Popularized by the participation of Senegalese troops in the War, African art was beginning to quicken the heartbeats of Parisians, via the red phallic totems of Paul Guillaume, but also Picasso's cross-hatched faces, and later, the black gods Nazmé, Mébère, and Nkwa that Milhaud would set to dancing in *La création du monde*, after he had returned from Harlem in 1923. "Jazz has such sublime, such heartrending accents," Morand confirmed, sensitive to the song of the descendants of slaves.[53] Cocteau would not have contradicted him; hadn't he anticipated, during the war, this confused desire to "be Black" that would steadily increase?

Covered one day in fetishes, totems, feathers, and straw, and the next day dressed as almahs or as wading birds from the Landes — or as playing cards or *Nouvelle revue française* covers, naked under plastic in the middle of winter, or decorated like Christmas trees in the middle of summer — Cocteau, Radiguet, Morand, Picasso, or Crevel would knock on the luxurious houses of the Beaumonts on rue Masseran, then the Noailles on the place des États-Unis. A spectacular season of balls was beginning during which Man Ray would be resurrected as a black man, Poulenc as a diva, Crevel as a sailor, Nancy Cunard as Irma Vep (the rubber-suited heroine of the Feuillade films), and Valentine Hugo as an allegory for the four continents — the symbol of the last decade when Paris was the place to be.

Cocteau's work before the war had been fueled by the frustration engendered by the routine of a flat, romanceless world. This time, however, it was the entire capital that seemed to be determined to realize its dreams. The need for metamorphoses that had long fueled Cocteau was taking over entire swaths of society; painters were changing into dancers, poets into filmmakers, clowns into playwrights, and Swedish dancers were freezing into columns for abstract ballets against the backdrop of sets by Léger. No role seemed fixed anymore in this prodigious aesthetic carnival that was in full swing during the house-warming party given by Milhaud (who had moved to the boulevard de Clichy) one July evening in 1923, which also was a celebration of Cocteau's thirty-fourth birthday. "Through the open windows," Milhaud would remember, "you could hear the music from the organ-grinders, the sounds of shooting, and the growls of caged wild animals, since the Montmartre fair was at its height." The bird theater that followed impressed Cocteau: the tame canaries and sparrows, after flying through the living room, would come to rest on the fingers, shoulders, and hair of their tamer; one canary fired a tiny cannon at a sparrow, which fell stiff onto a stretcher carried by two other birds. From that day on, the poet saw himself only as that bird tamer, one capable of commanding animals by his charm, like the pagan Orpheus or Saint Francis of Assisi.

Paraphrasing Talleyrand's saying about the pre-Revolution, Drieu la Rochelle would state in 1940 that anyone who had missed the postwar years had not experienced the full sweetness of life. It was more than a fountain of youth; it was a veritable springtime that Cocteau conveyed in sparkling images and whose first decline, two years later, was enough to propel Morand across the world. As Marinetti announced presciently in his 1909 *Manifesto of Futurism*, "We want to sing of the man at the wheel, the ideal axis of which crosses the earth, itself hurled along its orbit. . . . We are on the extreme promontory of the centuries!"

Cocteau decided to take advantage of this carnival atmosphere to exalt the radical ordinariness of daily life, through a musical spectacle that could draw comic, or even ironic, potential from habitual gestures and clichés. This theatrical ballet would be based on the rhythm of a wedding where everyday clichés—"beautiful as sunshine," "strong as a Turk," "fresh as a rose" (always a rose)—would emerge from the mouths of human archetypes—the general, the young bride—until they took on a miraculous reality when, from the camera of a photographer announcing, "watch the birdie," an ostrich, a swimmer, and a baby would emerge—then the lion that would devour the general.

Already during the time of *Parade*, Cocteau was announcing an art of the cliché that was meant to make everyday life situations seem unreal, much like the poems of Apollinaire, "where an ordinary word becomes unusual."[54] But Cocteau wasn't the only one to work in this direction. The entire modern movement was seeking at the time to blow out of all proportion social, psychological, or regional archetypes, those pillars of the "stupid nineteenth century," and to exploit the tendency of people and places to conform to the caricature of themselves: for instance, Normandy showing itself covered in cows and apple trees, and Corsicans posing with shotguns in the mountains. Cocteau wanted to give this intense ironic labor, whereby human tautologies were called out as inane, more of a laughable than an aggressive tone. By exalting ready-made phrases, the sort repeated at provincial weddings, and by giving them that charm given off by fairground chatter, he outlined a poetics of the cliché based on nonsensical replies. By making a man's accidental fall suddenly give him the status of a puppet, Bergson defined laughter as the liberating and hence validating outcome of dehumanization: that's the fate that befalls all the characters in Cocteau's mimed, danced wedding.

Cocteau paid particular attention to the speeches of his soldier, who owed much to General Clapier, that platitude-spouting machine he had invented on the front and whom the lion itself would deem indigestible after it had emerged from the photographer's camera. Like that old bad-tempered codger perpetuating anti-Boche hatred, Cocteau made his characters into automatons whose hypocrisies he commented on, in tandem with Pierre Bertin, through a card-board loudspeaker. In this way, he was able to take up the idea he hadn't been able to put into practice in *Parade* and use all the dialogues that Picasso and Satie had denied him. If his sketch owed much dramatically to Feydeau and to puppet theater—he had situated it in 1890, a completely outdated era—aesthetically it was close to the Douanier Rousseau, with its Eiffel Tower painted by Irène Lagut and its very "popular dance" costumes designed by Jean Hugo.[55] While still claiming to be a group of friends instead of an aesthetically minded group, Les Six on this occasion made a strong demonstration of unity.[56] Their shared taste for irony, farce, and parody was indulged to their heart's content through carnival music, military waltzes, popular quadrilles and ritornellos, July 14 parade music and wedding tunes, a thousand musical saws—even Gounod's *Faust*. All of these diversions blended into a potpourri in which the powerful delicacy of a Honegger, in his *Funeral March*, joined the resonant cheerfulness of Milhaud's *Wedding March*—whose underlying melancholy revealed its profound unity to these deliberately anti-romantic melodies. That is how *Les mariés de la tour Eiffel* was born, in the wake of *Parade*: it was a spectacle that was worked on so carefully that it seemed simple, or even dumb.

The premiere confirmed that Cocteau had enemies on the Right, like Henri Béraud, a journalist-novelist who accused him of being a little millionaire disseminating stupid pleasantries. But he could also count on his old allies. Tzara's troops, expelled from a *bruitiste* concert that they had wanted to sabotage, and wearing tails and suits in order the better to infiltrate the audience, invaded the Théâtre des Champs-Élysées on June 18, 1921, and didn't stop getting up and sitting down, like robots, throughout the entire performance, shouting: "Vive Dada!"[57] They also chirped like birds, and used trumpets and whistles, after handing out pamphlets saying, "Dada alone offers all guarantees against diseases of the personality, virtue, and other disorders of the scalp."[58] A few days later, Cocteau celebrated, in a supplement to the 391 of his true/false friend Picabia, their shared cure for the Dada "disease" and their simultaneous break with Breton—with whom Duchamp, Satie, and Varèse had linked themselves.[59] "Our heads are round to allow thoughts to change direction," the Franco-Cuban would say in another paper.[60] The aphorism expressed well the sinuous paths that Cocteau's developing intelligence liked to take: indeed, Breton's fine phrase about Picabia—"The man who takes our mind off Picabia the most is Picabia"—could also be applied to Cocteau.

Already evident in Futurist productions, which the ephemeral Dadaist theater was only prolonging, the desire for parodic mechanization in this *Mariés* assured it a lasting fortune, throughout the century, by way of the theater of the absurd—Ionesco in particular would say how much it had influenced him.[61] But thirty years later, thinking back on the spectacle, Cocteau saw how much he owed to the atmosphere of camaraderie and intense emulation that reigned in Paris at the time. "We were living through a veritable springtime of work, research, invention, friendship between the arts," Morand confirmed, thinking back on those times when Léger, Claudel, Matisse, or Cendrars mingled with each other in one of those ballets that followed the formula *Parade* had set out, adding, "You even saw writers liking each other!"[62] Lavishing his talents— drollery, instinct for graphic design, witty repartee—quickly and without reflection or calculation, "Cocteau-the-Pointed" saw in each creator he met an opportunity for friendly collaboration: "He annexes geniuses . . ., sees himself in everything his friends do, he lives in everything he does for them, and thinks he makes them do something original," said Maurice Martin du Gard.[63] Constantly surrounded and "collectivized," the "poet-orchestra" could now only conceive of existence as co-creation.

During the two years to come, Cocteau would amass poems, articles, novels, plays, and ballets—a demon seemed to be urging him to dance, drink, or marvel at the meanderings his own speech took on the telephone, and at night to extract from him in a few hours some poems about which he had sometimes been thinking for months. Did people wonder about the fecundity of an author whom no one ever saw at work? "The poet works while sleeping," he got into the habit of replying. His ideas were executed right away; mounting a horse with steaming nostrils, the Cocteau of the Gaya never searched, just found— like his friend Picasso. His talents acted despite himself; he designed clothes, created jewelry, played the triangle and drums; from his fingers emerged notes, phrases, and verses; images and sayings gushed from him. It was no longer his cortex but his hands that gave rhythm to an era that would rather have genius for an hour than talent for a whole lifetime. His style would flutter here and charge there, gather nectar and zigzag, at once telegraphic and amoral. You would see him pass by, but you wouldn't realize it until later: he was the thunderbolt and the locust, the mayfly and the canker-worm. Served by his lightning-quick intelligence, his electric cheerfulness, and that grace that Nietzsche had called for, Cocteau's gifts for ubiquity seemed to make him consubstantial with the air of Paris, which was so sought after that Duchamp would ironically put it in a bottle. For this capital already won over by the snobbism of being just a first name, he was no longer even Cocteau, but the "Jean!" one kissed in the hallways of a newspaper building or over cocktails at a gallery opening and who, overexcited by these perpetual encounters, signed his letters to his mother, "Jean, duc d'Anjou and prince of Paris."[64]

How could one regret that he didn't keep a journal at the time? In the center of all these currents, borne along by all the trends, Cocteau wouldn't have had time for it—he who traveled faster than his shadow. Morand wrote:

He couldn't miss the train because he was running in front of the locomotive. At the tip of everything, from the prick of metaphors to the nib of the pen, thanks to his arrow-phrases [*formules-flèches*] he became sharpness itself; his questioning chin, his screwdriver gaze, his spinning fingers, he lived "at the limit of himself." To rest would have been to lose his edge.[65]

In the middle of the horrors of the war and the suffering of the mid-1920s, those few hedonistic years were the happiest intermission in Cocteau's life. He had frequently wanted at all cost to be of his era, even if the era didn't want him: now, he was the very spirit of the time. "See everything. Hear everything. No one suspects," Cocteau wrote under a self-portrait as a detective.[66] Capable of feeling *all* current events, the Ariel of the 1910s became the inspirer of the 1920s, the *ambianceur* of that generation of guinea pigs that Morand would describe, in *Venises*, as "the only really cosmopolitan generation to have appeared in France since the Encyclopedists."

From all over the world poets and writers flowed to Paris who had come to seek out the man whom Picabia had ironically nicknamed "the Parisian," but whom they perceived as the capital's Open Sesame. It was Cocteau whom Ezra Pound visited, with Picabia and Joyce, during his move to the rue des Saints-Pères, in the spring of 1921, and Cocteau he would compare to that complete man the Renaissance dreamed of, in the letter he sent regularly to the *Dial*, a Chicago magazine, after having deemed Cocteau the most talented poet and prose writer in Paris.[67] It was Cocteau whom Edmund Wilson would make known in the United States, praising *Les mariés* in *Vanity Fair* (despite the fact that it failed in New York in 1923), and Cocteau again whom the Bloomsbury group would introduce to England, via Clive Bell; Cocteau's very particular concept of time, his seamless style, without "padding," filled the group with enthusiasm.[68] Did Cocteau already see himself, since they were speaking of a new Renaissance, as bringing together men and trends, in order the better to surpass both the avant-garde and official art, "equally absurd things" in his eyes? Maurice Martin du Gard thought so, but in any case, for all the foreigners in Paris at the time, Cocteau was "the wittiest and most popular poet," as Mayakovsky would assert during his first week-long trip to France, in 1922. This quintessence of virtues attributed at the time to Paris had become a kind of Diaghilev orchestrating the immense Parisian choreography.[69]

Since Mayakovsky didn't speak French, Stravinsky served as interpreter, but he struggled to render into Russian that curious language that was "le cocteau."[70] Ideology complicated the dialogue even more. Having been changed into a politician (like any poet in a country in the midst of a revolution, as Cocteau said), the Communist-Futurist Mayakovsky, deemed rude, "deplorably dirty," and alcoholic by Stravinsky, had only one obsession: to get from Cocteau, whom he believed still to be Dadaist, the exhaustive list of literary schools competing over Paris. Wanting to believe only in personalities, in keeping with the national genius, the author of *Le coq* ended up, with annoyance, acknowledging the existence of a "small Cocteau school." "Imagine the gaze directed at my slingshot by the giant Mayakovsky!" commented this phony David, in a postscript to *Le coq et l'arlequin*.

Translated in avant-garde journals, from the Atlantic to the Caucasus, Cocteau was now known among all the advanced literary circles. Cuba itself discovered the writer whom Glenway Wescott, a protégé of Gertrude Stein, called "the delight of Europe," and to whom Alejo Carpentier paid a visit that he would recount in *Social*, in July 1925.[71] Admiring *Les mariés de la tour Eiffel*, which he placed higher than Jarry's *Ubu Roi*, the future author of *El siglo de las luces* (Explosion in a cathedral) was struck by the intelligence of this modern anti-modernist, in whom he already saw a false chameleon and an authentic writer seeking to flagellate himself "with the salutary hair shirt of return to tradition, that is, to form," as if to hold on to a nature that, one guesses, in certain respects, could not be held. In other words, "To dance in chains," as Nietzsche said.

FIRST LOVER'S CHILL

The summer of 1921 was again one of serious study for Cocteau and Radiguet. The two spent it—first in Besse-en-Chandesse in the Auvergne, and then again in Piquey, on the bay of Arcachon—reading and writing. Encouraged by his strange eighteen-year-old tutor, the schoolboy that Cocteau had never been added Flaubert, Constant, and Balzac to his reading list, while convincing Radiguet to apply his analytical intelligence to writing a novel. Too concrete and critical to become a great poet, not wanting to abandon himself to pure sensation, despite his mentor's attempts at nocturnal influence, Radiguet took up his notes from 1919 and worked on a straightforward story of doomed love. Inspired by the affair he had had at the age of fourteen, with the wife of a soldier away at the front, *Le diable au corps* would culminate with the acceptance of "their" pregnancy by the soldier and end with the heroine's death in labor.

Ever since Valéry had railed against the genre of the novel, and his ex-disciple Breton had taken up the charge, calling character-based fiction a bourgeois pastime on a par with boulevard theater, novels had been unpopular. Radiguet, however, aware that the story of a real-life affair is interesting only by its trans-formation, applied himself to taking that distanced tone he so admired in *Les liaisons dangereuses*. Paring his tale to the bone to make it transparent, he staked everything on his own teenage cruelty and forbade himself any stylistic display: this was the time to write in ordinary prose, for this activist of nonoriginality.

This story belonged to him so strongly that he wrote it like a scribe under dictation. Never had he felt so sure of himself, so concentrated on the paper. He had a tendency for brilliant but slapdash work, but in this case everything flowed so easily that he felt as if he were entering wholly into his book: his sensitive intelligence, as well as his absolute indifference to the sufferings of the soldier that his alter ego was betraying, were totally absorbed by the paper—so much so that when he raised his head from his manuscript, his expression showed such strange coldness that it worried his mentor.

Cocteau, however, was outlining the text for a lecture he would give in December, "The Professional Secret," an indictment against the myth of the "maudit" artist—or "critical poetry in prose," as Max Jacob would say, and as Jacques Rivière would report positively, for once, in the *Nouvelle revue fran-çaise*.[72] Stylistically, then, Cocteau was working in an opposite direction from Radiguet, and the text he wrote for the lecture is so brilliant, and so difficult as well, that even today it gives readers a profound sense of their incompetence. Yet his attention was nearly completely absorbed by the adolescent who had already submitted to him, at the end of August, 120 pages of his novel. Cocteau studied the pages with growing enthusiasm and immediately began correcting the pace and style, noting hurriedly, "Make an absolutely psychological story from that." What he had just read was remarkable; a few more weeks of work, and this *Le diable au corps* would be on a level with Benjamin Constant's *Adolphe* or Mme de La Fayette's *La princesse de Clèves*.

How could Bébé write such wonders at an age when most boys know nothing of love, and sometimes even of friendship? It's as if he had had a previous life and kept perfect memory of it.

Everything progressed so easily that Radiguet began again to find writing tedious and to laze about on the beach, and dance fox trots with the *patronne* of the hotel, to the sound of a phonograph. Each time Cocteau had to lead the bird back to its nest and sit him down at his desk. Five times over the months that followed, he would advise Radiguet to resume working on the end of *Le diable au corps*; he even locked him in his room, after throwing part of his manuscript into the fire, to force him to rewrite the destroyed passage. When he wasn't simply overcome with terror about the task of finishing the novel, Radiguet would grumble, as if this laborious work wasn't worthy of him.

Upon his return to Paris, everyone noticed how much the young Radiguet had changed. Was it the "miraculous" experience of the summer or perhaps contact with the creators of the Mutual Admiration Society, many of whom were the same age as his parents? Radiguet, whom these members now called only "monsieur," or "mon petit monsieur," had truly acquired confidence. During a dinner at the home of Jacques Porel that spring, he had refused to leave his chair when Cocteau had shown his wish to leave; in June again, when he was celebrating his eighteenth birthday at Francis, a restaurant on the place de l'Alma, after the premiere of *Les mariés*, Cocteau had publicly made a scene with him. It seemed as if Radiguet were beginning to find it difficult to be every-thing for a man he didn't desire, and that he was impatient to prove himself on his own, like Nijinsky before him. Endowed as he was with the beginnings of a body of work and with an appreciable number of conquests, Radiguet wanted finally to enjoy the profits of his precocity.

Without Cocteau, Radiguet went to see the editor of *Les nouvelles littéraires* to offer him his plans for novels and his disdain for work. His myopia continued to soften his harsh, stubborn expression, by giving him "a charm from another world"—especially when he read impassively in the center of a room full of visitors—but his paralyzing shyness turned to insolence.[73] Staring coldly at his interlocutors, he interrupted them with a "Wait a minute!" or "Oh come on," or leaning toward them, "Just listen!," all the while puffing on an enormous cigar offered by Paul Morand, who thought him "implacable like a child judging his parents."[74] A gesture with his cane, a drawled "Really?," were enough to ruin the euphoria of the one talking—"to strike stupidity with lightning," as Cocteau said. Picasso heard him murmur, in front of a still life that a painter didn't know how to finish: "It would be humane to put it down." He would immerse himself in a sphinx-like silence from which he would emerge only to question Georges Auric or Jean Hugo, the most cultivated of their friends, about some oddities of language.

Cocteau felt pride at this arrogance, but he suffered from it as well: the more Radiguet asserted himself, the more his own role lost importance. Cocteau, who continually worried that the young man would catch a cold, get drunk, become scattered or forget himself—in short, that an accident would derail that wonderful literary machine—sensed him indeed growing remote from him. With other people, Raymond Radiguet remained delicate enough to be excused for the selfishness that made him seek out friendships he could return only with smiles, or short notes, but to his mentor he gave the impression of being only half there and of wanting to summarize life, rather than live it. "Lack of interest, selfishness, tender pity, cruelty, suffering from contact, purity in debauchery, mixture of a violent taste for the pleasures of the earth and of scorn for them, naïve amorality": you could find it all in Radiguet, according to the transparent portrait of the angel every poet has inside that Cocteau gave in his autobiography, *Le secret professionnel*.[75] At once blasé and childlike, as scornful of fake values as he was respectful of real qualities, and no longer aware if he was playing a role in a comedy or living his life in Cocteau's brilliant circle, Radiguet was beginning to worry Cocteau.

Cocteau did know that he was respected, but he feared one day having to pay for this adopted son, whose rare remarks were heavy with disdainful irony and a feeling of pointlessness. One evening at the Gaya, the Society was discussing the curious fate of a male descendant of Joan of Arc destroyed by drugs and Radiguet, who hadn't opened his mouth for twenty-four hours, shouted, "It's self-evident! The heroine!," then plunged back into his silence, engulfed in it.[76] Concerned to disprove the rumors that labeled Radiguet Cocteau's catamite, Radiguet sought every opportunity to "betray" him by becoming associated instead with one of the foreign women drawn in great numbers to Paris during these mad years. He spent his nights in Montmartre clubs, but for lack of money, he would often return alone and overwhelmed, at dawn, to one of the two little hotels on the rue de Surène and the rue de Castellane, near the rue d'Anjou, where Cocteau had rented him a room: "It was horrible . . . another virgin," he said to Georges Auric, four years his elder and his sole confidant.

In a hurry to reach his goal, the young vampire turned toward experienced women, like the eccentric Beatrice Hastings, an English novelist he had met in Brancusi's studio, and whom Modigliani loved enough to devote fourteen portraits to in two years. Parading in unlikely English hats, a basket full of live ducks under her arm, this cocaine addict who came from a sect inspired by Mme Blavatsky embodied freedom in the eyes of Radiguet: after living on several continents and marrying a professional boxer, she seemed to be able to survive only in the heart of Montparnasse bohemia. Radiguet was an ideal companion for an exile; he spoke little, slowly, and very clearly. By acquiring this "angel of grace and tenderness" a quarter of a century younger than she, Beatrice Hastings drove a final nail into Cocteau's heart.[77] Unlike Cocteau, though, this man-eater wanted Radiguet whole. Dazzled by his talent, she who had been the lover of Katherine Mansfield and who had contributed to the discovery of Ezra Pound began bombarding Radiguet with novels to read and ever more impassioned letters confessing to him, under the seal of secrecy, her

fear of losing all prestige: for the first time in fact, she was faithful to one man—
behavior that verged on catastrophe in 1921 Montparnasse.

The growth of this relationship put Cocteau off his stride. That his Radigo
physically needed the other sex, he could admit, but seeing him abandon his
legendary silence and become a chatterbox was too much. "Bébé est vicieux, il
aime les femmes," he confided bitterly to the young Hemingway, who was
passing through Paris.[78] Hastings, five years older than his mother—and ten
years older than Cocteau himself—seemed like a bottomless pit for whiskey,
and made herself look pathetic by her late-in-life love. Radiguet, suffocating
under her kisses—and her dream of collaborating on a literary project with him
so as to unite forever her name to that "ornament of the French race"—went
back to favoring his mentor, in order to keep this overwhelming mistress at a
distance. For although he knew how to nourish himself on Cocteau's love in
order to revive his own desire for women, he was not against making them suffer
in turn by going back to Cocteau. "Denise," a story written in 1920, describes
him deliberately kissing a boy in order to cut to the quick the woman he desires.
Beatrice Hastings begged him to "free" himself from his protector before it was
too late.

Cocteau might have thought his calls to order had convinced Radiguet to
drop Hastings. If so, he must have felt disillusioned when he saw Radiguet grow
close to the young Mary Beerbohm, a clinging vine with "legs of Venus" and
imploring eyes. A product of the establishment, and related to the Wildean
cartoonist Max Beerbohm, this twenty-one-year-old English girl managed not
only to break Beatrice Hastings's weakening heart, but also to inflict on Cocteau
a new and cruel denial of the love on which he had staked everything, for now
there was proof that Radiguet pathologically had no need for him. When he
came to understand that a person so important to him didn't love him, Cocteau
began not loving himself. Worse, he soon convinced himself that people in
general didn't love him—a change that marked the beginning of the end for the
former wunderkind, who feared being an anomaly after his transformation.

Yet Cocteau was used to suffering in love and, with the help of experience,
was better able to bear it than Alice, the pretty suburbanite who had inspired *Le
diable au corps*, and who was still overwhelming journalists from *L'intran*, at the
end of the war, with tearful confessions about Radiguet's ingratitude. Led to
suffer and give, believe and hope, Cocteau clung to the idea that Radiguet
needed him as a literary mentor and, trying hard not to follow Diaghilev's
example, repressed his jealousy in order the better to persist as Pygmalion. He
preferred to love rather than be loved, if he had to choose. Giving love made
him feel amplified to the point of the pain that surgeons call "exquisite," in all

the nuances of his sensibility; as the one who received love, however, he suffered, until he seemed inferior to the other, as he had with Christiane Mancini. He had been endowed with a talent for suffering. When Cocteau was young and had to stay in bed building a model theater, illness offered him his first joys as a child, and ever since he had drawn a certain positive energy from his unhappiness. He was even proud to be diagnosed with an illness that only the Chinese ambassador had contracted before him, or when he discovered that he had once again skirted mortal danger and deserved his nickname of "trompe-la-mort" (death cheater).

And he couldn't stop himself from loving cruel people. He belonged to the race of glass, and Radiguet of diamond; the fate of one was to bleed, that of the other to wound. This pitiless algebra would have made other people melancholic, but Cocteau had known since the Greeks that protesting would only worsen his case. Instead, accepting that suffering was an element of his fate, he claimed it, with a quasi-Nietzschean lightness: indeed, he would probably have ended up tolerating these affairs with women—he soon became mother-like in love—if Radiguet himself hadn't made that impossible.

Beatrice Hastings's aggressive jealousy started to exacerbate Cocteau's. He could no longer bear to see this hysteric distract Bébé from his work. Sensing Cocteau's frustration, she tried to make peace with her lover's mentor by sending him flattering letters, then myriads of quatrains, some celebrating her meetings with Radiguet, others complaining at his coldness or even suggesting to Cocteau a marriage that might stabilize the young man. Meeting with no success, Hastings began again to harass Radiguet, but nothing worked, including calling him a rabid ape and "extra-vulgar," threatening him with becoming a nun, and showing him in an ignoble light in a novel.[79] While running from Cocteau to women, women to his books, his books to alcohol, and alcohol to Cocteau's literary mothering, Radiguet threatened all who approached him. "He always went to the edge of the abyss, to look," said Pierre Bertin.[80]

THE CABARET OF LE BOEUF

Cocteau's situation was becoming delicate. In love with a minor who desired women, he couldn't openly express his jealousy, or even his anxieties. But this situation was stronger than he was; he would rather risk ridicule than denial, since every new conquest of "monsieur Bébé" placed ever more in doubt the reality of a relationship that was vital to him. Therefore, when at the end of 1921 Moysès decided to enlarge his club and obtained from Cocteau his permission to use the title of the American farce he had written with Milhaud to baptize a new bar, larger than the Gaya—and when on the evening of the unofficial opening, after Picasso and Olga, Marie Laurencin, Mary Beerbohm, and the whole Mutual Admiration Society had invaded the twin premises located on each side of the porte cochère on 28 rue Boissy-d'Anglas, he heard Brancusi say, "Let's go," and Radiguet reply slyly in kind—he could only accuse that "scandal-monger," that "policewoman" (Beatrice Hastings) of having plotted their escape, to justify his fury. It seemed that only that "monster" could have led Bébé to betray him so openly.

So it was with real relief that he received, after several days without news, a telegram from Corsica, where both men had gone in search of sex, and where they said they were having a lot of fun (the island still passed for a Frenchified bit of Italy). It was truly Cocteau whom Bébé wanted to reassure first, through this "little blue" (telegram) that Cocteau proudly exhibited during the official opening of Le Boeuf sur le Toit, on January 10, 1922, in the presence of an over-excited crowd. It served as proof that his rival had played no part in Radiguet's departure, and he was still the favorite. But when the two escapees finally returned, ten days later, soaking wet and disappointed at having met only men in bars and women in black on the streets, they were still forced to endure Cocteau's tantrum over it, staged in front of the whole Society gathered for the traditional Saturday dinner at chez Delmas.[81]

Moysès's new mahogany bar on the rue Boissy-d'Anglas immediately became the place to be seen drinking Alaskas or Manhattans. Jean Wiener played Gershwin, accompanied on the second piano by Clément Doucet—a fat Walloon who would down his beers or read a thriller with one hand as he played. Other spectacles that could be seen there were Radiguet and his mentor, thought to be on nonspeaking terms ever since Radiguet's flight, and girls of easy virtue come to try their luck. Jacques Porel writes:

> Cocteau and Radiguet formed an inseparable pair that we never tired of watching, Georges Auric and I. There was a kind of diabolic curiosity inter-mingled in this: We wanted to see how far Radiguet would follow his taste for freedom, how he would manage to free himself from the tutelage of his men-tor. We would watch him with women, with alcohol. We might even have encouraged him for a little while. It was a dangerous game.[82]

By increasing Cocteau's anxieties, this new bar that owed its name to him would also expand his influence. From Duchamp to Tzara, the entire avant-garde frequented this fief, with the notable exception of Breton and the hard core of the Certà. Yet despite the express orders of the leader, Desnos showed himself there; and Soupault saw Proust there, for his sole appearance in July

1922, when he complained about the boorishness of a neighbor, whom he even challenged to a duel; grumbled about an era when no one knew about the customs that he had made, in the *Recherche*, into a language as complex as Church Latin; and finally moaned about this spot that was "deadly" for his lungs—"Pastoral by its name, but nothing less than a roadhouse."[83]

Open until dawn, to the great dismay of the neighbors, Le Boeuf became, in a matter of months, "the crossroads of destinies, the cradle of love affairs, the hearth of discords, the navel of Paris," according to Jean Hugo.[84] Since Moysès was as generous as he was clever, he extended great amounts of credit to his regulars. Radical bohemians were soon joined there by industrialists out for a good time and Americans chased there by Prohibition. All were impatient to be seen among "le *Tout-Paris* that can't stay in place, gets bored, changes cafés ten times a night to escape something it will never escape," according to Léon-Paul Fargue. Buttoned up to the ears in a greatcoat reminiscent of Inspector Javert in *Les misérables*, Ezra Pound saw Caryathis dance there, on a tiny stage, in front of two of the assassins of Rasputin, Grand Duke Dimitri and Prince Yussupov, while an all-pink lady let a paying admirer bury an ecstatic face under her skirts and while beautiful snobs sang, after Tzara: "Drink bird's milk / Wash your chocolates / Eat calf!"

The gaiety, sexual tolerance, and wonderful excitement and romantic encounters that Le Boeuf gave rise to made the bar a comfort to Cocteau. Keeping one eye on Radiguet, and observing the newcomers with the other, he held court almost every night in the heart of this incredible birdcage whose sonorous ambiance Maurice Sachs would describe evocatively in *Au temps du Boeuf sur le Toit*: "The sozzled, friendly voice, the abrupt, friendly, drunken laughter of Georges Auric, the voice of Francis Poulenc that came out of his nose," the flow "of warm-water voices, icy voices, pedantic voices, gentlemen, comrades, arrivistes, surprised, self-sufficient voices," and the noise of broken windows produced by the enchanting voice of Cocteau.[85] Young people who had known nothing of the war except the excitement of air-raid alerts, the intoxication of movie theaters plunged into the darkness, the explosion of distant bombs, the absence of any paternal authority, and finally the almost sexual euphoria of victory, came there to finish their mini-revolution. As Maurice Sachs explained,

> The frivolity we had learned from our mothers, that "vacation-like" atmosphere, as Radiguet said, in which our school years had bathed, that noise of kisses, that smell of sperm, the jingling of easy coins, the habit we'd gotten into of venerating a crowd of heroes, the relaxing of morals that neces-

sarily follows a major human ordeal; all this contributed to making post-war young boys into cheerful, light-hearted, frivolous, easy, enthusiastic, and rather amoral beings. Life wasn't just to be taken: it was pillaged like a conquered city.[86]

For Cocteau the time and the place were a curious mixture of joy and terror, hysteria and melancholy, borne along by the jazz of Clément Doucet and Jean Wiener—experiences so popular that we still owe to them the French expressions "faire un boeuf" (to have a jam session) and "avoir un succès boeuf" (to be incredibly successful). For Radiguet the appeal was the certainty of finding bodies softened by Gershwin rags and Jérôme Kern, and mouths greedy to share a flaming Alaska. So Moysès's bar took the place of the Dôme and Maxim's, and became the mythical place of the 1920s, the Parisian equivalent of the Berlin Hop là!, just as the Café de la Régence had been for the generation of the Enlightenment, or Le Rocher de Cancale for Balzac's generation—a dozen tables, with wicks soaked in enough Tokay, absinthe, or Manhattans to be infused by the "new spirit."

THE RETURN TO ORDER

Vocabulaire was the first real poetic fruit of the four-hand aesthetic thought up by Cocteau and Radiguet. It is a collection in which Cocteau claims the right to speak from several mouths, "like Janus," and in which he praises the rose, Ronsard, "kind, green France," as well as mythology and Apollinaire, whose influence we can recognize here or there. But it's death that carries the most beautiful poem—a death that, "on the other side of our living selves," weaves our life, then withdraws from it—like an ice angel, lighter than cork, heavier than bronze, who has only to lie down on the desired lover to fix his heart in place, close his eyes, and make him forever deaf, better than love could do.[87]

Radiguet wrote of Malherbe and Baudelaire, in the article he would devote to this *Vocabulaire*, but its reception once again disappointed Cocteau. "It's the worst kind of garbage you can imagine," wrote Jacques Baron in *Littérature*, the organ of the Breton group.[88] (In the same issue, and while apologizing for even mentioning his name, Baron accused Cocteau of being a "genius of the meaningless," of producing an "intolerable malaise," but also of living on the "corpse" of Valéry and Marinetti—which would have been a better description of Breton.) Even though Edmond Jaloux described Cocteau as an authentic and infinitely treasured poet, and Pascal Pia solemnly announced that *Vocabulaire* was "perhaps the only book of classical poetry written since the seventeenth century," the insults coming from the Certà were enough to make Cocteau weep.[89] Was it a crime, he asked in his book, "To distribute one's rhymes / As much at the end of lines as in the middle"?[90] Obviously, it was.

What had he done to be so poorly treated? What stain from birth did they reproach him with? They had only to say, "Someone read to me your new collection yesterday," without any more detail, and immediately he would despair.[91] "My poor *Vocabulaire* is sinking like the rest of my books," he worried. "I won't write any more until the new order." Cocteau would soon write a grave, wounded plea in *Plain-chant*—"I have, to trick the offensive clock / Sung in twenty ways"—referring apologetically to his enigmatic personality over the years and to those demanding years of intense mutation. He who ten years before thought he was the luckiest of poets now had to admit that he was not loved, and that the joy produced by the Mutual Admiration Society fell away as soon as he found himself alone in his room.

Since Paris was inflicting such pain, Cocteau chose to withdraw again to the sea. Convinced that his work could wait, and knowing that Radiguet was flirting dangerously with death, he decided to take the younger poet with him again. Already "le secret professionel" was talking about those angelic poets who either committed suicide or died young, with the Beyond using love, opium, or murder to take them back: the more uncontrollable Radiguet became, or the more Mary Beerbohm or Beatrice Hastings regained their influence over him, the more Cocteau knew he had to act quickly.

This time the pair went to Lavandou, in the neighborhood of Toulon, on the French Riviera, and chose a little wooden hotel looking out onto the island of Port-Cros. "Electricity?" Cocteau worried. "We expect it any minute now," the bellboy replied. "Running water?" It had to be hauled up in buckets. The owners? Gone, but until when? Three days later, with the help of Cocteau's charm, the staff was doting on this strange couple occupying separate rooms.

Lavandou was another paradise of sand, bathed by a turquoise sea crossed at times by a warship. Silence here was master, and the rare vacationers who walked with bare feet on the little white seashells and golden mica knew nothing about the journal *Littérature*, Beatrice Hastings, or André Breton. "Seeing society degrades one, staying alone disgusts one," said Cocteau to Max Jacob, not long before his departure.[92] Alone with Radiguet, he was finally happy. Caresses? The sun took charge of that. Scarcely risen, it already pinned Cocteau to the ground, warmed him, then penetrated and burned him, without his having to ask. Never had a lover been so little demanding; never had a mistress given so much. Everything life had refused him was suddenly offered, beyond all expectations.

Three days of this treatment and, going beyond all his promises, Cocteau began again to write and draw, adapting for the Pitoëffs a play, *L'épouse injustement soupçonnée*, writing a comic-opera libretto for Milhaud, *Le pauvre matelot*, and even outlining his first actual novel, under the influence of advice he himself had given to Radiguet. First entitled *"La moitié d'ombre,"* then soon *Le grand écart*, this transposed story of his unhappy love for Madeleine Carlier brought him literarily, if not sexually, closer to Radiguet: reviving through a brief fiction his times of erotic ambiguity, close to those that Radiguet experienced in the end, Cocteau realized the dream of a desk for two that Flaubert had nursed before.

Cocteau would take great pleasure in writing this short novel of sentimental education—he, for whom poetry was suffering and criticism a game. "It will be a heart rich and pure mingled with the lowliness of a city, which walks on the edge the way sleepwalkers walk on the edge of a roof. A sensibility that desires in vagueness, finds a brief reply, and expends itself as if it were an eternal love," he explained to his mother. More simply, it was a matter of showing all the strangeness of a nature desirous of becoming the beloved man—or woman, more than possessing that person.[93] *Le diable au corps* would convey all the cold mastery in love of its author; *Le grand écart* would reveal all the emotional fragility of its author, and the constant imbalance life inflicted on him, like the difficult dance step—the "splits"—in its title. Seeking always to make fictional the reality he was living, Cocteau had scarcely felt the need to write a novel until then: just existing took charge of that. But the failure of *Vocabulaire* as well as the still secret success of *Le diable au corps* convinced him that a novel would be a better way than poetry to invite the public into his innermost thoughts. The facts recounted were already fifteen years old, and this distance helped him as he composed the character of Jacques Forestier, his double in many respects who, by trying to poison himself, sees his mother leaning over him, changing into the Germaine who made him suffer so passionately—or one of the "animals of his desire" glimpsed in a casino. Was seeing those "animals" his way of complying with the sexual and social ban placed by Mme Cocteau on Madeleine Carlier?

The novel occupied Cocteau fully for several weeks. About *Vocabulaire*, Max Jacob had said, showering Cocteau as usual with compliments, "Cocteau is focusing: I am convinced that with austere cruelty he is depriving himself of the abundance that would be natural for him, in order to rein himself in and concentrate on simplifying traits."[94] This was the same treatment he now applied to *Le grand écart*, a book as lean and sinewy as he, full of blinding lightning flashes and perilous glissades that are sometimes unbearably swift and true, as in this remark: "To love and be loved, that is the ideal. Provided it's the same person involved."[95] His own talents intrigued him, actually; it was no accident that his novel was advancing quickly. It was an uncontrollable force that, despite his original decision to take it easy, set him to work sketching the tarts getting their johns drunk in a restaurant in Pramousquier on the Riviera or drawing a flash outline of the profile of Radiguet the insomniac, when a mixture of fatigue, the open air, and unpasteurized milk had made him rest his head on his right arm, on the table where he was writing. This randomness that governed his actions was some cause of anguish to him, but already Cocteau was convinced that it governed all the movements in the world, from the rotation of the planets to the spawning of mullet. The idyllic landscape of the Mediterranean hid other realities that also refused themselves to him; he still didn't dare call them God but he couldn't reduce them to simple Matter.

In the evenings, the waning light would make him lift his eyes to stare at the sea. Was it sadness at sensing Radiguet mobilized by his sole book? Visions of the apocalypse assailed him: "The damaged, used-up earth, the sun becoming an Earth, everything is stained, displaced, disorganized. Very sensitive natures sense these death throes of the universe that are beginning."[96] This large moon that our planet will one day be deeply upset him, since that was also the fate that awaited the universe, whose fire was being absorbed into the horizon. He who had been laughing two hours earlier went to bed in misery, haunted by the fragility of what seems most lasting to us. An hour later he would get up, feverish to add to his novel, until he again lost both sleep and appetite for it.

Radiguet was working just as hard. But even though the manuscript of *Le diable au corps*, which Bernard Grasset had just enthusiastically accepted, wasn't finished, the "child-king" (so nicknamed by Max Jacob) already had another idea for a novel. In order to perfect himself, too, he insisted first on reading and "taking apart" not just classics, whose structures remained mysterious, but also rubbish, since the visible workings of bad novels seemed more instructive to him. "When I've read all the books," he wrote to Mme Cocteau, "I'll write one to have something to read."[97] This would be *Le bal du comte d'Orgel*, his second novel.

In this second novel, Radiguet would take his inspiration from the Parisian aristocracy to which Cocteau had introduced him—especially the Beaumont couple, whose style would contribute to giving the book its neo-eighteenth-century climate. Even more than a lesser Montesquiou with a falsetto voice, the Comte de Beaumont was the exact evocation, in Radiguet's eyes, of what the ancien régime would have produced, if it had continued till 1920: a colonel with a switch that mobilized ambulances in wartime, a huge dragonfly dreaming only of buzzing around in peacetime. The balls given in the mansion on the rue Masseran—where this giant comic could appear as a winged Cupid wearing a pink jumper, or as a Hindu dancing girl or a gypsy, threatening his guests with harmless arrows and then, under the lens of Man Ray, turning his gaze to the forever serene and deserted sky of high society—had left traces in Bébé's mind. His rigorous frivolity in organizing these dizzying changes of identity can be seen in the characters of Anne d'Orgel and the count, as well as in the silent passion of François de Séryeuse for Mahaut, the count's emotionally abandoned wife—"Mahaut" is as androgynous as "Anne," which was a masculine name in old aristocratic families. The count is so moved by Séryeuse's charm that he is troubled for the first time by his own wife: having caused such emotion in such a troubled boy has wreathed her in mystery. (In the end, Anne d'Orgel falls in love with her.)

To nourish this novel of chaste love, which he wanted to be as obscene as an erotic novel, Radiguet had only to use his memories of the Médrano circus or the soiree given for *Pulcinella* in Robinson; he placed his easel in front of *La princesse de Clèves*, the story of a deliberately suppressed passion. This classic should have intimidated him, but already he was responding with an unruffled confidence to objections, taking up Cocteau's phrase about how original artists assert themselves even more when they copy. Overall it was a transformative stage for the ex-Dadaist, who would come to tell his story like an omnipotent witness, and who in just a few months would go from "I" to "he," from adolescence to adulthood, from coarse sincerity to the game of mirrors of an ambiguous triangulation. But this novel also conveys his intimate alertness to the unhappy passion Cocteau had for him. It wasn't by chance that both chose as models Mme de La Fayette, Laclos, and Benjamin Constant: *La princesse de Clèves*, *Les liaisons dangereuses*, and *Adolphe* tell of passions burning with ice, stories in which one of the protagonists' inability to love turns infernal. By banishing their subjects to private pain, these impossible loves encourage them to perfect a very French manner of geometrizing love, and ruthlessly to prune the branches of this "rosebush," in order to compress tenderness and make internal bleeding come out—creating an aesthetic of great harshness that unites with the demoralizing art of the moralists. This is what the pair was effecting together in their "return to order," during that long neoclassical summer in which not only *Le diable au corps* and *Le grand écart*, but also *Le bal du comte d'Orgel* and *Thomas l'imposteur* blossomed.

While Cocteau's personality influenced Radiguet, what they were experiencing together also came to color the style of Cocteau. Each of Cocteau's books was born from a sense of dissatisfaction provoked by the previous one, leading to an oeuvre marked by dramatic contrasts (a fact that never failed to excite criticism of him). In addition, his books often reflected characteristics of his companion at the time. Each man, though, preserved his own universe. Radiguet fulfilled without fail his paradoxical plan to write like everyone else, so that any failure would prove his inimitable personality. By contrast, Cocteau couldn't keep from betraying his inimitable feverishness, in *Le grand écart* or *Thomas l'imposteur*, despite a few phrases that show the effect of his reading of Mme de La Fayette. One author was watching himself live, love, and punish; take pleasure, abandon, and betray—all with the calm of someone shaving. The other was breathlessly weaving together his constant confusions about love and shifting identities.

THE GREEK SUMMER

Sometimes, the four-handed organism of Cocteau and Radiguet would take a break in the sun. After a refreshing dip with the plump Auric, who had come to Lavandou with Pierre de Lacretelle (an aesthete met in the wings of the Ballets Russes whom Cocteau had found on the front in Sector 131), the group set off to walk the deserted shoreline barefoot as far as the delta, where a trickling brook was surrounded by leaning cattails that Cocteau changed into mysterious characters. One day their path met that of a couple on honeymoon, and the hairy "wife" took off her wedding dress to wriggle into the water before dancing with the fishermen. Everyone was surprised to see that the neighborhood beachgoers, who were used to seeing men go off "on walks" with other men, so good-naturedly admitted this man in drag on the arm of her proclaimed husband. "It's because it's common," Radiguet said, in whose eyes the fact that they were all a similar class—fishermen—was more important than the "difference" between the sexes.[98]

On Sunday, the group picnicked in a juniper grove. The great classical culture of Pierre de Lacretelle (the brother of Jacques, who was the author of the novel *Silbermann*) fed Radiguet's curiosity, who now began reading authors as unfashionable as Victor Hugo and André Chénier, despite the protests of Cocteau, who preferred to feast on *Fantômas*, but never had such drawn-out conversations about the art of writing. Having passed his thirtieth year, Cocteau, the devoted writer, rearranged his classes around this prodigious self-taught boy, who made him ashamed of his own ignorance of Greek and grammar. The one he already called his "examiner" impressed him by the brilliance of his analyses, which he deemed worthy of Boileau in *L'art poétique*: "Jean understood before reading; Radiguet read slowly, but he saw what Jean hadn't seen," noted

Bernard Faÿ.[99] On this point it was an ideal couple, with Cocteau showing Radiguet the same talent to make him write as Radiguet had to make him read. "Cocteau let his serious and profound side appear more clearly," wrote Jean Hugo, who had come to join them with Valentine.[100] The distance from Paris, the drastic fast from news and rumors, and Radiguet's inspired terseness all had such a calming effect on Cocteau that he came to envy Lacretelle's good moods. It was as if, by dint of loving and admiring Radiguet, he had abandoned that body so difficult to live inside in order more and more to integrate Radiguet's own, and under this carapace to begin a second life, more resistant and infinitely more serene.

Cocteau and Radiguet stimulated each other so much that they were two silhouettes walking in the twilight, their eyes shining with cheerfulness, wearing the same fisherman's blue canvas smocks, which Joseph Kessel, who had come on honeymoon with Sandi, on the recommendation of Jacques de Lacretelle, had discovered in early August. "They swam, worked, fed on the pagan, spiritual sap of the earth and the water," the young author of *La steppe rouge* said, charmed by the Virgilian atmosphere of Lavandou, by the asceticism radiating from the animated structure of Cocteau's face, as well as by his purebred bearing.[101] This even if Kessel, that man with the boxer's physique tempered by a gentle gaze, was himself impressed above all by the seer's myopia of Radiguet, five years his junior, which gave him an "infallible knowledge of the human machine in its most secret springs."[102]

When vacationers invaded the beaches of Lavandou, the couple moved to the neighboring bay of Pramousquier, which had remained wilder. François de Gouy and his boyfriend, Russell Greeley, soon joined them there. "Incredibly fat, as if he'd been inflated as a joke," as Maurice Sachs said, Georges Auric in turn settled into the villa Croix-Fleurie, a pension inhabited by a spiritualist convinced that its piano played by itself at night, when rats were the real cause of the racket.[103] The very young Drieu la Rochelle would visit them as well, along with Jacques Rigaut, that strange Dadaist and secretary to Jacques-Émile Blanche, whose self-destructive dandyism would inspire Drieu with the magnificent *Feu follet*.

By early October, this Adamic inlet, where sometimes tiny black flecks coming from a pinewood fire floated, was again deserted. "I remain alone with the silent one," Cocteau confided to his mother, who was already sending "sweet words" to Bébé. "He works—I work. He eats—I eat. He sleeps—I sleep—we don't exchange ten words."[104] At the end of each of these Trappist days, distracted only by the pigs being killed by their neighbor, Radiguet and Cocteau would go to read, naked on the beach, Balzac's *The Black Sheep* and Stendhal's *Charterhouse of Parma*. With *Le grand écart* finally finished, in less than three weeks, Cocteau had already started adapting an *Antigone*. The sun, the sea, the shepherd's crook a friend had just given him—he couldn't be closer to the ancient climate of Sophocle's play, the most beautiful one in the world, in Cocteau's opinion. "I call 'modern' what takes your breath away, and 'classical,' what gives it back to me," Florence Delay would say half a century later. From Cocteau's fingers flowed verses, drawings, and retorts, without order or reason. The process Proust had analyzed in *Sodome et Gomorrhe* was confirmed: Cocteau resembled those hermaphroditic species among whom both sexes cohabit in one individual, but who are prevented from reproducing by a barrier, until a third party (an insect for a flower or a boy here) helps their male aspect fertilize the female.

Plain-chant brought this rediscovered plenitude to its height. Stunned by the ease with which the poem burst forth, Cocteau exulted to Max Jacob: "I received (there are no other words for it) 40 pages of poetry."[105] His first reflex was to pay homage to the "angel" whom he clutched in his thoughts at night, so hard that the pair came to form a single mechanism, "With many heads and arms, like the gods / In temples in China." A twin who formed with him a tree with a single bark, a single color, "from which our kiss would be the sole flower"—the two-headed eagle, already. For even if grammatically Cocteau addresses a female muse, it was indeed Radiguet who inspired this love song, which had ripened during the hours spent watching him sleep with his mouth open. The erotic allusions to a single bed scattered throughout the poem might almost prove the nonplatonic nature of their relationship, but nothing reveals any consummation of it. It's Radiguet's sleep that Cocteau sings of, not his sexuality. Just like Proust's Narrator watching Albertine, Cocteau had tenderly kept watch over Radiguet as he dreamed.

On August 2, Radiguet had read to Cocteau an early passage from *Le bal* about the history of the d'Orgel family. Cocteau, already convinced that the novel was starting wonderfully—"more beautiful than Proust and truer than Balzac"—had written to his mother, "For a year, we've been seeing him reading the [Almanac of] Gotha—it was with this chapter in mind. I envy this faculty of silence and mystery."[106] To Mahaut d'Orgel, his heroine, Radiguet had in fact given origins close to those that Radiguet had claimed when he said he was descended, through his mother, from Joséphine de Beauharnais and through his father, from the Poissons, and hence from la Pompadour. Was he making that up? Indirectly placed in the position of a sovereign, Cocteau couldn't have been happier, but he preferred to believe, as always, these genealogical half-truths. His mother was promptly informed that Mme Radiguet was a Mlle. d'Audifrédy from Martinique—an origin that was supposed to justify the "Creole" behavior of a boy who slept during the day, smoked at night, and stuffed himself on sugar. One couldn't provide better justification for the handsome portrait of Bébé with his mouth erotically open that Cocteau attached to his daily letter.

Radiguet, however, had put a final period on that first version of *Le bal*—four hundred pages that stunned Cocteau. How had he been able to summarize the essence of these experiences in so little time? With what measuring instrument had he observed, then internalized, the adult motivations of these characters? It was as if Radiguet had taken notes, at each moment of his life, or placed his heart in front of a mirror, and coldly recorded all of its beats. "If I had the slightest pride, Radiguet's novel would be enough to stifle it in me," Cocteau wrote to his mother. "This incredible masterpiece puts to shame everything I compare him to, even my dear Stendhal."[107] A month earlier, he had confided to her that this book made him feel disgust for his own, just as Picasso's discipline had made him reject his own, in Rome. Confidence of judgment, originality of thought, independence of conception: Radiguet was a miracle—"the miracle of the Marne," he sometimes said. The young author might grope his way forward with a blind man's cane, but his internal eye forgot nothing, now retracting like a microscope, now stretching into telescopic view, always observing beings with precise clarity or novelistic vagueness, as required. A teenager and an old man cohabited in him, and this couple knew well the emotions caused by life. "He probably liked existence more for the documentation it provided him than for its charms," Marcel Raval confirmed.[108] Stravinsky would be more laconic, calling Radiguet a "thinking machine."

But *Le bal* was too long. Cocteau, whose literary eye never shut, encouraged Radiguet to shorten the action and the descriptions, then accelerate its too-regular style: in this way a little of his nervous essence passed into the book, which was already marked by his wit. Made fertile by this good example, as if this masterpiece had also become his own, Cocteau felt a new novel growing inside him. He began writing a book with the background of war as its canvas, but more by implication than in *Le diable au corps*, which he had truly wanted to be "deadly." Here again, he was sensing the feel of the times; the 1920s generation, which had been birthed with forceps by the conflict, was producing novel after novel about the subject—usually to show its horror. Cocteau approached the subject in a dreamlike, cheerful way that was half-realistic and half-pathetic, using his firsthand knowledge during the war of the soldier who had passed himself off as the nephew of the famous General de Castelnau—here renamed de Fontenoy.

Of Raoul Thomas—his name in the book—Cocteau made a new Fabrice del Dongo that moved like a tightrope walker through not the Battle of Waterloo but the battles of the Great War, a kind of Fanfan la Tulipe totally unaware of reality—including his own—and experiencing this dark period in utter, complete euphoria. The imposture interested him. Rich in poetic material, this existential lie in his eyes required more imagination, courage, and talent than the ordinary writing of a fictitious story—it was the romanesque made real, if one could put it that way. The conflict had given rise to many vocations of this kind, including that of Nadine Hoang, who had obtained the rank of colonel by posing as a man and fighting in the Chinese army. Indeed Cocteau had only to exploit his own memories as a fake Zouave to slip under the skin of his Thomas.

The book kept him awake day and night, for a month. Finished on October 27, *Thomas l'imposteur* was deemed a complete success by Radiguet, who had now taken on the role of censor. Cocteau could think himself happy; for the first time, he had managed to speak intimately about himself outside of the cryptic channel of poetry, and with more imaginative profundity than in his sketch *Le grand écart*. The constraining framework of the war had provided a real foundation to his unreality. Could it be that he needed to be tied up in order to be able to unravel himself in a productive way?

The twin births of *Le bal* and *Thomas* made Cocteau supremely happy. "You two are worth easily 12 Paul Morands," Max Jacob had written to him in the spring.[109] This kind of exaggeration had the power of making him cheerful for days, even though he suspected Jacob (whom they had nicknamed "God's clown") of saying the equivalent to Morand. The autumn, it's true, had been miraculous. Radiguet had finished two novels, as had Cocteau, who moreover wrote two plays, an opera libretto, a hundred or so letters, *Plain-chant*—one of his most beautiful collections of poetry—and *La rose de François*. Never had he seemed so serene, so full, so sure of himself. With his need to please fulfilled, he didn't even feel compelled to smile in front of the cameras of Man Ray and Martinie, whose photographs testify to this magnificent time when, aware of his good influence and certain of his talents, happy to love but also balanced by Radiguet, Cocteau imposed his image by the strength and concentration of his burning gaze, the opposite of the theatricality with which, later on, he would try to recapture these times that were passing him by.[110] Probably he was not the god he thought he was, during his Symbolist years, but with Radiguet, the concentration of possibilities and forms he had within him acquired a framework, an equilibrium, and almost a classicism that he would never find again.

THE FUNERAL OF THE PHANTOM

Cocteau and Radiguet hadn't been back a week in Paris before, on November 18, 1922, exhausted by fifteen years of intensive work, recurrent illnesses, and insomnia, Proust died on the rue Hamelin, in the 16th arrondissement. The embalmer of the Belle Époque had devoted his last remaining strength to dictating corrections of his nesting-doll manuscript to Céleste, his housekeeper, who added additional loose paper strips that sometimes reached six feet long. He also dictated some final letters to Mme de Chevigné complaining again about her silence and reminding her of their first meetings, which had caused him some small heart attacks, but left her like marble.

Daylight had become intolerable to him, so his final outings took place at night, for dinners where that fantastic insect, greedy to suck "matter to make his black honey," as Cocteau said, tried to appease his insane thirst for detail.[111] Preceded by an avalanche of phone calls from Céleste — "Is his herb tea ready? Are there any drafts?" — Proust had made one final appearance at the ball given by Édith and Étienne de Beaumont, for New Year's 1922. Dressed in the fashion of 1908, when he had taken to his bed, the now famous writer had appeared reeking of fumigations — puffy, pale, and powdered, like a ghost that had escaped from his book *À la recherche du temps perdu*, which he had borne for so long and in which the most vapid snobs sometimes attained a Homeric grandeur. Twenty years earlier, seeing him appear with his outdated cloak, Princess Bibesco thought he looked as if he had come to see her in his coffin outfit; now Proust seemed dead. Only his double, the Narrator, still had the strength to question some decrepit duke. "Look at him, he is working from life!," whispered Picasso, near Radiguet, who had come to put the final touches on his Comte d'Orgel, not realizing that some of those present would also be found in the "bal des têtes" in *À la recherche du temps perdu*.[112]

Actually, it wasn't Proust who had escaped from his book, but the book itself that had, by draining all his flesh, finally left him nothing but an empty envelope. Subject to the rhythm of the episodes that he continued to write, slavishly — he was still dictating clarifications about the death of Bergotte the day before his own death — his exhausted body, like the chrysalis at the end of its metamorphosis, had strength enough only to expel the last threads of its living work. Cocteau had often expressed the wish, during these last months, to see again the one he could regard as an old friend, since they had known each other well for twelve years. But Proust always argued overwork to turn him away, preferring to preserve his last strength to try one last time to extract some precious details from Mme de Chevigné. He was aware how much the two men could gain from seeing each other again, "questioning each other about the mechanism of the other's life," but if he still mentioned a visit to Cocteau, it was while pretending to fear that upon emerging in the middle of the night on the rue d'Anjou, he would find Cocteau like "an Egyptian vase depicting Ramses, hidden under a dressing gown."[113] Sometimes, as in that beginning of 1922, the author of the *Remembrance* even conveyed how much the slightest phrase cost him: "This simple letter, how many medications just to be able to lift my head to write it!," and when signing, exercised this indirect form of blackmail: "Your friend is sorry that you seem to doubt the pleasure there is in seeing you, but (if you're not convinced) resigned to this disappointment after all the disappointments each day brings me."[114]

A hostage of his cork mausoleum, a phantom that flourished only in the past, Proust had died for real this time. Cocteau would never again hear his quavering, exhausted voice, which came not from the throat but from the center, "the way ventriloquists' voices come from the torso." He would add, in the splendid text for the *Nouvelle revue française*, that Proust's voice "organized his narration into a system . . . of formal entrances, . . . pauses, politenesses, uncontrollable laughter, white gloves crushing his moustache to fan out on his face," which emerged from his stiff-shirted bosom.[115]

For a long time Cocteau watched at the brass bed where Proust's body lay, his eyes lined with mauve streaks. His long pointed beard, while he was alive, had camouflaged whatever flesh was left in his face; dead, it gave Proust the look of a great Assyrian priest with ivory skin, as if he had rejoined forever that distant Persia that used to fascinate them both. Looking up, Cocteau noticed the mantelpiece where the endless manuscript for *À la recherche du temps perdu* was stacked. "This pile of paper, on his left, continued to live like the watch on the wrist of dead soldiers," he said; in fact, the volumes would continue to come out, for five more years, as if their author still remained secretly perfecting, in the cellars on rue Hamelin, this truly monstrous work, at once the apotheosis of the roman à clef and his own tomb, in which a stylist of the old guard had become the modern demiurge. At the request of Robert Proust, Marcel's brother, Cocteau went to find Man Ray, who came quickly to photograph the "imperial" mask. Morand also took a picture of the sallow body that Reynaldo Hahn watched over; later, Dunoyer de Segonzac, after Helleu and many others, sketched the corpse's expression in India ink.[116] In a neighboring room, intimidated, Gaston Gallimard expressed to Cocteau for the first time a wish to publish him.

Preceded by a hearse overflowing with flowers, the funeral procession took off from the Église Saint-Pierre-de-Chaillot on the morning of November 21, "a grey day that dirtied the stones." Playing in the background was Ravel's "Pavane for a Dead Princess," whose title resonated strangely. Cocteau and Radiguet followed close behind monocle-wearing dukes, princes in button boots, balding ambassadors, and brilliantined members of the Jockey Club who had served as models, if not researchers, for the Narrator in the *Recherche*. A forest of suits and top hats protected between five hundred and a thousand people from a threatening rain, among them Barrès in old-fashioned splendor, Lucien Daudet and Maurice Rostand—"the *haute* red-headed Jew and the great Parisian pederasty reappearing, wearing make-up," as Maurice Martin du Gard said—as well as Mayakovsky, the leader of the Komfuts movement, who was visiting Paris.[117] It was like the funeral procession in *Entracte*, the Dadaist film, that Étienne de Beaumont, by his incredible height, had prevented from turning into a stampede.[118] The hearse emerged onto the Champs-Élysées as noon struck, passing by the Tuileries gardens on the avenue Gabriel where as a child the Narrator had played with Gilberte, in the *Recherche*. As they approached the rue Boissy-d'Anglas, Radiguet began to get impatient: was that prodigy of abruptness, trying to distance himself from the great master of the long phrase, whose *Sodome et Gomorrhe* he had so admired? The group around Cocteau discreetly detached itself from the cortege and stopped at the Boeuf sur le Toit. "Radiguet . . . immediately ordered some crêpes from Moysès and went off to make a phone call," continued Maurice Martin du Gard, who also went on to the Père-Lachaise cemetery in a taxi.

Six months earlier, in Lavandou, reading pre-publication excerpts from the second series of *Sodome et Gomorrhe*, thinking the pages about the grandmother wonderful, Cocteau had nevertheless reproached the book for being full of snobbism and handicapped by the obvious masculine origin of Albertine. "Compared to your books, everything seems boring. The last three are profoundly entertaining," Cocteau had written to Proust, not seeming to be aware of the reservations that his compliments concealed.[119] Did he ever read the *Recherche* in its entirety? Like all his literary judgments, the ones he gave after Proust's consecration—generally critical, sometimes unfair if not absurd—would lead us to guess at a reading that was both attentive and undermined by the shadow of the actual character that "le petit Marcel" was—or at least what Cocteau knew of him.

But the destiny of Proust the writer was just beginning. "He had already entered so far ahead into posterity during his lifetime" that his status wasn't really changed, Maurice Sachs noted.[120] "Leaving out three-quarters of Proust's oeuvre, one could still make an exquisite little book," Paul Souday could say in 1925.[121] A decade later, neither Proust's snobbism nor his style were the subject of criticism; fifty years later, Cocteau would remain one of the last readers to have reservations about his work, and to reproach him for hiding his homosexuality in it.

GENEALOGY OF A TRAGEDY

The sweetness of admiring ourselves, agreeing with ourselves,
answering ourselves exactly—we ask for the means, the motives—from
Others! We beg them to grant us the pleasure of loving ourselves.
—*Paul Valéry*, Mauvaises pensées et autres

GREECE AGAINST BRETON

A year earlier, in 1921, Cocteau had the idea of recounting, in *La noce massa-crée*, the two visits he had made during the war to Maurice Barrès. Since the postwar public now looked upon Barrès with a critical eye, Cocteau's story teased the egocentrism of the former anarchist who had gone over to nationalism. It waxed ironic about his supposed impatience to see the war end, so he could rediscover the Acropolis and a Greece already described, with "crystal blinders," in *Le voyage de Sparte*. But Cocteau was not in the least insulting, unlike the prosecutors for the trial the Breton group launched a month later, on May 13, 1921, against that same Barrès. Cocteau, paradoxically, had only a distant admiration for Barrès, unlike Aragon, who took on the role of defense attorney in the trial. Breton himself, who demanded the "death" of Barrès as the herald of the "cult of the self," had still liked him enough to have asked him, as late as 1919, for a preface to *Lettres de guerre* by Jacques Vaché (who if he had had a say, would probably not have appreciated this sponsorship, but he had committed suicide earlier that year).[1] This old allegiance, improved through shared experiences with Dada, had not calmed these feelings. On the contrary, the more that Cocteau distanced himself from Dada, the more Breton reproached him for his old links with Anna de Noailles (Barrès's idol), as if by doing so Breton were clearing his own name of past connections.

Having also broken up with Tzara, Breton summoned in March 1922 an "international conference for determining the directives and defense of the modern spirit." He undertook, subtly at first, to rally the Dadaists to his cause, then granted himself the power to decide on each person's right to speak and the amount of time granted them, and even, in case Tzara wanted to sabotage the conference, to ask for police intervention. Finally, in a communiqué published by *Comoedia*, a cultural journal with a wide readership, he denounced the actions of "a character known to promote a 'movement' come from Zurich" and the "calculations of an impostor greedy for praise." These were arguments worthy of that nationalist Right in which Barrès had become a leading member, and which testified to the hostility that Breton felt now for the Romanian he had welcomed like the Messiah two years earlier.

A band of artists, including Cocteau, Man Ray, and Éluard, had immediately gathered at the Closerie des Lilas to denounce the chauvinism of these attacks. Satie had fun parodying the prosecutor-like tone of Breton, whose journal had just accused him of exhibiting the portrait of Cocteau on his shirts: "An 'international' conference that reproaches someone for being foreign has no reason to exist," Tzara noted, with an unusual amount of common sense. Despite the unexpected support of Picabia, Breton felt isolated: he had to lower his flag and acknowledge having defamed his former idol. "Everyone is the director of the Dadaist movement," said the *Bulletin Dada*: obviously, Breton did not want to be everyone.

For his part, Cocteau, after having rediscovered Ronsard, had taken refuge in a Greece reinvented through Sophocles—an author who had been Cocteau's standard during his Noailles phase. Cocteau's adaptation of *Antigone* was already in rehearsal at the Théâtre de l'Atelier, which had just been revived by Charles Dullin, one of the directors who would revolutionize dramatic art as the head of the four theater companies known as Le Cartel.[2] But here again Cocteau had to confront the volcanic character of a man who was irritated by Cocteau's constant interventions, for Cocteau wanted to play all the roles and even replace the electricians, machinists, and set designers. Dullin, known for his Homeric rages, would rant about Cocteau, half-annoyed and half-admiring. The rehearsals were tense.[3] Cocteau's courteousness helped to smooth over the clashes between "external" collaborators: Picasso for the set and masks, Arthur Honegger for the additional music, Coco Chanel for the costumes in thick, coarse Scottish wool. But the gloomy presence, in the role of the soothsayer Tiresias, of Antonin Artaud, who was a bashful lover with the beautiful Génica Athanasiou, an Antigone with a shaved head and burning, kohl-lined eyes, added to the strain.[4]

The premiere, given on December 20, 1922, was violent. For having severely shortened Sophocles's play, Cocteau met with the protests of the traditionalist dancers of Raymond Duncan, Isadora's brother: wearing Grecian sandals, these apostles of a strict return to Greece hissed into tiny megaphones hidden under their peplums to protest this play of "savages." The critic Gérard Genette would write later of a "shrinking," in the sense of the shrunken heads of Jivaro Indians. Still not used to brutal "rereadings" of the classics, the public objected to the jerky diction of the actors, including the hesitant French of the Greek-Romanian Génica Athanasiou. They laughed as if they were at a puppet theater at the actors' faces, painted by Cocteau like Redskins, and at the Spartan short skirt that Haimon wore opposite the blanket that served as Antigone's dress.[5] Cocteau had so streamlined Sophocles' tragedy that his blueprint, which he compared to those photographs taken from an airplane that seem to reinvent the Acropolis, seemed simplistic, if not inhuman, to some. The same was true for the deliberately monotonous voice that commented on the action, playing the role of the ancient chorus: it was Cocteau's, through a hole made in the backdrop from which he observed, as if in a mirror, Antigone's inability to live. To those who accused him of treason, he replied: "You respect, I love," like Stravinsky had during *Pulcinella*. To others, shocked at seeing the neoclassical aesthetic that Cocteau had advocated short-circuited, if not electrocuted, he declared, with humor, "Sophocles will only be understood in thirty years."[6] Once back at home, Cocteau wrote another comeback: "You accuse me of causing laughter with *Antigone*, and I accuse you of laughing."[7] The controversy would continue until the hundredth performance, which was also the last. Gide would complain about the production: "Suffered intolerably from the ultramodern sauce with which this admirable play has been accompanied"—continuing, for the benefit of the adaptor: "Patina is the reward of masterpieces."[8] "Patina [glaze] is the make-up of bad paintings," retorted Cocteau.

The spectacle was just beginning to find its rhythm when, on the third night, a voice interrupted Dullin-Creon to shout: "It is wrong!" Cocteau retorted through the opening in the background canvas: "Get out, Monsieur Breton," before some young admirers, including Maurice Sachs, threw out the rabble-rouser and his troops. The critics followed. Ezra Pound was one of the most enthusiastic in the *Dial*, Radiguet praised in *Les feuilles libres* an adaptation "deplored only by those who like only the dust of an ancient work," and money flowed in.[9] Furious at seeing the young disciple that Artaud was place his talent in the service of the enemy, Breton forbade Artaud all acting activity—the very inventor of the Theater of Cruelty!—without the slightest success. After brilliantly participating in Dreyer's *Joan of Arc* and Abel Gance's *Napoleon*, Artaud would break, in 1926, with these "toilet paper revolutionaries [*ces revolutionnaires en papier de fiente*]." He began a long solitary journey toward madness, accompanied by the memory of that fatal Greek woman Génica Athansiou-Antigone, whom he still praised ten years later as a moan borne by a wave from the Mediterranean, "a day flooded in sun."[10]

Having broken with Tzara in order to employ his own methods, Breton started a salvo of criticisms against Cocteau, critiques whose ferocity could still today inspire court proceedings. Having decided to stop writing "once and for all," after Duchamp had said farewell to any actual artistic practice, Breton, co-author of *Les champs magnétiques*, dreamed of destroying literature, and so focused his aim at a man who could never do without it. Tzara's ukases were not only taken up again, but enlarged.[11] To the novel, journalism, and the decorative arts, already banned by his interpretation of the modern movement, Breton added theater and opera. Of course Breton hated the police, like a good policeman's son, but he was impatient to regulate artistic traffic. "The only talent of that sterile mind is knowing how to prick his friends' weak points to paralyze their creative force," Cocteau confided to Max Jacob.[12]

Cocteau, more an observer than a combatant, more cat than dog—there are no police cats, he would note one day—couldn't resign himself to outright ruptures; instead he'd speak of "muddles" that could eventually be "sorted out," even if it meant confirming Breton's prejudices about Cocteau's basic desire to compromise. It was a man whom Breton, the editor of *Littérature*, wanted to confront, but he would never find anything but a creator anxious to be loved. Cocteau's courageous companion in arms, Radiguet, was being similarly targeted by that same hatred, as confirmed by the young writer Joseph Delteil, one of Breton's protégés, summarizing what he knew about Bébé before their meeting in 1923: "He was Cocteau's fairy . . . headquarters had assigned him to me as my Enemy No. 1, something like a hereditary enemy."[13] This was because Cocteau represented, in the eyes of the Breton group, the artist whom they all feared becoming—sensitive, well-off but fragile, and dependent. He was the bourgeois who had been born with everything—well-connected relatives, money, and multiple talents—and whom Breton denounced all the more since he had himself just married an heiress, Simone Kahn, who was rich and generous enough to allow him to envisage the effective end of all artistic practice. The contributors to *Littérature* had to heal "from that wound Cocteau's oeuvre represents."[14]

Though confined solely to the artistic field, the battle was already taking its vocabulary from ideology: "It would not be bad for us to restore the laws of the Terror for the mind," Breton declared at the end of 1922. The destructive project was fortified by charges, accusations, and other judgments of Dada matinees, which demonstrated a "firm desire to appoint ourselves, above all, as a revolutionary tribunal," in the words of Aragon, who went on, "At the goal of our projects, there was the sun of the guillotine, and we were determined, if necessary, to do without legality."[15] Cocteau may have had a foretaste of this "delightful" auto-da-fé in early 1923: learning Cocteau would be present at a dinner given in honor of Ezra Pound, Robert Desnos, author of *Pénalités de l'enfer*, went with the declared intention of killing him—and only those unaware of the rages he was capable of thought the threat was a joke. Since the designated victim had in the end stayed away, Desnos wanted to plant his knife in the back of the American poet, whom a neighbor saved in extremis.[16] It seemed that the implacable bandit morality Breton was calling for had led this young recruit to become a zealous hired killer.

Tensions reached their height in July 1923, during the evening called "Coeur à barbe." This final Parisian Dadaist demonstration was held at the Théâtre Michel, where Cocteau had been invited by Tzara, who was already slowing down at the age of twenty-seven. Not wanting to hear themselves spoken of officially as artists, but still furious at seeing the name of Cocteau listed as one of them, Breton, Soupault, and Éluard came to forbid the reading of their own works. The arrival of Les Six, favorite scapegoats in the Dadaist screeds, curiously aroused no incidents; Breton and his people didn't even deign to interrupt the reading of Cocteau's poems by Marcel Herrand, for fear of annoying Picasso, very visible in the auditorium, whom they wanted to rally to their cause.[17] When the painter was called into question by the youthful Pierre de Massot (a friend of Picabia's and of Cocteau's), Desnos and Péret even climbed onto the stage to seize the young man and hold him firmly while Breton broke his left arm with a blow from his cane—a weapon that Royalist supporters also appreciated.

The crowd was threatening to take things into their own hands with Breton when the police arrived to expel the attackers. Man Ray's film *Retour à la raison* seemed to occur at the perfect time, but scarcely was the curtain raised over *Le coeur à gaz*, a sketch by Tzara, when Éluard ordered Tzara to explain himself about this forceful intervention—which he had not asked for. The police returned. Éluard leaped over the railing and hit the "crook" Tzara in the face— who would sue him in a *bourgeois* court—then attacked the young and cute Crevel, who was still wavering between the two camps.[18] Meanwhile Breton aimed a monumental slap at Jacques Baron. "Never have I seen such idiotic, narrow-minded hatred on people's faces. Breton's face, Desnos' face were abject . . . That poor little Jacques Baron, just before he had his face smashed in . . ., saying to me: Breton is too intelligent," Cocteau commented, spared for once by the cyclone, which left an auditorium strewn with broken seats, torn poems, and wounded men, including Éluard.[19]

The time when these geniuses of self-promotion—Cocteau, Tzara, Breton, and Picabia—needed each other was over. There could no longer be any confusion among members of the Dadaist "suicide club," the ex-doctors-in-training, and the hundred-armed "god." By his exaggerated sense of the absurd, the poetic black hole that was Tristan Tzara had succeeded at attracting to himself, with redoubled violence, final supportive troops. Then the whirlwind dragged him into the void. As Jacques Rigaut concluded in *Faits divers*:

> Yesterday in the garden of the Palais-Royal they found the corpse of Dada. Suicide was presumed (since the unfortunate had been threatening since birth to put an end to his days) before André Breton made a full confession.[20]

Even before the discovery of the body, people had predicted that once the springs of his destructive imagination had been exhausted, Tzara would throw himself out of the window, in order to make people talk about him one last time. Afterward, and after a little more time went by, Breton accused him in abstentia of "plagiarism" and disputed his invention of Dada—making surrealism go back to 1919. "Breton is a moron," Cocteau again confided to Max Jacob, in his letter dated August 1.[21] This ideologue, who had ordered him to stop writing and who hit anyone he didn't like, could be nothing but his enemy. The war was on.

THE DEVIL IN THE FLESH

The idyllic collaboration of the summer of 1922 between Cocteau and the young Radiguet did not last. *Le diable au corps* couldn't yet be sent to press because of the absence of Bernard Grasset, who was already rumored to have gone mad, and Radiguet, back in Paris after Proust's death, hadn't let two weeks go by before he had returned to his "bad" habits. "You have to do things," Apollinaire had told Radiguet, when visiting him in 1917: afraid of not fully using his life, he himself was living at breakneck speed and trying his hand at everything, so that he could one day describe it.

Having become Radiguet's only friend to use the familiar "tu" when addressing him, Joseph Kessel took him every night to bars where he, Kessel, drank majestically until dawn—at least when he wasn't fleecing his stunned partners at the poker table for forty-eight hours at a stretch. Kessel, a one-of-a-kind wildman, had only one criterion for friends: they had to be able to endure all excesses and know how to take the greatest risks. His excess fascinated Radiguet: it was not that of a man of letters, but of a Cossack living as if in wartime, capable of inviting to the table a Russian prince who had been changed by the events of 1917 into a night porter, then of flinging glasses off tables to terrorize the bourgeois, and finally of leaving before paying for five bottles of champagne. Totally foreign to Proustian insinuations, straightforward, direct, effective and raw, Kessel liked to touch bottom at the Yar, the most luxurious of the Russian clubs opened at Pigalle after the fall of the czar, where he got drunk with Radiguet while listening to a gypsy orchestra until the early morning—leaving the bill for the paper that employed him—then offering new rounds at the Palermo, a bar kept by a Corsican gangster. This lifestyle was his way of defying death, of leaping through rings of fire on the back of an untamed horse.

Cocteau's "adopted son" Radiguet had already gotten to the point of emptying both a bottle of whiskey and one of gin every day, and spending the night watching wasp-waisted Cherkessians dance to the sound of balalaikas, when an adventuress from Shanghai, Mme de Warkowska—a phantom in a samurai's outfit—initiated him into opium. The child with the soul of an old man who had been able to "taste" homosexuality relished the opportunity. He was always impatient to experience everything, with explosive substances if necessary: he had once even almost died of a massive dose of laudanum.

Cocteau fell physically ill from this turn of events. Radiguet, the prodigy whom he had contributed to setting on his feet, the child who in two months had conceived a wonderful novel, was in the process of destroying himself. Each day Cocteau's authority over him eroded a little more, and soon he had no other recourse but to ask Kessel to come to his room, where flu and then jaundice had pinned him, and tell him what was happening at the Yar, and what Bébé was doing at the Boeuf before going back in the wee hours to his little hotel on the rue de Surène, near the rue d'Anjou. All this was a tragedy for Cocteau, who for months had been preparing for the publication of Radiguet's *Le diable au corps* with as much energy and perhaps more conviction than he had put into launching his own *Le Cap*.

Already in January 1922, Cocteau was giving a reading from *Le diable au corps* at the Hugos' house, in the presence of the Picassos, the Serts, and the Beaumonts. Although the sweet Édith de Beaumont had fallen asleep under the monocled gaze of Radiguet, most of the listeners were enthusiastic and had encouraged Cocteau to suggest the book for the Balzac Prize. The secretary for the award had already informed Bernard Grasset, the anonymous sponsor of the prize, which was supported by the armament dealer Basil Zaharoff. "A masterpiece, a miracle," the publisher had exclaimed after reading the book, in Cocteau's presence, and then offered to pay Radiguet on a monthly basis for two years, at a rate equal to the best salaries offered in the publishing house. "A golden bridge," as his mentor said, but one that also had the disadvantage of making the protégé financially independent. After showering his family with gifts and buying himself a superb pigskin suitcase, Radiguet had officially left to add the finishing touches to his "jewel"—though actually to meet up with Mary Beerbohm—in a hotel in Fontainebleau where Brancusi had joined him. Cocteau judged severely the version of *Le diable au corps* that he had brought back, and Radiguet was once again locked up, this time at the beginning of February 1923 in a hotel in Chantilly, to perfect the ending of his "botched homework." After once again becoming elusive, a few weeks before its publication, Radiguet suddenly reappeared, as if to prove to his Pygmalion that he alone was master of his calendar. Hadn't Radiguet already shown, by recommending Cocteau's *Le discours du grand sommeil* to Grasset, that he, not Cocteau, was the one who could most help the other's career?

Although in this era writers generally seemed to know nothing about the publicity done for them, Radiguet supervised his campaign to make sure that his *Le diable au corps*, whose style he feared might be thought too reasonable after the Dada storm, would reach the widest possible audience. He even demanded from Grasset "odious advertising," so that the book would stand out despite the uproar that would be made about him: "Before," he added, "a book had to be classified, screened, damned by the rare few. Today it has to be done by advertising."[22] It was Radiguet who stated, in the third issue of *Le coq*, with the paradoxical ruling of a Breton: "In advertising, more than anywhere else, I place the future of the sublime, so threatened in modern poetry"—a point of view that Tzara shared, without drawing all its implications. Indeed, Radiguet began to learn all he could about advertising, so he could reach the greatest number of people. Anxious to prove to Radiguet that he was still indispensable, Cocteau engaged all his strength in the battle as well. He and Bernard Grasset sent a letter to all of the critics that exaggerated Radiguet's youth, referring to him as a "seventeen-year-old master," and announcing: "I do not think that such a literary phenomenon has appeared since Rimbaud."[23] The publisher extended its sales to kiosks at train stations and lobbies with a remarkable brazenness of promotion. Thousands of moviegoers, during the Gaumont newsreel before the movie, saw Radiguet, in a tight woolen overcoat, signing "live" the contract of the century that engaged him for ten years. "Grasset wasn't thinking," Cocteau confirmed; "he was madly in love with the book. He was the one with the devil in the flesh."[24]

Sales of *Le diable au corps* exceeded all their expectations, in part due to scandal. Revolted by this apologia for vice, veterans' associations violently denounced a work whose hero sees in the war only four years of vacation suitable for cuckolding a soldier. Armies of wounded veterans demanded that the novel be banned, as if to give back some meaning to the absurd conflict that had propelled them into metal wheelchairs. Roland Dorgelès, the author of the famous *Croix de bois*, confided to Radiguet his annoyance at a story that displayed from first to last page "an absolute lack of heart" (having known the man who had been the model for the heroine's husband on the front), and concluded: "If I am pleasantly surprised that at the age of twenty you were able to write such a book, I'm saddened that at that age you conceived of it."[25] In short, this man in his forties was reproaching Radiguet for lacking youth, while being surprised that a man less than half his age had experienced twice as much.

The novel had a phenomenal launch. Well-received literarily—although the editors of *Littérature* called it the worst book of the year—*Le diable au corps* was, as foreseen by Radiguet, criticized for its crass promotion: Aragon, Mauriac, and Berl called into question Grasset's huckster methods, making fun of the "nice little nine-year-old novelist"; the *Nouvelle revue française* didn't hide its disdain for the shopkeeper-publisher and his literary milieu, or its annoyance with the claque of "pederasts" that followed this precocious author, who was promoted like laundry detergent or laxatives. As the first writer to enjoy filmed publicity, in this case shown in movie theaters, "Bébé Cadum"—a nickname given to Radiguet taken from a very popular soap at the time—had just inaugurated, with calm cynicism, the media era. Cocteau experienced the praise that showered down on the young novelist as a consecration: when Valéry wrote that the book was "of a sufficing, perfect design," or when a critic credited Radiguet with having, by his cold presentation of love and the impassive control of his own precocity, instantly proven a mastery worthy of a Benjamin Constant, Cocteau applauded as if these compliments were addressed to himself, and had made him greater in force and talent.

A whirlwind surrounded Radiguet for some weeks. From girls who worked in bookstores to linotypists at printing shops, everyone wanted to get near him. Valentine Hugo, Picasso, Blanche, and Lipchitz had already done portraits of him, but now Marie Laurencin, whom he didn't like, was transferring his features to canvas, and Man Ray was photographing him. Parisians were unambiguously trying to associate themselves with his nascent fame, while the foreign press came to photograph the prodigy whose image already adorned all the bookstores. Radiguet's name was entering all of the houses, "quickly, like water rising," said Maurice Sachs, but all this clamor seemed natural to Bébé, to the great annoyance of the previous generation, which mistrusted success like the plague. The triumphant one, "never one gesture too many, always calm and slow," as Maurice Martin du Gard said, seemed as indifferent to the scandal as he was to the sales, and only anxious that he had let slip past a few mistakes of syntax that others now pointed out to him.[26] Already he could be found stopping by at *Les nouvelles littéraires* to correct an article with the precision of an old Swiss watchmaker, or thinking about the books to come and the style he would use for them, blending the intelligence of a Racine in the body of a male Lolita. Maurice Martin du Gard watched him observe this uproar "absolutely as if it concerned someone else."[27] Was that someone else Cocteau, who had done so much for him? One might almost think so, so much did Pygmalion's joy contrast with Galatea's composure. This fame he had waited for so long and that he himself would still need years to achieve Cocteau savored as if it were his own, watching the press shower praises on the son he had been pampering for three years. Cocteau's agitation verged on "strident exaltation," said Bernard Faÿ, secretary for the Prix du Nouveau Monde, as he watched *Le diable au corps* battle against a book by Soupault that was supported by Morand and Larbaud; when finally *Le diable au corps* won the prize, with a hefty purse attached, Cocteau was the more excited of the two.

The pair's influence on each other was reversed in Cocteau's mind. He was convinced that his early advice—"Be ordinary, write like everyone else," had in fact been uttered by Radiguet, probably because he had made better use of it than Cocteau. The author of *Le diable au corps* regarded himself neither as a miracle nor as a monster—just a talented young writer, having no imagination except of a stylistic kind. But Cocteau, by a reversal of which he alone was capable, ranked him among his own masters in a lecture he gave at the Collège de France on May 3 that Radiguet saw.[28] Urged on by his need to adore, Cocteau placed his disciple in the starry sky of precocious glories where, for a dozen years, he himself had held court. But this time, he was in love with his idol.

Cocteau's narcissism would never be satisfied: the unreal being that mirrors reflected, with its unattractive face and transparent body, could never be enough. Chosen to remedy this lack, Radiguet was becoming better than a double—instead he was the model for Cocteau as he relearned how to grow, and soon to believe in himself, after the semi-failure of his first transformation. Until then Cocteau had chosen his masters the better to surpass them, according to the definition that Lacan would give of hysterics; this time, he chose Radiguet in order to love himself better, to benefit from his aura and his success, and to curl up in the pantheon he had built for him. "Love is infidelity to oneself," said Mallarmé: Cocteau would not have disagreed. In the future he would introduce himself as Radiguet's student and would make the younger man into his indirect literary progenitor. He had always needed to venerate someone, but his gods, from Anna de Noailles to Picasso and from Stravinsky to Satie, had until then been his elders, whereas the present master wasn't yet twenty. As the brilliant Proust had called Reynaldo Hahn, four years his junior, "my little master" (in English), love was beginning to place Cocteau in a position of inferiority, and was making him describe himself as a craftsman dazzled by the "diamond-cutting machine" that was Radiguet. He always adored best at a distance: erotic remoteness added more to his enthusiasm. Proust, similarly, was never so happy as when he sent Reynaldo Hahn, his "lovable prince" who was reading in the next room, notes wishing him good night and praying that angel flights would rock him to sleep.

Soon the critical process began, aimed at making Radiguet, like Nijinsky before him, into a living myth. Because he preferred the ruses of reason to the resources of madness, and the yoke of style to the instinctual unleashing of the elemental, the author of *Le diable au corps* became the symbol for a disillusioned adaptation to the world. He was the exception who, while very few survive their precocity, made use of it to abolish all forms of romanticism—he was the archetype of the anti-maudit. Rimbaud had wonderfully satisfied "the tragic idea, brief and blinding, that people have of genius." But Radiguet was even more surprising because of his literary calm and the near-platitude of his genius. An immobile adventurer, Radiguet had no need whatsoever to escape to the Harrar, like Rimbaud, since he was "struck with an opposite madness, which is wisdom itself."[29] Tired of the rare and the extraordinary, the gods seemed to be pleased to introduce into the human game a contrary adolescent, impatient to write like the old ones by alternating methodical work and sensory indulgences—a classicist with sensitivity.

THE PROTÉGÉ AND THE SHE-WOLF

If there was one place where Cocteau wanted to be seen, after such a triumph, and one bar to remind people of the role he had played in it, it was Le Boeuf sur le Toit. All Paris was fluttering about this magic lantern that had offered its ephemeral aura, almost a kind of glory; even François Mauriac, who during the war claimed to want to attract attention no more than a cricket constantly chirping in its meadow, had become a regular. Several times already Mauriac had seen, with thwarted envy, the couple of the hour showing off at the bar. Blushing with pleasure at the slightest acknowledgment, Mauriac also admittedly reeled at the smallest cocktail—"He doesn't have enough health to be a pagan," Marthe Bibesco murmured. Mauriac had noted in his *Journal d'un homme de trente ans:* "The other night, at the Boeuf sur le Toit, C. was holding court with, on his right, R. Hieratic Antinous. And the black jazz player approached the august couple for a bit, and poured out his ballad, very close, into their ears."[30] Irritation had only increased over the months. Mauriac, the suitor who had so hated being rejected ten years earlier and then hated the sight of Cocteau's transformation, found Radiguet, a "wonderful upright owl, motionless and blind, on his stool," every time he risked going to the rue Boissy-d'Anglas. Always close to Radiguet was his protector, Cocteau, whom Mauriac saw as an insect with "metal wings" who was crushed by the prospect of being "the misunderstood genius of his time," or of remaining only Radiguet's "supplier of poisons." But Mauriac, who had finally separated from Barrès and who also feared, ever since 1917, the establishment of a world where he would have no place, always came back to the party. Recalling the time of their early friendship, Cocteau would write:

> Naïve, cheerful, sly, adorable Mauriac! He watched me squander myself with a little fear and quite a bit of kindly trust. Facing my artificial lights, he thought he was in the shadow. "Well," he exclaimed, "I'll write novels, and I'll launch them like Poulain chocolate!"[31]

What Cocteau had done for Radiguet again aroused the secret jealousy of the ex-suitor, who although he had saluted *Le diable* in the press, felt angry and frustrated by the "frightfully uncultivated" generation that hung out at the Boeuf. At the ripe age of thirty-five, he could no longer pass as a young author, and the licentiousness reigning at the rue Boissy-d'Anglas made him feel uneasy: sexually, Mauriac had made the opposite wager from Cocteau's—restraint and dissimulation—and had recently gotten married: "I only gave in a little. But that little was too much, already too much." Confronted with the burning temptations of sex and alcohol, Mauriac protected himself. "In my family, colors literally frightened us," he would say.[32] And there was no more colorful place than this harlequin-bar that he went to almost despite himself, in a matte top-hat, white foulard, and silk-lined overcoat, at an advanced hour of the night—it seemed that in order to conquer the demon, he had to defy it. Mauriac, the man from Bordeaux whom Morand would describe as a provincial "whom the success of the Parisian Cocteau kept from sleeping, and whose complexes no honors would appease," had finally made himself known, the previous year, after four novelistic failures, for *Le baiser au lépreux*, but the arrogance of the "authors" of *Le diable au corps* still irritated him.[33]

Despite his own partial complicity, Mauriac was a supporter of punishment who, in *Le mal* in 1924, then in *Ce qui était perdu* in 1930, would go back to that bar of perdition and to "sordid Paris, its *grandes dames*, its pederasts, its Sapphos, that universal whoremongering, that traffic of knicknacks, folding screens and fatherland," and describe, in a "Supplement to Souvenirs," written in 1940, the Boeuf as "a kind of paradise for dogs."[34] Shocked to see the name of Cocteau among the sponsors of the "Grand Transvestite Transmental Artists' Ball" given at the Bullier in February 1923, Mauriac again discovered with horror, a year later, the existence of "glorious and provocative sodomites" when he read Gide's *Corydon*. Such a phrase would never refer to the author of *Thérèse Desqueyroux* — he always stayed in the closet. Mauriac may have also suffered at seeing Bernard Barbey (a Swiss cultural attaché with whom he was secretly in love) having weaknesses for Cocteau.[35] "It was the eroticism of others we hated," he confessed to Jean Paulhan. "Everyone has his own, which he has or has not overcome."[36]

The games at the Boeuf, as well as the indirect success that Cocteau enjoyed from *Le diable au corps*, were not enough to satisfy Cocteau for long. An anxiety tinged with morbidity had long ago convinced him that this world was less in the hands of men than in the invisible but decisive hands of Fate; and Fate had decreed that Radiguet would not belong to him for long. Cocteau was always able to "see," hear, and even foretell; energized by his frustration in love, these gifts continued to expand. An unexpected fit made him roll onto the parquet floor on the rue d'Anjou on September 1, 1923; the next day, the press revealed that a powerful earthquake had just ravaged Tokyo. He happened to point out to Radiguet, on the Barbizon road, a couple of bicycle repairmen, saying, "They look just like the Stevensons," only to discover, in speaking to them, that they were in fact cousins of the author of *Doctor Jekyll and Mr. Hyde*. Cocteau's imagination was never at a loss: he could pick up a stone, sitting in the sun at Piquey, and turn it around in his hand until he lost all notion of time, seeing his body fall apart, his blood spread, and his limbs reshape a little later as an animal, and then he could become that animal, like shamans did. The feeling of unreality that inhabits most of his characters was profoundly his own: irrational, not classical, and anti-Voltairean, Cocteau had the conviction that serious things were happening elsewhere, beyond or beneath appearances — in the wings of reality, where past, present, and future were woven into a unique form of time that had infinite density and was almost stifling because of its potentialities.

Cocteau had learned the art of the séance early on in order to enter into contact with his dead friends. Just after the triumphant publication of *Le diable au corps*, Cocteau organized some séances to commune with spirits at the new home of the Hugos at the rue de Chateaubriand; he wanted to find out what Radiguet and he would become — as if he feared that his love would lose as much as literature was gaining. On April 21, at 11:00 p.m., Radiguet, Auric, and the Hugos took their places around the flowered black occasional table from which Cocteau had read *Le Cap de Bonne-Espérance* four years earlier. They agreed on the code—one knock for A, two for B, and so on. They then placed their hands on the table, with the tip of each person's pinky touching to close the circle, and began questioning the table, which responded by striking the floor with ambiguous messages and then aberrant replies. This threat addressed to Radiguet floated up: "Illness will grow with genius."

Taking Jean Hugo's place, Cocteau "heard" the spirit pronounce Radiguet's place of origin (the Antilles), its own surname (Beauharnais), and then heard it add: "He must love me because he loves nothing." "Are you a spirit that belongs to him?" Cocteau asked. "Yes." "Will you only come tonight?" "Yes." "Do you love Radiguet?" "Yes." "Will he meet you someday?" "No." The spirit added: "Flee," and when Cocteau asked it if that was because they were boring it, or because Radiguet was sitting there, twice it answered yes. The table then began to spin more quickly, and the knocking spirit gave birth to quatrains worthy of *Le coq*, which were aimed again at the Creole Radiguet: "Marthe inique / Fait la nique / Et fornique / Martinique"—then fell silent, at 2:00 a.m., after again suggesting, "He won't get the P," which everyone interpreted as "Radiguet won't get the Prix du Nouveau Monde," which he did in fact receive in May.[37]

Another séance took place the following week, in the presence of the same people, but with the addition of their neighbor, Morand. The table, recalcitrant, demanded the expulsion of those about whom the questions were asked, and finally exclaimed, "Toujours pour coq tôt le jour se lève où meurt l'étoile pour Cocteau se lèvera le jour où l'étoile brillera toujours" (Always for the early rooster—the day dawns where dies the star for Cocteau will dawn the day where the star will always shine.) Radiguet was granted only this cold sentence: "I say again hurry, the years pass, fame does not replace love even in death and I am death." Then the table that had betrayed everything that Cocteau forbade even himself from thinking began to spin at an inhuman pace. The participants became so uneasy that they decided to put an end to these soirées: the table was announcing nothing now but calamities. "In Jersey the table made verses as if by Victor Hugo," noted Jean Hugo, evoking his "grand-papa soleil," whereas "the one on the rue Chateaubriand made verses as if by Jean Cocteau."[38]

The triumph of *Le diable au corps* clearly had increased Radiguet's desire for independence. Wanting to remove all power from his protector, he crossed the Seine to settle into an upscale hotel on the boulevard Raspail and began again to go out, impatient to take advantage of the women who were now offering themselves to him without much coaxing—when alcohol allowed him the wherewithal. Never had anyone seen Radiguet so sure of himself, so irritating in his calmness, so demoralizing by his silences: "He made people nervous. He dominated," André Salmon confirmed.[39] His reputation grew so quickly that writers twice his age came to question him about some book or character; he would take his time, before delivering his reply, to wipe his monocle with a handkerchief, then wedge it into his eye socket. Kessel wrote:

> You could see first in all his features a sort of frown reflex, a kind of obvious germination of thought. Then, . . . the desire to see clearly, to get to the point, covered his face with a tense, almost harsh mask. In order to convince you, he would hammer out the words between his clenched teeth, without looking at you. And then . . . he would raise his head, smile, and you'd see on his entire face nothing but a focused appetite for life.[40]

Cocteau's literary mothering had made a strange, almost inhuman creature appear, which owed to Cocteau some traits of his intelligence, yet felt for him only occasional gratitude.

It was this owl that the fading Tristan Tzara, accompanied by a little sixteen-year-old foreign girl, met near the Closerie des Lilas on Mardi Gras in 1923, on his way to the Bullier ball.[41] "Thin, with a very pretty body, overflowing with a teenager's sulky vitality," the young foreigner so pleased Radiguet—she loved to dance—that as they left the ball he suggested they go for a ride in a boat on the Marne.[42] Her beauty was so strange and so rare, Maurice Sachs said, that she seemed unable to survive beyond adolescence.[43] She had a Siamese cat's blue-green eyes, in which mauve flowers blossomed, according to her mood, Denise Tual remembered—"the most beautiful woman I've ever seen," Buñuel would add in his *Memoirs*. Having arrived a year earlier from Anvers, via Germany, to study the piano, Bronja Perlmutter dreamed of becoming an actress after having taken part in a film by Jaque Catelain, the young lover of Marcel L'Herbier. Capable of being successively ten different characters, by turns "adorable as a kitten or cold, cynical, calculating," alternating shy childlike gestures with the expert looks of a she-wolf, Bronja instead had to be content with posing nude for Kisling and some of the Montparnos, a lonely status that pained her; hence her equivocal nature.[44]

Her appearance caused Cocteau much grief. With her pageboy haircut, and wonderfully dressed by Poiret or his sister Nicole Groult (for whom she sometimes modeled), the young vamp was appealing in all the ways that Cocteau would find most threatening: ambitious and direct, although clever enough not to compromise herself too much—Kiki de Montparnasse called her the Virgin—Bronja had a real curiosity for literature, the talents of a pianist, an ability to speak several languages, and a vivacity of wit that Gide himself was so impressed by that a Bronja would appear in *The Counterfeiters*.

Until then, Cocteau had tolerated Radiguet's affairs, as Cocteau's mother had tolerated his. But those flings didn't call into question the preeminence of his relationship with Radiguet; in fact, the certainty of being the special life-partner of his protégé allowed him to bear these relationships without too much pain. This time, however, it became difficult to mask the obvious: this teenager took the arm of his protégé, "shy and proud as a confidante of Racine's." Radiguet, the son of a French caricaturist, and Perlmutter, the daughter of a Polish rabbi, soon had to deal with Cocteau's overwhelming jealousy—a jealousy like no other, Jacques Guérin would say seventy years later.[45] It began with constant supervision, which forced the two lovers to develop stratagems to meet, and continued with ruses meant to damage their relationship, for instance, by inviting to each of their meetings Tylia, Bronja's sister, who was as blonde as her younger sister was brunette. "In every creator, there is necessarily a man and a woman, and the woman is almost always unbearable," Cocteau explained, in *Le coq et l'arlequin*: in this literary couple, though, it was Radiguet who played the role of the boy—and he had become indispensable to Cocteau's own creative force.

Thwarting all Cocteau's plans, Radiguet soon bedded Tylia as well, who said she also loved women. This "extra" must have reassured Cocteau, at least temporarily. But he suffered from hearing Bébé announce, like a real pasha: "My Chinese girls," referring to these sisters with slightly slanting eyes and mother-of-pearl complexions when they entered the Boeuf. Was Radiguet as in love as the young Dutch girl would later say? Wasn't it rather she who, while feigning remoteness, conceived of a passion for him, as suggested by the story by Djuna Barnes that their love affair inspired?[46] In any case Bronja disturbed Radiguet enough for Cocteau to still sense her presence even after he had managed to distance her from Radiguet. "I shared . . . the melancholy of parents, for whom, by a strange law of perspective, those they watch grow up become more distant," Cocteau was already writing at the age of twenty-seven.[47] Radiguet embracing Bronja in front of their friends was probably the cruelest spectacle he had to endure.

Again Radiguet changed hotels to settle at the Foyot, a very literary hotel on the rue de Tournon, where Bronja joined him.[48] They would both dine there among actors from the Odéon, fortified by fine wines; at times they were joined by Paul and René, Raymond's little brothers. Sometimes the nineteen-year-old novelist and the sixteen-year-old future actress would see an aging senator from the nearby Palais du Luxembourg come over to have his copy of *Le diable au corps* signed: the contrast in age stressed Bronja's adolescence even more, full as she was of self-destructive impatience: "I have no lifeline, I won't live, I'll die at twenty," she would say to Maurice Sachs, showing him her hand.

Only one place really counted for Cocteau: the bar at the Boeuf, where all rumors were born. He could be seen there, silent, in his usual place, leaning against Doucet's piano, with the haughty Radiguet next to him, and stuck in his eye a monocle "so big that when he removed it, it would pull at his lower lid."[49] Radiguet was flanked by a laconic Bronja, toward whom her sister leaned that night to ask in a low voice for something to drink—a desire immediately transmitted to Radiguet, who transmitted it to Cocteau, as if in a submarine. "Of course, we'll all have something to drink!" Cocteau replied, trying to smile, as his long hands came and went in his sleeves.[50] In vain Mme Cocteau had come to her son's rescue, pitying the poor Radiguet for having to put up with a "very boring Dutch girl."[51] Everyone else, however, sympathized with Radiguet—and sometimes even encouraged him. Hadn't he dreamed as a child of growing up to seduce women? Now he was so quickly successful that his plump mouth was sometimes deformed into a satyr's rictus.

All the conditions for tragedy were present, with Cocteau's lover's jealousy mixing with sexual frustration and a vague feeling of literary betrayal. He couldn't bear the woman-child who was stealing Radiguet away from him, and the Dutch girl hated the influential writer who scorned both her sex and her age, so much that she was afraid he'd force her to leave France, denouncing her as an alien. Between the two, Radiguet let himself be loved, while continuing his social life with Cocteau. There was neither trial nor revolver, as there was between Verlaine and Rimbaud. Cocteau did not have the bisexual leanings of Verlaine; Radiguet, unlike the Wizard from Charleville, did not at all think of himself as an exterminating angel. But there were still vindictiveness, spectacular scenes, and much suffering. As Cocteau had already written at the time of *Plain-chant*:

> I suffer a thousand deaths with my too-tender heart
> But an inflexible soul commands this hell
> In vain my heart swears it doesn't want to hear him
> It keeps him standing with its iron rod.[52]

Sometimes Radiguet took advantage of Cocteau's presence, as he had so often done in the past, to let Bronja know that she couldn't replace everything. In this way, Cocteau was able, in April 1923, to bring Radiguet to England— their first trip abroad—for important literary meetings. The Oxford campus dazzled them—"Lots of gazelles, Gothic, and Greek," wrote Radiguet, in a very

Cocteau-like letter mentioning a "paradise without Eve."[53] His mentor was only too happy to have gotten rid of Bronja and other "bitches," whose presence had the temporary effect of making him coarse. Their shared dandyism flourished in this land of privilege and literary snobbism, over which the ghost of Oscar Wilde floated. The two-headed eagle reshaped itself during their stay—after a lunch at the King's Head Hotel, Cocteau discovered, at a shop in Harrow, some walking sticks lodged in a golf bag of which strangely he had dreamed the night before. On the way back, the two writers would carry them while wearing the same woolen gloves as when Man Ray photographed them later.

THE IMPOSTOR'S NOVEL

Le grand écart received a less favorable reception than *Le diable au corps.* Cocteau's first novel, with its nervous narration—"a brutal onrush," said Max Jacob—even found some confirmed opponents. Gide above all, with whom the author had laboriously reconciled—although the reconciliation was not mutual—was annoyed by its "artificial" style, although "the extreme ingenuity of images and the clown-like brusqueness" of the descriptions amused him. Moreover, Gide didn't believe for an instant that Cocteau could have had a relationship with a woman, which wounded Cocteau, who had already had to read this about himself: "If Cocteau let himself go, he'd write vaudevilles."[54] Aragon denounced an "empty intellectual par excellence . . ., the garrulity of a concierge, an absolute absence of human feeling, an unspeakable meanness."[55] That was the tone of the times, especially for that Musketeer determined to make himself unpleasant everywhere.

But the book did find some enthusiastic readers. Charmed by the systoles of this wildly pounding heart, some of the regulars at the Boeuf perceived in the novel's ambiguous atmosphere an echo of their own sexual bohemianism. Moysès would name a new establishment after it; a month after its publication, the Grand Écart, a bar on 7 rue Fromentin in Montmartre, had received more visitors than the novel had readers. Proust's death had had at least one positive effect: finally acknowledging the role of Cocteau as one of the first critics to have praised *Du côté de chez Swann,* Gaston Gallimard offered Cocteau the chance to take part in the tribute that the *Nouvelle revue française* would make to honor Proust. Even though Cocteau would have to wait for the death of Jacques Rivière to publish regularly in the journal, the beautiful text that Cocteau submitted for Proust's tribute, "La voix de Marcel Proust," led to a change of attitudes on the rue Sébastien-Bottin. Rather than portraying him as the heir of De Max and Noailles, as the journal's editors had after publication of Cocteau's *Poésies*—scornfully writing that he may have been "endowed with more wit and talent than most of the people he imitates," but his "prodigious memory" was equaled only by his "ability to forget"—they gave Cocteau his due. After the author's years of fruitless attempts to break into the *Nouvelle revue française* circle, Gallimard finally published Cocteau's *Thomas l'imposteur*, the second novel born during the miraculous summer of 1922.

Cocteau, who knew the rules, submitted his manuscript to Gide as if to a "headmaster."[56] The co-founder of the *Nouvelle revue française* liked it enough this time to suggest a few corrections and to lead Cocteau to think it could be successful—"He unreservedly liked Thomas, because he thought my hero belonged to his myth," Cocteau would say. But the reception of the book, which Cocteau presented as an "old wives' remedy for modernism," brought him again only limited satisfaction.[57] Published just a week after *Le grand écart*, *Thomas* found even fewer reviews and readers. The press was hoping for *the* book about the war; instead it saw a "little" novel about a fictive man, a story composed of brief notes, dry phrases, petals pulled from the battlefields. If Radiguet had assured scandal for himself by pricking to the quick the virile patriotic pride of the survivors, Cocteau had managed to take the view opposite of everyone else's—just five years after the end of the conflict, he made French and German soldiers into "Siamese twins joined by a membrane of mud and despair." The literary Left didn't want novels anymore; the Right accused Cocteau of making the war too light-hearted and, by overusing metaphors, of making it into an absurd, cheerful episode without killers or orphans, and without goals or morals. The novelist was also stigmatized for not giving his characters enough depth and color. Readers reproached Cocteau for deboning the quail too much before serving it, and for not so much narrating a novel as stuffing a story full of aphorisms, like Wilde's *Portrait of Dorian Gray*. His style—biting and fragile as an insect's, gorged with blood and pollen, also irritated people by its fits and starts and by that sort of overuse of images that made them say in the eighteenth century, "Wit is good for everything and enough for nothing" (*L'esprit sert à tout et ne suffit à rien*). "Overly brilliant," was the most widespread verdict. "Brilliant as a tear," Cocteau replied, without convincing anyone. For hadn't Gide decreed that Cocteau was incapable of emotion?

"Critics look at it with detachment," Cocteau wrote to Valentine Hugo, before convincing himself that it was the fate of anything new to remain misunderstood by definition—when his real mistake, more likely, had been to publish two novels at once, and not to have realized he should first create a desire for them.[58] But he suffered from the response to his novel. This Thomas who had imposed his lie on an entire regiment, but then developed disgust for himself, was indeed his Siamese twin; this fake soldier who, just barely grazed by an enemy bullet, thinks he should pretend to be dead, in the hope of saving his life, is his submerged part: under this disbeliever's name, he hid his own credulity. "In him, fiction and reality were one," Cocteau wrote about his anti-hero: He could have said the same thing about himself, at every time in his life. As Proust once wrote to Gide, in January 1914:

> And if the words of a book are not entirely silent, if (as I believe) they are like spectroscopic analysis and inform us about the internal composition of those distant worlds that are other beings, it is not possible that having read my book you do not know me.

Cocteau again felt as if, beyond its simplistic narration, critics were rejecting the unease he caused, and that through this semi-stroboscopic cascade of visions, it was his own sensibility being condemned. Worse, he saw some friends, in the wake of the triumph of *Le diable au corps*, show more literary esteem for Radiguet than for him. Like Gertrude Stein, who would say "he spoke too well ever to write anything lasting."[59] Or some members of the Society, who already doubted he was capable of a powerful reconstitution and who judged his literary bone structure too frail, and his style too marked, for the reader to forget being the consenting hostage to his stylistic strangeness. His short sentences, though, had the gift of sculpting the space of war where his characters evolved, and thus gave this enlarged story a properly novelistic dimension, if not its eternal freshness. So it was with good reason that Cocteau refused to give up. Sensitive only in fits and starts to ordinary people, he knew he was condemned to writing for those strange beings who were already literary, so to speak. But he knew precisely how to restore the humanity of that group: by plunging them into a hostile reality that will drive them into mythomania and lead them to self-destruction. This pattern shapes almost all Cocteau's stories.

Arming himself with courage, Cocteau published, in *Les nouvelles littéraires* on October 27, 1923, a text defending his two novels. Six months earlier, too, Cocteau had tried to justify his new course, in his lecture at the Collège de France, by denouncing the race to invention with statements like "That's already been done" and "We must never do that again," and proposing the rehabilitation of simplicity, through a thousand detours, advocating "that profound elegance we call classicism." For the first time someone was openly calling for a return to antiquity, not to the scholarly Greece of symmetrical architecture, but to the bizarre peninsula where Nietzsche had heard the celebration of orgies and the rule of Dionysus and Apollo, and where poetry was a goddess ample enough to let herself be sung by Tristan Tzara as well as Anna de Noailles.

Aware that this improbable pair would irritate people, Cocteau had been led to acknowledge implicitly the hypersensitivity of his own work, to the times it traverses, and to describe himself as walking on a high wire, in front of a public awaiting his fall—the method is "not good for fame," he added, with a premonitory lucidity. Commenting on his new about-face as if he were observing himself from a twin trapeze, Cocteau had again aggravated his case by comparing "poetry to a card trick performed by the soul." At the same time, he prayed to be spared from the fate of that acrobat at the Médrano who, after working for four years on a dangerous jump that made him appear out of a large box, had remained stuck inside it. This was a little like what had happened to Cocteau, when he had emerged from his first transformation.

This time he had to acknowledge his feelings of confusion. Life seemed to permit him only to suffer, and while his contemporaries liked his personality well enough, they did not understand his books. He would not be the Apollinaire of the 1920s: his personality interfered with a body of work that demanded, in order to achieve its full poetic mastery, having to give no explanations except to its readers. Hadn't Apollinaire the Enchanter himself needed to die before he was truly loved? François Mauriac wrote at the time:

> Spent an evening at the Boeuf, at the table of the gods, at Jean's right and facing that sphinx Radiguet. What a frightful professional deformation poor Jean has undergone—speaking of the readers that *Thomas* and *Le grand écart* will have in a century. You feel you have to agree with him, not contradict him, flatter his mania . . . He winces at the merest mention of Montherlant . . . Wretchedness of a man without God.[60]

Cocteau, in his intense need for love, was already thinking about the other life that death would assure him: finally admired because idealized, everyone would pay homage to this second Cocteau on his bier. "One must be a living man and a posthumous artist," he said in *Le coq et l'arlequin:* he would never be convinced otherwise.

SUMMER OF THE STORM OF THE GODS

Cocteau managed to take Radiguet "on vacation" to Piquey, in the Arcachon basin, but the summer he spent there, from July to October 1923, increased his confusion even more. Cut off from the world in that little hotel, which was accessible only by taking a little *pinasse* from Arcachon, where they had already stayed twice, Cocteau was in the doldrums. "Auric, Radiguet, Gouy, share my solitude," he confided to Picasso, in a confession revealing the distance that had set in between Cocteau and Radiguet, who was busy trimming *Le bal du comte d'Orgel*, his second novel.[61] The immense pine grove overwhelmed the lover with dizzying melancholy when, at nightfall, nothing but waves could be heard pounding on this desolate moor. That was the time to light candles in the bedrooms and illumine the ground floor with an acetylene lamp, before sitting down to the long table covered in oilcloth, as Auric improvised an ephemeral little opera on the piano that a fat sailor had brought over. Another night of anguish and insomnia, then an awakening to the rooster's crow; Radiguet would dictate his novel to the mediocre typist Auric, in a clacking that the roaring surf mingled with the song of cicadas.

As always, inaction made Cocteau feel guilty, and finally awakened his fear of having lost all inspiration. Immediately he outlined a pamphlet on Picasso, but his anxiety increased so much that he felt almost relieved when a bout of rheumatism inflicted *real* pain on him. His beloved was still near him, cold and distant, and Mme Cocteau, the only person able to console him, was pacing through the large, dark rooms on the rue d'Anjou, even more solitary than he was. At least Radiguet came without Bronja, and he was working constantly, sometimes at the same table as Cocteau. Who could suspect, seeing them wearing the same English sailor's jacket, that the elder's heart, pierced with an arrow, was bleeding day and night?

The arrival of their dear friends "les Zugo" (the Hugos) changed nothing, and that of Bolette Natanson only made things worse. Small and tousled, the daughter of the editor of *La revue blanche* tried to express the love she secretly had for Cocteau, and Mme Cocteau was covertly encouraging the relationship.[62] But Bolette loved to serve, if not sacrifice herself, with a "Jewish humility" that disturbed Cocteau.[63] Already unimpressed by her looks—he thought she looked like a Sarah Bernhardt shrunken by the Jivaro Indians—he confessed to his mother how unwelcome, and even truly embarrassing, the attentions were of this fragile young woman, who had tried several times to end her life by eating lightbulbs.[64]

The arrival of François Gouy and Russell Greeley, two charming alcoholics, tempted Radiguet to drink again and took him away from his work. With anguish Cocteau watched him buy bottles in secret then circulate among the seven wood-paneled rooms in the hotel, all of which were occupied by the group, here gathering confidences from Bolette, there playing dominoes with the Hugos, never walking straight. In Paris near the end of June, Bébé had fled from an overly alcoholized dinner and had been found at one in the morning, asleep, on the grass in the Parc Montsouris; this time, some fisherman have saved him from drowning (he was not very athletic), which increased even more the unease surrounding the stay. It was hard to forget that just a month earlier, during a party on a Parisian *péniche*, Cocteau had amused himself by donning the captain's outfit and announcing in a lugubrious voice, lantern in hand: "We're sinking."

On August 18, a barber from Arcachon nicked Radiguet's right ear with a razor. This time Cocteau was certain that a fatality was weighing on the group. Passing the baker's carriage drawn by black horses galloping on the shore on its way to deliver his bread to the neighboring villages—Arès, Mestras, Andernos—Cocteau knew he had returned to Sophocles' Greece, and that the group was at the mercy of the slightest whim from Olympus: the tragedy he was experiencing was indeed worthy of Antigone's or Electra's. "We should go to Mass," Radiguet said one Sunday as he saw the *pinasse* leave taking a family to church in the Villa Algérienne. It was not a joke, in the mouth of "Monsieur Bébé," but a very Radiguet-like response to the conformism of the anti-conformists, or what Cocteau called, in *Le Potomak*, the "custodians of old anarchies." In keeping with this impulse, Auric, a real Christian who had been rewarded with the friendship of Léon Bloy, had Radiguet read books by Jacques Maritain, a young philosopher faithful to the rule of Saint Thomas Aquinas, before going off to offer his large body to the sun.

On August 3, Radiguet read on the inn's balcony *Le bal du comte d'Orgel* to a Valentine dressed in a mauve silk dress and black slippers. Hidden in his room, more out of curiosity than jealousy, Cocteau hadn't lost a crumb of the reading. "Valentine . . . thought she was the heroine, coughed, tittered, hid her face, etc.," he wrote to his mother.[65] Valentine, sure of being at the center of all masculine attention, thought Bébé was secretly in love with her, ever since he had sent her an obscene poem, "Les fiancés de treize ans."

Once again Cocteau helped Radiguet rewrite the opening to his novel—making it more lively, less explanatory—then convinced him to go over the entire manuscript before his departure for the army, which was planned for the end of the year. Reduced to half what it had been in the fall of 1922, *Le bal du comte d'Orgel* now seemed finished. Seized with a sudden need for order, the young novelist began to organize his poems and asked his brother René to do the same with the manuscripts he had left in Saint-Maur.[66] Cocteau read *Armance* by Stendhal, which he thought a masterpiece, and La Fontaine's *Fables*, but also the neoclassical Jean Moréas, whose long poem *Les stances* had the misfortune of pleasing him: Radiguet was so furious that he tore the volume away from Cocteau and threw it into the sea, as Satie might have done—and with an unforgettable assassin's look. You couldn't annoy Bébé, literarily: the now dominant student could, with a single "revolver" glance, slay the expectant lover. Indeed, Cocteau, already intimidated by the verdicts of a boy to whom he submitted all his texts, was not far from believing in the infallibility of the cruel Radiguet—who liked, to the great displeasure of Valentine, to torture razor clams, those long shellfish taken from the neighboring marshes. This, though, was the same "kid" that Cocteau found one night in tears, despairing that he could no longer receive a disinterested letter from his family, ever since his father started depending on him financially.[67] A hard heart, Cocteau would say, but not a dry heart, one that hated to be softened by chance since it saved itself for real tragedies.

The signal for departure was given in mid-September. The beauty of Bordeaux, to which they accompanied the Hugos, filled Cocteau with wonder after two months spent in the pines, though the scenery did not dissipate his anxieties. "The sky was heavy and grey; a sadness floated through the streets and wrenched the heart," Jean Hugo wrote.[68] Back in Paris, Cocteau was reunited with his mother, and Radiguet resumed his affair with Bronja, who had settled at the Hôtel Foyot. Bronja was profoundly vexed at having to compete again with the one she saw, from the height of her seventeen years, as just an old homosexual, and at seeing Radiguet resume his drunken escapades. Cocteau's tireless remonstrances—"Don't catch cold, go quickly back to your hotel"— would make Radiguet bridle even more against this infantilizing grip.[69] Already ferocious at anyone who prevented him from being what he wanted to become, the boy relished telling off his mentor, who was now less useful literarily. "Certainly not affectionate," Jean Hugo said about their relationship at this time. Determined not to end in the eyes of the world as "a forty-year-old man called Mme Jean Cocteau," Radiguet was seen more than ever on the arm of Bronja. "Cocteau, obviously, too obviously, suffered greatly from it," Auric said—without anyone being really surprised.[70] Described by some as dead-drunk half the time, violent as a peacock, "shot through with vanity" (Jacques Guérin), and capable of "killing absolutely all people present with his eyes" (Aragon), Radiguet had long been perceived as a troubling character.[71]

Cocteau endured, concerned only with helping Radiguet's genius blossom. He would do everything he could so that the chrysalis could destroy its silk cocoon and set its books free . . . and not care about anything else. If Radiguet was harsh with Cocteau, it was only because that's the way he was with the women he made fall in love with him, as well as with anyone who could help his development: "When B. has sucked for a long time on his peppermint stick and made it sharp he'll bury it in my heart. I must be prepared for anything," Cocteau had already written three years earlier, in a letter to Georges Auric.[72] What did Radiguet's "insensitive gaze," his unique disdain, and art of manipulating hearts matter? Cocteau saw only the seal of a prodigy's singularity—that is, his basic literary purity. The diamond race was made to dazzle, not to console; he had said as much during the time of *Parade* and Picasso.

Still, Cocteau made a few attempts at diversion, and chose to be seen with Yvonne George, the chanteuse. But far from being jealous, Radiguet redoubled his sarcastic remarks: "Look at that pretty couple," he said to Auric, emerging from a tense lunch and seeing Cocteau and George intertwined, before announcing to the composer that he was going to marry Bronja. Out of love, or against Cocteau? Bronja Perlmutter probably didn't know herself.[73] And Cocteau finally exploded, during an insane scene in front of Bronja and Radiguet: only Kessel was able to calm him, by placing his friendship at risk.[74]

Radiguet was sure enough of himself to let Cocteau compare him in public to Rimbaud, to Radiguet's advantage. Radiguet dreamed now only of sporting a beard and developing a potbelly—like the pre-1914 authority figures. "When I'm old," he kept repeating, as if he were impatient to be able to say someday, "When I was young." Wearing on every occasion an aggressive businessman's suit, determined to contradict one last time the too-predictable expectations of his sheep-like generation, the former Dadaist now venerated only Maurice Barrès and Paul Bourget—the least fashionable authors. Bronja's future husband now thought only of getting Abel Hermant, an academic writer in his sixties, to read his *Bal* and correct all the mistakes of syntax. After two years spent laughing at Mallarmé, finding Rimbaud "a drag," and piercing the bladder of Jarry's *Ubu*, Radiguet displayed, with cold irony, his desire to enter into the Académie. The leanings of Radiguet's father had led him to attack strikers, Jews, and Boches in the anarchist magazine *Assiette au beurre*; after having intellectually rehabilitated the ancien régime, Radiguet hoped to become, with full knowledge of the facts this time, that young man for old people that Cocteau had been until 1913.[75] With one exception: being old had lost much of its power.

Radiguet's decision to age more quickly—which Cocteau noticed first—had physical manifestations, too. Laughing and childlike during the day, Radigo's face became at night that "of a man who has lived an entire life in seven years."[76] Weakened by alcohol, disillusioned until he seemed fierce, the Bébé of the morning seemed, when he went to bed, to be going to his grave. A close friend had compared him as a fifteen-year-old to an old man; his life was unfolding so quickly now that he seemed victim of a genetically manipulated growth. "Raymond was born at forty," said Cocteau—and Radiguet nodded in silence. Weren't youth and old age the result of a kind of auto-intoxication? At any age, "one has both lived and one is beginning to live," said this premature being.[77] Nothing could better proclaim the life-feeling of Cocteau the Phoenix. Auric thought that, if there was a genius in the couple, it was Radiguet. And he was not the only one imagining him entering the Académie *before* Cocteau. Would Radiguet even vote for his mentor then? Many people doubted that.

THE ANGEL'S LEAP

Cocteau suspected, since the triumph of *Le diable au corps* and the mediocre reception of *Thomas l'imposteur*, that Radiguet's fate was to fulfill himself in an earthly way, while Cocteau's was to preserve something aerial, if not virtual. He still recognized himself in aviators or acrobats, and often had compared the activity of the tightrope walker with the perilous art of poets, the sincerity of the creator with the artifice that expresses it. This time again he let himself be caught up in the transvestite acrobatics performance given by a young American named Vander Clyde, under the name of Barbette, who was passing through Paris in that fall of 1923.[78] "An angel, a FAIRY, a bird," he wrote to Valentine Hugo," dazzled by that brother who flew, indifferent to the lewd noises rising up from earth, and the ill-contained fury of "real" acrobats.[79]

Barbette's performance may have seemed executed by a beginner, it's true—aside from the moment when "she" caught herself with one foot on her trapeze, emerging from a dangerous leap, to show upside-down her face of a "crazy angel." But the strange equilibrium the American maintained between the two sexes, and the slightly obscene passage where he removed his robe, on a bearskin-covered divan, to mime voluptuousness, seemed to Cocteau unforgettable. "He swung over the audience, over death, over ridicule, over bad taste, over scandal, without falling," Cocteau would say, as if he were speaking about himself, before returning to that performance in a beautiful text he gave to the *Nouvelle revue française*.[80] Ten times he returned to see Vander Clyde's transformation in his dressing room. Supplied with a sandwich and a hard-boiled egg, Cocteau watched the miracle unfold among the theater's reds and golds. He sat down in front of the mirrors bristling with lightbulbs to accompany the metamorphosis in a sacerdotal silence. His old familiar taste for "trompe-l'âme" (trick the soul) and existential bedazzlement found a miraculous reality when, adorned with a blond wig, pots of face cream, and metallic paint, the ambitrapezist tore a pin from his lips to fix his attire with a lazy gesture. Like those "Cambodian dancers who are sewn every night into the gold costume," Barbette then revealed himself in the form of a siren whose swaying walk provoked little shouts from the chorus girls in the wings. Only three performances were needed for Cocteau, who saw himself on the swing as an aerialist between genders, to add Barbette into his winged pantheon, joining Roland Garros and the Aérogyne from the Foire du Trône.

Cocteau talked so much about Barbette that, from Igor Stravinsky to Georges Auric, all of Paris went to watch the delicate butterfly emerge from the chrysalis of the transvestite-trapeze artist, who, after some loops, fell at the end back to his feet, removed his fake hair, and played a tough guy. The Jekyll and Hyde of sex, the ancestor of all the Victor/Victorias who would divide in order the better to get back together, Barbette summed up the desire for metamorphosis that was winning over the capital, at that dawn of the 1920s, and the prestige that homosexuality had suddenly acquired after the war. This other actor of his own life, Barbette, did nothing but exalt, in the eyes of Cocteau and the Mutual Admiration Society, the "supernatural sex of beauty" (Wilde); by his desire to be other, by the distorted avowals of his body as a lie, he suggested that any identity is in the end nothing but a role. Won over by Cocteau's enthusiasm, Man Ray also came to photograph from every angle this false hermaphrodite. On his negatives, we can still see Barbette rolling his vampish tights onto thighs free of all hair, or sticking out his chest in a dodgy street, wearing waistcoat and tails. The very young Maurice Sachs found on Barbette's bedside table, in a room in the Hôtel Daunou, Joyce's *Ulysses*, Cocteau's *Le grand écart*, and Havelock Ellis's *L'onanisme seul et à deux*—an entire life summarized in three titles.[81] Radiguet himself was anxious to come admire the flying transvestite, probably accompanied by Bronja, if we are to believe the commentary that the performance Radiguet attended inspired in Cocteau: "This ravishing creature killed the little women all around. They were extinguished, became ugly. It's because by playing the role of a woman, he summed them all up."[82] If only Radiguet had been able to experience the aphrodisiac powers of this erudite acrobat, Cocteau fumed! The second sex (including of course Bronja) would have lost any reason to exist, and life could have started over as before.

But Radiguet had been suffering from digestive disorders since their return from Piquey, as was Valentine Hugo, who had to be transported urgently to a clinic in Montpellier. Annoyed by the mothering recommendations of his protector, Bébé refused to consult a doctor and persisted, despite his corpse-like pallor, in spending his nights at the Boeuf, where he accumulated debt and insomnia. A furlough had just been granted him at work so he could finish *Le bal du comte d'Orgel*, and he would still find the strength to put on some tails and hide his pallid face under a bowler to attend the funeral of Philippe Daudet, Lucien's nephew, a fifteen-year-old anarchist whom his father Léon and all of the Action Française said had been killed by the police, whereas he had actually killed himself in a taxi. But Bébé was so blue and swollen that a disciple of Breton, present at the Boeuf, whispered later into Aragon's ear: "In six weeks, he'll be dead."[83] It was more than a shameful wish: the angel's leap that Barbette had prefigured would be carried out soon by Radiguet.

Seeing him keep to his room at the Hôtel Foyot, unable even to work on his novel, Cocteau summoned Dr. Capmas, in whom he had absolute confidence, although he had proved incapable of saving Apollinaire. Renowned for injecting distilled seawater into buttocks, the bonesetter diagnosed the flu and could come up with no treatment except asking Bronja to give him cups of herb tea and grog.[84] Helped by the incompetence of this charlatan, and despite the orange juice and fresh meat from Bronja, the disease found a home in the alcoholic liver of the young writer. When Joseph Kessel stopped by to bring Radiguet the first set of proofs for his *Bal du comte d'Orgel*, Bébé was slurring his words and unable to move from his bed. All Radiguet could do was throw Kessel an eager glance, through myopic eyes that were "at once vague and piercing, pale and profound."

Having been asked to change practitioners, Cocteau decided to summon Dr. Dalimier, Coco Chanel's personal physician, who immediately diagnosed typhoid fever—from contaminated oysters at Piquey? Dalimier administered a Fournier serum to Radiguet, then had him brought by ambulance to a clinic in the 16th arrondissement, with the manuscript and proofs for the *Bal* in his bag.[85] Still trying to reassure the sick man, Cocteau told him that two seraphs would look over him during his hospitalization. But these guardian angels—Misia Sert and Coco Chanel—along with Mme Cocteau, who brought a medal she had had blessed at Notre-Dame-des-Victoires and that was meant to work miracles, must not have been worshipping the right God. "Everyone is so kind to me," murmured Radiguet, seeing his own mother settle down near him on a little metal cot.[86]

When Bronja Perlmutter arrived, the door to her young lover was barred by Cocteau. The young woman withdrew. "I'm afraid," Radiguet stammered on December 9, kissing the medal from Notre-Dame-des-Victoires, that "in three days I'll be shot by the soldiers of God." Cocteau protested by claiming that the doctors had offered reassuring prognoses, but his tears betrayed him. "Your information is not as good as mine," retorted Bébé, whom typhoid was causing to hallucinate. "The order is given. I heard the order." The phrase froze Cocteau, who had heard at the séance table at the Hugos: "I still say hurry the years pass fame does not replace love in death and I am death." Radiguet still found the strength to babble, "There is a color walking abroad and people hiding in that color." When Cocteau asked if he could intervene, Radiguet replied discouragingly, "You cannot chase them away because you can't see the color," and then sank into torpor.[87]

Cocteau's last visits frightened him. Radiguet looked so little like himself, with his strained face, that he wanted to say to him, "What have I done to you?"

as if on the eve of a final quarrel.[88] But Radiguet would not open his eyes again except to look with surprise at his own hands, or stammer the names of his visitors—his parents, Chanel, or Misia: "The heavy angel who lies on the stomach of those who are about to die" was already weighing on his whole body; the haughty detachment he used to display at all times was followed by a mute form of terror.[89] Never had he so resembled the old man he had dreamed of becoming. The nurse on duty even had to leave the room: the spectacle of his sufferings was too terrifying.

Returning to the clinic with his mother on December 11, Cocteau was summoned to the "parlor": Mme Radiguet had just been contaminated by typhoid as well, and then confined to a neighboring room, so visits were now forbidden. Seeing the grave form and black robe of Abbé Mugnier, Cocteau burst into tears. Respect for orders, as well as fear of contagion, prevented Cocteau from being present at the last hours of the one who had been at once his son, his master, and in some way his lover—but that was the case too for all their friends. Radiguet died alone, from a heart attack, around five in the morning, at dawn on December 12, 1923. "I've never seen a face as desperate, as disappointed, as terrible," a female friend of the Hugos would say, discovering the expression of horror that disfigured the young novelist.[90] Cocteau fainted when he heard the news. He felt unable to go see the body with its waxlike complexion, which had been placed on a simple board among flowers. At Cocteau's mother's request, a priest came to give absolution to the dead man— Misia, returning that night, found his face peaceful—even though she was far from being a believer. "He didn't suffer. He didn't watch himself die," Cocteau wanted to believe, according to Radiguet's father.

Misia Sert took charge of the funeral, with Chanel settling the medical expenses. The Église Saint-Honoré-d'Eylau was nothing but a cloud of white, from the drapes to the flowers, including of course the albs; only a few red bouquets formed bloody spots on the catafalque also draped in white—the color reserved for stillborn babies and for minors. At the end of the service, Radiguet's mistresses, from Mary Beerbohm to Bronja, to whom Coco Chanel and Misia Sert offered a little black dress; as well as his friends and relations, from Picasso to Brancusi, and from Tristan Tzara to Paul Morand; and even his publisher and André Salmon, who had discovered him—got up to greet the family, including four of Raymond's brothers and sisters. Tears flowed in "the most tragic spectacle I've ever witnessed," Nina Hamnet would say.[91] Nothing was more poignant or incredible, Joseph Kessel confirmed. After just twenty years, four months, and twenty days of existence, that literary meteor had created nine hundred pages of novels, poems, short plays, pantomimes, and critical essays that his niece Chloé would gather together in full, seventy years later—a body of work that would make any seasoned writer envious.

Preceded by Vance Lowry and the black band from the Boeuf, the crowd wound through the streets of Paris in the December rain, with the hearse overflowing with white flowers, until the white parade horses disappeared in the fog. Radiguet's father was only half-exaggerating when he spoke of an apotheosis: all of artistic Paris followed the young man's body. Some accompanied him to Père-Lachaise cemetery, where they had already buried Proust a year earlier and where the young writer still lies, regular gifts of flowers adorning his headstone. Radiguet had been able to live without ever losing himself, to love while taking care to note everything down, and to read and read some more while keeping himself safe from mimicry, pillaging instead the hearts of his mistresses and the brain of his "lover." His early demise seemed to be an act of fate, as if it threw to the ground this prodigy who seemed to know more than anyone else about life, and then rushed to withdraw him from circulation.

Cocteau's absence was frowned upon—especially by those who usually accused him of showing himself everywhere. Too wounded to endure the ceremony, he kept to his bed, "amputated without chloroform," he would say, as if they had torn the dead man from his side. He would cry for three days, until he was empty. In this way he was like the beloved he had shown on a railway platform tying the string of her heart to the wrist of her departing marine, and who became completely unwound when the train pulled away, and ended up dying.[92] That heart, which Cocteau had made his symbol, and with which he signed all his letters, was now nothing but a pocket full of blood.

From the Abbé Mugnier to Russell Greeley, many came to present Cocteau with their condolences. The unknown disciples who crowded into his room, including the very young Nino Frank, found him sometimes in tears, sometimes motionless as a martyr. "He wasn't crying, he was dried up . . . and I can still feel his skeleton-like torso in my arms," wrote Mireille Havet, a young admirer.[93] So many "mourners" surrounded him that Boris Kochno, Diaghilev's new companion, thought he was entering a funeral chapel; Gide would leave without saying a word, as if he had just watched over a corpse; widowed by Nijinsky, Diaghilev himself came to pay homage to the widow of Radiguet.

Radiguet's father came by every day. "He is extraordinarily touching, and looks a lot like Raymond," wrote one of their friends to Valentine. "How horrible to think that now, to make a living for his family, he has to go back to those little cartoons 'to make people laugh.' "[94] Proclaiming to Cocteau his boundless gratitude, the father perpetuated their joint guardianship in death, by giving Cocteau all his son's manuscripts, then asking for Cocteau's photograph, as well as Poulenc's and Auric's: "He spoke to me with so much affection about you all," he wrote to Cocteau, "that for me your photo would be a reminder inseparable from his own."[95]

Then it was the brothers' turn to come, bringing Cocteau's malaise to its height, for every time it was Bébé who was revived as they told stories about times when he slept on the table at the Hugos', or in Juan Gris' studio, or among Brancusi's totems. "There is around this death an emotion, an extraordinary kindness," Cocteau wrote to Max Jacob, when he learned that Russell Greeley and François de Gouy had settled the bill left by Bébé at the Hôtel Foyot, and that Moysès had forgiven his tab at the Boeuf. Telephone calls and condolence letters poured into the rue d'Anjou, and Cocteau began again to talk at a dizzying rate: Maurice Martin du Gard came to talk to him about the prodigy, who was so tender and pitiful under his cruel and selfish airs, so worthy of every characteristic of the angels he himself described. A friend affirmed, like the remarkable literary critic Albert Thibaudet did later on, that this death killed in the bud "twenty masterpieces and the career of one of the greatest writers of the twentieth century."[96] What would this author "who would not age, of a book that will not be dated" otherwise have given us?[97] A new Stendhal—or another Morand? Didn't the moralist and the novelist balance each other out in him in a miraculous way? In any case, this enigma who observed his entourage with the skepticism of the scholar studying his fishbowl could certainly have written dozens more books.[98]

Christmas was approaching; everyone went to visit their families, leaving Cocteau alone and soon desperate. The Mutual Admiration Society was already on its decline; the death of Radiguet, their collective son, scattered at last this improvised tribe. "For Mama, I'm trying not to die, that's all," Cocteau wrote to Valentine Hugo.[99] Half-decapitated, the two-headed eagle was suffocating. Nightmares assailed him during the weeks that followed: he would escape from the clogged entranceways of dreams only to plunge back into sleep and engender new monsters. By killing Radiguet, fate had in one blow deprived Cocteau of that poor, unreciprocated love that had given meaning to everything and kept him busy the way a child keeps busy. Sometimes he saw again the large hall where the Beaumonts gave their ball and where Radiguet and Proust had gone, on New Year's 1922, to glean their royal jelly. The mirrors that every year reflected the slightly older faces of the disguised participants seemed to have drunk up the substance of the two writers; by stepping through these frozen lakes, Radiguet had gone beyond time to enter that hinterland where already were wandering Henri Bouvelet, Jean Le Roy, and Roland Garros—not to mention Raymond Laurent and Georges Cocteau, who had been taken by suicide.

One night, Cocteau dreamed that he and Radiguet were walking with a light step around the Place de la Bourse. "I'm doing very well," Radiguet whispered to him before turning a corner, where his face became transparent then vanished completely, as his jacket disintegrated into the night until it looked charred. A few hours later, Radiguet's father rang at the rue d'Anjou and told Cocteau that when he had opened the suitcase containing his son's things, he had discovered, among his intact clothing, a jacket that was shriveled like an old rag. But Radiguet had worn this coat only eight times. Was it a sign? It was through dreams that the dead, in ancient times, communicated with the living.

Thinking back, Cocteau was disturbed by other possible signs. At the end of their final stay at Piquey, Cocteau had been happy to see Radiguet organizing his manuscripts and affairs, with a meticulousness that had made Cocteau think of plans for a grand journey.[100] On this day, however, rereading the final pages of *Le diable au corps*, he was seized with doubt:

> A disorganized man who is about to die and doesn't realize it suddenly puts everything around him in order . . . He gets up early, goes to bed early. He gives up his vices . . . Thus his sudden death seems all the more unfair. *He was going to live happily.*[101]

Hadn't Radiguet also written, with his strange faculty for anticipation: "Happiness, I recognized you only from the sound you made as you left"? Hadn't he appeared at the Beaumonts' Louis XIV ball just six months earlier, disguised as a sick man spotted with measles? And what about when he had offered a scarf to Bernard Grasset a mere three months before dying, telling him, "Keep it with thanks, and also in memory of me"? Was it really by chance that he had also noted, a year and a half earlier: "It's a cliché, and consequently, a truth, and not at all a negligible one, that in order to write one must have lived . . . Doesn't the past tense logically imply death?"[102]

Cocteau came to believe that Radiguet's third eye had made him see the origin and end of his fate. The gods had willed neither his marriage nor his blossoming as an adult, not even the passionate support of his mentor—just his books, nothing but those. They had ordered him to live as intensely as possible, always keeping on the lookout, and to note down as quickly as possible his observations. Once this task was accomplished, the gods had called him back.

Cocteau's disturbed state was increased when he remembered having himself told Radiguet, in a story titled only with the telephone number of the rue d'Anjou, how Ganymede, the so desirable hero that Jupiter was pursuing, had been taken up to heaven as he was getting married on the Île d'Amour, on the Marne—where Radiguet himself came from.[103] Was it the gods or the devil who had arranged everything? Radiguet couldn't have arisen out of nothing. His incredible precocity could not have a simple human origin—either he had already taken time to observe life during a previous lifetime, or he had been "lent" to earth, in order to write in black on white what the gods above had said. After everything they had produced together, the celestial text had then rewound, like the ribbon called a scroll that emerges from the mouths of angels in Quattrocento paintings—and Bébé had climbed back up into the sky, his mission accomplished.

The troubling, "mad with suffering" letters with which Cocteau showered his friends made them fear for his mental health: "half of his person is in the underworld," noted Lucien Daudet.[104] "I appeal to your reason, don't mix up the diabolical with your suffering, and be careful with your poetic imagination," Max Jacob begged Cocteau.[105] Urged to see a priest, then to read the Gospels, as well as to take Communion, the way one goes to the doctor or takes an aspirin, Cocteau balked: "I have too deep a respect for the Church to use it like a drug or a fetish." He needed something more palpable.

THE WIDOWER ON THE ROOF

Radiguet's critical intelligence and Cocteau's poetic talents had produced one of the most creatively productive couples that ever existed. But nothing remained of it except a few books and the triple wedding ring that Cocteau had designed for them, which thousands of couples, not just masculine ones, still wear today.[106] The bubble had burst. The crystal factory had shattered. Gone was the Arizona-like paradise of Piquey, the African drunkenness of the Boeuf, and even the jealousy of the little mistresses, so all-encompassing in the end. The world was nothing now but a wounding illusion, an enormous prison of air, an atrocious, burning desert of mystics losing faith. A part of him was dead— perhaps the best part: the one who could write two novels in less than a summer and had "extracted" as much from Bébé, and the one who gave substance to *Le diable au corps*, and even more, *Le bal du comte d'Orgel*. Radiguet was a personality to be shaped, a masterpiece to be perfected, with entire days occupied; his death made Cocteau incomplete. Radiguet limped, but now Cocteau no longer knew how to walk, or where to sit: every chair was made of ice and every bed was soaking wet. But for Parisians, Cocteau was just the butt of jokes, the tin puppet who didn't deign to attend the funeral. "*Le bluff sur le moi*, the bluff on the self," gossip columnists were already calling Cocteau, seeing him as a plagiarist or a cheat.[107] Faced with that caricature of an inconsolable person drowning his insensitivity in false tears and real cocktails, they rebaptized

Cocteau "le veuf sur le toit" (the widower on the roof). His inspiration? A bar. His mourning? An operetta. "Jacques . . . knew that in order to live on earth one had to follow the customs and the heart plays no part in it," Cocteau wrote in the last line of *Le grand écart*.

It was not just Cocteau's mourning but also his responsibility that were called into question. Who was the source of the tragedy, if not the man who had overwhelmed an adolescent with relationships, trips, balls, and promises of money and fame—the one who had made him live too quickly and had been unable to take care of him? "He squeezed Radiguet's genius like a lemon, until it was completely expelled," Irène Lagut would say, sixty years later.[108] A murderer, from too much admiration, if not from an editor's zeal . . . and who knows, out of self-interest as a "puppeteer": Hadn't the tables Cocteau made talk at the Hugos' betrayed his secret wishes, by announcing the imminent death of Radiguet? "One doesn't have the heart to play in a world where everyone cheats," the young Emmanuel Faÿ had declared before dying, a few days before Radiguet: Cocteau was not far from thinking the same thing.[109]

Mirrors reflected his face sideways, revealing his starving dog's gaze, his airs of a premature old man. Deprived of his reason to live, with holes in his heart and incapable of looking after himself or holding his pen—yet still compelled by his constant search for legitimacy—Cocteau came to declare publicly that he would never write again. As if Radiguet's death had removed all of Cocteau's interest in literature, by reducing it to a solitary mania. His machine was new, mine was clogged up, he would say: might as well close up shop. For a few weeks, Cocteau lived a life colder than death, worthy of the torture suffered by the naked soul of Jewish mysticism, that bloody essence that wanders endlessly in the night, in search of a warmer body. Would he follow Radiguet into that frozen river leading, ever more quickly, to the kingdom of the dead? Overwhelmed with insomnia, the man was in pieces; all that remained was the orphaned "mother" just strong enough to thank friends for immediately recognizing the genius of his "poor child."[110]

Mme Cocteau thought it would be a good idea to send Marianne Lecomte Singer, his favorite cousin, to her son's bedside. But Singer, who had always thought of Radiguet as an arriviste using her cousin, said she was certain that this death was a lucky thing for Cocteau, which only added to his feeling of being misunderstood. Bronja herself had begun again to go out—she would pose as a naked Eve for New Year's Eve, next to a Marcel Duchamp dressed as Adam, in a remake of the Cranach paintings that Man Ray photographed.[111] As for Cocteau, he remained incapable of leaving his room, or changing his ideas. A trip? He'd never much liked them. Piquey? Without Radiguet, it was death.

His mother began dreaming again of a normal life for him, with a "real" job, family reunions, and vacations in the open air. A life where one worried about one's parents' health, discussed the usefulness of buying a sideboard, and in which one would not ask oneself if Radiguet, by insinuating a semicolon into a transposed portrait of Beaumont, was ruining his preamble. But that was the life for others, not Cocteau.

Finally Max Jacob intervened. Cocteau looked up to the author of *Le cornet à dés*, a former protector of Radiguet and a converted Christian, as an authority figure. Jacob's long letters, themselves overflowing with anguish, managed to convince Cocteau to start working again, or at least not to yield to his death wishes, so contrary to the will of Christ. And Cocteau ended up agreeing to go join Auric and Poulenc at the opera house in Monte Carlo, which was performing two of their compositions, *Les fâcheux* and *Les biches*, and where the Ballets Russes were staying for the winter.

Diaghilev gave Cocteau a warm welcome. Since Massine had been banished for having married a dancer, Cocteau, by sending articles to the *Nouvelle revue française*, helped to relaunch a troupe threatened with becoming institutionalized. The appointed choreographer of Les Ballets Russes had become Bronislava Nijinska, Vaslav's sister, but a new nineteen-year-old recruit from the USSR, Serge Lifar, was already distinguishing himself. While in Monte Carlo, Cocteau found Louis Laloy, a music critic previously linked with Debussy, as well as an amateur orientalist who had contributed to spreading the use of opium by publishing in 1913 *Le livre de la fumée*, a book praising the serenity that skillful use of the pipe had offered to European "barbarians" made numb by speed and machines. It was all the easier for Laloy to convince Cocteau that it would be in his own self-interest to escape from his body because Cocteau had already tasted this tranquilizer, first while in the entourage of De Max, and then during the war.[112] And so Cocteau shut himself away with the amateur Sinologist and the musicians in a room in their hotel, plugging up all the cracks, like conspirators.

Since their first attempt at smoking opium disappointed Cocteau, who thought it too bland, Laloy prepared other pipes for him, more full-bodied, and still others, which set him reeling. His nausea became so great that it gave his sickness a new dimension. "I am in an atrocious state. Worse than in the early days. I felt a kind of drunkenness at that time," Cocteau wrote to Jacob when he was back in Paris, concluding with these words: "I want to die."[113] He needed a lot of will, patience, and courage to get intoxicated. A hundred times he tried to absorb this Chinese sedative, more bitter than bromide; a hundred times he complained about not feeling any benefit from it. Finally after three months, the anguish fell away. His aching body could again take food, drink, and could sleep, after weeks of asthenia. The air he breathed in tended to empty him out, but opium numbed his panicky sense of loss. Having become insensitive to wounds, and foreign to nostalgia, Cocteau was evolving in a neutral space, isolated from time, a fishbowl of smoky air protecting him from the world. The bliss and Asiatic grace promised by Laloy were still to come, but at least he had set one foot outside of hell.

In the afternoon, Cocteau could be seen leaving the rue d'Anjou, looking like a traveling salesman off on his rounds, with the little briefcase holding his smoking necessities. Monopolized by the government, opium was officially forbidden to Europeans in the French Empire, but places for consumption were proliferating in Paris since sailors from steamers out of Saigon, French Indochina, had begun selling it in round boxes. Not in the least suspicious, the smoking room that awaited Cocteau was in the middle of Passy, in an apartment on the rue Raynouard that Marcelle George, Roland Garros's former companion (whom everyone called Marcelle Garros), occupied with the poet Mireille Havet, who had been sharing her life with her since 1920.[114]

The supplier would lift out of a bone box the chando, the paste from which the guests, armed with a scale, would take a ball the size of a pea. They would then cook the ball of paste over a flame while turning it on the tip of a polished silver needle—and finally use a jade ring to reshape the ball into a cone with which they covered their pipe bowl. Placing his headrest on the straw mats, Cocteau would stretch out alongside his tray, pull a thick blanket up to his chest, and lie down on his side to light his pipe at the lamp. The drug would gurgle in the bamboo bowls, giving off a nice smell of grilled cocoa; then the walls began to melt, and the ceilings to undulate. These sessions had the benefit of unknotting Cocteau's nervous system. His blood vessels dilated, his perception became sleepy, and the world abandoned itself to its ghostlike dimension—time itself came to be undone in the already sheltered world of the 16th arrondissement. Cocteau could no longer distinguish between himself and those around him, his arm and Marcelle Garros's, the walls and the pipe his lips sucked at; from the floor to objects, everything he touched became an integral part of himself. Even if his finger were cut off he would have stroked that little slug without suffering; curled up on his cot, the smoker was one with the world.

Gone were the spasms, skin eruptions, abscesses, and insomnia. If cocaine had made Cocteau feel as if he had "someone else's teeth," it was his entire body that was transformed by opium. His slowed breathing set him in tune with the elements so that sometimes he felt like a floating cork, and sometimes like the foam lapping the shores of the Orient, borne by a river of cream, far from enervating Europe. Sounds, shapes, smells reached him in an attenuated form, as if he were outside of life, looking in. Better than general anesthesia, better than the sovereign remedy against anguish that Artaud spoke of, opium offered a wonderful deliverance. Sometimes luminous filaments would penetrate him through every pore, then reemerge by piercing his epidermis and standing straight up like glowing hairs, so that his body became a night swarming with stars; at other times he felt his flesh imperceptibly fade away with the grace of India ink dissolving in water, so that everything around him became gentle, subdued, almost sensuous—and without the slightest importance. The drug didn't just bring an end to the despair caused by Radiguet's death; by detaching him from life, it temporarily made him forget his obligation to shine constantly, to be productive and brilliant, morning to evening, summer and winter.

Rather than using the fancy pipes of society people, Cocteau quickly came to prefer the old bamboo pipes of the Indochinese, with their simple white metal bowl, and instead of the Benares, the "Havana" of the snobs, he preferred a coarse mixture, the opium equivalent of good old caporal tobacco. The aesthetic dimension of the ritual was also of great interest: the choice of the alcohol lamp and the needle, indispensable for heating the paste, became objects of research; so did the scissors to trim the lamp's wick and the spatula to clean the pipe's bowl, once the chando had been reduced to ashes. The set of supplies he acquired was treated with great tenderness, with the ritual given cult-like attention and dignity. Cocteau's usual group was made up of remarkable people, from Georges Auric to the poet-diplomat Saint-John Perse, who often wouldn't exchange three words during the night. The communion was so intense that they were content to smoke in silence until they saw the first rays of light through the Persian blinds, and heard the trills of birds rising up from the garden shared with the house of Balzac: Colette, who didn't like to smoke, would remember this when she described the smoking room in *Le pur et l'impur*. Cocteau's body hadn't moved an inch, and yet he felt as if he had crossed the clouds and lived for years; he had floated over people and things, in a world without age or weight, like the blue god he had dreamed of being fifteen years earlier.

Opium is not a drug, he would often say, it's a form of life, almost a philosophy. Around this time, Roland Garros's "widow" Marcelle began to lavish onto Cocteau the affection he had once inspired in the aviator. She was so devoted, and Cocteau seemed so fragile! More and more this friend-admirer was seen at the rue d'Anjou, still just as nostalgically attached to the aviator, after six years, as Cocteau himself was to Radiguet. Finding her charming and already a good influence—Jean seemed to be getting so much better!—Mme

Cocteau began dreaming of a marriage in which Marcelle Garros also wanted
to believe, and which Cocteau again had to deny, upsetting everyone. Mireille
Havet herself was sighing in secret for the widower Cocteau, whom she had
known in the entourage of Apollinaire (when she was fourteen, Apollinaire had
published her first poems).[115] Aware for a long time that her passion would not
be reciprocated, this now twenty-four-year-old poet was content to follow
Cocteau in everything, to act and dress exactly like him. Indeed, she had so well
incorporated this impossible idol that she ended up resembling him in a
disturbing way. Colette, who knew her well, wrote:

> By imitation she squeezed her slender waist into a navy blue wool sweater,
> her thin cat's neck in a bowtie tight enough to strangle her a little, and on her
> feminine wrist turned over the sleeve of a man's shirt. In a word, she loved.
> Without reciprocation, except for friendship . . . But people assured me that
> [Jean Cocteau] was good and affectionate to the young girl . . . who extracted
> in broad outline and in tiny details the secrets of her superficial resemblance
> in contemplation of her already glorious "twin."[116]

Actually, Cocteau already needed nothing more aside from his daily dose, a
mat on which to lie down, one or two accomplices with whom to smoke, and
that smell about which Picasso said there was nothing more intelligent on
earth. Fernande Olivier, the woman who shared Picasso's life during the
Demoiselles d'Avignon period, would write about their nights smoking the
bamboo pipes:

> We talked, we were happy; everything became beautiful, noble; we loved all
> of humanity, in the skillfully attenuated light of the big oil lamp . . . The
> nights flowed by in a warm, close intimacy, stripped of all suspicious desires.
> We spoke of painting, literature, in a perfect lucidity of mind.[117]

It was the "chaste, sweet poison" of which Apollinaire had also sung; the
wonderful remedy that Baudelaire had praised, before growing tired of it; the
paradise of all the creators eaten away by dissatisfaction. The most devoted of
Cocteau's friends got used to bringing him little doses that the dealer would
drop off at his tailor's, in the neighborhood of the Madeleine. Cocteau's cheeks
hollowed out and his nose narrowed out into an "arrowhead," according to
Morand. He began to suffer from lack of the drug, and soon found he was
freezing in full sunshine. The fish was well and truly hooked—but at least he
was thinking of something else besides Radiguet.

THE ANGEL'S DREAM

The intimate genuineness of each minute, even when it offers a
series of apparent contradictions, traces a straighter, more profound line
than all the theoretical lines to which we are so often enjoined to
sacrifice the best part of ourselves.
—*Jean Cocteau*, Visites à Maurice Barrès

THE FLOWER OF SACHS

Radiguet's death had created many hopes. Alone and fragile, Cocteau had
become a dream goal for the many admirers who yearned to approach him.
Serge Lifar, whose precocious talent and dark beauty had made Cocteau loudly
wager on his future when Cocteau had discovered him dancing in *Les fâcheux*
in Monte Carlo, didn't hesitate to come down through the audience to sit near
Cocteau, until Diaghilev—reprising his role as protector—sequestered him in
the wings. But Lifar in this instance was only worried about his career—as he
confessed in his memoirs, he had never made love to anyone or anything except
a willow tree in Russia, by friction.[1] According to Morand many of these young
admiring men, curly-haired "as cabbages," who roamed the streets in 1925 and
spent their nights perched atop stools at the Boeuf in front of Manhattans, visited
Cocteau after Radiguet died: the author of *Le diable au corps* had become like a
fetish, after the triumph of his novel, and many dreamed of a similar fate. The
most precocious and least ordinary of these literary party animals, Maurice
Sachs, seventeen, had grown up in the shadow of Verdun and then of the liberating turmoil of the Armistice. Whereas he had until then adored only Gide,
already the liberator of three generations, a friend in common had given him the
urgent desire to meet the author of *Antigone* and *Plain-chant*—"There is no one

but Cocteau," repeated Gérard Magistry. Sachs, enthusiastic, had attended each performance of *Antigone* and afterward numbered among the crowd of admirers waiting at night, sometimes perched on lampposts, sometimes sleeping on the steps, for Cocteau's arrival on the rue d'Anjou.

Cocteau's doors were soon opened to this young fan. Sitting in his bed in black silk pajamas, his neck encircled by a tight red foulard, Cocteau, although still sick, showered the teenager with colorful stories about the famous people he had known. His "pale, long, very long hands, like the hands of the kings of Egypt" placed straight on the white sheets, the *veuf sur le toit* dazzled the little receptionist working at the Hôtel Vouillemont, a family-run inn nearby. Like so many others before him, Sachs was treated to a life-size reconstruction of Marcel Proust, with his "padded" voice; of Anna de Noailles, with her silvery timbre; of Barrès, with his peasant's accent; of the furious shouts of Tzara and the whispers of Satie—five geniuses for the price of one.[2] Departing with his arms full of gifts, which immediately became relics, Sachs returned the next day, and the next, both intimidated and impatient to receive his dose of wit. Cocteau knew wonderfully well how to make himself liked by newcomers: he gave them everything he had, but also placed his trust in them; he treated them right away as equals, and then encouraged them to do better. His energy had the power to awaken their numbed minds and sometimes their inhibited hearts; suddenly they felt uplifted in these lives made narrow by a lack of money, love, and confidence. "The enchantment was perfect, complete, spontaneous and delicious," Sachs confessed.[3]

Soon the little receptionist became the first of the courtiers gravitating around the rue d'Anjou. They would go see the master as soon as he got up, around eleven in the morning, to help with his dressing—although Sachs could arrive only when his work allowed. Climbing the steps with a beating heart, he would find Cocteau half engulfed under the towel held in place by a hat, like a photographer under his veil, soaking his face in steam in order to soften his beard, all the while saying charming things.[4] It was a wonder to see him set off these verbal fireworks as the vapor from the boiling water rose from the pot, and as a blind, long hand rose like a claw from the dressing gown, only to be waved by "that man-beetle with a chest made of golden silk."[5] Immediately his charm went to work: "impossible to encounter a quicker intelligence, a more acrobatic mind." As Sachs explained, "This virtuosity had as its springboard a cleverness of wonderful drollery, a great vivacity in puns, an innate sense of imagery, an obvious poetic instinct, an ardent taste for gossip and cruelty to which all the French are susceptible."[6] Once dressed, Cocteau made it his duty to amuse the little receptionist by reading his latest writings to him, between endless telephone calls, or take him to private film showings—with sometimes as many as fifteen admirers in tow. The films that Cocteau liked, as well as the books he recommended, were immediately praised to the skies by Sachs and the others; his judgments were sacred, his verdicts absolute.

Learning to have his hair cut at Milliat's, at the Madeleine, the young snob quickly learned *cocteau*, that language recognizable by its epithets—"prestigious," "astounding," "confusing"—as well as its "monsters," "madmen," "darlings," "angels of purity" or "of heaven"; contradictory attributes that all referred to Radiguet, Sachs soon realized. With the help of his wonderful talent for adaptation, the young man soon felt at home on the rue d'Anjou, even more than in the Hôtel Vouillemont on the nearby rue Boissy-d'Anglas where he worked and slept under the protection of the owners, the Delle Donnes. The elder poet's plans, his choices and dreams, progressively became Sachs's own—no one had a stronger desire for osmosis than he did, something that until then had been Cocteau's specialty. Convinced that he had met the equal of Ronsard and Villon, two of the greatest French poets, the young Sachs swore off Gide to place himself wholly at the service of Cocteau and his genius. "I took a vow of my own to attach myself eternally to him," he said, when discussing this meeting that would change his life:

> He domesticated us while making us, in the meantime, happy to serve him
> . . . We would walk in the street praising his verses, recounting his exploits,
> getting drunk on the greatness we attributed to him and that he conferred on
> us, more brilliant for having been presented to him, until we made it our
> food. Cocteau had formed a following for himself, a court, which served him
> while thinking he served it.[7]

More than love at first sight, it was a bewitchment. Sachs would explain later that physical attraction played no part in it for him, but he would also acknowledge, in the contradictory stream of his avowals, that Cocteau seemed "extremely handsome" to him, with his mobile face and his Oriental languor. Endowed with a very strong sexual appetite, Sachs, the one whom the daughter of the Delle Donnes nicknamed "Biquette" (nanny goat), began, as a way of dazzling his mentor and attaching himself even more, to shower him in turn with gifts and invitations, and to do everything as Cocteau did, except sharing his opium—drinking was enough for him. "His zeal for me is boundless," Cocteau soon gushed, before adding for his mother: "I admire his golden heart."[8]

But the writer remained wholly "taken" with the memory of Radiguet, and still saw his replacement as a betrayal, if not a way of killing him a second time. He felt Sachs's charms. But in part because he was devoted body and soul to opium, he preferred to play the part of father, mother, and tutor—a mixture that had succeeded with Radiguet—without ever seeking that of lover. Sachs knew, from feeling the devastating effects every day in mirrors, the disagreeable impression left by his flabby body, his damp hands, and his "oily" affability.[9] The rejection disappointed him, but didn't surprise him; he instead redoubled his admiration for Cocteau, and his ardent need for fusion. Sad that he didn't arouse his idol, the teenager wanted more than ever to enter into his life, take part in his books, commune in his genius, to be him in mind, since he was unworthy of his love and body.

Abandoned by his mother when she had divorced after some years of marriage, and surrounded by women of remarkable egocentrism and frivolity, Sachs had for a long time been living life as one man too many. From a cultivated, lazy, self-destructive family—a "Jewish House of Atreus," as his biographer Henri Raczymow writes—he had grown up shifting his need to admire others onto Jacques Bizet, a close childhood friend of Proust's who had become his grandmother's second husband. But morphine had changed Jacques Bizet, that son of Proust's muse and the composer of *Carmen*, into a phantom that shot the curios in his apartment before finally aiming at the desperate, vague being staring at himself in the mirror and killing himself.[10] Giving up his studies even before taking the *bac*, the young Maurice had since then accumulated odd jobs, from insurance salesman to night watchman, while frequenting the home of his grandmother Alice, who was part of the literary rear guard that Cocteau had fled in 1913. It was for this *bateau ivre* of a boy that Cocteau, starting in the spring of 1924, became the compass and the goal.

Sachs, however, was not content to be a communicant in the cult that Cocteau had made of Radiguet, whom he himself had glimpsed at the bar at Le Boeuf, isolated in his alcohol-fueled silence, like a "young god in mythology."[11] He instead asked to follow Cocteau in the dances for boys that were taking place openly at the time, like that "Faggots' Ball [*bal des Lopes*]" in Magic City, near the zoos and the Scenic Railway of the Champ-de-Mars, where two or three thousand masked men, wearing cape and opera hat, or in drag as "The Sparrow Kid" or as Madame de Pompadour, could dance in the shadow of the Eiffel Tower during Mardi Gras.[12] At the Bal des Colonnes on the rue de Lappe, a favorite of hoodlums but also of the upper crust, Cocteau introduced the young Sachs to Albert Le Cuziat, the owner of the baths at the Ballon d'Alsace who had served as the model for Proust's Jupien.[13] The teenager spent entire days with him, collecting memories about the hidden vices of the author of *Recherche*.

It didn't take long for Cocteau to discover the shady dealings, lies, and kleptomania of his zealot. Sachs's charm was so engrossing, and his passion for Cocteau so poignant, however, that Cocteau never took offense. Behind his disarming generosity and his verbal agility, Sachs was afflicted with an insatiable self-hatred, and nothing affected Cocteau more than that intimate leprosy with which he himself was so used to living, ever since the failure of *Le Cap*. Seeing how ashamed Sachs was of his job and his morning coat, and softened too by his slightly thievish side, Cocteau encouraged the young Sachs to tell people, in case their friends from the Boeuf surprised him in uniform at the reception desk of the Vouillemont, that he was just returning from a wedding. No one liked lying better than Sachs, and no one had such a visceral *need* to lie. Full of that generous and terrible feeling that Stefan Zweig named "dangerous pity," Cocteau hired this brilliant right-hand man first as an errand boy, then as a secretary in charge of both organizing the shop window that the Stock bookstore had dedicated to Cocteau at the Palais-Royal, and the first exhibition of drawings and manuscripts devoted to Cocteau in February 1925 by a gallery in Brussels—before including Sachs in the casting of his *Roméo et Juliette* at the Théâtre de la Cigale.[14] This promotion set Sachs on fire; he compared Cocteau's impulse to the summons that Christ had given Peter. The receptionist's little room, in the attic of the Hôtel Vouillemont, filled up with portraits of the idol before which he prayed and asked advice, every day . . . that is, when the idol didn't come over himself to smoke opium, far from his mother. Sachs would write in *Le Sabbat*:

> I will always be indebted to Jean Cocteau, for he was the first to make me feel those profound voluptuousnesses of the soul that mix together friendship, religious feeling, devotion to beauty, and veneration of greatness, and which are a kind of love that cannot arise in us except at a certain age, but which at that age is more necessary than bread and water.[15]

Losing all his reserve, abolishing any critical spirit, this child without a family, this collarless lost dog, devoted himself body and soul to this devouring kind of love that only saints or charlatans can arouse—Sachs himself would speak of "slavery." "Caught at every turn, believing in every despair, taking part in every tragedy, trembling at every love," Sachs delightedly underwent the spells on the rue d'Anjou, as well as that theatrical bedroom haunted by Cocteau, from whose ceiling hung the long tresses of a woman "recently sacrificed." If Cocteau told stories, Sachs believed them. If Cocteau cried, he wept. If Cocteau joked, he would laugh until the tears came. "When the curtain had fallen, we would all go dine at the Boeuf sur le Toit," Sachs writes. "Then we'd go to bed with regret, impatient for the next day to bring us our dose of enchantment."[16]

Sachs didn't even need to harass his idol with questions, with that Proustian eagerness that was already making some people worried; Cocteau would even answer the questions he didn't ask. Anticipating all his desires, magically fulfilling his expectations, the living ex-god rediscovered for this seventeen-year-old "naif" the extraordinary powers that fairytales attribute to their heroes: Never had Sachs been transported so far from rude Parisian reality. Seeing his mentor smoking in bathrobes that looked like dervish robes and brilliant silk scarves, the teenager grew convinced that it was his basic orientalism that had led Cocteau to opium, and not the other way around: the volutes of the drug helped that "prince worthy of a Persian miniature" to flee a country that was too cold, rational, and narrow to understand him wholly. Come from the kingdom of Scheherazade and the sultan Shahriyar, Cocteau was trying with all his strength to revive the mysteries of the Orient in the country least suited to them.

> Hence his blood-prince morning levées, hence his king's sensitivity, hence his prodigious interest in the aristocracy, his liking for parties, for the rare, the brilliant, the precious . . ., his habit of regarding as sacred anything that approached him and believing that everything he touched was miraculously transformed.[17]

Everything that surrounded Cocteau became pure and rare, including the little dazzled orphan. Sachs, who had always thought of himself as abject, suddenly saw himself transformed into a being of fairyland.

> This predilection for pomp, this need to be complimented, to talk for a long time about nothing before getting to the main point, this search for the strange (at bottom, much less strange for him than for us), this theatrical life, all announced an unconscious memory of splendor, palaces, kingdoms, colors, lights—an Oriental truth before which dank Paris, cold democracy, boring French avarice (an avarice for emotions as well as money) became unlivable. And when Cocteau cried out (Oh how many times!): "I am tied to the impossible," the impossible was . . . Paris, France, the French (the incredulous French).[18]

Once Cocteau's character had been internalized, thanks to that mimetic avidity that would serve as his foundation until his death, Sachs let himself be mesmerized by the books, with their phrases that fold in on themselves and unfold to say the opposite of what one expects. There was magic in this literature that abolished all obvious meaning in order to thicken the curtain of smoke surrounding its author. It was no longer a man but an oracle that he was reading, no longer a writer but poetry itself, with all that implies of the experience of suffering and presentiment of death. The blossoming of the teenager struck everyone: Cocteau had instilled in him not only his values, but also his obsessions and anxieties, until a version of Sachs emerged that was much more brilliant than the simple and "hideous" original. It was a real case of possession, Max Jacob would say. Sachs would confirm:

> These joys, so new for the young man, of understanding and being understood, the ineffable pleasure produced in the mind by the first intimate contact with a very lively intelligence, the selfish pleasure of devoting oneself to, taking part or thinking one is taking part in, a great work, the feeling of self-importance one has in contact with famous men, finally the provision of human experiences one accumulates in the milieus where the action is—all that was generously placed within my reach for several years. I got drunk on it.[19]

Cocteau, for his part, had never felt so well understood. Radiguet was probably a much better reader of his works, but Sachs had the gift of restoring his "magical" dimension, while making his emotional cords vibrate. Facing this adolescent, Cocteau was no longer the victim of the Breton group, or the "widower" that Paris laughed at, but the magician who could enchant life, as during the time of Anna de Noailles.

Sachs, meanwhile, was frantic to seem worthy of the fairy-like Cocteau. He borrowed large amounts of money to pay the greatest tailors to provide him with shirts and fancy capes made to order. The debts led him into a spiral of lies, thefts, then swindles. He began demanding twice the price for the theater tickets he would buy for clients of the Hôtel Vouillemont and then resell what he "found" to his new acquaintances. "Answer on your life for the objects that leave my room," Cocteau would write to him from Villefranche, when the teenager was gathering together items for the Stock shop window.[20] Sachs hurriedly took the oath, and the dance resumed: he felt so rich near Cocteau that he needed to show himself to be even more generous than him.

Cocteau's hold grew so quickly that Sachs soon had the illusion of harboring some of the actual essence of that incredible man. Previously convinced that fate had made the world good, with the notable exception of his person, he had never dared to grant himself the possibility of writing, but the powers his idol was conferring on him were changing his opinion. Yes, he would create books, like Radiguet.

LE BAL DU COMTE D'ORGEL

Cocteau had to admit the obvious: no afternoon spent with Sachs was equal to reading the poem that Max Jacob had dedicated to Radiguet. Neither drugs, nor money, nor the overflowing affection of Sachs could mask the fact that

Cocteau was actually thinking of only one thing, and internally uttering only one name, ever since he had begun perfecting the *Bal* that Radiguet had left unfinished. He worked on it with even more conviction since he knew each cogwheel of it, if not each key. He cut, condensed, and edited, as was his habit, with the help and consent of Bernard Grasset, whose stylistic "purity" kept him regularly correcting his authors. Kessel himself got involved, as well as the house copyeditor, and then Cocteau streamlined and condensed the manuscript even more. Everyone concentrated on making this posthumous novel into a masterpiece, and surprising the critics, many of whom doubted that the miracle of *Le diable au corps* could be repeated: it seemed more likely that the very young schoolboy, once his satchel was emptied, could have nothing more to tell.

The new novel's publication aroused strong opinions. Everyone acknowledged its strength and precision, but still didn't agree with Cocteau that it was more beautiful than Proust and more realistic than Balzac. Radiguet's psychological mastery, his disaffected distance, and his irony evoked rather the Laclos of *Les liaisons dangereuses* or even the Chamfort of the *Maximes*. His calculated cynicism disturbed people: he seemed to know everything about his characters in advance (Sartre would later reproach Mauriac for this), and was content to move them around, as a chess player does his pawns. The mature, *ex cathedra*, worldly tone that the book used to attack the licentiousness of the time and the pathological fear of being fooled that had prevented people at that time from believing in miracles caused suspicions to arise. Why had they waited six months to publish his book, when the invalid had the proofs of his book in hand on his hospital bed? True, Radiguet had died before he was able to begin his final corrections, but had he asked his mentor, in a will, to correct the proofs, as the collector Jacques Guérin asserted? Suddenly people noticed that while Radiguet, in *Le diable*, had written like everyone else, the *Bal* had that aphoristic tone that came spontaneously to the author of *Thomas l'imposteur*. The end, where Anne d'Orgel shouts at her spouse, in a fit of "grandiose frivolity," the phrase of hypnotizers—"And now, Mahaut, sleep! I want you to"—was so Cocteau-like that the rumor spread that Radiguet's mentor was behind the book.[21] "It's very good Cocteau," one critic even wrote in *Les marges*, adding that if *Le bal du comte d'Orgel* was not by Cocteau, "then the previous book by Cocteau was by Radiguet."[22]

Pressed with questions, Cocteau finally confessed that he had "piously" retouched the manuscript, and Grasset revealed that Radiguet, during their last meeting a month before he died, had spoken to him with anxiety about the imperfect state of his book. Did that justify a kind of post mortem beautification that took the form of a thousand corrections and the amputation of 9 percent of the text, as André Fraigneau said?[23] Half a century later, Georges Auric, who had typed the original manuscript, would denounce a "correction" that he had denied at the time.[24] The various manuscripts indeed prove a disturbing interference, and the large amount of work Cocteau did on the book.[25] But if the novel that Radiguet had originally planned was denser, more violent, and more disordered than the one we read now, Radiguet had during his lifetime already performed some major corrections. Was Cocteau the post mortem sire of the *Bal*, in his desire to make his love for Radiguet literarily concrete? "There is nothing of his genre, his multifaceted style, his literary clown ellipses," Léautaud noted in his *Journal*.[26] Even if the novel was performed by four hands, the composer was indeed Radiguet.

The book's launch required careful consideration. Since Radiguet remained suspect in the eyes of the literary Left—not to mention the Surrealists, who had taken a strong dislike to him—Grasset suggested to *Nouvelle revue française* that they publish it in its entirety in exchange for a small sum. Rivière agreed, though he prefaced the text with a rather scornful commentary—a final twist of the knife for Cocteau—to the fury of Grasset, who threatened him with a duel. By singing of that born writer, a Dadaist at the age of fifteen, patriot at seventeen, worthy of the Académie at nineteen, as wise at twenty as an old Mandarin, Cocteau wanted his dazzling fate to be the source of dreams for generations of runaways, rebels, budding writers. Kessel talked about the young man who had taught him so much—"one of the greatest sources of pride" of his life; Morand evoked the "indolent meteor" who regarded his own restlessness with annoyance, since Radiguet preferred internal voyages. In short, Radiguet was exalted as an embodiment of precocity, as Villon and Sade had been for crime or perversity.

There was, however, Joseph Delteil, Breton's protégé, who noted, "That old wreck of academicism whom we had so valiantly scolded . . . now that devil of a tyro has suddenly revived him . . . under the freshest and most exuberant kinds of classicism . . . It was infuriating."[27] But it was the literary Right, in the end, that seized hold of *Le bal du comte d'Orgel*. The Thomist philosopher Jacques Maritain praised a classic able to match the left-wing Protestants of the *Nouvelle revue française*, then encouraged Henri Massis, a literary critic with Thomist leanings, also close to the royalist Action Française, to shower praises on *Le bal du comte d'Orgel*.[28] This article moved Cocteau all the more since the arguments used were his own, which had been told in confidence to Massis.

Although Beaumont was horrified to see himself as the Comte d'Orgel, as Montesquiou was in recognizing himself as Baron de Charlus, sales soared.[29]

Radiguet's father took part in the promotion of the book, but Cocteau thought of himself as the sole person morally responsible for its success. Supported by M. Radiguet and Bernard Grasset, he even contested the authenticity of all but two poems in the book of erotic poems that had been published in 1925 under the title *Vers libres*, as well as the *Jeux innocents* that would be published a little later. Cocteau even threatened the "plagiarism" with a trial, even though, according to Valentine Hugo, he knew these poems from having illustrated them with obscene drawings.[30] Was Cocteau anxious, by dismissing a collection that was in fact uneven, to keep the prodigy's memory "clean," to use a word he liked? Or did he refuse to see the heterosexuality of his "son" revealed in broad daylight? *Les vers libres* in fact leave no doubt about the precocious and brazen desires of Radiguet.[31] For the poems in *Joues en feu*, however, which were also published posthumously, Cocteau made only a few typographical corrections, not wanting to dirty "these eternal primroses" that he would preface with the poem that Jacob had dedicated to the dead man.[32]

For the first time, with the success of *Le bal*, Cocteau acknowledged that he may not have lost everything: had he lived, Radiguet would have married the frightful Bronja and would have escaped from him in the eyes of the world; dead, he remained forever his literary lover, the angel he had sheltered with his wing—his "Bébé."

Then Paris stopped thinking about Radiguet. Sales of the *Bal* collapsed, and Cocteau rediscovered that terrifying void that the presence of young Sachs, at least some days, only emphasized. His affection was so sticky, and his admiration so overbearing, that the older man encouraged the younger to marry a young woman who said she was attracted to him—always this tendency to marry people off—then he returned more than ever to opium. Like the pious Muslim's day, Cocteau's day was punctuated by those meticulously held appointments that had him turning to an Orient of smoke, in Marcelle Garros's apartment, or in Maurice Sachs's room. Sublime peace was his. With opium's "heavenly kindness," he would say, he was only too happy to be able to escape finally from work and to attain serenity for a few hours. Words no longer gushed from his pen. His ideas remained in rough draft, or as drawings, but he drew a kind of tranquility from them. If opium lovers often imagine themselves producing masterpieces, they also feel no need to let anyone know: this excellence is only their concern.

At the same time, no one wanted to see Cocteau inactive. Weary of his title of king of the ballroom, Beaumont-d'Orgel encouraged Cocteau to take part in the Soirées de Paris, a series of performances he would give at the Cigale during the 1924 Summer Olympics. Taking out the adaptation of *Roméo et Juliette* he had written in 1916, Cocteau hired some actors, had them rehearse to a jazz background—which he later was forced to replace with airs from the sixteenth century—and supplied a black backdrop for the strawberries, diadems, and stars on Jean Hugo's embroidered costumes. The polychrome brilliance of the performance, with its *tableaux vivants* full of the craftiness and naivety for which Cocteau was applauded—he was stage designer and acted in the role of Mercutio—was in tune with the era and celebrated even by Gide; Maurice Sachs, too, appeared on stage in a harlequin's coat, under the name of Ségur.[33] Yet the omnipresence of black—"Very Borniol," said the stagehands—revealed the abyss in which Cocteau was still struggling.[34] "The tragedy unfolded like a big funeral ceremony, deadly and sublime. The sets, the costumes, the gestures, the movements, everything came from Jean, from his suffering and the efforts he was making to confer on that suffering a kind of mortuary symphony," Bernard Faÿ remembers.[35] With his waist cinched into his Renaissance carapace, Cocteau labored so much that he compared himself to those insects continuing to struggle once cut in half, and would even say he hoped to be killed during the duels peppering his *Romeo*. Learning that the *Nouvelle revue française* had published a text by Gide in place of his own homage to Radiguet, one evening Cocteau accosted the Immoralist when he arrived looking for Marc Allégret, whom Beaumont had hired as manager for these Soirées.[36]

The distance would continue to increase between Cocteau's personal despair and the collective fantasy of those years. Convinced that a fate weighed on him, that death was lying in wait for him, and that the gods wanted to take him young too—a premonition that more generally haunted that neoclassical period, in which people believed that fate turned against all heroes—Cocteau was still trying to flee his underlying desire to join Radiguet in death.[37] He was panic-stricken, like those chickens that run more quickly when their head has been cut off.

Even though Cocteau had sworn never again to depend on Diaghilev, he took the initiative and suggested to Diaghilev an operetta for Dolin, the new favorite whom the Russian wanted to launch. Charmed by a plot that set out to "say nothing," where an airplane passes by in the sky that one isn't supposed to see, the impresario gave his assent for Milhaud to compose the music for this third collaboration between Cocteau and Diaghilev.[38] Resolutely modern, frivolous, and luxurious, influenced by the gestural movements of tennis, golf, swimming, and other emerging sports as well as the acrobatic moves of a pair of dancers whom Cocteau had noticed at Ciro's, the ballet took the name *Le train bleu*, after a fast Paris–Côte d'Azur train that had begun service the previous summer. Having become the official choreographer for the Ballets Russes,

Bronislava Nijinska refused to give in to the suggestions of the librettist for whom she had danced *Le dieu bleu* ten years earlier. Cocteau wanted to show how tennis and golf champions, those modern heroes, instinctively rediscovered the rhythms of ancient statuary; hostile to that specifically Cocteau-like discovery, which would become a neoclassical cliché, Nijinska took her inspiration instead from the agile moves of Suzanne Lenglen, the famous tennis champion, who also inspired the costumes.[39] The conflict was never-ending during rehearsals at the Théâtre Mogador. Cocteau's plot evoked the venal opportunism and cynical humor of beachside affairs, with their gigolos and overexcited "chicks," but the librettist himself was no longer in a joking mood. The choreographer, too, just as stubborn and inept at French as her brother, didn't like luxe or laughter. Diaghilev thus often had to serve as a go-between for a Cocteau who was very sure of himself, a Nijinska in tears, and a Dolin feeling fiercely independent. The torrid heat, and the fairground-like music that was brushed in large strokes by Milhaud, finally discouraged Cocteau, who deemed the spectacle detestable, despite the immense stage curtain by Picasso, which featured strong bathers running on a beach, and had been made twenty-five times larger by an assistant.[40]

Exhausted by these two spectacles and by the abuse of opium, Cocteau again felt a need to leave Paris. He left to join the faithful Auric, Radiguet's closest friend along with Kessel, and the very devoted Marcelle Garros, in the Villa le Calme, a family inn in Villefranche, the little harbor near Nice on the French Riviera. "Here I'm trying to live," Cocteau wrote in August to Gide, whom he insisted on making confidant to his sufferings. "Or rather I'm trying to learn to live with the death that is inside me. It's atrocious."[41] The sun, usually so beneficial, this time only increased his malaise. He managed to reduce his consumption of opium, but saw himself all the more as a phantom during that burning August, and calls for help followed despairing confessions: "Write— have pity," he implored the Hugos.[42] The photos of Radiguet that Poulenc sent him only upset him more. "I'm trying to live without Raymond, but I'm not succeeding," he wrote to René, the dead man's favorite brother. Unable to write or even to concentrate, Cocteau wondered, in a letter to Radiguet's father, if his real role on earth was simply to help the genius of Radiguet reach the light of day.

Cocteau spent his days staring at his face in mirrors, when he wasn't making portraits of it from memory. He found his features horrifyingly thin, as the drawings and his captions testify; he published a collection of them as *Le mystère de Jean l'Oiseleur*.[43] By scrutinizing his own enigmatic visage, Cocteau finally pierced through the landscape of skin and joined, through a long, dark hallway, a world where time doesn't pass, where the same scenes are reproduced a hundred times, like a trauma, in a terrifying present without past or future, without cause or purpose. Scarcely had he returned to Paris than he left again for London in order not to have to celebrate the first anniversary of the fatal event. "Raymond's memory makes me sicker every day," he confided to Max Jacob, on New Year's Day 1925. "Every day deepens the hole into which I am sinking," he confirmed, two months later, to Étienne de Beaumont.[44] He sounded like a mother speaking of her dead child, mad with the fact that no one could join her in the desolate universe where she was condemned to live.

THE ANGEL HEURTEBISE AND HER SEX

Drugs no longer easily pacified Cocteau. The endless half-second naps they caused relaunched him into a heaven haunted by Radiguet. In the morning he no longer had the courage to unfold his body; the images his eyelashes let filter through were soon covered over by the memory of his sticky dreams. Reading the paper seemed beyond his strength. That printed testimony of universal agitation, with its brutal intrigues, its swift fortunes and incessant glories, was like a knife blow to Cocteau: the world showed so much energy, and his nebulous body produced so little. The first visitors would ring, forcing him to emerge from his lethargy, splash water on his face, and cover his cheeks with shaving cream. He would then plunge back into reality like those half-dead fish forced to live when they're thrown back into a sink. To escape his mother's reproaches—she seemed to have known all along, and acted more or less as if she couldn't understand—he began eating opium, but the morphine and the residue contained in the balls that he absorbed in ever more massive doses damaged his kidneys and overwhelmed his plexus. Tears came to him at every hour of the day, tears or mucus—so that he escaped one drowning only to be engulfed in another. For three years, his imagination had benefited from the stimulating and focusing presence of Radiguet, but great writing still remained as difficult when he worked alone. Stage fright, which he hadn't previously felt, overcame him, until it blocked the creative process. Only the night, which paralyzed all forms of social activity, imposing its little death on the entire city, was still livable for him; its sudden changes of subject and drifting dreams ensured him the respite that opium no longer offered.

A terrifying impression seized him one day, in the elevator that was taking him to Picasso's studio on the rue La Boétie: that of growing up side by side with "some sort of terrible, eternal thing."[45] A voice from nowhere whispered to him: "My name is on the plaque!," forcing him to lower his eyes to discover that

"Heurtebise" was the brand name of the elevator mechanism hoisting him up to the sky—and not Otis-Pifre, as was usual at the time. "But everything is a miracle!" exclaimed Picasso when Cocteau told him about this strange "encounter." "It's also a miracle not to dissolve in one's bath like a lump of sugar!"

But the angel brushed against in the elevator didn't stop bothering Cocteau. Was it the phantom of the dead man that was preventing him from living or the embodiment of Cocteau's lost fertility? This presence sought to force a passageway in him with such a rage that one night, despite the presence of his mother in the neighboring room, Cocteau thought of killing himself to end his sufferings. Finally at dawn, he threw himself onto his papers and began writing a poem under "dictation," against his own wishes and purely automatically. These crises followed one after another for a week, so brief and violent that they seemed to tear out his innards, so that he compared them to giving birth. At the end of the seventh day, at seven at night, Cocteau, exhausted, saw the angel. Haughty. Completely indifferent to him. "A monster of selfishness."[46] The young man who had been "lent" him by heaven had just been recalled to him, in the form of a seraph whose very name—half-clash half-kiss—expressed both violence and tenderness.[47] An angel of an incredible brutality, leaping again and again onto him, "bestial boy, tall flower . . . heavy male scepter," to whom Man Ray would soon attempt to give a face, via some "Rayogrammes."

It was March 8, 1925. The son (Radiguet) and supposed lover (Cocteau) had experienced a kind of Assumption, much like those that would determine the fate of almost all of Cocteau's heroes, from Paul in *Les enfants terribles* to Patrice in *L'éternel retour*. The pair had climbed to heaven for a week to relaunch their dream of co-creation.

When Cocteau came back to see Picasso on the rue La Boétie, the elevator had changed its brand name. The Spaniard was right: everything was a miracle. That week had been so exhausting that he swore to himself, emerging from the ordeal, never to write again. Wasn't there more courage in starting to live again than in perpetuating this flattering mourning? "How ugly is the happiness we want, / How beautiful is the unhappiness we have," we read in *L'ange Heurtebise*.

Cocteau obviously would not keep his promise. All his life, he would regard *L'ange Heurtebise* as the most beautiful poem he had ever written, the only one in which he couldn't change one letter, even at peril of his life—a watershed he liked to compare to that of *Les demoiselles d'Avignon* in Picasso's trajectory. An arguable evaluation but a revealing one: it was here that for the first time he made his disciples into angels, conferring mythical names on them—Heurtebise for Radiguet, Cégeste for Bourgoint, who had just entered his life. And it was starting from that stage that he would truly devote himself, like Apollinaire, to a poetry that was at once Promethean and Orphic, capable of crossing into the underworld to bring back fire, of entering into contact with the dead who know—with hostages of that other world, peopled with phantoms and angels, to which only seers have access.

His poem finished, Cocteau fell back into a kind of coma that came on slowly and insidiously. Nothing else really mattered to him now—as if the earth were no longer even his homeland. Or as if he too had been "lent"—but by whom, and to whom? Impatient to rejoin the heavens to which Radiguet had lifted him for a week, he confided to the Abbé Mugnier: "You know what I need, and it's not something that's obtained upon request." Opium and writing became more than ever a way to suspend everything.

When he withdrew, time abandoned all its empery to space, the everyday became the eternal, and anguish was relegated to a kind of soft peace. "Everything we do in life, even love," Cocteau would say, "we do on an express train headed for death. To smoke opium is to leave the moving train."[48] The hours went by at the speed of clouds; caressed by celestial hands, he felt like Barbette flying through space between the sexes. The pipe led him so far away from himself that he wondered sometimes to whom the body lying in front of him belonged. He obeyed other laws and took other forms, like a knife plunged in water. He no longer felt hunger, or desire for anything.

> The Chinese man floats on his back on the river Love
> Thanks to a profound, light machine
> And the huge ridiculous universe around
> Arranges itself, wise as the Flowery Kingdom.[49]

There was nothing picturesque, though, in these visions, no dragon spitting fire on transvestites plaiting their hair, nothing of the sensual Oriental dreams that sailors were bringing back from Burma or Cochin China: since opium produced no hallucinations, it was his own mythology that Cocteau found in the chandoo. It was after three opium pipes that René Clair got the idea in 1923 to film *Paris qui dort*, where the capital is sleeping under the sway of mysterious, paralyzing radiations; Cocteau needed no more for his intelligence and memory to be deployed with ease, wonderfully stimulated. Some people are able to write poems only under the influence of high fevers; by placing him right away in that trance-like state capable of making him into a medium, opium allowed Cocteau to live all year long at the necessary temperature to make him write verse. The ink flowed, without his even needing to move. Cured was the cowardice that had been blocking his fingers; gone was that limp anguish that made him idle; already he was composing poems, many of which express his gratitude for the poppy, that flower so clever at taking him away from the world. The others praise that royal path to the unconscious that he would explore, before Michaux or Leiris, in key works—from *Opium*, the journal of his detox- ification cure, to *Les enfants terribles*, the story of another kind of intoxication: by twins.

THE DREAM WAR

Breton's followers were at the same time practicing recounting their dreams. Faithful to the desire to explore the psychic abysses of Breton, the man who had contemplated becoming a psychoanalyst during his years studying medicine, and who had just established his doctrine in the first *Surrealist Manifesto* (1924), they increased their sessions of provoked sleep and stories meant to produce images in dream. But if the magnificence and atrocity of dream-like scenes also fascinated Cocteau, as much as did their logic pushed to the absurd; and if he dreamed a great deal, and almost always in color; he refused to translate into words the spontaneous genius of these images, preferring to let them accumu- late inside him to weave the threads of the poem already under way. On this point Cocteau was years ahead, since he had already been encouraging himself in 1913 to dream, for *Le Potomak*. But the result had somewhat disappointed him, and since then he was more interested in the way that dreams change according to the poses that the sleeper takes, or the swollen eyelids of the sleeper, than in his nocturnal "journeys." Indeed, Cocteau thought of dream as a wonderful organism that deserved to be filmed from a diving suit, but which in his opinion lost all its brilliance, like seaweed and coral, as soon as you tore it from the liquid mass of sleep to exhibit it in the open air. In short, if dream had interest, it was as an exercise of loss of self-control, or else as a substitute for the desire to fly, which the occult sciences, for once in agreement with psycho- analysis, liken to dreams of universal seduction. Sleep "takes the lid off our box," Cocteau would assert, and it was this aerialist "improvement" that he hoped for first.[50] All of existence stemmed in the end from a kind of sleep that knows only one awakening: death.

The competition between Cocteau and the Certà gang, which demanded exclusivity even in this domain, soon took a fierce turn. But sleep was one of the most sensitive places in Cocteau's imaginal environment, and he persisted in being the poet of active somnambulism, waking dreams, existential twilight, and lucid lethargy. Writing became more than ever "shedding light on the night," dreaming of the thoughts of sleeping boys.[51] Jacques Prévert, a new recruit to the Breton group, quickly gave Cocteau a nickname as funny as it was unfair: "The Déroulède of dream."[52] It was not Prévert but rather Aragon who had just warned against a "wave of dreams," as if one had to prepare for it the way one would for a wave of conversions or a military offensive.[53] Cocteau would compare the Surrealist art of sleep to the "exquisite corpses" that were circulating throughout the group.[54] This art, he thought, debased the mystery, by illuminating only the picturesque effects of the "petrifying fountain" that makes the sleeper into a being radically different from the awake subject, a stranger linked by veins to the supernatural world that presides over animate life.[55] This stranger was much more interesting to Cocteau than the fantastic quality of dreams, which so quickly became hackneyed — as Magritte and Dalí would prove.

The conflict was a matter of aesthetics, but also of temperament: Cocteau, whom opium, that "dream paste," made sleep standing up, was trying to introduce himself by force into reality. Breton, by contrast, so willful and lucid, was trying to break and enter into dream, but as a prisoner of that "harsh discipline of mind to which we mean to submit everything once and for all," which had made him so admire Valéry, he found it difficult to doze off during the hypnosis sessions he organized, and could not abandon himself totally to automatic writing.[56] He went back to his slightest attempts of unbridled poetry and reached delirium only with great vigilance. Cocteau was worse than a rival on this point; he was the aggressive image of what Breton dreamed of becoming — a poet "working while sleeping." Far from always being the inspired man he would complacently describe, Cocteau was however capable of making his imagination float, the way one blows glass. He censored this imagination so little that he didn't even fear ridicule in his search for the nameless, and finally left a body of work as verbose as it was uneven — a defect that Breton cannot be reproached with, since his superb prose has a metronomic regularity.

Psychoanalysis was another source of discord. Although Cocteau would readily adopt some of its intuitions, like "flight into illness" — "die Flucht in die Krankheit," said Freud — he would always keep himself at a distance from it, afraid of setting off in exploration of his own shadows with an overly explicit guide. He never sought to treat this suppurating core that fed both his poems and his illnesses, any more than he sought to decipher the primitive scenes, from his father's suicide to the mirror-love of his mother, that might have shed light on his feeling of incompleteness. While obsessively staging the character of Oedipus, Cocteau preferred to explore, without revealing anything intimate, that mythological unconscious from which Jung made his honey. Like many creators, Cocteau feared that pursuing a cure might bring into the open the neurotic source of his fertility, and make his imagination go stale, as Freud himself had suggested when Schnitzler had come to consult him. For a little while, he would have seen in the entire Freudian corpus a form of bad fiction, from which he had to defend himself by an excess of good fiction. "Psychoanalysis is a disease that takes itself for its own remedy," Karl Kraus said in that same period of time. Cocteau still preferred his own bad health, if we can put it that way; thus he was content with a chronic verbal therapy, which made him write, still and always—indeed, his entire body of work can be read like a long parade through his life. "The mystery begins after the explanations," he said in his *Lettre à Maritain.*

Breton and his group, however, dreamed of finding out more. Experimenting with trance and hypnosis starting in 1922, those methods first tested by the great Viennese doctor Crevel, Desnos and Breton gathered in the dark and joined hands around a round table, waiting for their "unconscious" to speak. Since genius was supposed to flow from madness, ever since German Romanticism and the theses of Dr. Lombroso, mental anarchy was compared to poetic fecundity by most everyone—and first of all Breton, who was still hesitating between a haughty refusal of any career and dreams of radicalized Romanticism.[57]

Here again Cocteau objected. He thought that madmen, like children, work in a way opposite to poets, by destroying the web that poets put a lifetime of patience into weaving. He believed in Penelope, they in Erostratus; his visions were born from his second, "reptilian" brain, but he wrote with the first.[58] "Poetry is diamond. Force the flame. It's coal," he said.[59] In other words, if inspiration is close to divination, writing itself remains a critical process: cooling stages are required for the free expressions of the unconscious. Ezra Pound perceived this reticence when he wrote in his *Pisan Cantos:* "'He won't,' said Pirandello, 'fall for Freud, he (Cocteau) is too good a poet.'"[60] Time would not settle things. Annoyed by the worldwide success of psychoanalysis, Cocteau would suspect it of wanting to give everyone a kind of poetic aura, if not repressed genius. "Freud was burgling poor apartments," he would say at the end of his life. "He would move a few mediocre pieces of furniture and erotic photographs around . . ., and set up a confessional for the unfortunate."[61] For Cocteau, creators were great only when they were able to express themselves "without opening their mouths," and to treat their "miserable little heap of secrets" (Malraux's phrase) like manure for fiction. The repression of those "trifling matters" could alone lead them to dominate art and to last.[62]

The conflict with the Breton group crystallized around the designation it took upon starting in 1924. It was in his preface to *Parade* that Apollinaire had used the word "sur-realist" for the first time, we remember, but Tzara himself had reused it in the second issue of *Dada*, in 1917. Other disciples of Apollinaire claimed it, too, including the poet Yvan Goll, who in 1922 used the term *Überrealismus*, and since then had continued to wave that standard in his journal *Surréalisme*, to the great displeasure of Breton—as well as Paul Dermée, one of the editors of the journal *Nord-Sud*.[63] Was Breton afraid that Cocteau, using Apollinaire's text for *Parade* as backup, might claim it for himself in turn? We can suspect as much when we see the intensity with which Soupault claimed, in *Profils perdus*, that their movement had been named in memory of another text by the Enchanter, *Onirocritique*, which he had belatedly called surrealist.[64] Any attempt to use this designation without Breton's imprimatur would be, in any case, harshly suppressed: with tactics drawn straight from the Berlin Dada movement, Valeska Gert was prevented, with rotten eggs, from giving "Surrealist dances" in Paris. In order the better to assert his legitimacy, Breton would go so far as to claim that he had cowritten the preface to the *Mamelles de Tirésias* where Apollinaire, for the first time, had defined what he meant by Surrealism. The word would poison Cocteau's life.[65]

Breton and Cocteau had, it's true, opinions about all the arts, with the notable exception of music, in which Breton heard nothing. Just like Apollinaire again, the two men counted on becoming exclusive distributors of fame and on attaching to themselves the talents they had launched. Following in the footsteps of Marinetti, that enemy of intelligence and reason, both also wanted, as Breton would say, "to undermine the walls of reality that surround us," to make us glimpse that "room at the bottom of a lake" evoked by Rimbaud, and to open up to the wonderful the generation emerging from the war. Sharing the same taste for clairvoyant chance and medium-like experience, they saw poetry as "a secular mystery"—a phrase of Cocteau's—and regarded existence as an art in itself, to the point of simultaneously calling for "several lives lived at the same time" (a phrase of Breton's, who wanted to see men re-learning how to live each morning).[66] Finally and above all, time seemed to them an arbitrary notion, with the rivers of the past, present, and future endlessly crossing; the infra-world they were surveying in writing seemed to be bathed in that timelessness unique to mysteries, whose ancient access paths so familiar to the Symbolists—spiritualism, chiromancy, spinning tables—they resuscitated simultaneously.[67] Cocteau was moreover convinced that great texts possess a hidden memory that the future must actualize, just as analysts see us obeying a fundamental unconscious and forgotten narrative through cryptomnesia. Breton, for his part, was certain of the anticipatory value of automatic writing, inspired again from the "oui-ja" of the spirits—that articulated pencil attached to a board that allows access to one's most secret intuitions, and Cocteau even asserted that a future action can provoke the dream announcing it, by a retrospective overflowing of energy; Breton would write in *L'amour fou* (1937) that without realizing it he had repeated, with a woman he'd met in the street, the Parisian trajectory he had already described in 1923. "Don't the minutes we've lived through leave concrete traces in the air and on the ground?" Man Ray would ask in *Les mystères du château du Dé*: Cocteau didn't see things any differently.

The competition was all the fiercer between these adherents of complete subjectivity who were equally fascinated by reading the stars, inkstains, tarot cards, and lines on the palm, as by learning about fairies and the succubi of Germanic legends. "I was defending the same causes as they were," Cocteau said once, "but I was working alone, while they were working in a group." One could argue about the extent of that kinship, and the isolation that struck the author of *Opium*. But it is disturbing to consider the overlaps, which were less of an issue with Éluard or Aragon, whom Cocteau thought of at the time as an arriviste of the marvelous, than with Breton, who was very sensitive to the "Pythian" dimension of existence, and was similarly convinced that it is up to the poet to produce the crucial gesture capable of reconciling rational knowledge and secret awareness. The ace of hearts that the painter draws in *Le sang d'un poète* would be countered with *Arcane 17*, a symbol of consoling Eve for Breton; the phantoms Cocteau believed in since childhood would be contrasted with the revenants wearing "fluidic costumes" in the *Minotaure*, the Surrealist review; and the poet's limping angels would come to face the dream-like accessories of Surrealism—naked mannequins and orthopedic shoes in display windows. Cocteau and the Surrealists also shared a taste for starfish and empty gloves, symbols of the fourth dimension, and for other "metaphysical" embellishments. "The only difference between the Surrealists and me is that I am surrealist," Cocteau eventually said.[68] There is more than a jest in this statement, made by a man convinced he was the plaything of obscure forces using our unconscious like an antenna. Didn't he think of Radiguet as one of those exceptional "gloves" by which heaven regularly probes humans, before suddenly withdrawing?[69]

True, Cocteau had stopped thinking of himself as modern, once the Dada episode had been overcome; but one could easily say the same about Breton, who was just as hostile to abstraction, minimalism, and geometricism as Cocteau. Fed on symbolism and, through it, on German Romanticism and esoteric tradition, via Nerval, the sensibility of the young Breton had been marked by his amazed discovery of Gustave Moreau, the painter of the Sphinxes, and of Salomes and Narcissuses.[70] Breton too would make great use of symbols and allegories, to the point of building around Theseus, the Minotaur, and the bullfight, during the 1930s, a mythology that competed with the one that Cocteau had created already around Orpheus, Oedipus, and the Sphinx.

From the exploitation of dream, the conflict extended to the use of drugs, about which the Surrealists claimed they were unequivocally hostile. Although drugs, along with fasting and asceticism, were one of the most widely used means of accessing superior knowledge or occult powers, Breton preferred to these "dishonest" substitutes the stoking of an inner fire also inherited from Symbolism before Aragon had rejected drugs in his *Traité du style* (1928)—with the opium smoker Crevel being the only exception.[71] Soon, Breton would want to dominate every terrain, encouraging a poetry that justified the nocturnal and primitive unconscious, was inspired by dark Romanticism, and promoted a kind of thinking utterly hostile to the Enlightenment. The man whom Prévert would call an "inspector of a palace of mirages and Grand Inquisitor of dreams" was more hopeful than ever of electing himself as exclusive heir to Apollinaire.[72]

BLAMING THE VICTIM

Cocteau would not be the only victim of this rise to power. Shoved to the margins—"since there are no Surrealist diplomas, they threaten us with blows," Tzara wrote in *Les nouvelles littéraires*—Tzara for his part seriously considered never writing again, something he had recommended to everyone two years earlier, it should be said.[73] But Cocteau's eclectic, airy, narcissistic nature undeniably irritated Breton's aggressive, compact, and centralized one. With an anger fueled by their thematic similarities, the gendarme's son, Breton, was overcome with veritable fits of rage as soon as Ariel—Cocteau—materialized in front of him to threaten his territory. Breton would welcome hysteria, during the fiftieth anniversary of its "discovery" by Dr. Charcot, as a supreme method to express the unconscious—but obviously he couldn't bear Cocteau's own hysteria, even though it was so fertile; it symbolized in Breton's eyes the art that he had sworn to destroy. The victim of this burning hatred came to define it, in confidence to André Germain, as a "mystical state."[74] Marcel Duchamp himself would confess that Cocteau's mind, his precocity, and his brio acted on Breton the way red affects a bull, arousing both his envy and his scorn.[75] The extraordinary talents and omnipresence of Radiguet's former protector, Cocteau, would continue to give the future contributor to *Minotaure* the desire to attack.

Duchamp as it happens was content to recycle the bullfighting metaphor that the Surrealists had used to define writing itself: Breton, like Leiris or Bataille later, compared the risks involved in composing literature to those the torero takes in entering the arena. It is his life a writer engages when he confronts the muzzle of desire, the horns of death; writing is not a spectacle, but a solitary ceremony in which one must consent to risk one's skin. Dressed in pink and gold, Cocteau became the little toreador whom the Surrealists confronted in a group. But he was also the little animal, vibrant and frail, who always returned to take his measure on the field, "with that dumbfounded pause of the bull emerging from the pen"—the one who answered their shouts, turning his head in every direction, before the picadors threw their lances into his spine, then ran at random, a "poor little tired bull who wants to be a matador too."[76]

Many people would question the personal roots of Breton's hatred. Georges Hugnet, who was connected to both camps, and whose hand his ex-Surrealist friends would break as well as tearing off half his ear, states that Breton could be by turns aggressive and obsequious, in the presence of well-brought-up, wealthy, or elegant people. He was annoyed to see Cocteau so at ease with, and even intimidating, Charles de Noailles, adds Emmanuel Berl.[77] "He had no agility of mind," writes Claude Roy. "No interest in discussion, in the famous, so Parisian mental swordplay."[78] Anxious to perfect his doctrine, Breton continually presented Cocteau as a mole of the bourgeoisie infiltrating the heart of the avant-garde and, in a play of words on "cocktail," reduced him to a human "petit-four." Soupault was already calling him a "silent butler" and an ashtray, under the name Poteau, in *Un bon apôtre*, a novel that had competed in 1923 with *Le diable au corps* and that called Cocteau "dry as a drum and crafty as a puppet."[79]

But it was more likely Cocteau's sexual tastes that were intolerable to Breton, that provincial who devoted a cult to Woman, in a "curious mixture of Symbolist idolatry and nonchalant dandyism," according to one of Breton's biographers.[80] "I accuse pederasts of offering to human tolerance a mental and moral deficit that tends to erect itself into a system and paralyze all the enterprises I respect," he would exclaim, during the weekly meetings that the Surrealists would devote to sexuality, before adding in a later meeting: "I am absolutely opposed to the discussion continuing on this subject." Since Aragon had suggested that there had never been a question of "praising pederasty," Breton said he was ready to "display obscurantism in this realm"—and he kept his word.[81] To a young poet who imprudently introduced himself at the Cyrano, the group's new headquarters near the Moulin Rouge, giving Cocteau's name as reference, Breton shouted, "So, Monsieur, are you a pederast?" before adding, to the stunned debutant: "If you aren't yet, you'll become one."[82]

Breton's desire to excommunicate people didn't stop there. Stating in a quasi-pontifical way that onanism, "insofar as it is tolerable, must be accompanied by feminine representations," Breton threatened a literary critic who had dared to praise his poetry at the same time as Cocteau's: "Monsieur, I am not a cock sucker!" So it was his virility, more than his pen, that had to block any comparison between his work and his rival's. One can only imagine the fury that seized Breton when Claudel called him in turn a "cock sucker."[83] Breton's homophobia made him particularly sensitive to this sort of attack. Not long before the conference in 1935 that would mark the divorce between Surrealism and Communism, Breton would even slap the Soviet writer Ilya Ehrenburg who had accused him of giving himself over "to pederasty and dreams" instead of working. Ehrenburg then decreed that anyone who relied on his fists was a fascist, and Breton retorted that "recourse to the most abject calumny" was also a form of violence (this time, Cocteau might have agreed with him). In short, because France was the only one of the large European countries not to suppress homosexuality legally; because the liberating explosion of the Armistice had softened public opinion; and because three of France's most visible writers — Gide, Cocteau, and Montherlant (to say nothing of the departed Proust) — loved men or teenagers, Breton defensively perpetuated, with a violence worthy of the Victorian era, ancient curses against this so natural form of pleasure.[84] In reconciling these acts with the profound affection this "Don Juan for men" bore for René Crevel, a declared homosexual, or his understanding of the masculine experiences confessed by Desnos, during those same sessions on sexuality (he even declared retrospective passions for the Marquis de Sade and Jean Lorrain, two Sodomites buried ages ago), people would say that it was possible because Breton knew how to settle things with his conscience, and decide who he could or could not tolerate.[85] Curiously, Desnos's hatred garnered energy from a very different argument: "They say you are a pederast," he wrote one day to Cocteau. "I forbid you to be one, since I am."[86] It was as if Cocteau, by his behavior, threatened to take away from Desnos the privilege of a minority sexuality, which Desnos practiced only very occasionally.[87] All of this made for many contradictory and confusing taboos.

Cocteau never knew how to react. He didn't understand, in his naivety as a former Parisian bourgeois, that one could reproach him for customs he had never claimed or denied, or for a birth he had not chosen. And the less he understood, the more he suffered — "What a misfortune to have such sensitivity!" Max Jacob confided to Marcel Jouhandeau at the time.[88] Refusing to make his social origins or his sexual preferences into criteria of value, he preferred to slip by, to become effective on the literary front, adding fodder to the anti-Romantic status of Radiguet, the first writer to have loved Cocteau's work deeply, against the Rimbaud myth orchestrated by the Surrealists. But appropriating Radiguet was to awaken old jealousies, as well as to diminish Rimbaud. Not wanting to "change life," hence going along with the established order, Cocteau worsened his case. His sexuality, his spontaneous "oneirism," as well as his strange inability to deal with the so-male matters of government or army, which the Surrealists were exploring at the time, made Cocteau the perfect scapegoat for the group. His "plain" humanity had the curious power to arouse the potential inhumanity of adversaries whose sensibilities were otherwise. If Cocteau had had the kind of natural authority that commands respect and arouses a desire for obedience, he could probably have defended himself better, but he lacked that phallic hardness to which certain heterosexuals too are sensitive — Breton first of all.

Having from the onset, against all morality and his education, made a Nietzschean choice in favor of strong personalities, Cocteau wanted to regard the Surrealists as excellent men of letters and refused to lower himself to the level of the insults they launched at him. If one of Cocteau's disciples dreamed of writing in *Littérature*, his request had only to be made politely to be accepted. "I ask you to forgive my character," Cocteau sometimes wrote to his own mother. Some of this masochistic lament showed in his face as he confronted Breton's men in his own way, by not immediately handing over to them their fill of raw meat, in the hope of appeasing them. Cocteau's fragility would make even the softest of them feel virile, and since hatred can be self-perpetuating, they were the first to throw a stone at him. Like the schoolboys chasing Dargelos in *Les enfants terribles*, Cocteau had become the man they loved to hate, the victim who makes others strong, someone even better than Jacob or Cendrars (who were also hated after having been honored), for closing the ranks. Referring to the scars left by the wounds he had received, Cocteau would one day say, "There is no literary school. There are only hospitals."[89]

Cocteau couldn't bear to be hated, though. Capable himself of ridiculing a once revered idol, he remained naïve enough to believe that he still deserved everyone's love — probably because he viscerally needed it. When insulted, he was convinced that a simple meeting would be enough to cause the scales to fall from the eyes of an aggressor. Cocteau would be the first to greet him, when chance placed him in his path, in order to prove that he wasn't angry with him, and to put an end to conflict. When he was answered, Cocteau considered the other party noble and tried to convince the other, if not to soften him. Like almost everything that Cocteau experienced, the wounds he had received would seem so unreal to him that he would not think of retaliating, or even of asking the reason for them. Fearing that he might cause more displeasure, he would quickly excuse someone who had "assassinated" him just the day before and would become convinced, seeing him be so natural, and finally so human, that he was dealing with a being as sensitive as himself. Immediately upon being hurt, he would set out to forgive, as a noble, unresentful victim—that is, when he wasn't suffering along with his torturer for the remorse he must be feeling. In a little while he would hope to take the tormentor into his arms, to help him depart with a lighter heart.

Cocteau could regret "this stupid mania of believing in hearts, fairies, miracles," but he was never able to conquer it.[90] Hating hatred, he would long continue to believe in compromise with men whose sensibilities were so close to his own. He so needed to be essential to his enemies that he couldn't even stop himself from asking Paulhan, the literary editor-in-chief of Gallimard, to send him secretly Éluard's most recent book.[91] He also sang the praises of Breton's *Nadja*, in 1928—adding that he found much more pleasure in liking the book of an enemy than that of a friend: a confession, one suspects, that only increased the aggressiveness of a group convinced that it was in Cocteau's nature to desire the strong. The persecution would then often intensify against the man who, by granting his pardon, thought he was asserting his moral superiority. Cocteau, a homosexual of Catholic origin, was pleased to suffer, for sure. . .

Cocteau became the animal that, banished a hundred times, still tries to join the herd; after being left for dead at dawn, he would be found that night prowling in the neighborhood, licking his wounds. Convinced that it all was just a bad dream, every time he would return to the fray, like those Don Juans obsessed with women who resist them. Cocteau, who had rebuffed Proust in another life, went so far as to hold out a humble hand to go-betweens who might reconcile him with his enemies. "You don't love me?" his gaze said: "That's all to your credit. It's because you understand me better than the others. How I love you, feeling you so close to me." Probably he would rather expose himself to blows than not expose himself at all. Hadn't he developed a secret taste for insults, as a child, after climbing onto the platform to receive minor prizes for gymnastics or drawing under "a fusillade of disapproving gazes"? If he was under fire, at least people were talking about him. If he was being riddled with arrows, his wounds were living proof of his singularity.

This need quickly became reciprocal, all the more so since the Surrealists, by dint of glorifying the fairytale woman and *l'amour fou*, were readily showing themselves to be masochistic in their pairings. Breton always returned to the "abject" Cocteau, and Desnos to the "despicable" heir of Edmond Rostand. Despite Soupault's resolve not to utter Cocteau's name anymore, he hurried to mention that "boy who thinks he's a clown because he was always getting kicked in the ass."[92] But this was probably better than silence for Cocteau, and who knows, perhaps he acted this way as a way of guaranteeing that his enemies would talk about him. "Having stones thrown at you is still the best way to get your bust made," he had asserted.[93] Thus he propagated, almost knowingly, his secret penchant for not loving himself.

Rejections got worse, blows multiplied, Cocteau loved himself even less — and the hatred was prolonged indefinitely. "The guilty one is the victim," said Franz Werfel, in a particularly apt phrase: just as self-love creates envy, so did the little esteem Cocteau had for himself make him incredibly easy to detest. Jung had asserted that the rumors surrounding a man instinctively convey what remains unconscious, repressed, or archaic in him, that they pursue him precisely because they are his shadow: and this double began to follow Cocteau everywhere. His spontaneous pacifism — one could almost call it "Gandhi-ism" — also led to a first back-and-forth of disciples. The cane that had broken the arm of Pierre de Massot, that fine mind, had convinced him that Breton was the stronger man: abandoning Picabia and Cocteau, that precursor victim of the Stockholm syndrome, rallied over to Breton body and soul to sign, in 1926, a public eulogy for Felix Dzerzhinsky, the founder of the Soviet secret police.[94] Fifty years later, Massot would still have enough masochism to praise the purity (worthy of Robespierre) of André Breton, and the terrorist virtues of that "septembriseur" about whom he said — with such pride! — that he could have made heads roll, once in power.[95] That was the conclusion Cocteau came to as well, remembering the guillotine to which André Chénier, the great pre-Romantic poet, had been led during the Terror.[96]

Since the vise was tightening, Cocteau gradually returned to the Right Bank, where his family had started out, a place indeed conventional and literarily old-fashioned, but morally much more tolerant. For example, Anna de Noailles, the only notable figure to have survived the big poetic housecleaning of 1916, continued to receive her ideological enemies at her home there if their conversation was worth the trouble, and asked nothing of "her" homosexuals except not to shock people openly. It wasn't long before Desnos imagined, in his dreams of the revolution, a procession of disemboweled officers and castrated priests marching to the scaffold, followed by "women of letters from la Noailles to Jean Cocteau, cleverly martyred by the executioners we could so well be." Desnos was already calling for the revolution, "that is, the Terror," hence for the great return of the guillotine — that "kind machine of deliverance."[97]

BOURGOINT AND THE CURE

It was doses of hatred, then, that the press and the mail passed on daily — and equivalent doses of opium that Cocteau smoked as a result. His bedroom became a pigsty that stank of the characteristic smell of burnt chocolate. Most opium smokers like a damp atmosphere where smoke from the pipes, by its thick warmth, unites their dilated minds. Cocteau added another criterion: he very quickly preferred to smoke in a very select group. Since opium produced the powerful phenomena of depersonalization and feeling two places at once, here again he had to be loved, or at least share an actual complicity.

A few weeks before the appearance of the angel Heurtebise, Cocteau had met a young man to whom, without warning, he had given "his first puff of opium in a kiss."[98] Jean Bourgoint, a boy with big blue eyes lost in the face of a straying eagle, with immense feet and nicotine-stained fingers, was living self-sufficiently with his sister, Jeanne, in a smoke-filled apartment on the rue Rodier, not far from an invalid, haggard mother. Like Siamese twins incapable of making a solo entrance into the world, the two beauties shared Apollonian features and a royal disdain for any form of work—though Jeanne did serve as a model for the couturière Madeleine Vionnet. Jean Bourgoint spent his nights walking endlessly throughout Paris. Dirty, unkempt, and recalcitrant, but possessing a real physical magnificence, he led a contemplative life worthy in every point of the sadhus, those Indian beggars who accept all donations in exchange for the example of detachment they give.

Cocteau, in his confusion, thought he had fallen in love with this mixture of an untouchable and a poor dandy—at least he wanted to believe so. He began showering the young opium-smoker with poems, encouragements, and letters—as many as three a day, not counting the pneumatiques—and dreamt of receiving as many. Convinced that Bourgoint lacked only discipline, just like Radiguet earlier, he encouraged him to submit to him first everything that he might write. "I beg you to believe me. You are the only one of the young to possess a writer's surprising genius," he added, to the silent despair of Sachs, who was present at the birth of this idyll.[99] Half-annoyed, half-flattered, Bourgoint went along with it. Back to his sole need to love, Cocteau increased the doses of letters, without any other result than getting the grumpy Bourgoint to lock himself away, that "little rooster of anger"—like so many other companions of Cocteau—still hesitating between silence and irony, a refusal to live and a need to be rewarded. These encouragements to work kept colliding with the inexhaustible passivity of that immense boy whose legs, standing or sitting, always seemed to be crossed. Like the parasol that "receives the sun and gives shade," in *La danse de Sophocle*, Bourgoint persisted in reading detective novels at night, before prolonging his torpor with steaming baths in which he would fall asleep until dawn—the book he was reading in the tub floating like a cork.[100]

Bourgoint's sleeping body moved Cocteau: with his long eyelashes closed, his face took on an angelic quality. He looked as if he were inhabited by the beyond, or had been won over by the spirit of Morpheus, one of the thousand children of Hypnos, whom that god of sleep sometimes ordered to take a human shape in order to appear in the dreams of sleeping people, and whose name had also baptized the beneficial morphine. Was this a new messenger from heaven? Both very thin, almost noncorporeal, Cocteau and his new seraph—Cégeste in *L'ange Heurtebise*—seem not to have shared the same bed very often, for, as Cocteau noted, if opium awakens the libido of women by stifling their emotionality, it has the opposite effect on men, often eliciting cool, mental desires. Soon after Cocteau's death, Bourgoint would confirm to a friend:

> Jean was of an exquisite temperance: He was—and this will surprise you— profoundly chaste. Just as he chastely smoked his opium like the wise men of China, so was he in his love affairs of a delicacy and temperance of heart to which most men and even poets are little accustomed.[101]

Did Cocteau see love in the fog in which Bourgoint hid himself? He at least wanted to believe that the young man, after coming up against the void everywhere, would end up seizing the hand that Cocteau held out to him. The gaping absence from which Cocteau himself constantly suffered, until he was transformed into a veritable "vacuum cleaner," as he would say, was also familiar to Bourgoint. If he could not leave Jeanne, that sister who, married to a businessman, would return a year later to barricade herself in their incestuous nest, with its "indescribable material and moral disorder" regulated in some way by drugs, Cocteau would help him to get out. When that sister was *very* unhappy, he would try to help her as well. But actually it was Cocteau who, at the end of his tether after Radiguet's "departure," was only awaiting a savior.

It was then that a shadow knocked on the door of the rue d'Anjou. Since the silent Jacques Maritain was not a man to come calling on the spur of the moment, Maurice Sachs had to hurriedly put away the pipes, the lamp, the needle, and the opium resin that was scattered over the floor.[102] But Cocteau had simply forgotten the appointment he had made the day before. This Christian philosopher, disciple of Saint Thomas Aquinas, had long admired Cocteau; already in 1919, he had used some aphorisms from *Le coq et l'arlequin* in a book called *Art et scolastique*, before publishing three years later "Antimoderne," an essay condemning the forced culture of progress, onto which Radiguet and Cocteau had fastened. Since the era was not one devoted to God, it had required the intervention of Georges Auric, in July 1924, to bring Cocteau around to the idea of a meeting. Immediately Maritain had perceived that Cocteau, younger than he by seven years, was an infinitely unhappy man—a tragic soul, permanently condemned to a suffering, unlivable existence. Cocteau acknowledged that opium provided him with only an illusory relief—"happiness in a mirror," he said—and was making him into a lie living inside a "nightmare."

Encouraged by Mauritan to follow a detoxification cure, Cocteau decided to take the step: more dependent every day on the drug, and hence on his mother, to whom he sent bills and requests for money, he no longer felt capable of piloting his own life. "Death was squeezing your throat, Mercutio," Maritain said to him, referring to the role Cocteau had played in his *Roméo et Juliette*. So on March 9, 1925, the day after "Radiguet" had dictated Heurtebise to him, Cocteau entered the clinic of Thermes Urbains, where he was forbidden to receive visitors or to speak to anyone for two weeks, or to take opium.

The weaning would turn out to be particularly cruel. Condemned to absolute isolation and double doses of "calomel," Cocteau went from ice-cold showers to electric baths, when he wasn't undergoing intestinal douches administered by assistants who pulled him by his feet to "baths of light," before placing his face on a box containing a thousand lightbulbs. Shot through in every direction with contradictory impulses, he felt as if his nervous system were being unraveled "into astrakhan," or as if a Chinese tree were being extracted from his vulnerable body. His legs, gone mad, began walking on the ceiling, then stretching out until they touched the opposite building; sometimes his skin was covered with leopard spots, sometimes it folded back, like a robe you lift to cross a puddle. A knife seemed regularly to be cutting up his hands, head, feet, or sex, or an axe was cleaving him in half like a tree trunk; dozens of conical pipes came out of his mouth and eyes; and a diabolical scientist—a madman with a fixed stare with the disturbing name of "Dr. Dereck"—seemed to be using his body as a guinea pig. "This suffering without suffering is atrocious. Ten thousand people in my legs are all awaiting, upright, for the box office to open, but it won't open," he wrote to Valentine and Jean Hugo, who were also living on the rue Chateaubriand, two doors down.[103] Delirious visions assailed him: One day Marc Allégret appeared to him in the form of ankle boots with buttons, and André Gide as rubber shoes; the next day, it was his own head on a painted cube that stared at him harshly, speaking into the void like a sibyl: a Surrealist vision, he noted, as if the terrible Breton were still behind this shock treatment.

Delirium was followed by despondency, the desire to cry, and a deadly sensation of abandonment. Torn from the gauzy ocean of smoke, he was suffocating as he paced his red-brick prison, for "without opium I float about / And my feet are no longer on the ground: / From the poppy I have cut the stem," he would write.[104] He lied to the doctors, spat up their pills without their knowing, and probably had balls of chandoo delivered to him, via packages sent by Maurice

Sachs. A mulatto doctor—also in treatment?—sometimes kept him company as he smoked, but Cocteau had trouble understanding what he said, and the phrases emerging from his own mouth scarcely had any more meaning: chaos reigned in his body disjointed by lack of love and smoke. The nurse who attended him day and night, even sleeping in a neighboring bed, helped him through this nightmare, in the second month. "Sublime in her patience," finesse and tact, this war widow was ready to cross Paris to unearth new editions of *Fantômas* for Cocteau, and then cut out pages for him to devour—an already less toxic form of dependence. Having dreams on purpose in order to recount them to Cocteau, when Cocteau couldn't fall asleep, the woman in white also guessed from the letters Cocteau received every day that the feelings that Sachs had for Cocteau were ten times more profound than those of Bourgoint: "He loves you for you, and Jean [Bourgoint] for himself."[105] But there it was— Cocteau preferred the boy who resisted rather than the one who gave himself, and this revelation only overwhelmed him a little more, pointing again to this flaw in his personality.

Just the day before, his world had been structured by absence and by drug-taking; one pipe was enough to tear him from hell and change him into a snowy cloud. Today he lay on the ground like an animal skin deprived of brain, nerves, blood. "China is taking its revenge," he said to Max Jacob. The crystal ball he had brought, in an excess of superstition, now announced nothing but catastrophes. Already he was getting ready for the worst; in letters he asked Sachs to make sure *Les nouvelles littéraires* treated him well, in case he died, and begged him to intervene with Jean Bourgoint, so that he would reply more profoundly to his letters—that is, with love, or at least tenderness. Did Cocteau sense how much he was wounding his page by asking him to sound the heart of that rival, and then to convince Mme Cocteau that Bourgoint was "good"? Did he see how much that fanatical young disciple was suffering from seeing him tormented by the coldness of Bourgoint, who had the audacity to like neither *Thomas l'imposteur,* nor *Le grand écart?* Obviously not. His first reaction was even to suggest to Sachs that they form a "love triangle" with Bourgoint, confiding to Sachs in a letter, among a hundred disjointed phrases, "I trust no one but you and Maman." Grateful for Sachs's role as intercessor, Cocteau at the same time reproached this "pureblood of friendship," this summit "of elegance and nobility," for never talking about his—Sachs's—debts.[106] This would have been small consolation for Maurice Sachs—who would have preferred Cocteau to have attributed to him a little talent, more than money, which was something he already knew how to make—when Bourgoint, who never even lifted his pen, was immediately labeled a genius.[107]

Whether due to the opium Cocteau took on the sly or the effects of Bourgoint's absence, the invalid began to be agitated again with trembling, and tears flowed from his eyes for no reason. "Jean is betraying me with his sister who's back. I sent a poem for her," he lamented in an umpteenth letter to Sachs, adding, "Without Jean, without you, I would collapse."[108] Mme Cocteau and her daughter Marthe were already scheming to obtain the right to visit him, but any letter from Bourgoint would have had more weight than their forced optimism: four words from his hand, or even the simple recitation from his mouth of the poem that Max Jacob had dedicated to Radiguet, were enough to cover him with tears of joy. Unable to write, except for letters, Cocteau still managed to express the violence of the states he was experiencing through admirable drawings that he published in *Carnet de santé*, in 1926. He thought with his eyes, Max Jacob would say, and this was never so true as during those days when he had to relearn how to breathe, eat, and live, like a child in an incubator.

After two weeks of isolation, Cocteau could finally receive loved ones and friends. Brought by Sachs, Bourgoint paid him a notable visit that launched the beginning of his true detoxification. Still hoping to reconquer his mentor, Sachs showed himself to be more than affectionate with Bourgoint, who in turn was all honey to Cocteau. Overwhelmed by this unhoped-for kindness, Cocteau spoke again of the "heavenly trio" they could form—Sachs, Bourgoint, and Cocteau—in that "absurd masquerade" that was the world.[109] A deluge of gratitude rained down on Sachs, who finally heard Cocteau say, after a letter described as a masterpiece, "What a writer you'd make!"[110] Thinking of everything according to Cocteau's lights, the hopelessly-in-love follower began conceiving of grand projects. Cocteau's skill in launching young talents, by associating them with greater ones, had been famous, ever since Les Six: Sachs had only to show that he was up to snuff to take the place of Radiguet in the heart of his idol. But already Cocteau was advising him to fall in love in his turn, promising him, with frosty lightness, that he would get thinner then, "like women."

The fact is, Cocteau was beginning to feel sexual desire again, for the first time in months, with an insistence that made him very impatient to live his love for Bourgoint. "I feel my feathers growing back," he confided, still to the unhappy Sachs; and poems began to gush from his pen:

They want me to relearn foreign life
And to invite girls to the ball to dance.
They want me to change my wings, in short.

I had wings of smoke in my mind
They want me to regrow my human wings.[111]

Cocteau took advantage of this newfound energy and clarity to correct the
proofs of *Joues en feu*, the poems by Radiguet, and for the first time, he walked
around his room, making a list of friends who had ignored him: "People bury
you quickly," he noted to Sachs. "But I will reappear like Fantômas. And they
will tremble."[112] Learning that Jeanne Bourgoint was knitting a tie for him in
preparation for his discharge, Cocteau had hope again. Perked up by a diet
based on shrimp rémoulade, he was already doing exercises to get back "his lost
body," was regretting that they hadn't prescribed an astrologer for him, and was
thinking of doing a karma cure. Evicted by the demolition of the clinic—from
the Hugos' apartment he would watch his room cut in half, about to be shattered—he went to rest in a hotel in Versailles, only to discover that he wasn't as
attached as he thought to Bourgoint: by losing its power over him, opium had
freed him of his illusions of love.

Aside from the few poems composed during the cure, Cocteau remained
incapable of carrying out a real literary project. He was at an even greater
impasse than before his discovery of opium, which had temporarily freed his
hand: the criticisms of Bourgoint, that "breaker of writing," hurt him too much.
Without any taste for life, unable to bear even the sight of a literary journal,
Cocteau took refuge again in sleep, but thought he was dying every time he
woke up. From his detox cure, he had emerged "weary and weakened," Bernard
Faÿ would say: "He left that part of youth there, made of unconscious happiness
. . . joy without reflection . . . which he then had to compensate for by that
incisive energy, with which he armed himself and which made another man of
him, young with a willed youth, an anxious, wrinkled youth."[113] To give him
courage, Dr. Capmas promised to prescribe opium for him in a medical form.
That was a relief: his only moments of happiness, since Radiguet's death, he
owed to the drug.

MARITAIN AND THE CROSS

Jacques Maritain hadn't stopped trying to comfort Cocteau at the Thermes
Urbains. On the only chair in the invalid's room, then on the divan in his own
house in Meudon, the austere, taciturn, "oafish" philosopher had lent an ear to
the story of the poet's semi-delirious ravings, then encouraged his confidences,
taking notes (he would find replies the next day, he said). The blue, clear,
straightforward gaze of Maritain had a child's gentleness; a halo of lightness

surrounded his handsome, pale face, conferring on him a kind of happy weight-lessness. "When he entered a room, the sun came out," said Julien Green, who like Maritain had been born Protestant and then converted to Catholicism, out of a need for wider vistas.[114] Cocteau in turn experienced the radiant kindness and magnetic serenity of this shy man who dreamed of devoting himself to writing, and whose mysterious silences reminded Cocteau of a fish in the depths of the ocean, "luminous and blind."[115] By his availability, his calm, and his gentleness, no one evoked better than Maritain the peace known by men in Christ.

The "anti-modern" theologian had an advantage; he did not belong to the world of letters and was completely ignorant of its low blows. The literary critiques he published in his journal, *Le Roseau d'or*, however, betrayed a surprising ability for empathy. Struck by his delicacy in listening, Cocteau remembered the praises he had reserved for *Le bal du comte d'Orgel* and began talking about the heavenly body of work that Radiguet and he had outlined, and the crystal factory that they had operated together. Maritain not only repeated how much he had admired their work; he also commented on it with a sensi-tivity that led him to find in his friends' texts dimensions of which they them-selves were unaware (a talent that had made him the close friend of Rouault, and then of Chagall, two painters concerned with religion). Who better than that "knight of the absolute," attracted to lost causes, could have spoken of God to Cocteau?

After believing himself the equal of Shiva and Vishnu, Cocteau now thought that artists were never anything but a failed god. Hearing Maritain make the distinction between the man of letters who apes God, in his omnipotence, and the poet who serves Him, by perfecting His work, Cocteau thought he had found the confirmation that heaven had sent him Radiguet to perfect him and make him into a masterpiece. Relieved to discover that everything he had done up to that point was obedient to a hidden plan, Cocteau continued to open his heart to the Thomist philosopher. Never had he confided in anyone so much. The flaws of this thirsty soul, deprived from the start of any form of stability, appeared more than ever to Maritain. But wasn't this sincerity, which could become pathetic, also Cocteau's greatest artifice? Didn't he have to tear off this mask made of real skin in order to let his authentic face be seen—that of the man full of sadness and despair, estranged from the earth for lack of faith? Yes, this soul stripped bare was not made for this world. Come from elsewhere, it aspired with all its strength to return there; this bleeding organ wounded by skin and hair like wiry wool sought to become one again with the single body where it could flourish—the one the Creator reserves for his stray sheep. These visions struck Cocteau: no one had looked into him so clearly except this man curious about all created things, who had passionately loved his friend Ernest Psichari, and who himself wrote at the age of eighteen, "It is absurd and dangerous . . . to look in oneself for the immutable, true self, to arrest the definitive traits of his person. You might as well petrify your cells. One is never oneself."[116] Or at least he wasn't himself until his decisive meeting with Raïssa made him a steady man who submitted to God.[117]

It had occurred to Cocteau, during his fits, to request prayers from the Abbé Mugnier, and then to take communion; he also offered candles in the churches in southern France, certain that they could stop the mistral and cure his rheumatism. He sometimes even prayed to the Creator to give him back the will to live, and had confided to the abbé, on a day of distress: "If I had faith, I would become a priest." How clearly we can recognize Cocteau in this impatience to speak about God to a clergyman who was not even interested in the subject! When it came down to it, Cocteau was not a believer. His fervor about heaven found no foothold, and his wandering aggravated him all the more. "I suffer at your expense, / Non-existent God, for if you truly existed, / I too would truly exist," Cervantes had written, and Cocteau could say the same. Wasn't he sad for being a nonbeliever, with a mind so inclined to believe? For being so alone and tender, faced with the indifference of a Bourgoint or the harshness of a Breton? How could he not envy the Christian convictions that Maritain showed in contrast to Breton, and the courage with which he asserted that he was Breton's adversary?

The Thomist acted in stages. He discussed the evil committed by certain thinkers, Protestants, and modernists, when they rushed the "happening of the self," and Cocteau, who had so tried to free himself of his own self, in the smoke from Asia, secretly approved. Maritain also told him that, in order to survive in this world, one had to have a hard mind and a soft heart. This was already Gospel for Cocteau, who had never been able to hurt others, but who believed in the sharpness of ideas. Actualizing the ancient Christian parables, Maritain spoke to Cocteau then about the "old man," of whom Saint Paul wanted to rid us, and the "new" man who would be born, sleek and virgin: nothing was better suited for Cocteau, that eternal candidate for metamorphosis. Cocteau, who had so many times proven the eminently pliable character of his nature, began to hope for an evolution. By dint of doubting everything, he had come, two years earlier, to "doubt his doubt," and to convince himself that someone, inside him, had always been hoping for a revelation.[118] Maritain's active compassion made him regret knowing nothing of that spirit that had carried his own mother to God: "I am heaven's quarry," he wrote, in the midst of his cure, while also noting, still to Max Jacob, that a force inside him also wanted to be occupied by the enemy.[119] A Christian, however, ordinarily wants to welcome only that great Friend that is God.[120]

Far from making Maritain grow cold, the writer's doubts delighted him. Having an intensely poetic perception of his faith, the Thomist revealed to Cocteau that he was living, like any baptized person, under the protection of an angel attached to his fate, and that Cocteau, for his own part, had only to acknowledge that angel fully. After asking many questions, Cocteau discovered that these guardian angels, by condensing air, could form clouds, rainbows, or even an aurora borealis, and that, while they were personally attached to humans, they were also interested in animals, at least in a collective sense: thus there was an angel of swallows, an angel of bees, an angel of elephants, which was true as soon as these species were created by God, in order to provide them with instincts indispensable for their survival. Cocteau could never resist this sort of interpretation of the world—and Maritain was lavish with them; in his youth, Maritain had envisioned a sort of division of labor where the most solid people would take charge of the perpetuation of the species, while the most subtle would spread "over humanity in effusions that were otherwise light and pure."[121] The Maritains displayed at every opportunity that artistic enthusiasm that would have Raïssa say, after the premiere of one of their new friend's plays, "What fills me with wonder . . . is the grandeur that beauty confers on those who are creators like gods."[122] Already convinced, as a child, that it was from heaven that storks secretly deposited newborns in cradles, Cocteau wondered if his sensibility betrayed a profound Christian inflection, and if his roots were in heaven, the way the farmer's are in the earth. He had made the rounds of all available aesthetics, without pausing at any one; what did he risk by trying the heavenly aesthetic, except the possibility of finding himself?

Love had placed Cocteau at the service of a young literary genius, Radiguet, who hadn't loved him as he had hoped. By introducing him to the ecstasy of initiates, opium had changed him into a slave. God might be more merciful, or at least more human, than these alternatives. Maritain took him at his word: Why not make the "crystal factory" in ruins into a temple to the glory of the Lord? And why not place himself under the protection of an angel who, this time, would not usurp his name? Wasn't the Church the sole earthly institution to lay claim to love and to choose the weak, the poor, and the lepers? "It's the mouth of a pistol or the feet of the Cross," Barbey d'Aurevilly had said, faced with the despair that Huysmans conveyed in *À rebours*.[123] Guided by Maritain's velvet grip, Cocteau leaned toward the second solution. The Thomist, whose grandfather had been one of the founders of the Third Republic, and who himself had dreamed of revolution before converting, knew how to lead his flock; arranging the lives of others was the great happiness of one who, while living like a man without roots, passing through life as if a stowaway, had come to regulate his own life in God.

Raïssa Maritain received the new recruit with overwhelming kindness. Born Jewish in the Crimea, the woman who had shared the philosopher's life for twenty years, but who in the meantime had taken a vow of chastity, together with him, opened wide the doors to their house in Meudon. This small, humble, frail woman reminded Léon Bloy (the writer through whose influence Raïssa, her husband, and her sister were all converted in 1906) of a lily of the valley bending under the effect of the sun; but Bloy also knew she was strong enough to split oak trees. In her eyes burned the same never-extinguished flame that burns in the pages of the Bible, said Maurice Sachs; it was she who gave Cocteau food and drink, listened to his words while holding his hands, and soon offered him the treasures of a boundless affection, which was only increased by the ministrations of her sister Vera, who had lived with the married couple for many years. Offering emotional and spiritual support through a kind of osmosis, this trinity wasn't content to offer relics brought back from Lisieux to the poor "widower," but instead overwhelmed him with love and encouragement. Their lives were made whole by communicating delicious certainties with the proselytizing enthusiasm of those who had themselves been saved. "The leader is a man who needs others," Valéry had said; but others soon came to need the Maritains. The burning faith of those wise people in God ended up touching even the most skeptical.

For Cocteau, it was all about the warmth of the isba and the samovar, after a long solitary walk in the snow; the joy of finding oneself among family, back from an endless exile in the cold. With its waxed parquet floor and its mirroring brass saucepans, its ideal cleanliness, and its always warm kitchen, the house in Meudon reminded the recruit of his own family house in Maisons-Laffitte: the same smell of corn-fed chicken, warm bread, and polish; the same wooden chairs and painted plates whose patterns, as a child, he would try to match with his glass. Cocteau had just rediscovered the "green paradise" of childhood loves, as Baudelaire sings, with its garden full of fruit trees. Raïssa and Jacques did indeed remind one of children, flinging crumbs at each other at the table or indulging in little lover's farces, replete with winks, under the complicit gaze of Vera. Truth, from their mouths, seemed to say to that other child, also raised in religion: "I've kept your place. Come back. Your mother is a believer? Join her. You lack love? Follow us, if you want to keep your candor and your innocence." Already the soot-filled soul of Cocteau was beginning to breathe again: even better than the Thermes Urbains, Meudon was the clinic that could purify him.

THE WORD INCARNATE

So shy when he was "officiating" alone, Jacques Maritain acquired next to Raïssa and Vera a surprising magnetism, as if the ardor of his wife and sister-in-law had the power to inflame his gentle, vibrant soul. The American-born novelist Julien Green, listening to him, thought he was in the catacombs, by the side of the first Christians; and "from the way his left shoulder fell a little . . . it was as if he had carried the Cross," wrote Maurice Sachs.[124] Cocteau wondered if Maritain's body might be a kind of clothing thrown haphazardly on that exceptional soul: the Thomist seemed to belong so little to current life, to have so little need to eat! His face looked almost like an imprint, like the one that Christ had left on the Veil of Veronica. Yes, they could be the features of the Crucified that appeared between the lines, under the short blond beard of a philosopher whom God seemed to have made a direct delegate on earth, like his Son before.

Seeing the power of Cocteau's aspiration, Maritain had him read about the lives of the saints, whose ordeals were so similar to those of poets. Cocteau drank in these sublime destinies until they took root in him, and soon began to follow their example. Hadn't he always acted as a "universal brother," spontaneously going toward the other with that "royal kindness" Jean Bourgoint would still marvel at, forty years later? Didn't he see in every wounded man his equal, in every victim a twin, to the point of going to console Marcel Achard, a playwright made bitter by the triumphant revival of Cocteau's so controversial *Antigone*, and confiding to Achard that he preferred the first performance, as if feeling guilty for his own success?[125] Hadn't he always thought it was evil to make others suffer by an excess of happiness? A strange feeling of lightness took over him, when he closed his books about the lives of the saints. He felt washed of his sins, cleared of illness, almost as if his thirst had been quenched. After all, didn't the name of Maritain rhyme with that of the good Samaritan—that helpful man who provided drink in the Gospel according to Saint Luke?

On June 15, 1925, after dining with the collaborators of the *Roseau d'or* and as he was waiting for the car to take him to the premiere of the new choreography of the Ballets Russes, a missionary from the Sahara appeared in the dining room in Meudon. Announced that very day by telegram, the appearance of Father Henrion petrified Cocteau: with the red heart shining on the bosom of his white burnoose, this successor to Father Charles de Foucauld seemed to be holding his head on his chest.[126] The gathered friends, the living room, the library, all vanished; only the hermit's cassock remained, like a white and red shape revolving in the sky, printed with that same heart with which Cocteau followed his signature, at the bottom of all his letters, and had ever since the end of the war.

Already this priest who lived in the Tunisian desert and who had been converted by Paul Claudel was talking about his decisive meeting with Claudel, as well as their pilgrimage to Saint-Maximin. And Cocteau drank in his words, envying his intelligence and kindness, the ease and joy that radiated from his face burned by the African sun. "The impression is considerable," Raïssa confirmed in her journal. "I see Jean Cocteau standing, silent, in the window enclosure, *hooked*. So this is God's very clear answer to our prayers."[127] Maritain himself had his breath taken away: such light filled the writer that he would bless God, forty years later, for having let him experience that moment.[128] The writer and critic Henri Massis, also a witness to the unforgettable appearance of the priest, which he would compare to the divine presence, foretold that it would break Cocteau's heart from within and overwhelm him with love.[129]

Subjugated by the priest's aura, Cocteau in fact saw his world turning upside-down. What did the gossip caused by his books matter, in the face of the sovereign calmness of this crusader? What could possibly be wrong with the conviction of this modern saint, except perhaps his "show-off charm"? When he saw the hermit leave, Cocteau suddenly suspected that his arrival had been "arranged." But Maritain was emphatic: if there was any conspiracy, it was made by the angels; they alone could have pushed the priest toward him, in a great swirl of silence, just as the angels had encouraged that same Charles Henrion to read *Le coq et l'arlequin*, a few months before his own conversion and departure to the desert. Was it his fault that the priest loved literature and had also been devoted to the work of Anna de Noailles?

A force drew Cocteau toward heaven, during the hours that followed. Wasn't that where Radiguet was waiting for him? He literally felt as if his soul were "kneeling," overwhelmed as it had been at the end of *Le sacre du printemps*, but in a way that was at once gentler and more terrible. What if God was the solution? What if He was going to help him rid himself of his painful body, to make him live by and for Him? Maybe even He was already guiding his steps, his thoughts, for hadn't humans always seemed to him to be pulled by invisible wires, like film characters, seemingly autonomous on the screen but actually just shafts of light emerging from the projector?

Convinced that in Cocteau he held the spokesman for young people to be reconquered, Maritain went to the rue d'Anjou the day after next, to encourage

Cocteau to go to confession, quickly, right away. Reverdy, who accompanied Maritain and had himself turned to mysticism two years earlier, questioned the poet he had slapped before *Parade*: "How could you understand anything without the sacraments? Just pick up the earphones! Pick them up!"[130] Uplifted by their enthusiasm, Cocteau promised to come back to speak with Father Henrion, for whom the Maritains had already obtained, without Cocteau knowing it, the authorization to hear confessions at home. The very next day, Maritain, with the implacable determination he used to bring stray sheep onto the straight path, parked on the rue d'Anjou, went up to get the poet, and, without even asking his opinion, brought him to Meudon, where Father Henrion was waiting.

Moved by a desperate need to submit himself, Cocteau fell into step with Father Henrion, a hermit who was indeed reticent but determined to fulfill his Christian duty. Urged on by an irrepressible force, Cocteau confessed at great length, then began to talk about the luminous world and the communion of love he had always hoped for. He described that harmonious, positive circle where everyone would love each other through all, a foretaste of which the Maritains had given him, and that alone could bring him peace. Dazzled by the "astounding" words he was hearing, Father Henrion blessed the writer who delayed leaving because he was also overcome by what he had just uttered. The scene marked the priest so strongly that he would always refuse to talk about what had been said, and would wonder at it still ten years later. Agnostic at the time, Jean Hugo himself expressed his stupefaction when he heard Cocteau discuss his "oracles": "He had reached heights that the contemplative attains only after a long winding path through brambles and thorns."[131] Struck also by the poet's premonitions, Maritain attributed to him the power of projecting his body into others in order to feel them better, like that very pure John—the evangelist—"who guessed the secrets of God out of love." Cocteau had penetrated the heart of Father Henrion.

Not for an instant did the Thomist Maritain doubt that he had found an exceptional "subject," one of those stray chosen ones whom heaven, in its infinite clairvoyance, is sometimes pleased to take back to make into a minister. Cocteau himself, who was already declaring in 1920 "I don't know how to live without a miracle," no longer doubted that a Light, a Spirit, an Idea was behind appearances: the sleeper, in his fog, had just rolled over to awaken in God.[132] All that remained was to make him officially return to the Church.

On June 19, the day of the Feast of the Sacred Heart of Jesus, Cocteau returned under bright sunshine to Meudon and entered the private chapel where Maritain had obtained from Pope Pius XI the special privilege for someone not a priest to administer the holy sacrament. Taking it from the monstrance on the improvised altar, the philosopher placed the body of Christ on the writer's tongue, in the light of the red electric votive lamp indicating the real Presence of God. Henri Ghéon, that pillar of the *Nouvelle revue française* who had just left Gide for God, as well as Louis Massignon the orientalist, took communion in turn, in profound contemplation. Thus began the reverse fall that would make Cocteau "fall into heaven," lifting him irresistibly up to the clouds, with the grace of a bird.

"Joy! Joy! Tears of joy!" Max Jacob exclaimed when he learned of Cocteau's return to God; for ten years Jacob had been praying for Cocteau every day and encouraging him to examine his conscience.[133] The author of *Cornet à dés* had secretly been hoping that Breton's hatred would bring Cocteau to God, but it was Maritain's love that had carried the day. "In Jean there is angel," Jacob wrote to Cocteau in the spring.[134] Cocteau hadn't been detoxified for three weeks before he was already responding to the call of religion, that "opium of the people" in the words of Marx, who saw in it the heart of a world without heart. But hadn't the detachment encouraged by the pipe prepared Cocteau to leave the flying carpet of drugs for the bread of angels?, Jean Hugo noted. Laloy had predicted it, describing the nirvana of opium addicts: "Even outside the smoking room, they remain there in thought; monks without profession or obedience, they move through the world and do not belong to it."[135] Opium addicts, it is said, are easily mistaken for saints.

THE SHOCK

Cocteau refused to speak of a conversion: baptized at birth, he was content to return to the cradle, after a long period of wandering. Poetry had helped him to live; religion would finally permit him to exist. Solicited by the group of the *Roseau d'or*, whose editorial committee—from the Swiss poet Ramuz to Henri Ghéon—awaited only his texts, Cocteau felt truly purified, like a child whose mother introduces him to God during baptism: a reborn Christian. And soon he came to commune in thought with the angel of whom illness had deprived him. Had Radiguet been sent to earth in order to approach him and see if his soul was light enough to make him a privileged interlocutor? Perhaps heaven, in this case, had finally withdrawn from the young man in order the better to fill Cocteau. He had sought for so long to put a name to his strangeness that already he wondered if God had chosen him to reveal to humans His plural nature, His polyphonic genius.

Paul Claudel, overjoyed by Cocteau's "conversion," which had occurred at the same time that Claudel was in Avila staring at the radiant face of Saint

Teresa, sent Cocteau an image of Saint John. Claudel found Cocteau entirely transformed when he saw him again: beneath his "worried, sensitive, fine" expression, a real light was now inhabiting this writer who no longer let a day go by without taking communion.[136] The author of *L'annonce fait à Marie* was not only a contributor to the *Roseau d'or*, but he also pestered Gide and had just precipitated the conversion of Jacques Rivière, another pillar of the *Nouvelle revue française*.[137] Others rejoiced as well. "No more neurosis, a calm, a serenity that does one good," noted Misia Sert, who was usually less charitable toward Cocteau.[138]

Encouraged by the incredible aura of Father Henrion and the joy of having rediscovered his faith, Cocteau thought about joining the disciples of Charles de Foucauld for a while in the desert. It was also rumored around that time that Cocteau was ready to retire to the Abbaye de Solesmes, together with Jacques Copeau, the director of the Théâtre du Vieux-Colombier who had also recently been converted. After years spent with Gide and the *Nouvelle revue française*, Copeau was ready to leave to become a confidant of God; to imitate the white-clothed priests "who consume themselves in the desert and whose love is a pious suicide," imagery that Cocteau would evoke in *Le livre blanc*.

Already those close to Cocteau were worried about this new about-face. Since Maritain had acquired the reputation of being able to "turn around" a soul in just a few minutes, they put Cocteau on guard against the risks of such a hurried move, many fearing that he would find neither equilibrium nor happiness in such a restrictive faith. The Abbé Mugnier himself showed a certain reserve: "Jean, now, is following his heart, for his head has always led him astray," he wrote.[139] But Cocteau was regaining hope, for the first time in two years. An inner force was working to make for him, in place of the cast-off left at the Thermes Urbains, a new skin, white and smooth as the saints'. What did he care if he were being thought imprudent or ridiculous, when God had just snatched him out of the horrible sterility that had been afflicting him since he had left the opium dens?

If people called him the Maritains' puppet, the opposite could also be argued. Won over by his elliptical style and system of imagery, Jacques Maritain was turning more than ever to literature; Raïssa was getting ready to write poems, and the *Roseau d'or*, the publication they had just created at the Éditions Plon, was about to publish and introduce Graham Greene, Georges Bernanos, and Nicolas Berdyaev, not to mention Louis Massignon, Julien Green, and Charles-Ferdinand Ramuz—the cream of the crop of that generation of converts. Convinced that he was fantasizing yet again, some friends pulled away, wearied by his irrepressible tendency to commit errors out of enthusiasm, and always to be fooled by new "myths." But nothing was more sincere than that rediscovery of faith by a man who, lacking a core "self," was looking for a strong, nurturing point of reference. Having doubted God for a long time, every Westerner is more or less confident of his own existence. But Cocteau—more of an Easterner on this point, since he was easily convinced of his unreality— was more inclined than some to believe in divine existence, or at least in the superiority of cosmic forces.

Cocteau's return to religion was immensely beneficial to him. He felt at peace, as he had never felt before. "I need to be limited," Cocteau confessed to Sachs, and faith provided him with a framework. With his bedroom decorated like a cloister, and with Maritain as his special confessor, his scattered nature had never been held in place so well. At night, he was no longer overcome with a desire to get up and flee his room; he was not worried about where to go: his life had finally found meaning, anchored by the "trinity" at Meudon, as well as by his old desire to act like a good boy. He was happy as a beggar who has finally been offered a plot of land. "A farmer of heaven," he wrote to Max Jacob.[140]

Maritain, for his part, was not inactive. Aware of holding a distinguished author in his hand, he began to send to the rue d'Anjou the young talents whom Meudon attracted, hoping to give rise to a modern, Christian literary trend, or at least an anti-materialist one, capable of setting itself up in opposition to the progress of Surrealism—as well as to the oversecular influence of the *Nouvelle revue française*, which was claiming a monopoly on classicism. It was still the imperial Cyprien who introduced these neophytes into the apartment on the fifth floor. They came to present their homages to Mme Cocteau, whom they found sitting in a little salon, feet snug in a muff, knees covered with a plaid blanket. And often they were surprised by the real curiosity of this woman in her seventies, by her universal indulgence and her "piety exempt from bigotry"—every morning she went to Mass. Finally the writer's doors would open, revealing, between his architect's table and his hotel bed "covered in a flowered eiderdown," relics from Cocteau's numerous lives: a portrait of a very Proustian Cocteau signed Jacques-Émile Blanche, another, from the 1920s, by Marie Laurencin; a dreamlike De Chirico; two paper dice painted by Picasso; some crystal balls taken from a palace in Peking; the busts of Radiguet and of Cocteau by Lipchitz; and the photographed faces of Verlaine, Apollinaire, Roland Garros, and the boxer Carpentier.[141] Meant to surprise, the ensemble also served as a test; seeing where the curiosity of the newcomer was directed, Cocteau could guess his nature, when he didn't force a confession from him. "Do you like boys or not?" he asked Jean Aurenche out of the blue, who would become a scriptwriter of "French quality" for the cinema, before adding, seeing his inscrutable face, "Fine, we won't talk about it anymore."[142] Then the visit would resume until the novice, already giddy from being admitted into the holy of holies, received, dazzled, the words of Cocteau.

Encouraged by Maritain to be the artisan of a spiritual and poetic renewal, Cocteau catechized with all his strength these young men, often sad and unhappy, who came to him. He encouraged them, expressing himself through parables and oracles, to open themselves up without fear to Love and spirituality. Familiar with his words and sometimes influenced by him in advance, some would leave weeping in silence, won over by the obvious grace that touched him and the intuition that they had finally arrived at the right harbor. To revive the honor of having received Cocteau's "confession," they in turn began to spread the good word and speak like him, sometimes pushing imitation to the point of idolatry. This was neither encouraged nor forbidden by Cocteau, who was content to give each his due and let him act according to his conscience, like a good prophet: "as a vesture shalt thou change them, and they shall be changed," says Psalm 102 of the Bible.

After Jean Aurenche, it was the poet Roger de Lafforest who rallied to Cocteau's side, then Pierre-Jean Robert, a disciple of Apollinaire and Max Jacob, whom Cocteau was also urging toward men, sexually. Already seminarians from Lyon were ringing at the rue d'Anjou to take that elevator that resembled a confessional to some; or else the callers were young disappointed Surrealists, ready to join that flotilla flying up to heaven. Unhappy at seeing his print run, after twenty years of activity, remain well below that of Morand, Giraudoux, and especially Proust, Cocteau was suddenly enjoying an influence that went beyond simple literature. "The stone he had thrown into the water inscribed infinite circles on the wave," Sachs wrote. "Some rushed to church doors to receive the sacrament, others hurried there to welcome the newcomers."[143] Cocteau exulted: his entourage now was not just about love and purity, creation and fertility; an invisible Church was forming around him, under the sole force of the attraction of his faith, as if he possessed powers in that domain as well. Just as a generation of believers had appeared after the Terror, the Vendée, and the Napoleonic wars, a generation of intellectuals was being touched by faith; the word of God and attention to the "other" seemed like the best way to renew one's ties with "real" poetry. After the slaughter of the war and the shouts of Tzara, a wave of love was unfurling over Paris.

One of the first to be touched by grace, the ex-avant-gardist Pierre Reverdy had just converted in turn the playwright Armand Salacrou; the misanthrope Drieu la Rochelle was planning on becoming religious, after his desires were exhausted; and the pleasure-seeker Morand had returned from the East converted to the immortality of the soul and the supremacy of God. Jean Hugo, meanwhile, had a dream of walking down a street in Meudon talking about God with a man he had never seen before; some time later, noticing Auric talking to that man from his dream, the painter asked him: "To whom were you speaking just now?" The answer—"To Maritain"—helped lead to his own conversion.[144] Excluded from the Surrealist group, and called a sworn enemy of literature and a "vulture," Antonin Artaud, too, a few months later took the path to Meudon. The host had become the special of the day; even the Boeuf sur le Toit was resounding with conversations about God.

THE MESSIAH OF ANJOU

It's an understatement to say that Sachs saw in Cocteau's Christian involvement a betrayal. How could the writer, who represented independence itself, bow down thus before God? And what did he find in these "stubborn, conquering, political, Maurras-ian, women-involved youth" who served as his new squadron?[145] Born abandoned and not taking well to being left aside again by this idol who claimed to treat him as his son, the young orphan began to despair after a year of obsessive passion. Fate, however, had given Sachs an illness similar to that of his hero. Cocteau's religious fervor, which had annoyed him at first, was beginning to disturb him, then to make him almost envious; after hearing Cocteau describe the miraculous arrival of Father Henrion and his own deliverance, Sachs wrote to Cocteau finally in July:

> Until today you have given me my only happiness, but near you everything is horrible, every comparison atrocious. There is nothing, nothing in life . . . Twice at the end of my tether, I kneeled down before your portrait, but I love you too much in life itself to draw from you an appeasement. Come to my aid. There remains faith. You have turned to it. Do not abandon me.[146]

Cocteau was leaving for Villefranche, where he was supposed to write a letter to Jacques Maritain for publication (in order to give the movement its key text), when Sachs asked to meet the Thomist. A meeting was set for August 2, 1925, the day after Cocteau's departure. Sachs recognized immediately in the warmth of the Meudon house the home he had never known, and in the suffering face of Maritain the legendary image of Christ. Taken charge of by the three Maritains, brooded over especially by Raïssa, who was overwhelmed by the confusion of the young de-Judaized Jew, Sachs was evangelized with even more energy than Cocteau. After learning the *Pater* and the *Ave* in just three days, he was sent to an accelerated catechism lesson with Father Pressoir, a close friend of Maritain's. Reading Max Jacob's *La defense de Tartuffe* had relieved Sachs of his final remorse about the faith of his distant ancestors, and every day at dawn he left his room at the Hôtel Vouillemont to attend Mass at the Carmelite church. After one month of this regime, the Maritains decreed it was time for him to renounce "the errors of the Jews." Sachs approved, with the zeal he would put into all his metamorphoses, of this verdict by that converted Jewish woman Raïssa, and that son of a Protestant Jacques, whom already he was calling "Dearest," like his idol.

Baptized on August 29 in Meudon, with Cocteau as his virtual godfather—he was praying for his salvation at the church in Villefranche at the same time—Maurice Sachs was confirmed by the Bishop of Versailles in person on September 13. The thin host of unleavened bread, melting in his mouth, overwhelmed him with an "unparalleled" sweetness, as if he were communing with his hero. Happy to be finally bound to him, Sachs hurried to share with Cocteau the lightning-fast progress of his faith and was convinced that the supernatural force that was filling him would finally manage to make him loved: since he had never been able to make Cocteau forget Radiguet, he would dazzle him by becoming a saint. The "Imitation of Jesus Christ" was well under way—Jean Cocteau had the same initials as the Messiah—and now that Sachs was united with the writer in the great mystical body of the Catholic Church, having become part of his flesh and blood by the grace of the Holy Spirit, he was incorporating himself with Cocteau with the chaste blessing of Maritain.

A flurry of letters to his mentor described the bliss Sachs felt in God, without mentioning the comparison he made between Christ and Cocteau. "How happy I am at your calm and the extraordinary effect of grace on you," Cocteau answered him, relieved to see his votary changing his object of adoration: the boy who oozed anguish had also found his way.[147] But he had an important task at hand. Between dips in the Villefranche harbor, Cocteau began writing his *Lettre à Jacques Maritain*, in a hurry to make public the reasons for his return to God, but also to embellish the story of his new transformation by offering up the image of a solitary man who had always been used to the wild joys of nature and introspection.

He never read the Thomist's philosophical writings, and that was probably for the best, since their dogmatic faith would have turned him cold—that is, if he had understood them. He preferred to concoct for himself a "homemade" Christianity, one able to catalyze the enthusiasm of the young by giving it weapons against Breton, but also capable of dynamiting a much too conservative French Catholicism. The former Dadaist had it in his head that he should renew the Church by opening it up to his century, making it "artistic" and modern, if not sensitive to subjects like drugs. Did he think for an instant, in the euphoria of his return to God, he was creating an ersatz personal faith, as Nietzsche in *Zarathustra* had dreamed of a religion without God? "The modern world is full of old Christian values gone mad," G. K. Chesterton had said; in his Messianic temptation, Cocteau may have been imagining a communion fed by his blood and his word, if not a "coctholique" rite for which Cocteau's body of work would have been the paper cathedral. His dogma, a direct answer to the Surrealists, stemmed from only one sentence: "I want intelligence to be recaptured from the devil and returned to God."[48] In other words, he wanted kindness to be as violent and persuasive as harshness. Cocteau's angelism was so radical that he went so far as to deny the existence of Hell and minimize the permanence of a malice, of which however he had daily proof. His Catholicism could seem impious, by dint of veering toward Platonism, because Cocteau wanted a religion of love, not of hatred and infernos. He was promoting the angelic lineage of a Christ whose holiness was physically engendered—unlike the God of the Jews, who was exclusively abstract.

Already it was no longer a question of writing to write, with this *Lettre à Jacques Maritain*, but of leaving literature to find a new language giving the key to heaven. Similarly, it was no longer a matter of searching the unconscious, that mirror-lined cellar, but of leaving the house, of leaving behind a way of thinking and being based on the sole desire to dazzle and possess, take pleasure or dominate. Thought of as being partially responsible for his own personal tragedy, Nietzsche was rejected for having played at being the Antichrist, and Rimbaud for having given weapons to the Surrealists by declaring, "Now the time of assassins has come." All this was done with as much energy as when Cocteau had attacked Wagner and Stravinsky in *Le coq et l'arlequin*. Thus this magnificent text of the letter, visionary at times, brought full circle the period of programmatic prefaces begun by *Le Potomak*.

Impatient to create an "art for God," Cocteau outlined a play, or rather a mystery, portraying the Virgin's enigmatic pregnancy, which of course was regarded as the fruit of adultery by the inhabitants of Nazareth. Having always found it difficult to believe he himself was the simple fruit of a fertilized egg, Cocteau was convinced that he more than anyone else, especially after the appearance of Father Henrion, could evoke the Annunciation from which Christ was born. Hadn't writing been for him, ever since the revelation of the angel Heurtebise, a meeting of word and body? Yes, it was time he returned to the service of the Word.

Prudent for once, Maritain remarked to Cocteau that God didn't demand quite so much, and above all wasn't seeking to make others talk about Him.

God's sole ambition was to be fully experienced in all languages: wasn't the best service that could be rendered Him actually helping Him to remain hidden, so He could continue to do good, as effectively as the devil harms? And so Cocteau changed his Virgin into Orpheus, a poet inspired by the devil via messages transmitted by a horse's hoof, before the providential arrival of a glazier, capable of remaining suspended in the air, and in a return to his pre-Christian "angels," the Annunciation was borne by Heurtebise. Thus, thanks to his "confessor," Cocteau did not become a Catholic writer. Distancing himself from the emergence of a religious art, Cocteau began to write, as he had always done, short, lacunary books, and to avoid attempting to create huge "masterpieces" that could rival the Creator, much like Persian weavers deliberately leave a defect in their Kilim rugs, since all perfection is reserved for God. Henceforth faith for Cocteau would be only a private affair, a pact of love between God and self, self and mankind.

Deprived of a literary loudspeaker, Cocteau's enthusiasm diminished. His appearances at church had already been less frequent since his departure from Paris; having asked the Abbé Mugnier to serve as his intermediary with God, he preferred to concentrate on the writing of his *Lettre à Jacques Maritain*. But this distancing made his faith more fragile, if we are to believe what he reported to Max Jacob: "I'm suffering from being a bad Christian, and my converts are giving me lessons."[149]

This is because Maurice Sachs had been joined by Jean Bourgoint, Cocteau's other guardian angel. Encouraged by the exuberant faith of Cocteau, as well as by the "winged tobacco" and aura of the Maritains, the dandy-beggar had taken his mystic flight in September of that 1925. Baptized in October in the private chapel in Meudon, with the Maritains as godparents, the cyclothymic had begun his military service on November 1 in a freezing barracks in Metz. "Without the Holy Virgin I would cry all night," he wrote at the time to Cocteau, before Cocteau had him sent to Nîmes, which has a more serene climate. After just a few more months the opium addict retreated to Solesmes so as to "rid himself of the old man" who was in him, as Saint Paul demanded—an experience that was so luminous that he thought at the time of entering the Benedictine order. And every time Cocteau went to the church in Villefranche, on a steep street "bordered with tomatoes and laundry," to pray for the salvation of his "angels." Maritain exulted from Paris, happy at having been able to lead to God Sachs and Bourgoint, those pink sheep he was convinced he had wholly shorn.[150]

Meanwhile, Sachs's fervor had continued to grow. Victim of a constant mirage, the new zealot felt his soul catching fire with each host, as under the effect of a great love. Impressed by the ardor of his faith, probably also secretly jealous at his exaltation, Cocteau announced to his mother, "Grace has made him into a thundering road."[151] Feeling his own faith weakening, he would confess to his young disciple that he knew neither how to love himself nor even how to concentrate his attention on God. The unreliable Sachs then saw himself encouraged to pray for the "poor rag in the sun" who was asking him, in veiled terms, to be the arbitrator for his impossible relationship with himself. "I believe God has placed me on your path so you could help me," Cocteau concluded, definitively reversing the roles—he had first written: "God has placed you on my path"—in order to make the adolescent his master, as in the time of Radiguet.[152] But when he heard Sachs speak about taking holy orders, Cocteau began to worry. Could he let a boy go to the convent who said he suffered cruelly from his absence and constantly demanded his return at this crucial moment in his life, all while apologizing for these "selfish" demands? Indeed, Sachs was an "exceptional" soul, as Cocteau had confided to his mother. But what if the novice were also seeking to escape his creditors, or to hide away an overexcited body whose blood was carrying sperm, as he himself would say?[153]

Already the Maritains were pushing this recruit to the monastery, and already Cocteau was fearing that they might be sending the devil there. Sachs's weak willpower had always urged him to say nothing but yes to everything; Cocteau was even beginning to think the strange "crisis of calm" that was striking his page was disturbing. His warnings about the shortcomings of the "clerical world," however, only reinforced Sachs's determination to raise an insurmountable barrier between "temptations" and himself. As for the protests of his family members, the young zealot thought they were self-interested: they all came from free-thinkers, Jews, and Protestants. Cocteau's final remonstrance arrived too late: freed from all anguish by the decision of the "trinity" to wipe away his debts, Sachs had left the Hôtel Vouillemont to go live at the home of the Maritains. Softened by the paternal authority of Jacques, dazzled by the sacred faith of Raïssa—one of "those Jews in whom the mystic flame rose and whose soul was vertical from Earth to Heaven"—Sachs prepared for his entrance into the Carmelite seminary on the rue de Vaugirard, near the Luxembourg gardens. He spent his days converting his entourage, from Jean Salomon, a Jewish friend of Aurenche, to the most unlikely writers—just as Cocteau had been doing three months earlier.

A single thought held the young man back from making the final step: that of losing his mentor forever or discovering how indispensable Cocteau was to him. Refusing to say goodbye forever to that former cult, "Biquette" went back over all the letters he and Cocteau had exchanged during Cocteau's detox cure. But the resurrection of this recent past threw him into another state; he laughed and cried warm tears, was moved and exalted, as if he couldn't entirely yet believe that he had been able to attract the attention of the great Jean Cocteau. And again he asked his idol for a signed photograph, and then that he sign all his books to him—including *Le bal du comte d'Orgel*. But Cocteau's return to Paris confirmed to the young Sachs his inability to make Cocteau forget Radiguet, the "atrocious anniversary" of whose death Cocteau was obsessively dreading.[154] By reopening the wound of nonreciprocity, this indifference reinforced Sachs's religious determination. "I've been eating at your heart for two years," he wrote, with a frightening frankness, determined this time to punish Cocteau, his failure in love, with his departure for the seminary.[155] The two men would still dine together at the Maritains' for Christmas, then would attend midnight Mass in the company of Jean Bourgoint; but finally, on January 2, 1926, Sachs presented himself at dawn at the Carmelites', his little suitcases in hand, and moved into a cell on the third floor where he was granted the exceptional favor—thanks to the intervention of Maritain—of being allowed to wear the cassock immediately upon entering the seminary (regulations stipulated that a novice had to wait four years before doing so), and to include in his cell the complete works of Cocteau, as well as his signed portrait.

Maritain could be content: the conversions he caused were the opposite of flashes in the pan. Cocteau himself—Cocteau above all—returned to Villefranche perked up, after having taken advantage of his brief stay in the capital to go to confession to the Abbé Mugnier. He had also met in Meudon the Abbé Lamy, the priest of the rag dealers and vegetable sellers from La Courneuve, a prefiguration of the Abbé Pierre who has acquired, even in Paris, the reputation of a saint, prophet, and thaumaturge. And the Abbé Lamy, between the fruit and dessert, had very naturally told Cocteau how, as he was saying Mass twenty years earlier, he had seen appear, crowned with a circlet of lilies and daisies, floating in a royal blue dress from which her bare feet emerged white and fragile as chalk, the Virgin, whose silhouette had provoked "a swirl of silver flakes as high as several buildings" as she brushed against the altar.

This first meeting had so impressed Cocteau that he had asked the Abbé Lamy to tell him how, when Lamy was doubting his calling, Mary had shown herself a second time over the path he was climbing, to curtsy to him mockingly and say, "And I! You always keep me busy" before "royally" making fun of him, of his red cheeks and his slightly coarse humility.[156] Again on September 9, 1909, the Queen of Heaven had shown herself to him in the Guyotte forest, near Violot, in the Haute-Marne. This time the priest had found her very brown of skin, of rather average size, with eyes going from periwinkle blue to brown and with hair just as changeable, intermingled with the oak branches dominating the plateau of Langres, itself dominated by "Our Lord." Suddenly the devil had fallen onto her, showing all his claws, to reproach her for the harm she had been causing him "since the dawn of time"; whereupon the Virgin had replied in a gentle voice, not without reason or humor, "I hadn't been born."[157] The vivacity of this retort had subjugated the Abbé, who had bought the former hunting lodge where she had shown herself before making it a pilgrimage site, renamed Notre-Dame-des-Bois.

These stories of apparitions of the good Mother crowned in gold, by satisfying Cocteau's sense of the marvelous, restored his faith. He had always sought to enter into contact with the beyond; now he began singing the praises of the Catholic, miraculous fairy—at the same time as Breton was enthusing over the appearances of the fairy Melusina. He was convinced he could soon, thanks to the cohort of angels surrounding the Virgin, cross through solids thick as his hand and enjoy the marvels of the wonderful Christian. "Through you I touch heavenly things and thanks to you I find support here below," Cocteau would say to Maritain. The tightrope walker had finally found a platform between heaven and earth. Who knows if, from there, he might not resume contact with Radiguet and serve in turn as his glove?

13

La Croix et la Bannière

"Ange asked that there be no violence. With skill you can do so much harm."
— *Louis Aragon*, Anicet ou le Panorama

GOD'S JESTER

Through his conversion, Cocteau drew even closer to Max Jacob, his elder by thirteen years, whose taunts, pranks, and way of justifying himself to God, after a long night of cruising, had initially made the younger man mistrustful. He soon recognized, however, that Jacob was a man with very little self-esteem who was trying very hard to cover that up. Born to Jewish parents in Quimper in 1876, Jacob had been drawn early on to the avant-garde, and followed them to Montmartre, where they gathered at that time. One night in 1909, Jacob saw the shining head of Christ appear on his bedroom wall. The vision was so impressive that he soon thereafter dedicated his life to God and had himself baptized under the name Cyprien, with Picasso serving as godfather. This scandalously swift conversion followed him wherever he went: some suspected that he had done it for the publicity, or as some kind of avant-garde performance. But despite all the opium and ether he was taking, the wild illumination that had showed him the face of God did not reveal itself again. Torn between his desire for purity and his sexual obsessions, and exhausted by twenty years of literary perfidy in Paris, in 1921 he finally retired to the countryside in Saint-Benoît-sur-Loire, in the shadow of a church where he would become a guilt-ridden pillar of the parish.

Although nearly unknown today, Jacob's work at the time inspired some fascination. He was "God's Juggler," half-pervert, half-anchorite, a tightrope-walker of the Word, a dervish. Michel Leiris would remember his unequaled verbal inventiveness and his mastery of the pun, demonstrating a gratefulness for it that approached plagiarism.[1] Jacob could have been branded a Surrealist avant la lettre (something Breton would never forgive, even after a period of idolizing him) but also a proto-Cocteau (which would have given the Surrealists, given as they were at the time to hunting "penitents in pink undershirts," another reason to persecute him). The forgotten helpmate of so many well-known artists, the poet they had been saying for half a century was due for a comeback, Jacob was in truth a better critic than Cocteau: because he read books through to the end, he less easily saw "angels" everywhere. Prodigiously eclectic, his taste was sure. After having precipitated the invention of Cubism by relentlessly critiquing Picasso's work ("still too Symbolist"), he also spotted, with a rare confidence, the talent of Blaise Cendrars and Marcel Jouhandeau, as well as Jean Dubuffet and Henri Michaux—not to mention Pascal Pia, with whom he corresponded as early as 1922.

The younger ones would continue to visit him, as a way of signaling to the world that they were embarking on a life in literature or painting. He would welcome them with an avid eye encircled by a monocle beneath the ivory dome of his forehead, and he would say to the newcomers, with varying degrees of success, "Poets embrace one another." With a nearly clairvoyant judgment he would sniff out the talented ones, and send them on to Cocteau. This process confirmed the men's role as a sort of two-headed godfather to young literary men—although, since Radiguet, Jacob tended to be more prudent. From Michel Leiris to Jean Dubuffet, Jacob baptized dozens of young men, regretting that he was unable to keep them all in his bed, and went immediately to confession when he could.

Since Radiguet's death, Max Jacob had continued to support Cocteau. If a new article accused Cocteau of plagiarism, Jacob was there to reassure him. "You are Cocteau. No one else has been or ever will be," wrote that "gardener in clogs" whose spirit, to hear him say it, made flowers grow everywhere.[2] Daily letters during Cocteau's detoxification, lyric missives to each of his publications: of all Cocteau's correspondents, only Jacob could respond to his compulsive need for approval. Jacob could also write up to thirty letters a day, even if he probably preferred Reverdy's poetry. Jacob was henceforth the poet and friend Cocteau loved the most. To him alone did Cocteau confess everything, or almost everything, from the abject void that his books left behind, to the feelings of plenitude that friendship brought; as well as the fear that Breton's hatred inspired in him, and the love he still felt for his mother. Their obsessive need to be loved led them to compete in sycophancy; they were both so poetically rich that Cocteau, who supported Jacob's work unconditionally, felt like "Rothschild faced with a Vanderbilt."[3] In turn, when he endured renewed attacks from the Surrealists, Jacob told him: "You alone have all the qualities . . . You dazzle everyone and force them to move aside . . . You are pope, king, emperor by birth."[4]

After having published Jacob in *Littérature*, André Breton now rated him lower than dirt, leading both Cocteau and Jacob to complain and launch jeremiads against those whom Cocteau called the "sub-realists." And if Cocteau came over in tears over a particularly vile article, Jacob would write to Jouhandeau, "He is part of history; one cannot speak of 1910–1925 without mentioning his name."[5] Endowed with the same wistful gaiety—Cocteau would speak of Jacob's Jewish melancholy—and the same tendency to exaggerate, they outdid each other in suspect humility, sincere masochism, and adolescent megalomania, as well as in cruel and lucid irony, sharp intelligence, and prescience. "I love you for loving me," Jacob told him one day.[6] Cocteau might well have said the same thing. Convinced that Cocteau instinctively possessed those "admirable Christian values" that some believers spend a lifetime trying to acquire, Jacob was already thinking of the good his friend would do for France, bringing its intellectuals to the Church with Maritain's help.[7] In his isolation, he also wanted to believe that the moment had come to unleash one of those storms of love that Christ's disciples dream will bear everything away with it. Seeing himself finally supported by a group, a journal, a publishing house, and aware of the opportunities this afforded, if not to him, at least to God, in May 1926 Cocteau hurried into print his *Lettre à Jacques Maritain*, which would be followed by a more tempered response from the philosopher. Love, for once, would conquer all.

A WAVE OF HATRED

To Cocteau's great surprise, the Christian community had a divided response to the *Lettre*. Léon Daudet congratulated himself on having encouraged this younger generation, which he perceived as already following the Thomist model in being reactionary and somewhat violent. Or at least so he hoped, in order to provoke a civil war, under the double aegis of Maritain and Maurras. An old intellectual understanding united Maritain, who dreamed of wiping out modernity and returning to the virtues of medieval ways, with Maurras, the director of Action Française, which after being condemned by the Pope in the winter of 1926 was about to be disbanded. Otherwise, the general response to this sudden return to God was confusion and embarrassment. Mauriac spoke of "divine imprudence" among his self-interested words of praise, while Reverdy emphasized the letter's overly literary quality. In spite of its sincerity, Julien Green judged its tone "unacceptable."

The agnostics were even less united in their response. Morand decreed it heartless, and accused Cocteau of being like the Surrealists and their dreams, trying to break into faith by force. "Religion is doomed, once men of letters move in," Valéry commented with irony, while Picabia suggested mischievously, "In trying to uncover God, they're going to make him catch his death." (The painter's metaphysics in seven words: "God helps us and makes shit grow."[8]) Guessing Cocteau's need to perennially keep the public informed of every development in his thought, the press made jokes about the fear of anonymity for a writer who, while a good tactician on occasion, remained a terrible strategist. "You don't tell the world when you're going to confess," one journalist noted, while another wrote, "you can't get to heaven with an ox on a roof."[9] Compared with his entry into the Dada group, and even his appeal to the Fratellini family during the war, Cocteau's return to Christ was perceived as having been somewhat indiscreet. It is true that sometime before his detoxification cure he had published a collection of self-portraits entitled *Le mystère de Jean l'Oiseleur*, whose title retrospectively associates him with those inspired beings who can speak to birds, in the image of Saint Francis of Assisi. And he was suspected of wanting to graft his own figurines—eroticized angels and androgynous trapeze artists—into a Christian pantheon that was already rich in seraphs, Christmas mangers, and other quasi-pagan figures, but was less open to intruders bearing an odor of heresy.

Anna de Noailles, too, who was capable of asking the Abbé Mugnier to visit her "without his last rites kit," was somewhat hostile to Cocteau's letter. She had been dubious earlier, when Cocteau confessed to her, "I was unhappy, but now I am content."[10] This time, she bitterly reproached him for his about-face as a "poet with frayed nerves, frayed senses, frayed life," and chased him out the door in his nightshirt, declaring, "If God existed I would be the first to know!"[11] Cocteau replied by reproaching her for being her own god unto herself—and ought to have been well aware she could have made the same reproach of him. But he could not face up to the mockery and attacks that came at him from all quarters. Even the enthusiastic letters he received from members of the church in his home on rue d'Anjou could not calm his mother's fears. Was it normal that in loving God, he had succeeded in making himself the object of man's hatred? "Gaffe to gaffe towards glory," he would say, at their Saturday dinners.[12] He confessed to Maritain the doubts that sometimes assailed him and his desire to revitalize himself at Lisieux, and to pray for guidance from Thérèse, his favorite saint.

A strong anticlericalism had always bound the Surrealists. As a student, Pierre de Massot had once amused himself on a suburban train in Lyon by brandishing the ink-blot Picabia signed "The Virgin Mary." Thrilled by the mixed response to the *Lettre à Maritain,* the group let loose against Cocteau's double "disgrace": the clerical black skullcap on top, the pink knickers below. Breton no longer even needed to react (he who could not so much as see a priest in the metro without pressing up against him and shouting "Have you finished fondling me yet? Bastard! Dirty pig!")—instead his lieutenants anticipated his saintly anger.[13] "Conversions are very much in fashion," wrote Ribemont-Dessaignes in *The Surrealist Revolution.* "The saintly bosom spreads itself like a vulva in heat [to receive] . . . the perfumed semen of worldly excess . . . Two days in heavenly baths? Not at all. It's a question of eternity . . . For centuries upon centuries they will consult the registers where the names are inscribed and the display cases where the concierges hang the skin and the grandest organ of the new tenant."[14] This imagery was meant to equate Cocteau's old skin with an obscene costume, and the baptismal water with those bathing establishments where he was said to offer himself to the first person to come along—following Max Jacob's example, "entering by the devil's backside and leaving through the mouth of God." For Breton, this was the very definition of infamy.

The rivalry, however, was mutual. The Surrealists, too, sought a way to access the deepest mysteries. Forbidding his followers to "dirty" themselves by writing for the theater or the newspapers, the High Priest Breton expected them to consecrate themselves to rebuilding the secret links between man and the occult powers ordering the universe. Surrealism wasn't only an aesthetic revolution or an ideological laboratory; in the Surrealists' desire to bring back the study of alchemy, they cast an envious eye toward the knowledge of the great initiates, from Boehme to Paracelsus. Desnos would go so far as to write in *Intentions* that Breton, through his moral preoccupations, was trying to restore meaning to the word "religion."[15] Walter Benjamin, too, was the first to note the at-once outdated and religious aspects of a doctrine that saw passion as a "profane illumination" and that would lead Breton to become impassioned by the "courtly love" of the reign of Louis VII when he first met Nadja.[16] Ten years later, Trotsky would still be reproaching Breton in their Mexican correspondence for keeping "a little window open to the great beyond."[17] In calling God a "pig," was he not giving in to the perjury of the crypto-believers? And was he not then also buying into the monopoly of good and evil? If he did not tolerate God—"the name alone could send him into spasms of anger," noted Ribemont-Dessaignes—it was because God was a serious rival.

When several faithful young Surrealists one by one defected to join up with
Cocteau (for example, Paul Sabon, whom Father Henrion had also impressed, or
André Grange, who converted in three weeks and died suddenly in January 1926),
total warfare broke out. "Jean Cocteau: an angel's turd. Max Jacob: Jesus' heart.
Raymond Radiguet: the shovel for angel's turds," Benjamin Péret had written
three years earlier.[18] Paul Éluard went a step further, writing, in a tone reminiscent of the Terror and the Church, "And then, without blushing, for we will one
day cut him down like a stinking beast, let us pronounce the name 'Jean Cocteau,'
a slab of meat who would be advised once again to go back to the 'bathhouse.'"[19]
Quite a subtle sales pitch, with its battery of allusions to "jesus"—a nickname
given at the time to queers—and one that the fascist writers Laubreaux and
Rebatet would adopt each in turn, under the German Occupation, with Rebatet
denouncing in *Les décombres* (1942) those "wankers who mistake baptismal fonts
for toilets, [and those] pederasts who look for God in little boys' assholes."[20]
Cocteau was henceforth the most detested man in Paris, even in Maritain's own
eyes. Aware of the philosopher's ideological leanings (he judged the revolution of
1917 to be "essentially Satanic"), Cocteau wanted to clear his own name in
affirming in his *Lettre*, on the subject of the Russian Revolution, "I absolutely
refuse to critique a people who shed their skin in such a manner." But the argument remained too personal to be convincing.[21] Especially in the eyes of Breton—
who after long disdaining political engagement (he pictured himself off in an
imaginary castle, hunting on the grounds with twenty-two of his closest friends, in
his first *Surrealist Manifesto*), and after denouncing, with Aragon, "Moscow the
senile old woman," totally reversed his position and began to call for the opening
of prisons and the dissolution of the army.

Tempers continued to rise when Cocteau had the paradoxical bad luck to
have his literary virtues extolled by Henri Barbusse, a conventional writer allied
with the French Communist Party, which Breton hoped to join. Cocteau had
recently published *Le rappel à l'ordre*, which brought together a number of
already published titles (*Le coq et l'arlequin*, *Carte blanche*, *Le secret professionel*) in which politics played a very small role but which was also unhappily
dedicated to Georges Auric, a friend of Breton's. Thanks to Breton, who
described Cocteau as the author of "vile patriotic poetry, of nauseating professions of Catholic faith," he would henceforth be known as an "arrant counter-
revolutionary."[22] Blending Maritain's Thomism with the reactionary doctrine of
Action Française, Leiris would go so far as to declare as "of a purely fascist
essence" the order Cocteau wished for, even though Cocteau saw it being "as
opposed to an outdated order as to disorder."[23] Breton not only wanted to rein-
vest existence with passion; he wanted to remake society itself, out of the ruins

of the old world, and against the indifference of someone like Cocteau, for whom belief in progress was nothing but "biological vaudeville."[24] The whims of nature would always win out, in Cocteau's view, over man's will.

Cocteau rounded up the troops and launched his squadron against Surrealist headquarters. While Breton was attracting young defrocked Catholics, Cocteau was gathering young Surrealists who hoped to return to written poetry. A war, fought by supporters, raged between the two self-appointed prophets of the modern movement, with the public taking sides: their two names could be found graffitied on the walls of Paris: "Vive Cocteau!" "Down with Breton!" Cocteau however lacked Breton's strategic instincts and regulatory authority. Too muddled to set himself up as headmaster, too subject to mood swings and reversals to impose a coherent program, he was reduced to claiming exclusive bonds with each of his followers—"I totally depend on my belief in you," he would write to them—while Breton demanded allegiance.

The strongest of Cocteau's followers drifted away. Sickened at seeing 1925 popularize the discoveries of 1913 and 1917, Morand left to travel the world; Jean Hugo took refuge in his estate in the Camargues; Les Six were divided among as many projects of their own; Radiguet was dead; and Sachs still hadn't spoken up. But on the other side, Breton's hauteur and closed-mindedness drew ever more brilliant recruits, like Leiris or Ponge. Breton, who held up his head as if in challenge, in Man Ray's view, not only reserved his humanity for the narrow circle who lived off his authority and charm, but also had strong organizational abilities, a rare quality in the Republic of Letters, which made him capable of renting a space or calling a meeting. How could Cocteau have possibly bested him? Already weakened by his neurotic kindness, Cocteau, "a giant, super-fluous appendage in the modern world," as Alejo Carpentier determined upon first meeting him, could no longer even hide his sensitivity.[25]

Moreover, Cocteau began to accept as true the hatred he had inspired, with a fatalism encouraged by the opium he was taking. "Each of us is created in the mold of his own sadness," remarked Frédéric Lefèvre in *Les nouvelles littéraires*, a journal that supported Cocteau and whose offices would be sacked in May 1926 by Breton and Aragon.[26] Christianity was only going to encourage Cocteau's submission to this pseudo-necessity. "I do not blame them, I pray for them," he told Max Jacob, who was himself convinced of the reversibility of suffering, a Christian principle by which the pain of the innocent would hopefully reduce the faults of the guilty in the eyes of God.[27] As if Cocteau had chosen the Surrealists to practice seeking forgiveness and to establish his literary sanctification.

This time Breton sent Cocteau personal letters full of insults, some to demand he stop writing; others to insult his sexuality. The letters "were the entrance to a revolting cesspit of sacrilege, pornography, etc, unleashing all its hatred on me," he wrote. His mind empty, his limbs broken, his body shattered, Cocteau wondered if his enemies were trying to cast a spell on him by these letters with their attached photographs. "I'm beginning to believe," he told his mother in February 1926, "that the strange hatred of the Surrealists isn't content with being simply hatred and that it is beginning to blend with magic, and enchantment. It is since their appearance (dada) that my life began to be unlivable. Only prayer can save me. Pray. Pray. Let us pray."[28]

Convinced that these letters belonged to some magical system, with secret codes and alchemical signatures, Cocteau burned this "disgusting" bundle and advised Jacob to do the same.[29] The group—"the bad gang," he called them— clearly sought to put a curse on the two men; after all, had not Breton written in *Les vases communicants* of his desire to influence other people's dreams in order to "act at a distance, gravely, upon his life"? This hypothesis would be confirmed in its way by a seminarian named the Abbé Gegenbach, who had been drawn to the Surrealists during a suicidal period, then encouraged by them to wear his cassock with a woman upon his knees. The Abbé Gegenbach would confess, when Cocteau's *Lettre à Maritain* was published, his wish to see the Surrealists exorcised.[30] Max Jacob, who also believed in magic—like Apollinaire before him—went further: the Surrealists were possessed! As apologists for cursed poetry and gothic romanticism, they had become practitioners of the occult sciences and black magic. Impatient to uncover the magic powers that, in Athens as in African societies, also belonged to poets—Rimbaud believed himself to be a magus—they had reclaimed Satan, the black god.[31]

Curiously, Breton lived with the same obsessive fear, but about Cocteau and Jacob. Unable to explain the departure of his recruits, he was convinced that Cocteau had somehow enchanted several of them, like Paul Sabon, who had converted to Catholicism under Cocteau's influence, and who was summoned to the Cyrano to be tried, then eventually excommunicated.[32] Did Cocteau have powers equal to those "great invisibles" that Breton believed were responsible for cyclones?[33] A suspicion of satanism would henceforth drive a quarrel already heavy with irrational, emotional, if not outright sexual, undercurrents. The writer and painter Alberto Savinio, the brother of Giorgio di Chirico, revealed to Cocteau that Breton had had someone buy one of Cocteau's works, when they were shown at the Galerie des Quatre-Chemins, in order to stab it with diabolical hairpins like voodoo priests with their dolls.[34] Savinio's wife recalls the Surrealists bursting into the gallery and making off with a canvas that would show up the next day at Breton's home. For once Cocteau was the victim, and not the thief.[35]

Things would get even more scrambled. A magazine published a fake interview in which Max Jacob questioned the veracity of Cocteau's conversion. Soon the rumor-mill had Cocteau saying all sorts of terrible things about Jacob. Some letters of dubious validity appeared on their desks, stirring things up between them, turning them against each other, reminding Jacob of all the poetic "borrowings" that Cocteau had taken from him. Finally it was rumored that Picasso had confessed to Jacob his loathing for Cocteau. How to tell truth from invention? Jacob was a hard man to pin down. His generosity was often tainted with perversity; he was excessively trusting yet paranoid; he needed to wound and also to be forgiven, and then he would lavish praise.

Cocteau had very few friends during this time. He was misunderstood, if not rejected outright, like many poets before him. It was a cliché that the modernist movement sought to do away with, but all the same, clichés do contain a grain of truth. He was inspired, solitary, and superior, therefore damned. "Since we cannot harden ourselves, let us become transparent, which is to say, invulnerable because invisible," he said three years later to Max Jacob.[36] He would emphasize this policy of confession, like Madame de Maintenon declaring "The most honorable behavior is the most skilled." Rather than hiding his contradictions, he showed them off, to the point of making himself incomprehensible, unknowable, and therefore invisible. All budding writers attempt to camouflage their potential goodness; Cocteau advertised his. Nietzsche placed the insatiable need for recognition at the very heart of the desire to create, but Cocteau preferred, on the contrary, to dissemble. Someone like Picabia would cynically, joyfully show off his desire to be famous; Cocteau preferred to speak, with a hypocrisy that was in part a legacy of his education, of the heart and of poetry—both of which were important to him, but were also not incompatible with the desire for fame.

A man is what he does and not what he hides, said Malraux. In his determination to cover his tracks, Cocteau would sometimes feign having no secrets at all. Incapable of making himself anti-social, difficult, severe, or intimidating, he preferred to attack from all sides, despite the catastrophic consequences this urge might have, and would confess so many truths that they would come to seem like as many deceptions. Lacking a clean, thorough, photographic sort of memory, he instead saw the world through the blurry lens of childhood and gave accounts of himself that were more or less in line with his whims, and showed his personality off to best advantage. He invented fictionalized versions of himself, which while not without their grains of truth, were adapted to the circumstances in order to mask whatever might prove displeasing in the original, and then he believed in his own fictions. Once these false selves became as unpopular as the preceding ones, they were pushed out to make room for others. "The more I am mocked, the more I want this faded self to be mocked," he said lucidly, and soon he was no longer sure who he was. Thus he tried always to find, in the other's gaze, a sign that he was not absolutely hated. He did everything he could to be loved as he used to be, in his twenties—even writing impassioned dedications to unknown people.[37]

THE END OF SATIE

The wave of conversions washing over the Great Prostitute that was Paris, in the eyes of certain believers, had an unexpected victim. Eaten away by cirrhosis after a lifetime of brandy abuse, in hospital with nothing but a horsehair brush and a pumice stone, Satie finally accepted a visit from Jacques Maritain—to everyone's surprise, since Satie could not hold back his tears at the death of Lenin, one year before.[38] Did the musician who had enrolled himself in his local Arceuil branch of the French Communist Party want to hear another version of the story or prepare for the future? Maritain wouldn't have an easy time of it with the unpredictable Satie, who, seeing him looking around his sickroom in vain, would shout at him: "What's the use of being a Catholic writer if you can't find a goddamn pot of jam?"[39] Nevertheless Satie agreed to receive a visit from the same Abbé Lamy to whom the Virgin Mary had appeared, in the Haute-Marne, and then the Abbé Saint. "I am happy to finally see a saint with my own eyes," he said, before dying in July 1925 having received unction and with Maritain praying by his side.

That Cocteau should shed tears for a composer was too much. "I nearly felt joyful at this death which was such a relief to him," he wrote to Max Jacob, "but at the Eglise d'Arceuil my sadness and weariness were without limit."[40] Satie had irrevocably fallen out with him, but Cocteau had never ceased to admire him for his unpredictable laughter and his childlike universe. The problems between them had in truth begun five years earlier. Weary of Cocteau's stiflingly protective reign, Satie began to find the writer's insistence on forever lauding Satie's genius a bit condescending. Cocteau would compare him to the Douanier Rousseau, who was a bit too naive for Satie's taste—he hated being called "nice" as much as he hated being called "crazy." Then he had become very angry when Cocteau announced that not only was he going to adapt into a light opera the little book that he and Radiguet had adapted from *Paul et Virginie*, which was true, but he was also going to give up music in order to devote himself "to the cause of the young composers," that is, Les Six. Satie, who was not as altruistic as all that, resented this move and vented his anger by setting to music a poem by Radiguet called "Adieu," in which an old admiral goes off, shaking a handkerchief in farewell, to tilt at the windmills of the past. Satie's second revenge would be more measured: although he mentioned the light opera with great enthusiasm each time he saw Cocteau, he composed just a sailor's chorus from the first act (a piece that was only found and published in 1997).[41]

Anytime Satie (who loved a farce or a cruel trap) was angered — and a simple tear in his umbrella could set him off — Cocteau forgave him, murmuring "He's a child!" Satie, too, would continue to visit Cocteau on the rue d'Anjou and borrow his nail scissors to trim his beard, while Cocteau shaved his own. Satie may have feared becoming Cocteau's official musician, if not his property, but he did hope that Cocteau would help promote his "furniture music" — melodies to play in restaurants, department stores, and markets as a way of stimulating conversations, appetites, and purchases, and which the composer dreamed of seeing declared a public utility, like municipal street lighting or central heating. Satie was as capable of paternalism as Cocteau in this case, even if his own style was more ironic: "Take care of this, will you, old boy?" he would order, concluding with the royal command: "Kiss my hand." But no doubt Cocteau was not a strong enough supporter of this zany forerunner of Muzak, which would definitively eliminate the presence of serious music in everyday life, for Satie again found revenge by declaring of Cocteau that "He's getting a bit of a paunch — morally speaking."[42]

In truth, Satie had never forgiven Cocteau for the opium-fueled friendship that had developed between him and Louis Laloy, the critic who had reproached *Parade* for "protesting against the sublime," and whom Satie considered a personal enemy. Although Laloy had even published an enthusiastic article when the ballet was restaged in 1920, Satie still declared himself betrayed in learning that Auric and Poulenc — already guilty of the offense of paying homage to Ravel — were spending time with Laloy in Monte Carlo. "Sexual blending, vomitous and insexual," he wrote when the "criminals" returned, before interrupting one of Cocteau's interminable monologues on music by thundering "imbecile!" with the expression of a man ready to throw a plate in someone's face.[43] From Satie's cosseted son and overprivileged propagandist, Cocteau had now become his public enemy number one. His epistolary efforts only aggravated Satie's violent desire for independence. "Cocteau adores me," he noted in July 1924, in the eighteenth issue of Picabia's journal *391*, "I know it only too well . . . But why then does he kick me under the table?"[44] Like Debussy before him, after thirty years of militant support and active complicity, Cocteau had been excommunicated by the former *Parcier* of the "Église métropolitaine d'art de Jésus conducteur," that ironic congregation of which Satie had been at once the Grand Inquisitor and the only believer.[45] The writer's disgrace was complete. Cocteau, who had risked prison for Satie during the *Parade* trial, became a "coward," a "bastard," the *"squelette omelette* of the rue d'Anjou."[46] The mere mention of Cocteau's name was enough to send toads flying from Satie's mouth. Overwhelmed with letters that "didn't exactly smell of roses," which he burned straight away, Cocteau could only keep his head down in the face of the fury of a composer capable of turning anything into a reason to argue; Cocteau could only distance himself from the man whose tornado of anger, flaring from "some obscure place inside of him," made the veins stand out on his forehead and a whirlwind of papers fly up around him.[47]

When Satie's funeral was over, his heirs broke into his apartment in Arceuil-Cachan, where no one had set foot in thirty years, apart from Satie himself. Inside, they found a hundred umbrellas waiting for them, undisturbed in their shop-wrappings, as well as dozens of dickey collars arranged in an immense spider's web, several identical mite-ridden velvet suits, two pianos with shackled pedals sleeping under a mattress of dust, and hundreds of letters of which many had never been opened. Not to mention jars full of dried-out bits of snot that Satie had conserved with the fastidiousness of the Locked-up Lady of Poitiers, who, according to André Gide, kept her feces in jars. Satie, who claimed to awaken each morning at 7:18 a.m., to give himself over to inspiration from 10:23 to 11:47 and then from 3:12 to 4:07, who ate for dinner only white food accompanied by fortified red wine from 7:16 to 7:20, had taken all his secrets with him to the grave.

"This man was a saint," wrote Cocteau. "Even we did not understand him, but his whims always had a noble foundation."[48] In this comment, Cocteau offered one last protective gesture for his difficult friend, whose music he had done so much to promote, but to whom God could not be given without confession.

FROM INK TO BLOOD

The news coming from the rue de Vaugirard was good: not only had little Sachs's behavior been irreproachable for two months, but, inspired by faith, he had come to discipline his days and indulge in grandiose thoughts worthy of any young missionary: "I dreamed of nothing less than converting the world and persuading Cocteau to enter a monastery," he said, victim to the strange process that led all of Cocteau's protégés to want to become his protectors.[49] This insistent desire to radically save him from evil filled Cocteau with joy, who was still at Villefranche in early 1926. But his faith was still hesitant, far from Maritain:

it had difficulty finding terrain in which to take root, rites that could give it shape. And although Cocteau was studious and solitary, this time that he had devoted to writing *Oedipus Rex*, which Stravinsky had commissioned, was far from being marked by assiduous religious practice: instead, Cocteau, who spent some of this time out at sea on his little boat (the *Heurtebise*), was left with a sense of unease.

Max Jacob had his own ideas about this straying. He knew from experience that Cocteau, in spite of the poetic élan that had inspired him to turn toward God, could be a truly religious person only if he renounced his homosexuality. He himself, out of fear of hellfire, had fought this impulse for years, without success, in part by trying to convert the young men he desired. "Pure one moment, full of appetites another," as Sachs put it, "more divided than anyone else and yet so simple in each of his incarnations," Jacob could try fleeing his contradictions in a sort of permanent self-parody, but inwardly he doubted, like Cocteau, his ability to satisfy divine expectations.[50] Maritain had never openly mentioned to Cocteau what were then still referred to as his "mores"; as long as he remained chaste, these did not bother Maritain. Likewise, Cocteau was able to slip some praise for Laloy's religious spirit into his *Lettre à Maritain*, after a defense of the correct use of opium, in which he advised that it could only be taken with great care, while stipulating that drugs were to religion what an illusionist was to Christ.

Cocteau's desire for abstinence, coupled with Jacob's torturous remorse and Breton's hate, combined to reawaken an ancient, gnawing sexual guilt, due as much to the presence of his mother as to the traces left by an incomplete religious education. Perhaps acting out the secret wishes of his mother, who grew more Christian by the day, he decided that in spite of his doubts he would go even further in his imitation of the saints, if only out of regard for his disciples and respect for Maritain. Aware of the example he must have set, Cocteau began to give sermons on purity, and soon began as well to declare his horror of "H couples"—that is, homosexual couples—and then to describe his sexuality as the vice he "hated most in the world."[51] The boy who had once dressed up as Elagabalus, with de Max, had become the most terrible judge of masculine love; the ancient Judeo-Christian condemnation came back to haunt the nephew of the diplomat who had been thrown out of Germany for casting a homosexual spell on Wilhelm II and his court. Self-hatred triumphed for Cocteau, the writer who needed to love in order to take his pleasure, but who had found very few companions willing to respond to his double desire.

In his genealogy of the "vice" since the damnation of Sodom, Proust believed that the angels' destruction of ancient pederasty in the Bible—ancient pederasty had been socially useful and perfectly accepted—had spared the progeny of the shameful sodomites, whom God's messengers, fooled by their "moral" disguise, had let escape from the city. Cocteau seemed to agree, as if he were belatedly experiencing the shame that Proust felt for all militancy, as well as for any desire to rebuild Sodom as others dreamed of rebuilding Zion. But Cocteau's will to pose as an example of purity, as a living testament to Christian virtue, was not free of personal ambition. "The saint has no self. This way, even his self is fulfilled," a Daoist poet wrote three centuries before Christ. This was Cocteau's gamble: in letting God invade those empty parts of him, in offering himself to His example and submitting to His law, he would be enriched by a multiplicity worthy of His genius. After consuming many successful personalities, which always left him dissatisfied, he would finally know fulfillment.

Heir to an outdated Romanticism, through the dying breaths of Symbolism, Cocteau had only ever conceived of a total, even sacrificial, artistic commitment. He had often asked himself if his destiny was to be a misunderstood poet, but he expected more of himself now. He wrote his books out of his blood, not just his ideas, and with his guts he made his poetry. "You have very Christian-ly blended your body with your books," Max Jacob confirmed to him, always prepared to bring him closer to God.[52] Cocteau would also opine that if "the exceptional man" that Renan spoke of, the religious artist who had given flesh to the God of the Jews—Christ—had been the secret model of Wilde, Gauguin, and so many Symbolists, it was up to every artist to be ready to die to prove his inspiration. This poem of flesh, this poet who signed his work with a cross of blood, this artist who disdained marble to work in living flesh—was, Van Gogh explained, the ancestor of all creators.[53]

But was this a question of God lowering himself to man's level, or man rising to the level of God? Jesus Christ was the first to take on the weight of the world, to say "I" on everyone's behalf, to believe down to the marrow his grandiose intuitions. In calling himself the King of the Jews, the salvation of humanity, and then the son of God, Christ too had demonstrated true megalomania before recognizing his mistake and dying repentant. Wounded by ten years of various disappointments, Cocteau's narcissism recognized itself in Christ's sufferings. Did not his literary career confirm that failure is the inevitable result of all earthly ambitions? Yes, solitude, bad luck, and hatred alone can lead to salvation; the grandeur of Christ's final defeat was the healthy counterpoint to the nauseating triumphs of Alexander, who died of an indigestion of glory. It was because he taught love, forgiveness, and charity that Jesus was able to inspire the humble to identify with him, and then become part of him. This failure of a man, without money, without arms, without property. This disheveled, unshaven man who had fallen out with his own people, with only the wealth of a few followers and the Word of God, who was reduced to doing magic tricks to convince onlookers and to scandals to make his name known. This Jew, who was disapproved of everywhere he went, who turned the other cheek when he was struck, and who was betrayed by one of his own. This was He. Did he not come from a far-off place with hints of the Orient, from some Persia neighboring Judea? Had he not also been abandoned by his father? Heaven had bestowed on him the divine power to make himself "other," while giving him the gift of all the human understanding that he usually enjoyed. Was Cocteau so different from Christ, who had come to earth to redeem all men, one by one?

Cocteau's fantasies did not remain abstract for long; even the most unlikely of them would soon be replaced with colors and images. He would remember that wonderful summer when he and Radiguet wrote with such ease, with truly divine grace. Did Bébé limp because he was God's left foot walking on the earth? And if he himself sought balance, could this be because the other man in the pair was the right foot? As soon as they "walked" together, at Piquey, they were close to becoming once more the God that Cocteau had believed he once was, but was no longer capable of being on his own.

WELCOME, ROOM 25

The Welcome Hôtel was not exactly the ideal place to carry out this imitation of Christ. During lunchtime, Cocteau's room was sometimes rented to young women who had come from the bordellos of Nice and Marseilles to distract American soldiers visiting Villefranche. The inn soon became a steamy hive of activity, filled with Yankee accents and Provençal moaning, under the watchful eye of Aunt Fifi—the madam, straight out of a Maupassant novel, who wore a wig and had tattooed knees, and who would settle on the terrace of a nearby café.[54] At night, sailors from the USS *Pittsburgh* would come and sing in chorus under Cocteau's windows, shoulder to shoulder, attempting to belly-dance and beating improvised drums. Then they would begin to hit each other with bottles of rum, shouting and frightening the girls. The police would come to arrest the ringleaders, evacuate the wounded, and from time to time, close the establishment. The soberest supported the drunkest as they undid their sailors' trousers to relieve themselves in the harbor, or hung out philosophizing on the quay, holding dialogues worthy of Antigone and Creon, or Jocasta and Oedipus.

Some friends of Christian Bérard, so-called neo-humanist painters hostile to abstraction who had turned the hotel into their Bateau-Lavoir, weren't avid churchgoers either. The halls of the Welcome perennially echoed, in 1926, with the noisy merrymaking of parties given there by seventeen-year-old Francis Rose, Leonid Berman, and Kit Wood, a young Englishman who was also an opium addict.[55] "A chaotic mix of gaiety and poetry," Jean Bourgoint wrote to his sister, as he was on leave and came and joined Cocteau. At the Welcome, the eccentric Lady Rose, wedged into a striped sailor's jersey that her son had decorated with flowers, would accost strangers in the street to read their palms.[56] There, too, the legendary Isadora Duncan wandered barefoot in search of sailors, who she would bring back to her flower-filled studio on the Promenade des Anglais, in Nice, over whose doorway Cocteau had engraved *Love*. "Life was not a series of parties, but one constant long party . . . impromptu dressing-up, processions, fireworks," said Glenway Wescott, a young American novelist.[57]

Cocteau would receive his morning visitors in silk pajamas or a dressing gown, a razor in one hand and his beard covered in shaving foam, greeting them under his *Débourre-pipes* sculpture, which hung from the ceiling. He welcomed everyone from Georges Hugnet, the poet and painter of collages who had introduced him to Bérard; to the young Man Ray, the "Ray-Man," who seemed to stifle his companion, the luscious Kiki de Montparnasse whose salacious remarks impressed even the whores; to the very young Christian Dior—a friend of Bérard's; to Mary Butts, who wrote books upstairs; not to mention Isadora Duncan, who would show up unannounced with her "pigeons," that is, two Americans carrying baskets filled with live lobsters intended for the dancer, who had begun to put on weight. While keeping them all apprised of his progress with God, Cocteau would take care of his correspondence, draft a poem, which he would abandon to move on to another, all in the heady odor of fish glue, which owed as much to the fisherman's nets as the sailor's relief.

Cocteau continued to stop by daily at the little church of Villefranche and to pray before the altar where he believed (he thought) to having seen the Virgin Mary appear, after his meeting with the Abbé Lamy. Christ overcome by the cross still inspired his ardent prayers, which strengthened his desire to behave morally. "He always treated me with the rigid severity of a Victorian father," Francis Rose would recall.[58] But how to remain untainted and free of sin in this port full of lusty sailors, to whom all Paris's snobs and bohemians fail to measure up? Already the gap between his real life, fraught with temptations, and his petitions for chastity were creating in Cocteau new and subtle feelings of guilt.

Religion, however, did not cost him his sense of humor. He could still tell brilliant stories, and compared Isadora Duncan dancing in his room to a "flabby Rodin."[59] At night, he would dine with a group in the cabarets of Villefranche before joining the impromptu sailor's orchestra at the Welcome, to make hail rain down on their drums. Once again he was the great god of noise that enchanted all of Paris, in the time of Gaya and the Boeuf; feeling their partners lose themselves in their arms, those brutes in striped shirts gave him looks of thanks, and he himself almost envied the night their companion would spend in their arms. But soon he would get ahold of himself, splash some cold water on his face, and climb back up to his room where he would recite an Ave Maria in front of an image of the Virgin and smoke one last opium pipe, to smother the longing that overcame him.

The bamboo ritual had started up again. A few sweet puffs and heaven opened up to him again. It wasn't where God sat on his throne, but a sort of cottony richness, which cleared some breathing room for him, helping him not to betray his own preaching and remain chaste, so he could become a being who existed purely for spirit, detached from the flesh and indifferent to death. Was not the poppy the Lord's plant, the vegetal complement to the ladybug? "By the rite of smoke, our sins will be put off, our filthiness cleaned, the state of grace returned to us," affirmed Louis Laloy in *Le livre de la fumée*. Maritain's Christianity promised nothing less, and the poppy soon sealed up all breaches of faith.

In truth, Cocteau had continued to smoke since his return to God. As early as the previous winter, he had only one hundred meters to walk, coming out of the Maritains' house, to get to Laloy's smoky home in Bellevue. The climates of the two houses combined to create a fatal serenity; who knows if God was only a dream, during those opium-laced months? At the first crisis of doubt, he raised his dosage. The night before meeting the Abbé Lamy, Cocteau confided to the Abbé Mugnier that he was a wreck. Then he pulled himself together in the lead-up to his show at the Galerie des Quatre-Chemins, in December 1926. Behind the closed blinds of the Welcome he had begun to create again—objects made out of cards, string, pushpins; bas-reliefs in candle-wax; figurines made of plaster, sheets, matches, and hairpins, which he painted by melting walnut stain and lipstick; and the overhead busts made of pipe cleaners, inspired by the faces of Orpheus, Oedipus, and Barbette. These busts, mobile-like creations that looked like cages freed of their birds, evoked both three-dimensional drawings and empty hanging sculptures, and represent some of his most extraordinary work in the medium of sculpture.[60]

His doses of opium doubled again. Three pipes in the morning, around eleven o'clock; four in the afternoon, at tea-time; three in the evening, after dinner. He claimed that this was a "reasonable" amount to consume, but it became unreasonable whenever he felt the desire to write, stimulated by smoking. "Opium is more yourself than you are," he said, summing up in one aphorism a lifetime of addiction.[61] Just as acrobats can only accomplish their feats in a state of semi-consciousness—if they were totally aware they would become afraid and fall—Cocteau needed this unconsciousness in order not only to abandon himself to his best impulses, but also to teach abstinence to those least likely to obey him, like Christian Bérard or Kit Wood.

These contradictions shocked Glenway Wescott, the young writer (and friend of Hemingway's) who had left Wisconsin to come and live at the Welcome with his lover Monroe Wheeler. Austere, intelligent, and gifted—the novel he wrote at the time, *The Grandmothers*, is still read in the United States—Wescott was a secular Protestant, taken straight out of a modern-day Victorian novel, who had witnessed, aghast, the increasing number of lies generated by the "conversions" of Cocteau, Bourgoint, and Sachs. Agnostic and out of the closet, Wescott was the opposite of Cocteau in his intellectual rigor and his moral convictions. How could Cocteau preach abstinence and the sacraments one moment, and the next spend his evening dancing with sailors at Isadora Duncan's? Declare one day that opium is the best cure for a deviant sexual nature, and call it a miracle the next? Teach the Roman Catholic values, and then declare that using opium is a way to "become close to God"?

No one like Cocteau would be able to resolve his contradictions through words alone. "He is impulsive, like you," Wescott wrote to Sachs, "but he explained what he has done with such magnificent ease, intelligence, and rapidity that the explanation seems to have been given before, and not after."[62] Sure that he was right as a man of reason, while Cocteau had only the dreams of an artist, Wescott, astonished, took it into his head to make him renounce his "lies" and to bring him back to the "straight and narrow," that is, the secular, sexual path. After all, Cocteau was a writer capable of producing *Orpheus*, which Wescott had already begun translating. "You're not Catholic, you don't understand," Cocteau would retort, lowering his voice: "You're too American." Deep down, though, he knew that the holy purity of the water that Maritain had made him drink in renewing his baptism had been diluted by the Côte d'Azur's free-flowing alcohol. Far from Father Henrion, the Abbé Lamy, and the Meudon Trinity, God could hardly compete with the poetry of the sailors, "coiled together, unspooled by the waltz."[63] Cornered into theoretical balancing acts by Wescott's needling, Cocteau resorted to negative theology, describing God by what He is not, arguing that evil and destruction are worth more than peace and health, because they bring one closer to the breaking point that leads to Him. Wescott was unconvinced.

Just then, Jean Bourgoint announced that he was coming to Villefranche on leave. Out of arguments, Cocteau "revealed" to Wescott that his conversion was doubtless just a means of escaping his love for Bourgoint, another opium addict, and then to keep him from killing himself, because he had to set a good example. Finally, Cocteau conferred on Wescott the task of "consoling" Bourgoint, sexually speaking. To Cocteau's great disappointment, Wescott ended up falling for Bourgoint, and Cocteau grew more jealous by the day. Revolted by Cocteau's "inauthenticity," Wescott confided to Maurice Sachs that he was ready to become "Jean's spiritual opposite."[64] Their entire entourage soon seemed "rotten," caught in the haze of an unhealthy magic. Wescott began to receive his own worrying letters from Bourgoint, declaring, "Glenway my dear . . . Last week I was at a marvelous monastery in Solesmes." A Protestant's worst nightmare began to take shape, composed of Cocteau the teller of large tales, Bourgoint the opium addict, and Sachs the seminarian, whose soul Max Jacob would compare to that of Thérèse de Lisieux ("with a little something more, perhaps").[65] With wild erections everywhere, the young seminarian began to doubt his vocation, and wrote to Bourgoint that he must reflect deeply before taking his vows. The remarkable letters with which Wescott inundated Cocteau's group had no effect; his arguments, made with his strong American accent, became incomprehensible in the smoke.[66]

Caught between a bitter awareness of his isolation and the crowd that invaded his bedroom every morning, Cocteau would, from time to time, experience moments of madness. Of course he had his defenders and his fans, to say nothing of the groupies who would cross Europe to knock at the door of room 25 at the Welcome asking him to sign one of his books, but all these pale boys were so odd, and so interchangeable, that they seemed less real than the marvelous drawings he made of them.[67] It didn't matter what Sachs and Bourgoint said or did, they could not fill even a quarter of the place that Radiguet had held in his heart. The gay nights of debauchery he passed in the bars could not conceal an ocean of despair: behind this heroic charade, Cocteau gave the impression of a crucified clown.

The Bérards, the Roses, and the Wheelers often heard him complain of his inhumane and unreal life, but drama seemed such an intrinsic part of his nature, and sickness so useful to his genius, that no one thought to tear the pipe from his lips. Cocteau was made a certain way, and it served him well artistically. Every day he wrote and sketched out drawings, depending on his mood. *Orphée* was almost finished, the poems for *Opéra* were accumulating, and the Welcome embodied all that he loved. "It's [there] that I finally found my own personal mythology," he confessed to André Fraigneau, a young writer. Villefranche was no hell, in any case. The news seller asked how he was, the taxi drivers murmured his name in the streets, and the sun warmed him every day, through the window of the Welcome, from which he could see the infinite sparkling stretch of the Mediterranean. When the USS *Pittsburgh* left, while an orchestra intoned a slow Marseillaise, the crossing beams of the searchlights revealed rows of tearful girls returning home to their "barracks" in Nice and Marseilles, leaving Cocteau alone at his worktable.

SACHS ON THE CROSS

Cocteau had confided his doubts and relapses of that winter first and foremost to Maurice Sachs. In fact, Sachs had received frightening letters in which Cocteau, sure that nothing could save him from himself because God could not reach him, turned his enemies' arguments against himself. "I only live by trickery . . . by ambush, by fleeing," Sachs read. "I disgust God. He has abandoned me. I disgust the devil. He likes people who are Very Bad. Whereas I . . . I am neither good nor bad. Help me, I love you."[68] An exaggerated version of Cocteau, who reflected back his doldrums, Sachs was better placed than anyone to understand these highs and lows. But in the euphoria of faith, he (Sachs) missed no opportunity to reprimand each return to intoxication with such energy that Cocteau described him as having "the hardness of a sheltered young man, judging an old poet on the front line." Proud, nevertheless, to have the nineteen-year-old Sachs for a mentor, Cocteau played the role of the defenseless condemned man. "If you, you of all people, cannot understand my trouble . . ., I want to die."[69] Only too happy to play the part of the "good man" and to fulfill the upright image Cocteau had of him, Sachs would become angry, so Cocteau would swear to him that he would take no more drugs, except in homeopathic doses. But the damage was done: susceptible to the least infection, Sachs was beginning to lose his faith in Cocteau, and his admiration for his powers. The writer had always had the air of self-esteem that he himself had lacked until that point; Cocteau had judged, dominated, set the tone. The strange weakness that had come over him changed things. The idol that Sachs had joined, via Christ, was slowly deflating in his eyes, now that he saw that Cocteau was as changeable as himself. "Jean is a deceptive angel," Wescott confirmed. "I sincerely believe that is his celestial mission on this earth."[70]

Finding himself even more alone and unprotected than before, Sachs began to feel that he had been dragged into religion by a man whose effusions turned out to be without foundation, and who emphasized his feelings like the tragic actors. His religious zeal suffered the consequences, and he himself began to doubt his monastic vocation. Desire began once again to haunt his great flabby body, and literature to keep him busy, now that he no longer had someone to

(left) Jean Cocteau as a boy. Comité Jean Cocteau

(below) Cocteau's mother, Eugénie, with her two elder children, Marthe and Paul. Comité Jean Cocteau

Jean Cocteau, or Fame at
the Age of Eighteen. Comité
Jean Cocteau

The Pythia Anna de Noailles, in her lair on the rue Scheffer.
Bibliothèque Nationale de France

(above) Cocteau with Marie Laure, a spiteful "Lolita." Comité Jean Cocteau

(right) The Dada Dandy succeeds the Frivolous Prince: Cocteau at the time of *Le train bleu.* Collection Christophel/ Photoshot

Cocteau (*left*) and Raymond Radiguet, seated on Georges Auric's lap, with Russell Greeley (*right*) looking on (Var, France, 1922): love at a distance, literary symbiosis, the obsession of a lifetime. Susan Nagy/Bibliothèque Littéraire Jacques Doucet, Paris

At the piano, Cocteau, organizer of Les Six, surrounded by (*left to right*) Darius Milhaud, Georges Auric (in the drawing), Arthur Honegger, Germaine Tailleferre, Francis Poulenc, and Louis Durey. Lipnitzki-Viollet/Getty

"My name is Erik Satie, like everyone else." Studio Hamelle,
Arcueil, 1909 © Archives de la Fondation Erik Satie

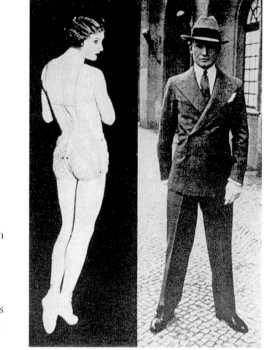

(right) Barbette, trapeze-artist transvestite, or the miracles of ambiguity (photo by Man Ray). © Man Ray Trust/Artists Rights Society (ARS)

(below) Igor Stravinsky, orchestral chameleon and mammoth titan, two years after *Oedipus Rex*. Stravinsky was a great role-model to Cocteau, as was Picasso. Lipnitzki-Viollet/Getty

(left) Jean Desbordes, Cocteau's first great reciprocated love, in 1929.

(below) "For a woman, glory is the gleaming grief of happiness," Madame de Staël once wrote. Cocteau seems to think this aphorism applies to some men as well (photo by Man Ray).

Enrique Rivero(s) diving into the mirror in his studio: going through the looking-glass,
joining the dead one has loved to try to bring them back to Earth and—who knows?—
change one's sexuality on the way back, like Orpheus. BIFI/Sacha Mansour

(left) Natalie Paley, the anguished princess: this self-portrait was taken in a wardrobe mirror into which she has slipped the poet's portrait (1932). Bibliothèque Historique de la Ville de Paris, Jean Cocteau collection

(below) Two knees, a cushion, a pair of felt socks: Cocteau could write only on the fly (photo taken by Jean Roubier in 1932, rue Vignon). Fond Photographique Jean Roubier

The entrancing rites of opium, caught in the act by Cecil Beaton. © The Cecil Beaton Studio Archive

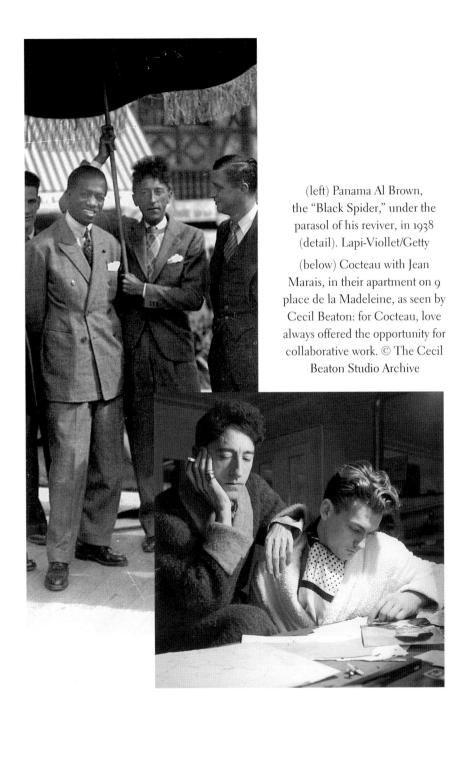

(left) Panama Al Brown, the "Black Spider," under the parasol of his reviver, in 1938 (detail). Lapi-Viollet/Getty

(below) Cocteau with Jean Marais, in their apartment on 9 place de la Madeleine, as seen by Cecil Beaton: for Cocteau, love always offered the opportunity for collaborative work. © The Cecil Beaton Studio Archive

The rue de Rivoli under the German Occupation. ©ECPAD/France

(above) The jailbird Jean Genet, whom Cocteau had launched at the height of his own glory. Brassaï took this photo a few months after the publication of Genet's *Le miracle de la rose*. © Estate Brassaï-RMN. Grand Palais/Hervé Lewandowski/Art Resource, NY

(right) Leaving the mines of Lorraine, Édouard Dermit became engulfed in the fairytale his Prince Charming concocted for him. Comité Jean Cocteau

The first male couple beloved by the public, Jean Marais and Cocteau
stayed together for photographers—here Serge Lido immortalized them on
the terrace of the Café Florian, St. Mark's Square, Venice, in 1947.
Lido/Sipa Press/Sipa USA

The six-armed god, too talented not to be suspect—or How Vishnu Came to Be Rejected by Paris (photo by Philippe Halsman). Philippe Halsman/Magnum Photos

(top) Pablo Picasso feeding Cocteau in Vallauris, France, in August 1955 (photo by Jacques-Henri Lartigue). Their sadistic friendship lasted almost half a century. Ministère de la Culture-France/AAJHL

(below) "I remain with you": Cocteau, one year before his death (photo by Luc Fournol). Luc Fournol/Photo12

emulate. In Sachs's disillusioned eyes, even God began to seem inconsistent. He imagined he could become a secular priest, in order to be able to participate in everyday life through confession, but this compromise proved overly ambitious. His need for someone to mimic became parodic. Lampooning the Carmelite monks who reproached him for "frivolously" spending his weekends at the Maritains', he thought only of donning silver-buckled slippers to light up his cassock and to give himself an air of clerical authority. After six months in the seminary, Sachs would flip his cassock, his "black dress," with a strange voluptuousness in the hallways of the monastery. "Black makes one appear taller and thinner, one can believe oneself beautiful in it," he would write in *Le Sabbat*.

Offering herself as a neutral chaperone, his grandmother suggested that they holiday in Juan-les-Pins, a seaside annex to the Boeuf sur la Toit, where all of Paris would come to sun themselves — and to see and be seen. She also proposed that Sachs spend the summer of 1926 on the Côte d'Azur, still in his cassock, which he had had lined with pink crêpe de Chine so as to realize a childhood dream of being a gay, light-hearted young girl, sexy enough to make the boys catch their breath — like the Abbé de Choisy in the old days.[71] Parisians had already learned, with a mix of astonishment and hilarity, of his entrance to the "seminary," which some mistook for the name of a new nightclub. Even Jean Wiener, the pianist at the Boeuf, nearly lost control of his car when, returning to Paris after several months on tour in South America, he saw Sachs crossing the Place Saint-Sulpice. The last time anyone saw him, through the opium haze of the rue d'Anjou, "Biquette" (nanny goat), as they called him, had a carnation in his buttonhole. Incredulous to see him in his new state, the Parisians roasting on the beach at Juan-les-Pins pressed him with questions, while Picasso, Marie Laurencin, and Rebecca West looked on, amused. Sachs would reply with homilies on Maritain's goodness and Cocteau's genius, but this barrage of questions, under the burning sun, with the immense sea before them and these inviting bodies all around, made his head spin. Sachs went crazy after twenty weeks of chastity and self-flagellation, of savage erections and nightly pollutions, falling deeply in love with a fifteen-year-old American called Tom Pinkerton who was there on vacation with his mother. "Like a cadaver brought to life in the midst of a carnival," he would say, describing the fever with which he clasped the adolescent to him on the beach, slipping his cassock around him like a bath towel as he came out of the water.[72] He managed to convince himself at first that he was only trying to bring religion to the child, who hated it, but his attempts managed only to amuse the crowd of onlookers, who were happy to see the absurdity of these one-minute conversions unmasked.

Sachs was so happy to have finally found his soulmate that he set off for the Welcome, to introduce him to Cocteau. Horrified to find him there, with his skin darker than his cassock, Cocteau ordered the novice to get back to the seminary on the double and explain himself to the priests. Sachs didn't want to leave the coast, where Picasso, perversely, encouraged him to stay, and where he was surrounded by young admirers who applauded as he danced on the tables of the Welcome, spinning his "dress" around to show off the pink under-lining. When he finally returned to Paris, his confessor told him he could once again take off his habit, since he still hadn't taken his vows. Sachs immediately went back to Juan-les-Pins to find his love, to the great anger of Mrs. Pinkerton, a dreadful Quaker who asked the Bishop of Nîmes to put his foot down.

The scandal was enormous. Threatened with charges of corrupting a minor (though Sachs was a minor as well), Sachs turned once again to Cocteau, who was furious with him and worried about his own reputation. Cocteau decided to send his unmanageable disciple to Max Jacob for spiritual protection, thereby reversing the chaperonage that had helped to launch so many beginners—"Jacob's ladder," as Jouhandeau called it. Still, Jacob was warned by Cocteau: "He's a charmer; he could charm even God."[73] Even more than Cocteau, Jacob would open his heart to just about anybody. "He would put his whole life at your service, tell you about it, offer it to you, not without adding that it wasn't worth a penny," said André Beucler.[74] The two men got along brilliantly, and Sachs spent the whole winter with Jacob at Saint-Benoît-sur-Loire. Taking heart from the example of Pierre Reverdy, who regularly retreated to the Abbaye de Solesmes, and lectured by Jacob, Sachs began once again to take communion every day. Cocteau wanted to believe that everything would be fine, in spite of the risks of a sudden return to the seminary, and that Sachs would suddenly submit himself once again to God. But Jacob was a strange Christian who, boundless in his contradictions, would spend the night confessing his anxieties to Sachs. "I can only paint if I've taken communion and I can only sleep if I've made love, so that in order to take communion, I don't sleep, and if fatigue keeps me from painting, to be able to sleep I make love, which keeps me from taking communion, so God takes away my inspiration."[75]

None of this was very encouraging. More and more people were saying that Sachs could only live if he were once again cut off from the world. Afraid to lose the little goodwill that remained toward him, especially with Maritain, who was more than angry about what had happened at Juan-les-Pins, Cocteau nevertheless insisted: "What I reproach Maurice for, because the devil conned us in letting him wear the cassock, is that he doesn't con the devil by keeping it," he wrote to Wescott, seemingly unaware of the madness of his argument.[76]

Renewed reprimands could not, however, prevent Sachs from going around declaring that his faith had been weakened, like that of his mentor, or from having the audacity to refer to himself and Cocteau in the first person plural, when speaking with Maritain. Sachs would swear to whomever would listen that he had embraced God only for Cocteau, and now wanted to leave him for the same reason. Sachs had held up a mirror to the one he loved in vain, and the face in the mirror now grimaced. "Maurice is a chameleon. He's afflicted with the malady of mimicry," Cocteau noted to his mother, who was alarmed at seeing her son lose all authority in the matter.[77]

Concerned that their future was at stake, Cocteau tried again to spare Sachs Maritain's judgment, arguing that this "poor child" was frivolous, credulous, and comical, not to mention unserious. But for the first time, Maritain's response was icy. These renegade members of the squadron were, he believed, his first lieutenant's responsibility, and Cocteau, repentant, had to swear to do all he could to bring Sachs back in line, knowing all the while that Sachs was a hopeless case. The situation contributed to a cooling in the relationship between Maritain and Cocteau. Already held solely responsible for Sachs's entrance into the seminary, Cocteau was also blamed for the Juan-les-Pins scandal. Their conversions were attributed to the blue eyes of Father Henrion, or the youthful body of Tom Pinkerton; since rumors of orgies surrounded the Welcome Hôtel, the exhibitionist Sachs was seized on like a magnifying glass to examine Cocteau's own weaknesses. The scandalous seminarian became the clown to Cocteau's tightrope walker, the exaggeration of the treachery that some judged inherent to both men's sexuality: Sachs was Cocteau to the nth degree, a little devil complete with horns and cloven hooves.

Soon Bourgoint, too, gave up. One visit to the seminary and a few letters from Sachs were enough to reveal his breathtaking lack of will. The monk-in-training took refuge with his mother and sister, and then left to do his military service in Nîmes. This was a new blow for Maritain, who, discovering the program for the show that Cocteau was planning for December 1926 at the Galerie des Quatre-Chemins, reacted violently. Cocteau knew that he himself was suspected of straying from God, and in order to prove his moral value went so far as to ask for a trial like Joan of Arc—as if a tribunal could finally decipher his contradictions. But Maritain wouldn't hear of it. He asked him to remove the "hermaphroditic" matchbox and the drawing of urinals that Cocteau was planning to exhibit. Cocteau refused, then managed to confirm Maritain's suspicions by writing to Sachs, "It's God's exhibit, which is to say the Devil's. Something criminal and deeply, magnificently ugly. I will be firm anytime anyone tries to round off the corners."[78] This marked the first sign of the discord between the poet and the philosopher who was secretly revolted by Sodom, though he had many homo-sexual confidantes, from Sachs to Green and from Mauriac to Ghéon.

Meanwhile Sachs had rediscovered his passion for literature, his need for money, his sexual bulimia, and his self-loathing. Once again disarmed by the young man's unhappiness, and feeling more guilty than ever, Cocteau arranged for him to translate a novel written by a nine-year-old British girl named Daisy Ashford, but discovered in the end that Sachs had merely plagiarized the earlier translation by Jean Hugo. (The leopard really can't change his spots.)[79] The infuriating cycle of demands, remonstrations, and apologies began all over again, and Cocteau gave in every time, without seeing the catastrophic influence of his permissiveness on Sachs. Jacob, however, had encouraged Sachs to write, and better yet, had disciplined him by sitting him down to his desk and forcing him to stay there, just as Cocteau had done with Radiguet. For the first time, it occurred to Sachs to draw a portrait in words of his former god, this seductive yet deceptive writer who was able to make the most of his weaknesses but could not impose his authority—unlike Jacob, who was a real father figure. Who knew Cocteau better than he did, in any case? Radiguet? But he was dead, and Sachs had sworn to make him forgotten. Glenway Wescott had given him some advice concerning the man who few could, in his view, love and admire at the same time.[80] This was if not the secret origin of Sachs's literary vocation, at least the most durable cause of his inspiration, which would lead him to write many portraits, half-loving half-hating, of this man whom he had venerated as a god and could now see only as an impostor.

Sachs was bitter. Having found Jacob to be a more accepting mentor than Cocteau, he insulted Bourgoint to no end—his jealousy far from diminished—and openly stole from the Delle Donnes (who had taken him in and got him a job at the hotel Vouillemont), until they no longer wanted to hear his name.[81] In trying to become an intimate of André Gide's, he spread venomous lies about Cocteau. "Be careful of the devil," Cocteau wrote to him that summer. "Don't joke—don't shrug your shoulders. Believe me: I am an oracle. A disaster would sink us all."[82] They were indeed headed rapidly in that direction. Cocteau's judgment on Sachs's first novel, Le voile de Véronique, made the young man see his idol in another light. "My dear Maurice," Cocteau wrote to him, "you can do anything you like, except for one thing: be a writer."[83] Sachs was stung by Cocteau's opinion of the book—the elder writer called it the work of a schoolboy—but even more so by the painful memories that Sachs had of Cocteau's past criticisms, which had been benevolent but severe. Cocteau thought he was too muddled to keep any of his promises, literary (about which Sachs was much in doubt himself) or otherwise.

The world was not as pure and enchanted as the prince of the rue d'Anjou had led him to believe. The gifts that Cocteau had seemed to attribute to him, when he had needed Sachs during the hard days of his detoxification, were brutally withdrawn, now that Sachs wanted to publish his work. The mirage surrounding the false messiah evaporated, revealing the blackest horizon. "I hate the world and all mankind and I am sorry I was ever born," Sachs wrote.[84] The pillars of his fragile edifice were collapsing; he wanted to destroy everything his Pygmalion had brought him, the good with the bad, everything he had described as "pure," "marvelous," "enchanted," and "sacred," as if impatient to discover under the Galatea sculpted by Cocteau the real Maurice Sachs who had been covered in clay. Maritain was also ruthless when it came to the novel, and he was assailed with ungrateful letters from the author. Cocteau received missives clamoring "Strike! Strike! Your blows feel so good!"[85] Sachs was a man possessed.

Only too happy to collect a bit of the passion that Sachs had felt for his former mentor, if not to revenge himself for Radiguet's betrayal, the ambiguous Jacob encouraged Sachs by promising that he would be an even more popular novelist than Cocteau, and that he would soon lead his generation. Sachs's frustration turned to vindication; convinced of Cocteau's literary cruelty, he stopped writing to him for a time, to the point that Cocteau believed Jacob had convinced Sachs to end their friendship. "God hates Cocteau," Jacob concluded in a letter to Maritain. Cocteau, one by one, lost his supporters. The writer "scolded" Sachs, as his mother had taught him, but he nevertheless maintained too lofty an idea of his responsibility toward the child to be able to really punish him. Taking on the role of mentor one last time, he persuaded Sachs that the military, unlike the seminary, would be good for him. And they came together again, to Cocteau's great relief. Sachs had a good heart. He often made blunders, was sardonic whenever possible, but he concealed a wealth of affection. He was unstable, but hardly more so than Cocteau himself, who wrote, to justify his differences of opinion with Maritain: "Let them ask me for love, and more love, but never for a system."[86]

He did bear some responsibility for Sachs's accumulating faults. When he found himself short of money (and therefore of opium) he wrote to him from Villefranche, asking him to sell certain rare books that belonged to him, and requesting that Madame Henri, his mother's housekeeper, let him into the rue d'Anjou. Later Cocteau would claim that Sachs had forged his signature on this letter, but all evidence points to the contrary. Numerous signed editions were sold: a *calligramme* poem in which Apollinaire had sketched his profile, the drafts of the main poems in Anna de Noailles's *Éblouissements*, several tomes of

Proust's À *la recherche du temps perdu* with marginalia in which Proust describes in verse how Cocteau leaped up onto the table at Larue's, "Like a sylph on the ceiling, like a ski on the snow . . .," or complains about the literary indifference of Madame de Chevigné. Cocteau publicly protested these "disappearances" in March 1926, in a complaint letter addressed to the director of the Librairie Gallimard, without providing the name of the thief. In a letter to Sachs that Henri Raczymow reproduces, Cocteau went so far as to accuse a friend of Sachs, someone called Robert, of being the guilty party, and to demand that Sachs make him return what he stole.[87] But since Sachs's mission was to procure the opium that made Cocteau so gentle and easygoing, it is difficult not to believe that the two men were at least complicit in these thefts. In the autumn of 1928, a letter signed by Cocteau again asks Sachs to go to his mother's to pick up three or four Persian vases, all the big blue bowls, and the gilded crystal carafes, and then send these items to him in Villefranche by a trustworthy packing service.[88] Raczymow found the letter in Jacques Guérin's archives; was it in fact a forgery by Sachs? "If he stole from me," wrote Cocteau in his *Journal d'un inconnu*, "in order to cover his tracks, it was to buy me gifts . . . I have always preferred burglars to the police . . . In any case trust must reign supreme. With Sachs there was trust. I tell you again, he gave more than he took and he only took to give."[89]

Doubtless Cocteau knew, and knew intimately, how unrequited love, self-hatred, and faltering mimicry could lead a man to steal from his idol. He loved to please too much to permanently alienate a boy whom he wanted to see happy, or at least more stable. "The more difficult the position, the better he came out of it," writes Emmanuel Berl . . . Maurice Sachs stole from him before his very eyes and he was happy. He said, "It gives me great pleasure. I am going to pretend not to notice."[90] Thirteen years later, Cocteau would add, "Deep down, I was only too happy to be relieved of my mess of papers."[91]

In November 1926, barely twenty years old, Sachs left to do his military service in Germany, inaugurating a new chapter in his extraordinary life. He became the lover of a barmaid in the garrison, staying with her until the spring of 1928. "There is no greater proof of Jean's grace than our vocations," he had written to Bourgoint a few months earlier.[92] Their joint estrangement from the Church only confirmed a drift that had begun long before. Their respective conversions ended in failure; all three discovered the muddy foundations on which they were built. "We were not searching for a way to become close to God so much as we were modeling ourselves on Maritain," Sachs would write, with his usual lucidity, in *La décade de l'illusion*. A few weeks more and Cocteau, already feeling the effects of his relapse, soon needed the advice, the massages, and the cures of a mysterious guru, the Yarma-Yogi. Aware of the unforgiving wheel of fortune to which he was strapped, he soon wrote to Max Jacob. "My life limps along. I don't live it to exist—I live it to become another—another whom I will never enjoy."[93]

THE DEVIL AND THE DEMOISELLE

Max Jacob gave Cocteau one last chance to practice his Christian virtues, that year of 1925. In the spring, he had spoken rather humorously to Cocteau of a young writer who shared their tastes—"a young, devout demoiselle with a terrible desire to marry"—then sent him to scratch at the door of Marcel Jouhandeau, who had shut himself up in the house threatening suicide after romantic disappointment.[94] To get to know the boy who so obsessed Jouhandeau, Cocteau voluntarily accepted the role of mediator, even though Jouhandeau had once insulted him under the influence of the Surrealists who were then courting him—perhaps to show that his insults were unjustified.

Cocteau's patience, generosity, and good interpersonal skills managed to convince the young man to make things up with Jouhandeau, the butcher's son-turned-Latin teacher whose incredibly frank autobiographical work would celebrate eroticism, God, and the abject, all in a style unequaled in its elegance. As the days went by, Cocteau developed passionate feelings for the school-teacher with his strange ardor, whose indirect torturer was an "extraordinarily beautiful" young actress called Kissa Kouprine.[95] She was the one monopolizing all the attention of André Jullien Du Breuil, the object of Jouhandeau's passionate affection, and Jouhandeau applied a particular sort of genius to reconfiguring the equation. "J. is a novel, a man-novel, and his tests are really 'proofs' let us help him correct them," Cocteau wrote to Max Jacob.[96]

Taking back his insults, Jouhandeau recognized that Cocteau could be straightforward and serious. Religion helped in this regard; Cocteau had the right to see this very strange man again. The boy had barely returned when Jouhandeau "cynically" insisted on sleeping with him, knowing full well that he would refuse, in order to make Cocteau fail badly in his role as mediator. "I love him now for the unknown evil I have done him," the redoubtable Jouhandeau confided to Jacob, accusing him of having brought him together with Cocteau to inflict "mutual humiliation" on them both.[97] Soon the paranoid Jouhandeau would view Cocteau his benefactor with horror, guilty of having wanted to bring him stability.[98]

Cocteau had once again awakened the sadistic impulses of a man who had instinctively seen how deep "the love of one's neighbor, the love of one's enemies, the love of love" ran in him, making him vulnerable.[99] Worse, when Sachs went to see Jouhandeau, taking his first novel with him out of the insistent desire to dedicate it to him, he was not content to hate out of principle Sachs, this "dirty pig" whom he held responsible, ten years later, for the birth of his anti-Semitism.[100] Jouhandeau would instead quarrel with Cocteau, whom he blamed for Sachs's turn to amorality, and whom he would call an "angel of lies." "You [Cocteau] remain the symbolic lightning rod," Jacob recognized, and he began to distance himself from Jouhandeau.[101]

14

"RAYMOND HAS RETURNED"

In life, the swindler fakes illness; in art, he fakes thought.
—*Vsevolod Meyerhold*, Le théâtre théâtral

THE CALL OF THE VOSGES

Cocteau's failed return to God reduced his prestige in only a few circles. Instead, after his forced months of abstinence and the departure of Sachs and Bourgoint for the military, a new generation of young men came hopefully to him, attracted by the sulfurous aura of drugs. More than ever, people were flooding Paris from abroad to take its temperature via Cocteau. He was part of "the myth of our international brotherhood," said Klaus Mann, the son of Thomas. "His name—like those of André Gide, Kafka, Picasso—had become a password which allowed the bright young things of our age to recognize each other, from Cambridge to Cairo, from Salzburg to San Francisco."[1] Yet Cocteau, much solicited and flattered, sometimes even showered with praise—this "villainous bird—so tenacious," at whom Satie had "taken aim"—hoped only for Radiguet's return.[2] Hadn't he already spent a good part of his time waiting for him when he was still alive? But in spite of the prayers and the pipes meant to bring Cocteau closer to heaven, the phantom would not come.

In autumn 1925, Cocteau had received a gushing letter from a nineteen-year-old boy from the provinces who had just devoured *Le grand écart* and wished to send him his own writing. The young man, who called himself Jean de List, enclosed a photograph of himself and closed his letter with a daring "My life is yours!" "My dear Jean," Cocteau replied almost immediately. "I have not behaved like the illustrious writer of your book. I have read what you sent

433

me. And I see there is some genius in it . . . Your inner fire sets the pages on fire. They burn. It's difficult to read. The smoke blinds you. . . . Calm down. You possess what no one in our time possesses: the intensity of depth."[3] This was word for word the message Cocteau had sent to Jean Bourgoint—except in this case there really was a book under discussion, as well as a writer.

Convinced that these "primitive ingenuities" and "burning ejaculations" ought to see the light of day, Cocteau took them to an editor, who would publish them as *J'adore*. This preternaturally pure young man perhaps lacked the genius that Radiguet had cleverly disguised as talent, but he had *some* genius, unlike the lazy, deceptive Bourgoint. Born in a village in the Vosges to a Protestant family, Jean de List—his real name was Desbordes—lived on a farm near Fontainebleau with his mother, a stern woman, and his two sisters, who loved him passionately. Brief excursions to Paris in the early months of 1926 allowed him to approach Cocteau, who found him to be a fresh, natural, and timid boy—three qualities that he himself was beginning to lack. He was so unedu-cated that he did not know the name Rimbaud, but he was also arrogant enough not to be vexed by what he didn't know, alternating between candid smiles and haughty stares. Desbordes lived far from society, unaffected and clumsy, awkward in a spontaneous kind of way.

Sure of having found Rousseau's noble savage, Cocteau took this naïve and volatile "kid," seventeen years his junior, under his wing. Having also been called to military service on his twentieth birthday, Desbordes was then sent to the navy in Brest. But Cocteau intervened, and with the influence of his cousins in the navy, managed to get him transferred to the Ministry of the Navy, in the rue Royale, just a hundred meters as the crow flies from Cocteau's place.[4] Desbordes might have strolled down the rue d'Anjou, the rue de Surène, and rue Boissy-d'Anglas, in "the most charming uniform in the world," his hair standing on end like a flame, with a stubborn (and therefore all the more desir-able) air.[5] Cocteau had fetishized the sailors whom he had met in 1914–1918; Desbordes's white uniform and blue stripes put him smack in the middle of that fantasy.[6] The photographs on Desbordes's naval ID cards seem to have been torn out of Cocteau's sketchbook; with his pompom hat, gaiters, and sailor's trousers, the young navy man of the city looked not only like one of those vaguely thuggish apprentice sailors who earn a bit of cash with homosexuals on vacation in Toulon, but also like the well-born children who, during Cocteau's adolescence, were so often photographed wearing sailor's outfits.

Desbordes took advantage of his first furlough, in early summer 1926, to join Cocteau in Villefranche. "He was an extremely timid, shy boy . . . so innocent that he would say any nonsense," Cocteau remembered thirty years later.[7] The group at the Welcome received him with reserve, this writer-in-training in search of a godfather. They found him fawning, banal, and to have the air of a "mid-level office worker," said Glenway Wescott. Paris would hardly be more welcoming to Cocteau's new protégé. Had Cocteau been a bit hasty in describing him as brilliant? For his part, Jean Hugo had loved Radiguet too much not to be reticent toward this new candidate; he found Desbordes likable but emotional and immature, praising everything arbitrarily, without the slightest critical spirit—not out of opportunism, but out of a lack of intelligence and personality. His main merit, in Hugo's view, was he was not effeminate.[8]

The military offices on the rue Royale had one advantage: they were not a dormitory. Desbordes could leave every day and go home to his hotel, sometimes in the company of other sailors. Cocteau liked to play dress-up with these sailors, or to put them in tutus. These games had been forbidden the previous two years, and it was delicious to play again. "If God condemns me, I accept it," he wrote to Max Jacob. "I love him to the point of madness, of heresy, etc., all the way to hell."[9] The desire was stronger than he was, and it made him go against everything he had until recently believed. Under the double influence of Desbordes and Yarma-Yogi, Cocteau had stopped being a saint. A letter from the Admiral Durand-Viel put an end to these dress-up sessions.

Still, Cocteau refused to betray *all* of his commitments to Maritain. Desbordes was permitted only to lie beside him, smoking opium. "Suddenly he would fall asleep, and speak of another world, where he flew, and walked on water," Cocteau noted.[10] Mouth open, body in a state of surrender, Desbordes would spend hours under Cocteau's gaze, and was trained purposely to fall into this "sleep of chance." Not content with this, Cocteau advised that Desbordes write down his thoughts when he woke up, and taught him to make the most of the visions that appeared to him in his sleep. Because Desbordes proved to be almost as gifted and disorganized as Radiguet, Cocteau decided to put his sketches in order, and give form to his lyricism—"might as well try to teach a nightingale its do-re-mi," he joked, adding, "I will never forget the discomfort my early advice inspired in that starry-eyed, unsuspecting boy." For a long time, this was the only form of intimacy between the two.

Had Cocteau promised himself not to be as weak with Desbordes as he had been with Radiguet? We may well think so, especially reading the portrait of the young sailor in "Le mystère laïc," and the dangers that he inspired: "A friend sleeps against us, flat as a firearm, the hammer cocked, the trigger on our side. One clumsy move from a dream would be enough."[11] Those disciples who turned up in droves at his home allowed him at least not to expect everything from Desbordes. The most audacious was a young man from the South of

France with remarkable cheek, who signed his letters "Noël," and who soon invited Cocteau to join him in Montpellier, graphically describing the postures in which he would await his arrival at the Hôtel de la Métropole. And one of the most promising, André Fraigneau, who lived with his mother in Nîmes, soon moved down the road on the rue d'Anjou.

Determined to move things along himself, at the end of 1926 Desbordes moved into the Hôtel de la Madeleine, into the very room that Radiguet had occupied during one of his furloughs. Putting his hands where Radiguet had once put his, getting drunk in the very room where Radiguet and Cocteau had spent so many hours, until he felt them come to life within him, he waited for the writer for days on end. But this did not prevent Cocteau from going down to Montpellier in January 1927 to meet Noël, whom he described as "an adorable boy—and that accent . . . a very lofty and stern and tender spirit . . . and remarkably honest."[12] This erotic intermission did Cocteau enormous good. "A sort of happiness in the void," with no newspapers, no Surrealists, it was "a miraculous relaxation after years of stress," he wrote to Jacob.[13] After seeing Noël for himself, Jacob replied that he had never seen such complete devotion: Cocteau was blood, life, heart, mind, stars, and God to the young man. It was "a case of possession" worthy of Sachs, whom Noël would go on to befriend.[14]

"Come back if you can," Desbordes wrote to him. "You will find me, and then Raymond."[15] This was certainly not the worst way to get Cocteau's attention, for he ran home at once.

THE MIRRORS OF ORPHEUS

It was no accident that Cocteau changed the Virgin in his play into Orpheus, after Maritain's remarks; mythology had always been more interesting to him, to the extent that he found himself powerless to control his destiny. In his view, men were certainly given free will, but they always chose for themselves destinies that happened to be exactly the ones that the gods had dictated. Four years earlier he had chosen to adapt *Antigone,* by Sophocles, who was the first Greek tragedian to believe this. Even Breton had been persuaded that our actions and our encounters were "dictated" by "objective chance," without being able to say by whom. Cocteau wanted to believe that the potions, the sphinxes, the angels, the seers, and the demons were mere intermediaries charged with applying the express wishes of the gods.

Theater adaptations of mythology had the advantage of being able to show characters without being specific about their age, their occupation, or their rank, as was required in classical tragedy or bourgeois drama. When it came to the vague or legendary beings of the demi-gods, Cocteau was able to make them say and do anything he liked, without worrying; they had the benefit of being already known, and so conveying a sort of universality. The ordeals he had recently experienced, too, led him to say much, if not too much, through the myth of Orpheus, which he insisted on giving a modern interpretation. The tragic hero, whom Greeks believed had invented poetry, was an ideal model: whether pronouncing his lines in verse, or singing accompanied by his lyre, his voice cast a spell over all the elements of the universe, men and women, plants and birds; prolonging celestial waves, it calmed storms and tamed forests, making the stones soften and the wild beasts calm, surpassing in sensuality even the Sirens' call. In descending to the Underworld to seek his beloved Eurydice — and in turning back to look at her in spite of the gods' orders, thereby bringing on her final demise — the enchanter thus incarnated the limits of mankind, however divine it might be. The bard of Thrace may have been able to charm the monsters of hell — Sisyphus, Tantalus, and the Danaïdes — and to silence Cerberus, that terrifying canine, but he was unable to keep his love alive, although he was a son of those Thracians who were said to be immortal.

After Orpheus's story was taken up by Ovid in the tenth book of his *Metamorphoses*, a tradition grew up according to which Orpheus no longer cared for women after having seen the masters of the kingdom of shadows strike down Eurydice ("But many women / Wanted this poet for their own"[16]). He was said instead to teach love to the young boys of Thrace, until the Maenads, furious at being disdained, tore him to pieces. His head, carried by the currents, washed up in Lesbos, where it was said to become an oracle fed by the secret knowledge he had gained in hell. This story led to the birth of the radical ascetic religion Orphism, which spread across the Mediterranean world not long before Christianity.

Cocteau believed existence to be a prolonged "catastrophe," and had the frequent sensation of descending into the Underworld, since that day in 1917 when he had crossed the world of the dead on the front. Never having been able to give a foundation to his life, or bring Radiguet back from the Underworld, he sometimes imagined that he was being punished for disobeying the gods. With Orpheus he could capture his feelings of being a man caught between life and death, a prisoner in a hall of mirrors. Under the Greek mask, his wanderings between heaven and earth, poetry and religion, could become not only noble but almost logical. "With his disguises, his travesties, his masquerades, adopted for celebrations, man tries to change himself into something else which is only the imitation, on the surface, of the phenomenon of the most profound mythological metamorphoses. That is why he lies to himself so often, unmasking only another mask," he would say, in a little-known text.[17] Thus did he return as a way of ordering and laying the groundwork for the neoclassical decade to come. After identifying himself for so long with those who made him look good, like Anna de Noailles, Picasso, and Stravinsky, he would come to recognize himself in the figures of Orpheus and Oedipus.

Magus, musician, but also a leader of the Thracian people, Orpheus had served as a standard for German and French poets impatient to recapture from priests, under Romanticism, the role of humanity's guides. Mallarmé had decreed that the very goal of poetry was the Orphic explanation of the earth, and in the midst of the excitement for the avant-garde, Apollinaire, as we know, had even created Orphisme, a school of which he was the only (or almost the only) master.[18] This school would inspire Orpheus's delicate *Bestiaire ou cortège d'Orphée*, ten short poems dedicated to the animals whom Orpheus's lyre had enchanted, which Cocteau would publish at the Éditions de la Sirène. This was an Orphism that the Enchanter could only gesture at, but of which Breton hoped to be the inheritor, a desire that would set him against Cocteau for fifty years.

Orpheus was, then, the perfect mask. He symbolized not only the fine line between life and death, between masculine and feminine, but also Cocteau's determination to flourish in all the arts, to hold up a flag to the youth who worshipped him, and to impose his colors on his infernal enemies (the Surrealists, of course).[19] The play that Cocteau created was doubtless his most lucid attempt to unite the rival models that he had set for himself: on one side, the prophetess like Anna de Noailles, with her incantations and great pagan powers; and on the other, the Rimbaldian Seer, the thief of fire turned explorer of his own psyche. For Cocteau, these two currents converged in the form of Heurtebise, the angel with glass wings inspired by Radiguet whose role Cocteau himself would play when it was revived in 1927—and who, dressed simply as a glazier in blue workman's overalls, comes to unveil Orphic knowledge to drowsing humans. In Orpheus, for the first time a composite mythology would take shape, one that would be Cocteau's trademark for the rest of his life: a poet surrounded by mirrors through which Death enters and leaves, and sometimes pulls him into its orbit, like the reflections in which he searched for himself. Consider the drawings for *Jean l'Oiseleur*: Death incarnated by a splendid young woman in rubber boots, with masked surgeons for assistants; a strict, prosaic Eurydice, whom Orpheus would seek in the Underworld but whom he would condemn to remain there, by deliberately turning toward her; a tribunal of Bacchantes ready to condemn him, as so many followers of Reverdy, Dada, and Surrealism had done so often. All the elements that would feed his most personal films after the war—*Orphée* and *Le testament d'Orphée*—are already there.

Orpheus premiered in June 1926 at the Théâtre des Arts. It was directed by Georges and Ludmilla Pitoëff, and attracted an elegant and cosmopolitan crowd of American, British, and even Japanese patrons. Determined to cause a commotion, the Surrealists booed not only when Orpheus (played by Marcel Herrand) made his entrance—the Comte Kessler found him "nauseatingly sweet" and seeming to emerge "fresh from a second-rate hair salon"—but also when the housewife Eurydice entered, played by a very pregnant Ludmilla Pitoëff.[20] Although the play was intended to be a "Cocteau-esque" retort to the Surrealists, their disruptions did not have the same effect as they had at the premiere of *Antigone*. Death, played by the very strange Mireille Havet in a pink muslin Chanel ballgown and chinchilla coat, was able to preside undisturbed. Havet, Cocteau's discovery, was an opium-addicted lesbian who had once been the lover of the British novelist Mary Butts and was secretly in love with Jean himself. She so profoundly embodied her role that several audience-members reported feeling a chill in their blood.[21]

The performances were plagued by ominous signs and omens. The bathroom mirror in the apartment where Marcel Herrand rehearsed his lines collapsed just as he said "With these gloves you will walk through mirrors as if they were made of water." While on their way to the premiere, Glenway Wescott and Monroe Wheeler were stopped by a mad white horse that broke a window on the boulevard Raspail.[22] Mireille Havet suffered so often from opium withdrawal symptoms that Cocteau had to regularly make a tour of the Pigalle nightclubs, call on Yvonne George in her dressing room at the Olympia, or make Havet sniff a bit of flour and sugar from a straw box before going onstage.[23] In Mexico, the actor playing Orpheus fell down dead after emerging from the mirror, and in America, the Angel died onstage, if Cocteau is to be believed.

Cocteau was genuinely convinced that the gods, through this constellation of signs, wanted to announce to all humanity the return of Orpheus to earth. In the magical thinking by which he navigated the world, there was no such thing as chance, only coincidence or plotting; there were hardly any accidents that were not the work of an unseen hand. The white horse that stomped its hoof onstage—one tap for yes, two for no—obeyed the same code as the séance table that had predicted Radiguet's death. The tragedies surrounding these performances could only be destiny's warning shots. Paul Morand, whose talent stemmed from an aerial, clinical observation of reality, understood immediately that Cocteau, who had once been a rival, had "opened the door to phantoms." In fact, Cocteau would isolate himself even more from the 1920s generation, whose humor and insight he had shared, in order to plunge himself ever more deeply into his own shadows. "Since these mysteries are beyond our understanding, let us pretend to rule over them," he wrote in *Les mariés de la tour Eiffel*. But this time he was no longer pretending; other powers had taken over him.

Cocteau's attempt to reintroduce Greek mythology would not generally be well received by the critics. It updated these ancient texts in a way that sometimes felt forced. The press found the mystery overwrought and deemed provocative, if not mediocre, the acronym formed by the words Madame Eurydice Reviendra Des Enfers.[24] They laughed at the men's legs that appeared through the horse's costume, tapping out its message—which brought back memories of *Parade*—at the exclamations uttered by the glass-winged angel, and at that "death in a pink tutu" ridiculed by Jouhandeau. But Cocteau had no fear of ridicule; on the contrary, he used it, he played with it, like a child, innocently. In short, that incongruous play despite itself brought the spectator, who felt somewhat at a loss, closer to its author. "He sticks our noses in our own wealth," judged the *Nouvelle revue française*, with an almost olfactive sense of phrasing.[25]

Cocteau was used to being reproached for this kind of eccentricity. "I make use of whatever I come across—and that includes my own heart," he responded, aligning himself with Picasso, but his heart was exactly the organ at which his enemies were aiming.[26] To those who criticized the overflow of symbols, he protested that this was part of the fundamentally personal nature of the play. "There are twelve years of tragedies thrown away hidden there," he wrote to T. S. Eliot, the author of *The Waste Land*, complaining of the misunderstanding that plagued this "emergency surgery."[27] But the Surrealists' hostility was enough to encourage glib dismissals. A second-rate critic, Léon Pierre-Quint, wrote to him when the play was published, "I am delighted to have finally received *Orpheus*, because I had to leave before the second act to which I believe you grant great importance"—though the play contained only one act.[28] Others admitted more freely that they hadn't understood much of it. This, however, was Cocteau's intention: to use a slightly esoteric language in order to capture the enigma of existence, and maybe, perhaps, allow access to the sublime. Like the Romans, who were usually so practical-minded, but who cast Greek actors to utter mysterious phrases during their banquets, so did the poet seek out what is complex, and difficult-to-understand, in order to remind us that there are some things beyond our control. For Cocteau, poetry should serve as a conduit to mystery. Perhaps he was too ambitious, but let us remember that Apollinaire believed himself to be the possessor of Orphic knowledge that allowed him access to the kingdom of the dead, and that Joyce sought to discover an Edenic language, with the babble of *Finnegans Wake* offered as a distant echo of this lost language.

Despite the lukewarm reception by the critics, the play was an immediate hit with theater-goers. Young people turned up at the rue d'Anjou in even greater numbers than usual to get a glimpse of the resurrected Orpheus. Those more timid simply sent him their manuscripts or amateur photographs of themselves, including nudes, begging for a role in Cocteau's next play, or in his life. That is, when they weren't blackmailing him to force his generosity. "Goodness, what strange people we're raising!" Cocteau wrote to Max Jacob. "They threaten things like suicide, saying things like 'give me back my photographs,' or 'I'm giving up literature,' etc." Rilke liked the play very much; he too had tried, three years earlier, to breathe new life into the Bard of Thrace. Virginia Woolf, too, called it "the greatest tragedy of our time."[29] Had Rilke, the author of *Sonnets to Orpheus*, begun translating *Orphée* when he died in December 1926, as Cocteau claimed? Struck by the presence of terrible angels in both of their works, the Klossowskis seem to have done all they could to encourage Rilke. Learning that his mistress—the mother of Pierre Klossowski and Balthus, who painted under the name Merline—was inviting Cocteau over, and regretting that he could not be there to meet him, Rilke sent her a telegram: "Do your best to channel my soul and make him feel the warmth of my admiration, he alone to whom poetry opens myth, whence he returns with a healthy glow, as if from the seaside."[30]

Cocteau's turn to ancient Greece was not adequately understood in France, where, unlike in Italy, mythology was generally a passion of the bookish.[31] Pleased to have finally found a world of imaginary but time-tested references, however, Cocteau continued to draw inspiration from it. Driven by some unseen force, he raided the costume shop of antiquity, full of stories, poetic oracles with their sibylline pronouncements, richly imagined characters, symbols, and images, sometimes to the detriment of their physical or moral reality. "Cocteau alone possesses the secret of investing the contemporary with a mythological character," Radiguet had said as early as 1922.[32] Cocteau would forever turn his eyes to the heavens, like a blind bard, listening for the genius the gods whispered to him.

For Cocteau was a genius, and would brook no doubts. The critics may have been skeptical, but it was this word he asked his friend Bernard Faÿ to use in his review of the play for the *Panorama de la littérature française*, no matter what he thought of it. He could not accept any other term, "like a child who doesn't understand that his mother might have to care for someone else," Faÿ would say of him.[33] Why suffer so greatly, if he weren't a genius? His fragility found an outlet in his megalomania. He was convinced that his novelty was shocking, not his eclecticism, and that *Orpheus* heralded an aesthetic that would replace Surrealism. Since the wheel of fashion made a complete revolution every thirteen years, Cocteau saw himself not only as the grave digger of the "suicide-club dada," but also as the initiator of a return to the classics. One must not only be cursed by the general public, but by the avant-garde, he wrote in *Le rappel à l'ordre*, a collection of critical essays that he published that same year. He would succeed at this goal beyond all expectations.

BAD COMPANY

It had got to the point that Cocteau could barely go anywhere without running into his enemies. Breton's men shared with him not only an imaginary rival, but also friends, books, and places. Even the Boeuf sur le Toit was no longer a safe haven; the stylish Aragon went there with the eccentric Nancy Cunard, the heiress of the Cunard Line, an English transatlantic ocean liner company. Often showing up at the Welcome, at Villefranche, were Crevel or Desnos, who had connections with some of Cocteau's painter friends. Cocteau was worried that the Surrealists were going to take over all of his favorite haunts when he saw Desnos frequenting the concerts given by Yvonne George, the singer who had played the role of the nurse in his *Roméo et Juliette*. A close friend of Les Six, and nicknamed "the Queen of the Boeuf sur le Toit" because she appeared there so often, George was already a close friend by 1924, the time she began to be known by a discerning public. Easily moving from bitterness to gaiety, with the violent sincerity of the sailors' chorus—"Dans les prisons de Nantes, goodbye, farewell"—George seemed as if she was several singers in one, and defined her art as "an excuse to be someone else."[34] Cocteau soon began to suspect that Desnos was not there only because he appreciated George's subversive or anti-colonialist songs; almost every night, he went to the singer's dressing room.[35] But Desnos could dedicate as many beautiful poems to her as he wished, and threaten to deck the audience members who complained about her songs praising mutinies on the Black Sea: his unrestrained passion was no match for her Sapphism. At that time she was the mistress of Violette Murat, the opium-fiend princess whom Radiguet had loved, and who could be found smoking in an abandoned submarine in Marseilles.

Yvonne George's dressing room became the only place where Desnos could meet Cocteau without insulting him, three years after his plan to murder him. He preferred to humiliate himself in front of his group's number one enemy rather than having to share his beloved's attentions, and would always leave when Cocteau entered. In time, witnessing the daily rites of this impossible love, Cocteau began to see Desnos in a different light. He felt sympathy for the relentless masochism of a man who was so unattractive he was compared to a sleepy clown, but demonstrated a truly supernatural sensibility during Surrealist meetings. He became especially sympathetic when Desnos, in order to have an excuse to return to George every night, made himself her personal supplier, and began himself to smoke opium, in order to lay down beside her. There was no further intimacy between them, however; instead it was as if he were simply prolonging the kind of Surrealist hypnotic sleeping sessions that had threatened his mental stability.

Desnos may have held on to some hatred of Cocteau, but opium accentuated Cocteau's natural tolerance, and he was unable to understand why they could not dine together, or discuss their books, their dreams, the drug they took. Life had become so difficult for him that he could not bear anyone to raise their voice; any disagreement seemed an unpardonable waste. He himself was often the first to be moved to tears when Yvonne George "sang of sailing ships, which her tenderness reduced to the size of the little barks retired sailors imprison in bottles," as Janet Flanner, the *New Yorker*'s Paris correspondent, put it.[36]

The atmosphere around Cocteau became suffocating. Although Breton's and Cocteau's books were displayed beside each other in the shops, laid out on green leather tables for fashionable readers, the two men's disciples would come to blows if they met in the street. Defectors were the most passionate, but each promised to return in kind the slap or the strike of the cane. The Surrealists often had the upper hand. "This gang works relentlessly, tirelessly, at trying to kill me," Cocteau wrote to his mother.[37] Sometimes, turning around in the street, he thought he saw a group of men staring at him. Sure he was being followed, he would run away as quickly as he could, taking one detour after another. When he finally stopped to catch his breath, he would turn around again to be sure there was no one behind him. "My bad dreams are casting a pall over my days," he wrote to Max Jacob.[38] "They overflow into everything, and make everything dirty." The evil twin who shadowed him, as Jung said, had found in Breton's gang a particularly cruel incarnation.

At least Cocteau kept his friends from the early days—Picasso above all, the monster of fertility to whom he loved to send erotic postcards. The painter had changed greatly since the days of *Parade*. Their stay in Italy had opened the doors of the theater to him, as well as the ballets of Diaghilev, and the anatomy of Olga the dancer had inspired him to study movement from close up. Picasso's desire to revisit the past was balanced (as always) with his desire to abolish it, and without totally ending his Cubist proclivities, he rediscovered the Mediterranean and the circus, antiquity and figurative painting, just before

Cocteau returned to the "French" novel, with his *Le grand écart* and *Thomas*. Having abandoned dance for a respectable bourgeois life, Olga made certain social demands that transformed the bohemian Picasso into a dandy, complete with Hispano-Suiza and liveried chauffeur. Those early days of cafés and poverty were gone; now an averred Royalist since that gold crown had united him to that beautiful White Russian, Picasso would associate himself only with the highest members of society. "His duchess period," said Jacob, who had been excluded from it. His apartment had become a dreadful place thanks to Olga, all sanded parquet floors and polished furniture. His paintings could now fetch the price of a Corot or a Renoir, and when Picasso looked at himself in the mirror, in a tuxedo and bowler hat, he compared himself to "M. Ingres," whose atelier he had glimpsed when designing the sets for *Parade* on the Via Margutta, in Rome.

Cocteau may have facilitated this transformation through *Parade*, but Picasso—the "hundred-handed" Hindu god—played his cards close to his chest. He set the standards; it was up to Cocteau now to fall in line. And Cocteau, who tended to want to become whomever he admired, fell. Habit gives rise to osmosis, and so in 1922 they produced as if with one mind the scenery for *Antigone*. Cocteau even developed the ability to reproduce Picasso's drawings from memory; the painter would then add a little note under the drawing of the Minotaur: "Jean made this Picasso."[39] Cocteau regularly visited Picasso on the rue La Boétie. Happily in love, triumphant in art, and blissfully satisfied with Pablito, Picasso's little boy, the painter no longer needed Orpheus to sing his praises; there were many others who were in charge of that. Since Cocteau's letters went unanswered, he was reduced to inviting the painter over through his mother, without any more success. "I am the comet; Cocteau is but a spark in my tail," Picasso commented, around the time of *Parade*.[40] You could not influence the Spaniard and be loved by him—unless you were married to him.

Cocteau had naively believed himself to be one of those rare contemporaries who could understand Picasso straight away; in his need to be loved he had thought he might take Apollinaire's place, and receive those feelings in his stead. But Picasso, artistic libertine that he was, needed to be admired by a continually renewed stream of zealots. There was indeed a "cross-fertilization of minds," as John Richardson has put it, but the exchange had become unequal: Picasso liked to take as much as Cocteau liked to give.[41] Their friendship declined; Picasso no longer took the time to sketch him on the rue La Boétie, as he had once drawn him between Olga and Satie; now that the sets for *Parade*, *Antigone*, and *Le train bleu* had been sent off to storage, Cocteau was already wondering what remained of their collaboration.

Picasso may have been irritated to see that Cocteau had been inspired by his sculptures for some of the pieces in the show at the Galerie des Quatre-Chemins. Or Cocteau's friendship with Bérard might have had something to do with it— Picasso hated his paintings.[42] Or perhaps it was simply due to the weariness Picasso already felt for the life of luxury that Olga was making him lead. Whatever the reason, Cocteau was flabbergasted to find in *L'intransigeant* on October 19, 1926, the French translation of an interview that Picasso had just given to *La publicidad,* a Catalan journal. Along with thousands of others, he read:

> Cocteau is a thinking machine. His drawings are pleasant; his literature is journalistic. If they made newspapers for intellectuals, Cocteau would serve up a new dish every day, an elegant about-face. If he could sell his talent, we could spend our whole lives going to the pharmacy to buy some Cocteau pills, and we still wouldn't manage to exhaust his talent.

Picasso would later prove even more cruel, but his indifference in this interview left Cocteau speechless. "Journalistic literature"! A performer of about-faces! Dishes to sell and medicine to distribute! How could Picasso say such things, and provide so much ammunition to the enemy? Cocteau's whole world was collapsing. The youngsters would think he had never been Picasso's intimate friend, just his supplicant; the Surrealists would more vehemently than ever accuse him of mythomania; the press would call into question his position as the leader of the new generation. He would have to rebuild everything.

The only person he could open up to, at that time, was his mother. She was all too aware of his weaknesses, and was always the first to feel sorry for him. He would still be writing to her, a year later, "Rock me to sleep, carry me as you carried me to my room, on the rue La Bruyère."[43] "My dear," he wrote to her, "Yesterday I received the harshest blow of my life . . . Picasso has spoken of me in the same way as my worst enemies . . . If I have not thrown myself from the balcony it is because of you and the church . . . I think I will never again have the strength to return to the city . . . Pray for me. I'm suffering horribly."[44]

Cocteau had believed that Picasso would never take part in the Surrealists' persecution—proving "his indifference to drama," he added—but Breton had been courting Picasso since 1918, and he was beginning to make headway.[45] A year after *The Surrealist Revolution* reproduced several of Picasso's paintings, Breton called Picasso an unaffiliated Surrealist, specifying that he had been one since 1909—a sort of retroactive achievement.[46] Of course, Picasso found their paintings insufferably academic, in their insistent turn to symbolism, but Breton was such a devoted fan that it wouldn't take long for Picasso to begin to exhibit along with them.

Cocteau thought things over. He had to appear still to be Picasso's friend. Perhaps the Catalan journal had made a mistake and interviewed that deviant Picabia, who was in Barcelona at the same time as Picasso . . . Perhaps the interviewer had mangled his name—written Picabio, for instance, which a Parisian typesetter had corrected to Picasso. That must be it. Yes, that was it! Picasso remained prudent in public, more out of indifference than anything else, but it didn't matter. And in any case he never granted interviews. With all the energy he spent defending his own lies, Cocteau got it into his head to convince Picasso of them as well. He encouraged Picasso by telegram to deny having said anything, but he did not receive a reply.[47] He therefore took up his pen to give his own version of events to *L'intransigeant*. A pathetic solution, but Picasso, as Cocteau knew, would otherwise have done nothing.

By chance, not long after, Mme Cocteau, Olga, and Picasso ran into each other at the theater in Paris. During the intermission they met up, surrounded by mutual friends, and Cocteau's mother told them how relieved she and her son had been to discover that the interview had not been given by him. "Isn't that right, it wasn't you?" she added. And Olga replied, "No, it wasn't him." Picasso confirmed this. The retraction, however dubious, was at least now made public.

Picabia, however, denied having said any of those things to *La publicidad*.[48] Cocteau then wrote to Picasso, and as usual received no response: "You who never speak of anyone—you who refuse to 'speak'—you have spoken. And of whom? Of someone who adored you, who was ready to die for you and yours."[49] Cocteau had nothing to do but to contort himself to kiss the hand that had stabbed him in the back. In a letter to "his dear friends" on the rue La Boétie, he apologized two months later for being too ill to come and hang little Paul's gift on the tree at Christmas. He received a telephone call on December 25. Then they didn't hear from each other for a while; it became more difficult to see Picasso than to kneel at the feet of the Pope, Maurice Sachs said.[50]

Years later, Gertrude Stein (a longtime friend of Picasso's) would give her version of the facts, which are likely close to the truth. In Barcelona, Picasso had run into a friend from childhood, who had become a press magnate, and he agreed to do an interview in Catalan, knowing there was little risk of it being translated into Spanish. The journal, however, made its way to Paris where it was translated. Knowing that Cocteau would demand an explanation, Picasso instructed his maid to tell him that he wasn't home when he called; then Olga had bailed him out, at the theater.[51] "Something of these betrayals of the heart still remains," Cocteau confided to Max Jacob, in early 1927. When they inadvertently encountered each other at the theater—Picasso was with Olga in

Diaghilev's box—Cocteau accepted their invitation to lunch. The meal was pleasant, even familial. And Cocteau immediately forgot his troubles. Upon rereading, the interview did stress the abundance and diversity of his talents— apart from that word "journalistic." And did it not demand a certain courage to remain so friendly, given the pressure Picasso must be under from Breton?

Having always avoided mandates—including, first, from the Cubists— Picasso kept his distance from Breton. Refusing to be enlisted, as he refused to work for anyone but himself, he was happy to turn to Paul Éluard, that excellent art critic, as his new "poet laureate." Almost as flexible and masochistic as Cocteau, Éluard was less generous with his praise, but through him Picasso gained the support of the whole group, who managed to turn him into the era's artistic Sun King. Soon the very young Marie-Thérèse Walter would succeed Olga in the role of muse, and the painter's "Metamorphoses" would betray the ever-growing influence of the Surrealists' supple and dreamlike forms, an influence that would continue to grow into the 1930s. Cocteau, an ally of the too-bourgeois Olga, receded into the past.

THE SWAN'S BETRAYAL

The 1920s were so promising at the dawn of the decade, but in time the epoch seemed to tire of Cocteau. He was no longer found to be joyful or inventive; his about-faces and his little tricks became tiresome—except, of course, to the young. Valentine Hugo herself had even begun to treat him coldly of late. She could no longer bear his exaggerations and his frequent cries for help, to say nothing of the mythomania a year earlier during which he had claimed to see Radiguet's features in those of an old picture of Buddha.[52] His return to God had seemed, to her, like a publicity stunt, pure and simple. At the same time, she was concerned about the influence of Maritain's group on her husband, Jean.

Cocteau at first blamed his friend's coldness on the nascent depression that kept her from working. Shocked at not seeing her at the opening of Orpheus— she retorted that she had not been invited—he sent her tickets. This time she agreed to come, called it a masterpiece, and then went back to speaking badly of him. Had she lost all feelings for him? When they ran into each other in public, she almost seemed ashamed to know him. Their wartime idyll, the times they had spent with the Ballets Russes, with Varèse and Satie, with Radiguet and Les Six, seemed never to have taken place. There remained only awkwardness and reproachful silence. "An evil spell has transformed Valentine Hugo . . . into my worst enemy," Cocteau wrote to a mutual friend.[53]

Once she joined the Communist Party, and Cocteau began to run into her, humble and blushing, in Breton's wake, he understood: she was secretly in love with the leonine Surrealist. The Swan of Boulogne had gone over to the enemy. He loved her so that he thought it must be a bad dream; the young woman to whom he had pledged his heart, as they walked along the Seine, could not abandon him so brutally. And she knew so many things about him that he had cold sweats imagining what she might reveal to Breton. Was she punishing him for not desiring her physically, she who preferred to believe that all men wanted her? That must be it. To beg forgiveness, Cocteau sent her two magnificent red and gold vases that his uncle the ambassador had brought back from Persia. "I don't deserve them," Valentine responded immediately. Since he insisted, she resold them, to the great displeasure of Jean Hugo—but both sides thought they might have a spell cast over them. Cocteau was determined to love her "in spite of herself," incapable of resigning himself to such a horrible betrayal from someone who had been so close that during the war they had thought they might marry.[54] Yes, in continuing to court the true Valentine, and not the woman whom Breton had enchanted, he would manage to make himself heard.

Breton remained wary of anyone formerly associated with Cocteau, as if this "society man" was contagious. Valentine Hugo, ten years older than Breton, was thus reduced to showing up wherever he went, begging for attention. If she seemed like an aloof seductress, she became tender and almost imploring when it came to the defender of "l'amour fou."[55] She may even have reproached herself for having hosted, ten years earlier, the reading of Le Cap de Bonne-Espérance, which had caused Breton's allergy to Cocteau. "I hate all that I seem to have loved," she assured him.[56] She could disavow her passionate friendship with Cocteau—that "angel's turd"—all she liked; Breton nevertheless continued to keep his distance.

Soon she was even dreaming of Breton, in the form of a crescent moon with blindingly bright points, so she went back to work, to glorify her new idol. Never had she shown so much talent. Marvels emanated from her brush, which only the Ballets Russes had been able to inspire to that point. Breton, this star who obsessed her days and illuminated her nights, became the center of a human constellation that he made dazzle with his supernatural aura. In her limitless love, she painted Breton's face as the Angel of Death in her illustrations for Achim von Arnim's Contes bizarres. Then she turned him into the prophet of a new Orphic cult, with a lyre under his arm. Saint Luc himself did not display as much ardor when he painted the first icon of the Virgin Mary.

Valentine Hugo would always play an understated role in the very masculine Surrealist world. Unlike the naked women who gravitated toward the masculine sky of Breton's "Poètes Surréalistes de 1932," she would only ever be a small moon reflecting Breton's light.[57] But the role of secret muse suited her. Was she—as Breton would say of Frida Kahlo—a ribbon tied round the Surrealist bomb? She didn't care: living in Breton's shadow was enough to keep her happy.

THE SEALS OF VILLEFRANCHE

After Paris, Villefranche was an oasis of calm, and a welcome relief. The Welcome Hôtel was a dizzying microcosm of the important things in life: upstairs, you could make love for a few francs, and sometimes new life was created; you could drink, sing, or even murder at the bar. In his room with a view of the sky, Cocteau wrote. He was distracted, in his purposeful solitude, by the sailors' bellowing love-making. But once in his room, he forgot his sufferings. The only news to reach him was whatever they printed in *Le phare de Villefranche*: strictly local and refreshingly insignificant. To relax, he would take the boat, row out to sea, and stretch out naked on the floor, letting himself float with the waves. "The sun is an old lover who knows how to play his part," he wrote in *Le livre blanc*. "It wraps its arms around you. It grabs hold of you, it turns you over, and suddenly, I would come back to myself, sluggish, my stomach covered with a liquid like mistletoe."

As for the Surrealists, he would repay them in kind, sketching out the arguments that would become "Mystère laïc," a defense of Giorgio De Chirico, whom the Surrealists had just brutally ejected from their ranks for abandoning metaphysical painting. Doubtless Cocteau had more than simply aesthetic reasons to support such a decision by the painter of sleeping cities and dreamlike factories—that "faithless believer" who so excelled at making objects and people seem strange.[58] De Chirico himself suspected as much, while praising Cocteau's courage.[59] Cocteau was so pleased at being able to thwart the group that had taken Picasso from him that De Chirico and even Dalí (who was himself blacklisted by the Surrealists) would eclipse the Spaniard in his *Essai de critique indirecte*. But Cocteau also recognized his own path in De Chirico's neoclassical evolution. Rather than painting dreams (as Breton demanded), De Chirico intelligently conceived of works that themselves "seemed to sleep," like Cocteau's poetry, and as time went on his drawings soon accumulated lyres, columns, and temples.

The nebulous atmosphere that De Chirico created was reminiscent of the days that Cocteau had spent with Christian Bérard stretched out on bamboo mats, feeling their limbs grow numb, one after the other. Behind the closed shutters of the Welcome, he thought he was floating on the river of the dead, like an Egyptian mummy sometimes obliged to return, in the space of a daydream, to the barracks of the living.

With his grubby nails and his slippers full of holes, his multicolored dressing gowns and his always congested head, Bérard monstrously embodied the fantasy of the era. Jean Hugo said that he would sleep on a mattress of fashion magazines, photographs, detective novels, cigarette ash, and opium residue. This dirty catchfly whose own fly sometimes gaped open in the middle of his stained dungarees had become Cocteau's inseparable companion on his journeys into the dark. Bérard would only interrupt these journeys to return home to visit his parents, in their villa in the 16th arrondissement. Later he would go instead to a cheap hotel in the rue Nollet, where Max Jacob and Maurice Sachs were also sometimes guests.

This was more than a friendship; it was one of those pure, knowing, and joyful relationships that are unique to homosexuality. Opium inspired them to ape the most absurd characters; belting his dressing gown and draping his little dog around his neck like a living fur collar, Bérard became a rich old lady confessing the worst obscenities to a general, a cousin of Clapier's who was violently attracted to him, but who, knowing nothing of homosexuality, understood nothing of what was happening to him. Together they pretended to be all sorts of people, from a famous German actress to a brilliant rival of Wagner's stifled by his talent for blustering. Sometimes they would contort themselves into fishing nets with cutouts for the eyes, ears, and nose; other times they would dress up like young ladies circa 1900, with a spray of tuberoses in one hand. They would dig out of the attic floral day dresses and antique hats worthy of Laure de Chevigné and imitate a pair of old ladies who went blithely to the casino in Monte Carlo to lose all their money, or they would pretend to be a pair of old chorus girls kicking their legs up one last time at the Folies Bergère before keeling over.[60]

Bérard's chubby cheeks earned him a nickname previously reserved for Radiguet: a second "Bébé" was born. Valentine Hugo, who saw herself as the guardian of Radiguet's memory, saw this as yet another reason to reject her old friend. With his half-complimentary, half-fatalistic sense of humor and a taste for the macabre that it would perhaps be too much to attribute to his mother, whose family owned the Borniol funeral parlors, Bérard was almost as gifted as Cocteau. Painting, set design, sewing, dance—he did it all, except for writing. A kind of gnawing laziness and a constant need for money, because of his opium habit, kept him far from his easel, selling his talent for cash instead. At the theater he would become Cocteau's right-hand man, and soon Louis Jouvet's best collaborator; in life, he would become Cocteau's third eye, always ready to draw him asleep, as Cocteau had done with Radiguet: Cocteau's Cocteau. The opium-saturated fantasies of Bérard's painting had their own strange charm. "I seek out malaise," he said, describing the woolly state created by smoking: the fanciful disease that had also inspired Picasso to paint his scrawny acrobats, and that ate away at the hybrid beings—half-fetal, half-elderly—which filled Bérard's canvases. The Surrealists accused him of painting ectoplasm, but Cocteau had a sensual love of those human seals washed up on beaches, to whom Bérard devoted his bulging little fingers and his corpulent figure, like that of an overgrown child. He too preferred to paint "sleepers over dreams," as Cocteau wrote to Max Jacob, before becoming the defender of these solitary beings on the edge of dissolving into the horizon, and so upping the stakes in the Breton-Cocteau war.[61]

Cocteau already loved animals. The tireless love Bérard inspired in his dogs was so infectious that he adopted a vivacious little Madagascan monkey. Bérard only had to put his lips on Biribi the Scottish terrier's muzzle to receive an outpouring of love, whereas Cocteau could simply hold out a banana to Gnafron, see him pick up a pen and try to write, or feel him wrap his arms around his neck while he slept, to once again have the sensation of being his generation's golden boy.[62] The scent of flowers surrounded him in his nightly walks around the port, and he felt himself turning back into Orpheus, the enchanter of the beasts and the plants, the King of Creation. In Nice on September 14, 1926, Isadora Duncan held a recital in her studio. Cocteau read Orpheus, Marcel Herrand read some of the poems from Cocteau's *Opéra*, and Duncan danced bare-breasted in the candlelight, moving to the music with "slow, splendid steps," as Janet Flanner wrote.[63] It was then that Cocteau began to believe that happy times had returned.

THE OEDIPAL LATIN MASS

There were hints that Cocteau's fortunes were improving, at least slightly. After Cocteau praised the achievement of Stravinsky's *Mavra* in the press, even though many critics had ignored it completely, the Russian composer warmed to him again. The stinging failure of *David* and the attacks made against Stravinsky in *Le coq et l'arlequin* (to which he had added a more than amiable 1926 postscript) were forgotten in a chance meeting in a train on the Côte d'Azur in 1925. "I had just seen his *Antigone*, and I had very much liked his treatment of the myth, and the way he updated it," Stravinsky said.[64] Taking advantage of this enthusiasm, Cocteau read him *Orpheus*, which the composer enjoyed as well.

They began discussing music once again, and discovered they were very much in tune with one another. Stravinsky had entered a neoclassical period himself with *Pulcinella* (1920), for which Picasso had done the sets. Stravinsky had rejected the pagan savagery of his work from the previous decade—*Le sacre du printemps* in particular—and hoped to find his way back to a more traditional use of melody. He imagined a Latinate work, clear, almost algebraic—a bit like that which Cocteau had espoused in *Le coq et l'arlequin*. Overwhelmed by the spiritual crisis that had recently brought him to Orthodox Christianity, Stravinsky went so far as to declare the ballet heretical because of the importance it granted the body. "In his self-refusal," Cocteau would quite logically say, "Stravinsky outdoes us all."[65]

The two were moved by their increased mutual interest in religion, and imagined collaborating on something together before they went to visit Maritain, in June 1926. From the port of Villefranche to the heights of Mount Boron, where Stravinsky lived, was no great distance, and the journey was well-suited to walks in the mountains. Stravinsky proposed that they adapt Sophocles' *Oedipus Rex*, a tragedy about exile and the terror of being without religious or geographic roots, as well as the fragility of man in the face of his destiny. The theme would have emphasized the maturity that Stravinsky had reached in his forties, and the suffering he felt from having left his birth country, as well as his desire to create a truly international work. It was also very appealing to Cocteau, who was then full of the convert's zeal, and more than usually willing to accept a proposition when he was not the one to make it. Since they were less interested in personal destinies than in the figure of Destiny itself, they decided they would stage only its pawns. The plot would be minimalist, and the characters less subjects with free will than living statues. There could not be a more neoclassical theme, but it was so new for Stravinsky that he would ask Cocteau to say nothing about the work, in public or private, before—and, moreover, after—the "Greek liturgy" had been performed, recalling the era of *David*, when Cocteau had blithely promised it would be a great success.[66] This was a promise no one could make.

Stravinsky believed that a specific language was called for in any material that hoped to reach the sublime. Saint Francis of Assisi had believed, for example, that French was necessary to express intensely religious and poetic emotions. Stravinsky decreed that the dialogues Cocteau would take from Sophocles should be translated into Latin by Jean Daniélou, a young seminarian from Maritain's circle.[67] This dead language, mysterious and immediately phonetic, capable of bearing the words of those who inhabited the kingdom of the dead who awaited Oedipus, symbolized the kind of constrained order to which Stravinsky, like Cocteau, had decided to submit himself in order to be revitalized. But if Cocteau aimed for *Thomas l'imposteur* to be a remedy for modernity, with *Oedipus Rex* he was transitioning to shock therapy.[68] Stravinsky was thereby convinced, as Cocteau said in *Le coq et l'arlequin*, that there was nothing better than a deliberately "ordinary" style to reveal the originality of its creator.

The two men worked separately. Stravinsky wrote the score between 1925 and 1927, letting himself be guided by the ancient rhythms, trying to create a work that would be "outside of time" and occasionally resorting, as a way of "Westernizing" it, to playful pastiches of Handel, Mayerbeer, and Tchaikovsky. His former opponent, by contrast, sketched out the reciter's speeches while revising the Latin he had learned. They compared their results every day for two months, and Cocteau sometimes had to try two or three times before he got his libretto right. Although he had been quite strict when they had worked on *David*, Stravinsky now approved of all Cocteau's ideas, like the sketches Cocteau drew for Stravinsky's son Theodore, who was in charge of the costumes and sets—sketches that soon changed into proliferating suggestions of how to stage the piece. "The hopes I had placed in Cocteau were wonderfully rewarded," Stravinsky said, delighted with the majestic style and sonorous power of the Latin text.[69] As for Cocteau, he found the music miraculously "gilded, coiling, looping," to such an extent that he went with Stravinsky to thank God in the churches of the Côte d'Azur. Encouraged in his little weakness, the poet felt obliged to add to the cast a commentator who would explain the myth to those who were unfamiliar with it. The antique references were beginning to go over the average mortal's head—Antigone and Orpheus had proved it—and this ringmaster would summarize, after every scene, the drama experienced by the offspring of Hades.[70] With explanations like "Without knowing it, Oedipus is entrapped by the powers that watch over us from the other side of death," we are reminded of the gramophone-announcer that Cocteau used in *David, Parade*, and *Les mariés de la Tour Eiffel*. Stravinsky approved yet again, and went so far as to offer the role to Cocteau. Delighted to have found an "unsentimental" and anti-individualist means of expression, as the Church had always preached, Stravinsky would praise Cocteau's genius for stagecraft eight years later in his memoirs.

Stravinsky's about-face was displeasing to most, except Cocteau. The use of Latin, amplified by a harp, hieratic chorus, and "medieval" trumpets, was intended to make the score perennially fresh and immune to wear and tear, but it gave the work a slightly rigid if not outright pompous air. In striving for a libretto that would be written in a deliberately conventional, almost ritualistic style, Stravinsky had ended up cutting out all the work's imagination, any "inspiration" or romanticism that might have come from its mythic-Catholic "still life." Pierre Boulez denounced Stravinsky's neoclassical "depravity" and it must be admitted that he proved himself to be a much more stirring, and paradoxically much more universal composer, in *Petrushka* or the *Le sacre du printemps*, which are pagan celebrations of his beloved Russia. It seemed as if this new "international" style was only a repentant step away from his original nationalist style.

Was Stravinsky right to resort to a language that was, as he said, not dead but "petrified"—that is, monumental, ageless, and therefore protected from falling out of fashion or into vulgarity? He had better success elsewhere, in other works with similar goals and also in Latin, like his 1930 *Symphony of Psalms*. It seems that some doubts were inevitable upon hearing Jocasta proclaim "Non n'erubeskite, reges, / clamare, ululare in aegra urbe / domestikis altercatonibus," knowing that it was being sung "by Russians, with Latin pronunciation, for a French audience," as Janet Flanner put it maliciously in her column for the *New Yorker*.[71] Saved by the composer's formalist power, the old-fashioned hodgepodge of musical archetypes did win its supporters, like Boris de Schoelzer, for whom "the anti-individualist ideal of order and discipline" to which Stravinsky had submitted himself made his music revolutionary (he then added, unfortunately, "much like what Charles Maurras is doing at the moment").[72] Which is to say that the oratorio, which had intended to make tradition the future, was not exactly progressive.

Meanwhile, *Oedipus Rex* was running out of money. It was meant to be a surprise gift for Diaghilev, to celebrate the twentieth anniversary of his work for the theater. But the great impresario, suffering from diabetes, suspected something, and undertook a sly investigation. Interrogating Cocteau as if he already knew the full story, he managed to get enough information out of him to piece together that the work was about Oedipus blindly headed toward his own downfall, and pronounced it a morbid homage. Cocteau protested, but Misia as usual had to pour fuel on the fire as the flames licked at his feet. "Be careful, they're singing in Latin. It's your death mass," a friend whispered, exacerbating an already paranoid Diaghilev—a man who refused to have his illness treated.[73] "Everyone knows that I don't like to sleep with women, and that includes old witches like Jocasta, even if she were my mother," Diaghilev confided to the musician Nicolas Nabokoff. Was this an allusion to Cocteau's incestuous tendencies, or a sign of Diaghilev's own weariness? He was so exhausted that doubtless he would have shut himself away in the palace of his ancestors to devote himself to his books, if the USSR had left him the money to do so. The Ballets Russes hadn't only ruined him; they had taken his health as well.

"We're waiting for you darling, you hold the purse strings!" Misia said when Coco Chanel returned from London.[74] But Chanel was hoping for a more flattering role, and the ballet had to be cancelled, and then the scenery and the costumes, because no one wanted to go into debt for a spectacle that was intended to run for only three or four performances. Only the generosity of Princess Winnie de Polignac could save it from total failure.[75] Cocteau, as always, suffered; after the opera-oratorio had been stripped down to a concert accompanied by singers in evening wear, Diaghilev even took away Cocteau's role as reciter and went so far as to forbid him from directing his "replacement," an actor who had been deliberately chosen for his youthfulness. "In his desire that the work fail—a cantata in his honor!—, Diaghilev is capable of anything," Cocteau confided to Stravinsky.[76] He was wrong, however, to give detailed reports of these intrigues to the musician, and to let slip how much Diaghilev detested the set that Stravinsky's son had designed. It didn't take much to reawaken Stravinsky's obsessive fears, knowing that he was at the source of the original "flight." "Silence is natural. Do you not sometimes feel the need for it yourself?" he said haughtily to Cocteau.[77]

The premiere was May 3, 1927, at the Théâtre Sarah Bernhardt. Stravinsky conducted with his customary passion, lurching his enormous arms up toward the galleries: "A vertical ant," as Cocteau put it.[78] Although it was sung by voices of unequaled power, his "austere vocal concert" suffered for being caught between two colorful ballets, and the reception was cold. Stravinsky was tempted to blame the piece's failings on Cocteau's reciter, whom the *Nouvelle revue française* had criticized harshly. Interviewed by Alejo Carpentier, Cocteau commented that Stravinsky's music was that of a shark who thinks himself a nightingale.[79] Thirty years later, in his interviews with Robert Craft, who had "converted" him to the twelve-tone scale, Stravinsky would still be accusing Cocteau of having "re-sentimentalized" and prostituted his work, when his reciter had on the contrary contributed an aloof distance toward the proceedings. But Stravinsky had always been quick to humiliate his collaborators, especially when their value could be proven through their fame, so he credited Cocteau only as a contributing writer to the libretto, displaying his name in small letters beneath his own.

Cocteau would never again collaborate with Stravinsky, who finally admitted to Cocteau that the passages he had written about him in *Le coq et l'arlequin* had driven him mad.[80] The more versatile artist of the two was not, perhaps, whom he believed himself to be.

THE REIGN OF DESBORDES

Cocteau's relationship with Desbordes, liberated by opium, had gone beyond simple literary mentoring. After having his cousin Darlan reform the young sailor, Cocteau (eroticizing, as usual, the object of his admiration) had come to confuse Desbordes's writing with his body, the savage lyricism of his texts with his physical aura. During the three years that Cocteau mourned Radiguet, Desbordes had become a new, idealized alter-ego, younger, handsome, talented—the "child-King." For a time, Cocteau felt guilty. His Christian readings had so convinced him that sex was dirty that he could no longer set foot in the Villefranche church without embarrassment. He had to admit that in spite of his saintly ideals, desire had never left him. But the affection that Sachs had dragged out of him and the fears Maritain had inspired in him were eclipsed by the attraction he felt for Desbordes, and he convinced himself that these other things were not, in fact, important. Why should Christ be offended to see his followers love each other, when His own doctrine was built on love? Was it not most important to do good, to love one's neighbor as much as oneself and to banish all evil?

Most of the boys who had infatuated him until that point had been reluctant. He had had to charm them with his words and his hands, until they became intimate with him almost in spite of themselves. But Desbordes willingly shared his bed. He may have been the third Jean to enter his life, after Le Roy and Bourgoint, but he was the first to reciprocate his love. Desbordes recognized no sexual taboos; he was capable of taking what he wanted anytime, any place, with either sex, with animals, or even with trees. He forced Cocteau to integrate the joys of the body into his Christian philosophy. "He laughed at my guilt, which he took for weakness," Cocteau said of Desbordes in *Le livre blanc*, through Desbordes's alter ego, H. Cocteau's abstinence—undertaken with difficulty during his time with Radiguet, then desperately defended when he returned to God—turned to prodigality; what a joy it was to rediscover the virtues of "this fabulous little sea plant, that had been crumpled up, dead, washed ashore by the sea foam, now come back to life, stand up straight, and hurl out its life-blood!"[81]

In a cold, hard generation, born to take nothing seriously, Desbordes never held back his enthusiasm or his feelings. "Jean loves himself, with all the awkwardness of passion," Cocteau wrote to Max Jacob.[82] Nicknamed Jean-Jean, to avoid confusing him with Bourgoint, Desbordes was exuberant in other respects. His very name—Desbordes, or "what spills over"—haunted his vocabulary, full of "lurches" and "floods": if his door was half open, there would be a gust of wind. Cocteau had freed himself from Radiguet through opium, from opium through God, then from God by a little more opium; Desbordes pushed him back into the kind of life he had had with Radiguet. Cocteau took Desbordes to the Luna Park with the remaining members of the Society of Mutual Admiration, where they made a pilgrimage to Violetta the Trunk Woman, a stubborn German woman with no arms or legs; they also wandered all over the Russian mountains and cried from the top of water chutes. Then they slipped down into a grotto where the red eyes of a panther gleamed at them and a naked young woman threw herself from a ladder into the basin. There they shot the same foam balls with plastic rifles, and laughed while they ate cotton candy, just as in the days with Bébé Radiguet.[83]

Jacob warned Cocteau that in shamelessly returning to pleasure, his time in Purgatory might be lengthened, or he might go straight to Hell. The Evangelist had been clear: only continence or expiation could banish sin; by violating this divine decree, he was offending Heaven. But Cocteau no longer wanted to turn his back on his own nature, or to imitate Jacob's self-sacrificing pose. Jacob could only bear it if his love were disinterested and his desires unsatisfied, in the manner of Christ addressing his disciples. But Cocteau was convinced that God demanded to be lived, not imitated: the Virgin herself would probably look on what believers like Jacob called "indecencies: shame, sex, etc." with the same distance as the stars. Sex was not dirty; it was beautiful, alive; as liquid and abundant as the Milky Way. Poor Max, whose guilt made him believe that the end of the world was set for May 28, 1928, when the earth would open and humanity would be swallowed up into Hell!

Yet it wasn't simply a question of pleasure with Desbordes, but of love and of literature. So what if he wasn't Radiguet's equal: a few on-the-job lessons would reveal his genius. "Cocteau had a kind of Cophetua complex," said Lee Miller, the photographer and companion of Man Ray: like the African king who did all he could to transform the beggar girl whom he loved, he took it upon himself to turn Desbordes into a real writer.[84] Soon he could be heard to say, "There has been a miracle from heaven—Raymond has returned in another form, and he often unmasks himself."[85] And in time, he would reproduce with Jean-Jean, according to the same implacable logic as with Radiguet, the abusive relationship his mother had with him. He was simultaneously Cocteau the writer; Jean the lover; and a suffocating, cultivated, and right-minded person whose personality he had adopted when he was very young. In Desbordes's young, svelte body, Cocteau quasi-incestuously united his own self with the Parisian lady and friend of academicians who sought to protect her son against the impurities of the world and the vices of his entourage. "My mother is like myself," he had written to Sachs three years earlier.[86] He did everything for Desbordes, in order to be everything for him—so much so that he could well have said: "Desbordes, c'est moi."

Only one person could find fault with this role-playing, and that was Mme Cocteau herself. She despaired at seeing Cocteau's Christian ardor diminish, and was shocked to see him encouraging and grooming a boy who quite clearly knew how to enjoy himself. For the first time, she outwardly opposed the arrival of one of Cocteau's new favorites. Though Cocteau might have thought he was doing her a favor in not inflicting a rival on her, and though he may have thought that his love, instead of proving to be "sterile," was giving her beautiful and talented new sons, she would not budge. He could not inflict such an affront on the Church, on Maritain, and least of all on herself.

A confrontation with his mother became less avoidable every day, so Cocteau decided to sever his material dependence on her. Taking advantage of the disruption caused by work that needed doing at the rue d'Anjou, he took a room at the Hôtel de la Madeleine, on the nearby rue de Surène. This was quite a risk for a writer with no regular income, but also a relief for a thirty-seven-year-old man to finally be able to make love the way he wanted to, and to openly smoke his pipes. His mother had continued, as she had when he was ten years old, to pay his lawyer's fees and his fines, as well as to send gifts to the women who invited him over and clothes when he needed them. But now she would cease to be the person he loved best and who loved him most, and instead would become a mother from whom one must hide certain things. The incredible openness which had marked their relationship, in which each seemed to live on either side of a two-way mirror, was over. For the first time since his adolescence, she did not receive a poem at the end of the year.

Hotel life was liberating. Radiguet's ghost, which had been maintained by a constellation of photos on the walls of the rue d'Anjou, was dispelled. "Memories of my room no longer gnaw at me," he wrote to Maurice Sachs, the first to hear of the end of this possession—which had not after all been diabolical but angelic. The dead no longer had a hold on him; he could breathe again among the living. If Desbordes longed for the country, they took themselves off to Chablis, a small town surrounded by vineyards, and then to the Midi behind the wheel of a Citroën B14, a gift from Moysès, who had just closed the Boeuf on the rue Boissy-d'Anglas to open a branch in Cannes. It was wonderful to drive with Cocteau. The trail of clouds and the vagaries of the wind excited his fantasies; the tortured silhouettes of the olive trees turned into dancing gypsies, and their car into a farcical character, the "Abbé Quatorze," who would drive across fields to deliver extreme unction, then into a hovel in Marseilles to give confession to a young girl, before spraying holy water on a gangster's body: an anti-Maritain who only loved louche places and joyous vices, ecclesiastical pomp and obscenities in a cassock.[87] It was one of those free-wheeling, boyish trips with no domestic or familial worries, where the spirit can throw its hat up above the windmills and laugh crudely at everyone, and where objects could have their own inner lives.

They spent a night in Aix, rocked to sleep by the sound of the fountains, then passed over the invisible border into a Greek version of France, where they were surrounded by vines and fruit trees. Through the car windows they could make out, as evening fell, the Camargue, "Arizona on our scale," where the couple stopped in the shadow of Jean Hugo's farmhouse.[88] They left the car to the side and bedded down on the terrace. Desbordes was half asleep, but Cocteau wanted to draw him from every angle before abandoning himself to a kind of half-sleep, which made his hand even more supple. It seemed that Cocteau was not content simply to transform Desbordes's way of life and personality into his own, and to give him his own values and quirks; he also wanted to perfect his desirable silhouette as he slept.[89]

These few days were like a dream, lived in a place that was neither earth, nor water, nor sky, but all the elements at once: a perfect definition of balance, for Cocteau.

NAVY BOYS

The "Abbé Quatorze" soon resumed its travels and deposited the couple in Marseilles, in the heart of a giant brothel, just behind the Vieux Port, that attracted sailors the world over. To encourage the sailors to follow them back to their rooms, the girls would steal their hats so they would chase after them. But Cocteau and Desbordes were bare-headed, and they could leisurely survey this improvised casbah where the interlaced bodies endlessly smoked and made love. Bérard, who had joined them, managed to worm his way into a gang leader's den, seemingly flea-ridden, but actually full of Kisslings and Derains — a real Ali Baba's cave.[90] Praying before the Maritain's Rouaults was somehow less exciting!

They set out for Villefranche before making it to Cannes, in order to help launch the Boeuf that Moysès had just opened, but it was at Toulon that they were happiest. The port was so beautiful that its harbor was compared to the Bay of Naples, or even Venice for its colors, and all the boats of Europe came there to moor. "Scenery by Puget and Vauban, with markets like Greek temples, and piazzas like ballrooms," Cocteau wrote to his mother.[91] Toulon was as old as Carthage or Tyr, according to Paul Morand, who admired the navy officers with sideburns, those "elegant, bare-necked, upright sailors, with narrow hips, carrying a boat-hook," and the young workers, market gardeners, and mussel gatherers from La Seyne or Tamaris, who shouted at each other and enlivened the quai Cronstadt.[92] The cousin of admirals and a lover of sailors himself, Cocteau took up residence near the port, which already boasted two hundred opium dens by the beginning of the century, and whose bars were teeming with sailors (twenty-five thousand lived there), Montparnasse painters (Picasso, Lhote, Kissling), Parisian homosexuals, and local transvestites, all eager to amuse themselves.[93] "It would be boring to describe the charms of this Sodom, where the fire of heaven falls without striking in the form of tender sunlight," Cocteau would write in Le livre blanc, but others were more willing to chronicle the unique atmosphere in the city, which would be destroyed in the bombings of the war to come.

Cocteau could often be seen at the fairgrounds, weaving in and out of the waffle sellers, the hucksters, and the "strongmen with their red pompoms." Soon he would have a drink with a sailor with a broken nose with "No luck" tattooed on his neck, then take him back to his hotel—this man who was a double for Dargelos, with his woolly hat set back on his head and "La Tapageuse" ("The Noisy" or "The Show Off," the name of his boat) written there in gold letters, who was making more and more pressing demands for money after a motorcycle accident.[94] Cocteau could also be found waltzing and singing with the soldiers on leave at the Clos Mayol, Bérard's regular hangout; the sailors would often ask a man to dance, if they couldn't find a female partner. Night would come over the little streets and would change "the most brutal convicts, the most frustrated Bretons, the most ferocious Corsicans into big girls with low-cut dresses, swaying their hips, decked out in flowers, who liked to dance and would take their partner, without hesitation, to the hotels along the port."[95] (That is, when the captain of the Prince of Lucinge's yacht didn't buy them first for his rich visitors.) In the morning, Cocteau, Desbordes, and Bérard would go and play on the quays with Petit-Cru, the dog he had bought as a companion for Gnafron, his little monkey. Then they would return to the Hôtel des Négociants, which was also a brothel, to smoke a bit while Gnafron too swallowed a bit of the smoke, before giving in to the sound of the water lapping at the boats as they bobbed in the inner harbor. Sometimes Cocteau preferred to hum the melody of Pauvre Matelot, the three acts of which Milhaud had composed out of despair, and which would be performed later that year at the Opéra-Comique.

After barely six months, Desbordes, like Bourgoint, had become a confirmed opium addict, and become addicted to cocaine. Cocteau took cocaine as well to counteract the soothing effects of the opium. Living intimately with a smoker without smoking was impossible, Cocteau recognized; it would be like living in two different countries in the same bedroom. Only one of his companions, Maurice Sachs, had escaped addiction, but that only resulted in a much more toxic love, one that Cocteau seemed curiously eager to feed. "I swear I have never changed," he wrote, thinking he should add: "I love you. My life has changed. You have nothing to do with this change. I live quite alone and devote myself to Jean Desbordes. You will find a place again in my home, wherever that home may go."[96] What was Sachs supposed to make of this shower of contradictory promises? It sounds like a letter written by a father who is about to remarry, the type of person in whom Sachs had long ago lost confidence. His former guardian angel had definitively changed into a dark angel, eager to deface his former god.

As in love as he had been with Radiguet, Cocteau could only speak of Desbordes. He presented him as the literary hope of his generation when they were invited to the parties that Coco Chanel gave at her *hôtel particulier* in the rue Saint-Honoré, whose gardens extended all the way to the Avenue Gabriel, near the U.S. embassy, in the place de la Concorde. Once the meal had been served, Marcelle Meyer, Les Six's soloist, played the piano and Cocteau sang the classic ballads he had learned from Reynaldo Hahn and Coco de Madrazo. That is, unless Stravinsky came to beg for the designer's attention; he had secretly loved her since 1921, with a masochistic shyness that she cruelly mocked.[97]

Born of the wandering affairs of a street vendor from the Auvergne, Chanel, who revolutionized the feminine silhouette, had since *Antigone* designed all the costumes and accessories for Cocteau's productions. Their collaboration had turned from artistic to commercial: he rewrote the interviews and texts she gave to the press, while sketching clothes and jewelry for her, when he wasn't busy helping with the window decor at the rue Cambon. On her side, Chanel was beginning to make money from the Eau Miracle de l'Impératrice Eugénie that Cocteau splashed on his face every morning—the recipe for which had been sold to her by Lucien Daudet, after being kept secret since the Medicis. It became an important part of her fortune, before the triumph of the famous N° 5. Like Picasso, everything Chanel touched turned to gold.[98]

Under the influence of Misia, who had created her taste, but helped along by sheer force of willpower (prompting Maurice Sachs to compare her to the heroines of the Fronde), Chanel—the "Great Mademoiselle," as the publisher Bernard Grasset called her—had changed from a milliner into a real Parisienne. She was purely a designer, something no dressmaker had yet managed to do, and she lived royally among her Coromandel screens, providing sumptuous pensions for her artist friends. She partly funded the ballets of Diaghilev; in fact, the austere Reverdy had become her protégé and lover—another inheritance from Misia, who, like the lead character in Mankiewicz's *All about Eve*, Chanel would eventually cast aside. Cocteau himself received ten thousand francs per month (about 600 dollars today), along with access to the little summer house in Roquebrune and the assurance that his patron would provide for his hotel bills, his detox bills, or simply his vacations.

Thanks to Desbordes's almost exalted love and Chanel's princely generosity, Cocteau's belief in his lucky star was restored. He made it his symbol that spring, when he arrived in Chablis with his companion at the Hôtel de l'Étoile—using a star with five wings to replace at the bottom of his letters the heart that had bled too much, and to remind the world of the distinctive sign that cast its light on him. "I'm living through a very calm, gentle, and lofty period," he told Max Jacob. Although the opium kept his weight around fifty kilos, or 110 pounds, he was reinvigorated by the cure prescribed by Dr. Carton, whom Stravinsky had recommended, and Cocteau felt light enough to join his vanished friends and float up among them like an angel. Dullin's triumphant revival of *Antigone* had "swept away like a tempest of love" all the hatred that had pursued him for years.[99] It was a relief for Cocteau, who as he approached his fortieth birthday could bear only comfort and applause.

Desbordes's naturalist ways also did Cocteau some good. The country had never really existed for him, but it now became vital, like journeys without destinations and spontaneous stopovers. Dipping his nose into the flowers of an apple tree, the "odor of reproduction" nearly caused him to faint. Just as every other time he had undergone a metamorphosis, the smell of his own sap wafted up at him everywhere he went. Every day Desbordes's vitality led him further astray from Maritain's ascetic Christianity, and closer to what he believed to be the solar essence of divine instruction. If he still spoke to the Creator, it was no longer through the confessional or the Host, but through the innocent creatures with which he had enchanted the earth, the monkeys, the lilies, the nightingales. "Cocteau remade his sensibilities with . . . Desbordes: he became a pantheist," noted Maurice Martin du Gard.[100]

Cocteau worked on Desbordes's writing with him, having encouraged him to put some pieces together with an eye to publication. He suggested some cuts, and then began to melt down entire phrases, adding his own turns of phrase. Relieved of a few "obscene" passages, this patchwork was submitted to Bernard Grasset, who gave it his approval; as soon as *J'adore* was published he began to plan with the editor—just as he had done for *Diable au corps*—how best to promote this fresh young thing, so ill at ease in Paris, in the literary world. And who knows—maybe they would make him as glorious as Radiguet, the angel he had replaced.

Opium bound Cocteau and Desbordes to each other as much as did ambition or love. Seeking it out, preparing it ritually, and finally consuming it, took the better part of their days, during the early months of 1928, which they passed in part at the Welcome Hôtel. "The typical, easily recognizable smell filled the hallways," said an American passing through, adding: "I remember wondering how it was possible to smoke so openly in a public hotel without the authorities catching wind of it."[101] By the end of the season, the osmosis was complete. They had the same long, pomaded, unparted hair, the same way of using mouthwash that turned their tongues and cheeks red; and Desbordes began to wear Cocteau's clothes, as Radiguet once had, including a blue ratteen overcoat with a pink lining.[102] Always up for the codependence that love encouraged, Cocteau absorbed his protégé's personality, until they formed a couple that transcended both their destinies.

A SOLITARY *OPÉRA*

Once again, upon the publication of his collection *Opéra*, written under the influence of opium, and then during his detox period, Cocteau found the Surrealists in his path. A perfunctory reading would reveal, among the numerous word games, the final echoes of an early twentieth-century childhood marked by the puns of the Vermot Almanack. But its poetic ambition was much greater: to prove the unsurpassable influence of words on our way of seeing the world, as well as the musical and organic links that join them. "L'ami Zamor de Mme du Barry," was Louis XV's mistress, who had been denounced in the Terror by her servant Zamor.[103] And of course there was this line: "G. touchant G. sans en avoir l'R. Selle et faix de mon âne archi-tranquille."[104] These linguistic riddles, with their echolalia and other pre-Lacanian non sequiturs, sometimes came from Cocteau's dreams; this was the first time he would use them to create a story, betraying how syllables profoundly influence and interfere with the very objects they bring to life.

Desnos claimed no other aim when he wrote: "Pourquoi votre incarnat est devenu si terne, petite fille, dans cet internat où votre oeil se cerna."[105] Leiris, meanwhile, wrote "Le sang est la sente du temps" and Duchamp: "Il faut mettre la moelle de l'épée dans le poil de l'aimée." By grappling with the poetic experience, Breton's friends also knew how powerfully the psyche could reduce the signifier and the signified to the same essence of sound, to some extent the original melody of language, if not to the unconscious itself. But Cocteau was feeling the pull of his own abyss behind these double-edged phrases—much like in a De Chirico where the shadows cast by the bars of a window at sunset, or the outline made by a broken windowpane, are proof that the dead and the angels are close to us, almost brushing against us. Beyond words lay the entirety of the atmosphere, made greater by these mysterious beings sent by the entity who weighs our value as He holds us in the palm of His hands.

Although originally autobiographical, Cocteau's poetry here would come to refuse its earthly origins and rise up to the level of a personal epiphany. He would affirm, in his mad desire for renewal, that *Opéra* marked the birth of his mythology. This was more surely the first gospel of a solitary religion, written by an apostle ready to make the ultimate sacrifice, when he wasn't explicitly identifying with heaven itself:

> Don't wake God, he sleeps
> Deeply, I am his dream . . .
> To awaken him would mean my death.[106]

Just as the rose had been before, now a statue served Cocteau as allegory. Half-man, half-god, this stone phantom delivered, by night, the most dangerous messages but also the rarest predictions. The revenge of the beaten child who comes back to life as an eagle in his dreams, the statue will never cease to be the image in which Cocteau will hide himself to live, glorious and powerful—the clairvoyant block that would protect him from being spat at and hit. "What does the marble think when a sculptor turns it into a masterpiece?" he asked as early as Orpheus. It thinks: "I'm being hit, chipped away at, broken, I am lost." It was thus for his own salvation that his enemies worked, in spite of themselves. Doubtless he had paid for this bust in his own blood, but he was convinced that for this reason he would be nourished by glory, that each drop of ink-blood spilled would feed him for centuries to come. "Stones thrown at me, you create my statue," he said here again, sealing his masochistic dependence on severity and blows.[107] For in his eyes the stones had in addition the advantage of making up for his tireless wandering, his "bounding from one world to another," as he described it. They weighed him down, preventing him from floating too quickly up to the heavens, like Radiguet before him; they grounded him in a way that was necessary for his work. They were salvation for a man in permanent revolution. No one since Nietzsche had confessed more bluntly the useful grandeur of suffering than this angel disguised in the body of a man, himself sheltering inside a virtual stone double. For this occasion he coined his most sincere aphorism: "I am a lie that only speaks the truth."[108]

Where this uneven and frustrating collection succeeds best is in its dreamy qualities, its air of weightlessness, in the middle of which floats Cocteau. No poetic place suited him more than the cesspool he sank into every night, the boundless territory where he could take root by the veins, and from which he could emerge only with the greatest of pain:

Do sleepers have legs?
Do they have an up and a down?
Are they in the air or in the water?
Is there bone in their limbs?
Is there air in their bones?[109]

There is no better way of phrasing the questions that Cocteau asked himself each day.

Opéra made no great splash. Cocteau would claim not to have sent it to any critics, sure that it could not please those who did not have the time to work out its enigmas; but it seems he was above all afraid of the Surrealists' vindictiveness, because he contemplated not even letting it go on sale. Desbordes took up the pen in defense of the collection, like Radiguet had at the time of *Orpheus*, and young André Fraigneau wrote that it was the foremost example anyone had seen for years of "pure poetry," that it brought "a taste of the absolute for which the readers of the period were dying of hunger."[110] Only the *Nouvelle revue française* broke the silence by devoting an unkind article to the "beautiful mask" who reliably produced spectacles, never events, before concluding: "The poetry he offers us is an insult to the poetry of which I am sure he is aware."[111] Though enthusiastic in his correspondence, Jacob privately complained that he had been plagiarized, because very early on, in *Le cornet à dés*, he too had used poetic wordplay. This was an understandable complaint from a man who was capable of writing "J'aime mieux descendre mon thé que monter des cendres" and whose bivocal phrases Michel Leiris, the most productive of his followers, would perpetuate, in works from *Glossaire, j'y serre mes gloses* to *Langage tangage, ou ce que les mots me disent.*[112]

Many readers of *Opéra* would laugh at the wordplay, as at the spoonerisms in their satiric weekly newspaper. Referring to Bergson, Cocteau was convinced that it was a response to the disquieting strangeness of his collection, the way one might sneeze out of anxiety. These pages were indeed not particularly funny; their sincerity is truly pathetic. It is troubling to imagine Breton reading the passages in which Cocteau compares himself to a cluster of mold continually surprised to find itself loved and embraced, and later, to an illiterate con man, with no knowledge of any language or dates, terrible at history and geography, building his reputation out of sheer brio.

The critical silence that greeted *Opéra* gave Cocteau the idea that he was the only one who could support his books, or appreciate them. His energy, his sense of intrigue, his talent for causing sensations still couldn't prevent them from being received with indifference. He wrote as early as *Thermes Urbains*,

I was only ever clumsy
And they all thought me graceful.
Left is my sole mistress
And they always put me on the right.[113]

Feverishness returned; the infinite promise of society's mirrors proved disappointing. The abyss yawned open once more. Why add another book to the thousands already weighing down the library bookshelves? After proliferation, emptiness, the monk's indifference, the nihilism of the hysterics, the pessimism of men without a penny to their names, nothing more existed, in such moments, beyond an unhappy conscience, which was made distraught by his total incapacity to be satisfied and to do without other people. "I love life, but it hates me," he said.[114] The publication of this collection only aggravated his situation. "To those who ask for much, much will be denied," said Horace.

Deeply wounded, Cocteau would practically stop writing poetry altogether, until the war. The pages of *Opéra* bled when they were cut, he swore. He came to detest *Plain-chant*, his most beautiful poem, which received so much praise, because it reminded him all the more how much this last publication had disappointed him.

THE RETURN OF SACHS

The only one of Cocteau's friends to understand and love *Opéra*, except for Desbordes, was Maurice Sachs, who seemed to find it contained his best-kept secrets. No sooner had Sachs returned from his military service than the former seminarian sent him a magnificent letter that made him believe for a moment that publishing that collection hadn't been a complete waste, that it had moved a soul as sensitive and delicate as his own. Cocteau had long ago forgiven Sachs his thieving; once again, their mutual weaknesses united them. Like those couples who need to drink together, Cocteau and Sachs renewed their intimacy—with Cocteau going so far as to tell Sachs the extent of his psychological suffering, and of the toll it was taking on his life with Desbordes. Which was a godsend for Sachs, who loved a chance to lecture his mentor, but was also a cause for suffering, given how jealous Sachs was of anyone who might have taken his place at Cocteau's side: Sachs was the promising disciple, too green to write anything really accomplished, the most affectionate of "sons" and the most miserable of lovers.

And so Sachs was reunited with Cocteau, along with alcohol, profligate spending, and visits to Albert Le Cuziats' steam baths. Like a golem returned to haunt his creator in order to find some semblance of reality, Sachs had decided this time to make himself useful and to earn his living honestly. Recently appointed editor of a prestigious series, his first decision was to obtain publication rights for "Le mystère laïc," the essay Cocteau had just written on De Chirico.[115] He soon discovered the existence of *Le livre blanc*, a short part-autobiography, part-fiction piece inspired by Cocteau's erotic liberation. Written in Chablis in December 1927, while there with Desbordes, the text was explicitly sexual, but in the end was restrained by a form of modesty (unlike the drawings that would one day accompany it: figures with erect phalluses and bulging muscles, carried along by a kind of obscene piety).

Cocteau had never outwardly approached the subject before; the word "homosexuality" was the only one he would not allow himself to use until then, preferring to let the "thing" emerge on its own from his work. Yet he guessed at the importance of this book, the most astonishing of his actual novels—"my best thing," he would say to Sachs. This indirect praising of homosexual love, experienced as "one of the most mysterious workings of the divine masterpiece," was the kind of work that might once have helped the adolescent Cocteau to rise above opprobrium and secure his self-esteem. Yet he refused to let the book be published in his lifetime. Sachs tried to shake some sense into him, evoking Proust's brilliant frankness in *Sodome et Gomorrhe*, which had inspired Gide to publicly assume his own sexuality in *Corydon*, a dialogue published in 1924 in which a gay man justifies his desires by "the hermaphrodism of the duck and the bisexuality of the snail"—that was Angelo Rinaldi's opinion—but in which he himself still plays the role of the supposedly "normal" man.[116] Unlike his illustrious predecessors, Cocteau persisted in not wanting to publish his book, both to protect his mother, already traumatized by the Sachs-Pinkerton scandal, and because he wanted to avoid exhibitionism. "To make his secrets known to the salons seems to me the height of vulgarity," he wrote a bit later to Jacob, and this was one point on which he would never change his mind.[117]

Nevertheless, he gave his confession an almost militant air, declaring with a flourish, "I do not accept being tolerated," after opening with "I have always loved the stronger sex, which I believe can be legitimately called the fair sex. My misfortunes stem from a society that condemns the rare as a crime and forces us to reform our inclinations."[118] Certainly Cocteau was in an incredibly privileged position; if he had anything to suffer, it was more from Breton's prejudice than that of his milieu. But he thought of all the boys in the provinces who were made to fall into line and who might one day come upon his writing, and to them he declared that their "inclinations" were not reformable, and must be accepted. Though he agreed with Gide that they allowed man to escape the duties of reproduction and the social conventions that accompanied them, unlike Gide he did not see them as a luxury, or as art for art's sake, as Thomas Mann said, but the result of necessity.

In the book, he recounts his precocious and irrepressible sexuality, awakened by a young farmboy riding nude on a horse (Botten, his first lover?), by the "gypsy lads" climbing trees naked as Adam, or the young servant to whom he had given a drawing of a naked woman before trying his luck "with an inconceivable audacity." But if the richness of his imagination caused him to see again and again the "scraped knees blazoned with scabs, mud, and ink" of his fellow student Dargelos, or think back to his aborted attempt to follow the other students to a bordello and "counterfeit his nature," submitting to the act itself was a more delicate matter. He even confessed in these pages a deep jealousy of those homosexuals who are able to enter a house of ill repute and immediately choose their prey. In the places of enjoyment—baths, nightclubs, bars—he always preferred "conversation to action," and proved incapable of "perfecting a vice" to make it easy to satisfy, in exchange for a little money.

> In me the heart and the senses are so inextricably bound up together that I don't quite know how to involve the one without the others following suit. It's this that leads me to overstep the limits of friendship and makes me fear a summary contact from which I run the danger of catching the disease of love.[119]

This indicates the extent to which Cocteau depended on those who entered his life, and how much he dreaded even still the "mute horror of unrequited love" he had felt with Madeline Carlier, Raymond Radiguet, and Jean Bourgoint.

The most troubling aspect of *Le livre blanc* lay in its description of Cocteau's father, whom he had never mentioned before then. "The homosexual recognizes the homosexual as infallibly as the Jew the Jew . . . It has always seemed to me that my father and I too closely resembled each other not to have this essential feature in common. He was probably unaware of his true bent; at any rate, instead of going down that path, he struggled to climb another"—a mistake that would explain his suicide, especially in the eyes of his son, who would add, with troubling sincerity, "to this exceeding blindness it may be that I owe the fact that I was brought into the world. Well, I deplore it, for it would have been to the benefit of us both had my father known the joys that would have spared me much sorrow."[120] As if the son were paying with his suffering for the timidity of his progenitor.

Hoping to spare Maritain as well, Cocteau decided to publish the book anonymously and almost clandestinely, at a print run of only thirty copies. But since neither he nor Sachs were particularly discreet about it, rumors were soon circulating around Paris. Catching wind of this "devil's project," even as Cocteau asked him to write an article on his "Le mystère laïc," Maritain tried to get hold of this erotic manuscript, just as he had managed to obtain a copy of *Corydon* from Gide. Since Bernanos had let *Sous le soleil de Satan* be heavily censored before it was successfully launched by *Le Roseau d'or*, Maritain was surprised to encounter a clear refusal on Cocteau's part. Cocteau was not likely to accept delaying publication of a work that the young editor would judge financially impossible, as he painstakingly explained in a letter addressed to the philosopher.

Maritain was horrified to find behind it all Maurice Sachs, his adopted son whom he had tenderly led to the seminary and who had shamefully betrayed his confidence. Deeply wounded, he offered to personally buy up all the copies of *Le livre blanc* and, in his fear of seeing the most prestigious of his friends rally to the side of the Devil, went so far as to ask the priest at the Madeleine for funds from his coffers. But Cocteau, once again, gave him an unqualified refusal. After all, the novel was being published anonymously; it was full of clues, of course, but any doors they might open led onto even darker corridors. Maritain reminded him of Wilde's fatal fall, and the disaster that always results from what he called "humanity's greatest wound." Sterile by definition, homosexuality was to love what magic is to life: a conjuring trick, an authentic trompe-l'âme, a trick of the soul, as Cocteau would have said himself. But Cocteau still resisted; he had already subscribed to the evil of which Maritain was accusing him, and this "devil's project" was going to see the light of day—his nature demanded it, with the force that accompanied each of his metamorphoses. "Poor Father Charles," murmured the Thomist, evoking Charles Henrion, the disciple of Charles de Foucauld who had precipitated Cocteau's return to God. And in August 1928, a lucky few could discover the pompomed supermales, the whores with hearts of gold, and the pimps who dyed their hair and lent color to the pages of *Le livre blanc*.

In order to avoid the hotel bills, as well as the interminable conversations with his mother at home on the rue d'Anjou, Cocteau moved nearby to Coco Chanel's *hôtel particulier*, at 29 rue du Faubourg-Saint-Honoré. His room was the most beautiful he had ever occupied. "From his bed, he could see the trees of the Champs-Elysées and the obelisk at the end of a large park," wrote a very impressed Jean Bourgoint.[121] It was there that he waited out the publication of *Le livre blanc*, calmly smoking his opium while the designer's masseur unknotted his "grand sympathique."[122]

Chanel and Cocteau, two refugees from the prewar period, understood each other perfectly.[123] He was amusing, brilliant, and talkative; she was intelligent, hard, and still happy to listen. When the sensationalist press predicted their marriage, Cocteau's mother, who bought the papers devotedly, was the only one to believe it. She so hoped to see her son put away the drugs and the vice! "Why not tell me, my poor little one, since it's in all the journals?" she said to him, as if he were still of an age to be secretive.[124] To open her eyes still wider, he would return to the question two years later in *Opium* by asserting that a normal man should be capable of making love to *anybody*, since vice began with choice: but this was a concept of virtue that was too singular for a woman who was becoming more and more religious with age.

Le livre blanc had a limited distribution and a negligible impact. While appreciating the charm of "certain obscenities," Gide professed to be shocked— "very shocked"—by the pseudo-religious sophistry, though he had made much more objectionable declarations in *Corydon*. In spite of everything, the work managed to reach homosexual circles; Marshal Lyautey, resident-general of France in Morocco, invited Cocteau over to congratulate him, then left him alone with one of his recalcitrant officers, adding: "You explain all this to him and tell him he mustn't dig in his heels."[125] The general public, however, knew nothing of the book, unlike *Corydon*, whose theses were discussed and sometimes judged to be out of fashion. The name "Cocteau" was mentioned, but of course he denied all paternity. Playing his part of the one who takes the blame, Sachs let Cocteau accuse him of stealing the manuscript and publishing it without Cocteau's consent.[126] Two years later, it was in these cryptic terms that Cocteau wrote to the editor of an illustrated reprint:

> It is said that I am the author of *Le livre blanc*. I suppose that is why I have been asked to illustrate it, and why I agreed. It seems, indeed, that the author is familiar with *Le grand écart* and has no disrespect for my work. But in spite of the good I think of this book—even if it were my own—I will not put my name to it, because then it would take the form of an autobiography, and I reserve the right to write my own, which will be more singular still.[127]

The Sound of the Fall

The only way to get rid of a temptation is to yield to it.
— *Oscar Wilde*, The Picture of Dorian Gray

FROM JESUS TO THE GOD PAN

Meanwhile, *J'adore* had been published. The windows of the bookshops were filled with photographs of the author in a sailor suit, surrounded by Cocteau's endorsements: "Jean Desbordes's book is an apparition." "Young man, do not kill yourself before you have read *J'adore*." "I would endure all ridicule to sell a few more copies of such a book." And that he did, in an all-out assault on the media proclaiming his lover's glory, adding, "ridicule only does in the weak." He had tried—unsuccessfully—to prepare his friends for the shock, beginning with Maritain, whom he would have liked to have seen publish the book in his *Roseau d'or* collection, but who, catching a whiff of sulfur in the air, had asked early on to see the manuscript. "It is brilliant and pure, a purity which will seem monstrous to you," Cocteau wrote to him, announcing the book's imminent publication.[1] Maritain dug in his heels at hearing the book called "divine" and at Cocteau suggesting, knowingly, "Maman loves it."

In his preface, Cocteau not only turns Desbordes into a wild child of the Vosges, raised in nature (one critic called him a "little wolf"), but he also drew inspiration from Claudel's opinion of Rimbaud: "a mystic in the savage state." He let it be clearly understood that Desbordes was going to save his generation from its deep-seated pessimism, which, like the desiccated intellectualism of the Surrealists, resulted from the deleterious effects of Freud. Desbordes gave many public readings from the book, with great success. A writer no less prejudiced than René Crevel, after running into Desbordes in Marseille, admitted,

"He is charming and has genius, according to those who have had the honor of reading his book."[2] Skimming the proofs, journalists would have seen, as page-headers, *J'adore* on the left, and phrases like "the most beautiful boys" on the right. *J'adore* . . . "making love in an isolated garden." *J'adore* . . . "the Bible." *J'adore* . . . "Jean Cocteau." And if some critic was reluctant with his praise? Cocteau would write to him immediately, congratulating him for seeing the genius in his protégé's book and providing him with some new arguments. "A miracle! A *cri d'amour!* A masterpiece!" he declared to Martin du Gard, editor of the *Nouvelles littéraires*, with the same anxious passion that du Gard had heard in his office just a few years earlier when Cocteau described his own book projects.[3]

The proud Desbordes soon ceased all public activity, out of fear of compromising himself. "Monsieur de Mont What?" he asked Gallimard, learning that Henri de Montherlant wanted to meet him; he didn't so much as bat an eye when Cocteau again compared him to the author of *Illuminations*, again in front of du Gard. Indifferent to this canonization, he let Cocteau brandish a sketch of him sleeping, "the North wind swelling an imaginary breast beneath his sailor's jacket," and produce an essay by Max Jacob comparing him to Adam in the middle of the Earthly Paradise.[4] "What about Eve?" du Gard snorted, causing a furrow of distress to appear in Cocteau's brow. "He was really suffering, he seemed about to cry," he added. Around this time du Gard promised to publish Jacob's essay in which the "divinely bestowed intelligence" of Desbordes was compared to that of Buddha or Jesus Christ, before eventually changing his mind.

Cocteau may have thrown all of his weight behind it, but *J'adore* didn't catch on. The comments made out of friendship by Morand, Chardonne, Kessel, or Julien Green may have indicated a critical enthusiasm, but the sales didn't follow. Cocteau noted in his preface that Desbordes's head had been turned by reading *Le grand écart*, but the readers of *J'adore* did not have their own heads turned. Finally Maritain received the book and discovered with horror that Cocteau's new protégé was ejaculating everywhere in nature. "Careful, dear friend," said Morand in welcoming Desbordes to the countryside, "don't make any holes in my garden!" Even more unacceptable, Desbordes affirmed that two true lovers had their own place on the cross, and that if a miraculous tenderness brought two beings together to the point that one would die for the other, "the Divine spirit is no longer in the Church but in the lover's spirit."

A great fury arose in Maritain. How could this sacrilegious amateur dare to include God in a wave of creative spirit encouraging "strange coitus," chronic masturbation, and "marriages with the self"? What right, for that matter, did

Cocteau have to encourage him—he was obviously behind all of this—to write that pleasure left one in the state of an extenuated angel? "It asks if onanism and pederastic love form a shrine worthy of the Names of Jesus, the Virgin, and all the saints," Maritain thundered in a letter. "He must have been out of his mind to think I would read such a thing without indignation."[5] To think that Cocteau had imagined he would greet the book's "delirious sensuality" with thunderous applause! Did he really believe that the Church would authorize replacing the Eucharist with Desbordes, and kneel down before a cross built by him alone? "In poetry you must create the world. In life you are in a world already created," Maritain had written to him a year earlier, already uneasy at seeing Cocteau reduce the miracles of Christ to fairytales and legends, and making Him a character in his work, midway between *Potomak* and *Orpheus*.[6]

Cocteau's emotional solitude had until then seemed a useful way, in the eyes of his "confessor," to bring him closer to the ethereal soul of the Elected. Seeing no one in his life, Maritain believed that he had cured Cocteau of what he perceived to be the narcissistic cancer of homosexuality. Everything had changed since the writer, loved and caressed, made *angel* ("ange") rhyme with *mire* ("fange"). Maritain was a born activist, always trying to straighten out his friends' lives and dreaming of making them less accustomed to pleasure. If all greatness came, as he believed, from Woman, then all purity derived from abstinence. Cocteau's erotic awakening had excited Maritain's love of propaganda, and provoked in Maritain feelings of jealousy that exceeded simple Christian love. Did he guess that Desbordes was trying to capture the influence that Radiguet had had over the author of *Thomas l'imposteur?* Desbordes was declared the principal cause of Cocteau's spiritual deviation. The suave, secular saint who could stir a dead soul to life was displaced once again by the philosopher of shock who had confessed, at the age of twenty, his terrible fear of living. Relinquishing his implacable gentleness, the theologian attentively reread *J'adore*, and this time turned against the man he had called, only weeks before, "Jean chéri." No longer was he God's messenger discoursing with a modern-day John the Baptist; he was Torquemada cooking a sodomite who had dared to claim Christ for his own under the pretext that he only had male disciples.

Betraying heaven for the love of a young social climber, to whom he whispered private arguments taken from Maritain's own letters to Cocteau! Maritain was appalled, even before the personal attack against him: "Jacques Maritain murmurs that love between men is a disfigured, violated one, grace betrayed. Love is royal. It reigns over the Versailles of our hearts. It stops Satan as fire does the wild beasts!" Indeed, Maritain could not believe that Cocteau had the audacity to ask him to publish this disgusting ode to sperm, and even to brag about it in *Roseau d'or*, and finally to complain to him about the campaign that he was leading against Desbordes, even believing him outright responsible for the failure of *J'adore*. Maurice Sachs was one thing, but the most renowned writer of the younger generation, the "star" meant to guide the spiritual renewal of France?

Maritain demanded an explanation. Invited to Meudon, Cocteau feigned total astonishment. Was he not asking the kinds of questions about life and love that were important to all Christians? Did not Maritain himself, in responding to his *Lettre*, cite Saint Augustine, who wrote: "Love, and do what you will"? Who had maintained that reproduction occurred during pleasure and by the sex, if not God? Was spring indecent by nature? If not, then why anathematize those words which make of semen the stamen of mankind? And why would Julien Green and Max Jacob, who were both Catholic, applaud the publication of *J'adore*, which the Abbé Mugnier compared to the writings of Saint Francis of Assisi? Maritain was inflexible: the Church would never accede to a discussion of the subject—not even the "advanced" elements that Cocteau claimed. These theses betrayed the contract of the Gospel; this sin crucified God. Desbordes's sensual paganism could only be seen as an attack on Catholic dogma; it contained the beginnings of one of those heresies against which the papacy had always stood. Spurred on by the violence that the unacceptable engenders in the obedient, the defender of revealed truth preached like Bossuet back from the dead.[7]

They were sitting down to eat when the young man in the sailor suit rang the bell. The Maritains refused to let him into their home, but Cocteau chose to stay in order to defend this "divine" book. Maritain, this time, was unable to contain himself. How could Cocteau dare compare Desbordes to the angels and other celestial beings? Radiguet was one thing, he was dead, but this blasphemer hungry for fame—this shameless hussy rubbing up against the world! And for the first time Cocteau rebuked him for his hostility to this particular kind of love. "It is nature who has no pity for homosexuals, Jean: it is the law of the race, the terrible reality of what is. Alas, it is sufficient to think only of the aging of pederasts!" the philosopher replied.[8] Does not the Gospel encourage men who bear this burden to castrate themselves, like Origen, before attempting to enter the Kingdom of God? Cocteau must chase the heretic from his house and publicly renounce this form of amputated love, turning away from the "empire of sex" and the "awful cruelty of Venus," from the ultimate sin, condemned for "eternal reasons," the vice whose practitioners Dante expelled to the third level of the seventh circle of Hell.[9] Cocteau, upon hearing this diatribe, left without saying a word.

The article in *Le roseau d'or* finally appeared. Maritain condemned in no uncertain terms this Rousseauian religion of love and the ridicule Cocteau had brought upon himself in proclaiming the author as "Adam before evil." A few days later, the philosopher asked his editor to cease publication of Cocteau's *Lettre* and his own response. This time Maritain was bitter: he had personally spoken for Cocteau before Christ and had the feeling he had been played from the very start. Remembering with rancor Cocteau's sudden conversion, as well as his first declarations of friendship, Maritain suspected that he had been the target of a vast public relations operation. "Was I wrong to look after all these men of letters?" he asked himself, even in front of Julien Green.[10]

The man of letters, for his part, began to think that the presence of the sacred sacrament at Meudon was giving Maritain ideas of omnipotence that were inconsistent with true Christian humility. Their duel, as terrible as it was loving ("as we can only imagine between angels," writes Maritain's biographer), went on for months, under pressure from Catholic quarters.[11] From Father Henrion to Paul Claudel, who flushed *J'adore* down the toilet, the outcry was loud and widespread. Mauriac, who was growing closer to the Church, found the book *very* shocking.[12] However Cocteau might mock his former friend, whom he sneered had "converted" out of the fear of "hellfire" to which "infamous" books were condemned—"he was cut from the Index," Cocteau joked—Mauriac's response was not unusual; in fact, all the Christian intellectuals mobilized against Desbordes.[13] The affair even reached the Vatican, where Maritain had twice gone to meet Pope Pius XI, because the philosopher saw Desbordes as the devil in disguise, tasked with leading Cocteau to hell by reawakening his oldest desires. "In Maritain's world the devil is always the subject," noted the Abbé Mugnier, who complained with all the tact he could muster that Cocteau was trying to force his hand.[14] Although he had indeed found some Franciscan qualities in *J'adore*, he still believed the work to be "seriously reprehensible" from a religious perspective.

Cocteau suffered. The attacks he had experienced for fifteen years were now coming at him from all sides at once. "God has willed me a dreadful path," he affirmed, still trying to soften up Maritain. This was a point on which Maritain was perfectly willing to concede: "You are an infinitely unhappy man, I know the tragedy of your soul."[15] Raïssa tried one last time to bring the wandering sheep to the path of righteousness, but with a dogmatism that only made him stray further. Beneath her martyr's wrapping, the Virgin of Meudon hid cogs of steel, and Cocteau, feeling himself cornered by a chaste happiness and repentant smiles, sensed awakening in him the child's visceral hostility to those who would punish or give out lessons. His conversion had been at gunpoint; even his mother knew it. Cocteau began to see the Maritains less and less frequently. Their marriage was too austere, too cerebral, and in the end a bit snobbish: "They have the Blessed Sacrament in their home, but they never miss a concert. They want to have it both ways," he said to his mother, as if that were the problem.[16] "Spiritual groups were as passionately linked as lovers," wrote Maurice Sachs. "After the embrace, they withdraw exhausted."[17] While remaining affectionate toward him, Catholicism's gatekeeper distanced himself from the writer who sought to dupe God. "Before the wave of love arrives, there will be simulacra," predicted the Virgin Mary at La Salette.[18] Maritain believed in her and her besmirched holiness more than ever.

Cocteau, meanwhile, rediscovered the vague deism that had always served him as a kind of faith, and the feelings of abandonment that were part of it: "God thinks us but he doesn't think of us" (*Dieu nous pense mais il ne pense pas à nous*), he would say, neatly summarizing his unhappy premonition of the hereafter.[19] It wasn't very difficult to prefer Christ to himself, but he began as well to prefer Desbordes, innocence itself, perfection incarnate, and therefore the true religion. "Even the sun has stains. Your heart has none," he would write, dedicating his book *Opium* to Desbordes in 1930. In three years, he could find not a single fault in him. When Desbordes published a new novel in 1931, Maritain sent the author a letter that Cocteau deemed atrocious. "God has put the purest, most noble, most perfect friendship on my path, the kind of son or brother that only exists in fairy tales, and . . . it is this unknowing, loving, credulous child, turned toward God, . . . who is the victim of your relentlessness," Cocteau wrote, indignant.[20] But Maritain knew exactly what he was doing.

Cocteau was suspected of turning to God in order to glean support from his Christian connections; but in fact he was happy to rid himself of their suspicious benevolence by reaffirming his inimitable singularity. "God created man in his image, and the closer one is to oneself, the closer one is to God," he declared. The new about-face was astonishing, and happened so quickly that the Abbé Mugnier, listening to him speak about theology and art, determined that he had a "disorder of the brain."[21] The contradictory violence of his clashing values would have led others to madness, but Cocteau kept it together. He had long been a friend to chaos.

BAD BOY

The angel feathers soon revealed dragon's scales: after declaring to Maritain that he would never touch wood again, Cocteau reverted to his superstitious ways and his interest in the occult. He had always found it necessary to collapse the boundaries between the real and the imaginary in order to survive, changing roles to escape his neurasthenia, dancing toward the furthest reaches of the self in order to keep from dying of boredom. "Without the devil," he joked, "God would never attract such a big audience." In the great drama of life, he would from now on need to remain in the camp of the sinners.

The distribution of Cocteau's *Livre blanc* was too small to alter his situation; of all the homosexual writers, his name was still the least scandalous. Gide wrote voluptuously about his pederasty; rumor had it Proust had needed to see rats tear each other apart to experience pleasure. Jouhandeau would soon bring out several volumes detailing his "vices." Cocteau alone seemed to have grown up in his mother's skirts, or a priest's. With retrospective adaptability, he began to invent stories about his childhood. Running away after his second failed attempt to pass the baccalauréat, which he had perhaps already confessed to Proust, became an epic: having decided, at the age of sixteen, to become a cabin boy, but quickly laid low by hunger, he found himself wandering the piers of Marseille's Vieux-Port until an elderly Vietnamese woman plucked him off the rue de la Rose—in a shady part of town where he had found work as a waiter in a Chinese restaurant. There he was among the riffraff dancing the night away at Aubagne. He first tried opium at a boys' bordello, where he found refuge and lived for a year—or two years, or even four, depending on whom you asked—using the papers of a young man who had drowned, without unduly worrying his family.[22] "We mustn't try to find him, this will help him find his feet," his older brother Paul was supposed to have said to punish the young vagabond, a detail included in order to illustrate the cruelty of the Cocteau family. Smoking opium with "a device meant to fool the police" (a small bottle of Bénédictine pierced with a hole, a gas pipe, and some hairpins), surrounded by spiders and cockroaches, he was said to have been schooled in crime by the Indochinese mob—before two gendarmes brought him back to Paris in 1905, his diplomat uncle having finally succeeded in tracking him down. "Were you happy in Marseille?" Roger Stéphane asked him before his death.[23] "Ah," said Cocteau, savoring the words, "it set me free."[24]

His mother's vigilance and the silence of the archives make this escapade improbable, but then Cocteau was ready to do anything to suggest a darkness behind the sweetness of his character, and to give himself an aura of being a "bad boy." Appropriately, he would choose the "terrible" Jouhandeau to tell, a little while later, how as a child he had almost put his mother behind bars, on their return from a trip to Switzerland. The story went that he had forced her to buy for their servant Auguste a big box of cigars, which he told her to hide in her dress as they approached the border. Faced with such a respectable-looking pair, the customs agent waved them through, but the young Cocteau is said to have called out to him, to his mother's indignation, "This woman is hiding a box of cigars in her dress!" Mme Cocteau was then undressed, frisked, taxed, and humiliated, thanks to her son, who was impatient, it would seem, to put the lie to his "angelic" reputation.[25]

A brilliant liar and a smooth talker whose career as an editor was faltering, Maurice Sachs was one of the possible inspirations for this new direction, which had been inaugurated by the publication of the *Livre blanc*. One might have sworn that he had taken it into his head to encourage his former idol toward Evil, just as Cocteau had once pushed him toward Good. No one, it is true, had understood as well as the former seminary student to what extent God needed the devil to bestow life on the world. When Cocteau took up with someone, nothing was too good for that person. Coco Chanel wanted a library in her mansion? Cocteau introduced her to Sachs, who took it upon himself to perform this favor for her, in exchange for sixty thousand francs a month.[26] Having become Mademoiselle's personal librarian, he began to live the high life. He moved to the rue des Eaux in the 16th arrondissement, hired a secretary and two servants, a masseur and a driver, who would wait for him at all hours to take him to the baths in the rue Nolle. Organizing Chanel's table-seating arrangements, he was received in the best houses of the faubourg Germain. The Marquise de Polignac wanted him to be her librarian as well, which enabled him to become the "intimate friend" of the Jockey Club members, who were all of the aristocracy, and Sachs to see himself as a cross between Julien Sorel and Rockefeller, the supreme successor to Balzac's dandy and the century's greatest captain of industry.

"Another fresh start!" Claudel remarked upon learning that Cocteau had given up opium smoke for Church incense.[27] What would he have said if he had discovered, like the rest of Paris, that Cocteau had traded the communion wafer for the bamboo? This about-face, the latest in a seemingly infinite series, confirmed at least for Breton the idea that Cocteau was nothing but a trapeze artist forever swinging from one extreme to another. Aware that Cocteau had lost his last defender, with Maritain, the Surrealist became even more aggressive. Not content to accuse Cocteau of living off the cadavers of first-rate poets, Breton compared his ambition to serve as a model with his inability to follow one. "No, you will never be a point of reference, for you are never *yourself*, just a reflection," Breton told him, in his monthly batch of insults.

The Surrealists were certain that alone Cocteau would not last long. Having understood that brilliance was not enough to make oneself loved, the darling of the Right Bank would discover that his high-wire acts were beginning to wear down the public, and that if they continued to follow him at all, it was with the cruel curiosity of circus-goers waiting for the misstep that would bring the tightrope-walker down to their level. The increasingly political nature of the Surrealists helped Breton to channel the energy of those early Dadaist days: "The simplest Surrealist act is to go out into the street, revolver in hand, and to fire at random into the crowd," he wrote in the *Second Surrealist Manifesto* of 1930. We now know that this promise went unfulfilled, but his scapegoats could see in it a renewed aggression—Cocteau above all, for whom Breton's hatred took an obsessive turn. "Those who dislike Jean Cocteau are those who speak of him the most," remarked Picabia as early as 1923.[28]

It had become a rite of passage: to enter the group, you had to prove your loyalty by settling the Breton's scores with Cocteau, just as Desnos had once done. Prévert thus climbed onto the stage of the Théâtre du Vieux Colombier to slap an actor who dared to recite some verses by Cocteau in the midst of Apollinaire's poetry, which supposedly belonged to the Surrealists, and some songs by Éluard, who had not given his permission.[29] Seeing the delicate thread connecting Cocteau to reality waver, the "gang" rejoiced, but his deep-seated self-regard always saved him, at the very last moment, from collapse. He did not want to end up like Serguei Essenine, Isadora Duncan's companion: he had killed himself in 1925, after saluting the Bolshevik Revolution by writing his final poem in blood.

Still, he had his moments of doubt. His best friends rejected him so frequently that he would sometimes wonder if something detestable dwelled inside of him. Maritain's anger against Desbordes, and then against him, even seemed to prove the "inhumane legitimacy" of the Surrealists' hatred of him.[30] And if he did manage to pull himself together, through some scrap of pride, it was rarely to face down his enemies themselves but more worryingly to borrow their methods when a work seemed degrading to him. This explains why he leaped up onto the stage of the Théâtre Sarah Bernhardt in June 1927 to denounce the frivolity of *Pas d'acier*, the mechanical ballet in which Prokofiev and Massine shamelessly recycled a Soviet aesthetic—factories, creaking wheels, and power-hammers—in front of Dukelsky, a friend of the composer, who had mounted a counterattack in announcing the death of "decadent, bland Parisian music." Dukelsky must have seemed a quintessential snob, though perhaps not the cari-cature the Surrealists had concocted of him, with his Louis XV cane and his top hat. In fact, hearing it put about that the Parisians thought he was a piece of shit, Dukelsky let himself be slapped without responding. "Come on then, hit me back!" Cocteau dared him, propped up by Desbordes. The taunt earned him the threat of a duel, to which he did not respond.[31] "I blame Massine for having turned so awesome an event as the Russian Revolution into the image of a cotillion to be purchased by the ladies at 6,000 francs for a box," Cocteau wrote apologetically to Boris Kochno, Diaghilev's secretary.[32] But did he have the resources to bring justice to this domain? Was he not swimming against the current since the publication of *Potomak*, offering poems in verse when he should have sung the glory of the machine, composing his *Lettre à Jacques Maritain* when the fashion was for blasphemy, and, imitating Breton, defending the Russian Revolution when Stravinsky no longer wanted to hear anything about it? "God and the devil loathe me alike," he had written to Jouhandeau, a year earlier.[33]

TOUT DÉBORDE

The failure of *J'adore* had profound repercussions.[34] Desbordes was disappointed in himself—he had thought he would win fame and fortune as quickly as Radiguet—as well as in Cocteau, who had turned once again to opium. Afraid to end his life stuck in bed, hostage in a smoke-filled room, with a fakir for a companion, Desbordes began to keep his distance. He did not want to let himself be devoured by literature like the man he lived with—a man who was incapable of resting, a man who, when asked, would snap into action to finish writing an article under the pressure of a deadline. He wanted to run at dawn in a field of oats and roll himself in a bale of hay, like a vigorous little country boy. Did he not confess in *J'adore* that he felt desire if a hand so much as lightly touched him? The two men continued to live together, but they slept apart; after two years of intimacy, they were no longer attracted to each other. They were still happy on the deeply symbolic trip they took in the Vosges and then in Alsace, in the summer of 1928, but Cocteau was beginning to suspect it would not last. "Something in the air told him love was flickering between other people," said Desbordes, who was already seeing someone else.[35]

Although Cocteau could understand the younger man's erotic fatigue, seeing him turn toward a woman who (however seductive) was also an opium addict, and much older than he, was insupportable. "Love ravages me. Even when I am calm, I tremble out of fear the calm will cease and the anxiety will return, which prevents me from feeling any kindness at all. The smallest snag undoes the whole work. It would be impossible for things to be worse," he noted in *Le livre blanc*, before adding, "Waiting is a kind of torture; possessing is another, out of fear of losing that which I hold."[36] Every absence felt like an abandonment. He began to grant more significance to the life Desbordes was leading elsewhere than to the one they led together.

Without a body to press close to, no presence in which he could root himself, Cocteau began to make more and more violent scenes. He wanted Desbordes to break with Geneviève Mater—who was tall, upright, sophisticated, self-possessed, and, to make matters worse, married to one of his friends.[37] Since his radical opposition led to failure, Cocteau gradually changed his tactics and tried to skirt round the obstacle instead. Rumors began to circulate. Mater liked women as well as men? Her best friends were decorators who liked boys? He tolerated her in his social landscape and soon established her in his bereaved kingdom. All the while, he covered up his suffering with a resignation that would find its way into the heroine of *La voix humaine*, a monologue for the theater that he was sketching out at the time. Opium brought together those who, under the influence of alcohol, would have flayed each other alive, imbuing them with the listless torpor for which the Greeks had a word— *narké*—which is not only the source of "narcotic," but also the name for what afflicted Narcissus after he began gazing at his reflection.

The Desbordes-Mater affair took such a passionate turn that the young "sailor," who had already stopped writing, left in December 1928 to return to the Hôtel Nollet, where Max Jacob and Maurice Sachs were living. Cocteau became truly ill. The angel Desbordes was not only the ideal mediator between the physical world and his own sense of unreality; he was also the collaborator without whose love Cocteau could not move forward. Part of his very being was torn from him, that earthly part of him, as it had been when Radiguet died. Rheumatism flickered on his face and affected his nervous system. "Poor guy, broken in half by pain," navel-gazing in spite of himself—thus did he describe himself to Paulhan (a friend of the Surrealists).[38] He smoked more and more: three pipes in the morning when he woke up, around nine o'clock, four in the afternoon, around five o'clock, and three in the evening, around eleven. In that state, he was neither warm nor cold; two plus two was no longer four, but twenty-two, or even 222222222; thousands of stars lit up the night, which sped by, though he did not move. He became once again the child with the fairylike power to change himself into whatever he liked, but he also anticipated his battered, dried-out old age, when all that was left to do was to numbly watch the time go by and his neighbors die off one by one. "Sleep, Cocteau, the earth is a bit tired of you," he himself would write in *Le crapouillot*.[39]

The drugs "made jealousy grow to the point of emasculating the smoker," he would write in *Opium*; he was almost happy to have replaced desire, "that fairly low kind of obsession," with the attempt to realize his artistic ideals. In the fog of his mind, everything had the same value: just as in *Les enfants terribles*, coarse Dargelos was mirrored by beautiful Agathe. He confused day and night, his limp body resting on the mat, head propped up by a cushion, legs curled up in the fetal position, as he raised himself up just long enough to suck on the bamboo while the opium crackled in the bowl of the pipe, like a diseased lung. Time froze, and with it the horrific sensation of driving at breakneck speed. Life reversed itself, and he felt as if he were moving backward, washed in the photo-development bath that turned the negative back into the image taken from reality. The pipe, held delicately between the tips of his fingers, was soon forgotten; it was not until the next day that, seeing his peignoir full of holes, he would become aware of having dropped it. The lyrical days were done; the imaginary saint was no more than an addled drug addict smoking away the little money he made. Aware of the miserable turn his life had taken, Cocteau, confined to his tiny bedroom, was also aware that he was courting death in small doses. The opium had withered his muscle mass; he no longer had the energy even to perform the small amount of exercise that allowed him to eliminate toxins. He had no appetite, was constantly constipated, and had lost circulation to his extremities. All the circuits of his body were slowing down. Protected by whatever bodily fluids the opium produced, he was no longer even susceptible to colds or germs. He had become a fossil: anyone seeing him would have sworn they were witnessing a living dead man kept going by the memories of his former life.

Though many an old Chinese man can attest that a well-managed opium habit is a good preservative, Cocteau was incapable of smoking in moderation. Had he been rich perhaps he might have resisted the poison, but his level of addiction and lack of funds obliged him to smoke even the most toxic bits of dross at the bottom of the bowl, sometimes even twice. His graceful, lively hands; the sparkling look in his eye; his brilliant repartee—all had perpetuated his youth beyond all expectation, but his exhausted face betrayed the truth: he was approaching forty, that fateful age after which the hourglass is turned back over, and one's work declines inexorably (without Cocteau's having ever produced any great books, as Picasso cruelly reminded him). His skin was beginning to detach from his body, like an ill-fitting suit; he developed a habit of slathering his face with ointments, or of framing it, whenever he was photographed, with African masks or bull heads, while moussing his hair, to distract attention from his wrinkles and to perpetuate the image of the ashen adolescent who, for the rest of his life, would regularly emerge from his features. He knew that his was the name that was always cited by Parisian drug dealers when the police interrogated them about their clients, in hope of getting off lightly. But he was no longer intimidated by the raids from the crime squad; it was with great resignation that he let himself be taken to the central police precinct, at the quai des Orfèvres, in May 1929. There he waited for Joseph Kessel, himself an opium addict, to intervene on his behalf with the prefect, Chiappe, who let him go with the assurance that he would seek rehabilitation.[40] But the drug had become an integral part of his life; he could not go on without this thick covering of deathlike repose.

Cocteau was really no longer a believer in God. "An absurd book, stricken from my list of publications," he retorted to an unwise admirer who had asked him about his *Lettre à Maritain.*[41] He had become so indifferent to faith that he amused himself by saying everywhere that he refused to go to Heaven if that boring so-and-so were going to be there. After spinning the wheel in his cage, the squirrel was back where he had started. Soon he could be seen imitating the Abbé Lamy recounting one of his visions in his Franc-Comtois accent: "He called her the Virgin Maury."[42] Thirty years later, Jean Bourgoint (who by then had become Brother Pascal) would call him Lucifer, repeating the comparison some had reserved for Sachs.[43] But wasn't Satan, in eschatological writings, that empty, flexible being who imitated goodness to better do evil, that supreme mimic who disguised himself as an angel of light in order to damn his victims? "I wonder if I failed in my work, if the devil fooled me from start to finish," Cocteau wrote at that time to his mother.[44] His life had, indeed, become truly hellish; definitively addicted, his nerves could not bear even the light tapping of a pigeon's feet on the zinc rooftop. Caught in a cycle of toothache and rheumatism, he was like a man electrocuted, a prisoner of his power socket.

THE PURGE

On December 5, 1928, Cocteau entered a luxurious clinic in Saint-Cloud, determined to undergo another round of detox therapy, having put it off for too long. The first twelve nights there, he didn't sleep a wink. Worse than the withdrawal was the solitude: feeling like a prisoner, he dreamed of the underground passages that would bring him close to Bérard or Jean Hugo, imagining they scrutinized him through the "transparent" walls of his bedroom. At times judgmental, at others compassionate, their gaze trapped him in a panoptical cell in which his heart was bared, examined, stripped. It was though this being-for-others were engaged in a sort of moral striptease in which he delivered himself to their judgment, to the point of depersonalization.

Without any word from the world outside—Desbordes was himself in detox in the same facility—by the eighth day he nevertheless found the energy to write to his friends, to the great astonishment of his nurse. Gertrude Stein's response overwhelmed him; Picasso's made him cry; he watered the plant that

Stein sent, and carefully kept the drawings that Picasso had enclosed, as if these fetishes would save him from hell. Brutally torn from his two months of hibernation, he was intensely sensitive; his hair smelled, his veins had become frozen siphons, his lips were stuck together from dehydration, and his eyes stared like a lizard's, all while his mouth sought out an opium cone, or sometimes a pipe. Being without it felt like a vast terrible nothingness—as if he could hear the cries of a plant as someone cut it—and at other times was overwhelming, as though he were being drowned by the cries of thousands of children calling to be breastfed. The mirrors he encountered drove him mad: his head seemed to double in size, and his body expanded on all sides, like the knave in a deck of cards caught in a funhouse mirror. His figure improved thanks to his new diet, but his mouth persisted in seeking out something to smoke. Where did he get his stamina? Was it a desire to survive, or the horrible pleasure he derived from extreme pain, whose unreal intensity helped him bear the unbearable? "That life is impossible despite boundless courage," he wrote then, "I have known from the beginning."[45]

The first symptom of detoxification was his renewed ability to tolerate the noise of the world. He was able once again to perceive the passage of time, and his memory returned; he could once again sneeze, yawn, and cry. His nights thickened: he could dream whole dreams again, shot through with rude dialogue or references to old, old dreams. As his body thawed, it took an uncouth turn; whereas he had become accustomed to the refined sensations afforded by the most subtle of drugs, he now experienced the carnal throbbing of a libido that would not be ignored. Savage erections would come on in unexpected moments, while another spurt of energy allowed him to keep a journal of his cure, embellished by astonishing drawings—which would provide the material, the following year, for *Opium*. Like life itself, he would frequently change subjects in the book, drifting from one image or idea to another, brushing it onto the paper as it emanated from his skin. The result is one of the most beautiful texts on drug use, along with Michaux's *Misérable miracle*.

Raising his eyes from his notes, Cocteau sometimes saw the room of another writer, similarly isolated: Raymond Roussel. Writing plays in a barely recognizable language, Roussel would switch letters in his words and words in his phrases, all the while dreaming of finding financial success in the boulevard theaters. That wealthy heir was probably the strangest human being you could encounter at the time. Roussel, even in his "normal" periods, would throw away his clothes the moment they were stained and ate only one meal a day, composed of twenty-two or twenty-three courses, in a servant-filled caravan in which he traveled around France. When his friends were thirsty, he was known to take them down to Reims to drink twelve orangeades.[46] He was a great influence on Marcel Duchamp; his books brim with minutely detailed descriptions of unusual objects, like the machine that spit out teeth of varying colors, or the "railway on calves' lungs" that appears in his *Impressions d'Afrique*. Identifying Roussel as a "genius in the purest state," Cocteau would also call *Locus solus* an unknown masterpiece.[47]

At first Cocteau and Roussel could only exchange letters. One note from Roussel would include lines of his *Mariés de la tour Eiffel*; in reply, Cocteau would compare Roussel's work to "a world of suspended elegance, of wonder, of fear"—almost a way of describing himself. The suffering they both had known soon convinced Cocteau that they were both paying the price for their struggle against a degrading mundanity and for their incongruous poetics, which had always been threatened with ridicule. It was a troubling coincidence: no one except the Surrealists paid any real attention to Roussel as a writer, unless it was to dismiss his work with a rationalizing laugh, but Roussel himself found the Surrealists "a bit obscure," and Cocteau was happy to snatch him away from them for a while. Roussel and their nurse helped Cocteau fight his bouts of distress and his crises of depersonalization; whenever he began again to see the world as spectral and shallow, they remained strangely *real*. The simple presence of the outlandish, wealthy Roussel could help him regain his strength. Was he not infinitely less alone than this hermit marginalized by his fortune— his family was ten times richer than Proust's—a man at the mercy of the workers who were paid to share his nights, then tried to blackmail him for it? Roussel had imagined, in *Locus solus*, a product capable of bringing back the dead; the cure for Cocteau was this "resurrectine."

Reading *Le grand écart*, which Cocteau had published in 1923 while at Stock, Jacques Chardonne had guessed that Cocteau nourished an anguished desire to finally write a masterpiece. "You are afraid of the blank page!" he told him. "Well, go on then, write anything, and then get the handle cranking."[48] Following his advice, Cocteau opened a notebook and put down these simple words: "The Cité Monthiers is situated between the Rue de Clichy and the Rue d'Amsterdam." Add a snowball thrown by cruel Dargelos in the little street where he had played as a child, and the novel that Cocteau had wanted to write since 1912 was begun. Having remained sterile for so long put him in a sort of rage. "When my patient writes, he turns into the kind of guy you wouldn't want to meet in a dark forest," their nurse confided to Raymond Roussel, who must have known what she meant. The pages accumulated so easily, those first days, that he tried to introduce a secondary character—Elisabeth's American husband—to say his piece about America, more as an essayist than a novelist.

The mechanism was brutally interrupted, and he had to wait two weeks for the book to resume its "natural" progress. By the time it was finished, to hear him say it, *Les enfants terribles* had been "dictated" to him in seventeen days.

His door opened. After Desbordes and Sachs, one of his most zealous visitors, Bérard and Max Jacob arrived. Morand came to advise him to follow his own way of life: awaken at dawn, exercise, and write during business hours, a life ordered by the clock. The deviant Jouhandeau and the faithful Caryathis, the dancer of Les Six, came to announce their unexpected engagement.[49] But Cocteau, like Sachs, who was also in the room, was struck by the disappointment etched on Morand's almost Eurasian features. His fabulous success seemed to cause him to miss Cocteau's dangerous but romantically bohemian life.[50] Julien Green was allowed to leave with a typewritten version of Cocteau's new manuscript. Even Gide came to visit, in an act of either kindness or sadism.

On March 19, 1929, after three and a half months in the clinic, Cocteau was permitted his first outing, by car, to read *La voix humaine*, a one-act play inspired by Desbordes's "betrayal," to the editorial committee of the Comédie-Française. Then he returned to the clinic, where he continued to feel better, in order to finish his novel, all the while keeping his door open to visitors. Hearing that he was seeing people every day, Chanel ran over to see him, and finding him in good shape, encouraged him to leave; her generosity as patron had its limits. Like a prisoner on the eve of his release, Cocteau was suddenly afraid. He took at random a room in a small hotel in Saint-Germain-des-Prés—the only time he would ever stay on the Left Bank—where he joined Desbordes, who was working in a bookshop, and tried to resume his life. But his tiny room would prove depressing, almost lifeless; it was so obviously made for love that to see it confined to unrelenting friendship—"a thousand times more exhausting"—seemed to him extremely sad.[51] Since the arrival of Geneviève Mater, Desbordes had lost the power to make Cocteau's days enchanting. "Healed," he wrote in *Opium*, "I felt empty, impoverished, nauseated, ill. I was unmoored." Wandering like a phantom in the city where he had lived, Cocteau sought out new points of reference that could help his life make sense without his pipe. "Coming back to life is very, very hard," he confessed to Maritain. Reality, in its basic state, was decidedly unbearable.

QUADRILLE

In May 1929, Cocteau left for Villefranche. But he felt so weak that the sight of the sun, the commotion in the port, and finally the sudden arrival of a group of English sailors made him melancholy. "I would like to be the ugliest of them and not to write books," he told a Swiss admirer.[52] He and Desbordes left for the Colline, the house that Chanel had lent them in Roquebrune, in the company of Biou, a Vietnamese servant hired for the occasion who would prove himself to be very good at managing money.

It was not a great idea. The relationship between Cocteau and Desbordes was fraying, but the two men could not manage to separate. Desbordes reproached Cocteau for his obsessive jealousy and his possessive interrogations, while to Cocteau, Desbordes's double life was a permanent betrayal. At night, the younger man took the B14 to gamble in Monte Carlo, but he drove so unevenly that Cocteau always feared catastrophe. The arrival of Pierre Herbart on May 17 only made the atmosphere more tense. "Our meeting had glorified his taste for violence, [as well as] the need for destruction we had within ourselves," Desbordes said of this twenty-five-year-old boy, who joined their circle soon after Sachs.[53] Obliged to return to Paris to correct the proofs of *Les enfants terribles*, Cocteau had no other choice but to leave Desbordes with Herbart while he went to live in the Madeleine-Palace-Hotel, in the rue Tronchet, which would be his new headquarters. But while Jean-Jean went on to embed their car in a tree, Herbart continued to send reassuring telegrams to Paris signed "Desbordes-Herbart."

These were days of madness. Desbordes's cure was not a great success, and he had taken up opium again. Each of his doses cost him, on average, 700 francs—then the price of a cottage in Provence. Entire villages, so to speak, went up in smoke during his stay. To cover his debts, he invented wild betting systems with which to play the casinos, but these only made him lose more money. Once the car was repaired, he went off again, leaving Herbart alone in the designer's villa. Cocteau found out what had been going on through a letter from Blanche, Geneviève Mater's mistress, who was as jealous as he. Desbordes was in fact far from the Colline, in Naples with Mater—and had left without a word, just as Radiguet had once done during his trip to Corsica. The scenes multiplied when Desbordes got home; Cocteau could not bear to see Desbordes so dependent on a woman and still remain tender toward him. Desbordes came to prefer spending his evenings with Mater, her husband, and Blanche—they were a gay trio, compared to the apocalypse that Cocteau was inflicting on him. "This is my wife's first husband," M. Mater would say at the beach, introducing Blanche, dressed in pajamas.[54] It was a theatrical atmosphere that Desbordes found relaxing, after the heartbreak of *Les enfants terribles*.

Cocteau's frustration took on frightening proportions. He had to regain control of this hot-tempered child at any cost. Desbordes himself was jealous of the affection that Cocteau still showed for Jean Bourgoint, not to mention his weakness for Sachs. He had to discredit in Desbordes's eyes Mater, this woman who occupied the symbolic function of her name, whom he had taken to referring to as "this great big woman with the frightfully small feet."[55] Cocteau caused scene after scene, fomenting drama—even Aristotle had attributed to tragedy the power to provoke a sort of catharsis. Sachs himself saw him disintegrating, then abandoning himself to fits of despair "in which actors and women were more than other subjects."[56] Having loved in vain, Sachs was now convinced of the duplicity of these demonstrations.

> He mistook tormenting desire for the urges of the heart, and was overwhelmed with an anguished, fevered, feminine desire to possess everything: secrets, devotions, beings and things. The sometimes excessive price he paid for this possession made him think he was in love. He burned, but as ice burns, without heat.[57]

The more Cocteau yelled, the more terrible Jean-Jean became. No longer seeing Cocteau's suffering, just his fear of no longer being the favorite, he judged Cocteau incapable of living in a state other than hysteria and pretense. He no longer believed in his melodramatic sentimentality, or in his convenient stories; he was tempted to throw back at him what Cocteau had said of one of their friends: "He's such a liar that you can't believe the opposite of what he says."[58]

Cocteau suffered even more given that Desbordes persisted in telling him the unvarnished truth. "He was capable of extreme cruelty and great, very great gentleness," he recalled, long after this interminable round of score-settling was over.[59] Everything that Sachs reproached Cocteau for in his books, Desbordes said to his face, but the underlying message was the same: if Cocteau was the man they dreamed of being, he could just as easily become the one they feared of becoming. Geneviève Mater herself could prove very fierce, as Desbordes was aware; he compared her eyes to those of an "angry miner."[60] Desbordes found a release from these scenes with Cocteau, just long enough to absorb his shock; but when Cocteau's anger was roused, Blanche did her best to fan it, eager to see things return to "normal," and the two original couples as they were.

Cocteau understood that he was becoming impossible to live with. "I would demoralize an angel—a hero made of gold and iron," he wrote to a young friend, adding, "Jean-Jean is sublimely patient and gentle."[61] They returned to Chanel's villa, accompanied by Biou, and Cocteau returned to his usual remedy. "I will smoke once more, if the work needs it," he predicted at the end of *Opium*; the mysterious machine that made him write required its dose of medicine. His jealousy relaxed, and the scenes became less frequent. The drug did have that advantage—it softened everything, making him as angelic as ever.

GIDE'S REVENGE

Of the small group that gathered around Cocteau, Pierre Herbart was doubtless the most unique element—except, of course, for Sachs. Blue-blooded, enigmatic, a vagabond in tweed with a superior, nonchalant air, Herbart had been the intimate associate of an aide-de-camp of Marshal Lyautey's in Morocco who had taught him to smoke opium. Ever since, Herbart had lived in the smoke-filled bubble that was Cocteau's universe, overshadowed by the sad history of his father—an insurance broker who, after sixteen years of marital life, had suddenly left one morning, without a *sou* in his pocket, only to be found dead in a ditch. The police had called Pierre to identify his body. Unable to settle down anywhere, Herbart, now a dandy and opium addict, alternated between sarcasm and despair, a shallow hedonism and the depths of nihilism.

Lean and lithe, Herbart had the moral makeup of an angora cat. Prodigiously indifferent, he could curl up in a blanket for days, then bound up to conquer the affection of a newcomer. Extremely gifted at understanding, feeling, and making up his mind, he was also very good at fleeing, out of fear of running into his shadow. "Very few people kill themselves as often as I do," he would write.[62] Capable of absolute generosity, but also of great cruelty, Herbart had loved girls when he was young, but discovering he didn't share their pleasure, turned to boys at age sixteen. As quick as Sachs to play the most unexpected parts, he spared himself the return to Christianity and was content to settle in Cocteau's "enchanted" world, which he observed from his nearby hotel room at the Madeleine-Palace-Hôtel.

One day, alone in Roquebrune, not long before Desbordes fled to Italy, Herbart, out strolling on the terrace, noticed an aging Arcadian shepherd in a cape and greatcoat. This was André Gide, the great glory of French literature. Disappointed at not finding Cocteau, Gide finally accepted a seat. With his green eyes, his ascetic, gaunt frame, and his air of a "troublemaker," Pierre Herbart reminded the writer of the character Lafcadio in his *Les caves du Vatican*, who threw a passenger off a train for no reason. Immediately taken, Gide suggested that Herbart travel with him. Having no other plans, Herbart agreed. "We fit together immediately," Gide said, not at all displeased at getting his revenge for the Cocteau-Allégret flirtation.[63] He lauded this irresistible being, this depraved individual with "all the charm of hellfire."[64] Cocteau felt betrayed. How many times had he consoled Herbart, after having heard him confess his doubts about his talent, or his attempts at detoxifying? "I don't like my skin any longer," he would say, or "My *massif central* hurts," or "Have you noticed how balanced Jews are, they have a kind of inner keel which protects them from shipwreck."[65] Remark after remark to which Cocteau had no idea how to respond, as with Sachs—so much anguish, which Gide was already beginning to ease.

Convinced that Cocteau was "one of the most pernicious [influences] imaginable" on Herbart, Gide became determined to save Herbart from opium and alcohol.[66] Although Cocteau had unsuccessfully recommended for publication *Le rôdeur* (Herbart's first novel) to Grasset, describing the author as a "young genius," Gide managed to get it published by Gallimard, for a good sum of money. This cordial competition for the future author of *L'age d'or* reinforced what had already divided the two writers for ten years. That someone like Desbordes had written to Cocteau first of all was a good sign; a decade earlier, he might have gone to see Gide. But Herbart then distanced himself from Cocteau and joined up with Gide, seemingly without the slightest bit of remorse. "Ever since Gide entered the house in Roquebrune, you have ceased to love, to live through my work," Cocteau reproached him in 1930, after receiving a cold letter from him concerning *Opium*.[67] But this was asking too much from someone as ego-driven and adaptable as Herbart, whom Gaston Gallimard would call a whore—and he had seen his share. Not content with becoming Gide's secretary, Herbart would marry in 1931 Elisabeth Van Rysselberghe, who was fifteen years his elder, and the daughter of the "little woman" who watched over Gide, and whom Gide had deliberately impregnated, nine years earlier—the child was called Catherine.[68] It was a way of keeping Herbart in the family, and maintaining fertility by proxy, helping cure him of his drug habit and getting him finally to settle down.

Cocteau was always one to take heart in spite of bad fortune. The two "couples" socialized often and Gide could not restrain himself from finding Cocteau and Desbordes "inexpressibly exquisite."[69] But Herbart would never make up with Cocteau, whom he described, years later, as being afflicted by a "Saint Vitus dance of seduction."[70] He would prefer to make a child with his wife in his turn, in the conventional way this time, before accompanying Gide on his famous tour of the USSR, leaving Cocteau to his regrets.[71]

All this, and the dramatic climate in which Desbordes made him live, was enough to convince Cocteau that the new generation didn't have much use for him.

LES ENFANTS TERRIBLES

When *Les enfants terribles* was published, Cocteau expected yet another failure. "I have written a book which will only interest four or five people," he said to Bernard Grasset, sure that the purity of the characters would be rejected by a microbial era. Quite the opposite: the book was a critical triumph. The press saluted a work they declared "poignant, light, fantastical and realist at the same time," and which they proclaimed was carried by the dramatic precision of its author, who possessed "the incomprehensible dexterity of a carver of fowl."[72] Albert Thibaudet devoted nine pages to this "extraordinary success" in the *Nouvelle revue française*, pronouncing this precious verdict: "None of his previous books, not even *Le grand écart*, were so inspired by his nature, his mission, and his profound pathos."[73] To the American readers of the *New Yorker*, the barb-tongued Janet Flanner called it "a little desert of subtle suffering dotted with stiff events and cactus-like descriptions."[74] Young people followed Cocteau again.

To write of these holy terrors, Cocteau had made use of the colorful stories that Bérard had told him of Jean Bourgoint and his sister, a lesbian opium addict. But he may also have recalled the strange language invented by Lucien Daudet and his sister Edmée—she called him Djônn and spoke in monosyllables—or the quasi-incestuous relationship between the son and daughter at the Hôtel Vouillement, which consisted of secret meetings arranged in secret languages—people said they were stitched together.[75]

The kind of incest that haunted this pair of fraternal twins living "in a vacuum container" had never touched Cocteau's life; his sister and brother were too old to have shared any kind of intimacy with him. Nevertheless, he poured his heart into the story of this couple isolated in a room that was a double for his own, its walls covered in photographs. Like him, Paul and Elisabeth had trouble living, taking shape, inhabiting themselves; having sheltered all the iterations of themselves since childhood, these Russian nesting dolls had to dream their existence, since they didn't know how else to be, and to imagine themselves in grown-up roles the way you play dress-up—for the fun of taking the costumes off. To this foundational couple, Cocteau added Dargelos. Already present in *Le livre blanc*, this imaginary school chum took on greater dimensions in becoming the idealized embodiment of the cruel sex-appeal that Cocteau prized. His white snowball and his black opium powder, equally lethal, would serve as the fatal revelation for the hero: Paul would find himself reduced to the state of those "lovesick larvae" that Cocteau describes in his memoirs before Dargelos's female double, Agathe, inspires Elisabeth's murderous jealousy and sets the drama in motion.[76]

Cocteau was living a fairy tale. His heroes had been adopted by thousands of young readers, especially in the provinces, where parents tended to exert the kind of authoritarian morality that in Paris had been swept away by the postwar period. The generation of readers who were fifteen years old in 1918, for whom Sachs or Herbart could have been the symbol, showered Cocteau with letters of admiration or even love. The lucky ones who lived comparably bohemian lives recognized themselves in the novel, seeing themselves as schoolchildren in search of their soulmates, aware of not being good enough, through their fragile ambivalence, except in the haven of their bedrooms. The others discovered in the novel the adolescence they'd never had. All who read it saw Paul and Elisabeth as realistic characters, and themselves as their forsaken siblings. Finding within its pages their attempts to impose their individuality on the impersonal adult universe, hundreds of adolescents claimed to be co-creators of the novel. Some were even indignant when Cocteau denied being inspired by them to write their story. "It's become the handbook for mythomaniacs and those who want to dream standing up," he would say, fascinated by the powers that fiction was finally giving him.[77]

Cocteau had always lived his life as if it were a novel, and now one of his stories was invading his life, through the hundreds of confessions it inspired. No doubt he lacked the ability that certain novelists have to take advantage of the way the world had disappointed them: creating a substitute reality. Instead, he managed to impose his own unreality, to the point that it became a legend.[78] The expression "enfant terrible" became part of everyday language, and remains so today. Moysès, superstitious as ever, proposed naming his new bar "Les Enfants Terribles," to capture the same kind of success as the Boeuf sur le Toit and Le Grand Écart; chronically in need of money, Cocteau sold the rights to his title, fearing all the while being accused of selling out.

His success restored his confidence. The young people who applauded him led him to announce to the Abbé Mugnier that a renaissance was imminent: "We are on the eve of lyricism, of romanticism."[79] In his impatience to take the lead in French literature, after Gide and Breton, Cocteau came off as a phony to the abbé, who was tired of seeing him bend everything to fit with his personal ideology; the only constant was his megalomania. But his triumph was ruined by the literal reading that some gave his novel. He himself had written, at the end of the text, that Elisabeth dragged her brother into the clouds "where flesh dissolves, where souls wed, where incest lurks no more," but he also suffered when some critics "dirtied" the purity of his heroes by attributing to them a taboo sexuality. The theatrical adaptation that was produced in Munich in 1930, far from pleasing him, plunged him into despair. *Geschwister* was produced by Klaus and Erika Mann, the novelist Thomas Mann's children who were known for their amorously close relationship.[80] The final stigma of his time with Maritain: he wanted his heroes to appear angelic.[81] There was no use reminding him that he had congratulated Desbordes, a few months earlier, for having written in *J'adore*, "Maternal love is carnal love," no use reminding him of the innumerable passages in which Freud argues that the repressed desire for incest is the basis of all sexuality. His mother, who was still alive, contributed to the silence that he maintained on such matters.

On Christmas Eve 1929, after a drunken night spent with her companion, the Princess Violette Murat, Jeanne Bourgoint, a model turned slattern who slept in dirty sheets, killed herself with a massive overdose of barbiturates. Though unrelated to the publication of his book, this act was largely blamed on Cocteau. The Bourgoint siblings hadn't even recognized themselves in the book, when he had read it to them, but the damage was done; Cocteau alone was blamed for this tragedy. His reputation for lightness became tainted with suggestions of diabolism. His fame "strangled" him, Morand noted.[82] Three years later, the idea of suicide occurred, in turn, to Jean Bourgoint.

THE CONTRARIAN ANGEL

If anyone deserved to be known as an "enfant terrible" in the generation that came of age after the Armistice, it was René Crevel. This promising young lad with the face of an angelic boxer was only fourteen years old when, his father having just hanged himself, his mother asked him to make his father's body stop swinging as she hurled accusations of cowardliness at the corpse. Brilliant, desirable, and restless, "carrying within him all the strangeness, the virtues, the disorder, and the poetry of the post-war period," as Sachs put it, Crevel appealed to Cocteau on many levels.[83] He was a talented young man shot through with fragility, an insatiable need to be loved, a luminous gaze, and winglike shoulder-blades that caused Marie Laurencin to call him a seraph. "Something in him trembled like a tear," Jouhandeau said, in reference to the tuberculosis that drove him to live life to the fullest, as fast as possible, from the underground rooms of bohemia to the ballrooms of high society.[84]

In fact, Crevel had appealed to Cocteau when he appeared in Maurice Sachs's wake in the rue d'Anjou; his square, sensual face, like Desbordes's, called out for a sailor's cap, complete with pompom.[85] As proof of his admiration for Cocteau, he had published (in *Aventure*, a Dadaist revue he edited) some of his work, alongside that of Breton and Tzara, until January 1922. He had expressed enthusiasm for *Thomas l'imposteur* in 1924, as well as for Cocteau's talents as an actor and playwright.[86] Cocteau's enthusiasm for Crevel cooled, however, when Crevel described the "prowess of the converted angel enthusiast" to the editors of the *Nouvelle revue française*, who were already ill-inclined to think well of Cocteau.[87] Crevel also found a master who would be stricter with him, and even an ideology that would give him more structure: "André Breton is my god," he confided to Jouhandeau—a god in whom he believed infinitely more than in himself, and with whom he had experienced hallucinatory sessions of hypnotic sleep.

Though he had disengaged from Cocteau, Crevel hadn't broken with the kind of snobs that Soupault had found intolerable, from the Prince de Lucinge to the Noailles family. Likewise, he continued to be quite public—imaginatively so—about his homosexuality, in defiance of the Surrealists' strictures, but in such an acrobatic way that some people saw him as the authorized "Jean Cocteau" of Breton's gang. Crevel's *My Body and I*, published in 1925 (just before Cocteau began visiting Maritain), told of a profound self-alienation. The author, whom Klaus Mann also loved in vain, sought refuge in opium during a course of treatment for his tuberculosis in Davos.[88] He was visited there, in 1926, by several close friends, including Bourgoint and the Princess Violette Murat, also good friends of Cocteau's. When he joined the Communist Party in 1927, like most of the Surrealists, the estrangement between the two men was solidified. Rejecting Cocteau for the fragility they had until recently shared, Crevel went beyond even Breton in his zeal. "I thought I would die of hatred for him, for myself, for the world," he wrote after an afternoon spent with him, at a rugby match at Colombes.[89] Although in 1929 he and Cocteau found themselves both serving as witnesses at the marriage of Caryathis and Jouhandeau, the suicide in 1930 of Crevel's friend Kit Wood, a habitué of the Welcome, only encouraged the younger man to flee the "diabolical" atmosphere surrounding Cocteau.

In the end, it was the more "sane" and "natural" of the two who would kill himself. Eaten away by a disease that kept him apart from those he desired, as he was by the open hostilities between the Surrealists and the Communists, Crevel returned home one evening in June 1935 and swallowed a handful of sleeping pills. He fastened a note to the inside of his jacket ("Please cremate my body. Disgust"), turned on the gas, and went to sleep forever.

THE HAVEN OF THE MUTUAL ADMIRATION SOCIETY

There was one group that kept apart from these tragedies, a haven where shelter could be found from these aesthetic storms and the thunderbolts of love. In the chaos in which Cocteau lived, and faced with the fate that precociously struck down all these angels, it was a pleasure for Cocteau to go back to the salons where he had his beginnings and where his talents and celebrity, his natural camaraderie and his desperate drollery, as well as his exquisite manners and his kingly generosity, immediately made him the center of attention. Transformed and modernized, the aristocrats he had known growing up had dwindled to a handful of lavish eccentrics and activist patrons, all of whom were infinitely more interested in literary and artistic endeavors than in the countesses his mother was friends with. This circle celebrated a host of overdressed rebels, sometimes to the point of playful decadence. So many balls and displays, so much banter—this kind of patronage was a godsend for the victims of Surrealism, as it was for those homosexuals discarded by the red flag. These were often one and the same: from Cocteau to Bérard, from Boris Kochno to Pavel Tchelitchev.

The Comte de Beaumont remained the most spectacular of the group. This specimen of the prewar period, at whose home Proust had made one of his last social appearances, and who had inspired Radiguet to create the Comte d'Orgel, was living out his dreams. He would have made a marvelous master of ceremonies at the court of the Sun King; he had put his *hôtel particulier* on the rue Masseran at the heart of all Parisian social intrigue. In addition to the sadistic pleasure he took in not inviting this one or that one (a proclivity inherited from Montesquiou), Beaumont reveled in choosing themes and the orders of entry for his balls, which never began before midnight and lasted well into the next day. The ambiance of these extravagant parties was reminiscent of both Lully's Versailles and a Montparnasse for aging Dadaists.

After four centuries of intense activity, this was the ultimate contribution of the French aristocracy to the arts, as played out by the Prince of Lucinge, whom Max Jacob called a "prince charming"; Daisy Fellowes, whose yacht sometimes sailed past Villefranche in order to steal Cocteau's opium; or Nicky de Gunzbourg, the patron and unforgettable star of Dreyer's *Vampyr*. But the ultimate burst of aristocratic energy was the work of Marie Laure de Noailles, the granddaughter of Madame de Chevigné, even if later it would look like a splendid act of sabotage. Even more than Beaumont, who remained fundamentally a nobleman, the heiress married to a distant cousin of Anna de Noailles liked to go tramping through the poorer sections of Paris, from the rue de Lappe to the slums of Clichy, where she felt as much at home as on the waxed floors of her *hôtel particulier* in the place des Etats-Unis. Although for many years she was hamstrung by a lingering shyness, she finally managed to emerge from her husband's shadow, whose family (dating back to the Crusades) had been one of the most-guillotined of the Terror. Ever since, she had given amusing dinner parties that were closer in spirit to the eighteenth-century celebrations than to the salons Cocteau had visited as an adolescent, where the boorish bourgeois had feasted under fake Louis XV portraits. If Charles and

Marie Laure de Noailles were inspired by the century of the salon, it was a version that followed the ironic, detached example of the *Bal masqué*, a "profane cantata" that the two commissioned from Francis Poulenc in which Madame la Dauphine ("fine, fine, fine") rubs shoulders with the Comte d'Artois, who, for his part, climbs onto the roof to "count the tiles."[90] As for the rest, the twenty-second Vicomte de Noailles, and his spouse, the heir to tramways in Brussels as well as to some dockyards in New York, asked only to be of their era.

Marie Laure had made some progress, then, since the winter of 1917 when Cocteau had stayed in Grasse at the magnificent villa belonging to her mother, the wife of the playwright Francis de Croisset. Only fifteen then, with a father who had died of tuberculosis when she was just a year old, the bereaved child had been cosseted and overprotected by nurses and tutors who feared a new infection. But the only illness that afflicted the little recluse, who would come into one of the greatest fortunes in France, was boredom. Shining with the success of *Parade*, the young Cocteau had told her stories of Paris, Apollinaire, Picasso, and Satie, as she sat naiad-like by the artificial lake. He introduced her to Nietzsche and Proust, the eternal "suitor" of her formidable grandmother, who lost no time in making her throw away the letters she received from that bore "petit Marcel." Did Marie Laure catch wind of the brief affair that Cocteau had in Rome with Marie Chabelska, the dancer from the Ballets Russes? Filled as she had been from childhood with fairy tales, sure that crowns grew from the heads of monarchs and that they bled when the crowns were removed, the romantic young woman had fallen passionately in love with Cocteau. The warnings she received from her grandmother, then from her mother—and even from Marcel Proust—could not change her mind.[91] The poor little rich girl had begun to daydream, under the lemon trees of the Villa Croisset, of an enchanted future by his side. "I looked like one of Raphael's self-portraits," she would say, but the painter was no doubt too feminine for Cocteau.

"Marie Laure is such a good girl, so gentle and unaffected," Cocteau wrote to his mother.[92] But this is the way a man speaks of a child, not of a woman, and in fact, Marie Laure would long regret not having been a boy. Cocteau was so adoring, calling her "chérie," or "bébé," that the pretty young girl was convinced, and declared to her grandmother: "When I am fifteen and three months, I will marry Jean."[93] The prospect of this bad match—bad on both fronts—inspired vehement cries of refusal from the old woman whom Proust had called "Corporal Plutarch." Convinced that Cocteau was trying to insinuate himself into her powerful family, she cold-shouldered not only him but also his mother, her neighbor, who in turn reproached her son for hanging around a woman who never paid her suppliers.[94] Marie Laure was nevertheless the only one, apart from Madame de Chevigné, who took the idea of this marriage seriously. Cocteau was not in the least aware of the force of Marie Laure's feelings, which would paralyze her until the end of the 1930s. "I did not love her," he confirmed, retroactively apologetic for having led on this child who idolized him.[95] Marie Laure confessed that she would only ever love him, only him, in 1923, when she was preparing to marry Charles de Noailles, in order to make Cocteau appreciate the damage he had done to her adolescent heart.

Two children were born of the brief encounters between Marie Laure and her husband, who was preoccupied with building an enormous villa high up in Hyères, designed by Robert Mallet-Stevens. Man Ray would go there to film *Les mystères du château du Dé*, and the couple had slowly been won over by the Surrealists. Marie Laure admitted to being distantly related to the Marquis de Sade, to whom Breton had recently paid homage, and she was preparing to replace the Beaumonts as the patrons of modernity. In fact, remarkable artists like Stravinsky, Poulenc, and Kurt Weill, as well as Dali and Picasso, would have agreed: the Noailles family was at the center of the "rebellious aristocrats." Built in the shape of an ocean liner, with portholes and gangways, the Villa Saint-Bernard looked like a ship that a modern flood had wrecked on the top of a peak overlooking the Bay of Hyères. Captain Charles de Noailles would ensure its smooth operation via telephone from inside the building, then disappear into the diamond shapes of his Cubist garden, which he maintained with the kind of passion that Marie Laure longed to feel.

It was there that Cocteau spent the winter of 1929 in the company of Jean Desbordes, Georges Auric, Marc Allégret, and André Gide. From his room, he could see the Giens Peninsula and the Island of Porquerolles, shrouded with fog or beaten by rain. The Noailles family had arranged everything necessary for the comfort of their guests. A British valet brought them breakfast in bed; during the rest of the day, a team of servants stood ready to satisfy their every whim. The villa's gymnastics teacher—"very friendly," Gide noted—was available to help them play volleyball; and for those who wanted to swim, a blue-and-white striped bathing suit and colorful balls waited beside a fifteen-meter pool that Mallet-Stevens had installed inside the house (the first such indoor pool in a home). Marie Laure dove in every morning, and the more athletic swung above it in a trapeze. She preferred to survey the bottom, with the help of two halters that kept her under the water while her air bubbles floated up to the surface.[96] In her liquid kingdom, she had added a bar, gymnastic equipment, changing rooms, and a sauna, not to mention a large gym wheel inside which she liked to spin during the "acrobatic teas" she gave, when she and her guests weren't amusing themselves playing leapfrog. One day she discovered her husband in the arms of their gymnastics trainer, having opened the door to his room, and she withdrew quietly, greatly disturbed by the strange fate that drew her to those men.

This island of luxurious insolence seemed a kind of haven to those who lived under the hard regime of literary competition—above all Cocteau, who loved to attach himself to it like a golden buoy, to flee his cyclothemia. It symbolized for him his carefree youth, modernized and sun-filled, with open-minded people, happy to display their bodies. Every evening the little group of guests would play wild games of charades, absurd card games, "portraits chinois," and games of truth; they would wear costumes and show rare films; or they would look at the stars from the roof, under the banner of the Noailles family arms.[97] One day Cocteau dressed up as an Indian princess; the next day he nailed a piece of fabric, some bits of newspaper, and some wrapping paper to a jute canvas and signed it "Picasso," before presenting his Cubist collage to Bernard Berenson, a specialist in the Italian Renaissance, and cornering him into not being able to say why this "Picasso" was so ugly while the metopes of the Parthenon were an example of eternal beauty—against a backdrop of laughter that drove the scholar away. At night, he would read aloud from a text he was writing, or he would improvise a plot from a play he was already planning to produce with the other guests. As much as the act of writing awakened his inhibitions—Posterity seemed to sit in the very room with him—so did the presence of an audience liberate him. The admiration he inspired filled him with the kind of warmth so cruelly foreign to the monastic practice of writing. Led by the flow of words and the gestures of seduction, he combined love and intelligence, individual and mob, seduction and "glory," as during those magic hours when he had been introduced at the Théâtre Femina. It was out of affectation that he denied knowing how to read or write, but he would unquestionably have lived better if he could have created his books in public, feeling the hearts in his audience beat and their blood pulse as his own ink flowed.

There were miraculous nights when allegories and histories, paradox and gossip, surged forth in his exalted brain as the curls of opium smoke made the Noailleses' guests lose control. Much like the way the spirit of Chamfort, before the French Revolution, left on his victims' necks the coolness of the blade that would soon cut them down, the words and energy of Cocteau acted like an opium fog that would make the visitors lose their sense of time and space. "He needs his Boswell," wrote Julien Green, impressed by Cocteau's monologues and referring to the biographer who had recorded everything of the life of Samuel Johnson, in the eighteenth century.[98] Conversation remained the only place where Cocteau's thoughts, his fancies, and his dramatic gifts came together. For two or three hours, the strangers he held captive in his web began to live through him, coming to share even the strange physical state in which he lived. He was not the only Jean Cocteau, that almost unbearable chimera, that symptom just barely clothed in flesh; instead others coexisted within his ailing body, supported his fragile frame, just as he somehow became them, worrying for their well-being and even for their future. The darker the night became, the more dazzling his exaggerations. It was as if he were creating calligraphy in luminous letters in the atmosphere, like a storyteller of mist. His listeners' eyes devoured him, their mouths drank in his words, while their mute bravos pushed him even further, removing his inhibitions. Sex became the subject; the systematic politeness of his writings gave way to an obscene reading of the world in which his words, ceaselessly reproducing, restored to him the pleasure of which Desbordes had denied.

Finally it came time to leave. Cocteau tried one last time to convince them to stay, hiding his Scheherazade-like fever that made him feel that by dispersing they were signing his death certificate. Back home in Paris, there was the pleasure of telling all the stories again, with a savage joy, to his friends there. But after just a few hours of solitude, his euphoria crashed—and a week later, the empty bed he woke up in, late in the morning, was cold as ice.

A TOO-HUMAN VOICE

After the failure of his last poetry collection, Cocteau was thinking about changing genres. In *Opium* he wrote about the theater, the circus, the cinema; this was a way of announcing his return to the theater arts, as if to remove the bad taste left in his mouth by *Opéra*. He had to somehow get around the critics in order to physically affect his audience, short-circuiting the clannishness that reigned in the literary world. He was too clever. Having grown up with the idea that a Parisian writer owed it to himself to be constantly at his best, he proved himself time and again to be brilliant and dreamlike, tense and spasmodic, a mental decathlete. Desbordes's betrayal encouraged him to simplify, and to articulate his anguish not in the form of a myth or a fable, but as a confession expressed to those crippled by love, in a language they would understand. It was therefore natural that his return to the theater would take the form of a monologue in which a woman, abandoned by her young lover for a younger woman after five years of living together, tries one last time to keep him. She calls him on the telephone and asks him for letters she has sent him, only to learn in the end, and after many interruptions in their connection, that he is lying in bed with the woman he will marry—she "sees" with her ears.

Formally, *La voix humaine* was an accomplishment, but it was not innovative. Sacha Guitry had already used the dramatic potential of the telephone in the theater, throughout the magnificent monologue of *Faisons un rêve* (1916), and in 1904 Henry Bataille had written *Maman Colibri*, a play that evoked the unhappy love of a woman for a boy the age of her son and included panting monologues that had shocked the audience.[99] Cocteau didn't want to shock anyone, except for the avant-garde (or what was left of it); instead he was hoping to provoke a "banal scandal" that might affect ordinary theater-goers. Yes this imploring woman is stuck in the past, and jealously checks hotels and counts kilometers, but her heart bleeds; she can no longer stand or swallow food. She cannot be alone, and in this she resembles anyone who while suffering prefers to degrade himself or herself rather than recognize the torturer's indifference. She begs her former lover to keep talking to her, to keep the blade from falling; this was the desperate response to the irony of the ballet *Les mariés de la tour Eiffel*. It was his first work to convey the dramatic solitude he had felt throughout the 1930s, a period far removed from the collective gaiety of the previous decade.

Cocteau was careful to cover his tracks by lending the phantom lover his own habits of drawing stars everywhere, and rolling up his jacket sleeves. Obviously, though, this victim who protests and lashes out, panting and complaining to the operators ("Hello? Mademoiselle? The line's gone dead"), forgiving even when she understands her lover's indifference to his betrayal — this was Cocteau himself. The lead character has Cocteau's possessiveness, his tact, his almost troubling capacity to put himself in other people's shoes — to such an extent that she invents lies to justify her own eviction. It is Cocteau who, through his character, begs his lover not to cut the ties that bind them; it is he who, throughout this too-human voice, expresses the suffering he feels at loving boys who also love women, as well as the way that he renews through them his bond with his mother. A blend of incest, Oedipus, and love makes this monologue the dramatic equal of *Les lettres portugaises*, that masterpiece by Guilleragues in which love, condemned to the greatest solitude, feeds on itself until it has been exhausted.

Accepted unanimously by the Comédie Française, while Max Reinhardt claimed it for Berlin (Cocteau wished it to be produced by the most outwardly conservative institution), *La voix humaine* was a real challenge for its director. The forty-five-minute-long monologue would benefit from the unexpected moments that occurred with manual telephones in those days: lines going dead, wrong numbers, incompetent operators, musical interference, nothing else. Cocteau had the good idea of asking Bérard to do set design — this would be the painter's first foray into the theater. He reduced the large space of the stage to a white box topped with an unmade bed and a table, in order to focus attention on the pathetic solitude of the woman dying under the dagger of her own questions. Berthe Bovy, a well-known French actress, rehearsed the role for a month, reading the single act to friends with such conviction and intensity that Bernard Faÿ would say: "We are all distressed at the idea that he could have felt, expressed, and set down such a particular and feminine form of human suffering."[100] Playing the role for a television adaptation, Ingrid Bergman called it "the most difficult thing to do": overexposed to the public, the actress had to play for two, without ever becoming mawkish.[101] Cocteau directed Bovy to play it impassively, in order to emphasize her suffering by contrast. Having no stage partner but a bakelite telephone receiver, the actress got to borrowing his intonations, as if internalizing the everyday heroism he had developed in his daily life. The tears he had rigorously forbidden her seemed to flow from inside her body, through the cord, to dampen the receiver—the only thing allowed to suffer.

The final rehearsal took place on February 15, 1930. Since he could only invite twenty people to the dress rehearsal, Cocteau got permission to make this "intimate" work session open to the public and invited two thousand people: the entire Parisian theater community would witness his return to the theater, four years after the critical failure of *Orpheus*. The curtain went up on the "scene of the crime" where Bovy, her hair in disarray, "standing on end like Cocteau's," waits in vain for her ex-lover to call before deciding to call him instead, to interrupt his new life. She hadn't been on stage for ten minutes before someone shouted, "It's obscene!" All heads turned toward the balcony where they saw a man with a hat brandishing pieces of newspaper. The same voice, a few minutes later, cried out again, "Enough! Enough! This is obscene! You're telephoning Desbordes!"[102] A glacial silence fell over the theater. Berthe Bovy held back genuine tears, and wanted to stop the performance. "It's Breton!" exclaimed an audience member, but the heckler's voice wasn't as imperious as Breton's. More likely it was Breton's second-in-command, Paul Éluard, whose outline could be made out in a box on the balcony, clad in a gray overcoat, chanting rhythmically, "Merde, merde, merde."[103] The crowd began to roar; dozens of disgruntled audience-members headed straight for the balcony. Cocteau stood up to call for silence, but a Comédie-Française subscriber, imposing and indignant, knocked off Éluard's hat. "The golden pince-nez went flying to the side, torn from their cord. Cuffs came off as the fists flew . . . Down below, in the dark, women were shrieking," Eisenstein wrote, who was in the balcony as well—right beside Éluard.[104] With people coming at him from all sides, Éluard escaped to the corridor, as the lights came up in the theater. A group of audience-members surrounded the Surrealist demanding he be thrown out, while an unknown hand put a cigarette out on his neck and another tore at his jacket.

The fisticuffs threatened to turn into a riot. Cocteau stepped in to "save" Éluard, and the audience clapped as Bovy took the stage once more. Once the curtain fell, the protagonists of this drama gathered in the theater manager's office. "Men only," Éluard demanded, before hurling at Cocteau, "One of these days I'm going to kill you. You disgust me."[105] Having been invited as Eisenstein's guest, in whose favor Cocteau had recently intervened with Berthelot and the Prefect Chiappe, Éluard stalked off into the night.[106] As for Eisenstein, he tried to make a discreet exit through the small lobby, but Cocteau was out there thanking his public, after the standing ovations the play had received and the accolades given to his leading lady. Then Eisenstein tried to leave by an emergency exit, wondering if Cocteau would be angry with him. But Éluard's disruptive presence had conferred success on him in the end. "Maybe he should even have thanked me?" added the director in his *Memoirs.*[107]

The same night as this "intimate" rehearsal, the telephone rang at the rue d'Anjou, and an anonymous voice informed Madame Cocteau that her son had just been run over by a car. The same voice, perhaps, that sometimes phoned her up to read her obscene quatrains of which her son was the hero.[108] Other calls placed to Anna de Noailles, Picasso, and Gide informed them that Cocteau had just committed suicide in a bar. Anna de Noailles told Madame de Chevigné, who went to comfort Madame Cocteau, her neighbor—though she had just been reassured by her son that he was very much alive. Picasso went running over next, enraged by the Surrealists. Gide was more of a skeptic; he didn't go over until the next day—while Éluard, in the ultimate defiant gesture, entered the Boeuf sur le Toit.[109] Anna de Noailles demanded his immediate removal before Cocteau could bail him out yet again.

"Jean is delighted. He has had his scandal. He's been dying for one for the past ten years," Valentine Hugo wrote soon after, without stopping to wonder how her new friends could have given such a "gift" to the "angel turd." No one would speak out as fervently against *La voix humaine* as this former friend of Cocteau's, whom he tried to avoid, though he ran into her not long after. "I understand marvelously well that you don't like the play or the actress . . .—but your opinion matters so greatly to me," he even felt obligated to write to her, to justify himself.[110] Then there was the question of the voice behind the anonymous phone calls. Many suspected Desnos, who had actually tried to kill Cocteau back in the Dada days, though he had since fallen out with Breton and Éluard. De Chirico confirmed that the Surrealists had already used the telephone in 1926 to punish Cocteau for taking his side in their dispute; Benjamin Péret seems to have been the one making those calls, and he had remained faithful to Breton.[111] Unable to know for sure, Cocteau preferred to believe that this time it had been "some little journalists" who believed themselves to be Surrealists and who had apparently confessed the whole thing to Yvonne George.[112]

Whoever the guilty party was, these antics seemed awfully familiar. As Picasso said to the Surrealists: "If it's not you, it's you all the same." Breton's men—Cocteau would find out after the war, via Aragon, that it was indeed Desnos—had wanted Cocteau's hide for so long that they would not have been surprised or disappointed to learn he had actually committed suicide. According to their twisted logic, you couldn't regret the loss of a non-person who, never having really left his mother's womb, was still agitating inside it, in taboo complicity. Perhaps the symbolic death of this homosexual would help them recover their own virility, which had been undermined by so much contact with these beautiful, hard, cold women (often rich it must be said), whom they placed on pedestals as idols of *amour fou*, and at whose feet they chastely laid down their arms. A pamphlet called *Un cadavre* was published a month later, announcing Breton's spiritual death.[113] For his thirty-third birthday, the "false revolutionary with the head of Christ" had been accused by twelve of his apostles of living off the cadavers of Vaché, Rigaut, and Nadja.[114] Under the revealing title of *Thomas l'imposteur*, Desnos made the phantom speak of his old God in order to bring him to his knees: "I simulate everything: love, poetry, a taste for revolution"—the very terms that Breton had always used to describe Cocteau.[115] The prose of the "groper, sacristan, in short: cop and priest" of Surrealism, whose conversion to Catholicism was already predicted, was, to Georges Bataille, reminiscent of nothing else but the "nauseating gardening of Jean Cocteau."[116] It's easier to understand the attacks against *La voix humaine*; its author remained one of the few common causes of the Surrealists and their dissidents.[117]

Cocteau received many messages of support. An anonymous fan wrote to him, "If only I could remove with a kiss all the bitterness that I know must burn on your lips."[118] And the controversy made the play a success: its author was applauded for having endowed this devastated woman with his most profound feelings. With Éluard's help, *La voix humaine* became a prime example of "camouflage," like Proust's *Albertine disparue*, but it is also the most performed of Cocteau's plays today, around the world, because it is the most accessible and the most touching. Since it only calls for one actress and a single set, the play serves as an ideal test for young companies, and stands in stark contrast to the psychological realism that would dominate Cocteau's own theater for the next decade. Just as *Le sang d'un poète* would be simultaneously a trial run and a masterstroke in the cinema, *La voix humaine* immediately attained the highest level of dramatic achievement, impressing a multitude of directors—and all because unrequited love was for Cocteau much more than a theme; it was an obsession.

The play was a triumph and Cocteau was again lauded by the public. Berthe Bovy was so poignant in the lead role—the photographs of Germaine Krull attest to that—that she even moved those who had never suffered an abandonment, who had never had to bless those who persecuted them. This bourgeois woman and her privileged troubles would even be transposed, seventeen years later, onto a working-class woman, played by Anna Magnani, who was in the middle of being left by the film's director, Roberto Rossellini (Cocteau served as adviser).[119] Thirty-nine years after that, the role would be reprised by Carmen Maura in one of Almodóvar's most beautiful films, *Law of Desire* (1986).[120]

TAEDIUM VITAE

The Surrealists' attacks once again managed to mar Cocteau's success. The more he wrote, the less he was liked, but the less he was liked, the more he had to say. He gave so much and received so little, and he was finding it more and more difficult to get out of bed in the morning. His life was so much like his heroine's that his friends themselves sometimes admitted growing weary of his doglike need of compliments. "They couldn't bear his delicate sensitivity, his perpetual need for affection, his amorous infatuations, the tears that could appear at any moment, his feverish appearance . . . his melancholic happiness. It all seemed like a pose."[121] These lines, written by Pietro Citati and referring to Proust, apply so well to Cocteau that they could provide the key to his friends' attitude with regard to his work and the life that work undid. Proust's advice finally struck home: literature was gnawing away at Cocteau's body like a tapeworm.

Diaghilev had recently died, eaten away by the diabetes that he resolutely refused to care for except through sugary foods, and leaving behind the mite-ridden Ballets Russes and two heirs, Serge Lifar and Boris Kochno, who kept each other at knifepoint. "I never imagined that death could reach him more than bailiffs, suppliers, etc.," Cocteau wrote to his mother, informing her of the "definitive" disappearance of this master of small pleasures. "I saw him living a false life, from hotel to hotel, from set to set."[122] It was not a bad description of his own life, a bloodless, loveless existence in which he was always on the run, from the clinic to a friend's villa, from a Parisian hotel room to a guest house in Villefranche. Success couldn't manage to restore Cocteau's joie de vivre. Unable to make himself loved by a single person, Cocteau seemed condemned, by wanting to belong to everyone, never to meet anyone.

He began to spend time again in the opium dens of Toulon, fleeing to that pale weightless planet where beings grow at the speed of plants. Was it really happening, was there really a giant phantom ship docked in the port of Marseille where sixty boys, faintly lit, smoked with tangled limbs, their faces convulsed in a kind of half-sleep—or was it a story someone had told him? His imagination had a tremendous power to invent; it carried him to the farthest shores as well as through the inside of his alveoli, in the accordion of his lungs, whose space amounted to two hundred square meters if it were spread out and ironed, he was told. He smoked so much in the autumn of 1931 that the police shut him up in his apartment, out of fear that he would run into his cousin, the Admiral Durand-Viel, who was showing the Arsenal to the minister of the navy. Desbordes still accompanied him sometimes, but since the failure of his novel *Les tragédiens*—a novel that described the tempestuous love between a mother and a son, and that Cocteau had partially rewritten and helped to launch with great fanfare—Desbordes had begun to be seen less as a writer than as the spokesperson for one.[123] Incapable of building a career (unlike Radiguet), Desbordes entertained the idea of becoming an antique dealer on the Côte d'Azur. Had it been a mistake to immediately introduce Desbordes as the new Radiguet? The thought never occurred to Cocteau, who probably would have keeled over if someone had dared to suggest that Desbordes was the anti-Radiguet, a writer who rambled on where the other was self-contained, and cried, "J'adore!" when Bébé would have said, with all necessary coldness, "I don't hate you."

By dint of abstinence, Cocteau's desire shifted. For lack of skin, his hand caressed paper. It sketched so many erections that it evoked those cults created in antiquity in which the streets leading to brothels were marked with phalluses: it drew thousands of angels, of sailors, and of Narcissuses thrusting their outsized members between the columns of a temple, in and out. The masculine organ became a talisman protecting him from evil, the scepter ruling the world and the symbol of inexhaustible human fecundity. Held hostage by the homosexual fear of aging, Cocteau was at that moment entrapped by his imagination as well, the survivor of a life that he had wished was enchanted, but had slowly revealed itself to be so disappointing that he permanently strove to reinvent it. It is hard to be one of those people who think everything is possible, but for whom nothing really exists.

THE TRAGIC YEARS

It is requisite for the ideal artist to possess a force of character that
seems hardly compatible with its delicacy; he must keep his faith in
himself, while the incredulous world assails him with its utter disbelief;
he must stand up against mankind and be his own sole disciple, both as
respects his genius, and the objects to which it is directed.
—*Nathaniel Hawthorne*

TWILIGHT: BETWEEN DOG AND WOLF

It is nine in the morning.[1] Or perhaps it is noon. Maybe, in London, it's tea-time; who even knows if the sun hasn't already sunk behind the horizon of the Madeleine. Two eyes try to pierce the protective darkness of the curtains; a hand gropes blindly in the air for an alarm clock. All around, lunar, disquieting objects gleam—a crystal ball, a grayish ball, a pipe cleaner in the shape of a head, other inhuman but disturbingly lifelike heads—to say nothing of the empty gloves and plaster cheeks streaked with tears brought from the rue d'Anjou. Unable to "unfold" the life it harbored, Cocteau's body was readying itself to descend back into a light coma when a car horn reminded him of the menacing presence of the city around him. Or was it the telephone that caught him—some publication awaiting his article, a mechanic calling about an unpaid bill, the police laying hold of a new drug dealer? A faraway yet friendly voice—Desbordes's or Bérard's, maybe even Bourgoint's—was in the next room, explaining that Jean Cocteau wasn't available.

Where did he find the strength to get up, when he was losing weight every day? His eyelids were already beginning to shut; he was surrounded by the thick, soft dough that the night had kneaded from dreams; it prevented any movement, leaving him unconscious and motionless, like those species who are terrified of day, such as the moth or the bat. Lighter, more childlike souls are the hardest to awaken! He needed to hear the cries of the street vendors near the Madeleine to cut the cord connecting him to the night. Emerging from his half-slumber, he would curl up at the end of his bed and see a cloud of dust dance gracefully in a ray of light up toward the window, whose diamond-shaped handle looked like a *calisson d'Aix*.[2] It was a child's gaze, more surprised by the black dots on a ladybug than by the outsized silhouette of the Eiffel Tower. It was the same look that, when his father died, had plunged him back into the game he was playing with his cousin, preventing him from grasping the whole picture, so he would glimpse, as flies do, only a number of discrete details arranged in facets.

Sitting up again, the ghostlike figure spies his naked torso in a mirror, but he is so emaciated that his skin looks like a creased suit. His hair sticks up as if in a bouffant, or a wig; it looks like a crown, perhaps like the one they had virtually fastened around his forehead the morning of the Femina. This nightmarish memory is enough to wake him up. Once again he must compose his face, assume the pinched mouth and the nose he hated. More than the self-confessed dunce or the impostor hunted by Breton, he feels himself to be a larval being—an urban zombie. "The nothingness of human things being such that, save for the being who is by himself, nothing is beautiful, but that which is not," as Pope said—though this being, existing by itself, was still not Cocteau.[3] He could leave his mark on everything he touched, desired, or described, but every year he was less and less convinced of the actual existence of *Jean Cocteau*. He might be called by his name, in a hotel or at a counter, yet this did not penetrate. It was not himself they were addressing, but someone else with his name, as foreign to his environment as a Louis XV armchair sliding down a glacier. Had he usurped the identity of the young poet who had died when he was eighteen, after making his début at the Femina? An acrobat bent on proving the genius of a man who didn't exist, the Surrealists had said of him then.

Many people of Cocteau's age felt themselves to be at a turning point, and behaved as adults resigned to living and dying by the rules. But that was one metamorphosis that was forbidden to Cocteau, this specialist in transformation: he could not become used to the decades that his body was accumulating. What force pushed him, at the moment when he was poised to become the Anna de Noailles of his generation, the futurist of the rue d'Anjou or the neoclassicist of Piquey, to change tracks, to call it all into question? Was it destiny that forbade him to "take" that track, that made him "the man you love to hate" of French literature? That made him create the "collection of [mirrored] reflections" that a critic called *Les enfants terribles*, or the "floating genius" that another called it, referring to its author as "neurotic, thin-skinned, hypersensitive to everything, to life, to words" [à fleur de nerfs, à fleur de peau, à fleur de vie, à fleur de mots]?[4] He had a difficult time, he knew, rising above the contradictory aesthetics of symbolism and the Baroque, Dadaist and dandy, which all lived inside of him. Although they had bestowed so many gifts on him in the cradle, the fairies forgot to give him the one gift that could magnetize them. "Eclecticism is so boring," he wrote as early as 1922. "The only thing that moves me is a narrow, deeply specialized intelligence."[5] This ably sums up what he was missing. What could be made of all these Cocteaus who reproduced like so many growths, like invading homunculi menacing the others? The sadness of the decade as it began left him a lot of time to reflect on the versions of himself that he had engendered. He sometimes felt like one of them, all of them, or none of them, like the hero of *One, No One, and One Hundred Thousand*, a recently published novel by Pirandello.[6]

Undeniably, Cocteau's progressive isolation also encouraged him to look for alter egos inside himself. Many of his friends had left. Jean Hugo had retired to his farmhouse in Fourques, in the Camargue, to watch the flight of the pink flamingos; baptized by the Abbé Mugnier and sponsored by the Maritains, he had grown close to God, to Valentine's great disappointment, and only wrote to Cocteau from time to time: this "subtle peasant, medieval monk" would now hunt the angel of the bizarre alone.[7] Morand was running around the world in search of the pleasures that Paris could no longer give him. Radiguet and Satie were dead, and Les Six had dispersed. Maurice Sachs had convinced Max Jacob to abandon Saint-Benoît-sur-Loire and to live off his gouaches in the capital. But though Jacob and Cocteau frequently wrote to each other from a distance, they also avoided running into each other, now that they lived only a half-hour apart. Jacob thought Cocteau was much too concerned about his reputation.

As for Sachs, he had shown himself to be very grateful that Cocteau had saved his life yet again, by introducing him to Coco Chanel. But Reverdy realized that Sachs was dishonestly filling the designer's library with non-first-edition books, and Cocteau could only support her when she finally fired Sachs. "We don't lack for victims, but for cheats," said Talleyrand, and indeed Sachs wasted no time in finding other dupes. After Sachs sold to an old woman a framed photograph from a magazine as if it were an original engraving by Chardin, Max Jacob discovered that Sachs was pocketing some, if not all, of the proceeds from his gouaches, which Jacob had put him in charge of selling. When Sachs decided to go and seek his fortune in America, thousands of kilometers away, Cocteau was undoubtedly relieved, but it still meant the loss of another friend.

Alone with his dreams of collective creation and his unquenchable thirst for glory, Cocteau had to ask himself: why did he no longer hear from those friends who, just five years earlier, had been there for everything he had lived through? Even the presence of Desbordes, in a hotel room next door, could not manage to soothe him. The attention of just one person—no matter how attractive and talented—was never enough for him; without visitors waiting for him in the hall, or the telephone ringing before he'd even had his coffee, through whose receiver he could hear a heart beating as if through a stethoscope, he felt totally disoriented. I love others and only exist through them, he said one day, before adding: without them I am only a ghost. To take shape, he needed outside stimuli such as fascinating times or dazzled onlookers. For his words to be made flesh, for his lack of being to reverse into overflow, an "angel" had to visit him. "He's a hungry skeleton," Reverdy said, giving him a vampiric reputation in *Le voleur de Talan*.[8] Nothing else existed when he needed this nourishment. With neither apartment nor automobile, deprived of the belongings that in spite of everything link men to the fiction that society orchestrates under the name of *reality*, so that it might serve as a shared reference protecting them from chaos, Cocteau lost all notion of the world. He wasn't really attracted to Buddhism, but a Tibetan maxim would no doubt have interested him: "The world exists, but it is not real." Nothing that happened on earth had any weight; even dramatic events seemed to float; for him the world was, as it was for Fichte, a "zone of not-I." At the heart of this illusion, the syllables "Coc-teau" couldn't even manage to support him.[9]

This name, whose evocative potential Cocteau had always made use of, was turning out to be cruel as the years went on. "Concoct" is to cook up a complex project, according to the dictionaries; borrowed from medical low Latin, "decoction" is a pejorative designation for a dull blend of elements. *Cocoter* ("You stink!") is used for overly perfumed coquettes, or for *cocottes* (tarts) who cackle. At times, Cocteau's problems seemed to stem from the very instability of his surname. Without the anchor of a steady meaning, a fixed label, everything escaped him, his productivity first of all. Sometimes inspiration might strike him at the most incongruous moments, and then in a mere ten days a book might be born, grow, and be expelled, along with its placenta; sometimes he spent entire seasons without writing anything, terrified of never again finding anything to say. Such highs and lows naturally made him suspicious: "Genius is a void which fills up by itself. Talent is a void which is filled up from outside: everything is outside of it," as the formidable Reverdy put it, about a character inspired by Cocteau.[10] What more terrible thing can be said against a creative person? "Wanting to avoid convention through obstinacy is wanting not to be understood," wrote Nietzsche.[11] By refusing this kind of advice, Cocteau had gone beyond its reach.

A small faithful group still remained, but they were mostly drug addicts, marginal creatures, or would-be writers who could only manage to reflect Cocteau's own view of the world. "Red curtains prevented real news from filtering through," he would say of his apartment on the rue Vignon, in *La fin des Potomak*; the more his lies were repeated back to him, the more he lost hold of reality. Of course people found him brilliant, but "like a tear," as he described his *Thomas*. His virtuosity was impressive, but his despondent air did not soften his audience's view of him. A genius has to have the strength to impose itself; we demand of a writer fully formed characters, not emotional pits into which the reader might fear falling. "My forehead is not strong enough to protect my brain," said Cocteau in his first collection.[12] He had come to envy those with more simple personalities, who were so much better at self-promoting—like Montherlant, who grew prouder and more entrenched with every book, or Picasso, that hunk of virility onto whom all could profitably project themselves.

Sometimes healthy, ambitious new recruits knocked at his door. The parade began: the queen gathered from their eyes the nectar of their admiration on which she sustained herself; she worried for their future, and promised to send their manuscripts to this or that editor; she confided in them the bitter aftertaste of her time with Desbordes, and even told them about "la Mater." As night fell, the recruits dispersed, leaving Cocteau totally refreshed. They, however, awakened in their cold little rooms, finding only useless snippets of promises. Like the Pentecostal tongues of fire, Cocteau left only blind witnesses. Having violated the writer's privacy (with his consent), they found themselves somewhat less impressed. When an editor rejected the manuscript that Cocteau had recommended, the novice began to reevaluate what he had just experienced. He went to complain to his friends, who sowed the seeds of doubt: had he perhaps not been taken in by the "lady of letters" who denounced the Surrealists whenever he got the chance? In a surge of virility, the young writer would declare that brilliance was not enough to make a writer. Culling the best of Cocteau's turns of phrase found in an interview or in a poem, he rejected a body of work whose freshness he had plucked.

And Cocteau would have spent the morning reassessing. Does any writer like to hear that his conversation is his masterpiece and his books mere secondary output? Slipping on his dressing gown, he would cross the few feet separating his room from where Bérard, Desbordes, or Bourgoint busied themselves with their pipes. He would lie down on the mat, while the opium cooked in the bowl of his pipe, and then he would swallow the smoke in deep draughts.

His limbs, and his dulled senses, sank into the cottony nothingness; the character-machine, the poetry-machine, the drawing-machine—all slowly wound down to motionlessness, and he no longer suffered.

For two hours, or maybe even five, he turned and evolved without moving, like a fetus in its sack. In that state of being, there was no longer an inside or an outside, neither himself nor not-himself; the wounds left by his transformation had been cauterized; the sense of his own strangeness had faded in a horizon of smoke, or gauze. He sometimes claimed that every man remade the world every morning, flowering at noon, before withering in the evening, to die at night—thanks to the opium, this pitiful illusion took on the force of reality.[13] Sometimes a shadow entered in the dark: without moving, without even looking at it, Cocteau would end up speaking to it. Then he would chatter with Bérard, or with Desbordes, dig little holes in the walls of their dimly lit hotel to spy on the caresses being exchanged in the next room, until night. Then they would go to the cinema to watch the doings of those they called "the people with black blood," and where they would sometimes stay for several showings in a row, to the point that they confused themselves with the figures on the screen, or that ghostly, solitary body Cocteau saw changing into a "block of ice"—Greta Garbo.

All Cocteau's agonies were now confined to the daytime. To avoid the "hour of the guillotine," when the first rays of the sun strangled him, he stayed in his room. Showing up spontaneously one morning to see Cocteau, the pianist Jean Wiener had difficulty recognizing him. His deathly pallor, in his black dressing-gown, the drawn features under his wild hair, his neck cinched with a charming black ribbon, Cocteau looked like a prewar beauty—as if he had brought with him not only his childhood bedroom, but also his mother herself.[14] The drugs helped, and he could spend hours lying in bed emotionless, dreaming, as he had under the sun in Piquey years ago. He managed to rise above his emaciated body to float on his back, like those flies that stand for hours on the ceiling, back to the floor. This frozen, upside-down life was pleasing to him; nothing was absurd any longer, in this etherized state, for now *everything* was: the most fantastic ideas, the most incongruous views flourished, unrestrained. It was the drunkenness of creation with no fear of punishment. He enjoyed the omnipotence of some unknown director who has the freedom to command the objects and beings that dwell at the heart of our dreams.

From this nebulous territory, Cocteau brought back *Le sang d'un poète*, his first film, and the most personal. Of medium length, its protagonists perform against the black background that had been his trademark since *Roméo et Juliette*, as if they were floating. It was a work that he wanted to be commercially unexploitable so that it might maintain its mystery—like the occult arts that in his view were so unlike public art, which was designed to serve the social order.[15] Like some kind of UFO, it would, over time, take on almost mythic status, and brought him closer to what would have been his best art—the tenth art—if he had been able to draw with a pen of light in the dark, as Man Ray would do in his *Space Writing*, seven years later. Did he not live like a human outline, sparkling in the night, a will-o'-the-wisp dazzling his audience?

LE SANG D'UN POÈTE

The cinema would give Cocteau a means of translating the somnolence that allows "our night to slip into full daylight, as if illegally."[16] He had admired cinema since the 1910s, and he had very early understood its poetic potential. In an article from 1919, republished in *Carte blanche*, he wrote:

> As soon as the cinematographer was discovered, he was co-opted by outdated ideas, seized by money-grubbing hands, slowed by them. It was basically photographed theatre . . . I wish for independent artists to take advantage of the perspective, the pace, sped up or slowed down, the ability to walk backward, an unknown world to which chance had cracked open the door.

From the very beginning he decided he did not want to tell any other story than that of the proliferation of the imaginary, the split second separating the moment between the explosion of a factory smokestack and its collapse. "Film could become the ultimate poem because it takes place in pure duration," a critic had written in 1925: that is precisely what Cocteau wanted to prove in this dense, mysterious, moving work, which though made with sound retained the astonishing physical power of the silent film.[17]

Cocteau's film begins with a painter discovering a speaking mouth in the palm of his hand, which he brings to his own mouth, and slides down over his chest and his stomach, culminating in an ecstasy from which he awakens to discover a human statue depicting *Glory*. The statue will itself encourage him to dive into a mirror which leads to the corridor of the Hôtel des Folies-Dramatiques, where, like a weightless voyeur, he observes room after room through their keyholes: a Mexican killed twice, and brought back to life each time; a schoolmistress forcing a little girl to fly with blows from her whip; the shadow of a Chinese man preparing his opium pipe, twirling the resin on the tip of a needle. An intercessor between hidden powers and that illusory appearance that is the world, the Symbolist poet wanted to open the door to all mysteries.[18] Here Cocteau uses a mirror as a liquid passage to explore his own labyrinth and to show the figures of his mythology. "I know the astonishment of one who sees in the mirror his own image open its mouth as he keeps his closed," he wrote in *Le Potomak*. This is the kind of fear that courses through *Le sang d'un poète*.[19]

At a time when many intellectuals looked down on the cinema—Georges Duhamel even described it in all seriousness as "an amusement for slaves"—Cocteau became the first French writer to make the great leap of picking up a camera.[20] Only too happy to express himself through this new medium, and not through the frequently too-polite French language, he was achieving the dream of many Surrealists, those heralds of a fantastical, populist cinema that would blend German expressionism and Hollywood comedies, for whom the seventh art is the ideal medium to promote "real life."[21] Cocteau had already made one attempt, three years earlier; a young actor who may have been his lover, Fabien Haziza, for whom he had written the role of Heurtebise in *Orpheus*, had encouraged him to pay homage to Chaplin. Like an illiterate man dipping his finger in an inkwell, he had wrapped his actors in wet sheets and guided them, like human statues, through a dreamscape. This film (*Jean Cocteau tourne un film* or perhaps *Jean Cocteau fait du cinéma*), now lost, might had been his sole cinematic foray had Marie Laure and Charles de Noailles not offered him, in the winter of 1929, a million francs to shoot an animation that turned into a film. (The couple were meanwhile suggesting the same thing to Buñuel, from which would emerge *L'âge d'or*.[22]) It was an artistic offer, but it could also be perceived as the ultimate act of love from a woman who could not resign herself to let Cocteau remain unaware of her feelings.

Cocteau was in charge of his expenses, and was able to choose his production team and his actors without consulting his "producers"; he was never so free as in this first film, made on a shoestring. Only two professional actors were involved, so filming (which began on April 15, 1930) was trying. The lead actor, Enrique Rivero (sometimes spelled Riveros), a Chilean gallant sometimes compared with Rodolph Valentino, would prove difficult to manage, like the young stagehand playing the student Dargelos, because he liked to break up the discipline of the set with fashionable dinners.[23] The jazz dancer Feral Banga, too, who looked like a black angel with his oiled body and steel insect wings, sprained his ankle during the first days of filming—so Cocteau gave him a limp, like Radiguet. Lee Miller, however, with whom Cocteau had spoken by chance at the Boeuf sur le Toit, was magnificently heroic in the role of the statue. Her face covered with plaster, her hands tied behind her back, having to remain still for hours under the floodlights that would cause her castor-oil-soaked dress to smoke, Miller, Man Ray's assistant and companion, suffered even more when the holes in her "armature" had to be sealed up with butter and flour, which quickly went rancid and stank up the set.

Determined to make a "realist documentary of unreal events," Cocteau left nothing to chance. In order to give those figures who explored the netherworld the flexibility of cameramen-divers filming the lives of algae, he thought to nail to the ground the set of the hallway where Enrique Rivero(s) wanders, and the doors whose keyholes he peers through, so that he dragged himself along instead of walking: he would only have to stand the scenery up, once it had been filmed, to tilt it back ninety degrees.[24] With no technical knowledge, but solidly supported by his camera operator Périnal, Cocteau had the idea of standing Rivero(s) on a moving plank and pulling him along—since he knew nothing of the existence of tracking cameras.[25]

The stagehands were already inclined to mock Cocteau's ignorance, but they cursed this neophyte who tried to show the extent of his power by using certain methods he'd lifted from Méliès when he wasn't comparing himself to those ancient priests—half-doctors, half-sorcerers—who made the statues of Thetis speak. Resentful at being reduced to odd jobs—they had to replace the broken horn of a steer that Cocteau had saved from the slaughterhouse at La Villette, then get a cowherd to come and lead the injured animal across the studio—they openly hated him when they began to be bit by the fleas and other insects that crept out of the mattresses with which he had lined the walls in order to soundproof the room. On the last day of filming, the most aggressive of them deliberately filled the place with dust as they were sweeping between takes—but Périnal, unfazed, said it gave the shots a mysterious aura.

Cocteau had emerged from his previous film shoot with bloodshot eyes and a fever of one hundred and four; weakened by the opium, every shot hit him like a bullet. Always present on set, to the point of literally sleeping on his feet, he caught a terrible case of sciatica, from stooping over to adjust the effects; frozen to the ground in pain, he would raise his voice only to ask his chief operator for "sordid lighting" or a "sick" ambiance. But if in the final weeks he came to feel he was witnessing the crucifixion of his dreams, he did not yield on his demands—except for during the nineteenth take of the card game scene, when Rivero(s) tore up the deck upon learning that Cocteau wanted to film a twentieth. Cocteau deliberately pushed his performers to the edge so they would give the impression, on film, of sleepwalking. "As a filmmaker, he showed the same fanatical concentration, the same disciplined brilliance, as when he worked on a drawing, a poem, or an essay," observed Klaus Mann, who visited the filming.[26]

During the creation of the film, did he think of his father, the man his mother had discovered bathing in his own blood? Cocteau showed with frightening precision the blood gushing from the mouth of the dying child-poet after the blow administered by Dargelos, the living allegory of beauty, and gave to his pain the liberating intensity of an orgasm. It is an unforgettable shot, capturing perhaps a primitive expression of his masochism, accompanied by the tune of *Va petite mousse* in Auric's score.[27] Cocteau haunted this film, which would appear, in retrospect, to be one of the first overtly autobiographical cinematic works, and perhaps the first to use a camera obscura to film the intimacy of a consciousness—another kind of dark room. It was his star tattooed onto Rivero's back, and his profile that is outlined by the pipe-cleaner sculpture; it was his voice that spoke from the mouths of all of the actors except for Lee Miller, and his own heart that beat on the soundtrack. It wouldn't have taken much more for him to have developed the precious negatives in his own blood.

Was *Le sang d'un poète* really the first film to be conceived from a purely cinematographic perspective, as the Italian journal *Futurismo* claimed?[28] There was Fernand Léger's *Le ballet mécanique* (1924), Man Ray's *L'étoile de mer* (1928), or Artaud's *La coquille et le clergyman* (1928)—to say nothing of *Entr'acte* by René Clair (1924), the most well-known of French experimental cinema, and of course Buñuel's *Chien andalou* (1929). A link in a chain begun by others, Cocteau's radical jewel could however be considered the swan song of the French avant-garde cinema that would begin to die out in the early 1930s, weighed down by ideology and a lack of funds.

THE MORT

Cocteau was still editing when the Noailles family decided, in 1930, to present a private showing of Buñuel and Dalí's *L'âge d'or*, to which Cocteau and Breton were both invited. Although the Surrealists thoroughly approved of the Spaniard, and had definitively converted him to their cause, the film was coldly received by the crème de la crème whom his patrons had invited.[29] Worse, its anti-religious irony and unrestrained brutality—the film depicted a bishop being defenestrated, an old woman being slapped, and a blind person being abused—provoked violent reactions when it was shown at Studio 28. The Patriotic League and the Anti-Jewish Youth threw stinkbombs into the theater and ink on the screen; they also tore the Surrealist paintings on display, including one of Dalí's, since the editors of *Le Figaro* were already leading a campaign to ban this "Âge d'ordure."[30]

These confrontations caused the first screening of *Le sang d'un poète* to be delayed until November 17, 1930.[31] Shocked at seeing themselves clapping at the stoning of a child (they were featured at the very end of the film, just after the poet had shot himself, applauding from two reconstructed theater boxes), the Noailleses and the Lucinges asked for the scene to be cut. In vain Cocteau swore it was the suicide of the painter they were applauding, but Charles de Noailles, fearing a new scandal, asked him to refilm the scene. After initially digging in his heels, Cocteau eventually relented and allowed the film to be reshot without these luminaries, replacing them with the transvestite Barbette in one box and a zaftig opera singer and some extras in the neighboring box. But word of this scandal, spread by Lucien Daudet, set all of aristocratic Paris against a film that many of them hadn't even seen; Mme de Chevigné put it about that Jean, that "dreadful person," was more than ever having a nefarious influence on her granddaughter. They wanted to see the film as an aggressive farewell to that rival form of the marvelous (Christianity) that Cocteau had followed via the Maritains, so they deemed "sacrilegious" the fourth episode, "The Profanation of the Host," which was based on a painting by Paolo Uccello, to whom the film was dedicated, and whom Artaud had already honored in an issue of *La révolution Surréaliste*.[32] Cocteau swore, however, that he had not included any symbols in his film, that he had not wanted it to be analyzed; rather, he wanted it to be *lived*: "I am a carpenter. I build a table. Up to you to make it turn and speak."[33] With the help of psychoanalysis, then, everyone set about interpreting his film.[34]

The prefect of police, Chiappe, tried to use the violence that had greeted the release of *L'âge d'or* to prevent Cocteau's film from being distributed. Afraid that he would be excommunicated, Charles de Noailles canceled another showing of *Le sang d'un poète* they had planned at their home, then—no doubt to his relief—the authorities refused to let it be distributed abroad.[35] Even the Beaumonts dropped out. They were threatened with being thrown out of the Jockey Club, and the Viscount cut his losses by resigning of his own accord. He and Marie Laure took refuge in their villa in Hyères, asking Cocteau to stop showing the film even in private. Its release was postponed for over a year.[36]

There were a variety of reactions to *Le sang d'un poète* when it was finally shown at the Théâtre du Vieux-Colombier in Paris, January 20, 1932, during a gala celebration including André Gide, Serge Lifar, the Maritains, and Moysès, owner of the Boeuf sur le Toit. According to Julien Green, Cocteau feigned shyness when he presented an edited version of the film, minus an erotic scene, and in which the child's death was cut short.[37] André Gide "grumbled his admiration" but thought it was in some respects derivative.[38] With word spreading that it was a "Surrealist" film, and possibly the first full-length French Surrealist film, Breton put out a call to arms during the month that *Le sang d'un poète* was shown in the theaters. In spite of their passionate interest in film, the group had yet to produce one.[39] Instead they set about blocking the path of this "cheater" who had had the gall to cast Man Ray's mistress and to film his hermaphrodite in front of one of Duchamp's mobiles—since both were close associates of the Surrealists.[40] They accused Cocteau of having ripped off Buñuel, who had been consecrated by the attacks on *L'âge d'or*, calling Cocteau's film a shameful counterfeit, a work of total plagiarism that put the Spaniard's work in a terrible light. Concerned that public opinion would be affected by the fact that both films were funded by the same patrons, and weakened by their recent eviction from the Communist Party, the Surrealists consoled themselves by attacking Cocteau.

Cocteau retorted that he had finished filming his film before *L'âge d'or* had been shown to him. Recognizing the partial truth of the argument, the Surrealists accused him next of having had spies on the set of *L'âge d'or*, which had been filmed slightly before *Le sang d'un poète*.[41] Cocteau protested that it wasn't true, but to add support to his case, claimed not to have seen the film at all, though in fact he had been part of one of its first audiences, and during a meal on July 9, 1930, had, according to Julien Green, "described the film to us from beginning to end with such great precision that it was as if we had seen it ourselves . . . Had someone else recounted a film in such detail it would have been interminably boring, but Cocteau can do anything he likes with words."[42] Likewise, Cocteau claimed not to have seen *Un chien andalou*, Buñuel's first film, until after he had finished making *Le sang d'un poète*, though in fact he was one of the first to see it during a dinner given by the Noailles family.[43] Moreover, in *Opium* (in October 1929) Cocteau had cited *Un chien andalou* as one of four cinematic masterpieces, adding this revealing detail: "Every time blood flows, in families, in the street, we hide it, we cover it up with gauze."[44] Pretending not to have seen these films until after his was done was undoubtedly childish, but his protests came from the same avant-garde anxiety of influence that caused Picasso to claim never to have seen any African sculpture until *after* he had painted *Les demoiselles d'Avignon*.

The two directors had little in common, in fact. Buñuel praised *l'amour fou* by filming waking dreams; Cocteau dramatized the absurd logic of creation, across the abyss into which his narcissism plunged him. The Spaniard profaned religious, military, and bourgeois ritual, in the cinematic equivalent of automatic writing; the Frenchman, by contrast, only profaned himself, through a narrative saturated with an oneiric symbolism like that which would flourish in the work of Bergman or Fellini, from *The Silence* to *8 1/2*. There remained strange coincidences between *Le sang d'un poète* and *Un chien andalou*, including the gaping hand, the smiles that are wiped away, and the flowing blood. In *L'âge d'or* as well, the marquis's tail-coated friends gather on a balcony to observe, as if in a theater, the body of a murdered child. Here, too, it was a question of mocking whatever was left of the bourgeoisie of 1900; the minister of the interior, after his suicide, is found stuck on the ceiling of his office, like the little girl in *Le sang d'un poète* during her flying lessons.[45] If the debt to Buñuel is obvious, it went the other way as well: In 1922–1923, Buñuel had belonged to the Ultraist movement, which idolized the work of Apollinaire, Reverdy, and Cocteau. As Buñuel himself would admit many years later, in his interviews with Max Aub: "Without Cocteau, *L'âge d'or* would never have existed. It was he who introduced me to the Noailleses, and he who insisted for days on end that they give me the money I needed to make it." Did Buñuel find it more useful to join up with Breton? "That's another story, which doesn't concern me," he replied with his breezy cynicism.[46]

The Surrealists began to flex their muscles, determined to alienate the "angel's turd" from the patrons that bought their work, paintings, and manuscripts. In their view, Cocteau was neither a man nor a filmmaker, so they went about mockingly calling his film *Le sang menstruel d'un poète*.[47] *Le Figaro* praised it, the better to call for Buñuel's "shameful" film to be forbidden; but the debate heated up as Cocteau hastened to praise Buñuel's film in the same newspaper; he did sincerely admire it. At least he had the consolation of being joined in his disgrace by Dalí, from whom Buñuel had become estranged during the preproduction for *L'âge d'or*. The painter had hoped to show in the film, in his own delirious way, the "splendor of the creation of Catholic myths," and Dalí was soon excommunicated by Breton. But the fight against Cocteau took a very physical turn. "Éluard, Aragon, and I kept watch (so to speak) over his door, near the Madeleine, to give him a beating," Buñuel noted in this same interview. "He always had much respect for me. But with homos, you never quite know where you stand." Why stand with them, then? The hunt for the "smooth-talking hermaphrodite" almost succeeded one day, when, spotted in the balcony of a cinema in Montmartre, Cocteau came very close to being thrashed by the athletic René Char, the film critic Georges Sadoul, and Pierre Unik, a young poet who was as disgusted by homosexuality "as by excrement."[48] The "desperate, impassioned cry for murder" that Buñuel revealed in his own *Un chien andalou* had found a convenient target.[49]

No one today questions the personal nature of *Le sang d'un poète*: knocking down walls, subverting space as well as narration, Cocteau's film is one of the strangest coded confessions in cinematic history. The film, he believed, was a challenge to the psychoanalysts; Freud had even supposedly written that it was like watching a man undress through a keyhole, and had deduced from it that

Cocteau's father had killed himself.[50] (The article in question is not included in Freud's *Complete Works*, and probably only existed in Cocteau's imagination.[51] He would have been only too happy to have scored this point against Breton, who in two decades of epistolary harassment received only brusque refusals from Freud, after a short visit to his Viennese consulting room.[52])

Breton would never give up. In 1935, in *Position politique du Surréalisme*, he expressed concern that the movement was spreading too quickly across the world, and was particularly indignant to hear that the "unnamable" M. Cocteau—once again named—had managed to get himself included "in Surrealist exhibitions in America, and in Surrealist publications in Japan," despite the fact that Cocteau had never set foot there (nor had Breton, for that matter).[53] It is not impossible, however, that without Breton's vigilant ban, certain bridges might have been formed between Cocteau and certain members of the group, as the *Manifeste jaune* proves; composed in 1928 by Catalan artists, including Dalí, it was signed by Desnos, Éluard, and Aragon, as well as Cocteau.[54]

Breton's obsessive fear would climax in February 1934 in the United States and then again during the war, when *Le sang d'un poète* was shown in New York between Man Ray's and Buñuel's films. It was received as a Surrealist film, and would continue to be, since the Cocteau-Breton feud was unknown there.[55] This was so traumatic for the French Surrealists that as late as 1965 Soupault would still claim that Cocteau, through his "counterfeiting" and cheating, had forever put the Surrealists off of filmmaking.[56] Oddly, Breton had banned Soupault from his group in 1926 for having dared to write novels.[57]

One particular turn of events made the situation even worse. After months of scheming, Valentine Hugo had managed to convince Breton to share her bed from time to time. The news crucified Cocteau, who, unthinkingly, had arranged to move into her building at 9 rue de Vignon, two floors below, sure that it was the best way to rebuild his relationship with his "sister," and perhaps even to pacify the Surrealists.[58] Valentine was outraged to have Cocteau as her new neighbor; the polemic surrounding *Le sang d'un poète* had only hardened her feelings against him. Cocteau would not stop ringing her bell to explain himself, and Valentine forbade him from coming to her door, out of fear that he would encounter her new lover. The "bloody poet" had to content himself with slipping letters beneath her doormat. Before Breton could even ask Valentine to move, she returned to the rue de Montpensier, then joined Breton at Castellane, before it was her turn to move into *his* building. Poignantly, in her boundless veneration of her new lover, she went so far as to sell her piano and all her sheet music—the very sight of them bothered Breton, who hated music.[59]

The thought of revenge did not occur to Cocteau. Never having had the kind of awkward, heavy, solid ego that had allowed Picasso to crush all but his admirers, he instead waited for the storm to settle before setting back out to sea. For years he tried to win back Valentine, convinced that the young girl he had met backstage at the Ballets Russes was still in there somewhere, under the Surrealist armor. "I didn't like Jean," she would say, "because he claimed to be more persecuted and unhappy . . . than he was. He charmed some people, he offended others, and those were the ones he wanted."[60] When Breton broke up with Valentine the following year, Cocteau was the first to try to console her, but she rejected his overtures, instead distancing herself even more from this troublesome witness to her own unhappiness.

FROM THE BEDROOM TO THE THEATER

The limited release of *Le sang d'un poète* bothered Cocteau. Condemned to smaller audiences because of the experimental nature of his work, but more than ever rejected by the avant-garde, he felt as if he were losing on all fronts. His notoriety went beyond the group of booksellers who sold his collections and his essays, without ever managing to sell more than five thousand copies; he was well-known abroad, and in France the tabloid magazines photographed him. But in terms of readership, he remained somewhat marginal, at forty years old. With no party, no group, no journal behind him, Jean Cocteau was a literary lightweight.

The jeers of someone like Picabia had spurred him on in the 1920s; but as time went on, the Surrealists' scapegoat began to wonder if he had the strength to live out the rest of his life in such a manner, without money or recognition. Paris was so hard, like an "old egg full of dead matter," he had written to Max Jacob ten years earlier.[61] He so loved praising others, and could not adapt to the brutal, quasi-Darwinian struggle for literary survival. He saw that there were too many demands and not enough offers, but could not tolerate the cutthroat atmosphere. Could he survive in this overcrowded environment, among the pen-pushers who set themselves up as little Robespierres, the better to kill off their rivals? Was he not like the suffering bird he had once saved on the Champs-Elysées, then brought home with him, only to have Colette wring its neck after examining it?[62] "I was born for the country, the provinces, slow weeks. I got caught up in this battle by mistake," he had written three years earlier, before adding, "Poetry be damned!"[63]

To rise in the morning, open the bathroom door, and stir up shaving cream for the thousandth time was an ordeal; socializing made him nauseated. He detected so many negative vibrations around him that he wondered if Breton hadn't put a curse on his apartment on the rue Vignon before Valentine moved away. Opium, like madness, inoculates against most maladies, he told himself; yet he caught every microbe that happened by. "I must have burned out my essential organs; my beautiful machine is now a nail," he wrote to his mother, sounding almost nostalgic for the days when she had carried him up to his bedroom on the rue La Bruyère.[64]

In the spring of 1931, an old shepherd healer diagnosed him with a terrifying cerebral anemia that he said had been in place for thirty years and whose aggressiveness made his survival a miracle. Treated for four days with red wine, sugar, and medicinal plants, soothed by fawning comments about the doctors of Paris ("They're not bad, but they just don't know"), Cocteau felt as if he had been brought back to life.[65] He finally knew the cause of his unhappiness. His life haven't been a long imaginary tragedy; instead he had been the victim of a terrible childhood illness that was not detected or treated. It was a very happy four days. In the habit of reading tarot cards, palms, and crystal balls, he was more than ever convinced that the space we inhabit is nothing less than a closed room, decorated by ourselves. The fourth wall of this box could be broken down only by the esoteric arts, which would reveal the immensity of the hidden world and the mysteries weaving our destiny.

A week later, however, his maladies returned; and three months later, in late summer 1931, a paratyphoid fever made him take to his bed. Having caused the death of Radiguet, this illness led him to make another prolonged stay in a clinic, where Thomas Mann wrote to him, with his usual coolness, "You are the kind of person who dies in hospital."[66] Friends once again agreed to pay the bill, but his health still was not restored six months later. "Cocteau arrived dressed in thick, enormous white gloves, and death came in with him," noted Raïssa Maritain during a concert revival of *Parade*.[67] This "leprous" lifestyle could not last. The drugs were dehydrating his body to the point where he had become a hardened shadow, a scrawny caricature of the statuesque figure that since adolescence he had dreamed of becoming. When his whole organism came to be paralyzed, illness was the only way out, according to the tragic cycle he had endured since childhood. Feverish and disconnected from reality, he accomplished his best work.

His country could not sustain him in this slump. He who was so cheerful and obliging, so polite, who had learned to be friendly and *never* to humiliate anyone, no longer felt at home among those "Italians in a bad mood," which is how he saw the French. He tended to magnify the existence of others, while they played it down. He believed in the power of dreams and divination; they kept up a bad-natured skepticism—except his worst enemies. He had a self-contradictory spirit; they demanded that a writer remain coherent and stable, with a clear political involvement, the heirs of 1789, the defenders of Reason. "France cannot bear a role that is contradictory. The miser will always be miserly, the jealous man always jealous. That is why Molière is so successful," he wrote in *Le livre blanc*.[68] But where then could he go?

To Italy? The customs agents had made an exception and let him through without a visa for a quick getaway to San Remo with the Citroën B14. This quick trip had reminded him of how beneficial it had been for Nietzsche to spend time in Turin, Genoa, or Rome—but what would a French writer do in the land of fascism and Mussolini? Should he go to Germany, where he spoke the language and where his works were well-received? The idea would not have occurred to him before the 1950s; he would have been too far from his group of friends.

He thought, then, of perhaps buying a cottage by the Mediterranean, and devoting himself to horticulture. He could see himself returning to the city to sell his flowers, a Rousseauian fantasy left over from the Desbordes days. But whoever enjoys hearing his name mentioned in France should be wary of leaving Paris; and Cocteau knew that he would spend most of his time inundating his friends with letters, in order to be kept up to date. And in any case, what good was it to try to flee an incurable, internal suffering? All he could do was stay and smoke, nestled behind the closed doors of his apartment.

Everything Cocteau needed to live was sent back to the rue Vignon; once enclosed in his bubble, he could dream, draw, invent jewelry, or sketch dresses or paint objects found in a dumpster—just as in his childhood bedroom he had re-created the colors of all the shows his mother attended, by painting small models of their sets. Unhappy in love and in art, Cocteau evaded the outside world, replacing it with creations of his own. His room became the only stage on which he could move the shapes and shadows that animated his life, which had always been more richly fictional than his own novels. He would ask himself if he might also break down the fourth wall separating him from the world outside, to present this strange scene to the audience. Could he remain inside, yet impose himself out there? If the mystery of life escaped him, he could at least pretend to be its orchestrator. If the world was rude to him, he could conduct it from his bed.

People were tired of hearing his name, he knew. Having become used to Cocteau's personality for over twenty years, the enlightened public thought it knew everything about him: should he continue to force-feed it, at the risk of being rejected once and for all, or should he sever himself from it, even if that meant letting the public get used to his absence? To escape from this dilemma, Cocteau usually adapted himself in some new way, and worked against the image the public expected of him. Beginning in 1930, encouraged by the success of *La voix humaine*, he preferred to return to the theater of his childhood, leaving film and poetry behind. This time, he no longer hid his nostalgia for the idols of his early years: Édouard de Max and Jean Mounet-Sully became divine emperors striding across the stage of the Théâtre Français, while Sarah Bernhardt added monologues of her own, as Napoleon II in Edmond de Rostand's *L'aiglon*. Cocteau could imitate these monologues with a stunning accuracy, adding vibrato as he liked, as if he were still the child he had been in 1903, and at the same time the actress who fascinated him.

Of all the art forms, theater, along with drawing, had most excited Cocteau early on. He was compelled by the magic of matinees at the Français, the blood-red velvet curtains and the footlights like diamonds, and the "sword of fire" that separated the fictional world from our own and was forever seared inside of him.[69] In Piquey, we will recall, he had very quickly composed a drama worthy of Bernstein, the author who had tried, in *Mélo* or *Le secret*, to raise boulevard theater to the level of Ibsen and O'Neill. After his fortieth birthday, he returned like Orpheus to his first love, to give in once more to the "red-and-gold sickness." Even if it meant giving the impression of being back where he started and having made a complete inventory of himself. Such is the case with every good revolution.

The theater had always served Cocteau well. His avant-garde productions had led Drieu la Rochelle to ask for a theater hall for him, in 1923. He said Cocteau was "the only Parisian who knows anything" about this art, who captured the "hard hope" of their generation, which he felt Cocteau achieved more in his theater works than in his prose or his verse.[70] Dada was dead and buried, having absorbed its own "call to order." Surrealism too had gentrified, ever since *Le minotaure* had begun to target rich collectors, and the group's works had entered the speculative art market. What was left for him to accomplish, if not a defiant return to the past? Finding the path blocked, a vehicle must back up, the better to continue on its way; reclaiming the theater of his youth would allow him to access the tremendous feelings it had inspired in him then. As Stefan Zweig wrote, "A child's imagination is the most powerful; it is only in the dawn of life that people invent myths and symbols." Cocteau would not have disagreed.[71]

For ten years, Cocteau dreamed only of successful plays, even when they weren't at all. Converging his gifts, he furnished Parisian stages with both the dining rooms of boulevard theater, in his impatience to reach the masses, and with dramatically lit columns, to provide a frame for his eclectic mythology and his very particular form of fatalism. On stage, he portrayed families torn apart with loving each other, figures with animal heads posing riddles, and statues come to life to seek vengeance on humans for inflicting the boredom of immortality on them. With *Antigone* and *Oedipus Rex*, Cocteau had been one of the first to break with the irony of the 1920s to recover an Apollonian spirit; from then on he demanded an "atmosphere of grandeur" to live on. But this new metamorphosis was less complete than the others. To this neoclassical model he grafted the rediscovery of the sentimental drama of Henry Bataille and the bourgeois melodrama of Bernstein, whose success had left its mark on the prewar period. To escape from ceremoniousness, the desire for grandeur was contradicted by a sort of provocative prosaicness. His plays were "huis clos" (closed-off rooms) charged with electricity and needing only a spark to set the drama in motion; but they also dramatized recognizably ordinary people. Caught in the nets of the gods as well as in the tangles of their own incestuous bonds, as in *La machine infernale* (1932), shut up in their caravan in *Les parents terribles* (1938), or caught in a tangled web of lies like the protagonists of *La machine à écrire* (1939), his heroes would live in the gap between the exalted imagination and the sometimes pathetic daily life of their creator.[72]

From his conversion to his drug addition, Stravinsky viewed all of Cocteau's reactions as theatrical ones. Cocteau's means of announcing his joy or sadness to the world were frequently "excessive" or "hyperbolic," it's true; his metallic, nasal voice aspired to the dramatic authority of the giants of his youth, or tried to re-create Sarah Bernhardt's swells of emotion and ability to command her audience. This theatricality, absorbed in childhood, was the very matrix of Cocteau's being, if not the ultimate refuge of a personality for whom the true and the natural were uncertain notions, and for whom, in order to appear, he had to forget himself—to betray, transform, and distort himself. Having become used to playing his life, out of a fear of revealing himself in some radical and destructive way, Cocteau had something in common with actors. The more that the roles he took on seemed to exceed his abilities, the more he would demand of his body and his voice, in order to impress the audience. It was therefore a natural course of affairs for Cocteau to return to the theater. Having thought through his plays well before writing them, he would always give more attention to their dramatic impact than to their literary value; for this reason, some of his works might be considered melodramas. The result might be judged uneven; no one could deny Cocteau had a talent for bouncing back, to a dizzying degree. Life had tossed him about so much that he could not imagine any tragedy without a series of theatrical twists.

THE DIFFICULT PRINCESS

For three months already, Cocteau had been working on *La machine infernale*, a play about the return of Oedipus to Thebes, when Marie Laure de Noailles introduced him to a childhood friend during a private screening of *Le sang d'un poète* in her mansion on the place des États-Unis. Natalie Paley— pale, with feline cheekbones and a beautiful, sad expression under her abundant blond hair—had already seen the film in a private screening, but the young princess was a fan of the cinema (she had seen *Shanghai Express* more times than any of her friends), and had asked Marie Laure to see it again, this time in the company of Serge Lifar, the dancer from the Ballets Russes who accompanied her everywhere.[73] The beautiful twenty-six-year-old was fascinated by Cocteau's film, this confession of an opium-eater.[74]

Born into the Russian imperial family, Natalie Paley did not readily play the princess or the poseur; frank and good-natured, she followed Cocteau into his den, sat down before his tray of pipes, and willingly consented, with a royal courtesy, to the practical exercises he suggested. Biou took out the necessary implements while they drew the black curtains over the window that overlooked the Madeleine, and lit candles. The flame softened the brown ball on the tip of the needle before they filled the bowl of the delicate wooden pipe in a subtle, almost luxurious ritual.

Was it a ritual to which she had already been initiated? Plunging into the smoke gave the young princess the feeling of reliving the internal voyage Cocteau had filmed. Everything became so light, so graceful, when she lay on the floor; the anxiety of existence gave way to an almost royal insouciance. Soon she was asking to "go away again," wrapped in one of her host's dressing gowns, stretched out beside him. Cocteau spoke so eloquently, his images were so poetic! The movements of the smoke seemed to give body to the flux of his words, carrying her to the ceiling with an almost Asian gentleness; like young Nemo discovering the kingdom of Slumberland, the young Russian saw herself entering an enchanted universe whose prince was the poet.[75] She who needed the euphoria of "society," and who only felt comfortable in her own lies, leaped at the chance to flee the real world even more.

Cocteau was always concocting and mythologizing, but this was precisely what pleased the young princess, who during the Russian Revolution had seen how cruel reality can be. There was something unreal about Cocteau, and this is what reassured the young woman. "Sometimes he had something stronger than opium," she said; "doubtless it was this cocaine that helped Cocteau emerge from his lethargy. Jean would not let me try any, but I am sure I would have adored it. I was mad for his spirit and his charm."[76] "Natalie let herself be carried along, enchanted," confirmed a vexed Lifar.[77]

The delicious fog thickened, in time. Cocteau and Paley left the house only to see Mistinguett sing at the music hall; to watch Garbo or Marlene prowl across the big screen (they knew their films by heart); to listen to Édouard Bourdet read from his *Fleur des pois*, an urbane comedy about the third sex that Étienne de Beaumont was still financing; or to hear Ravel play *Pavane pour une infante défunte.* "Natalie and Jean were captivated with each other; they were perfectly fused. They made a marvelous couple," remembered the granddaughter of the couple that had hosted the concert.[78] Deeply moved by such an unexpected acquaintance, and flattered as well by her high birth, Cocteau succumbed to her beauty, in whose marvelous proportions could be glimpsed a secret fissure. The granddaughter of Czar Alexander II, the "liberator," did not leave the rue Vignon all that winter of 1932. "It was our honeymoon," he wrote ten years later.[79]

Natalie Paley was a strange character. In public, she never showed the slightest feeling, but in private she revealed a taste for sadness and poetry, which she would define, in almost Cocteauesque terms, as "the freezing, blinding antechamber of death."[80] In general, she liked to please, to amuse herself, distract herself, or even take part in very crude conversations, with what would eventually become known as the "jet set"—but at some point her versatile face would always cloud over, until it made others uneasy. She was capable of going from laughter to despondency and from excitement to the most complete indifference without any transition. Her mouth, like that of a badly weaned baby, would return to its unhappy frown when she left a meeting, her eyes squinting as if the daylight bothered them. "It was as if she were in exile on this earth," the Prince de Lucinge wrote in his memoirs.[81] This quality is precisely what would have moved Cocteau.

On occasion Paley did have to return to the sumptuous cold luxury in which her husband made her live. Lucien Lelong was a forty-three-year-old unattractive but chivalrous fashion designer who was himself secretly in love with one of his models. The couple kept different bedrooms and different summer holidays, and only came together under the watchful eye of "le tout Paris," the paparazzi's lenses, which captured them in a Venetian gondola or at a ski resort where young Natalie, in form-fitting ski clothes, looked like "a fragile and victorious young archer."[82] No sooner had she acquitted herself of these duties than she would return to the artificial paradise on the rue Vignon. There the spoiled and unhappy young heiress could bury herself in the most complete unreality.

Like so many daughters of the exiled Russian aristocracy, Natalie Paley had begun as a model, then made her reasonable marriage at the age of twenty-one.

Guessing the arrangement, after seeing so many others, Paul Morand had fallen in love with her pale virgin's face and her catlike eyes. "Pretty women are easier than the rest," Morand's wife claimed; "having been so often solicited, their ability to resist is greatly diminished."[83] But Natalie Paley did not give in.[84] A fragile but damaged Narcisse who, according to Jean-Pierre Grédy, liked to lead men on, while approving them, she evidently preferred the company of men who were less sexually demanding, and often more amusing.[85] For this reason she was drawn to Serge Lifar, her indefatigable gallant, who encouraged in her the kind of nostalgia for the Romanovs she made fun of; as well as the likes of Cecil Beaton, Horst P. Horst, George Hoyningen-Huene, or any of the other photographers whose cameras illuminated her silhouette, so evocative of the lily, a flower that was already invading the pages of *Vogue*.

Natalie Paley loved to be loved, but her idea of love was that of the princesses the troubadours sing about: when the beautiful lady becomes bored, her courtly lover must put away his lute and retire. He could win permission to photograph her, to style her, to dress her, but rarely to undress her. She was so aware of her image that it sucked the lifeblood from her, said her biographer Jean-Noël Liaut; a perfect image of glacial beauty, she feared sex like some Japanese women the sun. "Natalie's approach to love could only ever be fraternal," confirmed an intimate source. Others said she had the sexual maturity of a twelve year-old girl, the age at which she may have been raped by Red Army soldiers.[86] Except for her first husband, Paley, the cousin of the last czar, had no lovers or friends who were not homosexual men. Princes and millionaires were also driven out if they demanded the proof of love that Lelong himself had had the tact to forget; in order to taste her childlike little mouth, she had to be the first woman to stir you—and Cocteau appeared to have belonged to this category. Leaving behind her life of privilege for an otherwise flattering penury, the sad, spoiled young woman gave herself over to the ascetic poet.

In order to desire, Cocteau had to love; and to love, his childlike faculty for astonishment demanded angels or saints, adventurers or heroes. Natalie Paley was born mythical: her father, the brother of Alexander III, had been one of Diaghilev's first patrons; her mother, a friend of the daughter of Mme de Chevigné, Proust's idol; her brother Vladimir was a poet whose talent was compared to Pushkin's, and whose figure was compared to the princes sketched by Léon Bakst for the first Ballets Russes; and as for her half-brother, the Grand Duke Dmitri, one of Rasputin's killers, he had been the lover of Coco Chanel, which was all it took for the former frivolous prince to see her as his romantic sister.

Her father having been declared persona non grata at court by his nephew, Czar Nicholas II, Natalie Paley was born in a *hôtel particulier* with a view of the bois de Boulogne—escorted into the world, so to speak, by officers of the White Guard. Once the grand duke Paul was back in the czar's good graces, she returned to live with the imperial family at Tsarskoye Selo, where she played with Yusupov, Rasputin's other killer, an "angel" who dressed up as a girl at night. She had an adolescence that in its splendor and its cruelty was worthy of any Russian novel. During the Revolution, her father was thrown into jail and drunken soldiers prowled around their home at night. She and her sister crossed over the border into Finland, on foot and in secret. Her beloved brother was thrown into a coal pit with sticks of lit dynamite, while her father, uncles, and cousins were all shot. "All the blood of the Romanovs curdled" and splashed onto the young woman, who desired to hear nothing further of Russia from that moment on, except for what *Vogue* reported.

Meeting her set Cocteau's imagination on fire. Queen Mary of England predicted that Paley would marry her son, the duke of Kent. She was one of those princesses whom society was still willing to cast in its greatest roles. In Natalie Paley's veins ran the blue blood of the Romanovs; in his, the red blood of poets. The princess's sad beauty, with her claw-like eyebrows à la Garbo, added to his pride at being seen on the arm of this survivor. For if her physique was the basis of her career, it was also her destiny; the Romanovs were known for their dangerous brilliance. Cocteau's heart, easily broken since it never learned to be cast in bronze as Chamfort recommended, was a bundle of nerves; Natalie Paley had only to touch him to ignite his desire. At the age of forty-three, Cocteau had fallen in love with this woman who wore a permanent look of surprise, as if she had just been woken up. Or at least he wanted to fall in love—which for him was the same thing—with this Sleeping Beauty, this shadow in search of a body, which was always terrified whenever it did present itself.

Was Cocteau trying to compete with Desbordes or to experience a form of love he had always envied in his lovers? Did he hope, having tried everything, without ever constructing a lasting relationship, that he had found balance, or even legitimacy? Did he sense that his emaciated body was losing more and more of its ability to seduce men? Whatever the case, he dove in. After having claimed in *Opium* that a normal man should be able to make love with anyone or (even) anything, he was going to prove he was completely normal, and therefore demonstrate his universal humanity.[87] He did all he could to manage, in spite of the opium and the habits he'd acquired with boys. "I can only make love to a woman if I hear Weill playing," he confided to a conductor; Natalie Paley therefore developed a passion for the German's music; *Threepenny Opera* had recently been adapted for the cinema by Pabst, and Yvonne George had sung the magnificent *Mahagonny Songspiel* in December.[88]

Cocteau had been so public about his preferences for so long that the news took everyone by surprise, especially Mauriac.[89] Those who had called him an acrobat doubted whether he could pull off *that* kind of tumbling. While he had a vague idea that all creators were in some sense androgynous, it was not the case for Cocteau's own sexuality, which had had nothing to do with women since the 1910s. For others, this rediscovery of the sex that at that time was still called the "weaker" was even more improbable than his return to God. "After boys, drugs, religion, is this not the final proof of his eternal reinvention?" suggested Jean-Louis de Faucigny-Lucinge, who was also close to the princess.[90] Had Cocteau not shown a certain ambiguity in his youth? And if he was estranged from women during the period he had dreamed of himself as a demigod, was it not because he saw them as a mundane obstacle to his will to omnipotence?[91] Twenty years later, with a few more battle scars, Cocteau saw in the princess's flattering unreality the best way out of his disarray.

Sixteen years younger than he, the enigmatic Natalie Paley would hold the key to Cocteau's destiny. She was the Sphinx that Bérard would sketch in red chalk on the walls of the rue Vignon, facing down Oedipus, eager to enter Thebes—by which he meant real life. Proud to show that he was able to get hold of himself, Cocteau took up a way of life that had previously been taboo. "Normal love, I thought, is not forbidden me. Nothing prevents me from having a family and setting myself on the right path," he said in *Le livre blanc*, before adding: "Without effort, nothing beautiful could exist." In fact, he had looked very well since he started seeing Natalie Paley. Apart from those who mocked him, only one person warned him against the "worldly pitfalls" in store for him: his mother. Natalie Paley might have symbolized everything Mme Cocteau could hope for her son, given her snobbish penchant for nobility, but she did not look kindly on adultery, which was the case for the princess at least. Cocteau attributed her attitude to jealousy, called her a killjoy, and resigned himself to being patient. Hadn't she eventually ended up welcoming Radiguet, and even Desbordes, in time?

From out of nowhere, Cocteau received a letter from Desbordes. "I thought you were safe from this kind of thing. Women, I mean," Desbordes wrote, before humbly reminding him that he still loved him, as strongly as at the beginning, and thought of him every moment. Wary of this "stupefying adventure," Desbordes, who in Cocteau's film had been indifferent to the poet's suicide, became concerned when he heard from Bérard that Paley was "crazy" about Cocteau.[92] Spying through keyholes on their meetings, Desbordes threatened to leave the rue Vignon to live with his sister Éliette, and made more and more violent scenes. Paley grew jealous as well; Cocteau tried to explain this old affair by persuading her that Jean-Jean was the reincarnation of her brother Vladimir, the poet. It didn't work. "When a woman loves you, she doesn't love your friends," he would write in a poem he would send to Kurt Weill. "In our hearts she wants to be the only one."[93]

Yet Cocteau was incapable of totally cutting himself off from his former life. "You know, my love, that my life is yours—yours and yours alone," Jean-Jean wrote to him, already proposing he return at whatever frequency Cocteau liked, sure that Cocteau loved him as much as he loved Cocteau—that is, completely.[94] Cocteau, at the same time, did not want to "destroy everything" in Natalie's life, as Desbordes dared him to do. Contradictory forces fired at him from one side or another, and it was impossible to tell where one ended and the other began. It was the trickiest of all his acrobatics; how could he physically yield to this new love (however deeply he needed it) when that part of him still belonged to the other?

With doubt clouding this new affection, he was also concerned to see how sensitive the young Russian was to the cinema's charms. The photographer Hoyningen-Huene had just directed her in a short film with Coco Chanel, and Marcel L'Herbier spoke of offering her a part in his next film. Did they see her as the next Garbo? She ran to tell him, with the pride of the young lover. But for once he did not behave as Pygmalion; he did not want a film star or a tomboy, but a *real* woman by his side.

Did she question the force of his commitment? He offered her the triple ring he had designed for Radiguet. She wanted to think it over before accepting this gift. It was a bit risky to bind herself to this champion of the about-face when she had a reliable husband by her side, and when she had much more credible suitors beside her, like Andy Embiricos, a wealthy Greek heir, or Jean-Louis de Faucigny-Lucinge. What should she make of the strange sexual limping of this forty-three-year-old man? Cocteau, however, seeing himself less as a solid form than as an idea, less as a body than as a line that could redraw itself, showed no doubts at all. "I HAVE THOROUGHLY CHANGED," he wrote to her, with obvious sincerity.[95] Galvanized by his new role, he demanded that she tell her husband of their affair. But Lucien Lelong showed himself more than magnanimous: he left her entirely free to act, within the limits of "respectability." "Sublime," was her response.

Convinced that this tolerance was his worst enemy, Cocteau pushed things further, and in order to force the princess to choose, asked her for a child. The time of adopting young boys had lasted long enough; now he wanted to give life, create one with his own features—it would only be a boy, of course. The heir to the greatest thrones, adding the czar's crown to that of poetry, the child quickly became a genius in his mind. Like the heir he had hoped to conceive with Anna de Noailles at one time, this "Jean Romanov" already shone with a supernatural glow. And one day, perhaps he would reign over all of Russia!

THE ANGEL-MAKER

With the opium's help, Natalie Paley also began to dream of a little "czarevitch." Soon she confessed to the poet that she was pregnant, and swore him to secrecy. But in his pride at finally becoming a father, Cocteau could not keep himself from announcing the good news to a few friends, and soon all of Paris knew about it. Their friends discussed the implications of this unexpected pregnancy. Cocteau's ability to marry was greatly in doubt, and it was hard to imagine the young Russian with a bottle at feeding time. Finding her more pale and unhealthy than ever, the Faucigny-Lucinges tried to dissuade her from actually carrying the pregnancy to term. Given her responses, however, they concluded that the pregnancy was imaginary, designed to flatter Cocteau or validate her own ability to reorient homosexuals. Lucien Lelong, however, believed there would soon be a child, and told his wife if she kept it he would ask for a divorce—in short, that she would have to part with her lifestyle. Soon after, Paley told Cocteau that Lelong was ready to claim the child as his own, which displeased the writer.

Every day the tension increased at the rue de Vignon. Too much electricity coursed through the apartment in which he was writing *La machine infernale*; it was a bit like Mount Olympus, where lightning announced the birth of a new demi-god. As we've seen, in childhood Cocteau never felt better than when a storm forced his family to snuggle up around the gaming table at their house in Maisons-Laffitte: the whole universe seemed finally to live at the degree of tension that he lived every day, awaiting the great release that would bring calm to the earth and peace to his nerves. If Lelong dug his heels in, the drama would play out accordingly. Natalie Paley, however, was more firm: knowing that she was not only going to give birth to the child, but also have to raise it, she was beginning to wonder if having it was the right thing. Could she really trust this man who had, according to her friend Marie Laure, disappointed every woman who approached him, from Valentine Hugo to Caryathis—not to mention herself? Could he possibly want a child in order to prove to the world the reality of their affair? In fact, was she entirely sure she was pregnant? And if so . . . by whom? Lying came so naturally to her that even today it is difficult to know which of her accounts to believe.

"I fell in love to the point of sickness (with complete reciprocity)," Cocteau told a friend.[96] "Jean, my love, I think of you all the time and I love you endlessly," she telegraphed him.[97] But the lovers were overshadowed by a husband who was no longer happy to play a bit role. Lucien Lelong's obstinacy and the procrastination of his "Imperial" mistress—she had "several centuries of indecision" behind her, he said—made Cocteau's dreams turn to legends. He saw himself as Tristan, and Natalie as Isolde, fatally bound by the love potion that is opium, but prevented from being together by the king, Marc-Lelong. As a way of reading the situation, Arthurian legend, itself founded on physical separation and heavenly reunion, was a useful one. Hadn't his passion for Radiguet been characterized by erotic distance and premature death?

Cocteau decided to go and finish *La machine infernale* on the Côte d'Azur. He was picking up on the clues that Natalie did not really want to keep their child. But how to pose the question without hurting her? And what reproach could he make of this young woman who panicked at the sight of him leaving and who ran to the stores to fill his suitcases? Even so, neither the South, nor Desbordes, who went with him, nor even Geneviève Mater, who stayed nearby, could distract Cocteau from his obsession. He was willing to do anything to have this child. He secretly encouraged Desbordes to write to Natalie to lure her with the prospect of a little family ready to warm her by the hearth, and then to welcome the newborn.

At the end of her rope, still weak from a bout of appendicitis, the ice princess left with her maid for Saint-Moritz, her bags full of books he had recommended, to care for her anemia, but more likely to reflect on the situation. "Every night before I sleep I reread *Plain-chant*," she wrote to him. "I go to sleep in your arms; a photograph of you (the one by Man Ray which is my favorite) beside me; I've hung from the bed . . . the amber necklace and the little monkey . . . it looks very sweet. Across the room, on my dressing table, I have the photograph of you taken from the film."[98] Part of the decor from the rue Vignon had gone into her bedroom. Natalie Paley mulled over her decision, during long walks across the glaciers, reflecting her burning coldness. "I have looked at these photos so much that nothing is left of you; I've absorbed it all," she added, a few weeks later.[99]

Cocteau read these letters in a state of joy and terror, next to the photograph of Natalie he had slid into the mirror of the armoire in his room. The world was empty without her; everything that was good and beautiful on the Côte d'Azur wounded him; he might have thrown in the towel without these astounding letters and the hope of the approaching birth. It was then that Petit-Cru fell ill. The puppy, which Cocteau had purposely named after the animal that Tristan had given to Isolde, was dying, and Cocteau took this as a bad omen. He came to believe that under pressure from her husband, Natalie Paley had gone to

Switzerland to one of those clinics that were illegal in France. She had killed the flesh of his flesh, his life's one hope!

Judging from the questions her friends were asking about her health, Natalie Paley deduced that Cocteau had put it about everywhere that she had killed their child. Devastated to see herself the object of the worst Parisian rumors, the young princess was outraged to discover that he was not lying when he wrote to her: "The one who loves writes on the walls." "How do you expect me to believe you, to trust you? . . . You don't know what it is to protect a woman, that the relations between people of two different sexes are infinitely fragile."[100] Did he think his indiscretions were unimportant, given the power of their love? She saw with horror how greatly their views of the world differed. "Love is not everything in life. You need total understanding, something we do not have."[101] Cocteau was too flighty.

But it was she who was flighty, Cocteau thought, refusing to begin this new life together, with a child beside them! It was she who spent her time playing golf with socialites, playing cards with imbeciles, dancing with gigolos. She only refuted his suspicions in order to thicken the fog of their combined lies: "I have never done anything bad only because God would not want me to."[102] Did she miscarry or had she simply anticipated his own desires by announcing a pregnancy that did not yet exist? Anything was possible with this young woman who could confess to him, "How do you want me to make plans, create new life, when I'm missing that essential thing, the desire to live?"[103]

Whatever the truth may have been, there was no more talk of a child. Did she really abort this "bastard," as she supposedly told Desbordes in a letter, or did she lose the baby?[104] Either way, nothing wounded Cocteau as much as this loss, one that nevertheless pleased his mother, twenty years after Madeleine Carlier's abortion.

THE HEAD OF THE MEDUSA

All that remained was for Cocteau and Paley to continue to live out their love, which neither of them questioned. But their relationship had taken such an intense turn that Natalie decided to go first to Switzerland and then on to Cernobbio, on Lake Como, to join the Noailleses. Marie Laure naturally became her confidant. From morning until night the two women could talk of one thing only: Cocteau, his poetic genius, his existential difficulties, his insatiable need to be loved. Seeing her foundational wound reopening, Marie Laure told the princess that though Cocteau was happy to demonstrate their affair all over Paris, he would have had great difficulty actually living it on a daily basis—and as for thinking himself capable of starting a family, that seemed impossible.

How could the young Russian not have listened to this "old" friend she so admired, and who had fallen brutally in love with Jean fifteen years earlier?[105] More intelligent, more inventive—more scheming as well—Marie Laure took advantage of her influence over the princess to make her more seriously doubt Cocteau's capacity to reform his sexuality in the long term. At the same time, Marie Laure was vicariously experiencing all the more intensely what was happening to Natalie. Frustrated by a husband whom she declared was made neither for women nor for men, but for flowers, she physically felt the same mixture of happiness and dismay that the younger woman experienced—Natalie was more beautiful and younger by three years, but drawn to the same kind of men. Not yet having dared to take a lover, she suffered at seeing the young Russian living out her own dream. Why did Natalie Paley fascinate Cocteau as she did? And why was she not the one chosen—why had she been rejected years ago? Was it because of her Jewish origins, which she did not even own up to?[106]

Her pride deeply wounded, Marie Laure took up her pen to intercede between the two protagonists, whom she had in fact introduced. Understanding in her letter that she was trying to set the princess against him, Cocteau wrote to the young Italian who accompanied Marie Laure to Cernobbio: "Tell Natalie for me . . . that I have given her my life, *once and for all,* and that she is free to use it as she sees fit."[107] The young Russian could throw his whole life into the fire, he would offer it to no one else—this life did not belong to him any longer. Natalie was free to return to her routine of flirtations reined in by her painful marriage; he would always wait for her. "I refuse to allow myself to believe that our relationship has been a failure," he concluded.

Cocteau's indiscretions awakened Marie Laure's frustrations; each passed judgment on this unusual liaison in Italy. The intimate drama turned to opera, commented on in real time by "café society." "Everyone is in an atrocious state of nerves" and Marie Laure is "devoured by pain and jealousy," the young Russian wrote in a letter to Cocteau.[108] A crepuscular feeling settled over the idyllic vacation spot where a brother of Luchino Visconti was also staying, a man whom Marie Laure described to Cocteau as a "Lucifer" ready to do anything to seduce Natalie.[109] A thousand gossips, heedless of the consequences, exacerbated the sadistic atmosphere that was "seeping with flesh, stones, and vegetation," as Marie Laure put it—the same Marie Laure who told Cocteau, in the midst of a sentence written jointly with her husband, "Both of us love you and me especially because I always have."[110] Did the woman who, as a teenager, was desperately in love with him, want to show herself worthy of her ancestor, the monster of La Coste, whose manuscript for 120 *Days of Sodom* she kept in a leather briefcase shaped like a phallus? More than the Marquis de Sade, it was Laclos's Madame de Merteuil whom she wanted to emulate, in her despair. Cocteau had ignored her love? She would force him to hate her.

Natalie Paley could well guess at the frustrations Marie Laure was exorcising, but she believed her to be sincere, if not chivalrous. Was Marie Laure not the first to show her the letters she wrote to Cocteau? One written on September 30 was the culmination of this stormy summer. "You must remember this in your heart: Natalie tells me several times a day with tears in her eyes *that she loves you*. It's the *truth* . . . But she is made to be loved and not to love."[111] The princess was, in her eyes, a marvelous plant, requiring mirrors and lights to flourish. Was he skeptical? She told him that all the men of Cernobbio were at Natalie's feet—Luchino Visconti included. Did he doubt it? She described the young Russian as the wondrous heroine of a novel, who must remain inside of it, who must continue to be, to use Cocteau's vocabulary, an angel of uprightness and purity—as if any hint of carnal love would sully her.

Cocteau no longer had one enemy, but two. And Marie Laure was the more dangerous, because her influence far exceeded that of Natalie's husband. The uncertainty in which Cocteau found himself was poignant; on one hand, the princess definitely loved him; on the other, he knew her to be the hostage of a man who had a lot invested in his reputation, and of a woman who had made the failure of his relationship with Natalie her own personal cause. To cut short his suffering, Marie Laure took it upon herself to tell him that Natalie had "more or less decided to return to Saint-Cloud" with her husband. The young princess quickly confirmed this:

> But since this is all infinitely painful, and because giving you pain is more unbearable than anything, I'm begging Jean-Jean to give you my letter, to explain with all the love he has for you, why I've decided to continue with my life as it is.[112]

This was her way of suggesting that she was not leaving him all alone. But Cocteau would not yield. Encouraged by the letter's final sentiments—"What I have given you, I cannot take back, it is yours, just as my heart and soul are yours. I kiss you and love you for eternity"—he asked to meet Lucien Lelong, who had returned to Paris. The interview took place on "neutral" territory, at the home of Faucigny-Lucinge. Cocteau pled his case extensively, piling up declarations and promises, but seeing himself unsuccessful, ended up asking, "If I die, would you let your wife run to my bedside?" Replied Lelong: "I would run there myself."[113]

Natalie Paley was in no hurry to return to her husband, and decided to prolong her absence by going to stay with the Viscontis in Rome, where she wrote to Cocteau:

> All my joys, all my emotions make me think of you, you are the most lumi-nous part of myself. My days are spent reading your poetry, as Madina V[isconti] knows it by heart, we are going to play records of you reciting it, you follow me everywhere, I live in your shadow and I feel this to be *eternal*.[114]

For his part, Cocteau was convinced that Natalie, far from Marie Laure, would come back to him, and that Lelong would be the first to give her her freedom, after rediscovering the abyss in their marriage that had only deepened while they were apart. He had finally told his friends about the tone of his meeting with Lelong, which he had wanted himself to keep secret. Lelong's iciness, like his own passion, won him their honest support; no one, except perhaps a few socialites, seemed to hope for the survival of a couple who were together only out of financial interest. Touched by his insistence, the princess could already think of nothing but the fabulous disorder of the rue Vignon, and the poetry of the *enfants terribles* in which the Viscontis also lived—all of which possessed a sublime beauty, "dramatic, violent, and incestuous." The letters arriving from Rome grew more passionate; Cocteau was once again the "Exceptional Being" whose love and genius illuminated her life. He confided to his friends, who then talked in turn, to such an extent that Marie Laure's jealousy flared like never before. Prepared to do anything to defy Cocteau, this time she made explicit advances on him.[115] When she was rejected once again, she became determined to erase all traces of Cocteau from her life, and threw away or burned everything he had given her—from books dedicated with draw-ings at Hyères, to a pipe-cleaner portrait, under which Man Ray had photo-graphed them, to the manuscript of *La machine infernale* that he had just signed to her. The patron had turned arsonist.

Marie Laure needed everyone to know that she had been the one to put a stop to their relationship; it was on the rue Vignon that she was finally able to do so, subjecting Cocteau to an atrocious scene in front of her husband and Natalie Paley. In her rage, she tore the dresses and destroyed the hats that the young Russian kept at Cocteau's home. The writer finally slapped this fury whose terrifying eyes and venomous mouth he compared to that of the Medusa, most terrible of the Gorgons.[116] "It was little Marie Laure from Grasse, spoiled, irritated," he said, adding—he who was never violent—that she deserved to be whipped in the town square.[117] In making this scene, Marie Laure convinced

Cocteau—who would refer to her henceforth as the "Viscountess Medusa"—that she alone bore responsibility for Natalie's abortion, and therefore for the murder of the "czarevich."

The young princess was not blameless. Why had she been so afraid of being hit by him, during that scene on the rue Vignon, if not out of guilt? She had been inconsolable, too, at the death of Petit-Cru, which certainly was a means of mourning for her own child.

Cocteau showed he was more determined than ever to win back the difficult princess. "I love you," he told her in October. "It's an invincible power. If you love me—another invincible power—it's useless and ridiculous to plan. Our stars have it all mapped out . . . I BELIEVE."[118] Nevertheless it was his own will, more than his feelings, that emerged from his declarations—unlike those of the young Russian. Some thought his confessions too theatrical to be sincere, or too inconsistent, seeing him reenact his interview with Lelong as if he were thinking of turning it into a Bernstein-esque drama. But that was also the way he had lived with Desbordes; he always expressed his pain theatrically. "He's an odd man," noted Lelong, at the end of their meeting.[119]

All sorts of rumors spread about Cocteau. One claimed that in his bedroom, under the framed photograph of his "fiancée," there was a photograph showing an actor, well-known for his flexibility and his virility, pleasuring himself.[120] People talked about Desbordes's omnipresent jealousy, according to which the princess of abortion deserved a beating, and about the arrival of a seductive young Kabyle man. Something wasn't right; a man who was really in love wouldn't gallivant about in such a manner. His sudden rediscovery of women, which happened even more quickly than his return to God, was spoiled by the attention it attracted. Natalie Paley herself would confess, anonymously,

> Cocteau was all spirit—and later, of course, all drugs. From the very beginning things happened mainly in his head, and then later too much opium extinguished any sexual life. He was certainly not like Oscar Wilde, capable of bisexuality.[121]

And yet their letters attest to an intimate, ardent relationship; as anxious as she may have been, the young Russian never seems to have doubted that she was loved, if not desired.

The love they had dreamed of, one freed from all contingencies, began its slow decline. Cocteau understood that Natalie Paley did not wish to destroy her figure and submit to the enslavement of maternity—she was the more narcissistic of the two, in the end. This beauty, who treated her body as a work of art by cultivating her cold, fashionable silhouette, could be attracted by poetry, but she did not have the calling for poverty or for playing mother. If Cocteau had more definitively sacrificed Desbordes, and all his friends along with him, Natalie Paley might have been more convinced. "She would have liked for Barbe to paint her in triumphant garb, on a mountain of death," he wrote in the end of *La fin du Potomak*.[122] But the writer could not live alone, even in a relationship. "The attraction he had for me was purely physical," she would say years later, contradicting herself again. "He wanted a son, but with me he was as efficient at getting one as any total homosexual stupefying himself with opium. All this was undignified and shameful. There was no love between us. I did not inspire a single one of his poems."[123] Not one, but ten, in fact, were dedicated to her, from "Looking for Apollo" to "Der Egoist," which describes his jealous love.[124] To say nothing of *La fin du Potomak*, which she haunts under the name of Princess Fafner, and *La machine infernale*, of which she is the cornerstone, in the figure of the Sphinx and in which Jocasta herself has a Russian accent. "Souvent femme varie, bien fol est qui s'y fie" (Woman often changes; foolish is the man who trusts her), wrote François I. The motto remained true, like its inverse, the one that the postwar "boys" liked to quote: "Souvent folle varie, bien femme est qui s'y fie" (A poof often changes; only a woman can trust "her").

Like Isolde in her small boat, in late 1932 the princess drew away from Cocteau and from opium. "I secretly weep every day for our ruined chances," she still wrote to him, a year later, as she grew closer to Kurt Weill, who had helped bring them together before helping to drive them apart. "Happiness was so close, so possible," she wrote to Lifar, breaking with him.[125] The fairytale was over: Marie Laure had taken it away.

His heart as well as his pride deeply wounded, Cocteau cried for a long time, prostrate. For once he had loved and been loved, outside of all ambition! Having been finally ready to lead a "real" life, he found himself with nothing. Was this affair only a dream, invented by this Isolde? Was their passion fed by opium? "If she thought me a liar, why did she not turn my lies into reality itself?" he confided to a friend.[126] Was this not a way of recognizing that he had acted as the author of fiction, that the power behind his love was theatrical in nature? Natalie Paley had undoubtedly inspired his love, but he was one of the rare men to believe himself capable of founding a "normal" family with her. "I dreamed what is," announces the heroine of *La voix humaine*, . . . "and when I knew it was true, that I was alone, that my head was not on your neck or your shoulder, and my legs between your legs, I felt that I could no longer . . . live."

Natalie Paley divorced soon after, moving into an apartment on the Esplanade des Invalides that she filled with Cocteau's books. She never had any children, and never seemed to regret it.[127] Her cinematic debut in L'Herbier's *L'épervier* was promising, and she was cast, in 1934, opposite Pierre-Richard Willm in *Le Prince Jean*—whose title must have unsettled Cocteau, superstitious as he was.[128] But the script he planned to write for her remained unwritten, and her career came to an end soon after an astonishing performance in George Cukor's *Sylvia Scarlett* (1935).[129]

Cocteau secretly mourned losing her until his dying day: the modern-day Isolde of his *L'éternel retour* would be called Natalie, and the spokeswoman for the kingdom of the dead in the film version of *Orphée* would be a princess. "I have loved boys and two women," he added in a manuscript for *Le livre blanc*, and boys had given him happiness—at least he wanted to think so—unlike the women.[130] But he wept more for the "angel" that the young Russian had "made" through her abortion; all his life, he would speak of it in doleful tones, but also with the wounded pride of an author whose small masterpiece has been refused by editors. Perhaps this unusual Pygmalion would have made a good father—he had so much to pass on. "It was the saddest period of my life," he told Markevitch.[131]

GOODBYE, JEAN-JEAN

This tragedy poisoned his relationship with Desbordes. The younger man could not bear the elder's exhibitionism, the scenes he made at the smallest provocation, or the lies he hid behind. It was not amnesia that led Cocteau to contradict himself at two-week intervals, but the opium that truly made him forget what he had said and thought—and therefore to lie, so to speak, in good faith. Keeping a secret was impossible for him; everything he lived seemed publishable, like a clue to his singularity; the confidences of those around him became fodder for the monologues that he developed and dramatized, or letters he recopied, sometimes word for word, for different correspondents—when he didn't turn them into a poem or a play. Desbordes no longer believed in the generosity of a man who always avoided paying at a restaurant, under the pretext that he would pay for his friends in words—that a poet shouldn't have to worry about such things. He saw Cocteau impatient to exploit the heart whose state he kept everyone up to date on, but which owed much more to his nervous problems than to real feelings. Yet as soon as Desbordes left, Cocteau fell apart. That Desbordes was "educating" young women under his nose, he tolerated, but solitude was the worst thing that could be inflicted on him.[132] Locking himself in his room, Cocteau stayed there for days without moving, frozen, embalmed—a kind of invalid who wondered why every attempt he made to be loved was cursed, and why everything he felt seemed like a lie. Basically, it was the earth itself that made him live falsely or condemned him to live a lopsided life, as if his true essence were located in the sky. "I love the truth," he confessed in a monologue. "But she doesn't love me. That's the true truth: the truth doesn't love me. As soon as I speak her, she changes her face and turns against me . . . But as soon as someone calls me a liar, hatred smothers me."[133]

Once again he allowed Bourgoint to visit him, as an antidote to solitude. With no income, no home, and no clothes, Bourgoint, who was definitively inept at working, had become a sort of vegetable, happy with the scrapings at the bottom of his friends' pipes, or making do with bottles of pastis or eau-de-vie, which he drank straight, without catching his breath, until he littered the floor with empty bottles. "His body emitted opium in the form of a black sweat," wrote Jean Hugo, who found Bourgoint "pale and defeated" in May 1932, like a corpse thrown in the dump. More depressed than ever since the death of his sister, the *enfant terrible* would take out Cocteau's smoking equipment, prepare his pipe, and dream beside him, falling asleep while reading a detective novel.

That is how Desbordes found Cocteau when he returned. The younger man was still jealous of his former lover, but had tempered his jealousy with a kind of sarcastic cheerfulness, as if he now knew Cocteau was incapable of true fidelity, and also knew, at the end of the day, that Cocteau was really only interested in himself. "Your love is vast and nonexistent," the frivolous prince had reproached Anna de Noailles; this is exactly what Jean-Jean thought of Cocteau now. Exhausted, bitter, and as disappointed as Sachs, the author of *J'adore* was nevertheless incapable of leaving for good. He continued to passionately love Cocteau, even if he did his best to prove the contrary. The writer had not only launched him; he had invented and molded him, and while it was easy to leave him for a month, it was much more difficult to start his life over, far from him. Geneviève Mater, however, no longer tolerated seeing him return to Cocteau again and again. Caught between the two of them, Desbordes decided to go with pretense, trying with one to affirm his virile strength, confessing with another his fear of just being a page or a "client." "For me she is not a housewife, or perhaps I am just a houseboy," he exclaimed indignantly one day.[134] But the air was so rarified, in the heights to which Cocteau had raised him up, that he preferred to be a good boy with her than a false genius with him.

At the same time, he could no longer bear his own back and forth. "There was inside of me a man and a woman," says his alter ego in *Le livre blanc*. "The woman submitted to you; the man reacted against this submission." For a little while, Desbordes blamed Cocteau for making him believe he was Radiguet's equal, in order to keep him close by. But then Madeleine Peltier, a pharmacy student and sister of a naval officer, took advantage of these hesitations to get closer to Desbordes. Neither pretty nor brilliant, but sweet and easy-mannered, Peltier knew that Geneviève Mater would never leave her husband, or even her mistress. Her candor touched Desbordes—she at least loved him for who he was. After seven years of tumult, Desbordes finally left Cocteau for good. Having received the "Abbé Quatorze" car as a parting gift, he returned to live with his mother who, out of love, had denounced his opium habit to the police.[135] Arriving fresh and naive from the country, the young writer had been eaten away by opium, ambition, and the debauchery of an insatiable desire.

Cocteau experienced Desbordes's departure as a tragedy. It was as if he had enflamed everyone without being able to satisfy anyone. His heart seemed to operate in a different way from other people's, and all the feelings he expressed seemed to emanate from a bizarre, almost incomprehensible, creator—the two-legged equivalent of a zebra, an anomaly striped with black and white ink. He pulled the curtains more and more frequently, sinking into the unreal thickness of the smoke. Seeking out the images that mirrors reflected back to him, scrutinizing the wounds left by his enemies, like Saint Sebastian caught in a hall of mirrors, he finally realized that he wanted to join, beyond the glass, this wounded enigma staring back at him, the one who seemed already to belong to the world of the dead. With his astonishing ability to leave his own body, he was able to rejoin all those he had lost, and to persuade himself that he belonged among them.

To give a semblance of life to the deserted, silent apartment, he played a recording that he had recently made. It spun in lieu of the monologue he usually offered his visitors, echoing in an empty corner of the room, offering his voice but in a more metallic form and issuing from a waxen disk reciting one of his poems in the half-dark—a phenomenon that Kessel would find terrifying on a visit to the wasted, torn-apart (*déchiré et déchirant*) Cocteau.[136] Reduced to the androgynous solitude of creators condemned to reproduce themselves in vitro, far from other people and their desire, Cocteau wept over his destiny, which so many envied all over the world. "Nothing human can cure the melancholy of the chosen ones," Colette would say one day; this was precisely how he felt.[137]

Opium blurred his thoughts; he fooled himself by thinking he was clarifying his poems, bombarding journals with letters of correction, ostracizing himself as a "genius of self-provocation." "Don't scold me, pity me," said this old child to Paulhan, which must have irritated him even more.[138] A few weeks of solitude were enough for him to reveal the vital energy that kept him going: it was a little ball, repulsive and hairy, sticky and rough, that was both animal and vegetable.

A kind of silkworm, driven by a mysterious force, was painfully weaving its threads in him, assembling them into ideas or phrases but following an aberrant design, as scientists have noted drugged spiders are prone to do. "Pupae, larvae, cocoons, chrysalides, the sleep of sleepwalkers working without knowing it, hypnoses, crimes of love, spasms, fatal efforts, a blind man's anguish, the struggles of a corpse that awakens living in the tomb," his insect-like fertility worked through him, until he lay his eggs, leaving him more disgusted still.[139]

After vomiting too much bile, Cocteau agreed to a new cure of serums, solitude, and health food, under the authority of one Dr. Rosenthal, a "genius" whom he thought might be able to restore his strength through a diet of animal embryos. He then went on to another stint in rehab, at the Salem clinic. This thousandth attempt to wean him from the drugs tested once again the limits of his physical and psychic suffering. "I have been through the worst," he told a friend, before leaving to try another cure of sleep, overeating, and sunshine in the countryside, from which he returned more disoriented than ever, his arms thin and legs feeling as if they were floating, "filled with a sadness that doesn't weigh enough to be reabsorbed."[140]

At the end of 1934, Cocteau left the deserted apartment on the rue Vignon and took a room in the hotel next door, the Madeleine-Palace. Once more, he was starting all over again—like a wounded bird that can't get its footing on land.

THE DECADENT ONE

Brothers who live after us,
Let not your hearts be hardened against us,
If you have pity for us poor men,
God will have mercy towards you.
— *François Villon*, Ballad of the Hanged Men

SACHS AND LOULOU

Maurice Sachs seemed to have an uncanny gift for reading his former mentor's soul. He knew Cocteau's weaknesses inside and out, and his own failings brought him inevitably to this "father" figure, for if Cocteau could not break with anyone he had loved, the inverse was equally true. Having attempted to set himself up as an art dealer in the United States, in spite of the Depression, and having dropped Gwladys Matthews, the woman he had married, more quickly than he had dropped his monk's habit (the daughter of an influential American Presbyterian clergyman, he had married her in an attempt to build a political career over there), Sachs had returned to Paris on the arm of a young American man, Henry Wibbels. For once he was in a happy relationship, but lacking funds he had naturally turned up at Cocteau's door, in November 1933.

He had gained almost seventy pounds and lost his hair by the handful, and anxiety seeped from every pore: one contemporary described him as "a bearded lady who had shaved three days earlier to escape incognito from a circus."[1] Out of pity, Cocteau took him in, this deflated version of the con man he had once been, before Coco Chanel and Max Jacob, the first victim, but Sachs seemed to be in as poor shape as he was. Sachs soon introduced him to Wibbels, "the love of his life," foregrounding Wibbels's deep passion for Proust. Cocteau found the young Californian so endearing that he opened up his box of treasures and insisted that he accept a note that Proust had sent him inviting him to tea, signed "Yours, Marcel." Wibbels couldn't get over it—he had been out of America for only three months and already Marcel Proust was his! Only a prince could make such presents.[2]

Sachs's rich imagination was awakened. Was not Proust his, in a sense, having been an intimate friend of his grandmother's? He returned to see Cocteau and brought up the old days at the Boeuf sur le Toit, which made the writer tear up at the memory of their shared conversions. He thus easily found out where Cocteau had filed his Proust and Apollinaire manuscripts, not to mention his letters from Natalie Paley.[3] Cocteau had forgiven Sachs's larceny eight years earlier, which Sachs took as an invitation to return to his old habits. He showed up wheeling a cart—which would turn into a truck as the years went by, in Cocteau's version—the better to transport this correspondence (including the uncorrected manuscript of *Le bal du comte d'Orgel*) to a second-hand goods dealer.[4] Cocteau had confessed to feeling almost relieved by Sachs's previous thievings—he would surely be even more relieved now!

Certain letters were so compromising—there were even some from François Mauriac, according to Cocteau—that the booksellers who were offered them rang up the rue d'Anjou, and all of Paris thought Cocteau was selling his secrets to finance his artificial paradise. Quickly informed of what was happening, Gaston Gallimard warned the writer, who didn't have much difficulty naming a suspect. The editor then called in Sachs, the former seminary student, to whom he had recently entrusted a collection of adventure novels, to dismiss him from the publishing house. Sachs left without protest, but once he had gone he concocted a letter from "Cocteau" begging him to sell all of his manuscripts and letters, and returned to brandish it before Gallimard, before taking out his lighter to set fire to this "damning" proof of Cocteau's duplicity. The editor wanted to believe he was innocent, but with Cocteau he laughed at the finesse with which their "protégé" had attempted to exonerate himself by destroying the false evidence he had created himself. Cocteau again refused to press charges; after all, these things could have happened the way Sachs recounted them. In fact, he preferred to buy back some of the letters, while Lucien Lelong offered to pay any price to get back his wife's. Sachs concluded from Cocteau's largesse that the writer was truly indifferent to his crimes—since even the worst thefts could not alter his attitude. And in any case, as Henri Raczymow asks, "is it stealing from one's father if one merely borrows a few objects belonging to him?"[5]

Back on his feet again, Sachs decided to publish the talks he had given in the United States, which would become *La décade de l'illusion*. First published by Knopf, in New York, the work included a flattering passage about Cocteau, where Sachs's reservations—"the man often exceeded the writing"—were compensated for by several allusions to his great lyrical streak and by this affectionate dedication: "To Jean Cocteau, to whom I owe the most exquisite years of my youth."[6] It was clear that although Sachs outwardly protested he had no writerly ambitions, in fact he was soliciting the literary mentorship that Cocteau had always denied him. But Cocteau would not budge, and the book would not be published in France until 1950. Having recently been convicted for debt, and abandoned by Wibbels, Sachs cut himself off from Cocteau again, and tried to reinsert himself at Gallimard, appealing to the all-powerful Paulhan by miming the agonies of Anna de Noailles, who had died the year before—a performance developed with Cocteau, in which the poet begins by complaining she is not as bald as Max Jacob and ends, gasping, "To think that I will soon know if the good Lord (whom Jean claimed to know so well, but hid from me like all his boyfriends) really exists."[7]

Sachs had never been so brilliant. Not content to bring up Cocteau every chance he got or to mythologize the 1920s, which he spent under his tutelage, he would entertain his visitors in a bathrobe, razor in one hand, and indiscriminately recite the names of his lovers—as if everyone were aware of all the details of his private life, as well as Cocteau's—and punctuate his monologues with "What? How's that?" interjections intended to keep his audience quiet. The dummy devoured the ventriloquist, with no great literary result: *Alias*, his first novel, would earn only a six-line review, and an insulting one at that, in Gaston Gallimard's *Nouvelle revue française*.[8] But this time, the portrayal of Cocteau (as "Adelair") was unkind. An art dealer and erotic procurer, this "society storyteller" featured all the faults that Cocteau's enemies attributed to the poet: ludicrous frivolity, abusive familiarity, being morally and emotionally indecipherable, and having a talent for self-parody that led him to make remarks during the *J'adore* days like this: "There is in men like me a great idiotic provincial poetess whose flesh stirs at birdsong." Insatiably jealous, Sachs reserved this last insult for Desbordes, invoking the proclivities of Adelair-as-Cocteau: "Every time he says of a new boy that he's not at all like that, that he's very pure and doesn't even know what it is, then we may be perfectly sure the boy in question is the worst of whores."[9] Sachs, from then on, expected no further dealings with Cocteau.

In fact, not just Sachs but all Cocteau's friends were turning against him. He began to feel like a pariah; and yet no one wanted the best for them more than he did. "To live in Jean's orbit, in the sphere of his radioactivity, was not without danger for a young man," said Jean Bourgoint years later.

> But he was dangerous the way a star is dangerous. He was a sort of "universal brother," with a kind of royal benevolence, of which his friends and anyone who approached him retained a dazzled memory, renewed at each encounter—this generosity of self profoundly deserved gratitude from those who benefited from it, because he was the most in need of it.[10]

The failure of Cocteau's relationship with Natalie Paley had not dampened all his hopes. He fell in love at first literary sight when the postman delivered *Sainte-Unefois*, the first book by an unknown young woman published by Gaston Gallimard. Richly innovative, fresh, and "ferocious, with an unbelievably light touch," the flamboyant universe of this young writer was worthy of his childhood fairytales. From Switzerland, where he was staying with Igor Markevitch, Cocteau wrote immediately to Louise de Vilmorin in the most exalted terms. He found a kindred spirit in the clever young woman, who so delighted in playing with words—"Je méditerai, tu m'éditeras" (I will meditate, you will edit me) she said to Gallimard, or "Je maigrirai, tu t'aigriras" (I will get thinner, you will become bitter). Her book told the story of a duke with no heirs who makes an oaken armchair his son and marries him to a girl made of snow and salt.[11] In his mind, he endowed her with all the best qualities; this genius "schoolgirl" that a great red balloon had lifted up to the heavens, this princess drawn straight from *Les enfants terribles*, soon became his confidant, and he confessed everything to her about his impossible love for Natalie Paley.[12]

Believing melancholy, sadness, and bitterness to be wounds that must be hidden, Louise de Vilmorin had a thousand recipes for better living, just as her sister, Mapie de Toulouse-Lautrec, had for better cooking. (Married to a nephew of the painter, in the 1950s and 1960s she would become a well-known food writer.) Imagining that this voracious water-spirit could wipe away the memory of the princess, or bring her back to life by becoming once and for all "his beloved of the snow-countries," Cocteau offered himself by letter, and invited her to visit him in Switzerland, in spite of the dreadful "general staff" of four brothers watching her, curbing her independence: "I think of you. I dream of you . . . I'm afraid I'm falling in love with you." Louise de Vilmorin's discomfited response reminded him to what extent this heiress to a seed merchant's fortune liked to be spoiled. "Small gifts maintain love, big ones create it," she said. "Oh! If I were rich I would be on my knees. I would beg you to want me, to marry me, to live with me, *don't laugh*," he wrote. "Like someone with an injured spinal cord who cannot sit down but persists in drawing chairs," Cocteau wrote of his fictional double in *Le grand écart*, "he dreamed of discreet wives who help men with their work and build a family." Stunned by a series of setbacks, Cocteau could think only of settling down. "What about Natalie?" asked Markevitch, who was behind in the news. "She dropped me. Typical of her family," said Cocteau. "They let an empire fall."[13]

Flattered by his offer but a bit startled by its haste, Louise de Vilmorin sugarcoated her rejection. Returning to Paris a few days before the *Nouvelle revue française* published his ode to *Sainte-Unefois*, Cocteau finally managed to meet the object of his epistolary crush.[14] Her friends shrieked that she was courting disaster, but the tall young woman turned up at the Madeleine Palace Hôtel. Cocteau found her more than beautiful: with her deep voice and her lanky allure, her cruel laugh and her feigned lack of education, she was poetry, humor, and fantasy incarnate—a feminine version of Jean Bourgoint, a chic version of Dargelos with eyes that were pale, "heartless and superb."[15] "He welcomed me as if I were both his sister and his betrothed," added the future author of *Madame de*; "I was moved, he seemed happy, and when he took me by the hand, I felt my heart beating."[16] Sitting side by side on his narrow bed, they drank their first coffee—"our potion," Louise de Vilmorin would say, already won over by her admirer's mythologizing.

Since he could not make her his wife, Cocteau instead baptized her "his little saint," his poetic twin, and he would never stop loving her, as he had Valentine Hugo at one time. This time, however, anticipating another failure, he preferred to admit his madness from the outset; he was even seen to poke fun at those who had been naive enough to believe in his plans to marry. In truth, he didn't know which register he was operating in—boulevard theater or high tragedy. "Did I lie in telling you I lied or in telling you I did not lie? A liar? Me? Deep down, I don't know. I'm confused," says the hero of one of his short monologues.[17] Only Louise de Vilmorin seemed to take him seriously. "Jean's tragedy is to have always needed a woman, but never to have found her as he wanted her to be," she confided to Jean-Jacques Kihm. This was no doubt excessive, but it had the ring of truth, at least at this moment in his life. As Cocteau confessed to her, secretly, "I no longer have a precise place on earth."[18]

THE FEMININE BEING

Curiously, Marie Laure's love was not extinguished by the scenes she inflicted on Cocteau on Natalie Paley's behalf. While preferring not to see him for a time, she still took it upon herself to tell Cocteau how much this abstention bothered her:

I do not have your strength, or your purity. I love you too much not to suffer from this with all my soul, and every time I have to return to the customary, the earthly, I hurt myself and I cause harm all around me . . . You have been present in my heart during such a long absence that I know that nothing in the world—except death—can change this feeling which is stronger than love: the almost divine friendship which will always keep me by your side.[19]

Although she had taken a lover for the first time (Igor Markevitch), it was in fact Cocteau whom she instinctively invited to join them—as if to show him that she was finally happy—when in the summer of 1934 she ran away in her Bugatti to a Swiss chalet at Villars with the handsome young Russian musician, eleven years her junior.[20] Reduced by opium to having to ask his mother for money to buy cigarettes and stamps, like a fifteen-year-old boy, Cocteau jumped at the chance to flee the debt collectors who were harassing him, and went off to join Marie Laure where she was playing Robinson Crusoe, learning to live without servants and to prepare food for her young lover.

Markevitch had loudly approved of the writer's arrival; he owed the lyrics for his 1930 *Cantate* to Cocteau.[21] Along with his hypnotic gaze and his captivating intelligence, the young musician (trained by Nadia Boulanger) was also gifted with prodigious self-confidence. At barely sixteen years old, he had played his first compositions to the elderly Diaghilev, who said they were passé. "I am not interested in yesterday or today, but in that which is eternal," replied the teen-ager, with an arrogance that deeply moved the sickly impresario. Aware that he was living out his final passion, Diaghilev smothered Markevitch with his feudal generosity, and Cocteau in turn succumbed to the charm of the boy, who was born the same year that Chinchilla (Diaghilev) had said to him: "Astonish me." As Markevitch would write in his memoirs, "a long and fraternal friendship began" between Cocteau and him.

Marie Laure had meanwhile become pregnant, and Markevitch asked her to get an abortion, as her husband did; the couple fought all summer as Cocteau looked on, powerless. Bitter at finding his star fading at only twenty-one years old—the premiere of *Rébus* (1931) had been disappointing—the composer Markevitch put up with his protector's shouting, but began to see her as despoiled, a poor little body skinned alive by its jewelry "whose life knocked against the mirrors that reflected an image she detested."[22] Cocteau was able to wear the calm face of the peacemaker, but this was exactly what Marie Laure did not want. "I love you too much to bear your presence," she eventually said to him, a year after writing to him: "My feelings of tenderness are always with you, alive, violent, eternal." In search of an outlet for her anger, the Marquis de Sade's descendent accused Cocteau of using his "diabolical" influence on the young musician to turn him against her, and then of secretly having an affair with him. Markevitch protested categorically, but his old affair with Diaghilev only fed Marie Laure's suspicions. "Doubtless M. Markevitch has received from M. Cocteau's own lips the recipe for his genius," a musical critic had insinuated, as early as the premiere of *Cantate*.[23]

Worse, when Markevitch decided to go home to his mother, at Corsier-sur-Vevey, Cocteau went with him—and stayed for months, spoiled by the old Russian woman who was enchanted by his stories. Oddly, Marie Laure accepted her defeat and even seemed ready to cut herself off from Cocteau for good. "Jean has rebuffed my love. I will spend my life seeking revenge," she hissed to Markevitch.[24] Cocteau had once again managed to make himself hated. And to round out her assault, the lonely heiress who as a child had believed statues bled from the nose could find nothing better than to show interest in the Surrealists.

These hysterical scenes, after Geneviève Mater's scheming and Natalie Paley's "betrayal," affected Cocteau for a long time. From a potential sister, woman had become a stranger, menacing, octopus-like—a Gorgon with a mouth full of hatred and a growling stomach—as if they all carried the bones and teeth of a dead little Cocteau. He who had dreamed of finding a faithful, devoted spouse in Natalie Paley and then Louise de Vilmorin began to yearn for the mores of the Orient, where the male dominates and adorns himself, reducing his wife to her genetic usefulness. He even began to take aim at "our European women, intoxicated by Mme Dietrich and the great Garbo," who seemed horrified by the idea of having children.[25] It didn't matter that he had been, by Natalie Paley's side, the first to applaud the appearance of these Northern stars; now the guilty party was a sort of embryonic feminism that spontaneously emanated from these narcissistic, sterile icons. "The female entity!" he complained during the war, to a friend who had confided that the prostitutes of Marseille demanded they be desired.[26] Compact and self-centered, this female entity had entered into conflict with his own masculine multiplicity.

LA MACHINE INFERNALE

Written during his tragic passion for the difficult princess, Cocteau's play *La machine infernale* marked his second attempt to express the implacable fate of failure and death. Just as the figure of Orpheus had allowed him to articulate the inexorable links that connected his nature to poetry, the mask of Oedipus, which he employed for the third time, would help him to approach the unknown cause, if not the secret link, that prevented him from succeeding in his love affairs and that organically deprived him of satisfaction.[27] Through Oedipus, an innocent heir condemned by oracle to kill his father and sleep with his mother, he could reflect on the maternal love that had so weighed on him during his formative years. Unlike Salvador Dalí, who three years earlier in his painting *The Enigma of Desire* had written "my mother" in each alveolus of the larval masculine body, Cocteau refused to own up to the slightest incestuous urge. Oedipus, in his opinion, was as innocent as the hero of *Les enfants terribles*; he could not be blamed, because he had never objectively desired his mother. He had married Jocasta because he had been tricked by the gods, the same gods who continued, in Cocteau's own day, to determine the course of events, which made Sophocles more contemporary and lucid than Freud. Yes, the world was an infernal machine, and nobody—not even the psychoanalysts—could make it deviate from its course by one iota.

By including the ghost of Laius, Oedipus's father, in his play, Cocteau nevertheless was aware that this kind of ghost always returns to haunt the places it once inhabited, in order to torment those who carelessly neglect its memory. He had always said the morning crowing of the cock that shared his surname sounded to him like "barking ghosts."[28] Still, he refused to admit that it was also his father he heard reminding him of his existence, or indirectly accusing him of his suicide; if he felt some degree of guilt because of the silence he and his mother kept on the subject of this paternal nonentity, he apparently felt that it was not the role of literature to express it. In short, Oedipus's blindness conveyed nothing but Cocteau's presumption and basic lightness, believing he was one of the gods' chosen ones, and realizing too late that if he was, it was in order to witness their crushing superiority. On this point, the play espoused his fate with troubling precision. Having begun like a game, the play ends with the "mathematical annihilation" of its hero, who increases the tragedy by gouging out his eyes with a golden brooch.

Nevertheless, it was a play, not an essay. In order to make its neoclassicism more appealing, and his atemporal plot more contemporary, Cocteau recycled certain conventions from popular theater, convinced that he was again going to catch his audience off guard, or even provoke a scandal. The audiences of 1917 had seen *Parade* as a night at the circus, and then had seen *Les mariés de la tour Eiffel* as a farce; those of 1934 were going to be deceived by the offhandedness of *La machine infernale*. The prince and princess of Thebes were portrayed with the kind of familiarity that the Faucigny-Lucinges and the Noailleses used among themselves. Calling her high priest Tiresias "Zizi," Jocasta would point out a guard to him in the first act, saying, "He's so handsome, Zizi, feel his biceps," as an audacious guest at the Noailleses' home might have done while fondling their gymnastics instructor.[29] Was the inclusion of this indiscreet Zizi intended to humorously discourage taking Freudian interpretation too far? Cocteau preferred to see Zizi as an offbeat, comic figure, one that he would associate with radical innovation. He wished to shock the audience in a very obvious way.[30] Just as Édouard de Max or Sarah Bernhardt had worn their excesses like a banner of pride, he decided to cloak himself in it, like Gribouille jumping into the water to avoid getting splashed.[31] If he was going to be continually reproached for being what he was, he might as well accentuate his faults and communicate his unease through laughter.

Jouvet was impressed by the dramatic power of the play, and agreed to perform it in his theater. But rehearsals were difficult; the director, who also played the shepherd, grew annoyed by Cocteau, who incessantly interrupted the group's work in order to address the actors.[32] Cocteau also had disagreements with Coco Chanel, who was designing the costumes. But Cocteau rediscovered his ideal alter ego in Bérard, whose geometric set designs were so like those of *Parade*—including the bed in which Oedipus is joined with his mother—and who proved himself gifted at blending boulevard theater and high tragedy, prosaicness and mythology.

The premiere took place on April 9, 1934, at the Comédie des Champs-Elysées, with an audience of five hundred largely composed of people who knew Cocteau. The conservative press was just shocked enough to be charmed by this return to the Greeks; Stravinsky was enchanted. Colette would write a ferociously intelligent article about it, which Cocteau would later call worthy of Baudelaire:

> Where does such an innovative artist turn? To the past. To mythological fables, to the marvelous classical era. He lunges forward, backwards. He returns to Orpheus, the Sphinx, toward that which is known, that which he perhaps knew. He-who-dislikes-Cocteau doesn't realize that his enemy belongs to a great tradition.[33]

Raïssa Maritain was deeply moved by the play, calling it "the best he's ever written, the purest, the most human."[34] It's "the most moved I've been at the theatre in a long time," confirmed Klaus Mann.[35] Everyone applauded the brilliant monologue given by the Sphinx:

> Greedier than insects, more bloodthirsty than the birds . . . more mindful than the snake moistening its prey with saliva, I secrete my thread; I pay it out, spin it back and wind it in; . . . My thread envelops you, binds you, quiets you in fine arabesques of drawn honey dropping into a pool of honey, Until you are numb as an arm you have slept on and deadened.[36]

It was as if Cocteau himself were speaking.

The audience was clearly uneasy as it watched this hybrid play, which is impressively authentic when it approaches Oedipus's drama sincerely, but hits a false note when it tries to show off. Something is a bit forced, if not abstract, in the figure of Oedipus, as in those of Orpheus and Eurydice; their speeches don't entirely humanize the legendary figures. Playwright Jean Giraudoux, who relied on affectation and offhandedness in his neoclassical creations, struggled with the same issues. Only with Jean Anouilh's *Antigone* would these Aegean narratives acquire contemporary resonance, precisely because Anouilh's Antigone is a real human being—in the midst of the Occupation, no less.

Having been the first to inaugurate neoclassicism with his own *Antigone*, twelve years earlier, Cocteau ardently resented those critics who accused him of climbing on the bandwagon because of Giraudoux's 1929 *Amphytrion 38*. He did not like it very much when Gide remarked that there was a veritable "oedipidemic" afoot, since he, Gide, had himself staged a modern adaptation of *Oedipus* in 1931. It was as if every time Cocteau ventured onto a new front, people would whisper to him, "Stop trying to reinvent yourself, it's just another role." Too recently developed not to be fragile, his new theatrical skin was not thick enough to protect him. He was indignant that he was expected to do the same thing all the time. That would have been, for him, the artificial thing to do. "The reason one creates something matters little in the long run," he wrote, anticipating these critiques. "A man simply tries not to die, to try at all costs to fix in place, by the cunning means of some visible form, the power that we lose in the void and that exhausts us." But how to make these journalists understand that he was a jumble of people forced into an unhappy solitude?

La machine infernale attracted a cult following among students and young actors, but most audiences turned away. "Only a thousand people have seen the play, but they're the same people who come back every night," said Cocteau.[37] For someone who dreamed of associating his future as a dramatist with that of Jouvet, like Giraudoux, it was truly disappointing. "It is difficult to imagine / How stupid and quiet success makes people," wrote Apollinaire.[38] But this was a problem that, once again, would not afflict Cocteau.

FRANZ THOMASSIN AND THE DEVIL

One day in 1932, at the dawn of his strange passion for Natalie Paley, Cocteau opened his door to a very young man, who was at the same time elegant, shy, and brazen. Like Cocteau, Pierre Thomassin came from a bourgeois family from Le Havre, but Protestant instead of Catholic; he lost no time in returning with his older brother Franz and his sister Christabel—"the youngest divorcée in France," he said. She was nineteen when she had fled an arranged marriage with a son of Geneva's high Protestant society. They were so strange, these three shy adolescents barely twenty years old, who lived together in little hotels so intimately that they seemed near to engaging in the kind of chaste incest that Cocteau had made famous. Just as the *enfants terribles* of his novel steal a watering can they have no use for from a shop in Deauville, the Thomassins entertained themselves by pilfering bunches of padlocks for the sheer beauty of the gesture, and brandishing pornographic pamphlets in the street just for the joy of shocking mothers and the elderly. They had the spirit of the Sachs-Bourgoint generation, with everything that implied: madness and challenge, open rebellion and familial score-settling.

The trio, born to a theosophist father who died in the war—but whose spirit was killed much earlier by military discipline—and an atrocious, partly mad, woman who ate her own veils, was as rich as she was miserly, and made her children pretend to have tuberculosis so they could flee to sunny climes, won Cocteau over immediately with their extravagant way of life. It was a delight to listen to Pierre describe their terrible jealousy of "Benjamin," their parents' favorite "child" (a giant golden ingot placed in the Le Havre branch of the Banque de France), or to hear Christabel tell of her "captivity in Switzerland"— that is, her marriage—or to watch François relive the pleasure he took in renaming himself Franz, to anger his Germanophobic mother. The Thomassins were better than characters from a novel, but they seemed straight out of one of Cocteau's. "Life imitates art," said Oscar Wilde, upon seeing enter his life Lord Alfred Douglas, the almost perfect incarnation of the cold, weak-willed character whose portrait he had just drawn under the name of Dorian Gray.

The Thomassins were received as intimate friends from the very beginning; it was their turn to be taken to see Marlene Dietrich at the cinema and Marianne Oswald in concert. They became the poet's "dear little rabbits," something like the children he would have liked to have had with Natalie Paley, that mysterious princess whom he was always promising to introduce to them, sure that she would love them "like a sister."[39] He became their "supernatural father," the ironic equivalent of Santa Claus, with his overflowing sack of gifts. They showed up at his door after midnight and sprawled all over the brass bed to hear him talk. Once the flood had run dry, Cocteau would make them read his poems, which they soon knew by heart, or give them the proofs of the books he was preparing. These they would mark up with the greatest honesty, before learning to moderate themselves, since Cocteau, despite seeming sure of himself, could be wounded by the slightest hesitation. Though discreet about his own sexuality, Cocteau was insatiable when it came to their experiences. He made Franz talk about how he mostly only liked macho types, or he would urge on Pierre, who liked both sexes but got bored very quickly, or, less often, he would encourage stories from Christabel, who used her shyness to protect herself. "It smells good here, like bitter chocolate," she said innocently when she first visited, but very quickly the opium ritual would no longer be a secret he kept from them. Biou would tear himself from the pipe he was preparing to murmur "Christabel crystalizes in sugar," before chanting in a language the Thomassins took for Chinese. Then he would project giant shadows on the walls with his hands, always with such grace that Cocteau believed he had special powers, including an ability to eat his handkerchiefs, which had a tendency to disappear. Everything got weird with Biou. "If we sent him to Versailles with a camera, he would return with postcards of his own country," Cocteau said of his faithful servant.[40]

The Thomassins managed to avoid smoking, unlike so many others, but they did learn to love the delicious smell of the opium, which kept them awake thanks to the vigilance of the "little odd-job men" who restocked Cocteau's supply. One day, harrowing cries came from the bathroom: someone was beating his or her head against the walls. "Don't worry," said Cocteau to Christabel, "that's Marie Laure, she's in love with me. Opium doesn't work for women." Another time the Thomassins heard Desbordes, then still Cocteau's favorite, protesting the presence of a rival, stationed in another room. Ever since, they eagerly explored this delicious fictional bubble, only stopping to observe through a spyglass the neighbors undressing across the rue Vignon.

Desbordes also succumbed to the charm of this fantastic trio, who received him in their family home in Magagnosc, near Grasse. First he was charmed by Christabel, who was "pretty and fresh as a peach." Then he was unsettled by the self-assurance of the strangely talented brothers, who were more unique in his eyes than the Bourgoint siblings—"the most prodigious beings on earth, the maddest, the purest, the more extravagant," he wrote to Cocteau, after meeting them.[41] Absolutely won over by their bizarre vocabulary, like the picturesque nicknames they bestowed on everyone, the author of *J'adore* adopted the Thomassins, who formed a little court around him, with the aim of "keeping" him beside Cocteau. The poet, thanks to them, knew *everything* that Desbordes did. They amused themselves by telling him how, when they were invited to see Geneviève Mater's mother in Toulon, they had burst out laughing seeing this proper bourgeoise woman pass out petits fours while her daughter, flanked by Desbordes, his little girlfriend from the Vosges, and a young naval officer, all smoked opium, before inviting them to lie down with them, as if to encourage partner-swapping. Cocteau hastened to recount these details to Desbordes, to make his mistress ("the big woman with the little feet") seem ridiculous.

Franz, the strangest of the three, became the most devoted, and soon took a room at the Hôtel de la Madeleine. Tall, thin, and muscular, with Slavic cheekbones and a piercing gaze that would inspire Matisse, this dilettante was overwhelmed with such paralyzing pride that his very nobility gave him complexes.[42] "The most Roussel-ian character since [Raymond] Roussel," wrote Sachs in *Au temps du Boeuf sur le Toit*, "but with tact and kindness, even an excess of kindness, like Proust, which hurt him: he had a beaten air, but a tender, proud, and congenial one."[43] Cocteau tried at first to "read" this living mystery, who would spend his whole life not writing the books he had promised to write. By turns obsequious and exhibitionist, Franz Thomassin protected himself from others with virginal modesty or audacious timidity. Such characters are often found in Gide's work, but Gide himself tried not to meet them in real life; Cocteau, however, happy to meet this living form of literature, welcomed him with open arms. Who knew? Perhaps he would be fodder for his next play, or inspire him to write another novel.

Helped by his generosity and his prestige, Cocteau became the object of veneration, everything that Franz Thomassin's severe Protestant education should have forbidden. Like Maurice Sachs ten years earlier, the young provincial would fall fanatically in love with the author of *Les enfants terribles*. Hostile to the "lordly" snobbery holding court on the rue Vignon, and jealous to the point of violence when he sensed a "rival" approaching, whether it be Desbordes or his brother or sister, Thomassin was nothing but sweetness and light when he was alone with Cocteau. As Proust said, "When we love someone, we love no one else." Seeing that the scenes he was inflicting on Desbordes displeased Cocteau, Thomassin befriended Jean-Jean, in the hope of being forgiven, and soon managed to tolerate the indirect source of his suffering. When Desbordes left, passion devoured Franz Thomassin. If Cocteau needed money, he would receive five-hundred franc bills rolled up in silk or folded into typewritten envelopes. If an awful toothache sent him to the dentist, Thomassin would pay the bills by dipping into his sister's alimony. If a friend attacked Cocteau calling him "someone who cheats in verse" or a "perverter of youth," Thomassin, his knight in shining armor, would ride out to defend his liege lord and quarrel with this overly critical friend.

Cocteau had always run after boys who were initially uninterested in him; by loving Cocteau wholeheartedly right from the start, Thomassin paradoxically lowered his own value. Like the young Proust, mooning after men who didn't want him and pushing away those who wanted him too much, Cocteau preferred to be rejected than to reject, and ruled in favor of those who did not love him; he who was normally so wounded by indifference would make his admirer suffer without even realizing it. He was the first to sing the praises of Franz Thomassin, to describe his "miraculous purity" and his "limitless goodness." If someone suggested to him, tactfully, that this "archangel" did not seem very happy, this proved that it was impossible to live a truly moral life in a contaminated world. But the more he celebrated Thomassin, the more he fled from him. In short, Cocteau did not know what to do with this young man who adored him.

Young Franz's jealousy took a wild turn. Everyone on earth seemed to compete with him for the man he loved. Even the favors Cocteau showed Franz's little sister and brother made him suffer so greatly that he demanded Christabel return the ring Cocteau had given her, made from an artillery shell from the First World War. Uncompromising and hot-tempered toward those he did not depend on, Thomassin could be perfectly pliable when it came to his chosen master. Cocteau could keep him waiting in a back room, and he never blamed him for it; a man of his fiber had to devote himself first and foremost to his work. In trying to reason with him, the other "dear little rabbits" only made him dig his heels in. Only Sachs seemed to understand what he was going through. Through his own suffering, Cocteau had developed a capacity for cruelty; hard toward his own weaknesses, he was even harder toward the greater weaknesses of others. He came to be annoyed by Thomassin's masochism, the doleful gaze that accused him in silence but which, with the least encouragement, would show an oppressive willingness to absolve him. "What I like the least in other people is me," Picabia had said. Adoration was exactly what Cocteau had always hoped for: it filled him with a secret pride, and he could not prevent himself from finding in it a bitter consolation. But he also needed not to see Thomassin. Understanding this, the young man excused himself a thousand times for the trouble he caused and promised not to follow him, on learning that the poet was about to leave for vacation. And Cocteau left, relieved that this shadow would follow him no longer.

One morning, though, as he strolled in the narrow streets of Saint-Tropez, coming home from the port, Cocteau ran into his lovelorn admirer, his cheeks hollow and his look imploring. Cocteau "grumbled at him in a friendly way," and asked him to please be reasonable; faced with such kind indifference, Thomassin decided to return to Paris on foot, across the whole of France. He was living in a kind of hell; he needed a release. A draconian diet wasn't enough; the young man, wandering in the rougher parts of the capital, took up with two gigolos, whom he brought back to his seedy hotel at Madeleine. The athletic young man took them up to his tiny room, took out three thousand francs in bills, put a kitchen knife on the table, and calmly instructed them to cut off one of his fingers. "It would be better if we made love!" but no, Franz Thomassin wanted his phalanx. They cut off his finger without antiseptic—"The operation had to be completed at the butcher's," said Charlotte Aillaud, a friend of Thomassin's.[44] He wrapped the stump in a handkerchief, placed it in a matchbox, and sent it via post to his idol.

The package horrified Cocteau. Pity turned to disgust; disgust to terror. Desbordes's protestations—this unhappy rival had softened him—had no effect: Franz Thomassin had become a madman to be avoided at all costs. Had Cocteau read Nerval's "La main du diable," the short story in which a failed painter buys an amputated hand meant to bring him fame and fortune, only to learn that the man who sold it to him was the devil? Terrified that he would be the next one to be knifed, Cocteau decreed that he would no longer see "these horrible children." Blacklisted by his liege lord, the knight in shining armor fell into such a deep despair that his mother had him committed. Christabel mentioned the name of Dr. René Allendy, one of the founding members of the École Française de Psychanalyse, who had already analyzed Maurice Sachs, as well as Antonin Artaud.[45] Allendy, finding no particular illness in the mutilated patient, prescribed a long rest. Later, when Mme Thomassin, in the summer of 1934, asked her daughter to bring Franz to the seaside, he decided on Le Piquey. Cocteau and Radiguet used to stay at the Hôtel Chantecler; the brother and sister took their own rooms there. Opening a drawer in the room that had been Radiguet's, Franz Thomassin found the draft of a letter to the young Bronja Perlmutter, with a photo of her—what better proof that destiny wanted him in Cocteau's life?

All of literary Paris soon heard the details of this cruel human sacrifice. After Radiguet's tragic death, Sachs's moral deviance, Jean Bourgoint's decline, and Bourgoint's sister's suicide, this new drama exaggerated Cocteau's diabolical reputation. People already thought him to be dry and frivolous, seeing him selling off remnants of his private life merely for shock value; now, seeing the state in which his disciples ended up, Desbordes first of all, they suspected the worst. After calling him an actor in need of an audience, they now denounced him as a vampire in search of fresh blood, a specter who rejected his victims once he had drained them dry—when it was more likely Radiguet who, through his death, had destabilized Cocteau. "At the very moment when he seems to care for you the most he kills you: he cuts you off from your roots one after the other, while he gives you water with the attentive air of a caring gardener," said Marie Laure de Noailles, at the worst of their dispute: "You only have to go near him to catch the germ of death. He's the devil . . . When he has lost a young man, Jean Cocteau seems, for a little while, revived. He is once again young, brilliant, in good health."[46]

Thus his dark legend was born, that of the monster who'd rip out your heart to feed his unhealthy hunger. If Gide was the demon accused of corrupting French youth, Cocteau was damned, denounced as a leper and a decadent by a population grown tired of the vices—sodomy, opium, and so on—that were associated with him.[47] No doubt those he socialized with during his opium-addict phase carried more risks than Bourgoint would admit. He is a "poet, like Orpheus, there is electricity in the air surrounding him, and lightning strikes and kills very close to him. One must not approach poets when one is weak," Sachs said; but he himself had some interest in putting it about that Cocteau was the one person responsible for Sachs's own failure, and that this "monster" had never given him real artistic support and instead spread death and destruction around him.[48] Sachs even went so far as to imitate, once again, Cocteau's handwriting, forging the poet's signature on the back of a photograph of Cocteau, dedicating it "To Maurice Sachs," and signing it "Lucifer."[49] Sachs showed it around, and it made Cocteau that much more ostracized. The pale, emaciated, bony poet, with so little flesh that he seemed no longer to project his shadow onto the earth, resembled the legendary Peter Schlemil, who had sold his own shadow to the devil and from whom men turned away in contempt.

Sometimes a friend would defend him. "He has managed to renounce all worldly things; he lives a life that is so detached, contemplative, and upright that he is the only man of my acquaintance whose door you could open day or night without knocking," wrote Joseph Kessel. But how could these noble declarations keep from provoking a smile when every day boys could be seen storming the smoky bedroom of the poet?[50] Raised, unhappily, to believe that he had to be upright, clean, and pure, Cocteau became more and more depressed at the idea that he was being taken for a vile, dangerous person.

THE CRISIS

The times were no longer in favor of permissiveness. The effects of the stock market crash that had hit Wall Street in October 1929 were beginning to be felt in Paris. "Here there is not the shadow of a crisis," Cocteau wrote in 1931 from Toulon; but by 1934, France was seeing its own long, snaking lines of bankrupt stockbrokers and unemployed workers in front of soup kitchens.[51] The financial scandals increased (it didn't take much) on February 6, when the patriotic leagues, followed by the Communists on February 9, nearly toppled the Republic, accusing it of chronic corruption.

During the Depression, the public was no longer in the mood for flagrant expressions of sexuality, or the formal experimentations of the avant-garde. The days of snobs applauding pseudo-Bolshevik ballets were over; there was instead a push toward "useful" art, clear responses to great problems, and writing that could reflect on an unpleasant reality and the crisis of civilization. Pure literature was seen as the purview of "dilettantes," and the poetic idols of the postwar years, from Lautréamont to Apollinaire, were effaced in favor of those thinkers, from Marx to Maurras, who offered a totalizing narrative. As early as the late 1920s, the younger generations, tempted by Communism or nationalism, were already reading essays describing the revolt of the masses or the betrayal of the intellectuals, the mechanization of mankind, or the death of bourgeois thinking; they demanded works that addressed the general sense of social decay, industrialization, or the anonymous way of life in America, which was accused of producing interchangeable wealth ad infinitum.[52] The decline of Europe, signs of which had been accumulating since the First World War, seemed to enter an irrevocable phase, if some people were to be believed. "Everything is screwed up," declared Drieu la Rochelle in 1927, in his obsession with decadence.

The upholders of moral order and solid ideologies took power; all anyone could talk about was the man in the street, and the leader in which he had placed his hopes. "Garçonnes" (mannish women) and other "hannetons" (homosexuals) were no longer in fashion; after the boisterous minorities, it was time for the silent majorities to hold their heads up.[53] This "fascist perversion," as homosexuality was described in the USSR, was again criminalized in Germany. Everywhere political parties were calling for a return to a demographic revival, hence of sexual mores, sure that the tragedy of existence could be felt only collectively. "Never again will any man be alone," promised a Nazi leader.

Architecture became more monumental in response to the crisis, in broad, almost caricatured homage to antiquity, as did painting. Léger included the outlines of workers in the objects they were manufacturing by the thousands, as if they themselves were the product of the assembly line. De Chirico's dream-like paintings, with their walking Roman statues; Dalí's flamboyant fantasies, featuring Lenin's head aureoled with fire on a piano keyboard: the dreams turned to nightmares. The unconsciousness freed by a Futurist Italy, the France of *Parade*, and Weimar Germany were taken over by ideologies that, from Berlin to Moscow, strengthened their totalitarian hold. The State became a would-be artist staging collective fantasies, mass demonstrations. "We are entering an age of capital letters, in which man becomes lowercase," Morand had predicted in 1917.[54] From Europe to the USSR, manipulated crowds were agitating in the limelight; the individual "self"—that malleable organ that Musil described as "colloidal"—became the central issue at stake in these mass ideologies.

The brutalism begun in 1914 had found its fullest expression starting when Hitler came to power in 1933. Violence would become the monopoly of the State in those countries in which, under the pretext of stemming that violence, dictators were installed. Germany's rearmament, which was intended as a means of baring its teeth as well as creating jobs, intensified the process. After the orgy of the 1920s and the "return to order" outlook of the early 1930s, the postwar period became the prewar period. Everyone had to choose sides. The totalitarian apparatus had little difficulty mobilizing not only those "useful idiots" whom Lenin had sought in his own time, but also great thinkers. Marinetti, for example, who was for years an apologist for mechanization and war, asserted himself more and more as a zealous spokesman for fascism; in Germany, a great number of essayists lined up to contemplate war or fetishize steel. In France, Georges Bataille still believed that literature could serve as a catharsis for violence, by daring to link sex, madness, and death—the "part maudite" (cursed side of life). But the time for Sade and Freud seemed to be over; it was now up to Nietzsche to make conceivable, if not desirable, the kinds of acts that for centuries had been repressed by civilization.

On the Left, things became even more radical. Violence had gone from being the luxurious privilege of the avant-garde in the 1910s and 1920s to the purview of the political machinery behind which many writers rallied. Two years after the attacks against the "false revolutionary with the head of Christ" in *Un cadavre*, Aragon pulled away from Breton and definitively entered the French Communist Party. Breaking as well with the Surrealists, who had become much too "artistic," Tristan Tzara joined up with Stalin; declaring that he was "married to large masses of rebels," in 1935 the former nihilist asked every poet to "give his life for the revolution." Having made a recent political shift—he had supported Action Française in the 1910s—Gide himself declared in 1931 that if he had to give his life to ensure the success of the USSR, he would do it on the spot. "How curious it is to see all these great bourgeois NRF [*Nouvelle revue française*] types, like Cocteau's Mortimers, decked out in luxury, hurling themselves en masse into the gaping maw of the Bolshevik Eugene!" remarked François Mauriac, who was soon criticized for his defense of the Spanish Republicans and other "priest-eaters."[55]

Marcel Duchamp, the last real avant-gardist, had stopped producing work in 1923, after having exhibited urinals and coatracks, and had taken refuge in the United States. Faithful to the disruptive slogans of Dada, to which he had never actually belonged, Duchamp preferred to play chess than to appear on the phantom (in his eyes) art scene, which was still dominated by what Max Ernst called "peinto-peinture." Curious about everything and indifferent to himself, alert, inspired, and courteous, even with Cocteau, toward whom he felt no rivalry, Duchamp would be one of the rare intellectuals to respond to the calls to political indoctrination with the Sphinx-like smile he offered all human endeavors.

As for Cocteau, he continued to concern himself exclusively with his day-to-day life, his impossible loves, and his reputation. The dollar could rise, the franc could fall, Germany could occupy the Rhineland, and China could hand over Manchuria to the Japanese—all this trouble was far from him. In twenty years of intense exchanges, he had never made the slightest allusion in his correspondence to the reparations imposed on Germany, the march on Rome, or Stalin's power grab. He was of course engaged in 1914 and had been able to demonstrate political opinions from time to time, but so erratically that it never would have occurred to anyone to ask him anything further about such matters. All attempts to reduce the world to an ideological grid left him indifferent; Cocteau remained, in the midst of the 1930s, attuned to waves emitting on a totally different frequency.

During this period of tension before the next conflict, Cocteau's talking mirrors, and his dreams with their black backgrounds, felt out of fashion. The opium addict who fought only on the front between his unmade bed and his overheated telephone would appear more and more out of step. "Now was the time for activists, the dynamic ones, the bards of action, of sacrifice, of adventure—people with spirits like Malraux, Hemingway, Saint-Exupéry—and young people were attracted to this," noted Klaus Mann, who himself joined anti-Nazi networks helping people leave Germany.[56] Out of instinct, in case of danger, Cocteau sheltered under his own more or less gilded private umbrellas, but only a firm or abusive ideology could contend with the storm that was about to devastate Europe. From democrats to libertarians, from radical Socialists to social Christians, most of the anti-totalitarians would be swept away. Less equipped than the average person to resist this planetary hurricane, Cocteau resorted more than ever to smoking, until he resembled a ghost of a happy decade, condemned to an intimate tragedy becoming more futile every day.

RETURN TO CHILDHOOD

Cocteau nevertheless felt the danger at the beginning of 1935. Describing the threats coming from the East, he declared "a new age of pestilence, signs in the sky . . . in which leaders will not enlist with haste . . . where the theater will demand the fire with which it once burned on the doorsteps of cathedrals."[57] Far from pledging himself to a useful sort of literature, however, he was already looking to measure himself against the prevailing tension by reawakening the violence of an imagination formed under the influence of Symbolism. Against the dangers of ideological distortion, he saw art more than ever as an individual kind of religion—an unhappy one perhaps, but an essential one in his view.[58] His only notable concession: the forces of the occult directing all desire would be more clearly evil and would take the form of fairies or sorcerers rather than gods. The setting would be less Greek and more Celtic-Germanic, the Breton tales and those of the Round Table having been indelibly marked by Wagner, in *Tristan und Isolde* and *Parsifal*.

In Germany itself, Expressionism had by the 1910s restored the power of medieval imagery, with its succubi and its vampires, but Hitler's rise to power had emphasized the hypnotic climate in which cinema lived over there. Everywhere you looked, there were stories of possession and control, mesmerizing eyes and obsessive victims. For who better than Cocteau could appreciate a land ruled over by Doctor Mabuse? That is how, in preparing a remake of his own film *The Cabinet of Doctor Caligari*, Robert Wiene offered Cocteau the role of Cesare, the born sleepwalker who walks on the rooftops of the city and sometimes kills those who slumber beneath them, before returning to take a well-deserved rest in his coffin.[59] In his response to Wiene, Cocteau foresaw that the era to come could be "hard, cruel, bloody, austere, punctuated with . . . nightmares and vengeance."[60] This was the atmosphere of Cocteau's medieval-inspired play *Les chevaliers de la table ronde*, which he had just written.

If Cocteau is to be believed, this play had not simply been dictated to him. He had jumped out of bed at the Salem clinic, the last day of the year 1933, after "attending" in his mind the three acts of a play entirely written and complete with set and costume design, bringing to life a period of which he knew absolutely nothing—and then he had immediately set it all down on paper, like a monastic scribe. In fact, he had been thinking of writing this play for three years, and it was at Corsier, Markevitch's mother's home, that he had begun work on it, encouraged by the musician, who saw him write a first draft (refined later) in just four nights.[61] *Les chevaliers de la table ronde* actually drew on four sources: the tales that had been read to Cocteau by his German nanny, in which ladies with unicorns encounter princes who have been changed into cats; the strange state brought on by opium and then the detoxification process; the by-now familiar sensation of being the object of a spell cast by his enemies or the gods; and of course the legend of the Holy Grail, and all it brings with it of Celtic mythology and Christian wonders. It was thus a sort of return to his sources for Cocteau, jumping back over the decades to a time when medieval music and sacred poetry were seen as enigmatic, and when he himself laughed, hearing Ezra Pound singing his opera about Villon at the piano, a genre he called *moult* or *j'avions*.[62] It was his childhood, as well as his state of disarray, that the permanently invisible character of Ginifer represented—he was a sort of valet who only existed if the sorcerer Merlin ordered him to manifest himself as someone else.[63] It was his uncanny ability to become other people that he dramatized, in this figure who could become a double for Gawain, the nephew and future son-in-law of King Arthur, a false Queen Guenivere or a clone for Galahad the Pure, who asked his master: "Do you think it's funny . . . never to be able to live in one's own skin?"

Cocteau was developing the fairylike aesthetic that would be his imprimatur during the war: in Merlin's castle, tables heaped with food advanced by themselves, chess pieces were moved by an invisible demon. These oddities anticipated episodes in *Renaud et Armide* and *La belle et la bête* that would bewitch audiences during the Occupation, and then during the Liberation. For the moment, this medieval imagery was out of style, not to mention ridiculous, but Cocteau had lost all hope of winning over the strong-minded, those who demanded that his work reflect their own abstract understanding of the world.[64] He was now interested only in charming those with simple souls, who, like children, or himself, "see fairies more easily than other people."[65] He found one of these in his mother, who helped finance him and tolerated his smoking; she, like Cocteau himself, felt and believed before thinking, and did not have any preconceptions about the past. "The sublime characters of classical mythology and medieval legend behave with the intense feverishness of contemporary neurotics, while the *enfants terribles* of a decadent bohemia style their suicidal games on the model of classical myth," Klaus Mann wrote in 1943, attempting a synthesis of Cocteau's work: audiences often understood this better than the critics did.[66]

From then on, Cocteau would navigate between epochs, the no longer all-encompassing present and the tantalizing past. Resorting to legends, his memories of Symbolism came flooding back from his childhood; his nervous system restored thousands of perfectly intact olfactory, visual, and aural sensations that he had recorded then. His eyes and ears, which took in everything, restored the world of his parents to life, and then that of his adolescence; Footit and Chocolat slapping themselves and Polaire throwing ice cubes at the "johns" on the skating rinks; de Max making his entrance nude on a chariot carrying him to Thebes; and Cécile Sorel calling Isadora Duncan "chérie," like an actress of yesteryear—a habit that he himself picked up, and even used on taxi drivers. A music box of reminiscences had opened within Cocteau, and out came the enchanting melody of the Belle Époque.

Stripped of melancholy, these memories were astonishingly detailed, though difficult to date, coming as they did from the limitless time of childhood, with neither past nor future, just the absolute present of the 1890s, shot through with the idea that society was simply a vague extension of his family. Stimulated by the success of Paul Morand's *1900* (1931), one of the first writers of the *années folles* to bring back the period from which they had emerged, Cocteau decided to make his own book. His *Portraits-souvenir* would be developed through friends and others who had lived through the period, but in truth they were stories he told himself in order to relive the enchantment of his early days. Claude Roy compared Cocteau the memorialist to a Madame de Sévigné who was her own daughter; there was some of that in these stunning evocations of a "time regained." It was his most brilliant book—almost too brilliant. Never had ink been so close to inspiring not only the vertigo generated by his words, but also the inability to relax that Gide reproached. "The reader may suffocate in this universe without fields, or cows, or poplars, or poor people," Claude Roy also said.[67] And so it was; Cocteau could not live normally. He needed excessive cities, captivating monsters, and all the artifice of civilization.

Cocteau dedicated the book to Marcel Khill, his new companion—a vigorous young man, full of fun and cheek, which for Cocteau were the highest virtues.[68] Uneducated but happy, lively and delicately featured—Jean Marais would later say he had the airs of a Persian prince—Khill had "a feminine beauty, without being effeminate," as Cocteau put it. Not an angel, still less a fairy, but an elf who could bring life to the haunted universe of the poet who was falling in love again. The son of a Kabyle father and a mother from Normandy—Mustapha Marcel Belkacem ben Abdelkader was his full name—restored Cocteau's ability to enjoy his skin, his mouth, his fingers. The declaiming poet became a murmuring lover. Khill had a marvelous temperament, free from prejudice, and the kind of body he embraced mattered less to him than the sexual role he played. Being able to dominate was enough for him to make himself infinitely available. And Cocteau, for the first time, allowed himself to follow this young man's lead. Khill liked to dance, to drive, and to amuse himself; overcoming the apathy into which the opium had plunged him, Cocteau began to go out at night, and to once again live a free, frivolous, joyful, and social life. In the summer they took a cruise on board a fishing boat, the Lancelot, from Villefranche to Toulon, via Cannes, the Lérin islands, Saint-Tropez, Port-Cros, Porquerolles, Saint-Mandrier—they had months of true happiness in the sun, a kind of happiness that Cocteau had not known for years.[69]

Cocteau could introduce as his sons Radiguet and Desbordes, well-educated as they were, but the most naive of mothers could never be in the dark about the role that Khill played in his life—Madame Cocteau most of all, who had become truly bigoted over time, under the influence of a Dominican priest. The Oedipal fiction cranked back into life, nevertheless. Faithful to his positive vampirism, Cocteau wanted to make Marcel Khill into the dazzling son that he had been for his own mother. Encouraged to paint and to write, Khill, before he knew it, found himself performing *La machine infernale* in front of a room of five hundred people. The role of the messenger from Corinth included maybe ten lines, it's true, but he couldn't do it for more than four nights. Aware of his remarkable powers of imitation, Cocteau also pushed him to do the set design for a one-act play he was writing for Arletty, *L'école des veuves*, before realizing that he was "spontaneously" outlining poems, for which Cocteau wrote prefaces after retouching them and putting them in the form of acrostics.[70] Did he believe he was flattering the young Kabyle by telling him he was amazed to discover he too spoke the language of poetry, like a man astounded to find his chauffeur read Aeschylus? For months, Paris heard its modern Orpheus sing the praises of this primitive poet, this "graceful savage" whose gifts he had managed to awaken.

Desbordes wasn't the only one to be incensed by Cocteau's unabashed idealizing of Khill, who was already sagging under the weight of his gifts; Franz Thomassin suffered like a martyr, discovering that his hero had found a new companion. He could be seen wandering, gloomy and alone, near the Madeleine, eating his heart out over Cocteau's display of happiness. Loyal Thomassin had learned to respect the wishes of his liege lord. And soon this young man, who had dedicated his life to an absent figure, offered his suffering as the ultimate proof of love. Overcoming his jealousy, he managed to grow close to the young Kabyl, in the hope of winning back his prince. Only too happy to play savior, Khill welcomed him with open arms and enabled him to return slowly to Cocteau's favor. Thomassin moved back to the Hôtel de la Madeleine, right next to where Cocteau lived, so afraid to disturb him that he sometimes did not respond to their invitations, which nevertheless made him very happy. So he lived in Cocteau's shadow, communing in thought with his idol and adoring him at a distance. Sometimes he could even laugh elegantly at his own veneration, as if a second Thomassin were lucid enough to smile at it all.

Suddenly a paragon of all the virtues, Khill acquired an enormous amount of power over this weakened man who candidly encouraged his virile pride. In loving Alfred Douglas, who was fifteen years his junior, Oscar Wilde had noted the eternal youth that falls on those who are maintained by someone older than themselves, on whom daily sexual domination is imposed. Marcel Khill would not have denied it; he soon took a certain pleasure in beating a willing Cocteau.

THE SONG OF THE PEOPLE

Encouraged by Khill's insatiable energy and the general climate of the 1930s, Cocteau began to hang out in sports arenas—velodromes, stadiums, boxing rings. Indoor cycling marathons were all the rage at the Vélodrome d'Hiver, in front of a crowd that occasionally fell asleep in their seats. The enthusiasm of the spectators was as impressive as the athletes' endurance; they could bear in triumph a cyclist who had gone round the track for twenty-four hours, or kiss the hands of a boxer who had made them cry. Far from the bourgeois, fickle, and stiff audiences who had given a mixed reception to *La machine infernale*, Cocteau felt more comfortable among the working-class people, those whom Maurice Chevalier sang about, who ran to applaud the stars who had emerged from their ranks and made a name for themselves thanks to their spirit and their tenacity. Twenty years after the trenches of Coxyde-bains, the common people were making a powerful comeback into Cocteau's life: the times had really changed.

Cocteau had faithfully attended Mistinguett's and Yvonne George's performances in the music halls (sitting very close to Robert Desnos), which in addition to his defense of the *bal musette* in *Carte blanche* (1919) was proof that he had long had a taste for the *chanson populaire*. Over fifteen years, however, the repertory had evolved a bit; the Parisian gaiety of the postwar period had given way, in the darker era of 1930s Europe, to much more dramatic melodies. The violence that threatened in all corners was intimately translated in song, perhaps its first release. One day, as they quarreled, Marcel Khill broke three of Cocteau's ribs. So Cocteau was not the only one moved while hearing Damia sing:

Quand je danse avec mon grand frisé
Il a une façon de m'enlacer
J'en perds la tête
J'suis comme une bête . . .
Il me cogne, il me démolit, il me crève,
Mais que voulez-vous moi j'aime ça
Après je m'endors dans un rêve
En me pelotonnant bien dans ses bras.[71]

Kurt Weill's music had an aphrodisiac power to which Cocteau was sensitive, as we've seen; he found him the most sophisticated of barbarians, perhaps the popular counterpart to the Stravinsky of *Le sacre du printemps*. But he was not up to the task when the musician asked him to work on *The Seven Deadly Sins* (1933), which would be his last collaboration with Brecht, and perhaps his most impressive. Thus, when Hitler's rise to power sent pro-Weimar refugees scuttling to Paris, Cocteau had been the first to offer his services to the German composer, in the early months of 1933.[72] Drawing on his great themes—sleep, lies, amorous suffering, as well as the danger of money, a clear allusion to Natalie Paley that must have troubled Weill—Cocteau wrote around thirty poems in German, and sketched out a musical comedy, *Alice*, as well as an operatic version of *Faust*, in which Marguerite, this time secretly in love with the old man, but greatly disappointed by his sudden return to youth, leaves him in the end.[73] It was a powerful subject that would have allowed Weill to hold forth on the illusion of love, showing that virtue could also reveal itself to be cruel—far from Brecht's brutal, cynical irony. Unfortunately, these two men who both hoped to appeal to the masses, one for reasons of ideology, the other for his desire for an audience, could not complete the project.[74]

Their collaboration did generate at least one song, steeped in lovelorn melancholy, which the men intended for Marlene Dietrich, another symbol of the Berlin cabaret.[75] Testifying to the ease with which they worked together, and their shared taste for spoken song, "*Sprechgesang*," "Es regnet—Il pleut—It's Raining" describes the short period during which Cocteau brought Lotte Lenya, Weill's wife and principal singer, to the lesbian cabarets of Paris, dreaming of a Paris *berlinois*.[76] The arrival of Marianne Oswald in his circle brought him closer to Weill's form of popular drama sung in German. Redheaded, electric, and depressive, Oswald, a born rebel who had also been chased out of Germany when the Nazis rose to power, seemed surrounded by a destructive aura. "A fiery red power lives in her, like the end of a cigarette, a torch, a lighthouse, a beacon, this flame-like determination . . . that form the effectiveness of this chanteuse," he wrote.[77] She had recently given a recital in Paris in which she sang the sailor's song that Sauguet had taken in 1933 from Cocteau's and Radiguet's *Paul et Virginie*.[78]

Onstage, Marianne Oswald always seemed as if she were about to faint. Her scratchy voice, her grimaces, her volcanic furies, and then her poignant tears created an unbearable discomfort; it was difficult to know how to place her— gypsy, madam, or madwoman. But though her voice was often off-key, her heart had perfect pitch—she had also sung Weill's *Threepenny Opera*. Often attacked, the "red whore fresh from the Berlin sewers," as the nationalist press denounced her, was as flamboyant as she was disorderly. That was enough for Cocteau to ask her to sing *Anna la bonne, Mes soeurs n'aimez pas les marins*, and *La dame de Monte-Carlo* (1934–1935).

Suzy Solidor's repertoire was more sexual, though equally dramatic.[79] Cocteau went with Khill to hear the Breton woman sing at La Vie Parisienne, a cabaret on the rue Sainte-Anne, near the Opéra, which had been given to her as a breakup gift from Yvonne de Brémond d'Ars, an art dealer; she sang under the portraits that Foujita, Van Dongen, Picabia and Tamara de Lempicka had done of her.[80] It was standard to see certain women singing songs written for men, but the sailor songs sung by Suzy Solidor were particularly audacious. Describing the woman she was fondling, from her navel to the "folds of her curtains," her gravelly, almost virile voice threatened in *Ouvre*, her masterpiece, to inundate the abyss she entered, and declared in *Obsession:* "Chaque femme je la veux / Des talons jusqu'aux cheveux"—with a frankness that had made her a heroine of the margins, after her 1932 record *Paris lesbien* was released.[81]

This "bird of the sea" with the long yellow beak became infatuated with Cocteau, and she would recite several of his poems in the middle of her recitals. Pronouncing them in a voice saturated with the sea spray of Saint-Malo, which seemed to emerge from her sex, she recited "Attendre" and "Mensonge," which describe masculine duplicity and romantic dependence—Cocteau's main themes as a lyricist.[82] When her recital was over, Solidor would go backstage and smoke opium in her dressing room with Cocteau. This blend of obscene language, rough music, and opiates gave Cocteau all kinds of ideas, and he began to speak of the possibility of having a baby with the singer. The child would be handsome like her, intelligent like him, and would sing his own songs and conquer Paris.[83] Suzy Solidor was not flattered enough to actually agree, however, and Cocteau found himself once again deprived of an heir.

This was not the case, poetically speaking, for a young singer from Perpignan who idolized his work, as well as Max Jacob's, had just shown up at his door. "The new poetry troubled, intrigued, disturbed this young man," Cocteau remembered, describing Charles Trenet, who was still singing with Johnny Hess, a Swiss composer, but through the Front Populaire would soon make his solo debut. The poet drew for the young singer the halo, stars, and wings that would make him, if not an angel, the "singing madman" that *Y'a d'la joie* would establish for good in 1937. Cocteau described him as "a flash in the pan that would last a long time"; chubby-cheeked Trenet would enjoy the limelight for seventy years.

This friendship with the stars would bring out one of Cocteau's oldest gifts. On Radio Luxembourg, he began to do impressions of Mistinguett, Maurice

Chevalier, Marlene Dietrich, even Marianne Oswald. His talent for exaggeration was so well received that he was asked to record these astonishing resurrections; he even managed, drawing on his rich sense of the past, to do Mounet-Sully, Sarah Bernhardt, and Marcel Proust, his masterpiece. Cocteau recreated the singer Tino Rossi's voice, which was like that of a suntanned eunuch at the height of his glory, as well as the cascading sound coming from Louis Armstrong's trumpet, with the help of a Gillette razor, a bit of rolling paper, a rubber band, and a glass lamp shade. The mimic secretly dreamed about becoming those he brought to life. The masses were the central protagonist of the decade, and he wanted to be as loved by them as the stars he envied. "What glory! That's what I'd love to have!" the Thomassins heard him exclaim before an advertisement on a Morris column of a smiling Tino Rossi. Cocteau had been the first to call Rossi an idiot, but the singer had the gift — unfortunately inimitable — of tapping into the excitement of a crowd, and receiving excellent notices from the critics. Igor Markevitch was not the only one to see Cocteau as a slave to popularity.

AROUND THE WORLD IN EIGHTY DAYS

If songwriting helped Cocteau reinvent himself, his drawings would soon reveal the limits of the neoclassical atmosphere: they would be overwhelmed with lyres, columns, and blind heroines, a jumble in which his graphic gifts lost a bit of their gracefulness. The magical mercury into which he had dipped his pen for twenty years had solidified. His long fingers with their "swollen veins," which Eisenstein had compared to those of Orlac (the pianist whose hands are replaced by those of a murderer in Robert Wiene's film), remained more or less independent from his brain.[84] They took advantage of his down time to sketch decoration ideas, as well as ideas for jewelry and accessories for Elsa Schiaparelli's themed collections, to the great anger of her rival, Coco Chanel. And while they blackened the paper, his mouth sang a sailor's ballad, through the windows with a view over the Madeleine. A poor nightingale, Cocteau hoped that Parisians would stop to applaud him. But Khill could not bear this stifling room, whose only alternatives were other somber rooms. He wanted to take advantage of his partner's fame and go out and see the world, not be the passive roommate of a typewriter. The complaint was no sooner out of his mouth, at a dinner given by the press mogul Jean Prouvost, than Cocteau had the idea to do a new version of *Around the World in Eighty Days*, sixty years after Jules Verne's novel had been published, respecting the same constraints and refusing to take an airplane.

For the first time he stopped the mental cruises offered by opium to board a ship stopping in San Francisco and to spend some time on a felucca headed for

Luxor. His instinctive loathing of traveling did not evaporate, however; nothing really surprised him, or disappointed him for that matter; everything was more or less as he had imagined it, and Kuala Lumpur looked like it sounded. Who knows if a map would have been as inspiring to him?

Dead civilizations impressed him, and the Roman Forum above all. At night the forest of columns was transformed into a ghost whose mythological aspects were accentuated in the moonlight. The "sunshine of ruins" lit up the site into a gigantic picnic that Jupiter and Neptune had abandoned at the first hints of an earthquake. "But these aren't ruins, everything is broken!" exclaimed Khill. This childlike expression warmed the heart of a man who had become too accustomed to thunder.

The Egypt of the pharaohs gave him visions. The pyramids, the Sphinx, the obelisks were so many hieroglyphs whose hidden meaning could be perceived only from the heavens, by the gods they praised. A supernatural punishment must have put an end to the demiurgical attempts of a people eager to be the equal of their idols.

In Alexandria, Marcel Khill wanted to visit the red-light district. Cocteau went with him, but at the last minute let Khill quench his own thirst for life, and returned to bed to smoke a pipe. In the newspapers, he was photographed beside his "young secretary"; did readers understand the role Khill played in his life? Regardless, this belated honeymoon was a joyful time. In Bombay, emerging from boutiques filled with goddesses "surrounded by a cruel fan made of arms," he went to see those terrible silent towers, those "castles of death" in which certain castes deposit their loved ones' dead bodies, where he learned that the vultures would sometimes drop a bit of ear or finger on the city. In Rangoon, he saw Sikhs who were forbidden to cut their hair and Chinese men going to the barber to shave their armpits, their chests, and their legs, like de Max had done at one time. Everywhere he went, he saw unsettling rituals and absurd customs, or so it would have seemed to another Western man; for him it was a joy to see these faraway people whose sense of poetry was intact. The deeper into Asia he traveled, the more he regained his habit of preferring beliefs to ideas, myths to facts, and tolerance to philosophy. This similar way of thinking was confirmed in his far-off "Asian" ancestors.

His boat, *President Coolidge,* was en route from Hong Kong to Shanghai when Cocteau spotted Charlie Chaplin, a god of the cinema in his eyes. He immediately sent a letter to Chaplin in his cabin and waited in vain for a response. A second attempt led the filmmaker, who thought someone was playing a joke on him, to verify Cocteau's presence in the ship's register, which eventually led to their meeting in the boat's dining room. The ambiance was awkward because Chaplin spoke no French, and Cocteau no English. But through the interventions of the bilingual Paulette Goddard, recently married to Chaplin, the two men were able to establish their mutual admiration, with the help of much gesticulating. "We spoke with our eyes and our hands," said Cocteau, in one of the accounts he would give of this divinely willed encounter. Cocteau had paid tribute to Chaplin as early as 1917, through the character of the young American in *Parade.* He called Chaplin, at first, "Charlie." As they were leaving dinner, Chaplin began to act out some of the scenes from his films.[85] "In the narrow cabin, he set up his scenery, instructed his extras, and transformed into himself," wrote Cocteau, amazed that everything in this genius fed his dramatic intentions. This little man, the former vagabond turned millionaire who was as popular with the masses as with critics and kings, by picking up pins in front of a camera, continued to inspire absolute veneration in Cocteau. No one better than this mustachioed "angel" could embody Cocteau's hopes for international popularity; this man, conductor and orchestra in one, was able to send his cinematic double everywhere, sliding into every culture. This inspired Cocteau to hope that one day his own body might serve as the raw material for his work.

If Chaplin is to be believed, the evening was exhausting. Cocteau made him mime every role in his next short film—a modern crucifixion that goes totally unnoticed in a New York nightclub. Tired of having to perform *Charlot* on his cruise vacation, Chaplin spent the rest of the trip avoiding this overzealous admirer, whose many gifts he often praised, but whom he perceived to be a caricature of himself, with his intellectual tricks and his cunning naiveté. Did he guess that this other born mime couldn't wait to imitate him, even his imitations, as soon as he returned to Paris? "Sometimes I saw him all the time, and then he would suddenly shut himself up in his room, and we'd see nothing further of him," said Cocteau. "He was afraid he had upset me, and so, at dinner, someone put their hands over my eyes": this game of hide and seek lasted the whole crossing.[86]

Together, they went to the cabarets of Shanghai, where Cocteau was sorry not to be able to examine close up the jars of oil, in which there floated "aging children" (likely fetuses of some kind) who were worshipped like buddhas, and whose heads alone seemed to grow over the years. Strangely, Chaplin wasn't interested in anything. During their stop in Tokyo, the actor stayed in his hotel to work, and during the projection of *Modern Times* in Yokohama, he couldn't take his eyes off a kitten as it wandered through the room, continually putting its paws in shafts of light coming from the projector. "Why are you always so sad?" Cocteau asked him. "Because I've become a rich man playing a poor one!" replied Chaplin. This kind of paradox delighted the writer, who was long convinced that genius was a disaster.[87]

From the geisha to the maître d'hôtel, from the sumo wrestler to the emissary from the Imperial Palace, the people of Japan gave Cocteau the royal welcome. Everywhere he was asked to sign autographs on gold-flecked paper. The press photographed him, with a big smile on his face, beside the man who had translated nearly all of his books into Japanese; in Tokyo, he went to applaud a fifty-year-old transvestite whom he saw transform into a young girl, and then an old lion. But he had to move more and more quickly; the twenty-fourth day was approaching, his spirit was soaring between centuries and worlds, passing through the walls of time and space. His greatest pleasure was to fall asleep on a Tuesday night, cross over the international date line, and wake up on Tuesday morning, losing a day: hadn't he always said that time was the fictional fruit of the delirium of human rationality? To keep up with Phileas Fogg, he had to cheat on the final leg of the journey and take a plane, supported by Khill's incredible resourcefulness—"all three musketeers in one."

Cocteau was most disoriented by his return to Paris. "It's funny," he said, "it's just like in Proust—there are no children or dogs."[88] After Malaysian magic and Hindu elegance, he was plunged back into the "rudeness, haste, bluster, machine-made junk" of Europe; after the Egyptian fans beating the torrid air came the rain and the cold; after the hypnotic crowds of Asia crept the freezing solitude of the Parisian writer.

Cocteau's own *Around the World in Eighty Days* (*Tour du monde en 80 jours*) greatly pleased Gide, who never failed to praise the reporter in him; but then, the book was dedicated to Gide. For others it was an almost asphyxiating narrative, a hail of images and sensations. None of the characters of the book, except Chaplin, had time enough, or place enough, to take shape given its compulsive, breakneck pace; only the strangest figures could tear themselves from the crowd, with a lightning flash of lucidity. "One day you reproached me for being too tense, for not letting myself go," Cocteau wrote in his dedication to Gide. It might still be said of this perpetually evolving narrative, which was like a film made by an insect with 360-degree vision. "Every ship is a romantic object, except that we sail in," said Emerson.

Often glorified, if not mythologized, throughout the book, the versatile Khill began to imitate the writer whom he dominated at night. Not content merely to trace Cocteau's drawings, he aped his mannerisms, his gestures, his way of telling a story; everyone was suddenly called "Chéri" or "Bébé"; every anecdote was punctuated by "for-mi-dable!" or "hal-lucinant!"[89] A second Cocteau thus led their group from bar to bar to shower them with his anecdotes and tire them with his imitations. "Have a cappuccino, we'll put it on Jean's tab," the Thomassins were told; it was the voice of his master, coming out of a body that had shed twenty years. Having been Cocteaufied, as the photographs taken by George Platt Lynes show, the young Kabyl soon began to make pilgrimages, and to spend two months in a retreat at Trappe. The real Khill, however, needed physical satisfactions; he secretly rented a maid's room far from the hotel, and began to lead his prey there; if Cocteau could converse with a chair, Khill could seduce it. Soon the phone calls from disgruntled parents began to arrive at Cocteau's, who had to cover up the abortion of one of Khill's "victims."[90] In becoming the master, the young secretary had managed to make himself almost as deliciously intolerable as his predecessor.

CONQUERING THE MASSES

General Franco's military coup against the Republican government in Spain, and the civil war that followed, meant that even those who were the most indifferent to politics had to take sides. Picasso finally spoke up in favor of the legitimate government, and even Maritain, getting over his flirtation with the ideas of Charles Maurras, joined *Vendredi*, a defiantly left-wing magazine. If politics had been more or less off the agenda, since the Dreyfus affair, it was now the only thing anyone could talk about—except in Cocteau's circle. His political indifference was certainly tempered at times by his preference for "subdued disorder" over "flat order," or by his rhetorical attacks against the "rich ladies of leisure, who, having everything, can only destroy; painted, golden idols whose insolent cheek attracts the workers' slap"—a phrase that appears (it should be said) at the end of a panegyric in praise of Louise de Vilmorin.[91] He had also noted, during his trip around the world, the constellation of stains on the walls of Rhodes that were imprinted on his retina in the shifting sunlight, before composing a portrait of Mussolini; in passing he had even complained of police harassment in a Japan that was becoming fascist; but these were merely picturesque details among many others, in the heart of an unreal land.

When Cocteau had returned home, the France of the Front Populaire was being paralyzed by the general strike and factory occupations, but writing his book, with its evocation of Oriental fatalism, had encouraged his natural bent toward uncertainty. "There are no injustices except superficial, temporary ones," he wrote in his *Tour du monde*. "Everyone has the place he deserves, through a system of checks and balances that functions at a deeper level than our own actions." The text must have sounded strange to the partisans of the Front Populaire . . . even if some would no doubt have approved of the passage claiming that a secret group, with a leader worthy of Fantômas that he called the Kings of the World, dominated the world economy and played poker with human lives.

Cocteau spent the summer of 1936 in the Camargues, on Jean Hugo's estate, capturing mice and chameleons, tree frogs and scorpions, then taming a giant lizard he would take for walks on a leash, thanks to a raffia harness woven by Khill. Officially in a state of detoxification, Jean Bourgoint was secretly having Khill give him opium injections. Khill would fall asleep beside a bat he had trapped, while the writer lovingly drew the insects he encountered as if they were brothers, the reincarnation of people he had loved.[92] "The life of the Pink Library. We are five years old," said Cocteau to his mother; he had stopped shaving or bathing, and ate with his fingers.[93] It was a life filled with magical creatures, the kind the modern Orpheus dreamed of; Jean Hugo described it in his journal, trying to capture something of its strange poetry. Neither right nor left ("on the ceiling," Jean Touzot joked), Cocteau continued to glide through China in his dreams, more interested in regaining his health than in rebuilding society.[94] Nevertheless, he ended up siding with the Front Populaire. The "bourgeois" image that followed him around, like the scandalous bohemia in which he lived, kept him from showing too much support for the "paid vacation" camp, but in his own way he showed his solidarity, discreet and guilty, while Breton and his lot remained slightly above the fray, ostracized by the Communists who regarded them with "the same suspicion they themselves had reserved for Jean Cocteau."[95]

Tzara led the support committee for Spanish intellectuals and wrote poems in rhyme again; only too happy to encounter the workers, Gide raised his own voice in meetings at the Maison de la Mutualité, a prelude to his trip to the USSR where he would meet Stalin, in the company of Pierre Herbart, who had turned Communist. Sachs himself composed a hagiography about Maurice Thorez, the "foremost Stalinist in France," while remaining in charge of Gallimard's Catholic imprint, an inheritance from the Maritain era.[96] Marie Laure de Noailles claimed to have rented several rows of an auditorium where there was meant to be a pro-Franco event, the better to disrupt it. But though a good number of rebellious aristocrats were enthusiastic, on the whole the bourgeoisie rediscovered its fear of the worker, and threatened to leave, even to emigrate. "Those on the Left remain in their homes; that's how you can recognize them," said Marie Laure. She continued to receive—a diamond hammer and sickle on her lapel, people said later—those mostly apathetic members of the right-wing, like Poulenc or Bérard. Auric, for his part, preferred to "squeeze his little fist" in public assemblies, upon hearing the "Internationale" sung.

Cocteau signed petitions and attended meetings; one time, he even dared to speak, but his words were greeted by gibes and derision, which wounded him.[97] No one could believe that a skeletal opium addict like Cocteau could carry any weight in such affairs. We can imagine how surprised he was to find that his old friend Maurice Rostand, still with his mother by his side and more than ever plastered with cold cream, could triumph over an electoral meeting, the magic of his surname finally winning him some kind of respect among the proletariat. The divisions that were tearing apart the Surrealists paved the way for Cocteau's turn to politics. Since all the Surrealists' firepower was being used to respond to Communist attacks, for the first time, after fifteen years of open war, Cocteau could imagine going out openly, without protection. "Do you think Aragon could see me without hating me?" he asked Gide, with a humility that makes one's blood run cold.[98] Taking note of Cocteau's interest in the Front Populaire, Aragon, the former dandy of the Certà who had become the champion of the workers' paradise, offered Cocteau a column in *Ce soir*, a journal with the political policy of *L'humanité* and the populist tone of *Paris-soir*. Entitled "Articles de Paris" (Items from Paris), it would allow Cocteau to "chat," in his way, with his readers—primarily workers.

This unexpected alliance was the first serious fault line in the blockade that Breton had built up against Cocteau, the "pelle à crottes" (shit-shovel).[99] For Aragon, it was doubtless a question of defying the stentorian poet to whom he had been so close—it was said that "Aragon's heart beats in Breton's chest."[100] Perhaps by publishing Cocteau's byline in his newspaper Aragon was getting his revenge for the novels that Breton had made him burn, not to mention the censorship he had imposed on their friendship. "Almost his whole life long, this incredibly cultured and intelligent man lived in the constant fear that Breton would discover his homosexuality," said Jean Aurenche.[101] Whatever the situation, the most talented of the Surrealist Musketeers didn't hesitate to call on the former scapegoat—the Communist Party was looking for prestigious fellow travelers. Aragon, however, very slowly became as kind as he had been in the beginning. He had told Cocteau, in 1919, before Breton clamped down, "Our friendship, no matter what he says, began like the Ninth Symphony."[102] Aragon never apologized, but he was friendly, which in this case was worth more. Eager to conquer the people of France, Aragon—whom Picabia compared, with a healthy dose of malice, to a modern-day Sévigné taking tea with Dada—slowly returned to his former love for Barrès. What right had he to critique Cocteau's discreet return to Symbolism? Éluard himself, when he joined the French Communist Party, turned Lamartine quickly enough.

Cocteau hastened to appeal to readers of *Ce soir* by writing about boxing, bull-fighting, and Charlie Chaplin, but also, more curiously, about political meetings. Contrasting the "white revolution" led by the Front Populaire with the Nazi's book-burning in Germany, or the bellicose appetites of fascist Italy, he congratulated the French people on their maturity and applauded the Republic for serving as a haven for the persecuted, just as Picasso offered to the victims of the German air attacks, in *Guernica*, a cross that "Franco will always carry on his shoulder." It was such a clear engagement that Romain Rolland asked Cocteau for autographs for Republican Spain. He replied by taking a bedsheet and in pencil and charcoal created an immense drawing entitled *La peur donnant des ailes au courage*, which he completed by cutting himself with his razor in order to stain with his own blood the bandaged wounds of one of the figures.[103]

However much Cocteau declared in *Ce soir* that he loved to work, which was true, and that he had always been a worker, which was less true—and however much he proclaimed that the artisan was the real aristocrat in France, the ideological issues of the Front Populaire escaped him. In the Communist meeting he attended for *Ce soir*, six months after the successful elections, he delightedly took note of one thing only: that the dominant color in the pennants, flags, and scarves was not red but pink, purple, and orange. Congratulating Gide on his *Retour de l'URSS*, the anti-Stalin bomb dividing the progressive camp, he called it "brave, noble, charming," as if it were a storyline for a ballet. Never having completed his studies, or defended his "positions" in an amphitheater, Cocteau would always be better at speaking about a Suzy Solidor recital than the "great" Stalin's latest work on linguistics. His politics—made of emotion, love, and childhood reverie—were the total opposite of the movement sweeping France. Perhaps his dealings with Aragon had opened his eyes. That other masked tightrope-walker, having nearly killed himself over Nancy Cunard, had signed an irrevocable pact with reality, putting himself under the protection of Elsa Triolet, "the blue-eyed sword," said Pablo Neruda. Indeed Aragon, who had sworn never to work and who, ten years earlier, called civil servants, workers, and servants "fellators of the useful" and "masturbators of necessity," had become a zealous Stalinist.[104] His ability to adapt quickly and completely, which allowed him to move between Dada and the GPU, the "Marseillaise" and "La Jeune Garde," Elsa and the boys, would henceforth be controlled by the Party.

Cocteau, by contrast, had only opium as a foundation, and unstable companions as his "sword." Khill eventually left him, partly because of Cocteau's weakness, and partly because he had met a young illustrator, Denyse de Bravura. Concealing his suffering, Cocteau tried as usual to persuade himself that he had wanted Khill to go for his own good. "In order not to acknowledge his

defeats to himself," said Gide of Robert de Passavant, Cocteau's fictional alter
ego, "he always affected to have desired his fate, and, whatever happened to
him, he pretended that that was what he wished . . . His emotions were never
too violent to keep under control . . . His affection weakened as soon as one
didn't need it."[105] One last trip to the Midi, in December 1937, and Cocteau,
true to his reputation, gave Khill his blessing if he wanted to leave. Alone once
again, more resigned to his fate than ever—they really did all leave, didn't
they—Cocteau holed up in a hotel room in the heart of the rue Cambon where
Coco Chanel, his benefactor, held court. He would smoke up to sixty pipes a
day, after seven detox attempts, all of which were as atrocious as the illness they
sought to cure. Thin as a fakir, sad as a clown, confusing names and dates,
sometimes calling for his mother at four o'clock in the morning, thinking he
was picking her up as she came out of Mass, Cocteau was a shadow of himself.
The most elegant, the most snobbish of drugs had made him into a derelict.[106]

Cocteau still found the energy to address a thousand boy scouts in short
pants at the Sorbonne, at a 1937 jamboree, telling them the future depended on
them. But Glenway Wescott, the American novelist from the Welcome Hôtel,
was horrified to find him in this state. The poet's outrageously madeup face was
as livid as that of the aged actor, his eyes full of tears of blood, who had just
recited some extracts from Cocteau's *La machine infernale*. Ten years had
passed since they had met at Villefranche, but it seemed like a century. The
word "decadent" did not do him justice; Cocteau was so evocative of bad luck
that in Rome or Naples no one would have spoken his name without crossing
their fingers. "I have lived half of my life / I no longer want to live," he wrote.[107]
He had so often confessed this weariness that no one listened any longer.

THE RETURN OF PANAMA AL BROWN

A few months earlier, during a freezing cold night when Marcel Khill had
again accused Cocteau of being too much of a homebody, they had gone out to
the Caprice Viennois, a nightclub on the rue Pigalle, where Khill and Roland
Toutain often went to see a former world-champion boxer conduct an all-black
orchestra, before doing a little tap dance as he jumped rope. The show was
pathetic. Panama Al Brown, the black idol whose fans paid to watch him train,
and beside whom Maurice Chevalier was proud to be photographed, was now
only a memory. "A human rag," Cocteau said, fascinated by his pipe-stem legs,
his wasp waist and his prominent ribs, his arms long and breakable like bread-
sticks—the physique of a Nubian marathon runner. Eaten away by opium,
syphilis, champagne, and tranquilizers, Brown was a ruin who was alive only

thanks to the medicine he took, having blown a fortune with these parasites in the greatest cabarets in the world. "A black diamond in the rubbish heap," added Cocteau, filled with compassion for this fallen champion who was as addicted as he himself was to opium.

It was during the rigged world championship in the Valencia arena, in the summer of 1935, that Panama Al Brown had been relegated to playing the fool. Knocked out by the narcotic that his adversary, Sangchilli, had poured into his glass just before the fight, the boxing genius resisted his blows for fifteen super-human rounds, then blacked out as the winner was announced. Discovering later that he had been poisoned by his own agent, who had been bribed by Sangchilli, he had sworn he would never put the gloves on again. In twenty years of boxing he had known only dishonest managers and brokers eager to put him in debt. He was a high roller, capable of playing baccarat for millions in Deauville, but he was fragile, and had had to sell the stable of also-ran race-horses he kept up at Maisons-Laffitte, Cocteau's hometown. He was such a dandy that he could change his clothes six times a day, from a fur given to him by his friend Maurice Chevalier to one of his Prince of Wales suits he had admired on Fred Astaire, his role model; he would then turn back into a ghetto kid and alternate moments of euphoria with crises of depression. He could treat a whole restaurant to dinner if he felt like it, yet he kept just enough money to buy opium.

Cocteau recognized himself in the former champion who hated giving anyone trouble, whose left knee was eaten away by arthritis and his lungs by the tuberculosis that only the drugs allowed him to forget. He persuaded himself that the boxer would still be able to win back his place, if not his title, and that a "guardian angel" would chase away his demons. The writer swore he would do for the boxer what he could not do for himself: get the fighter, who everyone said was washed up, back in the ring, in order to restore to him the pride that had given him an "icon's nobility."

Panama Al Brown refused outright. He felt only disgust for the violent sport, with its rigged matches and knowing crowds, which was becoming more and more like wrestling.[108] Why would he want to revisit this other kind of fight, like when he had been disqualified by the referee during the final round and had nearly been lynched by an angry crowd at the Vel d'Hiv furious that a "monkey" had prevented his white opponent from fighting? Bring back the blows that had broken his right hand, from the metacarpus to the wrist, and had required Novocaine injections? Find himself at the mercy of poisoners and con artists, and hear the spectators call him "ballerina"? He didn't want to do it any longer. "I don't want to be touched, my wrists are made of glass, they're as thin as yours," the "black wonder" said. The former star had only one desire: to live out peacefully his secret nightlife, in a cabaret that gave him as many drinks as he liked. Cocteau followed him to the nightclubs where he spent his nights getting boys to drink, whom he then dreamed of arousing, sometimes until eight in the morning. Tired of catching champagne bottles from tipping over, Cocteau tried again. How could a boxer think he was finished at just thirty-five years old? The boxer's resistance only increased Cocteau's resolution. Had he not spent fifteen years fighting a "gang" that was stronger than him? They were no doubt underdogs, both of them, but those are the ones who win in stories — otherwise the hare would have beat the tortoise.

It began to work, to a certain degree. Panama agreed to accompany Cocteau to watch, from the fourth row, two of his old rivals fight each other in a match. Dinner parties brought them together, and Brown eventually took his own room at Cocteau's hotel. When the boxer was nearly thrown out of the country for writing bad checks, Cocteau immediately wrote to the French president, who sent a letter back immediately, via a member of the Republican Guard cavalry, pardoning Brown.[109] One evening, having made himself late, Brown asked Cocteau if he could bathe at his place. Amazed that the white writer got into the bath he had just left, when most Americans would have hurriedly emptied the water that he had dirtied, Brown kissed Cocteau's feet, finally convinced he had found a true benefactor. Cocteau took advantage of the situation to demand that the boxer detox once and for all, something he himself had not been able to pull off; and Brown went in for treatment at Sainte-Anne, Cocteau having convinced Coco Chanel to foot the bill. Cocteau advised the boxer to bury his head in some pillows to endure the horrors of withdrawal. Cut off from drugs, alcohol, and, essentially, life — "he wanted to kill us when he got out," said Cocteau — Brown showed an unbelievable amount of courage, helped by letters that Cocteau asked readers of the sports papers to send to him, as a way of supporting Brown in his battle with himself.

Brown finally agreed to go (still at Chanel's expense) to take a cure in the great outdoors, at a restored farmhouse in the Cher, where he was overseen by a trainer, a team of boxer friends, and a mysterious gentleman. He made himself wake up every day at six o'clock for four months. He who had always hated training jumped rope, did push-ups, and, after a seven-kilometer morning run, alternated rounds of shadow-boxing with training with a punching bag. He got his weight up to fifty-eight kilos (128 pounds), beyond the maximum for bantam weight. Through sheer willpower he stopped smoking, worked up to weightlifting fifty-two kilos, and restored his arm extension and his ability to do the necessary legwork. To blow off steam he would shoot at chickens with a rifle, to the great displeasure of the farmers. For a boxer who had quit two years ago, it was a miracle. Stuck in Paris directing his *Oedipe roi*, for which he had also designed the costumes, Cocteau could only cheer on Panama at the Palais Berlitz, where he continued getting back in shape.[110] "Imagine . . . something (it is impossible to write 'someone') that is moving around, like lightning, like luck, like anger . . . like an epidemic," Cocteau said in the middle of a room full of boxers with punching bags, ecstatic at his protégé's resurrection.[111] Wings seemed to hold him up when he spun on his trampoline, spiraling through the atmosphere; beneath his winged feet, the ground fell away and then reformed itself, the ceiling "dove in and out"; he looked like the black angel in *Le sang d'un poète*.

The boxing world was convinced that Panama Al Brown would never make it to the end of a match again. Gamblers laughed at the effort of the aesthete who had never played a sport in his life trying to bring back this has-been who had never been able to make a real career; even the aficionados thought it was criminal to try to bring back a drug addict capable of burning a Bugatti on a sharp turn, just after having sunk all his winnings into it. As for the press, they laughed at the press conference that Brown held in his villa in the Cher, in which he pretended to have shed six years and predicted his imminent victories with a braggadocio worthy of Cassius Clay, thirty years later.

Cocteau persisted. Convinced that Panama Al Brown was a born star, "one of those beings who belong to the people and contain all their secret desires to conquer," he directed his "entrances," as he would have done with his actors, asking him for less haughtiness and more concentration, then reminded him of his duty: to win back the title of world champion. A challenge that verged on pure madness, this would be the most improbable episode in an already far from banal life . . . but there it was: Cocteau the opium addict was convinced that his passion was equal to the best trainers on earth. Brown was so endearing! Naïve, credulous, gay, fanciful: an imp with a joyful boxing style who could also play the sax, sing lead with a band, or sit down to a drum kit to improvise. A strange boxer, who hated the ring and couldn't stand the sight of blood (he fainted seeing Roland Toutain emerge from the wardrobe in his bedroom) and who was much more interested in evenings in nightclubs or chrome-plated two-seaters, Brown loved life to distraction, so much that he adopted a child at the height of his glory. But he both amused himself and destroyed himself with the same frenzied energy, seeming a more than worthy successor to Battling Siki, the Senegalese man with a thousand legs, a demi-god with closed fists. He was aware, as well, of the necessity of making blacks more visible on the world stage, after having been the forgotten people of history; like Josephine Baker and the

Noailleses, he was a patron of the legendary Dakar Djibouti expedition of 1931–1933, from which Marcel Griaule brought back many objets d'art (particularly from the Dogon tribe) to make a donation to the ethnographic museum at Trocadéro. This museum, which would later become the Musée de l'Homme, provided Michel Leiris with the material for his important study, *Phantom Africa.*

Brown's comeback match took place at the Salle Wagram, on September 9, 1937. He fought André Régis, a native of Algiers, a fighter made of pure granite who'd gone unbeaten for four years. Cocteau had given Brown only a few words of advice, telling him to avoid asking for champagne or a cigarette before the fight, crossing himself ostentatiously, or doing the grasshopper jumps that so horrified Parisian spectators. To encourage Brown, Cocteau gave him the triple ring that had already shone on the hands of Radiguet, Desbordes, and Natalie Paley, telling him that it brought good luck. The imp in Panama Al Brown was unleashed at the first gong. He moved so quickly that it was difficult to keep track of him: zipping this way and that, he was as hard to see as his jumprope when it whistled through the air during training. He stung the ex-champion of the French bantamweight division again and again; under the weight of the blows Régis softened, lost his breath, and then slumped like a piece of flannel. The bell brought the match to an end while the latecomers were still taking their seats: the single round had lasted for sixty-five seconds, knockout included. The audience was miffed at having so little believed in the boxer's return, and they remained incredulous, almost suspicious, as if some kind of trick were being played. Carried off in triumph by his core group of supporters, the Panamanian Lazarus made it to the locker room, then, once dressed, went to celebrate his resurrection at his hotel. There the boxer, born black and poor, kissed the writer, born white and rich, who had brought him back to life. He hid his tears badly.

The press unanimously saluted Cocteau and tried to call Brown a poet; but was this truly a compliment? The public continued to secretly resent this boxer whose disdain for training conflicted with the proletarian love of effort. Cocteau could brag of the "*enfant terrible* of the boxing ring," but the "people" detected a spoiled child, a big-time gambler with his sports cars showering the public with champagne, or worse still, an arrogant ex-colonial, thirsty for revenge, insidiously attempting to prove black superiority. Another match was organized between Brown and a former French champion, but this too was over quickly: it didn't last two rounds. A third sparring partner, too, found himself on the mat after just five minutes, trembling like an epileptic puppet. It was a real massacre, carried out by one of the most elegant figures that boxing has ever known. The half-starved drug addict, the also-ran of the Caprice Viennois, had become once again the lucky star of every stadium in France. People wanted to believe that if Cocteau was always in the front row of these devastating battles, it was to be better able to coach the boxer telepathically, but the writer was happy simply to fill a bottle of champagne with seltzer water (it was Brown's ritual to crack one open at the beginning of every match) in order to make his opponent think that Brown had gone back to alcohol and so make him drop his guard.

Fascinated by Brown's "mental" way of boxing, Cocteau began to write feverishly about not only the "terrible bronze grasshopper," but also the subtle psychologist who had a wondrous ability for mimicry. If the bleachers called for blood, tears, and butchery, Brown danced—delicate, airborne, intangible, almost nonchalant—even if it meant frustrating them. If his opponent lost his cool, he would float, a distant, crazed look in his eye, like a zombie waiting for his orders, or he would pretend to make mistakes, as if he were drugged. Then he would stare at his opponent, like a snake charmer with his flute, letting him circle around him, and then, once his face was close, he would uncoil his left boa and the stunned idiot would bite the dust. Born on the same day—July 5—thirteen years after him, with the same measurements, the boxer became Cocteau's black twin. He arranged his blows the way the others set out words, danced his corporeal poems as if he were staging Cocteau's writing; he became an artist with the calves of a hero, looking for the perfect blow. For Cocteau the ring became the ideal popular theater, a truly lethal counterpart to classical tragedy. More than song writing, another medium intended for "simple" hearts, boxing became the centerpiece of his new aesthetic, the heavy, serious counterpart to his fascination with acrobats. Panama gave the best of himself in front of a crowd that rooted not only for his success but also for his death.

On December 31, 1937, the ecstatic writer presented "his" champion to the audience at a Montparnasse cinema. "Once upon a time, there was a famous boxer," he began, as if Brown had been living a fairy tale. His smile broad, his hands open, his lips ready to sip champagne, the boxer was once again a favorite with the crowds. On January 11, 1938, Cocteau again praised him, this time in the pages of *Ce soir*, Aragon's newspaper, calling him a sorcerer capable of making himself into a zombie in order to put his opponent to sleep, and then to take on all the forms necessary—panther, smoke, swallow—to take hold of him, like the "loas," the divine voodoo spellbinders. Cocteau waxed truly poetic writing with the blood (like "black ink") of Brown; soon he had written so much about him that a collection *Le sang du boxeur* would not have been out of the question.

With all these accolades, the boxer began to neglect his training again, and gradually went back to smoking and drinking. While fighting Poppi Décico, he broke his right wrist and finished the match triumphantly with only his left fist. He had barely recuperated when he went up against a former world champion whom Sangchilli had just beaten. Cocteau could even win a little money betting with the journalists covering the match if he could tell them the exact moment when Brown would knock out his opponent, having been forewarned by the boxer that he would rub his nose with his glove as soon as he felt ready for the final punch. Now there was only Sangchilli himself left to take on.

The date for the Brown revenge match with Sangchilli was set for March 4, 1938. Wearing a white cap and blue corduroy trousers, Brown walked into the big arena at the Palais des Sports de Paris. Twenty thousand spectators saw him climb into the ring, ready to knock out Sangchilli, the cheat who had stolen his title, sending him to the mat for years, so to speak. But Brown, weakened by a cold, his liver eaten away by the champagne he demanded but could not tolerate, was not in great shape. After dominating nine rounds, he finally stopped fighting. Cocteau wanted to believe that if Sangchilli kept burrowing his hair beneath Panama's nose, it was because it was drenched with ether, or a sleeping potion, but in reality Panama was paying the price for the return of his demons. The alert young man was aging before his eyes; badly defended by his flannel legs and breakable fists, wincing against the uppercuts, and bleeding from everywhere, Brown wore a look on his face of a terrified child; Lazarus in his bloody robe seemed eager to return to the calm of the grave. "Al, I'm begging you," his "trainer" cried out, out of his depth and suffering himself with every blow, as if it were his own destiny being played out in the ring. The match was "fifteen savage rounds," he would write in *L'Auto*, "between a man who raged chaotically and a man who hated calmly." Finally the referee raised the arm of a distressed man: Brown had won, but only on points.

The room stood up to applaud a man who had come to retrieve the title of bantamweight world champion, to erase three shameful years. Just like his idols—the movie stars Raimu and Jean Gabin, the singer Tino Rossi, and the stuntman Roland Toutain—the audience celebrated the "black spider." A delegation from Panama bestowed on him the highest national decoration, and gave a standing ovation to the writer who had brought him back to life. Cocteau savored his triumph. The victory of Panama Al Brown was the revenge of the opium addict on the poisoner, the homosexual on his torturer, the ghost on reality—the negation of all the blows he had received since early puberty.

The press encouraged Panama to challenge other opponents. He was meant to fight Engelmann on April 13, and the agents and bookies made their bets. Only Cocteau tried to warn him, in an open letter published in *Paris-soir*:

Let go of boxing. You hate it. You wanted justice. The notorious elite, who remember four rounds of fatigue and forget eleven miraculous ones, aren't worthy of your exhausting yourself for them. The crowd has proven that they love you . . . Try something new.

Brown listened to him, but his need for money was so great that he agreed to fight Engelmann at the Palais des Sports. Cocteau applauded his legwork, but believed that from now on, his role was to discourage him. Brown was a grasshopper, not a tank; he was one of those insects capable of numbing a cow, not knocking over a giant. He was a Nijinski in satin shorts, not a Diaghilev in rhinoceros hide. It was time to hang up the gloves; this sickly man, approaching forty, had already fought 231 times, including twenty-three world championships. During the break before the eighth round, an exhausted Panama asked for champagne, which Cocteau administered. "Don't worry Jean, it's over," he said. Six seconds later, Engelmann was on his knees.

Brown was offered thousands of francs to fight Kane, but aware that he had come too close to catastrophe, decided to leave boxing, as he had promised Cocteau. This impresario, sent from heaven, and to whom he owed all his renewed glory, had more authority than the entire boxing world. There was an outcry in the press. "What does he think he's doing?" *L'auto* asked, indignant, after having praised Cocteau to the skies. But Brown wouldn't bend under pressure. He retired after squandering a million dollars, giving way to the next rising star, Marcel Cerdan, and was hired by the Médrano circus, thanks to Cocteau. Three days after quitting, Brown was jumping rope again to the sound of a trumpet, in the midst of tigers, seals, and clowns, tap dancing to swing music and boxing with his own shadow—in a performance of the training he so loathed.[112]

His mission accomplished, Cocteau grew distant. He was happy to have proved that his "protégés" didn't always end up in the hospital or the morgue, and that he himself, if not a living god as he had once believed, was not, for all that, the devil.

THE RESURRECTION

Every second, a living person is in the midst of disappearing.
"Creativity" gives the impression of reversing the process:
one feels oneself in the midst of appearing.
—*Claude Roy*, Somme toute

GALAHAD THE PURE

Panama Al Brown had barely crossed Cocteau's path when a young actor with a charming awkwardness, auditioning for a production of *Oedipe roi* that Cocteau was planning, caught Cocteau's eye. Tall, athletic, and friendly, Jean-Alfred Villain-Marais had until that point only been an extra in some of the films of Marcel L'Herbier, who was more attracted by his sexual power than his acting technique. But Cocteau chose him right away for the role of Oedipus, to the near-unanimous dismay of the other students, who were cast in the chorus. The novice, who called himself simply Marais, confessed with a charming directness that there was nothing accidental about their meeting: he was in fact studying acting with Charles Dullin, and had deliberately insinuated himself into the audition.[1] Four years earlier, Cocteau's name had been totally unknown to him, but having discovered, in the studio of a friend who worked at the Renault factory, how much he resembled the posters of masculine profiles hung on the walls, he became interested in this mysterious artist-writer whose name was whispered to him by the gay factory worker in Issy-les-Moulineaux. Marais picked up *Les enfants terribles*, then went to see *La machine infernale*, before crashing the audition.

With his demands for a deliberately jerky, outrageously unnatural diction, an attempt to create an atmosphere that would be worthy of the Greeks, Cocteau the author-director exhausted everybody during rehearsals, with the exception of his star beginner. The more they worked together, the more young Marais sustained his attention; a blend of cunning and unrealism, cruel resolution and sunny cheerfulness emanated from this gesticulating man-child. Lively, clumsy, and affectionate, at twenty-three years old Marais had something infantlike about him. The strips of cloth that Cocteau had devised to wrap his naked body underscored his instinctive sensuality; he was truly the incarnation of those fauns with sensuous lips and straight ears that Cocteau had drawn since the days of Nijinsky—a Greek animal straight out of *La machine infernale*, as well as Nijinsky's *Après-midi*.

Cocteau's work had attracted Radiguet and Desbordes to him; this latest chosen one seemed to have surged forth from within it, as if a living, joyful, desiring body had emerged from the Canson notebooks he drew in. "I didn't meet him, I recognized him," he would say. Had he not written six years earlier, in a poem dedicated to Natalie Paley, "Theatrical, as with his elbow he holds up his wild / Drapery, Apollo, buckled with gold, from the side. / Like a horse rearing up: his mouth, / And eye, dark sun, shining from its lashes"—and was this not the spitting image of Marais?[2] After only a few days he asked Marais, "as if he were speaking to the biggest star," whether he would agree to play the role of Galahad the Pure in the play he was planning to direct. Though unaware of even the legend of the Knights of the Round Table, Marais immediately said yes. Cocteau saw Marais's eager agreement as a sign that he was someone who said yes to life, whatever form that might take, whatever cost it might exact. Young Marais was invited to the Hôtel de Castille, where he saw Marcel Khill and Panama Al Brown slip into a neighboring room and Cocteau stretch out in a dressing gown full of holes to read aloud the first act of *Les chevaliers de la table ronde*, a bamboo pipe in his hand. The smoke that stank up the place did not prevent Marais from finding his role marvelous. He skipped home, sure that he would finally be discovered. He had always believed in his lucky star.[3]

He was given a second reading, this time privately. Cocteau warned him that he would have to audition in front of the theater's director, and then added, casually, "I should warn you that if you accept this role, everyone will say you are my boyfriend." "I would be very proud," replied Marais. The preview for *Oedipe roi*, at the Théâtre Antoine, was dramatic. Having come to see the costumes Chanel had designed, that society audience (described by Gide as "surélégant," or "overly elegant") was astonished to discover, that day in July 1937, Tiresias with his hair styled like Harpo Marx, women wearing Phrygian caps, and this young actor, naked beneath the gauze of a severely burned man, already handicapped by his frail voice and his strident way of acting, who either walked in a straight line or suddenly veered sideways. Marais was so scandalously presented, and so weak playing opposite the beautiful Iya Abdy as Jocasta, that the audience began to laugh, and then to boo. Cringing inwardly, the young actor stared down those who were whistling in the front rows, almost close enough to touch. Hiding behind the curtains, where he was beating a drum to set a rhythm for the play, Cocteau admired the way Marais stood up to such "ignorant idiocy." "Flames emanated from him and . . . he managed to overcome their stupid tittering," he said. The next day, *Vogue* and *Harper's Bazaar* sent photographers: Marais's image first crossed the Atlantic in a mummy costume.[4]

Even more than his courage, it was Marais's ability to calm the cast's jealousy that touched Cocteau. If an actor was saying bad things about him, Marais went to see his rival with a disconcerting amiability, and was able to put those accusations to bed. Thus did he acquire a reputation for kindness that would never leave him. Once the performances were finished, the cast dispersed and Cocteau vanished as quickly as he had arrived in Marais's life. Meanwhile, they were calling Marais the "worst actor in France." A few weeks later, he received a phone call. "Come right away, something catastrophic has happened!" Afraid of having lost the role of Galahad in *Les chevaliers*, Marais hurried to the Hôtel de Castille, where Cocteau confessed to him, in his dressing gown: "I am in love with you." "I am in love with you, too," replied Marais.

The young actor pulled off the lie with the radiant enthusiasm he brought to all his roles, even those he shouldn't have taken on. Marais was not discouraged by Cocteau's pitiful state, nor by his repeated wish to be finished with life, quickly belied by the certainty that Marais alone could save him. In the dark, he would join Cocteau's long, scrawny body, its neck strangled with a scarf and its cricket-like legs, and follow him, at the end of August, to the villa in Pramousquier where the writer and Radiguet had spent the summer of 1922. Thus did the unscrupulous social climber—a stranger to principle as well as to guilt, as he himself would later admit—become the companion of the living corpse. He rescued him, in what was almost a resurrection: if Cocteau was like the knights of his play, condemned to spend days without light and a sky without birds in the midst of a drunken court, Marais resembled Lancelot demanding "a true happiness, a true love, a true *château*." Having lived for so long in hell, the artificial paradises began to dissipate; emerging from his perpetual twilight, the writer again saw the sun when it rose and the moon when it set; he had the childlike feeling of being reborn into a new world, washed clean, of starting all over in a much younger body. Life was beginning to fill with new colors, after the black and white of the smoke.[5]

Born in December 1913 in Cherbourg, raised without a father by a voracious woman whose maternal fervor outstripped even that of Mme Cocteau, Marais had nearly always had his desires attended to. Nothing was too beautiful or too expensive for Rosalie Villain when it came to the son whom she adored. She demanded the red carpet be laid out for them anywhere she went, name-dropping a certain "uncle" who organized the president's travels, a strategy that sometimes allowed them access to the head of state's train. She never paid for a ticket on public transportation, and was wont to refuse to justify herself to a ticket inspector on the pretext that he was not wearing the required white gloves. Likewise, she had been known to strike a police officer who had dared attempt to prevent them from parking in front of the store where she had come to buy confetti in bulk. It is clear to see, then, how the young Villain-Marais had come to believe she was all-powerful. She was capable of dressing up as a burglar to amuse her friends, but also of faking the death of her nephew, a vial of poison at the ready, just for the pleasure of scaring her sister. She would, on occasion, abandon her children to head down to Paris (by train, of course) and return weighed down with enchanting gifts for them, but also with jewels from Cartier, Chaumet, and Van Cleef. To keep up with his older brother, who showered his girlfriends with gifts from the maternal coffers, the young Villain-Marais learned as well to lie and to steal from his aunt's purse, to rise above his fear and deny all authority, "a little monster with the face of an angel," he would say. His mother's disappearances sometimes lasted, with no explanation, for months on end, or he would suddenly have to change towns, houses, and schools—and sometimes even his last name. His "uncle" would take him to the cinema and tell him, when he was worried about his mother, that her job as a fur broker had taken her to the South.[6]

Time passed. The boy wrote to his beloved mother, but, not knowing where to send the envelope, imagined that she had already returned to heaven among the benevolent deities. She finally returned, resumed her "good" habits, and made it rain presents all over again. If men in uniform knocked at their door, she dressed as a servant, wearing a wig and a false nose, and went out as if she were going to do the shopping. Her creative son would await her return by making his own costumes in the attic, dressing as a girl to go to the butcher, or parading himself provocatively, wearing a dress, in front of a gym teacher who had looked after him but whom he hated—surprisingly, Marais was not at all athletic, though he was widely desired. One of his "uncles," one of his mother's lovers, sexually abused him in a hotel room. All he knew of his father was that his mother had kicked him out soon after the birth of their children, but he didn't know if he was still alive. Only his beloved mother, Rosalie, counted, no matter what. He alone had the power to make her happy, and just as he saw her as a kind of goddess who occasionally descended to earth, he began to see himself as a demi-god who amused himself by dressing as the child of a human.

After his haphazard education, the young Villain-Marais became a kind of private detective for a professional photographer. A news report on the Saint-Lazare prison informed him that the kleptomaniac whom they had locked up and tried to keep from him was in fact his mother. Arrested again shortly after she had been freed, Mme Villain-Marais swallowed needles so that when she was hospitalized she might send word to her son, who then broke into her room to help her escape in a taxi. Afterward, Rosalie, upon seeing her son set his heart on becoming an actor, a career that she did not believe to be serious, lost no time in involving him in her juicy escapades, like telling him to ask the sales assistants at Révillon questions while she wrapped sables around her waist in the fitting rooms, so that she looked pregnant. Marais thus had crazy stories to tell, so crazy they seemed tailor-made for Cocteau, who immediately believed them all. Marais had admitted to having spent his childhood making up stories, but they all seemed true to Cocteau—and so they were. This atmosphere of lies and fraud was so exciting, "Jeannot" was so dashing and his mother so creative, that Cocteau felt as if he were reading a mother-and-son version of *Les enfants terribles*.

In time, the haze of pathological lying in which Rosalie Villain lived affected Cocteau as well; forgetting that Marais was half his age, he fell completely in love with the actor, who, when he was five years old, had professed a great passion for Pearl White, the actress who scaled skyscrapers and had served as Cocteau's model for the young American woman in *Parade*. For once Cocteau had met a boy who actively wanted the best for him, as well as for himself. For his part, Marais, convinced he was Cocteau's good-luck charm, secretly hoped to help the writer to live the kind of sunny, carefree life he did. Cocteau was certainly open to it! Neither destructive nor a dilettante, Marais wanted to succeed, not simply to live; to act, and not only to be flattered. Aware of the influence he was gaining, he turned down the pipes the writer offered him, in spite of how fascinating he found the opium ritual. "Posing you is my only desire / I want to become your portrait," Cocteau told him, in a poem describing the drawings he was making of him.

Waking up with Jeannot was like a miracle to Cocteau, who felt as if he were drinking milk fresh from the farm, after years of tobacco consumption.

I slept one hundred years. Then came Prince Charming
He was gay, innocent, infallible, energetic,

But he awakened me from this magic slumber
I could not say how.[7]

The joy of feeling his body return to life in order to plunge once again into
the smells and sounds, the sweat and the cries, that belong to nights of love,
turned to euphoria. The ghost with the fragile arms had turned back into a
young, fresh organism, supple and ardent, endowed with vigorous organs and
the most beautiful face in existence. Rhymes came spontaneously to mind,
echoing the alexandrines of his happy childhood; he had never written such
inspired erotic poetry; he had never been so lyric in his love, or so touching on
paper:

Traveling the world was a pathetic jaunt
Compared to the journey I make with you
Every day I love you better and more
Wherever you live is my home.[8]

Gone were the mirrors through which Death slipped to take its prey;
banished were the gods so prone to blind their victims. Nothing remained but
their interlaced bodies, the "love pollen" they spat, and Jeannot's arms "of salt,
of honey, of pepper and amber."

Oh! I would like to run the risk
Of expressing these lines
Around your obelisk
At the center of our universe.[9]

He who had always dreamed of having the physical proof that he was loved,
who still thought of strength as an extreme homage, rediscovered the pleasure
of living, singing—almost braying.

When the artist sculpts my statue
He kills a bit of my death.
But when you . . . mold me, you create me
You do an unknown work
Knight, may your blond thighs
Tame the thin nude thoroughbred![10]

Marais's vigor made Cocteau feel as if he were as young as the actor. At the
theater, he would tenderly lay his head on Marais's shoulder, with the dreamy
gaze of a young girl in love; in the street, he would lengthen his strides to keep
up with Marais's athletic stride; when a friend photographed them holding

hands in front of a forest, Marais wearing a young sportsman's sweater and Cocteau in a tie like a child receiving his First Communion, he was the first to think that he looked like a schoolchild. All the looks of admiration (and even jealousy) he received while out with the young actor had a euphoric power. Life is so beautiful when you're in love!

One sign didn't lie: the ball of ambergris that Daisy Fellowes, the belle of all the Parisian balls, had given him was sparkling brilliantly, after having remained mostly dry over the previous few years.

BIRTH OF A DEMI-GOD

Pygmalion took it into his head to bring the young man to the theater and then to museums, in order to fill in the gaps in what the actor himself called his "crass illiteracy." As honest as gold, as moody as watered silk, Marais read Cocteau's poems—though Cocteau forbade him to look at the first three collections—and was prescribed a long list of books, from Dostoevsky to Stendhal, even Radiguet. Marais took on Cocteau's beliefs and superstitions, and soaked in his universe—as Cocteau himself put it, like those "insects who know how to disguise themselves as leaves." If Cocteau was fascinated by the iron red glove above a glovemaker's shop in Toulon, Marais climbed the house with his bare hands and took it down for him. At the same time, Cocteau helped Marais to channel the energy that had made people call the young actor "crazy" during his first audition, as if to forget the memory of the first roles that L'Herbier (who had secretly been in love with Marais) had lured him with years ago, in the hope of attracting Marais to his bed. But Cocteau did all of this tactfully, without ever seeming to want to change Marais. When, much later, a newspaper came to interview Marais, he was heard to say, parenthetically (since of course Cocteau rewrote all of his answers): "Jean Cocteau never told me how to say a line . . . or told me to make any gesture . . . His method is different. Living, speaking, seeing beautiful things together."[11]

Marais did more than just adapt. He learned to give advice to those whom the Thomassins called Cocteau's "all-purpose helpers." If one of his suppliers announced that he had had a child, Marais went with Cocteau and the Thomassins to break into the maternity ward crying, "Well fancy that, we're fathers!"—anything Cocteau liked. Goodness, creativity, humor, common sense, morality, erotic and culinary knowhow: Cocteau soon saw Marais as a paragon of all the virtues, like Galahad in the play he worked on daily. Fate had brought him a boy worthy in every way of the knight who had fought Merlin the wizard, detoxing in his castle, letting sunlight return and bringing the birds back to life, before heading off on new adventures—for "wherever love reigns, he may not remain." Cocteau was astonished by the coincidence, and came to identify their sexual particularity with a knightly order invested in demonstrating its excellence to the world. Marais would be the *preux chevalier*, and the Round Table the occasional table he had begun to consult once again to catch a glimpse of the future. Did he recall that thirty years earlier his uncle had been connected with a group of young members of the court of Kaiser Wilhem II—a group that the German press had denounced as a Byzantine clan whose ways were "against nature," or even a secret knighthood imbued with the spiritualism, which the press had called "the Round Table"? It worked the same way.[12]

Sometimes Marais protested; he was not the archangel Cocteau boasted about everywhere he went, but a calculating, dim-witted young man, capable of great unkindness. Cocteau told him he was wrong, and began again to campaign in his favor. He would never express the slightest concern about his latest envoy from heaven, whom he thought was beyond all human elements, built like a stag but with the spirit of the divine. The machine for making gods and angels was at work again. But at times, when Marais was less ardent, or less present, Cocteau's doubts would return.

> You love me. Is this God even possible?
> If I could have been a mirror!
> A thin David in black bronze
> I'll give you my sling-shot, I'll be your target.[13]

He remembered then that he was nearly fifty years old and that no one, in the state to which the opium had reduced him, could spontaneously desire him. He was thus all the more grateful to Marais for preferring him to the dazzling boys who offered themselves to Marais every day.

Jouvet had commissioned *Les chevaliers de la table ronde*, but he was critical of the play when he read it. "He was troubled by this being who doesn't exist and who is embodied in several different characters," Cocteau would say, describing Ginifer, Merlin's magical valet, who transforms himself into Galahad, Gawain, and the queen. Given Jouvet's reluctance, Cocteau took his play to the Théâtre de l'Oeuvre, where he would serve as director and designer. The opening on October 14, 1937, was received coldly; for an audience accustomed to subjects out of Greek mythology, this sudden departure for the Middle Ages and its imagery was disconcerting. Marais was described as "Radiantly beautiful in his gold and white armor" (Chanel's costumes broke out of their usual sobriety) and for the first time played important roles, both Galahad the Pure (called "Blancharmure," or "White Armor") and the false Galahad. But though his entrance to a Purcell trumpet fanfare was impressive, his acting was unconvincing. "He is handsome, that is all," concluded one critic. The actor, who did not like his own appearance, concluded that he was worthless.[14]

Probably Colette wrote the most enthusiastically about the play. Knowing that words like "enchantment" and "fairy" would not move a naturally skeptical audience, she wrote:

> I am not trying to convert to Cocteau's brand of theater those audience members who seek imitations of reality and an echo of their own passions. But for those who go [to the theater] to sit before illusions, docilely offering their necks to the magic ribbon, who enjoy giving in to magic charms, and gaining access to misleading dimensions, and the subconscious which tirelessly blends dream and reality, I can think of no work that will please them more than *The Knights of the Round Table*.[15]

The author of *Chéri* didn't stop with this praise; to better "popularize" an author who came off as obscure and difficult, she added these lines, which seem premonitory when we think of the aesthetic that reigned under the Occupation:

> The place Cocteau occupies in literature straddles two centuries (the nineteenth century only truly ended in 1914). Definitions of the man of letters and of the poet break down when applied to him, are shown to be too narrow, like the barks of certain species of early blooming trees. His curiosity and his influence extend to all artistic domains; he senses, often determines, the fashion in all his fields—no field escapes fashion . . . it is a certain kind of artisan who is able to make your armchair resemble your grandmother, and the piano a toad with a dislocated shoulder.[16]

With fewer than twenty people in the audience by the end of its run, for the hundredth performance, the play closed in late 1937, confirming for Cocteau that his name no longer guaranteed financial success. Someone close to him said his career was crumbling, that an air of snobbery clung to him. But this time Cocteau would not let himself be beaten. Marais requested a new role to play—a modern, exaggerated one in which he could laugh and cry but not be handsome, and Cocteau leapt at the chance. He left for Montargis to draft a new play, deeply inspired by the monstrous relationship between Marais and his mother, who lashed out in jealousy at anyone who dared to approach her son.

Marais's enthusiasm for the draft reassured Cocteau of his dramatic powers. After a period of despondence, Cocteau finished *Les parents terribles* in eight days. A sad little "angel" accompanied them in their walks along the canals formed by the Loing. Attracted by Marais's "golden lightness," and flattered by Cocteau's invitation, Roger Lannes regarded this superb, happy, liberated couple with paralyzing admiration. An amphigoric, knotty poet, Lannes would have given anything to have been a young athlete of Antiquity, covered with blood and dust, hailed by entire stadiums; as it was, he had to content himself with silently applauding this young Greek, whose beauty tortured him, and his generous protector. He was fascinated by Cocteau's inexhaustible productivity— he was capable of writing at the edge of the abyss—but more than anything he was impressed by Cocteau's romantic life, by the avalanche of gifted young men, built like gods, who had accompanied him all his life. Lannes could not stop contemplating Marais's perfection, "an unheard-of blend of virginity and sensual violence."[17] When Max Jacob came to visit Cocteau, surprising them in bed naked under their light dressing-gowns, Marais ran a hand through his unruly hair before kissing the poet, but he did not abuse his power. Marais, "handsome to the point of madness . . . sweet as a cat, like a fearful child, a sacred monster," tortured the young Lannes, who was struck with impotence.

In the spring of 1938, the couple moved to a small apartment at 9 place de la Madeleine. Marais went to the Tuileries gardens to steal the iron chairs; the blankets, the sheets, and the pillows were donated by the actresses whom Cocteau planned to cast in *Les parents terribles*. Atop a column of white plaster they placed a rusty rooster found at the flea market; the iron red glove hung from the wall that looked out on the impressive columns of the church of the Madeleine, whose environs Cocteau had barely left for forty years. A sailor's trunk served as a night table. On the unmade bed lay the Japanese fur-lined jacket that Cocteau wore when he read the palms of whoever sought his chiro- mancer's powers—sometimes he read three palms at once. It was the first time that Marais had slept so far from his mother—she would only forgive Cocteau much later—as well as the first time that the writer had lived with a man who was publicly homosexual, if not exclusively so. Paradoxically Cocteau suffered from their union; he had the recurrent confirmation that if Marais struggled to give him what he demanded at night, it was because, from then on, he was saving his "blond strength" for others.

> When we make love
> between heaven and hell
> I think it must be like
> Gold penetrating iron
> Hard gold, soft gold, alas . . . what do I know?
> It's cold, it's hot, it's snow.[18]

Marais wanted to take endless advantage of his luck and exert his lust for life on new bodies. But it hurt Cocteau to see him go out to meet friends some evenings; he would have liked to be able to fly, to follow him everywhere and protect him from bad influences. Cocteau was a regretful guardian angel, and he mentally hounded Marais, but nothing could restrain the young man's swaggering sexuality. Many took advantage of it (Marcel Khill first), and many fell in love with him as well. The others shared the fantasies of Horst P. Horst and Raymond Voinquel, the photographers who shot him nude framed by an oeil-de-boeuf, like an annunciating angel of pleasure.

Cocteau wanted to forbid Marais any sexual life outside of their own, but instead tried, more subtly, to destroy the actor's new relationships by putting down his newly chosen companion. "You betray me with opium," the actor retorted. No longer able to bear the dinners that Marais would inflict on him, with exes or future lovers, Cocteau would make scenes. "You only love drama and crises," Marais reproached him, slowly beginning to desert his bed. The writer suffered from this quarantine, which was as painful as a detoxification cure. His hypersensitivity put him in constant contact with Marais, and therefore with his flings. He kept track of their telegrams and tried to listen in on their phone calls like a "poor autumn stag" listening for his rivals' bellows.

They can give you their hard, robust bodies
Cruel, joyful, secret meetings . . .
Can they give you a palace of your own busts?[19]

Aware that his main qualities were his fame and his talent—"My happiness builds a temple / To your young antiquity" he once wrote to Marais—Cocteau developed the habit, during nights on his own, of writing poems or notes to Marais, slipping them under his door, then waiting, eyes wide open, for him to return. When he finally heard the key turn in the door, and Marais enter his room, Cocteau would hold his breath and try to guess, through the wall, what his companion might be thinking. "Sleep. It is sweet, Jeannot, to keep watch like that / And to let my blood flow under your door." The situation was a familiar one: a lover with passionate affairs, whom Cocteau managed to enjoy nevertheless by slipping into his dreams . . . and who was growing under his very eyes, the further away he got. Was it not better to be cheated on with many unimportant men, than to have a woman as his rival, as he had with Radiguet and Desbordes?[20]

An incredible flow of love songs issued forth, in hexameter and alexandrines.

Will we ever find more passionate letters?
Ink like sperm, and as quick to depart?[21]

But Marais went out so often that these very quatrains lost some of their impact.

This morning I hid the songs I offer you
They were yellow and strewn across the lid of the chest.
Is my angel becoming used to my verse?
Habit kills something inside of us.[22]

Scarcely had Marais folded up one poem telling him of these restrictions than he found another.

I say: you will only have one poem
And here I have slipped you another
One to tell you "I love you,"
The other: "I am your lover."[23]

The more Cocteau wrote, the more he seemed to be the only one nourishing the love that occupied all of his energy. Having returned to the bachelor pad he kept in Paris, Marais no longer put his arms around him except in front of the photographers, and would sometimes stay to lunch with him but then leave in search of other conquests. The pure knight was turning into love's executioner. But Cocteau was everywhere he went, and nothing could separate these twins united in the air.

My heart finds an answer to the eternal problem
You are me—I am you—we are us—they are them.[24]

JUSTICE, FINALLY

In July 1938, Cocteau brought Marais to Toulon, along with the ever-faithful Biou. The active, maternal decorator Coula Roppa, "an ardent follower of the cult of Lesbos," according to a police report, hosted them in her apartment, at 4 impasse du Quai-du-Parti.[25] Cocteau immediately took out the Berger lamp that had allowed him to cook his opium in the sleeping car of their overnight train while stifling the smell, then blocked all the doors with wet towels. The "trip" would last several days until, at dawn on July 28, six police agents broke into the smoke-filled apartment to confiscate the drugs, apologizing for doing their duty. Marais, who did not smoke, and Biou (whose real name was Nguyen Ngoc Hien, identified as a "subject from Tonkin") were charged, along with the Greek decorator (whose real name was Wassiliki Rompapa), with possession of narcotics. The prefecture's investigation, which had begun three months earlier with an interrogation of Marcel Khill, was a success.

No legal body had to that point felt the need to denounce the ravaging effect the drug had on Cocteau; he had taken care of that himself, in *Opium*. But this time neither his fame nor his "protectors" could prevent the press from fanning the flames of scandal. (His fame did carry some weight, however—every drug dealer arrested declared himself to be Cocteau's supplier, in hope of leniency.) Back in Paris, and fearing another raid, Cocteau hid his opium-related paraphernalia at his mother's and rented a maid's room where he could go to smoke. Having spent time in a correctional facility in Toulon, and threatened with prison (Coula Roppa had fully informed on him), Cocteau arrived demoralized at the trial seven months later. His physical condition was the prosecution's greatest weapon, as he was well aware. But the judges were perfectly courteous. In fact, the state prosecutor was very complimentary, and even said that Cocteau's presence was an honor to the city, and his repentance a comfort to justice. His lawyer declined to make arguments, in order to allow the judges the privilege of clemency. Their verdict was a fine of a thousand francs.[26] "It was marvelous," said Cocteau, who was used to much harsher "trials" at the hands of his enemies.[27] Meanwhile, *Les parents terribles* was a smashing success.

A man had followed the entire trial, supporting Cocteau with his very presence, sure that he would not bother him from such a distance. It was Franz Thomassin, emaciated and dressed as if he had been sleeping rough. He who had been so lavish with Cocteau was now dying of hunger. Cocteau was very moved to see him, and slipped five hundred francs into his injured hands, only to receive a basket of roses the next day that must have cost twice that.[28] Thomassin's love had never flagged. For years, the awestruck crusader had continued to write to Cocteau, calling him "Sir Jean the magnificent and formidable," struck by a passion that fed on itself, even more than Cocteau's for Marais.[29] "So much love gets lost in the world," Maritain had written in his *Réponse*.

Encouraged by Jouvet's initial response to his plot summary ("Admirable, it's ready-made!"), Cocteau had meanwhile been busy staging *Les parents terribles*. Though the title echoed that of his 1920s novel, *Les enfants terribles*, the new play's tone was very different. In the hope of giving Marais as well as himself a real success, he borrowed from the boulevardier tradition. He produced a text that was meant to be acted rather than read, filled with poisonings against a background of incest and thunderbolts. The aim, however, was the same as the earlier work: to reproduce that shut-in, hothouse sort of life that condemned its characters to the kind of psychodrama that he himself lived, from room to room. Just as weak as Monsieur Cocteau, the father of Michel, his hero, was also named Georges. He named his heroine (with whom both men are in love, though unaware of it) after Madeleine Carlier. And the role of the mother was inspired by Marais's mother, Rosalie Villain, and more distantly by Mme Cocteau and Mme Desbordes. Cocteau's ambition was to produce "material for great actors" capable of carrying on the legend of Édouard de Max or Sarah Bernhardt, in a play intended, this time, to reach a wide public and all the generations to come.

It was, however, very difficult to stage. This return to the boulevardier tradition, just as the Cartel's critical, detached direction prevailed, perplexed Jouvet when he read it; Marais's relative inexperience worried him as well. After Cocteau the Dadaist, the neo-Greek, the neomedieval, he was offering to the public "the Rolls Royce of families." "As my Aunt Léo says, let me contradict myself, it's my own confusion, my own luxury," he replied, but the theater directors fell into line behind Jouvet's refusal: "It won't bring in a *sou*." (Jouvet's mistress, Madeleine Ozeray, also did not like the character of Madeleine.) Cocteau was in serious financial difficulty, and nearly had a breakdown, threatening to burn his manuscript and for the first time seriously threatening suicide—telling Marais in passing that that was how his father had died. "I have never seen Jean so destroyed," noted Roger Lannes. "His eyes are dead." Marais ran to Chanel in the middle of the night, but the patron of the rue Cambon, tired of bailing out the writer, was unmoved by these threats of suicide. Cocteau, in tears, responded by tearing up all his photographs of the designer.[30]

The play was meant to be like a boxing match, he said, and it had gone against him. It should have been his comeback, after that of Panama Al Brown, but instead it had wounded him to death. After months of scheming and resubmitting, the play was finally accepted by the Théâtre des Ambassadeurs, whose director was Roger Capgras. The play would be directed by the actress playing Madeleine, Alice Cocéa, who was also Capgras's mistress. Basically, Cocteau took care of everything, as usual. There was great empathy in his love for the actors who shed blood for him every night on stage, only to be reborn the next day. That is no doubt how he found the strength to support the magnificent Yvonne de Bray, who had been the wife and muse of Henry Bataille, the playwright, but who arrived dead drunk at rehearsals and drank everything in sight, including the perfume in bottles. Yvonne de Bray was more than an actress; she was an organic entity, physically monstrous, but warm and affecting to such a point that Marais lost all shyness with her and managed to surpass himself. Her passion for Marais was so intense that the real Mme Marais felt she had to get involved: she could not bear anyone else playing her role, and she showered Yvonne de Bray with insults, as she did with Cocteau. Marais and de Bray grew so close that they even looked like each other onstage. One sleepless night was enough for Marais to develop bags under his eyes that matched the actress's, so swollen from drink that they looked like mosquito bites. Eventually the stumbling de Bray was replaced by Germaine Dermoz. A few weeks later, Marais collapsed in tears: his own mother had just been sent back to prison.

The dress rehearsal took place November 14, 1938, at the Théâtre des Ambassadeurs, with Khill, Desbordes, and Maritain in the audience; the premiere the next evening would draw Picasso and Stravinsky. To attract audience members' attention to the Oedipal drama and the mother's suicide, Cocteau kept his decor very pure, cut phone calls and servants, and ordered his actors not to smoke. The actors he treated like fighters in a ring, hoping to draw crowds. The price of the seats, however, drew a much less democratic crowd than Panama Al Brown. "All the bourgeoisie down to the most reactionary among them went to see *Les parents terribles*," wrote Sachs in *Au temps du Boeuf sur le Toit*; "at one time these parents, whose children admired Cocteau, threatened to disown them, but today they buy tickets. It's not that the parents have advanced, but rather that Cocteau has reversed towards them." It was a triumph. The audience shed its bourgeois reserve, laughing and crying at the same time. They witnessed onstage their family story, amplified and unbridled, with its tragedies, its jealousies, and its secrets, presented brilliantly by one of their own sons: the prodigal son returned to the fold.

For the first time, Cocteau was interested in the real life of millions of his countrymen, and they were grateful that he had "descended" to their level. From everywhere he received ecstatic letters of praise, requests for interviews, and free seats. The voluptuous Kiki de Montparnasse confessed that she had "bawled like a Mary Magdalene."[31] Franz Thomassin compared Cocteau to the great classic dramatists, proclaiming him the equal of Sophocles or Shakespeare. "*Les parents terribles* irrefutably earns Jean Cocteau his place in the highest ranks of French writers," wrote Aragon in *Ce soir*. Cocteau, once an underread poet, had become a popular dramatist at the age of (almost) fifty.[32] Gabrielle Dorziat won rave reviews as Tante Léo, but Marais also made a comeback as the ideal *enfant terrible* who was no longer a figure of conflict, like his novelistic brothers, but trapped by his filial passion. Remembering Coco Chanel's snub of Cocteau, Marais turned his back on her when she came to his dressing room, thereby earning her lifelong admiration—she only liked hard-headed people.

In the *Nouvelle revue française* on January 1, 1939, Paul Léautaud expressed some reserve, on behalf of a more literary audience, toward this "bourgeois tragedy." "It's skillfully constructed, which is precisely why it lacks interest. It's too perfect. It's too *finished*. His characters say too much, explain themselves too much, to the point of repeating themselves. There's no room for the audience."

In painting another portrait of a mother's weakness for her son, and the latent, murderous desire that accompanies it, Cocteau had made his popular debut into a deeply personal affair, at once sincere and contrived, deft and well-paced. Cocteau would eventually direct the film adaptation, ten years later, which would feature brilliantly in one allegorical shot—a shot highly praised by André Bazin, the famous film critic—the son's mouth and the mother's eyes. A polemic arose in the extreme right-wing press; Brasillach saw the play as a disgusting apology for incest, applauded by a "rich, rotting bourgeoisie come to applaud its own decay," as outrageous as the postwar Berlin audience. The author of *Les sept couleurs* even referred to the play as profane, adding that "if the word *garbage* means anything, it must be applied without hesitation to this author and this work."[33] The rest of the reviews were so glowing, however, that the "fire" didn't take.

The play was booked for weeks in advance, and made a million francs in four days. All of Paris ran to see *Les parents terribles*. At the end of the year, with Cocteau's encouragement, the director of the theater made matinees free for local students. This time, the invitation "to debauchery" provoked an outcry— *L'officiel* had already referred to the play as "demoralizing old age." The Ambassadeurs was in part publicly run, and the Parisian municipal authorities forced it to close the play, under hidden pressure from Henry Bernstein, who was jealous of the success happening on his turf. Cocteau, supported by Aragon, Kessel, the Communist press, and *Ce soir*, strongly censured the town councilors, who were behaving as if incest were actually committed onstage—an ignoble thing, he said, while noting that there is nevertheless "always incest between a mother and a son who adore each other, a mental incest."[34] It was true that in the first act, Yvonne's sister Léo (who is also in love with Georges) accuses her sister of "cheating" on her husband with her son, but this is merely suggested.[35] How to make these councilors in love with bawdy jokes (whom he called "collectors of obscene postcards") understand this distinction? "I have had enough of your ceaselessly throwing this parricide and incest in my face. I am innocent," he had already written in *Oedipe roi*, adapted from Sophocles. Cocteau wrote in vain to the prefect of police and even the president—he had even risked going to jail, six months earlier—and the scandal allowed Bernstein to take back the Ambassadeurs, which he had been coveting. But it was the intervention of Jean Zay, the minister of education despised by the far Right, who would save *Les parents terribles*. The play was transferred to the Bouffes-Parisiens, where Albert Willemetz, a friend of Sacha Guitry, welcomed it.

There was a second opening, which ended in another triumph, though a part of the audience this time was expecting an obscene play. Addressing the audience during the first intermission, Cocteau did not need to justify himself: the room was already won over. During the second intermission, a young British man and a very young, very hairy American slipped backstage asking to meet Jean Marais. The British fellow was a languid poet whom Roger Lannes had already met; the American was a handsome and limping nineteen-year-old wearing sky-blue pajamas and a fur-lined overcoat, drinking a bottle of brandy, two glasses in one hand and a silver box full of Chesterfields in the other. Visibly drunk, the young man demanded the box he had reserved by telephone, but his entrance in the theater made such a scandal that he cried, "Please, I want to see M. Cocteau!" He was brought to Marais's dressing room, where Cocteau sorted things out elegantly—"But of course," he said, "the play was written to be viewed in pajamas!"—while Roger Lannes took them to a screened-in box. When the curtain fell, Cocteau took the two intruders in Marais's Lincoln to the rue du Bac, where they had had to flee some friends who had stolen their clothing, according to Lannes. The young poet, David Gascoyne, would later say that it was on a whim that Denham Fouts had charged into the theater that night, wounded in the foot and furious that Marais had failed to come see him that afternoon, as he had promised.[36]

The play's success brought Cocteau and Marais closer together, and the actor went back to their conjugal apartment. When, in 1939, Marais came down with a double ear infection, Cocteau's own ears hurt so badly that he struck his head against the walls. Terrified that fate might act against the actor as it once had Radiguet, Cocteau refused to leave their apartment. Because of episodes like these Rosalie Villain finally learned to respect him—Cocteau was suffering like a mother—more than a lover—true suffering, down in his gut.

The handsome American from the theater, Denham Fouts, visited Marais, and when he left, kissed him "in the Russian style." Marais became infatuated with this disarming young dandy, a former packager in a General Foods warehouse who had his sights set on a horizontal sort of career, like Cléo de Mérode if Glenway Wescott is to be believed.[37] He was "a lavish, spoiled young man," said David Gascoyne, "gifted with a fragile and reasonably polished charm," and capable of pretending to shoot himself after a friend reproached him for belonging to a Nazi Youth group during his time in Germany. The quintessential *enfant terrible*, but without the depth and loyalty of the role, Fouts was a unique character who later inspired Truman Capote, Gore Vidal, and Christopher Isherwood—not so bad for a gigolo.

Cocteau tried not to become jealous, but he was overwhelmed. He suffered like a martyr on discovering Marais's bedroom empty in the middle of the night. It was an affront not only to their love, but also to the spirit of the Round Table;

it was like cutting the eagle with two heads in half. "You go out [with] a little group of society cheats, kept men, unworthy of you; your presence lifts them up even as it debases you," Cocteau wrote to him one day. "D.'s conversation isn't your style, nor is his taste or his lifestyle. You think him a prince charming, but ... he's just a poor kid, uncomfortable in his place in the world and lazy in the face of destiny."[38] Seeing Marais being overprotective of this heroin addict who thought himself Dorian Gray but didn't know anything about Oscar Wilde, Cocteau was afraid he was reliving that terrible time when Radiguet went about Paris on Bronja's arm. He thought of putting to good use the freedom that Marais was clearly granting him, but he was unable to enjoy the men and women who still wanted him "violently." As he confessed to Marais: "the idea of touching anyone other than you, addressing tender words to them, repulses me." He wasn't jealous of Denham Fouts in the strict sense of the term; instead he physically suffered every minute that Marais spent with him. Imagining him so close to another body was infinitely torturous.

> You must fuck me and bite me
> Replace and take back your ring
> And sometimes tie (around my neck) the order (of the golden fleece)
> from which a lamb's cadaver hangs.[39]

By spending his nights listening behind walls, he began to resemble the bloody nightingale that he had described during the First World War, the one who sang "the whole night stuck to the rose that pierces his heart."[40] Deprived of the thing that kept him alive, Cocteau suffered, as he had during his detox.

THE RETURN OF THE MONSTER

Two months before the opening of *Les parents terribles*, "no longer able to listen to the drums beat at Nuremberg," Cocteau left Paris for Dax, where he hoped to return for the first time in years to writing poetry, that "iridescence glistening on a swamp," that "white lily on the dirty pond." "L'incendie," the poem he would dedicate to Marais, described "the interminable, unbearable attacks" that France was enduring, and the tension that the Munich Accords would soon relieve, at least temporarily.

> All this to sum up
> is terrible, frightening, beyond all limits.
> This French torpor, heavy and light,
> Faced with a two-headed eagle like two horns.[41]

Sensing more than ever the strange waves that signaled the storm, as they had in 1913, Cocteau had the idea, in the spring of 1939, to write a sequel to *Potomak*. After Hitler's troops invaded Austria, Mussolini's took over Albania in March, and the sound of marching could be heard everywhere. When in September the Wehrmacht entered Dantzig, he claimed to have predicted the war.

Cocteau's willfully fairylike stories, with their tangents and wordplay, seemed light in this wider context. Current events filled this new *Potomak*, but in a farcical mode: Hitler meets a Maurice Chevalier type and a Jewish fairy, benevolent but ugly, vaguely inspired by Marianne Oswald.[42] Like so many other survivors of the butchery of 1914–1918, Cocteau had difficulty believing that a new war had been unleashed, when almost no one in France wanted it.[43] In whose interest was it to disturb the peace, anyway? But German aggression was so obvious that he had begun to worry for Jean Marais, who with his incredible insouciance seemed as ill-adapted as Cocteau was to the days of struggle that lay ahead. To forget the threats of war, he decided to bring him for a holiday in the Piquey, where he hadn't returned since the tragic summer of 1923.

They stayed in the very room where Radiguet had written his *Bal*, by candlelight, in the wooden shack that, when he joined them, had struck Roger Lannes as having a military character. It upset Cocteau, to be reminded of the trapper's life he had been leading at the end of the First World War, that miraculous season when he and Bébé had written so much. He awoke early, washed with a pitcher as he had then, and then sat down to Radiguet's table; Marais set up his easel to face the sea—he had a vague desire to paint—and Lannes read Conrad. It was a "family" life, ordered by the rising and the setting of the sun and the bell that signaled their meals, and they stayed for almost a month before leaving for Excideuil in the Dordogne, with Marais at the wheel driving 130 kilometers an hour, leading his passengers to ask themselves by what miracle he had been given a driver's license five years earlier. Always on the lookout for places to set up his easel, the actor nearly managed to drive them all into a ditch when a hornet flew into the car, but Cocteau didn't even look up from his notebook.

Cocteau's observations had a gift for making towns more beautiful, châteaux more magical, and encounters more incredible; Marais and Lannes felt as if a film were unfolding as they drove from Périgord to Corrèze. Thanks to Cocteau's powers of mimicry, they soon found themselves joined by a lady who spoke only of herself, of her physical success, her impossible servants, her magnificent hats, her sensational trips. As the car zigzagged through the countryside it seemed to have passed into the hands of this shameless coquette, frivolous and overly perfumed, whose simple-minded prattle was like laughing gas to the Lincoln's passengers. "He loved to make people laugh . . . He knew how to crank it up, that boy," the great Arletty would say of him.[44] Young Roger Lannes himself felt as if he had wings of lead next to the magnificent playfulness of these imitations.

They arrived in Tulle, a town that had been deeply affected by a scandal about a series of anonymous letters seventeen years earlier. Cocteau was thinking of turning the story into a play—it would become *La machine à écrire*—and he felt an unusual documentary impulse. From the post office to the bishop's palace, he wanted to see everything, but he didn't take any notes. Marais, who gesticulated wildly when he spoke, as if he were onstage, gave them a bumpy drive home. Disappointed by the sequel to *Potomak*, which struck him as a kind of involuntary self-pastiche, Lannes still took notes on it while sitting next to its author. Marais, on the contrary, found the book wonderful, and could not restrain himself from saying, naively: "My reign is producing miracles."[45] The passionate phase had ended, however; their kisses were no more compromising than those between a father and son, noted Lannes, and when Marais left for the weekend it was with Denham Fouts: although his name wasn't uttered, no one was fooled.

Cocteau finally set Marais free to live as he liked, but demanded that he remain the primary object of his affections, and made him promise always to tell him the unvarnished truth. The actor could love whom he liked, but Cocteau must be his sole confidante. "I cannot say that this decision was an easy one to make," he wrote, "because my adoration is filled with respect. It has a religious, almost divine quality . . . You are everything to me . . . Surely it is better to deprive myself of a small amount of my happiness and win your trust . . . I would be ashamed to place the slightest obstacle in your sunlit path."[46] Cocteau went around saying that their relations were "absolutely pure"; the Adonis was definitively transformed into a son, whose progress he would follow ever more closely, and who, in exchange, would help him to live "like a saint." As for Marais, he confided to whoever would listen that he no longer had any affectionate feelings for Cocteau. In concrete terms, it was a separation.

The year 1939 was the happiest of Marais's life. For Cocteau, it wasn't always easy. The miracle of resurrection was marred by frustrations, artistic as well as personal, that age only accentuated. Of course, the runaway success of *Les parents terribles* had allowed him to accomplish the goals he had set himself at the beginning of the 1930s. But although he was recognized in the street, according to him, it was because too often he was mistaken for Alfred Cortot, the pianist, or else congratulated on writing so well about Montmartre street life—it was Francis Carco they mistook him for—or they spoke to him about his theater, as if he were the theater director Jacques Copeau. Luckily, a young writer introduced himself in February with an idea for a journal aimed at "the young," then told him, not without awkwardness, that he wanted to write a book about his work.[47] Cocteau was very pleased: Valéry and Gide overwhelmed with critical works about them, Breton and Malraux too, but no one had ever thought to write about his own work. For the former man-god of the Noailles days, it was, if not the first sign of a consecration, at least the hope for a real rehabilitation, after the success of *Les parents terribles*. To add to his pleasure, the young beanpole addressing him—already the author of a noted study on Marcel Jouhandeau—was the son of François Mauriac.

Cocteau made his life an open book for Claude Mauriac. After showing him his apartment, and Marais's room, he invited him to the Hôtel de Versailles, where he had taken refuge to write.[48] He introduced him to the actor, took the young man into his room, warning him that he had just smoked sixty opium cigarettes there, and began to preach, disheveled and unshaven. "Like a poet of antiquity telling a story, embellishing the details every time he tells it," Cocteau told him he had just finished writing a new play in five days, *La machine à écrire*, and then began to read to him from his new *Potomak*, which was even more arcane than the previous one. "The voice is dry, clean, precise, inhuman," Claude Mauriac noted.[49] "I think Claude is slightly astonished," Cocteau confessed, taking him to dinner in the hotel restaurant with Roger Lannes and Jean Marais.[50] The foursome caused a chill to fall over the room as they entered: they were a "delegation from Hell," in the eyes of the retirees filling the room, Mauriac noted. Cocteau immediately began to chatter, in a stream of fables and speculation, "a lie as beautiful and poetic as a blackbird's song":

> The masters have real genius, the genius of childhood: Gide is the old English lady wearing a hat with a green veil who wants to see the Pyramids; Claudel, he's the Cadum baby, yes? and Valéry is a lazy child who raises his hand to be allowed to leave the room . . . Do you know what the doctors call a seton wound? A clean, fast bullet that goes through a part of the body without leaving any trace; the flesh closes over it by itself. It's the same with my work. It is so clean and speedy as to go unseen.[51]

Impressed by this actor who performed from the heart, taking up his enemies' worst accusations, and playing devil's advocate, Claude Mauriac convinced himself that Cocteau had been the victim, if not of a manhunt, then at least of an unfair evaluation. "There were three of us listening but he called us by the singular "tu" as if he had only a single audience member," he added.[52]

As soon as he left, the younger Mauriac was struck by doubt; reviewing the intricacies and contradictions of Cocteau's speech, he wondered: what was the point of it? Were these salacious anecdotes about Gide true, or just designed to lower Mauriac's opinion of him? Could Cocteau be believed when he said he had letters from Claude's father, François—very intimate letters—among the manuscripts that Sachs had stolen? Claude Mauriac was already intrigued by homosexuality, but since the subject was still taboo in his family, he made contact with Cocteau's entourage. Marie Laure was the most damning; the brilliant, inspired man she had known and loved now seemed to her a man possessed, bent on dragging each of his friends through the dirt, capable of disgusting actions. "I nearly succumbed as well," she confided; "I woke up one day on the edge of the abyss. He takes advantage of your weaknesses to push you further. Do you have a fault that no one knows about? He would soon detect it, in his appetite for corruption. He congratulates you on it. He persuades you that it is the best part of yourself."[53] Young Mauriac still wanted to meet Gide. The author of *Les faux-monnayeurs* heard him out, then, finding the young man's version of Cocteau too understanding, cut him off: "The true Cocteau does not suffer." In Gide's journal, which had already begun to appear in the Éditions du Pléiade (a first for a living author), he put it another way: "He is incapable of seriousness."[54] In other words, there was no authentic man behind the name. Finally, Claude Mauriac overcame an instinctive repulsion and met Maurice Sachs. The former seminary student seemed to him "seemingly without any ill-will," but he let slip a few key critiques and ended up offering, in veiled terms, to sell him some of the letters that Claude's father had sent to Cocteau. Claude refused "nobly," but the damage was done.[55]

Cocteau knew nothing of these meetings, but still endeavored to shine and laugh in front of young Mauriac, though his heart wasn't in it. Had he guessed that the young man's analysis was becoming less and less favorable? His face began to sweat as soon as he went outside. The young man's change in attitude after Marais's physical estrangement made him see how fruitless were his efforts. Cut off from vital support by "his" own young men, ravaged by opium, age, and sadness, Cocteau compared himself to a pen from which blood flowed in great waves. "Look at yourself," Colette said to him one day, when he reproached her for not yet having built an oeuvre in spite of her immense talent, and for talking a little bit about everything without writing: "As for me, I want to live, to have beautiful legs and a strong body! But you, you haven't even kept a folding chair to sit down on!"[56] He had wanted to *live* his work, and logically it was eating him alive. The existential masterpiece that he had dreamed of becoming had become a sad little pen pusher who had lost all his best friends. Was it during this period that he added a caption to one of his drawings: "Jean Cocteau is dead and lives to frighten you"?[57] This was just about what he had come to believe.

Having exhausted opium's literary resources, he began to inform friends like Joseph Kessel that he wanted to replace it with drink. But he had never had the luck to become an alcoholic. His hair was turning gray and his emaciated cheeks sagged, like the skin on his body from which his bones and skeletal joints protruded. His legs like a heron's, his interminable fingers, his nails yellow from smoke—all seemed so breakable. His weight fell below 110 pounds, and for a man who stood about 5'7", he looked, with his knotted fingers, like the old vine stock that still, by some miracle, produced superb grapes. Reduced to bone, the old young man of 1910 now looked like a ghost haunting his own destiny.

Some supernatural power prevented him, however, from taking his own life. It whispered to him that only second-rate artists actually killed themselves—that great artists prefer to shed their dead skin after each of their transformations. Claude Mauriac had witnessed this strange capacity for growing young again; emptied of all human substance, "saddled with an annoying remnant of false childhood," Cocteau's hardened, tortured mask, back in his hotel room, had given way to a handsome, youthful face in the shadow thrown by the lamps.[58] For the world at large he had become a caricature imitated by two different mimics on stage in 1939, one crude and hateful, wriggling his bum in Rip's annual revue—the other cultured and amusing, in Agnès Capri's revue, which included Jacques Prévert as one of its writers. Cocteau went to see the former, revealing to Claude Mauriac while watching the show his true face, "frozen with sadness and joy," responding with feeble, sad smiles to the prancing about that was attributed to him.[59] He then asked to meet, in private, a friend of the Thomassins who also did a keen impression of him since he had acted in *Oedipe roi*; this time he was so hurt that he refused to see this mimic ever again.[60]

Why did Cocteau inspire such ridicule and hatred? It was as if fate had chosen him as a universal foil, throwing him into a time and place that was incapable of understanding him, like Rousseau in his own day. He published a long text on Rousseau to make it clear that he didn't have a persecution complex, but had in fact been hunted down by Voltaire's gang.[61] "Notes on Hell": this was the title Claude Mauriac was planning to give his book, though Cocteau did not know it yet.

THE PHONY WAR

Marais decided to spend the end of the summer with Cocteau in a little hotel in Saint-Tropez called the Aïoli. "Don't deprive me of the inn / Where we only find one bed," Cocteau wrote to him the night before they left, in a poem slipped under his door.[62] The South had always been the best medicine; the presence of Marais always made him euphoric, the sun warmed him, the heights of the citadel on the Canoubiers beach, where Colette had her house, boosted his morale. It was a delight to follow the narrow customs road as it wound by the gulf toward the little Graniers beach outside of Signac's studio, en route to the Soleil, another little hotel where they went to stay after the Aïoli, where, at night, one could hear the mechanical piano playing at the Palmyre nightclub. When the little port emptied out, at the very end of August, it was paradise: the blue-green surface of the Mediterranean was no longer disturbed by the wakes of boats bringing back nets full of anchovies or sea bream.

On September 3, 1939, France declared war on Germany, ten days after Stalin's USSR, catching the rest of the world off guard, signed a nonaggression treaty with Hitler. Convinced that his country's strength could be found in its tradition of individual revolt, and not in its technical powers, Cocteau decided it was not necessary to fight. "Imposing a war on Germany to punish them is as idiotic as pretending to kill goldfish by sticking them in a tank," he told his friends; but the war had already begun.[63]

Marais was called up as a reservist, and left for Montdidier, in the Somme, eighty kilometers from Paris, but he had difficulty understanding the usefulness of this "transfer" that prevented him from responding to the numerous offers from the theater and the cinema that were already flooding in. He was totally unsuited to military life, and knew nothing of the stakes of the conflict—1918 was ancient history to him. Marais the soldier wandered in his garrison, learning his lines for *La machine à écrire*, as indifferent to the designated enemy as the young Californians who, thirty years later, would crisscross the Vietnamese rice fields. Cocteau did all he could to obtain leave for the actor to stay in a hotel and to keep the Havana-colored Matford car that he had bought for him, which soon was used by the whole regiment. The weeks that went by were unsettlingly calm. Montdidier was a hundred kilometers from the front, where the two armies calmly faced each other, without firing, like a "pacifist" remake of the great confrontation of 1914—one of those absurd bits of saber-rattling that brass love so much; the tanks and planes that gathered at the front were paraded like giant, expensive toys.

Cocteau himself was caught between extreme anguish and a total denial of reality. He couldn't believe this general mobilization, the noise of boots marching! Just a few months earlier a student from Montpellier had shown him an unusual short film, "Portrait of My Friend," in which the camera examined a boy's naked body from his head to his feet, his sex enlarged to the size of the screen.[64] Peace would surely be declared at the last minute, and this bad dream would dissipate. The more worried he became, the more Cocteau reorganized reality, dramatizing it to the point of mythomania. "Oh it's you my child, come in, come in . . . I'm dying . . . I am going to die in front of you," the actor Jean-Pierre Aumont was told when he visited Cocteau in October.

> It's nothing, you know, I have a cold, I ought to have an operation . . . but they don't operate on poets . . . People are monsters, all my life I've fought against aesthetics. Aesthetics, today, is defeatism. An extraordinary woman asked me if gas was bad for pearls—what should I have told her? . . . This war is an impressive game of chess. Hitler is like the fat mustachioed lady who plays the piano at Magic City [the ladylike annual ball in Paris] wearing a pink bow in her hair, it's like lions fighting ants, fighting bees, hey? Sorel told me: "This war is atrocious, it's cutting me down just at the beginning of my career," but Paris is admirable, the sandbags are more beautiful than the monuments, France has real genius . . . Stalin has appropriated Hitler's style, while Hitler is searching fruitlessly for a new one. I have a friend who made a pornographic film; Hitler bought it and has it shown to him every day for two hours: when you know that, it really clarifies things, doesn't it?[65]

Loneliness would soon temper the frivolity of these opinions. Finding it difficult to live in an apartment haunted by Marais's absence, Cocteau went to live at the Ritz, taking up Coco Chanel on her invitation to stay in her pied-à-terre. He grew more and more worried, though he couldn't bring himself to believe violence would ensue. All of Europe had mobilized; even Stalin had entered the fracas. "Keep reminding yourself that my heart beats in your chest. That my blood flows in your veins and that I am much less alone than some people because in spite of the distance that separates us, we are united," he wrote to Marais, while complaining about those who remained "neutral" for not loving with all their power.[66] He was already thinking of writing a new play for Yvonne de Bray, and of the films that Marais could star in, perhaps with him behind the camera.

With censorship reestablished, however, Cocteau did not receive permission to bring *Les parents terribles* back to the stage—the play was much too immoral for the time. The writer found himself without a project, in the middle of a country paralyzed by this "phony war" in which not a single shot had been fired. Marais hadn't been gone two months when Cocteau began to recreate him in ink and bronze. As before with Nijinsky, he turned Marais into a chimera, a gold and ivory statue, a demi-god and an Adonis with curls and horns, faun's ears and goat's feet, half medieval roebuck, half ancient cat or tree. "You are my only masterpiece, and I will only work for you from now on," Cocteau had confided to him a year earlier; this time, it was almost the truth.

Ah! Jeannot, I sing, I sing
To have you back the same tomorrow
For life seems too cruel
Without the touch of your hand.[67]

It was unbearable to know that Marais was in uniform, so close and yet so far, spending his days doing nothing, when he would have been so useful in Paris. Sometimes the military post would bring Private Villain-Marais four letters at a time, leaving him embarrassed in front of the other soldiers, who didn't have any.

In December, Cocteau left the Ritz and went to live with Bérard at the Hôtel de Beaujolais, in the Palais-Royal. "After a few days, his room looked like all the others he had ever occupied. It's like the shell of certain crustaceans: it always grows back [re-forms]," wrote Roger Lannes. The army forbade him from visiting Marais at the front for Christmas, so Cocteau turned to Violette Morris, a champion racecar driver known for having slipped into all-male races and for even winning a few, during the 1920s. Barred from entering the 1928 Olympic Games, this world recordholder for shot put and discus had a double mastectomy but since that still wasn't enough to get her accredited, had begun to organize world championships for women—in vain. "Chic" lesbians like Nathalie Barney disapproved of her, but, ever provocative, Morris had filed a desperate suit against the Fédération Féminine Sportive Française that had excluded her, while threatening to reveal the private lives of several of its members. She had then turned to the music hall, like Panama Al Brown. She could be seen in town, dressed like a man, on the arm of not only Josephine Baker or Yvonne de Bray, but also Jean Marais. Some said she was secretly in love with him.

Not for a moment did Cocteau stop to think about the risk he was taking by getting into a car with Violette Morris. Had he known that when she was invited to the Berlin Olympics she had been contacted by the German secret service and was now informing for them, he might have hesitated, but the possibility of seeing Marais again might have erased his concerns.[68] He lived for excessive love affairs; driving across the Oise as France called up its citizens fulfilled a certain fantasy. "Glory is nothing compared to love": he had never felt this deep truth—which he repeated to Marais—so strongly.[69] They arrived laden not only with gifts that Chanel had sent for her protégé, but also with flasks and cigarettes for the whole regiment, not to mention balaclavas, sweaters, and gloves from the atelier on the rue Cambon. Marais was informed that his brother Henri and a friend had come to see him, and the first shock for the soldiers was that the driver with the crew cut ("huge, dressed like a flabby schoolboy," said Lise Deharme) was a famous sportswoman.[70] The second surprise was for Cocteau, when he saw Marais in uniform: he was the spitting image of *Thomas l'imposteur*. The actor took him to see the belltower of Roye, the highest point in the neighborhood, where Marais (near-sighted though he was) spent most of his time watching the horizon for German planes, a military telephone in his hand. The planes did not always show up, so he made the terrace his solarium, where he sunbathed for hours in his underwear, hanging on to his telephone in front of a small bedroom where he pinned up photographs of Cocteau and Chanel.

LE BEL INDIFFÉRENT AND THE BLITZ

Written during the "phony" war, *Les monstres sacrés* was inspired in part by the tragic insistence with which Misia Sert wanted to live with her husband's young mistress, before their divorce ruined her dreams of a ménage à trois. Here Misia became an actress, the wife of an actor, and probably an expression of Cocteau's hidden hopes of finding a third man who might live "theatrically" between himself and Marais, without trying to play the lead. However artificial and quickly thrown together, it was still easier to stage than *Les parents terribles*. Violette Morris, who was offered a role as thanks for services rendered, unfortunately wound up traumatizing Yvonne de Bray during rehearsals. "An old person's play," Roger Lannes judged, coming out of the opening at the Théâtre Michel in February 1940, attributing the diminished quality to Marais's departure for the front. Cocteau had arranged a happy ending, for once, reuniting the initial couple at the end. Regardless of some disappointing reviews, there were enough ticket sales for the play to transfer to the Bouffes-Parisiens two months later, with, as a curtain raiser, *Le bel indifférent*: the monologue of a cabaret singer, played by Édith Piaf, speaking out against her man, a gigolo played by the impassive Paul Meurisse hiding his face behind a newspaper, with sets designed by Bérard.

Cocteau quickly saw that Édith Piaf was an unusually dramatic performer capable of sending shivers down the spines of her listeners: women were reminded of what they had endured, and men of lost opportunities. With a gaze like a blind person whose sight has been restored by the holy water at Lourdes, Piaf lived her art. Divinely talented, she stood on strong little legs, with her waxen hands crossed on her stomach; she had Bonaparte's forehead and Anna de Noailles's passion, Cocteau would say.[71] She had long admired Cocteau, praising the extraordinary intelligence with which he spoke about *chansons* and the music hall; she, the little sparrow, had fought to make her acting début in this proletarian version of *La voix humaine*. She identified with her heroine as much as Cocteau, who also hated when anyone read the newspaper in front of him, and who had confided a thousand times to Radiguet, Desbordes, or Marais what Piaf said to Meurisse: "In the beginning, I was jealous of your sleep." On stage, Piaf was like a wounded nightingale singing its guts out in the black night of abandoned love. Here, however, where she was permitted only to speak, the bird's wings seemed clipped, and though Cocteau was delighted with her performance, and would write another monologue for her (*Le fantôme de Marseille*), the recordings show that she was not as moving as Berthe Bovy was in *La voix humaine*.

Cocteau, however, increased his attempts to bring Marais back to Paris. The hostilities that had been declared eight months earlier still remained theoretical. The audience would have the illusion that the play was happening "in a special time in which the war might not be taking place," he wrote in his preface to *Les monstres sacrés:* the only time he knew. In May, however, the cannons began to sound. Spurred on by the relentless advance of Guderian's and Rommel's tanks, the German army invaded Holland and Belgium, and began bombing Paris on June 3.

Cocteau refused to be worried, except for Marais's safety. (Marais was alone in the village where he kept watch, all the other soldiers having fled). Cocteau's attitude stemmed less from indifference for his country than submission to his work, the point around which his life revolved. "Invade us, France will conquer you and in time will possess you," he declared, addressing the army from beyond the Rhine.[72] Whenever asked his opinion, he would reply, "We will win because we are weaker," before changing the subject. As early as the spring of 1938, he had signed a petition along with Paul Nizan and others calling for a left-hand solution to the ministerial crisis afflicting Blum's second cabinet. By nature a pacifist, he could not comprehend the mysteries of the conflict that was rapidly approaching, and preferred to wait for things to settle down on their own. "My France — is you — you are my country — my courage — my genius — my mischievousness — my patience — it's you and nothing but you," he wrote to Marais, leaving little room for complex historical reasoning.[73] "Jean Cocteau is a poet for whom the outside world doesn't exist," Jacques-Emile Blanche said in 1917.[74]

If there was a real tragedy, for Cocteau, it was the upcoming June issue of the *Nouvelle revue française*, which was featuring an excerpt from the book Claude Mauriac was writing about him.[75] Reading it took his breath away. The young man in whom he had confided for days on end had swallowed the worst lies his enemies had spread about him! Cocteau had disappointed Claude's father in love; the son was getting his revenge, probably with help from Marie Laure and Gide, who was on holiday in Malagar, staying with none other than François Mauriac. The same Gide who congratulated Claude on the accuracy of his portrait, writing: "It's excellent, it outdoes my wildest expectations."[76]

One of Cocteau's disciples found the poet shut up in his hotel room, curtains and shutters closed, after the article was released. "Jean, what's wrong?" "Leave me alone, I want to die." "I'm calling a doctor." "No, let me die." Then Bérard burst in on him, languishing in his stained robe, and brandished the *Nouvelle revue française* at him. "You're wrong, Jean, I'm telling you that he loves you."[77]

This blow, which had been carried out on behalf of two of his oldest enemies, increased the ambivalence that Cocteau felt toward his countrymen in the land of Voltaire, who criticized everything baselessly, for the sheer pleasure of complaining. He already was starting to feel like a foreigner wherever he went; the article was so painful that the suffering it caused blended with the worry he felt at the looming war. "My heart is once again a martyred country," wrote Ungaretti. He convinced himself that young Mauriac's belligerence, which reminded him of Sachs, was the result of a repressed romantic disappointment, and began to write to him again, to try to win him back. After all, the book hadn't yet been published.

THE OCCUPIED

Man is a creature that can become accustomed to anything,
and I think this is the best definition of him.
—*Dostoevsky*, The House of the Dead

"THEY'RE HERE!"

The Germans advanced at lightning speed. Cocteau, swept along in the exodus of ten million French citizens to the south, which left Paris as empty as it had been in that autumn of 1914, rushed to leave the capital to take refuge in Perpignan, on the Mediterranean, with a family of doctors, while the government moved to Bordeaux. The Great War seemed to be starting all over again, but this time no one thought it would be the "war to end all wars." All the authorities had more or less fled and the last officers standing were shouted down, disarmed, and sometimes even killed by the crowds, who already feared German reprisals. For every hundred heroes there were thousands of soldiers incapable of hating their opponents, and who, like Private Villain-Marais, only wanted to go home.

The Armistice was finally signed on June 22, 1940. The "best army in the world" had resisted the Wehrmacht's Blitzkrieg for only three weeks, and had lost one hundred thousand men—an unprecedented catastrophe in French history. The country was in a state of shock, like the victims of a car accident, Léon Blum said. The very next day, Hitler landed in Paris for a quick tour, guided by Arno Breker and Albert Speer, his favorite artist and architect. From the Trocadéro to Sacré-Coeur, and from the Opéra to Montparnasse, on that beautiful sunny day the Führer encountered a deserted, cataleptic city. In 1870 the German troops had raped, pillaged, and burned—not to mention, it was rumored, cut off many a hand; between 1914 and 1918 they had once again razed all the territories they occupied; what would these hairy, drunken, ferocious Prussians (as the press described them) do this time? The few Parisians remaining in the city asked themselves what they had let themselves in for.

The evening before the German army invaded, the surgeon Thierry de Martel (a distant descendent of Mirabeau) killed himself to avoid this humiliation.' Others preferred to close their shutters. As the first Germans arrived, they baptized Paris the "city without eyes." But to everyone's surprise, the Horsemen of the Apocalypse proved themselves to be clean, calm, clean-shaven soldiers who paid for their drinks in cash and were in no hurry to humiliate anyone. The soldiers who had just ravaged Poland, Holland, and Belgium set up camp in Paris like armed tourists. Unlike Warsaw or Prague, which according to the Third Reich had a population of "sous-hommes" (subhumans) subject to the cast-iron rule of the Wehrmacht, Paris had only people so here soldiers opened doors for women and asked passersby for a light in order to practice their French. Far from wanting to revenge themselves for the crushing defeat of 1918, these white-gloved burglars seemed to want to be accepted, if not appreciated, for the first time in the two nations' history. Disarmed by this goodwill, as well as by their defeat, Parisians elected to endure the ordeal of Occupation and wait for it to pass.

They detected an ulterior motive behind the Germans' restraint. If these oafs were going to behave in such a *korrekt* fashion, they must have been given orders to do so in order to lull the country into submission. Had they not just announced that the curfew would be pushed back to midnight from nine o'clock (as it had been during the early days of the Occupation) as a reward for the Parisians' "peaceful and understanding" attitude? Who knew but that by giving the illusion of normalcy, the Wehrmacht weren't attempting to stay for good? Some preferred to keep silent about their suspicions; others sounded the alarm. It was said that Goebbels, the Reich's minister of propaganda, wanted to humiliate France, then annihilate its culture. "From the beginning of the Occupation, our orders were to halt the development of French culture," Lieutenant Heller would later confirm, to underline the efforts he had made to the contrary throughout the war. That was where the real conflict would take place, and where the first "Resistance" would be staged.

From Charles Dullin to the cabaret owners, from Sacha Guitry to the director of the Concert Mayol, most of the Parisian directors reopened theaters and nightclubs in order to show the Germans the persistence, even the superiority, of the French art of living. Reciting verse, performing tragedies, laughing out loud to prove that nothing had ended; they loved, wrote, danced, and acted to drown out the sound of the boots and to affirm the powers of life over those of death. The Germans might control three-fifths of the country, but they would never control the spirit of Gavroche, or of Marianne.² The first show to be performed at the Théâtre des Optimistes, in August, was called *Chantons toujours*. Curiously, the generals and administrators that Hitler had sent to Paris were not hostile to this "Resistance." They were the first to laugh, to be moved, and to applaud these performances, even if it meant listening to pointed remarks about "doryphores," a kind of beetle known for its love of the potato, much like the German soldier. The skimpily dressed dancers and singers in boater hats exactly fulfilled the image they had of France. If these comments were the only form of protest the local population would wage, the occupiers were happy to bear them for the thousand years of the Reich that were supposedly beginning. Soon it became clear that these officers were in no hurry to destroy French culture; if anything, by reopening the Opéra and the Comédie Française, it seemed they were trying to give it new life. The Wehrmacht's trucks were ordered to broadcast lively popular songs, in French and in German, to keep up morale. It could seem strange, if not painful, but they were not acting out of anti-French sentiment. They didn't like the Jews, as everyone knew, or the Slavs, but the Parisians—the sons and daughters of Renoir and Toulouse-Lautrec—they loved.

The Germans' overwhelming victory had brought the City of Light to their feet; envied and resisted for a century, the Germans' hereditary enemy had been reduced to submission in only a few weeks. The cabarets and risqué bars, the Moulin Rouge and the Boeuf sur le Toit, the brothels and the gaming rooms—all reopened by the dozen. Mistinguett and Les Nouvelles Goulues sang for them, the Opéra dancers lifted their legs for them, the flirtatious come-diennes and curvaceous crooners flattered them, the orchestras came together to play Fauré or Saint-Saëns for them. All over town, the soldiers could gather in cinemas and theaters, browse in bookshops, attend opening nights where they could spot Danielle Darrieux or Micheline Presle (who were already famous in Germany), or go to art openings where they could run into Maillol or Despiau. There was good wine and good food, and plenty of perfume, cognac, and ladies' underthings! The land of the Sun King, of Marie-Antoinette and Bonaparte, relinquished all of its secrets, as well as its arms, its factories, and its banks. For the more sophisticated palates, there was jazz galore, Cubism in the galleries, Satie, and soon Messiaen in the concert halls, to say nothing of the many other art forms forbidden in Germany. How could these new masters not appreciate their privileged position compared with their colleagues stuck out in

Warsaw or Prague? Paris was the most prestigious posting for any German soldier. "Glücklich wie Gott in Frankreich" went an old German expression; in this case the officers of the occupying army could indeed be said to be as "happy as God in France."

When Cocteau returned to Paris in September, these "lucky devils" in lovat green had set up camp everywhere. His old neighborhood was covered with red and black flags flying the swastika. From the Madeleine to the Opéra it was all German cinemas, Soldatenkaffe (soldiers' cafés), Kommandantur (army posts), and armed guards. The Old England store on the boulevard des Capucines, where his mother used to buy his mufflers, was turned into the Heereskleiderkasse, which supplied uniforms to the Platzkommandantur officers. The grand hotels of the rue de Rivoli and the avenue de l'Opéra? The headquarters for various German military administrations. The École Polytechnique, on the Montagne Sainte-Geneviève? A barracks. The Lycée La Fontaine and the Lycée Michelet, at the doorway to the capital? Strongholds of the Kriegsmarine. The clocks were set an hour ahead, to German time. The German high command was so German-like, with their monocles, their sticks, and their black boots, that they looked like self-caricatures.

Soon the citizens of Paris realized that Berlin had sent the crème de la crème of their administrators to oversee their conquest. From the ambassador, Otto Abetz, a former art professor and committed but capable Nazi, to the supervisor of the Schrifttum section (in charge of literary affairs) at the Propagandastaffel, to a young Lieutenant Heller, who had studied in Toulouse and who would manage to spare French literature (but who wouldn't mention in his memoirs that he had joined the Nazi party in 1934), these Germans would seem to be unusually careful with French culture.[3] Instead of Prussians, Paris had received men from the Rhineland, with all the Francophilia and southern humor that often implied. They told anyone who would listen that they had not conquered Paris, but that Paris had conquered them. They would gather at the tomb of the unknown—French!—soldier and go about out of uniform, as civilians, if not friends, like the officer who requisitioned Mauriac's Malagar property, telling him, after admitting to having read his novels, "France's defeat is such a tragedy!" If Parisians continued to hate their conquerors, at least they disliked them a little less.

Their "stewards" tried to keep Parisians' spirits up, for the pleasure as well as the advantage it gave. On the advice of Friedrich Sieburg, author of *Dieu est-il français?*, Otto Abetz tried to persuade them that while Germany occupied a role like that of Rome at the height of its empire, France was like Athens, culturally valued. "They told us over and over that . . . after the war, France would be the schoolteacher to the rest of the world," wrote Jouhandeau.[4] Some Parisians allowed themselves to believe that their charms had worked: was it not said that the Athenians had managed to conquer their Roman conquerors? France might have lost half of its territory, but Paris was still the capital of the world. Its inhabitants continued to be important, sought-after players on the world stage, in this new era. Flattery helped Parisians to swallow the bitter pill of the Occupation. That was how Paris, for so long a beacon of light for all of Europe, initially managed to tolerate its captivity: misplaced pride.

Entire busloads of Germans were arriving, unloading battalions of men and women at the Eiffel Tower and Notre Dame—real tourists this time, with Zeiss-Ikon cameras around their necks. Of course, the officers who had preceded them were holding prisoner two million French soldiers and were undertaking measures to strip the country of its riches, but how, when they stooped to pick up the handkerchief you had dropped, could you refuse the cigarettes they offered with a smile? What could you do when, on a café terrace, a young lieutenant patted a young girl's cheeks, offered to share a bottle of champagne with her mother, and reassured her that her imprisoned husband would be home soon? Was he not in a hurry to return to his family as well, after months away at war? "You poor French citizens, you have been dragged into a deadly war by a government of scoundrels bankrolled by England"—or the Jews—the benefactor would murmur, kissing *maman*'s hand.[5] The most fortunate were already betting that things would slowly improve: "Hitler beat us, now we're going to civilize him."[6]

Maréchal Pétain, a prominent war hero of 1914–1918, was voted to power by the Chamber of Deputies and the Senate on July 10; in late October, he officially instituted the policy of collaboration with Germany, and so ended the strange transition period. With no soldiers left to defend France and so no other choice for its survival, the people of France—from the demobilized nurse to the farmer anxious to return to his seedlings, to the railway worker with his locomotives and the engineer distributing electricity—went back to work. The country had no idea that Hitler's encounter with Pierre Laval, on October 22, 1940, had convinced him to reduce France to a vassal state, one that would turn over its mines and its factories, while Germany awaited its workers and Jews. Like a sheep making good cheese and strong wool, France could become angry, rear up, but she would be milked and sheared within an inch of her life. The French were not fooled when Hitler repatriated the remains of Napoleon's son—"They take our coal and give us back the ashes!"—but they worked hard. Cocteau resumed writing, in his apartment in the apparently protected Palais-Royal, a hundred paces from the rue de Rivoli, where so many flags signaled the presence of the Occupier. There he applauded the Armistice that returned Jean Marais to him alive and in good health.

Charles de Gaulle, then a relatively obscure general and undersecretary of state for war in the last government of the Third Republic, had gone to London with a handful of faithful followers to call for continued combat with Germany. Some leaders of the Republic who had originally taken refuge in Bordeaux left for Morocco, and most of the fishermen of the Breton Île de Sein went to England to join the Free French forces. But the first group was placed under house arrest, and no one heard anything more about the heroic decision of the second. As for the patriotic university and high-school students, "Gaullists" and Communists alike, who defied the Occupiers for two hours on the Champs-Elysées on November 11, 1940, their demonstration was broken up with gunfire.

Cocteau had risked his life for his country during the First World War, but this time around he was fifty years old, more than a little late to pick up a gun, especially when he had been abandoned by everyone. Did he even know how to hold a gun? The fight continued in London, but very few writers went to join de Gaulle, aside from Albert Cohen and Joseph Kessel: the soldier from the nationalist Right did not inspire much confidence. Only a handful of literary types began a Resistance network that fall, calling themselves the Association des Amis d'Alain-Fournier.[7] The Right liked to follow authority, while the progressive intelligentsia cried, as they had for fifteen years, "Down with fascism!" and "Disarmament!" The two slogans continued to be incompatible, as Simone de Beauvoir observed.[8] After having called for desertion and conscientious objection for so long, the Surrealists now elected to go into exile rather than resist. Paralyzed by the pact between Hitler and Stalin, most of the Communists waited for more than a year to throw themselves into the fight.

Though they had been so active in the 1930s in the fight against fascism, Gide and Malraux made no public statements. After a decade of fighting fascism in Italy, Germany, and Spain, most writers, not knowing the damage it would wreak, felt that it had now won in France as well. History has been the judge since then, and our moral resolution has been reinforced, but the vanquished French of the time were operating in a fog: Nazism was not yet synonymous with definitive, absolute evil, as we know it, but an as-yet-incomplete evil, an evil-in-progress, we might say. Unable to bring themselves to submit their books for the German censors' approval, some writers chose to leave for the Free Zone, where it would be less compromising to publish; still others—like Maurois, or later, Breton—left for America.[9] But many did take up their pens, to show the world that French literature would continue, or out of the prosaic need to earn their living, or to keep a rival from taking their place or their books from disappearing from the bookshops. Although some writers, like René Char or Jean Guéhenno, continued to write but refused to publish under German control, or went elsewhere—like Malraux, who published his *Noyers de l'Altenburg* in Switzerland—most chose to compromise and submit their work for Otto's rubber stamp of approval, as did many publishers. By September 1940, the first Otto list of forbidden books was published and the bookshops were emptied of books by not only Jewish authors, but also Malraux, Nizan, and Koestler. Soon, as Guéhenno predicted, the writers would care only about the size of the font in which their names were printed.[10]

SCRUPLES

The social milieu in which Cocteau had been raised had no tradition of resistance. It had always managed to maintain a relationship with whoever was in power, whether radical or right-wing, in order to maintain its prestige and privilege, however much it may have ridiculed or denounced the government in private. The theory of six degrees of separation claimed that there were no more than six people between the president of the Republic and a garbage collector in Marseille; Cocteau, however, belonged to a circle that was never more than one step away from power. Until the war, the names of Pétain or de Gaulle, Laval, or Thorez were more or less interchangeable in his mind, and a letter or a message from him would easily reach them if necessary. Just as his mother could telephone general so-and-so to exempt him from military service, he would still write spontaneously to ministers to free such-and-such. But he would never revolt against their politics of collaboration. His pacifism was so deeply rooted that he seriously wondered for a long time if one day, looking back, France's great honor might have come from its "refusal to fight."[11]

Come what may, a writer's vocation is to write, not to get mixed up in politics; Cocteau had never strayed from this principle, even during the Front Populaire, when his articles were simple observations. What remained of the works that Racine had written as historian to Louis XIV? Of the pages Stendhal wrote in praise of Bonaparte or against the Bourbons? In his view, a writer had one duty: to travel his path as freely as possible, to fight against conformity in all its guises, reactionary and revolutionary. It was a logical choice for someone who hadn't read a newspaper since 1917, when *Parade* had been vilified by the critics, and who only asked one thing of those who were in power: that the indifference be mutual. Convinced that art and ideology were two parallel tracks that ought never to meet, Cocteau returned to developing his body of work, as he had always done. Helped by the opium, he buried himself in a murky drug-induced zone, the limits of his territory bordered by dreams, sealed in almost as hermetically as was Proust's cork-lined room. For a long time he behaved as if this war did not exactly concern him, not because he was indifferent to the fate of his country, but because he believed he had another kind of citizenship, one that spanned national borders. This was also his rationale in 1917 for withdrawing from the front so he could write *Parade* in the Roman sunshine, even as French soldiers were still being decimated by the thousands.

Cocteau was convinced that he was doing the right thing—after all, his work opposed that of the undertakers, the butchers, and the arms merchants. His sincere but distant utopia was a world without judges or police, without borders or nations, where painters, poets, and musicians lived together in harmony with acrobats, muses, and boxers. During the war, he could be heard to utter the most incongruous hypotheses: the youth would claim power; a World Union would arise. Suffice it to say that he was not entirely lucid when it came to this subject. The atrocious fighting he had seen in the trenches of Coxyde-les-Bains had purged his disdain for Germans. In spite of the anti-Wagnerian attitudes of *Le coq et l'arlequin*, in Cocteau's view Germany had again become France's natural ally, even a friend among nations. As early as 1921, he was calling for reconciliation, according to Kessler; in 1931, two years before the Nazis took power, he signed a manifesto against excessive nationalism and in favor of Franco-German understanding, which was then published in *Notre temps*.[12] Ten years later, he would continue to refuse to hate a nation whose authors, from Thomas Mann to Walter Benjamin, had always given his books a warm reception, or often, in the case of Max Reinhardt and Kurt Weill, had praised his sense of spectacle. This was not the Germany of the Nazis, one could argue, but Cocteau made no such distinctions: his vision of the world was more cultural than political.

The collective, barbaric, and controlling nature of the regime celebrating itself at Nuremberg disgusted Cocteau. As much as he loved crowds gathered around boxing rings, he loathed mass gatherings and the unanimity preached there. By 1938, he was wary of the envy and enthusiasm Hitler had inspired in some French people after the Anschluss.[13] "How sinister when a man is saluted like a god," he wrote that year.[14] When Chaplin had released his film *The Great Dictator*, Cocteau had made fun of the tyrant who, in Berlin, was reduced to imitating Chaplin. He had been so nourished by German culture, nevertheless, that he could not see the occupying army as thoroughly foreign. Its soldiers spoke a familiar language and sometimes hummed songs his nurse had taught him, along with fairytales from beyond the Rhine. "Et moi qui ne savais pas sentir la moindre haine / Contre un pays qui fut le pays d'Henri Heine" (And I could not feel the least amount of hate / For the country of Heinrich Heine), he had written two years before the First World War, in an atmosphere of much stronger patriotism; he might have said the same thing in 1940.[15]

Yet Cocteau never took part in the euphoria that took over certain parts of Paris. The 1930s had robbed him of much of his gaiety, and his art, during those gloomy years, had become rather dark. Having become more fatalistic since his neoclassical period, he channeled the pessimism of the masses. It was his *Oedipe roi* that prisoners-of-war at the Stalag IXA camp sought permission to perform, in March 1941. In some ways his life had taken on a tragic dimension, and the tragedy that Europe was experiencing matched his own mood. He returned to weaving an invisible web, through his many letters and drawings, dedicated photographs, articles that had yet to appear, and unpublished manuscripts. He didn't see that anyone with a public image who accepted the German yoke implicitly became its hostage, or understand that it is when people have the least amount of backbone themselves that they most demand moral fortitude from their public figures. The trap was about to snap shut.[16]

FOXHOLE IN THE HEART OF A GHOST TOWN

In spring 1940, following the advice of Emmanuel Berl, Cocteau rented a small apartment at 36 rue du Montpensier in the Palais-Royal, in the very heart of the city, but he settled there only after Marais returned. Though the neighborhood at first seemed worn out and melancholy, for Cocteau it was full of memories and friends: Berl, whom he had met through Proust, still lived there with a singer called Mireille; Colette reigned there as she had in her native province of Burgundy, finding "this little bit of country" more amiable and united than the other; and there were many reminders of Valentine Hugo and Paul Morand, who had lived there in the 1920s—it was at their home that he had read *Le Cap de Bonne-Espérance* and their spirits accompanied every move he had made, in this strange sense of timelessness in which he lived his life. Nevertheless, the gardens of the Palais-Royal were ghostly. So lively during the ancien régime, when they had served as both amusement park and public forum, they were devoid of activity by 1940: the ideal refuge against a disturbing reality. Yet the winds of history had often blown through this drowsy place; during the Revolution, heads were paraded on pikes in front of orators and journalists; this was where Charlotte Corday bought the knife that killed Marat. Near Cocteau's shoebox of a flat, on either side of the arcades of the Galerie de Montpensier and the street with the same name, Bonaparte had made his debut; twenty years later, Madame de Nucingen had taken Rastignac to play the tables in Balzac's *Splendeurs et misères des courtisanes*. It was a city within a city. Today the area is mostly calm, but back in 1940 it was a lively place where Cocteau came to know everyone, from the humpbacked concierge of the Théâtre du Palais-Royal to the overweight server at the Le Revel restaurant, to all the dogs in the neighborhood.[17]

The daylight barely filtered through the half-moon windows; Cocteau and Marais had to turn on the lights as soon as they woke up. Just off the entryway to their apartment was a little kitchen and dining room, with a view over the rue de Montpensier, and on the other side was the living room, with a white wooden drawing table on trestles and a sofa covered with animal skins where visitors would sit. They hung giant blackboards on the doors where they could write down appointments and draw while they spoke on the phone. Cocteau had a small bedroom on the left with a view over the gardens; then there was a small bathroom and a "spacious" bedroom, which doubled as a painting studio, where Marais slept. There was also the tiny, secret room into which Cocteau would burrow to smoke his opium. The Théâtre du Palais-Royal was on the other side of the wall; the arches of the Comédie Français were less than fifty meters away. Cocteau used gold nails to hang blood-red velvet curtains on the wall, the ultimate theatrical touch to this small space where Julien Green felt as if he were moving around in the back of a drawer.

The first rations had begun. Cigarettes, sugar, and chocolate were the first to become scarce, as well as coal for heat and cooking gas. They had to learn to pick up *décades* (ten days' worth) of loose tobacco and ration cards to exchange for meat and eggs. The price of black-market merchandise increased along with the traffic in ration cards, which were stolen with impunity in administrative offices: at the end of the winter, many impoverished elderly people had died of hunger. Marais warned Cocteau that ties to far-off colonies (Indochina in particular) were weakening and the opium supply would be tapering off. To continue to smoke under such conditions would be to increase his reliance on drug traffickers, to expose himself to the harsher Vichy laws (part of their moralizing policies), and to put himself at the mercy of the occupying army. Opium, which Cocteau perceived to be the opposite of vulgarity, would surely bring him into conflict with those whom he judged to be the "height of vulgarity": the police.[18] It was time to give it up. Marais, who wished Cocteau a happier, healthier life, had made him promise a thousand times to quit, and a thousand times he had reneged on his promise. This time, Marais surprised him with his stubbornness: the same stubbornness that had gotten Panama Al Brown to quit. And so, in the fall of 1940, Cocteau agreed to try a new cure, a more painful one no doubt, but Marais managed to get permission to visit every day, and like Galahad could say to him: "Nothing true could happen near you. Now the world is alive, everything is bleeding . . . The truth begins. It is hard. It will hurt you to wake up."[19] When Cocteau returned to the rue de Montpensier, Marais had destroyed all of his smoking paraphernalia and thrown all the drug addicts out of his entourage. Cocteau was deeply grateful to him, for it was the only way to prevent a relapse. A few months more and the actor proved to be the best caretaker for his mentor: indeed by early 1941 Cocteau had managed to completely kick the habit.

The outside world slowly began to exist for him again, but the form it had taken in his absence was almost more unreal than he had feared. Some people were raising wild chickens in their courtyards and kept rabbits in their households, or grew radishes on their balconies and carrots in the public gardens. The lack of gas and the establishment of an *Ausweis* forced the citizens of Paris to put away their cars—only seven thousand had the right to circulate. Parisians rediscovered the joy of walking. Since buses and motorcycles were also confined to the garage, the bicycle-taxi was invented, as well as the gasogene car (which ran on charcoal) and a front-wheel drive car cut in two and pulled by a horse—when it wasn't pulled by manpower. The stench of horse droppings took over empty streets, where grass began to grow between the paving stones. The older Parisians, who had grown up without motorcars, gas, or electricity, couldn't believe their eyes as they breathed the fresh air in Châtelet or bought garlic in the place de la Concorde as ducks took flight; with horse-drawn carriages traversing the rue de Rivoli, they almost thought they were back in the reign of Napoleon III, before the rise of this dreadful industrial civilization.

This collective regression happened under the reign of an old *maréchal* who—through a curious effect of national mass mimicry—reminded many people of their grandfathers. It was bolstered by Charles Trenet's cheerful, old-fashioned songs; mentions of "eternal France"; attacks against "those lies that do us so much harm"; the politicians of the Republic; and calls to return to the land, for "it [did] not lie." Though they resisted Vichy's agricultural fantasy, the Parisians learned to love the rain that watered the crops and the chickens that awoke them every morning to lay their eggs. Now that he was off the opium, even Cocteau seemed to have a healthier air. He gained back a bit of weight, chose his words more carefully, and lost something of his trancelike lyrical state. It was a new beginning, like a dip in the fountain of youth, after twenty years of addiction. Fairytales from Asia told of sleeping beauties who live the better part of their lives in bed, and die on awakening; Cocteau felt on the contrary that he had been resurrected.

His first trips outside astonished him. Paris had become almost silent. The motors and machines had stopped running; even the radio could no longer be heard, as official reports were greeted with suspicion. It was like a dead planet, noted Ernst Jünger, an officer in the occupying army. A young Jean Genet described the city as "a sort of Pompeii, without policemen at the crossings, a city dreamed of by thieves, when they are tired of inventing ruses."[20] It was a frozen city in which could be heard the far-off clatter of horses' hooves on the cobblestones, or the song of a partridge. The city looked like something out of a De Chirico painting, and Cocteau walked through it, confused and thankful, as if an invisible corridor had brought him directly to the night into which the opium had plunged him, in the 1930s, to that game of shadows animated by the Occupier. Stripped of its external signs of prosperity, Paris had acquired an almost poetic charm: empty shop windows, like something out of a Surrealist photograph, were filled with bottles, vials, and tubes as fake as the stockings that women painted onto their legs, the coffee people drank, the potatoes they ate.

Returning home at night to the Palais-Royal before the gates were closed, Cocteau felt as if he were slipping into a Forbidden City: not a soul stirred in the neoclassical architectural fantasy built two centuries earlier. The mind could rest, death withdrew, even fatigue abated—it was truly a dream carved in stone. In winter, the footprints of blackbirds, wood pigeons, and seagulls tracked across the snow, as if it were the North Pole. In summer, there was the song of the fountains and the wind in the trees. It was an enchanted place, where every bench awaited its princess. In an exhibit organized by the Galerie Charpentier in front of the now-deserted Elysée Palace, Cocteau had the chance to explain how this new city fascinated him, becoming by night a "moonlit Paris, like the statue of the commander . . . in the stereoscopes of our childhood, which showed me Saint-Petersburg in the snow."[21] This was what would inspire him to write *Léone* in 1942, a poem in which no hint of the Occupation appeared (except perhaps for the dizzying absence of any hint of *living* life).

They soon welcomed a third man to their little kingdom on the rue de Montpensier: Paul Morihien, the swimming instructor at the Racing Club pool that Marais went to, and a key figure on his water polo team. Morihien had a few things going for him. He sometimes worked as an acting extra (he would have quite the career in Marais's wake), and before the war he had been the secretary to the aircraft manufacturer Paul-Louis Weiller, who had been chased by German orders into the South. This ladies' man was won over by Marais's charm, and stayed overnight with him so often that he soon moved into the shoebox.

Cocteau warmly welcomed Morihien. Why deprive Marais of his pleasure, when they were no longer sleeping together? "Your happiness takes precedence over mine, because if you are happy, I am happy," he wrote.[22] If he missed being able to run his hand through the actor's hair, he kept it to himself. This new arrival was so complimentary about his work! Cautious, modest, discreet, capable, and a hard worker, Morihien quickly proved to be an ideal third man, and his physique was an added boost to Cocteau's pride. What's more, he proved able to sort out Cocteau's messy business affairs, and officially became his secretary in November 1941.[23] Marais, however, no longer spoke to Cocteau unless he had something specific to say, which saddened Cocteau; Morihien was the one who fed his hunger for conversation. Through sharing their meals, entertaining, and going out to the movies together, the threesome became a little family, so radiant and happy that Roger Lannes felt like a distant country cousin. It was easy to feel free with Cocteau. The maddest ideas could be trotted out before him and he would never find fault with them. "So will I," Cocteau replied, when, at dinner with the Jouhandeaus, Marais announced that he would be married within three years. Morihien asked what would become of him, and Marais replied: "You'll live part of the time with Jean, part of the time with me."[24] The trio could not imagine being separated.

Otherwise, Marais was insatiable; he had an endless stream of lovers, some who stayed the night, and some who hoped to stay for a lifetime. There was talk of a rich man, the owner of the Magasins du Louvre, who was ready to become a film producer to win him over. Cocteau's physical condition improved greatly, and he too found himself much in demand, but the most ambitious boys found their passion unreturned; after twenty years of opium, literature, and monologues, Cocteau had lost all erotic drive. The monk had acquired a reputation for licentiousness, and no one imagined he could turn down such tempting offers, but nevertheless it was true. He loved only Marais, and asked only to enjoy his *joie de vivre* and his contagious health.

Marais was so fearless, so ready to deny anything that disturbed him, that he almost seemed foreign to the great human emotions, to the city, and even to the stage. He didn't do well in roles that required a subtle psychological performance; he thrived instead in very physical roles, or very dramatic ones. Cocteau understood that Marais required excessive — heroic or adventurous — roles, and that he conquered his reputation for being a bad actor by going after outsized parts. Aware of his foolhardy, daredevil proclivities, Cocteau pushed him to rise above this and take on roles that might help him rival the actors of his childhood. Against all expectations, he set his sights on classical theater by staging Racine's *Britannicus*, though Marais had no notion of directing or of alexandrines. It would be a masterpiece or nothing.

VICHY MEDICINE

Vichy, a self-appointed National Salvation government, started off by reminding everyone of their duty, and not their rights, and instituted an ideology of sacrifice, obedience, savings, and effort. Not content to abolish the unions and republican parties, to make divorces quite impossible to obtain, and to harden the anti-abortion laws—these great depopulators of the old Gallic soil!—the machine to turn back time run by the Maréchal aimed to restore faith and the natural hierarchy, as well as prestige to the men in uniform who had been somewhat sidelined since the "moral revolution" of 1918. It was a "politics of the breadwinner" that aimed to create capable leaders and disciplined subjects. A rhetoric of contrition helped absolve the sins of the past, that is, the destructive effects of the Front Populaire, even of the French Revolution. It was a Boy Scout morality for a country on its knees. The defeat was portrayed less as the result of a misguided military policy and more as punishment for the mistakes of the past; the guilty parties were not so much the colonels who had fled, but those defeatist teachers who had demoralized the country beginning with its schoolchildren, the pacifist Left, the postwar cultural hegemony, the winos who had drunk the country dry, and the moonshiners who had destroyed their pregnant wives. Along with, of course, the Freemasons, whose network of influence had been fatal for the economy, and the Jews, the corruptors of the Republic who had infected the French state with their cosmopolitan interests and their business dealings with Anglo-American corporations. The Vichy regime, which poured 400 million francs a day into Germany's coffers to support the Occupation—more than half the national revenue—believed it had found those responsible for their country's defeat.

In late September 1940, the German authorities imposed a census on Jews living in the Occupied Zones north of the Loire; then, on October 18, they began dispossessing Jewish businesses. Posters reading "Jüdisches Geschäft—Entreprise juive" began to appear on the windows of non-"Aryan" shops in Paris. The Comédie-Française fired all of its Jewish actors and staff; a Jewish student could not win a prize at the Conservatoire d'art Dramatique. Marianne Oswald, Jean-Pierre Aumont, Reynaldo Hahn—all lost the right to perform or have their work performed onstage, as did Darius Milhaud, who left for the United States.[25] Vichy, meanwhile, forbade Jews from occupying positions of authority as civil servants, in the army, in organizations receiving public funding, or with influence in the culture industries (the press, the cinema, radio, and so on). It also kept Jewish people from practicing numerous liberal professions, and instituted quotas in areas like medicine where they were still thought to be useful.

Cocteau was descended from a pair of families who had ardently desired the condemnation of Captain Dreyfus, and would sometimes go around their house on the rue La Bruyère wearing "Yid masks." This social anti-Semitism, fed by the traditional Christian prejudice against the "chosen people," had marked him to some extent until the 1920s, at which point it reversed into a profound, actively voiced antiracism, which was perhaps his only political conviction. "Shake the hand of our Jewish comrades," he wrote as part of his agenda in his *Lettre* to Maritain, who was suspected of wanting to convert them. Prone to putting himself in the place of others, Cocteau in 1940 had the least racist temperament that could be imagined. As early as 1938, Cocteau compared Hitler to the anti-Semitic Wagner, whom Nietzsche had loathed in the end, and to an evil demiurge planning a Saint Bartholomew's Day massacre for Jews.[26] A month before France's defeat, on May 4, 1940, he signed in the "Droit de vivre," a petition circulated by the Ligue International Contre L'antisémitisme, which protested the rise of racism and anti-Jewish sentiment in France, and the "crimes being committed every day."[27] After having so often been "ashamed of his white skin" when seeing the situation of colonized peoples during his trip around the world in 1936, Cocteau had good reason to resent those who discriminated against people based on their color, faith, or customs.[28]

We don't know how Cocteau reacted to the first anti-Semitic measures—he was not yet keeping a journal. But evidently he could not imagine that the Vichy government would ostracize a minority that had enjoyed full rights of citizenship since 1791, or that it could be planning to purge France of its Jews; he had even more difficulty imagining that this would be the aim of these courteous, cultured German officers. "In 1939–40, in front of a Jewish friend . . . I said she was being hysterical about the concentration camps and the Jews . . . When one's own flesh and bone is not in danger, it remains unreal," Simone de Beauvoir would say. She, like so many others, was left incredulous by the rumors that started to swirl in 1940 that Polish citizens were being deported by train and gassed.[29] They remembered the propaganda during the First World War that incorrectly ascribed atrocities to the "Boches."[30]

Cocteau and Marais had both been baptized, but neither was safe from danger. Hungry for scapegoats, Vichy went after corruptors of youth, whom they blamed for France's defeat. "They indict literature, they accuse it of refinement, of trying to weaken them," wrote Gide in his journal on June 11, 1940. In particular Vichy took aim at the "bad teachers" who had encouraged the licentiousness of the 1920s, the disregard for the authority of the country, and an unnatural sexuality. Following Drieu La Rochelle's 1939 novel *Gilles*, which denounced the fad for self-flagellation with "those two feeble plagues: homosexuality and drugs," those Vichy supporters who wanted to right these wrongs went after loose women and "enfants terribles." Cocteau sensed the danger as it approached. "You know I love drama, but I dread the purifying bonfire," he wrote to Roger Stéphane, a young man of good family who was trying to build a career in Vichy. "They throw anything in there, daubs as well as da Vinci."[31] The note went all around the Hôtel du Parc, where Pétain's government was housed. "What is France?" he asked another day, in a clear allusion to the accusations aimed in his direction. "A rooster on a dunghill. Take away the dunghill and the rooster dies."[32] But Vichy was convinced that the defeat could have been avoided if before the war the country had sung of work, painted the family, boasted of the country, and produced moral or patriotic artists.

The campaign would be concentrated around four figures who had encouraged youthful rebellion, vice, and pleasure: André Gide, the author of *Corydon* and *Les caves du Vatican* whom devout Catholics truly believed to be possessed by the devil; the "Jew Blum," former president of the Counsel of Ministers whose mannerisms got him regularly accused of homosexuality, against all common sense, but who had the bad luck to have published in 1907 *Du mariage*, a dissection of that venerable institution, and who was thus accused of promoting a reduction in the birth rate, and therefore an ageing France, when Germans were doing nothing but having children and arming themselves to the hilt.[33] Then there was François Mauriac, the mannered writer from Bordeaux whose work was deemed unhealthy and corrupting, who had become the portrayer of breakdown, greed, and meanness with *Le noeud de vipères*. Finally Jean Cocteau, another of the devil's agents, who with *Les enfants terribles*, *Opium*, and even the selectively distributed *Le livre blanc* had supposedly instilled in French youth the poison of drugs and homosexuality, incest and suicide. He had championed "individualist self-abuse," as the head of the Collaborationist party would put it, all while provincial families had looked on aghast, seeing him, since the end of the last war, as a vampire preying on the young.[34]

According to this narrative, the defeat had less to do with the failures of the French army, or with the widespread pacifism inspired by the memory of the 1914–1918 massacre, and everything to do with three more or less openly gay men and one ladies' man whose misfortune it was to have been born Jewish and exquisitely polite, and to have ruled France on the left-wing. These four men were accused of being unnatural, and their work was found to promote weakness and irresponsibility, unbridled individual liberty and national spinelessness; they had created an environment in which "anti-French" bacteria could thrive. The argument was so unconvincing that Sennep, in a drawing for

Le Figaro, drew a sickly peasant pushing his plow, harnessed to a pair of emaciated horses, who is told by a country squire with a monocle, "If you hadn't read
so much Proust, Gide, and Cocteau, it wouldn't have come to this."[35]

Léon Blum was soon dragged before a court in Riom, in February 1941,
alongside others held responsible for the defeat. Mauriac fiercely defended
himself; Gide, however, did not immediately feel the ill wind blowing his way.
"Pétain's speech is simply admirable. 'Since our victory in 1918, the spirit of
pleasure-seeking has won out over the spirit of sacrifice. People claimed more
than they served,'" he did not hesitate to write in his journal, in June 1940, as if
he knew nothing of the Gide of before the war, or had abandoned him to
Vichy's paternalistic moralizing: he quickly left for the Midi, putting Cocteau
and Mauriac on their heels. Cocteau was more lucid, at least in the beginning.
The first time he took a position in public was an article addressed to young
writers, whom he encouraged not to lose faith in literature and to keep their
distance from politics. The article was published in December 1940 in Alphonse
de Châteaubriant's Collaborationist journal *La gerbe*, from which Cocteau
would slowly distance himself, showing his outrage at seeing men who had for
twenty years supported the prestige of France incriminated, and the interwar
period described as "rotten." "Walk all over us," he wrote, encouraging his
readers to attack old men like himself, literarily speaking, rather than the
pseudo-decadence denounced by Vichy. He would get his wish.

Suggesting "a literary purging," Camille Mauclair, a former disciple of
Mallarmé's, responded in January 1941 in the same journal, accusing him of
building a "literature of the defeated" along with Gide and Mauriac, and so
igniting a quarrel that would last for months.

LUCIFER'S SHADOW

It was at this moment that the perfect embodiment of the damned decadence he was accused of supporting reappeared in Cocteau's life. Four years
earlier, when he had been rehearsing *Oedipe roi* with Rouleau's students, an
obese revenant entered the Théâtre Antoine. Maurice Sachs was trying to cast
his latest play, and had taken to wandering among actors as if he were the
theater owner—that day he spoke to the cast so intently that he muffled the
drum Cocteau was playing.[36] For once, Cocteau was firm, and ordered Sachs to
immediately leave the theater. That very night, the amateur dramatist sent
Cocteau a stinging letter claiming that he had not left out of a "feminine"
demonstration of privacy, but due to a "solid, male, and serious hatred" for
Cocteau's meanness, his lies, and his perpetual game-playing. "And this hatred

comes from this," Sachs added: "that when you thought yourself a shepherd, you were in fact the opposite, and led the youth astray . . . You brought out the worst in everyone (and in me as well)."[37] Resolved to burn his bridges once and for all with his former idol, Sachs warned that the next year he would publish a book called *Le Sabbat*, and threatened to add a section that he would call "Against Jean Cocteau" (from an article he had submitted to the *Nouvelle revue française* three years earlier, of such violence that Paulhan himself had turned it down) if he were not immediately given a large sum of money.

At the time, Marais had encouraged Cocteau to respond to this shameless blackmail in the strictest tones, and Sachs had left him alone for a few months. But Marais did not take into account Sachs's terrifying loyalty: having been branded by his first love, he demanded at least to be hated in return. In 1939, he published an account of the 1920s, *Au temps du Boeuf sur le Toit*, and used Cocteau's name (as he had Gide's, devoting a pamphlet to him) to describe their unforgettable first meeting. Then, in a Cubist portrait inspired by Cocteau's portrait of Proust, he described the clothing of this "cockchafer of a man with a breast of golden silk . . . who gesticulates wildly with his enormous pincers." It was an apparently friendly, occasionally dreamlike description: "When the cockchafer sheds his skin, it seems as if a red skin is ready to fall from his face"—but it was weighed down with phrases claiming that "lies are unleashed within him at the same time as his voice vibrates" or "he has written nothing worthy of a half-hour of his conversation."[38] Meanwhile, in the background, there was the reproach that continued to grow: how could this thirty-year-old man, from whom Sachs had felt a "vague feeling of iciness and falseness," have encouraged him as a child of fifteen to see Cocteau as the Messiah? And the more deep-seated resentment that was implicit but that he could never put into words: how could Cocteau, immediately and without proof, believe in him in a way he had not yet been able to believe in himself, before taking it back the minute he wrote something? Cocteau had let him go on, convinced that these accusations were a defense against his own influence, the outbursts of a young man who had been in his shadow for too long, a sort of backhanded compliment, as he himself had paid to Stravinsky in *Le coq et l'arlequin* after having loved *Le sacre du printemps* too intensely. And once again he had forgiven Sachs, with a magnanimity that the younger man had found unbearable.[39]

The letter that Cocteau received that January of 1941, however, managed to worry him. Sachs no more informed him of his hatred, but lamented what had torn them apart, letting him know that *Le Sabbat* would not be published as planned, and that he was ready to take back the terrible chapter about him, in order to explain all the "wonderful and sweet" feelings he had felt for Cocteau. "May we see each other again, and forget the years of quarreling in order to return to our deep friendship of twenty years ago?" he asked, aware, at least, of the tone that had to be used with Cocteau—that of an imploring *enfant terrible* hoping to return to the bosom of his spiritual father.[40]

Marais protested, fought, threatened, but in vain: Cocteau "did not know how to hate," the actor would say, appalled by this vulnerability. Drawn to each other like filings to iron, or Satan to Christ in certain eschatological texts, Sachs and Cocteau met face to face, at a dinner at Maxim's. "The gods build the traps into which men fall, thinking themselves free, over and over without realizing it," noted Cocteau several years earlier. Sachs would prove him right once again. Hearing him justify the growing severity of his literary portraits by citing Gide's example, who had a dig at Cocteau in his journal but had always been charming toward him in person, Cocteau wanted to believe that Sachs was trying to alleviate his remorse. Hearing that he had adopted a German-Jewish refugee reignited the pity he had always felt for the little "orphan"; in spite of his terrible faults, there was something unique about Sachs; the earth may never before have produced such a generous, charming man. Everything Sachs said should be verified, but he said it so well that in his presence it was as if you were attending a private concert, in which everything contributed to the soloist's innate theatricality, including the flamboyance of his lies. Sachs's mastery of the social comedy, including his ease at extricating himself from difficult situations, reminded their mutual friend Yvon Beleval of the kinds of powers we usually only possess in our dreams.[41] Because he may have taken a certain amount of pleasure in being robbed by Sachs, Cocteau retained the flattering impression of having served an important purpose in the fiction of the young man's life. But though he may have ended the meal in a spirit of affection, Sachs did not share his sentiments. "One could not know which war had just ended," Sachs wrote later to Beleval. "Maybe the Franco-Prussian war, who knows. He's off the opium and still curiously intoxicated by the worst parts of himself."[42] Sachs put up a show of buying the old "antique," in any case, by paying for the meal they'd just enjoyed.

The war had made Sachs prosperous. Like so many have-nots ready to sell anything to a population under the thumb of growing restrictions, but determined to prolong the pleasures that Vichy blamed them for, he had taken advantage of the country's collapse and of the deleterious climate outside its closed shutters to slip into the back courtyards of Parisian buildings with cuts of beef, baskets of eggs, and ropes of salami. But the black market was no longer enough for Sachs; he had to burn off the devilish energy that denied him any sexual or moral calm. "Everyone gets bored, but the Jews are the only ones who know it": these words from Madame Simone applied to this early experimenter in a nascent form of fictionalized autobiography called *autofiction*, who greatly preferred the smell of sulfur to that of paper.[43] It was enough for Sachs to write to Marais in February 1941, "I know you have very few reasons to like me, and these are reasons I like and respect. Fifteen years ago, loving Jean as I did, and as you do, I would have hated anyone who had been to him what I was to him for several years. This does not prevent me from writing to tell you from the bottom of my heart how admirable I found your production of *Britannicus*."[44] But the next day, Marais coldly refused to see this suspicious admirer when he knocked on his dressing-room door at the Bouffes-Parisiens. "I had just applauded too sincerely to come to start a fight," Sachs wrote, offended, to Cocteau, reminding him of the publicity he had undertaken all over Paris for this production. "But what haughtiness, what disdainful self-assurance in such a young man who does not yet know how much muck and mire reside in the body and soul of man. He has involved himself in a quarrel that has nothing to do with him, or he is acting as a judge. We *always* judge indiscriminately. I do not resent him for it, but he has grieved me. What a shame. I hope that you and I will always be able to cast away the obstacles that always seem to crop up between us."[45] Was the traitor hoping for a return to grace, or was he trying to destroy whatever affection Cocteau still had for him? The unlikely blend of love and hate with which Sachs pursued him always managed to shake the writer out of his benevolence: to attack Marais, to attempt to sideline him, maybe throw him out altogether, was to attack a better version of Cocteau himself, to blaspheme what he considered to be most sacred.

Sachs pulled away once again, with his determination for revenge doubled. He was so dissatisfied with his fate that when Violette Leduc, the illegitimate daughter of a wealthy man from Valenciennes, fell in love with him, a few months later, he was astonished to find himself at the center of anyone's world, "me who had never been anything to anyone, not even myself."[46] Leduc, the future author of *La bâtarde*, could not reconcile the man she knew with his past; discovering before anyone else the incredible ferociousness of the portrait of Cocteau in *Le Sabbat* (which would be published only after the Liberation), she tried to make him revise it, or cut it, but Sachs replied, with the sentimentality he would confess was the weakness of cynics, "I have suffered too greatly."[47]

Marais's budding fame was taking up all of Cocteau's attention. Although the actor forbade him from attending rehearsals, for fear of being too influenced by him, his directing style was saturated with their intimacy. It was Cocteau whom Sacha Guitry congratulated on *Britannicus*, before an anonymous letter referred to him as the "greatest of gods" for having produced such a hero. "I have never seen a more physically or morally beautiful Nero than your friend," Paul Morand wrote to him in March 1941.[48] Though Marais triumphed onstage as the deluded, hot-headed despot filled with desire, rancor, malice, and regret, Cocteau was applauded for having given the actor the confidence to perform Racine, making his awkwardness and his diction part of his technique. Many men and women saw him as the physical ideal of their generation. For several weeks, Marais was Nero: the role took over the man, with the young "tiger" prowling about in a sort of hypnosis sustained by the thousands of eyes that followed him every night. It seemed there was nothing the outrageously healthy young man couldn't do. Watching him, Cocteau rediscovered the emotions he had felt in the family box watching the *monstres sacrés* of his youth, those wild animals shaking their manes and tossing their animal skins. It was another way of slowing down time, smoothing his already wrinkling skin and rejuvenating his heart, which had suffered so much over the last thirty years.

In 1941 Cocteau was interested only in the theater, which he brought to life in the articles he wrote for the weekly *Comoedia*.[49] These articles confirmed his unique ability to recreate voices, gestures, and smells, blending them in a sea of images, but they also conveyed a timeless vision of Paris, one without the German officers who sometimes filled up two-thirds of the orchestra seats at the Opéra. Some might have been written in 1840 or in 1871, so striking was their indifference to what was happening in the world. Cocteau also pointed out that the Parisian theaters had always been full, even at the most critical points of the Terror or the Commune. Current events were left outside; theatergoers had the chance to lock themselves up every night in that box of dreams. Cluttered with costumes, buskins, belts, and helmets, the apartment on the rue de Montpensier became a sort of annex to the Bouffes-Parisiens.[50]

THE ULTRAS

Pétain had thanked Laval, vice president of his Counsel of Ministers, by placing him under house arrest in December 1940. He was then brought back to Paris by a dozen SS officers headed by Otto Abetz, the German ambassador. Laval's supporters, who were in favor of full collaboration with the Reich, descended on the capital, determined to fight on a second front. It was no longer enough to coexist with Germany, or to play games with it, as the Maréchal was doing; they insisted on throwing their arms around Germany in the spirit of brotherhood, and seeking its help on a large scale to accomplish a national revolution worthy of the name.

Some members of the press supported this response; the most brutal, influential, and best-written journal in this camp was *Je suis partout*, which resumed publication in February 1941. Officially run by Charles Lesca and Alain Laubreaux, Brasillach took it over in April, and the journal went on to publish the most unabashed royalist and poisonous pens, becoming the official organ of French fascism. Eager to have done with the tedium of parliamentary debate, the frivolity of Parisian political gossip, the sites of a sullied democracy ("démocrassouille"), and the bacteria of Judeo-Marxism, its editors loudly voiced their doubts about Vichy. They did not for a moment believe this supposed offshoot of La France Éternelle would survive alone. This new order of Crusaders had been defending their outwardly revolutionary agenda since 1936, and took these Vichy "newcomers" to be old refugees from the sickly Republic, which had certainly infected them with its microbes: plutocracy, corporations, and Freemasons. The Maréchel's men, at Hôtel du Parc, were half-masked Catholics, or dirty politicos—a bunch of "asexual patrons, calculating, intriguing, feminizing."[51] Endowed with absolute power by the "ghetto-Bourbon" Chamber of Deputies (the phrase is Céline's) elected under the Front Populaire, Pétain himself was but the residue of a regime of worm-eaten politicians and varicose-veined military types who had led a great nation to defeat.[52] Pétain, in their view, was a reactionary, the epitome of the doddering old fool who in his fear of violence was prolonging the decadence. He was eighty-four years old, after all, thirty-five years older, on average, than the other German leaders.

As early as December 17, 1940, a gazette called *Le réveil du peuple* sounded its wakeup call: "Frenchmen, be men. / Frenchwomen, become mothers." Ambiguity had done too much damage; it was time for the sexes to return to their places; to reject all that was unkempt, equivocal, weak; to overturn the seamstresses' and pen-pushers' morality that Montherlant had denounced before the war; and to eliminate those bacilli who would transform the genetics of the nation. The old Gallic country was not to be preserved, but thoroughly purged in order to put an end to the cancer that had eaten away at Weimar Germany before 1933. France was swarming with Jews, profiteers, and Freemasons—it was decaying from within due to Judeo-Bolshevism, corruption, and democracy. The country needed to be ruled with an iron fist, not a wrinkled one. "It's about not being fucked by the Germans, like a woman, but about being able to look them in the eyes," Claude Roy, a former collaborator on the first *Je suis partout*, wrote in July 1941.[53] In short, the country needed pure, upright men with a healthy, correctly oriented sexuality—"nationalists" whose pulses would quicken when they heard the national anthem, who would rise at the sight of the flag; brave men burning with ardor for their nation and desire to reinseminate their country, not "froides queues" (cold dicks) according to the pun targeting the Croix-de-Feu, a very right-wing group that the *Je suis partout* group nevertheless found insufficiently effective.[54]

As the Maréchal's campaign against "bad teachers" lost steam, these ultra-right-wing Parisians (with Brasillach, Rebatet, and Laubreaux as their leaders) fanned the flames of the fight against Cocteau. Having seen him at all his opening nights in the 1930s looking wasted and unshaven, high on opium and a wreck, they adopted him as the perfect incarnation of "decadence," and since his public affair with Marais, the incarnation of the abject complacency of the Republic. They knew him to be a defender of the "fucking ethnics"—a phrase coined by the anti-Semitic "scholar" and eugenicist Montandon—whose film producers and brothel keepers had turned Frenchmen away from working and Frenchwomen from motherhood. Finally, they took him for a dedicated "negro-phile" for helping Panama Al Brown out of the gutter so the "black sissy" could throw good white French men to the mat. Their crusade was somewhat marginal, but they knew of Germany's racial laws and were counting on them to breathe National Socialist life into France. Fascist and proud of it, they dreamed of using their writing like swordplay, and hoped in time to see Germany take over the reactionary, religious gerontocracy of Vichy. With Céline's blessing, they set about creating a united anti-Jewish party and strengthened their party line when they saw the Nazi regime launch a comprehensive campaign to eradicate homo-sexuality in the ranks of the party and the Sturmabteilung (SA), in the summer of 1941. They were convinced that Germany would waste no time in taking off of France's hands the effeminate types whom they believed, following Céline (who called them "Prout-Proust," or "fart-Prousts"), were making the country less virile. Cocteau was, again, the perfect scapegoat.

The Occupiers did not, however, impose their anti-homosexuality laws, except in Alsace, which they had annexed, believing it to be part of Germany. Unlike Vichy, they had no interest in holding anyone "responsible" for the defeat, and they allowed France to carry on with its picturesque licentiousness, maintaining the scandalous cabarets that made Paris so charming, with their procession of easy women and feathered transvestites, which had the other merit of distracting their troops—and the French from more pressing problems. Homosexual life went on, then, with its baths and its places of welcome, like the bar on the Champs-Elysées that auctioned off gigolos once a week. Far from suffering due to the moral rigor demanded by Vichy, Parisian gays continued to live as before, when they had the means to do so. Some went so far as to eroticize the ideological fraternizing between French workers and "German workers in uniform" that the Stalinist press encouraged, that is, until Hitler invaded the USSR. Daniel Guérin, a pacifist-anarchist, never concealed the attraction that the Feldgrau had for him, and the Wehrmacht let it continue out of a desire not to frustrate the troops, and perhaps to encourage other forms of collaboration. "Paris has swallowed the German army, just as an ostrich stomach swallows a pair of scissors," Cocteau said in 1941. The ostrich, his head planted in the sand, was a metaphor for those Parisians who were still trying to amuse themselves, those happy to see German officers oblige them by speaking French at receptions at the ambassador's home on the rue de Lille, while bandstand orchestras played "Le régiment de Sambre-et-Meuse."

More "relaxed" when it came to social mores than Pétain—to say nothing of Berlin—the occupying authorities also tolerated art that would have been deemed "degenerate" and forbidden back home, judging from the paintings that were shown at the Salon d'Automne in 1941 at the Grand Palais. *Je suis partout* could rage against "Negro-Judeo-American" music, but the nightclubs in Pigalle openly welcomed black jazz bands, sometimes within the admiring view of the German soldiers. Even on the political front, Maurice Martin du Gard was surprised, upon returning to Paris, by the ease with which one could publicly declare oneself to be a Gaullist or a Communist, given the suspicious atmosphere that the Vichy government maintained elsewhere.[55] Though the press was muzzled, in private everyone expressed themselves liberally—from right-wing patriots suddenly calling for a new Europe, to the earliest Resistance sympathizers; from leaders of the Chantiers de la Jeunesse, launched by Vichy to replace the military service, crying "The Surrealists are with us!," to Communists who were impatient, in spite of their party line, to enter the fray against Germany; from a fringe group of the anti-Fascist Left, who would collaborate out of shared pacifism, to the tiny Worker's Party of France, who called for a blend of National Socialism and Communism.

The ambiance was so lax that Albert Speer himself, returning from Berlin, was disturbed enough to tell his chancellor about it. "Let them be degenerate then! So much the better for us!" Hitler replied, having written in *Mein kampf* that the French had fallen to the level of negroes.[56] It was another disappointment for the "ultras," who had been counting on the Wehrmacht to save the country from its individualist anarchy. They dreamed of morally rearming the old Gallic people, whereas the Germans wanted precisely the opposite.

LAYING CLAIM TO *LA MACHINE À ÉCRIRE*

A third front, invisible but noisy, opened up at the end of spring 1941. From the underling slashing the tires of the Mercedes 170 (German officer's car) parked in the Place Blanche, close to the cabarets at Sacré-Coeur, to the engineer sent by London to install secret transmitters in the Seine region, some were starting to chafe under the yoke. Invisible hands began to carve the Gaullist letter V for Victory into the walls; others prepared to attack German officers riding the metro. The press in the Occupied Zone kept quiet about these modest, freelance fighters; the general population had to learn from German posters that Jacques Bonsergent, an engineer accused of beating the first German soldier in front of the Gare Saint-Lazare on Christmas 1940, had been shot. It wasn't until the end of the war that it came out that Bonsergent had been innocent, though he was a friend of the man who, to protect his wife, had beaten the drunk German.

Already busy systematically bleeding the northern half of France, the Militärbefehlshaber went after this small army of shadows, whose threat had already managed to make incursions into the forty brothels the Wehrmacht had claimed for itself, from the rue de Provence to the rue de la Lune, less comfortable. The Group du Musée de l'Homme was dismantled, with seven members condemned to death; Jean Paulhan, Gallimard's *eminence grise*, was arrested before Drieu la Rochelle was able to get him released. The cycle of repression and resistance had begun. The soldiers who had been so careful and proper now demanded revenge, the officers who were so sorry to have to occupy the city of Mistinguett now loaded their Mausers before going to Pigalle. Jews and Communists were rounded up at random when those responsible for attacks weren't found, then shot in groups of twenty for every German soldier killed. Reduced to admitting that it was not, in fact, at home, the Wehrmacht showed its true colors: it was a brutal Occupier come to pillage its hereditary enemy with a revolver aimed at its temple. The ultra-Right Parisian press reinforced its attacks against the Judeo-Bolshevism that was driving the *saboteurs*; the Freemasons and worm-eaten politicians, the Jews and the corruptors of all stripes, had more than ever become bacteria to eradicate. "All French men demand . . . the death of those to whom we owe so much pain," wrote Brasillach in the autumn of 1941, in *Je suis partout*. The cultural pages of the newspapers impressed on their readers the importance of fighting decadence—a fight that would result in far fewer deaths than the war itself, but would take up nearly all the terrain that politics had left behind.

It was at this moment that Cocteau decided to submit to the German censors the text of a play inspired by Tulle before the war—the second of his "great plays of subtlety." Inspired by a news item as well as many detective novels, *La machine à écrire* depicts very young people who, to fight provincial boredom, accuse each other of writing anonymous letters that poison everyday life in their region, and end by calling for their own conviction. It was a play with characters worthy of *Les enfants terribles* living through a tragedy that recalled *Les parents terribles,* in which vice once again makes an appearance—the heroine calls the legitimate son of her adoptive mother "ma vieille" (sweetie)—and it would once again be a great success. If this drama, written in 1939, betrayed something about Cocteau's mind, it was his tendency to blame himself for the faults of his friends, or even his enemies, much like some characters in Russian novels. But the theme had become hotly relevant, since half of France was showering the gendarmerie and the German servicemen with letters denouncing their neighbors for being Jews, Communists, or Gaullists. In this light, the play became a clear denunciation of what was going on in the country, ever since Vichy had begun drawing up a list of those morally responsible for the country's defeat.

The play scandalized the Germans, if Pieral, an actor, is to be believed—they called it "insulting . . . to the French." In an unusual move, they submitted it to the prefect of police, who in late April banned it "in the name of morality" and on the orders of the ambassador of France—that is, Vichy—in Paris.[57] Read as a critique of the Occupation, if not an apology for desertion, Cocteau's new play was again suspected of suggesting that the new moral order had not settled everything, even if it did outlaw all mention of holdups or crimes of passion in the press.[58] Cocteau denied that he had written a political play, but in order to pacify the Vichy government agreed to delete the most shocking passages. He also submitted a text to the German censors in which he explained that his goal had been to portray the feudal bourgeois atrocities of the provinces—he even used the word "decadent" in his preface—in order to warn the young against the kind of novelistic hysteria born of watching too many films and news reports. Finally he sought the opinion of Suzanne Abetz, the French wife of the German ambassador, who admitted in her reply to feeling "distressed by all these rumors."[59] To cap off this counteroffensive, Jacques Hébertot, the director of the theater that planned to stage the play, intervened with the Propagandastaffel, where Lieutenant Heller worked, which unlike the army was still operating under a policy of openhandedness.

It worked. After refusing to "get involved" in French affairs, the German services intervened with the Vichy leaders. The Propagandastaffel got them to lift the ban in the name of "artistic freedom," which outraged the association of theater directors in Paris. This prompted Cocteau to write to deny having sought any German assistance, while letting slip this confession: "It is lamentable, I grant you, that justice is granted by the Occupier."[60] Letting Paris and Vichy insult each other was perhaps the best way for Germany to maintain its own control. A double censorship was thus enforced on all plays to be performed in Paris, as long as power was triangulated between Vichy, the Occupiers, and the French ultra-Right. Cocteau would be caught in the middle, and fight from this position for three years.

The play opened on April 29, 1941. Marais was unsettled by some last-minute changes Cocteau made (he had reworked the play twelve times, for purely literary reasons), and proved ill at ease in the role of the twin brothers. His restlessness, as he paced the four corners of the stage set that he had himself designed, as his mentor had encouraged him to do, exasperated the audience. Cocteau had proved his great talent for developing plot and maintaining dramatic tension in *Les parents terribles*; here, his characters' dramatic power was less striking than their stagey nervousness, their ability to "make scenes": short-tempered, irascible, with a tendency to outdo one another, they encouraged the spectacular, sometimes artificial, reversals that unfolded. Although driven by a Dostoevsky-worthy theme, the dramatic machine also tended to turn infernal.

To everyone's surprise, the next day further performances were forbidden. Hébertot was the most immediate victim of this about-face, and went to see the Germans to ask why they were going against the approval they had already bestowed. "It's logical," they said. "Either we will reimburse you for all expenses, or we will allow you to keep showing the play."[61] Two days later the play received permission to continue, on the condition that the epilepsy scene that concluded the second act be cut. The press went on full attack. Beneath the machinery of the drama and the pulleys of the set design, the critics detected the "emptiness" and "lies" of its creator. On May 3 the theater critic Alain Laubreaux wrote of the "nearly sublime" ignorance of diction of Marais, who shot back the accusation that Laubreaux had never even seen the play.[62] But this scornful article was nothing compared to the brutal review published by *Je suis partout*, under the title "Marais et marécage." "*La machine à écrire* is the pure type of inverted theater," claimed François Vinneuil, alias Lucien Rebatet, who accused "Cocteau the cheater, the maniac, the chef of the questionable" of summarizing twenty years of the debasement and vileness, physical perversions and "pathological" volatility that had made him play the convert with "rabbi Maritain" and then to discover "with the cries of a swooning guinea fowl," a corrupt schoolboy — that is, Desbordes. "This clown could have been charming," added Rebatet, but "at fifty years old, an age of full maturity for real men, he is a degenerate buffoon . . . The morbid agitation that characterizes the zoological species that Cocteau belongs to is the height of ridicule and ugliness." In so doing he accorded him pride of place next to the Jewish rats and the African monkeys in the racial museum they were preparing. Having already been found guilty, with *Les parents terribles*, of making money off the "decadent" morality of the Jewish boulevardiers, thereby prolonging the "financial slavery" in which they had kept the theater for forty years, Cocteau found himself portrayed as an "enjuivé" (Jewified) invert.[63]

In the same journal Laubreaux piled it on a week later. Cocteau replied via an article in *Paris-midi* to which the critic responded with new attacks on June 16, still in *Je suis partout*. A failed novelist convicted of plagiarism before the war, but a pugnacious polemicist, the emotionally disturbed Laubreaux had been one of the first collaborators in France, one of the rare few to have openly wished, before 1940, for a defeat that might lead to a regeneration for the nation. He had even been arrested in June 1940, along with a handful of supporters of Germany—of which there were very few at the time, much less than in the United Kingdom. At that time he had been attracted by the military ideology of Jacques Doriot's PPF, the more and more pro-German Parti Populaire Français (run by the former second-in-command of the PCF, Parti Communiste Français), and by the virile aura of a leader whom Drieu la Rochelle had praised as "a good athlete . . . who breathes health into everyone around him."[64] In turn, Laubreaux made Cocteau out to be the supreme incarnation of equivocation and "corruption." Within the ultra-right-wing press there was a fierce competition to vilify him. *Aujourd'hui* claimed that Cocteau's "theater of decomposition" had no place in a unified Europe; meanwhile *La gerbe* had denounced in 135,000 copies Jean Cocteau's "rotten" poetry, though it had previously published an article by him. *Au pilori* called his rootlessness and his sexuality into question. Cocteau was a catalyst for all manner of phobias, and was judged unable to simply be himself. Like the "Jew who imitates the Aryan" and the "born female impersonator," Cocteau the homosexual was presented as a kind of sexual "youpin."[65]

Laubreaux's articles were not only read by many people; they also often had real influence. His readers wrote to the prefecture—the most determined wrote to the Kommandantur—asking why these "enjuivés" were being published, or their plays produced, when good French people lacked the paper to write to their loved ones who had been taken prisoner. The second-in-command of the Institut Allemand, Karl-Heinz Bremer, had to warn his French friends on several occasions that Laubreaux was almost certainly submitting his articles to the Gestapo, an action that visibly shocked him.[66] To say nothing of the anonymous rumors, often started by Laubreaux himself, that the weekly paper printed on page two—real denunciations that quickly transformed into grounds for bans or arrests. "So many writers are afraid each week, when they open *Je suis partout*, that they will find their names printed there, supplied by treacherous gossip columnists to feed the Gestapo's curiosity," wrote Maurice Martin du Gard.[67] Like Henri Jeanson, who was arrested twice after being informed on in this way, or the actor Harry Baur, who had to publish a correction denying any Jewish origins. "I never had anything to do with the Staffel or the German censors," Céline claimed after the war, "but they [writers from *Je suis partout*] crawled around those parts, answerable to them, under orders."[68] No one had any illusions about the real bosses at *Je suis partout*, a weekly that had published 150,000 copies by the end of the year.

Seeing the virulence of the articles about him, Cocteau became very afraid. Any one of Doriot's thugs might recognize him in the street and hold him accountable for his vile theater, and for being in thrall to millions of Jews and the other "mongrels" who, as Céline had claimed in *Bagatelles pour un massacre*, possessed three-quarters of France's wealth. "If there is one right we claim," wrote Brasillach, "it is to point out those who betray us."[69] Throughout the war, this was no doubt the most-respected right of all.

THE HUNT

One evening in June, after Cocteau and Marais left the Théâtre Hébertot and were sitting down to dinner in a restaurant run off the black market on the boulevard des Batignolles, Jacques Hébertot called the actor to the upstairs room and introduced him to a man who did not give his name.[70] "This is Laubreaux," the director eventually told him. "If that's true, I'll spit in his face," Nero-Marais said, turning to leave. Laubreaux hesitated for a moment before replying, "Yes, it's me." Marais spat in his face. The critic rose to fight, but Marais struck him first, before the restaurant-owner pleaded with him to restrain himself. When the critic went downstairs a half-hour later, Marais followed him outside, in spite of Cocteau's protests, tore his knob cane from his hands, and threw it across the street, before hitting him again until he split the arch of his eyebrow and threw him to the ground. "Help! Police!" cried the critic, but he was ignored by the passersby, eager to catch the last metro.[71] Laubreaux was so disliked that when he returned to the restaurant to telephone the police, he found it unplugged, and the actor celebrating with champagne.[72] The rumor spread all over Paris that Marais the Decadent had knocked out Laubreaux the Superman—making Marais "a queer of steel," one of his friends would say later.[73]

Though the ultra-right-wing press would now unleash all its fury against the actor, it did not mention the incident, unflattering as it was to a fascist like

Laubreaux, who simply wrote of the "imitation poet" who was the actor's mentor: "M. Cocteau will collapse all by himself."[74] Marais only half-reassured Cocteau by promising that if anyone were arrested it would be him. Jeannot, too, was naive, convinced that nothing bad could ever happen to him. And two weeks earlier, Paulhan had written to Cocteau that his article in *La gerbe* the month before was beautiful and courageous.[75]

Cocteau was beginning to regret not having been more circumspect, though he continued to receive numerous expressions of support. Mauriac sent him a letter applauding Marais's left hook, soon after the Gestapo searched his house: "France has become the little town you describe, and a gang of bastards has stolen the Typewriter, and is using it."[76] Céline himself offered to serve as intermediary between Laubreaux and Cocteau, whom he had met at a party for *La gerbe*.[77] But Cocteau refused to meet the critic who had tried to have his play banned for offenses against morality. Did Laubreaux stop there or did he demand sanctions? Either way, the German authorities did not follow up with the case. "We owe our lives to the fact . . . that some employers disdain their employees," Cocteau would say later, going even further to defend his play: "A tragedy like that of 1941 brings the deepest tears, the deepest sludge, to the surface. All the dark swampy parts of humanity take advantage of it and lose no time taking over the sunny regions, making its long tale of resentment a hymn to public salvation. Purity will surely be the theme of this impure clique."[78] No one could have done a better job of analyzing the ultras' position.

The climate had become even more difficult during the summer of 1941. Hitler's sudden about-face—he invaded the USSR in June—had allowed the French Communists to break their usual reserve. On July 14 demonstrators were arrested at Place de la République; on July 19, a worker was shot for insulting a German soldier; another was shot on July 24 for singing the Marseillaise. Two more were shot during a demonstration on August 13 near the Porte Saint-Denis. The order came from London to stop shooting German officers, but instead grenades began to fall on restaurants or hotels serving the Occupiers, whose reprisals cost the life of the Gaullist d'Estienne d'Orves, as well as the Communist Gabriel Péri. After trying to make themselves loved, the Germans returned to their old tricks and made themselves feared and loathed.

It was then that the press announced the October revival of *Les parents terribles* at the Gymnase. Yvonne de Bray was finally in good enough shape to play the role that had been written for her, and Cocteau thought he would be able to put the outcry of 1938 behind him. But this was to underestimate *Je suis partout*'s vigilance toward anything reminiscent of the *enjuivé* prewar bourgeois theater, as well as Brasillach's hostility to a play he had called "decadent" when it was first performed. The disappearance of the father figure (which recurred in Cocteau's work) in his view explained the hero's vices, and, more generally, the ills that plagued the country. France needed strong heads of family who could instill authority in every home, following the example of leaders like Doriot or Déat, the former Socialist leader who now headed up the Collaborationist Rassemblement National Populaire. The Maréchal also wanted to return authority to fathers: "The Maréchal is virile and calm. Feminine public opinion is nervous," claimed *Le grand homme seul.*[79]

Once the play was running, Laubreaux called up the troops. "Here he is again, in the spotlight," he wrote of Cocteau. "He has a perverted need to spread around his vice and his excrement."[80] That was the signal: the members of the PPF launched an attack on the Gymnase, sending down an avalanche of stink bombs and pepper spray onto the stage. Yvonne de Bray was sprayed in the face with ink. Serge Reggiani was pushed into the orchestra pit by demonstrators whom he tried to fight off with his fists. On December 7, the tough guys came back, but this time half the audience got up and threw them out, "while the hack journalists and old bags applauded," *Je suis partout* reported. The next day, the play was banned for the second time, and officially judged to be "counter-productive to national resurrection" by Admiral Bard, prefect of police.[81] It was a new victory for Laubreaux, who spearheaded the "indignant, upright youth" leading the fray and who concluded, still in *Je suis partout,* "M. Cocteau, who so loves young people, should not be displeased that power has remained on the side of the law, when I saw that night the grandfathers of latrines and old queers ready for a quickie." The great cleansing had begun.

Not long after, when Marais was dining with his mother in a little restaurant on the rue des Pyramides at a table close to where Picasso sat with Dora Maar, he was recognized by a group of PPF militants. They called him a "pédé" (homosexual), and accused him of sleeping with his mother. The actor rose, preparing to rip them to shreds, but was stopped by Lise Deharme, who was at Picasso's table.[82] Cocteau, however, did not lower his fists. He decided to write to his cousin, the Admiral Darlan, Pétain's presumed heir and the second most powerful man in Vichy, to explain that he was living the irreproachable life of a hermit, and to ask him to repeal the ban. He changed his mind, however, on the advice of friends.[83] It seemed there was trouble ahead for Vichy, and Roger Lannes suspected that it would be "even more compromising to serve that regime than to work in a pro-German newspaper," as he himself did.[84] Laubreaux must have caught wind of these attempts, for he went to war again fifteen days later, turning his focus from sexuality to race:

The heroes of his play, as in *La machine à écrire*, are flabby, spineless creatures ... The author's inner thoughts are projected onto the stage, contaminated by the Semites that reigned on French stages before him.

> —So racism is the order of the day?
> —That is, precisely, my deepest conviction.[85]

This slogan came at precisely the right time, when the Berlitz Palace on the boulevard des Italiens was playing host to an enormous anti-Jewish exhibition that would draw a million visitors, no doubt intrigued not by their usual invitation to "Learn English in three weeks!" but rather "Learn to tell a Frenchman from a Jew!" The French police made progress as well, rounding up five thousand non-French Jews on May 15, and another 4,300 on August 20, in the 11th arrondissement. "The first withdrawal has been made; others will follow," the editors of *Paris-midi* promised. They were well informed.

Céline was initially hostile to those moralizing critics who targeted *Les parents terribles* for its depiction of incest, until he came across the article in which Laubreaux mentioned Cocteau's 1940 support for the Ligue Internationale Contre l'Antisémitisme (LICA). Then he made an about-face and sided with the critic in a letter published in *Je suis partout* on November 22. It was a decisive show of force for Laubreaux, who, like all the ultra, always coveted the prestigious support of Céline. The prophet of anti-Semitism had designated the "real" enemy as early as 1937, in *Bagatelles pour un massacre*, and the following year had called for a Franco-German alliance "for life, for death," in order to prevent a war that the Wall Street Jews were financing, the "Yiddish War"; it was a godsend for *Je suis partout*, a publication that regarded Céline as the greatest of French fascist writers, and even, as Rebatet put it, the "father of the homeland."[86]

Céline took it upon himself to write to Cocteau, the better to sweep away his arguments: "'I'm not interested in politics.' What a joke! That old excuse! Everything is politics!"[87] Then, describing the still-inconceivable liberation of France, at a time when the Wehrmacht was still marching from victory to victory, he set himself up as the victim of the racial hatred he was spreading about everywhere: "Are you *with* or *against* those who would hang me? Do you believe that the Jews are responsible for the war and for the state in which we presently find ourselves?" he asked Cocteau, adding: "Jewish fanaticism is total, and condemns us to an atrocious death that would be personally and poetically *total*." Finally, after Céline had added, "fuck all *parents terribles* and their children," he dared the "dear Poet" to create an Aryan myth. In his letter to Laubreaux, Céline was even less polite. "Cocteau décadent?

Tant pis. Cocteau licaïste? Liquidé" (Decadent Cocteau? Too bad. Pro-LICA Cocteau? Liquidated). In another version, he concluded: "Cocteau LICAïste? Shot."

These calls for the firing squad were not just a result of the rhetorical enthusiasm that Céline demonstrated; proud that he had not waited until the Jews were persecuted to denounce their deadly influence, Céline really believed it was necessary to go after anyone who continued to put France at the mercy of a swarm of "fucking ethnics." For the Jew was not only a cultural danger, or a social catalyst, but, for Céline (a trained physician, who had begun his career by researching vermicules), a bacteria that, through "genetic sympathy," was liable to work on Aryan cells, then slowly cause gangrene to the species and in time replace entire peoples. Through his shocking ability to impersonate a goy and mimic his identity, he had been able to impose "Ben Montaigne" and "Racine the Jew" as nationally acclaimed authors, and ever since had replaced struggling literary genius with cheap false genius, which the monarchy of the "Jew Louis XIV" and the "démocrassouille" had stamped with the label "France": who knew if some Jew hadn't seized possession of Cocteau? Obsessed with this fatal transfusion, Céline had reached the point, by 1938, that he counted Cézanne, Picasso, Stendhal, and Zola among the "chosen people"— the "youpinuim," he said; some because their mother or their grandmother was Jewish, even partially, others because they were decadents, like Stendhal, or too naive in love, like his friend Élie Faure, a perfect goy who even so had had all his books banned by the Occupier.[88] Céline even believed it "logical," in *Les beaux draps*, published in February 1941, to denounce the insolent and ever-increasing presence of Jews in Paris, counting among their number the thousands of sympathizing Aryans, like Cocteau, who were being eaten away from within by the "Yid" cancer. In the Free Zone, Vichy police confiscated this pamphlet, declaring it counterproductive to their own anti-Semitic fight, since it went beyond everything that was suitable, serious, and reasonable on the subject.[89]

The LICA, with its "real- and false-nosed Jews," was the victim of an unprecedented slur campaign, and Cocteau became afraid, seeing himself classified among the "weak" who had slowly been taking on "kike" values. He was perhaps the ideal prey for these invaders, who took advantage of their power first over women, those who were so hungry for luxuries and power, but also over their masculine doubles, the "womanly-men" greedy for costume jewelry and fame.[90] Bent on undermining the virility of the Aryan people, in order to reduce their genetic-demographic power and impose the power of their own "jizz," the Jew also supposedly was leading a noxious conspiracy to emasculate them in literature. Hence Cocteau's hysterical, "female" style was clearly the byproduct of Proust's "microscopic analysis of buggery"—in fact, Céline ceaselessly assailed the customs, race, and style of all of Proust's work, calling it "tortuous, arabescoid, a chaotic mosaic."[91] Cocteau was therefore vulnerable to the accusations of "enjuivement" sent out by the Institute for Jewish Questions, where Céline went regularly, and which he repeated in his pamphlet, calling for the eradication of both the "Yids" and the goys who protected them.[92] This threat might appear to have been defused by his buffoonish excess, but it was given a certain weight by the presence in Paris of thousands of German soldiers—not to mention the law passed on June 2 that restricted even further the Jews' sphere of activity, by penalizing in advance all those who might help them to escape it. The terms in which he discussed Cocteau in his public letter to Laubreaux left no doubt about it: Céline was determined to condemn any person hostile to the anti-Jewish laws to forced labor for the rest of their lives: "Reasons of race should trump reasons of State. No explanation necessary. It's very simple. Total fanatical racism or death!"[93]

Out of class-inherited habits and instincts that he had acquired as a member of the minority, Cocteau always sought a powerful protector whenever danger loomed. It was the law of the schoolyard, the kind that had allowed *La machine à écrire* to be performed: if he's being beaten, the weakest will look for a protector, and he may go so far as to seek one in the hated principal's office. If he's been called a "wrinkled old hag" and a "slatternly poet" by *La révolution nationale*, if he's been lumped in with the "judéo-blennorragiques" (gonorrhea-infested Jews) denounced by Brasillach and *Je suis partout*, he is going to knock at the Occupier's door.[94] If Céline had "bewitched" Karl Epting, the director of the Institut Allemand, well, then, Cocteau would go in search of his own referee, so as to protect himself as well as Marais, Laubreaux's "vanquisher."

In November 1941, Cocteau had met a few Germans through Gaston Gallimard at the home of Paul Morand. Ernst Jünger, a close friend of Lieutenant Heller and of the commander of the Place de Paris, had initially found Cocteau likable, although "tormented, like a man sojourning in an unusual, but comfortable, hell."[95] Cocteau, for his part, found the writer hard, and rather precious, in his lovat green uniform, but was relieved to find that he too detested everything emphatic and heavy-handed—from Wagner to Zola. Like many in France, Jünger had been in favor of the war in 1914 and against it in 1940; after having expressed his fascination with the liberating effects of the earlier war, in *Stahlgewittern*, published the same year as Cocteau's *Le Cap de Bonne-Espérance*, he had come to loathe Hitler's calls to arms. *Auf den Marmorklippen*, which Jünger sent Cocteau when it was published by Gallimard in March 1942, struck Cocteau with its independent spirit. How could this officer oppose the war so openly without putting himself in danger? Cocteau no doubt was unaware that in 1941 he had written the first draft of a work called *Der Friede*, condemning Nazism, which he had hidden in the safe of his room at the Hôtel Majestic; but through his "adorable and terrible" way of writing about flowers, or the aristocratic poise of his style, Jünger seemed to Cocteau to be as much at odds with his time as himself, and on discovering his curiosity about drugs Cocteau sent him a book he enjoyed, *Fumeurs d'opium, comédiens ambulants.*[96]

Like Lieutenant Heller, Jünger served as an intermediary between Cocteau and the occupying authorities, whom he knew were the only ones with the power to lift a Vichy veto. In order to encourage them to allow the revival of *Les parents terribles* to be staged, he published an article in *Comoedia* showing how, beginning in 1938, the "gentlemen of the [pre-1940] ancien regime," lecherous old men that they were, had tried to see incest in the play.[97] Meanwhile Cocteau behaved prudently. He turned down an invitation to lunch at the embassy with Otto Abetz, but did not turn down all the invitations of Karl Epting, who entertained Gaston Gallimard as well as Jean-Louis Barrault at the Institut Allemand. The result was not long to come: in mid-December Cocteau was given permission to stage *Les parents terribles*, which provoked the ultras' fury. The editorial team at *La révolution nationale* sounded the alert; Laubreaux, Rebatet, Azema, and Ralph Soupault, along with Radio-Paris, fanned the flames, and the Cagoulard Jean Filliol headed up a commando team of 150—basically the 17th squadron—to go and bomb the stage with tear gas.[98] "The entire auditorium reacted passionately in defense of the play," Lannes wrote in his journal, but the rats released into the orchestra by the 17th squadron (a harassment technique that Cocteau would describe to Jünger) sent the audience running.

Cocteau had good reason to be frightened of Filliol, who was nicknamed "the killer." As head of the information service for the Mouvement Social Révolutionnaire, which had succeeded the Cagoule (the violent, secret, prewar anti-Republican organization) "on the visible front," he had already executed two Italian liberals seeking refuge in Paris, the Rosselli brothers, on orders from Mussolini.[99] During the night of October 2–3, 1941, the former *camelot* of the Muette quarter had headed up the squadron that had thrown dynamite into seven Parisian synagogues, with the German Sicherheitsdienst's blessing.[100] The public was frightened by the repeated attacks of the 17th squadron against the actors of the Gymnase, and, defeated by the cabal of ultras, *Les parents terribles* was taken off the bill again. After the blows that had struck *La machine à écrire*, the Collaborationist press was convinced they had succeeded in silencing Cocteau for a good long while; it had published enough articles against him to fill an entire anthology of literary hatred, which was then reaching unprecedented heights.

In the spring of 1942, Laubreaux could finally praise a play for being strong and healthy: *Les pirates de Paris,* which dealt courageously with the Stavisky Affair and dared to call "a Jew a Jew."[101] The author was praised all the more since the playwright, "Michel Daxiat," was none other than Laubreaux himself. French theater was saved.

IN THE HEART OF THE FURNACE

The true reason of a war is never known until all who have fought in it are dead.
— E. M. *Forster*, Abinger Harvest

WORK OR COLLABORATE?

The campaign against decadence would prove fruitful. In August 1942, for the first time since the Revolution, Pétain introduced to the French penal code an article that would condemn anyone committing a sexual act that was "against nature" with a minor (anyone under twenty-one years of age) to prison for six months to three years.[1] Eager to restore masculine authority, Vichy had nevertheless—or consequently—proved to be a veritable "nid de tantes" (nest of homos). From the academician Abel Hermant, an old journalist for the Occupied press and a member of the Groupe Collaboration, to the minister of national education Abel Bonnard, nicknamed "Gestapette" by Pétain himself; from the secretary of state to vice president Benoist-Méchin to Jean-Paul Martin, mentor to the young François Mitterrand—a part of the "pink elites" stalked the "old fart's" hallways.[2] (As early as 1916, Proust's Charlus had been pro-German.)

The Parisian supporters of collaboration were no less affected: the great bard of the bullfight and the stadium, Henry de Montherlant, "was one of them," as well as four of the ten writers who would make the trip to Germany, from Marcel Jouhandeau, who fell in love with Lieutenant Heller, to André Fraigneau, Cocteau's friend. There was great suspicion about Brasillach, as well as Drieu, who of course had women draped on him at all times, but whose appetite for power had led him to write in 1934, in *La comédie de Charleroi*: "I admired the Germans who came at me from the back," and who was perennially involved in a virile game of one-upmanship against homosexuality.[3]

This porousness made the Collaborationist press react even more virulently against Sodom's influence: cartloads of hatred were printed, and liters of spittle and splutterings delimited by the "...!...!...!" of Céline gushed out of the newsstands.[4] Having survived the Surrealists' vindictiveness for seventeen years, Cocteau of all people knew what the armed and almost official hatred of the ultras could do to him, especially because they had colonized two of the biggest daily newspapers in the capital, *Le petit Parisien* and *Paris-soir*.[5] Some, like Paulhan, were able to benefit from the discreet protection of Drieu, the most visible intellectual among the "collabos," in the name of the close relationship they had shared in the 1930s. Cocteau, however, could not expect anything from Drieu, to whom he had written at the end of the Great War, "You're a good man, but a bit soft, a bit sick, a phlegmatic believing in cynicism, and whom I could not imagine either liking or loathing."[6] Drieu himself, having applauded Cocteau's talents as a dramatist in the early 1920s, had cruelly caricatured him in the figure of Urcel, the drug addict whom his hero visits in his 1931 novel *Le feu follet*; Urcel "subtly abased himself" and could only mislead others "because he was never himself."[7] That left only the occupying forces, whom Cocteau had begun to approach.

Socializing with Germans in uniform was frowned on as just this side of unacceptable. At Maxim's, which served as a window onto Parisian life for the Wehrmacht—Arno Breker would say that every evening was a "feast for the eyes"—the majordomo attempted to keep French celebrities away from the Germans, who, at least in theory, were confined to the Omnibus, the least fashionable area. But there were a number of occasions when the two sides could meet, for Cocteau in particular, who lived in the same building as Maxim's owners, especially since they had asked him to paint the walls with frescoes in exchange for a permanent spot at their table, if not always in their famous restaurant on the rue Royale. Cocteau was so used to his German contacts, in fact, that he didn't see any problem with having Gerhardt Heller visit him in uniform at his home. In a mischievous moment, which would amuse the lieutenant but give Marie Bell the scare of her life, he arrived at Prunier, where the actress was waiting to lunch with him, with Heller in tow; soon he was lunching (of course at Maxim's) with Albert Speer, the architect whom Hitler had charged with designing the future Great Berlin.[8]

Four months after the cabal had brought down *Les parents terribles*, Cocteau, from his seat at Maxim's, addressed the alcoholic in a clown suit at a neighboring table. An ex-Communist turned fascist with Doriot, and a personal friend of Pierre Laval and Otto Abetz, Jean Fontenoy had managed to convince Cocteau that he was pure, sincere, and willing to break the law—he took drugs—as well as to astonish him with his surprisingly "romantic" way of living. "I won't commit suicide anymore," he said, "Every time I do I'm ill for six months."[9] He was a member of Deloncle's Mouvement Social Révolutionnaire, and knew well "the killer" Filliol, whose shock troopers had just managed to get Cocteau's play banned; so it was probably with an agenda in mind that the writer agreed to see him one evening.[10]

Paris's rejection of the Occupation intensified in early 1942. People in the street could be seen walking with two cane fishing poles—"deux gaules" (a play on "de Gaulle")—and German officers once again were shot at in the metro. The Feldgrau in the 1940s posters, holding a baby in their arms—"All those who have been abandoned, trust the German soldier"—were pulled down in favor of plac-ards with blood-red stripes, the Bekanntmachung, which encouraged the people of Paris to inform on each other and threatened them with reprisals if the "terror-ists" were not found. It became a very delicate time of waiting and seeing—some would support the Résistance, whether the London kind or the Moscow kind— while some would remain silent, and therefore complicit with the repressive forces. Few famous writers, however, took any kind of action: notable exceptions were René Char, who joined the maquis in 1943, and Jean Prévost. Seeing that he did not have the means to start a Resistance network, Sartre set about writing *L'être et le néant* and at Malagar Mauriac worked on his biography of Saint Margaret of Cortona. With his experience of the war in Spain, Malraux believed that any armed resistance would be doomed to failure; without military might, pushing back against the Occupiers became a simple moral wager. A real ambi-guity reigned in the literary world until 1943. Aragon and Elsa Triolet published with "Occupied" houses like Gallimard, or Collaborationist ones like Denoël, and sent texts to the unofficial "Resistance" presses in the south or the clandestine publications vilifying the houses that had "sold out" in the north; Paulhan was able both to socialize with Heller and launch the clandestine *Lettres françaises*; and Desnos joined a Parisian Resistance network, while publishing a novel with Gallimard on the drugged-out hell into which Yvonne George had plunged him.[11]

According to Simone de Beauvoir, the pro-Resistance writers tacitly agreed not to publish in the Occupied Zone, nor to speak on Radio Paris, which the Germans controlled. They did, however, permit themselves to publish in the Free Zone and to speak on Radio Vichy, under French control.[12] This distinction did not prevent Sartre from submitting an article to *Comoedia*, which was published in Paris and whose director would recommend Beauvoir to the director of Radio Vichy, for whom she would write some sketches. This weekly journal, however, was anything but pro-Resistance, even if its articles were mostly about culture—Cocteau had published theater reviews with them in 1941.[13]

Members of Cocteau's entourage were themselves on both sides of the fence. Roger Lannes, who worked in the Vichy censor's office, and the very young François Sentein, who taught in a program to train electricians, opposed de Gaulle, while Roger Stéphane, who had saved Cocteau during the difficult time in June 1940, buying him containers in which to transport his opium, leaned the other way.[14] A monarchist at heart, seduced at one time by the Spanish and Italian fascists, Lannes, while revolted by violence, was disdainful of Pétain but even more so of the Résistance. Like Sentein, born into an Action Française family, he was influenced by Montherlant's haughty ideas, as well as his athletic pederasty. He believed in an enchanted circle, physical and literary, from which he could exclude, with impotent rage, Chekhov and Claudel, calling them mediocre—regarding Cocteau, he alternated between the gravest reservations and the most complete enthusiasm.

When he had to give an opinion, Cocteau would tend to agree with that of his interlocutor; with Sentein, he could say, convincingly, "At heart, we're all monarchists!"; but one remark from Stéphane was enough to awaken his indignation against Vichy. Pétain's government was absurd, he would never take that back; the rigged trial he was holding at Riom against those in charge of the ancien régime—Blum, Daladier—was shameful; it was shocking how they'd banned the "zazous," those extravagant crimped-haired creatures rounded up by the hundreds by the police, in the cafés of the Champs-Elysées, and taken to the fields to work—this "regime of criminal Boy Scouts and truncheon blows" really wasn't for him.[15]

Sometimes the slightest word could make him change the subject and describe, in front of his devoted listeners, the vicissitudes of his friendship with Proust, long asthmatic monologues at the ready. He would lead them narratively into Marcel's room, which was covered with dust, but where the windows could never be opened, behind an anxious housekeeper who would ask if they had ever been in contact with a perfumed woman or even with flowers. He would then evoke the marvelous obsessive himself, sitting up in bed, wearing yellow gloves to prevent him from biting his nails—a man who paid a fortune to corrupt the workers who made noise in the building, and who could only survive with the help of an army of medicine and inhalers next to his bed, along with his accordion-shaped manuscript.[16]

Forever harassed with phone calls, invitations to dinner, and requests to write introductions, Cocteau no longer knew where to seat the young people who thronged the rue de Montpensier—"it was like Socrates and the *ephebes*," observed one regular.[17] He greeted his visitors as if he already knew them, and allowed the shy ones to look at his blackboard while he made a phone call or read the letters that piled up while he went out to lunch; they would often then spend the day waiting for him to return, snacking in the kitchen. The last metro was at eleven o'clock, and they sometimes spent the night in conversation, light years away from the tragedies bloodying Europe. They would laugh at his legendary impressions of Bérard, or at the jokes of Doelnitz, a party animal for whom the curfew was just an excuse to prolong these impromptu parties all night. Cocteau himself would tell them about meeting an Aurenche's friend who had begun to live as a woman, in the middle of the Occupation, but who made sure to tell him that he wasn't at all gay—to which Cocteau had politely replied, "Perhaps, but you're on the right path."[18] These were their favorite moments, in which he delighted them with his interest in everyone and his disinterest in the past; with his sense of humor, which became less unkind every year; and with the flashes of wit that seemed to pass right through him (according to Sentein) before striking those at whom they were aimed—and of course with that courtesy, which was so emphatic that it became almost poetic. Everyone would have forgotten the war if not for the German soldiers who came every morning to play chess by the fountains.

"Wit became as important as air to the people in my country," wrote Sentein, fascinated by the vivacity of this man whose skin was a bit weathered, "marked, tight," and who from the moment he awoke found himself assailed by pompous young men, by ladies staging poetry recitals, and by high-ranking civil servants, themselves reduced to sitting on the floor and hearing stories told they'd heard a hundred times before. Cocteau's repertoire had expanded over time. Capable even of imitating the dead, he could improvise verse worthy of Racine with Auric; when the erudite musician shouted, with a twirl of his cap, "That's enough, dear sir, return to your hovel, *Boeuf sur Toit*, *Grand écart*, *Terrible enfant* who heaves!" he would continue his side of the game by monologuing in alexandrines.[19]

Cocteau decided to put this irresistible talent to use by writing a verse tragedy worthy of that which France was living through, in order to show that in spite of the failure of *Les chevaliers de la table ronde* and the repeated bans against his plays, he had lost none of his theatrical prowess. Setting himself up in the little room that he had once used for opium, he worked quickly—"1,800 verses in 17 days," Roger Lannes noted with some alarm—then submitted *Renaud et Armide* to the Comédie-Française, which received it joyfully in January 1942.[20]

Two days later, the secretary of state for national education and youth, the Latin scholar Carcopino, described the piece as "untimely" and its author as "undesirable," sure that he had been condemned to prison by the tribunal in

Toulon. Taking all the usual steps to prevent this, Cocteau drafted a respectful letter to Maréchal Pétain. His friends, however, convinced him that currying favor with a regime that had made him into the antithesis of all they believed in was not the best politics, and once again his letter was filed away in a drawer.[21] The Collaborationist press somehow caught wind of this letter, however, and their insults became even more descriptive. This time they decided he had a glandular disorder, said he had a "fetid" attraction for an "enjuivé" society in which he splashed around like "a monkfish in a drowned man's trousers." They called him a "homo" and a "puppet of the salon and the fart bars," and insisted that "le grand écart" (the split) was one of his favorite "positions." Reminding readers that he had played "the little queen in the flowerbeds of Judeo-Masonic tolerance," *Au pilori* concluded its Cocteau flaming with an explicit call for a ban, if not worse: "M. Cocteau . . ., who declared that Hitler was only jealous of the fame of the Jew Chaplin, has no place in the new Europe."[22]

Determined to save *Renaud et Armide*, Cocteau turned to Lieutenant Heller again, who had just come in February, with Ernst Jünger, to hear him read his play at the home of Gaston Gallimard's secretary; Gallimard was present as well.[23] "We all fell under its magic spell," the lieutenant would say, while Jünger described it as a "song woven of floating threads," "of a light yet irresistible power."[24] At the same time, Cocteau grew close to a group of German intellectuals who met at the home of the Valentiner brothers (two soldiers who served as interpreters) and lived in a studio under the rooftops of a building on the quai Voltaire.[25] It was an open, well-lit space, where Cocteau, relieved, heard outrage over Céline's racist rantings and laughter regarding *Au pilori's* insults against him—even if these Germans did not always understand his cast of mind. It was a warm haven, with a view over the bell tower of the church at Saint-Germain-des-Prés, above the rooftops, and where everyone was very aware of the role of public enemy number one that the ultras claimed he played. "If the newspapers were published on a postage stamp they'd still make room to insult you," Jünger said with a smile.[26] These Germans were such Francophiles that he felt more at home among them than among the "national" press. He confided to his journal, "A homeland is where men meet and find themselves immediately on the same page."[27] It was disturbing, in the middle of the war, to hear Germans describe a first edition they had found at the Seine-side booksellers, then discuss Tocqueville or Léon Bloy, but Gaston Gallimard, who had practically integrated Heller into his editorial committee, confirmed it: it was less difficult to get along with "good" Germans than with "bad" Frenchmen, easier to speak with Abetz than with Céline, who would complain of being mistreated by the literary world in his own country.

These "good" Germans officially refused to get involved in Franco-Vichy affairs; in truth, they offered "disinterestedly" to mediate between the two, if not to reconcile them, and readily took the more liberal side. As long as the matter did not concern the question of Jews and the image of Germany, it was delightful for the poison to play the remedy. These Germans were, however, in the minority, and without political power. Lieutenant Heller, seeing him at the home of the Morands, assured Cocteau of his personal protection, but meanwhile *Renaud et Armide* remained banned.[28]

For their part, the Valentiner brothers could make fun of "Hitler's circus" and allow Cocteau to see the doubts that were beginning to occur to the Occupiers, but the situation remained as blocked as ever on the theatrical "front." Cocteau finally asked Suzanne Abetz to become the play's sponsor, a role she apparently accepted willingly.

These collusions, however, exasperated the ultras more and more every day. They repeatedly protested Heller's "laxity," which Drieu called decadent. They also denounced Karl-Heinz Bremer, the second-in-command of the Institut Allemand who did not hide his admiration for Cocteau (he had taught at the École Normale Supérieure before the war), and so had him sent to the eastern front, where he met his death.[29] In Paris too everyone wanted to find out who would protect whom. What would the editors of *Je suis partout* have said if they'd learned that Captain Jünger spent his evenings listening to Cocteau tell about his visits to the "arabescoïde" Proust?

PICASSO'S OCCUPATIONS

In the spring of 1942 the war seemed to be getting closer to the capital. There were regular warnings for inhabitants to hide in shelters, cellars, and metro stations, which they would enter like ghosts with their lighters, and from which they would emerge to see the Feldgrau patrolling while singing the "Horst Wessel Lied," or tanks topped with very young, very blond soldiers crawling up and down the boulevards, gun turrets open.[30] Marked with signs written in German, covered with posters encouraging French citizens to go work in Germany to "save Europe from Bolshevism," Paris in some places seemed to have been deserted once again. Thousands of men had fled to the Free Zone for racial, political, or simply food-based reasons, while many others had been killed on the front. Not until December 1941 did Cocteau learn that Khill had died in Alsace, killed by a stray bullet on June 18, 1940, the day the Armistice was requested.

The emptiness of the capital brought Cocteau closer to Picasso, as it had in 1916. They began to lunch together again, most often at the Catalan, a chic, expensive bistro on the rue des Grands-Augustins, an oasis of civilization that was forced to close for a while for having served meat during the rationing days. Some days they met on the rue de Savoie, in the studio of Dora Maar, the painter's new girlfriend. The decline of Surrealism and the rise of the Front Populaire allowed the two men to confide in each other again. Picasso invited Cocteau to his openings, or showed him in advance his canvases, like *Guernica*, which had been commissioned for the Spanish pavilion at the 1937 World Fair. More than ever, Cocteau saw Picasso as the word of God made flesh, a kind of couple in which the male and the female lived tangled up together, he coarse and hard-working, she loving to be seen and flattered.

Marais's personality also helped to reunite Cocteau and Picasso. Though he could not love Marais's painting (though Cocteau had hoped he would), Picasso unreservedly admired his physique, and had so enjoyed *Britannicus* that he had sent Dora Maar to photograph it. But if Cocteau celebrated the faun in the actor, Picasso saw in him the courtesan that he would "set up" under Brassaï's lens, in the lustful pose of an odalisque, his arms crossed behind his head, at the feet of a female nude he had just bought. He then asked Dora to photograph this spectacular overgrown boy. Never had Picasso's latent homosexual desire—which he believed naturally stemmed from his virility—been so stimulated.

At the same time, these reunions highlighted the gap between the two artists' ways of being and acting. Whereas Cocteau put himself at Marais's service out of love, while allowing him to act in his own creative universe, Picasso jealously fed on Dora Maar, his model, his primary source of inspiration, his other self, and soon, his possession. Once Maar did Cocteau's portrait, and he returned the compliment with a charcoal sketch. Picasso, possessive down to the marrow of his bones, painted over Cocteau's canvas with a representation in oil of *his* Dora.[31] Cocteau, obviously, did not dare to say anything. He had always been weak with Picasso, whom he believed to be invulnerable. "Here," Picasso had written on the doorway on the rue des Grands-Augustins where Balzac placed the painter's studio in "The Unknown Masterpiece," like a demiurge ready to sign every object on earth: the immense loft with a view over all of Paris was the center of the world that Picasso was pleased to co-sign, on equal footing with the other Creator. Having repudiated the too-bourgeoise Olga, Picasso had gone back to his bohemian life, his jumble of brushes and tubes, and the familiar scent of his Afghan hound. Marais's elegance, and Cocteau's impeccable trousers, became a subject of mockery for a painter who now worked in his slippers. "For as long as I have known him," Picasso told Brassaï, "his pleats have always been perfect . . . Cocteau was born . . . ironed."[32] It was his way of being affectionate: ruthlessly visual and rich in sarcasm.

Sometimes they would attend a private screening for a film that Marais had acted in, or Cocteau had written—often they were one and the same. Then they would enjoy the good weather with a drink on a café terrace, making fun of ladies' hats—worthy of wedding cakes, made of boiled cardboard, reminiscent of the wigs of Louis XVI's reign. Picasso was so inventive in his cruelty that Cocteau wondered how Dora managed to live, locked up as she was in his personality. "Loves intensely and kills all he loves," said a graphologist, studying the painter's handwriting.[33] Indeed, Dora would soon abandon photography and take up a cycle of paintings that Picasso could have come up with on vacation one day.

In the midst of the Occupation, Picasso found himself in a strange situation. Having refused to leave France when the Germans arrived, as much through egotistical inertia as passive resistance, he had never stopped working but had been forbidden from showing his work. Since *Guernica* had censured Nazi Germany's support for Franco's troops, and thereby betrayed the collusion between "degenerate art" and Marxism, the censors had been able to order that one of his paintings be taken down from its place in the Galerie Charpentier. At the same time they could be found everywhere at the Galerie Louis Leiris; certain German officers, like Heller, even came to admire them in Picasso's studio, where Jünger tried to buy them. Picasso, to hear him tell it, merely offered them reproductions of *Guernica*. "Did you do that?" an indignant Gestapo officer asked him one day. "No, you did," he replied.[34]

Appointed by the Spanish Republic as director of the Prado—a job he never actually started—Picasso was obviously not sheltered from arbitrary events, by virtue of his status as a foreigner. Officers from the Wehrmacht regularly came round to grill him about his Jewish origins—his mother was half-Jewish—which certain ultra critics readily repeated when a suspicious photographer did not continue his report indefinitely, so that the hand of Hauptsturmführer Dannecker, the all-powerful chargé of Jewish affairs, was suspected. One day some Germans came by, called Picasso a Jew and a degenerate, and left after knocking over and destroying a few canvases. But a friend of Cocteau's, the former assistant director of the Sûreté Nationale, André-Louis Dubois, regularly stopped by to make sure all was well.[35] Dubois, despite having been dismissed by Vichy in 1940, still had numerous contacts at the Préfecture, including Maurice Toesca, another friend of Cocteau's, who extended his painter's visa.[36] The Spanish ambassador to Vichy, Lecquerica, also seemed discreetly to watch over Picasso. Consequently the painter had continued working without worrying too much about the situation.

Neither Picasso nor Cocteau had any love for Vichy, but it was not a subject worthy of their discussion. They preferred to discuss the strange, half-coercive, half-anarchist regime they imposed on themselves. "His secret is to incarnate his own politics, and to endlessly stage his own revolution," Cocteau said of the painter.[37] The phrase, which also applied to himself, indicated the bubble in which Picasso went through the war, to an even greater extent than Cocteau. "Where would I be better off than with friends, where stupidity, ugliness, vulgarity, and current events cannot find any point of entry?" the poet said, after a day spent with Picasso and Dora Maar.[38] They both saw each other as somehow above "that"—not being soldiers, they did not see why the war should infringe on their working time. By abolishing all dependence on popular prejudice, and, soon, all feelings of guilt about other people's opinions, they had managed to flourish artistically: the same reasons that had led them to create *Parade*, during a period of massacres in Verdun, would allow them to keep the Second World War at arm's length. "Together, seated here as we are, we will negotiate peace this very afternoon," Picasso said to Jünger: It was the incontestable truth.[39] "Events bore me," Valéry confessed to Lieutenant Heller. "Events are the froth of life, but I'm more interested in the sea."[40] The sea was all that interested Cocteau and Picasso, when they walked in Paris.

The painter occasionally suffered at the hands of his French rivals. In June 1942 a bitter Vlaminck accused his former Montparnasse neighbor of plagiarism, "the Stavinsky of painting . . . impotence incarnate."[41] This was an appeal to those prejudices that saw every Jew as an imitator and a con man. But soon Lhote took up his pen to support him, and Cocteau protested to the director of the paper. Picasso returned to work, reassured by his defenders' vigilance. They were rather quiet, however, about the November 1941 measures that stripped their friend Max Jacob of his copyright and royalties. It would obviously have been risky for the half-Jewish painter and *enjuivé* invert poet to protest publicly, but apparently it did not occur to them to help Jacob further. Jacques Rivière wrote at the end of the First World War, at a time when artists' moral attitudes were greatly debated,

> I believe that a great writer cannot be a great character . . . He must be preoccupied with himself; he is badly made for devotion and sacrifice . . . he must distance himself a little from his feelings to see them clearly, and so they are never . . . as real as they are for other people.[42]

Life went on, and life, for Picasso and Cocteau, was about painting and writing, about finding something to sell and publish—and on occasion about lunching on the avenue Foch with a couple of wealthy patrons, Marcello and Hortensia Anchorena, whom Jean Hugo renamed the Sanchezes of Alcatraz in his wonderful memoirs.[43] These eccentric Argentinians invited only poets and painters—including Paul Éluard, Valentine Hugo, and Dora Maar—mainly those of the Surrealist persuasion, though if anything seemed dreamlike in this time of scarcity it was the exuberance of their menus and their footman in livery. Built in the shape of an amphitheater, their living room led gradually to balconied loggias; hidden by rows of books in which *Mein Kampf* reigned under a portrait of Hitler, whom the Anchorenas took to be the greatest man of the century, the walls were framed by *trompe l'oeil* doors onto which Braque and Jean Hugo had painted characters scrutinizing the guests, in a kind of Hitler-Dalí-ism as imagined by De Chirico, who had also contributed to the decor. "Modern luxury in all its atrocious mystery," said Cocteau, who was at first approached to design the entire apartment, but who preferred to draw in chalk on a little piano made of hollow slate containing only a record player.[44] Picasso, who found the place even more hideous than Cocteau did—and said so very bluntly to their hosts—promised to do the door to the bathroom, which never ended up leaving his studio.[45] Thus did Cocteau and Picasso earn their entry to these jolly lunches, which they judged to be slightly "too rich with sauce," in keeping with the Anchorenas' tastes. Once there, Cocteau liked to trot out his favorite old stories while doodling on the piano, making Picasso and Maar laugh.[46] The Harlequin from *Parade*, the bird-catcher of 1922, lived again before the painter's eyes; he would sometimes stay as late as six in the evening to listen. The war was ravaging Europe, but the only human comedy was in the living room on the avenue Foch.

Picasso and Cocteau were seen together often that year. "Still young and svelte; not a strand of silver in his brush-cut hair," noted Brassaï when he ran into Cocteau with Picasso; "he is all nerve and muscle, without a single excessive ounce of flesh. His long hands with the bony wrists and elongated fingers, admirably highlighted—theatrically—by his jacket sleeves which are so narrow and short that they seem skimpy, flutter about and accompany the vertiginous volubility of his lips."[47] But Picasso also knew how to dampen the poet's enthusiasm. Hearing Cocteau exclaim, "Yesterday I made an enormous drawing and I'm very satisfied with it," he would reply, "You're very lucky."[48]

In truth, Picasso kept a certain amount of distance. He almost never came to the rue de Montpensier, where Cocteau had hoped he would contribute to his chalkboard drawings. The role of Picasso's personal poet laureate had been reserved since the late 1920s for Paul Éluard. After breaking with Breton in 1938, who reproached him for supporting Stalin, the Communist poet had founded a clandestine journal, *Les lettres françaises*, as well as a clandestine Resistance network, but he continued to publicly socialize with Picasso, sometimes going against elementary rules of prudence. In time Éluard would run into Cocteau at the painter's studio, lunch with him at the Catalan and at Zatoste, a Basque greasy spoon, and then encounter him at Lise Deharme's, so that his mere presence in her home earned her the nickname the "Queen of the Résistance." After twenty years of hostility, Cocteau had been released from his position of semi-pariah. Valentine Hugo, who was very close to Éluard, eventually made up with him as well; she even applied a fixative to the colors on the piano he had decorated for the Anchorenas. Another Surrealist who served as a mailbox for the Résistance, Georges Hugnet, also wanted to see Cocteau again, recalling the wonderful years at the Welcome. One could even find Robert Desnos, who at one time had spoken of assassinating Cocteau, having lunch with the former "angel turd," letting himself be "dazzled" by his conversation.[49]

Their hatred, if Cocteau is to be believed, had softened as early as 1925, when a reading of *L'ange Heurtebise* had greatly affected Éluard. Only Breton's threats of excommunication made Éluard sign an offensive article. The war had forced Breton into exile in New York, and Éluard reclaimed a "national" poetry, in rhymed verses; protected by Aragon, brought back to favor at Picasso's side, Cocteau ceased to be the enemy. He had already had the pleasure of receiving a signed copy of Éluard's last collection of poems; he would even have the satisfaction of having him pose for three days in front of his easel.[50]

ARNO BREKER AND KUBISM

From time to time there came to Paris a German sculptor, a cultivated, handsome man who willingly offered his services resolving problems that French artists might encounter. Arno Breker was not unknown in Montparnasse; he had gone to art school there before the war, with Maillol as his mentor, before marrying one of his models—"an intelligent, bohemian Greek woman," Jünger said.[51] Cocteau said they'd known each other since the 1920s, but Breker mentioned meeting him only at the Boeuf sur le Toit, with Fernand Léger. When Breker returned to Paris in the fall of 1940 in order to improve relations between the two countries, one of the first people he contacted, aside from Man Ray who would do his portrait several times, was Cocteau, the French writer whom the Germans knew best (even if Breker had evidently read nothing of his work, just as Cocteau knew nothing of Breker's sculptures).

Hitler was impressed with Breker's monumental works, in which outsized Greek heroes marched in place, staring out to the horizon in grandeur, and commissioned him to do his bust, then the entirety of the Grand Berlin work that Speer was designing. But when Breker opened up to Cocteau about his artistic projects in the Europe to come, he asked that Cocteau see him only as a Montparno, not as the representative of an occupying force. And when, in spring 1941, the ultra press unleashed its anger against Cocteau, Breker "spontaneously" arranged to be contacted "by a special line to Berlin, in case something serious happened."[52] A favor from one artist to another, Breker said—one that extended to Picasso, Cocteau said. The bond was established. How many times this special line was used, no one can say, but it probably explains the strange impunity with which Marais had struck Laubreaux.[53] Cocteau, nevertheless, had hidden Breker's intervention from the intrepid Marais, worried he would be against it; likewise, he declined Breker's offer to intervene on his behalf "in high places" to stop the insults from the fascist press, so as not to be too exposed. He wanted to be protected, not compromised.[54]

Upon getting back to work in April 1942, Laval organized an exhibition of Breker's works at the Jeu de Paume, in the Tuileries, to prove his goodwill toward Germany. To inaugurate this homage, some in Vichy thought of Cocteau, and sent Chardonne, the author of *Claire*, to sound him out ("The tragedy is his sculpture; it has to be mediocre," Cocteau confided in his journal), but then the leaders of Pétain's government changed their minds, probably due to fear of the ultras.[55] It was Abel Bonnard and then Benoist-Méchin who presented Hitler's favorite works, on May 15, to the Collaborationist elite. Cocteau was not part of the welcoming committee, but it is his worried face that can be seen behind a series of flat caps, including that of the General von Stülpnagel, elbow to elbow with Derain and Van Dongen, Maillol and Despiau, in front of the cluster of naked giants, so close to each other that Guitry was grateful, once outside, that they were not in heat; if they had been hard, no one could have ever moved.

Breker did all he could to honor his friend the writer; three days later, Cocteau returned to see the exhibition with the artist and his wife. Recognizing the body of a cycling champion whom he had admired in the 1930 Tour de France, Cocteau was complimentary about the musculature, the realism of the veins, and the "almost sensual taste for detail" of Breker's neo-Greek—if not pre-gay—statues. Did they remind him of a time when he worshipped humans as gods? Did they inspire one of his "aesthetic erections" that he would mention more and more, as he aged? Cocteau persuaded himself that he was in the presence of work worthy of Michelangelo and returned to see the show with Marais, thinking that Marais's physique might inspire Breker, and finally went so far as to applaud the sculptor in the press. Having refused to publicly acknowledge his admiration for the company from Munich that had just performed Goethe's *Iphigenie auf Tauris* at the Théâtre Français (which he watched from the box of Abetz, who was anxious to demonstrate that his actors were superior to those of the Comédie-Française, who were doing the same play at the same time), Cocteau preferred to think that this time he could demonstrate his courage, as well as his singular and entirely inopportune nature, by publicly praising an enemy artist.[56] The French were already protesting this foreign exhibition; against these chauvinists, he would prove that a German could be a good sculptor. For a while he thought he was lending a hand to a friend in need, an unappreciated artist, whereas all the key institutions of Parisian collaboration were celebrating Hitler's protégé: even Pétain sent him a note of congratulations. That was how a homage to a sculptor who helped Marais out of a tight spot was transformed into an internationalist manifesto, though no one had asked Cocteau to do anything—or maybe it was for this very reason.

Published on the front page of *Comoedia* on May 23, 1942, Cocteau's "Salute to Breker" reverberated loudly. Breker was not only the official sculptor of the Reich; he had also become a symbol of German plundering, from the zinc of the bistro counters to the bronze of public statues, which could be melted down and turned into not only cannons, but also, as some rumors had it, into his colossal pieces. Breker would later say that he had asked Hitler to spare all the great Parisian sculptures, including the Fontaine Carpeaux at the Observatoire, but he did acknowledge having used between sixty and eighty tons of bronze.[57]

Éluard was the first to reproach Cocteau for his article. His letter was sober, dignified, and just:

> Freud, Kafka, and Chaplin have been banned by the same people who honor Breker. You were believed to be among those forbidden. How wrong you have been to suddenly show yourself among these censors! The best of those who admire you and love you have had a painful surprise.[58]

His conclusion—"Trust us. Nothing further should separate us"—left the door open to reconciliation, although this time Cocteau no doubt deserved, for the first time, one of the violent reactions to which the Surrealists had made him accustomed. Éluard perhaps secretly hoped that Cocteau would intervene in his favor if he were ever arrested, through his "contacts"; Cocteau too perhaps thought that Éluard would protect him from potential enemies, when the Liberation came. Whatever the reason, by the fall Éluard and Cocteau had been reunited at Picasso's home; Aragon himself did not even seem to have protested against this "Salute to Breker" that Mauriac, and Paulhan after him, described as odious.

However compromising Cocteau's letter, it brought no grist to the Nazis' mill. While Laubreaux praised Breker's work as an example of art's fight against decadence, he included a poetic description of the nighttime arrival, on the deserted Place de la Concorde, of these enormous statues advancing in the moonlight "with the terrible step of the Vénus d'Ille."[59] Paradoxically, Cocteau was the only one of Breker's French sycophants not to celebrate the heroic virility of his figures. Cocteau may have been attracted to men, but not to force in and of itself; he had always rejected it. This view set him apart from others like Bonnard or Benoist-Méchin, for whom the giants of this crude National Socialism represented the master race that was supposed to dazzle "healthy" people and make tremble the degenerate races—Jews, Gypsies, Slavs, as well as homosexuals, the mad, and the handicapped—whom the Reich wanted to reduce to slaves, or ashes. Breker was evidently not Hitler's protégé by chance; his work was clear and accessible and offered viewers the impression of being themselves monumental, or at least worthy of the paroxysms of virility that they still lacked. Walter Benjamin saw this kind of identification as the essence of fascist art. "I always choose [my athletes] from among the most splendid men, belonging to a reborn, pure race," Breker confirmed in *Comoedia*.[60]

Cocteau defended himself. His "Salute" was meant to attack artificial boundaries in art, he said; as in the time of *Parade*, the true creators were indifferent to country, they were "above" the questions posed by the Germans' presence. In short, it was as brave to celebrate Breker in 1942 as it was to militate for "Kubisme" in 1915, or to introduce German Expressionism, after 1918, to an "anti-Boche" public—as if Germanophilia were a virtue in and of itself, against the nationalist Right of 1917 or the left-wing Resistance of their own period. It was a paradoxical kind of reasoning from someone who during the First World War had accused Wagner and Schoenberg of being heavy and megalomaniacal because they were German, though they had given proof of a genius that cruelly outstripped that of the sculptor of the Reich. There was an important difference of size between the two wars: the German army was ruling over Paris, and the frontiers had been abolished for its sole profit. If Laval visited the exhibition, lunched with Breker, and threw him a reception at the Théâtre Hébertot, it was less out of love for eternal beauty and more to please a country that had sent Goering to see the show, incognito. How was it possible to separate Breker's work from history, when soon thereafter, on June 22, 1942, Laval publicly claimed to support Germany's victory just before the exhibition was reserved, the entire month of August, for German soldiers?

"GÖTTERDÄMMERUNG"

Cocteau eventually came to trust Arno Breker, with their friendship solidified by this shared ordeal.[61] The sculptor, who was using some of his time to demand the removal of the head of the German censor who had dared to question Cocteau about the film he was already writing for Marais, and who was calling Berlin so the actor could obtain a visa immediately for Italy, where he was meant to present *Carmen*, was beginning to seem unusually generous to Cocteau. If anyone could protect him against further attacks from the ultras, it was certainly this pro-French artist, who was enthusiastic about building a kind of supranational republic of creative types. Later, Cocteau would justify his "Salute" by pointing to the French camera operators who had escaped forced labor in Germany thanks to his appeals to Breker.[62] The sculptor himself confirmed that a number of French prisoners owed their freedom, if not their lives, to him—including Dina Verny, Maillol's partner; the Jewish pianist of the singer Germaine Lubin; Madame Flammarion, who was also "of Jewish origins"; the poet Patrice de La Tour du Pin, who would in fact be liberated in November 1942; and Picasso, on whose behalf Breker had intervened with one of Himmler's men, who was a little too interested in his origins.[63]

But did Breker really do what he claimed to have done? Cocteau, as usual, believed it all, and was easily moved. This incessant desire to be of service transformed the sculptor into a true knight of friendship, and Cocteau would be the last to refuse to pose by his side—even when he later discovered that the photographer worked for *Signal*, the general interest magazine for the German army forces.[64] Cocteau opposed only Breker's invitation to come pose for him in Berlin; Jean Marais openly rejected the offer. And Breker became a true friend, a man with whom Cocteau could dine by candlelight, talking of the good old days in Montparnasse, and of the bright, enormous workshop like a factory where he worked in the German countryside, at Jäckelsbruch, seventy kilometers east of Berlin, where bronze and stone arrived by a little river that had been specially dredged and enlarged for the purpose.

Who else could have offered such favorable circumstances in which to work? Who else had built a little town of villas designed to welcome his artist friends, just to the side of a seventeenth-century chateau where French prisoners worked for the sheer joy of it? Who else would have given him carte blanche to create the sculptures for the new chancellery? Who else would have bought a bronze bust of Wagner from him for his Berghof chalet? Who wanted artists to live as happily as dukes? Hitler, the Chancellor of the New Germany. A generous, amiable protector, easygoing in his daily relations and showing astonishing artistic intuition. A born architect, prevented only by lack of money from learning the rules of art, but also a great lover of the cinema, who could watch films all night in his Bavarian retreat. To say nothing of music, of which the Chancellor had an intimate knowledge, to the point that he had even convinced Wagner's daughter-in-law, Winifred, upon hearing him sing, that he would return one day to Bayreuth as a tenor.[65] He had composed an opera in his youth, after all, and the Petit Palais had shown one of his busts in imitation bronze in 1941.

Did Cocteau believe, like all of France, that Hitler was only a little house painter? Breker told him of the brief but extraordinary trip that Hitler had made to a deserted Paris, in June 1940. He had made a thorough inspection by car, and from Trocadéro to Montparnasse, from the Étoile to the Concorde, the City of Light had dazzled the Führer. "It's the most beautiful theater in the world!" he had exclaimed when he saw for the first time the Opéra, whose plans he knew by heart. By the end of this visit, the Chancellor told Breker that Paris was *the* town where he would have liked to have studied, if he had had the means, like Breker, and he grew nostalgic for the days when his ambitions had been merely artistic. As emotional as a schoolboy, he returned to Berlin resolved to show magnanimity to the French, as if to prove to them that he had not arrived to conquer but to liberate. This was why the Wehrmacht had not organized the monstrous parade down the Champs-Elysées, and had ordered the immediate execution of any solder caught looting. If France had been so well-treated, if life in Paris continued to be relatively tranquil, in spite of certain incidents, if the German honor corps went round the Étoile playing "Tout ça ne vaut pas l'amour," it was because, encouraged by his favorite sculptor, Hitler had given the order to his officers to behave like visitors, not Occupiers.[66]

Cocteau finally understood the strange clemency that Paris had enjoyed. He who had always loved to know what was happening behind the scenes began to wonder if his countrymen hadn't misunderstood. "No one in Germany considered France to be vanquished," Breker insisted, and what a shame that Paris had rejected the Chancellor's proposal: two parallel marches on either side of the Rhine, with German and French troops throwing down their weapons. It would have put an end to their thousand-year war! Yes, it was because of such refusals, disrespect, and insults that Hitler had been almost forced to make war. He was a pacifist at heart, fundamentally Francophile, like Breker; though he had had to make certain sacrifices for his country, he still preferred artists to soldiers. After the Madeleine and the Trocadéro, had he not specifically asked to see the Montparnasse house where Breker had learned to sculpt? "It was the rue Joseph Bara, in the building where Modigliani once did my portrait," Cocteau confided to Paul Valéry, a more than troubling coincidence for someone who had never believed in chance. Cocteau listened, amazed, to the sculptor, like Little Red Riding Hood captivated by her grandmother's stories, in spite of her big hairy nostrils.[67]

Who knows what else Breker said? He was also a mythomaniac, to such an extent that he told Hitler that his Greek wife was descended from Phidias and had promised to tell him the secret of his method. He described to Cocteau the passionate conversations he had had with the Chancellor while traveling between Paris, Berlin, and his immense villa at Berchtesgaden, sheltered by a "heroic circle of mountains," while flocks of eagles soared in the mist.[68] That was where the Führer had confessed his wish to add the land of Napoleon to his triumphs, as well as his desire to instill a great cultural policy, in which he, Breker, would become the protector of all the true artists, in a Europe that would finally be united and prosperous, once the war was won. Was he not on the brink of abolishing borders and distributing European identity cards? "France has never seen such a sensitive man," Breker repeated.[69]

Flattered at having been chosen as the witness to such an exceptional friendship, Cocteau bought it hook, line, and sinker. Maurice Sachs judged Hitler to be gifted "to the highest degree with a sense for the drama of History," and Gide himself had revealed, in November 1940, "Who knows, perhaps we're doing Hitler a disservice in thinking his ultimate dream isn't world harmony."[70] Cocteau began to think the German leader was a marvelous patron who only abolished nations to bring artists closer together. It was as if his home were not Berchtesgaden, in Bavaria, but Neuschwanstein, the chateau where Louis II had watched over Wagner with loving vigilance. In the heart of the Reich, too, was the villa of Tribschen, where Nietzsche came with utter devotion to listen to the musician compose; it wouldn't take much for the Chancellor to unite the creater of *Parsifal* with that of *Die fröhliche Wissenschaft* (Gay science), fifty years after their falling out. This is how the anti-Wagernian of 1916 became psychologically unified with the sculptor he had saluted.

Hannah Arendt would compare the Nazis to a gang of déclassés who wanted to steal from others their sense of reality. Breker didn't have too much trouble robbing Cocteau of what little he had left. For decades he had lived in an opium fog, with no sense of the economic reality of his contemporaries, and he let himself be won over by the mythologizing haze that surrounded the official hypnotist of the Reich, "Kniebolo," as Jünger mockingly referred to him, Bismarck's mongrel Mabuse. His reign was an example of politics turned legend, the climax of history, fate hoisting itself up to the level of a lyrical Götterdämmerung. Cocteau restrained himself from making any further public declarations, but in the privacy of his journal he reproached his country for treating the German Chancellor with "absolute disrespect and ingratitude." Hitler became the victim of a heartless nation that had been underhanded and hostile toward artists, one arrogant enough to call this frustrated artist a "peintre au pistolet" (spray painter, or "painter with a pistol"), the son of a customs agent, and an apocalyptic failure when he had through total devotion turned himself into a patron of Olympic proportions.[71]

Breker's siren song drowned out the pillaging, the reprisals, and the executions of hostages, and changed Cocteau's view of the war as if with a magic potion. But which of Cocteau's friends could have opened his eyes? Not Fraigneau, who thought himself the most important of his disciples; he had returned a total enthusiast from his trip to Germany in autumn 1941. Cocteau's world had always been filled with exceptional people and demi-gods. "I go the way that Providence dictates with the assurance of a sleepwalker," Hitler declared in 1936: this was exactly the kind of statement that would have impressed Cocteau.[72] It was Cocteau's turn to be victim to the hypnosis that had enabled Speer, through his "cathedrals of light" and his lantern-lit processions, or Leni Riefenstahl, filming the criss-crossing leaps of the Reich's athletes, to orient the German people to Hitler's dreams. By aestheticizing his ideologies, Cocteau was living through these days in the most complete fiction. Intrigued to learn that Breker's Greek wife had willingly told the Chancellor's fortune, he was even more interested to learn that the head of the German state always told the sculptor to be careful when he drove, and that he never went to sleep without speaking to him on the telephone. More than a patron, Hitler seemed to be a pseudo-father figure. "Breker is his adoptive son," Cocteau noted, moved. "Like Jeannot is for me." He even wanted to see this as a secret of the Führer, who was not known at the time to have had any affairs with women and was still childless, at the age of fifty-three—he had managed, like Cocteau, to sublimate his sexuality into art and paternity. Identifying with Hitler in this way led Cocteau to write the maddest things in his journal that even a child would not have believed. But Cocteau was exactly like a naive schoolboy who (having been informed by his classmates) asks his mother if Santa Claus really exists, and is asked in reply: "Do you want him to exist?" Yes, he wanted him to.[73]

When Breker went back to Germany, the mirage tended to dissolve. The fascination that Cocteau had for the cloud of Nazism gave way, in his sleepwalking awareness, to the real war, with its irritating tendency not to be artistic. The 300,000 French workers whom Hitler demanded to support his war effort, and the roundups that led young people to avoid the metro out of fear of being sent to the compulsory work service, reminded him that the German army hadn't come to France to sponsor oboe competitions.[74] "A terrible weight, a vague malaise," he noted in his journal, the day after the publication of his "Salute to Breker." Camille Mauclair, too, managed to bring him down to reality by adding him to the bottom of his list of "merchants" and "aliens" who had brought on the current decadence in French literature, in *L'appel*. Cocteau found himself described as the idol of "inverts, swindlers, drug addicts," one of the "more or less famous literary whores of either sex," which included the playwright Bernstein and the "Jew Darius Milhaud" with his "unclean music." "The sophists and liars of history worthy of being included among those responsible for [the] Riom [trials]," concluded the critic. *Je suis partout* had not a word to say in protest.[75]

Cocteau, on May 28, had already fallen apart seeing Marais pack for Italy, where he would stay for four months. This time he felt he had truly been emptied from within.

A FIGHT TO THE DEATH

In late May 1942, all Jews over the age of six living in the Occupied Zone were required to wear a yellow star over their heart, as big as the "palm of a hand," with the word JEW written in Gothic letters. They no longer had the right to own a radio or a telephone, and they lost the right to leave their neighborhood; to do errands (except between three and four o'clock); to go to restaurants, cinemas, or libraries; to use public baths and toilets, pools, municipal gardens, and campgrounds; and even to play the national lottery. Merely being Jewish could lead to being arrested and detained. Though they had mostly kept quiet to that point, the Parisians began to find this treatment unjust. A number of people began to wear yellow stars on their clothes, with the words AUVERGNAT, BRETON, GOY, ZAZOU, or even PAPUAN and IDEALIST written on them. The Gaullist and Communist networks asked their members to greet Jews with signs of sympathy on June 7, the date they had taken the initiative to gather on the Grands Boulevards. More of a realist on this occasion, Cocteau saluted "Parisians' extraordinary tact" when faced with the appearance of the yellow star, and declared himself indignant at this stigmatizing of Jews, which he felt was straight out of the Middle Ages with its singling out of lepers. But it would have been more accurate to speak of their courage rather than their tact; all Parisians wearing these fake yellow stars were arrested.

Cocteau acted with dignity, given the situation. He was the first to warn his Jewish friends when he learned that the Germans were planning to re-arrest those who had managed to get out of Drancy, and continued to write to Roger Stéphane, *né* Worms, in the prison to which Vichy had sent him. Likewise, he would be one of those rare people who, with Picasso, attended the funeral of Chaim Soutine, whose "Jewish" expressionism was at odds with its time. On July 1, 1942, while dining out with Paul Valéry, Cocteau "cautiously murmured" his concern about Colette's fate, given that her husband, Maurice Goudeket (a classmate of his at the Lycée Condorcet) had been arrested with a thousand other Jews seven months earlier as a reprisal for the United States' having entered the war. Such was the general ignorance about the exact whereabouts of the deportees, however, that Colette was almost relieved not to jump with fright every time the doorbell rang, though she was also afraid of being forced to divorce. Cocteau himself said very little about these arrests in his journal.

The Final Solution was carried out in extreme secrecy, after being decreed in a villa on Wannsee Lake in January 1942. For the most part, at the time, deportation "only" meant the separation of families and forced labor in the Eastern territories. Nevertheless, people were clearly disappearing for no other reason than their ethnic origins. Their belongings were confiscated, their apartments given to "Aryans," and their loved ones generally heard no more from them. Cocteau learned that at the Compiègne camp, from which Goudeket returned after eight weeks, almost twenty pounds lighter, that Communists were shot four at a time, but that this camp was a "dream" compared to the one in Drancy, where René Blum (the brother of Léon; René would die there) had been sent. And Breker had let it slip that in the "boss's" mind, the anti-Jewish movement was a "fight to the death."[76]

From the twelve-page letter he had received from Max Jacob, in April 1942, Cocteau had learned more of the administrative humiliation his friend was suffering. The voracious reader who had praised Nathalie Sarraute's *Tropismes* when it was published in 1939 (he was the only critic to do so, except for the very young Jean-Paul Sartre), told him tersely that his brother-in-law was dead but still in the Compiègne camp, and that one of his brothers had had his shop in Paris taken away from him in June 1941. "Oh, these hostages!" exclaimed the wife of an officer friend. "They're only ever Communists and Jews!" "I call this phrase 'accessory to murder,'" said Jacob, this strange sacristan who had to attend the six o'clock Mass wearing a yellow star. Cocteau said of Jacob, in 1928, "He's a Jew so he's suffered a great deal—for several centuries, and for thirty years."[77]

In August 1942, Cocteau heard from Colette about the suicide of the Polish Jewish wife of a playwright who had just been informed of the death of her entire family. Sick of being made to wear the yellow star, she could no longer bear being "an obstacle to her husband's work." It took her four days and nights to die after taking Veronal in the bathtub. "We were never more free than during the German Occupation," Sartre would write, meaning that everyone was given the chance to defend their principles by making certain choices, to risk their lives, or to resign themselves to having their neighbors carried away.[78]

But Germany did not really ask the Vichy leaders what they thought, and they in turn did not ask the French for their thoughts. Public demonstrations were forbidden, and any isolated protest was considered extremely risky, especially after the General Von Schaumberg, commander of greater Paris, had been blown up. Of course in the Free Zone, Claudel could openly express his support for the grand rabbi of France without worrying for his safety, and several bishops could stand up in public and read a letter denouncing the persecution of Jews without suffering sanctions. But on this point the Germans were inflexible, and the continual attacks from the ultras limited possibilities of speaking out even further. Cocteau, the "enjuivé," had to grit his teeth, using all his energy to keep his work from being attacked by the ultras. Under these circumstances, it seems as though the Jews benefited a little less actively from his anti-racism than the blacks, his personal chosen people, so to speak, from the African infantrymen of Coxyde to Panama Al Brown.

As we've seen, his friends were not exactly the best candidates to open his eyes. Though Jewish, Maurice Sachs had gone from the black market to gold trafficking, with the obvious complicity of the German authorities. The thundering defeat of 1940 had freed the perversity inherent to his personality—that is, his ability to be indifferent and passionate at the same time—and had given him an unhoped-for field of action. All his energy went into meeting the needs for luxury that had torn his family apart, efforts that brought out his louche, evasive, prodigal, opportunist persona—his only true literary invention. Speculating with jewelry and rugs that he didn't possess, selling furniture and fake paintings, Sachs continued to steal with charm, the better to fill his beautiful apartment on the quai Conti with treasures, or to dazzle a boy with dinner at a luxurious restaurant. "Everything and everyone is fake," Cocteau noted in his journal. "Fake papers, fake declarations, fake tickets, fake artists, fake journalists. Only the swindlers can live comfortably."[79] Sachs had never been so happy, cheerful, and well-off as during those dark years. "But what about you?" a friend asked with surprise, when they were talking about the anti-Jewish roundups. "It's not the same for me, I'm a homo," Sachs replied, as if his sexuality would definitively protect him from the hazards of the German reality. When the price of gold fell in 1942, Sachs even chose to travel to Germany as a volunteer, throwing himself into the mouth of a country that only wanted to eliminate him. It was as if he were asking Germany somehow to shoulder the burden of the self-hatred, both "racial" and sexual, that he had dragged around with him since adolescence. "The individual is nothing, the species is everything; nature laughs at the individual; Hitler is great because of that," he would write a year later from Hamburg, where every morning he saw the sun rise from the top of the crane he was driving, perched twenty meters in the air, on a work-site of the Reich that wanted to last a thousand years.[80]

Sachs, then, could not make Cocteau see reason, but then neither could Marie Laure de Noailles, who had given a forced laugh in recognizing herself as the Vicomtesse Medusa in the second *Potomak*, and showered him all over again with invitations and gifts. She was "a quarter Jewish" according to the categories being enforced, but for a little while she had been the mistress of an officer of the occupying army, and was learning German with a translator who had taken refuge in Hyères; she dreamed of convincing Arno Breker to visit her. She wasn't at all pro-Nazi, or even in favor of collaboration; she just wanted to be fashionable.

Then there was Lise Deharme, once worshipped by André Breton, who would never have imagined that the persecutions could have anything to do with her, though she was born Hirtz and socialized with Éluard. Not to mention Emmanuel Berl, another French-Jewish citizen who could still think himself protected, in the Free Zone, by the speeches he had written for Pétain that included powerful, provocative phrases like "The earth doesn't lie," and "These lies that have done us so much harm." Or his cousin Lisette Franck, the wife of the French ambassador to Paris, Fernand de Brinon, whom the Germans had made an "Honorary Aryan"—a rare status that Colette was the first to request from Otto Abetz for her husband, Maurice Goudeket, when he was released from the camp at Compiègne.

All around him, friends were taking the plunge, like Suzy Solidor, who had previously shown so little interest in men, but now suddenly became the mistress of a German officer. Or Arletty, whose brand-new lover was the head of the military tribunal for the German air force, and could regularly be seen in Laval's car. "Arletty is Paris. She is occupied," said Cocteau, ready to forgive her if she were really in love—but perhaps he was also thinking of himself, in that moment.[81]

In 1942–1943, Cocteau was everywhere. At the Comédie-Française, at the Opéra, at the home of Alfred Cortot, the famous pianist who didn't refuse to tour in Germany, and at the home of Paul Morand, the ex-member of the Mutual Admiration Society who was now a close friend of Laval, the prime minister who would send him to Bucharest as France's ambassador. Cocteau, whom Jean Touzot would call the "firefly of the dark years," occupied all terri-tories, uneasy about finally enjoying the recognition he had sought for so long. His ideas were far removed from Morand's pro-German convictions, or the bounding Pétainisme of his friend Charles Trenet, and he was more reserved than Maurice Chevalier or Tino Rossi, who sang to rooms full of officers in lovat green; still, the Breker infatuation had left its mark. There must have been some difficult moments for those who had left everything to go to London or who lived in fear of being arrested, when they saw Arletty, the symbol of a cheeky, libertarian France, or Mistinguett, the beating heart of the French workers, rubbing up against the enemy. Piaf, it had to be said, was behaving well, and Gabin even better, in the ranks of la France libre.

Goering had complained to the commanders of the Reich in August 1942 that the French ate too much. The result was fewer deliveries of food from provinces like Normandy and Burgundy, which had already been plundered by the Germans. Parisians had to learn to put saccharine in their chicory and their barley juice, Jerusalem artichokes in their mashed potatoes, rutabaga in their desserts, and to use other ersatz usually reserved for the livestock. All anyone had the right to was a few grams of butter, two loaves of bread, and a liter of wine per week. The young people who hung around Cocteau (Sentein in particular, who had been given the job of compiling an anthology of Aeschylus for him), began to suffer cruelly from hunger. If they happened to come across a beefsteak, their stomach could no longer digest it. Cocteau himself was no longer able to offer them cigarettes—a commodity that had become so rare that someone set up a cigarette-butt exchange at place Maubert. But Cocteau didn't suffer too badly from the restrictions—not even from the lack of opium. He was well and truly cured of his addiction. There was always some lover of Marais to bring them a cockerel from the countryside, a young girl to run to the town hall for some ration cards, a wealthy woman to invite them to dinner—not to mention the improvised coolie who asked only for an autograph in exchange for taking him there in his bicycle taxi. If they needed soap—which was very hard to come by—Cocteau or Marais would go and steal some from the pharmacy. A resourceful Egyptian intellectual who had tried to meet him for fifteen years took care of the rest. Where on earth did this "violent and lofty soul" manage to find the dairy products, milk, meat, and the other fresh products that she would drop off in his absence, along with a little snack near his ironed shirt, as well as a spray of gladiolas and homemade preserves from the countryside? Did it have anything to do with the crafty Morihien's improvised black market? Or were all these things—chickens and eggs and butter—brought as offerings by his young admirers, like Pierre Barillet? At the same time, when in September 1942 a bomb went off in the Rex cinema, which had been turned into the Soldatenkino by the Wehrmacht, and 113 Jewish and Communist hostages were shot, leading to the curfew being moved up to three in the afternoon, Cocteau was still able to obtain a free pass, like many who worked in the theater. He could also walk the empty streets of Paris without being concerned about the patrols who frequently checked people's papers.[82]

THE END OF JOCASTA

Over the years, Cocteau had become his mother's mother. He was always reproaching her for not showing her feelings enough and instead offering money. Desbordes, Khill, or Marais would come and go, but she was his anchor—it's tempting to say his "inker"—the most important woman in his life—with all that suggests of a lover's irritation and suppressed hatred. But the energy with which the eighty-something-year-old leapt out of bed at seven in the morning, and that kept her going until bedtime, upright and busy, was declining. In 1939, Madame Cocteau had begun the slow road that led to the exit. Senility had made her unable to respond to Jean's letters, or even his arguments, so she went to live in a retirement home run by nuns on the rue de l'Assomption—and when he visited she would tell him stories about his room at Maisons-Laffitte and the homework he had to do, as if he were still in junior high school. Now, however, she was not even capable of recognizing him, and with her thinning hair, hollow cheeks, and dissipating muscles, bore little resemblance to the beautiful young woman she had been in the nineteenth century. Deprived of his oldest confidant, Cocteau began to keep a journal in the spring of 1942. These big notebooks received the overflowing thoughts of a man of letters who was obsessed with his position, and with his destiny—they became a complaints department stuffed with anecdotes and memories, but in which the best of himself, which had already been poured into his books, appeared only from time to time.

When his mother died on January 20, 1943, Cocteau spent hours drawing her emaciated profile, then composed one last poem in her honor. "I am not sad," he said. "Death never makes me sad."[83] Just as he had refused to attend Radiguet's funeral, he would not publicly mourn, and if he cried in front of her casket, at the church and then at the Montmartre cemetery, when they slipped his poem into her tomb, he was ashamed. "I buried Maman. She has been put away in a piece of furniture where I will one day join her," he wrote in his journal, convinced that he would cross the centuries lying next to the woman that his friends perceived as his physical double. As one last near-sacrilege, he noted that their tomb was within reach of the homeless men's stream of urine.

One of the last ties connecting him to his social milieu had been severed. His mother, whom he still called, at fifty-three years of age, "my adored sweetheart" or "my only love," and who had showered him with tireless, sometimes overwhelming love, had joined her husband in the void. Like Jean's father, Eugénie Lecomte became a ghost who returned to haunt his nights, or even to brush past his hand, in the middle of the phantom-like Palais-Royal. These events inspired "Léone," his most beautiful poem after *Plain-chant*, a rhymed narrative of recurrent dreams—"the dream was inside me as Léone was in him." He was haunted by this airy figure, as prone to metamorphosis as he: "For Léone when she walked was a chameleon / Adopting the shape and color of places / Léone walked on thieves' feet." It was a poem evocative of the movement, if not the music, of the carousel, and the endless cycles of its carnivalesque life: "If I knew that sleeper of tomorrow / In whom Léone would continue her path . . ."[84]

Already financially dependent on Marais, and more eager than ever to give the best roles to his partner, Cocteau began to think of returning to the cinema. Not as a director—*Le sang d'un poète* had brought him nothing but trials and tribulations—but as a screenwriter, which was a better paid position. After trying his hand at adapting *Le lit à colonnes*, Louis de Vilmorin's novel that would come out in June 1942, he turned to writing *Le baron fantôme* and took so quickly to it that the director, Serge de Poligny, asked him to embody—if we can put it that way—the title role of a ghost caught in the spiderwebs of his château, which he haunts while wearing a Louis XV wig.[85]

He who hated to get up early found himself taking at dawn the metro, and then the bus, only to confront the freezing cold Joinville studios for ten hours at a time. Rediscovering this "lunar" world in which artistic camaraderie thrived (in spite of the difficulties of rationing) was a deliverance, his own unique utopia. He who had always lacked enough flesh to totally inhabit himself, who granted himself the grace and perspicacity of angels on his good days, and the aphasia of ghosts on his bad days, secretly felt relieved from the tragedy that Europe was experiencing. Neither the war nor time existed on the banks of the Marne. Like all former thieves, Cocteau experienced a strong feeling of ownership, and he suffered from seeing his treasures, if not his imagination, pillaged by Marcel Carné in *Les visiteurs du soir*—in his journal, on December 6, he would accuse Carné of running a "black market of poetry." This larceny, however, would drive Cocteau even further in the direction of the cinema, and the end of the year would find him adapting *La princesse de Clèves*, though the vagaries of the production process would prevent it from being filmed until twenty years later.

THE TURNING POINT

The successful Anglo-American invasion of North Africa had pushed the Wehrmacht to invade the Free Zone on November 11, 1942. The Free Zone had been under the control of the Vichy government, which now was obliged to pay a daily Occupation fee of 500 million francs. The east had been annexed to Germany, the north blockaded, as was the Atlantic coast; Corsica, Savoie, and Provence had been taken over by Italy; and the Vichy bigwigs had been reduced to little more than train station managers. With the war taking a less triumphant turn for them, Nazi Germany recalled Otto Abetz, who was deemed to have gone too easy on the French. In September, a census had been taken of all French citizens from eighteen to fifty years of age, with the plan of exporting them to Germany to perform forced labor. This time the looting was on a large scale: factories, hotels, buildings, boats, bordellos, and hospitals, workers and transporters, trains and railway workers were all requisitioned for the war effort. French citizens' quality of life grew still worse, in the provinces as well as in Paris, where the most urgent products became scarce. From Lyon, where she had taken refuge with Louis Aragon, Elsa Triolet wrote to her sister, Lili Brik, that the lack of fat in their diet was making them rustle like dead leaves. A new definition of the Collaboration went around: "Give me your watch, I'll give you the time." Léon-Paul Fargue coined a new version of the famous Vichy motto "Travail, Famille, Patrie" (work, family, homeland): "Tracas-Famine-Patrouilles" (trouble, famine, patrols).

The Resistance grew. Éluard began to hide not only leaflets, but also men whom he was trying to help. In September 1942, certain writers overcame their reticence and published alongside Éluard in the first issue of the underground journal *Lettres françaises,* on the one hundred fiftieth anniversary of the battle of Valmy. *Je suis partout* immediately began to denounce the cafés where they gathered. Joining the Resistance were some of Cocteau's former disciples, from Franz Thomassin to Pierre Herbart, including Roger Stéphane, but Cocteau was of course the last to know. He would have been so proud of their decision that right away he would have said everywhere that he had very courageous "sons"; the next day they would have been heroic; a few days later he would have cited their first names and they would have been rounded up.

Franz Thomassin devoted himself entirely to his network, as he once had to Cocteau. The leaders of this modern crusade, realizing that Thomassin would rather be cut up into pieces than betray his cause, put him in charge of delivering important messages to the Free Zone, and then of helping deportees cross over the border into Switzerland. "God save him," Cocteau said a year later, learning he had to tried to enter North Africa. The ultras' attacks, Marais's blind audacity, and then Breker's tall tales convinced the poet to maintain his initial "pacifism," but he learned that resistance had its virtues, and that Thomassin's courage made up for many indignities. "We don't have the right to complain," he said to Pieral, the actor. "So many young men are dying, and in the most horrible ways."[86]

Part of Paris was accustomed to eating well off the black market, or to enjoying the girls who worked the streets under the windows of the Palais-Royal. Nevertheless, a feeling of solidarity arose in France, while Germany, after taking a beating for the first time, was rediscovering individualism. "The whole country thought of Hitler," Cocteau noted. "Now—for the last month—women think of women, daughters think of daughters, sons think of sons, soldiers interrogate each other."[87] When after six months of Dantesque battles the Germans surrendered at Stalingrad, in February 1943, and Hitler decreed three days of national mourning that coincided with the tenth anniversary of his rise to power, it was clear that the Reich was on the losing side.

Cocteau found this period difficult. The angel in him had to recognize that he was caught in the jaws of some very earthly contradictions. Was he wrong to stay? In Sacha Guitry's strange film *De 1429 à 1942 ou de Jeanne d'Arc à Philippe Pétain*, in which Cocteau gave his voice to Rimbaud, Sacha Guitry would remind viewers that Courbet, Degas, Cézanne, Renoir, and Pissarro had continued to paint during the first German occupation of 1870, but Paris, after capitulating, had still remained French.[88] And Cocteau asked himself again: was his very presence in the midst of the lovat green nightmare a cultural safeguard, as he still believed in 1942, or a mistake, if not a crime, as some were already beginning to whisper? One of his deepest-held convictions made him see France as an artistic miracle that had escaped the vagaries of History, making it a divinity to be served no matter what, like the Greek Athena or Mother India. But was this occupied territory still France? The infernal heat of the war was beginning to melt his rare certainties, and to make him perspire. The political question, which he had always avoided, took a metaphysical turn. It was no longer possible to be this and that—one had to *be*, full stop, with all this implied in terms of partisanship; it was basic, but it was healthy. His semi-legendary universe was disappearing under the ruthless domination of History, which demanded its measure of victims and of blood. No one in France could hope to escape it. This war was becoming ferocious even for those who refused to take sides.

"The German army followed me all the way down the Champs-Elysées," Marais worried, returning home one evening. "You couldn't keep walking as far as Berlin?" Cocteau replied, half in earnest, half in jest. Until this deeply hypothetical withdrawal came, there were bills to be paid, everyday life to be lived. "Beefsteak first, morality after," Brecht and Weill wrote in *The Threepenny Opera*—words that Sartre and Beauvoir repeated often. But Cocteau had to work to live, unlike Gide or Mauriac who had family money, and he convinced himself that he had no choice. To show the younger generation that he was even a rebellious author, and to demonstrate how much Carné owed him, in February 1943 he organized a showing of *Le sang d'un poète*, whose release the Noailleses were still blocking. The film was shown in the little room at 44 avenue des Champs-Elysées where Henri Langlois, the future director of the Cinémathèque, showed forbidden feature films that he sometimes hid in his bathtub. The most positive responses came from Misia, Bérard, and Poulenc, and the film was shown again on March 6, to an audience including Picasso and Jünger. Cocteau noted in his journal, "What depths! What contrasts! What sparkling lights!" before adding "I'm beginning to understand why Ch. Chaplin so liked *Le sang d'un poète*, and why he's showed it to all his friends in Hollywood."[89]

Decadent and opium-addled, the old Cocteau lived on, in a few dark auditoriums, but he cohabited with the new one, the healthy scriptwriter, in the far reaches of his personality. Picasso declared that for anyone who used them, the styles inherited from Lascaux, the Dogons, or Ingres became contemporary; for Cocteau as well, art moved neither forward nor backward.

RACINE HAS RETURNED

Cocteau had never stopped working to have the ban against *Renaud et Armide* lifted. But although he appealed to Heller, Jünger, and Mme Abetz, it was the son of the minister Carcopino who was able to do the most, having come across the manuscript at his father's home. He informed his father of its dramatic merit, and informed him that Cocteau was not in fact an ex-convict, so that the play might be performed at the Comédie-Française. The plot was taken from Tasso's *Jerusalem Delivered*, and was in the same register as *Les chevaliers de la table ronde*: frozen for love of Armide, the immortal queen of the country he has just conquered, and the victim of a spell cast by Oriane, a witch disguised as a lady's maid, the young French king Renaud has been turned into a human statue and placed in the queen's gardens where he finds he is struck with amnesia, and then with a split personality. If a bit of leftover opium smoke seems to float across the pages, it is because of the tragic power of the love that Armide discovers this time, in agreeing to exchange her own immortality for the captive's freedom and for the very temporary satisfaction of his passion.

Hoping to create "an impression of vastness—of suffering—of luxury—of eccentricity," Cocteau rehearsed his actors ceaselessly for a month and a half.[90] His stage designs, which were surprisingly realistic even as they suggested the world of magic, impressed them. "It's Racine at the Châtelet!" exclaimed Mary Marquet, who co-starred with Marie Bell. The actors had trouble, however, physically interpreting the evil spell that forbade them from taking shape, from touching each other, and sometimes even from talking to each other. Cocteau could ask them to walk like peacocks all he liked, but they did not know how to play a passion that could be burning and freezing at the same time. Cocteau had developed the play through a long series of readings, one of which had led him, along with Marie Bell and Jean Marais, to an important woman's home in the Palais-Royal. "It's a grrrrrreat classic!" Colette thundered, at the end of the first act, before nodding off in her otter skin, from which only her naked toes and her wild hair emerged. As they left, she said, "I will not tell you anything about your play; you know very well what you have done."[91] Colette had aged, but the weakening of the support on which he had always counted rekindled his doubts, which only grew when he saw his play turn "like milk" at the preview. Was this play not a true mess of irreconcilables? What would the audience think, discovering this tragedy whose tone evoked the reign of Louis XIV but whose author had made them grow accustomed to his Dadaist ballets, his neoclassical dramas, and his boulevard theatre?

Cocteau prepared his audiences for this new about-face by declaring, in an article for *Comoedia*, that since the young did not dare contradict him, he would do it for them. Recognizing entire pages of their school textbooks, readers persuaded themselves very simply that he had managed to reconcile the classical unities with Romantic élan, after two centuries of confrontation, as well as with the ghosts of Orpheus, Phaedra, and Tristan. "After the last act, the audience called me to the stage after the tenth curtain call," Cocteau enthused the day after the opening. "I came onto the stage with the performers and I saw that magnificent thing: a full auditorium on its feet and shouting. No one left the room. They brought down the curtain and raised it back up again to this thick wave of exclamations."[92] Helped by Bérard's dazzling costumes, the three-act play in alexandrines had convinced the audience, in need of subjects of national pride, that an infatuated Racine had returned to save France.

The performances confirmed the success of a play that seems, in retrospect, like the high point of the return to the past—medieval, Renaissance, or classical—that the theater and the cinema were experiencing under the German Occupation. The day after the premiere, Cocteau was almost smothered by a mob of fans demanding his autograph in the arcades of the Palais-Royal. Beaten on all fronts, reduced to eating ersatz potatoes while listening to false news reports, part of France had clung to their language, to the classic authors that had served it, to the modern ones that hoped to perpetuate it—the only escape allowed in the spring of 1943. Was it not the ignoble twentieth century that had given birth to barbarism?

Neither Vichy nor Germany wished to see contemporary subjects addressed on stages across the country. Goebbels set the stage in France, calling for "Light, empty, and if possible, stupid films."[93] The Continental, a German production company, had a much more intelligent policy, bringing out fairly serious films dealing with current events, like Clouzot's *Le corbeau*, inspired by the same events as Cocteau's *La machine à écrire*. But the country generally preferred to shore itself up against the German predator's appetite by making an inventory of its literary and artistic treasures, its only inalienable goods. Sacha Guitry, for instance, would spend part of the war filming his Henry IV manuscripts and his Clemenceau canes.

Cocteau's play was not without its reference to current events. The subject of heartache and rivalries at court served to convey the particular climate of the country, with its "little coaches drawn by pairs of cyclists" and its lovers going about in horse-drawn carriages.[94] No one heard the first line—"Awake, Renaud, and take up your weapon"—as an appeal to the Resistance; the evil spell cast over Renaud and Armide reflected, through a poetic prism, the submission imposed on the country. The critics could not see that far, and wondered what could have driven Cocteau to write a verse tragedy respecting the classical unities, which had fallen into disuse since the nineteenth century. "Quand Cocteau prend racine," said one, unkindly, in a pun that meant both "when Cocteau takes to Racine," and "when Cocteau takes root." Another called it a pastiche worthy of Edmond or even Maurice Rostand, contrasting him with the much more "serious" and "modern" efforts of the better-educated Giraudoux. "It's charming, I spent an enjoyable afternoon at the theatre," Giraudoux himself said.[95] Bernard Faÿ had a similar verdict: "A melody full of grace, at rest in this period of iron, fire, and blood."[96]

The fascist press gleefully returned to its favorite scapegoat. "L'autre soir, on battait des records de recettes / Les tapis poussiéreux ont besoin de tapettes," wrote one of Laubreaux's friends.[97] Men who since 1940 had demanded that the theater be filled with tragic grandeur, against the corrupt prewar boulevardiers, had to tone it down a bit; for once, Cocteau wasn't writing in the shadow of the "Jewish oak tree Henry Bernstein."[98] Céline, who was in love with Marie Bell, whose "heroic" acting style had long fascinated Cocteau, went so far as to say that the playwright would have come close to Shakespeare, if only he had put some humor in his play: "Not a single Jew is celebrated in it, except maybe a little of Ben Jesus, I can breathe," added the author of *Beaux draps*, who was otherwise unforgiving of the set design, the costumes, the music, and the overture.[99]

Laubreaux stood noticeably alone when he signed an article lambasting the "menopause" of Cocteau the chameleon, and his logical rise to the "temple of convention"—that is, the Théâtre Français—though he himself would covet its directorship, a few months later. "M. Cocteau has spent his life fleeing his bourgeois nature, only to sink deeper into it," concluded the star columnist of *Je suis partout*, the weekly paper that was becoming more and more committed to the "revolutionary" party line and now published 300,000 copies.[100]

At the age of fifty, the supposed corruptor of youth had nevertheless given himself a "cleaner" image. The ghost that had drifted through the 1930s, the sleepwalker living by night, served for the first time as a mirror for thousands of people in France, themselves in the midst of haunting the history of their fallen country as if struck by some unnamable malady. No play had as much of an impact on the Occupied Comédie-Française, except for Montherlant's *La reine morte* and Claudel's *Le soulier de satin*; no other was so quickly forgotten. With a few of his historic rivals in exile—Breton in New York, Gide at Sidi Bou Saïd, Tunisia—Cocteau even became the author of the year, in 1943. For the first time in his life, his fundamental eccentricity was in step with public opinion; his anti-contemporary aesthetic and the regressive movement of the arts during the Occupation were perfectly compatible. Many Parisians, as long as they were fed, thought only of the cinema, the theater, or the opera. In spite of the elevated prices and the power cuts, the freezing temperatures in the auditoriums, and the alarms, the waiting lines at the Comédie-Française snaked through the gardens of the Palais-Royal, with people using newspapers to shield themselves from the cutting wind and in order to read without losing their place, shifting their feet like horses at the station.[101] "Since 1940, many Parisians have been returned to the earth, but many more have been returned to the theatre," wrote Maurice Martin du Gard.[102] Whether musical comedy or straight drama, the stage had become the opium of an occupied people, and reading the best moral balm. Ronsard, Verlaine, and Rimbaud were all the rage, driving a steady market in secondhand books, in anything printed. "Never has poetry—I'm not talking about occasional verse—been consumed so enthusiastically," Breton himself would confirm in 1944. "It is easy to see in this phenomenon a manifestation of the need to take a detour from the essential, of the sort one feels every time one's individual existence is put in mortal peril."[103]

In the year 1943, Cocteau would go from success to success. In January he staged *Antigone* at the Opéra, designing the set and costumes as well, with music by Honegger; it was a triumph, a "Mass for the dead," according to Roger Lannes, who was fascinated by the cerebral luxury of its stage design. The recital that Cocteau participated in at the Théâtre Édouard VII, in which he read *Plain-chant* while Serge Lifer danced Apollo, won unanimous support. "Alone among the major Occupied countries, France continues to produce great works of art," the British weekly *Observer* had to admit in July. At that moment Cocteau found himself legitimized. It was as if he had a sixth sense for what the Germans call *Zeitgeist,* or was a fairytale princess who could detect a pea beneath a pile of mattresses and so had given the Parisians what they needed, and through them a part of the country. Did he owe his success to that marvelous box of life that is the theater? He celebrated it in a restaurant near the Palais-Royal, by the Molière fountain, in front of an accordion band playing nostalgic songs from the happy years, and finishing with French military marches, including the "Marseillaise," allied hymns, and even the "Internationale."[104]

THE PLEBIAN ANTINOUS

The legend of Tristan belonged to Cocteau's personal mythology; Wagner's opera touched him as much as did Piaf's love songs, and he had even imagined writing an all-male *Tristan und Isolde* when Marais had pulled away from him physically, as had Natalie Paley/Isolde in her time. This time, he decided to produce his legend for the cinema, situating "King" Marc's domain near a very contemporary-looking garage. The pure souls of Tristan and Isolde would do a bit of time traveling before encountering the king's refusal and the unkindness of those who envied them in the château, one of those imaginary refuges of Occupied France. With its stormy atmosphere and title out of Nietzsche, the project updated the story, making it relevant to a period in which the French, by informing on their neighbors, seemed first and foremost to be condemning themselves.

The financial and artistic obstacles were numerous. Ordered to appear before the German officer supervising censorship for the cinema, Cocteau had to account for the article he had published before the war, in which he accused Hitler of imitating Charlie Chaplin's *The Great Dictator,* as well as his alleged relations with Jewish ministers of the time.[105] The producers chose Jean Delannoy (*Macao, l'enfer du jeu*) to direct, and Cocteau was very humble with him in the beginning: "Every time I start a new project, I feel like I'm seventeen again, and I'm on bended knee trying to convince the director, the editor, the producer," he noted, astonished to see how insecure he became when he had to work with an "authority."[106] His arrival at Victorine Studios in Italian-occupied Nice had an almost imperceptible effect on the filming climate, though he mostly remained silent. The waves of energy he sent out influenced the actors' performances, beginning with Marais; it was a delicate moment for Delannoy, who already had seven films under his belt.

When *L'éternel retour* was released in October 1943, it was a great triumph. The audience gave it a standing ovation as if they were at the opera, and began to howl "like a dog at the moon and at death," said Roger Lannes. Every day for a month the lines for tickets stretched down the Champs-Elysées, and people rioted at the ticket offices, breaking glass, exchanging blows, passing out. Thousands of women recognized themselves in the tragic experiences of Isolde (Madeleine Sologne), who could be united with Tristan only in heaven, rising up to him like a torch toward the heavens. "Jean can only end things with an assumptive failure," Lannes said.[107] The entire country cried over these two heroes, separated by an aging king. After ten years of trying to "clarify" himself, Cocteau had finally achieved the success he had hoped for since the 1930s: he had finally moved the masses.

The triumph of this mythic tragedy blended with bourgeois comedy provoked a debate. Convinced that it was shameful to "die of love," an obscure member of the Institut attacked the film's anti-nationalist character, under the pretext that a French hero had to be a conqueror who preferred battle above his own feelings. But Rebatet himself, in *Je suis partout*, had to recognize the quality of the film, even if he attributed it to Delannoy rather than Cocteau, who was insulted once again. "We do not like M. Jean Cocteau," said the French state radio, "but we must concede that the film is remarkable." A gala was organized at Vichy in the presence of the Maréchal Pétain's wife, several ministers, and the ambassador of Japan. Marais attended, but Cocteau did not. Others, and not only in the postwar British press, would read Marais's Tristan as a nationalist, Celtic response—unlucky and masochistic—to the Aryan heroes of German cinema. The dark-haired dwarf Pieral was seen to embody all the human defects—jealousy, greed, cynicism—while the sculptural Marais, who was turned into a living, Breker-esque statue by the waves of light falling on his platinum blond mane, was all the virtues: bravura, joy, and passionate feeling. The film's plot managed to escape political readings, however, which is precisely what guaranteed its success—apart from Cocteau's enchanted world and Marais's smiling vitality, the audience fell in love with these characters that carried them far, far away from the trials they were withstanding.

Chosen for her resemblance to Greta Garbo, but also for her evanescence, Madeleine Sologne managed not to overshadow Marais; her ghostlike stare was reminiscent of Natalie Paley's icy éclat ("She looks sculpted," Cocteau said). She even shared the limelight with Moulouk the dog, who became a star as a result of this memorable film. Within a few days, Marais had become an icon of virility in Occupied France. The jacquard pullover of this "Tristan in a sweater" (*Je suis partout*) became the standard of the J3, the young people baptized by the acronym on their ration cards. All the hairdressers were asked to replicate his peroxided hair, and his character's name took over the maternity wards. Numerous babies in 1943–1944 would be called Patrice (Patrick when the GIs arrived)—like Patrick Modiano, winner of the 2014 Nobel Prize in literature—as if their parents wished to imbue them with the amoral health and appetite for living of an actor who seemed to be completely unaware of the war that was raging on.

One of the biggest cinematographic success stories of the Occupation, *L'éternel retour* confirmed the intimate understanding that Cocteau had of his audience. Having already incarnated the joyful electricity of the 1920s, he had managed to channel the somber mood of the 1940s. Above all, he was happy to owe his success to Marais, whom he called the "stag" as often as the "roe"—never had Pygmalion been so quickly rewarded, or his Galatea so happily triumphant. From this terrible actor with the jerky delivery and the gestures of a mad dog, he had managed to create a popular, noble hero, alive and hieratic. In spite of his gigolo-like tics and his voice like a dissolute violin—the description is Jouhandeau's—the most handsome boy of his generation had been able to become an Apollo of the stage, like the demigod his mentor had dreamed of becoming three decades earlier. Having emerged from Cocteau's oeuvre through his drawings, Marais would triumphantly return to it, five years later, to the point of overshadowing it.

Thousands of young women imagined themselves Isolde in his arms, without for a moment suspecting his homosexuality, though it was perceptible, or perhaps they just ignored it. Their older brothers might snicker at this sissy of a demi-god, but the girls called him a thousand times a day, buried him under passionate letters, and rang at the door on the rue de Montpensier to see the real Marais, pet Moulouk the dog, and sometimes collapse in tears. It was a delirium of offerings, flowers, chocolate, and clothes, of love letters and unauthorized visits, of marriage proposals, and even proposals of children: Jean Marais seemed as well to have acquired the magic power to change other people's lives. Having arrived at the height of his power, the emperor Hadrian decreed that his lover Antinous be deified throughout the Roman world. In this case it was Parisian audiences who made Marais into a living idol. His clothes became relics to be venerated; young girls kissed the saddle of his bicycle, which had so often rubbed against him, or attempted to climb the façade of the building that led to his room, in the gallery of the Palais-Royal. Neighboring bakers had to throw buckets of cold water on them to calm them, and the girls would become so irate at being rebuffed that they slashed his wheels. "He is everything!" exclaimed a friend of Cocteau's.

But the actor kept his calm, in spite of his sudden currency as a heterosexual heartthrob. He would do anything not to disappoint his fans, and this "plebian Antinous," as Jünger called him, let his cult following develop—but he also went out more than ever with Cocteau, out of gratitude. Not only was his career unaffected by this implicit confession, but it benefited from the quasi-brotherly, quasi-conjugal image the photographers published. Their relationship borrowed from the mythic aura that *L'éternel retour* had idealized, of a couple united until death, which would feed many more romances after the war, when society began to rebuild. For the first time in contemporary history, a male couple was applauded and consecrated, on the same level as Louis Aragon and Elsa Triolet would be, just after the war, perhaps even more warmly. Marais had understood that it was not possible to make Cocteau happy; his obsession with his work undermined any love relationship he might attempt. Marais was too balanced for him, too insouciant to have any real effect on his nature, so he was happy just to stay near Cocteau, without trying to intervene in his destiny.[108]

Cocteau suffered from the masses of fans who overran him in the stairway to their apartment, treading on his feet to get closer to Marais. Their imbecilic vampirism reawakened his misogyny, to which he would give free reign in the film version of *Orphée*, saddling Marais with a horribly prosaic wife and disheveled, voracious female fans. These Gorgons in the making, who dreamed of providing Marais with little heirs, these annoying little "bitches" he and François Sentein made fun of, had awoken the angel inside of him. This huge success had some effects, nevertheless; carried away by the myth he had restored to life, Marais got back in touch with the beautiful, frivolous Mila Parely, whom he had met in May 1942 on the set of *Lit à colonnes*. Then he "officially" introduced her to Cocteau, who encouraged them to marry, telling them they would have magnificent children, before Marais got scared off. Cocteau himself would take under his arm the very pretty Josette Day, a thirty-year-old actress whom her lover, Marcel Pagnol, had recommended to him, though she cheated on him with impunity. Cocteau was able to reunite the lovers a first time, then a second, but by the third time he was more, shall we say, involved: "Josette has asked me for a child," he noted in his journal. "This will no doubt be my next work, if God wills it."[109] As usual, nothing would happen.

The winter of 1943 was freezing. Imprisoned in their tanks, the fish agonized in the frozen apartments that the Parisians fled—the last metro was at 5:30, on the days there were reprisals—to drink coffee made from acorns, or occasionally chickpeas, in bistros that were rarely heated. All of France was hungry, except for a lucky few in the south or in Paris; all of France was cold and afraid. But Cocteau, having taken refuge in the Breton manor of Tal-Moor (whose name evoked the universe of *L'éternel retour)* with Marais, who smoked while he painted in an attempt to lower his voice, and Morihien, who chopped wood while Moulouk romped about, devoted himself to writing a new play inspired by the story of Sissi, the lonely empress of the Austro-Hungarian Empire who had been assassinated by an anarchist at the end of the nineteenth century. Cut off from the world more than ever, the threesome of the rue de Montpensier could have believed themselves in King Arthur's time, prisoners of the frozen winters blowing in from the sea of Cornwall. By Christmas, *L'aigle à deux têtes* would be finished.

The Universal Suspect

Great literature is simply language charged
with meaning to the utmost possible degree.
—*Ezra Pound*, ABC of Reading

FLOWER BOMB

It was the spring of 1942, eighteen months earlier. While browsing through the bookshelves of a *bouquiniste* on the quai Saint-Michel, one of the young visitors to the rue de Montpensier, Roland Laudenbach, had met Jean Genet, a curious ex-convict who worshipped Proust and Jouhandeau and made his living by stealing books. Laudenbach, intrigued, introduced Genet to his friend Jean Turlais, a young literary critic. As Genet and Turlais spoke, Turlais happened to mention a very beautiful edition of Corneille's complete works that he had glimpsed in the front window of Gibert, the bookshop on the Boulevard Saint-Michel. The thief Genet had immediately suggested that he go and "bury" one of the volumes, and that Turlais go back two or three days later to negotiate a lower price on the rest of the now incomplete set. Then he would return and "dig up" the first volume, to be bought in turn. Before they could carry out the plan, however, Genet, by this point nicknamed "Corneille," was sent back to the prison at Fresnes, where he wrote an erotic poem dedicated to the glory of a twenty-four-year-old murderer who had been guillotined in Rennes in 1939. Genet self-published "Le condamné à mort," creating a few dozen copies before destroying most of them.

Fast-forward to February 6, 1943, when Laudenbach arrives at Cocteau's to read the poem to the master:

Ton visage est sévère: il est d'un pâtre grec
Il reste frémissant au creux de mes mains closes.
Ta bouche est d'une morte où tes yeux sont des roses,
Et ton nez d'un archange est peut-être le bec.
[Your face is severe, like that of a Greek shepherd
It trembles in the hollow of my closed hands
Your mouth is that of a dead woman while your eyes are roses
and your nose is perhaps an archangel's beak.]

"Le condamné à mort." comprises sixty-six stanzas of four or five alexandrines that praise crime and sodomy, purity and infamy, in an almost liturgical style. They are verses of haughty insolence composed with stupefying ease and mastery, suggesting a kind of obscenity that is "never obscene." "A miracle!" "A splendor!" cried Cocteau.

Cocteau usually skimmed through a book and judged by intuition, but he could not put this book down. The thorny rose, standing on end, that Genet pictured lunging from the soldiers' fly was the Ronsardian emblem that Cocteau had resurrected twenty years earlier, with Radiguet. But Genet had the audacity to put this symbol in the service of masculine love, investing that love with an incredible poetry, whereas more conventional treatments had tended to portray only abjection, sterility, or derision. "I don't like literature . . . I try to wait for an accident, and if it happens, I fall in love with him," wrote Cocteau to the editor Robert Denoël, who had sent him Dominique Rolin's *Les marais*, which he would also help to launch.[1]

Trained in the school of hard knocks and crime, Genet was the dreamed-of accident. Sure that he was witnessing a literary event, if not *the revelation* of the Occupation, Cocteau read "Le condamné à mort" to everyone he knew, from his masculine disciples to the very reasonable Yanette Delétang-Tardif, a fairly well-known poet of the time. "Two hundred lines of unbelievable homosexual desire," said Roger Lannes, who was also blown away by this "unrepentant Villon" who had stopped regularly attending school at twelve years old and had entered the agricultural colony and penitentiary of Mettray, eventually joining up with the Algerian infantrymen and finally the colonial infantry of Morocco before deserting and fleeing Europe and the Orient. From there he had walked from Tirana to Tanger, half-bum, half-whore.[2]

"Corneille" thought they were making fun of him when he learned from Roland Laudenbach that Cocteau wanted to get to know him.[3] The meeting took place on February 15, 1943, in the deserted apartment of the Palais-Royal (Marais had left for Italy). The hairy ex-con with the boxer's nose who was sometimes in tatters, sometimes dressed to the nines, generally made people uncomfortable. Brusque and often imperious, he became reverential when confronted with those who had become his idols in the jails of the Republic; he took great care when he spoke to them, taking time to choose his words as if he were composing aloud, and in an incredibly polished style. Cocteau was immediately won over—"a quickness, a terrible mischievousness," he wrote in his journal—by this "prodigious maniac" who called him "Maître," hid behind a churchgoer's manners, and rose up against the incorrect use of the imperfect subjunctive. He had a look on his face that suggested he was "in between prisons," which Cocteau found striking, as well as a rough charm and a paranoid expression. Cocteau sketched a pencil portrait of the thirty-two-year-old beginner, then brought him to lunch at a hotel near the Louvre. Encouraged, Genet recited by heart "Le fils de l'air," a poem that Cocteau had recorded on vinyl, and then the "Boxeur endormi," one of his own compositions. The title, as well as the power of the images, impressed Cocteau; Genet's jubilant style made him break out into amazed, irrepressible laughter. Genet misunderstood, and thought the author of *Parade* was mocking him. "Do you know Giraudoux?" he demanded, in a reproachful tone, seeing him greet the author of *Amphitryon 38* at the coatroom.

The next day, Genet returned to the Palais-Royal to recite, standing, several provocative excerpts from his new novel *Notre-Dame-des-fleurs*. "He read well, without affectation, and was impressively self-assured in Cocteau's presence. It was as if he hadn't come to ask for an opinion of his work or to beg for advice, but to show off his masterpiece," said the painter Mac-Avoy, who happened to be at the rue de Montpensier that day.[4] It was the story of an effeminate, crafty young man living among the transvestites of prewar Montmartre, but who remembers as well his years in prison, where he had endured the most brutal, ignorant treatment. Genet described a world of pimps and queers; pistil-men who self-fertilize, through humid dreams and outlandish masturbations—a world led by an omnipotent libido, including all the characters from the cellblock, from the Virgin to the "matons," from the "lopettes" to baby Jesus.[5] It was a mysterious elegy to the greatest of criminals, for who else would introduce the voluptuous specter of death into the act of love? It was too much for Cocteau. "Terrible, obscene, unpublishable," he thought. Genet saw it in his eyes, and slipped out.

Twelve hours later, ashamed of having rejected him this way, Cocteau sent Turlais for the manuscript and to apologize to Genet. "His eyes, while he was reading, told me I was wrong," he added, as if he feared having already discouraged a genius in the making.[6] Cocteau spent the night reading the full manuscript, which he still found alarming, but this time out of his own enthusiasm. He was mystified by this resolute individual who had wandered around Europe for years, sometimes sleeping right on the ground, only leaving behind his intrinsic solitude when thrown into a prison cell, which he would cover with photographs of killers wreathed with white stars. How could such a chronic vagabond transform himself, on paper, into a demiurge capable of disturbing his own opera in order to undo his characters or even destroy them, reducing them to his own will with a totally unheard-of literary narcissism? That is, when he wasn't implicating the reader in the characters' "worst" practices, then demanding that those characters meet the kind of fate that they deserve? Genet, who could put the whole world behind bars, was truly the living incarnation of the enigma of literature.

At the same time, his world had a hidden resonance with Cocteau's. The tattooed convicts of his dramas could seem to be the noxious counterparts of Cocteau's Blancharmure in search of the Grail; the two chivalrous characters seemed to have a sort of original twinship, like the gods of good and evil for the Manicheans. Genet had the same ability to mythologize people he met in real life—except that his Dargeloses were stuffed to the gills with vitality, and his prose showed a disturbing absence of modesty or guilt. Black angels, pure chimeras, always ready to crack open the armor of their partners (who were preferably killers) to release them sexually: these three hundred pages, to tell the truth, gave Proust's prose the taste of rosewater, made Gide's only vaguely salty, and endowed his own with holy water. The desire that Cocteau had always covered up in the most flagrant of manners so as not to hurt his mother, Genet the orphan exhibited everywhere, like the red nails of the reliquaries he had admired in his childhood. The hard kernel of homosexuality was right there, in the strange fantasies and ab-human obsessions. This manuscript was the first true cause for scandal he had encountered in years.

Did he fear that *Notre-Dame-des-fleurs* would make his own ventures into incest, Oedipus, and Greece seem outdated, and show up the coded hypocrisy that had reigned in literature up until then? Did he regret not having written this monument to the "mythology of queers," as Edmund White would suggest?[7] One sentence early on in the book, too had dampened his enthusiasm: "Angels fill me with horror . . .: neither mind nor matter, white, filmy, and frightening, like the translucent bodies of ghosts."[8] Which in 1943 was the same as saying "Though I am born partly from his work, I am the anti-Cocteau. I will turn his culture of goodness and forgiveness into a cult of crime and abjection. His sailors and saints, transvestites and acrobats, his mirrors and his doubles, I will stuff them with flesh and blood and semen, and I will put them in the service of thievery, sodomy, and betrayal." But whatever his feelings, Cocteau was generous enough to overcome his hesitation. Genet—the first writer to designate orphans like himself as "the children of angels"—had to be helped.[9] Literature demanded it—and Cocteau had never had any other priority, from Proust's time to Radiguet's.

He talked about publishing the work, but Genet put his foot down and categorically refused to have his name appear in any journal. Cocteau insisted, aware that he had to be encouraging (in spite of himself) to the self-taught Genet, whose letters even five years earlier had displayed an incredible clumsiness, but Genet was unmoved. Cocteau then reread the manuscript line by line, in spite of the strange fatigue inspired by its almost explosive compactness, and let himself be carried away all over again. It was as if lava were washing down the page, spurting from an overheated unconscious. This "marvelous and unworthy" book haunted him, for it was of a stunning purity, "pure in the sense that Maritain said the devil is pure because he can only do evil."[10] Left alone in this world, this black hole evidently expected him to help him on earth, and find a way to reach other minds, in spite of the war. Genet's appearance in Cocteau's life seemed even more astonishing than Radiguet's.

The reading Cocteau gave to Marie Laure de Noailles and Roger Lannes on February 20 confirmed his judgment. "The male member becomes a scepter wrought to the point of madness," Lannes wrote, dazzled by Genet's "unbelievably poetic sperm." Bérard and his partner Kochno, Diaghilev's former secretary, were also present, and helped spread the word across occupied Paris: a thief who had spent part of his life in a cage had chosen to address his jailers in their own language, and had written a classic work of prison literature, one of the masterpieces of the century! Cocteau could speak of nothing else. Dining with Paul Valéry, he pestered him about *Notre-Dame-des-fleurs* to the point of "total nausea," then asked his advice about how to publish it.[11] "I would burn it," the old skeptic said calmly. "But you would immediately be punished by a high court!" Cocteau exclaimed, horrified by the "layers of dotage" that he believed he was discovering in the author of *Monsieur Teste:* how could he have thrown this mesmerizing book in the fire? A writer had fallen out of the sky—better, out of the penal colony—armed from head to toe and stuffed with vital energy, and he wanted him to play Maritain and commit "legal assassination"?

Thinking he would find a more indulgent listener in Jouhandeau, a man to whom Genet recognized his debt, he went for dinner at the home of the author of *Prudence Hautecharme*, read him the least obscene parts of *Notre-Dame-des-fleurs* in order to spare his wife, Elise, and left the manuscript with him. Jouhandeau, unlike Cocteau, immediately liked the book, but he had read only a third of it when Genet called him a few days later. The three men met at the rue de Montpensier, while Cocteau shaved in his steamy bathroom. "Now that I have talent, I am going to live by my pen," Genet announced proudly to his prestigious elders. "Steal, rather," Jouhandeau retorted, not without good sense, who alternated between the most contradictory opinions, now professing his admiration, now confiding his fear at having pushed, through his own immoral books, this futureless man into catastrophe.[12] Cocteau began to think he was the only one who could take charge of Genet's future, the only one who could help this visionary who'd grown up among the hovels and urinals and people who had no one to speak for them—unlike the whores and the pimps, who had the cinema and the detective novel. He was risking, on the one hand, being dragged through the mud once again by the ultras, accused of being a corruptor of youth and an agent of decadence, and, on the other hand, being told off for loving power, uniforms, and leather belts.

He stepped back into the role of trainer, at which he had excelled with Panama Al Brown, and began to lecture "Corneille": "You're a bad thief. You get caught. But you're a good writer."[13] This was a mistake: nothing angered Genet more than mention of his criminal deficiencies. Unable to reason with this suicidal arrogance, Cocteau decided then to ask Paul Éluard to read the manuscript, as well as Jean Paulhan, who maintained his influence over the reading committee at Gallimard, even if he had had to turn over the reins of the *Nouvelle revue française* to Drieu la Rochelle. When they said no, he sent it to Robert Desnos, then brought Genet to see his neighbor, Colette, who asked her maid to keep an eye on the thief. No success there, either. What editor would take the risk, in the middle of the German Occupation, to publish a book that was so obviously going to be banned? It was too sulfurous, especially for those who took pleasure in it—Gide himself, years later, would call Genet the "Arno Breker of literature."[14]

Cocteau, however, believed that it was critically important to publish the book. Genet might be arrested again, the manuscript might be lost, seized by the police, or destroyed in a bombing. They were covering the statues with sandbags, so this book must be cast in lead to be kept safe. Driven by his voracious altruism, Cocteau became the chaste protector of the wildly talented hooligan: was it not the destiny of Orpheus to go and find his heart's dearest in the underworld? Genet, curiously, did not seem in the least concerned by these negotiations. It was as if he found them beside the point, almost a bit vulgar— he who had always dreamed of making films, who had piles of screenplays in his drawers, like *Les guerriers nus*, but also plays, like *Pour la belle (Haute surveillance)* and *Héliogabale*, which he had written for Jean Marais, whom he admired intensely. He also had completed the first draft of the novel that would become *Journal du voleur*, and other drafts hidden in hotel rooms, or at the homes of his sometime lovers.

Seeing how little care "Corneille" took of his manuscripts, Cocteau decided to immediately buy the rights to *Notre-Dame-des-fleurs* and asked Paul Morihien, who had never shown any interest in publishing in his life, to get Genet to sign an agreement for *all* of his completed work to date—three novels, a poem, and five plays.[15] The contract was signed two weeks after they met, and no doubt back-dated; it allowed Genet to pocket thirty thousand francs (to be paid by Cocteau) and gave him the material means to write in the Esterel and at the Welcome, in Villefranche—a tribute, obviously. Genet did not for a moment seem surprised by this outcome. His work obsessed him, and he did not care who had allowed it to blossom: it would *exist*, that was all that mattered. If he had been sent back to prison forever, he would have received the news with the same indifference, and no doubt with more gratitude: for the literary miracle to occur, it had to be inspired by the groaning of a prisoner getting himself off in the cell next door, by the clinking of the keys the wardens dragged against the bars as they walked by, and their obscene watchful eyes. All this human heat gave the jail an almost maternal air. He might well call himself a devotee of Cocteau's in his letters to Sentein, adding that he had found "God in a dressing gown in the clouds of a too-hot bath." With Cocteau, his only friend, he was Jean Genet, and no other.[16]

When Marais returned from Italy for several days, tan and vigorous, "struck with a warm gold," as Lannes put it, Cocteau's first instinct was to invite Bérard over and spend the night reading him excerpts from Genet's novel. The Allied bombings, which could be heard rumbling in the distance, could no longer reach them. "We are far from these idiocies, in the eternal realm of genius," he wrote, radiant.[17] Compared to the power of *Notre-Dame-des-fleurs*, the war seemed characterized by "dramatic frivolity."[18] The ex-convict's work was the only kind that deserved to be called human and serious, compared with the monstrous game in which each pawn was worth thousands of lives. "We posthumous others," he concluded in a Nietzschean tone, hearing the planes leave, having dropped their bombs. He and Genet, and Marais—they lived in another world, like the Picassos and Jüngers, whose "untimely" novel *Auf den Marmorklippen* he had called the height of timeliness. Protected by his "marble forest," the Palais-Royal, like Renaud under Armide's spell, Cocteau recognized only one homeland, the kingdom of smoke from which poetry derived—as if he truly did live on another planet, where all that mattered were extreme individual destinies.[19]

The thief nevertheless grew confident. Returning from Nice in mid-April to see the final rehearsals for *Renaud et Armide*, he shocked Cocteau by saying to a countess who had bumped into him on her way to congratulate the actors, "Come on lady, calm down." Equally surprising were his perceptive remarks on the play. "He has seen everything, judged everything, understood everything," Cocteau noted, after hearing him say: "It's the realism of the unreal that is so charming. We all live in this fairytale."[20] Coming out of a dinner at the Hôtel du Louvre, guided by the sound of water, they walked along the Seine, beneath the magnificent moonlight, before arriving at the Hôtel de Suède, in front of the quai des Orfèvres, the police headquarters. They went up to Genet's room, where Genet read Cocteau a few passages from his new book.[21] Stunned once again by the power of his narrative, Cocteau solemnly asked him never to steal again. Curiously, Genet did not protest; he even promised to go and care for the lepers, after writing one or two more works. Under the façade of a tough guy who could imitate with obscene gestures the heady odor of a transvestite on the prowl dwelled a saint who dreamed of unlikely devotions.

Finally Cocteau found a publisher willing to make his dreams a reality. Denoël said he would publish Genet's novel, but illicitly, at a print run of 150 or 250 copies, without the name of the author or the publisher, in order to legally protect everyone. It was a godsend for Genet: Denoël had Céline and Rebatet in his stable, but also Artaud and Elsa Triolet, and was one of the most highly considered publishers of the period. Although paper was distributed in meager amounts by the authorities, for whom the young Marguerite Duras worked as a secretary, Denoël had reams of it. Bewitched by Céline, whose operatic anti-Jewish hatred Denoël readily celebrated, Karl Epting gave him tons of paper, while Fargue or even Valéry were often refused it for their work.[22]

François Sentein was asked to copyedit the manuscript (correcting the grammar and adding punctuation), which had just been typed up; Morihien was in charge of production, with the unofficial help of Robert Denoël. Cocteau's secretary hesitated to help publish a novel he didn't like, knowing he risked going to prison, but he eventually got involved as well. When Cocteau told him Denoël had said yes, Genet reacted in an unsettling manner. "I don't want to publish," he growled again, mortified that they were thinking of taking his name off the book. Adding that he wanted to publish the book only "for a few friends," he said: "I want to be published as a pornographer and make money," then commented: "Denoël is a coward to make me publish illicitly. He risks going to prison. Whereas I've spent my life in prison and I wrote my book there."[23] He was a true man of letters, with his contradictions and his arrogance, his backward asceticism and his secret proclivity for shock value. A real character, too, who would say later that he wanted to be read by Catholic bankers, vicious police officers, and nosy concierges—but not by established homosexuals. He was the "maddest" person Cocteau ever encountered (and God knows he had encountered a lot!)—someone who seemed even less concerned by the war than Cocteau was, except when the theater of shadows began, by some "miracle," to reflect his fantasies.

These attempts to publish him were truly painful for Genet, who told Sentein (referring to Cocteau), "I see less and less of him. He repulses me."[24] The author of *Renaud et Armide* was, after all, inextricably tied to the awful literary system, with its show-offs like Giraudoux. This was the reasoning of Genet, someone who himself was physically affected by the restrictions, but who also had rejoiced at the incredible beating received in 1940 by the French troops who wore the same uniform as the gendarmes who had put him in the penal colony at Mettray fifteen years earlier. Soon he began going to bookshops with his rigged leather suitcase, stealing from the few remaining booksellers who trusted him, including the famous Adrienne Monnier, James Joyce's editor. He reliably kept up to date with only one topic—himself—though he also sometimes paid attention to authors whom he admired and judges whom he encountered. "Picasso is lucky to always be with Picasso," he would say, with a straight face; this phrase would forever place him as halfway between a child and a madman for Cocteau, who would always be dazzled by Genet.[25]

"CORNEILLE" AND HIS UNCLE

Caught stealing a rare edition of Verlaine's *Fêtes galantes* in the place de l'Opéra and chased to the boulevard des Capucines, "Corneille" was out of prison only twenty days before he was sent back. "I told you I could only write comfortably from prison. God knows what he's doing and perhaps I should thank him for being so good to me," he wrote to Cocteau from the Santé.[26] Hassled by letters that were half-thankful, half-demanding, Cocteau was made to promise to go and get the things that Genet had left at the Welcome, in Villefranche, including some manuscripts. Jouhandeau, for his part, was asked for money, food, various material assistance—his saying "Steal, rather" having been blamed for this relapse. Although he found *Notre-Dame-des-fleurs* to be a wonderful book in the end, Jouhandeau tore up his letter, and Elise roundly reproached Cocteau for sending such a thug their way. Sentein was asked for butter, meat, tobacco, matches, and paper, with this obnoxious addendum, given that it was wartime: "I believe all of this is easy to locate." All of it had to be financed by selling the (obviously stolen) books that Genet had left in storage.[27] Moreover, Sentein had to intervene with the authorities so Genet could have a private cell in an overpopulated prison, given his complaint (one among many) that the Resistance fighters were sullying the criminal atmosphere of the jail with their idiotic belief in the strong moral foundation of their activities. It was not always easy to be Jean Genet's friend.

Cocteau worked all his contacts and touched base with Maître Garçon, a big-name lawyer, and then went to the Santé to visit the detainee with Marais and Morihien, who received the order to provide for all of his needs. To André-Louis Dubois, the former assistant director of the Sûreté Nationale, and to Maurice Toesca, head of the municipal police, he asked for the best possible treatment for the repeat offender.[28] These were not bad hands to be in: Toesca wrote in his free time, and Dubois loved "Le condamné à mort" so much that he asked Cocteau if he could meet its author. "Corneille," however, thought things were taking too long. Demanding that he be blindly supported in the prodigious literary efforts that were already capturing for all eternity the faces he'd met when he was free, he piled up his contradictory and unrealistic requests. "He could say anything, with a clear preference for errors," said François Sentein.[29] Placing himself at the top of a complex hierarchy, modeled on the prison's, but also on the titles of nobility and the rituals of the church—"Like you I am devastated that there are no more princes," he sighed to Sentein, the ex-royalist—the author of *Notre-Dame-des-fleurs* had become deaf to any reasonable advice, and was hardly grateful.[30] Of course he thanked Toesca, calling him the "representative of poetry to the prefecture," and gave Dubois's lover a small part, a few years later, when *Haute surveillance* was produced. But when he spoke to Cocteau, it was no longer to the writer whom he admired, but to his publisher. He had nothing but ingratitude to offer him. If he had any kindness, he saved it for Picasso, who received a letter asking for the number of the cell in which Apollinaire had spent ten days, in the same prison, when he was accused of stealing the *Mona Lisa*.

Cocteau accepted him as he was, as had many others before him. "Corneille" could be harsh, obtuse, or ungrateful, but he was a real writer, and no morality applied in this sphere, beyond human laws. Genius was a fact—it could not be discussed, and it had never been so apparent as in the letters Genet sent, describing how, in the stairwells of the Santé, he had come face to face with Our Lady of the Flowers—that is, the former inmate at Mettray who had inspired the character—"dragging behind him a vermillion satin tail, twenty meters long."[31] Cocteau did whatever was asked of him.

Genet had dedicated all his energy to wrongdoing; Cocteau had sworn to his mother never to inflict pain and always to be of service. The lines that bound the bad boy and the good boy were electrified; the two were fascinated by the abyss that joined them. One child was proud to set a bad example; the other was embarrassed to set a good example: they had as much in common as the fox and the sheep, but an irresistible force attracted them to each other. Genet resembled Sachs: the same lust for thievery and lying, the same need to show himself in the worst possible light; a borderline personality, as the psychiatrists say. When he was asked to get help, he worked with Dr. Allendy, who had already "treated" Sachs—and, as it happened, Thomassin. Genet was unlike Sachs, however, in that he had absolutely no desire to be loved, and immediately took pleasure in deceiving, wounding, repulsing, and presenting himself as the embodiment of theft, betrayal, and unkindness, exaggerating his vices to the point of claiming as-yet-uncommitted crimes. Just as he was at the same time the pimp and the queer, the superman and the madwoman he built into his novels, in the city Genet was always the first to "charge himself."

It was only as the trial approached that Cocteau became truly afraid. He was ready to stand as a guarantor, as Genet had requested, for a promising writer with a great future ahead of him. But how would the *collabos* respond, hearing him ask for indulgence for a twice-convicted thief, when their journals were full of complaints against the spectacular increase in all kind of illegal trafficking, and when the accused flattered himself as being the author of an obscene book, glorifying a way of life that was utterly abject?[32] "O machine gun so often caressed in dreams, faced with the ignoble herds of the Front Populaire, the platforms of Blum, of Thorez, of Daladier, of La Roque, the golden ghettos and the sodomites of very Parisian parties! . . . I fire like a god, voraciously," Rebatet had just written in *Les décombres*, the best-seller of the time, describing his military training before the war.[33] Cocteau's procrastination made Genet furious. He already blamed him for not having brought his manuscripts from Villefranche, and now he accused him of writing only flat, mean letters. "You can be sure that the cowardliness that Cocteau has demonstrated until now where I am concerned will never be compensated for by his very great talent," Genet fumed, in a letter to Sentein. "In fact you can show him this letter. I despise him, the way you despise losers. He is not great. And, believe me, I make fun of it—and even congratulate me, on having hurt him with my invective."[34] Some days later, Genet added: "He doesn't break, he lets go, like the knots the sailors call whore's knots."[35]

The trial took place in July. Judge Patouillard had just asked for the maximum sentence for a burglar accused of stealing a sack of flour. Patouillard vigorously interrogated the defendant: "Why have you stolen a volume of Verlaine?" "I like Verlaine." "Do you know the price of this book?" "I don't know the price, but I know the value." "Are you yourself a writer?" "Yes." "What would you say if people stole your books, instead of buying them?" "I would be very proud." This was Genet: crude, laconic, arrogant, almost as inspired as Joan of Arc, his great heroine, confronting Bishop Cauchon. He even told the judge, after a previous stint of shoplifting, that he owed his culture to his pillages but also to his confidence in the choices made by the Goncourt judges, that every year he "procured" himself a copy of the winner, with a consistency he believed was laudable: "I can tell you who won every year . . . How many critics could do as much?"[36] He had a marvelous repartee, which Cocteau hastened to repeat to Jünger at a lunch given by Florence Gould, the wife of an American multimillionaire, at whose home a Resistance supporter like Paulhan and a Germanophile like Jouhandeau could both find themselves seated next to Lieutenant Heller.[37]

It was time for the defense's remarks. Maître Garçon read a letter written by Cocteau that called Genet "the greatest writer of his time" who "stole to feed body and soul," and concluded, after having showed his deference to the court, "We cannot condemn Rimbaud." That was how Genet, judged by the court psychiatrist to be "deprived of will and moral sense," was given only three months in prison (and this from the fourteenth chamber, known to be "the most detestable") in the name of a "genius" to which only five people could testify. And this in the middle of the German Occupation, during the harshest period of Vichy censorship. Sitting near Garçon on the lawyers' bench, in front of the insolently tanned Marais and Morihien, Cocteau sighed audibly with relief. Genet might have been sent away for years! Condemned to three months and one day, all his reprieves should have become immediately effective. The author of the most obscene book of the century, who could go on and on about the penal colony of Cayenne that according to him had been "unfortunately" closed since 1938, seemed almost disappointed by the verdict. Suspecting this, Judge Patouillard himself told Cocteau that he feared he had done this new Rimbaud a disservice. Hadn't Genet himself said he worked better in prison? And in fact these three months of incarceration at the Santé were spent writing *Miracle de la rose*.

It was predictable, but the trial put Cocteau, the head of French decadence, back in the hot seat, thoroughly denounced as the godfather of all the "queers" of France and Navarre. "Cocteau/Genet? Maybe they're uncle and nephew?" suggested *Je suis partout*, then at the height of its influence.[38] *Notre combat pour une nouvelle France socialiste* described Cocteau, "wreathed with Satanic poetry," leaving the tribunal as proud as a brigade general.[39] The only notable exception was *Comoedia*, which saluted Genet's nascent genius and asked that he take his manuscripts with him when he left prison. This time, Genet understood the generosity of Cocteau's gesture. "I've read the papers," he wrote from the Santé.

> I will no longer mock the precautions you take to avoid insult, for I know what it is to see one's name used in a shameful fashion by railing idiots . . . You dared utter an affirmation whose seriousness does not escape me, Jean, to divert me from an extremely perilous path, from a deadly path, for I had decided to off myself if I were sent back to the penal colony. I do not know if I am the greatest writer of our era, and I do not know if you think so (I hope not) but you said it to save me, and this is what stuns me and puts me before you in the situation of a proud guy who [lets himself] be crushed by a gesture of love more beautiful than gestures of pride.

Genet would not write many letters like this one. This passage would particularly touch Cocteau:

> As soon as I get out, I'm going to the country. You will see me very rarely, and only in an intimate setting. I have an unpolished intelligence, Dr Claude was right, and it is too late to civilize me. Deep inside, I am still a crook. I should have understood this, and loved you only from afar. But since committing the error of indelicacy is too difficult for me, I tell myself I did so only because you persisted in asking me to come and see you so often. As if we needed that! I've loved you for ten years and you had no idea.[40]

But Genet would not stop hassling his hero. Having fallen in love with the man in the neighboring cell, a twenty-three-year-old car thief who would become Bulkaen in *Miracle de la rose*, he sent a poignant letter to Cocteau asking him to send bread, sugar, butter, and meat to this young boy with no family, who was slowly dying of hunger. "He's never received a package. Nobody writes to him. One word from you would make him so happy!" Genet added. Writing that he was ready to steal something to reimburse the writer, he concluded his letter with: "I am afraid you will refuse. So I believe I will become terribly ferocious."[41] This time, Cocteau gave up; Sentein had to get up at dawn to take the requested package to the Santé, addressed to the young and pretty Guy Noppé, who had gone to the penal colony at Mettray at the age of eleven. Seeing Cocteau's energy flagging, Genet turned to Marais to ask him to protect yet another lost young man, "very beautiful," this one—a young Trotskyite who had joined the Résistance, who would serve as the link between the convict and his protectors on the rue de Montpensier, and eventually inspire *Pompes funèbres*. Since the actor had other things to do, it again fell to Sentein to look after

Jean Decarnin. And the defense of those attacked by Vichy (including Cocteau) that Sentein was trying to write never saw the light of day.[42]

Fascist papers had nevertheless revisited the scandalous judgment accorded Genet, as well as the indecent presence, in the middle of the courtroom, of his protector, surrounded by "long-haired favorites in zoot suits . . . such that we can imagine them engaging in unpleasant activities in apartment building foyers."[43] The indulgent outcome of the case had confirmed for the ultras that the Third Republic lived on, with its salacious judges and arrogant inverts, under the protection of the "old coot" in Vichy. It was an insult for Doriot, who, helped by his experience with Stalin and his zeal for Hitler, dreamed of replacing Laval, with Berlin's support, to impose a new order. Cocteau was too accustomed to these insults to react. Believing in *Notre-Dame-des-fleurs* as he did, he shut himself up more than usual in the timeless world in which he, Genet, and Picasso were meant to live, and spent the month of August 1943 supervising the music for *L'éternel retour*, then playing in *La malibran*, Sacha Guitry's film. It was a month so hot that the war itself seemed to have gone on vacation.

On August 27, as Cocteau was walking to the metro at Concorde, the drums of a military marching band made him turn around to see the battalions of the Wehrmacht goose-stepping up the Champs-Elysées; the auxiliaries of the Légion des Volontaires Français Contre le Bolchevisme were leaving for the eastern front, wearing the German uniform. His stupefaction at seeing them waving the tricolor was not lost on the security personnel whom Doriot had hired, those he had named, as they returned from the Russian front, the "French guard."[44] Cocteau had just enough time to see a hat fly past belonging to a man who did not "spontaneously" uncover his head at the sight of the flag, when he was blinded by a fist. Having been recognized by an agitator who cried his name as if he were brandishing a trophy, and whistled at by the crowd that had come to see the parade, Cocteau was knocked to the ground by a group of men who then went off to break the windows of a "zazou" café on the Champs-Elysées. The men continued to knock over anyone who refused to remove his hat, including policemen in uniform, whom the Germans had ordered not to intervene.[45] The "raid" would claim 152 victims. Laubreaux had his revenge: the "uncle" who had arranged for clemency for the scoundrel Genet had bit the dust.

Éluard praised Cocteau's act, but Cocteau was no hero: he just could not believe that the French would march in enemy ranks when Germany was demanding thousands of young people to work for their war machine, and when it was taking by the dozen hostages whose deaths were announced on lists available everywhere.[46] "But you're very hurt!" cried a woman passing by, seeing him try to stand up, covering his eye with a bloody handkerchief, to wander like a sleepwalker across the place de la Concorde and knock at the door to Maxim's, deserted at that hour. A pharmacist bandaged him up, and a bicycle taxi took him back to the Palais-Royal, where one of his actresses discovered, under the bandage, his eye covered in black and blue bruises.[47] The "Lesionnaire's" parade had luckily only left him with a black eye, which he would call his "compère-doriot," and not a "loriot," as they said in the slang of the time.[48] The ultra press took advantage of the nickname to unleash its bitterness toward this "notorious Gaullist, rabid pro-Semite, and insulter of the flag," and published a caricature decorated with his star and his heart, embellished with an anchor and a Star of David—suggesting that the writer knelt down only before Jewish people and sailors. The head of municipal police called the next day to see how he was, said how appalled he was that his agents hadn't done anything to defend him, and offered his rather flat apologies. "Strange times," Cocteau commented, receiving the play that Toesca had just written and sent over, in the hope of getting Cocteau's help producing it—for the chief of police as well, theater counted more than anything.[49]

Genet was freed three days later, and came to see Cocteau with his next-door cellblock neighbor. Galvanized by his time behind bars, as well as by the presence of the young man who also admired the police and whom he already suspected of being a *donneuse* (informer; another reason for his excitement), Genet proudly announced that he had just forbidden Denoël from publishing his book without his name on it. To his great surprise, Cocteau agreed, though Denoël thundered that he had spent twenty-five thousand francs for nothing. Genet found himself penniless, but refused all the advances Cocteau offered him. "He rebels against all attempts to help him," Cocteau noted, without too much surprise at Genet's folly. He was growing every day more sure of his genius, going around preaching the "good" word, a finger raised to heaven, like Sachs at one time—"but shaking it at the ceiling with a comic glint in his eye," Sentein said.[50]

In late September, while taking a nap, Cocteau was awakened by inspectors brandishing a copy of *Le grand Meaulnes*. Arrested at a bookshop near Trinité, with a pass and false papers in his pocket, the thief Genet had claimed he had checked the book out of the library on the rue de Montpensier. Cocteau played along until the police demanded the name of the bookshop where he had supposedly bought this copy of Alain-Fournier. When they left, he looked out the window and caught a glimpse of Genet handcuffed to a policeman. He had waited barely three weeks to return to his old tricks, and that very night he was sent back to the Santé. The next day, Cocteau received a letter from Genet giving him endless, vague instructions, mostly threatening, denouncing Dubois and Toesca for not having done anything, a few hours before the very same Dubois informed him of the fury of the police prefect who had personally intervened in Genet's favor. Cocteau was still not discouraged. "He will always steal. He will always be unjust. He will always inconvenience those who compromise themselves to come to his aid," he wrote in his journal. "I (sincerely!) regret ever having met him," Genet wrote about Cocteau. "He ruined the secret I wanted to save for my work." Cocteau was no longer wanted. To Marc Barbezat, a young Lyonnais industrialist who wanted to get into publishing, and was hoping Genet would write something for his journal, Genet wrote: "Send one hundred francs," before asking Sentein to go and ask Cocteau for the four plays he had assigned to him, in the name of their contract.[51]

The new trial took place in December. Genet hassled Cocteau to testify, but this time he did not want to. Sentenced to a mandatory sentence of four months, at Christmas Genet was transferred to the former barracks of Tourelles, where regular inmates, Jews, and *résistants* were crammed together under the watchful gaze of the Militia, a security corps created at the beginning of the year with the goal of straightening up the country's social and intellectual morality.[52] Tourelles was a kind of internment without end, the first step to deportation, guarded by tough guys used to the worst exactions, in whom Rebatet saw the happy fruit of the uniting of the French national socialists.[53]

Everyone was very depressed at the rue de Montpensier. Now subject to the most arbitrary of authorities, Genet risked paying a very high price for his irresponsibility. That very night, Cocteau asked Sentein to appeal to a member of his family who knew the head of the Militia, but Sentein refused to compromise himself with Darnand: as a runaway from the Service du Travail Obligatoire (STO), Vichy's compulsory work service, he also could be arrested. Genet was much less concerned: he immediately ordered that Sentein go and see Darnand, to whom Sentein finally wrote, offering to serve as personal guarantor not only to Genet's literary genius but also to his political indifference.[54] This time Cocteau solemnly informed Genet that he could do nothing further for him should he steal again. Genet agreed without too much conviction; after all, it was his ninth arrest since 1939. Faking tickets and stealing shirts, wallets, suitcases, vouchers for bedlinen, books, and the complete works of Proust had earned him three years of prison in all, since the beginning of the war, and prison suited him so well.

Cocteau was in a panic. What had happened to the proofs of *Notre-Dame-des-Fleurs*, which Genet had taken back from Denoël? No reason to worry,

Genet responded—he left everything at the hotel where the police arrested him. Moreover, he had no more faith in the novel, which he felt suffered from "childlike lyricism, bad architecture, facile psychology, a pretentious, screeching, unbearable tone."[55] He never wanted to hear anything further about that misbegotten book—writers always publish too quickly. The book he was currently writing would be much better; it would dazzle everyone. To Cocteau, in turn, he ordered that he go and get the second half of *Le spectre de la rose* from an abandoned suitcase at Jean Decarnin's, as well as buy some paper, and a big school notebook, so he could write on his knees, since his room was overrun with "thirty loud guys" and did not have a table. He was like Vautrin, pulling all the strings from prison, via Europe and Asia, in Balzac's *Splendeurs et misères des courtisanes.* Cocteau asked Sentein to go instead, then called Genet's hotel and tried to secure new support for him: a true wartime godmother.[56]

Cocteau had hardly begun when Genet bombarded him with letters complaining of his silence, reminding him that he, Genet, was writing one of the most beautiful books in all French literature, or telling him they were going to send him to a concentration camp. Was there really talk of sending him to Alsace or Poland? With Genet everything so quickly turned unreal: wardens, detainees, or visitors became the extras in a fantasy in which he played the magic lantern; his consciousness projected Platonic shadows onto the walls that surrounded him—shadows of crime, pleasure, and death, whose relentless parade kept him stable.

Cocteau took these risks very seriously—and one could always get what one wanted by making him feel guilty. Once again he begged Toesca to intervene in Genet's favor, to make him free, in spite of his damning file; after twenty years of penal colonies, vagabondage, and lies under oath, however, the multiple offender could not demonstrate the minimum required income. Aware that it would be a shame to deprive France, "reduced to living by its glory," of a Rimbaud in training, Toesca agreed to give him some paper and arranged for his novel to be taken out of Tourelles so it could be typed up—unaware that the novel in question was a celebration of betrayal and sodomy, but who could wait for an ode to work, family, and homeland from Genet?[57] Genet insisted that Cocteau get a fake health certificate in his name from Dr. Henri Mondor, a doctor who was a close friend of Paul Valéry's, while apologizing for speaking rudely to him and writing letters only to ask for things. It was a touching apology from an overly proud convict who nevertheless let it slip that if his letter went unanswered, he would try to escape, because "à la guerre comme à la guerre" (a soldier's got to do what a soldier's got to do).[58] And Cocteau, once again, had to convince Mondor that Genet was a modern-day Villon. The doctor told the prefect that he had diagnosed a kidney disorder in the patient, and signed a prescription ordering him to be transferred to the Hôtel-Dieu hospital in Paris. In private, Mondor confided to Toesca that he had detected an "evil flame" in the eyes of the detainee, on behalf of whose fate the highest authorities had intervened with such zeal as had rarely been seen for the Jews and Resistance fighters piling up at Tourelles.

Clandestinely published by Morihien, the first copies of *Notre-Dame-des-fleurs* began to circulate illicitly, in spite of the author's unwillingness, Genet having renegotiated the rights with Marc Barbezat. Three months later, Genet accused Cocteau of dropping him.[59] That very night, by some strange coincidence, Genet crossed the threshold of a prison for the last time. It was March 14, 1944, and the police prefect's influence had finally paid off. "He will start in again and we'll be back where we started," Cocteau noted in his journal, before adding: "He doesn't care about anyone else; he alone is pure; he alone has rights, etc., etc."[60] Genet, in fact, picked up his self-promoting speeches where he had left off, returning to the rue de Montpensier. An avalanche of false scruples and acrimoniousness, excuses and claims descended on Cocteau. Genet, paranoid and always ready to reproach those who had helped him, was concocting new plans to accuse the social order and all the traitors who had sent him to prison—a few days later, he had fake papers made for himself and returned to semi-obscurity.

For once, it was not Cocteau who spoke, but the indefatigable convict, who permanently reinvented his fate and proudly described himself as the "negation of man." Cocteau had met mythomaniacs and thieves, but he had never seen them have such illusions about the world they lived in. *Notre-Dame-des-fleurs* seemed to be the almost literal transcription of the complex mythology that was Genet's reality. More than a case study, it was a form of successful psychosis.

Cocteau spent hours listening to the thief claim that he had been baptized "Genet" in homage to the field of flowers where his birth mother had abandoned him, in Tiffauges, where Gilles de Rais, Joan of Arc's brother-in-arms, buried the adolescents he raped.[61] Nothing could be ordinary in the destiny of this once-shy, effeminate, and studious child who devoured the serials of Paul Féval, with their capes and swords, escapes and crimes, and who, plunged into total darkness for three months in Mettray, had lost all sense of time and space. Genet was also the name of one of Marie-Antoinette's chambermaids who had written her memoirs—the convict passing effortlessly from the queasy dungeon of bloody semen to the boudoir of the Petit Trianon, and he was off again, in his delirium, this time to the old roués of the Enlightenment, with their red-heeled shoes and their lace collars. Cocteau called him his "genêt d'Espagne" (Spanish broom), after the horse of one of the Dumas's Musketeers; "Corneille" wrote to him as "mon petit Jean"—as if he saw himself as the protector of this writer who had looked after him a little too much.[62] He too was capable of becoming a thousand fabulous characters—one day John the Baptist, the next day Christ— to say nothing of the movie star he swore he would become, in Egypt or in Hollywood. No one better illustrated what Rimbaud said about the convict: "And he alone is witness to his glory and his reason."

A few weeks after Genet was freed, Barbezat's journal published a chapter of *Notre-Dame-des-fleurs*, among other texts by Sartre, Claudel, and Leiris. Before it had a whiff of snobbery to it; now the name Genet became suddenly well-known. The day of the Normandy beach invasion, *Notre-Dame-des-fleurs* was being passed from hand to hand, and women were crying as they read "Le condamné à mort," Cocteau claimed. A whiff of brimstone emanated from his praise of Marie Antoinette and the troublesome Mignon, blessed with "the penetrating force of the blond warriors who've been steadily doing us in the ass since June 14, 1940." Nevertheless the book was disturbingly successful.[63] Vichy's old-fashioned morality was as violently beaten as the new one, which celebrated the martyrs of the Résistance.

THE BEGINNING OF THE END

"The day the Germans pull back, they'll pull out all the stops," Cocteau said, during their speedy victory; for once he had perceived correctly.[64] After the successive defeats in the East, the flight to the *maquis* in the Dauphiné of thousands of young men who had refused to go to the STO in Germany, and the increasingly murderous actions of the Résistance had brought on ever more bloody reprisals: whoever walked in Paris without an *ausweis* (pass) after curfew was threatened with being shot within the hour, if another German officer had been shot by the "francs-tireurs" (resisters). "The hide of a rabbit is worth more than the hide of a man," Léon-Paul Fargue commented.[65] Germany lost its power in the sky as well. The ongoing Allied bombings of the outskirts of Paris, of the large train stations, and of the Bourget and Villacoublay airports had made it difficult to send provisions to the city. The press's lies of omission were compounded by the spread of false news, which added to the confusion and fear. On such-and-such a day the Germans and the Russians were preparing an Armistice; on another, the British were said to have bombed the Vatican. There hadn't been so many crazy rumors afoot since the Terror in 1793; never had there been so many armed assaults in Paris.

"Do you know what happened the other night by the Luxembourg Gardens? At 9:20 a Jew killed a German soldier, cut him open, and ate his heart."

"Nonsense. A German doesn't have a heart. A Jew doesn't eat pig. And at 9:20, everyone was listening to British radio."[66]

Cocteau, as usual, only believed the least probable rumors. Learning that the Germans were planning to bomb from the stratosphere, he was convinced they would mistake their target, and, because time slows down so far from the earth, end up hitting the World Fair of 1900 or a yet-to-be-built skyscraper. Seen from his "box" on the rue de Montpensier in the heart of the ghost-city of the Palais-Royal, into which the light of day only filtered by refraction, the conflict became more incredible every day. Though he wholeheartedly applauded Mussolini's fall—"a terrifying idiocy that is finally diminished"—the possibility of a total collapse of the Axis powers worried him.[67] "We will be considered criminals for having stayed in France and continued our work," he wrote in his journal on July 30, 1943, before pointing out, with premonitory anguish, "Our misfortunes will count for nothing." A number of Vichy officials and fence-sitters were already beginning to rewrite their personal histories by making contact with the Résistance; Cocteau, however, turned away more than ever from current events to the ever-shifting mist of his world away from politics.

When Cocteau wasn't working on his poem *Léone*, he spent his days reading fairytales or giving a reading of *L'aigle à deux têtes*—a play that drew from *Götterdämmerung* folklore—at the home of the decorator Coula Roppa. When one of the actresses he planned to cast gave her critique, as if he were just starting out, he confided to his journal: "We have no shortage of heroines"—but he was talking about theater, not politics. The more Europe sagged with bombs, the more he took refuge in candlelit rooms, spending his time auditioning, rewriting, and rehearsing. The world was reduced to those red and gold boxes from which he emerged only at night, thanks to the precious *ausweis* he sometimes lent to his protégés. Hiding in the home of the owners of Maxim's, to flee Marais's fans, he wrote the dialogue for Robert Bresson's *Les dames du bois de Boulogne*, a film that had to be partially filmed at night to avoid the power outages that were still plaguing the city.

The Occupiers, who had protected Cocteau on and off since 1942, tried to outwardly compromise him. The head of German censorship proposed that he stage Kleist's *Le prince de Hombourg*, with Marais in the main role, but he was evasive, and in his journal cites this line from *L'aigle à deux têtes*: "Is that how the police chief gives orders?" His refusal left no trace, unlike the photographs that showed him with the German film star Zarah Leander, who was filming in

Paris. A clandestine Resistance journal, *Bir-Hakeim*, called for his arrest and trial in the August–December 1943 issue. This time, it was the BBC denouncing him, as payback for his *"Salut à Breker."* They called him a "collaborator" to their many listeners, while the French "national-socialists" called him a Gaullist. No doubt he is the only writer against whom both sides were ready to take measures.[68]

The roundups increased as the great confrontation approached. Otto Abetz was reinstated as ambassador, though this time with instructions to be firm, and at the end of 1943 he announced forty thousand arrests for Gaullist, Communist, and anti-German activities. On December 15, Max Jacob sent a letter to Cocteau telling him that his older sister Delphine had died of a broken heart; that his brother Gaston, arrested a year earlier in a Quimper park that was forbidden to Jews, had been sent to prison somewhere in Germany—in reality to Auschwitz—and that he himself lived in permanent fear of being arrested. He still prayed every day for Radiguet, twenty years after his death. This time, though, there was no more question of taking refuge in a literary Valhalla.

To celebrate the New Year in 1944, Pétain invited Darnand, the head of the Militia, to join his government, along with Henriot, a journalist and Militia sympathizer who gave influential speeches on the radio. The ultras, with the support of Germany, had finally made headway in Vichy. Cocteau himself understood that the days to come would be terrible, but he was the first to restrain Marais from going to Berlin to pose for Breker: he said he would ask to meet Hitler and assassinate him! "My poor Jeannot," Cocteau replied, "you will disrupt all the Allies' plans."[69] "Since these mysteries are beyond our understanding, let us pretend to rule over them."

On January 20, 1944, another letter from Max Jacob informed him that another of his sisters, Myrté-Léa, had been arrested after the death by torture of her husband, no doubt at Compiègne. Having learned that Cocteau had just played in Sacha Guitry's most recent film, Jacob asked him to appeal to the film-maker, reminding him that his family had been established in Brittany for over a century, and that his brother, who was still alive, was just a peaceful shopkeeper, "neither poor nor rich." Jacob's sister was deported to Germany and died in the camps. Neither Guitry, nor Misia Sert, the bishop of Orléans, the archbishop of Sens, or the superior of the Pierre-qui-vire monastary could do anything for her.

The Russian army's advance accelerated, and the ultras themselves began to fear defeat. Eager to show they were not "chicken," they flexed their muscles a bit. It was no longer the time for "fascists in rabbit skin" or "braggarts in slippers," but for real men.[70] Suspected of being too moderate, Brasillach had to leave *Je suis partout*; as a goodbye letter, he wrote in *La révolution nationale* this revealing phrase: "These last few years, Frenchmen of some thought will have more or less slept with Germany, not unwillingly, and the memory will be sweet to them."[71]

Two weeks earlier, Max Jacob had written again to Cocteau to thank him for intervening on behalf of his sister, an "imprisoned lamb," this time with Coco Chanel, the mistress of a German officer. Cocteau did not have the time to respond before a black front-wheel drive slammed on the brakes in front of the home of the sacristan of Saint-Benoît-sur-Loire. "Go out the back," hissed a doctor who was present in his bedroom. Jacob refused to run away, and preferred to be arrested at his work table, as a French poet and a Catholic of Jewish family. "I trust in God," he wrote to the priest of Saint-Benoît. "I thank him for the martyring which is beginning." The roundup of the last Jews in the Loiret had just begun. On February 29, after a brief stay in the German military prison in Orléans, "God's clown" left for the station.

> Dear Jean. I'm writing to you from a train car through the generosity of the gendarmes who are holding us. We will be at Drancy soon. That's all I have to say. Sacha, when we spoke to him of my sister, said, "If it was him I could do something!" Well, it's me. All my love.[72]

Cocteau rang at Guitry's door, who was still on good terms with the German authorities, and that of José Maria Sert, Misia's husband, who had become the Spanish ambassador to the Vatican. He contacted Georges Prades, a press baron connected to the Germans, and to the "head of Jewish prisons," and simultaneously intervened with Jouhandeau through Gerhardt Heller, who tried to obtain a liberation order from his ambassador, then contacted the SD, the German security service. Finally, Cocteau wrote a petition addressed to Abetz, which Paul Morihien took around Paris on a bicycle:

> For many years [Max Jacob] has renounced the world and hidden in the shadow of a church. Young French people love him and call him *tu*, respect him and see his life as an example . . . His age and his attitude, so noble and dignified, command us to try with all our hearts and our minds to do all we can to free him.[73]

Did Cocteau really offer himself to the Gestapo in Max Jacob's place, as he claimed?[74] In any case, he did everything he could to free Jacob from the clutches of the Gestapo, whose name Jacob pronounced *J'ai ta peau*, "I have your skin."

Only Coco Chanel refused to sign Cocteau's petition. Picasso seems to have signed it, then removed his name at the last minute, to avoid angering the

Germans, according to Georges Prades, who adds, "Picasso, from whom I was politically distant, nevertheless put himself entirely at my disposal."[75] Henri Sauguet, the musician of the École d'Arceuil, confirms having gone to see Picasso at the Catalan with Pierre Colle, another close friend of Jacob's, and having heard the painter reply, offended, "that we shouldn't worry about Max, that he was an angel and he would jump over the wall," or, according to Jacob's biographer, "He doesn't need us to fly out of prison."[76] If Picasso knew of his former protector's anguish, faced with such persecution, he nevertheless no longer replied, apparently, to his letters since seeing several of his poems appear in pro-Franco journals. "I have confidence in Cocteau," Jacob wrote to him, after his sister's arrest; "I am counting on his acumen and his goodness, which is genuine." Was this a way of saying, for Jacob, that he had less confidence in that of the painter?[77] "The myth of Picasso the egotist is completely false," Cocteau protested. "Not to know that he has always helped his friends, without making the least show of it, is not to know him at all."[78]

The petition was in German hands when Max Jacob died at Drancy on March 5, murmuring to the doctor, "You have the face of an angel." Was this an effect of his fascination for Christ, whose Passion he relived every day in the church of Saint-Benoît?[79] He did not try to fight off his double pneumonia, choosing instead to devote his last energy to converting his neighbors, Jews like himself, before apologizing to them for having embraced Catholicism. Convoy 69, which he was meant to be on, left for Auschwitz with 1,601 Jews on board, 170 of whom were children. Upon arrival, 1,311 were gassed.

Cocteau learned the "horrifying" news just as the liberation order was signed. It was for the "child" whom God had just called back to him, as much as for his unfortunate poetic double, that Cocteau mourned. *Je suis partout* announced the death of a writer who was "Jewish by race . . . Sodomist by practice," and like the rest of the legal press said nothing about the circumstances of his death. "This personage was the most characteristic figure of the Parisian that one could imagine, of this Paris of putrefaction and decadence whose most blatant disciple, Jean Cocteau, remains an equally symbolic specimen," the pro-Nazi journal added, before concluding, with the humor that made it such a success, "for, alas! After Jacob, we can't pull away the ladder."[80]

The liberation order delivered at the last minute by the occupying authorities confirmed for the ultras that they were full of liberals disguised in lovat green. "The Nazis themselves never took racism seriously," wrote Céline in the spring of 1947. "They used it like election bait to rally a few enlightened men of my kind—which meant a few more votes . . . They had a horror of French national-socialists . . . under the German boot the French theatre was more luxurious than ever—they fetishized French culture, Claudel, Cocteau, Mauriac, Colette, and all the others were literally pampered by the Nazis . . . the Germans are flunkies."[81] Convinced that if the Reich had to cede territory, it was because the Jews had infiltrated them, Céline revealed to the officers and the hosts of the Institut Allemand that they had even managed to replace the real Hitler with one of their own men—always the theory of the invaders—in order to prepare their definitive world domination. This "intuition" supposedly made the Germans turn white at the idea that the servants might inform the Gestapo of it.

The announcement of Jacob's death, so soon after Desnos's deportation—apparently it was Laubreaux who denounced Desnos—inspired profound disgust.[82] The mass given in the poet's memory at the Église Saint-Roch was followed by a profound silence. Around thirty people attended, including Éluard, in spite of being actively sought by the Gestapo, as well as Coco Chanel and Misia Sert, who risked nothing. Only Mauriac took communion, according to André Salmon, another old friend of Jacob and Apollinaire. Picasso, who according to Henri Sauguet was afraid to enter the church, hid in the doorway of a neighboring building: "He was persuaded that the Germans were going to go in and arrest everyone."[83] He chatted with friends on the sidewalk, when Salmon, whose hand no one wanted to shake—he had become more Vichy than Vichy—went up to the painter and advised him not to stay, that the police were threatening to come. "But the police are already here, because you are," Picasso retorted.[84] Others reported seeing him slap Salmon. Six months later, an old Breton friend of Jacob's died under torture. They called him Max, named after his old friend, but he is better known today under the name Jean Moulin, the first president of the Conseil National de la Résistance.

D-DAY

The city had taken a crepuscular turn. Electricity was available only around eleven in the morning and five o'clock in the evening; there wasn't enough coal, and there was talk of turning off the gas; it was so cold in the houses that Cocteau put his clothes on over his pajamas. Marais and Morihien had left in March to go skiing, leaving him painfully alone on the rue de Montpensier, in the heart of the capital, where from the Lutétia to the Raphaël to the Crillon to the Meurice, banners waved, emblazoned with geometric black spiders that seemed to be drinking from a large flask of blood. German pressure increased as the Allies advanced; the drain of humans was compounded by the seizure of all dogs likely to have been trained to detect land mines. There was talk of a retired doctor, a certain Dr. Petiot, who had fled his house in the avenue Foch, leaving behind his still-smoking boiler in which his Jewish patients, hoping to escape to Latin America, had burned, leaving him their cash and jewelry. "Evil Paris has returned to the jungle," noted Roger Lannes.[85] "People fled cafes, cinemas, anywhere public where people were rounded up and arrested." Aragon, Éluard, and Mauriac hid, or constantly changed hideouts, like Paulhan; the historian Marc Bloch was shot with twenty *résistants* on the side of a road; Victor Basch and his wife were killed by the Militia in the middle of the night and abandoned in a ditch—just like the former ministers Jean Zay and Georges Mandel. When the anti-Semitic "ethnologist" Georges Montandon, and then Admiral Platon, who headed up the fight against the Freemasons, were shot by the Résistance, everyone predicted that a civil war was imminent.

On April 12, Cocteau was offered the post of director of the Comédie-Française. "I prefer Fresnes!" he exclaimed.[86] Laubreaux's name had met with an outcry, and he complained that he was being persecuted, like more of the ultras. *Je suis partout* even accused Laval of working with de Gaulle—"that vile Laval, that mixed-blood Jew and Gypsy, that bit of junk conceived behind a caravan," wrote Drieu in 1942.[87] On April 26, for the first time since he took power, Pétain went to Paris to demonstrate his sympathy for the victims of the Allied bombings. Thousands showed up to applaud him when his car drove through the capital, with Laval by his side. Jean Marais, however, went to tell Picasso, in a style irresistibly reminiscent of his mentor's, that a woman affected by the bombs falling around La Chapelle had flown out of a fifth-floor window, only to land safe and sound on the ground: the hot air had acted like a pillow."[88]

The weather softened, and the Parisians received permission to swim in the Seine, between the Pont Royal and the Pont des Arts. "The lovely cyclists wore enormous *entremets* (dessert-like hats) on their heads; the hackney drivers waved at each other with their whips, the fishermen lined the quays," said Jean Hugo: there had never been such a beautiful spring in Paris, some said.[89] The high point of this false-seeming spring was the return of the music hall performers. Cocteau went to see at the Théâtre de l'Étoile the unbreakable Mistinguett, who claimed to have taken away his innocence fifty years earlier. The verdict? "Unchanged." "Hardly bearable," said Lannes. "Miss Ravaged, her face on all wrong, her continuing to tread the boards is as ridiculous as old Pétain remaining center-stage in France." The "old fogeys," however, would soon be given the hook.

In May, Marais performed in *Andromaque*, while also serving as director, set designer, costume director, and producer. Hoping to restore "savagery" to

Racine's play, the hero of *L'éternel retour* played the role of Orestes, his legs bare under his little peplum tunic, his arm brandishing the scepter that Picasso had forged for him. The youth welcomed this very "couture" version of Racine, overflowing with red wigs and violet tunics, bare thighs and suspicious poses—the men wore less clothing than the women—with Django Reinhardt providing background music. "France is shamed!" Laubreaux declared, when he went to see this sickening production "stamped with the seal of Corydon," against which "the honor of being a man" must rise up.[90] The whistles, the cries, the smoke bombs, and the teargas bombs began to fly once again from the thirty seats reserved for the members of the PPF, the fascist party. Marais replied with a courage that underlined, in Cocteau's eyes, his own weaknesses.

Marais was not Laubreaux's only target. Behind the "invert" sullying the classics, behind his actors with their "gyrating stomachs, as if they were giving birth to a tapeworm," once again stood a writer—the same as always—and an ideology, this time more surprising.[91] The "man with Cocteau between his teeth" was not only guilty of making Racine a eunuch, a true "female acrobat"; he had also become a "terrorist in a Greek tunic," the effeminate equivalent of the bandits ravaging the Vercors—in other words, the exact opposite of the German troops who showed, through their impressive bearing, to what grandeur France might aspire one day.[92] This was an absurd argument that surprised Marais above all, but which encouraged the Militia to put the finishing touches on the anti-Socratic trial brought against Cocteau in 1940.

Cordoning off the theater, machine guns on their shoulders, Darnand's troops beat up the concierge who tried to deny them access, then went in search of Jean Marais, whom a group of young girls had surrounded with their bodies, as he was putting on his makeup in his dressing room. The war had invaded this ultimate bastion of "eternal" Frenchness. In his radio program on May 28, Philippe Henriot had accused Marais, without having even seen the play, of damaging the country by massacring Racine, doing more harm than all the English bombs that had "assassinated the cathedral of Rouen or that of Orléans." Eager to put himself in charge of "France's intellectual protection," the regional head of the Militia complained to the prefect of police, declaring that his troops would occupy the theater if he dared to reopen it. The next day, *Andromaque* was banned. Laubreaux's campaign had been successful.

Marais was not shot, as the actress Marie Bell seems to have suggested out of anger, but he was not permitted to respond to his detractors in the press. Fearing arrest, he took refuge in a friend's apartment near the place de l'Étoile. "I have just learned that Cocteau and Jean Marais have been knocked out," wrote Roger Lannes in his journal, no doubt metaphorically. Declared a public enemy of the French state, the most oblivious actor of his generation became a *zazou* in the eyes of the swinging young. Recognized by a group of students in the Bois de Boulogne, Marais was torn from his bicycle and carried triumphantly to the porte Dauphine, while the students cried "Henriot, you shit . . . Laubreaux down the toilet!"[93] Radio-Alger, which was in Allied hands, voiced its support, while the BBC said, "Be patient, Jean Marais, we'll be there soon." Did he think of joining the Résistance when Louis Jourdan asked him to? The networks apparently rejected his request because of Cocteau's big mouth, but his belated support for de Gaulle must also have been only half-convincing. On June 6, the Allied forces landed in Normandy. A month after *Andromaque* was banned, Philippe Henriot was assassinated by Résistance fighters dressed as Militia. Cocteau convinced himself that Marais had contributed to his downfall. On June 17, the always-prophetic Céline fled to Germany.

JEAN-JEAN'S MARTYRDOM

Desbordes was part of a group of writers who refused to publish during the Occupation. Recruited by Parisian networks of the Polish Resistance as early as 1942, he had ever since been in charge (under the nom de guerre Duroc) of the network Marine F-2, which supervised naval movements in the Channel from submarine bases, as well as the arsenal, fortifications, and aviation fields of Cherbourg.[94] He very likely had no idea that one of the officers in the army he was fighting, Ernst Jünger, was reading, in the fall of 1943, *Le vrai visage du marquis de Sade*, the work he had written in 1939, on the basis of family documents supplied by Marie Laure de Noailles.[95]

The information transmitted by the Marine F-2 network to London contributed to the success of the June landings, and as a result German surveillance tightened.[96] On July 5, leaving the apartment on the rue de Rivoli where he was hiding, en route to the place de la Madeleine where he had so often strolled with Cocteau, Duroc-Desbordes was arrested and then brought to the Gestapo's Paris office.[97] At the same time, his wife was picked up in her pharmacy in Saint-Ouen, and then deported. He was the tenth member of the F-2 network to fall; twenty-four followed him the same day, including Christian Dior's sister.

Cocteau was retrospectively afraid that Desbordes might have called him to the rue de Rivoli headquarters. Desbordes's sister Eliette, with whom he had left all his microfilms and cameras, four days earlier, alerted him, and the writer immediately sent a letter to Otto Abetz, whose secretary replied, laconically, that if her brother were to be shot, Eliette would receive her brother's clothes and effects within five days. In fact, Desbordes was already dead, after having been tortured for hours on the rue des Saussaies and then the rue de la Pompe, the Gestapo headquarters; some comrades who had been arrested the night before found his naked body abandoned in a corridor, branded with an iron, his hands torn to bits. Cocteau was horrified, but also proud to discover that his former companion, who could not receive a shot or see a horse die without turning his head, had not given up a single name. "The Résistance is glory, and you get paid for it," the naïve Desbordes exclaimed in front of Franz Thomassin.[98] It was the man missing a finger who emerged safe and sound.

His supervisor, a man called Grégoire, confirmed to Cocteau soon after the Liberation that Desbordes had not talked, even after six hours of torture. The Minister of the Interior told him that Rudy de Mérode, Desbordes's torturer (a Frenchman whose real name was Martin), was reported to have fled to Saint-Sebastian, in Spain.[99] Desbordes's body was disinterred to receive a proper tombstone at Mont Valérien, among others who had died in the name of a Free France. One of the rare French writers to have paid for his resistance with his life, along with Robert Desnos and Jean Prévost, the author of *J'adore* was fated to remain an unappreciated hero: for the Communist Party, the Polish Resistance based in London and hostile to Moscow was nothing to be proud of.[100] "He was denied the glory of his heroism," Cocteau would say almost twenty years later, saying that he was still looking for his murderers, whom he believed to have taken refuge in Spain.[101]

On July 20, a bomb went off at Hitler's headquarters in Rastenburg, part of a failed plot led in part by the general commander of Gross Paris, von Stülpnagel.[102] Two days later, the ultras demanded that the German authorities crack down more forcefully against "terrorists" and Jews, increasing the denunciations in the press. The Marats of 1944 had become more zealous national-socialists than the Occupiers themselves. "These Germans, who do not believe strongly enough in Hitler, were charged with indoctrinating some Frenchmen, who believed too much in him," Drieu la Rochelle said, more bitter about the Germans, whom in 1942 he had seen as "democrats by birth and by nature," if not decadent "enjuivés."[103]

Paris was brutally awakened by the announcement of the imminent arrival of Allied troops. Entire boulevards were used to build barricades at strategic intersections, as they had been during the insurrections of 1830, 1848, and 1871. Tricolor flags were hoisted at the windows in "liberated" neighborhoods, but a curfew was established for two o'clock in the afternoon. On August 19, Cocteau left the walls of the Palais-Royal with a little tricolor cockerel pinned to the inside of his jacket, while Marais obtained a revolver and a Gaullist armband. From the Senate to the Opéra, the Invalides to Concorde, the Germans held only ten posts connected by vehicles that were regularly assaulted by machine guns and Molotov cocktails. In a final echo of the "idyllic" summer of 1940, General von Choltitz would not obey orders to blow up the City of Light, orders given by the chancellor who had so "passionately" loved the Opéra.

If the Germans defended themselves methodically, the ultras gave in to panic (except for the hotheaded Militia, who had to contend with an insurrection after the Germans' departure). The French national-socialists made a beeline for the last trains out of town, headed for Sigmaringen, a fortress in southwestern Germany that had become the capital of a phantom "French" state, where they had to coexist with Vichy "old farts," exfiltrated on authority of the Wehrmacht in a hatred fed by failure. The overcrowding and feces spilling out of the clogged toilets would inspire a hilarious masterpiece by Céline—this time free of incitation to murder—*D'un château l'autre*. Laubreaux fled to Spain, and *Je suis partout* (I am everywhere) was rebaptized *Je suis parti* (I have gone). Drieu hid in Paris—a logical punishment for a man who had for a long time thought of himself as "a decadent, theorizing decadence," but who did not have the courage to do away with himself.[104]

Finally Paris went out into the street, in spite of the stray bullets, to see the fall of the last German strongholds, and Cocteau found himself in the heart of the celebrations, as during the summer of 1914. On August 23, coming out of what is now the rue Danielle Casanova, with Marais and Moulouk the dog, he crossed the deserted avenue de l'Opéra. "The Résistance must have sacked . . . *Je suis partout*," the actor said, seeing the avenue blanketed with papers, when suddenly a barrage of gunfire surprised them as they reached the corner of the rue des Petits-Champs.[105] A spurt of blood shot out from the back of a man walking in their direction. The Militia's snipers had deliberately aimed at those they held "responsible" for Henriot's death—or so Cocteau and Marais wanted to believe.

After celebrating his twenty-fifth birthday at the rue de Montpensier on the 19, Roger Stéphane had cycled the writer over to the Hôtel de Ville, which he had helped to seize by leading a provisional FFI group, and during which he had been wounded in the arm. Ever since he had been commander of the Place, and soon a captain in the Résistance. On August 24, he heard, like Cocteau, the church bells ringing to welcome the liberators, who received a few last fusillades. On August 25, Leclerc's troops drove von Cholitz to surrender. Half of the city went out into the street to welcome the French liberators, who just preceded the Americans. Experiencing his first insurrection, Cocteau ran everywhere, as excited as a schoolboy, bristling when he saw a crowd at the Hôtel de Ville getting ready to attack a line of German prisoners—but he was also angry with himself for feeling pity. "Too many people [have] experienced German torture," he would acknowledge.[106]

Along the way he was separated from Moulouk, but found the dog again in front of Notre Dame (the animal seemed to find it completely normal that they would be reunited this way). He then came upon de Gaulle, back in France after four years of exile and struggle, getting out of a tiny car before appearing on the balcony of the Hôtel de Ville. "Everyone was cheering for him. His style is perfect, anti-dictatorial . . . de Gaulle is very tall, very slim, everything about him stands out: his nose, his eyes, his ears, his gestures. He's a star. Larger than life."[107] The demi-god showed through under the top brass; the idyll would not stop. The walk up the rue de Rivoli deeply affected Cocteau; as you walked between two columns you might stumble over the body of a German soldier bathing in his own blood; but there were also half-naked women with their heads shaved, sometimes in chains, who were being dragged to the Hôtel de Ville, where Roger Stéphane would give them shelter. The Crillon and the American embassy, too, had just been liberated by a group that included Paul Morihien.

The next day, he saw de Gaulle again, walking up the Champs-Elysées under the bright sun, followed by a joyful crowd and women wearing the colors of the flag. Seated at a window in the Crillon, an unbeatable place from which to behold the Arc de Triomphe, the place de la Concorde, and the Seine, he witnessed the euphoric procession. A sudden round of shots fired from the rooftops provoked a response from the tanks surrounding the head of Free France, and the cigarette hanging from Cocteau's lips was cut in two. He and Morihien threw themselves to the floor. "Get down! Get down!" they shouted to Marais. They had been mistaken for the snipers.

Roger Lannes had his own fright, a little while later, discovering a police unit deployed in front of Cocteau's building on the rue de Montpensier, before Cocteau himself arrived in a mysterious car. Two hours later, Marie Laure de Noailles saw him in the avenue Kleber, playing the soldier on a U.S. Army tank with some film stars. One of the first Americans to enter Paris, in the wake of France's second armored division in Leclerc's army, the war correspondent Ernest Hemingway had "kidnapped" Cocteau to bring him to a victory celebration at the Ritz, whose wine cellars he "liberated." "You shouldn't have gone," Éluard warned him. "He wrote against Spain. If the Communists knew you had seen him, they would turn against you." This made him realize just how much power Stalin's followers had acquired during the three last years of the Résistance, while confirming the goodwill he had gained with them, beginning in 1937 with Aragon's *Ce soir*. Since he had known Hemingway, like Breker, in the 1920s, he lost no time in convincing himself that there would be new sanctions for "collaborating" with the Americans. "Things never change," Picasso confirmed when Cocteau went to see him in his studio. "Our kingdom is not on earth." This reaction comforted him, but also earned murmurs of disapproval from those who had come to see the painter illustrate the work that the Résistance writers were going to offer to de Gaulle.[108]

THE LEGAL PURGE

The troubles really began in late August, when the principal members of the Académie Mallarmé, including Paul Valéry and Henri Mondor, composed a text they signed "the five who stayed French," thereby suggesting that others— like Cocteau—had not. The next day Cocteau's name was added to the list, but the damage had been done: his "Salute to Breker" was being held against him. His support of the sculptor who had saved so many, "thanks" to whom France had not been treated like Poland, became proof of Cocteau's cowardice, if not his capitulation to the German presence. Despite the overt calls for his work to be banned, the covert calls for his arrest, the tear gas bombs and the blows he'd received, the insults from the *Je suis partout* gang, and the fact that Doriot's brutes had made him nearly lose an eye, the only thing anyone remembered was Breker. As if Cocteau had written in *Deustchland-Frankreich*, or celebrated the German victory in 1940 and the "swastika, which is the solar wheel," like Montherlant.[109]

He decided not to give in. Breker was his friend in his time of glory, and so he would remain in time of adversity, not because of ideology but because he cared. Had Breker become the official artist of the USSR, as Stalin had proposed, via Molotov, during the Nazi-Soviet Pact, Cocteau would have defended his sculptures with the same ardor, just as he would have welcomed his stories about the generosity and patronage of "Uncle Joe," the so-called father of the people, with the same exaltation. But soon a young cinema actor associated with the *résistants* of the Comédie-Française was putting it about everywhere that Marais had also behaved badly. All over Paris, *franc-tireurs* went around conducting searches on the basis of rumors and commandeering petrol without orders to do so. Crowds went after innocent people—like the Tuals' Vietnamese cook, who was suspected of being a Japanese man firing on the crowd and nearly lynched.

Some *résistants*—real ones—went to pick up Sacha Guitry in his hôtel particulier on the Champ-de-Mars to bring him to the Vel d'Hiv, then to Drancy; the FFI, however, had their eye on Bérard, who was living as a recluse on the rue Casimir-Delavigne, smoking sixty pipes a day, as he had before the war. The pipes were prepared for him by "No Luck," the sailor Cocteau used to see in Toulon in the 1930s.[110] Even the ex-Dadaist Picabia was threatened for having claimed, in 1941, that Maréchal Pétain was younger than the "vile" deputies who had exploited France.[111]

Since the Enlightenment, French artists had enjoyed a rare impunity; now they saw themselves suddenly called to account for their actions. Having written good books was no longer an excuse, but aggravating evidence. *Parade* was applauded in 1918, but in 1944 it would have been seen as infamous. "You know, I love moments of crisis, but I fear the purifying flames," Cocteau had said after the defeat of 1940; the observation held true. He was perfectly aware of having been neither courageous, nor consistent. "My politics are non-existent," he told François Mauriac, who didn't need convincing. But he did not think he had committed any crime, and so did not even black out the mentions of Hitler from his journal, which he had made under Breker's influence. Having devoted all his energy since the age of twenty to producing and promoting his work, he had spent the dark years protecting it, a benign mistake that, in his view, the Résistance should ignore. But it was an era in need of people to blame, in some cases no matter what their real responsibilities.

What could he claim to have done? Published Genet the convict? That wasn't an act of resistance. Tried to save Jacob? That would suggest that he had contacts among the Germans—and in any case Jacob had died. Been a scape-goat for the French national-socialists? At the time, neither being homosexual nor being denounced as an "enjuivé" counted as virtues. He had of course published in the journal *Fontaine*, which included authors who had resisted in Algiers, and its editor, Max-Pol Fouchet, had mentioned his name among those who had ensured the "French victory."[112] But more people in Paris had been reading *Comoedia*, under German control, in which reviews of Cocteau's theater productions had been published. "Jean . . . told me he could not turn his mind away from the events," Roger Lannes wrote in his journal.

A captain from Leclerc's army told Marais to join up. "I almost urged him to go," Cocteau wrote, "to leave my companionship and to escape my paternal control, which no one manages to understand, and which, to outsiders, must look like one of those households of boys that I loathe and that wound what you might call my bourgeois reserve, my sense of grandeur."[113] The ultras, after the Surrealists and Maritain, had managed to make him ashamed of his desires.

Marais climbed into the jeep, the dog Moulouk trembling in his arms, and left his room to Roger Stéphane, the liberator of the Préfecture. The rumor spread across Paris that Marais had joined up. "Playing what role?" Marc Doelnitz asked ironically. Cocteau, like Genet, fell out with him. Genet had also distanced himself from the right-wing group that had launched him, in which François Sentein and Thierry Maulnier rubbed shoulders with Roland Laudenbach and Jean Turlais—with Turlais being the first critic to have mentioned his "work" in a deliberately provocative way by including it next to that of the real Corneille and Plutarch, in his "Introduction to the History of Fascist French Literature." Was it the posthumous political influence of the young *résistant* Jean Decarnin? Genet went around saying, "One must be Communist," forgetting that he had been so charmed by the Feldgrau. Now the black GIs were the ones who monopolized his romantic attentions.

When Sentein wrote to tell Genet that the letter he had written in support of him to the head of the Militia was causing him problems, Genet simply replied, "Too bad for you! You shouldn't have been associating with people like that." Cocteau, who had heard "Corneille" making fun of Decarnin's Trotskyist sentiments, finally said to him, "Remember what you said to me that day in the corner of the Théâtre-Français—that a poet who spends time on anything besides poetry is a scoundrel."[114]

Bernard Grasset, the publisher, but also Pierre Fresnay, the actor, whose behavior was less flagrantly dishonorable, would go to prison; both times Cocteau telephoned their wives, then hung up, shaking, before the call went through. Marais's absence added to his anguish; he thought the actor would be shot, and die shouting with pain, alone, far behind the line of tanks. When the Société des Auteurs sent him a questionnaire, he listed the press campaigns that had targeted him, the bans that had been applied to his plays, and pointed out the strictly apolitical character of his writings for *Comoedia*. Word got out that he had had a hard time, but this was almost a point of pride in the neighborhood; everyone in the Palais-Royal would defend his morality.[115]

Cocteau nevertheless decided to place his honor in the hands of two men: "old" Éluard, who had become kindly, and young Sartre—whose *Huis clos* he had passionately defended, having been to see it with Genet, while secretly reproaching the author for having put the kind of people into his hell that the Church would have sent there anyway. Sartre had been warm when they had met at a conference on dramatic art; they had also been brought together by Genet in a bar on the Rue Jacob, before ending the night by the Seine, under the spray of rockets provided by the DCA (France's anti-aircraft regiment). Simone de Beauvoir had heard Cocteau plead political indifference and rail against the Americans as much as the Germans: "We did not agree," she pointed out, "but we were sympathetic."[116] Picasso, who had just caused a stir by joining the Communist Party, was not mentioned. But perhaps Cocteau did not fully trust him—unless he did not want to bother him.

Who could be absolutely sure of having behaved well during the Occupation? Sartre? He had supported the Résistance, but he had seen his play *Les mouches* performed in the former Théâtre Sarah Bernhardt, renamed Théâtre de la Cité—since the actress was Jewish—before an audience well-stocked with German officers, and seen it praised by *Signal* and the *Pariserzeitung*; he had also done all he could to get Céline to attend. Camus? Through his contacts in the Combat movement, he had contributed to numerous patriotic publications since the end of 1943. But it was thanks to Heller's support that he had staged his own *Malentendu*, in July 1944. Simone de Beauvoir? She had narrowly missed the Goncourt, in 1943, for *L'invitée*—a book that had made Cocteau praise her "extraordinary talent," but whose erotic frankness had shocked him. Eugène Guillevic, one of the pillars of the Comité national des écrivains, who presided over the first "trials"? He had published in his protector Drieu la Rochelle's *Nouvelle revue française* before joining the ranks of the Communists. Maurice Blanchot? He had ended the war well, but only after having been on the extreme Right for a long time, having become, in 1942, Drieu's subeditor at the *Nouvelle revue française*, where Éluard himself had seen his own signature printed next to the names of notorious collaborators.[117] Picasso? During the insurrection of Paris, he was at home painting a *Bacchanale* inspired by Poussin.

Éluard unambiguously defended Cocteau. Ignoring the "Salute to Breker," he reminded people of Cocteau's refusal to salute the LVF flag. He did point out, however, to Cocteau: "Never talk about wiping the slate clean, that is a crime."[118] Sartre was more subtle in his defense. Cocteau prudently decided to leave for the country, far from the mounting accusations, and the possible risk of arrest.

When he returned, his heart sank, seeing the trunks into which Max Jacob's executor had placed his belongings. He found the books they had dedicated to each other, the letters they had exchanged, and even remembered some of the clothes he had often seen him wear. Two days later, Picasso was indignant to see Christian Bérard, whom he hated, proudly wearing Jacob's trousers. Michel Leiris heard about it, and denounced this act of "intolerable frivolity" in *Combat*. For a while, Cocteau and his friends were accused of having symboli-cally murdered Jacob.[119] Such was the climate of the purge: the slightest detail was suspicious.

In the winter of 1944, during the most dangerous period, Genet nevertheless proclaimed Cocteau the greatest living poet, against the latest Surrealist attacks led by Leiris. At the same time, the author of *Notre-Dame-des-fleurs* wrote a preface to a reprint of *La machine infernale*, which Cocteau called "magnifique": the former prisoner was defending the poet who had saved him in the middle

of the Occupation. Genet soon sent him *Pompes funèbres,* his novel that drama-
tized the arrest of Jean Decarnin, who had died during the liberation of Paris in
August, but that fetishized the militiamen who had killed him: through his
Nazi lover, Germany and Hitler were raised to the level of phallic divinities.
Cocteau was enthralled by the novel's audacity: "It's pure genius. And of a
freedom so terrible that the author is unimpeachable, perched on some devil's
throne in an empty sky in which human law no longer reigns." Hitler and the
French Militia, "kids of sixteen to twenty years old" whose terrorizing of France
for three years he had had the "subtle joy" of witnessing, were harbingers of evil,
whom Genet ventriloquized, then cannibalized in an erotic ritual hallucina-
tion. In 1939, Sartre had reproached Mauriac for playing with his characters
like God with his subjects; with Genet it was the devil who acted. The novel
was published a full three years later, anonymously and with a small print run—
which was probably best for Cocteau.[120]

On November 28, 1944, Cocteau was asked to appear before the Comité de
Libération du Cinéma Français. He slipped in front of Henri Jeanson, Marcel
Aymé, and other suspects to present himself to the president, a lily in his hand.
When criticized for befriending Breker—an action to which he fully owned
up—he replied with disarming aplomb: "Breker is right this moment doing the
bust of the General de Lattre de Tassigny!"[121] The committee acquitted him; the
president of the ad hoc tribunal himself had published in *Comoedia,* and as late
as 1944. Aragon having spoken up on his behalf, Cocteau did not even bother to
show up before the purge committee of the Comité National des Écrivains, of
which Éluard was also an eminent member. The two Communist writers
played a key role in the literary purge, and there again Cocteau was exonerated,
after several articles he wrote during the war were analyzed. It was a logical
decision, since he did not fit under any of the four categories of guilt established
by the committee: he had not joined any group favorable to the Collaboration,
he had not traveled to Germany, he had received no money from the enemy,
and he had not helped to spread Hitlerian propaganda.

The influence of the Communist Party helped, and Cocteau regained a
certain amount of respect. His name had already appeared in *Aurélien,* the
masterpiece that Aragon had found the time to write during the war. "He is
funny, he's creative, he's lively," said a society lady whose son imagined himself
his disciple.[122] He could also be found regularly in *Les lettres françaises,* the
cultural organ of the Communist Party, to which Aragon asked him to contribute
both writings and drawings. Cocteau could now consider himself safe. Soon
Éluard was suggesting that he and Cocteau work together to choose among the
poems left by Jacob, while Pierre Seghers, another important member of the

party, commissioned a study of him from Roger Lannes.[123] It was a strange twist of fate to have been saved from the "patriotic butchery" he so feared by two Surrealists who twenty years earlier had persecuted him.

Some remained skeptical, like Maritain, who accused him of not having contributed to the Résistance, which was undeniable, or Kessel, who had fought in the war, and because he suspected Cocteau of having links with Germany refused to shake his hand. In December, Cocteau decided to start a mutual aid society for the benefit of imprisoned soldiers, having been informed of their situation by Marais. He published an "Appeal to Knitters" in *Femmes de France* and demanded that the invincible owners of Maxim's send care packages to the front.[124] Then he befriended the new British ambassadors, Duff and Diana Cooper, whose protection had managed to whitewash even Louise de Vilmorin.[125] He seemed to be on steady ground, even to Maritain who, after keeping Cocteau at a distance, happily reunited with his old friend.

As Christmas approached, the wind turned. With the Germans' aggressive counter-offensive in the Ardennes, rumors flew in a terrified Paris that the Wehrmacht would be back by the end of the year. Bombs fell on the Tuileries, and Brussels was supposed to have received the V2. "If the Germans returned, what would you do?" Cocteau asked Picasso. "So what [winking, nudging], you haven't understood?"[126] Supported by Leclerc's and de Lattre's troops, the American speedroller took two weeks to fix the situation.

Volunteers surged to join the French 2nd DB (armored division), which had become a machine for laundering one's name, and everywhere Moulouk the dog got the star of the film *L'éternel retour* recognized and applauded; no one had thought to see Marais in uniform. Roger Lannes had been right: happiness converged around the carefree Marais. Headed to combat with the fervor and the courage he demonstrated in all he did, he exposed himself to enemy fire with his proverbial obliviousness. Convinced of his heroism, Cocteau came to believe that the French would give themselves to him if he fulfilled their fantasy of riding up the Champs-Elysées on a white horse. Marais was everything he never could have been. To Gide he confided that he was only half of Jean Cocteau; the other was off in Alsace with Marais's comrades. "My dream would be to make him happy in all things," he wrote in his journal, with that disarming altruism that could provide him forgetfulness, if not peace.[127]

In February 1945, Cocteau was denounced by letter for having participated in German "propaganda," and Marais for having been hired by the Comédie-Française in 1941. Moreover, Cocteau's brother, Paul, a stockbroker, had been suspended for six months for financial dealings with the occupying authorities—and this time it was true.[128] The Renseignements Généraux led an inquiry into Jean Cocteau's attitude, but could not establish any evidence against him, even if the suspicion persisted.[129] These threats did not prevent him, in January, from signing a petition—along with Camus, Mauriac, Valéry, and Claudel— asking for mercy for Brasillach, the former editor-in-chief of *Je suis partout*. He had every reason to hate the novelist's ideas; Brasillach had encouraged the deportations and had been an accessory to the worst campaigns against him. But he hated to see writers muzzled, banned, or condemned, and rejected cruelty, whether state-sponsored, party-sponsored, or private. Brasillach was executed in February 1945, the editorial team of *Je suis partout* was brought to trial in November 1946, and Laubreaux was sentenced to death (for refusing to appear in court) the following year, but none of it brought him the least plea- sure. The desire for vengeance was so foreign to him that he could even be heard to murmur "poor Laubreaux."[130] He would sign another petition asking for mercy for Rebatet, who hadn't thought to spare him, and for Pierre-Antoine Cousteau, the brother of the famous commandant who was condemned to death during the first trial.[131] There was no doubt that he would rather have seen the French suppliers to the Wehrmacht in the Santé.

Ezra Pound, banished and imprisoned for shouting on Mussolini's radio, received in 1947 *La crucifixion*, the poem Cocteau had just published through Morihien. Pound, the poet who was ostracized by his own country, would always be grateful to Cocteau. Pound's translations had introduced Cocteau to the United States, and not many people at the time had tried to pierce the circle of silence that surrounded Pound. Cocteau even defended Céline in 1950, soon before he was tried for collaboration, even though the author of *Bagatelles pour un massacre* had called for his execution in 1941 (Decadent Cocteau? Too bad. Pro-LICA Cocteau? Liquidated.). "Céline violently reproached me for not being anti-Semitic, but these things have nothing to do with a man's freedom," he declared to the judge, asking for clemency.[132] At the same time, he would remain loyal to Arno Breker, who had protected him so well during the dark years. "My only politics is friendship," he told Mauriac.

PARIS WILL ALWAYS BE . . .

The Armistice brought an end to a war that had claimed 55 million lives, from Auschwitz to Stalingrad, Dakar to Honolulu. Every day mass graves like something out of the Apocalypse were uncovered, revealing heaps of corpses, gold teeth, broken glasses, lampshades made of human skin. "Five years of hatred, fear, waking up in the middle of a nightmare. Five years of shame and mud. We were splattered, made queasy down to our souls," Cocteau would say.[133] The first to escape from the camps returned, their eyes devoured by the horrible secret they tried to transmit to an incredulous crowd, a secret that Cocteau, this time, would frequently describe in his journal: a people had tried, and almost succeeded, in wiping another off the face of the earth. Every day he learned of more deaths, including that of Lili de Rothschild, in whose home he and Marais were still dining at the end of 1943, and who had been arrested while waiting for Charles Trenet—not being Jewish by birth, she had thought she was safe—before being deported to Dachau and reduced to ashes in the ovens. Everywhere around him, the devil had spit his flames, and Cocteau had happened to stumble into its shadow, without truly understanding what a horrible task it was undertaking. "Hell exists, and it is History," he would say to Julien Green.[134]

Marais would return from the army to have lunch on the rue de Montpensier with Mila Parely at his side. Parely complained of being betrayed by a constellation of boys, while Cocteau, "irreparably alone," bitter, and annoyed, looked on, according to Roger Lannes. Marais the soldier still belonged to him a little, but Marais the civilian was impatient to share his fame a little with everyone.

In May, Claude Mauriac's book *Jean Cocteau ou la vérité du mensonge* was published, after the first chapter had been released by the *Nouvelle revue française* in June 1940. It was a sensitive indictment, intelligent but unforgiving of his "debased literature," and of his having turned away from the "strict commandments of tradition," and of being, through this literary drifting, "one of those chiefly responsible for this degeneration." Treading the furrows of the Liberation with Vichy clodhoppers, Mauriac Jr. set himself up as a public prosecutor in the preface: "As is the way with all revolutions, the guilty parties, no matter how highly positioned, no matter how grand their authentic titles of glory, must be denounced."[135]

Of course Mauriac paid homage to the author of *Plain-chant*, and to his talent as a novelist and playwright, but the trial carried out against this painful but fake character, such an easy target!, in its mimetic function and its basic malaise, was the cruel synthesis of the triple portrait that Mauriac Sr., the Surrealists, and *Je suis partout* had sketched: the young literary heir, who in 1936 had declared that he was ashamed that his country was governed by a Jew named Blum, had not finished sowing his right-wing oats.[136]

The wound was reopened, the pain increased by the balm that Claude Mauriac, in good Catholic form, applied as soon as the flesh was gouged out. Though the book evinced real depth of literary analysis, Cocteau was above all hurt by what Mauriac wrote about his terrible solitude, his muddled appetite for the "supernatural," and his inability to set himself a direction—Mauriac described him as one who "could not exist—and be authentic—except through a cycle of self-denial."[137] Too unstable to really believe in Christ, too narcissistic to know love, too weak not to prefer opium to God and illusion to reality, in this portrayal Cocteau saw himself condemned to the hellfire of his foundational void. If *Tartuffe* was synonymous with "hypocrite," Cocteau was the sincere liar who dwells in us all, this fake personality that God in heaven would relieve us of: for in order to enter heaven, one must be dead to oneself.

Cocteau asked François Mauriac what could have possessed his son to treat him so harshly. "But Claude is an idiot, you can't listen to anything he says," Maurice responded, amused—a way of reducing the importance of this offshoot, too quickly gone to seed, without confessing that he had whispered to him some of these accusations.[138] Indeed, to Roger Stéphane, Mauriac confided, "Have you read my son's book yet? . . . He didn't show me the passage in which he talks about decadent literature. That's the harshest bit, and I would have made him take it out. But at heart he's right. There is a permanent lie about Cocteau."[139] Had he not claimed for a long time that borrowing from other writers' work would never make Cocteau a writer? Had he not been one of the first to say that far from helping the young, he was helping them to an early grave? "I have always had problems with this family," Cocteau concluded, half serious, half joking.[140]

Life went on. Cocteau could be seen at all the opening nights, beside Picasso and Marlene Dietrich, but also in the British ambassador's box, or at the screening of *Les enfants du paradis*, a film whose credits proudly showed, under the heading "collaborators within the Résistance," the list of Jewish, Gaullist, or conscientious-objector technicians who had worked on it, but which Cocteau judged to be deplorably bad.[141] With Marais, he spent the summer of 1945 by the harbor at Arcachon, in the village of Le Piquey that Radiguet still haunted— even if their vacations seemed as long ago as the flood. Walking at night on the sand, under the false daylight of a half moon, Cocteau physically felt the power of the storm that had devastated Europe. An empire had crumbled, entire towns had been reduced to dust, millions of lives had been lost, but the little Hôtel Chantecler was still standing, and the sandy beach continued to sparkle, under the renewed assaults of the sea.

THE DEATH OF THE DEVIL

Those who had escaped to America began to return. Breton made it back to Paris in 1946 and reestablished the Surrealist headquarters, but not his influence. Crevel and Desnos were dead; all the great Surrealist names, from Artaud to Dalí, were flying solo; and Tzara was already accusing Breton, in the name of the Communist Party, of desertion. As for Éluard and Aragon, members of the same party, they praised the France of the music halls, big families, and patriotic charcoal far from the defeatism, abortion, and internationalism that reigned at the Cyrano. As late as the 1960s, Breton was still saying that even on a desert island, he would never again speak to "Sir Aragon." Born to decree, bless, wound, fascinate, and hate, Breton was reduced to entertaining light-weights at the Café de Flore. Six years away had dug a trench between Paris and the sensual disorder that he was still calling for.[142]

Maurice Sachs did not return from Germany, where, under the more "Aryan" name of Ettinghausen, he had served as a crane operator in Hamburg.[143] The books he had left behind began to be published under the authority of Yvon Belaval, Cocteau's ex-lover. They revealed an unusual figure, as well as a memorialist; his hypnotic glibness, the candor of the unloved, and his diabolical trickery could be felt through the paper. Rarely had a text embodied so much of its creator: every page exuded his erotic and financial gluttony, like that of an abandoned pasha, with no rules or structure, no court or valets. You could almost see his mouth greedy for alcoholic milk, and beyond, his heavy, mocking gaze. Poor "Biquette" had become a writer.

A few books were enough to transform this existential catastrophe into a legend; confessions from a group of French homosexuals working for the Gestapo, with whom Sachs had lived communally in Hamburg, rekindled the rumors about his death. It came out that he had spied on foreigners staying in the strategic port and even denounced double agents, before being denounced in turn. But these unbelievable stories reawakened old suspicions: he had worn the SS uniform, then turned spy, before being arrested; his Russian cellmates in the Hamburg prison had lynched him, when they found out he worked for the Gestapo, before turning his pulp of a body over to a group of German shep-herds; others claimed he had been deported and shot by the Germans. The success of his books fed the imagination; rumors flew that he had been able to escape from prison at the last minute; someone said they had seen him begging, covered by a long beard, on the boulevard Saint-German, two steps away from the cafés where Cocteau, his Catholic godfather, hung out. Decked out with braids and cloven hooves, the image of the wandering Jew, alone—with the Maritains as his only support, always praying in secret for his soul—continued to fuel the anti-Semitic prejudice of the prewar period.

In 1949, someone said they had seen Sachs in the Middle East, where he was said to have fled the American army. The novelist Philippe Jullian said he saw him at the head of a homosexual harem next to the Red Sea.[144] Like Hitler's secretary Martin Bormann—or like Christ, with certain sects believing that he had led a second life in India, once he got down from the cross—Maurice Sachs would be spied throughout the world, even among a group of devil-worshippers, even on a different continent. Much later, in 1968, this ghost of the Collaboration would haunt the young writer Patrick Modiano, who, born in the same building that Sachs had lived in on the quai Conti, imagined him as a broker in Antwerp, or a pimp in Barcelona, in his first novel *La place de l'Étoile.*

It would take years to establish what had really happened. Sachs had indeed joined the Reich's secret service, for eighty marks a week, and his downfall had been warning a young Jesuit, with connections to London, that he was going to denounce him to the Gestapo. Locked up in the prison of Fuhlsbütell, in northern Hamburg, he had effectively served as a "sheep" spying on the other prisoners, before being evacuated, along with all the other detainees, in the face of the British advance, and then killed by a Flemish SS agent during their forced march on the road to Kiel. His great flaccid body had been transported to the Wittorferfeld cemetery, where he remains to this day. "When you have had enough of life, you press there, like that, and it's all over," Jacques Bizet, his grandmother's companion, had said to him, pointing a revolver into his mouth. Sachs had preferred to have himself killed.

These revelations turned him into a myth. The author of *Sabbat* became an effeminate Nero in a German uniform watching as Europe burned. What were his real motivations, he who had become a passionate reader of the Bible—for real, this time—in the service of the Nazis? And what would have become of him had he survived the fall of Germany? All evidence suggests that Cocteau would have defended him warmly at his trial, but would not have been able to prevent his being condemned to death.

The books eventually published under Sachs's name maintained the idea of him as enigma. After *Le Sabbat* came *La chronique joyeuse et scandaleuse*, in which Cocteau appears under the revealing name of "Sanqueur" and then more allegorically, "Duvant."[145] The boy he had "adopted" and looked after, without managing to become his father, had returned after death to denounce him one last time. Cocteau was linked with the tendency to create books with no basis, and to a genius for promoting other people's talent, appropriating it when necessary. The author of *Parade* and *Le sang d'un poète* was mocked as a recycler of formal revolutions and other poetics developed elsewhere, hated by those whom he claimed as friends. The creator of the *Mariés de la tour Eiffel* and *Les enfants terribles* was belittled as a pyrotechnist whose false lightning dazzled only momentarily, a Monsieur Loyal whom the poor bohemian of

Montparnasse and hard-nosed avant-garde had greeted with disdain, all men "greater and truer poets than he": in short, Sachs brought to light everything that Breton had been saying for a quarter century about the show-off of the Right Bank.[146] The gift Cocteau had not been able to detect in Sachs, the literary authenticity the younger had so ardently coveted, was taken away from the elder in Sach's own descriptions. Cocteau's varied work was belittled as no more than a potpourri of "petals torn from many different flowers which all dried out in his hands"—an odorless old bouquet, fading and always the same, throughout his fake moltings.[147] Cocteau was accused of talking endlessly about love but being unable to practice it, and compared to an illusionist who made people's hearts disappear only to pull a rabbit out of his hat—hobbled by an "almost monstrous insensitivity" by Iago/Sachs, in one final thrust of the knife.[148] Cocteau underwent a form of lynching with every book by Sachs that mentioned him. As if, not having been able to make himself truly loved, or having come to regret his passion for Cocteau, the author of *Le Sabbat* had decided to pillage from beyond the grave all the kindnesses he had received from him, fixing Cocteau's dark reputation in writing.

Cocteau reacted by comparing Sachs's behavior to suicidal self-defense. "The more he lashes out, the more he hits himself," he wanted to believe.[149] It was Sachs's own inability to perfect a book that he was denouncing, through Cocteau, just as by reducing him to his verbal prowess, Sachs was trampling on his own conversation—which, according to Violette Leduc, was "his most successful book," adding: "to hear him is to steal the best of his talent."[150] The more Sachs accused Cocteau of leading astray anyone who approached him, the more he denounced his own strategy of playing the mimicking groupie: Sachs, this identity thief, was still that orphan who had stolen from Cocteau so many times out of love, only to return the most beautiful gifts. And he was still that offspring who, lacking a real moral system, had constructed himself as Cocteau's negative—as Genet would do, even more energetically.

There was only one argument for which Cocteau had no reply. Sachs blamed him in advance for his own tragic death, reminding him that though death had stalked him since the trenches of 1917, it had looked after him, spared him, preferring to use him as a "recruiter."[151] So if the SS had shot Sachs like a dog, it was because Cocteau, this false protector, had wished him dead. Continuing to turn his demonic eye on him from the far reaches of the German earth, Sachs seemed to whisper, "You loved Bourgoint, but I was the true character; you promoted Desbordes, but I was the true writer." Thus the memories of the debauched *collabo* were a hit, while the works of the heroic *résistant* fell into oblivion.

The stack grew taller. *La chasse à courre* appeared in 1949, *Tableau de moeurs de ce temps* in 1954—Cocteau began to wonder if Yvon Belavel was not beginning to add his own thoughts to these printed attempts at vengeance. The dead published more than the living—eight books in nine years!—and the figure of Cocteau appeared more and more like the black hole retrospectively structuring this autobiographical oeuvre. What had he done now, to be so hated? He recalled the last words that he and Sachs had exchanged. It was October 1941, more than a year before Sachs left for Germany, and eight months since their previous encounter at Maxim's.

> He called me in the morning. He was dying at the Hôtel de Castille. He begged me to come . . . I found him in bed, very pale. "I have only ever loved you," he said. "Your friendship suffocated me. I wanted to get away from it. I wrote lies and insults about you. Forgive me. I have ordered them all to be destroyed."[152]

Yet as he left France in November 1942, Sachs had asked that the portrait of Cocteau be reinserted in the manuscript of *Sabbat*: six atrocious, grandiose pages that concluded with the confession, "I have never felt worse than I have with Cocteau."

There was one small consolation for Cocteau: a year after Gide's death Pierre Herbart, who had become something like his adopted son, got his own revenge by claiming that the Immoralist was neither a great novelist, nor a thinker of any stature, but an egomaniac who made, during a life without passion, books without morality or the least imagination.[153] One must always be wary of secretaries.

THE UNFASHIONABLE

One day we'll know what I was building and where I was going.
— *Jean Cocteau to his mother, September 25, 1919*

HOW TO BECOME A "GERMANOPRATIN"

The end of the war unleashed a new wave of American fever, as it had in 1918—from the sticks of chewing gum offered by the GIs to the combat uniforms they exchanged for military surplus uniforms. And then, once again, there was the jazz. Nightclubs opened in all the old wine cellars of Saint-Germain-des-Prés, a neighborhood that Picasso had helped to make fashionable around 1935, and where, during the war, the "zazous" had promoted their bohemian lifestyle, halfway between the Incroyables of 1795 and the punks of 1977. Cocteau, a budding "Germanopratin," or denizen of Saint-Germain-des-Prés, had a superficial knowledge of these streets, having lived there for a few weeks before the war; he took to them immediately, with the same energy as when he took Montparnasse by storm in 1916. He could be seen at the Flore with Genet and his new friends, Violette Leduc, who had so loved Sachs, and Simone de Beauvoir—"I was the only heterosexual in the group, pure perversion on my part," she would say, excitedly.[1] Then they would walk up the rue Bonaparte together, joined by Sartre, toward the Palais-Royal, where Paul Morihien had his little publishing company.[2] On the café terraces, they exchanged glances with the young people who every night, from the Tabou to the Sphinx, thrilled to the trumpet of Boris Vian and the Assyrian face of the chanteuse Juliette Gréco.

Forgetting the difference in age, Cocteau wanted to be one of them. He could be seen chatting to the be-bop dancers from the Antilles and the chic young women of the neighborhood in Vichy skirts, then playing for Alexandre Astruc's "camera-pen" the flattering role of Homer in a film that has now been lost, *Ulysse ou les mauvaises rencontres,* in which Juliette Gréco plays Circe and Boris Vian and Anne-Marie Cazalis are part of the ancient chorus.[3] Cocteau even managed, once again, to play the role of godfather and big brother: Vian's play, *L'équarrissage pour tous,* would be compared to Apollinaire's *Mamelles de Tirésias* as well as *Les mariés de la tour Eiffel*—and Vian was himself praised for his insolence and his gift for "making his breath take the form of a trumpet."[4] How could the author of *Les enfants terribles* resist this kind of juvenile emulation? "It was very hard for him, no longer being a rising star," noted François Sentein.[5] The youngsters in the nightclubs viewed him with some circumspection; he was too dynamic not to be lying about his age. He may have contributed to the fashion for the duffle coat, the hooded Oxford cape that would for a long time give him the air of the eternal student, but they were skeptical of his dance of the seven veils. Gide accused Passavant/Cocteau, in *the Counterfeiters,* of always writing prefaces to his books in order to wipe away the memory of the previous ones, too clearly meant for a time gone by; in his desire to conquer each generation that emerged, Cocteau seemed to prove him right.

At the same time, he could not believe in the radical singularity of a generation of young people who were rediscovering Gershwin and sexual ambiguity, nightclubbing and cocktails, twenty-five years after the Boeuf sur le Toit. The decor at the Tabou seemed a reconstruction in which extras in plaid shirts (paid by the same Alexandre Astruc) were recreating the golden age of the rue Boissy-d'Anglas. When Juliette Gréco was photographed in bed with Annabelle, who would marry Bernard Buffet, her hotel room, with its film stars tacked to the wall and its studied disorder, seemed the exact copy of the cell in *Les enfants terribles.* Of course the handsome Jean Babilée had all the savage grace of Nijinsky, with his cheekbones and his Russian mane, but his leaps, too, seemed deeply indebted to the dancer who had brought so much glory to Russia, in *Le spectre de la rose.*[6] History was repeating itself like something out of a farce, as Marx had predicted. You could even find at Les Deux Magots one of Radiguet's improbable "nephews" who had "inherited" his sole proclivity for drink.

Already well-known before the war for *La nausée* and *Le mur,* but brought to greater public attention by the polemic surrounding *Huis clos* in 1944, Sartre had become *the* writer to read for this generation. Attempting to impose his supremacy over the novel, the theater, and the essay, to say nothing of the cinema (where he would prove to be less happy), this philosopher by training was naturally exposed to the same reproaches as Cocteau, but his intellectual stature, his eagerness to take on the great problems of the world, and the prestige of his theory of existentialism made him an infinitely more solid figure. In 1948 Céline accused the novelist of being a tapeworm who had crawled out of his intestines, a talentless "headcase" ("agité de bocal").[7] But his extremely rare conjunction of gifts had allowed Sartre to supplant the subtle domination that Gide and Breton had exercised over French literature for almost half a century. He was won over by Cocteau's charm and intelligence, as well as by his humanity and extreme sensitivity, which were so far removed from the brutal genius of someone like Genet, whom he also began to see socially.

Simone de Beauvoir herself came to find Cocteau amusing, seductive, and more than amiable; his kindness surprised their close friends, especially J.-B. Pontalis, who was accustomed to the abrasive maliciousness of some homosexuals, his brother in particular, a friend of Sachs and Genet. "Like Picasso, he tended to monologue, but words were Cocteau's medium, and he made use of them with the skill of an acrobat. I would follow, fascinated, the movement of his lips and hands," said Beauvoir.[8]

Like his fellow graduates of the École Normale Supérieure, Paul Nizan and André Herbaud, the young Sartre was deeply affected by reading Cocteau in the mid-1920s. "Their turbulent trio . . . fell under the influence of an extraordinary book, *Le Potomak*. The 'whole world' that Sartre wanted to reach was shared, for Cocteau, between two families: the Eugènes, helmeted monsters with crocodile jaws, and the Mortimers, innocents with a soft air about them . . . the three young men wrote, drew, danced, clowned, as dictated by *Le Potomak*. Cocteau was a Eugène. Raymond Aron, a classmate but not a partner in crime, was a Mortimer."[9] It would turn out to be a fruitful passion. One day, as Herbaud scribbled in class some Eugènes, his neighbor spoke to him, moved that someone "at the Sorbonne loved Cocteau." Intrigued, Herbaud introduced the young Simone de Beauvoir to Sartre, who found her "nice, pretty, but badly dressed" and dubbed her a Mortimer—but one of the tough Mortimers, capable of swallowing up rivals "by sheer speed of breath." In this way, "le Castor" (the Beaver) entered his life.[10]

Sartre, however, kept his distance, in literary terms. It was no longer the era of the gratuitous absurdity of *Le Potomak*, or the disconnected poetry of *Les enfants terribles*, but a time for all manner of engagements, after the wait-and-see years of the war. The generation of the 1920s was trying to translate the euphoria of the Armistice into art. The post-1945 generation, by contrast, intellectually rejected the eclectic pleasures it was living in daily life to discuss the austere arguments of Sartre or Blanchot, the death of art, or the impossibility of writing poetry after Auschwitz. Much more compromising than his associations with the Germans was the "apolitical nature" of Cocteau's work, during these days of existentialist interrogation and Stalinist engagement. For Sartre, however, the ambition to rethink the "whole world" was shadowed by a similarly immodest desire for artistic efficiency. Cocteau, a survivor of the 1910s, might have interested him, in terms of his know-how, or even touched him with his vulnerability, but most often Sartre's curiosity was expressed through Genet. If Beauvoir would say that the ex-convict "would let no one attack Cocteau in front of him," it was, no doubt, because Sartre was doing it. Yet when the author of *La nausée* said, "You have to admit that Cocteau hasn't known how to get on," Genet could only agree with him. When Cocteau found out, he could only suffer from this casual, lucid judgment, as well as from this blossoming friendship that excluded him.[11]

The smallest meeting or detail was enough to remind Cocteau of his advancing age. Running into Paul Léautaud at the home of the wealthy Florence Gould, they would reminisce about the days of Anna de Noailles, of Catulle Mendès, and of de Max, but all of that seemed so far away that he would immediately add "when I was a boy," as if he had accidentally grown up in this timeless milieu.[12] The denizens of Saint-Germain-des-Prés were not fooled; from the back Cocteau blended in, but from the front he looked three times their age. He had to admit it: that sad old man whose photograph was regularly featured in the press was indeed himself—a relic from before the war, from before even the First World War. With his stock of incredible stories and his quirky expressions, Cocteau was trying for one last comeback among the habitués of the Tabou, but if they read poetry at all, they preferred Prévert, who had just published *Paroles* and whose work was more in line with their detached, sardonic style. Cocteau often mistook his wishful thinking for his appearance, and his dreams for reality; this illusion remained until the end. For nothing pained him more, in his almost canine need for recognition, than no longer having influence over anyone.

These night owls' parents rewarded a play he'd written during the Occupation with critical acclaim and financial success. The rehearsals for *L'aigle à deux têtes*, which was staged in Brussels in 1946, and then the first performances at the Théâtre Hébertot, in late December, took up all of his energy. Every night he would walk to the theater and past the concierge's office like a child "whom the investigating judge has authorized to descend to Hell." Then he would settle into Edwige Feuillère's dressing room to watch her get her makeup done, and would leave only once the bell had made the walls vibrate, to climb up at the last minute to the gallery from where he had a high-angle view of the proceedings, like an archangel keeping heaven informed.[13] The anarchist in short leather trousers played by Marais and the solitary queen played by Feuillère were his final attempt to animate the heaven in which Wagnerian demi-gods endlessly loved and argued. "A myth is human passion that, in contact with the earth, provokes a natural phenomenon," Pirandello wrote.[14] Such was the thunderous climate in which Cocteau hoped to surround the young sovereign in pursuit of freedom and the rebel sent to assassinate her, before succumbing to her charm and then stabbing her after he had swallowed poison.

Thunderbolts, in antiquity, were seen as the result of the gods' angry clashes. The "theaterbolts" that set the rhythm of *L'aigle à deux têtes* pleased those who had lived through the 1930s, Marie Laure de Noailles above all, who believed she had inspired the caprices of this young empress, who was in fact modeled on Sissi. But for others, the rolling thunder that Cocteau orchestrated from a distance (like that volcanologist who called himself a "poet of fire" but refused to scale the erupting craters) struck a hollow, even false, note. Since the time of Anna de Noailles, Cocteau had always turned to myth to elevate himself far from reality, but the Nazis had made it difficult, for a time, to use this kind of drama, featuring exceptional characters with vast powers. Though acceptable in the era of the Eternal Return, it was somewhat less so after the war, with "liberated" ears hearing in it the final echoes of the *Götterdämmerung* that had ravaged Europe. A work written in French, but conceived in German, Cocteau himself said of his *L'aigle à deux têtes*, a reproach that could also have been made of Sartre's existentialist writings, which were greatly inspired by Husserl and Heidegger—but Satre's works had the merit, at least in the eyes of the Germanopratins, of seeming more innovative and less kitsch. After having become fashionable in the middle of the Occupation, Cocteau suddenly found himself out of fashion for having wanted, after the "family drama" of *Les parents terribles*, to create a drama of the gods in the German tragic tradition.[15]

THE PRINCE AND THE LEPER

Cocteau was more than ever besotted with fairytales, which he had rediscovered during the war. His readings were voluptuous, almost placental, not only because they sent him back to childhood, but also because all of life was contained there, bathed in the marvelous. Cats could prance about dressed as noblemen, and unloved princesses sleep for an eternity, before being reawakened even more fresh than the moment the spell was cast. Endowed with magic powers, men and beasts enjoyed the gift of metamorphosis that had made his life somewhat fabulous, but they were never reproached for it. What earth could compete with this world where all the Hop o' My Thumbs, through a blend of cunning and candor, manage to fell terrifying ogres?[16]

These stories had another advantage: they were happy, and made people feel lighthearted. Myths embodied a pessimistic, aristocratic version of the world, while fairytales and legends were more optimistic and democratic: a shepherdess could marry a prince, children save their parents, simple countryfolk be turned into great chamberlains. The extraordinary presented itself in the most unaffected of manners, and horror itself could be transformed into the marvelous. Love was unconquerable, promises eternal, charm and kindness always rewarded. Just the thing to delight this fifty-six-year-old child.

A short tale by Mme Leprince de Beaumont made him want to return to the cinema. It told of the sad life of a Beast who was powerful but ugly, a recluse who lived in a palace surrounded by a forest, and the equally sad story of a poor, beautiful, Cinderella figure, victim of her older sisters' jealousy, who goes to the Beast's kingdom in order to save her beloved father's life after he wanders by mistake into the Beast's lair. The Beast's suffering softens her, and she falls in love with him, which transforms the leper into a handsome Prince Charming. But in order to turn into a film *La belle et la bête*, this "fairytale without fairies," Cocteau was going to have to visually create the castles and monsters that seem so immense to children, without disappointing the imagination or awakening the skepticism of a culture that had lost all sense of exuberance or naiveté and instead had fallen into the habit of admiring well-wrought, reflective, premeditated works. For France, at the end of the war, was less than it ever had been a country for children—and you'd have to be one to picture yourself an animal. Instead it was a refuge for nitpicking teenagers, too aware of their superiority to be tricked.

Cocteau hunted for moated castles in the Touraine with a small team, until he came across the manor at Rochecorbon. Then he was able to obtain permission from de Gaulle for Marais, who was still in the French 2nd DB (armored division), to play the Beast, but also, instinctively proving his ability to make multiple use of his resources, the roles of Prince Charming and Avenant, the suitor turned down by Belle. Convinced, like Genet, that Marais would only win definitive recognition by playing an ugly man, Cocteau decked him out first with a roebuck mask. Soon convinced by Bérard that a long-haired animal would have a greater effect, he thought up a set of features that were half-dog, half-Persian cat, underlining the fact that Marais's beauty had something strange in it, something unsettling, and which made him look as if his dog Moulouk had been genetically modified while he lapped at the water in a pond. The actor's voice contributed further to the metamorphoses: so much drinking and smoking had made it deeper, while relieving none of its stridence, so that he sounded as if someone had given him the vocal cords of a cat.

Curiously, Cocteau approached the film with much less confidence than *Le sang d'un poète*. Aware of the great financial risks that he was taking on for his producers, he took what happened on set too much to heart, forgetting the flow of the film and piling up continuity errors. He began to think that he was no filmmaker at all, and sought out the technical assistance of René Clément, who had just completed *La bataille du rail*, a film celebrating the Résistance.[17] Filming was made even more delicate by the particularly unstable climate in the Touraine, as well as power outages and equipment that kept breaking down. Every morning, three full hours were required to apply the hideous hairy mask that did not allow Marais's skin to breathe or cool down, then another hour to apply hair to his hands and his wrists. The fangs meant that he could only eat pureed food during those twelve-hour days. The actor bore the general sense of irritation with a Roman stoicism, and it lent a poignant truth to his performance, but behind the mask his face was red with boils from ear to ear. Marais was hardly recognizable.

Cocteau in turn contracted a horrific skin disease, worthy of an evil spell in a fairytale. Some mosquito bites, followed by a sunburn caught in the Bassin d'Arcachon, were enough to make an army of boils stand out on his torso and face that would turn into anthrax, then would form little blotches of eczema. He had to hang a black veil with two holes in it over his hat to shield him from the projectors and drafts, and allow him to set up his shots and direct his actors. This excessively empathetic reaction to Marais's suffering seemed to be a self-inflicted punishment for exposing him to such an ordeal. His skin reached a frightening level of ulceration, and became a mask of "blisters, ravines, irritations" that sometimes burned and sometimes froze—a journalist said it looked like two different faces layered over each other.[18] As the heat grew worse, the wounds on his forehead and then his neck began to weep and "shone with serous fluid," which dried into crust at night.[19] Though he secretly identified with the naive young heroine in her unwillingness to leave her dear father to expose herself to the risks of sexuality, the filmmaker recognized himself more and more in the poor beast who can only be loved by giving endless proof of love and sacrifice, as he himself had done before the war to win over the real Marais.

On October 23, 1945, filming had to be interrupted. The director's suffering was so severe that he seemed dead on his feet. "Miserable, destroyed, ravaged, aged a hundred years," having lost twelve kilos and suffering from abscessed teeth, tracheitis, in addition to the boils and the lymphangitis—"emptied of hot blood, barely real, burning with fatigue"—Cocteau was immediately hospitalized at the Hôpital Pasteur. There, mostly confined to bed, a penicillin shot in each canker, his face covered with cold lard, he worked on *La crucifixion*, the short, beautiful poem in twenty-five "stations," without rhyme or alliteration, that represented a return to his Apollinaire phase, and captured the strange, secular saintliness of the filming.[20] He was spoiled: flowers and cigarettes, bottles of champagne, pâté—he was even allowed live chickens, a real luxury, since the wartime restrictions were still in place. The love letter sent him by the staff at Saint-Maurice studios particularly warmed his heart: the camera operators whom he had entertained with imitations of General Clapier as they waited around between shots loved him even more tenderly than some of his friends. "Don't let yourself be kissed by Cocteau," Picasso said to John Richardson, one of the painter's future biographers: "he caught a skin disease by going about with Germans."[21] This was an unforgiving interpretation of Cocteau's belief that he was purging, through his pores, the five years of anguish they had just experienced: he had to share the martyrdom of the extras playing caryatids or torches who stood immobile for hours, their faces covered with talcum powder.

Incapable of staying in one place, on November 3 Cocteau rose like a bedsore-covered zombie and, to the consternation of his doctor, tried to leave. He wanted to return to filming, which would last another two months. The experience would leave him as ill as ever, with eyes burned by spotlights and the boils exacerbated by the hairs of a beard that was impossible to shave. Nevertheless he accomplished these agonizing trials with a strange lightness. The on-set life of a movie team was the closest thing he could imagine to a utopia, in which all the workers and technicians hurried to build a fictional world. From the gaffer to the sound person, from Henri Alekan, the head operator, to Mila Parely, one of the evil sisters, each helped to sculpt in time and space the images he had invented, to shape the human time that weighed so heavily on him in ordinary life. Scenes that were set months apart were filmed at the same time; the time of the fable took precedence over that of reality; the child he could not have with Josette Day became the film she offered him, in playing the role of Belle with "grace and exquisite intelligence."[22]

The film began to contaminate the reality surrounding it. Marais went to lunch at the home of the owner of the Château de Raray, near Senlis, where filming had moved, wearing his Beast mask, and left an impression on her two daughters for life. Uncomfortable in his own skin, his heart raw, Cocteau went to the Halles to find a dead roebuck, whose throat he slit himself and bathed in its blood, before the cameras could capture its "agony." The team was able to anticipate his desires: René Clément absorbed his style so completely that he could have continued to film in his absence; Alekan himself, who would later try to take credit for it, began to understand his demanding concept of light and dark. His old dream of being one among many was realized; while the team waited for the sun to return to film a shot, he would sometimes lie down in the grass, close his eyes, and let himself work on his poem, plunging into inter-weaving dreams, sometimes not emerging until early evening. Some nights he found the energy to keep a filming journal—one of the most poignant and true descriptions of the intimate genesis of a film, the "ribbon of dreams" that Orson Welles would describe—then wait for sleep for hours. "I coughed. I dreamt that the cough was an editing mistake, that if I cut it, pasted it, inserted things around it, I could almost sleep peacefully. I woke up, coughed, and the dream continued, in my half-sleep."[23]

Cocteau guided the film's release (for which Auric composed the music, as usual) with a new humility. In his heyday, he had shown himself to be so arrogant that he piled up confessions of doubt and precautionary apologies. Now, he claimed only the status of a worthy artist, or an elite artisan. Éluard supported him by declaring on the radio that in order to love this film, you had to prefer your dog to your car. Owners of four-wheeled vehicles were in the minority, and *La belle et la bête* was a slow but lasting and profound success. Once again Marais shone, in the role of the Beast who turned at the last minute into a blond arch-angel. Once again the final illumination saved the hero from darkness, which made it the last great feature film of the Occupation.[24] But it was as usual the black set design that highlighted the nightmares he was trying to evoke, as had been the case in the *Roméo et Juliette* he had directed for the theater as well as in *Le sang d'un poète*. The film was received coldly at the first Cannes Film Festival, in September 1946, but praised warmly by filmgoers and awarded the Prix Louis-Delluc. With the success of *L'aigle à deux têtes*, the triumphant revival of *Les parents terribles* at the Gymnase and the good word-of-mouth about *Le jeune homme et la mort*, a ballet for the star dancing couple of the day, Jean Babilée and Nathalie Philippart, 1946 was a year full of suffering, but also of rewards.[25]

By this time Cocteau had gone for hydrotherapy at La Roche-Posay, but beyond the normal boredom of the spa—he felt as if he were being drowned "in shallow water"—the treatment had caused a new kind of pain, a sort of "liquid flagellation," he told Gide, so terrible that Roger Lannes had expected to find he had developed stigmata. This time his doctors ordered him not to do *anything* for a while. This forced period of rest stunned him. It was impossible for him to stop talking, to breathe, to stop inventing. Cocteau went to visit Colette who saw beneath his haggard appearance his impatience to shake things up, even to suffer, or at least to be seen, to feel alive. Seeing his neigh-bor's good spirits, Cocteau wondered how she kept in such good health, and by what fluke nature had bestowed all manner of anguish upon him and spared others sickness, fear, and insomnia. Must he suffer so these lucky few could flourish? If he was like the weasel who, unhappy with his lot, dresses up as all the other animals, Colette (to continue with La Fontaine's fables) was like the cat who licked her lips at the sight of milk being poured. She was a force of nature that, apparently, didn't take the trouble to do much except live.

When the opium appeared again, no doubt via Bérard, his relief was immediate. His pain evaporated; his body began to lead a life of its own. Reality lost all of its edge.

THE GOOD, THE BAD, AND THE UGLY

It wasn't long before Cocteau began to envy the influence that Sartre had over the young, through his ideas about existentialism. It was as if he had signed an exclusivity contract with anyone under thirty years old. The scandalous popularity that Genet gained by publishing his *Le spectre de la rose* in 1946 was more painful to him still, for he had truly wished for it. The sexual essence of creation had never appeared to him so clearly. The ex-convict's novels had a way of breaking and entering into his readers—his own swathed them in words and images until they were dizzy, in a convulsive dance of the seven veils. Genet's genius was tense as a fist; his own, diffuse as gas. Where was his place, among the giant Proust, the omnipresent Gide, and this rising star? Sartre was cleaning up everywhere, with a consistency he had never known. What could he lay claim to: an easy, fantastical brilliance? From then on, there was Boris Vian for that.[26]

Sartre and Simone de Beauvoir had at first been wary of Cocteau's unrelenting enthusiasm for *Notre-Dame-des-fleurs*. The discovery of that unusual novel, the audacity of its author's judgments, the reach of his erudition and the originality of his views—totally unlike what was expected of an autodidact— had convinced them. Genet perhaps described slightly too emphatically, when they gathered at the Café de Flore, his role as Poet, sitting across from Sartre the Philosopher, but he was so powerfully imposing that the couple were soon infatuated with him. Thus did the glory of Genet spread, while that of Cocteau waned, like the law of Saturn in retrograde, which, according to Max Nordau, sees the begetter plunged into darkness while the begat appears in the full light of day. Genet was already praised by new reviews like *Les temps modernes*, and, most flattering of all, sought after by Parisians like Colette, Picasso, and Éluard. Betrayal, crime, and inhumanity personified, if he was to be believed, the self-created son of a braggart and a prostitute was now the idol of the society that had banished him for so long. Patrons, ministers, and important detectives vied to receive Genet in their homes, in spite—or because—of the risks they ran in welcoming him. "The bourgeoisie, they're never happy unless I steal something from them," Genet groused, with the sarcastic humor that made him say, pointing to a still-empty alcove in Jean Babilée and Nathalie Philippart's new apartment, "There's the place where Jean and Nathalie will keep the precious objects that Jean Genet will steal from them!"[27]

Cocteau, on the contrary, was less and less frequently honored with a visit, and began, to tell the truth, to dread them. Not for the thieving, which he had always patiently tolerated, but because Genet, returned to glory, had taken it very badly when he dared to critique *Pour la belle*, which then became *Haute surveillance*, a play that the "old" ex-con had written for Marais. With no patience for anything but praise, Genet had immediately torn up the page in question, and then the entire manuscript. "You should keep a second copy," Cocteau said, accustomed to these tricks. This was indeed the case, and Cocteau managed to convince himself that many of Genet's scenes were feigned, or at least forced, like the behavior of a character who had invented himself from scratch.[28] Ever since, Genet had taken every available opportunity to show Cocteau the extent to which their ideas about literature differed. An author, in his eyes, should not be satisfied to see his characters live, or worse, complain about them, as Cocteau did. He had to take responsibility for their sins, and somehow spread around their virtues and their vices in *real* life—even if it meant paying for it in a Christ-like fashion. Thus did the former prisoner who looked like a "prosperous auto-repairman"—he made enough money to have his shirts monogrammed—catechize the host on the rue de Montpensier, guilty of being bound by his desire to do the right thing; Genet, by contrast, was convinced that he went right to the heart of things by showing the evil within.[29]

The problems had begun as early as 1943, when Cocteau had met a chubby, ringleted sixteen-year-old poet who had never set foot in school but whose conversation already rivaled his own. Having walked the forty-two kilometers between his grandfather's country house and the Palais-Royal, Olivier Larronde came to read his first writings with a cheekiness that was promising, but also with enough emotion that he provoked a tear from Genet. "You are not strong enough for poetry, seek out another calling, son," Cocteau declared, to the indignation of Genet, who took the precocious poet under his wing, then became infatuated with his doll-like physique. Cocteau, remorseful, published one of Larronde's poems in the prestigious review *Fontaine*, then financed, via Paul Morihien, a luxurious edition of his *Barricades mystérieuses*, a beautiful collection illustrated by André Beaurepaire, another of his close friends, in whose paintings he would salute "the most naive use of the marvelous."[30]

Although Larronde dedicated one of his most beautiful poems, "Soigner les roses," to Cocteau, Genet continued to reproach Cocteau for his injustice. His real mistake had doubtless been to influence him a bit too much, at one time. Was this a way of minimizing the taste of the man who had "discovered" him? Genet went around telling everyone that he didn't care what Cocteau thought of his work, because nothing counted more than the sublime Larronde's opinion—he was the "only true poet." Moreover, Cocteau was assailed by vague reproaches, and purposefully needled, in a way that reminded him of Proust's harassing, quibbling manner. Genet was even heard to say, in a moment of sacrilegious exaggeration, that one night, strolling in the gardens of the Arènes de Lutèce, he had sodomized the author of the Livre blanc—a doubly improbable act, but be that as it may; he was offending the man who had committed the mistake of preventing him from being sent to a work camp for life, when the Germans were in charge. While Cocteau tended to a sort of "pointless saintliness," Genet refined his stature as the cardinal of crime. "Let him steal, let him rage, let him leave us. He's right even when he's wrong," Cocteau noted in his journal. "He has acquired all rights to murder, ingratitude, idiocy." It was true: genius could allow itself anything, as the sole justification of a species that had shown, during the war, exactly how much cruelty it was capable of inflicting.[31]

Marais was less tolerant. Having made the mistake of refusing to act in all the plays that the ex-convict wrote for him, he had the honor of hearing, as he walked onstage for a poetry matinee at the Théâtre Hébertot, "In the name of Rimbaud, throw him down the toilet!" It was Genet's voice. The man whom Sentein had called a "peasant out of Verlaine" had turned infernal.[32] If someone let loose a stray remark suggesting that Genet was not the most precious being on the planet, he would be spoiling for a fight—"he threw away friends like Kleenex," said Edmonde Charles-Roux, editor of Vogue at the time.[33] Having been born alone, having grown up on the margins of society, then having been tossed into prison the minute he came of age, Genet hated anyone who tried to include him—and no one was more of an includer than Cocteau. "Dehumanizing myself is my most profound tendency," Genet wrote in Notre-Dame-des-fleurs.

In the winter of 1946, the police once again knocked at Cocteau's door. This time they were after a young man apprehended for stealing silver flatware from the Grand Hôtel du Louvre nearby—a man who had given them his address. Cocteau had no doubt that Lucien Sénémaud, who was later sentenced to eighteen months in prison for the crime, had been spurred to do it by Genet, whom Marais had introduced him to a few months earlier, and whose lover he had become.[34]

As fate would have it, Cocteau would be next to get into trouble with the law, in early 1947: photographed by the press among a group of drug addicts called before the judge, he once again escaped being found guilty—but it was not through the efforts of the glorious Genet that he managed to avoid imprisonment.[35] (Though the author of *Le journal du voleur* would not have been the best-placed to intervene, even if he had tried.)

Sometimes Genet would come back, remorseful. "I am odious, please forgive me," he would say to Cocteau, who of course defended him against himself. But this friendship was too much of a reminder of how he started out, and Genet preferred more and more to meet up at the Flore with Sartre, with whom he could talk endlessly about himself, describing yet again the completely fabricated harshness of his adoptive parents, the very real horror of the Mettray penal colony, and the liturgical choice he had made to put himself at the service of evil. Fascinated by his past as a glorious traitor, Sartre soon became Genet's new literary mentor. Then at the height of his intellectual fame, the philosopher signed the text that was used to launch *Le spectre de la rose*, and in January 1947 dedicated his very fine "Baudelaire" essay to him.

The great organizer of the dream in which he was at once the poet, the choreographer, the director, and the art director, Cocteau nevertheless remained one of Genet's secret role models. The thief's writings for the stage indicated a similar belief in a Greco-Racinian theater, whose heroes would be both the agents and the victims of their destiny. Genet showed the script for *Les bonnes* to Cocteau, and accepted his suggestions that the play be condensed into one act and end in self-destruction. But he did so only because he was eager to surpass his theatrical prowess by capitalizing on his know-how. After willingly lending himself to this operation, Cocteau zealously promoted it to Jouvet, suggesting that Bérard do the set design. Their shared experience gave Genet the courage to face up to Jouvet, who was a formidable director, though this was the first of his plays ever to be performed.[36] It also made, as Cocteau would write, "the singular bedroom where Madame and her maids move about so superbly, and with such debauchery" so unforgettable in April 1947.[37]

The two men continued to share certain themes and myths, from the sailors whom Cocteau would draw for the illustrations in *Querelle de Brest*, published by Paul Morihien in 1947, to "Funambule," a poem that Genet would write in 1955 which had much in common with Cocteau's "Numéro Barbette" of 1923.[38] At the center of a ballet Genet wrote in 1948, *'Adame miroir*, with music by Darius Milhaud, was a ship's boy kissing his reflection in a bedroom mirror, a scene that inarguably recalled those parts of *Le livre blanc* when the narrator, while in a public bath, sees a young worker passionately kissing his image through a one-way mirror, before pressing himself to the mirror, and, knowing he cannot be seen, enjoying the lips that offer themselves to him.[39] Beyond this obsession with mirrors, they both shared an impatience for death that verged on desire.

When Genet was threatened with being sent back to prison for an old condemnation that had been reprieved, Cocteau quite willingly agreed with Sartre that they should band together to protect Genet from his own excess. The petition they drew up and circulated in 1948, and eventually submitted to the President of the Republic (only Aragon, Éluard, and Camus refused to sign, for ideological or moral reasons) won him a permanent pardon. Genet now understood how lucky he had been to meet Cocteau; he even acknowledged that he would have had much more difficulty becoming famous had he been a Rothschild. And when someone asked him what the most important human quality was, in his opinion, the ex-convict would reply: "kindness." He felt fulfilled, seeing Cocteau and Sartre come to visit the house in the Midi that he was building for Lucien Sénémaud and his little family.

In 1950, Genet was filming the last shots for *Un chant d'amour* in the forest near Cocteau's house in Milly. The black-and-white medium-length film had sprung fully formed from his autoerotic imagination—the materialization of fantasies born of a single dilated moment. Cocteau's cinematographic influence is perceptible in this film: the hero of *Le sang d'un poète* seems to have come to open one last door, in the hallway of the Hôtel des Folies-Dramatiques, to discover a row of cells where convicts breathe out the smoke of their cigarettes through the walls, through a simple straw, and dance while pleasuring themselves. Genet made no secret of his desire to surpass Cocteau as a filmmaker; though we may doubt whether he managed to do so his first time around, he did manage to create a level of dreamlike perfection unequaled except perhaps by that conjured by Rainer Werner Fassbinder, when he in turn adapted *Querelle de Brest*. Far from being offended, Cocteau filled up the auditorium when Genet screened his film, which was quickly banned from release.

The magnificent article that Genet contributed to a special issue on Cocteau for the Belgian review *Empreintes* in 1950 was the peak of their strange relationship.[40] He paid vibrant homage to Cocteau, whom he described as "thin, knobbly, and silvered like an olive tree," as well as to his work, which he compared to a "light, airy, stormy civilization, suspended in the heavy heart of our own." He sanctified the dry elegance and abrupt brevity of the poet, filmmaker, and playwright by hailing him as "Greek!," praising Cocteau's intimacy with the somber, wild, and almost delirious aspects of Antiquity. "Having freed himself from a material which he sends shattering into a spray of shards,"

Cocteau appeared as a classic—someone "brief, hard, shining, comically unfinished," like an elegantly disordered temple whose every "bole and pedestal" had been rigorously reworked, then, "it would seem, broken and abandoned." This was the swan song of what had been much more than a simple friendship. After this moment Genet, the man for whom the Germans under Hitler had managed to be at once the police and the crime, pulled away for good from Cocteau, a writer who hated to reprimand or cause pain.

Genet would soon disavow his Cocteau period, as Cocteau did that of Noailles. Relegating this universe of gauze and mirrors, of incestuous chastity and feverish purity, to his developing years, he made Cocteau a witness to a sinking world—that of literature before Genet. The errant child of public services, who would deferentially call a reader who didn't share his tastes or values "vous" (not "tu"), hoping to earn their loathing through sheer force of arrogance, no longer wanted to be looked after by the once-cosseted offspring of the Parisian bourgeoisie, who tended to include his reader in an authorial "we," in the always-thwarted desire to make himself loved.[41]

STALIN'S MUSTACHE

Sartre respected the thief's literary opinions so much that he sent Cocteau the text of his play *Les mains sales*, as Genet had done with *Les bonnes*. Although the move surprised Cocteau, Sartre trusted his talent for the theater, and followed all of his advice. Cocteau, flattered, was even asked to direct the play, when Sartre, overwhelmed by events, was obliged to get rid of all of his actors at the last minute in February 1948. Cocteau was given carte blanche to recast the play and to rethink the set design. As usual, he went at it with excess. He hired Bérard to do the costumes, and took charge of rehearsals. While Sartre admired his inventiveness, Simone de Beauvoir was astonished by his generosity: "Never has a fellow playwright so looked after a colleague's success, or tried to help him so earnestly!" she said. There was so much humanity and humor in the stories that Cocteau told, at dinner in the evenings, about the old whores of the Palais-Royal, that she and Sartre were soon charmed. "I will never forget the purity you have given to my *Mains sales*," he wrote in the corner of a tablecloth.[42] "His lack of pettiness is so rare!" Beauvoir added, used to navel-gazing authors. If, for the Sartre of *Huis clos*, "Hell is other people," for Cocteau, it was Paradise.[43]

Flattered to learn that the couple had enjoyed seeing Marianne Oswald sing *Anna la bonne*, and then Yvonne de Bray in his *Monstres sacrés*, proud as well to hear that they were "delighted" when Marais knocked out Laubreaux, Cocteau believed they had become not just colleagues but friends.[44] He had

invested himself so ardently in *Les mains sales* that he made the mistake, after
the dress rehearsal when everyone was celebrating an unhoped-for triumph, of
congratulating himself a bit too loudly for the part he had played. The self-
indulgence of his "How marvelously I have helped you!" shocked Simone de
Beauvoir, almost as much as the empty-headedness of those who surrounded
him, including Marais and his lover of the time: "cretinous, hungry young lads
who let themselves be adored by old men for money."[45] Cocteau had made the
mistake of letting it be known that he had saved Sartre's play from going under.[46]

After being mistreated by Genet, prey to what he would soon describe as the
"tyranny of the Flore," Cocteau thought he had finally found a new family with
Aragon and Éluard. The Communist Party, in a hurry to transform the artists it
had saved during the purge into fellow travelers, was lavishing him with attention. In Picasso's wake, the Central Committee had placed him on the side of
the *true* France, and he did not hesitate to sign a petition in 1949 supporting
Aragon, who had just been stripped of his voter's card, since Aragon's newspaper, *Ce soir*, had been accused of spreading false information. He was even
seen standing beside Maurice Thorez, "the strongest supporter of Stalin in
France," during Picasso's openings. The French Zelig, without even knowing
it, had become a Communist sympathizer.

The war had been a lesson to him, however. In 1953 Aragon could not get
him to sign a petition claiming innocence for Julius and Ethel Rosenberg,
accused of spying on the United States for the USSR; nevertheless Aragon knew
how to force his hand, by announcing after their execution that Cocteau had
taken the initiative to circulate a petition for the case to be reexamined.
Although Aragon, supported by Fernand Léger, evoked his membership in the
most favorable terms, Cocteau continued his passive resistance and refused
even to vote, as he had always done. "De tous les partis mon parti / Est le seul
que je veuille prendre" (Of all the parties, my party / is the only one I will
support) he replied in *Clair-obscur*. Sartre himself, having himself grown closer
to the Communists, could not drag him to the conference on the Mouvement
de la Paix, which was controlled by Moscow, only managing to get him to
contribute a letter of support. And though he did convince him to give a talk at
a meeting in support of the liberation of a Communist sailor who had protested
the war in Indochina, he could not get him to publish his speech in the book
Sartre published afterward, *L'affaire Henri Martin*.[47] Bernard Grasset was even
refused point blank, when he asked Cocteau in 1952 to visit the Kremlin for
fifteen days and write an "Intimate Portrait of Stalin."[48] Nevertheless, Cocteau
would describe the dictator as the "only great politician of the era," and alongside Roland Barthes was one of the rare critics, in 1955, to praise Sartre's

Nekrassov, an overtly pro-Soviet play.[49] In 1960, after having nationalized the French properties in Cuba, Fidel Castro said: "France is nothing in my opinion but Picasso, Cocteau, Aragon, Braque, and Sartre."[50] But Cocteau was altogether too politically indifferent, and, henceforth, prudent, to take up arms within a party that in spite of its real power could not help him regain his lost youth. In any case, as Éluard put it, "the Party doesn't like homosexuals because between a man and the Party, the homosexual will always choose the man."[51]

MILLY, OR THE DIFFICULTY OF BEING

Dealing with issues of narcotics and social conduct, the Brigade Mondaine, in January 1947, raided the rue de Montpensier. Cocteau convinced them that he hadn't smoked for eight years. The prefect even issued a letter of apology, which allowed the opium den to get back down to business. But the drug had lost its anesthetic power. Wounded by Paris, disappointed by France, Cocteau, after forty years at the heart of the literary world, felt that it was time to get away for a while.

Along with Marais and Morihien, he went off in search of a peaceful spot, far from the Palais-Royal, where they lived under a constant onslaught of telephone calls and visitors, their home visible to strollers in the gardens, behind the half-moon windows of their shoebox. They decided to buy the former residence of the bailiff of Milly-la-Forêt, a true village house with a vast garden full of flowers. Cocteau would spend weekends there that soon stretched into entire weeks, and it helped him feel less scattered. He felt encouraged to take stock of himself and to write a book about the strangeness of his existence. Full of princes and fairies, sphinxes and crowns, the work he had published during the war perhaps suffered from being crammed with images. He left the heads of Anubis and the magic swords behind to give himself over to the crudest sincerity. "It is by hewing close to oneself that we may reach many others," said Goethe. Through his *Difficulté d'être*, Cocteau would not win a large audience, but he would leave behind an exceptionally lucid testament.

Cocteau had often evaded, with the sweep of a barrister's sleeve, entire swathes of truth; as he grew older, he decided to serve as his own counsel in the trial he had endured for half a century. He had put off this moment for so long that he confessed more weaknesses than most would admit, and explained how deeply disgusted he was by his permanent state of anguish. Aware of being misunderstood, and of the loathing he inspired, he admitted as well that he suffered from his almost absurd view of life, and came quite close to blaming his physique—his worst enemy.

My hair has always grown every which way, and my teeth, and my beard hair. Even my nerves and my whole soul must be like that. This is what has made me insoluble to those who only go one way and cannot understand a tuft that sticks out. This is what perplexes those who should rid me of this mythological scourge.[52]

It is difficult to put such profound unease more soberly, or to describe with more lightness this "poorly secured cargo" that had afflicted him since birth. One of the more revealing chapters was entitled "On My Escapes." His body was a prison, and consistency a condemnation; Cocteau avowed his repeated attempts to escape "out the hatch." At the same time, incapable of following one idea for too long, he owns up to his dreams of transcendence, no longer as a demi-god, but as a wounded man, eager to leave this world but aware that there is no place for him in heaven. He had adopted so many aesthetics, adhered to so many beliefs! Once the euphoria had passed, they all revealed their constraints. "I sought myself, I thought I had found myself, I lost sight of myself, I ran after myself, I found myself out of breath. Hardly was I under one charm than I hastened to contradict it."[53]

He was so cruel to himself that he did not know how to be unkind to others, and he began almost to say too much. Though he confessed his faults with his customary elegance, and a nearly Montaigne-like humor, he ran the risk of feeding further attacks on him, or seeming insincere. "You can see that he is weak, cowardly, that he can only imitate, that he readily lies—he's the first to admit it!" Cocteau fully accepted these risks and continued to explore his unconscious with the courage of a war correspondent. Five years later, the magnificent confession of human fragility that was *La difficulté d'être* was followed by the equally touching *Journal d'un inconnu* (1952), which is doubtless one of the most beautiful examples of self-analysis, along with the journals of Julien Green or Marcel Jouhandeau—as if the admission of his failure was the last success he could crave.[54] As late as 1961, he persuaded himself to write another memoir, and in *Le cordon ombilical* he executed one of his acrobatic monologues in which by telling his own story he pauses to describe one of Stravinsky's works, or Picasso's lines. Then his invisible boat was pushed to the shore he walked along as a child, from which a balloon rose to the vaults of the Théâtre des Champs-Elysées, in the time of the Ballets Russes, before the wind brought it back to the strange rower he was. Every book opened up new paths, as if the virulence of his contradictions made all summaries impossible. Or possibly, as if he lived with the secret hope that one of his readers would finally write to him, and reveal to him the key to his personality.

These autobiographical essays are among Cocteau's finest work. His style coils and condenses until it attains the mysterious clarity of the oracle, although he is apparently only relating anecdotal memories. "It's in minor literature that we spent most of our genius," he confessed to Aragon.[55] In conversation he could talk about anything, weaving from place to place and epoch to epoch without ever losing his thread. In his confessional books, he achieved a high level of formal freedom, in which he was able to make his confusions seem dazzling, and stylistically overcome the abysses where he clashed: his hand was in the sky while his body was at the bottom of a well.

In July 1947, Cocteau met a young man from Lorraine at Morihien's book-shop. The twenty-two-year-old was a pit miner in Bouligny who painted in his spare time. Handsome, healthy, and well-built, Édouard Dermit met the world with a disarming smile, full of kindness and availability. Cocteau suspected he was a character in search of an author, so he hired him as gardener at his new home in Milly. "Here is your house," he told him immediately. The son of a Slovenian peasant stopped filling wagons with iron ore many feet below the earth, as he had done since the age of fourteen, and began to water azaleas and hydrangeas. The fairytale had begun.

Dermit lived at the house and did all he could to make himself useful: answering Cocteau's phone, driving Marais's car, making appointments for Morihien. He became the manager of the place, and warmed up the solitude of the prince who with one flick of the wand had altered his destiny. Cocteau loved to draw attractive bodies, and with Édouard Dermit he was not disappointed: he was marvelously made. A ghost could not have found a more beautiful "armor of flesh" to inhabit.[56] Yet he believed it ridiculous, at his age, to think that such a boy could desire him, and although he obviously was drawn to Dermit, he would not permit himself to sleep with him. He was almost proud of this abstention. "I think that beyond a certain age, such acts are depraved, they no longer allow for an exchange and become laughable, whether with one sex or the other," he wrote in *La difficulté d'être*.[57] All of Paris might be talking of how "disgusting" it was to see him go about with such a beautiful young man without enjoying him, but he dismissed the rumors of his debauchery. It was enough for him just to watch Doudou (as he now called him) swim, paint, play ping-pong, ride his motorcycle through the woods around Milly, and lead that sensual, animalistic life that he had always refused himself. The young man's ignorance would have bothered him in the Radiguet days, but now seemed a sort of miracle. When Doudou fell asleep over a detective novel in the flowerbed he had just trimmed, it was as though he had discovered the recipe for happiness.

The young Yugoslavian learned how to obtain opium, then to prepare it. Regularly holding the sticky black liquid over the flame until it hardened into a little marble to be inserted into the pipe, he became an inveterate smoker. Already partial to lying still without speaking, the fairytale hero often seemed to be sleeping in the middle of the day. His passive nature avidly absorbed the smoke, which stoked his laziness; his spirit took refuge in the nothingness where he flourished like a well-watered plant. His dozing body offered itself to Cocteau's pencils. To keep from waking the young gardener, so desirable in his charmed abandon, visitors to the house spoke in a whisper until three or four in the afternoon.

A thousand invisible strands linked Doudou to his prince, strands woven from affection, money, and opium. The young man was so calm, and he so intensely admired his "inventor," that he acted like a balm on Cocteau's anguished soul. Doubtless at one time Cocteau would have experienced the feminine desire to blend himself with Doudou's luminous beauty, in the hope of creating a superior, divine being. But now, his soothing existence was enough to calm him.

> Tes mains, jonchant les draps étaient mes feuilles mortes
> Mon automne aimait ton été.
> Le vent du souvenir faisait claquer les portes
> Des lieux où nous avons été.
> [Your hands, scattered across the sheets, were my dead leaves
> My autumn loved your summer.
> The wind of memory slammed the doors
> of the places we have been.][58]

The young man had as much freedom as he liked to come and go, but oddly he didn't take much advantage of it. He stayed at Milly morning and night, near Cocteau, stunned by the dream life he had been given. "How could I not love him, I owe him everything," he said sometimes, as if he couldn't believe what had happened to him. From Radiguet to Desbordes, and from Khill to Marais, all of Cocteau's companions had quickly learned to betray him. The poet, this time, felt he was truly loved; the young exile's heart belonged to him, as his belonged to Doudou. He didn't even need to hear the words to reassure himself: he could see into the young man as easily as he saw through walls in his dreams. "I enter him like water into a sponge," said Armide of Renaud, in the eponymous tragedy.[59] The writer's desires were forever sublimated. Tirelessly drawing the object of his affection, he learned to content himself with the solitary eroticism that the sleep of those he desired had always inspired in him. The monk in the duffle coat had, after all, always said he was better at friendship than love. Having become used to painting, Doudou took up Marais's easel to outline landscapes or sketch a portrait of his god.

> Grand ouvert est le temple
> Où j'ai su t'enfermer
> Mon amour est l'exemple
> De comme il faut aimer.
> [Wide open is the temple
> in which I hold you
> My love is the example
> of how one should love.][60]

Paul Morihien was the first to move a bit farther, to the rue de Beaujolais, in the Palais-Royal, but on the same floor, above the bookshop/gallery where he showed canvases by Picasso, Jean Hugo, and Marie Laure de Noailles. Jean Marais, reassured to know that Cocteau had someone, but wounded that he was no longer incomparable and unique, used a need for light as an excuse to go and live in a houseboat on a stagnant branch of the Seine, near Neuilly. Cocteau now lived alone with the delicate young Dermit, and would hate himself for the rest of his life for making him cry the day after he moved to Milly, by harshly criticizing him for breaking the architect's table that he had worked at for many years.

Édouard Dermit was goodness itself, but he could not make Cocteau forget his literary isolation. Cocteau's bid to take over in Saint-Germain-des-Prés had brought back old memories from the early days of Surrealism, and sometimes he worried that history was repeating itself. He had more influence than he realized: "It was not explicit, but it had repercussions, like an echo even the hard of hearing couldn't escape, sometimes intoxicating, sometimes irritating," said Bernard Minoret, a young writer who would soon meet him.[61] From time to time Cocteau received letters from young men in the provinces, imploring him to help them, adding: "I would be loyal to you, I would live your work, you would be everything." Instead of Radiguets, however, he found talentless schoolboys, novice actors, or gold-diggers, including one who had won first prize at a transvestite's ball and to make him jealous threatened to go off with another man "to hunt lions and giraffes somewhere in Africa."[62] When *the* daily newspaper of the time, *Combat*, asked its readers in 1948 who were the best living French writers, Cocteau came in seventeenth place, far behind Jules Romains or Martin du Gard, half-forgotten nowadays. Camus, Sartre, and Malraux were at the top of the list, after the unsinkable Gide, born in 1869.[63]

THE GREAT RETURN OF ORPHEUS

At the same time, Cocteau could not blame the young; this would have forced him to accept that he had aged, a sacrifice he was still incapable of making. He preferred to try to win them back through filmmaking, in which he veiled and unveiled himself, always and again, in the guise of a modern-day Orpheus. Prey to the hostility of a group of literary types whose leader resorted to too-easy formulas, like Breton, but also the young *germanopratins* and the angry girls—the maenads—who already sounded like feminists, the misunderstood poet would privately find himself caught between a prosaic Eurydice and his own death, incarnated by a foreign princess whose Rolls Royce sent cryptic messages like those of Radio London during the war, and fed his poetry.

Cocteau had great difficulty securing financing. He applied to an official aid-granting commission, but they demanded certain modifications that he refused to make. No one understood what the Rolls was meant to symbolize. He did not deign to allude to the poem he had dedicated to Isadora Duncan, after the accidental death of her two children: "and the gods, today, no longer send eagles / Their hands turned the wheel of an automobile."[64] What good was it to speak of Jupiter to the contemporaries of Fangio, the champion Formula One driver of the time? He opted to borrow from the banks and hire actors in a profit-sharing scheme—they would not be paid unless the film made money.

Cocteau had always seen the theater as a healthy constraint and his plays as intended to show off his actors' gifts more than his own. The cinema, by contrast, was his own creature, a way of writing a poem not only with words but also with eyes and hands. In the end, it was the art that most closely fit Da Vinci's idea of it as a "cosa mentale." The camera had to pull the viewer out of his seat and project him into the twists and turns of the imagination, changing him not into a desiring body or a beating heart, but into a ubiquitous eye, that of the voyeur he himself essentially remained. The actors here were no more than puppets in the hands of Cocteau the demiurge. Their diction, their emoting, their movements were under his control, and their very existence, too, through the editing process: the film was not designed to make them stars, but to reveal to the public the strange poetic workings of a filmmaker's personality.

Cocteau used only special effects, instead of lab effects, as he had in *Le sang d'un poète*, and brought back the mirror as the antechamber that leads Heurtebise (François Périer) to the zone separating the living from the dead—a magnificent scene that conveyed the journey he had so often made after Radiguet's death. He asked his actors, from Maria Casarès (as the Princess) to Marie Déa (Eurydice), to speak in a tone that was neither tragic nor comic, and this helped Marais to act unnaturally. The very subject prevented a realistic adaptation; he encouraged the actors instead to sculpt their lines in order to achieve a kind of "dry supernaturalism" that would make the already strange myth stranger still.[65] Juliette Gréco played the role of Aglaonice, the head of the maenads, and Édouard Dermit played Cégeste, the fashionable young poet who drank too much and became violent, and whose arrival precipitates the decline of Orphée (played by Jean Marais).

It was a work intended to ward off the dreary life he might have led if he had made the choice to marry. The film *Orphée* betrays a childish misogyny, one that, contrary to all appearances, is more defensive than aggressive. Eurydice is reduced to an unquestioning mother who, after giving birth, withdraws into the domestic sphere, only to emerge with an excess of ordinariness. For a long time Cocteau had privately considered that his affairs with women had systematically nipped his sons in the bud, so to speak. If he had to go looking for someone in Hell, it was less likely to have been Madeleine Carlier or Natalie Paley than one of the "angels" they had given, then taken away. Isn't Limbo, in the Orphic tradition, meant to be the domain of stillborn children? The court that Orphée confronts, in the heart of that zone, also bore a resemblance to the very intimate one that for thirty-five years had defended his adversaries with rare cruelty. "In general, I was very insulted," Cocteau would say to William Fifield. "Well! I should say that I was rather . . . I leaned rather in favor of those who judged me and contradicted me."[66] This terrible acquiescence inspired one of the most curious scenes of the film, in which Claude Mauriac plays a witness for the prosecution.[67]

Filming was once again very painful for Cocteau, who by the end was nearly paralyzed with sciatica. Doudou, who was made more insecure by serving as both secretary and chauffeur to Cocteau, became intimidated by Marais's poise, so Cocteau encouraged him, in the kind of gentle voice used to speak to children in the dark. This did little to relieve the young man's anxiety. Cocteau then hired Claude Pinoteau, "his shadow" who had already worked on the set of *Parents terribles*, to assist him. But the technicians still looked askance at this director who made his actors walk backward in order to create the impression, after editing, that they were walking into a mirror that breaks.[68]

The film was a failure. Apart from a loyal few, several of whom would become the filmmakers of the French New Wave, including Jean-Luc Godard, the disoriented audience laughed in the wrong places, and occasionally hissed. "*Orphée* has the effect on the audience of a hypodermic needle," said a film critic. The dialogue sounded strange to the ears of the younger generation, who had been brought up, cinematically, on Italian neorealism and were little disposed to believe that the Thracian bard had returned to earth in the middle of Saint-Germain-des-Prés. "The French language banishes fantasy," Morand would say on another occasion.[69]

Cocteau was deeply disappointed. He was wounded by the criticism, without seeing how it could be confusing to take in his hybrid object—half boulevard theatre, half experimental film, as if he had blended *Les parents terribles* and *Le sang d'un poète*. Interviewed as if he were truly a star, Doudou showed so much modesty and sadness that the journalists tiptoed away, restoring his anonymity. Cocteau's celebrity prevented the film from going away quietly, and it won him the international prize at the Venice Film Festival in 1950—but he suffered from seeing himself so misunderstood in general. He had thought he was bringing back his own character, one much like Orpheus charming the birds, but he woke up as a scarecrow frightening them away.

Cocteau began to question how many years he had left. His nature, it seemed to him, was made for a brief, stinging destiny. Dead at thirty, like *Thomas l'imposteur*, he could have remained a genius; struck down in his prime, he could have become a myth like those he had helped to build, from Radiguet to Marais to Genet. At fifty-five, however, death would have dragged out the brief triumph he had known during the war; it seemed like his longevity began to turn against him. The more years went by, the less respect he received. The more he offered the public—plays, poems, drawings of films—the less he was awarded prizes. Proust, Gide, and Sachs had fed their work from his character, but it was always his ghostlike appearance that they caricatured—the flight of his hand gestures, or the strange powder puff that floated around his cranium like a sparrow's nest—never his personal life. His long-lost friend Blaise Cendrars from the Apollinaire days had even turned his hairdo into the star of a passage from *Bourlinguer*, in which his "cabalistic hairpiece" becomes the embodiment of a spell that Picasso cast on him when he did his portrait, before Cocteau, unable to get rid of it, made the mistake of bleaching it.[70]

Very early on Cocteau had made a slightly ridiculous impression, and nothing he had done since 1908 could erase it. His death, doubtless, would solve everything; until then, to console himself, Cocteau reread Nietzsche and mused over the phrase that so pleased Picasso: "the best hiding place is a precocious glory." He didn't need much more to convince himself that he was the greatest unknown of his time.

LES ENFANTS [NOT SO] TERRIBLES

The young people whom Cocteau could no longer reach, who seemed weary of him, quite unexpectedly rediscovered his *Enfants terribles* sometime around 1950. Like the generation just after the First World War, or the one that would gobble down Salinger's *The Catcher in the Rye*, they recognized themselves in the incestuous pair playing at love and death, or drugs, which was as foreign to the grownups as Martians. Cocteau may have seen the youth as copies, but in his novel they recognized their way of being, half-flamboyant, half-destructive, and totally against the morality and utilitarianism preached by Europe as it rebuilt itself. Although *Les enfants terribles* remained his favorite of his novels, he knew that his readers would only be disappointed by seeing its semi-mythological heroes brought to life on the screen. Did Jean-Pierre Melville force Cocteau's hand by offering him a sort of co-directing role, or was Cocteau the one who was struck by the young filmmaker, who had just won great acclaim for *Le silence de la mer?* Melville, himself a former student of the Lycée Condorcet, had long admired Cocteau as a filmmaker, and the three months they spent adapting the novel were idyllic.

Les enfants terribles was filmed on a shoestring in November 1950, at several locations: in the Théâtre Pigalle, in a space abandoned by the *Petit Journal*, in a restaurant on the Champs-Elysées, and in Jean-Pierre Melville's private studios in the 13th arrondissement. Before the war, Cocteau dreamed of casting Greta Garbo as Élisabeth, but the role would go to Nicole Stéphane, who was so unforgettable in *Le silence de la mer*, and whom Melville loved in vain. Melville also cast an unknown actress in the dual role of Dargelos the student, and Agathe, Paul's fiancée. Cocteau designed the set, and pushed Doudou into the limelight, in spite of the reluctance of both Melville and the terrified young man, who had to learn every line by heart.[71] Cocteau was there for every take and involved himself in every scene, armed with a technique he had finally picked up under the Occupation; he had the misfortune, the first day, in the middle of a tense shot, of crying "Cut!" to Melville's indignation. Melville forgave him—on the condition that he keep quiet—when Cocteau added, "I'm sorry, I was saying the same thing yesterday" (on the set of *Orphée*).

Cocteau resigned himself to letting his wishes be known concerning the set, the costumes, and the acting through letters or telephone calls to Claude Pinoteau, the assistant whom he had forced on Melville. Yet true conflict broke out on the fifth day of filming. Furious at being echoed endlessly, Melville, who was a proud man, rained down thunder. Cocteau slipped out and spent the night waiting for Doudou in a little café on the rue d'Enghien, where Melville was picking him up the next day. He didn't return for fifteen days, this time in small doses and most often at dinnertime—his advice and stories adding to the bohemian charm of a set where Doudou slept on set, the better to absorb the atmosphere of his room. Melville and Cocteau learned to tolerate each other, and a certain complicity was established. Distracted by a love affair, the director was called away more and more often, and Cocteau replaced him behind the camera. Genet saw him filming, which provoked Melville's immediate return.[72] Viewing the rushes brought back all the problems. Melville called Doudou "a catastrophe," to which Cocteau replied indignantly, "I have never seen an actor play so well since Mounet-Sully."[73] He haunted the editing room, this time convinced of Melville's ineptitude—half-eager, half-delighted that he had to do "everything" for him. "Which one do you prefer?" Melville asked Nicole Stéphane, showing her two versions of a close-up in which she shouts "Paul!" when she learns that Agathe loves her brother. "This one," she said first, indicating the one Cocteau had suggested, though not set up. Melville insulted her so badly that she slapped him, and he punched her back.[74]

The prosaic quality of life under the Fourth Republic infused the realist scenes, and damaged the mythic impression left by the book. The film was "defenestrated" by the critics, as Cocteau put it. The notices for Doudou were especially cruel, and his astonishing resemblance to Nicole Stéphane only highlighted that he was anything but a professional actor. Today this is precisely what saves his performance. Like Nora Gregor, the heroine of Jean Renoir's *La règle du jeu*, to whom the young François Truffaut (at the time a critic for the *Cahiers du cinéma*) compared him, the former miner gave a certain freshness to his character—a suicidal character who was a hostage of the incestuous confinement organized by a sister who could not love anyone who did not share her blood. Stéphane was impressively ambiguous in her role as a Machiavellian man-eater. *Le silence de la mer* had showed her to be intrepid, tenacious, ferocious; her androgynous beauty fed off the film to the point of monopolizing its latent eroticism. She was so unforgettable in the part that it became difficult for her to find other roles, and this Élisabeth-for-life had to turn to directing, and eventually producing. Wounded by the harsh reception of the film, Melville renounced it for a while, blaming the writer for the failure, which had also led to financial losses for him as co-producer. As for Cocteau, he found the energy to preside over the Festival of Cursed Films in Biarritz, which he had helped to found in 1948 with Robert Bresson and Orson Welles.[75]

HEALTH THROUGH FRANCINE

Taking up opium again hadn't done much for Cocteau's health or his finances. Generous with gifts, time, and affection, he had developed a tragic fear of doing without. More than ever, as his sixtieth birthday approached, money represented comfort, sun, the complicated health of his thirty daily pipes—life itself. He had always avoided asking for the check at restaurants—because he spiritually nourished his guests, it was their job to do the same for him, physically—but now he systematically refused to pay. His exhausted body demanded to be spoiled.

Fate, in the form of Jean-Pierre Melville, introduced him to a young woman who was nearly as beautiful, elegant, and admiring as Natalie Paley, but much easier to live with. With a slender figure and a gracefulness that seemed to extend from her tulle dresses, Francine Weisweiller immediately established herself as an unaffected presence in the poet's cork-lined world. Her limousines, her houses, her servants, her money, which had already helped to "round out" the budget for *Les enfants terribles*—Francine Weisweiller put everything she had at his disposal, including her mansion in the place des États-Unis, where she occasionally lived with her husband, one of the heirs to the Shell fortune.[76] Cocteau liked to eat at the Grand Véfour, where Raymond Oliver, the premier chef of the day, cooked; she made sure that he had an open table there. She indulged his preference for Hungarian caviar, omelettes with alevin, pig's trotters à la Sainte Menehould, making sure they appeared whenever he dined at the place des États-Unis, in the middle of a plate garnished with mesclun picked at dawn by old women. She saw to his vital need for the sun and the Mediterranean by inviting him to her summer home, the villa Santo Sospir, at Saint-Jean-Cap-Ferrat. At once protective and comfortable—Francine Weisweiller was the type of person whose papers are always in order—this friendship revived Cocteau when he thought all hope was gone. His life suddenly became luxurious, if not peaceful; his hostess's life benefited from basking in his aura. He introduced her to his brilliant acquaintances and thoughts; she introduced him to her brother, Gérard Worms, with whom she shared part-ownership of the Éditions du Rocher publishing house, who soon became his agent. He had always had to sell his letters from Proust and Apollinaire to pay for his opium addiction; she put an end to this, and soon accepted the pipes he offered her—she had already tried it once.[77]

Everyone became accustomed to seeing them together—dining at the Grand Véfour, after an evening at the Opéra, or at the private screening of a film, near the Champs-Elysées, flanked by young Doudou. So much ease, wealth, and beauty restored Cocteau's confidence. Cared for by this spoiled younger sister, the athlete regained his power. The love he was not able to bestow on himself, Francine Weisweiller provided a hundred times over. No one could ever call her especially cultured, but her way of caring for her champion, and the generosity with which she took charge of Émilienne, Doudou's sister, and soon their parents, fulfilled Cocteau's old familiar desires. The pocket money his mother gave him had never been enough to sustain total autonomy; this time, he had nothing to worry about. They were a fake couple, but a better match than so many real ones. Since Marcel Khill, Cocteau had become accustomed to living with a "simplified" entourage. Age had taught him that devotion like Doudou's or tact like Francine's were sometimes preferable, in the long run, to emotional coarseness like Radiguet's or supreme ingratitude like Genet's. He would have doubtless preferred to be in a "relationship" with Louise de Vilmorin, that unique, amusing woman who sometimes entertained them at her home in Verrières, but the author of *Madame de . . .* was not short of men who liked women — she had just made the glorious conquest of André Malraux, who had been her lover before the war and would be again until her death.[78]

This return of vitality proved to Cocteau that his magic still worked on the "young" — Francine Weisweiller was thirty-three when he met her. Truly tenacious, he was determined to win over audiences again through a new play, which, unusually, he decided would be "à thèse" (a "problem play"), in the hope of winning over the critics and possibly restoring an intellectual reputation worthy of his talent. The era called for an existential problem, but also a historical mirror in which it might recognize itself. He decided on the religious schism that had ravaged Christian faith and had seen a reformed religion emerge in Europe, against the Golden Calf, four centuries before Communism. This time he did the research, reading piles of books on the Reform, Martin Luther, and the German principalities, in order to intellectually bolster his drama. As in the days of Maritain, the goal was to bestow on God the intelligence attributed to the Devil. Cocteau worked so hard to contradict Luther, who believed that God was stupid, and Paris, for whom kindness is dumb, and in December 1951 he arrived at the opening night of *Bacchus* full of confidence. Watching the audience swarm into the Théâtre Marigny, through a peephole looking out on the auditorium, he murmured, "I order you to see this as a masterpiece."[79]

The audience reproached *Bacchus* for being inspired by Sartre's play *Le diable et le bon Dieu*, which had just been performed, and which also dealt with metaphysical problems during the Renaissance. Learning of this strange coincidence nine months earlier, though the idea for *Bacchus* had come to him as early as 1946, Cocteau had swooped down on its author ("that old clown suddenly thought that Sartre was competing with him," Beauvoir wrote) before admitting that their projects didn't have much in common.[80] The few readings the philosopher had recommended to him were enough to make Cocteau call him a cuckoo, the bird that lays in other nests with the aim of getting better eggs, but Sartre himself had already been accused of stealing from Genet: he pushed Goetz, his German condottieri in search of the Absolute, to the depths of evil and treachery.

Overall, Cocteau's final attempt at a comeback received a mixed reception. Featuring a strong construction and well-delineated characters—like its hero, an idiot who wakes up a prophet (is he faking it? does he want power?)— *Bacchus*, in spite of its eloquence, lacked the ease that would have made it truly personal. Both sincere and faked, provocative but obscured by its panache, this drama—which flirted with the young without speaking their language, and while engaged pleaded for disengagement—was not entirely convincing.[81] It seemed more like the libretto for an opera than a play.

Thinking it was an attack on his religion, seeing the bishop get laughs with the word "pater"—blasphemers from the Lettrist International had interrupted services at Notre Dame, a few months earlier—François Mauriac noisily left the theater, then violently attacked Cocteau in the press. "HELL DOESN'T EXIST. MAY AMUSE YOU. WARN CLAUDEL. GIDE," said a mysterious telegram sent to Mauriac at the death of Gide. By all accounts, Mauriac did not listen. "I've seen your act for nearly half a century. You have more than one trick up your sleeve, I know them all. You are the hardest and more fragile creature there is. Your harshness is like that of an insect, you have its protective armor, all it takes is to push a little harder, but no matter . . . but no I won't push," wrote the devout Christian in *Le Figaro littéraire*, adding: "*Bacchus* gives us a glimpse of Jean Cocteau in the light of Sartre, the same Cocteau we remember from 1910, bathed in the glow of Rostand's final flames . . . Forty years have gone by. Now is the time of 'God is dead.' This is the kind of thing that's in the air, and you've spent your life catching draughts."[82] Mauriac, who knew Cocteau intimately, suspected him of wanting to besmirch his old Mother—the Church. Cocteau replied by accusing him of having an ugly soul, implicitly referring to the envy that Mauriac had always felt where Cocteau was concerned: "JE T'ACCUSE, because you ceaselessly remind me that you are an overgrown child, of having retained from childhood only its snide cruelty . . . You declare that if you did not speak out, the stones would. A stone has spoken: it's you."[83]

The polemic raged on, but Mauriac was certainly the more relentless of the two, his rival's "religious" path, from Maritain to Genet, having been murky at best. Overwhelmed at finding himself a target once again, Cocteau didn't care to remind him that in their youth, when Mauriac was in love with him, he, Cocteau, had fascinated and terrorized Mauriac at the same time. "He would sometimes even run away shouting," Cocteau told Claude Mauriac, about his father. "He called me a demon, he hated me. And then he would come back and say he was wrong."[84]

In the end, the public grew tired of the controversy, and then of the play, after about thirty performances. These old men scratching each other's eyes out about faith did not provide the best publicity.[85] Cocteau, who was already lamenting that he hadn't been able to persuade Marais to take the lead role, was saddened to see the audiences weren't capable of letting themselves be taken out of their own time, of forgetting their own identity. They analyzed when they should have felt, which was always the case in France. A few guessed that Cocteau, mortally wounded, had just written his last serious work for the stage, and would never again try to recapture the mythic young man he had been.

SAINT GENET, ACTOR AND MARTYR

The tremendous book that Sartre had devoted to Genet after months of conversations stunned Cocteau. He read the doorstopper of a book in the summer of 1952, seven hundred pages reconstituting the interior journey of a forty-two-year-old man who had already published four novels and two plays.[86] He immediately thought it was magnificent. He himself excelled at the brief portrait and the poetic photograph; with his outsized intellectual gifts, Sartre had just invented a new literary genre, the philosophical portrait in three dimensions. The real Jean Genet, a hairy, bad-smelling ex-convict whom he had picked up in the middle of the Occupation, didn't have much to do with the phenomenological purity of the case study analyzed by the author of *L'être et le néant*. The actual Genet would sit down in front of you and demand, arrogantly, "What do you think of me? I'm pretty great, don't you think?" while the hero of Sartre's novels was Sartre's alter ego, someone condemned by fate to grow up in a "practical-inert" world, but who confirmed all the philosopher's intuitions. Totally reinvented, the book thief became the foundational saint of a theory of absolute existentialist freedom of choice. The book turned the idea of Genet into an issue of free will, and had an enormous impact. For most of the reading public, Sartre became the inventor, if not the discoverer, of Genet — Sartre, who was inventing schemes to get his plays performed in 1943, the same year that Cocteau was fighting to keep Genet from being sent back to the penal colony. Already left out of their friendship, Cocteau was also wounded, in the most insidious fashion, that in this "monumental portrait" he appeared only a few times, as if Genet's work relegated his own to the spheres of lofty ethereality. Of course, Sartre pointed out, without naming names, Genet defended his friends "with a warmth that is very rare in the literary world, sometimes even when it has been dangerous to support them," but the thief's route was only described in conjunction with that of the writer Jouhandeau, another bard of abjection.[87]

Cocteau brutally assessed the tenuousness of his critical position. Had he not also deserved a place in Sartre's project, through his unique capacity for self-fashioning? From *Thomas l'imposteur* to *La machine à écrire*, Cocteau's work was overrun with heroes unable to accept their truth, but also destined, through an excess of lies or false accusations, to reinvent themselves, in a way that fascinated the author of *La nausée*. If his idea was that man was "condemned to be free," to recreate his own humanity every moment, to be responsible for all that he would do and become, without ever becoming it, who better corresponded to this existential idea than Cocteau, the great master of transformation?[88] Was he not living proof that the self is created only through interactions with others, and irrefutable proof of the old saying "Esse est percipi" (To be is to be perceived), which was the foundation of Sartrian thought? His own life was closer to the definition Sartre gave — "one is not born, but becomes ugly" — than that of Genet.[89] It had always been other people, throughout his life, who had defined him as homosexual, the better to ostracize him; he himself had always let things float. More than young Genet, he had depended on his enemies to define him, sometimes to the point of conforming to the image they made of him. They had the advantage of having more distance from him, allowing for a better overall vision.

A year earlier, Cocteau had tried to interest Sartre in his case. He had invited both Sartre and Simone de Beauvoir to a restaurant to tell them about his projects for plays and films, as well as about the biography of Marais that he was putting together. The philosopher was "so generous, so interested in everything"! Cocteau talked for two hours straight, as Genet had done with Sartre, or Violette Leduc with the "la Grande Sartreuse" (Simone de Beauvoir), but without their cheeky way of referencing their homosexuality — a subject that particularly pleased the couple.[90] "Deadly boring, because he guessed that no one is interested in him any longer, not in France, and not anywhere else," Beauvoir concluded when Cocteau left.[91] The result: Sartre's book *Saint Genet, comédien et martyr* (Saint Genet, actor and martyr), which barely mentioned him. Had his youth been too comfortable, his metamorphoses too frequent, to interest a philosopher fascinated by this man who created himself out of what others had made of him? Had his conviction that everything was more or less dictated to us alienated Sartre, this master of free will? Then why make the extremely fatalistic Genet an existentialist in spite of himself? Cocteau had naively believed that one day a kind of saintliness would be recognized in him, but he soon learned that it would be only a gift against the grain, an acknowledgment of a place in the devil's entourage. It would be a gift that did not reward the blood that one had lost, but the blood that one had spilled. The son of Eugénie Cocteau belonged to the old world, one ruled by the Judeo-Christian codex and the Greek and Latin myths; the orphan Genet was a product of the neo-pagan universe that would gain so much importance, in which the body and the humors would predominate.[92] Was this why he deserved only the moralizing literary observations of Claude Mauriac, while the author of *Querelle de Brest* was canonized by Sartre? Radiguet was right: nonconformity had become the dominant means of conforming.

It all seemed so unfair, and Cocteau grew disgusted by this work that turned the impure (the unclean but also the anti-pure), the ignoble (but also the non-noble), the infamous, and the unknown into the absolute peak of a new morality. It was his turn to reject Genet, the author he had helped to establish, at a time when doing so meant incurring very real risks.

This critical apotheosis had another victim: Genet himself. At first exultant and proud to have inspired so many pages so early in his career, he soon felt exposed, stripped naked by someone other than himself. By taking away his being, Sartre had turned to nothingness his dreams of becoming the ultimate philosopher of his time. The miraculous flood of inspiration was already abating; Genet had written nothing for three years. It slowed to a trickle as he struggled to write a poem that would surpass the book that Mallarmé himself could only manage to outline. Genet's genius seemed to have totally deserted him in order to inspire Sartre to create this massive work, the most powerful and devastating ever devoted to a living author. Cocteau could have served as a literary and cinematic mentor, Mallarmé and then Sartre as poetic and philosophic models, but in trying to outdo them all, he had exhausted himself. He had told his savior, during the war, that he wrote only to get out of prison; once he had his liberty, thanks to the presidential pardon that Sartre and Cocteau had procured for him, he had difficulty recreating a universe entirely determined by the enveloping damp of his cell. The air of the outside world seemed to have corrupted his imagination, like those ancient frescoes that disappear as soon as they're exposed to the light of day. His genius lost all resilience far from the jail-pressured world; the "consciousness stuffed with itself, like the prunes of Tours" to which Sartre referred, was rotting from the inside.[93]

More than Sartre, however, Genet went after the man who had gotten him out of prison and turned him into a famous writer. He who hated literary careers and the vile prostitution it implied raged against this pseudo-benefactor who had allowed him to be adopted by a social order he abhorred, introducing him to his highly ranked friends in the police, and the prefects, and had forced him to be a human being like anyone else—an untenable position for Genet, who was a born thief, and who missed the days when Mauriac would call him an "étron" (piece of excrement) or even a "suppurating Cocteau."[94] The raging desire that enabled him to fetishize each of the individuals who brought the sordid world of prison to life was broken. It was less Sartre who had killed Genet than Cocteau, that pure product of a liberal bourgeoisie who was the incarnation of everything the thief hated most in the world: whiny, indulgent when it came to crime, and fearing prison more than anything in the world, unlike the thundering judges, his only friends. They were ready at any moment to send him back to prison where he could play with the other inmates like dolls, turning the prison wardens into his personal guards and where everyone, so to speak, was at his beck and call.

A furious Genet returned to Cocteau to accuse him of sacrificing morality to friendship, of compromising himself in mainstream cinema and commercial theater, of having become in the last ten years a vulgar boulevard author trying to become a star. Dragged by the ear like a disobedient student, the older man examined these insults, and for once chose not to listen to them. No, he was not a corrupt author, and certainly not a prostitute; Genet was the one who couldn't finish his plays, and who was undergoing other influences. It was Genet who, by refusing to admit that *Notre-Dame-des-fleurs* may have been his masterpiece, endlessly rewrote his plays, until he became the prisoner of an oeuvre from which he slowly eliminated his editors—the cruelest of all the prisons in which he had been incarcerated.[95]

Things took a nightmarish turn. Barely had Genet decreed that their ways of life were too different, and that he was going to break with Cocteau, than he came to reproach him for refusing, in the middle of the Purge, to have dedicated to him *Pompes funèbres*, Genet's novel that was sympathetic to the Militia.[96] Then Genet began to shout that he had nothing left to say, that literature disgusted him, that he had burned—or no, *torn up*—everything he had written for the last five years. Others would have asked Genet why he should destroy writings that he no longer cared about, but seeing the actor behind the saint, like Sartre, Cocteau bore it all stoically. He was so used to being rejected by those whom he had helped that he rightly found it regrettable that the ex-convict would give himself over to self-hatred. He understood that what Genet feared most of all was to see his work self-destruct, and therefore was angry with Cocteau, his elder, for remaining so productive. Cocteau continued to see in Genet only the great writer—"the greatest moralist of our time," he would say to Violette Leduc. He was as blind in his support as others were in their hatred.

Genet, however, needed an outlet for his fury. Since unlike Sachs he had never had romantic feelings for Cocteau, he contented himself with stealing from him, or rather with taking back the manuscript for *Notre-Dame-des-fleurs* that the writer had bought from him in 1942, when he had been a lone voice of support. Since Genet could not repay that debt to Cocteau, it was a way of erasing the proof of it, while at the same time paying one final, paradoxical homage to him: by sacralizing the friend in the stolen object, stealing the manuscript put a bow on the ties that bound them together. "You will find me ungrateful," Genet wrote to the author of *Les enfants terribles*. "I owed you so much. I no longer owe you anything."[97] But then his resolution began to waver, as if he could not decide to kill his mothering mentor. Although his quarrels tended to be definitive, he was no longer sure if it was Cocteau's work or the writer himself whom he rejected. "You and Sartre have turned me into a statue. I am someone else. This someone else must find something to say," he wrote one day.[98] The next day, Cocteau found him prostrate, like a "terrified baby," ravaged by doubt and fear.[99] A few days later, and Genet had pulled away again, his "eyes filled with an extraordinary kindness and mischievousness." That was Genet, unfeeling and independent; someone for whom others only existed part-time. Then Cocteau received an apologetic letter in which Genet, encouraging Cocteau to be as frank as possible, assured him of his very great affection, his unwavering respect, and his admiration for his *Journal d'un inconnu*. "You are wrong to believe you are alone, for everyone loves you—and often very intelligently—everywhere in the world," Genet added, before concluding, with a tenderness rare from his pen, "and I will always love you."[100] This was generous enough to win Cocteau over for years. "You have to love someone to make them suffer," wrote Sartre in *Saint Genet*.[101]

STEP FORWARD, PETER PAN!

Cocteau's daily life was no longer busy enough to sustain his prewar levels of euphoria. He had entire days in which to think about his life, and to keep a written record, between two canvases and five drawings, of his state of mind—encouraged by the calm that reigned over the villa Santo Sospir. A nagging worry began to invade his journal (which well deserved the name he would give to it, *Le passé défini* [Past tense]). The young had become uncultured, vulgar, living from moment to moment, with no thought of what might have come before—they were drunk on themselves and on their supposed preeminence. Of course he was angry with them for rejecting his last two films, but he suffered more deeply watching them consider themselves separate from the human race, every year a little more. "The young have this unique attribute," he confided in Roger Stéphane. "They are racist in the sense that there is a race of young people and a race of old. They don't realize they will one day become old."[102] There was truth in his complaint. But getting carried away with the idea (and what happened next would prove him right), wounded at feeling he was no longer in fashion, Cocteau recovered the attitude of the men who were old when *he* was an adolescent, when they were still in power—and even that of his former self, the young-man-for-old-people, who at seventeen was already, in a 1906 letter to his mother, denouncing his schoolmates' weakness, that is, "the crowning of human idiocy and the atrophy of the modern generations."[103] The stupidity of the radio shows that Doudou listened to while he painted, or the magazines that Francine read distractedly, gave him the impression of falling without ever hitting the ground. It was a Niagara of empty statements and silly songs, shrill advertisements and word games, in which armies of the ignorant won more money in a week than he had earned in a lifetime. The hollow debates that were being conducted everywhere gave him a tragic view of the times: stupidity had begun to think, loudly and freely. In his youth, he had heard a hackney cab driver say to his horse, when he knocked over a bag of oats, "How stupid you are! It would only be worse if you could speak."[104] And so it had come to pass. A never-before-seen species of simple-minded people, with big ears and big mouths, happy in their ignorance, had taken over the place. The Nazi debauchery and the Soviet severity had been succeeded by a society of chatty termites, multiplying, with no individuality, who badly needed the insecticide of the atom bomb. "A religion without hope," he called poetry; and now more than ever these words described Cocteau himself, an aging child who sang in the dark to calm his fears. The friend of Proust, of Picasso, of Stravinsky was not content to criticize the ravages of stupidity, and the general collapse of the level of discourse, declaring "As machines improve, the soul declines"; he took to denouncing the generation that danced to be-bop in Saint-Germain-des-Prés, pawed at each other in the middle of the Villefranche port, sunbathed bare-breasted at Saint-Tropez, and then skipped off to Monte Carlo only to wrap a car around a plane tree.[105] Hearing the radio and the press extol the poetry of a seven year-old girl who had already been compared to Radiguet, he declared, "All children have genius, except Minou Drouet."

Yet there was something reassuring about the culture gap. Knowing that the more "of his time" a writer is, the more likely he is to die within it, he tried to see his alienation as a guarantee of his longevity. His own fragility, after half a century of struggle, seemed proof of his unsinkable character, as well as his "live-wire" health. Yet he truly suffered from being rejected by these young people whom he so resembled on the inside. When he was an adolescent, men began to disguise themselves as old men by the age of forty-five to make themselves seem more prestigious. He was twenty years older than that, but seemed less inclined to show off how old he was, since aging had lost its mythic aura. Out of step with his time, Cocteau began to be just as out of step with his birth certificate. "I am not a child, but almost," he said in his *Journal d'un inconnu.* "That's what makes people believe I am young, although youth and childhood are two different things."[106] Caught between youth and old age, Cocteau was split ("le grand écart") once again.

The failure of *Bacchus* dissuaded him from turning to theater, and he didn't see the point of novels anymore. Only poetry attracted him, but it took him a longer time each year to write a poem. His machine was becoming unreliable; though Édouard Dermit was sweet and generous, he could not really stoke his artistic flames. Cocteau, who so needed other people in order to create, felt very much alone and cold inside. Putting the great literary genres aside, he began to pile up books of memoirs, but they served only to reinforce the impression he gave of belonging to the past. Worse, he started to repeat himself from one book to the next, less out of self-indulgence or of senility than by an inability to proof-read or to recharge his batteries. He was running low on energy, as he used up his ink. "My nights are becoming solitary," he wrote in 1953, before adding, poignantly, six months later, "The guitar is out of tune; the strings sag."[107]

He preferred to draw, almost in spite of himself, curves and loops on Canson paper, faithful translations of the systoles of his heart—the desires that still beat there, his latest dreams, like the lines on an electrocardiogram. Although Picasso's bullish eye had always dissuaded him from painting, he tried it for the first time, producing figures of Christ and Antigone, and others from Christianity or antiquity, often from the Noailles days, all part of his personal mythology.[108] The result was unconvincing, with a few near exceptions, but the goal above all was to keep Doudou company, while facing his easel. Soon, like Picasso at Vallauris, his little star, his legendary profile, and his Masonic eyes could be seen on plates, scarves, and pottery. Was it the childish love of drawing or the desire to cover the world with his pen? Unlike writing, which had brought him pitilessly face to face with himself, drawing allowed him to escape by his own hand, freeing him from his old wounded body to become the canvas he painted, the paper he filled, the walls he drew on, until, in the shadow of the pines at Santo Sospir, he felt at one with nature. Francine Weisweiller also picked up a paintbrush, under the tutelage of Doudou, who put all his pride into teaching this delicate heiress, firmly guiding her wrist. Cocteau encouraged the young woman as well, and persuaded her that she had talent, with the tireless energy that made him, in this sense, the opposite of Breton, who forbade others the arts he could not practice himself. Those in the neighboring villas spent their time playing bridge; the trio in Santo Sospir spent theirs brushing oil onto canvas in an atmosphere hazy with the smell of opium and the fragrance of tuberoses.

Always up for a game of pétanque (French bocce) or sunbathing on the deck of the *Orphée*, Francine's yacht, Doudou, unlike those who had preceded him, was an angel, truly docile. Deliciously trussed and gagged by compliments, he gave in to the agreeable feeling of being infantilized, and sought no autonomy whatsoever. Cocteau could watch him through his binoculars for hours painting bare-chested, sitting up straight in his chair. The elder man had already gained a few of the powers that his own mother had over him. More of a Pygmalion than ever, he went around bragging about the numerous gifts, superhuman qualities, and angelic soul of his last adopted son. The very honorable "Monday painter," as he had at first nicknamed him, became the equal of Vermeer and the Douanier Rousseau—although in truth his paintings looked as if they had been painted before the Douanier's. Doudou, in return, regarded Cocteau more than ever as the unknown star of the twentieth century. Reflected in these flattering mirrors, any imperfections either one might have had were erased.

Cocteau sometimes looked for Doudou's faults, but couldn't find any. He was "thoroughly pure," soaked in goodness, of an unequaled humanity, the dream companion. Those who were jealous called him average, mediocre. But Cocteau, touched by his kind smile, declared him a supernatural being, like Francine. Doudou could not ignore his beauty, wrote James Lord, for it had changed his life, "but in a strange way, it doesn't seem to have changed him."[109] He was not in the least narcissistic. Was he the best painter of his generation, as Cocteau liked to say? Surely not, but how could Cocteau be dissuaded when even Aragon praised "the paintings of the quietest young man in the world"?[110] Doudou's naiveté was worth a thousand times more than the cynicism of the more established artists. Sachs and Desbordes had gone away disappointed; Doudou remained under the charm of the magician who had pulled him out of the mines of Lorraine and moved him into this hiding-place of the gods. Things had come full circle: Cocteau now lived with a good, sweet painter, who—like Cocteau's mother at one time—had a nearly absent personality.

In the summer, the two men took a tour of the Mediterranean aboard Francine's yacht. Since he still did not know how to swim, Cocteau went in search of the cities of antiquity. Helped by the opium, the two men breathed the same air with no sense of time or the calendar. They were caught in the bubble where Cocteau had lived for so long, like deep-sea divers on decompression platforms, all while the little ball crackled in the mahogany pipe. The countries they visited, the birthplace of mythology itself, looked like film or theater sets, as they smoked. "Greece is an idea we develop," he wrote in *Journal d'un inconnu,* "to such an extent that we wonder if it really exists, if we exist when traveling there." These trips no doubt did him good physically, but they increased his sense of being in exile, as well as his fear of becoming nothing. After living so intensely for half a century, he had the sense, on this unknown shore, of being a film extra playing a vacationer, or a latter-day Flying Dutchman, condemned by the gods to wander indefinitely until someone sacrificed his life for him, thereby restoring him to reality.

When Cocteau returned to his shoebox apartment in Paris, he was reenergized. His need for publicity returned, and in his impatience to win over the public, he went to every opening night he could, and pressed his cheek to those of the starlet du jour. Such enthusiasm was intriguing in a man already so well-known; it was as if he only felt legitimate with other famous people looking at him, as if they were the true custodians of "Jean Cocteau." They alone could give him consistency. He always seemed about to announce to them, like Sartre's Kean, "I don't really exist; I'm just pretending. To please you, ladies and gentlemen." If he encountered one of his enemies, he hastened to confide something that could be turned against him, to make sure that enemy would agree with him. "It's an all-too human trick," Radiguet had said years before, "to believe only in the sincerity of those who accuse themselves."[111] In a way, Cocteau overused this strategy.

Something hadn't taken in Cocteau; he lacked the glue that could have unified all his incompatible selves. Aware that it was evolving in too-fragile a container, his genius always seemed about to come apart from his insubstantial body. When Elias Canetti, the author of *Crowds and Power,* met Cocteau, he said he felt as if he were walking through a transparent being, with "his too-narrow hands, the elegant network of wrinkles, the mass of grey curls . . . a man made of nerves and silver wire" like Cocteau's pipe-cleaner men of the 1920s.[112] He evoked a mixture of air and water, and this slight resistance made others aggressive, for this emptiness seemed proof that he had not managed to become someone. Didn't he try out each of the arts a little bit, without embodying any of them; try out all the slogans, without keeping to any of them? "At sixty years old, Cocteau still didn't know if he should write poetry like Anna de Noailles or Max Jacob, if he should paint like Ingres or Picasso, imitate Racine or Georges de Porto-Riche," Malraux said.[113]

Wandering was all right for the man in the street, but it wasn't tolerated in a man of his stature. Even the least conservative expected him to take root in an idea, if not a land, yet the author of *Thomas l'imposteur* seemed eager to be on the move. "It is as if Cocteau had been condemned to play life on a checkerboard, his opponent the specter of Anonymity, perpetually scheming to reach the end squares so that, crowned, he might continue moving, in any direction he pleased, for the sake of moving," Frederick Brown, Cocteau's second American biographer, would write.[114] Was Cocteau fleeing some long-repressed primal scene, some foundational trauma—or his own void? Freud compared hysteria to a deformed work of art, imprisoned in itself, yet somewhat paradoxically Jean Cocteau's complex poems and unique films were always attributed to his many-sided hysteria. His verse and his *calligrammes*, his sets and his staging not only did not allow a general idea to be formed of him; they did not even resemble each other. The ink in his books seemed to change color over time; like Virginia Woolf's Orlando, Cocteau had lived across the centuries and the sexes to the point of erasing all traces of who he had been. "It's doubtless because we have everything inside of us, and the more man is completed by his diversity, the more he is incomplete in the multiple fractions of his being," Maurice Sachs wrote in *La chasse à courre*.

After half a century, Parisian faces often showed hardness or bitterness. Cocteau's own betrayed instead an immense weariness. He had spent his life wasting his talent, his mind, his belongings, and he felt so much resentment. His generosity had not paid off; he would have been better off denouncing his era and oppressing his contemporaries. His acts of selflessness almost made him look mad, as Emmanuel Berl would say affectionately. There was no better nature than that of Berl, a friend of Proust whom Cocteau had met at Anna de Noailles's home. Tolerant of everything, even the anti-Semitism of Drieu la Rochelle, the author of the 1952 book *Sylvia* was one of those rare writers whom Cocteau could move. Berl liked that curious neighbor who dreamed of seeing charity offices open in the Palais-Royal and who, upon seeing the bellboy at the Véfour shiver under his worn peacoat, could not refrain from offering him, like Saint Martin or Proust himself, his own luxurious coat.[115] "Jean," Berl would say one day, "I would like to find a doctor who could lower your rate of kindness, like excess urea."[116] But the best specialists couldn't fight the strange weakness in the writer's immune system, whose kindness Berl judged "almost monstrous": Cocteau could not tolerate disappointing anyone.[117] His friend Cecil Beaton, who had photographed him many times, published his memoirs without mentioning his name once; still he could not keep from praising that viper's "golden heart" at a reception at the British Embassy.[118] Berl knew, however, how sensitive Cocteau was in secret, as if "devoured by a giant insect." Cocteau himself would describe the scene in a Proustian manner, declaring that if Beaton didn't feel ill-at-ease, it was because he was an idiot, which, after all, was not impossible.[119] A terrible taboo prevented Cocteau from expressing his suffering, but Berl was allowed to glimpse the truth: "One day when I was pitying him," he wrote, "he said to me, 'You know, I'm used to it, I have never felt good in my own skin,' with so much simplicity and grace that his words went right through me. They left a scar that neither the years, nor his words, nor his writing could ever erase."

Knowing he was incapable of holding onto anything, Cocteau's older brother managed the small amount of money that his mother had left him, but Cocteau was not exactly born to own things. Near the end of his life he found himself without belongings or artwork, with a few exceptions, including the portrait of his mother attributed to Joseph Wincker. He had never had the means to buy any of Picasso's works—and Picasso had been more generous to Éluard (who never even needed his generosity), and to so many others before him, than to Cocteau.[120] Typical of the grasshopper believed to be a millionaire by those who hung out in Montparnasse in 1916, Cocteau had only the letters that Sachs hadn't stolen from him. One of the portraits that Modigliani had done of him in 1916 turned up around this time in the United States. The dead-drunk bohemian, he remembered, had wanted to give it to him, but he had insisted on paying for it, and then, since he could no longer afford to call a hackney cab, had left it in Kisling's studio just before going back out to the front. Up to his neck in debt, Kisling had used it as a security deposit with the director of the Rotonde, who had hung it above the banquettes in his brasserie, and then eventually sold it. The portrait, by this time, was worth 250,000,000 old francs, and Cocteau still didn't have a sou.[121]

Picasso and Stravinsky were making a fortune; Dalí could declare, in a grand, hilarious gesture to the students of the École Normale de Saint-Cloud, "When September begins to september, I go to the Perpignan train station. Gala [Dalí's wife] writes up an invoice for my latest masterpiece to send it to America (the more of a failure it is, the more it costs!)." Everyone found that funny—and everyone paid up. Cocteau, however, had difficulty finding a gallery to show his work, and made almost no money from his drawings. "How can you propose to sell them, when you give them away?" Colette's husband protested.[122] "One of my secrets is without a doubt being inflicted with selflessness," he wrote to a very young Aragon, during their friendship in 1918. "A passion for the things of this world, a parasitical passion, but no 'earthly' papers in my pocket. An angel all alone."[123]

Why, then, had he always preferred to work for nothing but the sole pride of seeing his name in print? Because there was nobody behind the till, in his mind? Or because on the contrary his command post was occupied by a legion of pretenders, who were likely to take a variety of forms but were unlikely to agree— "Cocteaux" by the dozen who had spent their lives sapping whatever would have enabled their unification? He was not enough to have, said Denis de Rougemont of Don Juan. Conversely, Cocteau seemed too much to keep: the letters of admiration, the gifts, and the declarations he attracted seemed to fall into a bottomless well. Yes, he asked for too much, wrote too much, paraded about too much—to the point of going to dine at the maternal home of one of the young people who surrounded him, just to please him. Doing these things always turned out badly for him. But that's how it was; he had to engage with the greatest possible number of souls, and at dinners seduce his neighbors and even the foreigners who ignored him. "I've dreamed more than I've lived and it has taken on terrible proportions. The spectator can barely notice I'm like an actor in someone else's play. And even this other is under orders from a mysterious schizophrenic who lives in us all, that most people manage to exorcise, or in whom they refuse to believe."[124] This schizophrenic, as late as 1957, would make him write a poem, "Avec des si," using the methods of serial music that had excited Stravinsky—him again—and driven by the same old desire to start again from scratch, or to demonstrate that his genius was still fresh. "If you want to stay young, keep beginning," he wrote in *Le coq*, in 1920; thirty-five years later, Cocteau could expect "the same sarcasm and the same insults," but didn't let up.[125] He sometimes went looking to see where the saddle might have chafed. At the Femina matinee? Success was always a disappointing drug, so he accused those who had made the mistake of applauding too early. Paris coats its victims in honey before delivering them to the ants, he said one day. That is, he had been celebrated in order to be destroyed.

After hitting so many walls, which were always closing in, he dreamed of being able to fly out of time to a world directly above his own, one peopled with magi and fairies. The Cannes Film Festival in 1953, over which he presided, had a happy surprise in store for him, thanks to Disney Studios: the spectacle of Peter Pan flying under the protection of Tinkerbell to the palace in Never Never Land. In his *Journal d'un inconnu* he wrote that he recognized himself in that enthusiastic elf with the endless childhood. "My parents spoke of my future as a man. I escaped and met fairies," confided J. M. Barrie's bird-angel to Wendy, the young Londoner, before offering her "flying lessons above the land of 'Make Believe.'" This was, in a nutshell, Cocteau's life, which could also be used to name a psychoanalytic complex. The young Cocteau (Peter Pan) had wanted to make everything he touched wonderful, but he had difficulty convincing his contemporaries that Francine was Tinkerbell, and Doudou, Wendy. Those dreams were starting to attract fewer disciples, given that opium had become rarer after the loss of Indochina.

Despite his fear of decline, Cocteau knew that he possessed a kind of brilliance, and like all talented people, this single certainty enabled him to carry on working, to survive at all costs, to continue to write a little everywhere—on invitations, record jackets, cigarette boxes, theater programs, book covers. He might doubt the usefulness of this excessive production, but he never doubted its value, in the long run; he might wonder if he had been wrong to love poetry too much, to devote too much energy to his work—and even come to believe it looking at the glory of Duchamp, who had done almost nothing, already extending throughout the century—but it was his karma. He *had* to work.

WHO IS THE GREATEST
GENIUS OF THE CENTURY?

He could not let himself go, because there were too many individuals within
him. He went from one to the other . . . It is possible that his case was unique.
—*Jacques Porel*, Fils de Réjane, *referring to Cocteau*

NOT MUCH OF A TRIUMPH

Gide's death contributed much to Cocteau's bitterness. The Immoralist,
whom he had sincerely admired but to whom he never had anything to say,
received unanimous tributes when he died. From *Le Figaro* to *L'humanité*,
members of the press had lamented the modern-day Voltaire with one voice,
closing their eyes to the man who ran after young boys and who fifty years later,
should have been threatened with prison. For Cocteau, the need to celebrate
had always trumped his wounded pride; but this time, with a blind sense of self-
defense, he was convinced that they were praising a "living fraud," a literary
impostor. Gide liked to say that Cocteau was never better than when he was in
reporter mode; Cocteau called him an "anti-poet" after mentioning the
"monstrous stupidity" of Gide's journal in his own.[1] Gide had declared that he
could never take Cocteau seriously, after forty years of occasional socializing;
Cocteau had retorted by calling Gide a born liar and a bad priest, pointing to
his old Symbolist versatility and the way he lusted after the avant-garde, and
denouncing his dryness and his misguided ways, his duet with Stalin and then
the Germans, the cruelty of his unconsummated marriage, and his constant
apology of pedophilia.[2] Gide did not disguise his distaste for Cocteau's too-
obvious version of homosexuality; Cocteau suggested, in turn, that the old

maggot had engaged in much more scandalous affairs than the little Arab boys he owned up to. He implored Gide to delete the more disagreeable passages that concerned him from his *Journal,* without the least effect, and he revenged himself by imitating, in front of Morand, the old man "with the bitter, tightened lips" whom he had surprised in his hotel room, a little elevator operator on his knees, saying, against all evidence, "He's sewing a button back on," turning each word over in his mouth like disgusting hard candies.[3]

Gide and Cocteau each embodied a very different version of desire than the other: one still ran after young heartthrobs long past his eightieth birthday; the other had stopped actively desiring men at the age of sixty. Imagining the old fogey's maniacal maneuverings filled Cocteau with disgust; in his final fury, Cocteau refused to wear the gown that the University of Oxford wanted to lend him to receive its honorary doctorate, under the pretext that Gide had already worn it. The final encounter of the two men, in Taormina in 1950, was catastrophic. There by chance, Truman Capote had seen "il Vecchio" (Gide) daydreaming in the town square of the Sicilian village that was perched like an eagle's nest on a cliff overlooking the sea, a paradise for boys at the time, and Cocteau interrupted his rest. "Thirty-six years had gone by since the wartime tea party, yet nothing in the attitude of the two men toward each other had altered. Cocteau, still eager to please, was the rainbow-winged and dancing dragonfly inviting the toad not merely to admire but perhaps devour him. He jigged about . . . he effused, enthused, he fondled the old man's knee, caressed his hands, squeezed his shoulders, kissed his parched Mongolian cheeks . . . until at last he croaked, 'Do be still. You are disturbing the view.'"[4]

Because Gide said everything about himself while he was alive, Cocteau wanted to believe that now, after his death, no one would be interested in hearing more about him, which is almost what happened. Would this final disinterest guarantee that more attention would be paid to Jean Cocteau? That he too would get to see his complete works published by the Pléiade and awarded the Nobel Prize, with all the universal respect that this honor had brought Gide in 1947, Mauriac in 1952, Camus in 1957, and Sartre, who turned down the prize seven years later?

What happened after Genet's canonization was demoralizing for Cocteau. The more Genet sinned, the less resistance he encountered; he could not be attacked without having his genius praised. After dragging him through the mud, Mauriac himself defended him against the latest attacks in *Le Figaro.* The ex-convict's books were carried under every arm, like backward Bibles, and in spite of the depression into which he was sinking, Genet still found the strength to visit Cocteau, in order to ask for the thousandth time what he thought of his work, adding, "in any case, I've written a book that no other comes close to, *Pompes funèbres*. I owe the title to you, but even you haven't written anything like it."[5] Why was this "underworld Orpheus," this "inspired onanist" whose way of working even Mauriac recognized belonged to "Jean Cocteau's clock-making," more respected than he was?[6] Was it because he had the infernal courage to point out the worst in mankind? Why had Cocteau not taken advantage of the scandal of *Bacchus*? Why did he blush like a schoolgirl when he was finally complimented? Why did he break down upon reading that if you could find pearls in Cocteau, you could find ingots in Genet?

Breton had rapidly transformed into a sovereign patriarch; Aragon had instinctively known how to make himself feared, calling on forces that went beyond him; but Cocteau remained alone, with the pallor that made people fear contagion. He had been a diabetic of celebrity since 1908. A poor old aging dragonfly, flitting terrified around flickering lightbulbs, passing from a quick tribute to Ronsard to stale memories of the Boeuf sur le Toit, still singing of his love for Eurydice and the death of Iseult while screaming teenagers were discovering rock and roll. "The public loves me," said Orpheus, defending his film. "But they're the only ones," a neighbor retorted. Worldly and cursed at the same time, his ethereal character always seemed to impose itself between the public and his books, depriving them of their own independent existence, even of all their weight.[7] He was a ghost who was the opposite of a cuttlefish: his image disturbed his ink, which ended up dissolving in the ocean of his publications. Thinking of his powderpuff hairdo, Cocteau's potential readers put his books down. He was looked at but never truly seen, because he was too obvious, like Edgar Allan Poe's purloined letter. Harassed by fatigue and parched for recognition like a man crossing the desert without water, Cocteau asked himself, after fifty years of solitary journeying, why the skies refused to quench his thirst.

DESCARTES THE IDIOT

Cocteau sometimes wondered if he was a victim of the French fetish for geometry: each of his poems reactivated the old machine of rational defiance against the great unknown. He could barely mention the existence of other realities, or other worlds, without someone trying to gag him. A man of hot unreason and an electroshock aesthetic did not have a place in the down-to-earth land of skepticism, cold reason, and well-ordered intelligence. What could he say to the partisans of prolonged naturalism, or Socialist realism? That he preferred the flight of Melusine to the worker's dreams of paid vacation leave? How should he reply when, upon leaving a screening of *La belle et la bête* at the Saint-Maurice studios organized by Marlene Dietrich, Jean Gabin, her lover, said to him, "So now will you make us a *real* film, with bistros?"[8] Those two did not speak the same language.

He was fêted abroad. *Bacchus* had been a hit in Germany, when he visited in 1952; Hamburg had applauded *Orphée*; the Munich Pinacothèque had exhibited his canvases and tapestries; and some of his graphic work could be seen in Berlin. In a country that could accept a certain degree of irrationality, his popularity was at its height.[9] The same was true in Switzerland, where a group of students had carried him in triumph out of one of his speeches, and where he had received admiring letters from Thomas Mann, whose son Klaus had planned to translate *La machine infernale*, before his suicide.[10] He only had to set foot in Italy, give the talks that were asked of him in Turin, Genoa, Milan, and Rome, for the cameras to hunt him down, and when he went to Spain, university students flocked to the cinema to see *Orphée*. Princes and aesthetes fought to receive him in the spring of 1949 when, accompanied by Marais and Doudou, he had followed a company of twenty-two actors to Egypt, Lebanon, and Turkey, to perform *Les parents terribles*, *La machine infernale*, and *Les monstres sacrés*.[11]

Probably the Americans did not completely understand Cocteau's *Aigle à deux têtes* when it had been performed before in New York; on this return visit, in his *Lettre aux Américains*, he had bragged about the French spirit of anarchy. But the brilliant *New Yorker* correspondent Janet Flanner took every opportunity to praise his genius to her American readers, and they had been able to see almost all of his postwar plays and films. Ever since, younger Americans had celebrated him as the filmmaker and playwright of the avant-garde, from Tennessee Williams, long an admirer, whose *Streetcar Named Desire* Cocteau would stage in France, to Julian Beck and Judith Malina, the founders of the Living Theater, who would take *Orphée* to Broadway in 1954. A young musician like Ned Rorem, who often spent time in Paris, made sure to express his admiration.[12] Hans Richter, a member of the original Dada group, asked him to be in a film, 8X8, with Alexandre Calder, Max Ernst, Yves Tanguy, and Marcel Duchamp—creators who knew that art, as he liked to say, was just a game whose conventions changed as the players grew tired; in his enthusiasm, Cocteau even conferred his American rights to a literary agent, behind Gérard Worms's back, in the hopes of acquiring the glory there that he had been denied back home.

In Amsterdam, the whole auditorium stood up to sing the "Marseillaise" at a screening of *La belle et la bête*; Great Britain was deeply impressed by a writer who could also draw, paint, make films, and design sets and costumes. W. H. Auden, the friend of Christopher Isherwood and Stephen Spender, had just translated *Les chevaliers de la table ronde,* and a young film director had remade *Les parents terribles.* Auden had taken advantage of the occasion to praise the miraculous convergence of his gifts: "His drawings are drawings, not uncolored paintings; his theater is theater, and not reading matter in dialogue; his films are films, not photographs brought to life."[13] But what did the French know of the great Auden?[14] Haunted by the idea of becoming a world-famous figure, like Chaplin, Cocteau dreamed of going to Japan, where he had fans who regularly sent him letters. "Last year," wrote Emmanuel Berl, "as I was talking to my wife at the port of Helsinki, two Hindus asked us, 'Are you French? So where is Jean Cocteau?'"[15] The writer's life was envied everywhere in the world, except in France, where Cocteau's jealous peers had been given only one or two gifts in the cradle, and continued to see him as the would-be aristocrat he no longer was, a golden pariah.

He began to hate Descartes, the visionary who believed his Method would make him live for 250 years, and in the name of which his own visions were derided. That idiot had got it all wrong. Yes, if France thought in squares and did not permit itself to exceed common sense, it was Descartes's fault. "I do not think, therefore I am," became Cocteau's personal motto, reversing Valéry's own slogan to declare "Intelligence is not my forte."[16] He who refused as a child to imagine that the practical object below the Christmas tree was a gift for him considered unpoetic a country that dreamed only of sending its sons to the École Polytechnique. The only obstacle that kept him from moving to Italy—that warm, colorful country, less cerebral and guarded—was the language. Take southern Italy, for instance, with its lively, credulous people who adored their gods even as they laughed at them!

Sometimes a critic writing about Cocteau's work suspected his inner conflict and tried to give him an existential dimension. Cocteau would feel enormously grateful, as if he were finally being offered shelter, if not a new body. He would send the critic an emotional letter with poignant confidences: "I have almost always lived *entre chien et loup,* one leg on earth and the other in the abyss," he told Pierre de Boisdeffre.[17] "The result is some works in which I fight against my own conflict, others in which I accept it, still others in which I fail clumsily."[18] Other times, when he would go looking for a missing piece of clothing, he would discover an old press clipping and pieces of his past would flow back to him through those yellow lines. There were the wonderful phrases that Proust had devoted to Cocteau's first collection, for instance, or the article that Colette had published after the opening of *La machine infernale:*

The ring of fire encircling the long familiar prodigies like a cloud promising thunder has not yet gone out for Jean Cocteau. He knows serenely that hell is a certain shade of violet, that to move from life on earth to death is to lean gently on the molten silvering of an indescribable mirror, that in order to fly it is enough to wave one's hands, to lightly raise one's heels and confer oneself to the air.

The author of *Chéri* added, after noting the magical quickness of Cocteau's intellect and his inexplicable nature,

> I am content to watch him, and envy him, as if he had retained the gills human beings are born with, in their amphibian beginnings, and which are destroyed the moment the newborn takes its first breath. Jean Cocteau's audacity predates earthly life. He doesn't invent, he remembers.[19]

At the time it was written, this "admirable" article had been lost amid the mass of reviews inspired by his play, but now it brought him to tears. No one else had read his heart with such sensitivity. To his neighbor Colette, who was grouchy with a coarse appearance and rough accent, but who was adept at spotting what was unique and wonderful about him, his skin and bones seemed to be made of glass. Cocteau the "crystal factory," suddenly warmed by this unexpected fuel, began to work even more.

SANTO SOSPIR, OR THE SOLITARY RETREAT

With the friend of his dreams, the son of his dreams, a staff of cooks, and unlimited chauffered rides in a Bentley, Cocteau abandoned the rue de Montpensier and his house in Milly to spend most of his time at Santo Sospir, close to Cap Ferrat. The days were spent either on the deckchairs on the grass, on the hundred steps carved into the rock that led steeply down to the sea, or in the dining room overlooking hibiscus flowerbeds. If he needed to be alone, there were twin beds in his bedroom (christened "la chambre des sages," or bedroom of the well-behaved), which, while discouraging of erotic shenanigans, allowed him to lounge at his leisure or write on his knees. If he wanted to read as the sun set, the park offered him its shady nooks, rich with the scent of wild strawberries. He had long needed a dramatic climate to feel fully alive. But the fire that "endlessly lit up in [his] rooms that [he] fle[d] while stealing the fire," seemed, in retrospect, a misery, compared with the calm and simplicity that reigned over Santo Sospir; this life amid the elements calmed his complex spirit, and he was all too happy to see the enchanted sun of the Mediterranean chase away for good the funereal ambiance of the war.[20]

Francine Weisweiller soon asked him to decorate their villa to his liking. He bought a pair of overalls, some primer, some matte and some shiny paints, and began to "tattoo" the walls of the house and stairwells with unicorns and fishermen. He woke up at 8 a.m. every day to get to work after answering his letters. Francine got up at 11 a.m.; Doudou at 1 p.m., right before lunch; and in the afternoon everyone came together to paint. Cocteau was impressed by Doudou's progress; he had become more precise without losing his enthusiasm. Whereas the fashions of the time encouraged painting by bursts, Doudou took all the time he needed to work out a detail. In the evening, he could often be found trying to perfect one of his "divine" paintings in a silence that was sometimes interrupted by his voluble mentor, who was frequently wanted on the telephone. When the sun, as it had every evening for millions of years, began to set off the coast of Cap Ferrat, Cocteau's heart sped up. Between this woman of the world, beautiful and loving as a godmother without children of her own, and this gifted young worker, had he not gathered together all the products of a successful life? Was he not, in that moment, a man blessed by the gods, who since 1950 had seen fit to make him truly a star, appearing in color in all the magazines?

After several months of work, the villa had become a reflection of his unique universe, down to the mosaics on the floors. Here Orpheus played his lyre, there the Greek gods frolicked, elsewhere a group of Villefranche fishermen gathered. The tables, the chairs, and the sideboard made of bamboo cane recalled the pipes they smoked and that lightened their summer happiness; it was like being on endless holiday. The villa took on an almost mythological air when the sun changed the sea into an enormous red expanse. The gods and kings of Greece themselves seemed to have assembled on that windy perch to escape the idiocy of the times: Doudou was Eros, and Francine, Croesus. Colette had doubtless steered her boat more wisely—she who had never even thought of writing when she started out had ended in total literary respectability, by giving herself the luxury of seeming to disdain fame. But Colette had never managed to do what Cocteau had done. Stuck in bed with arthritis of the hip, like a great mammal scratching at the air with her pen, she was waiting for death in her apartment in the Palais-Royal while Cocteau enjoyed the sun, the wind, the birds, the elements, setting out to sea in the afternoon and eating the best lobsters in the Mediterranean.

Linked by their reflections in the mirrors and the opium smoke, he, Doudou, and Francine were like an adoptive family. When they went to the Harcourt studios, they were photographed as three couples. But to see them in the blue light of evening, Doudou painting on the terrace, Francine in the garden, and Cocteau a little farther up, drawing both of them, like three points on a magic triangle, they resembled one entity, an eagle with three heads. Invitations for events, too, were sent to them as a group. Doudou, it was said, went to join Francine at night. But how to be sure? Did Cocteau ever wonder? He didn't ask Doudou any questions when he saw him return at dawn from the nightclubs. He wanted to believe that their platonic relationship was enough for Francine — that she was satisfied, as he was, by the brilliant life he was helping her lead. "He didn't want to know anything about his friends' deeper feelings, worries, or aspirations," said James Lord, a young American who helped liberate France, who was not close to them, it's true.[21] Did the two younger people know themselves what they were doing? It is so easy to mistake one's desires — or one's lies — for reality, under the effects of the opium.

Be that as it may, Orpheus was happy at Santo Sospir. Sometimes the Bentley driven by the cap-wearing chauffeur — "Fernand isn't a servant, he's a friend!" said Francine — silently crushed the palm leaves that had fallen to the asphalt to bring them to dine at the heights of Èze, the village that Nietzsche so loved, where the square with its kiosk hadn't moved since 1900, then left them in front of the Welcome Hôtel in Villefranche, where Cocteau had so many memories of the 1920s. Usually, though, meals were family affairs at the villa, where those attending were lulled by the pure silence of luxury — never a difficult conversation nor a dispute.

In Paris, Cocteau's long-term entourage deplored the influence of this young woman who lacked the intelligence of Marie Laure de Noailles, the talent of Coco Chanel, the singularity of Natalie Paley, the wit of Louise de Vilmorin. But what could Cocteau do? Marie Laure, whose mansion had a view of the Weisweillers', hated him again in secret — "he cheated on me by going across the street," she said, accusing Francine of holding him hostage; Coco Chanel was less and less available; Natalie Paley lived in America.[22] Which one could compete with the frail opium-smoker whose implacable organization gave him the courage, every morning, to keep going? Francine was helping him live the kind of life he'd dreamed about in his very first collection:

> Oui, je veux ignorer tout ce que la terre a
> De laideurs, tout le mal qu'en ses flancs elle porte.
> [Yes, I want to ignore all the ugliness in the world, all the evil it carries in its side.][23]

To thank her, or to help her forget the coarseness of Doudou (who was very Mediterranean with women), Cocteau showered her with manuscripts, paintings, and jewelry that he had designed.[24] His presence, however, was the truly priceless prize; where else could Francine Weisweiller have found such a captivating companion? But she had to share him; happiness is not only good for two people, it's better for three or even more, so the house was made available to guests: for example, Genet, en route to Italy to marry one of his lovers to a rich heiress, or Chaplin, staying with his family on the Côte d'Azur.

They left this paradise only to go to a gala in Monte Carlo, or to the Cannes Festival, which Cocteau presided over three times in the 1950s. The photographers began to show up, surprising him as he walked down the Croisette in a tuxedo, or in the revolving door of a grand hotel, or in the middle of a cocktail party on a yacht. He didn't run from them; he had even approached the ones from *Paris-match*, whom he came to know well. To please Francine and Doudou, he invited them to come to Santo Sospir. Hiding his old puppeteer's sadness beneath a huge, desperate smile, he posed in leather trousers, espadrilles, and a sailor's cap, holding up one of his canvases; or he held a finger in the air, to try to seem imposing and turn the attention of disbelievers in his favor, through the intensity of his aura and the magic of Kodachrome. But these vampires, far from enriching his life, stole the bit of substance he had left.

Balzac had been convinced that human beings were made of a superimposition of ghosts, "foliated into infinitesimal layers of film," and that repeated camera shots removed successive layers until nothing remained but a phantom. There was no better confirmation of this strange vision than Cocteau. Opening the newspapers in the days that followed, he was horrified to see himself in the role he had fled for half a century: that of the toast of the town, the favorite son of socialite gods. He had led the life of a hermit devoted to literature, but one photographer had managed to bring back the frivolous prince! He was wounded to be turned into a puppet this way. It got worse when the interviews were released. The mediocrity of the articles that were created by his interviewers, even after they had showered him with ideas, confidences, and memories, inflicted atrocious wounds to his pride. They never wrote about his poems, his plays, or his autobiographical writings, and they barely mentioned his films and drawings; the article was always about the photos of "stars" he had pinned around his office, the residents of Cap Ferrat he hung out with, his dietary habits, and other gossip for hairstylists. When he was allowed to mention his ideas about poetry, or his long friendship with Picasso, his statements were practically deformed, sometimes through clumsiness, but more often through malice. The reporters were only perpetuating the clichés he had always dragged behind him—acrobat, tightrope walker, and so on—even if it meant denouncing those same clichés elsewhere.

The Cannes Film Festival nevertheless contributed to making Cocteau known around the world. The television news showed him showering the crowd with carnations (back when the battle of flowers was part of the competition) next to the voluptuous Martine Carol, the heroine of *Caroline Chérie*, or the wealthy Bégum, the French spouse of Aga Khan III. Although he brought in less money, the poet became a French export, halfway between Brigitte Bardot and the Renault Quatre Chevaux—a symbol of national excellence. He was recognized everywhere, from gas stations to the airport counter at Orly, from restaurants in Geneva to ports in Andalusia. Though they were often admiring, these people were stupefied to find a celebrity moving among mortals, instead of in a golden sphere. Accentuating the feeling of unreality that had followed him like a curse since adolescence, his notoriety made him feel more disassociated from himself, he who was already so apt to self-divide. He was invited everywhere to describe the Roaring Twenties or the Boeuf sur le Toit, but his true art, his poems and his films, was not very widely accessible. He remained an esoteric poet—although too well-known to be sincere, in the eyes of his rivals.

More than other people, young Cocteau had dreamed of being universally discussed, but now that it was happening, he found himself totally unconnected to the image people had of him, and almost unacquainted with his fame. The Cocteau of the journalists was not the *real* Cocteau, but an aging clown always made to tell the same stories. His fame had slowly become unbearable: the more the fake Cocteau proliferated through press coverage around the world, the more the real Cocteau lost substance. Wandering in the air-conditioned hell of his legend, the poet felt divorced from this being who shared his outline and his voice, but who went around degrading him. The fake, cheap Cocteaux were so widely spread in the press that by dint of spouting ridiculous platitudes, they were slowing down the day when his real work would finally be considered. He could deny them all he wanted; these impostors continued to sap the life from him. "But these are your words!" the editors would reply to him (when they didn't ignore him altogether). "Our reporter didn't make them up, he's not crazy!" As if he were the one out of his mind.

The luxury of the Villa Santo Sospir at least had the merit of putting an end to this awful duplication. The opium soothed his anguish, as well as his already-guarded relations with Doudou and Francine. He was using it in a healthier way than before the war; Francine's money meant he could exclusively smoke *chandoo*, whereas in the past he had been reduced to smoking leftover dross, which was the source of major intoxications. Dreaming during the half-seconds that stretched into eternity, under the gaze of a mynah bird who sometimes woke up to shout "Vive de Gaulle!," the trio were like the sleepers of Ephesus that a fountain had plunged into a supernatural slumber. When the summer came they would go on a cruise on the *Orphée*, and Francine would ask Fernand to join them in the car, at certain stops, to replenish their supply of opiates. Luxury had given to this otherwise very practical woman a sort of irresponsible nature. "She had a little screw loose," said her sister-in-law Jeannine Worms, who wrote plays for the Theater of the Absurd—but that is exactly what Cocteau liked about her.[25]

It was a different world, a "principality," that sometimes reminded him of the atmosphere at the Villa Cyrnos, at Cap Martin, where around 1910 he had met the Empress Eugénie, Napoléon III's widow. More than forty years had gone by, but that part of the coast remained the same. Hearing the waters of the Mediterranean lap against the shore, he sometimes wondered what year it was. Was he in his early years, under President Fallières, when he had whispered to Berl, his partner in Proustiana, "My only friends are very wealthy women and very poor boys"?[26] Had he somehow returned to the middle of the 1920s, that decade that some of them—like Georges Auric, Joseph Kessel, or Jean Hugo— had tried to perpetuate through opium?

IN THE ARENA OF THE MINOTAUR

Helped a little by Communist instructions, Paul Éluard publicly praised the very French poetry of Jean Cocteau. In private, however, Picasso's poet laureate used Cocteau's ambiguous attitude during the Occupation as a pretext to drive a wedge between him and the painter. "You're not going to say hello!" he said in a threatening tone, when, from a café terrace in Saint-Tropez, he saw Cocteau disembark from the *Orphée*. Picasso told Éluard that he could leave, if he was offended, nevertheless he remained frosty toward Cocteau as long as Éluard was there, and even after, for he felt that Cocteau hadn't shown enough enthusiasm for the Liberation.[27]

Cocteau suffered from this for himself, but also for Picasso: since the death of Apollinaire and especially of Jacob, wasn't Cocteau the best placed to comment on the work of the man he had known for forty years? Although the "ravishing waters" of Éluard's poetry were very personal and abundant, in Cocteau's view they did not qualify him to evaluate the violent work of the Spaniard. Hadn't the ex-Surrealist rated Picasso's painting a paltry two out of twenty, in a 1921 issue of *Littérature*—five years after Cocteau had published his own *Ode to Picasso*?

Cocteau had thought he had been let out of this semi-quarantine in 1950, thanks to James Lord, the young American whom Picasso had sent to him, and his friend Bernard Minoret, who was on vacation in Villefranche, but one visit to Vallauris put a stop to his dreams. While an obscure photographer was given a superb piece of reddish drawing chalk, Cocteau was given a shard of pottery whose only merit was that it was signed by Picasso—one of those sadistic gifts the painter so liked to make. Then Picasso insulted Lord for having brought along that "whore" (Cocteau).

In the summer, Cocteau was invited for the inauguration of Picasso's *L'homme au mouton* in the market square at Vallauris.[28] With Doudou, Francine, Minoret, and Lord, he stood in a balcony overlooking the platform where Picasso and Françoise Gilot, his companion since the war, Éluard, and Tzara were sitting among Communist Party officials. During the car ride home, Cocteau railed against Picasso's Stalinist associations; according to Françoise Gilot, he had shouted his own personal tribute to the statue in between each official speech.[29] "He was always sick with Picasso," confided one of his close friends.[30]

When Éluard died, in November 1952, the Party invited Cocteau to lead the cortège taking the body to Père Lachaise, a group that would include Éluard's wife, Picasso, Aragon, Léger, and Tzara, and Party officials. "Naturally the Party organized this to turn a little stream into a great tide; they want this to be Victor Hugo's funeral," Cocteau commented, with that slight tone of bitterness that would henceforth taint his literary judgment.[31] With the poet laureate slot open, he returned energetically to Picasso's side, with the active support of Françoise Gilot, who was herself a painter. The intelligent and determined Gilot had recognized the astonishing humanity of Cocteau—the only area in which Picasso did not attempt to shine. Using the power she had over the painter, whose social life she ran, Gilot (who was even more beautiful than her predecessors—"As a lover, you follow the canon of classical forms; as a painter, you don't," Braque told Picasso) opened the gates wide to Cocteau.[32] Only too happy to be reunited with the champion of his youth, the writer had once again allowed himself to be galvanized by his ability to appropriate forms and materials to create his own art: all the dishes in the world, broken but glued back together, turned to gold between his "miracle hands"; he could make a jute bag and a bicycle seat immediately a bull's head, then the pride of someone's art collection.[33] An adaptable demi-god—not for nothing did he illustrate Ovid's *Metamorphoses*—this Proteus with no inherent style infinitely remade himself.[34] Picasso, as incapable of not producing as Cocteau, knowing fatigue only when he lay down, once again became the writer's flattering mirror. The two artists were both mediums that Painting and Poetry made use of as they searched for new forms, unlike those laborers who have only one thing to say. "One is never more sensitive to the *Cocteau* side of Picasso than in front of Braque," Paulhan said before the war: the art of Georges Braque, who was still faithful to the Cubism that he had aired out and gentrified, only highlighted the links between the two harlequins.[35]

Picasso, protected by his genius, his money, and his dogma; actively supported by Wall Street, Saint-Germain-des-Prés, and the Kremlin; and possessing the prestige of rebellion and the interest in his celebrity—a Rimbaud with the life of a Hugo—seemed to be the living incarnation of the bull worshipped by Crete.[36] Cocteau had to agree; at a time when he himself found inspiration only in fits and starts, the painter went out every morning to start painting a new canvas, and still worked relentlessly. The appearance of lyric abstraction in the United States had no doubt aged Picasso's aesthetic; his Minotaurs in India ink could even seem out of fashion, like Cocteau's Narcissus, but no one dared to tell him. From East to West he was hailed as the prince of art even, and perhaps especially, when his painting wasn't liked; devoted to the proliferating reproduction of his genius, Picasso was more than ever the unassailable unit that *Parade* had consecrated—at once the twin and the opposite of Cocteau.

The painter's glory, in some corners, took an obscene turn. Sanctified by the precocious union of the critics and the market, something neither the Impressionists nor the Fauves had been able to bring off, his name had become value itself, subject to infinite speculations. Ladies with cat-eye glasses begged gallerists by telephone for his paintings, several months in advance; activists brandished his dove of peace in front of all the ministries in the West; from the bistro owner demanding to be paid in a signed tablecloth to the naiad who refused to wash herself once Picasso-Jupiter had drawn on her back, the whole world celebrated his fame.[37] Beyond the artist, it was the celebrity itself that had been visited, bought, and interviewed—and with every encounter it grew. Marx would have been flabbergasted: value was increasing all by itself. Though Picasso had admitted to having broken a few rungs because he could not climb the entire ladder of painting, he was on his way to becoming the ultimate painter, from Miami to Vladivostok.

The man in the street was not alone in applauding this phenomenon: overcoming its frustrations, the whole art world tried to fulfill the wishes of the man whom everyone secretly envied. Reproaching his tendency to repeat himself would have been to let on that they resented him. Picasso had become a kind of taboo, someone who could call one of his paintings a failure—but only to add, with a modesty that brought the naysayers to his side, "I always make mistakes, like God."[38] Nothing could have pleased Cocteau more. The demigod he had dreamed of becoming, in the Noailles days, stood before him, of course more rustic and lewd than he could have imagined, but just as laconic and malicious, rich and triumphant, not to say adulated. "I don't say everything, but I paint everything," said Picasso, who could even draw a crowd with his silences. For this "fairground barker who was so dazzling that one no longer felt it was necessary to enter his tent," as Berl would say of Cocteau, it was a constant subject of envy.[39] How Cocteau would have liked to abandon his airy physical envelope to slip into the virile, hairy body of this double Cyclops with the terrible eyes!

Sometimes, however, Cocteau felt fate was unjust. "They say in advance that what you do is magnificent. In advance what I do is detestable." Fully aware that anyone who spoke of Picasso won fame, and that he was taking a risk in praising him, the writer looked searchingly into his hero's eyes. "It is sad, all the same," Picasso conceded, before returning to his paintbrush.[40] Yet Cocteau had only to hear the painter tell him again how much he valued his plays and his films, and his graphic work before the war, to regain hope—"usually poets draw so badly," Picasso added, naming two of his former flatterers, Apollinaire and Jacob. When the Spaniard had finally told their potter in Vallauris that "only he and I possess the same capacity for work," Cocteau was ecstatic: this royal "we" enchanted him.[41] Picasso became once more his compass and his guiding light; at once variable and pulled together, changing and implacable, the fertile egotistical monster reimposed himself in his eyes as the greatest painter in history.

Picasso's work delivered shots of energy to the viewer: Cocteau couldn't see one of his exhibits without wanting to kiss the walls. It was the very essence of creation that was expressed there with an intense joy—the fruit of the sexuality that made him send, even past the age of sixty, alluring postcards to the painter that were intended to enflame his virility. "Picasso is best friends with life. As for me, I'm best friends with death," he confided to Maurice Martin du Gard, in a clear allusion to his angels, who had so often had difficulty living.[42] Françoise Gilot was expecting a son? They already said that he would be marvelous, like everything else "Pablissimo" did. The bull had balls of gold.

The painter lost no time regaining his former enthusiasm for Cocteau's quick spirit and verbal eloquence, which the Liberation and Paul Éluard had hidden from him. "His Andalusian peasant side, which he played up as necessary, felt a certain amount of admiration for Cocteau the young bourgeois," noted Bernard Minoret.[43] "Whatever was no use to him didn't matter," Gilot said of the man who needed to be the best at everything: one last time the "dandy" who had so impressed him at one time became useful again. Cocteau recorded the best of their conversations in his journal, or hurried to give talks about him abroad, as in Rome in 1953. Helped by his own versatility, the painter respected all the more the constant criticism of someone like Michel Leiris, the author of *L'âge d'homme*, but Cocteau added an almost amorous dimension to his praise. Showered with words, and drawings, and poems, like those heady days in 1916, Picasso came to "borrow" some of Cocteau's best catchphrases, including "the lie that tells the truth," which was his definition of art. Genet then reproached Cocteau for inventing the words that he lent to Picasso or himself, but that was just how things were; Cocteau's greatest pleasure was to improve his friends. "It's my job as a storyteller," he would say: "making animals talk." Moreover, the painter acknowledged Cocteau's supernatural powers, his rich visions: "clouds in which you could embed nails," he would say of them.[44] Initiated into mysteries by Max Jacob and Apollinaire, whom he called the "Hermes Trismegistos," Picasso believed as much as Cocteau in signs and numbers. That's how he knew, the minute he learned François Gilot's surname, that she would become his partner: Gillette was the name of Poussin's mistress in *Le chef-d'oeuvre inconnu*, the novella in which Balzac situates the main character's atelier exactly where his own studio could be found. "Everything is written above," the two men believed.

Picasso was never the one who had to ask for anything; it fell to Cocteau to request their meetings, via letters and telegrams; once the painter had been flattered enough, the request was accepted. Since he hadn't responded to anyone's letters for years (not even to Cocteau's), Gilot negotiated the conditions for the writer's visit, while feigning indifference toward Cocteau, to keep from awakening the bull's jealousy. Disheveled though he was, Picasso's life was nevertheless finely tailored. In Paris, visitors hoping to pay their respects to his old friend Braque could do so only after visiting Picasso; in Vallauris, Cocteau could have access to him only between certain hours; and Picasso was certainly not going to make the trip to Santo Sospir. "With me, friends are never 'thick as thieves,'" the painter said. Though he received guests in espadrilles, Picasso had as many rules of precedence "as the court of Louis XIV."[45] Not for nothing had he titled one of his self-portraits *Yo, el Rey*.

Picasso was in the habit of "rehearsing" with Gilot his professional meetings. If he was waiting for a dealer, he would ask the young woman to play him, and he would play the gallerist, in order to anticipate what hidden agenda this would-be buyer might have and what tactics he, Picasso, might employ in order to unhinge him when he knocked at the door. Cocteau's visits did not require this kind of simulation, because he had never asked for (or received) anything. But Cocteau did have to conquer some leftover timidity, as the day for their meeting approached. The older he got, the more Picasso's vigor inspired both excitement and fear. Given that they both tended to monologue, separately, the opening moments were usually awkward, and the sight of his "cher magnifique" made his heart race. Respecting to the letter the protocol of this king in shorts, Cocteau would try to create an appropriate atmosphere. His interlocking anecdotes would finally draw a little pearl of cruelty from Picasso, which would then awaken that fabulous power of imitation that had so impressed Cocteau's mother's friends. Proust, Satie, and Stravinsky lived again through Cocteau's words and gestures, when Claudel's gravelly voice wasn't yelling at Gide for the "dirty little things" sprinkled throughout his work.[46] All the prewar geniuses gathered around them in Picasso's court, and they lost their heads listening to the lubricated mewling of Simone Simon, the actress from Jacques Tourneur's *La féline*, whom the writer mimicked perfectly.[47]

To further amuse his liege, Cocteau said that one of his Italian admirers, the wealthy Mme Favini, had gone to extraordinary lengths to obtain the right to visit him—and perhaps even to move in at Vallauris—and then "recited" a series of letters in which this imaginary Genoan shoe manufacturer's widow confessed her undying love for him, with a priggishness that made the painter cry with laughter. Mme Favini was such a snob that she listened only to Schoenberg, and was so crazy for the Soviets that she went on a hunger strike when Stalin died, before being driven with insecticide spray from her pallet by her reactionary daughter, who was furious at seeing her fritter away their fortune.[48] Éluard hadn't been buried for six months before the climate became as joyous as in the *Parade* days. With age, Picasso began to let himself go. Impressed by Chaplin's fame, the painter decked himself out in a mustache, a bowler hat, and a cane, and Cocteau did his own impression of Chaplin. Harassed by photographers who lurked as closely as the gardens of Vallauris, the painter took advantage of his simian features to mimic other faces and wear costumes: now wearing a silly hat, there a feathered mask, this Harlequin—whose painting subjects Cendrars said wore eye masks over their faces—would disguise himself as a Sioux Indian chief, an African king, or a shadowy gypsy, before pretending to be a faun playing on the pipes.

For Doudou and his sister Émilienne, as for little Carole, Francine's daughter, it was marvelous to see these extraordinary "grandfathers" playing cowboys and Indians; for Francine Weisweiller, it was a unique opportunity to hear the legendary beginnings of these men who had survived two wars and married off Apollinaire, made *Parade* with Satie and *Le train bleu* with Diaghilev; stayed in Rome with the Futurists and in Naples with Stravinsky—through their energy and their imagination they incarnated the golden age of the century. Gilot herself laughed at them because they reminded her of the old comic teams Gog and Magog, Footit and Chocolat: "When Jean Cocteau is looking forward, he's still in profile; when Picasso is in profile, he's still looking forward," she said, like a true painter.[49] Galvanized by this good audience, Cocteau and Picasso began to play bullfight, Cocteau with his index finger up to his forehead—imitating Chaplin imitating the Minotaur—while the painter would fetch a wooden spoon and a tea towel to play toreador. Cocteau mimicked the old queens who would play the gamine one more time before the arthritis set in, and Picasso the aging skirt-chasers who wanted to prove they were still young: "an old Grock whose hour of glory was past," said John Richardson, his biographer. Who was the clown, and who the king in this strange team—more than a hundred and forty years between the two of them—where were the young harlequins that *Parade* had brought together? The question, once asked, would have been sacrilegious: "Pablo, who was often ironic, had little tolerance for other people's humor," said Françoise Gilot, who had learned this lesson the hard way. Cocteau avoided laughing at the painter whom he both admired and feared: he would never betray the secret code that kept Picasso safe from all criticism.

Bullfighting became the theater in which he and the painter rekindled their friendship, with Picasso rediscovering the classical combat games his father had introduced him to as a child, and Cocteau overcoming his aversion to the sport. In 1918, Cocteau had fearfully described the defeat of a bull spiked with lances that fell to its knees, its tongue dropping down to the sand, and the bloodthirsty Spaniard women stamping with joy on their cloven feet, then throwing their fans to the matador.[50] Since then, however, the oversensitive poet had learned to take pleasure in the drama that almost always ended with the spasms of beasts lacquered with blood. The arena had become the site for a decisive ritual illustrating the hermaphroditism that characterized all forms of art, in particular the femininity of the toreador who courts death and steals virility from the beast, which offers itself to fate.

Though the roles were interchangeable in the arena, they were not between the two friends: Picasso charged and Cocteau evaded. Picasso had to wound to win; knowing himself to be prey, Cocteau had no choice but to submit, hoping to make the most of the service. The bullpen became the center of Picasso's heartless world. On corrida days, they both went into the arena followed by their court—Picasso would sometimes drag as many as twenty people, moochers included. They set themselves up in the first row of bleachers, applauded the best "faenas" (passes), and shouted with the crowd when a horn just missed a thigh. When the matador had finally captured the bull's ear he offered it to them, after dedicating its death to them by throwing them his hat. In exchange

Picasso threw back a watch in which the hours were marked with the twelve letters of his name. Cocteau, the following week, threw his Rolex, whose lesser financial value was compensated for by the earrings that Francine added.[51] Then they let themselves be photographed arm in arm.

In the streets of Nîmes or on the terrace of the Hôtel Nord-Pinus, in the shelter of the plane trees in the delicious Provençal town of Arles, the pair became as legendary as Bogart and Bacall. People came to take their picture, ask for an autograph, extract a drawing, until they chased them to Douglas Cooper's magnificent Castille château, where the two men ran into Michel Leiris, who still felt cool toward Cocteau—but El Rey had decided it would be otherwise. Thus did the idols of the 1920s walk shoulder to shoulder in their fight against old age.

PICASSO THE SLACKER

Back at Santo Sospir, Cocteau would once again sport his Orphic crown. Taking advantage of the Spanish genius's aura, he became a sort of oracle among Francine's guests. Showing off the superb painted ceramic tiles that Picasso had just given him—a first—he got back to drawing, to designing new kinds of pottery, and to recycling the Spaniard's influence into curious canvases and no less dubious tapestries.[52] Learning about this through a third party, the painter felt the irrepressible need to wreck these paintings and ceramics that were so obviously inspired by his own. If Cocteau was going to steal from him, the bull would turn against the frail "banderillero," as Spain had nicknamed Cocteau in homage to his art of driving phrases into his audience's mind. Returning to Vallauris, Cocteau heard some horrible things. He discovered that Picasso, in encouraging James Lord and Bernard Minoret to make his acquaintance several months earlier, had said, "And that way you'll save some money. You won't have to buy his next book."[53] Or he was presented with Picasso's statements in print, which made him feel like a target, as in the interview the painter later gave to Geneviève Laporte: "Every artist is a woman and must be a dyke. Homosexuals can't be real artists because they like men. Since they're women, they lapse into normality."[54]

One day he learned that the Spaniard had called him "the hunchback" and when he published a book or gave him a drawing, amused himself by calling the least imperfection "the shadow of the hump." Some time later, he saw Picasso fix his mesmerizing stare on him before pronouncing the favorite phrase of his father (who was also a painter): "I can only bear my friends when they leave."[55]

Alarmed by Picasso's harshness, who thirty years earlier was already calling him the "tail of his comet," the writer went off without saying another word, taking refuge in Francine's little paradise, then woke up angry. How could Picasso treat him like that—Cocteau, his oldest friend, after Sabartès and Braque—when he could put up with flatterers, bores, and parasites for hours? Sent away like a servant! Cocteau began to loathe the painter. "He can invent form but he has no sense of poetry," he confided to the painter Mac-Avoy, before describing Picasso's divine stupidity, and accusing him of regarding any thinking man as his enemy, like Napoleon the despot.[56]

They had come close to quarreling in 1953, when Cocteau came to announce that he was going to Spain, where Picasso had refused to set foot as long as Franco was in power. For an entire summer, Cocteau had publicly called the painter a brute, and refused his "law of the jungle" in which only the strong gained his respect. Picasso didn't care about anything and reconciliation came swiftly, with Cocteau even subsequently earning the privilege of being able to visit the painter's sister.[57]

Another time, he learned that Picasso had whispered to his visitors, "What Cocteau does best is write prefaces"—as if he hadn't written anything important, but had only been the barker for a phantom work—and this after half a century of friendship, effort, and creativity. Sometimes too a difference of opinion would emerge from a simple aesthetic question: Picasso raged against a painter whom Cocteau had the misfortune of liking, and they rediscovered the abyss separating the naked Cretan women painted by Picasso who would have liked to have made their armpits smell and the ethereal Orpheus that Cocteau was sketching. Cocteau generally gave in during these spats, but once, at the end of a long day of filming in front of Clouzot's camera—it was the first time he had seen Picasso paint continuously—the Spaniard refused an autograph for the director of the studio's daughter, and then gathered up all his sketches, causing Cocteau to have second thoughts about Picasso's rigorous efforts to maintain his quoted value.[58]

So what if Picasso was signing fewer canvases than checks? And what if he was less of a creator than a kind of broker, ready to get in ahead of the demand? When a gangster settled down, in the police novels Cocteau devoured, it was always a Picasso he hung on his wall, and Chanel perfume he offered his moll—obviously not a copy of his *Plain-chant!* And why? Because Picasso had no taste. Let him paint Mediterranean landscapes for galleries in Cannes, sign bronze monkeys for traveling salesmen, engrave women's figures spreading their legs wide to excite old men. The whole world no longer dared to represent beauty. In New York, in the nursery of the Museum of Modern Art, the kids were slapped when they dared to draw something recognizable.[59]

Comforted by the lights of Santo Sospir, Orpheus had begun to look at his own work with a fresh eye. Was he not a far more sincere "artiste" than this destroyer of forms and enemy of beauty? Was he not an artist with a subtler line and a richer palette than this elephant who was still breaking the china, at more than seventy-five years old? They laughed when Jean Marais clumsily imitated him, with his paintings and his sculptures, but what were Picasso's girlfriends doing, and the zealots who plagiarized him? How could one still admire his repetitive paintings, which became more rushed every year? "There rarely exists . . . a true Picasso painting, there are periods painted," he noted.[60] The Spaniard painted in lumps, just as he loved in bulk, without seeing the marvelous qualities of the women who shared his life. The races he organized at "his" arenas in Vallauris? Just "corridacoca-colas" meant to fool his flatterers; touristy substitutes that made Picasso not the hidalgo of Seville that he imagined himself to be, but a kind of Don Juan-les-Pins, a pickup artist with a chain bracelet and the chest of a monkey, genetically doomed to vulgarity.

Who was the true genius of the century? Cocteau, who could draw like the masters of yesteryear! Cocteau, who behaved like a gentleman with women, lending grace to his ceramics and feeling to his paintings! No one else was worthy of the title during the century. Not even that chameleon Stravinsky, who wanted to compose serial music like the younger musicians. The frescoes that he, Cocteau, had created for the Villa Santo Sospir, those were a masterpiece! They emphasized the "deplorable poverty" of the chapel that Matisse had painted for the Dominican order in Vence, which had nevertheless inspired him to do the ones in Villefranche. The tapestry he had lent to the Musée des Antibes outdid all of the Spaniard's paintings, he said, as if he were completely objective. "A painting of mine is an accumulation of destruction," Picasso acknowledged.[61] Picasso was the first to say that he was worthless: Picasso was a slacker!

After throwing his idol to the ground, then sitting on his empty throne, the humbled child got hold of himself. Who would follow him down that slope? Who would dare to say with him that the painter's genius was spent, and shout before the world, "the Emperor has no clothes"? It had been so long since people had thought less of Picasso's canvases than his frightening ability to accumulate them, less of his goal than his movement, less of his aesthetic than his ability to change it. "He is what is known as an abyss, a chaos," Max Jacob had written to Cocteau thirty years earlier, before adding: "Picasso does not exist, he makes himself, as Vico said of God."[62] What good was it attacking that kind of entity? Picasso, at seventy-five years old, was not going to change.

So Cocteau returned to Vallauris, as if nothing were amiss. Encouraged by Gilot, who had made the writer her ally in the game of chess she was playing against the painter, the friendship between Cocteau and Picasso resumed, come what may. Filled with gratitude toward his "chère merveilleuse" who did all she could to spare him the natural aggression of his oldest friend, Cocteau paid homage to the power of Picasso's genius, as one kneels down before a jealous god. The painter was friendly once again; all Maurice Thorez had to do was speak admiringly of Cocteau at one of his openings for Picasso to regard him once again with amazement, then embrace him in front of the photographers, declaring to anyone who would listen how happy he was to be his friend. "I am the only person for whom Picasso feels a sort of passionate friendship," Cocteau wrote: "That is perhaps why he has so often conducted himself towards me in an unworthy fashion."[63] That was it: just as a lion does not apologize for being a lion, Picasso was Picasso—magnificent one day, ferocious the next. Capable of murdering one of Cocteau's paintings with one word, but also of saying to him, parenthetically, "You paint better than I write."[64] Their bonhomie was restored, as lively and ambiguous as the first day they met. A radiant Picasso went around saying everywhere that Cocteau was his "favorite scapegoat."[65]

Stravinsky had reappeared in 1952, when the composer Nicolas Nabokov, the novelist's cousin, had convinced him to perform *Oedipus Rex* at the twentieth-century arts festival. The Russian not only wanted to use Cocteau's Latin libretto, but he also wanted him to play the narrator, which in fact Cocteau had wanted from the beginning, as if to sign the aesthetic casing of the oratorio. Cocteau's costumes and masks—from which emerged the great egg-shaped eyes, made of ping-pong balls soaked in ink-blood—had been received with wild enthusiasm by the audiences at the Théâtre des Champs-Elysées.[66] But this audience, which was more visually than aurally inclined, awakened Stravinsky's aggressive feelings toward his librettist, who had been only too happy to stage the production jointly, since it had been conceived that way. The next day Cocteau discovered to his great sadness severe articles in the press, and then heard part of the audience jeering, which forced him to break out of his role to ask the audience to respect a work created by two men who had always respected the audience. Six months later, he was the only one who still suffered from this little scandal, which had ruined the production for him.

How he lacked Picasso's stony indifference—for Picasso, painting was just a way of exploring his own genius. Or the grasp of finances of the composer who continued to camp out on his ego as on a pile of gold, in spite of his growing alcohol consumption (some had rechristened him "Strawhisky"). When Radiguet died, Cocteau had thought to find a home with the Maritains, but everyone had spat on him; when Stravinsky himself returned to religion, and then to Mother Russia, everyone bowed down. When, made fragile by the

German Occupation, Picasso had abruptly chosen to join the Communist Party, everyone respected his choice; when the portrait of Stalin he had given to *Les lettres françaises* upon the dictator's death in 1953 was judged disrespectful by the Party, Aragon was attacked as the director, but Picasso was the one to whom Thorez apologized.

Cocteau continued to wonder about this difference of treatment. He was the only one not to have received official training, unlike Picasso and Stravinsky, but he was also the only one whose modernism and genius was called into question. Maybe he had been wrong to show off, during his society period, and to be prideful to the point of "ridiculousness."[67] His early years were still with him; half a century later, this elderly, unhappy man could not wipe away the memory of the frivolous prince. "In Paris, those whom one believes to be the most evolved, the most liberated, the most free belong forever to their milieu," Cendrars said right before the war. "One of them is the son of a great bourgeois . . . the other has just arrived from the provinces . . . and both of them are 'marked' for life."[68]

Cocteau saw Picasso again a year after Françoise Gilot left with Claude and Paloma, their children. The painter, who had never been abandoned, wanted to mark the occasion; he demanded that the Louise Leiris gallery break off their contract with Gilot, then threatened to take it to court. Cocteau was one of his very few friends, with Braque and Giacometti, to dare to stay in touch with her. This kind of "noble neo-Christian" gesture was ordinarily met with severe sanctions, but Cocteau had behaved the same way with Dora Maar, and Picasso had gotten over it.[69] Once the honeymoon was over, Picasso rediscovered how much he loved to destroy the faces of his mistresses. By contrast, Cocteau remembered how respectful he had been toward Marais's beauty. "The woman in Picasso loves men more than the man in Picasso loves women," he wrote, knowing full well how difficult it was to be a third wheel to that couple.[70] This was true even though he had been "reinstated" as poet laureate after a twenty-seven-year hiatus—a privilege denied any of Picasso's former mistresses.

Picasso soon became interested in a young woman who worked for the pottery makers in Vallauris, firing their ceramics. His Parisian entourage, led by Michel Leiris, found her beautiful though hardly the equal of Dora Maar or Françoise Gilot intellectually. But Cocteau gave a warm welcome to the new arrival, who made herself indispensable by organizing the domestic life of the man whom she literally treated like a monarch, calling him "Monseigneur." Bombarded in turn with letters and telegrams, Jacqueline Roque unreservedly befriended Cocteau, who proved to be a precious means of bandaging the wounds inflicted by the bull. Cocteau could be found more than ever at the painter's home when he and Jacqueline did up the Villa Californie, atop the heights of Cannes. The former queen Géraldine of Albania had lived there in exile, and the writer amused himself by imagining her relationship with the former king Zog, dreaming up more and more outlandish exploits for them. Returning from Rome, Cocteau talked about having seen the cardinals at Saint Peter's, whose trains had been shortened on orders from Pope John XXIII, and how they had looked with envy at the cardinal who had recovered all their scraps and sewn them to his own robe. Then Picasso, who listened to him while smoking his pipe, would slap his thighs, as Stalin used to do—neither Leiris or Aragon told such good stories.

For some, Cocteau was on his way to becoming el Rey's fool, the blood of an old vampire who, when he had his fill of admiration, would go and work through the night. But nothing made Cocteau more proud than seeing his presence encourage the genius's work. Had he not demonstrated his powers to Radiguet, and then to Genet? The strong must be protected, said Nietzsche. Also, when James Lord asked the painter of *Guernica* to break his silence, in an open letter to *Combat* published when the Soviets were crushing the Budapest uprising—between three thousand and ten thousand people died—Cocteau was the first to defend Picasso. "These things should be debated between us, face to face, never in public," he wrote to Lord.[71]

It was decidedly impossible to attack Picasso. A few months before his death, recounting his life for Roger Stéphane's camera, Cocteau could not keep himself from adding, after describing both how he first met Picasso and Jacqueline's protective shadow: "I love them, and I know that they're watching me right now."[72] The painter's gaze hung over the atmosphere, anywhere he was mentioned. Not in the way of the Christian God whom Dora Maar had begun to worship in the hope of forgetting him, but like the Aztec gods who are worshipped with human sacrifices.

THE CHIAROSCURO OF A JOURNAL

Cocteau's renewed confidence led him to pay homage to the geniuses who had influenced him, from Picasso to Rilke, or those whom he had only briefly encountered, from Kafka to Gaudí, in order to add a new stone to the anti-original aesthetics he had developed with Radiguet. As in the *Plain-chant* days, he wrote in rhymed verse, relying on the total sincerity of the confession and the rigor of assonance, which he carried out by invoking two great poets, François de Malherbe and Charles d'Orléans. He had very early on made the alexandrine form his own, and it blossomed with astonishing ease in his verse while he wrote *Clair-obscur*, though he also used his ability to manipulate words in all directions, as in the eye of a kaleidoscope, to escape both the "dead order" that threatened any poem in alexandrines, and the dreaded "fatal disorder" that he fought against.[73]

For *Clair-obscur*, he not only wrote a preface, but also went so far as to write the articles that he had hoped the critics would write about this "unique" collection. The reviews, as he expected, were mediocre and wounding. He reexperienced the "salty wave of nausea that invades the mouth after a ripening book falls from its branch and splits in two on the ground . . . and the birds rush to peck at it."[74] Morand was one of the few to understand and love the collection, which he compared to a freshwater pearl beside a lake: "What beauty, touched . . . by your precious genius. And so *young*, fresh as snow."[75] It was a balm that could not soothe a bloody heart, in spite of the admiring letter sent by Gaston Bachelard, the critic who nevertheless preferred to cite Éluard in his works, when he mentioned a writer of that era. Claude Roy, too, took advantage of the occasion to write a text—"Pour servir à un portrait de Jean Cocteau"—which remains, along with that of Claude Mauriac, one of the best analyses of Cocteau's work written while he was still alive.[76] Much more favorable than *La vérité du mensonge*, this brief essay wounded Cocteau, however. He saw only the negative aspects of it, writing "That's bad!" in the margin of the passage where Roy wrote of his "gentle heroism," of his small masterpieces, and of his "truly amusing and sometimes moving work.'" He was not even happy to see himself compared to "a grown-up who had sworn to a child to make his dreams come true": it all smelled too much of haphazard scribbling.

Cocteau had always been generous toward his peers, but so many of them had returned the favor with unfair criticism and ridicule that he began to be intolerant of the criticism he received. His indefatigable drive to write also made him regret, for some time, having made his protégés famous, more than himself. He was not so much exhausted by his exuberant life as humiliated by the poor response he had received. The more his critics and fellow artists pulled him down, the more he craved justice. The great writer of the time was Jean Cocteau, he would say forever. "If (by some miracle) you discover who I am and what I have done, you will die of shame," he wrote in 1961 to Maurice Martin du Gard.[77] No one was worthy of him, neither his rivals nor his friends, whether he had praised them, like Valéry or Sartre, or had always been severe toward them, as with Giraudoux or Malraux.

He believed that Proust had too dark a vision of his characters, that he discarded them like a painter's empty tubes. In real life, Marcel had ended up infecting with bile all the letters of praise he sent to his idols, for lack of responses worthy of his genius, and to revenge himself on the members of the faubourg Saint Germain who had so unjustly kept him at a distance. So Cocteau deemed Proust's work "fake" and the man himself a hypocrite. Not for one moment did he guess that he too was poisoning all the praise he had lavished on his friends. The whole world could be in ecstasy over the prodigious work of the *Recherche*, but every year Cocteau became more reserved. Literary criticism may well judge the question of sources to be taboo, but Cocteau was in a good position to know that Proust hadn't made any of it up, in spite of his modifications: the duchesse de Guermantes was quite literally their friend Mme de Chevigné, without the yellow teeth or the salty language; Baron Charlus was quite simply Montesquiou, who was known to be arrogant and royal but after *Parade* became "paunchy, made-up, dyed, wriggling his derrière"; Albertine the "prisonnière" was none other than the stupid bellboy whom Proust had "housed" and forced to paint—a vulgar boy who had confided to Cocteau, "We're dying in there!" before feminine wiles lured him away from poor Marcel.⁷⁸ Knowing the true mediocrity of the people whom Proust had tried to mythologize, Cocteau would not cease to deprecate the *Recherche*, after having once been its most ardent and precocious defender.

It is true that Charlus, like Françoise, was an unforgettable character, but the rest were fundamentally incoherent—saying impossible things, with badly worked transitions and characters summoned suddenly then abandoned. This was not the pinnacle of twentieth-century literature, the ultimate masterpiece of interlocking stories in the tradition of Balzac, but rather a stifling amplification of the fragile short stories about socialites that Proust had written in *Les plaisirs et les jours*. It was "a heap of absurdities, mixed in with slices of bravura," offered up in such an asphyxiating atmosphere that it was tempting to wear a mask, he added.⁷⁹ The striking incoherence of the "historical" figures of the faubourg Saint-German as deployed by Proust had a very simple explanation: "He wanted these ghosts to be what they no longer were, to bring them back to life," he noted.⁸⁰ But why turn his lovers into women on paper, as if his mother were still spying on him, and why, on the contrary, lend all of his "vices" to the other characters in the *Recherche?* Everyone turns out to be gay, with the sole exception of the narrator, in *Le temps retrouvé*. More than the sentences bristling with whiches and whoms and but-thats and by-whiches, more than the labyrinth of parentheses that would have made a marathon runner asthmatic, it was the dissembling that Cocteau could not forgive. Thirty years after his death, little Marcel was still lying about his sexuality to the whole world, as he had that long-ago day when he challenged Jean Lorrain to a duel for having "denounced" him.

Especially infuriating for Cocteau was that the sickly Marcel had found the ultimate literary remedy for his ills and was assured, like Nietzsche, of robust posthumous health with his *Recherche*. How could someone so fragile— someone colonized by so many other minds, from the aesthete Ruskin to the dandy Montesquiou—have so expertly used them to his advantage? How could such an idler, someone infinitely less precocious than Cocteau, have made himself so unassailable, when his books could be read as a collage of pastiches of Saint-Simon and Madame de Sévigné? And why had Jean Cocteau, on the contrary, that tense and slender genius, with such similar sensibilities, been able to produce only a crumbling literary monument? "Anything important, we have learned from anxious people. It is they and not other people who have founded religions and composed masterpieces," Proust wrote.[81] Did Proust's offense lie in overshadowing that other neurotic author, Cocteau, to such a degree that, after Proust had finished his cycle of frescoes of recurrent characters, he would cast a lasting shadow over the modern novel?

Sachs's revelation that, by the end of his life, Proust needed to see rats gnawing at themselves in a trap to get off, was the nail in his coffin for Cocteau.[82] He remembered Marcel demanding that a photograph of his mother be visibly displayed in his bordello room on the rue de l'Arcade, in order to achieve pleasure—a detail that seemed to be confirmed by the recurrent theme of the sullied mother in the *Recherche*. All this, along with the frightful complications that Proust added to their friendship, in which he had no longer believed, and the "sickly snobbery" that made him esteem too greatly the puppets of faubourg Saint-Germain, yet plunge him into an unhealthy ecstasy whenever he met them, an experience that would always end in horrible fits of denigration. "Poor, poor Marcel," wrote Cocteau, as his mother might have. "Poor sickly boy with the eye of a madman. He never knew love. He only knew the demonic tortures of his lies and jealousy."[83]

Cocteau still admired the writer, but could not absolutely dissociate the man from the narrator as could Berl, who at one time was also very sensitive to the worrying amorous pessimism of his former friend, and to the inconsistencies of his narrative.[84] By this point only tolerant of those he considered upright individuals whose work was "pure," Cocteau confided to friends, perfectly assured of his "moral cleanliness," that Proust's work was a "mountain of shit."[85] Sachs's perversity, or the pleasure that Gide took in leading a child in rags from his attic room to give him the Socratic treatment, repulsed him as much as Céline's scatological obsessions and his macabre reply to the feminine joy of childbirth did. The omnipresence of Evil haunted Cocteau, this man who was also happy to have a "healthy" sexuality directed toward consenting adults.

Proust mythologized the aristocrats of the noble faubourg in order to watch them dissolve in his analytic acid, like Genet with his pimps and fags in the penal colony. As for Cocteau, he was proud to have brought angels, not garbage, to life. He was reproached, through mentions of his brother-son-lovers and other eroto-literary alter egos, of playing himself over and over. But who were Genet's characters if not puppets whose master had stuffed them with sawdust and brought them to life with false passions—entirely patched-together creations, dramatized and fetishized by an omnipotent narrator! The "love songs" of a man who had never loved anyone were mere products of his fantasy, cultivated to the point of autism.[86] Proust had never managed to have a relationship worthy of the name, in spite of the thousands of toadying letters that had made naive boys believe he was love itself—letters that Cocteau, in the end, read as pure fictions, and had always refused to see published. When Sachs stole them, it had not even bothered him.[87] Why did people extol the cruel novels of these men, and not his own books, which were so much more human? Because they remained sketches, rather than paintings? But then why was Satie so celebrated, when all he had done was sketch out his frail music? Why the Pléiade for Proust, and silence for him?

Cocteau's marvelous *Plain-chant*, in which he spoke of his jealousy of the bodies that Radiguet encountered in his dreams, seemed to him infinitely more "Proustian" than the absurd rantings of a narrator who preferred to see Albertine go to the Trois Quartiers rather than to the Bon Marché, a bigger department store where she would have attracted more desiring gazes.[88] Because he had often loved, Cocteau knew very well that love was not the "policed illness" that Proust endlessly called it, but the desire to fulfill the other, hoping to be fulfilled as well.[89] Only Radiguet and his masterpieces in which everything was said of desire, without being too crudely showed, escaped this kind of massacre. Radiguet's *Le diable au corps*, in all its adolescent cruelty, was worth more than all of Genet's jigsaw novels; Radiguet's *Bal du comte d'Orgel* described infinitely better than Proust the social and amorous functioning of those survivors of the upper classes. To say nothing of the novels that Bébé would have written, if destiny hadn't torn him away at twenty years old . . . How could the critics dare, in praising the first Robbe-Grillet they came across, to steal bread from the brilliant child whom Cocteau had carried within him?

After having spent his life praising his rivals, the poet now unleashed his vitriol without hesitation. They had all usurped their glory; all reputations being made were the result of a trick or of chance, of vice or ignorance. Honestly, there was only Cocteau who mattered, in this circle, so he didn't want to read anything other than police novels and science fiction. Anything else, in literature, no longer interested the former altruist. How could a writer admire anyone besides him? "He would write what that person does," he said, in a final confession of his own mimicry.[90] His books had become his only reality, their future his only worry, their glory his ultimate desire. But wasn't this exactly what Proust had wished for him, back in 1913?

AMONG THE "IMMORTALS"

Cocteau's life was exhausting. After participating yet again in the Cannes Film Festival, which tied him to his seat with "kilometers of film," he left for Spain to attend the "feria" in Seville, where the bullfighter Damaso Gomez dedicated one of his bulls to him. In June 1954 he suffered a heart attack when he was going with Jouhandeau to the place de l'Étoile; he found the energy to convalesce at Santo Sospir, but the strong medicine had terrible side effects. He could not reread the notes he had taken during the feria, and had to call on a young writer to transcribe his hieroglyphs. "His enormous mouth, thin, tense, was like a gash in his face," recalled the young writer. "The famous nasal voice with its metallic inflections sounded like the screeching of a grasshopper, or a cricket. Thin, nervous, peeled alive, an insect waved its antennae, feeling the air, palpating my face."[91] An old healer who lived in the Midi came to visit, on the young man's recommendation. Mario only had to show up and the goodness in his face began to act on Cocteau, who immediately felt the astral waves emitting from his body, and after a few meetings, began to perk up and thought he was healed. Paid in manuscripts, the healer left calling him "cher maître." But the true remedy came when Cocteau learned that he had been elected to the Royal Academy of Belgium, taking the place of Anna de Noailles (as well as his friend Colette, who was the first successor but had just died). In another time, he would have been bothered by a consecration from this order, but this turn of events made him very happy. His body was going to sit in the place of the woman whom he had so admired when he was just starting out, as well as one who had supported him for so many years.

Two months later, he was elected during the first round of considerations to the Académie Française, after a quick campaign led by André Maurois and Pierre Benoit. The "Immortals" consecrated his unpredictable spirit, his rich command of language fed by an "extraordinary mind," his hard work, and the "almost unprecedented" courteousness of his visits, all gestures that the Academicians found admirable. "Tired of being taken for a tightrope-walker, Jean Cocteau desires to sit down," as Maurice Martin du Gard put it.[92] It was a true deliverance for the writer who still sought, at sixty-six years old, a literary family, and suffered from his orphan status. The Académie was a haven, the perfect foundation for a comeback. "The dragonfly whose wings have vibrated above our heads for half a century, this ravishing and irritating dragonfly who would never land, has finally landed on the back of one of our forty seats," noted François Mauriac, wryly. He who had occupied his own seat for twenty-two years, at the thought of this enthronement, suddenly found the energy to fight these academic sessions in which "two old men come to blows over censers and cries of victory."[93] He displayed an admirable amount of vigor for a Christian who as early as 1935 had replied to a first mention of Cocteau with "the Académie does not want poets," and who, left embittered by the squabble over Bacchus, had loudly voiced his indignation in finding in *Clair-obscur* poems with erotic connotations.[94] But it was typical of this "mean ladybug on a grape leaf," as Cocteau called him.[95]

"Consult one last time, dear Jean, the mirror in which your life is over and done with," Mauriac added, as if casting a spell, but the wicked witch with the broken voice could do nothing to stand in his way: by awakening the big shot so clever at "working" the room, the preparations for his reception had physically rejuvenated Cocteau. Happy to finally give public proof of his future glory, intoxicated by the letters and telegrams being dumped on his "head like a dowager duchess," with his hair "arranged in a tiara," he drew the whole world around him again.[96] "He who was famous before being known," as Marc Lambron said, seemed to have finally found a new equilibrium.[97]

In his euphoria, he even sent to Vallauris annotated sketches of his academician's sword, which Picasso "had" to design for him. Now that he was thought important again, Cocteau reacquired the imperious tones that he had had during the preparations for *Parade*, when the rising star of French letters had directed with great discipline the very first dramatic attempts of the poor Spanish painter. Picasso put him in his place by sending him sketches like something out of Arcimboldo, for the hilt of his sword: the croissant, the little spoon, the long butter knife, and the coffee cup he drew for the handle would have caused quite a stir among the Immortals if the Vallauris dentist had agreed to melt them into gold, as Picasso suggested.[98] With one thrust of his horns, Picasso reminded Cocteau that although he knew how to be generous with those he disdained, he also took a keen pleasure in torturing those he loved. "El Rey" was ready to be adored, not to sponsor Cocteau's glory.

Cinched into the uniform that gave him a green wasp-waist, like a young man of (three times) twenty-three, the new academician presented himself with his own sword constructed of a lyre, a star, a profile of Orpheus, and other kitschy objects. Meanwhile Picasso, refusing as usual to go anywhere, sent instead Paulo, the son he had had with Olga after *Parade*—a somewhat ambiguous tribute, since his son, who was nearing forty, had never thought of becoming anything other than his father's chauffeur. Cocteau had barely been elected when he said, during dinner, "As an academician, I have control over everyone, except a cardinal and, of course, Picasso."[99] The painter would later retort, to someone astonished that Cocteau hadn't even had to wait a minute to be accepted into the elite group, "That's because he'd been applying for a hundred years."[100]

When Cocteau was young, the great Sarah Bernhardt had invited him to recite his poems in her home. He had arrived damp with fear, and the public had laughed so hard that he believed his reputation was ruined. But on the spot he had a burst of courage: "Ladies, Gentlemen, it is my honor to perform for you a monologue entitled 'Stage Fright.'" It was a brilliant pirouette, and because of it Édouard de Max noticed his genius. Some of the Immortals expected an entertainer, if not a socialite ready to shock; instead they received a grave, brilliant, and individual moralist. "To a stateless person, you provide identity papers, to a vagabond a rest, a ghost a form, an illiterate person a dictionary, a seat to a tired person, to a disarmed hand a sword," he said in a dry, metallic, and almost anguished voice.[101] Without mentioning his predecessor, one of the Tharaud brothers (which was slightly insulting), he talked about himself and about others in endlessly varied ways, relating his memories like a virtuoso. If he listed those who had sat in the chair before him—"I am like an acrobat balancing on a large pile of chairs"—it was to claim more strongly his feeling of being an outsider, constantly desirous of taking part in the reign of the living, and regularly rejected by them.

He added the necessary amount of color to this meeting by inviting Genet the ex-convict and Arletty the pariah—she had been arrested in 1944—before having his speech translated into prison slang ("tas de ouistitis," or "bunch of monkeys") by the official translator of Peter Cheney, the author of the detective novels he most admired—as if when he joined the Immortals, so did all the urchins and street singers he had so loved. Not to mention the two queens, one in exile and the other in retirement, Marie-José of Italy and Elisabeth of Belgium, whom he had also invited, along with his two last companions, Jean Marais and Doudou. The Immortals had demanded that the former thief's name be removed from his speech, but he encouraged them to make amends for having refused Balzac, as well as other (as they put it) riffraff, the inheritors of Villon and other "sublimely disobedient subjects" who had brought glory to France. How better to pay homage to the genius of the penal colony who sat on public benches, "small, sturdy, like a sailor just off his boat who hasn't yet regained his land-legs"? Finally, the speech aired on the radio and the text published by Gallimard kept, in all its glory, the name Genet, which was still considered sacrilegious under the cupola of the Académie.

The meeting attracted so many people that the invitations were sold for a hundred thousand francs on the black market. Actors, musicians, and ladies rushed for a chance to see this moment — "as if Jean . . . had decided to start an Académie," noted Maurice Martin du Gard.[102] The petition that Cocteau had just signed against repression in Algeria did not dampen anyone's ardor — no one had ever taken his politics seriously — and the absence of Mauriac didn't surprise anyone. The man who had dedicated his last book to him ("to Jean, from his enemy who loves him") didn't want to lose any of the delicious ability to harm that made him write, until his last day on earth, letters warning Cocteau that the horrors he had spread around about him, according to this or that journal, were "pure inventions."[103]

Cocteau pulled himself away from the public's ovations and the photographers' flashes to hop into Francine's Bentley and make his way to the reception she was holding for him at her home in the place des États-Unis. There he found Robert Bresson and Marcel Jouhandeau, as well as Claude Mauriac, the "son" he had forgiven (and future author of *Le temps immobile*, a long-term diary), who told him that his own child would one day visit him so that it could all start over again a third time — "minus the wounds."[104] More literary than the Académie, the queen of Belgium asked to be introduced to Genet. Marie Laure seemed jealous of the glory that Francine received from this crowning. "I love you," the Viscountess was still writing to Cocteau as late as 1917. She resembled more and more a pregnant Louis XIV, according to John Richardson.[105]

Then Cocteau returned to the south and rested while he watched the sun rise (or the mistral make *Orphée* bob in the water) between the pines of Santo Sospir. He made the effort to reply personally to all those who had congratulated him on his election, famous or anonymous. He noted that though it had received positive commentary in the press and on the radio, the serious literary journals, like the *Nouvelle revue française* or the *Temps modernes*, had ignored what they apparently considered a nonevent. The titles he had just received began to lose a little of their reality; soon the Académie was relegated to a corner of his strange memory, as if it dwelled in another place in the space-time continuum, as foreign to his Mediterranean existence as the Cardinal Mazarin was to Sacha Distel, the star crooner that year. After three months in the Midi, Cocteau found himself more or less as he was before he had left, surrounded by the friends of his dreams, but feeling fundamentally separated from them, in spite of his crown of fresh laurels. He was alone, as the infernal Sachs had predicted: worse than alone, in a relationship with himself, as only writers can be, or sometimes homosexuals. "There is something comic to surmount in your name," one of the directors of the *Revue blanche* had warned him in 1914.[106] A victim of the cocktails and the "coqs tôt" (early birds) that echoed behind him, he was back where he started, forty years later.

He had long suffered from being less mainstream than authors like Morand; now he began to believe that he was the victim of a "conspiracy of noise," which was more dangerous for his reputation than silence, for at least silence evoked mystery; instead his legacy was being eroded by the questions that the press asked him, which every year were more stupid. The glory he had dreamed of gave way to an ersatz bitterness; all the letters he had received after his election couldn't take the place of those that true love and admiration would have sent him for eternity, or even of a simple municipal decree bestowing his name on the Cité Monthiers, where he grew up and where the snowball fights of *Les enfants terribles* took place. When a visitor would arrive to extract him from his solitude, his eyes still managed to smile, but his mouth—thin and red as a wound—barely moved. Reduced to his cricket-like exoskeleton, he was like those old men who are human orchestras, playing the drums and the pipe without believing in the music, having played alone for too long. He thought of the miraculous lightness of the *Mariés de la tour Eiffel*, the rivalry of the Mutual Admiration Society, and the joie de vivre of working with Les Six, not to mention Radiguet's endless inventiveness, and his throat tightened. Everyone had lived in symbiosis then; shows had been produced together, forms and ideas mixed among members of the group, bodies and minds loved each other, while today there was only silence and solitude, ambition and a one-man show, mediocrity and an abuse of authority.

He began to dream of a community where he and Morand could work together on a ballet that would be danced by Babilée and choreographed by Roland Petit, where Auric and Poulenc could compose the music for a film he would make with René Clair or Marcel Duchamp, unless they preferred Stravinsky or Hindemith, with whom the writer had planned to work.[107] Maybe none of them had this nostalgia; who knows but that these creative people might be the first to flee this convent of sixty-somethings. During the time of the Saturday dinners, it was Cocteau who rallied the troops and put the absent members on notice. As if all this effervescence hung on his swinger's dreams, in which each would swap his personality for his neighbor's—the way he felt on Sundays, during lunchtime, as a child.

In fact, he was still a child, with his too-short shirtsleeves. The decades could not do away with the ultra-sensitive little boy who remade the world from his sickbed. One day in 1957, he told Aragon he had gone back to the rue d'Anjou;

hardly had he made it past the concierge's apartment than he began to worry, "Oh dear, I'm late for lunch, Mother will be furious."[108] A few years earlier, walking up the rue la Bruyère, he had run his hand along the walls and lamp-posts and heard, as if putting a gramophone needle to a record, the exact timber of his grandfather's voice, the name of the classmate he was walking with, the sound of his cape rubbing against his leather bookbag. That child had never been weaned. He still dreamed of the plays his mother would see, of the actresses whose photographs were in the programs. A number of stars whom he had worshipped before the war had become his friends, thanks to the Cannes Festival. But this meant that those lofty divinities who had been Greta Garbo or Marlene Dietrich (to whom he once said, "Your name begins with a caress and ends with a horsewhip") had lost their mythic radiance.[109] When you know everyone, you can no longer idolize anyone.

To soothe him, a Madonna would have had to whisper in his ear, "You know that you are loved, it's a wonderful thing to have so many friends, to know how to write and always be published, to receive the greatest awards and be admitted to the most private clubs—wasn't it my dream to see you join the Académie?" But this mother figure had died, without being able to quench his thirst. "Poems, essays, novels, plays, the whole crackling body of work," Genet wrote of him in 1950, "it's through the fissures that the anguish enters. An extremely complex and mournful heart that would like both to hide and to blossom. Does a profound intelligence make this work infinitely sad? It trembles."[110] Every night Cocteau trembled in his little schoolboy's bed.

1900 FADES INTO MEMORY

In January 1954, the founder of the Arcadie group—its name an homage to Poussin's shepherds—asked Cocteau to come to the rue du Château-d'Eau to preside over the opening of the only masculine place that would be both joyful and militant. He had responded warmly to this tribute, and wished them good luck. Although Jouhandeau was much more sexually audacious—he reproached the author of *Le livre blanc* for proceeding in this realm "in half-measures"—he had been much less courageous, or at least less generous; he had even predicted the imminent closing of a gay venue that would nevertheless remain open until 1979.[111] At the same time, Cocteau's books won a cult following among a group of American youngsters who, fifteen years later, would play a key role in the emergence of gay culture.

Though always ready to help those who felt alone with their desire, Cocteau did not want to give too clear an impression in this domain. In the preface to the

1957 reprint of *Le livre blanc*, he recalled never having wanted to specialize in his own sex, even if he knew these tastes were a large part of his identity. In this area, everything was permitted in his eyes, for everything was both healthy and absurd. "The bitches mount the studs. The cows mount each other. Disorder is sometimes its own order. The natives of the islands recognized it through their own laws, before the missionaries showed up," he wrote in *La difficulté d'être* before adding, laconically, "A dog married my leg." Some sense of modesty prevented him from going further, and made him deplore the tribute to sodomy that Jouhandeau had just (anonymously) made in *Tirésias*. Likewise, if he wrote of "the family we cannot either brag or complain about, for far from being a privilege, it is linked to a fatality that Verlaine would call a curse," he would never share Proust's atrocious pessimism for the outcasts of Sodom, or agree with the stricken statement that Genet had just made: "the homosexual lacks continuity."[112] And he would never join in the sentiments of Mauriac, who had spent half his life cursing a sexuality that supposedly sterilized its "victims."

Seeing that the younger generation lived more freely, the guilt that weighed on him faded. As is often the case with those who are aging, he feared that too great a liberty would decrease the appeal of the "thing," but he was aware as well that it wasn't really his place to moralize, especially not at his age. Hearing himself on the radio, he thought that his voice sounded like a metallic quacking, and thought he detected the nasal timber of the Sarah Bernhardt years. By turns trumpeting, suave, and declamatory, his voice was always ready to be effusively modest but betrayed the national feeling of superiority that was already waning. It was the last trick of the great prewar illusionist, a survivor whom the Académie Française had made respectable and whom Oxford had turned into a false professor. He alone could still detect a hint of youthfulness in it.

How many people were still alive who could remember the 1910s? When he came across a drawing by Sem, he realized that all the subjects were dead except for him. Mistinguett, too, had just died, before he could see her again—though he had paid tribute in the press to that voice which had given itself to the glaziers and the grinders until it had become the soul of the Paris to which he himself belonged. Fate had led him, two years earlier, to give a speech at Colette's funeral in Brussels: he had revived the adventuress he had met in his youth, when she was only Mme Henry de Jouvenel, "a hairy boa constrictor wrapping itself around the world's neck" (as the young bourgeois Cocteau had written, wary of the Amazon who had danced naked with Missy, her patron, but had been able to free herself to open a shop selling beauty products and to write dozens of books).[113] Nijinsky had died in London in 1950, after thirty years of living in an asylum, in a vegetative state; Misia herself had left the stage.

Following a trajectory begun under Mallarmé's guidance, Misia, a morphine-addicted specter, had ended up beside another ghost, her secretary Boulos Ristelhuber—"the ashes of the duke of Reichstadt," as Cocteau nicknamed him. In 1950 Coco Chanel came to dress her one last time, and then they left to bury her, thirty years after Diaghilev. Étienne de Beaumont had also died, taking to the grave his exaggerated profile, his counter-tenor's voice, his hiccuping laugh, and his friendly disdain.

The survivors of the 1920s and 1930s were hardly getting on better. After the war Cocteau ran into Barbette the androgyne, his lip split by a trapeze accident, his figure stooped. Cocteau had organized a fundraiser at the Boeuf sur le Toit to help him; afterward the pale, shy young man, ill and impoverished, had left for the United States, and ever since had lived alone in Austin, unknown, faded, like an angel whom heaven has forgotten to call home.[114] Jean Bourgoint had finally managed to stop smoking opium. Struck by a divine calling when a fire ravaged Jean Hugo's library in Fourques, he had taken a vow of silence and become Brother Pascal, in one of the strictest monasteries, and kept pigs in the Abbaye de Cîteaux. Devoted to his patron saint, the mystical hobo Benoît Labre, the Trappist was finally "enjoying" the fruits of his first return to God, in 1925, which had been even more fleeting than that of Sachs. Cocteau even received surprising letters from him, when he had thought he was still loathed— Cocteau had said about Bourgoint that all his poetry had been expressed in the book he had inspired Cocteau to write, *Les enfants terribles*. Bourgoint had made peace with himself, and in spite of a few moments of doubt, he would dedicate the rest of his life to God, in deepest Africa, as a missionary.[115] "One thing only is necessary," as Christ had predicted.

As for Maritain, his faith was more proselytizing than ever. Appointed as representative of France to the Vatican at the end of the war, he had tried, according to Cocteau, to convert Pope Pius XII, using a quote from Saint Thomas. "But the Pope is also Catholic, *monsieur l'ambassadeur!*" the sovereign pontiff protested.[116] As for Maritain's wife, Raïssa, Cocteau had made it to the hospital in time to see her enter eternity, forty years after she had brought him back to God. Condemned to silence at the Liberation, Coco Chanel had reopened her fashion house in 1953 and was able, by who knows what miracle, to resume her imperial status. But by dint of solitary struggles, the Grande Mademoiselle found herself unable to love, an attribute that Cocteau had in spades, though "under the effect of a fatal numbness," as Edmonde Charles-Roux said.[117] The designer had always been royally generous toward Cocteau, but he had a hard time believing that the woman he had launched at the theater, praised a hundred times in the press, and had never once given up on, could call him an "insect" to her dinner companions, or say she was "really tired of his antique bazaar"—she who had made all the costumes for all his Greek plays! To say nothing of the articles in which, scratching at "his aphorisms fallen from a stony heart," she had called him "a snobby little fag who's done nothing his whole life but steal from other people," before recycling with impunity one of his own phrases, which he had made up precisely for the benefit of her work: "Fashion should look beautiful first and ugly later. Art should look ugly first, beautiful later."[118]

Franz Thomassin still regularly knocked on Cocteau's door. Although the housekeeper, Madeleine, had sometimes made him wait in the bathroom/ waiting room of the apartment on the rue de Montpensier among a procession of cats, he was no longer discouraged. Whatever Cocteau was doing, it was gospel for this writer without writings, who worked relentlessly but would not permit himself to publish anything, preferring to collect all the articles that appeared about Cocteau, fighting still and always with anyone who dared to say anything bad about him. "He would walk into cannon-fire, if a friend asked him to," said Joseph Rovan, who knew him during their days in the Résistance, when he was in love with a boy who died in Dachau.[119] Cocteau was still a role model to the chaste, secretive young man, who had converted to Catholicism, and whose intelligence and erudition prompted Chris Marker (the director of *La jetée*) to compare him to a mandrake, the magic plant with a root like the human form.[120] "In the end, you are the only one who really loved me," Cocteau would sometimes tell him, before leaving Thomassin, a thin man with a half-finger who lived off of invitations to stay in his friends' homes, crossing Europe on foot to stay with a man who didn't want him.[121] At last, tired of leaving his innumerable manuscripts in trunks in the care of friends, Thomassin condescended to publish *Vie et mort de Richard Winslaw*, an Elizabethan novel, under a pseudonym. Cocteau wrote the preface, lending his name to this book by "Franz Villiers," which was soon sent to the shredder. It is some of the only evidence we have, along with a few sketches by Matisse and Gilles Aillaud, that such a singular creature ever lived.[122] Pierre Herbart had begun to take drugs again, after Gide's death, and he also lived off of gifts and invitations, in a prideful state of mendicancy.

Panama Al Brown was up to his old tricks. The number that Cocteau had choreographed for him had gotten old; he had opened a nightclub called Kit-Cat in Toulouse, then when the war broke out had returned to New York, where he had lived off of drug trafficking, been arrested, and then started training again, only to be knocked out during his first fight. Long past his fortieth birthday, the "black wonder" had found himself training young guys who massacred him for a dollar a round, and was now washing dishes. "A walking cadaver," said the rare journalists who remembered the prodigy, who was sometimes awakened at dawn sleeping in Central Park. Cocteau went to see him during his visit to the United States in December 1948, the year of Al's last fight in a third-rate ring.[123] He kissed the "old Negro" on both cheeks in the lobby of his hotel, to the surprise of its exclusively white clientele—segregation was still an issue—then, returning to Paris, Cocteau had asked Edith Piaf's partner, Marcel Cerdan, who had become a middleweight champion in 1949, to take the former boxer under his wing. But the newly minted idol's plane crashed in October, and eleven months later Panama himself fell down on 42nd Street, eaten away by tuberculosis. The "old" champion was taken to a clinic on Staten Island, where he died five months later, not even fifty years old.[124]

Natalie Paley regularly sent Cocteau letters or telegrams, to let him know she loved him and was thinking of him. She had remarried, soon after divorcing Lelong, but had never forgotten Cocteau; she not only had *L'aigle à deux têtes* translated, but she also encouraged her new husband, Jack Wilson (the former companion of Noël Coward), and David Herbert (cousin to the queen of England) to produce the play on Broadway. Cocteau was just as faithful, and sent her every one of his books. Thus did they fall back into the strange era when they had both felt things they didn't know how to name. In the summer of 1948, the Russian princess had spent another night dreaming of him with worrying precision. "You have been so indispensable to my mind and heart, that I feel like a little girl again . . . May God always keep you," he read the next day.[125] Seeing her arrive not long after at Milly, with her magnificent lynx eyes, he had thought with intense nostalgia of the "little Romanov" they had almost conceived together, of the poetic-dynastic masterpiece who would have been twenty-three years old in 1956 but who, in his imagination, would have had the same tragic fate as Pushkin; for many years afterward, any mention of the poet's death could make him cry.[126]

Roger Lannes continued to suffer from the sad impotence that before the war had made him the third wheel of the Cocteau-Marais couple. After having published a book on Cocteau, a study that wasn't without its merits but followed him a bit too closely, he had a difficult time finding his own way as a poet. His sexual infirmity isolated him more and more, and he seemed only to live for and through the journal he kept, which remains unpublished to this day. "He didn't die, it's worse," said Cocteau of a man who, during his solitary life, obsessively went to see Visconti's *Death in Venice*, where he found his own stations of the cross.

Profoundly wounded by the Liberation, which nevertheless left him intact physically if not morally, Morand was more affectionate than ever toward

Cocteau, one of the rare writers who had refused to ostracize Morand in 1945. Even better, this survivor of the 1920s continued to treat him like the natural leader of their generation, the god with a thousand arms of the Boeuf sur le Toit, an establishment that the sister of Moysès, who had recently died, now ran. Morand, nevertheless, was aware of the great Cocteau's weaknesses, which in time he tended to attribute to a homosexuality that he finally hated.

Julien Green continued to send vibrant letters of affection; Cocteau had always been the first to show enthusiasm for his novels. Finally there was the unsettling, seductive, gifted lyrical novelist Aragon. A man who possessed a torrent of words (sometimes interrupted by a serpent's hiss), the grace of a court abbot, and a captivating blue gaze, Aragon, the author of *Aurélien*, ignored the Party's muttering and Elsa's tutelage to join Cocteau in the Orphic territory of poetry. Often accused of inconstancy or betrayal, but put on this earth to sing until their gifts were spent, these nightingales implicitly understood one another. Both had begun by dreaming of being a national poet, like Barrès or Anna de Noailles, before being reborn into the avant-garde, during the First World War—and both had returned to their first ambition, endlessly in dialogue with Apollinaire.[127] They had the same gifts for mimesis, the same hidden nostalgia for the lyrical heights of Ronsard, Musset, or Hugo. If Pierre Lepape could say that Aragon had reinvented "all of French poetry since the troubadours, without separating creativity from pastiche," the same could also be said of Cocteau, including his plays.[128] And if Éluard had still been alive (for he too sang of his multiple identities) the three men could have formed as credible—if improbable—a trinity as that which had joined the two Surrealists to Breton before the war.

A real game of mirrors arose between Cocteau and Aragon, each a Narcissus ever more aware of being caught between two generations. "There are not many of us who still know certain things," Aragon said to Cocteau.[129] They quoted themselves clandestinely, through their poetry, creating a strange echoing effect: "Si vous saviez d'où je déplonge / Et l'ombre qui me suit partout / Si vous saviez ce qui me ronge / Si vous saviez ce qui me cloue" (If you knew from how deep I undive / and the shadow that pursues me everywhere / If you knew what gnaws at me / If you knew what pins me down), Aragon wrote in *Le fou d'Elsa*. "Si vous saviez d'où je déplonge . . . / Je ne me suicide pas / Je m'acharne / où tous / se résignent" (If you knew from how deep I sink . . . / and I don't commit suicide / I strive onward / where everybody / else gives up), Cocteau had written fifty years earlier in *Le Cap de Bonne-Espérance*. "Who is this one they're taking for me?" asked Aragon, master of self-betrayal, in *Le roman inachevé*. This was a question that nagged at Cocteau, master of self-proliferation, who could have replied, "Theatre is the name of that interior place within me where I place my dreams and my lies."

Both capable, in the end, of describing anything passionately and in many different styles, Aragon and Cocteau sometimes had difficulty finding themselves in their work. Aragon's creations evoked a kind of mercury flowing constantly from the thousand pens that time, aesthetics, and ideology offered him; Cocteau's writings were like a rhizome capable of giving, depending on the season, generous greengage plums, endless salsify, or coriander sprouts. It was he who best summarized their situation, writing to Aragon at the end of the First World War, "I hardly ever approve of what I write—but one must be oneself to the very end, even if one envies other kinds of souls."[130]

The jealousy that Emmanuel Berl had once detected in Aragon had totally disappeared: the author of *Le paysan de Paris* now saw Cocteau as merely the survivor of his own youth, or the reflection of his beginnings; from Aragon's home in the rue de la Sourdière, to the Palais-Royal, their two monologues continued to intersect.[131] In time, their understanding took a truly affectionate turn. *Les lettres françaises* honored each of Cocteau's declarations. And if someone close to them spoke badly of Cocteau's last poem? Aragon's dry voice would immediately interrupt.[132] His former enemy had become his valiant defender, and would even write a new preface to *Anicet*, his 1920s novel, to indicate his new distance from the "haughty tone"—in demand at the time with the Surrealists—with which he had earlier described Cocteau, under the pseudonym of "Ange Miracle." Aragon was the perfect friend, Cocteau would say before he died. In 1957, the two men were meant to publish a book of interviews—Breton must have choked when he heard—about paintings in the museum of Dresden, which was then in East Germany. In the interviews, Cocteau now seemed the more modern of the two, with Aragon claiming to be hostile to abstract painting and instead supportive of his friends Matisse and Picasso. Sometimes Elsa Triolet, Aragon's wife, would ask Lili Brik, her older sister, to send caviar from Moscow for Jean, instructions that Brik, Mayakovsky's former lover, followed zealously, in memory of the trip that the "Komfut" (Communist-Futurist) poet had made to Paris in 1923. In exchange, Cocteau praised Elsa's latest novel (although her work was somewhat stifled by that of her husband) so that everyone was happy.

Aragon's friendship, after Picasso's endorsement, brought back to Cocteau almost all the leading lights of Surrealism, who had one by one left the group. Cocteau became socially acceptable again, for Max Ernst, who had once been called a "prostitute" by Breton's gang after designing a set for Diaghilev; for Miró, whom Breton had also threatened with hellfire; and even for Ribemont-

Dessaignes, who had just recorded radio interviews with Cocteau. To hear them say it, they realized that their "mysterious hatred . . . was just blind obedience to the leader."[133] In the Communist journal *Europe,* Pierre de Massot himself saluted the release of *Clair-obscur* as being on equal footing with collections by Éluard and Aragon. Apollinaire had supposedly scorned Cocteau, but this was now forgotten; symbolically, Cocteau gave Aragon the portrait he had done of Apollinaire, the author of *Calligrammes.*

Buñuel himself was more than friendly when he ran into Cocteau here and there, whether the two men had to pose for a photographer or do a television show together. Far from reproaching him for borrowing from *Un chien andalou* and *L'âge d'or* for *Le sang d'un poète,* the Spaniard showed on every occasion his artistic goodwill.[134] He even confessed that in Mexico, where he lived, *Le sang d'un poète* was sometimes attributed to him, and *Un chien andalou* to Cocteau. When he presided over the Cannes Film Festival, Cocteau never lacked support for Buñuel films, one has to say.

Abandoning the limp phalli of his paintings with their telegraphic forks, Dalí sometimes emerged from his spatiotemporal bubble to meet Cocteau. His theories on phoenixology, the so-called science of permanent resurrection, intrigued the poet, as we can imagine. Passionate about Christian Science and the irrational, cryogenics and holographs, all methods intended to make genius eternal, Dalí was convinced that humans were soon going to be able to be cloned out of our fingernail clippings, the cells of our skin, and "de-ox-y-ri-bo-nu-cle-ic" acid—bellowed with Dalí-esque rollings of the tongue. These Sunday scientists made each other out to be a rare breed: the writer was "the sharpest pencil in the world," according to Dalí, while Cocteau compared the painter to Vermeer and Velázquez, which basically put him on Doudou's level.[135] "I wanted to convince people of my genius," Dalí confessed to him one day, more observant than he appeared; "modesty and politeness always drove you to convince people that you were not a genius, but you are pure genius and this modesty is only a mask of pride. Take it off and they'll lick your boots."[136] Soon the painter whom Breton had rechristened "Avida Dollars," an anagram of his name, would pose with Cocteau, which only increased their fame. Using up the rest of his latest mimetic ink, Cocteau went so far as to be photographed beside him wearing a fake Dalí mustache. The painter, who styled his mustache with toad sperm and acacia honey, revealed to Cocteau that Breton, "that primitive petit-bourgeois," feared him like the plague. "It was strictly forbidden to describe a dream memory concerning, for example, Mary mother of Jesus—whom I often dreamed about—or even that I was obsessed with ass hair," Dalí would say, after declaring, "Shit scared him."[137] But did this console the former "angel turd"? Soon Cocteau pulled away, exhausted by this true madman who was "pretending to be mad," as Picasso would say, and who was furious that "his" poet laureate was interested in another painter.[138]

They were all old men or ladies in furs now, from Man Ray to Dora Maar to Lise Deharme, whom Cocteau sometimes met at the Hugnets'. It was probably there that Valentine Hugo reappeared, sometime around 1951. Nostalgic and crippled with debts, Satie's muse and the illustrator of the Ballets Russes lived by selling off her memories or through charity—when she wasn't killing her mother a second time to ask her new friends for money to cover the burial fees.[139] Solicited in turn by the woman he would call "the little sister of the rich," Cocteau immediately helped her, although he was in debt to Marais. This simple request for money, after all, was an olive branch.[140]

And Tzara? Having become the indefatigable intellectual servant to the French Communist Party, the former Attila of language sold *L'humanité* on the steps of Montmartre and militated at the France-USSR association. "A man of our time, lucid and of good faith," Jean Cassou had said of Tzara at the end of the war, in a preface to his *Morceaux choisis*, before calling his poetry "romantic" and "epic"—an insult that would have driven the young Dadaist to destroy the author's flat and go off laughing maniacally.

Having only ever obeyed the sibylline messages that he himself sent out, Marcel Duchamp had never stopped sending Cocteau signs of distant affection and courtesy, with an irony that made him closer to Buster Keaton than to Robespierre. This intangible fidelity, coming from a man whose subversive shadow would cover the whole century, but who, in the field of visual arts, had announced the future more than Breton, did Cocteau a lot of good. It was a relief for him to no longer see, when he saw his face in the mirror, "the painful grimace of a soul begging for mercy, flagellated, insulted, alone in the midst of a crowd of enemies threatening him with their fists," as during the height of the "gang's" reign.

Only Breton and Char continued to hate him as in the "good" old days of the Breton band, which had long ago been dissolved in the cascade of exclusions. Though there was also Soupault, the nephew by marriage of the wealthy carmaker Louis Renault, who, as late as 1961—like those forgotten Japanese soldiers who still traipsed around the Burmese jungle—reproached Cocteau for being a bourgeois haunting luxury hotels. Since insults from the Occupation had durably discredited allusions to race, features, or sex, their attacks had lost their violence; but Cocteau-hunting remained a useful activity for exalting membership in the declining tribe.[141] The painter-calligrapher Dotremont, for instance, had been threatened with exclusion in 1946 for having dared to write favorably about the writer who had supported and financed him throughout the war, and all the Surrealist anthologies continued to insult the author of *Le sang d'un poète. Orphée* allowed Cocteau access to the group of filmmakers banished by the band—Dreyer, Bresson, and Rossellini—so not such bad company. Like the insect preserved in amber for millennia, Cocteau continued to ring shrilly, intact, in Breton's mind.

He only reproached the survivors for one thing: for taking away his reasons to say positive things about them. He would so have liked to continue to admire than to have only pure, disinterested feelings toward them! In his spontaneous, opium-infused Buddhism, he almost suffered *for* them for the unkind things they did: he wanted to believe that these unkind acts weighed on their consciences. He knew he was as repugnant to them as the Beast in his film, but at the bottom of his heart, he was convinced that he would win them over, and soften them: "I am surprised they remember the evil they did me and that I had forgotten," he wrote in *La difficulté d'être.*[142] At least they hated him through conviction, not weakness, interest, or blind conformity, like Ernst and Buñuel—those former enemies who had become friends, but whom he respected much less.

HIS HEART TURNS THE OTHER WAY

Cocteau still was not taken seriously on an intellectual level. Leiris and Paulhan, Gallimard's *eminence grise,* and others like them might pretend to be friendly when they ran into him or wrote to him, but he felt keenly that he did not belong to their club—their books never mentioned his name, and their publications never mentioned his work, as if he had no real literary existence for them. They considered him a celebrity, not an important writer, like Proust or Genet; not even an exceptional individual, like Nijinsky or Radiguet. The critics excluded him from the little group of initiates whose name, like their work, would recur throughout languages and centuries. The chosen ones he had so often written about did not include him in return. The frequency of his appearances in festivals or great public gatherings to which he was meant to lend weight or prestige encouraged them to see him as a figure with no specific value, like the joker in a deck of cards. How else could his old "friend" Paulhan have declared to Dotremont, who would become one of the leaders of the Cobra group, "I don't worry too much about Cocteau. He's not made of the stuff of the dead"?[143] Because he wasn't made of the stuff of the living, either?

Complex as they might be, these people with diplomas and these bookworms could not integrate Cocteau into their ways of thinking. Cocteau couldn't be put into a box; he escaped Euclidian geometry. Too chaste to benefit from the scandal of his customs, too protected by luxury to deserve the monk-like aura that he had staked out for himself, he fit nowhere. "My heart turns the other way from yours," he confided in *Vocabulaire*, forty years earlier, adding: "Oh! how I ache." Radiguet, then, spoke of "this colored mask half-hiding, out of pride, an incurable sadness"—but Radiguet was a genius, while these people understood nothing about his impulsive and credulous way of being, or about his taste for magic and the occult.[144] How to explain to them that he could attend Mass one Sunday in Milly, driven by a mysterious impulse, but was also interested the next hour and for the same reasons in the Grand-Duchess Anastasia, the circles of Stonehenge, or the hierarchy of extraterrestrials? Was this not precisely what it meant to inhabit the world poetically? Did one have to be stupid to believe in clairvoyants and radionics to the point of hoping to find through them Radiguet, whose memory he celebrated every year with a text, a preface, or the publication of something he'd had in a drawer?[145] If so, then so be it: he was stupid.

Cocteau easily guessed whom Sartre was targeting in his preface for *Le traitre*, an essay published by André Gorz in 1958:

> A literary journal asked the prince of counterfeit money what he hated the most; he did not hesitate in replying: "Intellectuals." I feel some friendship for this counterfeiter; he is a true poet and a good man, but I had to ask myself what fly had stung him that day. Everyone knew of his paranoia, his monologues about destiny, and time, and life, extracts of a perpetual, supplicating apology, these verbal traffic jams in his throat, his charming hands which are themselves words, which turn, palms out, to protest his grace, that harassed, choked way of thinking, which still continues, jumping nimbly from one thought to the next, without realizing it is running in circles in its cage, those dazzling impressions whose framework can be found in the previous night's writings and which, when they are finished, allow one to glimpse the incurable sadness of an icy look.[146]

Cocteau withstood this new blow. Sartre, who was one of the most generous writers he had ever known, could not resist the easy pleasure of attacking him. These lines may not have been insulting, but they betrayed a strange, not to mention disobliging, commiseration: everything Cocteau did or wrote seemed fundamentally useless. "Sartre was the only one who spoke of him to me with warmth and sympathy," Bernard Frank would say; but Jean Cau, then the philosopher's secretary, said that "Sartre considered him an acrobat and a mandarin who didn't deserve his respect." It seemed that five years of friendship, in the end, had only led Sartre to reproduce these prejudices.[147]

Cocteau only replied to Sartre in order to make one point: he reproached him for using the insult "counterfeiter," arguing that Sartre had forgotten how poets created medals with their own effigies on them, "whereas the counterfeiter stamps his own with the effigy of the Banque de France"—a way of saying that he was his own man, all the same. But the damage was done; Sartre had cast him into the bad faith camp. He had been presented as one of those men who lie to themselves, without the courage to face themselves; one of those impostors who think they have created themselves, but claim at the same time that the gods have guided their fate; one of those reactionaries who overestimate individual liberty, but also social fatalism. "Past the age of thirty, we have the face we deserve," Sartre said. Cocteau did not love his face, so in that sense he did not freely accept his destiny. But why was it necessary to find marvelous a face that time had covered with wrinkles? Must one answer for one's physique as well as one's work? And did Sartre like the way *he* looked?

Cocteau, it's true, sometimes did not recognize himself. His nose had become hooked, like his grandfather's; if he combed his hair, he looked pathetic, so he let it grow every which way, and then was accused of poetic affectation. His legendary flexibility had aged; dozens of literary pregnancies had deformed his hips and curved his back; his side cracked when he bent over to cuff the hem of his jeans. He claimed he was three years younger in interviews, and in order to recuperate the centimeters he had lost would wear a cap that, along with his striped sailor's shirt, made him look like Popeye without his spinach. All of this, in the body of a sixty-five-year-old, betrayed the man who was seven years old at heart.

He had often compared creation to organic secretion; as he grew older, he realized he could no longer produce books and poems with ease. Exhausted by half a century of fighting against anonymity, boredom, and banality; by floods of ink and avalanches of stage productions; by a Niagara Falls of poems and memoirs, letters and sketches, ballets and oratorios, paintings and operas, his extenuated body sometimes perfectly evoked the ruin that he and Man Ray had gone to photograph on Proust's deathbed. During the Occupation, he had felt that he no longer knew if he resembled a young man lost in old age or an old man imprisoned by youth. When he looked in the mirror now, he thought he saw a mask of skin beginning to hang from his skull. Of course he could be part of the small group of people who survive every blow, returning by the window when they've been thrown out the door, but his machine had filmed, produced, sang, decorated, and drawn so much since 1907—the greatest testimony of productivity the century had known—that every day he risked the fate of the electric heating elements of the time, which could remain red for years on end, but were now giving in.

Sartre's verdict, however, drove him to touch up the face that no longer corresponded to the way he felt inside. Already accustomed to having his hair blued at the Hôtel de Monte-Carlo—to the point of confessing, when he caused too much surprise, "Léon went a bit too far"—he resorted to other tricks.[148] A photographer came to capture the fresco he had worked on for a year, with an illustrator called Moretti, and he asked Moretti to drop his cigar ash on his head, to hide the gaps between his roots. Since this method had its limits, he went for a skin tightening procedure. The facelift froze his smile and hollowed out his cheeks, but it did manage to bring out his adolescent face—a small resurrection.

Even if Cocteau went around saying he had kicked his drug habit, including in his diary or to his friend Dubois, the prefect who pitilessly hunted down opium smokers, the poppy had once again become (in spite of Marais's protests) the panacea that helped him through all his ills—the fevers, hay fever, stomach cramps, facial tics, skin diseases, sciatica, and crippling jaundice that had since childhood plagued this man born askew. As indispensable to him as water or bread, these "extreme" naps also had their price: he could forget a name in the middle of a conversation, go off on a tangent, then drift light-years away from the subject or even sit without saying a word, struck by brief moments of aphasia that seemed to anticipate the moment when he would stop talking once and for all.

Since childhood, Cocteau had been familiar with death. His first poems were full of morbid visions of dying teenagers and corpses clicking their bones. While believing himself destined to always be reborn from his ashes, at twenty-one years old he decided death was beautiful and sweet and life harsh; sharply aware of inhabiting his own skeleton under the thin protection of his skin, he lived in fear of his imminent death.[149] "Look at your whole life in the mirror and you will see Death working like bees in a glass beehive," he wrote in *Orphée*, the film destined to halt this merciless corruption—even if the cinema can record, through the bodies of the actors, only "death at work."

Professor Soulié had recommended, against the whole faculty's advice, that Cocteau take a cure in the mountains to help make new red blood cells after his heart attack.[150] Ever since, Francine Weisweiller had regularly brought him to Saint-Moritz. Crunching the snow beneath his feet, playing the only sport that mattered to him, conversation, Cocteau regained the enchanted atmosphere of Leysin, where he and Stravinsky had worked together on *David*, in 1913, in the intoxication of their combined genius. Sils-Maria, the village of Engadin where Nietzsche liked to spend time, was very close. Dressed in a warm duffle coat that swaddled his long, monklike face, Cocteau went walking on pilgrimages through the valleys: the snow and the cold seemed to dilate the landscape, as if to freeze time. Arriving at the pension where the "philosopher with the hammer" had stayed, he fell to his knees to kiss the front steps, took away a bit of snow, and ate it in memory of the solitary walker. This communion perked him up.

Nietzsche was more than ever his philosophical idol. An enemy of idle chatter as well as false science, a sworn opponent of readymade thoughts as well as nationalist ponderousness, Nietzsche had always encouraged him to think quickly, alone, and far ahead, in an untimely way if necessary. Everything pleased him about the lofty morality of the solitary thinker: his growing disgust for Germany, which he integrated into his own refusal of France, and his disdain for his contemporaries' prosaic way of thinking. What a joy it was when he opened one of his books to a random page and read: "a great man . . . is colder, harder, more resolved, and without fear of 'opinion'; he lacks all the virtues which are connected to 'respect' and to being respected, absolutely everything that has to do with the virtue of the herd. If he cannot lead, he goes alone."[151] Something in him responded to Nietzsche's final delirium, when he confessed to his friends, or to Cosima Wagner, that he had been Buddha, Dionysus, Alexander the Great, Shakespeare, and Wagner himself, one after the other! Though *Zarathustra* seemed to Cocteau a little overwritten, a little too "poetic," he continued to believe that *Die fröhliche wissenschaft* was the height of lively sermons, a supreme anti-Bible for the great wounded men of life. Capable of bringing together a million contrary thoughts—the source of harmony, according to the Pythagoreans—Nietzsche had this incommensurable virtue: he tried to express himself in the most succinct way possible. It was the best gift a writer could offer his reader—a sort of sacrifice through leanness. Finally, he knew that the true lyric poet is a disinterested medium, charged with conveying the tension of the world and making concrete the suffering on which it is founded—a kind of relay transmitting, at lightning speed, his own sensitivity.

Cocteau continued to walk, like the "indefatigable chamois" Nietzsche who frolicked on the sides of the summit of the Engadin, reaching the top of a peak or stopping at the edge of the abyss. Invigorated by the icy cold, and with his back turned to civilization, he scanned the magical horizon of the Rhaetian Alps and began to assess things. His life had no doubt been harsh, sometimes even terrible, but the blows he had received had reinforced him. Whatever doesn't kill you makes you stronger, observed Nietzsche, who himself had become a great critical poet when he had failed to become the god of poetry and music. What did it matter if he had seemed to take pleasure from his suffering, and so shocked the conformist hypocrites? Sacred pain! Divine incomprehension! How beautiful it is, blood spreading against the snow! And how much more tonic was this reversal than the miserable glory he had dreamed of at first! Destiny was jealous of the frivolous young prince's many talents, and had deliberately peopled his way with enemies, in order to compress his soul down to its core, like the hairshirts worn by saints—even if his own saintliness had no goal other than his work.

Every insult made Cocteau grow a bit more; every negation was a source of profit; every blow made him bounce back, stronger and better armed. Didn't he love to rewrite every lost text, redraw every stolen drawing, thirty years later if necessary? He was the eternal return incarnated, one of those "mother-men" who give birth and are endlessly re-inseminated, the chosen one in whom Creation, drunk on its own powers, replayed ad infinitum, and who could not be made to contradict himself either by cries or by failure, until it was exhausted. Death itself had no importance, in the end. The sun will go out one day, the earth will become a moon; life will begin again elsewhere, in another form; the same would be true of Cocteau and Breton, Nietzsche and Wagner—nothing would remain of those who had borne these names. How could a man who composed himself entirely through his work ever complain of life, in any case? "The aesthetic of failure is the only one that lasts," he had said in *Opium*. "Failure, the shipwreck of . . . souls built on an exceptional model has the force of law," the solitary walker of Sils-Maria had said, in *Jenseits von gut und böse*. Cocteau would make this Christ-like credo his own until the end.

THE SURVIVOR

oh how beautiful life is
sometimes for no reason
the immortal divine
in the good and the bad
— *Brigitte Fontaine*

TAKING STOCK

Cocteau had lost. He would not be recognized, after Apollinaire, as *the* French poet of the century. The Surrealists had won out: all the books, catalogues, and theses passed on their version of the facts. It seemed as though the quarantine into which Breton had placed him might last forever. Relegated to the role of the sad clown of modernity, Cocteau was alarmed at having to meet death, and posterity, in this position. Apollinaire had called him the "king of poetry," Proust had praised the way he brought together the highest truths "under a flamboyant sign," Drieu and Morand had been inspired by his character to create others based on him—but everyone preferred Char's intellectual poetry, Michaux's oddities, Ponge's portraits of animals or vegetables. Rilke had paid tribute to him and Pound, an attentive reader, had translated him—"You have saved France!" he had exclaimed, reading *Léone*, and would always regret not having written an essay on the poet, whom he believed to have been the best European writer of the century.[1] And yet Cocteau continued to be treated like the class clown.

After editorially supporting him for many years, Chardonne made an assessment that was even crueler than his destiny: "He believed himself to be the Great Poet, and wanted to invent everything," adding, with his customary clarity, "the danger is to want to surpass oneself. One must remain just short of oneself." He then concluded: "The most dangerous mistress is fame. She'll make you her puppet."[2] Of course, Cocteau's name had come to signify a particular type of person, as he had always dreamed it would, but not in the way he'd hoped. A "real Cocteau," it might be said of a good host during a successful dinner party—never a budding genius or a future Da Vinci. "He's doing his Cocteau routine," they would say of someone putting on airs, or appropriating others' property. His fame was like that of a visitor who had his picture taken in all the funfairs on earth, sticking his head through a hole like an "enormous painted ruff" so it looked as if he was on an ocean liner, or an airplane, but that no one would recognize in real life, a ghost wandering somewhere between ubiquity and inanity.[3] Unbearable, for him.

If he had any influences, the many layers of his consciousness had always filtered them out, like the rocks of mountain streams, only keeping those that added to his development. Had he spent his whole career fighting in the lightweight division? For half a century France had stopped producing men who were made to write great novels, like Thomas Mann or Dos Passos, Robert Musil or William Faulkner. But if he had always jumped from branch to branch, at least he had kept to the same tree. Gide liked to joke that his favorite vegetable was the "mange-tout" (literally "eat-everything," known in the United States as the string bean), but this was perhaps the only thing they had in common: their work was not faithful to one fixed idea. They echoed the proliferation typical of the world around them.

Cocteau was given credit for sometimes having been the catalyst for an era, and the midwife of some geniuses, but he was tacitly reproached for not releasing a remake of *Les enfants terribles* at regular intervals. Readers wanted to meet a strong personality with a determined aesthetic. Not having the time or the means to express themselves, perhaps suspecting something left unfinished within themselves, they demanded a reassuring mirror—and the author of *La difficulté d'être* offered them an even less reliable image than their own. "We recognize ourselves to be *cocteaux* and we blush," noted Claude Mauriac in *Jean Cocteau ou la vérité du mensonge*. His way of being everywhere all the time had become a bore, like the images he fired off. Was he read, then? Except for one or two titles, he doubted it. "My written work is like flotsam and jetsam," he confided to his journal.[4] Perhaps the readers feared the slight disappointment that Julien Green shared at his death: "a bit of the best of himself passed into the conversation, and this best is intangible."[5]

Always ready to critique him for being scattered and fickle, artistically speaking, the women who still ran salons in Paris—Marie Laure de Noailles,

Lise Deharme, Valentine Hugo, Élise Jouhandeau, and others—reduced his work to a thin saga in which he haunted all the roles, from the narcissistic painter in *Le sang d'un poète* to the abandoned woman in *La voix humaine*, not to mention the jealous mother in *Les parents terribles*. They denounced his inability to create life, in literary terms, all the more easily since they were intimately aware of doing so—they all had wanted to marry him, he wrote in his journal, to explain their eagerness to abort. A critic who had never spared him dedicated a book to him, signing himself "the executioner with no hard feelings."[6] And in London, in the offices of the BBC, a journal designating the hundred geniuses of the century indicated, under his portrait, "Result of a snobbery that has not yet lost any of its power." Prince Rainier himself, after soliciting an ode from Cocteau commemorating his marriage to Grace Kelly, refused this ancien régime compliment, "through modesty, no doubt," he wanted to believe. And Rebatet, whose forgiveness Cocteau had had the weakness to request at the Liberation, began to insult him again in *La Parisienne*.[7] At times they all seemed unanimously against him. "The slightly legendary doctrine that is used against him seemed of public utility, given that it has been contributed to by so many individuals and collectives," wrote one critic.[8] It was as strong as ever, in spite of the "honorable spanking" that he had received in the wake of his election to the Académie. "Nature is horrified by Gide," wrote Béraud, at the time of *Si le grain ne meurt* and *Corydon*; but the culture was horrified by Cocteau.[9]

Of course he still had a few defenders among the young. Encouraged by André Fraigneau and Michel Déon, who sometimes came to see him with Coco Chanel, the Hussards, a group of young right-wing writers, after marching under Morand's banner, had now "rediscovered" him.[10] The slightest favorable article was enough to give him hope. Returning to Paris, he left his door wide open, as in the blessed days on the rue d'Anjou, receiving young writers and once again giving them tips. The debutant herself was encouraged like the young men of years gone by. "Go on, the train never comes twice," Edmonde Charles-Roux, who was invited to become editor of *Vogue*, remembers being told; stripped of all erotic agendas, his availability took on stupefying proportions.[11] The man who, in his early career, had received encouragement from Théophile Gautier's son-in-law would receive in 1962 a letter from Johnny Hallyday, the French Bill Haley, thanking him for taking care of his fan club.[12]

Helped by the "needle-like sensitivity" that Max Jacob noticed, Cocteau could also see the kind of unease he was passing on. "I know there are those who avoid me out of some kind of fear of vampirism. They guess that I need their reality in order to create one for myself," he noted.[13] In the hope of covering up the void inside of him, which already threatened to make others seasick, he gave in to all the young people's desires. He systematically took the side of those who exposed themselves through writing (as Truffaut saw). The mediocre artist was worth more in his eyes than the best spectator, though he was afraid that they would one day learn that he had also given the royal welcome to one of their rivals.[14] He promised to write prefaces to their books when they were published, and showered them with so much attention that they left singing his praises. Cocteau the forgotten was suddenly rediscovered, once again made the heir to Ronsard and Apollinaire. He had become the last virtuoso of the French language, which was so intimately linked to the soul of its speakers that it was, in some parts of the world, the very language of literature.

Once again Cocteau received the treatment he deserved. The djinn that haunted his body but now rarely visited his spirit returned to life. Capable of waking him up in the middle of the night to grab a pen, but also of making him sleep through the day and walk on rooftops in his dreams, the poet within him sat up straight.

> Prince d'une bonté sans doctrine ni pompe,
> Riche de la minceur du figuier dans le fruit,
> Masqué par ton visage et voilé par ton bruit,
> Si la corde où tu marches, Jean, vient qu'elle rompe,
> Dieu l'arrange aussitôt, pour toi comme pour lui.
> [Prince of a goodness without doctrine or ceremony
> Rich with the thinness of the fig tree in fruit
> Masked by your face and veiled by your voice
> If the tightrope you walk upon should break, Jean
> God would take care of it, for you and for him.]

Thus did the poet and playwright Audiberti write to him when *Clair-obscur* was published.[15] That was indeed his way of being in the world.

The wave of solicitations eventually made him nauseous: why spend so much energy convincing beginners of his exceptional nature and why continue to write poems so the critics could jeer at them? His desire to please, he now knew, almost always turned against him. "Cocteau was very brilliant the last time we met," said T. S. Eliot to Stravinsky in 1951, "but he seemed to be rehearsing for a more important occasion."[16] He would take a seat; he was exhausted. He was like the old general in the Edgar Allan Poe story whose valet gets him ready, but who disintegrates into dust the moment his young visitor leaves.

He remembered that Proust had often described the artist's path to becoming himself, truly himself, in the enclosed space of his creation, with only the help of "perishable man, equal to his contemporaries, full of faults, to whom a true soul has been chained, and against whom it protests, tries to escape, to deliver itself through work." This soul was trying to kill him.[17] Even his work was impatient to see him dead so it could live: he had been too noisy announcing it, too noticeable, too desperate a ringmaster. He had clashed his cymbals too many times—it wanted to live on its own merits. His work was aware of the intelligentsia's disdain, like that of theater-people for the circus, and had convinced itself that Cocteau needed to be "a living man and a posthumous artist." A living poet was a contradiction in terms, almost an anachronism, he realized—when he wasn't staggering from dive bar to dive bar under a hail of sarcasm, like Verlaine at the end of his life. A true poet, a *good* poet at least, was a dead one. Well, it would all be sorted out soon.

Afraid that his entire edifice would crumble, he ended up leaving, haggard, for Milly. The house was empty except for silent Doudou. The white of the irises, the green of the lawns, the ring of the postman reconciled himself with himself; his nerves unknotted as he opened the mail. The telephone rang; an observation, a funny thought, and he began to laugh with all the energy that his turned-off sexuality afforded him. Stopping to look at Doudou's latest canvas, he realized in a flash, "Never has good painting been so close to bad painting," but at the same time he was amazed: this was the source of all "art naif," was it not?[18] They shared a good mushroom omelette and a few glasses of Morgon wine, took a little walk around the garden and visited the flowers that had bloomed in his absence. But already the letters he had received—more than fifty a day—began to work their odious blackmail. Where would he find the energy to reply to such a mountain? And what could he say to the friend who, in an outwardly favorable article, once again noted the way his work was studded with bits and pieces of other people's creations?

Night fell, and the nightmare began again. Nietzsche had been greatly inspired by Schopenhauer and had stolen from Pindar his legendary "Become who you are," but Nietzsche could get away with anything. Picasso had pillaged Braque and Matisse, the Futurists, and all the classical artists since Velázquez, but Picasso could also get away with anything. Not Cocteau. "The same will be true of you," wrote Epictetus, eighteen centuries earlier. "Today you are a fighter, tomorrow a gladiator, the day after an orator, and finally a philosopher, without having ever truly been anything. Like a monkey you imitate everything you see: today this pleases you, tomorrow that. You get to work without reflecting, you do not consider the subject from several angles." These accusations were vile—therefore they took root in him.

Scattered and many-sided, his work did recall, it's true, these "difficult to pick up objects" that were presented in wedding and banquet catalogs. From that to writing to him, as Igor Markevitch had, to encourage him, assuring him of his deep affection, to finally put "on paper the masterpiece that is yourself!" As if he had never managed to, when everyone accused him of only ever writing about himself!

If "a personality is only a persistent error," as Radiguet said, then the only guilty party was Cocteau.[19] He was the only one to have drained his reputation. Incapable of being, he had diluted himself in doubles, shadows, reflections, and phantoms; he was a man with a cut-off head, dreaming of being at the top of the class and waking up at the bottom. Such a ridiculous person, with his slice of a nose "stuck on his face like a recumbent statue's nose," said Cau, Sartre's former secretary, that the real Cocteau said several times that he would have refused to shake his own hand if he had met himself in the street.[20] That was the point: he always ended up becoming what he was accused of being. Hardly had he finished reading a hostile article than, putting himself in the journalist's place, he exaggerated his remarks: "I think that I would strike more accurately, that the steel would be buried up to the hilt and all that would remain would be to bend my legs, stick out my tongue, and fall to my knees in the arena," he admitted in *La difficulté d'être*.[21]

They accused him of being scattered? He was the first to say he was the "Paganini of the *violon d'Ingres*" (amateurs). After dedicating himself to glory, God, and opium, having loved men and several women—in short, after having learned all there was to know of the human condition—he wondered if he had done too much, if this profusion had somehow prevented him from truly existing. Laurent Tailhade had compared him in a lecture fifty years earlier to the hero in the *Thousand and One Nights* who finds a pile of treasure in a cave before finding himself locked in: that was exactly what had happened to him, and he was the only one to blame. Cocteau, a born target, was one of those of whom Sartre spoke, someone who can't take refuge in themselves—the enemy had already set up camp.[22] He was like the *enfants terribles* of his work, who fought tooth and nail but never managed to overcome a feeling of guilt; or the little cherry thief who had lived in remorse and ended up a religious zealot, whom Saint Peter lets into heaven precisely because she has stolen. "This man seeks a tribunal for the express purpose of corrupting it," Sartre wrote. "If you meet him, you will be both judge and jury, he will not forget a single detail of his conduct, and will not let you go because you have not acquitted him. But do not be fooled, he knows everything: he knows he has assigned himself the sentence he has fled since the beginning of the century; he knows he is a convict and he has been serving his time for fifty years, for he is condemned in old age to plead the cause that his adolescent self judged to be without appeal."[23]

The Psychopathology of Failure, a book published in 1939 by one of the founders of the Société Psychanalytique de Paris, had already made Cocteau reflect on the roots of his neurosis during the war. Perhaps he had lacked confidence in himself in the sexual arena; for the book's author, Dr. René Laforgue, this lack of assurance was related to the "anguish of the act," the fear of diving into the water, of tackling the world head on, of writing the play one envisions; of replying to letters—and even to taking refuge in a fear-based disorder. Had he lacked the essential courage that would have allowed him to tackle solitude, and to choose his own personality? The only secret to escape unhappiness was not to want to be someone else, said Schopenhauer. Was *that* the cause of his troubles?

Alarmed by the abyss widening within himself, Cocteau sat up on his little bed and began to answer the letters. He called everyone "chéri," showered his correspondents with the affection he chronically lacked, and for a few moments recovered the feeling of existing. He told them all how much he needed them and how much he cherished their encouragement, feverishly overdoing it in ways that led them to believe he was just an exalted stranger who didn't care, who bombarded the world with the same formulaic messages. "I would like to be everyone's friend," he had written in *Le prince frivole*, back when he dreamed of being the favorite child of all creation. Our destiny, according to some analysts, is set in motion by a psychic sequence that structures our unconsciousness. If true, Cocteau's psychic sequence might have been this: as God, I contain you all; as a human being, I owe you all my apologies.

Sleep brought him only temporary respite. He began to have torrents of dreams that opened many strange doors through which his guilt surged. Under the arcades of an unrecognizable town, he ran into the shade of Radiguet, who refused to speak to him. Had he hurt his feelings? He ran after him until he was out of breath, managed to catch him, and was kicked by a foot that turned him into a dog, whose baying at the moon made him wake with a start. He turned on the light to read, certain the whole world knew he had killed Radiguet.[24]

A FAILED GOD

The good weather always sent him walking in the streets of Villefranche. He knew every corner of the little port, from the rue Obscure where he ran into his double in *Le testament d'Orphée*, to the shed where the fishermen kept their nets. It had recently been restored, and revealed a marvelous Romanesque chapel, impressive in its purity, which he decided to paint and reconsecrate. If the faith Maritain had awakened had gone out, he remained convinced that all forms of belief were worthy of interest; no longer able to act as a Christian, he acted as an artist, and managed to impose his project on the fishermen (though they were reluctant) and the town council. Building sets by hand, filming the transformation of man into beast, as in the final scene of *La belle et la bête*, had always given him physical pleasure. What was at first only a hobby soon consumed him. Did he recall that the heroes of *L'éternel retour* died and went up to heaven in a boathouse? He not only devised "frescoes" to cover the walls, but also redid the ceiling and the apse, as well as designed the altar, the candelabras, the door, and the Jesus overlooking it all. Carried away by his work, he began to spend entire days at the top of unstable scaffoldings, as fishermen and the curious looked on. Dressed in simple worker's overalls, tied with a scarf that made the blood rush to his head, he lived only for the present moment.

Sleep tired him out; Cocteau's nights were filled with such terrible dreams that he emerged exhausted, and he never slept more than two or three hours on average. But work gave him an incredible energy. His body, in hibernation, released a spectral double that, like the mystics, could no longer be affected by fatigue or thirst. He forgot how long he had been at it, what time it was, the meals that awaited him, and rediscovered, intact, his brilliant gifts for design that had already been evident when he was ten years old. The child took the upper hand over the man whom death was beginning to undermine. Feeding off the walls he had covered with his paintings, he became the chapel, blending his body with the colors, painting his tense but beatific face with the plaster. Some days he was so full of joy that he looked like a fetus daubing the world with his placenta. As he painted, he forgot himself and became a living element, capable of feeling in his flesh the tempest that had just ravaged the coast of Dunkirk, but also as light, serene, and finally, "anonymous" as the seagull he heard crying in the port, or as the little boats drifting past maritime customs, near the Welcome Hôtel. His wounded megalomania had reversed into radiant modesty. Having lost his arrogance, the King of Paris and Duke of Anjou had become a little soldier of life, proud to participate in the great work: an empty being who served as a sensitive membrane to a full world and whose only ambition was to be able to hear its noise, to translate into points, lines, and colors the waves that came from the sky above. Having become a simple atom among billions, he painted at the heart of the cosmos, which was bombarding the earth with photons.

After the chapel of Villefranche was inaugurated, he began work on the one in Milly. The Milly chapel had been dedicated to Saint Blaise, a sort of Christian Orpheus who had brought about many miracle cures for the faithful as well as for the animals who ran to see him, thanks to the "herbal simples" he crushed in his mortar. The orders poured in for Cocteau's renovations. He was asked to decorate the wedding room at the Menton town hall, which he did in a style blending Greek classicism with African scarification, reminiscent of Bakst and comic-book graphics. Next was the chapel to the Virgin at Notre-Dame-de-France in London, and the outdoor theatre in Cap d'Ail, near Monte-Carlo. He soon hired assistants—honest, direct workers who showed him another face of humanity. Unlike Picasso, who always pushed himself further, they sang as they painted, taking satisfaction from the smallest achievement; living and breathing the love of a job well done. Safe from any creative vanity, these assistants, like the potters who heated his ceramics, the weavers who worked on his tapestries, or the machinists who worked by his side in the cinema, seemed to have a privileged access to happiness. For the first time, surrounded by unknowns, Cocteau found true comfort in daily work. Their ability to marvel made him forget the bitterness of the geniuses with whom he had spent his life—the jealous vigilance of the intellectuals, the civil servants of criticism ("art's bachelors," as Proust said). He believed these artisans possessed true wisdom, along the lines of the sublime candor of Félicité in Flaubert's *Un coeur simple*. Like Doudou, who didn't care if his paintings were shown, these anonymous people were happy just to do their work.

It was almost the same revelation when Pierre Chanel told him, soon after, that Dargelos was living peacefully in the Seine-et-Oise with his wife. Now an employee in a public works business, his former classmate at the Lycée Condorcet was obviously happy with the daily life society had given him in exchange for anonymity; like the millions of other lives that unfurled far from Paris, he appreciated the calmness and the protections that chance would never disturb. He was very happy to have inspired the writer whom he had known in his youth. There was something intriguing about having the man who had made him into an eroto-literary myth choose such tranquility and solitude.

There were profiteers, like in Villefranche, among the fishermen, but the men who assisted Cocteau the painter treated him with affection, even admiration. More than the star or the member of the Académie Française, they liked the man capable of spending ten hours on a scaffold, drinking out of the same bottle as they did and wiping his hands on his overalls as they did. They became his brothers, living for the same work of beauty, as he became himself a mason, forgetting the books he had written and the stirs he had caused. They became artists thinking with their hands, like Matisse or Picasso. Just as an orchid tries to imitate the insect that will fertilize it, Cocteau reflected the workers who carried out his work. The Soviet filmmaker Andrei Tarkovsky would cite as the limit of art those Japanese painters of the Middle Ages who, at the height of their success, withdrew from the public eye, changed their names and provinces, and painted their next masterpiece in the style of the new region.²⁵ Cocteau imitated them in his way, though he kept his initials.

Fame no longer really interested him. In his youth, he had called Fame "the terrible lady [making] with her wings a silence or an intolerable noise," a phrase borrowed from Byron.²⁶ The gods had whispered the truth to him from the beginning, as was their wont, before making him live according to the fate they had assigned him. And this time he did not really want to wear the "crown of laurels / More fierce than thorns."²⁷ It was better to live each moment to the fullest. Sometimes at the end of the day in Villefranche he would close the doors to his chapel, lie down on the scaffold, and savor the silence. The evocation of eternity made him visit mentally Jean Bourgoint, now Brother Pascal, in his little cell. The "enfant terrible" had said that he had found Truth, "the secret of secrets, the hidden truth which blinds the world," while presenting himself as an "old novice escaped from the labyrinth," where he had almost died "of hemorrhaging from lost time."²⁸ This was Cocteau's feeling as well. Proust would have been proud of him: he had not lost his time.

Sometimes Cocteau became very serious, thinking of the words of Chamfort, whose pessimism had deeply affected him: "We say that long reigns are always the most deplorable. God is eternal. Judge for yourself." But the sun only had to crack through the door and suffuse his decorations, the next day, for the desire to create to return. A passing journalist was astonished by his fresh inspiration, and he felt a surge of pride and ecstasy. Maybe he was only a mason, but in this case it was the cosmos that inspired him. What a joy to think that these walls would preserve the essence of his being, that in the next millennium people would come and admire them! Sealing the marvels his hands had made, he thought of the walls that Michelangelo and Raphaël had "tattooed" at the Vatican. His chapel was worthy of the Sistine; once the Villa Santo Sospir had fallen into ruins, his "frescoes" would be worthy of those of the Palace at Knossos. Won over by the aura of the Christ he had painted, giving him some of his own features, he shyly recovered his oldest dreams. Of course he hadn't yet founded a religion, as he had dreamed of doing, but he remained a hidden source of inspiration, which was no doubt much better. "You have been your own dupe," people whispered to him in the 1930s, reminding him that having inspired a Judas doesn't make you a messiah.²⁹ All right, he wasn't Christ, but neither was Breton a dream, or Aragon, France. "The artist is a failed god," he wrote to his mother.

With the help of opium, which tended to embalm him alive, the chapel of Villefranche became a dream refuge against reality. The days he spent there had a stupefying power of anticipation; he imagined himself crossing the centuries just as frail, lively, and tenacious as the little red light that signaled a divine presence; it was almost his mausoleum he was building, while he waited to join the beyond, like the pharaohs within their pyramids. Hadn't an Egyptologist told him that the architects of the great dynasties had built into the pyramids' foundations blocks taken from earlier temples, but arranged in a different order—wasn't this what he had done, contradicting his work at every step of it? Having come to the end of the cycle of birth and death, the aging demi-god gave himself something approximating immortality.

SCIENCE FICTION

Born with a talent for mathematics, Bertrand Russell explained that as his abilities weakened, he turned to philosophy, then, in his old age, found he was suited only to literature. Cocteau lived through this progression as well, but in reverse. The scientific discoveries of the 1950s had an enormous influence on his imagination. Pushed along by the Cold War, the thousands of researchers working around the world on atomic states began to understand more about chemical reactions; and the more that biologists saw how cells renewed themselves, or how the immune system identified enemies and began to secrete antibodies, the more Cocteau was persuaded that we are acted upon. Human beings lived as they had to live, just as his books wrote themselves: "Existence exists," said Kierkegaard. For a long time, he had taken a "classically" esoteric view of himself. According to this tradition, we pass through the different bodies that are given to us according to a certain temporality. Too-agitated lives, too-anxious natures, or too-violent deaths prevent this natural migration of souls, and may expel the soul prematurely, making it wander across the world looking for its body of origin. Thus did Cocteau regard himself as a member of a separate caste, caught in the cycle of his metempsychoses, or rather blocked halfway—someone who, always searching for a body, dressed and acted like other people but would have done anything to be them.

Then his horizons were broadened. He came to understand that our complex universe was surrounded by an infinity of others. This meant to him that though the ancient gods were utterly empowered over humans, they feared other gods, from other more powerful solar systems, who themselves feared other, still more powerful gods, and so on. Like the first Matryoshka doll of a series of embedded Russian dolls, each of us circulates among n degrees of reality, only seeing our own; the body of Cocteau was only a bit of dust surrounded by stars, but it also contained constellations and suns, moons and planets, that housed other microscopic Cocteaux; even plants lived in another space-time continuum, bound up with our own, as a sped-up time-lapse film showing their growing and blooming had shown him.[30] "The mountains breathe, move, slip one under the other, climb over and penetrate each other, and the secular slowness of their pace escapes us," he wrote in *Portraits-souvenir*.[31] Like the reader of the Torah, the author of *La difficulté d'être* circulated across forty-nine degrees of meaning, asking himself if God was the fiftieth, his infinite body encompassing all the others, or if he was the hypothesis allowing all these worlds to proliferate. His sensitive readings expanded the incredible reach of our solar system, making the earth a pebble turning around a ball of fire, itself dancing around a mega-star, which came from inside a galaxy evolving between a myriad of other universes, and so on into infinity. Time was only a convention; he already saw the solar system collapsing, and the Milky Way continuing out to the farthest edges of the universe that he traveled in his mind. He felt like Goya, whom he compared to a sorcerer traveling through the future on his broomstick.[32] While the Surrealists had long since given up their research into dreams and alchemy, Cocteau wandered more than ever through the depths of his inventive psyche.

Everything was so mysterious! Science spoke of traveling through faraway galaxies, where it should be possible to see, through a telescope, what would become of the earth in a few centuries. These inversions of time and distance fascinated his acrobatic intelligence: far-flung galaxies from our own, billions of light years away, burned in the sky, though they had already gone out; the smallest segment of his pinky finger, under the microscope, was the size of the Milky Way. Space was infinity folded, eternity folded, and all of us live inside these folds, blinded by their borders. The only way to escape despair, for Tolstoy, was to project himself into the universe: this is what Cocteau did as well. The whys of our existence intrigued this born diviner to the point of dizziness. His instinct was to turn things inside out like a glove: he considered what animates us, and measured the richness of the "silence" that reigns in our bodies. Is not the source of the world, in quantum physics, an active void charged with energy? Is not movement, wavelike, the only certifiable form of life? From movement alone comes light, and therefore life, whose sinusoidal variations produce matter and anti-matter, reality and unreality, truth and lies; it is thanks to movement that a body, entering a mirror, can transform into its opposite, and that someone in New Zealand, seen from France, walks upside down.

When he was young, Cocteau believed himself the lost prince of a kingdom located at the far reaches of Persia and India; then, defeated by the inherent cruelty of the "human race," he began to identify with those intermediary beings suspended between earth and heaven—acrobats, angels, ghosts, zombies.

As he grew older, more than ever he felt as if he were floating, and suffered from never being able to put himself down: "I would give anything to tread solid ground once again," he would confide in *Le testament d'Orphée*, aware of his strangeness. Hélène Rochas, whose husband Marcel had designed the costumes for *L'éternel retour*, confirmed, "He seemed to have come from another planet, or better still, from the stars."[33]

He sometimes tried to reassure himself by thinking that he was just ahead of his time—that one day all of humanity would float like him. A wise man would be able, then, to use the deforming power of mirrors to more radically detach human beings from the power of gravity and help them to travel in space. They would remain "umbilically linked to the Mother, to the maternal soil," but once gravity had been conquered, everything would become possible, including the fight against time, and therefore against aging. That is, unless biology, through a period of controlled disintegration, could encourage the vital matter of these beings to escape through some secret drain to go zooming through space and take shape once more in the neighborhood of a star.

And what if life had come from elsewhere, taking advantage of meteorites to sail past the clouds? It would have arrived here by accident, and without warning begun to flourish like dandelions, lichen, or vermin. It would have ended up adapting to the waves of cold and heat, would have developed wings when the water began to freeze and legs when the oceans got too salty. These thoughts infinitely reassured Cocteau: all the earth's inhabitants were descended from extra-terrestrials, rejected from another planet that had cruelly cut off all contact. He could not, then, be the only one to feel like a foreigner here on earth. If he were different from other men, it was perhaps his sharp awareness of this departure, and the laws of survival that Lamarck had analyzed, which led him to conclude that transformation and adaptation were natural animal responses. Human beings might drape themselves in conservative dignity, but in so doing they were denying the chameleon-like interplanetary nature that had taught them to stand on two feet.

With the enormous success, in 1958, of *Le matin des magiciens*, by Bergier and Pauwels, then the founding of the journal *Planète*, which popularized the first studies that tried to prove the existence of extra-terrestrial life, Cocteau did not have much difficulty convincing himself that there were beings trying to make contact, and that even if they couldn't or wouldn't speak clearly, they used codes and symbols. He and Doudou were already gorging themselves on scientistic and para-mystical works, as well as science fiction. Ever since the young Slovenian had spotted a string of unidentified objects flying over the coast, somewhere near Cagnes, the quavering of flying saucers over the four corners of the earth was no longer mysterious to them. They were convinced that a single lost ship, full of panic-stricken aliens, could be responsible for all the documented appearances, and collected testimonies concerning an American pilot who had been pulverized because he went hunting for one of them. Cocteau imagined this extra-terrestial species as being so peaceful, so exquisitely refined, that its curiosity for us had turned into terror at our vulgarity: the aircraft had flown from this "soft roe of the heavens, this heavenly caviar" that is the Milky Way carrying representatives from a superior race who secretly shared Jean Cocteau's feelings, finally! Convinced, since the First World War, that history is the result of a fairytale written by a mathematician, Cocteau didn't have much trouble convincing himself that the earth had once been ravaged by a catastrophe that had killed off, along with the brontosauruses, civilizations much more developed than our own, and that there was more destruction to come: the fictional world Cocteau had lived in, for half a century, was trying more and more to replace the real world, and he had just found a new way of gliding over it, making the planet unreal.[34]

Doudou was crazy about the work of a certain René Bertrand, author of *La tradition secrète*, and Cocteau became his most fervent supporter. There were other authors: Lieutenant Plantier explained life through cosmic energy, while Aimé Michel, after Captain Clérouin, claimed that flying saucers traveled through time and not space. He bought both of their books, which sometimes featured prefaces by a general of the air force as proof of the extreme seriousness of these studies. An honest baker had been followed home by a gnome covered with hair, with eyes as big as a crow's eggs. Cocteau imagined that the giants of beyond had their ships flown by a race of dwarves, catching them in garages situated beneath the immense, oval-shaped ones they inhabited. And when he learned that one of the German inventors of the V2 rocket believed these aliens were plants that could think and that had developed extremely advanced technology, he flung himself down this new line of thought with renewed passion.

Cocteau had always been sure that there was a sympathetic accord among the elements of the cosmos. Human beings were not simply in constant contact with the ore and salts making up the earth, the ether and the gas present in the air: they were part of a microcosm of functions that have counterparts throughout the universe. Even bodies that have been in contact only once continue to interact a long time afterward, like twins who live in symbiosis. That is why a human effigy, with real nails and hair—even an original photograph—could have a beneficial effect on the subject. More than ever he called on the healers who work on photographs and radionics experts to cure his lumbago. Bonesetters of all sorts and magi of all stripes paraded through Santo Sospir to restore his health, but Soulié de Morant was his favorite: the doctor had only to lay on his left hand to calm Cocteau's spleen or unblock his bladder. The relief lasted only a few days, but this meant a great deal to him. No one, however, could soothe his horrible chronic sciatica. He contacted Dr. Ricoux, a pioneer in ultrasound treatments, and began his "silent" therapy. And since Dr. Marjorie De La Warr was conducting important radionics studies at her laboratory, he began an enthusiastic correspondence with her. There were also suspicious savants, crooked atomists, and ostracized researchers with whom he became besotted just as quickly.

He believed everything, absolutely everything, that he read. If someone mentioned the harmful effects of atomic radiation, Cocteau became convinced that the monstrous boils that had plagued him during the filming of *La belle et la bête* were the result of radiation unleashed by the U.S. nuclear experiments in New Mexico and Arizona: the zombies working in those atomic laboratories were the sentinels sounding the trumpet of the great explosions that would soon lead to the Apocalypse predicted by Saint John. If he heard that a flying saucer had landed on the roof of Curzio Malaparte's house in Capri, he deduced that the two new satellites spotted thousands of kilometers from earth were used by aliens as hotels. He straightaway accepted that the monumental terraces of Baalbek, Lebanon, where *La machine infernale* had been performed, had served long ago as an airfield for interplanetary vehicles: there was no doubt in his mind that their vertical landings had the power to paralyze witnesses, empty drinking troughs, and make animals flee. The narratives of the modern-day witnesses to these apparitions, always very descriptive when it came to the gestures of the little green men, were an extension of the fairytales of his childhood, when tightly gripping a magic rock was enough to transport him to other times and places.

As *Planète* described the experiences of Lopsang Rampa in *Le troisième oeil*, he imagined himself to be the hostage of a brain that had dreamed him since childhood, but was incapable of waking up and letting him live his own life freely. Or he imagined that he existed only in the mind of Doudou sleeping in the next room, but was absent to himself and others. "God thinks us, but he doesn't think of us," he wrote in his journal during the Occupation; he might have said the same thing of all of his friends. Real life existed only in other people's fantasies; that was even the only place where it was livable. Who knows? Maybe one of the saucers flying over Provence would one day land on the terrace of Santo Sospir to bring all three of them—Doudou, Francine, and himself—at the speed of light, to the enchanted world whence came this French Peter Pan.

THE ULTIMATE IMITATION

For a long time, this angel fallen to earth with a bag full of "spare wings" had seemed able to make himself into anything he wanted.[35] Cocteau's eruptive nature would take in the admired other, sometimes to the point of swallowing it entirely, and he would brim over until his collective outline was reshaped, the way lava reforms a volcano. But Cocteau had now reached the age when one can no longer fundamentally change. In addition, as Proust said, our past, preserved by habit, weighs so heavily on us, conditioning our actions, that at every moment of our lives we are the descendants of ourselves. No longer wishing to learn anything from the Picassos, the Stravinskys, or the Chaplins, Cocteau would henceforth find his spine in the hostility he engendered, and in the fascination he inspired.

The damage was initially physical. His organism no longer had the strength to operate the fruitful migrations that Plato calls metempsychosis; his love for Doudou contained no need for imitation; exhausted by fifty years of metamorphoses, like the illness that had ravaged him during the filming of *La belle et la bête*, his skin had ceased to renew itself. This stasis also gave him, for the first time, the freedom to reflect on this strange capacity:

> Superficial critics have often believed my ability for mimicry to be voluntary, that it comes from a kind of annihilation of myself when faced with someone who interests me. I become it, somehow, to the point of playing the part of the anesthesia to the pain . . . It is possible that this makes itself felt in certain poems where I didn't have the patience to wait for a total return to myself. But it is rare that I'm not aware of it on the brink of a good piece of work.[36]

He gave this faculty for alteration a troubling justification that exceeded aesthetics or biology and verged on ontology: "I could not live without exchanges — but I do not demand to be given much. The point is that I give everything and someone gives me a helping hand. I make use of it and find myself leaving my skin like an uncomfortable suit."[37] This time, he would wear his clothes to the grave.

We could sum up the heterosexual of the 1950s — it would be arbitrary and vulgar, and a hundred counterexamples could be found, but we're nearing the end, let's indulge ourselves — as an a priori stable and sufficient identity until the seemingly less-definite personality of a woman dragged him into her orbit and absorbed him into her life cycle, whereas the homosexual of the time would be the reflected self, who, after having actively sought a double who could dazzle him, finally accepted himself as incomplete. This was the point at which Cocteau had arrived. There was only one last thing to do, for this human fiction (who existed for and through others, living off of imitations and thefts): to create his own painful truth, made of everything he had been precisely unable to become. Having come to the end of the cycle of births and deaths that the Hindus call *samsara*, the author of *Thomas l'imposteur* had finally become Jean Cocteau, or rather, only Jean Cocteau. Born multiple—"one of those men who seem to conjugate in the plural form," said Léon Bloy—he ended singular, as Valéry promised would happen to each of us.[38]

The effects of this stabilization could already be felt: the larger public immediately recognized his style, no matter what the nature of his creations, and he didn't even need to add his signature. His aesthetic was fixed. If style is, according to Proust, a written, audible, or visual revelation of the qualitative abyss separating our respective perceptions of the world, but which, without art, would remain each person's eternal secret, Cocteau's style had arrived. He had probably been wrong, in his youth, to claim his models so loudly. "Genius slits the throat of those from whom it steals," said Rivarol; on this point, Cocteau still had not always been a genius. Rather than killing his prey, like Picasso, he stifled it under silk handkerchiefs, then at the last minute turned away. But the name Cocteau now meant only one thing.

It was partly because the famous Cocteau was now a star, admired from Japan to Brazil, that the humble, pained Jean spent his time reproducing the fauns, the Orpheuses, and the unicorns that had built his fame. The old man of Santo Sospir went around making Cocteaux, drawing Cocteaux, creating Cocteau plates, signing Cocteau's initials. A hostage of his own making, he came to imitate, then to plagiarize himself in close to a caricature, drawing Oedipuses and his Antinouses on programs, napkins, paper tablecloths. Was his style frozen? Faithful to the process that he had never truly mastered, he continued without protest to make Cocteaux, like a good soldier in the service of his own strangeness. As Sachs, his nemesis, had put it only too well before leaving for Hamburg: "It's not that we don't remake ourselves. Alas, we only ever remake ourselves."[39] Thus bloomed the bad Cocteau, whose work still today takes up too much room in certain galleries.

He thought of himself, for a long time, as a schizophrenic maintained by his social skills. But an anomaly seemed to isolate him more every day, like the glass bell jar under which he had let himself be photographed during the filming of 8×8, Hans Richter's film—in which he also wore the paper crown from a *galette des rois*, like a sovereign foreign to our land, or a magus straight out of the science fiction films that Ed Wood was making at the time in the United States.[40] "Genius is a class with only one student in it," said Bachelard in *L'air et les songes*. But Cocteau did not find himself alone when he opened the panels of his mirror, which was covered in photos and drawings from times gone by. He instead found the first Cocteau—the one who had hung out with Édouard de Max but had also known the true Grand Duchess Anastasia during the First World War—the young girl who had disappeared during the massacre of the Russian Imperial family, as she pretended, but had since reappeared in the United States in the body of a Polish woman, who did not speak Russian.[41] Or the mirror reflected the second Cocteau, the one from the Radiguet years, who maintained a following faithful to *Les enfants terribles*—"this era that clings to my skin like the Shirt of Nessus," he would say.[42] The third, who had not left much of a mark, with his medieval plays and his Racinian tragedies, aside from *L'éternel retour*, had already been eclipsed by the one from the 1950s. But these numerous clones he had engendered, throughout his life, to the point where it seemed he had stitched together a patchwork quilt of unfinished selves—"botched, slapdash," would have said President Schreiber, the para-noiac analyzed by Freud—were so many "others" who would not have easily recognized each other.[43]

Who was he really, in this crowd of lookalikes? Had he not always acted like the American woman afflicted with multiple personality disorder, raped when she was one of her twenty-one identities, but whose rapist would claim to have been sleeping with another, who was willing? They'd thrown heaps of vitriol on the last Cocteau, but the real one didn't feel the burns—he enjoyed total psychic anonymity. Maybe he was essentially a crazy man who had fallen into a mirror as a teenager, and had mistaken himself ever since for Jean Cocteau? He who had only been able to get through it all by abusing opium was now interested in the research that Timothy Leary (among others) was doing on LSD 25, which at the time was considered a potential cure for schizophrenia. But seriously, who could believe themselves to be themselves? A young painter back in the day, Emmanuel Pereire, wrote in his *Livre des anges*, "Each man is the sum of all possible identities, except his own." Wasn't this definition the most realistic? Had not Breton himself, the tireless enemy of Jean Cocteau's unreality, confessed, after meeting Trotsky in Mexico in 1938, to having been struck speechless before the man he admired, to the point of not being able to work on the manifesto they had planned to write together? "I felt all of a sudden strangely deprived of means, prey to a perverse need to conceal myself. It's what I call, in memory of King Lear, my 'Cordelia complex'; don't mock, it's completely fundamental, organic."[44] This complex, named in tribute to Shakespeare, stemmed from a sterile veneration, unlike those, usually so productive, that nourished Cocteau. Humanity, then, was made of a chain of half-empty selves. Some, through love or power, managed to fulfill others with them, but they themselves remained always open to an invader, a leader, or who knows, God. We are only links in a chain.

THE SHIP OF FOOLS

The more nebulous the universe became, the more tempted Cocteau was to find a hidden meaning in it, to make the lattice of coincidences in which he had always lived into some kind of system. As a child he had dreamed of becoming an "ingénieur" (engineer), but pronounced it "ingénieux" (ingenious). Now he was learning about numerology, the science based on a pyramid founded on the numbers three (for the Trinity), four (like the paws of a mammal), and seven (like the wonders of the world and the invisible walls around our astral bodies). Convinced that he had broken through six of these walls, and had gotten stuck just before the exit, he acquired the same relationship to texts as an astrologer to the sky or a seer to the writings of Nostradamus: he abandoned their obvious meaning to interpret them according to a numerical system founded not on the number ten, but on twenty-six, corresponding to the letters of the alphabet, like the decoding machines that decrypted German messages during the war. At the same time, strange specialists, supporters of "cryptomnesia" (hidden, predictive meanings) used a grid that used a similar logic, along with the predictions contained in his poetry collection *Vocabulaire*, to "discover" that these meanings very clearly presaged the Second World War, the full powers conferred on Pétain, and the tragedy of Pearl Harbor.[45] Flukes, lapses, and coincidences are hidden in a superior logic, whose gigantic reach exceeds us, but which some clairvoyants, often without their knowing, can clearly predict: everything obeys a text, which some can guess at and a very rare few can read. Initiates, as always, suppose that the only temple to be built that would be worthy of this name, to be in contact with God, is already within us in the form of mathematical figures, the bones of the body serving as columns. The real work would consist of changing these figures into numbers, and these numbers into poems—while waiting for disciples to translate these messages clearly and reveal to the world who Jean Cocteau really was, and what his work, so poorly understood, was worth.

Cocteau had attracted many imposters after *Thomas* was published. A crooked impresario had managed to con him out of his royalties to *La voix humaine* and then to convince him to do the portrait of Maria Lani, a German actress he had invented with Bérard, who had become a "well-known" actress in Germany, and whose profile had been painted by the greatest artists, except for Picasso. A woman posing as Cocteau's wife had managed to extract thirty million francs from honest people, under the pretext of staging one of her "husband's" plays. And at the Salon du Comité National des Ecrivains in 1952, a young man had sat down behind a pile of his books and signed them in his place, then made off with the cash.

Cocteau's declarations in favor of numerological research widened his "public." The half-starved young people who had come to Cocteau to be knighted, who were capable of throwing themselves down the stairway if they found the door closed on the rue de Montpensier, gave way to amateurs dazzled by his radio broadcasts about the bundles of fiberglass falling from the flying saucers only to melt, like angel hair, in the hands of witnesses. Researchers fascinated by lunar eclipses, Napoleonic anniversaries, and reversible dates or symbols—808, 1961, 666—got in touch with him. Helped by his taste for the occult and his frequent allusions to the apocryphal Aquarian Gospel, the knights of the Order of the Temple of Jerusalem, via the Marquis de Luca, ordered Cocteau to decorate a chapel in Fréjus, dangling as bait the prospect of a villa in the Midi as payment.[46] Rumor had it that he had been made Grand Master of the Order of the Priory of Zion, a brotherhood close to the Rosicrucians, and was then initiated by the Knights of the Holy Sepulcher. His nature led him to say yes to everything, and some used his name without asking his permission. Thus did he become, without knowing it, president of many associations and signatory to many petitions.

Fake Cocteaux were pointed out here and there—imposters who got themselves invited to opening nights, con artists in search of subsidies, failures who wanted attention. Every time one was discovered, the real Cocteau was devalued a little more, as if he were dematerializing like the "tulpas," those ghostlike beings whom the Tibetan mystics believe have the power to take form and live, and who, without being aware of it, behave like anyone else.[47] Fascinated to see him cross through mirrors and lies, dreams and tales, opening all the doors to the vestibule leading to all the occult powers that control us, these "erudites" began to write to him letters to reveal to him the alchemical keys to his work. In the meantime, these irrational folk named him, without any contest, the greatest psychiatrist of the era. One begged him to accept beside him, as Christ had done, the wicked thief crucified by his vices who had the humble honor of writing to him; another identified him as the visionary keeping the link in place between the earth and the collective unconscious. As if Cocteau were a white shaman capable of putting himself in a trance to inhabit other bodies or travel in the kingdom of the dead, or able to speak in tongues.

A viscount called Cocteau flypaper and signed his letter "Your friend in Sodom."[48] Another man confessed his conviction that he was one of the appendages to the enormous centipede that was God. A woman reminded him of their first tryst, with underlying menace; another demanded he marry her. Found with a knife in his hand and committed "by dark forces," a Belgian mental patient demanded that he intercede with these forces on his behalf. Suspected of madness by reasonable people, Cocteau had come to be seen as a healer by the mad. God knows that between Sachs, Genet, and Marais (the son of a kleptomaniac), he had seen boys who were accustomed to evade reality; but this avalanche of the disturbed was really touching. Some, having come in contact with mystical forces, wanted to see him as a demi-god serving a shifting religion, like Vishnu, who made regular trips down to earth in order to promote spirituality, in the form of different avatars: one century Krishna, the next Buddha, sometimes Christ and sometimes Mohammed, forming an immense chain linking the great religions across the centuries. Others had a truly original vision; an unusually brilliant madwoman sent Cocteau one of the most beautiful texts ever written about him. Impressed, he went out of his way to get it published, but without success, and soon the poor woman "knew" that he didn't like the essay and was in fact secretly jealous, believing that he had written to all the publishers to prevent it from being published, and to encourage them to destroy it. Even among this limited group, his goodwill ended up drawing resentment.

Alarmed by so much vindictiveness, he bunkered down in the countryside and waited for the storm to pass. John Nash himself, one of the great mathematicians of the century, tried to get in touch with him, in the midst of the schizophrenic whirlwind. Convinced that he too was the left foot of God on earth, the future winner of the Nobel Prize in Economics probably wanted to confess the mystical secrets that had been revealed to him, or the numerological calculations that had allowed him to decode, through the headlines in the newspapers, the messages that aliens were sending him—or perhaps something about his own homosexuality.[49] But on the Princeton campus, where the old scholar wandered in search of his past glory, no one could give him Jean Cocteau's address.

TESTAMENT OF ORPHEUS

The real Cocteau, thank goodness, still had true supporters. He was "elected" by the editors of the *Cahiers du cinéma*, a revue that pushed back against the cinema that reigned in France, whose aesthetic and psychological shadows had barely evolved since the 1930s. The *Cahiers du cinéma* critics, who were on the verge of becoming filmmakers themselves, called into question the power of the screenwriters, the studios, and the high-ranking actors (like Jean Gabin and Michèle Morgan), and turned to Cocteau's films to promote a different kind of filmmaking. With other writer-filmmakers like Guitry and Pagnol, Cocteau soon became the heart of this "band of four" whose originality the *Cahiers* would praise as an antidote to the corporate inflexibility of the Qualité Française label. One of his major coups was to have cast real people in *Orphée*, like the Italian neorealists had done.

Starting in 1949, Cocteau had been saying he preferred to shoot on 16mm, a format that was easier to use, and a hundred times less expensive, than 35mm. At the festival of "Cursed Films" in Biarritz, where he had helped numerous badly funded or patched-together films, he had wished out loud that the big companies would make copies in 35mm of films shot in 16mm, so that new filmmakers could still show their work in mainstream theaters. Sure that the era of large-scale industrial film production was at an end, he had predicted that cinema, contrary to the other arts, would move toward a smaller distribution model. When they became filmmakers, if the Cahiers group did not entirely agree with his preference for 16mm, which he had just used to make on a shoestring *La villa Santo Sospir*, one of the first autobiographical films, they still regularly paid homage to the materialized dream of *Le sang d'un poète* as well as the opiate strangeness of *Orpheus*; in the journal, Jean-Luc Godard would praise these films as being a perfect mix of "magic" films and of documentaries.[50]

Jacques Demy was the most enthusiastic admirer. He began to adapt for the screen *Le bel indifférent*, the brief monologue that Piaf had performed, and then filmed Cocteau opposite his wax double, multiplied by the mirrors of the Musée Grévin—before Cocteau in turn encountered, in *Le testament d'Orphée*, this other Cocteau whom he had loathed in the end, who was everyone's puppet. If *Les parapluies de Cherbourg* established a very personal aesthetic, playing with the conventions of musical comedy and the fotonovela to create a kind of light tragedy, *Les demoiselles de Rochefort*, with its sad, dancing sailors, and *Peau d'âne*, with its impish fairies, would keep the memory of the poet alive for a long time. François Truffaut revered *Les enfants terribles*, which he considered one of the rare "olfactory" works in cinematic history—you could smell the teenagers' rooms, he said. He who had been half-abandoned as an adolescent, loved the "hospital poetry" that film unlocked, as well as the untutored quality of the nonprofessional actors whom Melville and Cocteau had cast. From this admiration was born *Les quatre cents coups*, in which a very young Jean-Pierre Léaud plays a neorealist schoolboy Dargelos. Cocteau, a member of the jury, made Truffaut win Best Director at Cannes in 1959, which triumphantly launched the filmmaker, and his young star. Other filmmakers adored Cocteau as well. Alain

Resnais was among the most devoted, and Godard, in his elliptical, citational style, never failed to pay tribute to him. He, along with Renoir and Epstein, formed a trio of "uncle Jeans" in his film buff's deck of cards. In his eyes, Cocteau had baptized French cinema: bizarre, inventive, and minority-focused.

Meanwhile, the name Cocteau remained prestigious in America. *Le sang d'un poète* continued to be shown exclusively at the Fifth Avenue Playhouse in New York, where the audience would not even let a copy be made, so attached were they to the original, which had become so worn that it was like watching a film shot in the middle of a monsoon. The film students saw him as the great innovator of their art, along with Buñuel and Man-Ray; from Maya Deren to Gregory Markopoulos, there were many underground filmmakers who claimed him as an influence. Kenneth Anger's first impulse in 1948 was to send his sulfurous *Fireworks* to Jean Cocteau, who admired and praised it all around, then showed it in the Festival of Cursed Films in Biarritz, in 1950. Fashion, on the West Coast, had already seized hold of his universe, and on the more literary East Coast, the name Cocteau was a very valuable brand. Andy Warhol was still a nobody (and in a certain sense this would always be true); fascinated by this Frenchman who had managed to become everything, he would be greatly influenced by Cocteau's simple lines when it came time to draw his virile profiles. Helped by his overactive passivity, Warhol would also demonstrate a sense for the seismic shifts of the time. He would make an art of being a chameleon, as Cocteau did, and he would show an astonishing artistic flexibility and a formidable talent for encouraging just the right kind of publicity. Warhol would launch the Velvet Underground and film the micro-stars of the Factory, from Ultra-Violet to Joe Dallessandro, just as Cocteau had once patronized Les Six and filmed his lovers.[51]

Cocteau knew almost nothing of this effervescence. Touched by the shows of appreciation he received from America or the New Wave, he had difficulty liberating himself from his persecution complex. The youth of his admirers was both an homage and an affront: he suffered when reminded that he had been born in the previous century. If there was a group he felt at home with, it was the Gypsies of Nîmes and of Arles, whom he sometimes met with Picasso, and some of whom would be featured in his *Testament*. The Gypsies, who had no material attachments and were accused everywhere of thievery and lying, and sometimes of kidnapping children, represented to Cocteau childhood itself. "We are born young or we are born old," Cocteau would say to Roger Stéphane. Incapable of working for anyone or bending to any authority, the Gypsies were born young, like himself; their wives only had to start stamping the floor to the sound of the guitars, as if they were trying to put out a fire on the floorboards with heels soaked in gas, for him to want to join them. Seeing them fight against the "angel of epilepsy," hearing them roll between their hands the "little death-heads rattling their teeth," he was transported back to Seville, Grenada, or Cordoba in the great aridity of Andalusia, and felt the genius of a people that knew how to live with fire and passion, and that had inspired such beautiful poems from him in the *Cérémonial espagnol du Phénix*, which he dedicated to Lorca.[52] Like those who celebrated in 1918, the Gypsies cried in the shelter of their circular caravans, "Death to death!" Between them and de Gaulle, there was almost no one; only this people of princes disguised as beggars and the ultimate political demi-god stood out from this standardized world in which crowds of the incurious jaw their chewing gum and watch soap operas. And since he rushed to the smallest flamenco dance given in the Camargue, Cocteau applauded every speech given by the hero of Free France, and encouraged him with a disturbing candor to defy the world through the sheer power of rhetoric. "I love you," de Gaulle would have read in the last letter he received from the writer, although by that point they were already embalming him.

As the end approached, Cocteau's dreams were tinted with history. He thought about the world of his childhood, the Third Republic that had incubated so many unique souls under the bell jar of conformity. Then he imagined turning up at the Versailles of Marie Antoinette, just after the two Englishwomen who were surprised, walking in the gardens of the Petit Trianon on August 10, 1901, to "encounter" the queen and her retinue, although she had left the château for good on October 6, 1789.[53] He had always been fascinated by these moments when the fabric of life is ripped open, allowing one to catch a glimpse of an endless beyond. Having become younger by one day, passing over the International Date Line during his trip around the world in 1936, he had ever since thought of those born on February 29, who only officially aged every four years. Or of the twenty-nine-year-old American who upon being hypnotized in 1952 had explained in great detail the life she had lived in Cork, Ireland, at the end of the eighteenth century. Convinced that it would soon be possible to travel backward in time, as well as to visit the future, he lost no time writing a play imagining Molière explaining to Louis XIV the scandal caused by his *Bacchus*, three centuries in the future—a quick sketch intended for the Comédie Française but which would be performed in Japan. This would be Cocteau's last contribution to the theater: his nomadic spirit, eager to collapse the fourth wall of the rooms that housed him, had pushed at the partitions of time, and they had given way.

Cocteau suddenly wanted to make a film that would dramatize these wanderings, a film in which he would play the role of a little marquis in the time of

Louis XV—a time that he fantasized about for its poetic gaiety, like that of the Sun King for its literary grandeur, but which he had to some extent experienced, in his youth, in the pastiched version of the Third Republic balls, covered with fleur-de-lys. Francine Weisweiller could appear under a parasol, like the beauties of the 1900s, in order to prolong the historical moment that had so dazzled him, when the aged Empress Eugénie, the last survivor of the Second Empire, had leaned over to pick a bunch of white daphne and had whispered to him, "I no longer have the power to decorate poets, but I can offer you this."[54] The scene already seemed old-fashioned in 1911; in 1957, it seemed to belong to the distant eternity that Cocteau dreamed of visiting.

He imagined his film as a testimony in images, in order to articulate the strangeness that had always lived within him. *Le sang d'un poète* was an allegorical biography whose flux of images imitated the sloshing waves of dreams; his new film would initiate the audience into the mysteries of his poetry and immerse them in the surprise, fear, and excitement that the Ancients felt in the temple of Sibyl of Cumae—each scene, then, had to pull the audience into this superior dimension where existence reveals its secrets. Hoping to repair his damaged reputation, and perhaps to erase the terrible portrait that Maurice Sachs, his Judas, had left of him, Cocteau thought this might even be the time to try again to launch the sort of cult he had tried to create: "His name was Jean. He wasn't light, but he tried to give light its chance to speak," said a first version of the script, before light was changed to shadow.[55] It was no longer the voice of a prophet, but that of a belated apostle no longer trying desperately to immortalize the initials J.C.

Cocteau's meetings with producers resulted in a wave of promises and empty wishes that kept him in suspense for months, if not years. Believing himself the victim of a spell designed to make the film "unreal," Cocteau decided to borrow money from the bank and to create a production company, with shares to be given to friends. Truffaut, who had already coproduced an adaptation of *Anna la bonne* by Claude Jutra, invested some of the proceeds of *Les quatre cents coups*; Francine Weisweiller and her brother added their contribution to that of the nominal producer. The budget was still very small, so Cocteau decided to ask celebrities to donate their time as actors. Picasso, Yul Brynner, Charles Aznavour, Lucia Bose—almost everyone he asked agreed to be in the film, which would be the strange filmmaker's last. Cocteau let himself be convinced to take, for the first time in his life, the lead role.

The film posed so many more problems: what phrases was he going to make himself say, and in what form would he appear, bearing in mind that these words, and these images, would survive him for eternity? What kind of look would he give to his prophetic poet tasked with introducing the audience to the mysteries of his psyche? Determined to surprise them by showing the range of his magic powers—from the supernatural restoration of a hibiscus with torn petals to Édouard Dermit's miraculous "undiving," snatched from the Mediterranean like a torpedo—he had false eyes painted on his eyelids, which he lengthened and underlined with kohl, until he looked like an Egyptian king.[56] Gazing straight ahead and pointing at the sky, to show his familiarity with the powers on High, he began to intone his sibylline phrases and his paradox in the almost inhuman voice of an automaton, and gave the impression of supplying a compendium of the stupefying "Jean Cocteau." At the same time he decided to give himself a "young" look, tousling his hair and never removing his suede jacket. The man who always sought to be definitive yet to renew himself, to become a statue and to start all over from the beginning, found himself at the height of his dilemma. Roger Caillois defined imitation as an incantation frozen at its peak, where the sorcerer is stuck in his own trap; Cocteau's approach, in this final feature film, would not have surprised him.[57] Behind his prophetic appearance, the filmmaker keenly evoked those fragile animals who take on the appearance of a feared species to escape their predators.

Returning to the Victorine Studios in Nice, where *L'éternel retour* had been filmed, he didn't recognize anything. The ghost town, where so many films had materialized and then dissipated, reflected his own destiny: a waiting room. The filming was intoxicating. For sixty-five days, some kind of magic bound together this team of men who ate at the same table and slept at the same hotels; the stagehands had never seen such a thoughtful, joyous, inventive director. Cocteau was always the last to bed. "Everyone asks where my energy comes from, and by what miracle I wear out giants during filming, stubbornly demanding a thousand drudgeries though they are begging for mercy and can't go on. It's because a production, a job, fascinates me to the point that I leave my own body."[58] The most thrilling scenes were filmed at Baux-de-Provence, a historic village whose mysterious quarries had inspired part of Dante's *Divina Commedia*. Forgetting the "uncomfortable suit" of his own skin, banishing his difficulty of being and his nervous spasms, confusing days and nights, time and space, Cocteau took his whole team into the hidden grandeur of this subterranean cathedral. Happy to finance "such a cobbler," Truffaut came twice to watch him direct the "actors" that Lucien Clergue photographed and was impressed by the precision of his directions—all the shots seemed already to have been composed in his mind—and by the way he took advantage of the accidents that happened during filming, including an unexpected jet flying over at the exact moment he was receiving Minerva's lance in his body.[59] More than ever this extraterrestrial was taking his orders from the heavens, where the gods who ruled over our destinies dwelled.

The last day was agony. To see two months of life together broken with a "see you later" that never turned out to be true made Cocteau crazy, separation-phobic as he was. He had to mourn once again his old dream of living in a community, and would wander for entire days like a sleepwalker brutally awakened, before coming back to Paris and getting back into the studio. He was worried, watching the rushes; had there been other people watching, he would have asked them to excuse his idiocy. It all seemed so outlandish, a potpourri that threw together the young Jean-Pierre Léaud and Oedipus, Serge Lifar and Minerva, Francine Weissweiller and centaurs! Fearing that it would come across as sententious, he sprinkled the film with "tragic gags." But what if the spectators began to laugh, seeing him materialize in a classroom in ancien régime attire, and reappear in his nylon shirt-jacket like Kim Il-Sung in the Villa Santo Sospir, before watching his death "live" in the Val d'Enfer in Beaux?

He had had his doubts during filming, but the team had convinced him to keep everything. Something wasn't working in his mystical comedy. Tightened to the point of breakage by another facelift, his face had difficulty sweating and in its inexpressiveness resembled a mask created by Jean Cocteau; cruelly contradicted by his sunken mouth, where death was already beginning to show, the apparent youth of his figure anguished him: he looked as if he was incapable of taking form and sticking to it. You could see both the messiah without worshippers and the beginner anxious to be believed, the god he had always hoped for and his horrible fear of being nothing. Outdone by this new avatar, losing all understanding of his personality, the director watched, stupefied, this transhistoric Cocteau that film had frozen for eternity.

He asked Robert Bresson to come and see a first edit, explaining, "You are perhaps the only one who knows me well enough to tell me if my ambitions of resurrection are just a dream."[60] The austere director of *Pickpocket* told him that he had made an abstract film, just as Rothko painted abstract canvases, and he immediately felt slightly better. *Le testament* lasted only fifty minutes, the "spontaneous" duration settled on by Cocteau the filmmaker—who as a novelist never wrote more than a hundred and fifty pages—but this meant it would not be able to be commercially distributed. He decided at the last minute, then, to shoot the scene in which the poet, at the tribunal of the Zone, must confront the pitiless prosecutors played by Maria Casarès, who had been the princess in *Orpheus*, and François Périer, in the role of Heurtebise. These two were professionals: it was shot in three days, and was the best scene in the film. The princess character was a tribute to Natalie Paley, and Heurtebise to Radiguet; all the figures in his personal pantheon would figure henceforth in *Le testament*, from Édouard Dermit as Cégeste, Orpheus/Cocteau's guardian angel, to Jean Marais as blind Oedipus. Picasso was given a private showing; he compared the film to a verse poem with mathematical rigor, but the strange Jouhandeau stood up right in the middle of the screening, and Cocteau became more worried than ever as the premiere approached.

The young wolves of the New Wave heaped praise on his film, more out of friendship than conviction, with the exception of Godard and Truffaut. The young readers of the *Cahiers du cinéma* went to see it as if they were going to Mass, in Tergal trousers and black wool polo shirts, and their reverence warmed his heart. Morand sent him a magnificent letter thanking him for the brilliant present he had just given to all those who loved him: "You jump through gravestones [*crever*] like paper hoops," he said, praising the succession of deaths that always left him more alive than ever. "Destiny has chosen well; you are the only gift to our era, to our generation," he concluded.[61]

Sensing death approaching the director, the critics were almost unanimous in their praise of this strange film. But the audience, after becoming accustomed to seeing him mistreated, detected complacency, and two weeks later, there was no one left in the theaters. Cocteau had once again chased away the crowds. "Who else amongst our contemporaries could permit himself such an exhibition without sinking into ridicule?" Jouhandeau wrote to him, meaning to cheer him up.[62] Morand himself noted, ten years later, "Astonishing after all this time! Cocteau almost seems like the Sacha Guitry of Surrealism."[63]

REQUIEM

Cocteau would direct one last time, starting rehearsals of *La voix humaine* for which Poulenc had just composed the music. He decided to take charge of the direction of the lyric tragedy, performed at the Opéra-Comique in February 1959, under the baton of Georges Prêtre. A week was enough for him to learn the score by heart, and he needed just a few more days to direct Denise Duval, who had already sung *Les dialogues des Carmélites*, also by Poulenc, a few months earlier.[64]

It was a musical miracle. Without ever stifling or betraying the text, the music managed to amplify the abandoned woman's amorous confusion. Poulenc adapted the drama with astonishing ease, and without giving the slightest impression of blind conformity. Duval's candor, subtlety, and humanity lent dramatic truth to a love that provides every excuse for the woman's executioner, who strangles her with the deadly cord of the telephone while she asks him only to squeeze harder. Poulenc's "dear tearful nightingale" seemed to die a thousand deaths, and to know nothing of the audience that took in all of her haggard affection. "Her eyes widening at the approach of the inevitable, Denise Duval has true pathos, is marvelously simple, and has found the role of her life," wrote one critic, reviewing a show that would tour the world.[65]

While he was rehearsing the cast in Nice, advising Duval to sing as if her blood were literally spilling onstage, Cocteau began coughing up blood. Treated for an internal hemorrhage and transported to Santo Sospir, he floated "on the river of the dead" for months, in a semiconscious state that made him feel like a fly glued to the ceiling. In spite of his doctors' strict orders, he began scribbling notes, lying in bed, with an eye toward writing a long poem. He was suspicious of traditional medicine—he was convinced that the antibiotics were attacking the germs of his poetic singularity—and he managed to get Dr. Soulié, who prescribed blood transfusions, to agree that one should not change the blood of poets. Cocteau then decided to renew his personal Grail through another stay in Engadin, where he continued to draft his poem, soon to be called *Requiem*. The benches placed at intervals all the way to Sils-Maria made him think of placing breaks in the poem to give it a certain rhythm. His extreme fatigue had contributed to the dreamlike qualities of *Le sang d'un poète*; this forced bedrest, by removing his critical vigilance, allowed him access to his unconscious. Moreover, the illness allowed him to realize anew how much he was loved, and even that he didn't fear death all that much. War, the occult, drugs, dreams, and religion had one by one ferried him onward. His body was now ready to discover the next world by itself; after death, he knew he would continue to fly.

It took three months for Cocteau to decipher his notes, with help from a few friends, and longer still to organize them. More than seventy years old, he sweated and puffed and panted amid the heap of papers, but four thousand verses emerged from the chaos of scrawls, which he reworked until they formed the fluvial surge that would lead him to his final home. "Dragging all the memories of a lifetime through these waters," as Michel Décaudin wrote, *Requiem* would be the longest (two hundred pages when it was published), and the last, of his poetry collections, with a clear testimonial value.[66] Finally, in 1962, the river of ink had found its bed of paper.

His poems were dedicated to the glorious living: Stravinsky, Malraux, Giacometti, Sartre, Marcel Duchamp, and even the young Françoise Sagan.[67] But aside from Aragon at *Lettres françaises*, who understood the importance of bringing back the alexandrine, the press left this ghost of another era alone to swim in his own blood. There were so few articles about *Requiem* that Cocteau had to ask Jeannine Worms, Francine's sister-in-law, to write one for *Le Figaro*, and the friend of Caillois and Cioran responded by praising "this towering work, expressive of French genius," a phrase that Cocteau crossed out, scribbling "of *his* genius."[68] He then called upon Alain Bosquet, who finally thought it was better to "assassinate" *Requiem* on the front page of *Combat*. "I offer you this river which people are spitting into," Cocteau wrote when he signed the young Pierre Bergé's copy.[69]

The era was so conventional that he was hardly surprised it kept such a solitary genius at a distance, as if he had a contagious illness; he was even expecting the reaction to be worse.[70] The twist, convertible cars, hitchhiking to the South with a fake Bardot and a guitar on your back: that was okay. A Johnny Hallyday concert where bottles were thrown and chairs broken, no problem. The deafening sound of jukeboxes and the whines of the pop singers: perfectly acceptable. But poems invoking Endymion and King Solomon, verses celebrating Nietzsche and the spring, dreams and Paracelsus, Nicolas de Staël and multiple dimensions?

As he himself had written, in this collection:

À force de vivre au-dessus
Des moyens de mon époque
Elle m'a fort mal reçu
C'est faute d'avoir su
D'où vient ma fortune équivoque.
[Because I have lived beyond
The means of my era
It has not received me well
It's because it didn't know
Whence came my ambiguous fortune.][71]

His time really had passed. Genet himself belonged to another time; the press only wanted to hear about Robbe-Grillet, Beckett, Duras, or Sarraute, writers of the *nouveau roman* who strove to cure the reader of his dependence on plot, character, metaphor, and psychology. Cocteau looked like an ancien régime fop by comparison. All the media did was praise this or that new debut, and the literary supplements were crawling with articles that didn't so much as mention his name—he wasn't even worth attacking! "Life is a horizontal drop," he had written in *Opium*.[72] Grown profoundly bitter, Cocteau was convinced that everything was going wrong and in decline—France, youth, literature, and therefore humanity, which had become an ungrateful and unlettered thing, which only cared about its "wheels" and betting on the horses. How many generations would it take before readers would be born who might appreciate his value — or who could rise above the effect of the "mysterious hatred" that still weighed on him?

Three years earlier, on June 5, 1959, while inaugurating a monument to Apollinaire in the square de l'Abbaye, alongside Saint-Germain-des-Prés church, with Apollinaire's widow, Jacqueline, and André Salmon, Apollinaire's best friend, Cocteau's gaze had met Breton's resentful glare. The old Surrealist was standing near the bust sculpted by Picasso in homage to his first poet laureate, and had come to interrupt the ceremony, along with Tristan Tzara and Gabrièle Buffet-Picabia, the ex-wife of the ex-Dadaist Picabia. Forty years had elapsed since Apollinaire's death, but his inheritors' hatred for one another had not dimmed. Twenty years after Aragon and Éluard had patched things up with Cocteau, Breton continued to loathe him. The era of Boeuf sur le Toit, the Maritain period, the crowds of the Front Populaire, the years of the Occupation, and the bars of Saint-Germain-des-Prés all belonged to history, but "Rimbaud the policeman" still had one hand on his nightstick.[73]

A year later, Cocteau's hurried election as the Prince of Poets by two hundred and fifty people who had telephoned the organizer of a poetry fair maximized Cocteau's paranoia. The title still had enough prestige that Breton rounded up his vassals and had them sign a manifesto contesting the election, to which Francis Ponge and Ungaretti affixed their initials. Even Paulhan, who had been linked to Cocteau for twenty years, encouraged him to step down to allow for a new election to be held, in which he would not be a candidate. Recalling that Aragon, Tzara, Soupault, Éluard, Artaud, Prévert, René Char, and Breton himself had promised each other, in 1920, never to waste their time on Cocteau, Breton got to work trying to convince readers of *Le Figaro*, a right-wing newspaper, that Cocteau should be considered an anti-poet, a born cheat and a typical imposter. "The contents of his verse, though there is no need to consult psychoanalysis, are the sort of thing one reads on the walls of a urinal," concluded the author of *Nadja*, whose haughty lyricism had eroded over the years.[74]

Cocteau had declared, during the war, that he preferred to be a scapegoat rather than nothing at all. When he learned that a counter-election had put Saint-John Perse in his place, it seemed at first as if he would change his mind and let the matter rest. But after seventeen years of being hunted by the Surrealists, four years of Collaborationist hatred, and almost half a century of concealed disdain, he decided to rebel. When Perse renounced the crown, Cocteau took up the battle to take it back, drawing strength from the thousands of messages of support he had received, the article Aragon had written denouncing the "prehistorical hatred" being used against him, and the welcome by students of Cadix, where he had gone to inaugurate the university.[75] He succeeded. But it was such an effort, and he received so many insults, that the crown began to seem as if it were made of thorns. Once again, Breton had managed to ruin his life.

In 1962, the journal *Arts* organized a trial, with the indefatigable Philippe Soupault serving as prosecutor. One critic called the author of *Les enfants terribles* a fact of civilization, but his voice was drowned out in a storm of insults. Cocteau had only a few months left to live. In August of that year, Breton warmly congratulated Alain Bosquet on his annihilation of *Requiem*, saying, with regard to Cocteau, "A serious tactical error on the part of the poets of my generation was to deliberately remain silent about him, judging his name unworthy even to be spoken. He certainly could have been crushed back in 1918."[76] Luckily Breton had assured Tzara that same year, still talking about Cocteau, "and hatred isn't my forte." These new attacks would be harmful for Cocteau's reputation. Arriving in Socialist Poland at the age of seventy-three with a group of French poets, he would be reduced to begging the young translator who accompanied them to convince another member of the delegation (who was still spreading around horrors about his poetry) that the young Poles loved his work.[77]

Cocteau's exhaustingly productive life had left him with no illusions, and if he still believed in Santa Claus, he no longer expected presents. Renan's phrase "It is possible that the truth is sad" echoed endlessly in his mind. Age had made him so tender and emotional that he would burst into tears if fate struck one of his friends, or even carried away a figure to whom he had been close in the 1920s. But they were discreet tears that no one was allowed to see. If hysteria results from a fear of enjoyment counterbalanced by an artificial euphoria, he had exhausted its energy: all his flesh had become part of his books, and his reputation was in tatters. His work had made him a memory.

Sometimes someone could still get him to smile, telling him that Madeleine, his devoted servant, had very seriously said to a priest, "Monsieur Cocteau? He's the good Lord . . . but better!"[78] He remembered how prestigious he had been, and how many hearts he had touched, and sometimes even burned. He knew, however, that there was no one left to revere him, besides Madeleine—and still she joked! Ambitious men and fools, yes, badly informed provincials, yes, but he was far, very far, from the ardor that had made Maurice Sachs's contemporaries climb the lampposts on the rue d'Anjou. He had become so used to the blows that he was almost embarrassed to come across a young writer who admired him unconditionally, as did Jean-Pierre Millecam, and he had to restrain himself from telling him he wasn't worth it. When a young poetess exclaimed, taking his hand, "How beautiful you are! Now I believe in the gods," this fawning made him so disgusted with himself that he truly wanted to vomit: "And why did I want to be loved / When I did not love myself," he wrote in *Requiem*.[79]

His archives were in shocking disarray, and every day he lost a letter or a poem, carried off by someone or another with or without his authorization: he was so discouraged that he didn't much look after whatever he kept. He loved Milly, but if someone asked what he would save from a fire, he would reply, "The fire!"[80] What good was it to prolong the myth of the Promethean poet, bringing together the earth and the sky, and writing under dictation from the gods, as Apollinaire described it? Busy as he was pontificating about the foreign policy of the USSR, Freud as a bourgeois, or the military strategies of Bonaparte, even Breton himself no longer believed in it.[81]

Cocteau's doctors were pulling out their hair, but he continued to smoke cigarette after cigarette, as well as to blithely drink whiskey and red wine, which Dr. Soulié had recommended for his heart. He was told that he risked cutting his life short, but he had become so used to visiting his dead friends in his thoughts that he now felt comfort rather than fear at the idea of joining them. A stranger to this earth, the child who came from outer space, Cocteau mentally prepared his funeral, just as Sarah Bernhardt used to spend time in a coffin to get used to her future circumstances. If he had been alone, he would have feared death without a doubt, but with Doudou steering his little boat, he wasn't afraid to cross the Styx. Why fear a condition we are born to, which will eternally survive us? Death had always been a part of his life, carried in his tears and his blood; wasn't it, even now, hollowing his cheeks, eating at his lips, thinning his neck? Had he not learned to tame it, through each mutation, each small suicide? He didn't have to die, because in a way he already had. Lucretius said that the tricky gods had concealed from mankind that the greatest pleasure is death. Cocteau wasn't far from agreeing with him.

"What would you do if you found out you had only fifteen minutes left to live?," people asked him. "I would use them so that the people who love me don't realize they're going to lose me," he replied.[82] What was there left to expect, now that he no longer had the energy to get up to watch the sun rise, to renew himself, to hope to be loved? If he feared one thing, it was leaving Doudou alone; he knew his companion was too earnest for this epoch of sound and fury, too fragile to live his life alone. Doudou himself dreamed of "leaving" at the same time as him, in a car accident for example. Then they would go up to heaven together and weather eternity side by side.

The scents that emanated from his palette sometimes reminded Cocteau of the smell of oil paints that had surrounded his father, whom he had spoken of so infrequently, but with whom he had spent hours as a child, fascinated by his facility with a paintbrush. Why had he killed himself? He still didn't know, but he described it for the first time to several friends (he had only previously trusted Marais enough, to that point) in a detached voice, adding only: "Without Doudou, I would have had enough of life."[83] He pointed out that his insurmountable mental fatigue had nothing to do with the causes that had driven his father to kill himself, but nevertheless, he made this troubling confession: "The idea of suicide is inherited as an action without the reasons that motivate it."[84] As if he were reserving the final right to hasten his departure.

What would he gain by clinging to life? Hadn't he said, like the heroine of *La dame de Monte Carlo*, which Poulenc had just set to music,

> Quand on est morte entre les mortes
> on se traîne chez les vivants—
> Lorsque tout vous flanque à la porte,
> Et la ferme d'un coup de vent,
> Ne plus être jeune et aimée . . .
> Derrière une porte fermée,
> Il reste de sauter dans l'eau.
> [When one is dead among the dead
> One wanders among the living
> When everything kicks you out the door
> And closes it in a gust of wind
> No longer to be young or loved . . .
> Behind a closed door
> All that is left is to throw yourself in the water.][85]

He did not believe in life enough, no matter what form it took, to actually take his own; life seemed as unreal to him as the dream he had had the night before or the Zone he was going to reach. The abolition of personality? He had already experienced that during the centuries that had preceded his birth; he was ready to bear those that would follow his death. Life and death were just two sides of the same coin, for a mind that had always lived opposites as interchangeable, and for whom human destiny was nothing, on the scale of Creation, but the spasm of a gnat. Hadn't the fourth wall separating us from the other world always taken the form of a mirror to him? Once through the mirror, everything would change; his flesh would become marble for all eternity; he would become a real being, surrounded by love and success. The final metamorphosis would be the right one.

He began to dream. He saw himself wandering, happy and translucent, in the jasper city of Saint John: either he would awaken in a body of crystal, shimmering and blinding, as in Persian mythology, or a gust of wind would carry him away to then turn into a fish in the water, or a bird in the sky, under the nuances of a rainbow . . . unless death were just a long sleep broken up by colorful dreams, lacking only the waking state, which he found so painful. He hadn't made so many beautiful plans for the future even as a teenager.

CHASED OUT OF PARADISE

Over the years, Marais had grown closer to him. His voice roughened by cigarettes, his face having become craggy, his body kept in shape by the Fantômas, the Iron Masks, and the Captain Fracasses he had hurled from the chandeliers to the dungeons, the actor had got it into his head to encourage the career of a young American dancer with whom he had fallen in love. Georges Rech was looking for a theme that could sustain several ballets? Marais made up the plots, sketched the costumes, designed the mock-ups, ended up directing—and then found himself cornered into being the producer. The dancer felt uncomfortable in his houseboat? He broke into his piggybank to build him an American Colonial–style house. But the little tenderness he had managed to glean from Rech cost him so much that he was beginning to understand, twenty years too late, the suffering he had inflicted on his own Pygmalion. "At the end of *Les chevaliers de la table ronde,* the first real Cocteau play I acted in, I said: 'You have to pay, and pay, and pay.' Well, I was paying for what I had done. Maybe it was the ransom for the pain I caused Jean," he would say in his memoirs.[86] As lively and athletic as ever, Marais continued to lock horns with anyone who dared say anything bad about Cocteau, but the poet was the first to forgive his enemies and to make him believe that that attitude was the height of disdain. Marais got carried away, and the quarrels began again, as in the old days. The Knight of the Round Table still burned to fly to his aid, but Cocteau didn't move. Despite the fact that the Germans had been gone for a solid fifteen years, he still feared reprisals.

Marais had lost some of his legendary joie de vivre; his happiness had gone. His life with Cocteau seemed, in retrospect, to have devalued any other way of living, and though he was over forty-five years old, the hero of *L'éternel retour* was still nostalgic for the miraculous years when, with Cocteau's magical help, the lisping young actor had suddenly, in the middle of the war, become a demigod. Finally appreciating the value of the love that Cocteau had given him, with a generosity surpassed only by his mother, Marais also saw how badly he had let him down, by always resisting his advice out of a fear of being too influenced. Having become the more rich and famous of the two, he suddenly confessed to Cocteau how much his teaching had supported him, and how proud he was, even awed, to have inspired a book nearly two hundred pages long bearing his name.[87] So what if audiences were booing his new production of *Britannicus* at the Comédie-Française: he took heart, thinking of all the attacks that Cocteau had endured during the Occupation.

Marais was the first to tell Cocteau's stories, to perpetuate his way of seeing things and his good points; from every tour he sent Cocteau enthusiastic letters telling him about the acclaim his plays received, in the provinces or abroad; from every vacation he tried, via the post office, to send him a bit of sunshine. The lying whisper "I love you too" when Cocteau had spontaneously declared himself became the truth, too late: a few years after leaving him, Galatea fell in love with Pygmalion. Cocteau had always hoped that one day his partners would watch over him, maternally; the actor Marais finally satisfied this hidden dream. Marais's solicitude confirmed to Cocteau that he had been a good father, more than a good lover. Learning that the actor's mother was stealing more than ever, Cocteau seriously considered marrying her not only to legally adopt Marais, who had never had a father, but also to bring Rosalie back to the straight and narrow. The actor persuaded Cocteau that it was a doomed plan: she would swallow him whole.[88]

Cocteau's view on life took a strange turn. He wanted to believe, and make others believe, that his love for Radiguet, Desbordes, and Marais had nothing to do with homosexuality. According to this new presentation, Cocteau's desires were simply those of the androgynes we had been in heaven, before being condemned to take bodily form in one sex, according to Plato; just as humans before Adam mentioned in the Kabbalah are born of the sexual hesitation that preceded the birth of the stars, Cocteau was the child of a world before the Fall, in which the two sexes, blended into one, could give each other all the pleasure in the world without God having anything to say about it. Soon he persuaded himself that his true calling had been to found a family; children would have given him a goal, even roots; he would have led a real life, in a real house, like the Maritains in Meudon. And because the women he had loved had deprived him of a child, he had instead adopted readymade sons: Madeleine Carlier and Natalie Paley were solely to blame for his homosexuality. The man who until five or six years earlier would still copy out (on Villa Santo Sospir notepaper) one of the beautiful erotic poems he had written in the past, now expressed himself as Maritain would have liked him to have done . . . forty years earlier.[89]

Wearing leather sandals in summer and a thick monk's robe in winter, the artist-saint refined his illuminated manuscripts in the modern monastery of Santo Sospir. He no longer bathed, less through neglect than because there was no use; his skin emitted the smooth odor that in the Church designates a person who will be canonized. Though his retreat was disrupted by television, he described with good-humored irony the many luminaries he had encountered, and spoke of them only with the most perfect goodwill—especially when he poured out horrors about them in his journal. He no longer went to the theater or the cinema, and wrote only occasional pieces. But while having his hair permed at Alexandre's salon, he would cover entire sheets of paper with the profiles of enchanting young men, lyres of Orpheus, or the rear ends of fauns, which he gave out by the handful, in order to thank those who had restored the glory of his plumage.

Cocteau did everything he could to adopt Doudou, because it was the only legal means at the time for a man to give his male companion an inheritance. It didn't work, in spite of years of legal proceedings; Francine thought perhaps Doudou could marry Carole, the little Shell heiress, who was now eighteen years old. Though he was at first surprised, Cocteau supported this socially acceptable form of incest, in line with the vision of love set out in *Les enfants terribles*. These plans fell through as well, and since he could not find an alternative, he made Doudou his sole legatee.

Until that point Francine Weisweiller repeated everything Cocteau said. Now, however, from one day to the next the things she said were molded by ideas about life and art held by her new "chosen one," a writer of detective novels—the last books Cocteau could bear to read. Weisweiller's new man had shown himself to be more than agreeable regarding Cocteau, but the status quo didn't last for long; soon Cocteau was asked to move out, chased from paradise by someone he nicknamed, in archaic, ancien régime style, the "mirliflore" (ridiculous dandy). The writer returned to the rue de Montpensier and to Milly, where his former protectress sent boxes of the things he had left behind at Santo Sospir. The press said he was living in the street, wandering without a cent.[90] Profoundly wounded at having been forced, like Orpheus, to leave the heavens without returning, the writer once again tumbled back into reality with Doudou. It seemed to him like he was "falling off a cliff into the night."[91]

This time, death really was drawing nearer. Cocteau experienced sudden and terrible pain in the middle of the night, attacks that inflicted "blemishes of distress, ulcers of unhappiness" on him; life suddenly seemed too vast, then too small; too long, then too short—in a word, unlivable. He changed rooms, went back to Paris, left again for Milly, but nothing helped. "The place I had wished for, where I used to hide, soon became a trap. I escape and am caught again, over and over."[92] The entire universe was speeding up Orpheus's final escape. Floating about in his dressing gown, an opium pipe in his hand, he looked like the sweet and naive king of the vagabonds from his 1909 poem—a king who wandered far from his kingdom, a lyre in his hand, and was found dead one morning.[93] He had never reversed his decision to disown his first three collections; when Francine Weisweiller bought the manuscript of *La lampe d'Aladin*, to take it out of circulation, he regretted only that this gesture could not retrospectively erase his false start. "One's talents marry the first form they meet and . . . this form risks being the right one," he wrote, at the end of the First World War. "Mine was the wrong one."[94]

Nevertheless, he wanted to celebrate the woman who had left her mark on him as he was starting out, whom he had so loved before disowning her poetically, and who filled him with tenderness whenever he thought of her. He too now understood in retrospect how much Anna de Noailles must have suffered at the end of the 1920s, seeing herself abandoned by the world, in a literary sense. Destiny seemed to have the same punishment in store for him; the gods had used her as a way of warning him what was to come. As always, he had not been able to see this. Death was approaching and the seasons he had shared with Minerva—the nights spent arguing, laughing, enthusing with her—now seemed the most intense, even the happiest ones of his life; those days were blessed, when they were exalted by their own gifts, and managed to fuse through language until they formed a sort of radiant androgynous divinity, almost sufficient unto itself. Those were the days when Edith Wharton, D'Annunzio, and Marinetti believed he was a prodigy, and Proust himself sought him out to flatter him as a writer who was more accomplished than even himself. He decided to pay tribute to Anna de Noailles through a book, which would be the last he would write.[95] Every year the work of the poet was fading a bit more from memory, but he wanted to believe that he could reverse destiny. "The Angel of the Bizarre" who had guided the poetry that came after 1918 had grown tiresome, like Surrealist painting. But Cocteau decided that Rimbaud would be forgotten and the Countesses' alexandrines celebrated—and then, perhaps, his would be as well.

He had written so much! So many poems in free verse, acrostics, quatrains, calligrams, and impromptus; did they really belong to one period or another? He himself sometimes had difficulty answering this question. Every skin he shed took with it entire patches of memory, and he wandered now in a temporal labyrinth, no longer able to place the people he had met into the appropriate periods. "I have been blended with such a large quantity of things that they fall from my memory, not singly, but in groups of fifty," he admitted in *La difficulté d'être*. Beloved names and voices, however, remained engraved in the wax of his heart—and even centuries could not erase them. When one evening in 1961 Proust's niece organized a soirée in memory of her uncle, he imitated Marcel's stifled, asthmatic voice so well that everyone, from Céleste to Mme Simone, had the disturbing sensation of being transported fifty years in the past. Cocteau himself was time regained.

With his mummy's hair—the mass on top of his head was now just a twisted bundle of dead tresses—Cocteau embodied another era. The French he continued to speak, just a few months before the Beatles were breaking out, became a bit difficult to follow and seemed to have escaped from the museum containing the dead luminaries he imitated so easily. At the same time, his child's heart was ageless. Many of his contemporaries no longer knew that Anna de Noailles had ever existed, but they could have said of him, as they said of her in 1927, "Anna wants a dead woman's career, but at the same time she wants to be the youngest, the most beautiful!"[96]

In the fall of 1960, Mishima arrived from Japan to visit him. The author of *Confessions of a Mask* found Cocteau's face wrinkled, but did not feel disappointed. "Cocteau did not age like most mortals," he wrote. "It seemed to me rather as if I were seeing a man suffering from an incurable disease called 'age,' contracted by accident and most inconveniently."[97] Even better than the French, the Japanese man had spotted, beyond the writer he admired, the man who had wanted to be a god, but lacking the seriousness to take on the role, had ended up a fallen angel with a truly poignant youthfulness about him. Cocteau had not become Vishnu, Shakespeare, or Alexander the Great, but humanity itself—always incomplete, always interrupted. With Cocteau's inexhaustible appetite for life and his dull longing for death, he was like the earthly twin of Kant's dove who, tired of being constrained by the air that carries him, dreams of a sky free of gravity.

Cocteau's brother, Paul, had died in December 1961, after his sister, Marthe, leaving him the sole survivor of their tribe; then it was Poulenc's turn. Every day another witness of that period died, and every day Cocteau wondered what he was still doing hanging around. "A closing door always makes us jump," he had said, ten years earlier.[98] Then, in April 1963, he had another heart attack.

He went to convalesce at Jean Marais's home and didn't move for several weeks, like those stick insects that become cataleptic and play dead for entire days to escape their predators. "We amuse ourselves and play cards in an express train bound for death," he wrote, after the war; this time, the train was slowing down.[99] To see him in his dressing gown, silently watching television, one would say he had already gone. He had refused, after his first infarction, to recuperate at the actor's home, out of fear of revealing that he still smoked opium; Marais told him that he already knew and that he was not offended. A few days earlier, the actor had dreamed that his mentor had died in his mother's room, and that he had taken him in his arms to carry him through his child-hood dining room, had patiently massaged his feet, and had managed to bring him back to life. He scrupulously played this role in reality.

Marais's vital presence comforted Cocteau, reminding him of that other happy time, interrupted by the war. He had suffered so much from their separa-tion! For years, he would burst into tears upon finding a pair of gloves that Marais had left behind at Milly. They lived that way for three months, a little extension of their life together before the great voyage out. Moved by Cocteau's "overwhelmingly" tender gaze, sure as well that he suffered more than others and felt everything more strongly, Marais demonstrated a tireless devotion. He prayed for Cocteau to get well again, for the gods to let them change places— the most effective of transfusions.

Soon Doudou came to live in the house in Marnes-la-Coquette, his suitcases filled with everything that made up Cocteau's little world, whose room had begun, once again, to resemble every other he had ever occupied. Soon he was receiving visitors, from Jean Rostand, the other son of the author of *Cyrano*, to Maurice Chevalier the crooner. "But it's too soon, dear madame, much too soon!" Satie had croaked, when an admirer burst into his hotel room laden with flowers, three months before his death. Cocteau was not quite ready yet either.

Cocteau returned to Milly with Doudou, and came back to life in the bailiff's house, where Louise de Vilmorin came to see him in August. "He was admi-rable," she wrote to her brother André; "all alone, very pale, very attentive and resigned. It seemed as if he were tired of all he knew, thought, and had thought, and of all he had created."[100] In September, it was the Jouhandeaus' turn to visit. They were his oldest friends after Picasso; forty years, and never had a cloud shadowed their friendship. Every season saw a new volume of *Les journaliers*, the diary in which Marcel spread horrors about Élise, but she did not read them. Out of fear of being hurt, or perhaps of recognizing herself, Cocteau wondered, seeing the two old people leave.

THE FINAL TRANSFORMATION

After killing five hundred thousand people, the Algerian War came to an end in mid-1962. The first beatniks appeared in the United States, where Bob Dylan had released his first album. Godard had become a star three years earlier with *À bout de souffle*; Truffaut had confirmed his own success with *Jules et Jim*, inspired by a novel by Henri-Pierre Roché. Cocteau, who had known Roché in 1916, tried one last time to belong to the times. He had tightened his skin so much that it didn't seem possible to patch it up any further, but he took up this final challenge: "There's no risk Jean wouldn't take to drink at the fountain of youth," Picasso said to James Lord.[101] The surgeon had asked him not to take any anti-coagulants, in advance of the new facelift, and a clot formed in his arteries.[102] Victim of a treatment that should have given him, like Wilde's Dorian Gray, eternal youth, he kept to his room several days, in Milly. The morning of October 11, 1963, he was told that Edith Piaf had died, but he felt so weak that he told Juliette, his cook, "Today is my last day on earth."[103] Around noon, the radio paid homage to the singer whose songs had so touched him, that he had recorded just a few days earlier, when Piaf was very ill. Then his heart gave out, for the third time. The doctor found him lying down, one hand on his stomach, as in *Le testament d'Orphée*—but this time for real. The heart that had circulated the blood of the poet had stopped beating. In a final transformation, he was sent to be reborn in the Zone.

In the mirror of an armoire, Marais saw the body that had just been embalmed, and saw himself helping Cocteau put on his green suit, the day of his reception in the Académie Française. "I felt as if I were dressing a child for his First Communion," he had said, touched by the contrast between this frail being and the weighty institution. The body now seemed curiously lifelike, and in a way much more appropriate to the situation. With his eyelids closed and his lips pursed, Cocteau seemed about to get up, with all the dignity that involved, in order to enact this backward birth that was death.

Genet was the first to visit the house. The former thief prayed over the body of the writer who had so influenced his fate, and whose work he had compared, in 1950, to a statue eaten away by anguish. He warmly embraced Madeleine, who had fed him during the Occupation, and went away in silence. Marais watched over the body all night, convinced that his "perishable [body, which had] gone, had, in an enormous task, taken away a message which in transcending it had perhaps crushed it."[104] He had a tendency to fall asleep easily, so to stay awake he stared at Cocteau's long, creative hands, which had first touched him in 1937, giving birth to him for a second time at the age of twenty-four, and which later slid under his door hurtful letters, little drawings captioned "Forgive me for the hurt I did not cause you," or a verse like

Je mourrai, tu vivras et c'est ce qui m'éveille!
Est-il une autre peur
Un jour de ne plus entendre auprès de mon oreille

Ton haleine et ton coeur.
[I will die, you will live, and that's what keeps me awake!
Is it another fear
That one day I will no longer feel against my ear
Your breath and your heart.][105]

Picasso was shocked—as were General de Gaulle and Morand—to receive one final letter from Cocteau the day after his death was announced. More than an old friend who knew how to flatter him, Picasso had lost the last witness of his marriage to Olga, the catalyst for his social success, and, along with Apollinaire, the most brilliant of his poet laureates. Robert Craft, Stravinsky's musical and spiritual adviser, had been present other times when the composer had learned of the death of a friend, but he had never seen him so distressed. The Russian composer cried.[106]

There were more disagreeable visits to come, for Doudou. A musician from Les Six demanded that cuts be made from Cocteau's wartime journal; Auric was afraid he had alluded to the contacts he had made with producers from the Continental, a film development company during the Occupation, created by Goebbels and funded by Germany. A friend of a former intimate friend demanded to see the journals for the last two years and members of Cocteau's own family got involved, but the manuscript stayed safe. "One more enemy lost, what a bore," said Marie Laure de Noailles.[107] Once the immediate tributes were over, everyone wondered about the strange hostility that Cocteau's name incurred. "How I would have loved this man-journal, capable of producing (with equal mastery) essays, scholarly articles, columns about this or that? . . . it was unfair competition," Paulhan said, ironically, questioning the ambivalence of his feelings toward the man who had helped get him into the Académie.[108]

The hearse was preceded by firemen in copper helmets, and followed by five thousand people. Cocteau had dreamed of a cortège led by ten young poets; he was given instead a handful of academicians, including the filmmaker René Clair, who was sixty-five years old and came without Bronja, his wife and Radiguet's last fiancée. Marlene Dietrich and Coco Chanel were there as international and Parisian ambassadors, and Paulo Picasso came in place of his father. The ceremony was held in Sainte-Blaise-des-Simples, where the silhouette of Serge Lifar was outlined against Marais's double profile flanking the face of Christ in the frescoes Cocteau had painted.

Finally the body was placed in the earth. Having gone on to the other side of the gate, Cocteau observed those who were leaning over his coffin. Like Narcissus, whom death turned inside out "like the finger of a glove," it was finally his turn to serve as a mirror.[109] A varied crowd of young people, workers, and simple villagers marched in silence; the child of the great Third Republic, the spoiled symbol of the 1920s, was no longer lacking ardent supporters of humble origin. "His famous star has gone up to join the others who wait for him, fraternally," declared Montherlant.[110] "It's an enormous swathe of my past," said Emmanuel Berl, "of the past of Paris, of literature worldwide, of all the arts, that is collapsing," describing the "separation of everything and everyone" due to the industrial age.[111] Morand added the description of a friend who had always lived at the summit of life: "Poetry was the only force behind the exploding shell that went through us."[112]

The only false note came from a Catholic writer, who was astonished that Cocteau could do something as natural, as unorchestrated, as dying. "Never has a dragonfly been so clearly condemned to remain a dragonfly," said François Mauriac, recalling Maritain's incapacity to change the insect into an angel; after believing himself stronger than the storm, up to the very end, this Cocteau "who so made us laugh" but who lacked a sense of guilt, and therefore the capacity to rise above himself, had returned to nothingness.[113] (Or to his hell? Out of Christian charity, Mauriac forbade himself from saying it; but four years earlier, he had remarked on the subject of his old "friend," "God cannot condemn a hunchback because of his hunch."[114]) It didn't take long for a scandalous writer, Roger Peyrefitte, to report to the press the amorous letters that Mauriac had written to Cocteau before the First World War. "It's not because we once did things together that he must treat me this way," Cocteau once said.[115]

From New York to Hamburg and from Tokyo to Madrid, the radios announced the almost simultaneous deaths of Piaf and Cocteau. The singer's notoriety vastly overshadowed Cocteau's, but they were both well-known outside of France. Learning of Cocteau's death, a young fan threw herself under a train.[116] When President Kennedy died a month later, riddled with anonymous bullets, everyone stopped talking about the poet. Lying at Saint-Blaise, leaving an empty seat behind him in the Académie Française, the white-haired Cocteau discovered the "fatal boredom of immortality." Christ, when he rose to heaven, announced to his followers, "I am with you always, even unto the end of the world."[117] Cocteau was content to have engraved on his tombstone a simpler message: "I remain with you."

THE MOURNED

Doudou forced himself to go on. Instinctively picking up the paintbrush of the prince who had created him, he decorated the chapel of Notre-Dame-de-Jérusalem in Fréjus according to Cocteau's designs, illustrated *La belle et la bête* and *L'aigle à deux têtes*, then began to keep a diary in his honor, *Le futur défini*, in which he would write to Cocteau for the next twelve years. "I was only ever happy with you, every day was a celebration," he wrote one day; he opened his notebook a month later to add: "Are you a man or some god disguised as a human?"[118] He missed Cocteau so much that he tried to make contact with him by any way he could imagine. By day he consulted mediums and listened to the radio subliminally; at night, he left the house at Milly after two o'clock in the morning and before dawn, taking with him a diviner's pendulum or a hazel wand, and waited for the radiesthetic messages that Cocteau might be trying to send him. A clairvoyant whom Doudou visited on the rue des Pyrénées, knowing nothing of his life, came close to the truth by describing the physique and the personality of the man he thought of constantly, who then spoke through her mouth, which made Doudou cry. Cocteau also appeared to him regularly in his dreams, but he was always silent. To see him without hearing him, or being able to tell him what he was thinking, was horrible.

He sometimes reread "Visite," the poem Cocteau had composed in 1918 upon returning home from the war:

I have some very sad news: I am dead. . . . for us, speed is much more important than for you . . . We are not seen, we are not heard, we can be walked
through without being hurt . . . I am speaking to you, I am touching you.
It's good to touch a real body! I remember my real body. I was some
water that took the shape of a bottle and judged everything according to this
shape. Everyone is a bottle that gives a different shape to the same water.
Now, having returned to the lake, I am part of its transparence. I am We.
You are I.[119]

The former miner didn't know how to live without Cocteau's enveloping presence, without the man who had praised everything he did, all of his paintings. He did everything to keep Cocteau's memory alive, to make his plays known, to encourage translations of them. Cocteau had told him that every time an American woman or a Japanese man read *Thomas l'imposteur*, *La difficulté d'être*, or *Le journal d'un inconnu*, these books ceased to be books, but became rather his own soul on paper, crying out to be delivered and spilling into their souls, being reborn in their bodies, where he would finally reach a kind of balance. Let's hope they did not close the book before the end! Life is beautiful in an organism that doesn't suffer . . .

Doudou's work as a beneficiary, however, was difficult without Cocteau there. "I am hungry for you, and will be for life," Doudou wrote in his journal, adding, "I know that in any case I will never be happy, because of you. I miss you too much."[120] To be close to him, he began to read and reread *Le passé défini*, Cocteau's diary, before asking Gallimard to publish it. Everything he read had the power to put him in the place of his "father," which was troubling, but the more he read, the more convinced he became that this man would always remain a mystery. In the end, he married, as Cocteau had encouraged him to do. His wife's name was Éliane ("Tania") Dubroca. A model for Dior, she quickly entered the enchanted, smoky circle. Their two children would be named for their "grandfather": Jean-Cégeste's godfather would be Jean Marais, and Jacqueline Picasso his godmother; the second-born, Stéphane-Orphée, had for godparents Pierre Bergé and Francine Weisweiller, with whom Doudou had reconciled. When he died in 1995, the former miner was buried in the Chapelle Saint-Blaise-des-Simples, where he lies next to Cocteau. Then Pierre Bergé, Yves Saint-Laurent's companion and a longtime friend of Cocteau's, took over the poet's legacy, because he already ran the Comité Cocteau. Cocteau couldn't have dreamed of better casting.

Jean Marais kept the flame burning with tireless devotion. He was the inconsolable widower, the son and Galatea. When he described Cocteau he did so with all the sacred enthusiasm his lover had used to celebrate Radiguet, until he became to seem like the curator of an imaginary museum. For forty years his zeal had no limits; everywhere he sang the virtues of the man who had made him, and ended up giving him, after his death, more than he had been able to by loving him when he was alive. He staged his plays and monopolized his memory, pastiched his paintings and sculpted his fauns, to the point of exaggerating through imitation the aesthetic decline of his last years. In spite of himself, the actor began to harm the memory of the genius he worshipped. In 1965, he had twenty songs composed based on Cocteau's poems, and recorded an album that would forever associate their two names on equal terms. It was a questionable homage on the part of this masculine Bardot, who once said, regarding his mentor, "He believed I had all the qualities, that was his only fault."

The height of this posthumous passion was reached in 1983, when Marais actually became Cocteau during a one-man show he composed based on Cocteau's poetry, thereby once again uniting their two names (this time, as "Cocteau-Marais"). For months, that singular spirit who had so loved and desired Marais lived again onstage. Nothing would have made Cocteau happier than to have learned that Marais embodied him every night. "He was truly my creator," the actor told a journalist, "as God is your creator. He was my god on earth."[121] In turn, Cocteau became an entity beyond all faults, incapable of lying or even having a negative thought. To pass on the legacy of this perfection, the actor had already adopted a fatherless young Gypsy in whom he instilled all his gifts; the child turned out to be "a painter, a sculptor, an actor, a singer."[122] The circle was complete: he imagined that upon his death, this "son" would pass on what he had learned, and perhaps carry on Cocteau's indirect line. But then the child's mother tried to blackmail him, and the dream was broken.

THE AFTERLIFE

Filmmakers had always loved Cocteau, and many paid tribute to him, either in words or in images, including Antonioni and Almodóvar, Joe Dante and David Lynch, Parajanov and Tarkovsky, Xavier Dolan and Léos Carax. But his literary reputation declined. Thousands of teenagers continued to discover *Les enfants terribles*, *La difficulté d'être*, and *Thomas*, but critics who could properly appreciate him were rare. In France, Angelo Rinaldi regularly applauded him as a deeply human stylist who in his life knew how to "never be too weighty, . . . to silence what goes without saying" — like Mme Geoffrin, who murmured on her deathbed: "It's nothing, everyone has greatly exaggerated."[123] Dominique Fernandez praised the man who did not try to hide his desires.[124] Genet would mention, in his conversations with Michel Foucault, the esteem he had for "that upright, generous, funny man," but he did not defend his literary work.[125] In 1975, the German writer Hubert Fichte interviewed Genet one last time:

> *HF*: You were a friend of Cocteau's. He defended you, I think?
> *JG*: Yes, but that is part of a little pseudo-literary story, without interest, or importance.
> *HF*: Do you respect Cocteau as a poet?
> *JG*: No.[126]

Genet denied his other mentor as well by saying, "Sartre no longer counts." In so doing, he kept the promise made in his first book — "I sow devastation" — so well that when his acrobat friend, Abdallah, killed himself, two years after Cocteau's death, Sartre had the insight that Genet's remorse had less to do with sadness than his inability to feel it.[127]

Sometimes, you can still meet in Paris people who knew Cocteau. You will recognize them by their way of opening their doors wide, by their warm, knowing voices, by the happiness they feel in introducing you to someone who will perhaps leave their mark on your life. They will talk until you lose all sense of reality and project yourself into that weightless world from which all anguish is banished, where only the pleasure of learning and laughing matters. That is what happened to me in 1977, and life changed forever and for the better. I was no longer the same, after this encounter; it was as if Cocteau had indirectly put a spell on me. But can writing a book ever repay such a debt?

We haven't yet finished with Cocteau.

NOTES

The following abbreviations appear in the Notes:

BHVP   Bibliothèque Historique de la Ville de Paris, Jean Cocteau collection

CJC   *Cahiers Jean Cocteau*

IMEC   Institut Mémoires de l'Édition Contemporaine, Paris

LM   Jean Cocteau, *Lettres à sa mère*, vol. 1: *1898–1918* and vol. 2: *1919–1938* (Paris: Gallimard, 1989, 2007)

PD   Jean Cocteau, *Le passé défini*, vol. 1: *1951–1952*; vol. 2: *1953*; vol. 3: *1954*; vol. 4: *1955*; vol. 5: *1956–1957*; and vol. 6: *1958–1959* (Paris: Gallimard, 1983–2011)

NRF   *Nouvelle revue française*

OPC   Jean Cocteau, *Poésies (1917–1920)*: *Oeuvres poétiques complètes* (Paris: Gallimard, Bibliothèque de la Pléiade, 1999)

INTRODUCTION

1. The "coc" in Cocteau will typically remind a French speaker of the phrase "coq-à-l'âne," which is a sudden change of subject, hence a flightiness. Literally, it means "[from the] rooster to the donkey."—Trans.
2. Paul Claudel, *Journal*, vol. 2: *1935–1955* (Paris: Gallimard, 1969), pp. 866, 792.
3. He was accepted into the Université Paul-Valéry in Montpellier and the University of Bruxelles (Belgium).
4. *OPC*, p. 193.
5. Pieral, *Vu d'en bas* (Paris: Robert Laffont, 1976), p. 118.
6. Henri Sauguet, *La musique de ma vie* (Paris: Séguier, 1990), p. 168.
7. See Chapter 24.
8. Francis Steegmuller, *Cocteau* (Boston: Little, Brown), p. 462.

9. Jean Cocteau, *Opium* (Paris: Éditions Stock, 1930), p. 249.

CHAPTER 1. THE CHILD PRODIGY

1. Jean Cocteau, *Portraits-souvenir, 1900–1914* (1935), also in *Articles de Paris*, ed. Pierre Georgel (Paris: Le Livre de Poche, 1977), p. 126.
2. See Francis Steegmuller, *Cocteau* (Paris: Buchet-Chastel, 1973), p. 17.
3. Jean Cocteau, *La lampe d'Aladin*, in OPC, p. 1264.
4. Cocteau, *Portraits-souvenir*, p. 52.
5. Ibid., p. 72.
6. Ibid., p. 82.
7. Ibid., pp. 53–54.
8. See Roger Stéphane, *Portrait souvenir de Jean Cocteau* (Paris: Éditions Tallandier, 1964), p. 34.
9. Cocteau, *Portraits-souvenir*, p. 63.
10. Ibid., p. 99.
11. Jean-Jacques Kihm, Elizabeth Sprigge, and Henri C. Béhar, *Jean Cocteau, l'homme et les miroirs* (Paris: La Table Ronde, 1968), p. 34.
12. "La main passe," *La Gerbe*, February 6, 1941.
13. Cocteau, *Portraits-souvenir*, p. 100.
14. Jean Cocteau, *Opium* (Paris: Éditions Stock, 1930), p. 182.
15. Cocteau, *La lampe d'Aladin*, p. 1266.
16. Interview with Madeleine Bouret in *Cocteau*, special issue of the newspaper *Libération*, 1982.
17. Stéphane, *Portrait souvenir de Jean Cocteau*, referring to an interview by Stéphane in the spring of 1963.
18. We also read in *Le grand écart*, Cocteau's most autobiographical novel, about the father of Jacques Forestier, the hero of the book: "If we erase M. Forestier, it's because he erased himself. Young, he suffered from a demon similar to the demon that tormented Jacques. He had brought it to heel it by study and marriage. But a demon is hard to curb. His straight nature atrophied. It felt all askew. M. Forestier guessed Jacques' troubles, he recognized them, he lost heart from them like a victim of sarcoma who, having cured his illness in his shoulder, sees it reappear in his knee."
19. Stéphane, *Portrait souvenir de Jean Cocteau*, p. 36.
20. Maurice Sachs, *La décade de l'illusion* (1933; Paris: Gallimard, 1950), p. 170.
21. Cocteau, *Portraits-souvenir*, p. 71.
22. This was a version of the story told to Desbordes around 1928, according to Kihm, Sprigge, and Béhar, *Jean Cocteau*, p. 28.
23. Steegmuller, in *Cocteau* (Buchet-Chastel), p. 17, quotes the name of Marcel Dieulafoy, whose wife, always dressed as a man, supposedly urged him to find consolation with the very feminine Mme Cocteau. This may account for the story about the "socialite archeologist."
24. Quoted by Monique Lange, *Cocteau, prince sans royaume* (Paris: Jean-Claude Lattès, 1989), p. 57.

25. Jean Cocteau, "La machine infernale" (Paris: Le Livre de Poche, 1970), p. 56.

26. Jean Cocteau to his sister-in-law Mme Paul Cocteau, February 6, 1962, in *Jean Cocteau et son temps*, catalogue compiled by Pierre Georgel for the Jean Cocteau exhibit at the Jacquemart-André Museum, 1965, p. 5.

27. Ibid., pp. 11–12.

28. See "L'amour du théâtre," n.d., BHVP, box 8.

29. This detail is from Cocteau's grandniece Durand-Viel, interview with the author, 1998.

30. Jean Cocteau, *Le Potomak*, in *Oeuvres complètes*, vol. 2 (Lausanne: Marguerat, 1947), p. 28; see also the text on *Les enfants terribles*, in BHVP, box 71.

31. "Venise vue par un enfant," *La Revue hebdomadaire*, May 1913, quoted in Kihm, Sprigge, and Béhar, *Jean Cocteau*, p. 33. Cocteau wrote of the hero of *Le grand écart*: "He mourned the fact that he was not the city. Heliogabalus, in his worst caprices, never demanded as much."

32. Cocteau, *Portraits-souvenir*.

33. Self-portrait as a youth under the name Jahel, winter 1910, quoted in P. Caizergues, ed., *Jean Cocteau aujourd'hui* (Paris: Méridiens Klincksieck, 1992), p. 268.

34. Hermione Lee, *Virginia Woolf* (New York: Vintage, 1999), p. 767.

35. André Berne-Joffroy, interview with the author, June 21, 1999.

36. Jean Cocteau, *Le Potomak*, in *Oeuvres complètes*, vol. 2 (Lausanne: Marguerat, 1947), p. 147.

37. The hero of *Le grand écart*, having seen a desired couple leave coughing and limping, also began to cough and limp out of love.

38. Jacques Brosse, *Cocteau* (Paris: Gallimard, 1970), pp. 46–47.

39. Cocteau, *Portraits-souvenir*, p. 134.

40. Jean Cocteau, *Mes monstres sacrés* (Paris: Éditions Encre de Nuit, 1979), p. 160.

41. "I am the woman-torpedo." — Trans. Mistinguett (Jeanne Bourgeois), *Toute ma vie*, 2 vols. (Paris: Julliard, 1954).

42. Steegmuller, *Cocteau* (Buchet-Chastel), p. 24.

43. Cocteau collection, BHVP.

44. See *LM*, pp. 70–71, 457.

45. Cocteau, *Portraits-souvenir*, p. 154.

46. In *Saying Life: The Memoirs of Sir Francis Rose* (London: Cassel, 1961), p. 11.

47. Cocteau, *Portraits-souvenir*, p. 158.

48. Maurice Beaumont, *L'affaire Eulenburg* (Geneva: Edito-service, 1973), quoting a 1930 letter he had received from Jean Cocteau.

49. Paul Morand, *Journal inutile*, vol. 2: 1973–1976 (Paris: Gallimard, 2001), p. 482.

50. Cocteau, *Portraits-souvenir*, p. 129.

51. *LM*, p. 64, letter dated August 16, 1907, and p. 71, letter dated August 28, 1907.

52. Ibid., p. 64, letter dated August 16, 1907.

53. Ibid., p. 65, letter dated August 17, 1907.

54. Jules Renard, *Journal* (Paris: Gallimard, 1960), p. 266, entry for March 1, 1895.

55. He had just published, in 1908, *Le chemin mort, roman contemporain*, recounting the decline of a young bourgeois homosexual who was richly kept then abandoned when he grew old.

56. Alphonse Daudet also had great affection for Reynaldo Hahn, who had written a musical score for him.

57. The comparison is Maurice Duplay's. See his "Mon ami Marcel Proust," in *Cahiers Marcel Proust*, vol. 5 (Paris: Gallimard, 1972), p. 48.

58. Charles Baudelaire, *L'art romantique* (Paris: Calmann-Levy, 1885), p. 167.

59. Joséphin Péladan, "Message aux visiteurs du sixième salon Rose-Croix" (Paris: Galerie Georges Petit, 1897).

60. *OPC*, p. 1834. Tailhade had lost an eye in 1896, during an anarchist attack on the hotel restaurant Foyot, near the Senate House. A few months earlier, he had celebrated the bomb that had exploded at the Assembly, saying: "What do the victims matter if the gesture is a fine one?"

61. Steegmuller, *Cocteau* (Buchet-Chastel), p. 29.

62. The hero of *Le grand écart* confessed that he inherited his father's "pathological lack of interest."

63. Jean Cocteau, *La difficulté d'être* (Monaco: Éditions du Rocher, 1947), p. 17; *LM*, p. 38, letter dated September 6, 1906.

64. Cocteau, *Lettres à sa mère*, p. 71, letter dated August 28, 1907.

65. In the novel, a young journalist reveals to the hero that he is going to kill himself in two hours, but the hero doesn't believe him because suicide in Venice was at the time a cliché, like suicide from the top of the Eiffel Tower would be later on.

CHAPTER 2. ARIEL

1. Dates could prove him wrong, since Rilke had stopped working for Rodin in May 1907, but apparently he kept his studio in the Hôtel Biron.

2. Jean Cocteau, *Le prince frivole*, *OPC*, p. 1378.

3. *Chevalier de la manchette* literally means "knight of the hanky."—Trans.

4. Account of Robert Rey, quoted in Francis Steegmuller, *Cocteau* (Boston: Little, Brown, 1970), pp. 40–41.

5. The Catholic press would denounce the holding of Black Masses in the once-consecrated site of that chapel, where the actor had had a marble bath and floors installed.

6. Frederick Brown, *An Impersonation of Angels* (New York: Viking, 1968), p. 33.

7. Éric Marty, *Louis Althusser: Un sujet sans procès* (Paris: Gallimard, 1999), p. 15.

8. According to Cocteau, the two of them together rented, "for a few pennies," his bachelor flat in the Hôtel Biron, but apparently she always lived on the boulevard Pereire.

9. Quoted by Dominique Marny, *Les belles de Cocteau* (Paris: Jean-Claude Lattès, 1995), p. 36.

10. Ibid., p. 37.

11. Jean Cocteau, "Sadisme," *La lampe d'Aladin*, *OPC*, p. 1298.

12. Jean Cocteau, "Le crépuscule," *La lampe d'Aladin*, *OPC*, p. 1312.

13. *Mercure de France*, May 1, 1909, article by Pierre Quillard.

14. This according to Maurice Sachs, *La décade de l'illusion* (1933; Paris: Gallimard, 1950), p. 168.

15. Roger Stéphane, *Portrait souvenir de Jean Cocteau* (Paris: Éditions Tallandier, 1964), p. 49.

16. Jean Cocteau, *Le grand écart* (Paris: Éditions Stock, 1923), p. 49.

17. Jean l'Oiseleur, "Ad usum delphini," sales catalog, Couturier-Nicolay auction house, Drouot, February 14, 1990.

18. Henry Bernstein, letter dated April 9, 1910, Gérard Langlet collection, quoted in Jean Touzot, *Jean Cocteau* (Lyon: La Manufacture, 1989), p. 173.

19. Jean Cocteau, "Les sonnets de l'Hôtel Biron," *Le prince frivole*, OPC, p. 1382. Pierre Chanel thinks this poem refers rather to the memory of Christiane Mancini. In *Le grand écart*, Louise consoles the hero, who thinks he is still not desired by Germaine, saying to him, "Poor little boy!"

20. Dedication written on the photo exhibited at the Musée Jacquemart-André in 1965.

21. Quoted in Pierre Caizergues, ed., *Jean Cocteau aujourd'hui* (Paris: Méridiens Klincksieck, 1992), p. 264.

22. Ibid., p. 154.

23. Her own mother, Émilie Lecomte, née Renaud, had married her husband as she was pregnant from an Irishman. Dominique Marny, interview with the author, April 23, 1998.

24. Quoted in Caizergues, *Jean Cocteau aujourd'hui*, p. 145.

25. "En biais," *Comoedia* (November–December 1910): 274. When he wasn't hiding under the name of Jim, the artist was presented in 1910 by *Le Témoin*, a journal edited by Paul Iribe.

26. Jean Cocteau, "Par lui-même," *Opéra*, OPC, p. 518.

27. Jean Cocteau, *Embarcadères*, OPC, p. 147.

28. Jean Cocteau to Pierre-Jean Robert, n.d., IMEC, Jean-José Marchand collection, MRC2, A35.

29. Jean Cocteau, *Le portrait surnaturel de Dorian Gray* (Paris: Olivier Orban, 1978), a play adapted with the help of his friend Jacques Renaud.

30. François Porché would publish in 1927, with Grasset, an essay on homosexuality entitled *L'amour qui n'ose pas dire son nom* [The love that dare not say its name].

31. Jean-Paul Sartre, *Saint Genet, comédien et martyr* (Paris: Gallimard, 1952), p. 81.

32. "En biais," pp. 268, 270.

33. The three plays were *La princesse lointaine* (1895), *La samaritaine* (1897), *L'aiglon* (1900).

34. *The Complete Works of Oscar Wilde*, vol. 2: *De profundis*, "Epistola: in carcere et vinculis" (Oxford, Eng.: Oxford University Press, 2000), p. 95.

35. Marcel Migeo, *Les Rostand* (Paris: Éditions Stock, 1973), p. 125. *Ballets bleus* are sexual orgies involving male minors. — Trans.

36. Author of *La chanson des gueux*, Jean Richepin, Tiarko's father, was regarded as the leader of the naturalist Parnassian school.

37. Jean Cocteau, *Portraits-souvenir*, OPC, p. 139.

38. Jean Cocteau, *Lettres à sa mère* (Paris: Gallimard, 1989), p. 84.

39. Jean Cocteau to Anna de Noailles, September 14, 1912, *CJC*, vol. 11 (Paris: Gallimard, 1989), p. 82.

40. Maurice Rostand, *Confession d'un demi-siècle* (Paris: La Jeune Parque, 1948), p. 122.

41. *Jean Cocteau et son temps*, catalogue compiled by Pierre Georgel for the Jean Cocteau exhibit at the Jacquemart-André Museum, 1965, p. 30.

42. François-Réne de Chateaubriand, *Mémoires d'outre-tombe*, vol. 1 (1849; Paris: Le Livre de Poche, 1979), p. 514.

43. Max Nordau, *Dégénérescence* (Paris: Félix Alcan, 1894), pp. 47–48.

44. Jean Cocteau, *Opium* (Paris: Éditions Stock, 1930), p. 164.

45. Maurice Martin du Gard, *Les mémorables*, new ed. (Paris: Gallimard, 1999), p. 599.

46. Marcel Proust to Jean Cocteau, January 1922, in Marcel Proust, *Correspondance*, ed. and comp. Philip Kolb, 21 vols. (Paris: Plon, 1970–1993), vol. 21, p. 42.

47. Proust, *Correspondance*, vol. 5, p. 80, as well as vol. 21, p. 29, which contains the letter to Walter Berry, January 6, 1922.

48. The quotation is from the first known letter from Marcel Proust to Jean Cocteau (December 1910?), in Proust, *Correspondance*, vol. 10, p. 231.

49. *L'intransigeant*, September 21, 1910. Active since 1842, Théodore de Banville had made a name for himself as the leader of the Parnassians calling for art for art's sake and defending Théophile Gautier.

50. Proust, *Correspondance*, vol. 10, pp. 233–234.

51. Marcel Proust to Jean Cocteau, May 1911, in ibid., p. 286.

52. Marcel Proust to Reynaldo Hahn, March 1911, in ibid., pp. 261–262.

53. *L'intransigeant*, September 1910. See also ibid., p. 232, and Jean-Yves Tadié, *Marcel Proust*, vol. 2 (Paris: Folio-Gallimard, 1996), p. 116.

54. Jean Cocteau, "Opium," *NRF* 201 (June 1, 1930): 795.

55. *Jean Cocteau par Jean Cocteau*, interviews with William Fifield (Paris: Éditions Stock, 1973), p. 136.

56. Lucien Daudet, quoted in Cocteau, *PD*, vol. 1, p. 308.

57. Marcel Proust to Jean Cocteau, December 1910, in Proust, *Correspondance*, vol. 10, p. 234.

58. See Jean-David Jumeau-Lafond, ed., *Robert de Montesquiou, Marcel Proust, professeur de beauté* (Paris: Les Billets de la Bibliothèque, 1999).

59. Marcel Proust, "Fête chez Montesquiou à Neuilly," in Proust, *Écrits sur l'art* (Paris: Garnier-Flammarion, 1999), p. 162.

60. Léon Daudet, *Souvenirs des milieux littéraires, politiques, artistiques et médicaux*, in Daudet, *Souvenirs et polémiques* (Paris: Robert Laffont, 1992), p. 119.

61. Jean Cocteau to Robert de Montesquiou, April 1, 1912, private collection of Jacques Polge. The count's voice supposedly pierced through idiots, "from the frog to the bull."

62. Montesquiou cited in *Têtu* 40 (September 1999): 53. Also in the "La treizième rencontre des chauves-souris," we read: "The effeminate man often tames the woman and the man/ Without being dominated . . . /Can you please tell me where the weak lies, actually?"

63. On exciting rumors, see "To more than one prepubescent/In the shadow of a lamp-post/The Comte de Montesquiou/has shown his prick . . ." according to one quatrain. Paul Jean Toulet, *Vers inédits, 1880–1919*, available at http://www.crisco.unicaen .fr/~stage/Verlaine/index.php?navigation=textesauteurs&auteur=TOU_2&code _text=TOU243_6 (accessed December 30, 2015).

64. Élisabeth de Gramont, *Les marronniers en fleurs*, in Gramont, *Memoirs*, vol. 2 (Paris: Grasset, 1929), p. 239.

65. André Germain, *De Proust à Dada* (Paris: Kra Press, 1924), p. 116.

66. Unpublished diary of Jacques-Émile Blanche, October 14, 1913, quoted in *CJC*, no. 11, p. 160. Curiously Gide would make almost the same confession in his *Journal*, thirty years later, remembering having said to Claudel: "I am made of rubber, don't trust me . . . as soon as I am alone, I resume my shape." André Gide, *Journal*, vol. 2: *1926–1950* (Paris: Gallimard, 1997), p. 825.

67. Cocteau, *Opium*, pp. 220–223.

68. Jean Cocteau, *D'un ordre considéré comme une anarchie*, in *Le rappel à l'ordre* (Paris: Éditions Stock, 1926). Elsewhere, Cocteau would express his fascination for the parrot, a man changed into a bird but not yet fully inhabiting this metamorphosis.

69. Otto Weininger, *Sex and Character* (1903; New York: G.P. Putnam's Sons, 1906), p. 195, available online at http://www.theabsolute.net/ottow/schareng.pdf (accessed September 30, 2015). The first French translation of this book didn't appear in Lausanne until 1975, but Otto Weininger's text radicalized many ideas that were circulating at the time throughout Europe.

70. Women, according to Weininger, could not have access to this art, the most abstract of all, the only one too that is not fed by imitation.

71. Gabriel Tarde, *The Laws of Imitation*, trans. Elsie Clews Parsons (New York: Henry Holt, 1903), pp. 77, 87, emphasis in original. The first French edition was published by Alcan in 1890.

72. Weininger, *Sex and Character*, p. 65.

73. Steegmuller, *Cocteau* (Little, Brown), p. 87.

74. See Jean Lorrain, *Pélléastres: Le poison de la littérature* (Paris: Albert Mérican, 1910).

75. Paul Morand, *Venises* (Paris: Gallimard, 1971), p. 98.

76. Porché, *L'amour qui n'ose pas dire son nom*, p. 18.

77. *L'action française* was a right-wing journal founded in 1899 to counter the leftist supporters of Dreyfus. —Trans.

78. In Steegmuller, *Cocteau* (Little, Brown), pp. 39–40.

79. For the quotation see Maurice Duplay, "Mon ami Marcel Proust," in *Cahiers Marcel Proust*, vol. 5, p. 57.

80. On her hoarseness, see Princess Bibesco, *La duchesse de Guermantes, Laure de Sade, comtesse de Chevigné* (Paris: Plon, 1951).

81. Ibid.

82. See Paul Morand, *L'allure de Chanel* (Paris: Hermann, 1976), p. 89.

83. Marcel Proust, *Les plaisirs et les jours* (Paris: Gallimard, 1993).

84. Élisabeth Greffulhe and Geneviève Straus also served as models for the Duchesse.

85. Homosexual heir of a family of bankers, Germain had married Lucien Daudet's sister.

86. Jean Cocteau, *Portraits-souvenir*, in *Oeuvres complètes*, vol. 11 (Lausanne, Éditions Marguerat, 1951), p. 139.

87. Jean Cocteau to François Mauriac, n.d. (1910?) in Jean-Jacques Kihm, Elizabeth Sprigge, and Henri C. Béhar, *Jean Cocteau, l'homme et les miroirs* (Paris: La Table Ronde, 1968), p. 61.

88. "Jacques-Émile Blanche," *Les nouvelles littéraires*, August 4, 1923.

89. Pierre Chanel saw this poem in the Milly house, but he couldn't swear that the lips in question were Cocteau's; Claude Mauriac refused its publication. Pierre Chanel, letter to the author dated November 25, 2002. A Savoyard priest is also said to own some love letters from Mauriac to Cocteau: see Matthieu Galey, *Journal*, vol. 1: *1953–1973* (Paris: Grasset, 1987), p. 335.

90. François Mauriac, *Lettres d'une vie* (Paris: Grasset, 1981), p. 44, letters from Spring 1911. Mauriac added: "Dear little ephemeral angel—singing, leaping soul—who are in these sad days my sole joy—who have still given me nothing but joy . . . my most precious friend." To R. Vallery-Radot, who asked him to stop seeing Cocteau, he replied on April 2, 1911, evoking that "poor little worried and frighteningly lonely soul, who hovers round me, not to lose me, but to save me" (p. 388, n. 23).

CHAPTER 3. THE LIVING GOD

1. Lady Ottoline Morell, *Ottoline* (London: Faber, 1963), p. 227.

2. Jacques Rivière, "Le sacre du printemps," in A. Rivière, ed., *Études (1909–1924)* (Paris: Gallimard, 1999), p. 361.

3. Jean Cocteau, *La difficulté d'être* (Monaco: Éditions du Rocher, 1947), pp. 69–70.

4. Quoted in "Le théâtre et la mode," *Masques, revue internationale* 1, no. 1 (March 1945).

5. Quoted in letter to Cocteau's mother, *LM*, September 2, 1920.

6. Vaslav Nijinsky, *Six vers de Jean Cocteau, six dessins de Paul Iribe* (Paris: Société générale d'impression, 1910).

7. Roger Stéphane, *Portrait souvenir de Jean Cocteau* (Paris: Éditions Tallandier, 1964), p. 76.

8. Paul Morand, *Venises* (Paris: Gallimard, 1971), p. 168. The "Misia" here is Misia Sert, née Godebska. a famous cultural arbiter of the time.—Trans.

9. Jean Cocteau, "La princesse de Bormes" et "La ferme," in *Thomas l'imposteur* (Paris: Gallimard, 1923).

10. Proust told Céleste, his governess, about a similar scene in which Cocteau, seeing him, had jumped onto the tables in Larue, shouting, "It's Marcel!," then had come over and sat down next to him, to his great embarrassment. The scene inspired the one in *Le côté de Guermantes II* in which Saint-Loup brings the Narrator the vicuña coat of the Prince de Foix.

11. Philip Kolb, the editor of Proust's correspondence, thinks the poem is by Cocteau himself, unlike George Painter, who attributes the verses by "mirliton" to Proust alone.

12. "Afin de me couvrir de fourrure et de moire,/Sans de ses larges yeux renverser l'encre noire,/Tel un sylphe au plafond, tel sur la neige un ski/Jean sauta sur la table auprès de Nijinski/C'était dans le salon purpurin de Larue/Dont l'or, d'un goût douteux, jamais ne se voila." Quoted in *Lettre plainte*, 1926, and Jean Cocteau, *Opium* (Paris: Éditions Stock, 1930), p. 168.

13. Cocteau, *Opium*, p. 164.

14. Jean Cocteau, *Le discours d'Oxford* (Paris: Gallimard, 1956), p. 35.

15. Cocteau, *PD*, vol. 2, p. 275. "Marcel spoke like this, with one hand in front of his mouth," Cocteau would tell Jean Cau. "He read *Sodome et Gomorrhe* to me in white gloves because he wanted to stop biting his nails. He kept bursting out laughing: 'I hope no one will understand a thing . . .' and then he would laugh even more." See Jean Cau, *Croquis de Mémoires* (Paris: Julliard, 1985), p. 54.

16. Frédéric Lefèvre, "Une heure avec . . .," 1st ser., *Éditions de la Nouvelle revue française*, 1924, p. 107.

17. Jean-Yves Tadié, *Proust: La cathédrale du temps* (Paris: Gallimard, 1999), p. 103.

18. Marcel Proust to Jean Cocteau, late December 1918, in Marcel Proust, *Correspondance*, ed. and comp. Philip Kolb, 21 vols. (Paris: Plon, 1970–1993), vol. 17, p. 531.

19. Ibid., pp. 243–244. M. de Sacy was the Jansenist head of the nuns of Port-Royal, under Louis XIV.

20. Pietro Citati, *La colombe poignardée* (Paris: Gallimard, 1997), p. 34.

21. André Gide, *Journal* (1951; Paris: Gallimard, 2012), pp. 109–110, entry for January 20, 1910.

22. Jean Cocteau, *Portraits-souvenir* (Paris: Grasset, 1935), p. 209; Léon-Paul Fargue, "Pour l'inauguration du jardin d'Amphion," *Le Figaro*, July 30, 1938; Jean Cocteau to Anna de Noailles, Summer 1911, in *CJC*, vol. 2: *Jean Cocteau et Anna de Noailles, Correspondance (1911-1931)* (Paris: Gallimard, 1989), p. 55.

23. Jean Cocteau, *Portraits-souvenir*, in *Oeuvres complètes*, vol. 11 (Lausanne: Éditions Marguerat, 1951), p. 197.

24. Emmanuel Berl in *CJC*, vol. 11 (Paris: Gallimard, 1989), p. 24.

25. Cocteau, *Portraits-souvenir*, p. 225; Proust, *Correspondance*, vol. 10, p. 244.

26. "Le temps de vivre," republished in Jean Cocteau, *La comtesse de Noailles, oui et non* (Paris: Perrin, 1963), p. 28.

27. Quoted in Claude Minot-Ogliastri, *Anna de Noailles, une amie de la princesse Edmond de Polignac* (Paris: Méridien-Klincksieck, 1986).

28. Anna de Noailles to Jean Cocteau, August 21, 1912, after *La danse de Sophocle*, in *CJC*, vol. 11, p. 78.

29. Cf. "La solitude" and "La lampe et les phalènes," in Jean Cocteau, *La danse de Sophocle, OPC*.

30. Jean Cocteau, *Essai de critique indirecte* (Paris: Grasset, 1932).

31. Mme Simone, *Ce qui restait à dire* (Paris: Gallimard, 1967), p. 106.

32. The snarky nickname for the balding lady was inspired by a three-horsepower car that Citroën sold in the 1920s. [The phrase can be translated literally as "the three-haired lemon." — Trans.]

33. Bernard Faÿ, *Les précieux* (Paris: Perrin, 1966), p. 266.

34. Princesse Bibesco, "Jean Cocteau et son étoile," *Revue générale belge* (December 1963).

35. Jacques Porel, *Fils de Réjane*, vol. 1: *1895–1920* (Paris: Plon, 1951), p. 348.

36. Edith Wharton, *A Backward Glance: An Autobiography* (New York: Simon & Schuster, 1998), p. 285.

37. Faÿ, *Les précieux*, p. 265.

38. Quoted in Porel, *Fils de Réjane*, vol. 1: *1895–1920*, p. 348.

39. Gérard de Nerval and Guy de Maupassant were both treated in Dr. Blanche's clinic in Passy.

40. Unpublished journal by Jacques-Émile Blanche, entry for September 3, 1913, n.p.

41. *LM*, p. 106, letter dated August 1912.

42. Jean Cocteau, "Les solitudes," in *La danse de Sophocle*, OPC, p. 1433.

43. "Le visage," in *La danse de Sophocle*, OPC, p. 1415.

44. Arthur Rimbaud, "Alchimie du verbe, Délires II," in *Une saison en enfer* (Paris: GF-Flammarion, 1973), p. 130.

45. All quotations in this paragraph are from Jean Cocteau, "La danse de Sophocle," OPC, pp. 1384–1451.

46. This comment is an allusion to *Remembrance of Things Past*, on which Proust had been working for three years.

47. Marcel Proust to Jean Cocteau, n.d. (a little after June 20, 1912), Proust, *Correspondance*, vol. 11, pp. 147–148.

48. Unpublished notebook, BHVP, box 16.

49. Ibid.

50. *LM*, vol. 2, pp. 89–95.

51. Cocteau sent his "Saadique" verses to Anna de Noailles.

52. In Jean Cocteau, "Les Vocalises," OPC, pp. 1453–1474.

53. Letter to Jean Cocteau, March 20, 1912, quoted in *LM*.

54. Journal kept from June 28, 1911, to April 1912, unpublished manuscript belonging to M. Bernard Loliée, with the quotation given by Pierre Chanel in his edition of *Vocalises de Bachir-Selim*, OPC, 1972.

55. This comment is from the margin of *Vocalises*, OPC, p. 1474.

56. Cocteau would retell the scene differently to the dancer Jean Babilée: "I want my Kodak," Nijinsky supposedly said. It was as if Diaghilev had been physically hit. "No, no, dear, concentrate. Concentrate." "I want a Kodak or I'm leaving." "You'll have it! But you know very well I don't have any money." "I want a K-O-D-A-K!" "Fine, you'll have it, you'll have it!" See Sarah Clair, *Jean Babilée ou la danse buissonnière* (Paris: Van Dieren, 1995), p. 66.

57. Anna de Noailles said one couldn't sit down without being touched by the sculptor.

58. Paul Morand, *Journal d'un attaché d'ambassade* (1947; Paris: Gallimard, 1996), p. 79.

59. A painter now and then, Madrazo left a portrait of Cocteau as well as one of Laure Hayman, the model for Odette de Crécy.

60. An earlier work for four hands, *La patience de Pénélope*, a "lie" in one act, with verse by Jean Cocteau, prose by André Paysan, and music by Reynaldo Hahn, had been performed at the home of the couturier Jacques Doucet, on Thursday, February 10, 1910 — "ancient dress, Greek or Roman, is *de rigueur*," said the invitation. Published in Chanel, *CJC*, vol. 9, pp. 25–96, this comical framework is preserved in BHVP.

61. Jean Cocteau, note on ballets in *L'art décoratif de Léon Bakst* (Paris: Maurice de Brunhoff, 1913).

62. *Dancing for Diaghilev: The Memoirs of Lydia Sokolovska*, ed. Richard Buckle (London: Murray, 1960), pp. 36–37.

63. Martine Kahane, *Les Ballets Russes à l'Opéra* (Paris: BN/Opéra de Paris/Louis Vuitton, 1992).

64. Anna de Noailles to Jean Cocteau, June 25, 1912, *CJC*, vol. 11, p. 70.

65. André Gide to Jean Cocteau, August 6, 1912, in Jean Cocteau, *Lettres à André Gide avec quelques réponses d'André Gide*, ed. Jean-Jacques Kihm (Paris: La Table Ronde, 1970), p. 30.

66. Ibid., p. 31.

67. Nathaniel is the main character in Gide's *Fruits of the Earth*.

68. "Les poèmes," by Henri Ghéon, *NRF* 45, September 1, 1912, pp. 507–511.

69. Ferdinand Bac, *Souvenirs inédits*, book 4, quoted in Ghislain de Diesbach, *Proust* (Paris: Perrin, 1991), p. 618.

70. *LM*, p. 121, a letter dated September 26, 1912.

71. Quoted in Maurice Rostand, *Confession d'un demi-siècle* (Paris: La Jeune Parque, 1948), p. 175.

72. Cocteau, *La difficulté d'être*, p. 70.

73. Cocteau told to Jean Babilée in Clair, *Jean Babilée*, pp. 66–67.

74. Georges Liébert, *Nietzsche et la musique* (Paris: Presses Universitaires de France, 1995), p. 106.

75. In *L'art décoratif de Léon Bakst*.

76. Abbé Mugnier, *Journal (1879–1939)* (Paris: Mercure de France, 1985), December 9, 1910.

77. Jean Cocteau to Anna de Noailles, April 28, 1913, quoted by Claude Minot-Ogliastri in *Anna de Noailles: Une amie de la princesse Edmond de Polignac* (Paris: Méridien-Klincksieck, 1986), p. 287.

CHAPTER 4. THE MOLTING

1. Marcel Proust to Jean Cocteau, November 21, 1913, in Marcel Proust, *Correspondance*, ed. and comp. Philip Kolb, 21 vols. (Paris: Plon, 1970–1993), vol. 12, p. 330.

2. Abbé Mugnier, *Journal (1879–1939)* (Paris: Mercure de France, 1985), p. 259.

3. By contrast, Maurice Rostand worried Proust by comparing him straightaway to Plato, Shakespeare, Leonardo da Vinci, Pascal, Goethe, Shelley, and Dostoyevsky.

4. Marcel Proust to Jean Cocteau, June 1919, in Proust, *Correspondance*, vol. 18, p. 267.

5. Report published in Frank Lhomeau and Alain Coelho, *Marcel Proust à la recherche d'un éditeur* (Paris: Olivier Orban, 1988), pp. 255–262.

6. *Le Coq* 1 (May 1920).

7. This is the opinion of George Painter, in his *Proust* (Paris: Mercure de France, 1992), as well as of Auguste Anglès, in his *André Gide et le premier groupe de la Nouvelle revue française*, vol. 3 (Paris: Gallimard, 1986), pp. 227–229.

8. *NRF*, January 1, 1914, pp. 139–143.

9. Having decided at the age of forty that she no longer needed to follow the dictates of fashion, Mme de Chevigné had actually stopped replacing her hats. To avoid being "dated," however, she no longer kept the ones that fascinated Proust—in particular a velour toque adorned with Parma violets, about which he still devotedly talked to Céleste, his housekeeper, after the First World War.

10. Marcel Proust to Jean Cocteau, July 1913, in Proust *Correspondance*, vol. 12, p. 222.

11. Paul Morand, *Journal inutile*, vol. 2: 1973–1976 (Paris: Gallimard, 2001), p. 57.

12. In Marcel Schneider, *L'éternité fragile*, vol. 2: *Innocence et vérité* (Paris: Grasset, 1991), p. 297, and vol. 5: *Les gardiens du secret* (Paris: Grasset, 2001), p. 139.

13. As much as he wanted to meet Proust, Maurice Rostand still refused a meeting at six o'clock in the morning in front of Notre-Dame.

14. Jean Cocteau, *Opium* (Paris: Éditions Stock, 1930), p. 168. George Painter, in his *Proust*, dates this scene as August 1911.

15. Pietro Citati, *La colombe poignardée* (Paris: Gallimard, 1997), p. 15.

16. The quotation is from Jean Cocteau, "Le sacre du printemps," in *Le rappel à l'ordre*, *Oeuvres complètes*, vol. 9 (Geneva: Éditions Marguerat, 1950), pp. 43–44.

17. *Le sacre du printemps* would be received with enthusiasm during the performances that followed, as well as when it was played in concert form, in Paris and abroad.

18. Arthur Gold and Robert Fizdale, *Misia* (Paris: Gallimard, 1981), p. 186.

19. Cocteau, "Le sacre du printemps."

20. Stravinsky would deny the existence of this ride to the bois de Boulogne, which, if we are to believe him, highlighted Cocteau, whom Diaghilev did not like. This protest should be taken with skepticism, since Stravinsky always tended to minimize the sincerity, role, or competence of others, as he did cruelly with Nijinsky, whom he accused later of not understanding the music at all.

21. Cocteau already mentioned what would become *David* in January 1912, in his unpublished journal. See Jean Cocteau, *Lettres à André Gide avec quelques réponses d'André Gide*, ed. Jean-Jacques Kihm (Paris: La Table Ronde, 1970), p. 48.

22. Anglès, *André Gide et le premier groupe . . .*, vol. 3, p. 274.

23. Jacques Copeau, *Journal 1901–1948*, vol. 1 (Paris: Seghers, 1991), p. 690.

24. Letter, n.d. (May 1914), in Cocteau, *Lettres à André Gide*, p. 52.

25. "Les poèmes," by Henri Ghéon, NRF 45, September 1, 1912, pp. 507–511.

26. Jean Cocteau, *Le Potomak*, in *Oeuvres complètes*, vol. 2 (Lausanne: Éditions Marguerat, 1947), p. 21.

27. Guillaume Apollinaire, "Zone," in *Les Soirées de Paris*, December 1912. English translation by Charlotte Mandell, available online at http://www.charlottemandell.com/Apollinaire.php (accessed September 30, 2015).

28. Cocteau, *Le Potomak*, p. 16.

29. Roger Stéphane, *Portrait souvenir de Jean Cocteau* (Paris: Éditions Tallandier, 1964), p. 28.

30. Cocteau, *Le Potomak*, p. 157.

31. "Projet de lettre à François Mauriac après la querelle de *Bacchus*," in Jean Touzot, *Jean Cocteau* (Lyon: La Manufacture, 1989), p. 239.

32. *Disque Perry*, unpublished autobiographical monologue (1958), quoted in Francis Steegmuller, *Cocteau* (Paris: Buchet-Chastel, 1973), p. 113.

33. Cocteau, *Le Potomak*, p. 15.

34. Cocteau most likely saw the films *L'arroseur arrosé*, *Le bock*, and *Bébé au bord de l'eau*.

35. Abbé Mugnier, *Journal*, p. 295, entry for December 5, 1915.

36. For the "hopscotch" comment, see ibid., entry for June 14, 1914.

37. Unpublished journal by Jacques-Émile Blanche, March 1912, Bibliothèque de l'Institut de France. See also *CJC*, vol. 11 (Paris: Gallimard, 1989), p. 155.

38. But the dance was also indebted to Roerich, great connoisseur of the pagan rites of the ancient Slavs.

39. Cocteau, *Opium*, p. 52.

40. "Cocteau said that Paris, at that time, was very small, that it comprised four restaurants, four theaters, three *demi-mondaines*, and two bad poets — Maurice Rostand and him." See Emmanuel Berl, *Interrogatoire par Patrick Modiano* (Paris: Gallimard, 1976), p. 111.

41. For the drawing, see the manuscript of *Le Potomak* kept at the Bibliothèque Royale de Belgique in Brussels.

42. *LM*, letter dated March 20, 1914.

43. Cocteau, *Le Potomak*, p. 13.

44. *Persicaire* is persicaria, or lady's thumb; *bourdaine* is alder buckthorn; and *Argémone* is a pun on "aigremoine," agrimony, and a species of puppy in Mexico and South America. — Trans.

45. Tristan Tzara, *Sept manifestes Dada* (Paris: N.p., 1924).

46. Sigmund Freud, *Essais de psychanalyse appliquée* (Paris: Gallimard, 1933).

47. "Adieux aux Ballets russes," *La revue musicale*, December 1, 1930, p. 307.

48. Juliette Roche Gleizes, *Mémoires*, unpublished manuscript quoted in Steegmuller, *Cocteau* (Buchet-Chastel), p. 88.

49. Abbé Mugnier, *Journal (1879–1939)* (Paris: Mercure de France, 1985), entry for January 12, 1914.

50. Ibid.

51. Mme Simone, *Sous de nouveaux soleils* (Paris: Gallimard, 1957), p. 209.

52. Unpublished text on *David*, BHVP, box 44, hardback brown notebook that includes an outline of *Thomas l'imposteur*.

53. Nijinsky had hired Marie Rambert, Dalcroze's assistant, to assist him in the choreography of *Le sacre du printemps*.

54. Thévenaz gave the Count, a ballet lover, gymnastic lessons in a black leotard: his arms and legs formed, in the French-style garden at the *hôtel particulier* on the rue Duroc, lines and circles worthy of the optical researches of the post-Impressionists.

55. Quoted in Touzot, *Jean Cocteau*, p. 176.

56. Jouvet was already having Copeau's troupe do gymnastic limbering-up exercises, during their retreat in Limon, in the summer of 1913.

57. See Anglès, *André Gide et le premier groupe . . .*, vol. 3, p. 53.

58. Jean Cocteau to Igor Stravinsky, February 17, 1914, quoted in Steegmuller, *Cocteau* (Buchet-Chastel), p. 75.

59. In a fictional story by Hugo von Hofmannsthal, "Die Entstehung der Josephs-Legende," available in Harry Kessler, *Künstler und nationen: Aufsätze und Reden, 1899–1933* (Frankfurt am Main: Gerhard Schuster, 1988). Count Kessler imagines that Hofmannsthal's short story "The Origin of the Joseph Legend" is based on Diaghilev's search for a biblical subject disclosed during a very late dinner at Larue's restaurant around May 12, when Cocteau had the idea for his *David*. Hofmannsthal likewise

sought and found *The Legend of Joseph*, which Richard Strauss set to music. See Laird M. Easton, *The Red Count, The Life and Times of Harry Kessler* (Berkeley: University of California Press, 2002), p. 203.

60. *LM*, letter dated March 10, 1914.

61. Jean Cocteau, "Cet amour des hauteurs," in *Embarcadères*, *OPC*, p. 137.

62. Jean Cocteau to André Gide, March 1914, in Cocteau, *Lettres à André Gide*, p. 47.

63. Libretto to *David*, kept at the Carlton Lake collection at the University of Texas, Austin.

64. Jean Cocteau to Henri Ghéon, April 10, 1914. See Anglès, *André Gide et le premier groupe . . .*, vol. 3, p. 327.

65. Stravinsky to Copeau, March 15, 1914, in Igor Stravinsky, *Selected Correspondence*, ed. Robert Craft (London: Faber, 1982), vol. 1, p. 82.

66. Thévenaz had previously completed two connected portraits of Cocteau and Anna de Noailles, both of which could be described as "high society-futurist."

67. Quoted in Francis Steegmuller, *Cocteau* (Boston: Little, Brown, 1970), p. 103.

68. Jean Cocteau to Igor Stravinsky, October 4, 1915, in ibid., pp. 82–83.

69. Quoted in Marcel Marnat, *Stravinsky* (Paris: Seuil, 1995), p. 20.

70. Jean Cocteau to André Gide, n.d., Bibliothèque Doucet, Gide collection, Y-547–15, and quoted in Cocteau, *Lettres à André Gide*, p. 49.

71. Anna de Noailles to Jean Cocteau, July 18, 1914, in *CJC*, vol. 11, p. 111.

72. Abbé Mugnier, *Journal*, p. 264, entry for June 20, 1914.

73. François Mauriac, *Journal d'un homme de trente ans: Oeuvres autobiographiques* (Paris: Gallimard, 1990), p. 221.

CHAPTER 5. THE WAR AS OPÉRA

1. "Arcole . . . and Valmy" refers to two famous battles, one won by Bonaparte, the second during the French Revolution.

2. Jean Cocteau, *Le Potomak*, in *Oeuvres complètes*, vol. 2 (Lausanne: Marguerat, 1947), p. 23.

3. Quoted in the unpublished diary of Jacques-Émile Blanche, August 1, 1914, *CJC*, vol. 11 (Paris: Gallimard, 1989), p. 113.

4. Jean Cocteau, "Le convoi," in *Thomas l'imposteur* (Paris: Gallimard, 1923).

5. Paul Morand, *Journal d'un attaché d'ambassade* (Paris: Gallimard, 1963), p. 83.

6. Jean Cocteau, "La princess de Bormes," in *Thomas l'imposteur* (Paris: Gallimard, 1923).

7. André Gide, *Journal*, vol. 1: *1887–1925* (Paris: Gallimard, 1996), pp. 846–847.

8. *Les cahiers de la Petite Dame*, June 1921, in *Cahiers André Gide*, vol. 4 (Paris: Gallimard, 1973), p. 80.

9. [The phrase means, literally, a woman defaced by an acid attack; *vitriolée* is a pun on the word for stained-glass windows, *vitraux.*—Trans.] Abbé Mugnier, *Journal (1879–1939)* (Paris: Mercure de France, 1985), November 27, 1914, and April 23, 1917. Marcel Proust to Louis d'Albuféra, March 1915, in Marcel Proust, *Correspondance*, ed. and comp. Philip Kolb, 21 vols. (Paris: Plon, 1970–1993), vol. 14, p. 71. Kolb, the editor of this correspondence, thinks that Cocteau is using a phrase of Proust's, but the dates speak in favor of Cocteau, who had seen the disfigured cathedral with his own eyes.

10. "La grande pitié des victimes de France," *Le mot,* January 30, 1915, *OPC,* p. 1507.

11. See Jacques-Émile Blanche to Jean Cocteau, January 27, 1919, in Jean Cocteau, Jacques-Émile Blanche, *Correspondance* (Paris: La Table Ronde, 1993), p. 141.

12. "La grande pitié des victimes de France." At the end of his life, Cocteau could assert that his name meant "collector of eggs." See Jean-Pierre Millecam, interview with the author, May 15, 1998. [*Coq,* "cock," plus "teau," reminds us of "Cocteau."—Trans.] "Coqueteau" also sounds like "petit coq," as well as a "louveteau," a young or tiny wolf.

13. Although these acrobatics have been called into question, Cocteau did fly with the aviator during the brief period when Garros was assigned to the Aérodrome de Villacoublay. Gautier-Vignal remembered only one flight; his sister, however, spoke of several expeditions, starting in November 1913. Cocteau probably mythologized these experiences, as was his habit. He placed the first flight in October 1912—but his correspondence does not mention it. See *OPC,* p. 1555.

14. Roger Stéphane, *Portrait souvenir de Jean Cocteau* (Paris: Éditions Tallandier, 1964), p. 74.

15. "Dans le ciel de la patrie," in Jean Cocteau, *Lettres à sa mère* (Paris: Gallimard, 1989), p. 511, letter dated January 1, 1918.

16. "Journal de la princesse Bibesco, janvier 1915," in *Revue générale belge,* December 1963, p. 51, quoted in Frederick Brown, *An Impersonation of Angels* (New York: Viking, 1968), p. 102.

17. Imitated and improved by the Germans, who took Garros prisoner with his plane intact in 1915, this invention allowed them to conceive of the formidable Fokker.

18. To this list Frederick Brown adds Pierre de Lacretelle and Bernard Faÿ. According to M. Martin du Gard, *Les mémorables,* new ed. (Paris: Gallimard, 1999), p. 179, Mauriac was also one of them—but he went to Salonica, to the other end of the front.

19. Bernard Faÿ, *Les précieux* (Paris: Perrin, 1966), p. 31.

20. *Cahiers d'un artiste,* ser. 2 (November–June 14, 1915): 148, January 9, 1915; Jacques-Émile Blanche, *NRF* (1916): n.p.

21. Letter from Jean Cocteau, quoted in Misia Sert, *Misia* (Paris: Gallimard, 1952).

22. Marcel Proust, *À la recherche du temps perdu,* vol. 4 (Paris: Gallimard, 1989), p. 322.

23. A former sketch artist for Lalique, Iribe had already illustrated the brochure that Cocteau had devoted to Nijinsky; he later went on to have an affair with Coco Chanel, then became a film director in Hollywood.

24. Barrès sharply opposed this tip of the cap to Nietzsche in an article he wrote for *L'écho de Paris,* published August 2, 1915.

25. Since Cocteau was unable to display the photos of mutilated children that he claimed to have in hand, Gide suspected him of lying.

26. *LM,* letter dated April 24, 1918.

27. Rough draft of the "Dedication" to Cocteau, *Le Cap de Bonne-Espérance, OPC,* p. 1565.

28. The Cartel was a group of four major theater companies that revived the dramatic arts by endowing a director with creative power—before that an actor was chosen to direct the others.—Trans.

29. Louise Varèse thought the intermediary was rather Jean Crotti, the future brother-in-law of Marcel Duchamp.

30. Valentine Hugo to Georges Hugnet, September 6, 1958, quoted in Ornella Volta, *Satie/Cocteau: Les malentendus d'une entente* (Paris: Le Castor Astral, 1993), p. 142.

31. Pablo Picasso, *Propos sur l'art* (Paris: Gallimard, 1998), p. 149.

32. For the comment by Caizergues, see preface to Pablo Picasso and Guillaume Apollinaire, *Correspondance* (Paris: Gallimard, 1992), p. 5.

33. Jean Cocteau to Pablo Picasso, September 25, 1915, Musée Picasso.

34. Cocteau, *Le Potomak*, p. 124.

35. Picasso persisted in drawing Harlequins armed with sticks. Refusing a kinship that fifty years of friendship would confirm, he would reuse, with his usual perversity, Cocteau's costume to make it the outfit of his famous *Seated Harlequin*; Cocteau would claim that his portrait as Harlequin was finished, unrecognizable, on a Cubist canvas.

36. Jean Cocteau, "Malédiction au laurier," in *Discours du grand sommeil, OPC*, p. 420.

37. *Michel Strogoff* was a novel by Jules Verne dealing with a Tatar rebellion against the Czar; Wilhelm stands for the Germans, Marianne for the French.—Trans.

38. "Mon cher Pablo la guerre dure/Guerre bénie et non pas dure/Guerre tendre de la douceur/Où chaque obus est une fleur." Poem-letter from Guillaume Apollinaire to Pablo Picasso, July 12, 1918, in Picasso and Apollinaire, *Correspondance*, p. 169, and Pablo Picasso to André Salmon, May 1915 (p. 133).

39. Jean Cocteau, *Discours du grand sommeil, OPC*, p. 406.

40. Jean Cocteau, "Température," *Poésies, OPC*, p. 159. For "pink inside," see Jean Cocteau, "Batterie," in *Poésies, OPC*, p. 170; for "like coral at night," see Cocteau, "La douche," *Discours du grand sommeil, OPC*, p. 416; for "gold typewriter" of their teeth, see Cocteau, "Trois surprises," a variation on the poem "Batterie," BHVP, box 24.

41. *LM*, letter dated May 29, 1916.

42. Jean Cocteau to Madeleine Le Chevrel, quoted in Francis Steegmuller, *Cocteau* (Paris: Buchet-Chastel, 1973), p. 109.

43. "It wasn't without some amusement that you read on the sign: Concorde, in the midst of the ruins of a casino," Cocteau would write in *Thomas l'imposteur*.

44. First version of Jean Cocteau, *Le Cap de Bonne-Espérance, OPC*, p. 86.

45. See Abbé Mugnier, *Journal (1879–1939)*, January 12, 1914, p. 259.

46. Jean Cocteau, "Visite," in *Discours du grand sommeil, OPC*, pp. 444–445.

47. Quoted in Éric Marty, *Louis Althusser: Un sujet sans procès* (Paris: Gallimard, 1999), p. 16.

48. The empress's rejuvenating lotion was sold on the boulevard de la Madeleine, chez Félix Milliat, Cocteau's barber. Lucien Daudet gave him the recipe.

49. Letters from Cocteau's mother, February 27, 1916, and June 26, 1916, quoted in Jean-Jacques Kihm, Elizabeth Sprigge, and Henri C. Béhar, *Jean Cocteau, l'homme et les miroirs* (Paris: La Table Ronde, 1968), p. 92.

CHAPTER 6. THE ORDEAL OF BOHEMIA

Epigraph: "La poésie ne mène à rien—à condition de ne pas en sortir."—Trans.

1. Satie had already refused to use for the occasion the piano monologues from his *Trois morceaux en forme de poire* (Three pieces in the shape of a pear), which had been composed thirteen years earlier.

2. Général de Castelnau had been nicknamed "The savior of Nancy" after a decisive battle.

3. Jean Cocteau, "Entretiens avec André Fraigneau," *Bibliothèque* 10, no. 18 (1965): p. 14.

4. Roger Stéphane, *Portrait souvenir de Jean Cocteau* (Paris: Éditions Tallandier, 1964), p. 73. This episode is even less likely since the Coxyde sector, according to the press, was calm at the time. Information provided to the author by Pierre Chanel.

5. The Quai d'Orsay is the French foreign ministry.—Trans.

6. Highly coveted by writers, this appointment allowed one to escape the front.

7. Letters from Erik Satie, April 25, May 18, and August 4, 1916, in Erik Satie, *Correspondance presque complète*, ed. and comp. Ornella Volta (Paris: Fayard/IMEC, 2000), pp. 239, 244, 251.

8. The name was a pun on *satirique*, satirical.—Trans.

9. Ornella Volta, "Une relation peu explorée, Blaise Cendrars et Erik Satie," in *Cahiers Blaise Cendrars*, vol. 3 (Boudry-Neufchâtel: La Baconnière, 1989), p. 96.

10. Ibid., p. 10.

11. "Le vieux hautbois dormant," in French. The pun refers to "la Belle au bois dormant," Sleeping Beauty.—Trans.

12. The *zutistes* were a group of late nineteenth-century poets including Rimbaud, Verlaine, and Charles Cros.—Trans.

13. *Le Pilhaou-Thibaou*, July 1921. Note that the translation of the Greek *Gymnopédies* is "naked children." [A *piano à queue*, literally a piano with a tail, is a grand piano; *queue* is also slang for penis, so it would translate as "with a big prick."—Trans.]

14. Christian Soleil, *Le bonheur fabriqué*, vol. 2: *Le pluriel et le singulier* (Saint-Étienne: Arts Graphiques, 1995), p. 204.

15. Preface by Georges Auric to the four-hand piano edition of *Parade*, 1917, quoted in Volta, "Une relation peu explorée," p. 27. Russolo, author of the 1912 manifesto *The Art of Noises*, launched concrete music by making strange instruments—a whistling buzzer, a hiccupping gurgler, a meowing stridulator—after modifying an airplane engine for the futurist aerial theater of Azari.

16. Paul Morand, *Journal d'un attaché d'ambassade* (Paris: Gallimard, 1963), pp. 79–80, entry for November 22, 1916.

17. This phrase appears in Panckiewicz, *Kisling and His Friends*, exhibition catalogue of the Musée du Petit Palais in Geneva, 1996.

18. "Parigot" is slang for Parisian.—Trans.

19. Jean Cocteau, "Le dernier chant du prince frivole," in *La danse de Sophocle, Mercure de France* (1912): 30–34, and *OPC*, p. 1390; also reprinted, in the latter edition, under the title "Le petit prince est assis à la terrasse du Fouquet's bar"—see Cocteau, *Poèmes de jeunesse épars, OPC*, p. 1477.

20. Jean Cocteau to Valentine Gross, August 12, 1916, quoted in Francis Steegmuller, *Cocteau* (Paris: Buchet-Chastel, 1973), p. 124. [The Pont d'Arcole is one of the most famous of Bonaparte's victorious battles.—Trans.]

21. Henri-Pierre Roché, unpublished diary, August 12, 1916, Henry Ransom Humanities Research Center, University of Texas at Austin. He did, however, translate the portrait that Gertrude Stein wrote of Cocteau in 1911.

22. Jean Cocteau, *Parade, genèse d'une création: Autour de la reprise par Angelin Preljocaj* (New York: Plume, 1993), p. 56.

23. The quotation is from Morand, *Journal d'un attaché d'ambassade*, p. 84, entry for November 26, 1916.

24. "Symphonie en rose à Vérone," *La lampe d'Aladin*, OPC, p. 1281.

25. Jean Cocteau, *La comtesse de Noailles oui et non* (Paris: Perrin, 1963), p. 97.

26. The quotation is from Blaise Cendrars, *Moravagine* (Paris: Grasset, 1992), p. 229.

27. Letter to Albert Gleizes, August 13, 1916, quoted in Billy Klüver, *Un jour avec Picasso* (Vanves: Hazan, 1994), p. 83.

28. He saw Kisling at 3 rue Joseph-Barra.

29. By reusing Kisling's old canvas, Modigliani would also make a portrait of Cocteau in oil that is erratic and touching, probably one of the most Modiglianesque there is. It is at The Henry and Rose Pearlman Foundation, Princeton University Art Museum, Princeton, NJ. Another portrait would be found, painted over, forty years later, but it turned out to be a forgery.

30. André Salmon, *Souvenirs sans fin*, vol. 2: *Deuxième époque, 1908–1920* (Paris: Gallimard, 1956), p. 263.

31. The portrait is now at Petit Palais, Musée d'Art Moderne, Geneva.

32. "Kiki" was Alice Prin, also nicknamed the "Queen of Montparnasse."—Trans.

33. Stéphane, *Portrait souvenir*, p. 46.

34. Bernard Faÿ, *Les précieux* (Paris: Perrin, 1966), p. 34.

35. Morand, *Journal d'un attaché d'ambassade*, October 7, 1916, p. 28.

36. The Futurist Manifesto is viewable online at http://www.unknown.nu/futurism/manifesto.html (accessed December 30, 2015).

37. Marinetti would put his words in action by attacking, in April 1916, the Socialist newspaper *Avanti!* with a gang.

38. *Sic, International journal for communisation* 2 (February 1916).

39. The "French 75" was a 75 mm field gun.—Trans.

40. Arthur Gold and Robert Fizdale, *Misia* (Paris: Gallimard, 1981), p. 231 (August 1916).

41. Cocteau recorded each stage of that magnificent day, thanks to the Autographic Kodak brought back from the front, from the instant when he found Picasso on the Rotonde café terrace, wearing a taxi driver's hat, with his companion Pâquerette, star model for Poiret, very elegant in her rosewood dress and bicycle-racing hat, to the moment when, getting up to go to lunch at the home of Baty, Picasso had met his assistant, the painter Ortiz de Zarate, then Max Jacob, who feigned obscene gestures behind his back under the sinister gaze of Henri-Pierre Roché in uniform. Kisling, Modigliani, and André Salmon were also recorded by his camera, as well as Marie Vassiliev, who had just emerged from her studio-canteen: published by Billy Klüver, these photos bear witness to Cocteau's almost medium-like prescience of the moment.

42. Jean Cocteau to Valentine Gross, August 31, 1916, quoted in Steegmuller, *Cocteau* (Buchet-Chastel), p. 125.

43. In his *Dictionnaire Picasso* (Paris: Robert Laffont, 1995), p. 195, Pierre Daix thinks it was as he was accompanying Satie back to Arcueil that Picasso discovered the house in Montrouge to which he moved in October 1916 in order to flee the haunting memory of Eva.

44. Erik Satie to Henri-Pierre Roché, September 5, 1916, in Satie, *Correspondance presque complète*, p. 257.

45. Morand, *Journal d'un attaché d'ambassade*, p. 28, entry for October 7, 1916.

46. "Cube tic tic tic tic au centième étage un ange a fait son nid chez le dentiste tic tic tic Titanic toc toc Titanic sombre avec éclat sous les vagues . . . glace au soda Pullman tic tic." (Cube tic tic tic on the hundredth floor an angel has made his nest at the dentist's tic tic tic Titanic toc toc Titanic sinks brilliantly beneath the waves . . . ice with soda Pullman tic tic.)

47. "Venez! Venez voir la vérité sur l'Amérique, les tremblements de terre, les courtscir-cuits, les détectives de l'Hudson, le ragtime, les usines, les trains qui déraillent et les bateaux qui sombrent! Un instant d'hésitation et vous êtes tous perdus!" (Come! Come see the truth about America, the earthquakes, the short-circuits, the Hudson detectives, the ragtime, the factories, the trains that derail and the boats that sink! One instant of hesitation and you're all lost!)

48. Jean Cocteau to Valentine Gross, September 4, 1916, quoted in Steegmuller, *Cocteau* (Buchet-Chastel), p. 127.

49. Ibid.

50. Jean-Christophe Averty reestablished this text in his own way, in the form of subtitles, in the *Parade* he promoted on French television in 1978.

51. Erik Satie to Jean Cocteau, January 1, 1917, in Satie, *Correspondance presque complète*, p. 271.

52. Erik Satie to Valentine Gross, January 5, 1917, Henry Ransom Humanities Research Center, University of Texas at Austin.

53. Gertrude Stein, *The Autobiography of Alice B. Toklas* (New York: Penguin, 1933), p. 87.

54. Jean Cocteau to Valentine Gross, February 15, 1917, quoted in Steegmuller, *Cocteau* (Buchet-Chastel), p. 132.

55. According to Richard Buckle, Diaghilev's biographer, Cocteau would never get back the advance he had paid Satie, for lack of a sufficient number of performances: only Picasso seems to have profited financially from the affair. See R. Buckle, *Diaghilev* (London: Weidenfeld and Nicholson, 1979).

CHAPTER 7. THE PARADE OF PEACE

1. Jean Cocteau to his mother, February 20, 1917, *LM*.

2. "Depero sees now that he has been more or less plagiarized by everyone, whether it's Picasso . . . for Erik Satie's *Parade*, or Larionov," a witness would report three years later.

3. Jean Cocteau, *Picasso* (Paris: L'école des lettres, 1996), p. 183.

4. Ibid., p. 34.

5. Ibid., p. 86.

6. Ibid., p. 33.

7. Jean Cocteau to his mother, March 16, 1917, *LM*.

8. Already comprised of works by Picasso, Braque, and Gontcharova, this collection, which was expanding to the Italian Futurists—Giacomo Balla, Carlo Carrà and Fortunato Depero—would be exhibited in Rome during that same season.

9. Cocteau had discovered the American actress Pearl White in 1915, when she performed with Edgard Varèse and Valentine in *The Mysteries of New York*, a 1914 musical film.

10. Jean Cocteau to his mother, February 22, 1917, *LM*.

11. Arthur Gold and Robert Fizdale, *Misia* (Paris: Gallimard, 1981), p. 224.

12. Quoted in Douglas Cooper, *Picasso et le Théatre* (Paris: Éditions Cercle d'Art, 1967), p. 24.

13. Cf. Ernest Ansermet, *Écrits sur la musique* (Neuchâtel: La Baconnière, 1971), pp. 25–26.

14. Jean Cocteau, *Carte blanche, Oeuvres complètes*, vol. 11 (Lausanne: Éditions Marguerat, 1951), p. 129.

15. Jean Cocteau to Guillaume Apollinaire, March 1917, in Guillaume Apollinaire and Jean Cocteau, *Correspondance*, ed. Pierre Caizergues and Michel Décaudin (Paris: Éditions Jean-Michel Place, 1991), p. 24.

16. Jean Cocteau, Manuscript of "Prologue," "Documents," *OPC*, p. 1646.

17. Francis Steegmuller, *Cocteau* (Paris: Buchet-Chastel, 1973), p. 175.

18. "Programme," poem accompanying a profile in India ink of Picasso, 1917, part. coll., reproduced on p. 2 of the catalog from the "Parade pour Parade" exhibit in the Centre Georges-Pompidou, December 1986–February 1987. [*Marievaudage* is a pun for marivaudage, a term used to describe the literary style of Pierre de Marivaux, an eighteenth-century novelist and dramatist who described intersecting erotic pairings.—Trans.]

19. Cocteau would have been content to pick a clover for his mother in the pavilion at the Vatican where Benedict XV liked to play bridge.

20. Jean Cocteau to his mother, March 3, 1917, *LM*.

21. *La statue retrouvée* is an animated scene in which a figure sets off to meet two women. Set to music by Erik Satie, based on an idea of Cocteau's, this "divertissement" for organ and trumpet would be played on May 30, 1923, at the Baroque Ball, an event inspired by the era of Louis XIV and hosted by the Beaumonts. The costumes were by Picasso, and Olga was one of the performers.

22. Jean Cocteau, "Rose des vents," handwritten poem, BHVP, box 16; also from *CJC*, no. 1 (Paris: Gallimard, 1969), pp. 12–15, reprinted in *CJC*, n.s. 1 (Paris: Passage du Marais, 2002), pp. 202–205.

23. Paul Morand, *Journal d'un attaché d'ambassade* (Paris: Gallimard, 1963), May 23, 1917, p. 246.

24. Jean Cocteau to Pablo Picasso, March 13, 1917, Musée Picasso.

25. Jean Cocteau to Pablo Picasso, March 17, 1917, Musée Picasso.

26. Letter dated Easter 1917, in Jean Cocteau, *Lettres à André Gide avec quelques réponses d'André Gide*, ed. Jean-Jacques Kihm (Paris: La Table Ronde, 1970), p. 59. A nymph is a newly hatched insect that will gradually grow to adult size.

27. Jean Cocteau, "Le mystère laïc", in *Oeuvres complètes*, vol. 10 (Lausanne: Éditions Marguerat, 1950), p. 33.

28. Guillaume Apollinaire, "Cortège," in *Alcools* (Paris: Poésie/Gallimard, 1966), p. 49.

29. Jean Cocteau to Guillaume Apollinaire, n.d., in Apollinaire and Cocteau, *Correspondance*, p. 99.

30. *La Parisienne*, January 1954; ibid., p. 132.

31. Guillaume Apollinaire to Pablo Picasso, April 4, 1917, in Pablo Picasso and Guillaume Apollinaire, *Correspondance* (Paris: Gallimard, 1992), p. 154.

32. The cousin was little Françoise Durand-Viel, who was still alive in 2003, the year the French edition of this book was written.

33. Guillaume Apollinaire to Jean Cocteau, March 13, 1917, *Catalogue de la Bibliothèque Jacques Guérin*, Ader-Trajan, May 20, 1992, lot no. 18, quoted in Ornella Volta, *Satie/Cocteau: Les malentendus d'une entente* (Paris: Le Castor Astral, 1993), p. 40.

34. Pierre Reverdy, *Le voleur de Talan* (Paris: Flammarion, 1967), p. 170 (published with the assistance of Maurice Saillet).

35. Jean Cocteau to Guillaume Apollinaire, Spring 1917, in Apollinaire and Cocteau, *Correspondance*, p. 43.

36. Jean Cocteau to Jacques-Émile Blanche, March 1917, in Jean Cocteau and Jacques-Émile Blanche, *Correspondance* (Paris: La Table Ronde, 1993), p. 91.

37. "Satierik" is a play on *satirique*, satirical.—Trans.

38. Roger Stéphane, *Portrait souvenir de Jean Cocteau* (Paris: Éditions Tallandier, 1964), p. 59.

39. Ibid.

40. *L'Excelsior*, May 18, 1917.

41. Published in *L'Excelsior*, May 11, 1917.

42. Cocteau would avenge himself in private, saying to the Abbé Mugnier: "Apollinaire is a Pole who has genius once a year."

43. Cf. the illuminating analysis by Ornella Volta in *Satie/Cocteau*, p. 43.

44. *L'Excelsior*, May 18, 1917.

45. André Salmon, *Souvenirs sans fin*, vol. 1: *Première époque 1903–1908* (Paris: Gallimard, 1955), pp. 343–344.

46. Silent films were shown at the Châtelet, "sonorized" by this machine, which was capable of imitating the sound of an express train, a stormy sea, or a machine gun.

47. Guy Noël, in *Carnet de la semaine*, May 27, 1917.

48. "Cocorico" is a rooster's cry, used as an expression of French national pride.—Trans.

49. *Der Querschmitt*, Berlin, 1922.

50. Amédée Ozenfant, *Mémoires, 1886–1962* (Paris: Seghers, 1968).

51. Morand, *Journal d'un attaché d'ambassade*, p. 366.

52. In other versions, all retold by Cocteau, it's a man.

53. In Cocteau's own words, quoted in Georges Auric, *Quand j'étais là* (Paris: Grasset, 1979), p. 77.

54. "Picassotises" is a play on Picasso and "sottises," which means silliness, foolishness.—Trans.

55. "Senegalese tam-tam" is quoted in Léo Poldès, *La Grimace*, May 1917.

56. Pétomane was a popular French music-hall performer who "delighted audiences with his farting skills." (*Péter* means "to fart.")—Trans.

57. Erik Satie to Jean Poueigh, May 30, June 3, and June 5, 1917, in Erik Satie, *Correspondance presque complète*, ed. and comp. Ornella Volta (Paris: Fayard/IMEC, 2000), pp. 289–290.

58. When the *Mona Lisa* was stolen in 1911 by an Italian handyman, both Picasso and Apollinaire were brought in by the Paris police for questioning. Innocent of the theft, they were, basically, guilty of having stolen other art from the Louvre: in Picasso's dresser lay hidden several ancient Iberian statue heads that had been stolen in 1907 by Apollinaire's secretary, probably on commission from Picasso himself.

59. Guillaume Apollinaire to Jean Cocteau, July 18, 1917, in Apollinaire and Cocteau, *Correspondance*, p. 53.

60. Morand, *Journal d'un attaché d'ambassade*, December 1, 1917, p. 436.

61. The audience rioted during the play's premiere, on February 25, 1830.

62. Faithful to her character, the Lolita Marie Chabelska fled to the United States, where she would live for the rest of her life.

63. Erik Satie to Jean Cocteau, October 22, 1917, in Satie, *Correspondance presque complète*, p. 312. [*Crâne-poli* means "bald head."—Trans.]

64. Morand, *Journal d'un attaché d'ambassade*, May 23, 1917, p. 246.

65. Erik Satie to Valentine Hugo, December 13, 1920, in Satie, *Correspondance presque complète*, p. 430.

66. A. Gide, *Journal*, vol. 1: *1887–1925* (Paris: Gallimard, 1996), January 1, 1921, p. 1196.

67. *Parade* would finally be repeated with *Le sacre du printemps*, during a Picasso soirée, but without the noises, whose restitution Cocteau would demand again in 1923, seven years after its creation. It was a triumph. Today, the ballet is still performed and recorded *with* the noises.

68. *Nord-Sud* (June–July 1917). The essay, however, appeared in the absence of Reverdy, who had let Paul Dermée edit this issue of the journal.

69. Marcel Proust to Jean Cocteau, May 19 or 20, 1917, in Cocteau, *Correspondance*, vol. 16, pp. 139–140.

70. See the wonderful *Band Wagon* by Vincente Minelli, who never hid his admiration for Cocteau. In the film, gunshots ring out in a dreamlike atmosphere.

71. See the *Piccadilly pour piano seul* that inevitably accompanies any silent film.

72. Cf., for this entire passage, the rough draft of Cocteau's dedication to Garros, *OPC*, pp. 1564–1568.

73. Morand, *Journal d'un attaché d'ambassade*, June 15, 1917, p. 266.

74. Ibid., May 3, 1923, p. 413.

75. Marcel Proust to Jean Cocteau, July 1916, in Marcel Proust, *Correspondance*, ed. and comp. Philip Kolb, 21 vols. (Paris: Plon, 1970–1993), vol. 18, p. 593.

76. "I am no longer capable of anything," Proust wrote Cocteau as an excuse. "My manuscripts, having waited too long, have yellowed, gotten torn, are forming an irreparable lace, and my brain more worn-out because it is no longer able to provide a new framework." Letter dated June 1917, in ibid., vol. 16, p. 161.

77. Morand, *Journal d'un attaché d'ambassade*, June 15, 1917, p. 267.

78. Jacques Porel, *Fils de Réjane*, vol. 1: *1895–1920* (Paris: Plon, 1951), p. 349.

79. André Beucler, *De Saint-Petersbourg à Saint-Germain-des-Prés* (Paris: Gallimard, 1980), p. 245.

80. Quoted in Morand, *Journal d'un attaché d'ambassade*, August 12, 1917, p. 349.

81. Marcel Proust to Marie Scheikévitch, August 4, 1917, in Proust, *Correspondance*, vol. 16, p. 202.

82. François Mauriac, *Journal d'un homme de trente ans: Oeuvres autobiographiques* (Paris: Gallimard, 1990), August 14, 1917, p. 242.

83. Jean Hugo, *Le regard de la mémoire* (Paris: Babel-Actes Sud, 1983), p. 115.

84. Bernard Faÿ, *Les précieux* (Paris: Perrin, 1966), p. 270.

85. "Le futurisme mondial manifeste à Paris," *Noï* (September 1924), quoted in *OPC*, p. 1559.

86. Article by Fernand Vanderem in *La revue de Paris* 2 (January 15, 1919).

87. Proust too would at last give in to brute fascination with metal. Struck by the spectacle of biplanes seen from a balcony at the Ritz as he was leaving a dinner followed by a hypnotism session, with air-raid sirens wailing—"another one who has walked at the foot of the Eiffel Tower," Cocteau had murmured—Proust in turn praised, in *Le temps retrouvé*, the beauty of planes taking off at night to intercept German bombers.

88. Abbé Mugnier, *Journal (1879–1939)* (Paris: Mercure de France, 1985), January 27, 1919, p. 349.

89. Jacques Vaché to André Breton, October 18, 1917, quoted in Pierre Ostier, *Le Robert dictionnaire des citations françaises*, vol. 1 (Paris: Le Robert, 1992), p. 706.

90. Quoted in Morand, *Journal d'un attaché d'ambassade*, May 27, 1917, p. 249.

91. Carlton Lake collection at the University of Texas, Austin.

92. Jean Cocteau to Guillaume Apollinaire, n.d. (July 1917?), in Apollinaire and Cocteau, *Correspondance*, p. 49.

93. "Prologue," fragment no. 10, in *Discours du grand sommeil*, *OPC*, p. 397.

94. Jean Cocteau to Jacques-Émile Blanche, spring 1918, in Cocteau and Blanche, *Correspondance*, p. 126.

95. Jean Cocteau to Louis Aragon, February 1919, quoted in Aragon, *Papiers inédits: De Dada au surréalisme (1917–1931)* (Paris: Gallimard, 2000), p. 263.

96. Quoted in Mauriac, *Journal d'un homme de trente ans*, p. 256 (April 1919).

97. *OPC*, p. 1571.

98. Jean Cocteau to his mother, July 20, 1917, *LM*.

99. Jean Cocteau to André Gide, August 24, 1918, in Cocteau, *Lettres à André Gide*, p. 71.

100. Jean Cocteau to his mother, July 6, 1917, *LM*.

101. The first ones would appear in an appendix to *Le coq et l'arlequin* under the title "Fragments of 'Igor Stravinsky and the Ballet Russe' (The Bartered Bride)," and the second ones, in *Le Gaulois* on April 27, 1919—and would be reprinted in volume 1 of *LM*.

102. They would be published in vol. 2 of *LM*, collected by Pierre Chanel.

103. "De la France," in Jean Cocteau, *La difficulté d'être* (Monaco: Éditions du Rocher, 1947), p. 36.

104. Jean Cocteau to his mother, April 24, 1918, *LM*.

105. Since Marcelle George, Garros's companion, never contradicted Cocteau, it is possible that the aviator had brought with him one of the copies of publisher's proofs

given to the author for corrections. Garros, after all, may have been flattered by the homage made to him, while he was alive, by a poet who was obviously destined to be a lasting name.

106. Marcel Proust to Jean Cocteau, in Proust, *Correspondance,* vol. 17, p. 531.

107. Divers eventually fished Agostinelli out of the water. He was a prisoner of his rubber suit, his "eyes eaten by fish," said Céleste, Proust's future housekeeper.

108. He did not confide in Gide, however, about the more than thorny case of Marc Allégret.

109. Jean Cocteau to his mother, June 7, 1918, *LM;* Jean Cocteau to Georges Auric, May 24, 1918, in Georges Auric, *Correspondance avec Jean Cocteau* (Montpellier: Pierre Caizergues, Centre d'études du XXe siècle, Université Paul-Valéry, 1999), p. 29.

110. *La Parisienne,* January 1954, quoted in Apollinaire and Cocteau, *Correspondance,* p. 131.

111. Quoted in Erik Satie to Jean Cocteau, April 7, 1918, Satie, *Correspondance presque complète,* p. 326.

112. She supposedly had "blue blood" because one of her grandmothers was seduced by a Marquis de Mailly-Nesles.

113. Jean Cocteau, *Journal (1942–1945)* (Paris: Gallimard, 1989), p. 232.

114. *Les écrivains célèbres,* vol. 3 (Paris: Mazenod, 1953), p. 165.

115. Guillaume Apollinaire to Jean Cocteau, May 1918, in Apollinaire and Cocteau, *Correspondance,* p. 83. To earn a living, Apollinaire was working at the Ministry of Colonies; hence the reference to "colonies."

116. Cocteau, speech given on June 5, 1959, in the square of the Abbaye, place Saint-Germain-des-Prés.

117. Pablo Picasso, *Propos sur l'art* (Paris: Gallimard, 1998), p. 157.

118. Ibid., p. 135. In *The Difficulty of Being,* Cocteau attributes these words to Oscar Wilde.

CHAPTER 8. WITH RADIGUET

1. Marcel Boussac made a fortune in textile manufacturing.—Trans.

2. Paul Morand, *L'allure de Chanel* (Paris: Hermann, 1976), p. 45.

3. Almanach Vermot was a daily publication founded by Joseph Vermot in 1886, featuring puns and plays on words.—Trans.

4. Reginald Bridgeman, quoted in Francis Steegmuller, *Cocteau* (Paris: Buchet-Chastel, 1973), p. 227; Maurice Sachs, *Au temps du Boeuf sur le Toit* (1939; Paris: Grasset, 1987), p. 87.

5. Paul Morand, *Venises* (Paris: Gallimard/Le Cercle du nouveau livre, 1971), p. 115. [La Fronde, also called the War of the Lorrains, was a civil war that took place during Louis XIV's monarchy, and was directed mainly against his main minister, Cardinal Mazarin.—Trans.]

6. Abbé Mugnier, *Journal (1879–1939)* (Paris: Mercure de France, 1985), February 9, 1915, p. 281.

7. "The next day, the concierge would receive triple that sum," Cocteau pointed out.

8. Morand, *Venises*, p. 25.

9. Westerns by Thomas Ince were already popular before the war. Cocteau would be especially infatuated with his *Carmen of the Klondike.*

10. This was published in January 1921.

11. Jean Cocteau to Albert Gleizes, January 30, 1918, Bibliothèque Jacques Doucet.

12. The "raw meat" quotation is from Stéphane, *Portrait souvenir de Jean Cocteau*, p. 103.

13. Mugnier, *Journal (1879–1939)*, April 23, 1917, p. 309.

14. Ibid., May 18, 1916, p. 299.

15. Jean Cocteau to Louis Aragon, December 2, 1918, quoted in Aragon, *Papiers inédits*, p. 248.

16. Liane de Pougy, *Mes cahiers bleus* (Paris: Plon, 1977), July 16, 1919, p. 31. [*Encoctoqués* combines *intoxiqué*, intoxicated, and *toqué*, crazy, with *Cocteau*—Trans.]

17. "Réponse à de jeunes musiciens," *Le mot* 12 (February 27, 1915).

18. The ballet had been performed in Madrid, before the King of Spain; in Barcelona; and then in Rio.

19. Jean Cocteau to his mother, August 10, 1918, *LM.*

20. This was in a note edited out of the proofs of *Le coq et l'arlequin*, BHVP, box 59. In February 1915, in issue 12 of *Le mot*, Cocteau outlined a revealing parallel between Stravinsky and Schoenberg. If "the lucid cold helps Stravinsky free himself of an Oriental poetry," he wrote, Schoenberg "persists in German glue, wants to be avant-garde, comes up against the old notes, blames himself for loving *Tristan and Isolde*, composes on a machine." In 1918 as well as in 1915, Cocteau spoke of Schoenberg solely by hearsay: it was Georges Auric who had told Cocteau about him. Not a single work by Schoenberg had been performed in France. It was in December 1920, during Jean Wiener's second "Salad Concert," that the first part of Schoenberg's *Pierrot Lunaire* (created in Berlin in December 1912) was given, in a French version by Benoist-Méchin, with Marya Freund, Jean Wiener at the piano, and an instrumental ensemble conducted by Darius Milhaud. The first integral performance, by the same performers, would take place in the Salle Gaveau on January 12, 1921, and the work would be performed again on March 10, 1922. On Cocteau's aesthetics at that time, see Jean Cocteau, *Entre Picasso et Radiguet*, ed. and comp. André Fermigier (Paris: Hermann, 1967).

21. "Le marteau sans maître" (The hammer without a master) is a composition by the composer Pierre Boulez, set to a surrealist poem by René Char.—Trans.

22. Bernard Faÿ, *Les précieux* (Paris: Perrin, 1966), p. 271.

23. To these musicians, we should add Jean Wiener, the pianist for Darius Milhaud's *Boeuf sur le toit* who would adapt "Aéronautes," a poem by Cocteau; Vance Lowry, a black musician who in 1928 would set to jazz Cocteau's "Voleurs d'enfants"; Georges van Parys, who set several of his poems to music, from "Îles" to "Fête de Montmartre," which Milhaud also orchestrated; not to mention "La danseuse"—the melody itself likens her to a crab—for which Satie would compose a tune.

24. Jean Cocteau to Darius Milhaud, August 16, 1919, in Jean Cocteau and Darius Milhaud, *Correspondance* (Montpellier: Pierre Caizergues and Josiane Mas, Centre d'études littéraires françaises du XXe siècle, Université Paul-Valéry, 1992), p. 14.

25. Picabia sometimes even called Cocteau Jean *Cocquebin*, a word meaning a young idiot.

26. André Gide, "Lettre ouverte à Jean Cocteau," *NRF*, June 1, 1919.

27. André Gide to Jean Cocteau, July 11, 1919, in Cocteau, *Lettres à André Gide*, p. 99.

28. André Gide, "La nouvelle parade de Jean Cocteau," *Les écrits nouveaux* 3, no 22 (October 1919).

29. Cf. Ornella Volta's excellent book *Satie/Cocteau: Les malentendus d'une entente* (Paris: Le Castor Astral, 1993).

30. Gide, after a year, had sold only 354 copies of *Les caves du Vatican*.

31. Jean Cocteau to Georges Auric, January 23, 1919, in Georges Auric, *Correspondance avec Jean Cocteau* (Montpellier: Pierre Caizergues, Centre d'études du XXe siècle, Université Paul-Valéry, 1999), p. 53.

32. Z 2 (March 1920). ["Noix de Cocteau" is a pun on "noix de coco," or coconut.— Trans.]

33. On Man-Ray, see *Les feuilles libres*, April 1922; on Brancusi, see Jean Cocteau, "Pour la tombe d'Erik Satie," *Comoedia* 20, no. 4891, May 17, 1926, quoted in Satie, *Correspondance presque complète*, p. 700. ["L'Homme-Rayon" is the literal French translation of Man-Ray.—Trans.]

34. Quoted in André Beucler, *Plaisirs de mémoire: De Saint-Pétersbourg à Saint-Germain-des-Prés*, vol. 2 (Paris: Gallimard, 1982), p. 14.

35. André Gide, *The Counterfeiters*, trans. Dorothy Bussy (New York: Vintage, 1973), p. 202. (Translation slightly modified.)

36. *Correspondance André Gide-Dorothy Bussy*, appendix A (March 1921), in *Cahiers André Gide*, no. 9 (Paris: Gallimard, 1979), p. 502.

37. Jean Cocteau to André Gide, August 24, 1918, in Cocteau, *Lettres à André Gide*, p. 71. [*Poulain* can mean either "colt" or "protégé."—Trans.]

38. Since the old edition of Gide's *Journals* designated her by the letter C, most people thought that referred to Cocteau, until Éric Marty's edition, which restored her exact, complete patronymic: Catherine Krüger.

39. André Gide, *Journal*, vol. 2: 1926–1950 (Paris: Gallimard, 1997), p. 1116.

40. *Les cahiers de la petite dame, 1818–1929*, May 1923, in *Cahiers André Gide*, vol. 4 (Paris: Gallimard, 1973), p. 182.

41. "Un entretien avec André Gide," in *Hommage à André Gide*, special 1951 issue of the *NRF*.

42. Jean Cocteau to Jean Paulhan, February 22, 1951, IMEC, Paulhan collection, folder 3.

43. From the title of the last novel published by this "corruptor" of youth, *La barre fixe*, we can see another allusion to Cocteau's *Le grand écart* [*faire le grand écart* is to do a split—Trans.]. There is also a pun on Passavant's name: L'homme qui *passe avant* tout le monde, i.e., the man who tries to overtake anyone.

44. Cf. Claude Mauriac, *Conversations avec André Gide* (Paris: Albin Michel, 1951), p. 108.

45. Gide, *The Counterfeiters*, p. 98 of the French. After a meeting with Gide in 1950, Cocteau would write in his journal: "He had asked me to take charge of Marc and show him a little of Montparnasse, the Cubists, Les Six, etc. I didn't see Marc much

but Marc made him think he saw me constantly. In that way he made Gide crazy and set him against me without my suspecting anything. Gide confessed that to me (the day before I left for Egypt), adding, 'I didn't yet know Marc's true nature, and I'm sorry for it.'" (*PD*, vol. 1, p. 29).

46. Jean Cocteau, *La difficulté d'être* (Monaco: Éditions du Rocher, 1947), p. 31.

47. Jean Cocteau, "Souvenir," in *Hommages, Oeuvres complètes*, vol. 11 (Lausanne: Éditions Marguerat, 1951).

48. *Avec Stravinsky* (Monaco: Du Rocher, 1958), p. 46. For his appearance, see Maurice Martin du Gard, *Les mémorables*, new ed. (Paris: Gallimard, 1999), p. 173.

49. B. Cendrars, "Paris par Balzac," *La table ronde* 22 (October 1947).

50. De Pougy, *Mes cahiers bleus*, p. 128.

51. André Salmon, *Souvenirs sans fin*, vol. 1: *Première époque 1903–1908* (Paris: Gallimard, 1955), p. 344.

52. Jean Hugo, *Le regard de la mémoire* (Paris: Babel-Actes Sud, 1983), p. 130.

53. Jean Cocteau to Irène Lagut, n.d., *Lettres de l'Oiseleur* (Monaco: Du Rocher, Monaco, 1989), pp. 169–170.

54. Cf. du Gard, *Les mémorables*, p. 176.

55. *Jean Cocteau par Jean Cocteau*, interviews with William Fifield (Paris: Éditions Stock, 1973), p. 77.

56. Poem written in the summer of 1919 by Jean Cocteau to Raymond Radiguet, quoted by Marie-Christine Movilliat in her *Raymond Radiguet ou la jeunesse contredite, 1903–1923* (Paris: Bibliophone Daniel Radford), 2000, p. 175.

57. "Profession of faith" letter from Raymond Radiguet to Jean Cocteau, summer 1919, quoted in Keith Goesch, *Raymond Radiguet*, foreword by Jean Cocteau (Paris: Éditions Palatine, 1955).

58. Jean Cocteau to Maurice Radiguet, November 16, 1919, quoted in Movilliat, *Raymond Radiguet ou la jeunesse contredite*, pp. 176–180. The "hotel" was the Hôtel de Surène, next to the rue d'Anjou.

59. Jean Cocteau to Maurice Radiguet, November 27, 1919, quoted in Steegmuller, *Cocteau* (Buchet-Chastel), p. 190.

60. Ibid., November 3, 1920, p. 200.

61. *Le coq parisien* 3 (July 1920).

62. *Sic* is an acronym for "Sounds, Ideas, Colors." Close to the Futurists, the *bruitistes*, and then the *nunistes* (from the Greek word for "now"), this journal had been founded in 1916 by Pierre Albert-Birot, a friend of Apollinaire's.

63. Quoted in André Salmon, "Les dix-sept ans de Radiguet," *Les nouvelles littéraires*, August 2, 1924.

64. This is what Georges Auric suggests in *Quand j'étais là*: "I have no reason to try to find out what actually happened between Cocteau and him: that has nothing to do with us. What I do know, on the other hand, is that at the age of twenty, nothing would have any importance for Radiguet anymore" (p. 144).

65. Interview with Robert Craft in *Avec Stravinsky*, p. 46.

66. Raymond Radiguet, "Désordre," "Ébauche," in Radiguet, *Oeuvres complètes*, ed. Chloé Radiguet and Julien Cendres (Paris: Éditions Stock, 1993), p. 847.

67. Ibid. and Monique Nemer, *Raymond Radiguet* (Paris: Fayard, 2002), p. 202.

68. "Raymond Radiguet," in *CJC*, no. 4 (Paris: Gallimard, 1973), p. 106, and *OPC*, p. 553.

69. "À propos du 'Diable au corps,'" in *CJC*, no. 4, p. 39.

70. Cf. Max Jacob to Jean Cocteau, April 12, 1927, in *Max Jacob and Jean Cocteau, Correspondance 1917–1944*, ed. Anne Kimball (Paris: Paris-Méditerranée/Écrits des Hautes-Terres, 2000), p. 529.

71. Jacques de Lacretelle, "Raymond Radiguet," *NRF* (January 1, 1924): 100–102.

72. Quoted in Cocteau's adaptation of *La princesse de Clèves*, filmed by Jean Delannoy.

CHAPTER 9. ALL AGAINST DADA

1. Jean Cocteau to Louis Aragon, January 20, 1919, quoted in Aragon, *Papiers inédits: De Dada au surréalisme (1917–1931)* (Paris: Gallimard, 2000), p. 259.

2. Draft of a letter from Jean Cocteau to André Breton, February 23, 1919, Harry Ransom Humanities Research Center, University of Texas, Austin.

3. Aragon, *Papiers inédits*, pp. 241–242.

4. Louis Aragon to Jean Cocteau, January 22, 1919, in ibid., p. 261.

5. See Aragon, *Papiers inédits*.

6. Breton was the son of a French gendarme.

7. Georges Auric, linked to both groups, had already brought about a reconciliation in the summer of 1919. Aragon wrote to Cocteau, but the presence of Radiguet between them ended up complicating relations. Cf. Louis Aragon, *Projet d'histoire littéraire contemporaine*, ed. Marc Dachy (Paris: Mercure de France, 1994), pp. 287–288, and Monique Nemer, *Raymond Radiguet* (Paris: Fayard, 2002), pp. 252–253.

8. Published in *L'anthologie dada* (1920), this poem was presented by *Le Crapouillot* as a pastiche. Cf. Jean Galtier-Boissière, *Mémoires d'un Parisien* (Paris: Quai Voltaire, 1994), p. 461. [Rough translation: Ticla our golden age Pipe Carnot Joffre/I offer to anyone with neuralgia,/Giraffe Wedding a hello from Gustave/Ave Maria by Gounod Virgin with Crown of Roses. — Trans.]

9. For the announcement, see "Carte blanche," *Paris-midi* (April 1919).

10. The letters sound like "Elle a chaud au cul" [or "She is hot in her ass." — Trans.].

11. Hugo Ball, quoted in Hans Richter, *Dada art et anti-art* (Brussels: La Connaissance, 1965), pp. 19–20.

12. See Maurice Martin du Gard, *Les mémorables*, new ed. (Paris: Gallimard, 1999), p. 128.

13. Tristan Tzara, "Manifeste dada 1918," *Morceaux choisis*, preface by Jean Cassou (Paris: Éditions Bordas, 1947), pp. 49–56. In English, see http://www.391.org/manifestos/1918 -dada-manifesto-tristan-tzara.html#.VHfczDHF8qQ (accessed October 27, 2015).

14. *New York Dada*, April 1921; Marc Dachy, *Dada et les dadaïsmes* (Paris: Gallimard, 1994), p. 147.

15. Living as the black angel of Romanian Symbolism, Tzara had founded, with Ion Uinea and Marcel Janco, who followed him into the Dada adventure, a journal called *Simbolul* (The symbol).

16. Tzara, "Manifeste dada 1918," pp. 51 and 48.

17. The phrase, used also by Germaine Everling, is by Pierre de Massot—see his "Souvenirs," *Verve* (May 1921). Cf. François Buot, *Tristan Tzara, l'homme qui inventa la révolution dada* (Paris: Grasset, 2002), p. 95.

18. For the quotation, see Tristan Tzara to André Breton, September 21, 1919, quoted in Michel Sanouillet, *Dada à Paris* (Paris: Flammarion, 1993), p. 485. Cf. also his "Lettre ouverte à Jacques Rivière," quoted in Dachy, *Dada et les dadaïsmes*, p. 65.

19. Man-Ray called the cardboard outfit a lampshade.

20. Cf. the testimony of Irène Lagut, in Buot, *Tristan Tzara*, p. 97.

21. Cf. Germaine Everling, "C'était hier Dada," *Les oeuvres libres* 109 (June 1955): 151. Mme Lara was an actress in the Comédie Française whose son, Claude Autant-Lara, founded at the time an ephemeral avant-garde journal, under Cocteau's patronage; the son would settle his accounts with Cocteau seventy years later, when, having turned sour, he would accuse Cocteau of having prepared the destruction of France via *Parade* by rallying the avant-garde over to popular Yankee culture.

22. Cf. the testimony of Soupault, in *André Breton, 1896–1966, NRF* 172 (April 1967): 668.

23. Jean Cocteau, "Le secret professionnel," in *Poésie Critique*, vol. 1 (Paris: Gallimard, 1983), p. 22. His wife was Gabrielle Buffet-Picabia, and in all, he owned a total of 127 automobiles in his life.

24. Duchamp was the author of the very first *L.H.O.O.Q.*—a portrait of a mustachioed Mona Lisa.

25. Paul Morand, *Venises* (Paris: Gallimard/Le Cercle du nouveau livre, Librairie Jules Taillandier, 1971), p. 134.

26. Paul Morand, *Journal inutile*, vol. 2: 1973–1976 (Paris: Gallimard, 2001), p. 476.

27. Liane de Pougy, *Mes cahiers bleus* (Paris: Plon, 1977), p. 82.

28. Adrienne Monnier, "Mémorial de la rue de l'Odéon," *Le Littéraire*, June 15, 1946, quoted in Jean-Jacques Kihm, Elizabeth Sprigge, and Henri C. Béhar, *Jean Cocteau, l'homme et les miroirs* (Paris: La Table Ronde, 1968), p. 411.

29. Morand, *Venises*, pp. 132–133.

30. Satie was also at play here: he thought he had been slandered by *Le coq*—God knows why—and Cocteau's text was supposed to be about him.

31. Aragon, *Anicet ou le panorama, roman* (1920; Paris: Gallimard, 1983), p. 122.

32. Martin du Gard, *Les mémorables*, p. 134.

33. Apollinaire protested Fraenkel's joke, according to Cocteau.

34. Jean Cocteau, *D'un ordre considéré comme une anarchie*, in *Le rappel à l'ordre* (Paris: Éditions Stock, 1926).

35. *Éphémérides*, May 13, 1920, in *Paul Morand écrivain*, comp. Michel Collomb (Montpellier: Centre d'études littéraires françaises du XXe siècle, Université Paul-Valéry, 1993), p. 293.

36. This is a reference to Perrette, the Milkmaid of La Fontaine's fable "La Laitière et le pot au lait" (The milkmaid and the pot of milk); see http://www.aestheticrealism.net/poetry/milkmaid-milk-lafontaine.html (accessed October 28, 2015).

37. Cf. André Breton, "Ombre non pas serpent mais d'arbre," in *Perspective cavalière* (Paris: Gallimard, 1970), p. 37.

38. Philippe Soupault, *Mémoires de l'oubli*, vol. 1: *1914–1923* (Paris: Lachenal et Ritter, 1981), pp. 34–35.

39. Philippe Soupault, *Mémoires de l'oubli*, vol. 2: *1923–1926* (Paris: Lachenal and Ritter, 1986), p. 81. Aragon would point out that Apollinaire spoke of Cocteau only in a scornful tone.

40. See also Breton's statements in *Le Figaro littéraire*, September 14, 1960.

41. Cf. Guillaume Apollinaire, *Le poète assassiné*, ed. Michel Décaudin (Paris: Poésie/ Gallimard, 1979), p. 286. The real model is probably the fashion designer Paul Poiret, according to Décaudin, one of the chief authorities on Apollinaire.

42. André Breton to Tristan Tzara, December 26, 1919, quoted in M. Sanouillet, *Dada à Paris*, p. 105.

43. Jean Cocteau to Jean Hugo, October 30, 1919, in Jean Cocteau, *Correspondance Jean Hugo*, ed. Brigitte Borsaro and Pierre Caizergues (Montpellier: Centre d'études du XXe siècle, Université Paul-Valéry, 1995), p. 49.

44. Aragon, in turn, would claim to have drawn Cocteau's attention to Radiguet, at the matinée in homage to Reverdy. Cf. Aragon, *Projet d'histoire littéraire contemporaine*, pp. 51–53.

45. Raymond Radiguet to André Breton, August 19, 1919, quoted in Marie-Christine Movilliat, *Raymond Radiguet ou la jeunesse contredite*, *1903–1923* (Paris: Bibliophone Daniel Radford, 2000), p. 185.

46. The poem he didn't like was "Emploi du temps," which was actually very thoughtful.

47. This was a first attempt at automatic writing, composed by Breton and Soupault, which had just been published. The idea, according to Soupault, had been forged by the psychiatrist Pierre Janet, but two years before *Les champs magnétiques*, the Futurist Carli had also published *Notti Filtrate*, "ten moments of lyrical somnambulism in which memories and images coalesce in essence, letting the useless taste of links of coordination filter through."

48. Raymond Radiguet to André Breton, January 2, 1920, published in Valentine Hugo, "En 1918 et 1919 Raymond Radiguet cherche le chemin de la poésie," *Actualité littéraire* 55 (March 1959), quoted in Movilliat, *Raymond Radiguet ou la jeunesse contredite*, p. 187.

49. Ibid.

50. Jean Cocteau, *Picasso* (Paris: L'école des lettres, 1996), "Témoignage," p. 91.

51. *Le coq parisien* 3 (July 1920).

52. Le Chien Qui Fume (The smoking dog) was an old restaurant in the heart of Paris.— Trans.

53. Lustucru is a character in a popular French comic song called "C'est la mère Michel."—Trans.

54. Raymond Radiguet, "Règle du jeu," in Radiguet, *Oeuvres complètes*, ed. Chloé Radiguet and Julien Cendres (Paris: Éditions Stock, 1993), p. 435. Cf. also *Le Gaulois*, February 21, 1920, quoted in Radiguet, *Oeuvres complètes*, p. 401.

55. For the quotation, see Paul Léautaud, *Le théâtre de Maurice Boissard*, vol. 2 (Paris: Gallimard, 1926), p. 127.

56. Quoted in Darius Milhaud, *Ma vie heureuse* (Paris: Belfond, 1986), p. 99.

57. Letter, n.d., quoted in F. Steegmuller, *Cocteau* (Boston: Little, Brown, 1970), p. 245.

58. Jean Cocteau to Raymond Radiguet, June 1920, quoted in Nemer, *Raymond Radiguet*, p. 318.

59. Paul Souday himself was still talking about a "nervous aesthete, slightly morbid, almost feminine."

60. Marcel Proust to Jean Cocteau, dated (incorrectly?) end of May 1917 in Marcel Proust, *Correspondance*, ed. and comp. Philip Kolb, 21 vols. (Paris: Plon, 1970–1993), vol. 16, p. 143.

61. Marcel Proust to Lucien Daudet, March 7, 1915, in ibid., vol. 14, p. 66. The director of the newspaper *Figaro* had been murdered in 1914 by the wife of a politician named Caillaux.

62. The whole argument was made via the intermediary of Lucien Daudet, to whom Proust, that enemy of Sainte-Beuve, wrote, "If there is communication on the 'way out [*aller*],' from life to literature (life nourishing literature), there is on the other hand no communication, no 'way back [*retour*]' from literature to life."

63. Dedication from Proust to Mme de Chevigné. See Princesse Bibesco, *Laure de Sade, duchesse de Guermantes: Lettres de Marcel Proust à la comtesse de Chevigné* (Paris: Plon, 1950).

64. Nietzsche had written the same phrase in the margin of an article about him in *Musikalisches Wochenblatt* (October 25, 1888).

65. Quoted by Laurence Benaïm, *Marie Laure de Noailles* (Paris: Grasset, 2001), p. 100. Cf. also Marcel Schneider, *Les gardiens du secret* (Paris: Grasset, 2001), p. 139.

66. The comte Robert de Fitz-James was the embodiment of the "best" Parisian society.

67. Marcel Proust to Armand de Guiche, June 17, 1921, in Marcel Proust, *Correspondance*, vol. 20, p. 349.

68. Aside from the Chevigné case, Proust had taken poorly certain attacks by Cocteau against Gallimard, his new publisher.

69. Undated letter, *CJC*, no. 1 (Paris: Gallimard, 1969), pp. 75–76.

70. About the connections between Octave and Cocteau, cf. Jean-Yves Tadié, *Marcel Proust*, vol. 2 (Paris: Folio-Gallimard, 1996), p. 132, and Marcel Proust, *À la recherche du temps perdu*, vol. 4 (Paris: Gallimard, 1989), pp. 184 and 227.

71. One troubling detail: Proust adds in this same passage that Octave, dismissed from school, had lived for two months in the brothel where Charlus thought he surprised Morel. Had Cocteau told Proust about his dismissal from the Lycée Condorcet, where Proust had also studied, and his improbable flight to Marseille? Or did he invent this flight after reading Proust? Cocteau's desire to make his life into a novel came from encountering Proust's desire to make an entire novel from his life.

72. Cocteau, *D'un ordre considéré comme une anarchie*.

73. Jean Cocteau to Francis Picabia, March 29, 1920, in *Cannibale*, April 1920; reprinted in *Lettres de l'Oiseleur* (Monaco: Du Rocher, 1989), p. 205.

74. *Littérature* 9 (November 1919).

75. Tzara revered Satie's *Piège de Méduse*. Satie had also conceived in 1893 of *Vexations*, a piece for piano that the performer had to repeat 840 times, over a period ranging from twelve to twenty-four hours.

76. *Le coq* 1 (May 1920).

77. For "still the best way to be," see *Comoedia*, December 21, 1920.

78. Radiguet, *Oeuvres complètes*, p. 395.

79. At the same time, Auric was composing *Adieu New York*.

80. *Le coq* 1 (May 1920).

81. Abbé Mugnier, *Journal (1879–1939)* (Paris: Mercure de France, 1985), June 5, 1920, p. 367. "Le satisme ne saurait exister [Satie-ism couldn't exist]," asserted Satie.

82. Frédéric Lefèvre, "Une heure avec . . .," 1st ser., *Éditions de la Nouvelle revue française* (1924), p. 11.

83. Was this feeling inspired by Malevitch, when he went back to Cubist-Futurism, then to representation, after his famous white square on a white background?

84. "Documents," *Poésies 1916–1923, OPC*, p. 1647.

85. Frédéric Lefèvre, "Une heure avec . . .," 1st ser., *Éditions de la Nouvelle revue française*, 1924, p. 106.

86. Raymond Radiguet, "Le préjugé du succès," Fall 1920, in Radiguet, *Oeuvres complètes*, p. 445.

87. Interviews between the author and the poet Jacques Borel, March 6, 1999.

88. Monique Nemer notes that Radiguet's watchword—"Try to be ordinary"—is an answer precisely to the "Astonish me" launched by Diaghilev at Cocteau in 1912.

89. Raymond Radiguet, "Conseils aux grands poètes," *Le coq parisien* 4 (November 1920).

90. *391* 14 (November 1920). ["Coq-Auric-haut" sounds like the French sound for a rooster's cry, "cocorico."—Trans.]

91. Ibid.

92. *Pilhaou-Thibaou* (July 1921).

93. From the Dada Manifesto, available in English at http://www.391.org/manifestos/1920 -dada-manifesto-feeble-love-bitter-love-tristan-tzara.html#.VID6VzHF8qQ (accessed October 28, 2015).

94. This is a technique that Bryon Gysin and William Burroughs would remember, as we know.

95. *Dadaphone* (March 1920): 5.

CHAPTER 10. THE MIRACULOUS YEARS

1. Vaslav Nijinsky, *Journal*, fourth notebook written between January and February 1919 (Paris: Actes Sud, 2000). ["Coc iyage" sounds like *coquillage*, "shellfish."—Trans.]

2. Jean Cocteau, "Vaslav Nijinski," in *CJC*, no. 10 (Paris: Gallimard, 1985), p. 64.

3. Jean Cocteau, *Plain-chant, OPC*, p. 377.

4. Cf. Jean Cocteau, "À la mémoire de M.S.N. mort pour l'Angleterre," *OPC*, p. 163.

5. Jean Cocteau to Georges Auric, July 28, 1920, in Auric, *Correspondance avec Jean Cocteau* (Montpellier: Pierre Caizergues, Centre d'études du XXe siècle, Université Paul-Valéry, 1999), p. 71.

6. Jean Cocteau to Maurice Radiguet, September 5, 1920, quoted in Marie-Christine Movilliat, *Raymond Radiguet ou la jeunesse contredite*, 1903–1923 (Paris: Bibliophone Daniel Radford, 2000), p. 218.

7. Jean Cocteau to his mother, August 13, 1920, *LM*.

8. Jean Cocteau, *Plain-chant, OPC*, p. 360.

9. Ibid., p. 361.

10. *Le gendarme incompris* would be performed during the comic spectacle given at the Théâtre Michel, in 1921. This parody of a 1900 playlet, with a Marquise in drag as a priest, rested on the deposition of a prudish gendarme nicknamed "The Penultimate," who had surprised the priest, in a corner of the bois de Boulogne, performing acts unworthy of that "ecclesiastic": wearing that "special robe worn with the confidence that one is everything for oneself, even one's wife," the priest,"apart from witnesses, was responding to the solicitations of the grass"—the vice of the Faun. Annoyed spectators saw in this hilarious deposition, with its learned nonsense and its unspoken obscenities, nothing but a parody of the "gendarme" style: Cocteau revealed five days later, by way of the press, that it was taken from "L'ecclésiastique," a prose poem by Mallarmé in *Divagations* (1897).

11. Manuscript in the collection of Francine Weisweiller. The play was published in the Pléiade volume devoted to Jean Cocteau's theater (Paris: Gallimard, 2003).

12. Paul Morand, *Venises* (Paris: Gallimard/Le Cercle du nouveau livre, Librairie Jules Taillandier, 1971), p. 142.

13. Thora de Dardel would inspire Sveva, the little Swedish girl in *Le Diable*. Her husband, Niels, also liked boys. A mediocre painter and honorable designer of Swedish ballets, he tried his luck with Radiguet.

14. Jean Cocteau to Maurice Radiguet, November 3, 1920, quoted in Francis Steegmuller, *Cocteau* (Paris: Buchet-Chastel, 1973), p. 201.

15. Filled with automatic signatures gathered from the end of 1920 through the two New Year's parties given by Picabia and the singer Marthe Chenal, at the end of 1921, this painting is exhibited today at the Musée d'Art Moderne in the Centre Pompidou.

16. Charles Baudelaire, preface to Edgar Allen Poe's *Oeuvres complètes* (Paris: Gilbert Jeune, 1953).

17. Maurice Martin du Gard, *Les mémorables*, new ed. (Paris: Gallimard, 1999), p. 292.

18. Raymond Radiguet, *Vers libres et jeux innocents*, in Radiguet, *Oeuvres complètes*, ed. Chloé Radiguet and Julien Cendres (Paris: Éditions Stock, 1993), p. 34.

19. Jean Cocteau to Valentine Hugo, March 24, 1921, quoted in Movilliat, *Raymond Radiguet ou la jeunesse contredite*, p. 238.

20. Jean Cocteau, "Les mésaventures d'un rosier," in *Vocabulaire, OPC*, pp. 322–328.

21. Jean Cocteau to Valentine Hugo, March 29, 1921, Jean Cocteau, *Correspondance Jean Hugo*, ed. (Montpellier: Brigitte Borsaro and Pierre Caizergues, Centre d'études du XXe siècle, Université Paul-Valéry, 1995), p. 71.

22. R. Radiguet, "Une carte postale: Les quais de Paris" (August 1919), in *Devoirs de vacances* (Paris: À la Sirène, 1921).

23. Cocteau, "Les mésaventures d'un rosier."

24. Jean Cocteau to his mother, March 1921, *LM*.

25. Quoted in Princesse Bibesco, "Requiem pour Jean," *Les nouvelles littéraires*, October 17, 1963.

26. *Le crapouillot* was a satirical magazine started during the First World War.—Trans.

27. Jean Cocteau to his mother, March 30, 1921, *LM*.
28. Ibid.
29. Jean Hugo, *Le regard de la mémoire* (Paris: Babel-Actes Sud, 1983), p. 150.
30. Du Gard, *Les mémorables*, p. 214.
31. Arthur Rubinstein, *Grande est la vie*, vol. 2 (Paris: Robert Laffont, 1980), p. 118.
32. Du Gard, *Les mémorables*, p. 171.
33. Jean Cocteau to Darius Milhaud, April 5, 1920, in Cocteau and Milhaud, *Correspondance* (Montpellier: Pierre Caizergues and Josiane Mas, Centre d'études littéraires françaises du XXe siècle, Université Paul-Valéry, 1992), p. 22.
34. Gyraldose was an antiseptic used in feminine hygiene products in the 1920s. — Trans.
35. Élise Jouhandeau, *Le spleen empanaché* (Paris: Flammarion, 1960), p. 122.
36. Hugo, *Le regard de la mémoire*, p. 191.
37. Jean Cocteau and Darius Milhaud, *Ma vie heureuse* (Paris: Belfond, 1986), p. 84.
38. Cocteau, "Miss Aérogyne, femme volante," *Vocabulaire*, OPC, p. 303.
39. *Éphémérides*, May 23, 1920, in *Paul Morand écrivain*, comp. Michel Collomb (Montpellier: Centre d'études littéraires françaises du XXe siècle, Université Paul-Valéry, 1993), p. 297.
40. Jean Cocteau to Georges Auric, July 28, 1920, in Auric, *Correspondance Jean Cocteau*, p. 71.
41. Jean Cocteau, *D'un ordre considéré comme une anarchie*, in *Le rappel à l'ordre* (Paris: Éditions Stock, 1926).
42. Paul Morand, *Journal inutile*, vol. 2: 1973–1976 (Paris: Gallimard, 2001), p. 154.
43. Paul Morand, *Journal d'un attaché d'ambassade* (Paris: Gallimard, 1963), October 11, 1916, p. 33.
44. Morand, *Venises*, pp. 135–136.
45. He was also compared to the Comte de Beaumont.
46. *Éphémérides*, May 17, 1920, in *Paul Morand écrivain*, p. 295.
47. *Lettres de mon moulin* (Letters from my windmill) was a collection of short stories by Alphonse Daudet, Lucien's father. — Trans.
48. Cf. Jean Cocteau to Darius Milhaud, September 16, 1920, in Cocteau, Milhaud, *Correspondance*, p. 33.
49. Léon-Paul Fargue, "Le Boeuf sur le Toit," in *Le Piéton de Paris* (Paris: Gallimard, 1993).
50. Cocteau, *D'un ordre considéré comme une anarchie*, pp. 212–213.
51. Ibid.
52. *L'horizon* (Brussels), July 16, 1921.
53. Morand, *Venises*.
54. Jean Cocteau, *La difficulté d'être* (Monaco: Éditions du Rocher, 1947).
55. Cocteau didn't want Picasso to make the sets, from fear they would distract the public's attention, as they had during *Parade*.
56. The only person missing was Louis Durey, who would soon leave the group.
57. The Dadaists failed to give credit to the Futurists in another way as well, since it was a question of making heard, for the first time in France, instruments invented by Russolo, of which Cocteau had given a foretaste through *Parade*.
58. Claire Goll, *La poursuite du vent* (Paris: Olivier Orban, 1976), p. 134.

59. *Pilhaou-Thibaou*, July 10, 1921.

60. The other newspaper was *La pomme de pin*.

61. By contrast, Jean Anouilh would return to his vocation for poetic theater after reading the *Mariés* at the age of eighteen.

62. Morand, *Venises*, p. 141.

63. Du Gard, *Les mémorables*, p. 176.

64. Jean Cocteau to his mother, August 22, 1921, *LM*.

65. Morand, *Venises*, p. 135.

66. Jean Cocteau, *Le mystère de Jean l'Oiseleur* (Paris: Champion, 1925), caption for self-portrait No. 10.

67. Obviously, Ezra Pound had been sensitive to the use of ancient forms in Cocteau's modernism, and to the vortex aspect—or "fusion of ideas endowed with energy"—of *Le Cap*. Not content to use the English translation of that poem made by Jean Hugo, Pound encouraged his companion, Olga Rudge, to translate "Le mystère laïc," and would later often quote Cocteau in his *Cantos*.

68. At the home of Picasso and Olga, Cocteau had met Clive Brown, the brother-in-law who was secretly in love with Virginia Woolf (a wonderfully "Ingresque" drawing testifies to the meeting). Brown would publish in *The Little Review* the Hugo-Pound translation of *Le Cap*.

69. Vladimir Mayakovski, *Du monde j'ai fait le tour*, trans. Claude Frioux (Paris: La Quinzaine/Louis Vuitton, 1997), p. 95.

70. "In vain Stravinsky tried to enrich the Russian sentences and impoverish my own," Cocteau said without modesty.

71. Alejo Carpentier, "Jean Cocteau et l'esthétique du mouvement," *Chroniques* (Paris: Gallimard, 1983), pp. 17–27.

72. Jacques Rivière would recognize in Cocteau the art of conveying the nausea aroused by the presence of death behind us.

73. For the quotation, see Du Gard, *Les mémorables*, p. 171.

74. Paul Morand, *Monplaisir . . . en littérature* (Paris: Gallimard, 1967), pp. 107–110.

75. Jean Cocteau, *Poésie critique*, vol. 1 (Paris: Gallimard, 1959), p. 39.

76. Jacques Porel, *Fils de Réjane*, vol. 1: *1895–1920* (Paris: Plon, 1951), p. 352. Comte Jacques de Maleissye, who claimed to be a descendant of Joan of Arc, and his wife, Ketty, were a couple of extravagant drug addicts: they committed suicide a few months apart, in 1930 and 1931.

77. Born in England and raised in South Africa (1879–1943), Beatrice Hastings drew from her stormy relationship with "Modi" a novel that has since disappeared called *Minnie Pinnikins*.

78. Ernest Hemingway, *Death in the Afternoon* (New York: Scribner's, 1996), p. 41. Cocteau must have met Hemingway in Ezra Pound's entourage.

79. Apparently this novel was never written.

80. *Les cahiers du comte Kessler, 1918–1937* (Paris: Grasset, 1972), p. 193. Eventually Beatrice Hastings killed herself and her white mouse in a gas oven in 1943.

81. Hugo, *Le regard de la mémoire*, p. 211, and Francis Steegmuller, *Cocteau* (Boston: Little, Brown, 1970) p. 277.

82. Porel, *Fils de Réjane*, vol. 2: *1920–1950* (Paris: Plon, 1952), pp. 352–353.

83. Jean-Yves Tadié, *Marcel Proust*, vol. 2 (Paris: Folio-Gallimard, 1996), pp. 471–472. Tadié writes that the scene occurs in June, but Painter describes it in more detail and places it in July.

84. Hugo, *Le regard de la mémoire*, p. 210.

85. Maurice Sachs, *Au temps du Boeuf sur le Toit* (1939; Paris: Grasset, 1987), pp. 128–130.

86. Maurice Sachs, *Le Sabbat: Souvenirs d'une jeunesse orageuse* (1946; Paris: Gallimard, 1979), p. 186.

87. Cocteau, "L'endroit et l'envers," in *Vocabulaire*, OPC.

88. *Littérature* 4 (n.s.) (September 1922).

89. *Le disque vert* 1, no. 5 (September 1922): 131. Cf. *Le disque vert: Revue mensuelle de littérature* (Brussels: Jacques Antoine, 1970). According to a letter from Cocteau to his mother dated June 28, 1922 (*LM*), Pia also wrote a very nice article on Cocteau in *Les cahiers idéalistes*, Desjardins's journal.

90. Cocteau, "M'entendez-vous ainsi?" in *Vocabulaire*, OPC, p. 341.

91. Jean Cocteau to Georges Auric, May 23, 1922, in Auric, *Correspondance Jean Cocteau*, p. 83.

92. Jean Cocteau to Max Jacob, February 2, 1922, in Max Jacob and Jean Cocteau, *Correspondance, 1917–1944*, ed. Anne Kimball (Paris: Paris-Méditerranée/Écrits des Hautes-Terres, 2000), p. 76.

93. Jean Cocteau to his mother, July 1922, *LM*.

94. Quoted in Sachs, *Au temps du Boeuf sur le Toit*, p. 167.

95. Jean Cocteau, *Le grand écart* (Paris: Éditions Stock, 1923), p. 31.

96. Jean Cocteau to his mother, July 23, 1922, *LM*.

97. Raymond Radiguet to Mme Cocteau, May 28, 1922, quoted in Movilliat, *Raymond Radiguet ou la jeunesse contredite*, p. 271.

98. Hugo, *Le regard de la mémoire*, p. 211. Cocteau must have told this story to Genet, who would tell it to Sartre, who would adapt it in his *Saint Genet*.

99. Bernard Faÿ, *Les précieux* (Paris: Perrin, 1966), p. 274.

100. Hugo, *Le regard de la mémoire*, p. 213.

101. Joseph Kessel, *Des hommes* (Paris: Gallimard, 1972), p. 16.

102. Ibid., p. 97.

103. Maurice Sachs, *La décade de l'illusion* (1933; Paris: Gallimard, 1950), p. 36.

104. Jean Cocteau to his mother, October 6, 1922, *LM*.

105. Jean Cocteau to Max Jacob, October 18, 1922, in Jacob and Cocteau, *Correspondance*, p. 138.

106. Jean Cocteau to his mother, August 2, 1922, *LM*.

107. Jean Cocteau to his mother, October 27, 1922, *LM*.

108. Marcel Raval, "Raymond Radiguet," *Les feuilles libres* 34 (November–December 1923).

109. Max Jacob to Jean Cocteau, March 29, 1921, in Jacob and Cocteau, *Correspondance*, p. 64.

110. Cf. the cover photo.

111. *Jean Cocteau par Jean Cocteau*, p. 127.

112. Hugo, *Le regard de la mémoire*, p. 206.
113. Marcel Proust to Jean Cocteau, August 1920, in Marcel Proust, *Correspondance*, ed. and comp. Philip Kolb, 21 vols. (Paris: Plon, 1970–1993), vol. 19, p. 399.
114. Marcel Proust to Jean Cocteau, January 1922, in ibid., vol. 21, p. 43.
115. "La voix de Marcel Proust," *NRF*, January 1, 1923.
116. Man-Ray made three copies of his photograph: one for Robert Proust, one for Cocteau, and one for himself. Morand apparently burned his negative while developing it.
117. Du Gard, *Les mémorables*, p. 265.
118. De Max died the same year and was buried, wearing makeup, in the toga he wore in the role of Nero.
119. Jean Cocteau to Marcel Proust, May 22, 1922, in Proust, *Correspondance*, vol. 21, p. 215.
120. Sachs, *Au temps du Boeuf sur le Toit*, p. 166.
121. Quoted in Morand, *Journal inutile*, vol. 2, p. 109.

CHAPTER 11. GENEALOGY OF TRAGEDY

1. The death of Barrès would not occur until two years later.
2. Le Cartel, a group of four theater companies directed by Baty, Dullin, Jouvet, and Pitöeff from 1927 to 1940, was influential in the development of modern French stagecraft. Dullin was a defector from Copeau's Vieux-Colombier Theater. — Trans.
3. "I understand why actors weren't buried with others," Radiguet noted, in an ironic allusion to the excommunications that actors suffered under the ancien régime.
4. According to Cocteau, Athanasiou's name meant "daughter of immortals."
5. The face painting was done on Picasso's orders. During the second premiere, Cocteau would cage them behind fencers' masks.
6. Raymond Radiguet, "Antigone de Sophocle, adaptation libre de Jean Cocteau," *Les feuilles libres* 30 (December 1922).
7. Unpublished manuscript, BHVP, box 2. Duncan and his disciples returned during a revival a few months later. This time they invaded the stage, from which Creon's guards, armed to the teeth, pushed them back.
8. Cocteau, *PD* (n.p.), p. 1205.
9. Radiguet, "Antigone de Sophocle."
10. "Never will I forget the golden, trembling, mysterious voice of Génica Athansiou-Antigone making her farewells to the sun," Artaud said in that same "Lecture on Post-War Theater in Paris," given on March 18, 1936, in Mexico, and published in his *Messages révolutionnaires* (Paris: Gallimard, 1971), p. 56.
11. Tzara was going in the opposite direction: he started a serialized novel, *Faites vos jeux*.
12. Jean Cocteau to Max Jacob, October 2, 1922, in Max Jacob and Jean Cocteau, *Correspondance, 1917–1944*, ed. Anne Kimball (Paris: Paris-Méditerranée/Écrits des Hautes-Terres, 2000), p. 132.
13. Joseph Delteil, "Radiguet vu de 23," in *CJC*, no. 4 (Paris: Gallimard, 1973). Cf. also Joseph Delteil, *Le sacré corps* (Paris: Grasset, 1976), p. 198. [*Tante*, literally "aunt," like the English "auntie" — is an offensive term for a male homosexual. — Trans.]

14. Interview with André Breton in *Le journal du peuple*, April 7, 1923. As for Tzara, in 1925 he would marry a wealthy Swedish heiress.

15. Louis Aragon, *Projet d'histoire littéraire contemporaine*, ed. Marc Dachy (Paris: Mercure de France, 1994), pp. 103, 105.

16. Humphrey Carpenter, *A Serious Character: The Life of Ezra Pound* (London: Faber and Faber, 1988).

17. Other testimonials place that moment as the origin of the fighting. Aragon left a detailed account of the evening, without, one imagines, much objectivity, in *Projet d'histoire littéraire contemporaine:* he asserts that fear prevented Bertin—and not Herrand—from reciting Cocteau's poems.

18. He was "acting" in *Le coeur à gaz*, in a costume by Sonia Delaunay.

19. Jean Cocteau to Max Jacob, August 1, 1923, in Jacob and Cocteau, *Correspondance*, p. 162.

20. Quoted in Marc Dachy, *Dada et les dadaïsmes* (Paris: Gallimard, 1994), p. 214. Rigaud would commit suicide in November 1929.

21. Jean Cocteau to Max Jacob, August 1, 1923, in Jacob and Cocteau, *Correspondance*, p. 162.

22. Quoted by Cocteau, "Une entrevue sur la critique avec Maurice Rouzaud," *Les Amis d'Édouard* 145 (July 1929): 15.

23. Seventeen, however, was in fact the age at which Radiguet had written the first version of *Le diable au corps*.

24. Jean Cocteau, *D'un ordre considéré comme une anarchie*, in *Le rappel à l'ordre* (Paris: Éditions Stock, 1926).

25. Roland Dorgelès to Raymond Radiguet, July 2, 1923, quoted in Chloé Radiguet, "Jean Cocteau, Raymond Radiguet: Fragments, traits, portraits," *Regard* 7–8 (1988): 52.

26. Forty thousand copies were sold; Cocteau himself sold about a thousand.

27. Maurice Martin du Gard, *Les mémorables*, new ed. (Paris: Gallimard, 1999), p. 293.

28. Cocteau, *D'un ordre considéré comme une anarchie*.

29. Ibid.

30. François Mauriac, *Journal d'un homme de trente ans, Oeuvres autobiographiques* (Paris: Gallimard, 1990), December 18, 1922.

31. Quoted in François Mauriac, *La rencontre avec Barrès, Oeuvres autobiographiques*, p. 268.

32. François Mauriac and Jacques-Émile Blanche, *Correspondance (1916–1942)* ed. Georges-Paul Collet (Paris: Grasset, 1976).

33. Paul Morand, *L'allure de Chanel* (Paris: Hermann, 1976), p. 82.

34. Jean Touzot, *François Mauriac* (Paris: Cahiers de l'Herne, 1995), p. 133.

35. According to Paul Morand, who hints at this story in his *Journal inutile*, vol. 1: 1968–1972, p. 423 and vol. 2: 1973–1976 (Paris: Gallimard, 2001), p. 347, at times he cites Mauriac by dotted lines, at other times, Barbey.

36. François Mauriac and Jean Paulhan, *Correspondance, 1925–1967* (Paris: Claire Paulhan, 2002), pp. 143–144.

37. Marthe is the heroine's first name in *Le diable au corps*. The lines translate as: "Marthe unfair/Thumbs her nose/And fornicates/Martinique."

38. Jean Hugo, *Le regard de la mémoire* (Paris: Babel-Actes Sud, 1983), pp. 219–223. Cf. also Valentine Hugo, "Il y a trente ans," *La parisienne* (December 1953).

39. André Salmon, *Souvenirs sans fin*, vol. 2 (Paris: Gallimard, 1955), p. 45.

40. Joseph Kessel, "Raymond Radiguet," *NRF* 124 (January 1, 1924): 100–102.

41. Telephone interview between the author and Jacques Guérin, June 12, 1999.

42. Robert McAlmon and Kay Boyle, *Being Geniuses Together* (New York: Doubleday, 1968).

43. Maurice Sachs, *La décade de l'illusion* (1933; Paris: Gallimard, 1950), p. 42.

44. Thora Dardel, *Jag for till Paris* (Stockholm: Bonniers, 1941), quoted in Bill Klüver and Julie Martin, *Kiki et Montparnasse* (Paris: Flammarion, 1989).

45. Jacques Guérin interview.

46. Djuna Barnes, "The Grand Malade," *Selected Works of Djuna Barnes* (New York: Farrar, Strauss and Giroux, 1962).

47. Outline for Jean Cocteau, *Le Potomak*, in *Oeuvres complètes*, vol. 2 (Lausanne: Marguerat, 1947), p. 17.

48. Joseph Roth stayed there as well, during the 1930s—like so many exiles. It was during an anarchist attack on the Foyot that Laurent Tailhade, the poet who had enthroned the young Cocteau during the Femina matinee, was blinded.

49. Paul Morand, *Venises* (Paris: Gallimard/Le Cercle du nouveau livre, Librairie Jules Taillandier, 1971), p. 103.

50. Quoted in Jacques Nels, *Fragments détachés de l'oubli* (N.p.: Ramsay, 1989), p. 68.

51. Abbé Mugnier, *Journal (1879–1939)* (Paris: Mercure de France, 1985), December 6, 1923, p. 426.

52. Jean Cocteau, "En marge de *Plain-chant*," *OPC*, p. 377.

53. Raymond Radiguet to Valentine Hugo, April 16, 1923, quoted in Valentine Hugo, "Il y a trente ans," *La Parisienne*, December 1953.

54. André Gide, *Journal*, vol. 1: *1887–1925* (Paris: Gallimard, 1996), May 18, 1923, p. 1216.

55. Louis Aragon, "Une année de romans (July 1922–August 1923)," letter to Jacques Doucet, *Projet d'histoire littéraire contemporaine*, p. 150.

56. Jean Cocteau, *Gide vivant: Paroles de Jean Cocteau*, illus. Julien Greene (Paris: Amiot-Dumont, 1952), p. 35.

57. Quoted in Frédéric Lefèvre, "Une heure avec . . .," 1st ser., *Éditions de la Nouvelle revue française* (1924): 112.

58. Jean Cocteau to Valentine Hugo, November 23, 1923, in Jean Cocteau, *Correspondance Jean Hugo* (Montpellier: Brigitte Borsaro and Pierre Caizergues, Centre d'études du XXe siècle, Université Paul-Valéry, 1995), p. 94.

59. Bernard Faÿ, *Les précieux* (Paris: Perrin, 1966), p. 275.

60. François Mauriac to Jacques-Émile Blanche, October 31, 1923, in Mauriac, Blanche, *Correspondance*, p. 105. Henry de Montherlant (1895–1972) was a renowned novelist and a successful playwright at the time (*The Girls*, *Chaos and Night*).

61. Jean Cocteau to Pablo Picasso, July 25, 1923, unpublished, Musée Picasso.

62. The editor of *La revue blanche*, Alexandre Natanson, was also one of the founders of the journal and Misia's ex-brother-in-law.

63. Jean Cocteau to his mother, September 3, 1923, *LM*.

64. She would finally succeed on December 11, 1936.

65. Jean Cocteau to his mother, n.d. (August 1925), *LM.*

66. Preface by their publisher, Bernard Grasset, to the 1925 edition, p. 5.

67. Georges Auric, *Correspondance avec Jean Cocteau* (Montpellier: Pierre Caizergues, Centre d'études du XXe siècle, Université Paul-Valéry, 1999), p. 148.

68. Hugo, *Le regard de la mémoire*, p. 233.

69. Maurice Martin du Gard, *Feux tournants* (Paris: Camille Bloch, 1925).

70. Auric, *Correspondance avec Jean Cocteau*, p. 148.

71. Jacques Guérin interview; text sent to Jacques Doucet, quoted in Louis Aragon, *Papiers inédits: De Dada au surréalisme (1917–1931)* (Paris: Gallimard, 2000), p. 290.

72. Jean Cocteau to Georges Auric, July 28, 1920, in Auric, *Correspondance Jean Cocteau*, p. 71.

73. She was still alive when the French edition of this book was being written. She finally died in June 2004, without having told anything of this story, except to Jean-Pierre Grédy and Pierre Barillet, the playwriters. Cf. Pierre Barillet, *Bronia: Dernier amour de Raymond Radiguet* (Grandvilliers, Fr.: La Rour Verte, 2012).

74. Yves Courrière, *Joseph Kessel; ou, Sur la piste du lion* (Paris: Plon, 1985), p. 230.

75. "Ever since 1789 I've been forced to think. I have a headache from it," he said in the first issue of *Le coq.*

76. Valentine Hugo, "Il y a trente ans," *La Parisienne* (December 1953).

77. Raymond Radiguet, "Mon premier roman: *Le diable au corps,*" *Les nouvelles littéraires* 21 (March 10, 1923).

78. "Barbette" is a pun on the French word for beard, *barbe*, with a feminine ending.—Trans.

79. Jean Cocteau to Valentine Hugo, November 23, 1923, quoted in Francis Steegmuller, *Cocteau* (Paris: Buchet-Chastel, 1973), p. 232.

80. Jean Cocteau, *Le mystère de Jean l'Oiseleur* (Paris: Champion, 1925), caption for self-portrait No. 16; "Le numéro Barbette," *NRF* (July 1, 1926): 33–38.

81. Maurice Sachs, *Au temps du Boeuf sur le Toit* (1939; Paris: Grasset, 1987), p. 199.

82. *Le mystère de Jean l'Oiseleur*, caption for self-portrait No. 16.

83. Maxime Alexandre, *Mémoires d'un surréaliste* (Paris: La Jeune Parque, 1968).

84. Cf. Henri Raczymow, *Maurice Sachs* (Paris: Gallimard, 1988), p. 94.

85. Sachs, *La décade de l'illusion*, p. 98.

86. Maurice Radiguet to Misia Sert, letter written a few days after Raymond Radiguet's death, quoted in Arthur Gold and Robert Fizdale, *Misia* (Paris: Gallimard, 1981), p. 288.

87. Coco Chanel would insinuate later that these "poetic" phrases were by Cocteau himself, but Radiguet's father, present during his visit, would confirm Cocteau's version in a letter to Poulenc. Preface by Jean Cocteau to the *Bal du Comte d'Orgel* (Paris: Grasset, 1924).

88. Roger Stéphane, *Portrait souvenir de Jean Cocteau* (Paris: Éditions Tallandier, 1964), p. 68.

89. Cocteau, *Le Potomak*, p. 130.

90. Chloé Radiguet, "Jean Cocteau, Raymond Radiguet: Fragments, Traits, Portraits," *Regard* 7–8 (1988): 49.

91. Nina Hammet, *Laughing Torso* (London: Virago Press, 1984), p. 301.

92. Jean Cocteau, "L'adieu aux fusiliers marins," in *Discours du grand sommeil* (Paris: Gallimard, 1967).

93. Mireille Havet to Ludmila Savitsy, probably from January 1924, quoted in Monique Nemer, *Raymond Radiguet* (Paris: Fayard, 2002), p. 489.

94. Letter from Valentine Hugo, December 20, 1923, quoted in Hugo, "Il y a trente ans."

95. Maurice Radiguet to Francis Poulenc, September 11, 1924, in Poulenc, *Correspondance, 1910–1963* (Paris: Fayard, 1994), p. 238.

96. Albert Thibaudet, "La psychologie romanesque," *NRF*, August 1, 1924.

97. Preface by Cocteau to the *Bal du comte d'Orgel*.

98. Radiguet's death both marked and inspired the Japanese writer Yukio Mishima, who thirty years later wrote a story—halfway between fiction and reality—bearing a name that was homonymous with Radiguet's.

99. Jean Cocteau to Valentine Hugo, December 18, 1923, Cocteau, *Correspondance Jean Hugo*, p. 96.

100. Cf. Matthieu Galey, *Journal*, vol. 1: 1953–1973 (Paris: Grasset, 1987), p. 44.

101. *Le diable au corps.*

102. Radiguet, "Mon premier roman."

103. "Élysée 08–74," *Le coq* 3 (n.d.).

104. Lucien Daudet to Étienne de Beaumont, June 27, 1924, IMEC, collection of Étienne de Beaumont, quoted in Nemer, *Raymond Radiguet*, p. 422.

105. Max Jacob to Jean Cocteau, December 27, 1923, in Jacob and Cocteau, *Correspondance*, p. 180.

106. The jeweler Cartier, in the meantime, has commercialized this ring.

107. A pun on Le Boeuf sur le Toit.—Trans.

108. Irène Lagut, interview for the Italian magazine *Panorama*, October 22, 1984.

109. Quoted in Gide, *Journal*, vol. 1, November 21, 1923, p. 1233. Brother of the Bernard Faÿ mentioned earlier, Emmanuel Faÿ had been very close to Radiguet, as well as to Marc Allégret and André Gide.

110. Jean Cocteau to Jacques-Émile Blanche, September 1924, in Cocteau and Blanche, *Correspondance*, p. 166.

111. This was a fantasy thought up by René Clair, the film director of the Dadaist *Entracte*, who became Bronja's lover. Asked for her hand in marriage by Mondrian and Buñuel, Bronja would end up becoming Mme René Clair, and would spur her husband into the Académie.

112. One of the letters that Cocteau wrote from the front alluded to the "little lamp," and notably described very realistically an experience of taking cocaine, with the sensation of a "bitter paste" on the stiff tongue. See Cocteau, *Le Potomak*.

113. Jean Cocteau to Max Jacob, January 29, 1924, in Jacob and Cocteau, *Correspondance*, p. 187.

114. Passy is a well-off neighborhood in the 16th arrondissement.—Trans.

115. Her poems were published in *Les Soirées de Paris*, in 1913.

116. Manuscript signed "Colette," Biblothèque National, N.a.fr 18703, folios 274–276, quoted in Claude Pichois and Alain Brunet, *Colette* (Paris: Fallois, 1999), p. 238.

117. Fernande Olivier, *Picasso et ses amis* (Paris: Éditions Stock, 1933), pp. 56–57.

CHAPTER 12. THE ANGEL'S DREAM

1. Serge Lifar would complain about finding this detail in *J'adore*, the first novel by Jean Desbordes. Cf. Francis Steegmuller, *Cocteau* (Paris: Buchet-Chastel, 1973), p. 287.

2. A young writer will recreate that experience, in the late 1920s: see André Fraigneau, *Cocteau par lui-même* (Paris: Éditions du Seuil, 1961), p. 14.

3. Maurice Sachs, *Le Sabbat: Souvenirs d'une jeunesse orageuse* (1946; Paris: Gallimard, 1979), p. 83.

4. Maurice Sachs, *La décade de l'illusion* (1933; Paris: Gallimard, 1950), p. 176.

5. Maurice Sachs, *Au temps du Boeuf sur le Toit* (1939; Paris: Grasset, 1987), p. 85.

6. Ibid., p. 88.

7. "Contre Jean Cocteau," private collection of Madeleine Castaing.

8. Jean Cocteau to his mother, November 17, 1924, *LM*.

9. The adjective is Marcel Arland's.

10. The muse was Geneviève Halévy, the future Mme Straus.

11. Sachs, *La décade de l'illusion*, p. 97.

12. "La môme Moineau" was Lucienne Suzanne Dhotelle, a French chanteuse of the 1920s.—Trans.

13. A waiter at the Ritz before he became Proust's chauffeur, Le Cuziat ran a brothel on the rue de l'Arcade, which his former boss frequented and where he even installed some furniture that came from Proust's mother's house. He is a model for the character of Jupien in *Remembrance*.

14. For "dangerous pity," see Zweig's best-known novel, *Beware of Pity*.—Trans.

15. Sachs, *Le Sabbat*, p. 84.

16. Ibid., p. 90.

17. "Contre Jean Cocteau."

18. Ibid.

19. Sachs, *Le Sabbat*, p. 83.

20. Letter, November 8, 1924, in *Cahier Jean Cocteau*, vol. 12, from *Correspondances avec Jean Cocteau* (Paris: Non Lieu Éditeur, 2014), p. 58.

21. The phrase was in fact Cocteau's, who had written to his mother, on October 20, 1922: "I gave it the final sentence."

22. Eugène Montfort in *Les Marges*, July 1924.

23. André Fraigneau, "Cocteau, Radiguet et la genèse du Bal . . .," *CJC*, no. 4 (Paris: Gallimard, 1973), p. 63.

24. See Georges Auric, *Correspondance avec Jean Cocteau* (Montpellier: Pierre Caizergues, Centre d'études du XXe siècle, Université Paul-Valéry, 1999), p. 148, and Paul Léautaud, *Journal littéraire*, vol. 1 (Paris: Mercure de France, 1986), p. 1476, June 30, 1924.

25. One can judge this by the critical edition of the *Bal* produced by Andrew Oliver and Nadia Oudouard for the Éditions Lettres Modernes/Minard in two volumes (1993 and 1999), where all versions of the text are presented—including one in the state Radiguet had left it, which Grasset published in 1924 in a run of twenty copies for Radiguet's friends (not for sale).

26. Léautaud, *Journal littéraire*, June 30, 1924.

27. J. Delteil, "Radiguet vu de 1923," in *CJC*, no. 4, p. 33.

28. The praise appeared in a Royalist publication that Massis had founded with Bainville, *La revue universelle*, August 15, 1924.

29. An amazing 35,000 copies were sold during the first two weeks.

30. Raymond Radiguet, *Gli inediti*, preface by Liliana Garuti Delli Ponti, ed. *Jean-Claude Lattès*, 1973, quoted in the preface to *Vers libres et jeux innocents*, in Radiguet, *Oeuvres complètes*, ed. Chloé Radiguet and Julien Cendres (Paris: Éditions Stock, 1993), p. 18.

31. "En jupe-culotte/Un soir à Joinville/Vénus la salope/M'a sucé la bite," etc. ["In culottes/One night in Joinville/ Venus the whore/Sucked my cock," etc.—Trans.]

32. Jean Cocteau to a friend, May 1, 1924, quoted in Marie-Christine Movilliat, *Raymond Radiguet ou la jeunesse contredite, 1903–1923* (Paris: Bibliophone Daniel Radford, 2000), p. 309.

33. This was also the name of a telephone exchange that had been newly renamed from "Saxe." Gilbert Lély, the future biographer of de Sade, had the role of a bagpipe player.

34. Jean Hugo, *Le regard de la mémoire* (Paris: Babel-Actes Sud, 1983), p. 242. [The Maison Henri de Borniol is the oldest funeral company in France.—Trans.]

35. Bernard Faÿ, *Les précieux* (Paris: Perrin, 1966), p. 277.

36. Henri Sauguet, *La musique, ma vie* (Paris: Librairie Séguier, 1990), p. 204.

37. For a sense of the mood of the era, see *Le pauvre matelot*, a short opera performed in 1927. It was written by Cocteau for Milhaud and is one of their great shared successes.

38. In 1921, Diaghilev had planned with Cocteau an avant-garde performance called *Plastic Hall*, in which experimental films would have accompanied alternative choreographies.

39. Isadora Duncan had contributed to this Cocteau-like discovery in the beginning of the century.

40. "La course, ou deux femmes courant sur la plage" (The race, or two women running on the beach) is today one of the centerpieces of the Musée Picasso, Paris. Diaghilev was so pleased with it that he would use it as a stage curtain for all his future ballets, and Auric was asked to compose a trumpet call to announce its appearance.

41. Jean Cocteau to André Gide, August 1924, in Jean Cocteau, *Lettres à André Gide avec quelques réponses d'André Gide*, ed. Jean-Jacques Kihm (Paris: La Table Ronde, 1970), p. 140.

42. Jean Cocteau to the Hugos, August 7, 1924, quoted in Steegmuller, *Cocteau* (Buchet-Chastel), p. 246.

43. Cocteau had just published with Éditions Stock *Dessins*, about a hundred drawings and portraits of Anna de Noailles, Stravinsky, and himself. It was republished in 2013, still with Éditions Stock, with a preface by Claude Arnaud.

44. Jean Cocteau to Étienne de Beaumont, February 1925, quoted in Steegmuller, *Cocteau* (Buchet-Chastel), p. 251.

45. Jean Cocteau, *Opium* (Paris: Éditions Stock, 1930), p. 57.

46. Jean Cocteau, *Journal d'un inconnu* (Paris: Grasset, 1953), p. 51.

47. *Mi-heurt mi-bise; heurt* means clash or conflict; *bise* means either kiss or North wind.—Trans.
48. Cocteau, *Opium*, p. 48.
49. "Le fumeur chinois," unpublished poem, BHVP, box 47.
50. "Ceux qui savent . . .," November 18, 1946, *CJC*, no. 10 (Paris: Gallimard, 1985), p. 128.
51. Quoted in Jean-Jacques Kihm, Elizabeth Sprigge, and Henri C. Béhar, *Jean Cocteau, l'homme et les miroirs* (Paris: La Table Ronde, 1968), p. 147.
52. Paul Déroulède was a poet of France's "revenge" against Germany, a founder of the League of Patriots, and a bombastic nationalist orator from the 1900s.
53. *Commerce* 2 (Fall 1924).
54. In the "exquisite corpse" game, a piece of paper would be passed around, folded up, on which one person would draw, for example, a pig's head, another a man's torso, a third a duck's feet, with each person not knowing what the previous one had done; then the paper was unfolded. The poetic equivalent also existed; this could produce phrases like "Winged steam charms the locked bird" (*La vapeur ailée séduit l'oiseau fermé à clef*).
55. Jean Cocteau to Anna de Noailles, n.d., in *Jean Cocteau et son temps*, catalog compiled by Pierre Georgel for the Jean Cocteau exhibit at the Jacquemart-André Museum, 1965, p. 22.
56. André Breton, *Second manifeste du surréalisme*, 1930, in *Manifestes du surréalisme* (Paris: Gallimard, 1966), p. 144. Breton needed Soupault's psychic suppleness to compose *Les champs magnétiques*. Breton was quickly irritated when faced with Aragon's monstrous facility; eventually he punished Soupault's novelistic tendencies by excluding him.
57. Cesare Lombroso (1835–1909) was the founder of the Italian School of Positivist Criminology. Lombroso's theory essentially stated that criminality was inherited, and that someone "born criminal" could be identified by physical defects.
58. Erostratus burned down Diana's temple in Ephesus.
59. Gérard Rosenthal, *Avocat de Trotsky* (Paris: Robert Laffont, 1975), p. 39.
60. *The Cantos of Ezra Pound*, no. 77 (New York: New Directions, 1993), p. 489.
61. Cocteau, *Journal d'un inconnu*, p. 39.
62. Jean Cocteau, "Le mystère laïc," in *Oeuvres complètes*, vol. 10 (Lausanne: Éditions Marguerat, 1950), p. 43.
63. The term was published in October 1924.
64. Breton would mark his wish for copyright even more clearly when he added, in the first *Surrealist Manifesto* (1924): "I believe that there is no point today in dwelling any further on this word and that the meaning we gave it initially has generally prevailed over its Apollinarian sense."
65. Henri Béhar, *André Breton le grand indésirable* (Paris: Calmann-Lévy, 1990), p. 52.
66. André Breton, *Manifeste du surréalisme*, 1924. For an English translation, see online: http://ir.nmu.org.ua/bitstream/handle/123456789/21862/1282e41ff8593e92c75ab5c0f828 48ad.pdf?sequence=1.
67. Thus Breton would assert, in 1930, in the *Second Surrealist Manifesto*, that the conjunction in the sky, between 1896 and 1898, of Uranus and Saturn, "which only

happens once every forty-five years," was responsible for the close-together births of Aragon, Éluard, and himself; an astrologer had foretold the arrival of an "investigator of the first order" and a "new school of science."

68. Cocteau would also say to Claude Mauriac: "In the room I lived in with my mother, Surrealism was born, but without my realizing it." Mauriac, *Une amitié contrariée* (Paris: Grasset, 1970), p. 29.

69. For once flattering, but obviously to excess, Mauriac wrote at the end of Cocteau's life: "He was truly the prince of this world in which the Surrealists constituted the wheeling flank. Despite their camping on the wildest frontiers, and holding the frivolous prince in great scorn, they were an integral part of his empire." François Mauriac, *Nouveaux mémoires intérieurs*, 1965, in *Oeuvres autobiographiques* (Paris: Gallimard, 1990), p. 746.

70. Breton, who was still running after the last Symbolist poets in 1913, had called Cocteau, in *Littérature*, after the publication of *Le cap de Bonne Espérance*, a "genius of disidealization"—a clear insult.

71. "I actually took hashish only one time, many years ago, in a very small quantity," Breton, a little ashamed, would confide in a note in *Vases communicants* (Paris: Gallimard, 1955). Jacques Vaché, one of his heroes, however, was an opium smoker.

72. Quoted in Alejo Carpentier, *Essais littéraires*, trans. Serge Mestre (Paris: Gallimard, 2003), p. 190.

73. René Crevel, "Voici Tristan Tzara et ses souvenirs sur Dada," *Les nouvelles littéraires*, October 25, 1924, quoted in François Buot, *Tristan Tzara, l'homme qui inventa la révolution Dada* (Paris: Grasset, 2002), p. 190.

74. André Germain, *La bourgeoisie qui brûle* (Paris: Sun, 1951), p. 275.

75. Cf. Steegmuller, *Cocteau* (Buchet-Chastel), p. 167.

76. Cocteau, *Opium*, p. 155; Glenway Wescott to Maurice Sachs, November 16, 1926, private collection of Carlo Jansiti.

77. Emmanuel Berl, *Interrogatoire par Patrick Modiano* (Paris: Gallimard, 1976), p. 112.

78. Claude Roy, *Somme toute* (Paris: Gallimard, 1976), p. 407.

79. Philippe Soupault, *Un bon apôtre* (Paris: Garnier, 1980), pp. 123–124.

80. Marc Polizzotti, *André Breton* (Paris: Gallimard, 1997), pp. 69–70.

81. *La Révolution surréaliste* 11 (March 15, 1928): 33 and 38, describing meetings on January 27 and 31, 1928.

82. Quoted in Victor Crastre, *Le drame du surréalisme* (Paris: Du Temps, 1963), pp. 80–81.

83. Maurice Martin du Gard, *Les mémorables*, new ed. (Paris: Gallimard, 1999), p. 582.

84. In France, any person who has reached the age of puberty has a right to make love with the person of his choice.

85. The phrase "Don Juan for men" is Jacques Prévert's, but Alejo Carpentier, who knew the group well, adds in his *Essais littéraires*: "for men without character." "We are the ones who decide who is or is not Jewish," Goebbels would declare to Fritz Lang, who was only half-Jewish, to encourage him to work for the new Nazi regime.

86. Desnos's sentence is cited in Jean Cocteau to Max Jacob, April 8, 1925, in Max Jacob and Jean Cocteau, *Correspondance, 1917–1944*, ed. Anne Kimball (Paris: Paris-Méditerranée/Écrits des Hautes-Terres, 2000), p. 239.

87. The homosexual passages in Desnos's book *La liberté et l'amour* would be censored in 1927.

88. Max Jacob to Marcel Jouhandeau, May 8, 1925, in Max Jacob, *Lettres à Marcel Jouhandeau*, ed. Anne S. Kimball (Geneva: Librairie Droz, 1979), p. 194.

89. Quoted in Joseph Kessel, *Des hommes* (Paris: Gallimard, 1972), p. 266.

90. Jean Cocteau to Max Jacob, October 2, 1922, in Jacob and Cocteau, *Correspondance*, p. 132.

91. Jean Cocteau to Jean Paulhan, November 1926, IMEC, Paulhan collection.

92. "One does not talk about what one scorns," he wrote. See *La revue européenne* (April 1, 1925): 66–67.

93. Dedication to Philippe Berthelot, 1921, quoted in Jean-Luc Barré, *Philippe Berthelot, l'éminence grise* (Paris: Plon, 1998), p. 373.

94. *La révolution surréaliste* 8, December 1, 1926, p. 15.

95. Pierre de Massot, *André Breton le septembriseur* (Paris: Le Terrain Vague, 1967). During a Stalinist period, Massot had, however, denounced, in 1946, "the shadowy dictatorship Breton wielded"—but that was only the better to praise Tzara's Socialist activities. Cf. Buot, *Tristan Tzara*, p. 373.

96. The "Septembriseur," sans-culottes, killed (*brisèrent la vie*) hundreds of prisoners in September 1792, after the European monarchies declared war on France.

97. *La Révolution surréaliste* 3 (April 15, 1925).

98. Jean Hugo, quoted in Kihm, Sprigge, and Béhar, *Jean Cocteau*, p. 166.

99. Jean Cocteau to Jean Bourgoint, November 28, 1926, in Kihm, Sprigge, and Béhar, *Jean Cocteau*, p. 178.

100. *La danse de Sophocle*, OPC, p. 1406.

101. Jean Bourgoint to Jeannette Kandaouroff, in Bourgoint, *Le retour de l'enfant terrible: Lettres 1923–1966* (Paris: Desclée de Brouwer, 1975). Radiguet had often "betrayed" Cocteau; Bourgoint was, in his own way, faithful to him.

102. Henri Raczymow, *Maurice Sachs* (Paris: Gallimard, 1988), p. 94.

103. Jean Cocteau to the Hugos, March 1925, in *Correspondance Jean Hugo* (Montpellier: Brigitte Borsaro and Pierre Caizergues, Centre d'études du XXe siècle, Université Paul-Valéry, 1995), pp. 101–102.

104. "Mystère de l'Oiseleur," on the margin of *Opéra*, OPC, p. 574.

105. Jean Cocteau to Maurice Sachs, n.d. (posted March 19, 1925), *Cahier Jean Cocteau*, vol. 12, p. 72.

106. Jean Cocteau to Maurice Sachs, March 15, 1925, *Cahier Jean Cocteau*, vol. 12, p. 66.

107. Bourgoint did, however, leave some beautiful letters.

108. Jean Cocteau to Maurice Sachs, n.d. (posted March 19, 1925).

109. Jean Cocteau to Maurice Sachs, n.d. (probably March 21, 1925), *Cahier Jean Cocteau*, vol. 12, p. 78.

110. Jean Cocteau to Maurice Sachs, March 16, 1925, *Cahier Jean Cocteau*, vol. 12, p. 67.

111. OPC, p. 525.

112. Jean Cocteau to Maurice Sachs, n.d., *Cahier Jean Cocteau*, vol. 12, p. 94.

113. Faÿ, *Les précieux*, p. 279.

114. Profile of Julien Green by Frantz-Olivier Giesbert, *Le Figaro*, July 22, 1993.

115. Cocteau, *Opium*, p. 118.

116. Jacques Maritain to Ernest Psichari, September 21, 1900, quoted in Jean-Luc Barré, *Jacques et Raïssa Maritain, les mendiants du ciel* (Paris: Éditions Stock, 1995), p. 65.

117. This was Raïssa Oumançoff, a Russian Jewish émigré whom Maritain met at the Sorbonne; they married in 1904.—Trans.

118. Jean Cocteau to Max Jacob on September 26, 1922, in Jacob and Cocteau, *Correspondance*, p. 126. In *Prière mutilée*, a poem written in Lavandou in 1922, which the NRF would publish in June 1925, we read: "Doubt, invade me until it charms away doubt,/Destroy the thorn-covered veil of Jesus Christ."

119. Jean Cocteau to Max Jacob, mid-March 1925, in Jacob and Cocteau, *Correspondance*, p. 210.

120. Letter, n.d., mentioned in the unpublished journal of Roger Lannes, IMEC, on August 9, 1936.

121. Jacques Maritain to Ernest Psichari, November 23, 1901, quoted in Barré, *Jacques et Raïssa Maritain*, p. 65.

122. *Journal de Raïssa Maritain* (Paris: Desclée de Brouwer, 1963), p. 217, entry for April 10, 1934, after the performance of Cocteau's *La machine infernale*.

123. Barbey d'Aurevilly, *Le constitutionnel*, July 29, 1884, quoted in *Le XIXe siècle: Des oeuvres et des hommes*, ed. Pierre Petit, vol. 2 (Paris: Mercure de France, 1964), p. 343. Barbey had used this phrase first in 1857, in an article on *Les fleurs du mal* by Baudelaire, which *Le pays* had refused to publish.

124. Sachs, *Le Sabbat*, p. 110.

125. Cf. Jean Cocteau to Max Jacob, May 1927, in Jacob and Cocteau, *Correspondance*, p. 534.

126. Father Charles de Foucauld (1858–1916) was a Catholic missionary who lived in North Africa; he founded the Little Brothers of Jesus, a religious order.

127. *Journal de Raïssa Maritain*, p. 167.

128. Clément Borgal, *Jean Cocteau ou de la claudication considérée comme l'un des beaux-arts* (Paris: Presses Universitaires de France, 1989), p. 166.

129. Postscript to *Lettre à Jacques Maritain* (Paris: Éditions Stock, 1926).

130. Note by Jacques Maritain in *Journal de Raïssa Maritain*, p. 168.

131. Hugo, *Le regard de la mémoire*, p. 431.

132. *Le coq parisien* 3 (1920).

133. Max Jacob to Jean Cocteau, June 18, 1925, in Jacob and Cocteau, *Correspondance*, p. 317. Those were the very words that Pascal had recorded, during the night of November 23, 1654, in his *Mémorial*, which was found after his death sewn into the lining of his doublet. They marked the announcement of his second and definitive return to God.

134. Max Jacob to Jean Cocteau, March 19, 1925, in Jacob and Cocteau, *Correspondance*, p. 211. [*Ange*, angel, is similar to the letters in *Jean*.—Trans.]

135. Quoted in Max Milner, *L'imaginaire de la drogue* (Paris: Gallimard, 2000), p. 239.

136. Paul Claudel, *Journal*, vol. 1: 1904–1932 (Paris: Gallimard, 1968), p. 698, December 22, 1925.

137. An unbeliever in his youth, heavily influenced by Rimbaud's poetry, Paul Claudel (1868–1965), brother of sculptor Camille Claudel, experienced a sudden conversion

at the age of eighteen on Christmas Day 1886 while listening to a choir in the cathedral of Notre-Dame de Paris.

138. *Les cahiers du comte Kessler, 1918–1937* (Paris: Grasset, 1972), January 2, 1926.

139. Abbé Mugnier, *Journal (1879–1939)* (Paris: Mercure de France, 1985), p. 462, November 23, 1925.

140. Jean Cocteau to Max Jacob, in Jacob and Cocteau, *Correspondance*, p. 349.

141. For the quotation, see Sachs, *La décade de l'illusion*, p. 170.

142. Interview of the author with Denise Tual, November 19, 1999. Jean Aurenche reports this first meeting in almost the same words, in *La suite à l'écran* (Paris: Institut Lumière/Actes Sud, 1993), p. 28.

143. Sachs, *La décade de l'illusion*, pp. 180–181.

144. Hugo, *Le regard de la mémoire*, p. 324.

145. Sachs, *Le Sabbat*, p. 121. The recruiting of the squadron, as we've seen, was more complex, but there were ties between the Roseau d'or and the Action Française, the Royalist Party, which was influential at the time, and whose leader was Charles Maurras. "With the optimism of youth, we were composing a synthesis of those often disparate elements," writes Jean-Pierre Maxence, in *Histoire de dix ans, 1927–1937* (Paris: Gallimard, 1939), p. 58. "A nationalism that was widening to the universal in Catholicism; a Catholicism that, offering a living order, respected and fortified the person: that, in short, is what we drew from Maurras, from Massis, from Maritain."

146. Maurice Sachs to Jean Cocteau, July 15, 1925, quoted in Raczymow, *Maurice Sachs*, pp. 96–97.

147. Jean Cocteau to Maurice Sachs, August 29, 1925, in *CJC*, vol. 12 (Paris: Gallimard, 1993), p. 108.

148. *Lettre à Jacques Maritain.*

149. Jean Cocteau to Max Jacob, October 1925, in Jacob and Cocteau, *Correspondance*, p. 360.

150. Jean Cocteau to his mother, August 12, 1925, *LM*.

151. Jean Cocteau to his mother, October 15, 1925, *LM*.

152. Jean Cocteau to Maurice Sachs, October 14, 1925, in *CJC*, vol. 12, p. 116.

153. Sachs, *Le Sabbat*, p. 107.

154. Jean Cocteau to Max Jacob, December 8 or 9, 1925, in Jacob and Cocteau, *Correspondance*, p. 373.

155. Maurice Sachs to Jean Cocteau, December 10, 1925, from Meudon, *CJC*, vol. 12 (Paris: Gallimard, 1993), p. 119.

156. Cocteau, *Journal (1942–1945)*, p. 231.

157. Recounted in Abbé Mugnier, *Journal (1879–1939)*, May 20, 1926, p. 471, and Hugo, *Le regard de la mémoire*, p. 417.

CHAPTER 13. LA CROIX ET LA BANNIÈRE

1. Michel Leiris would write, "I would have gone to the point of sharing his vices if that had been the means of acquiring his genius." Leiris, *Manhood*, trans. Richard Howard (Chicago: University of Chicago Press, 1984), p. 129.

2. Max Jacob to Jean Cocteau, May 6, 1925, in Max Jacob and Jean Cocteau, *Correspondance, 1917–1944,* ed. Anne Kimball (Paris: Paris-Méditerranée/Écrits des Hautes-Terres, 2000), p. 279.

3. Jean Cocteau to Max Jacob, September 19, 1922, in Jacob and Cocteau, *Correspondance,* p. 122.

4. Max Jacob to Jean Cocteau, April 29, 1925, in Jacob and Cocteau, *Correspondance,* pp. 265–266.

5. Max Jacob to Marcel Jouhandeau, May 8, 1925, in Jacob and Cocteau, *Correspondance,* p. 194.

6. Max Jacob to Jean Cocteau, October 24, 1925, in Jacob and Cocteau, *Correspondance,* p. 362.

7. Max Jacob to Jean Cocteau, February 3, 1922, in Jacob and Cocteau, *Correspondance,* p. 78.

8. "Dieu nous aide et fait pousser le caca," 391 14 (November 1920).

9. Jean Cocteau to Jacques Maritain, July 10, 1926, in Jean Cocteau and Jacques Maritain, *Correspondance (1923–1963),* CJC, no. 12 (Paris: Gallimard, 1993), p. 114.

10. Cf. Claude Mignot-Ogliastri, *Anna de Noailles, une amie de la princesse Edmond de Polignac* (Paris: Méridiens Klincksieck, 1986), p. 355.

11. Jean Cocteau, *Portraits-souvenir,* in *Oeuvres complètes,* vol. 11 (Lausanne: Éditions Marguerat, 1951).

12. Maurice Martin du Gard, *Les mémorables,* new ed. (Paris: Gallimard, 1999), p. 215.

13. André Gide, September 1, 1931, in *Journal,* vol. 2: *1926–1950* (Paris: Gallimard, 1997), p. 301.

14. *La révolution surréaliste* 8 (December 1, 1926): 23.

15. Quoted in Michel Carouges, *André Breton et les données fondamentales du surréalisme* (Paris: Gallimard, 1967).

16. See Walter Benjamin, *Mythe et violence* (Paris: Denoël, 1967), p. 300.

17. André Breton, "Visite à Léon Trotsky," in *La clé des champs* (Paris: Sagittaire, 1953). Michaux also noted Breton's stubborn tendency toward religious competition, and how he opposed poetic grace to divine grace ("Recherches dans la poésie contemporaine").

18. *Littérature* 5 (October 1922).

19. *La révolution surréaliste* 6 (March 1, 1926): 3.

20. Cf. *Jésus-la-Caille* by Francis Carco, which would have an impact on Jean Genet; Lucien Rebatet, *Les décombres* (Paris: Denoël, 1942), p. 554.

21. It was especially hard to believe given that Cocteau added, with his particular taste for one-upmanship, "My fondness for Robespierre and Saint-Just is well known."

22. André Breton, *Légitime défense;* cf. *La révolution surréaliste* 8 (December 1, 1926): 33. In *A Corpse,* the Surrealist pamphlet against Anatole France published in October 1924, Aragon was already attacking a "literary man saluted at once by the imbecile Maurras and by idiotic Moscow."

23. Michel Leiris, *Journal (1922–1989)* (Paris: Gallimard, 1992), entries for September 1926.

24. Jean Cocteau, *Le Potomak,* in *Oeuvres complètes,* vol. 2 (Lausanne: Marguerat, 1947), p. 29.

25. Alejo Carpentier, "Jean Cocteau et l'esthétique du mouvement," *Chroniques* (Paris: Gallimard, 1983), p. 25.

26. They were not, however, mistreated by the editors. Cf. Frédéric Lefèvre, *Les nouvelles littéraires*, September 18, 1926, interview with Anna de Noailles.

27. Jean Cocteau to Max Jacob, late July 1925, in Jacob and Cocteau, *Correspondance*, p. 324.

28. Jean Cocteau to his mother, February 28, 1926, *LM*.

29. Jean Cocteau to Max Jacob, late February 1926, in Jacob and Cocteau, *Correspondance*, p. 393.

30. Cf. ibid., p. 418 (note).

31. This is what Breton would suggest in *Arcane 17*—the seventeenth trump card in the tarot deck features a star named Lucifer.

32. Paul Sabon would die of an illness in 1933.

33. These entities, unlike men, "could escape undetected thanks to a kind of camouflage which . . . the study of mimetic animals alone might explain," Breton would write in his "Prolegomena to a Third Surrealist Manifesto," *VVV* 1 (June 1942).

34. "No, no, stop, you're going to destroy him," Mme Breton reportedly said. Cf. the unpublished journal of Roger Lannes, in *CJC*, no. 10 (Paris: Gallimard, 1985), p. 165.

35. Maria Savinio describes the painting: "We see a face appear, eyes lost in a dream, behind a Japanese doll's head, resting on the body of a man who has a kind of scarf in his hand." *Aux côtés d'Alberto Savinio* (Paris: Sabine Wespieser, 2002), p. 70.

36. Jean Cocteau to Max Jacob, August 16, 1922, in Jacob and Cocteau, *Correspondance*, p. 103.

37. The story has been told of an auctioneer who, after the war, announced the sale of a first edition of Cocteau, "without drawings or a dedication, in rare condition," and sold it for a price beyond all estimates.

38. Pierre de Massot, once a follower of Picabia and now devoted to Breton, served as go-between.

39. Cited in Ornella Volta, *Satie/Cocteau: Les malentendus d'une entente* (Paris: Le Castor Astral, 1993), p. 78.

40. Jean Cocteau to Max Jacob, early July 1925, in Jacob and Cocteau, *Correspondance*, p. 324.

41. Published by Salabert, with a postface by Ornella Vola; the booklet would go on to circulate among Francis Poulenc and Nicholas Nabokov, without going any further. Henri Sauguet set the chorus to music under the title *Chanson de marins* (Paris: Smyth, 1993), and Marianne Oswald would have her first success singing it that same year.

42. This furniture music consisted of samples repeated ad nauseam and taken from his loathed colleagues: Saint-Saëns, Ambroise Thomas, as well as Jean Poueigh, the "ass without music," who had the gall to criticize *Parade*—see 391 17 (June 1924).

43. *Paris-Journal*, February 15, 1924; "Ah, that's better," Satie said, sitting back down and adding, according to Auric, "this is one of the strangest and most disconcerting performances I've ever attended" (pp. 26–27).

44. Picabia had just written the book *Entr'acte*, which Satie was setting to music.

45. *Parcier* is an old form of *partiaire*, sharecropper; Satie wanted to convey he was a share-cropper of God.—Trans.

46. Erik Satie to Mme Guérin, September 29, 1924, in Erik Satie, *Correspondance presque complète*, ed. and comp. Ornella Volta (Paris: Fayard/IMEC, 2000), p. 634.

47. Ibid., p. 727; "Jean Cocteau: Deux de mes collaborateurs," in Jean Cocteau and Darius Milhaud, *Correspondance* (Montpellier: Pierre Caizergues and Josiane Mas, Centre d'études littéraires françaises du XXe siècle, Université Paul-Valéry, 1992), appendix 4, p. 67.

48. Jean Cocteau to Francis Poulenc, July 14, 1925, cited in *Correspondance de Francis Poulenc*, ed. Hélène de Wendel (Paris: Seuil, 1967), p. 69.

49. Francis Steegmuller attributes this phrase to *Sabbat*, but I have not been able to find it in this book. See Steegmuller, *Cocteau* (Boston: Little, Brown, 1970), p. 359.

50. Maurice Sachs, *Le Sabbat: Souvenirs d'une jeunesse orageuse* (1946; Paris: Gallimard, 1979), p. 145.

51. Handwritten letter from Glenway Wescott to Maurice Sachs, September 18, 1926, private collection of Carlo Jansiti.

52. Max Jacob to Jean Cocteau, March 29, 1926, in Jacob and Cocteau, *Correspondance*, p. 411.

53. We could even include Picasso, who saw himself as Jesus before mistaking himself for Dionysus before ending up as the Minotaur. Cf. interview with Jean Cocteau by Rouzaud, in Jean Cocteau, *Oeuvres complètes* (Geneva: Éditions Marguerat, 1950), p. 363.

54. *Saying Life: The Memoirs of Sir Francis Rose* (London: Cassel, 1961), p. 65.

55. Kit Wood threw himself in front of a train in 1930.

56. Francis Rose brought his mother to live at the Hôtel Welcome year-round.

57. Cited by Steegmuller, *Cocteau* (Little, Brown), p. 372.

58. Francis Rose was the most eloquent, if not the most accurate, witness of the unbeliev-able atmosphere at the Welcome. Cf. *Saying Life*, p. 56.

59. Recounted in Cocteau, *PD*, vol. 1, p. 367. "She really is from Greece," he said cruelly of the dancer. "She's very greasy" (*Elle est vraiment de la graisse*). Cf. *Continual Lessons: The Journal of Glenway Wescott, 1937–1955* (New York: Farrar, Strauss, Giroux, 1990), p. 69.

60. This was one of the objects that Breton wanted to turn into a voodoo doll.

61. "*L'opium est soi en soi*," untitled poem in *En marge d'Opéra*, OPC, p. 575.

62. Handwritten letter from Glenway Wescott to Maurice Sachs, September 1926, private collection of Carlo Jansiti.

63. *Opéra*, OPC, p. 525.

64. Handwritten letter from Glenway Wescott to Maurice Sachs, March 16 (probably 1926), private collection of Carlo Jansiti.

65. Max Jacob to Jean Cocteau, February 21, 1926, cited in Henri Raczymow, *Maurice Sachs* (Paris: Gallimard, 1988).

66. Wescott would serve as inspiration for the character of Robert Prentice, in Hemingway's *The Sun Also Rises*. After he returned to the United States, he continued to write and

to live in a ménage à trois with Monroe Wheeler, director of the Museum of Modern Art in New York, and the photographer George Platt Lynes. Cf. Anatole Pohorilenko and James Crump, *When We Were Three* (Santa Fe, NM: Arena, 1998).

67. This number is indicated in one of Jean l'Oiseleur's drawings. Set at an angle on the first floor, this room had a balcony with a view over the port. The Welcome Hôtel is still open, and praised by Cocteau's devotees.

68. Jean Cocteau to Maurice Sachs, n.d. January 1926, in Jacob and Cocteau, *Correspondance*, pp. 123–124.

69. Jean Cocteau to Maurice Sachs, March 1, 1926, in Jacob and Cocteau, *Correspondance*, p. 127.

70. Handwritten letter from Glenway Wescott to Maurice Sachs, "Monday morning, the . . . 27th, I suppose," March 16 (probably 1926), private collection of Carlo Jansiti.

71. Linked to La Rochefoucauld and Mme de La Fayette, author of religious works, the Abbé de Choisy (1644–1724) liked to dress as a woman.

72. Maurice Sachs, *Alias* (Paris: Gallimard, 1935), p. 178.

73. Yvon Beleval, preface to *La chasse à courre* (Paris: Gallimard, 1948).

74. André Beucler, *Plaisirs de mémoire: De Saint-Pétersbourg à Saint-Germain-des-Prés*, vol. 2 (Paris: Gallimard, 1982), p. 143.

75. Sachs, *Alias*, p. 196.

76. Cited in J. Bourgoint, *Le retour de l'enfant terrible: Lettres, 1923–1966* (Paris: Desclée de Brouwer, 1975).

77. Jean Cocteau to his mother, October 11, 1926, *LM*. To try to explain Sachs's behavior, Cocteau wrote again of "this Jewish need to shock the world and, thinking themselves stable, find they are merely making camp."

78. Handwritten letter from Jean Cocteau to Maurice Sachs, kindly photocopied by Nadia Saleh. For more information, see N. Saleh, "La correspondance de Jean Cocteau/Maurice Sachs, ligne de vie, ligne de l'oeuvre," in *Dalhousie French Studies* 44 (Fall 1998).

79. Although he was horrified by the episode at Juan-les-Pins, Maritain still published the book in his *Roseau d'or* collection, at Plon.

80. Handwritten letter from Glenway Wescott to Maurice Sachs, "Monday morning, the . . . 27th, I suppose."

81. Jean Cocteau to Maurice Sachs, courtesy Nadia Saleh.

82. Jean Cocteau to Maurice Sachs, July 8, 1926, courtesy Nadia Saleh.

83. Yvon Beleval, preface to *La chasse à courre* (Paris: Gallimard, 1948), p. 12.

84. Maurice Sachs to Jacques Maritain, November 5, 1926, cited in J.-L. Barré, *Jacques et Raïssa Maritain, les mendiants du ciel* (Paris: Éditions Stock, 1995), p. 336.

85. Jean Cocteau to Max Jacob, November 1926, in Jacob and Cocteau, *Correspondance*, p. 457.

86. Jean Cocteau to Maurice Sachs, October 1926, courtesy Nadia Saleh.

87. Henri Raczymow thinks it was Robert Le Masle, a young medical student at the time, who would become known as a collector and who would leave several pieces to the Museum of Modern Art. He was also in contact with Max Jacob. See Raczymow, *Maurice Sachs* (Paris: Gallimard, 1988), p. 146.

88. Brought back from Persia by his uncle the ambassador; see ibid., pp. 148–149. Cocteau's letter to Sachs is undated. It was Jean Touzot who dated it in the second volume of *LM*.

89. Jean Cocteau, *Journal d'un inconnu* (Paris: Grasset, 1953), pp. 102–103.

90. Emmanuel Berl, *Interrogatoire par Patrick Modiano* (Paris: Gallimard, 1976), p. 115.

91. Cf. Mauriac, *Une amitié contrariée* (Paris: Grasset, 1970), p. 47.

92. Bourgoint, *Le retour de l'enfant terrible*.

93. Jean Cocteau to his mother, January 28, 1926, *LM*.

94. Max Jacob to Jean Cocteau, May 6, 1925, in Jacob and Cocteau, *Correspondance*, p. 278.

95. This is according to Jouhandeau himself. Cf. Jacques Danon, *Entretiens avec Élise et Marcel Jouhandeau* (Paris: Pierre Belfond, 1966), p. 76.

96. Jean Cocteau to Max Jacob, December 8 or 9, 1925, in Jacob and Cocteau, *Correspondance*, p. 373.

97. Marcel Jouhandeau to Max Jacob, early December 1925, in Jacob and Cocteau, *Correspondance*, p. 376.

98. In 1927 André Julien Du Breuil would publish *Imprudence*, a novel suggesting that Jouhandeau's only fault was to be overly impatient.

99. Jean Cocteau to Max Jacob, December 8 or 9, 1925, in Jacob and Cocteau, *Correspondance*, p. 373.

100. This opinion is obvious in several articles published in *L'action française*, in 1936 and 1937. It seems that Jouhandeau was above all furious at having been recognized by Sachs, who had previously run into him in a "bad place."

101. Max Jacob to Jean Cocteau, November 14, 1926, in Jacob and Cocteau, *Correspondance*, p. 450; "[As for] Maurice [Sachs], we only interest him insofar as a representation of what does or does not irritate him, or is helpful or useful to his modulations," Max Jacob to Jean Cocteau, November 22, 1926, in Jacob and Cocteau, *Correspondance*, p. 455.

CHAPTER 14. "RAYMOND HAS RETURNED"

1. Klaus Mann, *Le tournant, histoire d'une vie*, trans. Nicole Roche and Henri Roche (Paris: Seuil, 1986), p. 291. See also the English version: Mann, *The Turning Point* (Princeton, NJ: Markus Wiener, 1984). Klaus Mann met Cocteau when he was eighteen years old, during a trip to Paris in 1925. His "generational" model was Radiguet.

2. Erik Satie to Valentine Hugo, January 5, 1917, cited in Ornella Volta, *Satie/Cocteau: Les malentendus d'une entente* (Paris: Le Castor Astral, 1993), p. 29.

3. Jean Cocteau to Jean Desbordes, December 1925, cited in Jean-Jacques Kihm, Elizabeth Sprigge, and Henri C. Béhar, *Jean Cocteau, l'homme et les miroirs* (Paris: La Table Ronde, 1968), p. 185.

4. His cousins in the navy were Admiral Georges Durand-Viel (1881–1942) and François Darlan (1875–1942), marine officer at the time and chief of staff of the Minister of the Marine, and who under the Vichy Republic was Marshal Pétain's designated successor.

5. Preface to Jean Desbordes, *J'adore* (Paris: Grasset, 2009), p. 6.

6. Cf. *Discours du grand sommeil, OPC*, p. 23.

7. Roger Stéphane, *Portrait souvenir de Jean Cocteau* (Paris: Éditions Tallandier, 1964), p. 54.

8. Conversation between Jean Hugo and Francis Steegmuller; see Steegmuller, *Cocteau* (Boston: Little, Brown, 1970), p. 382.

9. Jean Cocteau to Max Jacob, May 1926, in Max Jacob and Jean Cocteau, *Correspondance, 1917–1944*, ed. Anne Kimball (Paris: Paris-Méditerranée/Écrits des Hautes-Terres, 2000), p. 418.

10. Preface to Desbordes, *J'adore*.

11. Jean Cocteau, "Le mystère laïc," in *Oeuvres complètes*, vol. 10 (Lausanne: Éditions Marguerat, 1950), p. 26.

12. Jean Cocteau, undated (April 1927?), in Jacob and Cocteau, *Correspondance*, p. 524. See also Yvon Beleval, "La rencontre avec Jean Cocteau," in *CJC*, vol. 3 (Paris: Gallimard, 1972), pp. 69–107.

13. Jean Cocteau to Max Jacob, probably mid-January 1927 in Jacob and Cocteau, *Correspondance*, p. 482.

14. Jean Cocteau to Max Jacob, April 27, 1927, in Jacob and Cocteau, *Correspondance*, p. 532.

15. Cited in Pierre Chanel, "Cocteau-Desbordes," in Jean Cocteau, *Album Masques* (Paris: Masques, 1983), p. 28.

16. Ovid, *Metamorphoses*, trans. Rolfe Humphries (Bloomington: Indiana University Press, 1960), p. 236.

17. Jean Cocteau, "De la fête," *United States Lines* 5 (1960), Université Paul-Valéry, Montpellier, Cocteau Collection.

18. He would describe the painting of his friend Robert Delaunay as "Orphic," a description that Delaunay's wife, Sonia, like Kupka, echoed.

19. To this day Orpheus is sometimes credited with inventing the lyre or the zither, or with having built it with nine strings, in homage to the nine muses.

20. For the comte's comments, see *Les cahiers du comte Kessler, 1918–1937* (Paris: Grasset, 1972), pp. 204–205, June 15, 1926.

21. Mireille Havet died prematurely of drug abuse at a sanatorium in Montana, on March 21, 1932. Her diary has been partly published, in France, by Éditions Claire Paulhan.

22. Jean Cocteau, *Opium* (Paris: Éditions Stock, 1930), pp. 58–59.

23. Madeleine Milhaud, interview with the author, February 2, 1999.

24. Literally "Madame Eurydice will return from the Underworld"; the acrostic spells *merde* (shit). — Trans.

25. André Beucler, "Orphée, de Jean Cocteau," *NRF* (July 1, 1926): 112–116.

26. Cited in a letter from Jacques-Émile Blanche to François Mauriac, June 19, 1926, in François Mauriac and Jacques-Émile Blanche, *Correspondance (1916–1942)*, ed. Georges-Paul Collet (Paris: Grasset, 1976), p. 137.

27. Letter from November 1926, cited by Steegmuller, *Cocteau* (Buchet-Castel), p. 279.

28. Cited in Jean Cocteau to Max Jacob, March 1927, in Jacob and Cocteau, *Correspondance*, p. 513.

29. Cf. *Jean Cocteau et son temps*, catalog compiled by Pierre Georgel for the Jean Cocteau exhibit at the Jacquemart-André Museum, 1965, p. 95.

30. Rilke sent him this telegram after Max Reinhardt produced *Orpheus* for a one-night engagement in Berlin, Cocteau said in July 1926. Cf. Cocteau, *Opium*, p. 53—in which the quotation is almost exactly the same; Pierre Chanel, *Album Cocteau* (Paris: Veyrier-Tchou, 1970), p. 76, in which the telegram is reproduced, and Kihm, Sprigge, and Béhar, *Jean Cocteau*, p. 182, where it is cited in a paraphrase.

31. The Renaissance may have inspired learned poems and the seventeenth century many tragedies, but those that touch us most deeply are not about demi-gods, but real people: desperate queens, power-hungry men, abandoned children.

32. *Les feuilles libres* 25 (February 1922).

33. Bernard Faÿ, *Les précieux* (Paris: Perrin, 1966), p. 287.

34. English in the original.—Trans.

35. "To be released the day revolution breaks out in France," said the label on the master recording of "Adieux chers camarades." See the CD *Yvonne George, Kiki de Montparnasse, 1925–1940*, Succès et raretés, Chansophone, no. 114: "L'étoile de mer" (starfish) and "J'ai tant rêvé de toi que tu en perds ta réalité" (I've dreamed so much of you that you've become unreal).

36. Janet Flanner, *Paris Was Yesterday: 1925–1939* (New York: Harcourt Brace Jovanovich, 1988), p. 67.

37. Jean Cocteau to his mother, November 13, 1926, *LM*.

38. Jean Cocteau to Max Jacob, February 1927, in Jacob and Cocteau, *Correspondance*, p. 498.

39. Cocteau, *PD*, vol. 1, table 2, p. 56, and Jean Cocteau, *Journal (1942–1945)* (Paris: Gallimard, 1989), p. 143. Sir Francis Rose, in *Saying Life: The Memoirs of Sir Francis Rose* (London: Cassel, 1961), p. 112, tells the same story, but about a drawing of a wheel made of three human gyrating legs, like a Tibetan mandala.

40. Cited in Kihm, Sprigge, and Béhar, *Jean Cocteau*, p. 100.

41. Author's conversation with John Richardson. See also, J. Richardson, *A Life of Picasso: The Prodigy, 1881–1906*, vol. 1 (New York: Random House, 1991), p. 205.

42. Picasso hated it all the more since Gertrude Stein, who had done so much to promote his work, aesthetically and financially, had gotten it into her head to support Bérard and the other neo-humanist painters in order to make rivals of them. Then she became besotted with Francis Rose, who really wasn't worthy.

43. Jean Cocteau to his mother, August 1927, cited in Jean Touzot, *Jean Cocteau* (Lyon: La Manufacture, 1989), p. 97.

44. Jean Cocteau to his mother, October 29, 1926, *LM*.

45. Cf. Jean Cocteau, *Picasso* (Paris: L'école des lettres, 1996), "Témoignage," p. 91. Breton hoped in vain that Apollinaire would introduce him to Picasso; he always refused out of jealousy.

46. In doing so, he included Picasso's *Les demoiselles d'Avignon*. See *La révolution surréaliste* 4 (July 15, 1925).

47. Telegram from Jean Cocteau to Pablo Picasso, October 24, 1926, Musée Picasso.

48. Picabia's denial was reported by Gertrude Stein (n.p.).

49. Jean Cocteau to Pablo Picasso, October 25, 1926, Musée Picasso.

50. Maurice Sachs, *La décade de l'illusion* (1933; Paris: Gallimard, 1950), p. 233.

51. Gertrude Stein, *The Autobiography of Alice B. Toklas* (New York: Penguin, 1933), pp. 240–241.

52. Valentine Hugo had accused Cocteau of having totally invented this vision, but Georges Gabory, who knew Radiguet well, described him as an "elderly fifteen year-old" with a face like a "Greco-Buddhist child like something out of Gandhara." Marie-Christine Movilliat, *Raymond Radiguet ou la jeunesse contredite, 1903–1923* (Paris: Bibliophone Daniel Radford, 2000), p. 29.

53. Jean Cocteau to the Baronne d'Erlanger, "3 j. 1926" [month unknown], *Lettres de l'Oiseleur* (Monaco: Du Rocher, 1989), p. 105.

54. Jean Cocteau to Jean Hugo, November 1926, in *Lettres de l'Oiseleur*, p. 110.

55. Breton had published a novel called *L'Amour Fou* (1937), or *Mad Love.*—Trans.

56. Letter of August 25, 1930, Harry Ransom Humanities Research Center, University of Texas, Austin, cited in Marc Polizzotti, *André Breton* (Paris: Gallimard, 1997), p. 399.

57. These poets were Breton, Éluard, Tzara, Crevel, and Char.

58. Cocteau, too, would refer to his painting as a "sacred foreigner to faith."

59. Giorgio De Chirico, *Memoirs*, trans. Margaret Crosland (London: Da Capo Press, 1971), p. 119. "I am very grateful to Jean Cocteau for the interest he has shown in me, but I must say that I do not in fact approve of the kind of praise he accords me and the interpretation he likes to put on my pictures," De Chirico wrote. The painter explains Breton's hostility to his turning away from metaphysical painting by the number of canvases he (Breton) had acquired during his metaphysical period a few years earlier, and his desire to increase their value.

60. Laure Marie Charlotte de Sade, 1859–1936, the great-grand-daughter of the Marquis de Sade and wife of the count of Chevigné, would partly inspire the character of the Duchesse de Guermantes in Proust's *In Search of Lost Time.*—Trans.

61. Jean Cocteau to Max Jacob, late February–early March 1927, in Jacob and Cocteau, *Correspondance*, p. 503.

62. Geneviève Mater would give him another little monkey called Pompon in the summer of 1931.

63. Flanner, *Paris Was Yesterday*, p. 32. "Somewhat unpleasant flashing of breasts," Cocteau noted on the program he meant to send to his mother. A year later, to the very day, the dancer would be strangled to death by her own scarf, driving on the Corniche.

64. Igor Stravinsky, *Chroniques de ma vie* (Paris: Denoël, 1962), p. 192.

65. Jean Cocteau, *La difficulté d'être* (Monaco: Du Rocher, 1947).

66. Igor Stravinsky to Jean Cocteau, October 11, 1925, in Igor Stravinsky, *Selected Correspondence*, ed. Robert Craft (London: Faber, 1982), vol. 1, p. 94, a copy of which Pierre Chanel published in *Album Cocteau*, p. 74. See also Volta, *Satie/Cocteau*, p. 70, and also Cocteau, *PD*, vol. 1, p. 415.

67. In retrospect, we know he would become a cardinal, then a member of the Académie Française, and that he died under suspicious circumstances at the home of a Parisian prostitute. His brother Alain, who danced under the name Dunoeli, would become Maurice Sachs's lover a few years later.

68. On *Thomas l'imposteur* being a remedy for modernity, see dedication to Stravinsky, BHVP, box 44, reproduced in *CJC*, vol. 2 (Paris: Gallimard, 1971), pp. 95–96.

69. Stravinsky, *Chroniques de ma vie*, p. 195.

70. Cocteau himself did not know mythology well, and was not a serious reader of Aeschylus, if we are to believe François Sentein. Nevertheless, he had dictionaries of mythology in his personal library, and ranked Aeschylus sixth out of the 352 authors he would choose, when asked by Raymond Queneau in his inquiry, *Pour une bibliothèque idéale* (Paris: Gallimard, 1956).

71. Quoted in Flanner, *Paris Was Yesterday*, pp. 58–59. [Jocasta says, "Do not blush, O kings, to weep and cry out at the family squabbles in a plague-stricken city."—Trans.]

72. "Chronique musicale," *NRF*, August 1, 1927, pp. 244–248. [Maurras, as we know, was a writer and poet as well as the leader of Action Française, a Catholic, monarchist, right-wing group, as well as a notorious anti-Semite and Vichy collaborator.—Trans.]

73. "La présence," essay published in *Vogue* upon the death of Diaghilev, in September 1935. See *CJC*, vol. 10 (Paris: Gallimard, 1985), p. 110.

74. Cf. Jean Cocteau to Igor Stravinsky, April 2, 1927, in Stravinsky, *Selected Correspondence*, p. 106.

75. *Oedipus Rex* was then performed throughout Europe, as far as Leningrad. Einstein and Hofmannsthal attended one operatic performance conducted by Otto Klemperer in Berlin, in February 1928, at the Kroll Opera House. In 1948 Stravinsky would rescore his orchestrations in the United States.

76. Jean Cocteau to Igor Stravinsky, April 26, 1927, cited in Francis Steegmuller, *Cocteau* (Paris: Buchet-Chastel, 1973), p. 282.

77. Igor Stravinsky to Jean Cocteau, February 10, 1917, in Stravinsky, *Selected Correspondence*, p. 102.

78. Nicolas Nabokov, *Cosmopolite* (Paris: Robert Laffont, 1976), p. 254.

79. "It's the final bridge between *Les noces* and maniacal classicism," Cocteau would say in 1953; see *Past Tense: The Cocteau Diaries*, trans. Richard Howard (London: Hamish Hamilton, 1983).

80. They would never again collaborate, but the composer nevertheless thought of asking Cocteau to do the book for *Jeu de cartes* in 1936. See Stravinsky, *Selected Correspondence*, p. 114.

81. Jean Cocteau, *Le livre blanc* (Paris: Le Livre de Poche, 1999), p. 78.

82. Jean Cocteau to Max Jacob, February 1927, in Jacob and Cocteau, *Correspondance*, p. 493.

83. Jean Hugo, *Le regard de la mémoire* (Paris: Babel-Actes Sud, 1983), p. 294.

84. Francis Steegmuller, *Cocteau* (Boston: Little, Brown, 1970), p. 409.

85. Jean Cocteau to Bernard Faÿ, undated, cited in Kihm, Sprigge, and Béhar, *Jean Cocteau*, pp. 188–189.

86. Jean Cocteau to Maurice Sachs, undated (between November 8 and 14, 1924), with the header of the Hotel Beauvau in Marseilles, in *Cahier Jean Cocteau*, vol. 12, in *Correspondances avec Jean Cocteau* (Paris: Non Lieu Éditions, 2014), p. 58.

87. This is a pun on the name of the car, "la B14," and the name of an imaginary priest, "L'abbé Quatorze."

88. Jean Hugo to Jean Cocteau, October 14, 1919, in J. Cocteau, *Correspondance Jean Hugo* (Montpellier: Brigitte Borsaro and Pierre Caizergues, Centre d'études du XXe siècle, Université Paul-Valéry, 1995), p. 46.

89. Along with the illustrations for *Oedipus Rex*, these portraits were initially exhibited at the Galerie des Quatre-Chemins, in the rue Godot-de-Mauroy, and then published in Jean Cocteau, *25 Dessins d'un Dormeur* (Lausanne: Mermod, 1928). Some were reproduced in *Le sommeil ou quand la raison s'absente*, the catalog for a show at the Musée Cantonal des Beaux-Arts, Lausanne, October 1999–January 2000.

90. Hugo, *Le regard de la mémoire*, p. 330.

91. Jean Cocteau to his mother, 1931, cited in Pierre Chanel, *Album Cocteau* (Paris: Veyrier-Tchou, 1970), p. 92.

92. Paul Morand, *Méditerranée, mer des surprises* (1938; Monaco: Jean-Paul Bertrand, 1990), p. 74.

93. In spite of ample military surveillance, naval authorities feared the many sailors would in an intimate moment give away "secret strategies."

94. Cocteau's behavior was described by Boris Kochno, in his work on Christian Bérard, for whom No Luck subsequently worked as a servant. No Luck's real name was Marcel Servais; after being confused with a colleague during the mutiny of the *Ernest-Renan*, he was sent to the naval prison at Calvi, like Maxime in *La machine à écrire*, Cocteau's play.

95. *Le livre blanc* (New York: Macaulay Co., 1958), p. 75. Also available as *The White Book*, trans. Margaret Crosland (San Francisco: City Lights, 1989).

96. Jean Cocteau to Maurice Sachs, n.d., courtesy Nadia Saleh.

97. Cf. Paul Morand, *L'allure de Chanel* (Paris: Hermann, 1976).

98. Lucien Daudet sold her the recipe for six thousand francs. It was Georges Liébert who called her the "Midas from Auvergne."

99. Jean Cocteau to Max Jacob, May 1927, in Jacob and Cocteau, *Correspondance*, p. 534.

100. Maurice Martin du Gard, *Les mémorables*, new ed. (Paris: Gallimard, 1999), p. 604.

101. Testimony of Wesson Bull, cited by Steegmuller in *Cocteau* (Little, Brown), p. 389.

102. Jean Galtier-Boissière, *Mémoires d'un Parisien* (Paris: Quai Voltaire, 1994), p. 636.

103. Or "The friend, Zamor, of Madame du Barry," which doubles as "La mise à mort de Madame du Barry": the putting-to-death of Madame du Barry.

104. Or "G. touching G. without having the R. Saddle and burden of my very tranquil donkey," which doubles as "J'ai tout changé sans en avoir l'air. C'est l'effet de mon anarchie tranquille," or "I have changed everything without seeming to. This is the effect of my tranquil anarchy."

105. These word games are very difficult to translate. Timothy Adès has ventured: "What set your complexion withering, little girl, boarding where your eye came by another ring?" See Adès, *Papers of Surrealism* 9 (Summer 2011): 3; http://www.surrealismcen tre.ac.uk/papersofsurrealism/journal9/acrobat_files/Rrose%20Selavy%207.09.11.pdf (accessed November 14, 2015). Alternatively: Why is your blush so crushed, little girl,

is it rushing to work makes your eyes gush? (Desnos); Blood is the path of the past (Leiris); Plunge the marrow of the arrow into the curls of your girl. Plunge the marrow of the arrow into the liver of the lover (Duchamp).—Trans.

106. Jean Cocteau, "Le bon élève et l'apprenti," *En marge d'Opéra*, OPC, p. 562.

107. Jean Cocteau, "Procès de l'Oiseleur," *En marge d'Opéra*, OPC, p. 579.

108. Jean Cocteau, "Le paquet rouge," *En marge d'Opéra*, OPC, p. 540.

109. Jean Cocteau, "Joueurs dormant à l'Hombre," *En marge d'Opéra*, OPC, p. 519.

110. *Les feuilles libres*, December 1927–January 1928, cited in Marcel Schneider, *Les gardiens du secret* (Paris: Grasset, 2001), p. 128.

111. *NRF*, February 1, 1928.

112. The quoted line is a somewhat nonsensical play on "descendre monter que monter descendre," which literally means "I prefer to take down my tea than to rise up from the ashes."—Trans.

113. Jean Cocteau, "Testament," OPC, p. 583.

114. Jean Cocteau, "Oh! Là Là!," *Opéra*, OPC, p. 542.

115. Sachs was appointed editor by the Librairie des Quatre-Chemins, with his friend Raoul Leven.

116. Gide's work was published anonymously in 1911, with a print run of twelve copies, then in 1920, just as modestly. See *L'express*, September 30, 1983.

117. Jean Cocteau to Max Jacob, May 1927, in Jacob and Cocteau, *Correspondance*, p. 536.

118. Cocteau, *Le livre blanc*, p. 58.

119. Ibid., p. 79.

120. Ibid., p. 62.

121. Jean Bourgoint to Glenway Wescott, cited in Steegmuller, *Cocteau* (Buchet-Chastel), p. 285.

122. Maurice Sachs, *Au temps du Boeuf sur le Toit* (1939; Paris: Grasset, 1987), p. 84. [That is, his sympathetic nervous system.—Trans.]

123. Coco Chanel had started out as a dressmaker in 1912, at a time when women were wearing feathered hats.

124. Cocteau, *Journal (1942–1945)*, p. 22.

125. Michel Larivière, *À poil et à plume* (Paris: Régine Deforges, 1987), cited in Christin Gury, *Lyautey-Charlus* (Paris: Kimé, 1998), pp. 72–73.

126. Cf. "Cocteau/Sachs, Haro sur le baudet," Édouard Roditi, preface to the reprint of Cocteau's *Letter-plainte*, in Chanel, *Album Cocteau*, p. 87.

127. Letter from Jean Cocteau, May 1930. *Le livre blanc* was reprinted with the Éditions du Signe in 1930. It was reissued by the Éditions du Passage du Marais in 1992.

CHAPTER 15. THE SOUND OF THE FALL

1. Jean Cocteau to Jacques Maritain, February 9, 1928, in *CJC*, vol. 12 (Paris: Gallimard, 1993), p. 164.

2. René Crevel to André Gide, October 1927, in René Crevel, *Lettres de désir et de souffrances*, ed. Eric Le Bouvier (Paris: Fayard, 1996), p. 70.

3. Maurice Martin du Gard, *Les mémorables*, new ed. (Paris: Gallimard, 1999), p. 604.

4. Ibid., p. 606.

5. Jacques Maritain to Jean Cocteau, July 6, 1928, in *CJC* vol. 12, p. 180.

6. Jacques Maritain to Jean Cocteau, August 11, 1927, in *CJC*, vol. 12, pp. 153–154.

7. "Mind had become chapel," wrote Jean-Pierre Maxence, in *Histoire de dix ans, 1927–1937* (Paris: Gallimard, 1939), p. 61, on the subject of *Le roseau d'or* in 1928.

8. Jacques Maritain to Jean Cocteau, June 15, 1928, *CJC*, vol. 12, p. 169.

9. Jacques Maritain to Jean Cocteau, July 6, 1928, *CJC*, vol. 12, p. 149.

10. Julien Green, *Journal*, 19 vols. (Paris: Gallimard, 1938–2001), May 1, 1929.

11. Jean-Luc Barré, *Jacques et Raïssa Maritain, les mendiants du ciel* (Paris: Éditions Stock, 1995), p. 377.

12. He would eventually be won over, along with the critic Charles Du Bos and the philosopher Gabriel Marcel, by a second wave of conversions made possible by the Abbé Altermann. Cocteau would once again feel that he had paved the way.

13. Abbé Mugnier, *Journal (1879–1939)* (Paris: Mercure de France, 1985), p. 521, entry for January 22, 1930. [This is a pun on the word for forefinger ("l'index"), which is also slang for penis, but refers at the same time to the Index, the list of the books forbidden by the Church.—Trans.]

14. Ibid., p. 500, entry for July 6, 1928.

15. Jacques Maritain to Jean Cocteau, June 30, 1928, in *CJC*, vol. 12, p. 178.

16. Mugnier, *Journal*, January 16, 1929, p. 506.

17. Maurice Sachs, *La décade de l'illusion* (1933; Paris: Gallimard, 1950), p. 182.

18. Mugnier, *Journal*, July 16, 1928, p. 499.

19. Jean Cocteau, *Journal (1942–1945)* (Paris: Gallimard, 1989).

20. Jean Cocteau to Jacques Maritain, April 2, 1931, in *CJC*, vol. 12, p. 210.

21. Mugnier, *Journal*, p. 500, entry for August 6, 1928.

22. This drowned man would be called Jean Bourgoint, and would therefore be an almost perfect homonym for the *enfant terrible*, a detail that reveals a bit more his desire to enrich his personal mythology.

23. Bénédictine is an herbal liqueur.—Trans.

24. Roger Stéphane, *Portrait souvenir de Jean Cocteau* (Paris: Éditions Tallandier, 1964), p. 47.

25. Letter to Marcel and Élise Jouhandeau, May 1933, *Lettres de l'Oiseleur* (Monaco: Du Rocher, 1989), p. 157.

26. According to Henri Raczymow, *Maurice Sachs* (Paris: Gallimard, 1988), p. 169. This would be worth 24,000 euros today.

27. Jacques Maritain, "Réponse à Jean Cocteau," *CJC*, vol. 12, p. 310.

28. Quoted in Michel Sanouillet, *Dada à Paris* (Paris: Flammarion, 1993), p. 531.

29. Prévert was arrested, as well as Breton, and then very quickly released. See Yves Courrière, *Jacques Prévert* (Paris: Gallimard, 2000), p. 136.

30. As Jean Cocteau would put it in his *Letter to Jacques Maritain*, April 2, 1931, in *CJC*, vol. 12, p. 212.

31. The next day, Dukelsky rang the bell at the rue d'Anjou, accompanied by two officers

from Wrangel's army, and returned the slap. He subsequently became famous in the United States under the name Vernon Duke, and composed the music for *April in Paris.*

32. Cf. Cocteau, *PD*, vol. 2, pp. 70–71; *Boris Kochno, Diaghilev et les Ballets Russes* (Paris: Fayard, 1973), p. 261, and Richard Buckle, *Diaghilev* (New York: Atheneum, 1979), pp. 577–579.

33. Letter from early 1926, in *Lettres de l'Oiseleur*, p. 151.

34. The heading for this section, "Tout déborde" (everything goes wrong), is a pun on Desbordes' name.—Trans.

35. Cited in "La vie et l'œuvre de Jean Desbordes," program hosted by Pierre Chanel, Radio-Lorraine-Champagne, August 3, 1959.

36. Jean Cocteau, *Le livre blanc* (New York: Macaulay Co., 1958), pp. 75, 89.

37. She had been married to a law clerk from Bordeaux who had been a witness at Jean Hugo's wedding.

38. Jean Cocteau to Jean Paulhan, May 1928, IMEC, fonds Paulhan.

39. *Le crapouillot*, June 1928.

40. Yves Courrière, *Joseph Kessel; ou, Sur la piste du lion* (Paris: Plon, 1985), p. 320.

41. Jean Cocteau to Pierre Duflos, December 3, 1928, in Cocteau, *Simple est un miracle*, ed. Arnaud Seydoux (Paris: N.p., 1993).

42. [Or, in French, "*la Sainte Vierge.*"—Trans.] Jean Hugo, *Le regard de la mémoire* (Paris: Babel-Actes Sud, 1983), p. 324.

43. Georges Lauris, *Itinéraire d'un enfant terrible, de Cocteau à Cîteaux* (Paris: Presses de la Renaissance, 1998), p. 38.

44. Jean Cocteau to his mother, November 5, 1928, *LM*.

45. Jean Cocteau to Anna de Noailles, December 8, 1928, *CJC*, vol. 11 (Paris: Gallimard, 1989), p. 143.

46. Maurice Sachs, *Au temps du Boeuf sur le Toit* (1939; Paris: Grasset, 1987), p. 171.

47. Jean Cocteau, *Opium* (Paris: Éditions Stock, 1930), pp. 190–202. Cf. as well his praise on the publication of *Nouvelles impressions d'Afrique*, in *NRF* (September 1, 1933): 464–465.

48. Stéphane, *Portrait souvenir*, pp. 18–19. Cf. as well *Jean Cocteau par Jean Cocteau*, interviews with William Fifield (Paris: Éditions Stock, 1973), p. 91.

49. Cocteau had contributed to this engagement by praising them to each other.

50. Sachs, *La décade de l'illusion*, p. 80.

51. Cocteau, *Opium*, p. 65.

52. Jean Cocteau to Andreas Walser, undated (late April 1929), in *Andreas Walser* (*Chur 1908–1930 Paris*) (Basel: Stroemfeld/Roter Stern, 1994), p. 41.

53. Castor, *Cahier des Saisons*, no. 33, cited in Kihm, Sprigge, and Béhar, *Jean Cocteau*, p. 200. Pierre Herbart was introduced to the group by the manager of the Quatre-Chemins bookshop, Raoul Leven.

54. Philippe Julian, *La Brocante* (Paris: Julliard, 1975), p. 34. Her name was Blanche Fort.

55. Christabel Thomassin-Levanti, interview with the author, January 17, 2000.

56. Maurice Sachs, *Le Sabbat: Souvenirs d'une jeunesse orageuse* (1946; Paris: Gallimard, 1979), p. 90.

57. Ibid., p. 89.

58. Lilianne de Rothschild, conversation with the author, November 1999. Cocteau was referring to Étienne de Beaumont.

59. "La vie et l'oeuvre de Jean Desbordes," program for Radio-Lorraine-Champagne, August 3, 1959.

60. Christabel Thomassin-Levanti interview.

61. Pierre Herbart, *Textes retrouvés* (Paris: Gallimard, 1999), p. 46.

62. Jean Cocteau to Andreas Walser, undated (Summer 1929), *Andreas Walser (Chur 1908–1930 Paris)*, p. 49.

63. *Les cahiers de la Petite Dame*, May 1923, in *Cahiers André Gide*, vol. 4 (Paris: Gallimard, 1973), p. 155.

64. Ibid., p. 156.

65. Pierre Herbart, "Letter to Jean Cocteau," 1929, in *Textes retrouvés*, pp. 110–111. [The Massif Central is a mountainous region in south-central France, and, here, a symbol of the heart.—Trans.]

66. André Gide, *Journal*, vol. 2: *1926–1950* (Paris: Gallimard, 1997), p. 243, entry for January 15, 1931.

67. Ibid., p. 242.

68. Élisabeth Van Rysselberghe had already been Marc Allégret's mistress and had even believed in 1920 that she was carrying his child.

69. André Gide to Jean Cocteau, December 26, 1931, in Jean Cocteau, *Lettres à André Gide avec quelques réponses d'André Gide*, ed. Jean-Jacques Kihm (Paris: La Table Ronde, 1970), p. 168.

70. Charlotte Aillaud, interview with the author, January 16, 1999.

71. Little Jean Herbart died when he was three days old.

72. Robert Poulet in *Nord* 3 (1930). The phrase beginning "poignant, light" is Raïssa Maritain's.

73. Albert Thibaudet, *NRF* (September 1929).

74. Flanner, *Paris Was Yesterday*, p. 61.

75. Marie Delle Donne continued to sleep in the room adjoining her brother's, in the family hotel, long after she had married a man she had met while visiting Maurice Sachs in the seminary. Elisabeth, in *The Holy Terrors*, had a habit of sleeping with a clothespin on her nose and raw cutlets on her cheeks, to make her nostrils thinner and her complexion more rosy. Cf. Raczymow, *Maurice Sachs*, p. 81, and Denise Tual, interview with the author, November 19, 1999.

76. For "lovesick larvae" see Jean Cocteau, *Portraits-souvenir*, in *Oeuvres complètes*, vol. 11 (Lausanne: Éditions Marguerat, 1951).

77. "De la lecture," in Jean Cocteau, *La difficulté d'être* (Monaco: Éditions du Rocher, 1947).

78. For years, adolescents would shut themselves up with this book, incubating its miasma, until they became the young lords of that enclosed space that Cocteau had filled with his fetishes.

79. Abbé Mugnier, *Journal*, p. 513, entry for January 22, 1930.

80. In spite of the scandal, this adaptation flopped, if we are to believe Klaus Mann, *Le tournant, histoire d'une vie*, trans. Nicole et Henri Roche (Paris: Seuil, 1986). Thomas

Mann's two children had, in 1925, acted in *Anja et Esther,* a play inspired by their own adolescence, directed by Gustaf Gründgens, Erika's homosexual husband. "They were 'a child prodigy, funny and impressive, with two heads, four legs, and a brain full of European whims and unusual knowledge," wrote Linda Lê, without providing the reference for her citation, in the preface to Klaus Mann's *La danse pieuse* (Paris: Le Livre de Poche, 1995), p. 2.

81. Cocteau, *PD*, vol. 1, p. 358.

82. Paul Morand, *Ma légende* (1929), reprinted in *Papiers d'identité* (Paris: Grasset, 1931), p. 12.

83. Sachs, *Au temps du Boeuf sur le Toit,* p. 198.

84. Marcel Jouhandeau, *Souffrir et être méprisé, journaliers,* vol. 23 (Paris: Gallimard, 1976), p. 89.

85. Crevel was also friends with Marc Allégret.

86. See *Les nouvelles littéraires,* June 7, 1924, regarding Cocteau's adaptation of *Romeo and Juliet,* for which Cocteau was classified as one of the "rare writers who understand the way the stage works."

87. Jean Schlumberger, *Notes sur la vie littéraire, 1902–1908* (Paris: Gallimard, 1999), p. 152, entry for October 28, 1927.

88. Mann, *Le tournant.*

89. Letter to Marcel Jouhandeau, April 1928, in Crevel, *Lettres de désir et de souffrances.*

90. This is a play on "Comte d'Artois": he says he's gone to the roof to make a "compte d'ardoise."—Trans.

91. If we believe Pierre Bergé in *Les jours s'en vont, je demeure* (Paris: Gallimard, 2003), p. 56.

92. Jean Cocteau to his mother, January 30, 1918, *LM.*

93. Steegmuller, *Cocteau* (Buchet-Chastel), p. 152.

94. Cocteau, *PD*, vol. 1, p. 290, and vol. 2, p. 279.

95. Cocteau, *Journal (1942–1945),* p. 236, entry for January 13, 1943.

96. Hugo, *Le regard de la mémoire,* p. 302.

97. "Portraits chinois" is a game in which someone pretends to be a famous person and the other players have to "guess who" by asking a series of questions.—Trans.

98. Green, *Journal,* January 8, 1947.

99. "It is possible (I didn't know *Faisons un rêve*) that he used the telephone before I did," Cocteau said of Guitry. "But innovation doesn't count as much in art as the way it is sculpted. Even if I had known *Faisons un rêve,* I would have written my play . . . Everything has already been done" (*PD*, vol. 2, pp. 237–238). Maman Colibri's monologues had greatly contributed to the play's success, as Leon Blum's very complimentary account attests: "during those great dramatic moments, when Colibri's son discovers his mother's secret, or when she resigns herself to having to leave her young lover who doesn't care for her enough, it is a fresh sort of poetic litany, broken and sobbing, composed of terse statements, barely juxtaposed, but endowed with sufficient art that they suddenly take on an evocative, incantatory power, like music, or verse." Léon Blum, "Critique dramatique," November 1904, in *L'oeuvre de Léon Blum,* vol. 1 (Paris: Albin Michel, 1962), pp. 215–216.

100. Bernard Faÿ, *Les précieux* (Paris: Perrin, 1966), p. 283.
101. Quoted in Steegmuller, *Cocteau* (Buchet-Chastel), p. 294.
102. Martin du Gard, *Les mémorables*, p. 720.
103. That is, "Shit, shit, shit."—Trans.
104. S. M. Eisenstein, *Mémoires*, preface by Jacques Aumont, Bernard Eisenschitz, and Barthélemy Amengual (Paris: Julliard, 1989), p. 267.
105. Hugo, *Le regard de la mémoire*, p. 328.
106. Cocteau thought he remembered that the intervention concerned raising the ban on Eisenstein's film *Old and New*. In his *Mémoires* (pp. 261–271), the director only mentions that he was threatened with deportation, during an anti-Soviet campaign in the press, and that Cocteau spoke to Berthelot and Chiappe, the prefect of police with links to the extreme Right, who considered Brancusi to be a pornographer, but who had protected him from drug charges. Receiving Eisenstein in his home, Cocteau begged him to "excuse France" for its vulgarity, and for the offense it had caused him, and then he promised to intervene as well in favor of Mary Marquet, the prime minister's mistress, who was acting in Merimée's *Le carrosse du Saint-Sacrement*, at the Théâtre Français, which was playing alternately with *The Human Voice*. *Old and New* was a banned Soviet film that accompanied the lecture Eisenstein would give at the Sorbonne on February 17, which had been banned.
107. Ibid., p. 268. "We ought to make a movie together in Marseille," Cocteau wrote later. "We will never manage to make the dates work." See Jean Cocteau, *Du cinématographe* (Paris: Belfond, 1973), p. 62.
108. According to François Sentein, Pierre de Lacretelle knew several by heart.
109. *CJC*, vol. 11, p. 147.
110. Jean Cocteau to Valentine Hugo, February 20, 1930, cited in Steegmuller, *Cocteau* (Buchet-Chastel), p. 295.
111. It was Bernard Minoret who identified him for Marc Polizzotti, one of Breton's biographers.
112. Cocteau, *PD*, vol. 1, p. 292.
113. One equally insulting pamphlet had already been published under this title: Breton, Aragon, and Éluard published it upon the death of Anatole France, in 1924.
114. The apostles included Desnos, Vitrac, Queneau, Prévert, Baron, Leiris, and Ribemont-Dessaignes.
115. Breton had decreed that Desnos was spending too much time with Yvonne George, to the detriment of their movement, and Aragon accused him of verbal incontinence to such a point that he had plagiarized Cocteau. When he came across a photograph of Breton, Desnos rarely missed a chance to stab it with a knife. Breton would revenge himself by accusing him later that year, in the *Second Surrealist Manifesto* (1930), of lowering himself to the level of journalism, of having recited alexandrines on a trip to Cuba, and of having participated in naming a nightclub in Montparnasse "Maldoror," in homage to Lautréamont—instances of Cocteau-esque sacrilege.
116. *La critique sociale* 7 (January 1933). The phrase "groper, sacristan, in short: cop and priest" was coined by Ribemont-Dessaignes.

117. Eisenstein, to whom Breton was often cold, and who preferred the authors of *A Cadaver*, had thus invited Éluard, who had warned him he might make a scene.

118. BHVP, box 6.

119. Titled *Amore*, the film was made in 1947.

120. See the interview with Almodóvar (whose *Women on the Verge of a Nervous Breakdown* was directly inspired by *The Human Voice*) in *Les cahiers du cinéma* 535 (May 1999).

121. Pietro Citati, *La colombe poignardée* (Paris: Gallimard, 1997), p. 19.

122. Jean Cocteau to his mother, August 20, 1929, *LM*.

123. The tribute he published in the *NRF* in May 1931 particularly celebrated the passages he had rewritten.

CHAPTER 16. THE TRAGIC YEARS

1. "Entre chien et loup" (between dog and wolf) is the French idiomatic expression for "twilight."—Trans.

2. A "calisson d'Aix" is a lozenge-shaped sweet made of iced marzipan.—Trans.

3. Cited by Jean Genet in *Our Lady of the Flowers*, trans. Bernard Frechtman (New York: Grove Press, 1994), p. 131. Frechtman notes: "These are not Pope's exact words, but a translation of the author's misquotation, from memory, of a French version."

4. The critics in question were André Rouveyre and André Rousseaux; see Jean-Jacques Kihm, Elizabeth Sprigge, and Henri C. Béhar, *Jean Cocteau, l'homme et les miroirs* (Paris: La Table Ronde, 1968), p. 202.

5. "La nouvelle musique en France," *La revue de Genève* 21 (March 1922): 397–398, cited in Jean Cocteau, *Lettres à André Gide avec quelques réponses d'André Gide*, ed. Jean-Jacques Kihm (Paris: La Table Ronde, 1970), p. 115.

6. Pirandello's novel was published in Italy in 1926, and first published in English translation in 1992.

7. Jean Cocteau, *Arts*, June 19, 1957, cited in Jean Cocteau, *Correspondance Jean Hugo* (Montpellier: Brigitte Borsaro and Pierre Caizergues, Centre d'études du XXe siècle, Université Paul-Valéry, 1995), p. 174.

8. Pierre Reverdy, *Le voleur de Talan* (Paris: Flammarion, 1967), p. 171.

9. "Opium teaches only one thing," Malraux wrote in *The Human Condition*, "and that is, outside of physical suffering, there is no reality."

10. Reverdy, *Le voleur de Talan*, p. 171.

11. *Le voyageur et son ombre*, § 122.

12. "Faiblesse," in *La lampe d'Aladin*, *OPC*, p. 1315.

13. Abbé Mugnier, *Journal (1879–1939)* (Paris: Mercure de France, 1985), entry for January 12, 1914.

14. Interview by Jean Wiener with Frederick Brown, author of *An Impersonation of Angels* (New York: Viking, 1968), p. 287.

15. Introduction to *Le sang d'un poète*, BHVP, box 25.

16. Jean Cocteau, *Du cinématographe* (Paris: Belfond, 1973), p. 151.

17. André Beucler, *Cahiers du mois*, cited by Alain Virmaux and Odette Virmaux, *Les surréalistes et le cinéma* (Paris: Seghers, 1976), p. 20.

18. In *Nadja*, published two years before filming and which Cocteau said he enjoyed, Breton describes the old auditorium of the Folies-Dramatiques, as Milorad notes, in "Le sang d'un poète, film à la troisième personne du singulier," *CJC*, vol. 9 (Paris: Gallimard, 1981), p. 295.

19. *Oeuvres complètes*, vol. 2 (Lausanne: Éditions Marguerat, 1947), p. 121.

20. Marcel Pagnol would not begin until 1933, and Sacha Guitry in 1935—*Ceux de chez nous*, filmed in 1914, was only a silent documentary.

21. Apollinaire believed this.

22. They also approached Jacques Manuel, one of Marcel L'Herbier's assistants, who would produce the deceptively named film *Biceps and Jewels*.

23. Enrique Rivero(s) appeared in many Swedish and French films of the time, including Gustaf Edgren's *The Ghost Baron* (1927), and Jean Renoir's *Le tournoi dans la cité* (1928) and *Le bled* (1929).

24. Cocteau had been very impressed by Jean Painlevé's documentaries on marine life, which Maurice Bardèche and Robert Brasillach mention in their *Histoire du cinéma*, vol. 1: *Le cinéma muet* (Paris: Le Livre de Poche, 1964), p. 305.

25. Cocteau sent a pneumatic message to twelve different cameramen; Périnal was the first to reply.

26. Klaus Mann, *The Turning Point* (Princeton, NJ: Markus Wiener, 1984), p. 296.

27. At least it was this way during the screening that Julien Green attended. See undated article by Prampolini, BHVP, box 25. [A well-known song from the French operetta *Les Cloches de Corneville*, by Robert Planquette. The lyrics translated into English are "Go bit of sea-foam, wherever the wind may push you, wherever the waves carry you."—Trans.]

28. Ibid.

29. One year earlier, Buñuel filled his pockets with stones at the first public screening of *Le chien andalou*: Breton became hysterical at the label "Surrealist" being applied to a film by an unknown. He later gave it his blessing.

30. Or "age of garbage," a play on "Age d'or."—Trans.

31. "Cocteau didn't want to come because he was unhappy with several details and this made him suffer like a martyr," wrote Julien Green in his journal entry for November 17, 1930. Apparently "they had to restrain the poet from jumping out the window." See Julien Green, *Journal*, 19 vols. (Paris: Gallimard, 1938–2001).

32. See "Uccello, le poil," an article dedicated to Artaud's lover, Génica Athanasiou in *La révolution surréaliste* 8 (December 1, 1926).

33. Jean Cocteau, "Secrets de beauté," in *Oeuvres complètes*, vol. 10 (Lausanne: Éditions Marguerat, 1950), p. 359.

34. "Three hundred young girls in a Catholic psychoanalytic center see a phallic symbol . . . instead of a smokestack," Cocteau remarked drolly in his *Entretiens autour du cinématographe*. Let us note that certain critics found in *Le sang d'un poète* an allegory for the Passion of Christ, or at least recognized his last attempt at sketching out a personal religion.

35. A trip to Rome with his mother, the princess of Poix, seems to have prevented Charles de Noailles's excommunication.

36. Though he did go to Hyères to show his support, Cocteau also believed that the Viscount could have fought a little harder. Buñuel would refer to him as a patron with an exemplary sense of tact.

37. When the film was first shown at Billancourt Studios, Green noted that it included "very beautiful scenes including one which was furiously erotic."

38. Robert de Saint-Jean, *Journal d'un journaliste* (Paris: Grasset, 1974), p. 79. For the quotation, see Green, *Journal*, January 20, 1932.

39. A year earlier, Breton had in vain tried to adapt one of Barbey d'Aurevilly's *Diaboliques*; none of Desnos's full-length scripts would be filmed.

40. "Mobiles," a precursor to Duchamp's "rotoreliefs," attempted to go beyond the two sexes, as well as beyond all time and meaning.

41. Cocteau filmed from April 15 to mid-September 1930. Buñuel showed his film in July of that year.

42. Green, *Journal*, July 9, 1930.

43. In Jean Hugo's *Cahiers* (1917–1933), July 10, 1929, published in *Jean Hugo, peintre-poète*, ed. Pierre Caizergues (Montpellier: Paul-Valéry, 1996), p. 115. Cf. *Lettre aux Américains, Entretien avec André Fraigneau* and *Entretiens autour du cinématographe*.

44. The other "masterpieces" are Buster Keaton's *Sherlock Holmes Junior*, Charlie Chaplin's *Gold Rush*, and *Battleship Potemkin* by Sergei Eisenstein (Jean Cocteau, *Opium* (Paris: Éditions Stock, 1930), p. 206. Also in *Opium*, pp. 207–208, Cocteau praises *L'âge d'or*, in a 1930 note, for being the "first masterpiece of the anti-plastic."

45. To say nothing of the steer that appears at the end of *Le sang d'un poète*. But Cocteau's film may equally have influenced the structure of Dreyer's *Vampyr*, which came out in 1932. The vampire (Nicolas de Guinzburg), moving through a haunted house, finds in each room a new, fantastic scene; the house becomes a metaphor for the unconscious and for dreams.

46. Buñuel, however, would never recognize the formal debt he owed to Artaud (*La coquille et le clergyman*), who would complain of this for a long time. It must be repeated that Artaud had also become persona non grata in Breton's group. See Luis Buñuel, *Entretien avec Max Aub* (Paris: Belfond, 1991).

47. Jacques B. Brunius, *En marge du cinéma français, L'âge d'homme*, 1987, p. 348, cited in Virmaux and Virmaux, *Les surréalistes*, p. 36.

48. "Recherches sur la sexualité," meeting of January 27, 1928; see *La révolution surréaliste* 11.

49. Four years earlier, the very same Pierre Unik had physically assaulted Antonin Artaud for having directed Strindberg's *The Dream* — in Breton's view, the theater, like English cigarettes, was off-limits.

50. Cocteau mentions this article several times: in *Entretiens avec André Fraigneau, Du cinématographe, Entretiens autour du cinématographe*, and *Journal d'un inconnu*.

51. Thanks go to Martine Bacherich and J.-B. Pontalis, who did not believe Freud was at all interested in cinema, and tried to find this text for me, in the English and German editions.

52. "I am in no state to clarify what it is that Surrealism wants to be," wrote Freud to Breton, in December 1932. "Perhaps I am not made to understand it, since I am at such a distance from art" (cited in *Les vases communicants* [Paris: Gallimard, 1955], p. 176). Only Dalí earned a warm welcome from Freud, who wrote to Stefan Zweig the next day, "Until now, I was willing to consider the Surrealists, who have apparently chosen me as their patron saint, as complete fools" (cited in *Comment on devient Dalí*, ed. André Parinaud (Paris: Robert Laffont, 1973), p. 148.

53. Man-Ray would have a spat with Breton concerning the photographs he took during the filming of *Le sang d'un poète* and his mistress's participation in the film. Lee Miller, whom he tried to dissuade from working with Cocteau, would leave him. Man-Ray would distance himself from Cocteau, though he had been the means by which he met the Surrealists.

54. Cf. Jean-Louis Gaillemin, *Dalí* (Paris: Éditions Le Passage, 2002).

55. Welcomed with great fanfare at the avant-garde film festival in Los Angeles, in 1943, *Le sang d'un poète* was shown exclusively in a small art-house cinema in New York, the Fifth Avenue Play House, for seventeen years.

56. Interviews with Philippe Soupault by J.-M. Mabire, in *Études cinématographiques* 38–39 (1965): 31.

57. Breton would pick on Soupault's agitation, comparing him to "a rat in the ratodrome" [a place designated for fights between dogs and rats—Trans.] in André Breton, *Second manifeste du surréalisme*, 1930, in *Manifestes du surréalisme* (Paris: Gallimard, 1966), p. 88.

58. The apartment had once been occupied by Pierre Reverdy.

59. "And yet Breton owned a gramophone," observed Alejo Carpentier, who knew something about music. "It allowed him to express his total loathing for music. He would only play the following records: 'How to care for a Lebel rifle,' by a French army captain; 'Les p'tits pois,' by Dranem; a sermon on love, by the Reverend Father Samson, and stupid songs by Georges Milton." See Alejo Carpentier, *Essais littéraires*, trans. Serge Mestre (Paris: Gallimard, 2003), p. 195.

60. Valentine Hugo to Georges Hugnet, September 3, 1958, in *De Valentine Gross à Valentine Hugo, Boulogne-sur-Mer (1887–1968)*, ed. Béatrice Seguin, published by the Town of Boulogne-sur-Mer, 2000, p. 97.

61. Jean Cocteau to Max Jacob, December 28, 1921, in *Max Jacob and Jean Cocteau, Correspondance, 1917–1944*, ed. Anne Kimball (Paris: Paris-Méditerranée/Écrits des Hautes-Terres, 2000), p. 72.

62. Cf. Green, *Journal*, May 25, 1929.

63. Jean Cocteau to his mother, January 28, 1927, and an undated letter, *LM*.

64. Jean Cocteau to his mother, October 28, 1928, *LM*.

65. Cf. Green, *Journal*, May 11, 1931.

66. Jean Cocteau, *Démarche d'un poète* (Paris: Grasset, 2013), p. 43. See also "*La belle et la bête*," *journal d'un film* (Paris: Jean-Paul Bertrand, 1989). Cocteau greatly admired *The Magic Mountain*, according to Pierre Chanel, and had probably known the author through his son, Klaus Mann.

67. *Journal de Raïssa Maritain* (Paris: Desclée de Brouwer, 1963), p. 198, entry for December 15, 1931.

68. Cocteau, *Le livre blanc*, p. 80.

69. Ibid., p. 258.

70. "He is the only one who takes risks in every genre and tries to bring all the arts together," Drieu added. See *NRF*, November 1, 1923.

71. Stefan Zweig, *Trois poètes de leur vie* (Paris: Belfond, 1983), p. xv.

72. Each play is listed by year of conception.

73. Probably this was at a party on January 20, 1932, when Cocteau showed the film at the Théâtre du Vieux-Colombier: Julien Green noted in his journal that the princess was in attendance.

74. Natalie Paley had already met Cocteau at a ball at the home of the Pecci-Blunts, at which Man-Ray had shown an old film by Méliès on a mobile "screen" of dancers dressed in white.

75. Nemo is in the wonderful drawings of Winsor McCay.

76. Francis Steegmuller, *Cocteau* (Paris: Buchet-Chastel, 1973), p. 308.

77. Serge Lifar, *Les mémoires d'Icare* (Paris: Filipacchi, 1989), p. 59.

78. Maryse Goldsmith-Dansaert, cited by Jean-Noël Liaut, *Une princesse déchirée* (Paris: Filipacchi, 1996), p. 142.

79. Jean Cocteau, *Journal (1942–1945)* (Paris: Gallimard, 1989), p. 177.

80. Interview with Natalie Paley at Cinémonde, August 17, 1933, cited in Liaut, *Une princesse déchirée*, p. 75.

81. Jean-Louis de Faucigny-Lucinge, *Un gentilhomme cosmopolite* (Paris: Perrin, 1990), p. 139.

82. *Vogue Paris*, August 1930, p. 53.

83. Paul Morand, *Journal d'un attaché d'ambassade* (Paris: Gallimard, 1963), p. 57.

84. "What a waste of cum and time," noted Morand after three unconsummated months of courtship, in his journal, dated July 2, 1931; see Morand, *Journal inutile*, vol. 1: *1968–1972* (Paris: Gallimard, 2001), pp. 561–571. Saint-Exupéry would also try his luck in 1942.

85. Jean-Pierre Grédy, interview with the author, January 1999.

86. Maryse Goldsmith-Dansaert, cited by Liaut, *Une princesse déchirée*, p. 127.

87. Cocteau, *Opium*, pp. 136–137.

88. Maurice Abravanel was the conductor to whom Cocteau confessed he needed Weill's music to make love to a woman. Cf. Pascal Huynh, *Kurt Weill ou la conquête des masses* (Paris: Actes Sud, 2000).

89. "We have returned from death's door to learn that Jean Cocteau loves a lady," Mauriac would say. See de Saint-Jean, *Journal d'un journaliste*, p. 93.

90. Faucigny-Lucinge, *Un gentilhomme cosmopolite*, p. 136.

91. Cf. the book for *Le Dieu bleu*, available at Bibliothèque de l'Institut National d'Histoire de l'Art, Jacques Doucet collections, Paris.

92. Jean Desbordes to Jean Cocteau, undated (late March 1932), shared by Pierre Chanel; Desbordes played the role of "camarade Louis XV."

93. "L'égoïste," in the margins of *Poèmes écrits en allemand*, *OPC*, p. 610.

94. Jean Desbordes to Jean Cocteau from Toulon, dated April 3, 1932. Kindly shared by Pierre Chanel.

95. Jean Cocteau to Natalie Paley, June 1932, cited by Liaut, *Une princesse déchirée*, p. 146; *Catalogue Drouot*, sale of December 4, 1991.

96. Jean Cocteau to Richard Thom, June 1932, cited by Steegmuller, *Cocteau* (Buchet-Chastel), p. 309.

97. Telegram from Natalie Paley to Jean Cocteau, July 16, 1932, BHVP.

98. Natalie Paley to Jean Cocteau, August 18, 1932, BHVP. With thanks to Laurence Benaïm, who sent me a transcription of these letters.

99. Natalie Paley to Jean Cocteau, undated, on Hôtel Excelsior notepaper, BHVP.

100. Natalie Paley to Jean Cocteau, August 27, 1932, on Suvretta House notepaper, Saint-Mortiz, BHVP.

101. Natalie Paley to Jean Cocteau, September 2, 1932, BHVP.

102. Paley to Cocteau, August 27, 1932.

103. Paley to Cocteau, September 2, 1932.

104. This was written in a letter that Cocteau said he later burned—which was not at all like him.

105. As we have seen, the family connections went very far back. Marie Laure's grandmother, Laure de Chevigné, had been the Parisian contact of the Grand Duchess Vladimir, Natalie's aunt by marriage, who agreed to become Marie Laure's godmother in 1902.

106. Her father was the banker Maurice Bischoffsheim. Originally from Amsterdam, the family had established itself in Paris around 1850. From him Marie Laure had inherited parts of the Brussels tramways and the New York dockyards.

107. Jean Cocteau to Giorgio Ottone, dated August 1932, private collection of Jacques Polgès.

108. Natalie Paley to Jean Cocteau, September 1932, BHVP. To top it all off, Marie Laure had become infatuated with Giorgio Ottone, the young Italian man who accompanied her, and who treated her cruelly.

109. Cited by Laurence Benaïm, *Marie Laure de Noailles* (Paris: Grasset, 2001), p. 257.

110. Marie Laure to Jean Cocteau, September 30, 1932, BHVP.

111. Ibid.

112. Natalie Paley to Jean Cocteau, October 3, 1932, BHVP.

113. Jean Cocteau, *La fin du Potomak*, in *Oeuvres complètes*, vol. 2 (Lausanne: Éditions Marguerat, 1947), p. 186.

114. Natalie Paley to Jean Cocteau, undated, on Excelsior Roma notepaper, BHVP.

115. We learn this from a confession Cocteau made two years later, when he suggested that his only crime toward Marie Laure had been "to love another and to refuse the offer made him to betray her." Jean Cocteau to Denise Bourdet, September 1934, *Lettres de l'Oiseleur* (Monaco: Du Rocher, 1989), p. 174.

116. "She . . . drew on the doors of her riddles with lipstick, and tied her gloves to the candelabras," he would say about the Viscountess Medusa in *La fin du Potomak*.

117. Cocteau, *Journal (1942–1945)*, p. 236, entry for January 13, 1943.

118. Jean Cocteau to Natalie Paley taken from the Drouot auction catalog, December 4, 1991, cited by Liaut, *Une princesse déchirée*, p. 155.

119. Mme de Ravenel, daughter of Jean-Louis de Faucigny-Lucinge, interview with the author, April 29, 1998.

120. Yvon Belaval remembered seeing Roland Toutain, in a restaurant in Nice, take out his penis and wrap it around his glass. "La rencontre avec Jean Cocteau," in *CJC*, vol. 3 (Paris: Gallimard, 1972), p. 93.

121. Cited in Steegmuller, *Cocteau* (Buchet-Chastel), p. 24.

122. "Barbe" is a nickname for Bérard.

123. Cited in Steegmuller, *Cocteau* (Buchet-Chastel), p. 309.

124. On the dedication of "Looking for Apollo," see *Allégories*, *OPC*, p. 617. For the dedication of "Der Egoist," see the margins of *Poèmes écrits en allemand*, *OPC*, p. 610.

125. Natalie Paley was citing Pushkin (Lifar, *Les mémoires d'Icare*, pp. 68–69).

126. Jean Cocteau to Louise de Vilmorin, November 21, 1934, in *Lettres de l'Oiseleur*, p. 217.

127. Lelong had a child from his first marriage.

128. The film *L'épervier* was adapted from a play by Francis de Croisset, Marie Laure's stepfather.

129. The same year she would also film Roy del Ruth's *Folies Bergère*, with Maurice Chevalier, and in 1936 *Les hommes nouveaux* by Marcel L'Herbier, her cousin by marriage, which starred Harry Baur, and in which Jean Marais appeared as an extra.

130. He was referring, of course, to Madeleine Carlier and Natalie Paley. From the unpublished journal of Roger Lannes, July 19, 1937, IMEC.

131. Igor Markevitch, *Être et avoir été, Mémoires* (Paris: Gallimard, 1980), p. 302.

132. Cf. de Saint-Jean, *Journal d'un journaliste*, p. 106.

133. Jean Cocteau, "Le menteur," *Théâtre*, vol. 2 (Paris: Gallimard, 1948), p. 573.

134. Jean Desbordes to Jean Cocteau, undated (March 1932?), on Hôtel des Négociants notepaper, Toulon, shared by Pierre Chanel.

135. Christabel Thomassin-Levanti interview.

136. Joseph Kessel, *Des hommes* (Paris: Gallimard, 1972), p. 17. The recorded poem was "Les voleurs d'enfants."

137. Speech given at the Académie royale de Belgique, in *La comtesse de Noailles oui et non* (Paris: Librairie académique Perrin, 1963), p. 199.

138. Jean Cocteau to Jean Paulhan, November 1934, IMEC, Paulhan collection, folder 2.

139. "La chair nouvelle," BHVP, box 37.

140. Kessel, *Des hommes*, p. 30.

CHAPTER 17. THE DECADENT ONE

1. Édouard Roditi, cited in Henri Raczymow, *Maurice Sachs* (Paris: Gallimard, 1988), p. 225.

2. Cf. Francis Steegmuller, *Cocteau* (Boston: Little, Brown, 1970), pp. 429–430.

3. To Claude Mauriac (*Une amitié contrariée* [Paris: Grasset, 1970]), Cocteau would speak of a woman called O, with whom he had not had an affair, but to the Thomassins, he would mention the Russian princess by name.

4. The stash of correspondence consisted of two hundred letters from Proust, three hundred from Max Jacob, and books from Apollinaire stuffed with missives, Cocteau told Roger Stéphane, forty years later. But his memory, which often failed him, mixed up this episode with the earlier one, in which Sachs had given his mother a forged

letter that absolved him of responsibility—"He imitated my handwriting expertly," Cocteau would write in *Journal d'un inconnu* (Paris: Grasset, 1953), pp. 102–103. Acquired by Jacques Guérin, some of these manuscripts would be given by the great collector to the Bibliothèque Nationale.

5. Raczymow, *Maurice Sachs*, p. 217.
6. Maurice Sachs, *La décade de l'illusion* (1933; Paris: Gallimard, 1950), p. 178.
7. Raczymow, *Maurice Sachs*, p. 227.
8. *NRF*, March 1, 1936.
9. Maurice Sachs, *Alias* (Paris: Gallimard, 1935), pp. 66, 94.
10. Jean Bourgoint to Jeannette Kandaouroff, in Bourgoint, *Le retour de l'enfant terrible: Lettres 1923–1966* (Paris: Desclée de Brouwer, 1975).
11. Louise de Vilmorin, *La fin des Villavide* (Paris: Gallimard, 1937).
12. "My beloved persists in behaving like a madwoman, mad and cruel, and in living without love. I asked her to be light, light as snow, and to continue to fall around me," he confessed to her in a trance. See Jean Cocteau to Louise de Vilmorin, November 12, 1934, in *Lettres de l'Oiseleur* (Monaco: Du Rocher, 1989), p. 217.
13. Jean Cocteau to Louise de Vilmorin, written from Corsier, late 1934, cited in Jean Bothorel, *Louise, ou la vie de Louise de Vilmorin* (Paris: Grasset, 1993), p. 90; Jean Cocteau to Louise de Vilmorin, November 1934, in ibid., p. 219; Igor Markevitch, *Être et avoir été, mémoires* (Paris: Gallimard, 1980), p. 306. [The pun here is on *laisse tomber*, to dump someone, which literally means to let someone fall.—Trans.]
14. *NRF*, January 1, 1935, pp. 143–145.
15. Jean Cocteau, *Journal (1942–1945)* (Paris: Gallimard, 1989), p. 34.
16. Louise de Vilmorin, "Autre poids, autre mesure, Jean Cocteau," in her *Promenades et autres rencontres* (Paris: Gallimard, 2000), p. 154.
17. "Le menteur," *Théâtre*, vol. 2 (Paris: Gallimard, 1948), p. 576.
18. Jean Cocteau to Louise de Vilmorin, November 1934, in *Lettres de l'Oiseleur*, p. 221.
19. Marie Laure de Noailles to Jean Cocteau, March 1933, BHVP.
20. She had first tried her luck with Edward James, who financed *Le minotaure*, Breton's new journal, but the English aesthete, secretly in love with Dalí, proved incapable of moving beyond flirting.
21. Markevitch, *Être et avoir été*, p. 203.
22. Ibid., p. 231.
23. The critic in question was Jules Casadesus. See ibid., pp. 204–205.
24. Jean Cocteau to Denise Bourdet, September 1934, in *Lettres de l'Oiseleur*, p. 74.
25. Cocteau, *La fin du Potomak*, p. 188.
26. François Sentein, *Minutes d'un Libertin (1938–1941)* (Paris: Gallimard, 2000), p. 141, entry for August 24, 1940.
27. At the same time as he was writing the libretto for Stravinsky's *Oedipus Rex*, Cocteau wrote his own theatrical adaptation of *Oedipus*, loosely based on Sophocles, like *Antigone*.
28. Early draft of *Cap de Bonne-Espérance*, OPC, p. 88.
29. ["Zizi" is childish slang for "penis"—Trans.]. One guard called another "Ma vieille" ["my old lady," a slangy term of endearment—Trans.] But this kind of familiarity was

reminiscent of Offenbach's operettas, which Cocteau greatly admired. "Perhaps the queens of operetta are more real than the queens of tragedy, if we are to believe the admirable exchange of letters between Rasputin and the Tsarina, which was an inspiration for the relationship between Jocaste and Tirésias," wrote Cocteau in a preface to sixteen drawings that were published as "Le complexe d'Oedipe" in the numbered, original edition of *La machine infernale*.

30. Francis Ramirez developed this thesis during his talk at the May 1998 conference organized by Pierre Caizergues and the Université de Montpellier on the subject of Cocteau and the theater.

31. Preface to *Les parents terribles*, BHVP, box 8.

32. The actors were Jean-Pierre Aumont (playing Oedipe), Pierre Renoir (Tirésias), Marthe Régnier (Jocaste), Lucienne Bogaert (le Sphinx), and Robert Le Vigan (Anubis). "Vous serez mon Oedipe," Cocteau said to Aumont, after having invited him over.

33. Article dated April 15, 1934, in *Colette: La jumelle noire* (Paris: Ferenczi, 1934), later published in *Colette, Oeuvres*, vol. 3 (Paris: Robert Laffont, 1989), pp. 1086–1089.

34. *Journal de Raïssa Maritain* (Paris: Desclée de Brouwer, 1963), p. 216, entry for April 10, 1934. She added: "Cocteau is undoubtedly the only tragic writer of our epoch."

35. Klaus Mann, *Journal, les années brunes 1931–1936*, translated from German by P.-F. Kaempf (Paris: Grasset, 1996), p. 205.

36. *La machine infernale*, trans. Albert Bermal, in *The Infernal Machine and Other Plays* (New York: New Directions, 1964), pp. 50–51. [The translation has been modified slightly.—Trans.]

37. Cited in Jean-Pierre Aumont, *Souvenirs provisoires* (Paris: Julliard, 1947), p. 45. See also Jean-Jacques Kihm, Elizabeth Sprigge, and Henri C. Béhar, *Jean Cocteau, l'homme et les miroirs* (Paris: La Table Ronde, 1968), pp. 214–223, which provides a detailed summary of the relations between Cocteau and Jouvet.

38. Cited by André Breton in "Limites non frontière du surréalisme," *NRF* (February 1, 1937): 200–215.

39. Christabel Thomassin-Levanti, interviews with the author, January 10, 17, and 24, 2000.

40. Yvon Belaval, "La rencontre avec Jean Cocteau," in *CJC*, vol. 3 (Paris: Gallimard, 1972), p. 101.

41. Jean Desbordes to Jean Cocteau, late March 1932, shared by Pierre Chanel.

42. See the catalogue "Henri Matisse: Writers on Paper, Selected Drawings and Prints from The Pierre and Tana Matisse Foundation, November 2–December 21, 2010," La Maison Française of New York University.

43. Sachs and Matisse had met at the home of one of the Cazalis sisters, who were so dear to Mallarmé.

44. Charlotte Aillaud (Juliette Greco's sister), interview with the author, January 16, 1999.

45. He was a founding member with Marie Bonaparte, Evgénia Sokolnicka, René Laforgue.

46. Claude Mauriac, *Une amitié contrariée* (Paris: Grasset, 1970).

47. "When Jean Cocteau came to see me in Saint-Tropez, during the summer of 1936," wrote Colette, "the automobile that brought him stopped in front of my door on the

little road, and the poet who signs his name with a little star bounded out of it in a way only he has mastered. He was dressed simply, as slim as those who can walk through mirrors, a purple silk tie around his neck. On his head he wore a Tuareg hat in full bloom, as he had pierced the straw with a hundred black chicken feathers. Thus did he go about the Provençal countryside, which had seen worse. But my gardener recognized him immediately—since everyone knows the black chicken is evil—and jumped into the air crying 'Lucifer!' " See "Les chevaliers de la Table ronde de Jean Cocteau," at the Théâtre de l'Oeuvre, October 24, 1937, in *Colette: La jumelle noire*, p. 1328.

48. Sachs, *La décade de l'illusion*, p. 174.

49. The card was reprinted in an article by Frédéric Gaussen, "Cocteau et Maurice Sachs, le voyou pardonné," *Le monde* (May 4, 2000). Pierre Chanel believes that Cocteau may well have signed this card, to make fun perhaps of Bourgoint, who had compared him to Lucifer after his "sacrilegious" imitations of the Abbé Lamy. It was about this time that the devilish Sachs, according to Cocteau, had turned Max Reinhardt and Gustaf Gründgens away from the apartment in the place de la Madeleine. They had come to ask for the German rights to *La voix humaine* and *La machine infernale*.

50. Undated article for *Les Annales*, on the screening of *Le sang d'un poète* at the Vieux-Colombier, BHVP, box 25.

51. Jean Cocteau to Richard Thoma, cited by Steegmuller, *Cocteau* (Buchet-Chastel), p. 306.

52. This is a reference to Julien Benda's *Le trahison des clercs* (1927), translated by Richard Aldington in 1928 as *The Betrayal of the Intellectuals* (Boston: Beacon Press).—Trans.

53. Le Mercure de France denounced their "rebellion."

54. Paul Morand, *Journal d'un attaché d'ambassade* (Paris: Gallimard, 1963), p. 291.

55. Tristan Tzara, "La main passe," in *Morceaux choisis*, preface by Jean Cassou (Paris: Éditions Bordas, 1947), p. 211; "Initiés et précurseurs," *Commune* 23 (July 1935), cited in François Buot, *Tristan Tzara, l'homme qui inventa la révolution dada* (Paris: Grasset, 2002) p. 323; François Mauriac to Jacques-Émile Blanche, September 1, 1932, in François Mauriac and Jacques-Émile Blanche, *Correspondance (1916–1942)*, ed. Georges-Paul Collet (Paris: Grasset, 1976) p. 166.

56. Klaus Mann, *Le tournant, histoire d'une vie*, trans. Nicole and Henri Roche (Paris: Seuil, 1986), p. 292.

57. "Sainte-Unefois, par Louise de Vilmorin," *NRF*, January 1, 1935, pp. 143–145.

58. Curiously, in *Le minotaure* Breton had acknowledged that Symbolism had the merit of having been psychically enriching, in its denial of reality.

59. See the announcement of this second version in *Paris-midi*, BHVP, box 25. See also the article by Cocteau in *Paris-midi*, December 1934, reprinted in Jean Cocteau, *Du cinématographe* (Paris: Belfond, 1973), pp. 78–80.

60. Jean Cocteau to Robert Wiene, undated, BHVP, box 25.

61. In his memoirs, Markevitch writes that after returning to Paris a second time, Cocteau returned to Corsier with a boy with a scar on his face speaking *argot* (slang): Pierrot Nicolas, who had spent two years in the penal colony in Calvi, a sort of double for No Luck. A letter from Nora Auric informed the musician of the boy's suicide in January 1936.

62. Jean Hugo, *Le regard de la mémoire* (Paris: Babel-Actes Sud, 1983), p. 207. ["Moult" is Middle French for "maint," meaning "many"; "j'avions" is also Middle French for "j'avais," the imperfect form of "I had," still used in Acadian French. —Trans.]

63. Some of Cocteau can be found in the illustrious Merlin, "an old sorcerer, brilliant and cruel," so skilled at "sterilizing and putting to sleep the place he adopts, whose sap he sucks out . . . like a spider in the middle of its web."

64. Giraudoux wouldn't produce *Ondine* until 1939.

65. Preface to *Les mariés de la tour Eiffel*.

66. In Klaus Mann, *André Gide ou la crise de la pensée moderne* (Paris: Grasset, 1999), p. 23.

67. Claude Roy, "Pour servir à un portrait de Jean Cocteau," BHVP, box 60A, 1954, published in *PD*, vol. 3, p. 429.

68. Cocteau had met Khill in 1932 when he was quite young, at the home of his protector of the time, Tranchant de Lunel, an opium addict who belonged to Marshall Lyautey's homosexual circle when the Moroccan Protectorate was organized (he directed the Beaux-Arts). When Tranchant de Lunel died, Marcel Khill became Cocteau's "secretary," and then officially his partner.

69. The cruise would inspire *Retrouvons notre enfance*, a series of ten articles that Cocteau would publish in *Paris-soir* from August 6–16, 1935, and collected in Jean Cocteau, *Poésie de journalisme, 1935–1938* (Paris: Belfond, 1973), pp. 11–63.

70. Pierre Chanel, according to Milly's journal, believed that Cocteau did not alter the acrostics.

71. Christabel Thomassin-Levanti, interview with the author, January 24, 2000. [A rough translation: "When I dance with my curly-headed man/He has a way of wrapping his arms around me/I lose my head/I'm like a fool . . . /He hits me, he destroys me, he kills me/But what can I say, I like it/Afterward I fall into a dream/ As I nestle in his arms." —Trans.]

72. They may have met at the home of Marie Laure de Noailles, one of Weill's patrons, or through Darius Milhaud.

73. These poems would be published in 1934 in *Die Sammlung*, the anti-Nazi journal edited by Klaus Mann.

74. Cf. Pascal Huynh, *Kurt Weill ou la conquête des masses* (Paris: Actes Sud, 2000).

75. Dietrich had come to work with Weill in Louveciennes in 1933, for a musical film that Sternberg was supposed to direct. In the end she did not sing "Es regnet."

76. It can be heard, sung by Brigitte Fassbaender, on *Kurt Weill, die sieben todsünden, chansons*, Radio-Philharmonie Hannover des NDR, conducted by Cord Garben. Harmonia Mundi France, CD, HMC 901420.

77. Georges Peeters, *Les monstres sacrés du ring* (Paris: La Table Ronde, 1959), p. 162.

78. Cf. Jean Cocteau and Darius Milhaud, *Correspondance* (Montpellier: Pierre Caizergues and Josiane Mas, Centre d'études littéraires françaises du XXe siècle, Université Paul-Valéry, 1992), p. 46.

79. She also sang Weill's "Pirate Jenny," then, in 1937, his *Threepenny Opera*, with Yvette Guilbert.

80. By the end of her life Suzy Solidor had 225 portraits on display in her cabaret in Cagnes-sur-Mer.

81. Cf. *Têtu* 40 (September 1999): 73. ["I want every woman/From her heels to her hair."—Trans.]

82. Suzy Solidor, *La fille aux cheveux de lin: Succès et raretés, 1933/1939*, CD, Chansophone, no 121, 1992.

83. Account given by Suzy Solidor, cited in Kihm, Sprigge, and Béhar, *Jean Cocteau*, p. 239.

84. *Les mains d'Orlac*, directed by Robert Wiene, 1922.

85. Cf. as well the article of April 28, 1919, reprinted in Jean Cocteau, *Carte blanche*, *Oeuvres complètes*, vol. 11 (Lausanne: Éditions Marguerat, 1951).

86. Roger Stéphane, *Portrait souvenir de Jean Cocteau* (Paris: Éditions Tallandier, 1964), p. 110.

87. Ibid., p. 111.

88. Hugo, *Le regard de la mémoire*, p. 441.

89. "Marvellous!" and "Crazy!"—Trans.

90. Christabel Thomassin-Levanti interviews, January 2000.

91. "Sainte-Unefois, par Louise de Vilmorin."

92. Hugo, *Le regard de la mémoire*, p. 442. Cocteau's drawings would be shown at the Galerie des Quatre-Chemins, 19, rue de Marignan, in February–March 1937: "Dessins sur le thème: mandragores et mains chevalines."

93. Jean Cocteau to his mother, September 1936, *LM*.

94. Jean Touzot, *Jean Cocteau* (Lyon: La Manufacture), p. 111.

95. José Corti, *Souvenirs désordonnés* (Paris: Librairie José Corti, 1983), p. 220.

96. At least he was in charge, until the bishop of Paris protested.

97. François Sentein, *Nouvelles minutes d'un libertin (1942–1943)* (Paris: Gallimard, 2000), p. 85.

98. Jean Cocteau to André Gide, November or December 1936, in Jean Cocteau, *Lettres à André Gide avec quelques réponses d'André Gide*, ed. Jean-Jacques Kihm (Paris: La Table Ronde, 1970), p. 175.

99. Artaud had already offered him a role in *Les Cenci*, in 1935. Cocteau declined for health reasons.

100. T. Fraenkel, *Le coeur à barbe* (April 1922).

101. Jean Aurenche, *La suite à l'écran* (Paris: Institut Lumière/Actes Sud, 1993), p. 41.

102. Aragon to Jean Cocteau, January 14, 1919, in Louis Aragon, *Papiers inédits: De Dada au surréalisme (1917–1931)* (Paris: Gallimard, 2000), p. 256. He is referring of course to the Ninth Symphony by Beethoven, which begins in a state of uncertainty, hesitating between major and minor keys. "The understanding we have between us is unresolved," Aragon says later in this letter. Jean Aurenche (ibid., p. 29) maintains, unconvincingly, that Cocteau and Aragon had an affair, before Breton began his anti-Cocteau campaign.

103. Unpublished journal entry by Roger Lannes, January 12, 1938, in *CJC*, vol. 10 (Paris: Gallimard, 1985), p. 161. See also Pierre Chanel, *Jean Cocteau poète graphique* (Paris: Chêne/Stock, 1975), p. 115.

104. Jerrold Seigel, *Bohemian Paris: Culture, Politics, and the Boundaries of Bourgeois Life, 1830–1930* (Baltimore: Johns Hopkins University Press, 1999), p. 381.

105. *Les faux-monnayeurs* (Paris: Gallimard, 1951), pp. 411 and 415; for a translation see *The Counterfeiters*, trans. Dorothy Bussy (New York: Vintage, 1973), p. 324.

106. In the 1920s and 1930s, all of artistic and upper-class Paris smoked somewhat regularly.

107. From "Merci," a poem dedicated to Jean Marais and published in *Histoires de ma vie* (1975; Ramsay poche cinéma, 1994), p. 260.

108. Cocteau, *PD*, vol. 3, p. 125.

109. Cocteau, *PD*, vol. 2, p. 171.

110. Written in 1925, at the same time as the *Oedipus Rex* he was writing for Stravinsky, published in 1928, the play debuted July 12, 1937, at the Théâtre Antoine.

111. Cited in Eduardo Arroyo, *Panama Al Brown* (1982; Paris: Grasset, 1998), p. 231. For more on this boxing phase, see *Les monstres sacrés* and *Swing*, by Stefano Jacomuzzi, translated from Italian by Alain Sarrabayrouse (Paris: Climats, 1990).

112. Panama Al Brown would perform next at the Amar Circus in Douai.

CHAPTER 18. THE RESURRECTION

1. Raymond Rouleau's students had just formed the Jeunes Comédiens 37 troupe.

2. "Théâtral, relevant du coude une farouche/Draperie, Apollon, bouclé d'or, de profil./On dirait un cheval qui se cabr: la bouche,/Et l'oeil, soleil obscur, rayonnement de cils." See Jean Cocteau, "Cherchez Apollon" (1931–1932), in *Poèmes, 1916–1955* (Paris: Gallimard, 1956), p. 87.

3. Jean Marais, *L'inconcevable Jean Cocteau* (Monaco: Éditions du Rocher, 1993), p. 44.

4. Chanel had designed the women's costumes, Cocteau the men's; they were made by Ira Belline, from an article cited in ibid. [The Phrygian cap was a soft conical cap worn in ancient Greece and a symbol of liberty during the French Revolution—Trans.]

5. The Croix-Fleurie villa had been renamed Kia Ora ("welcome" in Tahitian) by its new owner, Titana, the pen name of Élisabeth Sauvy, the reporter who had published an interview with Hitler in *Paris-soir* in January 1936. During his stay, Cocteau decorated an interior room of the villa and painted images of the saints Tropez and Maxime on the doors. See Jean Cocteau, *Les chevaliers de la table ronde*, in *Théâtre*, vol. 1 (Paris: Gallimard, 1948), p. 96.

6. Cassagnac and Morel were two of the many fake family names that Marais had to adopt when he and his mother had to flee. See Jean Marais, *Histoires de ma vie* (1975; Ramsay poche cinéma, 1994), p. 18.

7. "Prière des animaux," cited in ibid., p. 261.

8. "Le tour du monde était un bien pauvre voyage/À côté du voyage où je pars avec toi/ Chaque jour je t'adore et mieux et davantage/Où tu vis c'est mon toit." Untitled poem cited in ibid., p. 257.

9. "Ah! j'aimerais courir le risque/De pouvoir exposer ces vers/Tout autour de ton obélisque/Au centre de notre univers." Cited in ibid., n.p.

10. "Quand le sculpteur fait ma statue/C'est un peu de ma mort qu'il tue./Mais quand tu . . . me moules, tu me fécondes,/Tu fais un travail inconnu/Cavalier que tes cuisses blondes/ Dressent le maigre pur-sang nu!" From "Le pur-sang rétif," cited in ibid., p. 274.

11. Jean Cocteau, *Jean Marais* (Paris: Calmann-Lévy, 1951). This can be seen in Gisèle Freund's famous portrait of Cocteau; see Marais, *L'inconcevable Jean Cocteau*, p. 121.

12. Author's interview with Christabel Thomassin-Levanti, January 17, 2000; introduction to *Les chevaliers de la table ronde.*

13. "Tu m'aimes. Est-ce Dieu possible?/Si je pouvais être un miroir!/Un David maigre en bronze noir/Qui te donne sa fronde et veut être ta cible," from "David." Cited in Marais, *Histoires de ma vie*, p. 266.

14. Roger Stéphane, *Portrait souvenir de Jean Cocteau* (Paris: Éditions Tallandier, 1964), p. 126; Marcel Schneider, *L'éternité fragile*, vol. 2: *Innocence et vérité* (Paris: Grasset, 1991), p. 223; Pierre Brisson, in *Le Figaro*. See Marais, *Histoires de ma vie*, p. 70.

15. October 24, 1937, repr. in *Colette: La jumelle noire* (Paris: Ferenczi, 1934), later published in *Colette, Oeuvres*, vol. 3 (Paris: Robert Laffont, 1989), p. 1331.

16. Ibid., p. 1329.

17. Roger Lannes, journal entry, February 23, 1938, in *CJC*, vol. 10 (Paris: Gallimard, 1985), p. 170.

18. "Quand nous faisons l'amour ensemble/Entre le ciel et l'enfer/Je pense que cela ressemble/A de l'or pénétrant du fer/Or dur, or mou, hélas . . . que sais-je?/C'est froid, c'est chaud, c'est de la neige." From "La colonne," cited in Marais, *Histoires de ma vie*, p. 268.

19. "Ils peuvent te donner des corps durs et robustes/Des rendez-vous cruels, joyeux et clandestins . . . /Peuvent-ils te donner un palais de tes bustes?" From "Ils," cited in Marais, *Histoires de ma vie*, p. 282.

20. "Ton silence," and "Ma nuit," cited in Marais, *Histoires de ma vie*, pp. 101, 265.

21. "Trouverait-on un jour des lettres plus brûlantes?/Encre au sperme pareille et si prompte à partir?" From "Mes lettres," cited in Marais, *Histoires de ma vie*, p. 261.

22. "Ce matin j'ai caché les chansons que je t'offre;/Jaunes, elles jonchaient le couvercle du coffre./Mon ange serait-il aux vers habitué?/Par l'habitude, en nous quelque chose est tué . . ." From "Un poème, un!," cited in ibid., p. 93.

23. "Je dis: tu n'auras qu'un poème/Et voilà que j'en glisse deux/L'un pour te répéter: 'Je t'aime'/L'autre: 'Je suis ton amoureux.'" From "Les autres," cited in Marais, *Histoires de ma vie*, p. 93.

24. "Mon coeur trouve réponse à l'éternel problème/Toi c'est moi—moi c'est toi—nous c'est nous—/Eux c'est eux." From ibid.

25. Police archives, February 10, 1943, police precinct of the 5th arrondissement of Paris, document 233.807, file Cocteau.

26. This would be a little more than thirty euros today.

27. See Claude Mauriac, *Une amitié contrariée* (Paris: Grasset, 1970), p. 44.

28. Thomassin had also begun to write for the theater: the brilliant polyglot, to whom a million paths opened but who wanted none of them, had adapted *Macbeth*, which was performed at the same time as Cocteau's *Oedipe roi* by the Jeunes Comédiens 37, of which his brother Pierre was a member, as was Gérard Oury, the future director of *La grande vadrouille*. Having learned along the way that Marais, who was acting in both plays, had become his new rival, Thomassin had to keep his head once again. "I wish I were wealthy," he wrote to Cocteau, upon learning that his play was in trouble. "You

know that I am sweet and angelic, but I am full of savage hatred toward those who would censor *Oedipe*." I wish I could torture them," he added, appalled that his *Macbeth* could still continue its successful run (letter sent from Chantilly, BHVP, box 6).

29. Franz Thomassin to Jean Cocteau, undated (1936 or 1937), BHVP, box 41.

30. Preface to the program for *Parents terribles*, Théâtre des Ambassadeurs, 1938; Roger Lannes, journal entry, April 27, 1938, *CJC*, vol. 10, p. 182; "In her sudden moments of anger, Chanel—that symbol of seduction and supreme elegance—was unrecogniz-able; she . . . would nervously pull on her pearl necklace . . . and looked like a little monkey who was furious at having been dressed up like a lady. But in general these venomous outbursts were followed by a rush of kindness and generosity," wrote Boris Kochno in *Diaghilev et les Ballets Russes* (Paris: Fayard, 1973), p. 34.

31. Kiki to Jean Cocteau, unpublished letter, BHVP, box 8. [Kiki de Montparnasse's com-ment is a play on the name of Cocteau's character and the expression "pleurer comme une Madeleine," or "cry like Mary Magdalene"—Trans.]

32. One could still find copies of the original print run of *Plain-chant*, in 1940, published by Éditions Stock.

33. *La revue universelle*, December 1, 1938, cited in Jean Cocteau, *Les parents terribles*, ed. Jean Touzot (Paris: Gallimard, 1994).

34. Stéphane, *Portrait souvenir*, p. 126.

35. "I carried him in my belly and chased him out of my belly, my child. These are the kinds of things of which you know nothing and which are more powerful than your nonsense," replied Yvonne four scenes later.

36. Roger Lannes, unpublished journal, IMEC, entry for January 1, 1939. See also David Gascoyne, *Journal de Paris et d'ailleurs, 1936–1942*, trans. Christine Jordis (Paris: Flammarion, 1984), p. 308. After helping to promote Surrealism in Britain with his 1935 essay "A Short Survey of Surrealism," and having translated Éluard, Aragon, and Tzara, Gascoyne published his own poetry collections. Suffering from depression, he was hospitalized for a long time, and rescued by a nurse, whom he later married.

37. *Continual Lessons: The Journal of Glenway Wescott (1937–1955)* (New York: Farrar, Straus, and Giroux, 1991).

38. Jean Cocteau to Jean Marais, undated, cited in Marais, *Histoires de ma vie*, p. 97.

39. "Tu dois me baiser et me mordre/Remettre et m'ôter ton anneau/Et quelquefois me passer l'ordre/Où pend un cadavre d'agneau." Cited in ibid., p. 102.

40. "La grande pitié des victimes de France," *Le mot* 8 (January 23, 1915).

41. "Tout cela somme toute fait peur/Atroce et dépasse les bornes./Cette française, lourde et légère torpeur,/Devant un aigle double et pareil à deux cornes." From "L'incendie," in Cocteau, *Poèmes, 1916–1955*, p. 94.

42. Cocteau met the singer through Panama Al Brown's entourage.

43. After the signing of the Munich Accords, Daladier was voted in by the Chamber of Deputies on October 4, 1938, 537 votes to 75 (73 Communists, the nationalist Henri de Kerillis, and a Socialist deputy, who voted against his party line).

44. Interview with Bruno Villien, *Masques*, in Pierre Chanel, *Album Cocteau* (Paris: Veyrier-Tchou, 1970), pp. 116–117.

45. Roger Lannes, unpublished journal, entry for May 24, 1939, IMEC.

46. Jean Cocteau to Jean Marais, undated, cited in Marais, _Histoires de ma vie_, pp. 96–97.

47. The journal, which was to be entitled _La politique des lettres_, would have been edited by Claude Mauriac, Roger Lannes, and Jacques Audiberti (who would remain close to Cocteau). It never saw the light of day.

48. Mauriac, _Une amitié contrariée_, p. 26.

49. Claude Mauriac, _Conversations avec André Gide_ (Paris: Albin Michel, 1951), pp. 64, 66.

50. Roger Lannes, unpublished journal, entry for May 24, 1939, IMEC.

51. Mauriac, _Conversations avec André Gide_, p. 71.

52. Ibid., p. 73.

53. Mauriac, _Une amitié contrariée_, pp. 81–82.

54. André Gide, _Journal_, vol. 1: 1887–1925 (Paris: Gallimard, 1996), August 20, 1914, p. 846.

55. Mauriac, _Une amitié contrariée_, p. 47. Author's interview with André Berne-Joffroy, June 21, 1999.

56. Cited in Mauriac, _Conversations avec André Gide_, p. 73.

57. The drawing was dedicated to Paul Poiret, the fashion designer, and filed at the Galerie Laurent Teillet under number 203 D. Annie Guedrars generously provided a photocopy.

58. Mauriac, _Conversations avec André Gide_, p. 70.

59. Ibid., p. 75.

60. Christabel Thomassin-Levanti, interview with the author, January 24, 2000.

61. Published in the _Tableau de la littérature française_ (Paris: Gallimard, 1939), with a preface by André Gide. Cocteau's "Rousseau" could be found alongside François Mauriac on Pascal, Jean Giraudoux on Racine, Paul Valéry on Montesquieu, Pierre Drieu la Rochelle on Diderot, and Paul Morand on Beaumarchais. "I won't try to convince anyone that Jean-Jacques Rousseau wasn't a madman with a persecution complex," Cocteau wrote. "But knowing myself how methodically we persecute poets, I think it my duty to make my experience count for something and to show that if Rousseau was hypersensitive, he had reason to be, for he was persecuted" (p. 264).

62. "Nous nous sauverons de Paris, de Paris," cited in Marais, _Histoires de ma vie_, p. 103.

63. Quoted in Roger Stéphane, _Tout est bien: Chronique_ (Paris: Quai Voltaire, 1989), p. 118.

64. Roger Lannes, unpublished journal, entry for May 4, 1939, IMEC.

65. In the 1920s, transvestite balls were held in the Magic City. Born in 1873, the actress Cécile Sorel began acting in 1889. She joined the Comédie-Française in 1901, and left it in 1933 for a career in the music hall. Jean-Pierre Aumont, _Souvenirs provisoires_ (Paris: Julliard, 1947), pp. 99–100.

66. Cited in Carole Weisweiller and Patrick Renaudot, _Jean Marais le bien-aimé_ (Monaco: Éditions du Rocher, 2003), p. 89.

67. "Ah! Jeannot je chante, je chante/Pour t'avoir le même demain/Car la vie a l'air trop méchante/Sans la caresse de ta main." From "Mon chef-d'œuvre," cited in Marais, _Histoires de ma vie_, p. 94.

68. Cf. Jean-Philippe Renouard, "Violette Morris, le destin d'une sportive révoltée," _Têtu_ 40 (September 1999).

69. Jean Cocteau to Jean Marais, undated (1939?), cited in Marais, *Histoires de ma vie*, p. 115.

70. Lise Deharme, *Les années perdues, Journal (1939–1949)* (Paris: Plon, 1961), p. 52.

71. Cf. Jean Cocteau's article in *Paris-midi*, April 19, 1940.

72. Marais, *L'inconcevable Jean Cocteau*, p. 170.

73. Jean Cocteau, *Lettres à Jean Marais* (Paris: Albin Michel, 1987).

74. Jacques-Émile Blanche, *Cahiers d'un artiste*, series 6 (December 1916–June 1917) (Paris: Émile-Paul, 1919), p. 157.

75. *Jean Cocteau ou la vérité du mensonge* would not be published in its entirety until 1945.

76. Mauriac, *Conversations avec André Gide*, p. 249.

77. Stéphane, *Tout est bien*, p. 263.

CHAPTER 19. THE OCCUPIED

1. He was also the son of the novelist Gyp (*Le mariage de Chiffon*, 1894), famous for her descriptions of society milieus.

2. Gavroche is a street urchin in Victor Hugo's *Les Misérables*. —Trans.

3. Heller was the potential censor for anything published in France, and was also responsible for the anti-Jewish campaign in the domain of literature.

4. The original title of Sieburg's book, *Gott in Frankreich*, repeated the German saying previously cited: "Glücklich wie Gott. . . ." Sieburg had also published, in 1939, *Éloge de la France par un nazi*. For the quotation, see Marcel Jouhandeau, *Que la vie est une fête*, in *Journaliers*, vol. 8 (Paris: Gallimard, 1966), cited in Gerhardt Heller, *Un Allemand à Paris* (Paris: Seuil, 1981), p. 72.

5. Henri Amouroux, *La vie des français sous l'Occupation*, vol. 2 (Paris: Éditions J'ai Lu, 1965), p. 334.

6. Cited by Marie-Madeleine Fourcade in her preface to Gerard Silvain, *La question juive en Europe* (Paris: Lattès, 1985), p. 10.

7. They soon united with the anthropologists and linguists of the Musée de l'Homme network.

8. Simone de Beauvoir, *La force de l'âge* (Paris: Le Livre de Poche, 1960), p. 170.

9. Of the few writers who chose not to speak out, we might mention Tzara and Reverdy.

10. Following the requirements of the German-Soviet pact, Germany banned anti-Soviet works as well. According to Lieutenant Heller, 2,242 tons of books were destroyed; see Jean Guéhenno, *Journal des années noires, 1940–1944* (Paris: Gallimard, 1947), p. 59, entry for November 30, 1940.

11. Jean Cocteau, *Journal (1942–1945)* (Paris: Gallimard, 1989), p. 111, entry for May 5, 1942.

12. From a journal edited by Jean Luchaire, who became a pillar of the collaboration and whose French secretary married Otto Abetz. A copy of the journal is available at the Bibliothèque Nationale de France.

13. "Légèreté," April 12, 1938, BHVP, box 51.

14. "Articles de Paris," from Jean Cocteau, *Portraits-souvenir*, in *Oeuvres complètes*, vol. 11 (Lausanne, Éditions Marguerat, 1951), p. 318.

15. "Les bucoliques basques," *Poèmes de jeunesse inédits*, OPC, p. 1545.

16. "To compound our misery, we can take no step, or eat, or even breathe, without making ourselves complicit with the Occupation," Sartre wrote. "Before the war the pacifists explained to us more than once that an occupied country must refuse to fight, and practice passive resistance. It's easy to say, but for this resistance to be effective, the conductor must refuse to drive his train, the farmer refuse to till his field. The conqueror may be annoyed, though he can always stock up in his own country—but the occupied nation will most certainly be eradicated as quickly as possible. We had to work, then ... only the slightest activity served the enemy who has struck at us, attached its suction cups to our skins and begun to live in symbiosis with us ... Everything we did was ambiguous; we never knew if we were doing right or wrong; a subtle venom was poisoning even our best enterprises." See "Paris sous l'Occupation," *France libre* (1945), repr. in *Situations III* (Paris: Gallimard, 1948). To Alain Bosquet (*La mémoire de l'oubli* [Paris: Grasset, 1990], p. 240), who criticized his attitude during the occupation, Sartre responded very simply: "I ignored the Germans."

17. Boulos Ristelhuber, unpublished journal, December 21, 1940.

18. Cocteau, *PD*, vol. 2, p. 118. The arguments made by André-Louis Dubois, a former assistant director of the Sûreté Nationale, whom we will meet during the Occupation, also greatly helped Cocteau to overcome his addiction. See Dubois, *Sous le signe de l'amitié* (Paris: Plon, 1972), pp. 116–117.

19. Jean Cocteau, *Les chevaliers de la table ronde*, in *Théâtre*, vol. 1 (Paris: Gallimard, 1948), p. 168.

20. Jean Genet, *Miracle de la rose*, in *Oeuvres complètes*, vol. 2 (Paris: Gallimard, 1951), pp. 224–225.

21. Preface to the exhibition "Scènes et figures parisiennes," 1943, available online at http://www.ebay.fr/itm/Catalogue-galerie-Charpentier-Paris-Scenes-et-figures-parisiennes-1943-Cocteau-/151061878771 (accessed December 30, 2015).

22. He wrote this in 1942. See Jean Cocteau, *Lettres à Jean Marais* (Paris: Albin Michel, 1987).

23. After the war, Morihien would be one of the founders of Club Med.

24. Marcel Jouhandeau, *Portraits* (Brussels: Jacques Antoine, 1988), p. 17.

25. All it took was for the editors of *Meyer Lexicon*, published in Germany, to call Satie a Jew for his biography to be banned in Occupied France.

26. "Légèreté," April 12, 1938, BHVP, box 51.

27. "That vile Jewish rag run by that swine Bernard Lecache," said Jouhandeau. Cocteau wrote in his message: "As a matter of principal, a poet's spirit is too anarchic to take a position, even a revolutionary one. But given the crimes that are being committed every day against the freedom of body and soul, it would be cowardly not to do anything," signing himself "The winged poet, the dramatist, who is not afraid to take sides against racism." Cited by Jean-Jacques Kihm, Elizabeth Sprigge, and Henri C. Béhar, *Jean Cocteau, l'homme et les miroirs* (Paris: La Table Ronde, 1968), p. 268, n. 1.

28. Cocteau, *PD*, vol. 1, p. 73.

29. Letter of December 14, 1950, Simone de Beauvoir, *Lettres à Nelson Algren* (Paris: Gallimard, 1997), p. 424. See also *A Transatlantic Love Affair: Letters to Nelson Algren* (New York: New Press, 1999).

30. Beauvoir, *La force de l'âge*, p. 498.

31. Jean Cocteau to Roger Stéphane, July 1940. Cf. Roger Stéphane, *Portrait souvenir de Jean Cocteau* (Paris: Éditions Tallandier, 1964), p. 10, and *Tout est bien*, in the middle group of photographs. Enraptured by Marais during the 1939 performances of *Les parents terribles*, Stéphane was soon invited to dinner by Cocteau, and called "darling." See Roger Stéphane, *Tout est bien: Chronique* (Paris: Quai Voltaire, 1989), p. 113.

32. Jean Marais, *L'inconcevable Jean Cocteau* (Monaco: Éditions du Rocher, 1993), p. 170.

33. An editor at *Au pilori* (October 18, 1940) thought he remembered seeing him walking along the quays of the Seine "tenderly holding two ecstatic youngsters around the neck." He left at the École Normale the "flouncing memory of his transvestites," according to *La révolution nationale* (March 1, 1942).

34. "You're going to see Cocteau!" cried a prominent Montpellier doctor in earshot of François Sentein, who then cautioned: "wear metal shorts." He was addressing Jean Fontenoy. See Cocteau, *Journal (1942–1945)*, p. 93, entry for April 19, 1942.

35. Stéphane, *Tout est bien*, p. 154.

36. He was playing it with the actor Pierre Fresnay. The play was *L'écurie Watson*, after a play by Terence Rattigan, *French without Tears*.

37. Maurice Sachs to Jean Cocteau, June 14, 1937, Madeleine Castaing archives, cited in Henri Raczymow, *Maurice Sachs* (Paris: Gallimard, 1988), p. 278.

38. Maurice Sachs, *Au temps du Boeuf sur le Toit* (1939; Paris: Grasset, 1987), pp. 84–86.

39. Nevertheless Cocteau forbade Marais from reading Sachs's work.

40. Raczymow, *Maurice Sachs*, p. 358.

41. Preface to Maurice Sachs, *La chasse à courre* (Paris: Gallimard, 1948), p. 10.

42. Maurice Sachs to Yvon Belaval, January 1941, Yvon Belaval archives, cited in Raczymow, *Maurice Sachs*, p. 358.

43. Simone Le Bargy was an actress and friend of Cocteau's, known by her stage name, Madame Simone.—Trans.

44. Jean Marais, *Histoires de ma vie* (1975; Ramsay poche cinéma, 1994), p. 131.

45. Letter from February 1941, in *CJC*, vol. 10 (Paris: Gallimard, 1985), pp. 108–109, Raczymow, *Maurice Sachs*, pp. 359–360, and Marais, *Histoires de ma vie*, p. 132.

46. He wrote this in the unpublished first draft of *L'Asphyxie*, by Violette Leduc.

47. Klaus Mann, who had been received on the rue d'Anjou by a "pudgy" Sachs wearing his cassock, would write in *Le tournant, histoire d'une vie*, trans. Nicole et Henri Roche (Paris: Seuil, 1986), p. 292: "The malice with which he accuses and caricatures the Master, his onetime friend, is as excessive as the admiration he displayed during our first conversation."

48. Paul Morand to Jean Cocteau, March 8, 1941, BHVP, box 71.

49. Some of these have been reprinted, with other prewar essays from Aragon's *Ce soir*, in *Le Foyer des artistes*. Pierre Georgel included them in his edition of *Portraits-souvenir*.

50. Boulos Ristelhuber, unpublished journal, February 16, 1941.

51. Marc Augier, *Les Partisans* (Paris: Denoël, 1943), pp. 195–196, cited in Pascal Ory, ed., *La France allemande: Paroles du collaborationnisme français (1933–1945)* (Paris: Gallimard/Julliard, 1977), p. 144.

52. According to Céline, the French deputees sat, until 1940 — and still sit today — in the Palais Bourbon.

53. Claude Roy to Maurice Martin du Gard, July 19, 1941, cited in Maurice Martin du Gard, *Les mémorables*, new ed. (Paris: Gallimard, 1999), p. 998, n. 1.

54. By refusing to take the Chambre des Députés, Colonel de La Rocque's Croix-de-Feu had saved the Republic, on February 6, 1934.

55. Maurice Martin du Gard, *La chronique de Vichy* (1948; Paris: Flammarion, 1976), p. 215.

56. Albert Speer, *Au coeur du Troisième Reich* (Paris: Fayard, 1971), p. 263.

57. Piéral, *Vu d'en bas* (Paris: Robert Laffont, 1976), p. 168.

58. Maxime, the main character, has been accidentally arrested during a mutiny, and sent to the penal colony in Calvi.

59. Suzanne Abetz to Jean Cocteau, May 10, 1941, BHVP, box 4.

60. See Gisèle Sapiro, *La guerre des écrivains, 1940–1953* (Paris: Fayard, 1999), p. 47; letter from Jean Cocteau, May 1941, BHVP, box 4.

61. I am following the version of events given by Jean Marais in his *Histoires de ma vie*, p. 134.

62. Laubreaux's article was published May 1941 in *Le petit parisien*.

63. Bernstein, Tristan Bernard, and Porto-Riche were all accused of wanting to make the biggest profit.

64. Laubreaux's father, a prison warden, had given him one of the inmate's manuscripts, which Laubreaux published under his own name. Doriot had been excluded on Stalin's orders for having called too early for a unitary politics across all left-wing forces — going against the "class against class" tactic set by Moscow — two years before the Front Populaire; see *L'émancipation nationale*, August 20, 1937, cited in Pascal Ory, *Les collaborateurs, 1940–1945* (Paris: Seuil, 1977), p. 210. Drieu la Rochelle had been a militant member of the PPF from the party's earliest days in June 1936. He resigned on January 6, 1939, and returned, out of defiance, on November 7, 1942.

65. "Youpin" was derogatory French slang of the period for "Jew," similar to yid, kike, etc. — Trans.

66. Cf. Herbert Lottman, *La rive gauche* (Paris: Seuil, 1981), p. 315. See also Herbert Lottman, *The Left Bank: Artists, Writers, and Politics from the Popular Front to the Cold War* (Chicago: University of Chicago Press, 1981).

67. Martin du Gard, *La chronique de Vichy*, p. 335, regarding February 1943.

68. It could only be *Je suis partout*. See Céline to Albert Paraz, June 22, 1957, in *Lettres à Albert Paraz (1947–1957)*, Collection les Cahiers de la NRF (Paris: Gallimard, 2009).

69. Cited in Beauvoir, *La force de l'âge*, p. 546.

70. The restaurant was Le Relais de Porquerolles.

71. The fight would inspire a scene in François Truffaut's film of that name, *Le dernier métro*. Piéral, *Vu d'en bas*, p. 168.

72. Marais, *Histoires de ma vie*, pp. 134–135.

73. Pierre Bénichou, "Fearless Jean/was buried Friday at Vallauris," *Le nouvel observateur*, November 8, 1998.

74. Cf. Hervé Le Boterf, *La vie parisienne sous l'Occupation*, vol. 1: *Paris le jour* (Paris: France-Empire, 1974), p. 187.

75. This article could not be located. After his "Adresse aux jeunes écrivains" on December 5, 1940, Cocteau published on January 2, again in *La Gerbe,* "À ceux qui nous ont écrit: réponse de Jean Cocteau."

76. François Mauriac to Jean Cocteau, June 17, 1941, BHVP, box 4.

77. Cf. François Gibault, *Céline: Délires et persécutions, 1932–1944,* vol. 2: *Mercure de France* (Paris: Broché, 1985), pp. 324–325. Lucien Combelle thought he remembered Cocteau walking around Céline, who was barely civil. According to Philippe Almeras, it was Cocteau who had asked Céline to play arbitrator: see his *Céline, entre haines et passion* (Paris: Laffont, 1994).

78. Manuscript, "Jean Marais," BHVP, box 54; typewritten text, 30.07.41, BHVP, box 51; typewritten text, 30.07.41, BHVP, box 51.

79. René Benjamin, cited in Brassaï, *Conversations avec Picasso* (1964; Paris: Gallimard, 1997), p. 90.

80. *Je suis partout,* October 25, 1941.

81. On February 2, 1941, many émigrés who had fled the Nazis, including Klaus Mann, could see the play performed in German at the Austrian theater in New York (see Mann, *Le tournant,* p. 556).

82. Testimony from Lise Deharme, gathered by Frederick Brown in his *An Impersonation of Angels* (New York: Viking, 1968), p. 353.

83. He had written to him once before, fifteen years earlier, to try to avoid sanctions against Desbordes, when he did his military service in the navy.

84. Roger Lannes, journal entry for November 21, 1941, IMEC.

85. "La querelle des *Parents terribles,*" *Je suis partout,* November 15, 1941.

86. Lucien Rebatet, "D'un Céline l'autre," in *Louis-Ferdinand Céline, Cahiers de l'Herne,* vols. 3 and 5 (Paris: Éditions de l'Herne, 1963), p. 231.

87. Céline to Jean Cocteau, undated (late November 1941), published in *Cahier Céline,* vol. 7 (Paris: Gallimard, n.d.), pp. 230–231. One page was reprinted by Pierre Chanel in *Album Cocteau,* p. 146.

88. In Louis-Ferdinand Céline, *Bagatelles pour un massacre* (Paris: Éditions Denoël, 1937).

89. In *Les beaux draps* (Paris: Nouvelles éditions françaises, 1941), p. 115, Céline accused Catholic morality of having prepared, over twenty centuries, an invasion in the name of a religion "founded by twelve Jews"—for once his facts were accurate—and asked that Jews be grabbed by their "strings" ["tzitzit," the "strings" that hang from the four corners of the prayer shawl—Trans.] and strangled with them. "We've been stuffed enough as it is by all the apostles, all the Evangelists. All Jews, you know, since Peter the founder, right up to the Pope, via Marx!" he belched in 1938, in *L'école des cadavres.*

90. According to José Germain. Cf. Ory, *La France allemande,* p. 226.

91. *Au pilori,* April 11, 1943, and *La révolution nationale,* December 20, 1943.

92. "Faut-il exterminer les juifs?" *La gerbe* and *L'appel* asked at the same time, to which Céline would reply favorably on October 30, 1941. Cf. Almeras, *Céline,* pp. 225–226.

93. *Les beaux draps*; *Je suis partout,* November 21, 1941. The letter is also partially cited in Frédéric Vitoux, *La vie de Céline* (Paris: Grasset, 1988), p. 376.

94. Cf. Hervé Le Boterf, *La vie parisienne sous l'Occupation*, vol. 2: *Paris la nuit* (Paris: France-Empire, 1974), p. 239.

95. In July 1941 Jünger had been assigned to Germany's censorship unit; his job was to examine the letters sent to officers by their friends and families.

96. Ernst Jünger, *Journaux de guerre* (Paris: Julliard, 1990), p. 241, entry from November 23, 1941. *Auf den Marmorklippen* was published in Germany in the fall of 1939; later, Jünger would remember a political discussion between himself, his friend Carl Schmitt, the famous jurist, and Cocteau, but could not recall what it was about. Cf. Ernst Jünger, with Antonio Gnoli and Franco Volpi, *Les prochains titans* (Paris: Grasset, 1998), p. 98; *Fumeurs d'opium* is by Jules Boissière, and was published in 1896. See Cocteau, *Journal (1942–1945)*, p. 61, n. 2.

97. *Comoedia*, December 20, 1941.

98. Cf. Henri Amouroux, *Les beaux jours des collabos: Juin 1941–June 1942* (Paris: Laffont, 1978), p. 360.

99. Directed by the well-known Eugène Deloncle, the Cagoule's general staff included Eugène Schuller, the founder of L'Oréal, and the writer Raymond Abellio. As for its paper, *La révolution nationale*, it would be, with *Je suis partout* and *Au pilori*, one of the strongest voices of the anti-Cocteau campaign.

100. See Robert O. Paxton, *La France de Vichy* (Paris: Seuil, 1974), p. 243 and Ory, *La France allemande*, p. 99. A rival of Déat's and Doriot's, Deloncle, the head of the Cagoule, sought to prove that he was Germany's greatest ally, while hoping that the Occupier, grown weary of Pétain, would finally install a French National-Socialism — with the aim of restoring the country of Clovis and Charlemagne, perhaps even recreating their Franco-German kingdoms. Two months later, Filliol would be one of ten speakers at the conference that Céline would organize to discuss the elimination of Jews from French life — along with Deloncle and Dr. Montandon, who recommended removing Jews' noses to make them more easily recognizable. See Maurice Vanino, *L'école du cadavre, l'affaire Céline* (Paris: Creator, 1952); excerpts can also be seen in *Louis-Ferdinand Céline*, in *Cahiers de l'Herne*, vols. 3 and 5 (Paris: Éditions de l'Herne, 1963), p. 488.

101. Alexandre Stavisky was a Russian Jew living in France who was accused of embezzlement in 1934 — the biggest scandal of the prewar era. — Trans.

CHAPTER 20. IN THE HEART OF THE FURNACE

1. This article also forbade all "normal" relations with anyone younger than sixteen. This interdiction was maintained by de Gaulle, and later overturned by Mitterand.

2. We will recall that Abel Bonnard visited Cocteau thirty years earlier, in his bachelor pad in the Hôtel Biron. With Larbaud, Jacques Benoist-Méchin (1901–1983) was the translator of the first chapter of Joyce's *Ulysses*, and a fleeting member of the École d'Arcueil, a group of musicians patronized by Satie. Before the war, Benoist-Méchin was the noted author of a book on music in the work of Proust and a history of the German army, which had long-lasting success. After the defeat of 1940, he was in favor of collaborating with Germany, and served as a member of Darlan's and Laval's cabinets (1942). At the Liberation he was condemned to death, but his sen-

tence was commuted to life in prison and he was freed on parole in 1954. He then turned to working on a history of the Arab world (*Printemps arabe*, 1959).

3. "Throughout articles by Châteaubriant, Drieu, and Brasillach [there are] many curious metaphors which present relations with Germany as a sexual union in which France plays the role of the woman. And very certainly the feudal relationship of the collaborator to his master has a sexual aspect," Sartre noted in his "Qu'est-ce qu'un collaborateur?," which was first published in August 1945 and then reprinted in *Situations III* (Paris: Gallimard, 1948), pp. 43–61. As early as 1939, the best short story in *Le mur*, "L'enfance d'un chef," was about a young man from a good family gone astray, seduced by Bergère, a Surrealist-influenced poet, who rapidly turns into a Fascist, anti-Semitic "bastard."

4. He would himself denounce *Je suis partout* as "an over-excited cenacle of politically ambitious little queers," in a postwar letter to Albert Paraz. See Louis-Ferdinand Céline, *Lettres à Albert Paraz, 1947–1957* (Paris: Gallimard, 2009).

5. Cf. Pierre-Marie Dieudonnat, *Je suis partout, 1930–1944* (Paris: La Table Ronde, 1973), p. 349.

6. Draft of a letter from Jean Cocteau to Drieu la Rochelle, April 12, 1918, BHVP, box 24.

7. Pierre Drieu la Rochelle, *Le feu follet* (Paris: Gallimard, 2000), pp. 120–123.

8. Gerhardt Heller, *Un allemand à Paris* (Paris: Seuil, 1981), p. 58; Albert Speer, *Au coeur du Troisième Reich* (Paris: Fayard, 1971), p. 228.

9. Maurice Martin du Gard, *La chronique de Vichy* (1948; Paris: Flammarion, 1976), p. 276.

10. Head of propaganda for the Légion des Volontaires Français Contre le Bolchevisme, Fontenoy would finally kill himself, wearing the uniform of the Waffen SS, in the 1945 street fighting in Berlin.

11. Robert Desnos, *Le vin est tiré . . .* (Paris: Gallimard, 1943).

12. Simone de Beauvoir, *La force de l'âge* (Paris: Le Livre de Poche, 1960), p. 593.

13. See the June 21, 1941, issue of *Comoedia*, devoted to Melville's *Moby Dick*. *Comoedia* would always publish glowing reviews of Sartre and Beauvoir's work.

14. He had been socializing with Cocteau since September 1941; in May 1941 Roger Stéphane organized the talk that Gide would give in Nice on Henri Michaux, the one that the Légion des Volontaires Français Contre le Bolchevisme would try to get banned.

15. François Sentein, *Nouvelles minutes d'un libertin (1942–1943)* (Paris: Gallimard, 2000), p. 253; Jean Cocteau, *Journal (1942–1945)* (Paris: Gallimard, 1989), p. 387, entry for October 20, 1943.

16. Cf. Ernst Jünger, *Journaux de guerre* (Paris: Julliard, 1990), p. 272.

17. Marc Doelnitz, *La fête à Saint-Germain-des-Prés* (Paris: Laffont, 1979), p. 108.

18. Jean Aurenche, *La suite à l'écran* (Paris: Institut Lumière/Actes Sud, 1993), p. 119.

19. Sentein, *Nouvelles minutes d'un libertin*, p. 271, entry for December 22, 1941; Jean Hugo, *Le regard de la mémoire* (Paris: Babel-Actes Sud, 1983), p. 500.

20. He set himself up on a little folding table that had belonged to Henry Bataille, Yvonne de Bray's husband, whom *Je suis partout* had accused him of imitating. See Roger Lannes, unpublished journal, entry for November 25, 1941, IMEC.

21. Ibid. One of these drafts would later help him sketch the face of Éluard, one of the Parisian supporters of the Resistance.

22. R. M. Féchy, *Au pilori*, March 12, 1942, reproduced in Cocteau, *Journal (1942–1945)*, p. 656. With 90,000 copies published per week, *Au pilori* would soon give the list of names of those who had been interned at Drancy. Its patron was the Parti Français National, which had been created at the request of the Propagandastaffel, whose thugs had cracked down on Jewish stores since the early days of the Occupation.

23. His secretary was Mme Boudout-Lamotte.

24. Heller, *Un allemand à Paris*, p. 57; Jünger, *Journaux de guerre*, p. 266.

25. Klaus and Max Valentiner were the sons of the famous Christian August Max Ahlmann Valentiner, a U-boat commander in the First World War. Klaus, a corporal, was assigned as an interpreter to the air force, but spent most of his time, according to Jünger, entertaining in their studio.

26. Cocteau, *Journal (1942–1945)*, p. 28, entry for March 12, 1942.

27. Ibid.

28. These comings and goings were analyzed in great detail in Jean Touzot, *Jean Cocteau* (Lyon: La Manufacture, 1989), p. 133.

29. Heller, *Un allemand à Paris*, p. 44; Cf. Martin du Gard, *La chronique de Vichy*, p. 284. In his *Journal*, Drieu la Rochelle would go so far as to describe Achenbach, head of press relations at the German embassy, as a "traitor to Hitler's Germany."

30. Most of the vigorous young soldiers were on the eastern front.

31. This is the well-known *Portrait of Dora in a White Blouse* (October 9, 1942).

32. Brassaï, *Conversations avec Picasso* (1964; Paris: Gallimard, 1997), p. 195.

33. Max Jacob to Jean Cocteau, June 24, 1942, cited in Cocteau, *Journal (1942–1945)*, p. 167.

34. Pablo Picasso, *Propos sur l'art* (Paris: Gallimard, 1998), p. 44.

35. Cf. André-Louis Dubois, *Sous le signe de l'amitié* (Paris: Plon, 1972), p. 145.

36. He was the director of the prefect of police's office, according to Dubois, and head of the municipal police, according to Cocteau.

37. Cocteau, *Journal (1942–1945)*, p. 554, entry for September 19, 1944.

38. Ibid., p. 58. In 1943, in an article on Greco, Cocteau would say, "Picasso demonstrates that royal magnificence with which beings who oblige all objects and forms to obey them move. Everything they touch, everything they break, everything they destroy, everything they collect, everything they buy, everything they are given, everything they join together, everything they attempt, everything they put in order and disorder, and the very dust itself, rise to a superhuman level of dignity. Nothing is neutralized. Nothing accepts insignificance." Jean Cocteau, *Le Greco* (Paris: Le Divan, 1943).

39. Ernst Jünger, *Journaux parisiens* (Paris: Julliard, 1991), p. 316, entry for July 22, 1942.

40. Heller, *Un allemand à Paris*, p. 127.

41. *Comoedia*, June 6, 1942.

42. Cited in Gisèle Sapiro, *La guerre des écrivains, 1940–1953* (Paris: Fayard, 1999), p. 698.

43. Jean Hugo, *Le regard de la mémoire* (Paris: Babel-Actes Sud, 1983), p. 535.

44. Cocteau's piano would be "inaugurated" in January 1943.

45. Matisse also painted several doors for them. Cf. Frederick Brown, *An Impersonation of Angels* (New York: Viking, 1968), p. 12 of the photograph notebook, which reproduces a document showing Cocteau and Picasso, in 1943, at the home of the Anchorenas, in front of the piano "decorated" by the writer.

46. Cocteau, *Journal (1942–1945)*, p. 239, entry for January 17, 1943.

47. Brassaï, *Conversations avec Picasso*, pp. 190–191.

48. Cf. Dubois, *Sous le signe de l'amitié*, p. 146.

49. Cocteau, *Journal (1942–1945)*, p. 172, entry for July 1, 1942. Cocteau had already encountered Desnos in the corridors of *Ce soir*, at the time of the Front Populaire.

50. Cf. Cocteau, *Journal (1942–1945)*, p. 25, entry for March 11, 1942.

51. Jünger, *Journaux de guerre*, p. 268.

52. Cocteau, *Journal (1942–1945)*, p. 112, entry for May 6, 1942.

53. This is also André-Louis Dubois's hypothesis, which he outlines in his memoirs (*Sous le signe de l'amitié*, p. 122)—he was very much aware of Cocteau's "secret" affairs, which Herbert R. Lottman confirms in *La rive gauche* (Paris: Seuil, 1981), p. 333. Dubois even specifies that this number corresponds to a service telephone assigned to the general staff of the Wehrmacht.

54. Cocteau would go so far as to say that Breker saved his life. Cf. Cecil Beaton, *Diaries, 1944–1945: The Happy Years* (London: Weidenfel and Nicholson, 1972), p. 12. Carole Weisweiller and Patrick Renaudot, in *Jean Marais le bien-aimé* (Monaco: Éditions du Rocher, 2003), p. 111, confirm that Jean Marais learned only years later from Paul Morihien how much Breker had protected him.

55. Cocteau, *Journal (1942–1945)*, p. 112, entry for May 6, 1942.

56. Cocteau did confide his enthusiasm to his journal, which would be published only forty years later and not right away, as Marie-Agnès Joubert seems to believe in *La Comédie-Française sous l'Occupation* (Paris: Tallandier, 1998), p. 444.

57. Arno Breker, *Paris, Hitler et moi* (Paris: Presses de la Cité, 1970), p. 136.

58. Paul Éluard to Jean Cocteau, July 2, 1942, cited in Cocteau, *Journal (1942–1945)*, p. 175.

59. "La Vénus d'Ille" is a short story by Prosper Mérimée in which a statue (La Vénus d'Ille) comes to life and kills the son of its owner.—Trans.

60. "Arno Breker vous parle," *Comoedia*, December 4, 1943, cited in Gilles Ragache and Jean-Robert Ragache, *La vie quotidienne des écrivains et des artistes sous l'Occupation, 1940–1944* (Paris: Hachette, 1988), p. 129.

61. Breker would invite Cocteau to the farewell dinner that his French hosts organized. The writer would be seated not far from Arletty, his interpreter in *L'école des veuves*, and Brasillach, his accuser in *Je suis partout*. But the list of Breker's guests, friends amassed during his stay in Paris, was dizzying: it extended from Le Corbusier to Pierre Benoit, the author of *Atlantida*.

62. If very few technical and administrative staff left the theaters, it was likely because of the Germans' desire to maintain intense artistic activity in Paris as a smoke screen.

63. In the wake of the retrospective, Madame Flammarion's husband had published a monograph on Breker's work, which included 120 engravings, including portraits of Albert Speer, Goebbels, Mme Martin Bormann, and Mlle Edda Goering. "La Tour

du Pin, better not. He was liberated under mysterious circumstances," wrote the Swiss mediator Lachenal in the summer of 1943, when he had to recruit authors for the Resistance press. And it was not Breker who gave an account of this intervention for Picasso in his book, but Hervé Le Boterf—see his *La vie parisienne sous l'Occupation*, vol. 2: *Paris la nuit* (Paris: France-Empire, 1974), p. 59.

64. See Brown, *An Impersonation of Angels*, p. 359, where the references to this issue of *Signal* are not cited.

65. Cocteau, *Journal (1942–1945)*, p. 128; Abbé Mugnier, *Journal (1879–1939)* (Paris: Mercure de France, 1985), p. 545.

66. Cf. John Toland's analysis in *Hitler* (Paris: Laffont, 1983), esp. p. 605.

67. Cocteau, *Journal (1942–1945)*, p. 129, entry for May 18, 1942; Henri Mondor, *Propos familiers de Paul Valéry* (Paris: Grasset, 1957), pp. 142–143. In his memoirs, in which he never fails to put himself in the best possible light, in spite of his limited intelligence, Breker writes, "Hitler wanted to go as far as the boulevard du Montparnasse to get a sense of the place where I spent years working. We drove as far as the famous café La Closerie des Lilas."

68. Beginning in 1939, an "intimate friend of Hitler's" had made an idyllic portrait for Cocteau of the atmosphere at Berchtesgaden, according to Claude Mauriac—see his *Une amitié contrariée* (Paris: Grasset, 1970). Was it Breker?

69. Cocteau, *Journal (1942–1945)*, p. 138.

70. Maurice Sachs, *La chasse à courre* (Paris: Gallimard, 1948), p. 62; *Les cahiers de la petite dame*, in *Cahiers André Gide*, vol. 3 (Paris: Gallimard, 1971), p. 205.

71. The pun was Marie-Louise Bouquet's.

72. Ian Kershaw, *Hitler, 1889–1936: Hubris* (Paris: Flammarion, 1999), p. 1168.

73. Cocteau, *Journal (1942–1945)*, p. 138, entry for May 29, 1942.

74. Hitler's attitude, at first, appears in directive 490, which he gave on July 9, 1940: "We can only consider the armistice given to France, terrible for the conquered, generous on the part of the conqueror, as a set of general rules and as a peace treaty during which France, spared up to this point, will become a kind of 'larger Switzerland,' a 'land of tourism, which may eventually be in charge of some production in the field of fashion'" (cited by Henri Amouroux, *La grande histoire des Français sous l'Occupation*, vol. 1: *1939–1941* [Paris: Laffont, 1997], p. 531). "Hitler had been equivocal about his true feelings toward France for as long as it had seemed useful," as P. Andreu and F. Grover note in their *Drieu la Rochelle* (Paris: Hachette Littérature, 1979), pp. 497–498: "He did not want to collaborate with France, Goebbels said, in his journal, that for Hitler, 'all this talk of collaboration is only provisory.' On April 30th (1942), he notes: 'If the French knew what the Führer meant to demand of them, they would shed all the tears in their bodies. That's why it's better to dissimulate for the moment, and take what we can from their delaying tactics.' Otto Abetz, much like Drieu in this respect, had for a long time tried to maintain his illusions regarding Hitler's sincerity, on the possibility of a Franco-German alliance. The ambassador was thus able to play a useful role for Hitler." See also Barbara Lambauer, *Otto Abetz et les français ou l'envers de la collaboration* (Paris: Fayard, 2001). This book shows how Abetz was a master at manipulating the opinions of intellectuals, those who worked in economics, and of course, government officials in Vichy and in Paris.

75. Cocteau, *Journal (1942–1945)*, p. 133, entry for May 24, 1942; "Littérature de vaincu," *L'appel*, June 25, 1942, cited in Pascal Ory, ed., *La France allemande: Paroles du collaborationnisme français (1933–1945)* (Paris: Gallimard/Julliard, 1977), p. 78.

76. In the very beginning of 1944, Desnos, arrested for resistance fighting and sent to the camp in Compiègne, wrote to his wife, Youki, "I assure you that I am delighted to spend several months in a German camp. It will make for some wonderful reporting." Cf. Jean Galtier-Boissière, *Mémoires d'un Parisien* (Paris: Quai Voltaire, 1994), p. 828. Goudeket was released thanks to the intervention of José Maria Sert and Hélène Morand; see Cocteau, *Journal (1942–1945)*, p. 138.

77. In October 1941, Jacob received a visit from a plainclothes German officer, an art critic who was outspokenly negative about the Nazis. "If anything happens to him, let me know right away," the officer said to a mutual friend. A few days later, German police raided Saint-Benoît. See Max Jacob to Jean Cocteau, April 5, 1942, in Max Jacob and Jean Cocteau, *Correspondance, 1917–1944*, ed. Anne Kimball (Paris: Paris-Méditerranée/Écrits des Hautes-Terres, 2000), p. 590; Jean Cocteau to Pierre Duflos, December 5, 1928, cited in Pierre Duflos, *Simple est un miracle* (Paris: Arnaud Seydoux, 1993).

78. Cocteau, *Journal (1942–1945)*, p. 194; "La République du silence," *Les lettres françaises* 20 (September 9, 1944).

79. Cocteau, *Journal (1942–1945)*, p. 343, entry for September 3, 1943.

80. Maurice Sachs to Yvon Belaval, cited in Henri Raczymow, *Maurice Sachs* (Paris: Gallimard, 1988), p. 62. Even the most zealous Communist intellectuals did not go so far, in their fight for the workers' homeland.

81. "Isn't it beautiful to see that this woman of forty has not changed since she was sixteen years old, and is still faithful to me," Cocteau wrote in his journal, when he was once again a regular guest in the house in the place des États-Unis. Lise Deharme ended up hiding in a house in the Glacière neighborhood; Marie Laure received a visit from the Gestapo. Cf. Dubois, *Sous le signe de l'amitié*, p. 167. Léon Poliakoff (*L'étoile jaune* [Paris: Éditions Grancher, 1999], pp. 62–63), did not recognize the writer under the name Caulette—a fact also cited in Gérard Walter, *La vie à Paris sous l'Occupation, 1940–1944* (Paris: Armand Colin, 1960), and Cocteau, *Journal (1942–1945)*, p. 321, entry for July 17, 1943. "This intimate detail of the life of a woman . . . who never had anything to do with politics, does not shock me," Simone de Beauvoir said five years later.

82. This Aeschylus publishing project would never come to anything. One of the cockerels was called Victor, and neither Marais nor Cocteau had the courage to strangle it; they wound up offering it to Jouhandeau, who knew what to do; author's interview with Jacques Loyau, November 17, 1998. Fanfan Berger, whose father ran the Hildich and Key shop on the rue de Rivoli, where Cocteau et Radiguet lived, was the young girl who ran to the town hall for ration cards; author's interview, April 29, 1998; Cocteau, *Journal (1942–1945)*, pp. 191–192, and François Sentein, interview with the author, April 5, 1998. Morihien received so many calls that Cocteau said: "I am my secretary's secretary"; see Dubois, *Sous le signe de l'amitié*, p. 120, and Barillet, *Quatre années sans relâche* (Paris: Fallois, 2001).

83. Cocteau, *Journal (1942–1945)*, p. 243, entry for January 20, 1943.

84. Cocteau, *Poèmes, 1916–1955* (Paris: Gallimard, 1956), pp. 103–140.

85. *Le lit à colonnes* starred Jean Marais, Mila Parely, and Fernand Ledoux.

86. Author's interview with Joseph Rovan, whose parents were saved by Franz Thomassin, March 18, 1999; Cocteau, *Journal (1942–1945)*, entry for October 11, 1943; Pieral, *Vu d'en bas* (Paris: Robert Laffont, 1976), p. 138.

87. Cocteau, *Journal (1942–1945)*, p. 226, entry for January 5, 1943.

88. This film, which celebrated the Maréchal's work as well as that of Henri Bergson, whom everyone knew was Jewish, would be shown during a gala event at the Opéra de Paris, May 4, 1944.

89. Jean Marais, *Histoires de ma vie* (1975; Ramsay poche cinéma, 1994), p. 160; Cocteau, *Journal (1942–1945)*, pp. 263 and 265.

90. "Renaud et Armide," letter from Jean Cocteau to Marie Bell, August 1941, in *CJC*, vol. 10, p. 119.

91. Hugo, *Le regard de la mémoire*, p. 500.

92. Cocteau, *Journal (1942–1945)*, p. 297, entry for April 15, 1943.

93. *Journal de Joseph Goebbels*, vol. 1: 1943–1945 (Paris: Éditions Tallandier, 2005), entry for May 19, 1942.

94. Cocteau, *Journal (1942–1945)*, p. 114.

95. Quoted in Hugo, *Le regard de la mémoire*, p. 521.

96. Bernard Faÿ, *Les précieux* (Paris: Perrin, 1966), p. 289.

97. [This literally means "The other night, sales records were broken/The dusty carpets need to be beaten," but there is a double entendre because the word "tapette" means both "tap" or flyswatter, and is slang for homosexual.—Trans.] Pierre Ducroq, *La Révolution nationale*, April 17, 1943.

98. Laubreaux, *Je suis partout*, May 26, 1941.

99. Philippe Almeras, *Céline, entre haines et passion* (Paris: Laffont, 1994), p. 258.

100. *Je suis partout*, April 23, 1943.

101. Colette, *De ma fenêtre* (Paris: Ferenczi, 1948), p. 111.

102. Martin du Gard, *La chronique de Vichy*, p. 214.

103. André Breton, *Arcane 17* (Paris: Éditions 10/18, 1965), pp. 18–19.

104. Lise Deharme, *Les années perdues, Journal (1939–1949)* (Paris: Plon, 1961), pp. 153–154, entry for June 27, 1943.

105. The accusations probably came from *Au pilori* or *Je suis partout*, to judge by the reference to Chaplin.

106. Cocteau, *Journal (1942–1945)*, p. 121.

107. Roger Lannes, unpublished journal, entry for September 9, 1943, IMEC.

108. "Plebian Antinous" is a reference to the *Andromaque* that he would produce at Théâtre Édouard-VII. In antiquity there were several mythic male couples: Castor and Pollux, Achilles and Patrocles. Parely was performing the "punaise" in Renoir's *La règle du jeu*.

109. Cocteau, *Journal (1942–1945)*, pp. 548–549, n. 2, entry for September 12, 1944, lines scratched out.

CHAPTER 21. THE UNIVERSAL SUSPECT

1. Dominique Rolin, *Plaisirs, entretiens avec Patricia Boyer de La Tour* (Paris: Gallimard, 2001), p. 18.
2. Roger Lannes, unpublished journal, entry for February 12, 1943, IMEC.
3. After the war the nephew of the actor Pierre Fresnay, whom Cocteau had known at school, would become the director of Éditions de la Table Ronde.
4. Edmund White, *Jean Genet* (Paris: Gallimard, 1993), p. 209. In his memoirs, *Le plus clair de mon temps, 1926–1987* (Paris: Ramsay, 1988), Édouard Mac-Avoy nevertheless claims to have met Cocteau for the first time in 1944.
5. "Maton" means prison warden; "lopette," queer.—Trans.
6. Interview with Édouard Mac-Avoy, 1988, in Albert Dichy and Pascal Fouché, *Jean Genet: Essai de chronologie, 1910–1944*, IMEC, 1988.
7. Jean Cocteau, *Journal (1942–1945)* (Paris: Gallimard, 1989), p. 269; White, *Jean Genet*, p. 210.
8. Jean Genet, *Oeuvres complètes*, vol. 2 (Paris: Gallimard, 1951), p. 10; Jean Genet, *Our Lady of the Flowers*, trans. Bernard Frechtman (New York: Grove Press, 1963), p. 52.
9. Genet had initially thought he would call *Miracle de la rose Miracle des enfants de l'ange*, and then *Les enfants des anges*.
10. Cocteau, *Journal (1942–1945)*, p. 272, entry for February 22, 1943.
11. Roger Lannes, unpublished journal, entry for February 23, 1943, IMEC.
12. Marcel Jouhandeau, *Que la vie est une fête*, in *Journaliers*, vol. 8 (Paris: Gallimard, 1966), pp. 101–103.
13. Harry E. Stewart and Rob Roy McGregor, *Jean Genet* (New York: Peter Lang, 1990), p. 115.
14. Told to Roger Stéphane and cited in White, *Jean Genet*, p. 371.
15. It included *Tonnerre de brest*, a first draft of *Querelle de brest*. Genet wrote to Cocteau on the manuscript: "The trust you have placed in me by requesting a dedication compels me to choose it for you from among many. I cannot better express my gratitude to you except by the joy I feel in knowing a reader for whom fetishes are a religion. May this manuscript serve you as an amulet." See Arnaud Malgorn, *Portrait d'un marginal exemplaire* (Paris: Gallimard, 2002), p. 41.
16. Jean Genet, *Lettres au petit Franz (1943–1944)* (Paris: Gallimard, 2002), p. 25; also p. 39 (letter of June 5, 1943).
17. Cocteau, *Journal (1942–1945)*, p. 283, entry for March 14, 1943.
18. Ibid., p. 335, entry for August 18, 1943.
19. Jünger's novel would show two brothers, both soldiers, retiring to the country after bloody encounters at war, to collect plants and put them under the microscope before the Great Forester—that is, Hitler—devastates everything. See Jean Touzot, *Jean Cocteau* (Lyon: La Manufacture, 1989), p. 149.
20. Cocteau, *Journal (1942–1945)*, p. 296, entry for April 13, 1943; also p. 297.
21. Possibly *Miracle de la rose*, according to Edmund White.
22. When Duras started, she was put in charge of readers' notes; in *Le cahier jaune*, according to Gerhardt Heller, *Un allemand à Paris* (Paris: Seuil, 1981), p. 133. The editor also published "Comment reconnaître le juif" by Dr. Montandon.

23. Cocteau, *Journal (1942–1945)*, pp. 303–304, entry for May 3, 1943.

24. Genet, *Lettres au petit Franz*, p. 32, letter dated May 20, 1943.

25. Cocteau, *Journal (1942–1945)*, p. 626, entry for February 21, 1945.

26. Ibid., p. 310, entry for June 11, 1943.

27. Genet, *Lettres au petit Franz*, p. 35, letter dated June 3, 1943.

28. As we've seen, Dubois maintained numerous contacts within the police, and was named head of the reconstruction in the Préfecture de la Seine. Moreover, he worked for a film production company run by the Tuals.

29. Author interview with François Sentein, April 5, 1998.

30. Genet, *Lettres au petit Franz*, p. 55, letter dated June 5, 1943.

31. Ibid.

32. There were 35,000 declared thefts in 1938, and 115,000 in 1942.

33. Lucien Rebatet, *Les décombres* (Paris: Denoël, 1942), p. 279.

34. Genet, *Lettres au petit Franz*, p. 66, letter dated June 28, 1943.

35. Ibid., p. 86, letter dated July 17, 1943.

36. White, *Jean Genet*, p. 180.

37. Ernst Jünger, *Journaux de guerre* (Paris: Julliard, 1990), p. 530, and Cocteau, *Journal (1942–1945)*, p. 322.

38. *Je suis partout*, July 23, 1943. For circulation numbers, cf. Pierre-Marie Dieudonnat, *Je suis partout, 1930–1944* (Paris: La Table Ronde, 1973), p. 346.

39. Jean-Jacques Kihm, Elizabeth Sprigge, and Henri C. Béhar, *Jean Cocteau, l'homme et les miroirs* (Paris: La Table Ronde, 1968), p. 276, and White, *Jean Genet*, p. 237.

40. Cocteau, *Journal (1942–1945)*, p. 327, letter dated July 26, 1943.

41. Jean Genet to Jean Cocteau, Harry Ransom Humanities Research Center, University of Texas, Austin.

42. Decarnin ran the booksellers' box on the quai Saint-Michel where Laudenbach had met Genet; author interview with André Berne-Joffroy, who was associated with the project, June 21, 1999.

43. *Le cri du peuple*, cited in François Sentein, *Nouvelles minutes d'un libertin (1942–1943)* (Paris: Gallimard, 2000), p. 376.

44. Cited in Gérard Walter, *La vie à Paris sous l'Occupation, 1940–1944* (Paris: Armand Colin, 1960), p. 233.

45. Cf. Sentein, *Nouvelles minutes d'un libertin*, pp. 385–387, and Cocteau, *Journal (1942–1945)*, p. 338, entry for August 31, 1943.

46. The LVF was recruiting "by authorization of Maréchal Pétain and the agreement of the Führer"; ten years later, paying posthumous homage to Éluard, Cocteau would tell the story of how, on the day of the attack, he was carrying, in the pockets of his coat, packets of books published by Éditions de Minuit (which at the time was a clandestine publisher) that Éluard was to pick up the following day. The Doriotistes did not find them. "Better to be beaten than frisked," Éluard replied, though he was not there to say for sure.

47. Cocteau, *Journal (1942–1945)*, pp. 338–339, entry for August 31, 1943; Cocteau, *PD*, vol. 2, p. 367; and Roger Lannes, unpublished journal, entry for August 27, 1943, IMEC.

48. A "compère-loriot" was slang for a black eye, boil, or a wart. —Trans.

49. Pierre-Marie Dieudonnat, *Je suis partout*, September 24, 1943; cf. Cocteau, *Journal (1942–1945)*, p. 693 (appendix 13); also Dieudonnat, *Je suis partout*, September 1 and 3, 1943, pp. 339 and 344.

50. Cocteau, *Journal (1942–1945)*, p. 356, entry for September 8, 1943. It was a strange destiny for a gesture passed from Saint John the Baptist to Montesquiou, and from Cocteau to the thief.

51. Ibid., *Journal (1942–1945)*, p. 367, entry for September 26, 1943; Genet, *Lettres au petit Franz*, p. 204, October 22, 1943. Cf. as well Sentein, *Nouvelles minutes d'un libertin*, October 22, 1943, p. 428; Jean Genet, *Lettres à Olga et Marc Barbezat* (Paris: L'Arbalète, 1988), p. 237.

52. Patrick Modiano would walk around this prison looking for traces of Dora Bruder in his novel of that name (Paris: Gallimard, 1999).

53. Dieudonnat, *Je suis partout*, December 24, 1943.

54. Cf. François Sentein, *Minutes d'un libéré* (Paris: Gallimard, 2002), pp. 20–24, and author interview with François Sentein, April 5, 1998.

55. Jean Genet to Jean Cocteau (n.d., 1943), sent from the Tourelles prison, Harry Ransom Humanities Research Center, University of Texas, Austin.

56. Cocteau was exactly the same age as the mother who had abandoned Genet.

57. Maurice Toesca, *Cinq ans de patience* (Paris: Éditions Émile-Paul, 1975), p. 203.

58. Letters from Jean Genet to Jean Cocteau, written from the Tourelles prison, Harry Ransom Humanities Research Center, University of Texas, Austin.

59. His reply is unknown. Like Satie, Genet threw away the letters he received.

60. Cocteau, *Journal (1942–1945)*, p. 487, entry for March 15, 1944, and p. 488, entry for March 24, 1944.

61. "Genêt" means Scotch broom. — Trans.

62. Jean Genet, *Journal du voleur* (Paris: Gallimard, 1949), p. 49 (note); Jean Genet, *The Thief's Journal*, trans. Bernard Frechtman (New York: Grove Press, 1994).

63. Jean Genet, *Notre-Dame-des-Fleurs*, in *Oeuvres complètes*, p. 51; Genet, *Our Lady of the Flowers*.

64. Roger Stéphane, *Portrait souvenir de Jean Cocteau* (Paris: Éditions Tallandier, 1964), p. 10.

65. Brassaï, *Conversations avec Picasso* (1964; Paris: Gallimard, 1997), p. 171.

66. Quoted in Henri Amouroux, *La vie des français sous l'Occupation*, vol. 2 (Paris: Éditions J'ai Lu, 1965), p. 321.

67. Cocteau, *Journal (1942–1945)*, p. 329, entry for July 27, 1943.

68. Dieudonnat, *Je suis partout*, October 13, 1943.

69. Jean Marais, *Histoires de ma vie* (1975; Ramsay poche cinéma, 1994), pp. 150–151.

70. Speech by Cousteau given at the conference; "Nous ne sommes pas des dégonflés" (We are not cowards), given by the editors of *Je suis partout*, January 1944. Cf. Amouroux, *La vie des français sous l'Occupation*, p. 347.

71. *La révolution nationale*, February 19, 1944.

72. Max Jacob to Jean Cocteau, February 29, 1944, in Max Jacob and Jean Cocteau, *Correspondance, 1917–1944*, ed. Anne Kimball (Paris: Paris-Méditerranée/Écrits des Hautes-Terres, 2000), p. 600.

73. Cocteau, *Journal (1942–1945)*, p. 482, entry for February 28, 1944. Pierre André, in *Vie et mort de Max Jacob* (Paris: La Table Ronde, 1982), gives a different version of the text, p. 291.

74. Cocteau, *Journal (1942–1945)*, p. 569, entry for October 17, 1944.

75. Indeed, the petition was signed (for reasons of efficiency, above all) by those well-known people who had good relations with the authorities: Guitry, Utrillo, Salmon, Braque and Mac Orlan; Pierre Cabane, nevertheless, claims that Picasso saw the manifesto as a "provocation"—Cocteau was thought to have been too close to the Germans (cf. Pierre Daix, *Dictionnaire Picasso* [Paris: Robert Laffont, 1995], p. 197). Cabane is not very reliable on this question; he believes that Cocteau did not visit Picasso in his studio, out of fear of running into Gaullists there. See also, on this issue, Hélène Seckel's catalog for the exhibition *Picasso/Jacob* (Paris: Musée Picasso, 1994), p. 194.

76. Henri Sauguet, *La Musique, ma vie* (Paris: Librairie Séguier, 1990), p. 361; Pierre Andreu, *Vie et mort de Max Jacob* (Paris: La Table Ronde, 1982), p. 293. "Max? But he's an elf! He'll fly off!" said the painter, according to François Sentein (*Minutes d'un libéré*, p. 149).

77. Max Jacob to Pablo Picasso, February 9, 1944, cited in Seckel, *Picasso/Jacob*, p. 273, and in Daix, *Dictionnaire Picasso*, p. 197.

78. Jean Cocteau, *Picasso* (Paris: L'école des Lettres, 1996), "Témoignage," p. 75.

79. "I envied JESUS CHRIST who had the joy of dying for mankind," he wrote to Cocteau, in April 1927.

80. *Je suis partout*, March 24, 1944.

81. Céline to Milton Hindus, April 16, 1947, *Louis-Ferdinand Céline*, in *Cahiers de l'Herne*, nos. 3 and 5, pp. 110–111.

82. Lieutenant Heller confirms this; Gilles Ragache and Jean-Robert Ragache, in their *La vie quotidienne des écrivains et des artistes sous l'Occupation, 1940–1944* (Paris: Hachette, 1988), question it.

83. Henri Sauguet, *La musique, ma vie* (Paris: Librairie Séguier, 1990), p. 363.

84. Cf. Lise Deharme, *Les années perdues: Journal (1939–1949)* (Paris: Plon, 1961), p. 179.

85. Roger Lannes, unpublished journal, entry for March 21, 1944, IMEC.

86. Quoted in Maurice Martin du Gard, *La chronique de Vichy* (1948; Paris: Flammarion, 1976), p. 335. [Fresnes is the second-largest prison in France, located outside of Paris.—Trans.]

87. Cocteau, *Journal (1939–1945)*, p. 303, entry for November 8, 1942.

88. Brassaï, *Conversations avec Picasso*, p. 171.

89. Jean Hugo, *Le regard de la mémoire* (Paris: Babel-Actes Sud, 1983), 542.

90. The expression comes from Jean-Pierre Grédy. Sentein refers to "music-hall Racine," in *Minutes d'un libéré*, p. 77; *Je suis partout*, May 26, 1944. Cf. Cocteau, *Journal (1942–1945)*, pp. 699–701.

91. The actors described this way were Alain Cuny, Annie Ducaux, and Michèle Alfa.

92. These arguments were, as ever, made by Laubreaux. "The man with Cocteau between his teeth" is a pun on "Cocteau/couteau [knife]," an oblique reference to a

Communist, caricaturized as a man with a knife between his teeth. See http://www.
gettyimages.fr/detail/photo-d%27actualit%C3%A9/the-man-with-a-knife-between-
his-teeth-anti-stalin-photo-dactualit%C3%A9/113490531 (accessed December 5, 2015).

93. Jean Marais, *L'inconcevable Jean Cocteau* (Monaco: Éditions du Rocher, 1993),
p. 113.

94. His commanding general was based in London.

95. Jünger, *Journaux de guerre*, p. 571.

96. Report by Léon Sliwinski, F-2 agent, in his *Revue historique de l'armée* (N.p., 1952),
kindly shared by Piotr Kloczowski.

97. Cocteau would say that he was arrested by the French Gestapo, while riding his
bicycle, his pockets full of compromising documents.

98. Christabel Thomassin-Levanti, interview with the author, January 24, 2000.

99. Cocteau was convinced that he had torn out Desbordes's eye in order to crush it
under his boot.

100. Cocteau would affirm that de Gaulle cited him among the soldiers of the army of
shadows, without saying when and where.

101. Cf. Stéphane, *Portrait souvenir*, p. 54.

102. Having arrested 1,200 Parisian SS immediately following the mistaken announcement of the successful attack, he let them go after the announcement of its failure,
then tried to kill himself the same evening he had invited Ernst Jünger to dinner.
Jünger, *Journaux de guerre*, p. 686.

103. Reported by Robert Aron in his *Histoire de l'épuration*, vol. 1 (Paris: Fayard, 1967),
p. 285. "We are dealing with aristocrats who let us know with a wink that they were on
our side, and that if they were obliged to talk a big talk, it was because they had the
Gestapo's pistol at their backs," Morand would claim, in *Journal inutile*, vol. 2: 1973–
1976 (Paris: Gallimard, 2001), p. 479; Pierre Drieu la Rochelle, *Journal (1939–1945)*
(Paris: Gallimard, 1999), p. 307.

104. Julien Hervier, preface to La Rochelle, *Journal (1939–1945)*, p. 13.

105. Marais, *Histoires de ma vie*, p. 167. *Je suis partout*'s offices were located on the rue des
Pyramides.

106. Cocteau, *Journal (1942–1945)*, p. 536, entry for August 25, 1944.

107. Ibid., p. 533.

108. That is, Hemingway wrote against the Spanish Stalinists, during the Spanish Civil War;
Cocteau, *Journal (1942–1945)*, p. 535. Some would refer to this period as the "American
Occupation"; see Cocteau, *Journal (1942–1945)*, p. 536, entry for August 25, 1944.

109. H. de Montherlant, *Le solstice de Juin* (Paris: Gallimard, 1976), October 1941.

110. Cf. Boris Kochno, *Diaghilev et les Ballets Russes* (Paris: Fayard, 1973).

111. Marc Dachy, *Dada et les Dadaïsmes* (Paris: Gallimard, 1994), p. 384.

112. His efforts included a "Discours sur Mallarmé," given at the Société des Gens de
Lettres to mark the poet's centenary, that *Fontaine* would publish in May 1942. Cf.
Cocteau, *Journal (1942–1945)*, pp. 651–654, appendix 1.

113. Cocteau, *Journal (1942–1945)*, p. 552, entry for September 16, 1944.

114. Cf. Sentein, *Minutes d'un libéré*, p. 156. "The living and the dead whom we have
turned into fascists in spite of themselves are worth more than those who pretend to

be on our side in spite of us," added Turlais, who, after having rallied to Free France at the last minute, would be killed in Germany, wearing the uniform of Leclerc's troops (*Les cahiers français* 6 [May 1943]). Cf. Sentein, *Nouvelles minutes d'un libertin*, p. 323, and Pascal Ory, ed., *La France allemande: Paroles du collaborationnisme français (1933–1945)* (Paris: Gallimard/Julliard, 1977), p. 228. Hans Mayer, in *Les marginaux* (Paris: Albin Michel, 1994), refers to a German work on Genet's "fascism": Walter Heist, *Genet und underer, Exkurse über eine faschistiche Literatur von Rang* (Hambourg, 1965). François Sentein, interview with the author, April 5, 1998; Sentein, *Minutes d'un libéré*, p. 147.

115. Sentein interview.

116. Simone de Beauvoir, *La force de l'âge* (Paris: Le Livre de Poche, 1960), p. 675.

117. Éluard signed "Blason des fleurs et des fruits"; *NRF* (February 1, 1941). He defended himself by saying that Drieu just had to rifle through Paulhan's drawer, which was full of his poems, to find a signature to use.

118. Cocteau, *Journal (1942–1945)*, p. 545, entry for September 8, 1944.

119. Cf. J. Galtier-Boissière, *Journal 1940–1950* (Paris: Quai Voltaire, 1993), pp. 440–441, and Sentein, *Minutes d'un libéré*, pp. 149–150.

120. White, *Jean Genet*, p. 372. Genet's text was never published and is considered lost; see Cocteau, *Journal (1942–1945)*, p. 614, entry for January 25, 1945. J. Genet, *Pompes funèbres, Oeuvres complètes*, vol. 3 (Paris: Gallimard, 1953), p. 59. *Pompes funèbres* was published in winter 1947, at a print run of 470 copies, without the name of the publisher, which was Gallimard. "His book inspires hate and love at the same time," said Simone de Beauvoir, who was also alarmed by this extremely daring novel that made the Militia a model of a society that was both criminal and military. If Picasso, through his painting, was so intimidating that he earned a reputation comparable to that of Stalin, Genet established himself as a mini-Hitler through his own mental cruelty.

121. This is the account Breker would give of this appearance; Cocteau would later reproach him for never having showed him this bust. Like Thomas the Imposter, Cocteau would end up believing in the truth of his lie. See Arno Breker, *Paris, Hitler et moi* (Paris: Presses de la Cité, 1970), p. 293.

122. Louis Aragon, *Aurélien* (Paris: Gallimard, 2003), p. 62.

123. There were enough poems to fill three wardrobes, and Cocteau managed to avoid working with Éluard on the project.

124. In the return issue of *Nouvelles littéraires*, in April 1945, Cocteau would publish an article describing the Liberation titled "25 Août 1944." Cf. Kihm, Sprigge, and Behar, *Jean Cocteau*, pp. 290–291.

125. Louise de Vilmorin, the wife of a wealthy Hungarian named Count Pálffy, had never shown much enthusiasm for the Allied cause.

126. Cocteau, *Journal (1942–1945)*, p. 598. According to Pierre Cabane, Cocteau, surprised, had added: "Now you've just signed up for the Communist Party!" and Picasso had replied, "Don't you see that it was a joke?"

127. Cocteau, *Journal (1942–1945)*, p. 569, entry for October 17, 1944.

128. After their mother's death, Paul Cocteau (1881–1961) looked after his younger brother Jean's inheritance.

129. Cocteau Archives, Musée de la Préfecture de Police, Paris.

130. Pieral, *Vu d'en bas* (Paris: Robert Laffont, 1976), p. 168.

131. Paul Léautaud, *Journal littéraire*, vol. 3 (Paris: Mercure de France, 1986), p. 1501, entry for December 12, 1946.

132. The Morihien publishing house had its headquarters under the arcades of the Palais-Royal, and employed part of the water polo team for Racing, a famous Parisian sport club. In 1957 Cocteau would also sign, with Stravinsky and Graham Greene, a petition in favor of Ezra Pound. Held in contempt of court, Céline was condemned to only a year of prison, a 50,000-franc fine, and national humiliation; see F. Gibault, *Céline, Cavalier de l'Apocalypse, 1944–1961*, vol. 3 (Paris: Mercure de France), p. 229.

133. *La belle et la bête: Journal d'un film* (Monaco: Éditions du Rocher, 1989), p. 112.

134. Julien Green, *Journal*, in *Oeuvres complètes*, vol. 4 (Paris: Gallimard, 1977), p. 513.

135. Claude Mauriac, *Jean Cocteau ou la vérité du mensonge* (Paris: Odette Lieutier, 1945), p. 16.

136. Cited in "Un garçon en désarroi," in J. Roussillat, *La vie de Marcel Jouhandeau, le diable de Chaminadour*, vol. 2 (Paris: Bartillat, 2002), p. 394.

137. Mauriac, *Jean Cocteau ou la vérité du mensonge*, p. 114.

138. This hypothesis was confirmed by Suzy Mante, who was married to Claude Mauriac: cf. Morand, *Journal inutile*, vol. 1, p. 453.

139. Roger Stéphane, *Tout est bien: Chronique* (Paris: Quai Voltaire, 1989), p. 263.

140. François Sentein, interview with the author, April 5, 1998.

141. Cocteau, *Journal (1942–1945)*, pp. 628–630.

142. His *Prolégomènes à un troisième manifeste du surréalisme ou non*, published in 1942, did not even mention the war. In 1947, invited to debate with a Stalinist tzara at the Sorbonne, he discovered the efficacy of his own methods and got himself thrown out and beaten by Communist henchmen.

143. It was his father's surname, also Jewish.

144. Philippe Jullian, *La fuite en Égypte* (Paris: Julliard, 1968).

145. "Sanqueur" is a play on "sans coeur," or heartless; "Duvant" means "du vent," or "just hot air." — Trans.

146. Maurice Sachs, *Le Sabbat: Souvenirs d'une jeunesse orageuse* (1946; Paris: Gallimard, 1979), p. 85.

147. Ibid., p. 85.

148. Ibid., p. 87.

149. Jean Cocteau, *Journal d'un inconnu* (Paris: Grasset, 1953), p. 105.

150. Unpublished chapter from *L'asphyxie*, cited in Henri Raczymow, *Maurice Sachs* (Paris: Gallimard, 1988), p. 400.

151. "Contre Jean Cocteau," unpublished manuscript.

152. Cocteau, *Journal d'un inconnu*, p. 104. Cocteau lived at the Hôtel de Castille during the 1930s.

153. Pierre Herbart, *À la recherche d'André Gide* (Paris: Gallimard, 1952).

CHAPTER 22. THE UNFASHIONABLE

1. Simone de Beauvoir, *Lettres à Nelson Algren* (Paris: Gallimard, 1997), p. 39, June 28, 1947.

2. Morihien would publish Sartre's *La question juive*, Beauvoir's *L'Amérique au jour le jour*, and Genet's *Querelle de brest*.

3. Genet, who was meant to be Cyclops, withdrew at the last minute. See Marc Doelnitz, *La fête à Saint-Germain-des-Prés* (Paris: Laffont, 1979), p. 169.

4. *Paris-Théâtre* program, issue 66, November 1952, collection Noël Simsolo.

5. François Sentein, interview with the author, 1999.

6. Cocteau presented *Le jeune homme et la mort* as if it were a new *Spectre de la rose*.

7. The phrase means "excited in his jar," like a goldfish, and it is used to call someone an idiot or overly excited.—Trans.

8. Testimony obtained by the author, May 4, 1998, at Gallimard, on the rue Sébastien-Bottin, where J.-B. Pontalis directed at the time the collections Bibliothèque de l'Inconscient and L'un et l'Autre; Simone de Beauvoir, *La force de l'âge* (Paris: Le Livre de Poche, 1960), p. 674.

9. "L'incursion prodigieuse de Samy Frey dans la conversation de Sartre et Beauvoir," Michel Cournot, *Le Monde*, September 28, 2001. Cournot makes just one mistake: he calls Herbaud the man who would nickname Beauvoir "the Beaver," then "le Castor"; in fact, it was René Maheu, another of Sartre's friends, who did so.

10. Simone de Beauvoir, *Mémoires d'une jeune fille rangée* (Paris: Le Livre de Poche, 1958), p. 441.

11. Beauvoir, *La force de l'âge*, p. 595; Jean Cocteau, *Journal (1942–1945)* (Paris: Gallimard, 1989), p. 542, entry for September 8, 1944.

12. Paul Léautaud, *Journal littéraire*, vol. 3 (Paris: Mercure de France, 1986), p. 1715, entry for July 10, 1948.

13. Jean Cocteau, *La difficulté d'être* (Monaco: Éditions du Rocher, 1947), p. 52.

14. Abbé Mugnier, *Journal (1879–1939)* (Paris: Mercure de France, 1985), p. 459, entry for July 14, 1925.

15. Unlike audiences, the critics were pitiless toward the play, which was staged "full of hams." Its "counterfeiting creator" was also accused yet again of pastiching Victor Hugo and Victorien Sardou.

16. "Petit Poucet," known in English as "Hop-o'-My-Thumb," was a character in Charles Perrault's story by that name.—Trans.

17. The film was released in March 1946.

18. *La belle et la bête: Journal d'un film* (Monaco: Éditions du Rocher, 1989), p. 91.

19. Cocteau, *La difficulté d'être*, p. 109.

20. Roger Lannes, unpublished journal, October 22, 1945, IMEC; *PD*, vol. 3, p. 348.

21. John Richardson, interviews with the author, March 1999.

22. *La belle et la bête: Journal d'un film*, p. 41.

23. Ibid., p. 235.

24. Marais had suggested that Cocteau use candlelight for his shots, remembering the images of Philippe Henriot's funeral at Notre-Dame. Sometimes filmed in the middle

of the night, the film derived its crepuscular aspect and its cavernous aesthetic from this choice.

25. *Le jeune homme et la mor*t was a ballet with a book by Cocteau, who also did the choreography, assisted by Roland Petit: there was Babilée, in stained overalls, with one strap broken, quivering like a bird caught by the neck, wings flapping in fear and suffering. Kenneth Anger, the director of *Scorpio Rising*, would adapt it to the screen in 1951. See: http://www.nytimes.com/movies/movie/290729/Le-Jeune-Homme-et-la-Mort/overview (accessed December 30, 2015).

26. Boris Vian's novels (the most notable of which was *L'écume des jours*) are known for their complex use of language and for their surrealistic plots.—Trans.

27. Edmund White, *Jean Genet* (Paris: Gallimard, 1993), p. 266; Jean Babilée, interviews with the author, April 21, 1998.

28. Genet had already torn up a manuscript—*Héliogabale*, which he had written for Marais—when Marais said he didn't like it. There were other copies circulating, however, until the end of the 1950s. As early as the summer of 1944, Genet had turned up at the home of Cocteau—who was still his editor—to demand *all* his manuscripts so he could destroy them, yet hadn't destroyed a single one. Cf. François Sentein, *Minutes d'un libéré* (Paris: Gallimard, 2002), pp. 105–106. Jacques Loiseau, telephone interview with the author, November 18, 1998.

29. J. Delpech, "Jean Cocteau," *Les nouvelles littéraires*, May 9, 1946, cited in White, *Jean Genet*, p. 275.

30. Jean Cocteau, "André Beaurepaire," *Revue Graphis* 15 (May–June 1946). Born in 1924, André Beaurepaire had designed the beautiful sets for *L'aigle à deux têtes* when it was staged at the Théâtre Hébertot.

31. White, *Jean Genet*, p. 272; Jean-Pierre Lacloche in "Brève vie d'Olivier Larronde," introduction to the *Oeuvres complètes* of Olivier Larronde (Paris: Gallimard, 2002), p. 25; Jean-Pierre Grédy, interviews with the author, March 3, 1999; Cocteau, *Journal* (*1942–1945*), p. 615, January 25, 1945.

32. "Quand le condamné à mort s'est éveillé," introduction to Jean Genet, *Lettres au petit Franz (1943–1944)* (Paris: Gallimard, 2002), p. 14.

33. *Paris-Match*, August 9, 2001, p. 64.

34. He would play the lead role in *Un chant d'amour*, the only film Genet made.

35. *Franc-tireur*, January 23, 1947.

36. This was according to Genet himself, in an interview with José Monleón for the Spanish journal *Triunfo* in November 1969. Cocteau thought Jouvet was as poor an actor as he was a director—his rejection of *Les parents terribles* had left a scar. Although infinitely superior as a play, Genet's *Les bonnes* did recall Cocteau's vengeful monologue *Anna la bonne*—which also took place in the close atmosphere of a bedroom—to say nothing of the Oedipal behind-closed-doors plays *Enfants terribles* or *La voix humaine*.

37. "Les bonnes," *La bataille* (March 10, 1949), p. 5, reprinted in Pierre-Marie Héron, "Genet et Cocteau," *CJC*, n.s., vol. 1 (Paris: Passage du Marais, 2002).

38. Genet was sued in 1954 for pornography, which would lead Cocteau to censor slightly some of his drawings.

39. The episode had been inspired by a story told by No Luck (the sailor from Toulon who now worked for Bérard)—a story that Cocteau wanted to adapt for the cinema.

40. *Empreintes* (May–July 1950).

41. The life Genet subsequently led betrayed the profound influence he had absorbed. His lovers also became his adopted sons, and he would first attribute all his talents to them, then, subject to the fantasy of his formative omnipotence, cannibalize their work for his own creations. If Lucien Sénémaud was doing some home repairs for him, "he was Mansart, Frank Lloyd Wright and Le Corbusier all at once," said Edmund White. Was young Abdallah a gifted acrobat? His Pygmalion asked him to use his gifts to make a sculpture of air. He tried to turn a petty car thief called Jacky Maglia into a great driver—better even than Cocteau with Panama Al Brown. A poor barber from Tanger became a Parisian taxi driver, intimate with Haussmann's map and the poems of Mallarmé, as if he too were going to reach the summits where there dwelled one Jean Genet, a truant turned Shakespeare. Stolen from by some, who lacked Maurice Sachs's talent, Genet would see others die tragic deaths, and was almost always accused, like Cocteau in his time. Dreaming as well of being visited by exterminating angels, he was the first to tire out his young lovers. In order to grow up, an angel has to submit to being plucked, tattooed, and wounded: was this not the treatment Genet had inflicted on the effeminate child of Public Services that he had been?

42. Cf. Jean-Jacques Kihm, Elizabeth Sprigge, and Henri C. Béhar, *Jean Cocteau, l'homme et les miroirs* (Paris: La Table Ronde, 1968), note on p. 292.

43. Beauvoir, *Lettres à Nelson Algren*, p. 175, February 12, 1948.

44. Beauvoir, *La force de l'âge*, p. 559.

45. Beauvoir, *Lettres à Nelson Algren*, p. 198, April 4, 1948.

46. He would sketch a poster suggestion for a revival of *Les mouches* the same year.

47. *L'affaire Henri Martin: Commentaire de Jean-Paul Sartre* (Paris: Gallimard, 1953).

48. Bernard Grasset had taken back his publishing house when he was released from prison, where he had been confined as a result of his pro-Hitler sentiments. His first letter had been to Cocteau, one of the few writers who had worried about his fate during the Purge. Obsessed by the memory of Radiguet, the only writer who had given him the impression of nascent genius, the editor had asked Cocteau if he might lure over this young man of whom he had heard so much, this Jean Genet, whose glory he seemed not to realize had been well established for a few years.

49. Cocteau, *PD*, vol. 1, pp. 54, 163.

50. Declaration to the *Times*. Cf. as well the letter from Cocteau to Paulhan of August 9, 1960, IMEC, fonds Paulhan, folder 3.

51. Quoted by Diane Deriaz, who was Éluard's mistress, in *La tête à l'envers* (Paris: Albin Michel, 1988), p. 120.

52. Cocteau, *La difficulté d'être*, p. 14.

53. Ibid., pp. 44–45.

54. To *La difficulté d'être* and the *Journal d'un inconnu*, he added *Démarche d'un poète*, trans. F. Bruckmann (Munich, 1953), bilingual edition.

55. Louis Aragon and Jean Cocteau, *Entretiens sur le musée de Dresde* (Paris: Cercle d'Art, 1957), p. 79.

56. *Renaud et Armide*, act 1, scene 6.

57. "Des mœurs," in Cocteau, *La difficulté d'être*, p. 184.

58. Jean Cocteau, "Un ami dort," *OPC*, p. 717.

59. *Renaud et Armide*, act 1, scene 6.

60. "Lundi," poem signed Jean (September 13, 1954), cited in Pierre Caizergues, *Jean Cocteau-Édouard Dermit, un demi-siècle d'amitié, 1947–1995* (Montpellier: Centre d'études du XXe siècle, University Paul-Valéry, 1998), p. 31.

61. "Les fantômes de Villefranche," Cocteau exhibit catalog, Pompidou Center, October 2003. Bernard Minoret had published *La Camarilla* with Plon, in 1954, and *Les Morot-Chandonneur* in 1955.

62. Anonymous letter from a young actor who lived in Passy, 1947, BHVP, box 27.

63. *Combat*, September 12, 1948. Cf. Touzot, *Jean Cocteau* (Lyon: La Manufacture, 1989), p. 203.

64. Jean Cocteau, *Poèmes de jeunesse inédits*, OPC, p. 1516.

65. Text on *Orphée*, undated, BHVP, box 28.

66. *Jean Cocteau par Jean Cocteau*, interviews with William Fifield (Paris: Éditions Stock, 1973), p. 18.

67. Having become de Gaulle's secretary, he would refuse to say "I don't give a crap about national glory."

68. Genet visited the set with Java, his new boyfriend, whom Cocteau introduced to Marie Déa. Java harassed the young actress so relentlessly that she finally gave in and let herself be dragged—to Genet's great displeasure—to the men's bedroom. The set was disturbed for a while by Java, whom Albert Dichy called an "innocent scoundrel"— a man who made women work for him after having fought on the eastern front with German troops, and a man whom Cocteau would help to clandestinely cross the Italian border in Francine Weisweiller's yacht a couple of years later.

69. Morand, *Journal inutile*, vol. 1: *1968–1972* (Paris: Gallimard, 2001), August 28, 1969, p. 257.

70. "This Voltairean mulatto hair pulls on the red brick and now people see nothing but it, which makes me sad when I meet the Prince Charming of Paris," Cendrars wrote maliciously. See Blaise Cendrars, *Bourlinguer* (Paris: Denoël, 1948), p. 234.

71. Claude Pinoteau, interviews with the author, June 29, 1999.

72. Nicole Stéphane, interviews with the author, June 8, 1999.

73. Jean Mounet-Sully was a great tragic actor of the nineteenth century, and Sarah Bernhardt's lover.—Trans.

74. See "Melville," film portrait by André S. Labarthe in *Cinéastes de notre temps* (documentary collection), broadcast 1970; Cf. Cocteau, *PD*, vol. 1, p. 339. The Cocteau-Melville dispute would last ten years.

75. The festival was organized by "Objectif 49," a movement created by, among others, René Clément and Claude Mauriac, and whose jury included André Bazin and Alexandre Astruc, who would go on to play a key role in the New Wave. It would put Cocteau in touch with the Lettrist International, led at the time by Isidore Isou, who would cast him in his *Traité de bave et d'éternité*, for which Cocteau would draw the poster, and which he would defend outside the festival at Cannes, as the crowd booed with Guy Debord present in the audience. Later, Jean-Pierre Melville would use his

genius to film thrillers and create gangster figures as erratic as they were tragic: *Le doulos, Le samouraï*, and *Le cercle rouge* starred major actors like Alain Delon.

76. Nicole Stéphane, to whom she was related, would introduce them.

77. Jeannine Worms, interviews with the author, April 24, 1999.

78. It was adapted as the celebrated film *The Earrings of Madame de . . .* (1953), directed by Max Ophüls and starring Charles Boyer, Danielle Darrieux, and Vittorio de Sica.

79. Cocteau also studied Holbein and Dürer for inspiration in directing the film, and for designing the costumes and the set.

80. Jean Touzot, preface to *Bacchus* (Paris: Gallimard, 1998), p. 10; Beauvoir, *Lettres à Nelson Algren*, p. 444, April 11, 1951.

81. Touzot, preface to *Bacchus*.

82. *Le Figaro littéraire*, December 29, 1951.

83. *France-soir*, December 30, 1951.

84. *Journal de Claude Mauriac*, February 2, 1939, cited in Claude Mauriac, *Une amitié contrariée* (Paris: Grasset, 1970), p. 35. François Mauriac would confirm that his Catholic friends were horrified to see him under Cocteau's thumb.

85. *Bacchus* had thirty-eight performances. The play was stopped when the Renaud-Barrault company left on a foreign tour; they had not planned to perform it on tour. Jean-Louis Barrault considered *Bacchus* to be one of his company's near-successes. See *Cahiers de la compagnie Madeleine Renaud-Jean-Louis Barrault*, fifth notebook (Paris: Julliard, 1954), p. 61.

86. Sartre could have written two thousand pages, with all the Maxiton he was taking— toward the end of his life, the stimulant would cost him his vision.

87. Jean-Paul Sartre, *Saint Genet, comédien et martyr* (Paris: Gallimard, 1952), p. 240.

88. Jean-Paul Sartre, *L'existentialisme est un humanisme?*, 2nd ed. (Paris: Nagel, 1968), p. 37.

89. Simone de Beauvoir's famous declaration in *The Second Sex* (1949)—"One is not born but rather becomes a woman"—echoes this.—Trans.

90. Cocteau, *PD*, vol. 2, p. 145.

91. Beauvoir, *Lettres à Nelson Algren*, p. 421, December 10, 1950.

92. In fact the situation was more complicated: Genet also owed much to this tradition, which associated sodomy, in all its torture and ecstasy, its abjection and redemption, with a sort of dark sanctity, not by elevation but by abasement; Michelangelo mixed his sperm into his paints, in place of egg whites, according to Cocteau himself. With regard to Genet, Sartre described "the urgency of his quest, which is to surround with religious respect the most denigrated of men" (Sartre, *Saint Genet*, p. 108).

93. Ibid., p. 254.

94. Cocteau, *PD*, vol. 1, p. 325; Cf. Arnaud Malgorn, *Portrait d'un marginal exemplaire* (Paris: Gallimard, 2002), p. 33.

95. "Genet is like a ghost; if he seems alive at all it is with the larval existence which certain people ascribe to their loved ones in the grave," Sartre wrote on the second page of *Saint Genet*. Sartre had understood: just as Cocteau's literary universe was consubstantial with his childhood bedroom forever reproduced in his adult apartments, Genet's depended entirely on the cell, always the same one, where he taped up pictures of boxer-killers, in one of the complex erotic rituals encouraged by these convents full of violent men.

96. Cocteau confirmed, on the contrary, that his own name had been replaced at the last minute with Decarnin's.

97. Jean Genet to Jean Cocteau, August 5, 1952, in Cocteau, *PD*, vol. 1, p. 318.

98. Ibid., p. 391.

99. The expression is from Jan Kott, who was among others who saw Genet during rehearsals. White, *Jean Genet*, p. 419.

100. Undated letter from Jean Genet to Jean Cocteau, in Cocteau, *PD*, vol. 2, p. 39.

101. Sartre, *Saint Genet*, p. 174.

102. Roger Stéphane, *Portrait souvenir de Jean Cocteau* (Paris: Éditions Tallandier, 1964), p. 28.

103. Letter dated September 6, 1906, in *LM*, pp. 37–38.

104. Reception speech, Académie française, October 20, 1955.

105. Jean Cocteau, *Le discours d'Oxford* (Paris: Gallimard, 1956), p. 16.

106. Jean Cocteau, *Journal d'un inconnu* (Paris: Grasset, 1953), p. 35.

107. Cocteau, *PD*, vol. 2, p. 136; ibid., p. 329.

108. He had made a tentative beginning, in 1937–1938, after Picasso's *Guernica*.

109. J. Lord, *Des hommes remarquables, Cocteau, Balthus, Giacometti*, trans. Claudine Richetin (Paris: Séguier, 2001), p. 25.

110. Ibid., p. 10.

111. "Mon premier roman: *Le diable au corps*," *Les nouvelles littéraires* (March 10, 1923).

112. Testimony obtained by Raphaël Sorin in *Elias Canetti* (Paris: BPI, Centre Georges-Pompidou, 1995), p. 51.

113. Quoted in Pierre de Boisdeffre, *Contre le vent majeur: Mémoires, 1368–1968* (New York: Grasset, 1994), p. 294.

114. Frederick Brown, *An Impersonation of Angels* (New York: Viking, 1968), p. 94.

115. Oddly, when Cocteau encountered the bellboy a few days later, he was still wearing his old peacoat, out of fear that Cocteau's fine coat would keep him from receiving decent tips.

116. Denise Bourdet, *Pris sur le vif* (Paris: Plon, 1957), pp. 131–132.

117. Emmanuel Berl, *Le temps, les idées et les hommes: Essais* (Paris: Julliard, 1985), p. 115.

118. He would however be mentioned in some of the *Diaries* that Beaton would publish with Weidenfeld and Nicholson: *1922–1939, the Wandering Years*, and *1944–1948, the Happy Years*.

119. "Ce grand pan qui tombe," *Le nouveau candide*, October 1963 (at Cocteau's death), reprinted in Berl, *Le temps, les idées et les hommes*, p. 411.

120. Cocteau did, however, have some graphic art Picasso had given him, including a Cubist *papier collé* and his portraits from 1916–1917. One of them, sketched in Rome at Easter, 1917, is still in the holdings of the Comité Cocteau.

121. This amount would be nearly six million euros today. The portrait is one of the masterpieces of Henry and Rose Pearlman's collection at the Princeton University Art Museum.

122. Berl, *Le temps, les idées et les hommes*, p. 411.

123. Jean Cocteau to Aragon, November 25, 1918, cited in Louis Aragon, *Papiers inédits: De Dada au surréalisme (1917–1931)* (Paris: Gallimard, 2000), p. 247.

124. Cocteau, *Journal d'un inconnu*.

125. Jean Cocteau to Jean Paulhan, October 27, 1957, IMEC, fonds Paulhan, folder 3.

CHAPTER 23. WHO IS THE GREATEST GENIUS OF THE CENTURY?

1. Cocteau, *PD*, vol. 1, p. 29, entry for August 25, 1951.
2. Claude Mauriac, *Conversations avec André Gide* (Paris: Albin Michel, 1951), p. 48; Jean Cocteau, *Gide vivant: Paroles de Jean Cocteau*, illus. Julien Greene (Paris: Amiot-Dumont, 1952).
3. Paul Morand, *Journal inutile*, vol. 1: *1968–1972* (Paris: Gallimard, 2001), p. 253.
4. This is an allusion to the episode, registered in Gide's journal, in which Cocteau had told him, to amuse him, of his early exploits driving an ambulance at the beginning of the First World War (see Chapter 5); see Truman Capote, *Portraits and Observations* (New York: Random House, 2007), p. 282. The American novelist's testimony is questionable, however; Cocteau went to Sicily in 1951, the year Gide died.
5. Cocteau, *PD*, vol. 5 (February 2, 1956).
6. François Mauriac, "Le cas Jean Genet," *Le Figaro littéraire*, March 26, 1949, p. 7.
7. *OPC*, preface by Michel Décaudin, p. xvii.
8. Cocteau, *PD*, vol. 3, pp. 169–170.
9. The following year, on May 9, his ballet *La dame à la licorne* premiered in Munich. It would be performed again at the Opéra de Paris in 1959.
10. Interview with Édouard Mac-Avoy, 1988, in Albert Dichy and Pascal Fouché, *Jean Genet: Essai de chronologie, 1910–1944*, p. 170, IMEC.
11. Cocteau had brought back a travel journal, *Maalesh* (Paris: Gallimard, 1950), which, however, only pleased half in Egypt, a country he described as a little too miserable, populated by "fanatiques." Étiemble, who taught in Alexandria at the time, panned it in his "La mouche malèche," *Les temps modernes* 54 (April 1950), reprinted in René Etiemble, *Hygiène des lettres*, vol. 1: *Premières notions* (Paris: Gallimard, 1952), pp. 82–96.
12. Cf. N. Rorem, *Other Entertainment, Collected Pieces* (New York: Simon and Schuster, 1996), pp. 80–101. See also *The Paris and New York Diaries of Ned Rorem, 1951–1961* (San Francisco: North Point Press, 1983).
13. "Jean Cocteau," *Flair* (February 1950): 101–102.
14. Wystan Hugh Auden (1907–1973), a British writer and naturalized American citizen, poet, and prose-writer inspired by Brecht before the war (*Poems*, 1930, *The Dance of Death*, 1933), next turned to a Christian existentialism (*The Double Man*, 1941). He was also the "passport husband" of Erika Mann when she fled Nazi Germany for England in 1935.
15. Emmanuel Berl, *Le temps, les idées et les hommes: Essais* (Paris: Julliard, 1985), p. 411.
16. "Intelligence, that small thing at the surface of ourselves. Deep down we are emotional beings," said Barrès, *Mes cahiers, 1896–1923*, edited by Guy Dupré, preface by Philippe Barrès (Paris: Plon, 1963), p. 53.
17. "Entre chien et loup" means literally between dog and wolf; figuratively, twilight; Cocteau seems to want to emphasize the transitory nature of his existence. — Trans.
18. Jean Cocteau to Pierre de Boisdeffre, November 20, 1956. De Boisdeffre's comments on Cocteau, in the many stories and literary anthologies he would publish, would be almost entirely negative.

19. Cf. Cocteau, *PD*, vol. 3, pp. 344–345.

20. Cocteau, *PD*, vol. 1, p. 397.

21. J. Lord, *Des hommes remarquables: Cocteau, Balthus, Giacometti*, trans. Claudine Richetin (Paris: Séguier, 2001), p. 43.

22. Laurence Benaïm, *Marie Laure de Noailles* (Paris: Grasset, 2001), p. 397.

23. "Révolte," *La lampe d'Aladin*, *OPC*, p. 1273.

24. The jewelry included a golden "bull" made by François Hugo, Jean Hugo's relative.

25. Jeannine Worms, *Avec ou sans arbres* (Paris: Actes Sud Papiers, 1985), and *Archiflore* (Paris: Actes Sud Papiers, 1989).

26. Berl, *Le temps*, p. 411; he confided this in 1912.

27. Françoise Gilot, interview with the author, April 26, 1999; "Éluard was seen as too gentle," said Jean Aurenche of the time before the war, "and maybe even a little simple. He was the only one who didn't hate Cocteau, which, in the Surrealists' eyes, was proof of semi-idiocy"; Jean Aurenche, *La suite à l'écran* (Paris: Institut Lumière/Actes Sud, 1993), p. 39.

28. Lord, *Des hommes remarquables*.

29. Bernard Minoret, interviews with the author. See also ibid. and Françoise Gilot and Carlton Lake, *Vivre avec Picasso*, 2d ed. (Paris: Le Livre de Poche, 1974).

30. Francis Steegmuller, *Cocteau* (Paris: Buchet-Chastel, 1973), p. 146. See also Gilot and Lake, *Vivre avec Picasso*, p. 379.

31. Jean Cocteau to Jean-Pierre Millecam, November 19, 1952, cited by Millecam in *L'étoile de Jean Cocteau* (Paris: Critérion, 1991), p. 133.

32. Gilot and Lake, *Vivre avec Picasso*, p. 342.

33. *Jean Cocteau par Jean Cocteau*, interviews with William Fifield (Paris: Éditions Stock, 1973), p. 67.

34. "We must kill modern art," Picasso confided, "because once again it has stopped being modern . . . This also means that we must kill ourselves if we want to continue to be able to do something." Hélène Parmelin, *Picasso dit . . .* , cited in Pablo Picasso, *Propos sur l'art* (Paris: Gallimard, 1998), p. 148.

35. Jean Paulhan to Marcel Jouhandeau, April 1939, in *Choix de lettres de Jean Paulhan*, vol. 2 (Paris: Gallimard, 1992), letter 72.

36. Cocteau, *PD*, vol. 3, p. 177.

37. "Do you have any Picassos?" "I have three." "I'll take the most expensive ones." "They all cost the same." "I'll take all three." "But, madame, you haven't even seen them!" "When I buy gas from Shell, do I ask to see the Suez Canal?" Jean Cau, *Croquis de Mémoires* (Paris: Julliard, 1985), p. 53.

38. Cocteau, *PD*, vol. 1, p. 47.

39. Berl, *Le temps*, p. 413.

40. Cocteau, *PD*, vol. 1, p. 344.

41. Cocteau, *PD*, vol. 2, p. 77.

42. Maurice Martin du Gard, *Climat tempéré* (Paris: Plon, 1964), p. 74.

43. Bernard Minoret, "Les Fantômes de Villefranche," trans. Trista Selous, exhibition catalog, Cocteau, Centre Georges-Pompidou, October 2003 (London: Paul Holberton Publishing, 2004).

44. Gilot interview.

45. Ibid.; Gilot and Lake, *Vivre avec Picasso*, p. 346. These rules applied to Matisse himself; when Picasso was worried what his historic rival (who had slowly become a friend) was up to, Cocteau hurried to arrange a meeting between the two giants, neither of whom wanted to take the initiative, out of fear of looking too eager.

46. Jacques Borel, interview with the author, March 6, 1999.

47. She was the official mistress of Alec Weisweiller, Francine's husband.

48. Gilot and Lake, *Vivre avec Picasso*, p. 378.

49. Gilot interview.

50. Jean Cocteau, *Discours du grand sommeil*, OPC, prologue, fragment 35.

51. J. Richardson, *The Sorcerer's Apprentice* (London: Jonathan Cape, 1999), p. 199.

52. Lord, *Des hommes remarquables*, p. 53; It will be recalled that his attempts at copying Picasso had already made the painter turn cold at the end of the 1920s. Cocteau had already made great use of pipe-cleaner sculptures whose invention "he owed to Picasso." Jacques-Émile Blanche, *Les arts plastiques* (Paris: Les Éditions de la France, 1931), p. 261.

53. Minoret, "Les Fantômes de Villefranche."

54. G. La Porte, *Si tard le soir* (Paris: Plon, 1973), cited in Pable Picasso, *Propos sur l'art* (Paris: Gallimard, 1998), p. 131.

55. Cocteau, *PD*, vol. 3, p. 293.

56. Mac-Avoy interview, p. 248.

57. Leiris himself was allowed to go to the land of Franco; Cocteau was thrown out of Spain, in July 1961, after signing a petition supporting refugees of the Civil War. He later received an official apology.

58. Henri Clouzot's film was *Le mystère Picasso* (The mystery of Picasso), 1955.

59. Jean Cocteau, *Lettres aux Américains* (Paris: Grasset, 1949), p. 17.

60. Cocteau, *PD*, vol. 4, June 9, 1955, p. 1.

61. Cf. M. Picasso, *Grand-Père* (Paris: Denoël, 2001), p. 97.

62. Max Jacob to Jean Cocteau, in Max Jacob and Jean Cocteau, *Correspondance, 1917–1944*, ed. Anne Kimball (Paris: Paris-Méditerranée/Écrits des Hautes-Terres, 2000), p. 454, entry for November 22, 1926.

63. Ibid., entry for August 6, 1955.

64. Millecam, *L'étoile de Jean Cocteau*, p. 193.

65. Emmanuel Berl, *Interrogatoire par Patrick Modiano* (Paris: Gallimard, 1976), p. 116.

66. The performance dates were May 19 and 20, 1952.

67. Cocteau, *PD*, vol. 2, p. 236.

68. "Une page de souvenirs de Blaise Cendrars," *Les nouvelles littéraires*, July 8, 1939.

69. Gilot and Lake, *Vivre avec Picasso*, p. 433.

70. Cocteau, *PD*, vol 4, pp. 138–139, entry for May 28, 1955.

71. Letter dated December 6, 1956, *Lettres de l'Oiseleur* (Monaco: Du Rocher, 1989), p. 186. Tzara, this time, had been more courageous, approving of the insurgents on the spot—before, it's true, remaining silent on his return to Paris.

72. Roger Stéphane, *Portrait souvenir de Jean Cocteau* (Paris: Éditions Tallandier, 1964), p. 56.

73. Second introduction to *Clair-obscur*, BHVP, box 22.

74. Cocteau, *PD*, vol. 3, p. 309.

75. Paul Morand to Jean Cocteau, December 19, 1954, in ibid., p. 315.

76. Reproduced in ibid., pp. 414–431.

77. Jean Cocteau to Maurice Martin du Gard, March 27, 1961, kindly provided by Claire Martin du Gard.

78. Cocteau, *PD*, vol. 1, pp. 271, 305.

79. Ibid., pp. 302 and 306.

80. Ibid., pp. 275.

81. From the tirade that Dr du Boulbon, Bergotte's friend, addresses to the narrator's grandmother after the attack. See *À la recherche du temps perdu*, vol. 1: *Le Côté de Guermantes I* (Paris: Gallimard, 1988), p. 601.

82. The confidence came from Albert Le Cuziat, the director of the baths on the rue de l'Arcade and the model for Jupien.

83. Cocteau, *PD*, vol. 1, p. 305, entry for August 8, 1952, p. 305. Cocteau was rereading the *Recherche* "out of order."

84. Proust quarreled with him when Berl was championing love.

85. Jean-Pierre Millecam, interview with the author, Montpellier, Spring 1998.

86. This is an allusion to *Un chant d'amour*, the unique film by Genet.

87. Cocteau, *PD*, vol. 1, p. 275.

88. Ibid., p. 302.

89. Ibid., p. 303.

90. *Jean Cocteau par Jean Cocteau*, p. 45.

91. J.-M. Magnan, *Cocteau invisible et voyant* (Paris: Marval, 1993), pp. 17–18.

92. Maurice Martin du Gard, *Les mémorables*, new ed. (Paris: Gallimard, 1999), p. 1053.

93. "Jean Cocteau de l'Académie française," *Le Figaro littéraire*, March 12, 1955, reprinted in François Mauriac, *La paix des cimes: Chroniques, 1948–1955* (Paris: Bartillat, 1999), pp. 531–534, and in François Mauriac, *Cahiers de l'Herne* (Paris: Éditions de l'Herne, 1985), p. 399; article published in *Le Figaro littéraire*, March 12, 1955, and reprinted in *François Mauriac, Cahiers de l'Herne*, pp. 399–400. "A word from Barrès on Jean de Tinan gives us some idea of the charming Cocteau of that time," added Mauriac, describing their meeting: "I'm thinking of Jean de Tinan, of his visit to Neuilly, of the way he sounded like a young page, so much lovable noise, kind bragging, all that empty buzzing of the twenty year old. It's the sound of the bee against the window.'"

94. Robert de Saint Jean, *Journal d'un journaliste* (Paris: Grasset, 1974), p. 153; Cocteau, *PD*, vol. 3, p. 140.

95. Notebook "Poèmes," 1958, BHVP, box 13.

96. Matthieu Galey, *Journal*, vol. 1: *1953–1973* (Paris: Grasset, 1987), p. 42.

97. M. Lambron, "Cocteau, l'éternel retour," *Carnet de bal II* (Paris: Grasset, 2003), p. 225.

98. Cf. unpublished Cocteau-Picasso letters at the Musée Picasso, and Cocteau, *PD*, vol. 4, pp. 287, 399–400, entry for October 1955. Another project showed a rooster stuck between the horns of a harlequin's hat, with its tail as a handle.

99. Cited by Richardson, *Sorcerer's Apprentice*, p. 7.

100. Cited in Jean Cocteau, *Le discours d'Oxford* (Paris: Gallimard, 1956), p. 20.

101. Jean Cocteau, *Poésie critique*, vol. 1 (Paris: Gallimard, 1959), p. 141.

102. Martin du Gard, *Les mémorables*, p. 1054.

103. Cocteau, *PD*, vol. 3, p. 159.

104. Ibid., p. 302. In *Une amitié contrariée*, Claude Mauriac tells how Cocteau had refused to be received by his father — "I do not want to be responsible for the increasing fatigue in his voice. He should not push it on my account" — a concern that amused the elder Mauriac, who had just murmured to his son enough rude things about Cocteau that would have been "sufficient to set our two families at war for the next ten generations." See Claude Mauriac, *Une amitié contrariée* (Paris: Grasset, 1970), pp. 217–219.

105. Richardson, *Sorcerer's Apprentice*, p. 119.

106. Cocteau, *PD*, vol. 3, p. 274.

107. Cocteau's composer friends, except for Stravinsky who was then flirting with serial music, were rejected by the avant-garde movement led by Pierre Boulez. Also, on January 13, 1954, at the Théâtre du Petit-Marigny, the first concert of the Domaine musical took place, conducted by Boulez (on the program: Bach, Nono, Stockhausen, Webern, and Stravinsky). All of artistic Paris was invited, but not Cocteau, who, along with Les Six, symbolized the neoclassical aesthetic against which the organizers were fighting. Cocteau, irritated, invited himself anyway and attended the concert, sitting on the floor in the front row. (See J. Agiula, *Le domaine musical* [Paris: Fayard, 1992], pp. 54–55.) The concert was a great success. According to Ned Rorem, who also attended, Cocteau, who "approved of the music," was bothered by the nonreaction of the other spectators. "But what should they have done, *cher maître?*" he (Rorem) asked. — They should have booed!" replied Cocteau. See N. Rorem, "Cocteau and Music," 1981, in *Setting the Tone, Essays and a Diary* (New York: Limelight Editions, 1984), p. 179.

108. Louis Aragon and Jean Cocteau, *Entretiens sur le musée de Dresde* (Paris: Cercle d'Art, 1957), p. 75.

109. "Tribute by Jean Cocteau to Marlène Dietrich," given by Jean Marais at the Bal de la Mer in Monte-Carlo, August 17, 1954. See Cocteau, *PD*, vol. 3, p. 355.

110. *Empreintes* 7–8 (May–July 1950).

111. "Today," wrote Jouhandeau, "these tastes which have become my own, though I keep them under control, have become so promiscuous, such an odious vulgarity surrounds them . . . that I am not at all proud of them; I am almost ashamed. There is a long road from my lack of hypocrisy to the ridiculous place you are in the midst of opening. Don't worry, they will close it, and with great to-do."

112. Reception speech at the Académie Française, October 20, 1955; Cocteau, *PD*, vol. 2, p. 252, August 1953.

113. *LM*, March 28, 1912.

114. Francis Steegmuller had discovered him in 1966: born Vander Clyde at Round Rock and at the time sixty-two years old, Barbette told Cocteau's biographer how he had been with him and Maurice Rostand in a bordello in Marseille known for showing "special" films. "Ah, Monsieur, we do have a film of that kind, and everybody asks for

it," replied the manager, when Cocteau asked for a film with boys, "but unfortunately it's being repaired." See Steegmuller, *Cocteau* (Little, Brown), appendix 14, p. 528.

115. "He had never washed outside or inside, neither body nor soul. He lived off of everyone and wanted to do nothing in exchange. Lucky that he found this Trappist order," wrote Cocteau in his journal; see Cocteau, *PD*, vol. 1, p. 411, December 1952.

116. P. de Boisdeffre, *Contre le vent majeur* (Paris: Grasset, 1994), p. 297.

117. E. Charles-Roux, *L'irrégulière* (Paris: Grasset, 1974), p. 400.

118. "His aphorisms fallen . . ." is from Paul Morand, *L'allure de Chanel* (Paris: Hermann, 1976), p. 7; "a snobby little fag" is cited in Steegmuller, *Cocteau* (Buchet-Chastel), p. 285. "He owed her his life," suggested Michel Déon, who knew them both, alluding to the detox cure she had almost forced him to follow, "but Mademoiselle Chanel's character was so merciless that she could not forgive him for having abandoned himself at one time in her life. She was his guardian angel, yes, but with a sword of fire." See Déon, *Pages françaises* (Paris: Gallimard, 1999), p. 210.

119. J. Rovan, *Mémoires d'un Français qui se souvient d'avoir été Allemand* (Paris: Seuil, 1999), p. 166.

120. Chris Marker, interview with the author by telephone and fax, March 9, 1999.

121. Christabel Thomassin-Levanti, interview with the author, February 4, 2000.

122. Chris Marker remembers that these trunks contained thousands of pages of novels and poems; Thomassin also published, with Chris Marker's encouragement, a volume on Portugal in the Petite Planète collection, at Seuil. The two men were still translating together, under the pseudonym Fritz Markassin, a work by Will Cuppy in which Thomassin's almost excessive erudition was impressive.

123. Cocteau was visiting the United States for the opening of the film of *L'aigle à deux têtes.*

124. Teaming up to (fraudulently) claim his body at the hospital, the boxer's last friends transported it in the back of a truck for two nights straight as they begged for money in Harlem for a grave worthy of his forgotten name. Having slowly drunk away the money, they ended up bringing the coffin back to the hospital, where the "black marvel" headed back to the "garbage," from which a miracle named Cocteau had extricated him before the war. Brown died listening to the recording of the speeches the poet had made about him, which some journalists from *L'équipe* had brought him. This is at least what Cocteau claimed, though thanks to the opium he didn't know if it had been the boxer's body who had inspired his drawings, by making hooks and uppercuts in the air, or the other way around. In time, Panama would join Dargelos, Heurtebise, and the other heroes who were the products of his imagination. In the end Panama Al Brown was buried in his own country.

125. Natalie Paley to Jean Cocteau, August 11, BHVP.

126. Jacques Borel, interview with the author, March 6, 1999.

127. "A modern Mme de Sévigné who took tea with Dada," said Picabia of Aragon.

128. Pierre Lepape, "La sortie de l'artiste," *Le Monde*, April 14, 2000.

129. Aragon to Cocteau, February 1954, cited in Cocteau, *PD*, vol. 2, p. 37.

130. Jean Cocteau to Aragon, December 11, 1918, cited in Louis Aragon, *Papiers inédits: De Dada au surréalisme (1917–1931)* (Paris: Gallimard, 2000), p. 252.

131. Berl, *Interrogatoire par Patrick Modiano*, p. 113.

132. Edmonde Charles-Roux, interview with the author, April 22, 1998.

133. Cocteau, *PD*, vol. 3, January 13, 1954.

134. Cf. Luis Buñuel, *Mon dernier soupir* (Paris: Robert Laffont, 1994).

135. Cocteau, *PD*, vol. 2, p. 354.

136. Cocteau, *PD*, vols. 4, 5, November 1955–February 1956.

137. "What is more human, however," added the painter, innocently, who prided himself on preciously guarding "the charming record of a flatulist," and who would narrate his hilarious spats with the surrealist Centrale in his *Comment on devient Dalí, les aveux inavouables de Salvador Dalí*, ed. André Parinaud (Paris: Robert Laffont, 1973), esp. p. 137.

138. Cocteau, *PD*, vols. 4, 5, Fall 1955 and February 1956.

139. Galey, *Journal*, vol. 1, p. 247.

140. After his death, she ended up composing a *trompe-l'oeil* in homage to *Parade*, blending his face with Satie's, Picasso's, and the letters they exchanged at the time, in a hodge-podge that recalled the walls covered in pinned-up pictures in Cocteau's bedrooms.

141. Sartre would perhaps be the last to resort to this, describing, when Franco died, his "head like a Mediterranean bastard," a comment that was hotly criticized.

142. Jean Cocteau, "De mon physique," in *La difficulté d'être* (Monaco: Éditions du Rocher, 1947), p. 38.

143. Cocteau, *PD*, vol. 3, p. 224.

144. "Les matinées poétiques de la Comédie-Française," *Comoedia*, March 21, 1922.

145. *La règle du jeu*, in which Radiguet had begun to find his feet as a poet, was published in 1956.

146. Jean-Paul Sartre, preface to André Gorz, *Le traître*, 2nd ed. (Paris: Seuil, 1978), p. 30.

147. Bernard Frank, *Vingt ans après* (Paris: Grasset, 2002), pp. 62, 245; Edmund White, *Jean Genet* (Paris: Gallimard, 1993), p. 279.

148. Lord, *Des hommes remarquables*, p. 38.

149. "À Mendelssohn," in Cocteau, *La lampe d'Aladin*, OPC, p. 1277.

150. *Jean Cocteau par Jean Cocteau*, p. 81.

151. Friedrich Nietzsche, *La volonté de puissance*, § 962, and *Oeuvres philosophiques complètes*, vol. 11: *Fragments posthumes, automne 1884–automne 1885* (Paris: Gallimard, 1982), p. 180.

CHAPTER 24. THE SURVIVOR

1. Cited in a letter from Cocteau to Mary Hoek, January 15, 1950. Cf. Francis Steegmuller, *Cocteau* (Boston: Little, Brown, 1970), p. 452.

2. Jacques Chardonne to Roger Nimier, September 1, 1950, in Jacques Chardonne and Roger Nimier, *Correspondance 1950–1962*, ed. Marc Dambre (Paris: Gallimard, 1984), p. 22.

3. Jean Cocteau, *Portraits-souvenir*, in *Oeuvres complètes*, vol. 11 (Lausanne: Éditions Marguerat, 1951), p. 42.

4. Cocteau, *PD*, vol. 1, p. 407.

5. Julien Green, *Journal, 1949–1966* (Paris: Plon, 1969), p. 13.

6. Cocteau, *PD*, vol. 1, p. 93.

7. Ibid., p. 133, June 1953. Cocteau had designed the cover of the review founded by Jacques Laurent.

8. Jean Touzot, *Jean Cocteau* (Lyon: La Manufacture, 1989), p. 11.

9. "La nature a horreur du vide" means "Nature abhors a vacuum" and led to a new pun: "La nature a horreur du Gide" (a pedophile).

10. Cf. A. Blondin, "L'aigle à une tête," *Certificats d'études, Oeuvres* (Paris: Robert Laffont, 1991), pp. 795–802.

11. Edmonde Charles-Roux, interview with the author, April 22, 1998. Cocteau was at his best with young foreigners, like Alberto Arbasino, who wrote a remarkable book about his trip in *Paris, ô Paris* (Paris: Gallimard, 1997).

12. Johnny Hallyday's letter, dated July 27, 1962, was a response to an encouraging letter that Cocteau had sent him. In October 1963, for Johnny Hallyday's November tour, Cocteau wrote, "Hi Johnny, cock of a new morning"; and this text was on his desk on November 11, the day Cocteau died. (Information kindly provided by Pierre Chanel.)

13. Cocteau, *PD*, vol. 5, p. 39.

14. François Truffaut, "Jean Cocteau, *Le testament d'Orphée*," in *Les films de ma vie* (Paris: Flammarion, 1975), p. 228.

15. *Arts-Spectacles* 493 (December 8–14, 1954), quoted in Cocteau, *PD*, vol. 3, p. 396.

16. Robert Craft, *Dialogues and a Diary* (New York: Doubleday, 1963).

17. Marcel Proust, *Écrits sur l'art* (Paris: Garnier-Flammarion, 1999), p. 303.

18. Cocteau, *PD*, vol. 4, p. 251.

19. Raymond Radiguet, "Art poétique," *Oeuvres complètes*, ed. Chloé Radiguet and Julien Cendres (Paris: Éditions Stock, 1993), p. 468.

20. Cau is quoted in the beautiful portrait of Cocteau in his *Croquis de Mémoires* (Paris: Julliard, 1985), pp. 51–58.

21. Jean Cocteau, "De mon style," in his *La difficulté d'être* (Monaco: Éditions du Rocher, 1947), p. 22.

22. Jean-Paul Sartre, *Saint Genet, comédien et martyr* (Paris: Gallimard, 1952), p. 30.

23. Jean-Paul Sartre, preface to André Gorz, *Le Traître*, 2nd ed. (Paris: Seuil, 1978), p. 32.

24. Cocteau, *PD*, vol. 3, p. 288.

25. Andreï Tarkovski, *Le temps scellé* (Paris: Cahiers du cinéma, 1989), p. 188.

26. Epigraph to "La gloire distraite," in *Poèmes de jeunesse épars*, *OPC*, p. 1482.

27. "De tous les partis . . . ," *Clair-obscur*, *OPC*, p. 838.

28. Jean Bourgoint to Jean Cocteau, December 8, 1954, cited by Georges Lauris, *Itinéraire d'un enfant terrible, de Cocteau à Cîteaux* (Paris: Presses de la Renaissance, 1998), p. 111. [*Temps perdu*, "lost time," could also be translated as "wasted time."—Trans.]

29. Jean Cocteau, *La fin du Potomak*, in *Oeuvres complètes*, vol. 2 (Lausanne: Éditions Marguerat, 1947), p. 192.

30. Jacques Forestier already believed this in *Le grand écart*.

31. Cocteau, *Portraits-souvenir*, p. 109.

32. Cocteau, *PD*, vol. 2, p. 201.

33. Hélène Rochas, interview with the author, January 8, 1999.

34. "Soft roe . . ." is from Cocteau, *PD*, vol. 3, p. 84.

35. "À la mémoire de M.S.N. mort pour l'Angleterre," in *Poésies*, *OPC*, p. 163.

36. Cocteau, *PD*, vol. 1, p. 284.

37. Cocteau, *PD*, vol. 3, p. 28, January 1954.

38. "Man is a creature who makes images of himself, and then comes to resemble that picture," said Iris Murdoch.

39. Maurice Sachs to Gaston Gallimard, October 1942, Gallimard archives, cited in Henri Raczymow, *Maurice Sachs* (Paris: Gallimard, 1988), p. 408.

40. The film 8×8, we will recall, was inspired by a game of chess. Duchamp, Calder, Arp, and Tanguy all played as well. The photos of Cocteau under a glass bell jar were on-set photos taken during filming.

41. "This young M. Cocteau is priceless," the Emperor's daughter said at the time; "unfortunately I forget everything he said. I'm going to buy a little notebook."

42. Jean Cocteau to Élise Jouhandeau, April 10, 1960, cited in *Jean Cocteau et son temps*, catalog compiled by Pierre Georgel for the Jean Cocteau exhibit at the Jacquemart-André Museum, 1965, p. 72.

43. *Jean Cocteau par Jean Cocteau*, interviews with William Fifield (Paris: Éditions Stock, 1973), p. 17.

44. André Breton to Leon Trotsky, August 9, 1938, Houghton Library, Harvard University. Cf. A. Schwarz, *André Breton, Trotski et l'anarchie* (10/18) (Paris: Union générale d'éditions, 1977), p. 76.

45. The Surrealists were also interested in the occult at one time. As for Tzara, he would spend the last years of his life decoding Villon's poems using a similar method.

46. Pierre Chanel, interview with the author, March 12, 1998, and Dominique Marny, interview with the author, April 23, 1998.

47. Cocteau, *PD*, vol. 3, p. 324.

48. Roger Lannes, unpublished journal, August 5, 1946, IMEC.

49. Cf. S. Nasar, *Un cerveau d'exception* (Paris: Calmann-Lévy, 2001), p. 370.

50. *Cahiers du cinéma* 152, February 1964. Truffaut was much less enthusiastic: see his *Correspondance* (Paris: Le Livre de Poche, 1988), p. 85.

51. Did the protean albino see *Le testament d'Orphée* with its "Get Famous in Five Minutes" machine? Did he know that Cocteau, after spreading so much of his archive around, by the end of his life held onto absolutely everything that concerned him—letters, photos—in the journal where he recorded his every word and action? He would have smiled, since he too recorded every manifestation of the phenomenon that he was, an icy visionary at the end of painting and the industrialization of art.

52. Cocteau, *PD*, vol. 2, p. 22.

53. Cocteau would go so far as to republish and write the preface to their work: see A. Moberly and É. Jourdain, *Les fantômes du Trianon* (Monaco: Du Rocher, 1959). Cf. ibid., p. 267.

54. Cocteau, *Portraits-souvenir*, p. 188. We will recall that the encounter took place on Easter 1911.

55. "Poèmes" notebooks, BHVP, box 6.

56. The hibiscus is Cagliostro's flower, with the red color of the blood of the poet.

57. "Mimétisme et psychasthénie légendaire," *Le Minotaure* 7 (1935).

58. Cocteau, *PD*, vol. 3, p. 28.

59. Truffaut, "Jean Cocteau, *Le testament d'Orphée*," pp. 228–233.

60. Jean Cocteau to Robert Bresson, January 2, 1960, cited in *Jean Cocteau et son temps*.

61. Paul Morand to Jean Cocteau, n.d., 1960, *Paul Morand écrivain*, comp. Michel Collomb (Montpellier: Centre d'études littéraires françaises du XXe siècle, Université Paul-Valéry, 1993), p. 233.

62. Cited by Marcel Jouhandeau, "Que tout n'est qu'une illusion," in his *Journaliers*, vol. 4 (Paris: Gallimard, 1963).

63. Paul Morand, *Journal inutile*, vol. 1: *1968–1972* (Paris: Gallimard, 2001), p. 247, entry for August 6, 1969.

64. Denise Duval to the author, March 1, 1999.

65. Bernard Gavoty in *Le Figaro*, February 9, 1959.

66. Jean Cocteau, *OPC*, p. 1803.

67. "I know Giacometti for his solid, yet light sculptures, reminiscent of the snow retaining the footprints of a bird," Cocteau is said to have written in a journal he kept in 1929; see it cited in James Lord, *Giacometti* (Paris: Jean-Claude Lattès, 1997), p. 113.

68. Jeannine Worms, interview with the author, April 24, 1999.

69. Pierre Bergé, *Les jours s'en vont, je demeure* (Paris: Gallimard, 2003), p. 30.

70. Interview between Jean Cocteau and Gabriel d'Aubarède, *Les nouvelles littéraires*, July 26, 1962.

71. See *Requiem*, OPC, p. 1096.

72. Jean Cocteau, *Opium* (Paris: Éditions Stock, 1930), p. 39.

73. Picasso's bust of Apollinaire had the face of Dora Maar; it was sawn off and stolen after her death in 1997, then replaced by a copy.

74. *Le Figaro littéraire*, September 14, 1960.

75. *Les lettres françaises*, October 20, 1960.

76. Alain Bosquet, *La mémoire de l'oubli* (Paris: Grasset, 1990), p. 345.

77. Later, Jerzy Lisowski would translate Gombrowicz's *La pornographie*, and publish a remarkable three-volume, bilingual *Anthologie de la poésie française* (Warsaw: Czytelnik, 2000 and 2001).

78. Cocteau, *PD*, vol. 3, p. 355.

79. Cocteau, *PD*, vol. 2, p. 97.

80. *Jean Cocteau par Jean Cocteau*, p. 42.

81. André Breton, *Vases communicants* (Paris: Gallimard, 1955).

82. *Le dernier quart d'heure* . . . , ed. Pierre Lhote (Paris: La Table Ronde, 1955), p. 61.

83. Cocteau, *PD*, vol. 6, p. 194.

84. Ibid., p. 146 (May 11, 1958).

85. See Cocteau, *OPC*, vol. 8, p. 407.

86. Jean Marais, *Histoires de ma vie* (1975; Ramsay poche cinéma, 1994), pp. 213–214.

87. Ibid.

88. Ibid., p. 216.

89. "Branle ton sexe à pleine poigne/Jeune cycliste musculeux/Bientôt tel un cri tu t'éloignes/Recapuchonné ton gland bleu," or in English: "Rub your sex with a firm grip/Young muscular cyclist/Soon like a cry you grow remote/Re-hooded your blue glans," he wrote in "Été" (*Érotiques*, OPC, p. 1022).

90. "They threw me out, quite literally . . . My trunks were in the road," he said to Morand, who added, "This was a mortal blow; he died of it." (*Journal inutile*, vol. 2, p. 120).

91. Cocteau, *La difficulté d'être*, p. 208.

92. Ibid., p. 209.

93. Jean Cocteau, "Conte simple," in *La lampe d'Aladin*, OPC, p. 1266.

94. Jean Cocteau, "Du travail et de la légende," in *La difficulté d'être*, p. 25.

95. Jean Cocteau, *La comtesse de Noailles, oui et non* (Paris: Perrin, 1963), was sold after his death in late 1963.

96. Maurice Martin du Gard, *Les mémorables*, new ed. (Paris: Gallimard, 1999), p. 562.

97. "La mort de Cocteau, Ange et lion," *Mainichi* (October 15, 1963), trans. Peggy Polak.

98. Jean Cocteau to one of his translators, February 23, 1951, cited by Jean-Jacques Kihm, Elizabeth Sprigge, and Henri C. Béhar, *Jean Cocteau, l'homme et les miroirs* (Paris: La Table Ronde, 1968), p. 329.

99. Cocteau, *La difficulté d'être*, pp. 136–137.

100. Louise de Vilmorin to André de Vilmorin, August 1963, cited by Christian Soleil, *Le bonheur fabriqué*, vol. 2: *Le pluriel et le singulier* (Saint-Étienne: Arts Graphiques, 1995), p. 75.

101. James Lord, *Des hommes remarquables: Cocteau, Balthus, Giacometti*, trans. Claudine Richetin (Paris: Séguier, 2001), p. 10.

102. Hélène Rochas, interview with the author, March 11, 2000, and P. Morand, *Journal inutile*, vol. 1, p. 293.

103. Green, *Journal*, vol. 5, p. 337.

104. Jean Marais, *L'inconcevable Jean Cocteau* (Monaco: Du Rocher, 1993), pp. 37–38.

105. Jean Cocteau, *Plain-chant*, OPC, p. 15. ["I will die, you will live, and that's what keeps me awake!/ Is it another fear /That one day I will no longer feel against my ear/ Your breath and your heart."—Trans.]

106. Steegmuller, *Cocteau* (Little, Brown), p. 360. But Craft also points out the irritation Cocteau inspired in the musician, and the way he frequently bad-mouthed him.

107. Laurence Benaïm, *Marie Laure de Noailles* (Paris: Grasset, 2001), p. 388.

108. Jean Paulhan to Marcel Jouhandeau, 1963, in *Cahiers Jean Paulhan*, vol. 6 (Paris: Gallimard, 1989), p. 489.

109. Jean Cocteau, "De Narcisse," *Vocabulaire*, OPC, p. 320.

110. Cited in Touzot, *Jean Cocteau*, p. 212.

111. Emmanuel Berl, "Le grand Pan qui tombe," in his *Le temps, les idées et les hommes: Essais* (Paris: Julliard, 1985), p. 410.

112. Pierre Caizergues, "Sur l'amitié de Paul Morand et de Jean Cocteau," in *Paul Morand écrivain*, p. 19.

113. François Mauriac, *Bloc-Notes*, vol. 3: *1961–1964* (Paris: Le Seuil, 1993), pp. 412–416 and 427–430, October 11 and 16, and November 14, 1963.

114. Mac-Avoy interview, p. 213. "Mauriac could not keep from disinterring the body to spit on it," Morand observed in his *Journal inutile* (vol. 1, p. 404). "Poor Mauriac," Cocteau himself noted, in *PD*. "When he dies he will have had it all, except for everything." François Mauriac told his son Claude how much Cocteau had dazzled him when he arrived in Paris, before disappointing him with his pretentions—"With *Thomas l'imposteur*, I have given France its version of Mozart's *Don Juan*," Cocteau said to him. By 1970, however, Mauriac had changed his mind: "He will live longer and better than any of those who disdained him would believe." Cf. Claude Mauriac, *Une amitié contrariée* (Paris: Grasset, 1970), p. 267.

115. This is from a letter to Pierre Gaxotte, partly cited in M. Galey, *Journal, 1974–1986*, vol. 2 (Paris: Grasset, 1989), p. 112. Mauriac's subsequent comments concerning Cocteau would be much less venomous and would become almost affectionate—as if a great weight had been lifted from his shoulders.

116. José Corti, *Souvenirs désordonnés* (Paris: Librairie José Corti, 1983), p. 200.

117. Gospel according to Saint Matthew, 28:20, King James Version.

118. Pierre Caizergues, *Jean Cocteau-Édouard Dermit, un demi-siècle d'amitié, 1947–1995*, Centre d'études du XXe siècle, University Paul-Valéry, 1998, p. 89.

119. Jean Cocteau, *Discours du grand sommeil*, OPC, p. 444.

120. Caizergues, *Jean Cocteau–Édouard Dermit*, pp. 91, 95.

121. Interview between Jean Marais and Brigitte Salino, *L'avant-scène du cinéma* 307–308 (May 1983).

122. Dedication, Jean Marais exhibition, May 28–September 5, 1999, "Hommage à Jean Marais," Musée de la Vie Romantique, Paris, 1999.

123. Angelo Rinaldi, "Cocteau en trompe-l'oeil," *L'express*, May 19, 1989.

124. Dominique Fernandez, preface, *Le livre blanc* (Paris: Le Livre de Poche, 1999).

125. Edmund White, *Jean Genet* (Paris: Gallimard, 1993), p. 558.

126. Hubert Fichet, *Jean Genet* (Frankfurt: Qumran, 1981), p. 102. "You may think whatever you like of Cocteau, but he was my friend," Monique Lange heard Genet say in the 1970s.

127. White, *Jean Genet*, p. 570; Jean Genet, *Notre-Dame-des-Fleurs*, in *Oeuvres complètes* (Paris: Gallimard, 1953), p. 69. It will be noted that there are two groups of *société des amis* dedicated to Cocteau; the Société des Amis et Lecteurs de Jean Genet was founded only in 1998.

Additional Resources

Compiling an exhaustive list of all the work written, filmed, drawn, painted, sculpted, and spoken by Cocteau would require an entire volume in itself. The following books and other resources, however, provide excellent inventories and insights.

GENERAL LISTS OF WORKS

IN ENGLISH

Jean Cocteau Committee Official Site, "Bibliography," http://www.jeancocteau.net/ oeuvre_bibliographie_en.php.

Jean Cocteau Committee Official Site, "Complete oeuvre," http://www.jeancocteau.net/ actu_librairie_en.php.

Media Resources Center, Moffitt Library, University of California, Berkeley, "French Cinema: A Bibliography of Books and Articles in the UC Berkeley Libraries," http:// www.lib.berkeley.edu/MRC/frenchbib.html#cocteau'ùùù=.

IN FRENCH

Brosse, Jacques. *Cocteau*. Paris: Gallimard, 1993, pp. 223–239.

Chanel, Pierre. Bibliographies at the front and back of Gallimard's editions of works by Cocteau, and for the publication for the fiftieth anniversary of Cocteau's death. See http://www.jeancocteau.net/images/commemoration/commemoration.pdf.

Kihm, Jean-Jacques. *Cocteau*. Paris: Gallimard, 1960, pp. 151–201, 279–290.

Kihm, Jean-Jacques, Elizabeth Sprigge, and Henri C. Béhar. *Jean Cocteau, l'homme et les miroirs*. Paris: La Table Ronde, 1968, pp. 436–443.

Touzot, Jean. *Jean Cocteau*. Paris: La Manufacture, 1989, pp. 379–390. List put together by Peter Hoy.

SELECTED ENGLISH TRANSLATIONS OF WORKS

Art of Cinema, The (Du cinématographe). Ed. André Bernard and Claude Gauteur. Trans. Robin Buss. London: Marion Boyars, 1992.

Beauty and the Beast: Diary of a Film (La belle et la bête: Journal d'un film). London: Dennis Dobson, 1950.

Cocteau on the Film: Conversations with Jean Cocteau Recorded by Andre Fraigneau. Trans. Vera Traill, new introduction by George Amberg. New York: Dover, 1972.

Diary of an Unknown (Journal d'un inconnu). Trans. Jesse Browner. New York: Paragon House, 1988.

Difficulty of Being, The. Trans. Elizabeth Sprigge, with contributions by Ned Rorem. Brooklyn, NY: Melville House, 2013.

Eagle Has Two Heads, The (L'agile à deux têtes). Adapted by Ronald Duncan. London: Vision Press, 1947.

Erotica: Drawings by Jean Cocteau. London: Peter Owen, 2002.

Holy Terrors, The (Les enfants terribles). Trans. Rosamond Lehmann. New York: New Directions, 1966.

Human Voice, The (La voix humaine). Trans. Carl Wildman. London: Vision Press, 1947.

Infernal Machine and Other Plays, The (La machine infernale). Trans. W. H. Auden, E. E. Cummings, Dudley Fitts, Albert Bermel, Mary C. Hoeck, and John K. Savacool. New York: New Directions, 1963.

"Maalesh": A Theatrical Tour in the Middle East. London: Peter Owen, 1956.

Miscreant, The (Le grand écart). Trans. Margaret Crosland. London: Peter Owen, 2003.

My Contemporaries: Personal Reminiscences of Apollinaire, Radiguet, Proust, Gide, Modigliani, Picasso, Chaplin, Piaf. Illus. Jean Cocteau. London: Peter Owen, 2008.

Opium: The Diary of a Cure. Trans. Margaret Crosland and Sinclair Road. London: Peter Owen, 2001.

Opium: The Diary of an Addict (Opium). Trans. Ernest Boyd. London: George Allen and Unwin, 1933.

Opium: The Diary of His Cure. Trans. Margaret Crosland. London: Peter Owen, 2013.

Parents terribles, Les. Trans. Jeremy Sams. London: Nick Hern Books, 1994.

Past Tense: Diaries. Vol. 1. London: Mariner Books, 1988.

Past Tense: Diaries (Le passé défini). Introduction by Ned Rorem. New York: Harcourt Brace Jovanovich, 1987.

Past Tense: The Cocteau Diaries, Vol. 2. Boston: Houghton Mifflin Harcourt, 1988.

Professional Secrets: An Autobiography of Jean Cocteau (Le secret professionnel). New York: Farrar, Straus & Giroux, 1970.

Souvenir Portraits: Paris in the Belle Époque (Portraits-souvenir). Saint Paul, MN: Paragon House, 1990.

Tempest of Stars: Selected Poems. 1997. London: Enitharmon Press.

Thirteen Monologues. By Georges Feydeau and Jean Cocteau. Trans. Peter Meyer. London: Oberon Books, 2011.

Thomas the Imposter. Trans. Dorothy Williams, introduction by Gilbert Adair. London: Peter Owen, 2006.

Toros Muertos. With Lucien Clergue and Jean Petit. New York: Brussel & Brussel, 1966.
White Book, The (Le livre blanc). Trans. Margaret Crosland. San Francisco: City Lights, 2001.
White Paper, The (Le livre blanc). Paris: Olympia Press, 1957.

LISTS OF COCTEAU'S FILMOGRAPHY

IN ENGLISH

Jean Cocteau Committee Official Site, "Films Written and Directed by Jean Cocteau," http://www.jeancocteau.net/oeuvre_filmographie_en.php.
Jean Cocteau Committee Official Site, "Available Works Published in France," http://www.jeancocteau.net/actu_dvd_en.php.
Internet Movie Database (IMDb) page for Jean Cocteau: http://www.imdb.com/name/nm0168413.

IN FRENCH

Brosse, Jacques. *Cocteau.* Paris: Gallimard, 1970, pp. 242–244.
Kihm, Jean-Jacques. *Cocteau.* Paris: Gallimard, 1960, pp. 202–210.
Kihm, Jean-Jacques, Elizabeth Sprigge, and Henri C. Béhar. *Jean Cocteau, l'homme et les miroirs.* Paris: La Table Ronde, 1968, pp. 436–443.
Touzot, Jean. *Jean Cocteau.* Lyon: La Manufacture, 1989, pp. 405–407.
To this list I would add the "Poésie cinématographique" section in the bibliography compiled by Pierre Chanel, and the already outdated study by René Gilson, *Jean Cocteau.* Paris: Seghers, 1964.

LIST OF THEATER WORK (IN ENGLISH)

Jean Cocteau Committee Official Site, "Theatre Oeuvre," http://www.jeancocteau.net/oeuvre_theatre_en.php.

LISTS OF GRAPHIC, PICTORIAL, AND MURAL-BASED WORK

IN ENGLISH

Cocteau, Jean. *Drawings: 129 Drawings from "Dessins."* Trans. Édouard Dermit. New York: Dover, 1972.
Jean Cocteau Committee Official Site, "Beaux Livres Oeuvre," http://www.jeancocteau.net/oeuvre_beaux_livres_en.php.
Jean Cocteau Committee Official Site, "Oeuvre Lieux," http://www.jeancocteau.net/oeuvre_lieux_en.php.

IN FRENCH

Brosse, Jacques. *Cocteau.* Paris: Gallimard, 1970, pp. 246–247.

Chanel, Pierre. Bibliographies at the front and back of Gallimard's editions of works by Cocteau, and for the publication for the fiftieth anniversary of Cocteau's death. See the online resource http://www.jeancocteau.net/images/commemoration/commemoration.pdf.

Cocteau, Jean. *Dessins.* Introduction by Claude Arnaud. Paris: Éditions Stock, 1913.

Fulacher, Pascal, and Dominique Marny. *Jean Cocteau le magnifique, les miroirs d'un poète.* Paris: Gallimard, 2013.

Weisweiller, Carole. *Les murs de Jean Cocteau.* Paris: Hermé, 1998.

LISTS OF CHOREOGRAPHIC WORKS

Brosse, Jacques. *Cocteau.* Paris: Gallimard, 1970, pp. 245–246.

Kihm, Jean-Jacques. *Cocteau.* Paris: Gallimard, 1960, pp. 210–217.

LISTS OF AUDIO AND MUSICAL WORKS

IN ENGLISH

Jean Cocteau Committee Official Site, "Published by French Record Labels," http://www.jeancocteau.net/actu_cd_en.php.

Shapiro, Robert. *Les Six: The French Composers and Their Mentors Jean Cocteau and Erik Satie.* London: Peter Owen, 2011.

IN FRENCH

Brosse, Jacques. *Cocteau,* Paris: Gallimard, 1970, pp. 247–250.

Chanel, Pierre, bibliography, the "avec les musiciens" section. See the online resource http://www.jeancocteau.net/images/commemoration/commemoration.pdf.

Kihm, Jean-Jacques. *Cocteau.* Paris: Gallimard, 1960, pp. 298–309, 310–311.

Touzot, Jean. *Jean Cocteau.* Lyon: La Manufacture, 1989, pp. 395–403.

ARCHIVED COLLECTIONS OF WORKS

Jean Cocteau in Francis Steegmuller Papers, 1877–2002, in Columbia University Library: http://findingaids.cul.columbia.edu/ead/nnc-rb/ldpd_4079364/dsc/7.

Jean Cocteau in Wallace Fowlie Papers, 1939–1998 and undated: http://library.duke.edu/rubenstein/findingaids/fowliewallace.

Jean Cocteau letters in University of Florida Smathers Libraries: http://www.library.ufl.edu/spec/manuscript/guides/cocteau.htm.

Jean Cocteau papers in Houghton Library, Harvard College Library: http://oasis.lib.harvard.edu/oasis/deliver/~hou00754.

Jean Cocteau papers in Montreal and in France: http://www.jeancocteau.net/archives_fonds_fr.php.

Jean Cocteau papers in Syracuse University Libraries, including correspondence (letters to Sergey Diaghilev, Max Jacob, Violette Leduc, Ezra Pound, Maurice Sachs . . .), holograph poems and essays, and drawings: http://library.syr.edu/digital/guides/c/cocteau_j.htm.

Jean Cocteau Papers, Jean Cocteau Art Collection at the Harry Ransom Center at the University of Texas at Austin: http://norman.hrc.utexas.edu/fasearch/findingaid .cfm?eadid=00292.

CATALOGS OF CORRESPONDENCE WITH JEAN COCTEAU

Jean Cocteau Committee Official Site, "Supplements" (in English), http://www.jeancocteau.net/cahiers_ancienne_collection_en.php.

Jean Cocteau Committee Official Site, "Cahiers Jean Cocteau" (in French), http://www.jeancocteau.net/wiki/doku.php?id=cahiers-jean-cocteau.

BIOGRAPHIES AND OTHER WORKS ABOUT JEAN COCTEAU

The works that have been most valuable to this biography are generally cited in the endnotes. In addition, the volumes mentioned at the end of Frederik Brown's *Cocteau* and Francis Steegmuller's *Cocteau: A Biography* are essential, along with the following few studies of Cocteau's work that have been published in recent years.

IN ENGLISH

Brown, Frederik. *Cocteau*. New York: Viking, 1968.

Evans, Arthur B. *Jean Cocteau and His Films of Orphic Identity*. Philadelphia: Art Alliance Press, 1977.

Gilson, René. *Jean Cocteau*. Trans. Ciba Vaughan. New York: Crown, 1969.

Steegmuller, Francis. *Cocteau: A Biography*. New York: Little, Brown, 1970.

Stravinsky, Igor. *Selected Correspondence*. Vol. 1. Ed. Robert Craft. New York: Knopf, 1985. Includes correspondence with Cocteau from 1913 to 1962.

Williams, James S. *Jean Cocteau*. London: Reaktion Books, 2008.

IN FRENCH

Aumont, Jacques. *La belle et la bête*. Paris: Éditions École et Cinéma, n.d.

Azoury, Philippe, and Jean-Marc Lalanne. *Cocteau et le cinéma*. Paris: Éditions Cahiers du Cinéma/Éditions Centre Pompidou, 2003.

Bergé, Pierre. *Album Cocteau: Bibliothèque de la Pléiade*. Paris: Gallimard, 2006.

Borgal, Clément. *Jean Cocteau, ou de la claudication considérée comme l'un des beaux-arts*. Paris: Presses Universitaires de France, 1989.

Brosse, Jacques. *Cocteau*. Paris: Gallimard, 1970, pp. 239–242.

Burgelin, Claude, and Marie-Claude Schapira. *Lire Cocteau*. Lyon: Presses Universitaires de Lyon, 1992.

Caizergues, Pierre. *Jean Cocteau et l'image*. Paris: Presses Universitaires de la Méditerranée, 2013.

Caizergues, Pierre, ed. *Jean Cocteau et le théâtre*. Montpellier: Centres d'Étude du Vingtième Siècle, Université Paul-Valéry, 2000.

Caizergues, Pierre, and Pierre-Marie Héron. *Le siècle de Jean Cocteau*. Toronto: University of Toronto, 2000.

Chaperon, Danielle. *Jean Cocteau, la chute des anges*. Lille: Presses Universitaires de Lille, 1991.

Guédras, Annie. *Ils, dessins érotiques de Jean Cocteau*. Paris: Le Pré aux Clercs, 1998.

Gullentops, David, and Malou Haine. *Jean Cocteau: Textes et musiques*. Paris: Éditions Mardaga, 2015.

Gullentops, David, and Serge Linarès. *Europe* 894 (October 2003), special "Jean Cocteau" issue.

Gullentops, David, and Ann Van Sevenant. *Les Mondes de Jean Cocteau, Poétique et Esthétique, Jean Cocteau's Word, Poetics and Aesthetics*. Paris: Non Lieu, 2012.

Kihm, Jean-Jacques. *Cocteau*. Paris: Gallimard, 1960, pp. 291–294.

Kihm, Jean-Jacques, Elizabeth Sprigge, and Henri C. Behar. *Jean Cocteau, l'homme et les miroirs*. Paris: La Table Ronde, 1968, pp. 443–446.

LGBT Project Wiki, "Jean Cocteau," http://lgbt.wikia.com/wiki/Jean_Cocteau.

Linarès, Serge. *Cocteau, la ligne d'un style*. Paris: Sedes, 2000.

——. *Jean Cocteau le grave et l'aigu*. Seyssel: Champ Vallon, 1999.

Magnan, Jean-Marie. *Cocteau, l'invisible voyant*. Paris: Marval, 1993.

——. *Cocteau, mots et plumes, sept ans d'amitié*. Paris: Autres Temps, 1999.

Marny, Dominique. *Jean Cocteau ou le roman d'un funambule*. Paris: Éditions du Rocher, 2013.

Mauriès, Patrick. *Le Style Cocteau*. Paris: Assouline, 1998.

Millecam, Jean-Pierre. *L'Étoile de Jean Cocteau*. Paris: Criterion, 1991.

Ramirez, Francis, and Christian Rolot. *Cocteau, l'oeil architecte*. Paris: ACR Édition, 2000.

Schiffano, Laurence. *Orphée*. Neuilly-sur-Seine: Édition Atlande, 2002.

Steegmuller, Francis. *Cocteau*. Paris: Buchet-Chastel, 1973.

Touzot, Jean. *Cocteau à coeur ouvert, les dernières années*. Paris: Édition Bartillat, 2013.

——. *Jean Cocteau*. Lyon: La Manufacture, 1989, pp. 390–394.

——. *Jean Cocteau, le poète et ses doubles*. Paris: Bartillat, 2000, pp. 270–271.

——. *Jean Cocteau, qui êtes-vous?* Lyon: La Manufacture, 1990.

Finally, *Les Cahiers Jean Cocteau*, published in 1969 and 1989 by Gallimard, are a goldmine of information, cataloging studies that mention Cocteau, as well as the various editions and productions of his work. A new series of these resources, published by Éditions Passage du Marais, was launched in 2002 with an excellent issue dedicated to the relationship between Cocteau and Genet, including previously unpublished material. Then published by Michel de Maule, and now by Non Lieu, the last issue, *Cahiers Jean Cocteau* 13 (2015), is entitled "Jean Cocteau et le Théâtre."

ACKNOWLEDGMENTS

Pierre Chanel has published numerous posthumous works by Cocteau, and has replied to my questions with a wealth of details during the four years I worked on this book. I am very grateful for the care he took in reading the proofs. Bernard Minoret knows that beyond his memories, his erudition, and his books, with which he has been so generous, it was his personality that enabled me really to enter Cocteau's world. He went over this book with a magnifying glass, and his perfectionism greatly improved it. Patrick Modiano shared numerous details regarding the Second World War, and Pierre Le-Tan kindly offered me access to the treasures in his collection. I warmly thank them here.

After informing me that Christabel, Franz Thomassin's sister, was still alive, Charlotte Aillaud encouraged me to get in touch with Chris Marker, the film-maker, and Joseph Rovan, the specialist in German history. They both remem-bered with great feeling this astonishing man Franz, who had died in the middle of the 1980s, and whom Marker had convinced to write a book about Portugal. One year later, in the early days of the year 2000, in the turquoise water of a beach in Jacmel, a small port in southern Haiti, I met the bureau chief for Agence-France-Presse in Port-au-Prince. He told me his mother had known Cocteau well, and mentioned the name (which didn't mean much to me) that she had taken when she married the second time, Gabrielle Levanti. Listening to his story, I realized he was the son of Christabel Thomassin, the younger sister of the man with the missing finger, whom I had tried to find in vain. With her lively sense of irony, her infallible memory, and her great literary intelligence, which had earned her Cioran's friendship as well as Cocteau's, Christabel Thomassin was a living ambassador from the 1930s. I spent marvelous hours listening to the octogenarian's mischievous way of speaking, half-posh, half-prole — "les Amerlos" (slang for Americans), "son marido" (Spanish for husband), "[j'en ai] rien à foutre" (I don't give a damn, but more crude)—and to her stories about "brother Franz," "brother Pierre," and Cocteau's little "odd-job men" in the smoky rooms on the rue Vignon.

François Sentein met with me twice, late in the evening and for part of the night, in his garret facing the church of Saint-Germain-des-Prés, which smelled of Occupation-era pot-au-feu, made with carrots and Jerusalem artichokes. At the center of the small living room, inside a mansard roof, hung his upside-down bicycle, like a souvenir of the curfew; on the wall was the same blackboard that had served as a partition for Cocteau in his apartment on the rue de Montpensier. I will never forget those nights I spent talking about Cocteau, Genet, and Jacob with that athletic eighty-year-old, who had recently published with Éditions du Promeneur the four-volume diary he had kept during the war as *Minutes d'un libertin, 1938–1941*, then *Nouvelles minutes d'un libertin, 1942–1943*.

Françoise Gilot's memories helped me to understand the roots of the friendship that had joined Picasso and Cocteau for half a century; I could not have asked for a better witness to the 1940s and 1950s than this painter who always had as much affection for Cocteau as she had felt the first day she met him.

I would also like to thank Yann Beauvais, who enlightened me as to the influence that Cocteau exerted on avant-garde American cinematography; Laurence Benaïm, who helped me untangle the relationship among Marie Laure de Noailles, Natalie Paley, and Cocteau; Pierre Bergé, Cocteau's literary executor, for generously granting me permission for unlimited consultation, and Fanfan Berger, for opening her gallery to me; André Berne-Joffroy, for sharing his reminiscences about the war years, and Pierre Borel, for relating the way he bonded over poetry with Cocteau; Claudine Boulouque, who guided me through the Cocteau collection at the Bibliothèque Historique de la Ville de Paris, with its cache of letters and unpublished work—a veritable treasure trove that is waiting to be mined; Pierre Caizergues, who keeps the memory of the writer alive through the Comité Cocteau, at the Université Paul-Valéry in Montpellier, and through numerous publications; Edmonde Charles-Roux, whose memories and various works on Coco Chanel encouraged this book; Emmanuelle Chenevrière, who facilitated my research at the Institut Mémoires de l'Édition Contemporaine (IMEC), as well as Albert Dichy, who knows so much about Jean Genet; Philippe Demanet, who greatly facilitated my task with the Comité Cocteau and with Éditions Gallimard, and Christian Dumais-Lvowski, who allowed me to read the then-unpublished notebooks of Nijinsky's *Journal*; Jean Derens, director of the Bibliothèque Historique de la Ville de Paris, who gave me a warm welcome; Madame Durand-Viel, who wrote poems when she was five years old that her uncle, Jean Cocteau, read aloud, on the rue Huyghens, in the presence of Apollinaire, Erik Satie, and Paul Morand, and who, when she was ninety years old, shared her family memories with me; Bernard Eisenschitz, who pointed out all the Cocteau references, explicit or implicit, in the work of Jean-Luc Godard; Jean-Pierre Grédy, the co-author of *Fleur de Cactus* and *40 Carats*, who shared his memories of Natalie Paley; Annie Guédras, who organized Cocteau's graphic work for the museum Maison Jean-Cocteau at Milly-la-Forêt, which opened in 2010, just before another opened in Menton in 2011; Yuko Hitomi, Yuji Masuda, and Katsuhiko Sugihara, who helped me access the articles that Mishima wrote about Cocteau; Carlo Jansiti, Violette Leduc's biographer, who gave me some precious documents he had inherited from Jacques Guérin, the great collector, including letters from Glenway Wescott to Maurice Sachs; Martine Kahane, then chief curator at the library-museum at the Opéra, who allowed me to watch videos of the ballets on which Cocteau collaborated; Anne Kimball, who allowed me to read her edition of the correspondence between Cocteau and Jacob before it was published by Éditions Paris-Méditerranée; Daniel Lander, who spontaneously offered me his photographic documents; Éric Le Bouvier, who suggested unpublished photographs for the plates in this book; Jean-Noël Liaut, Natalie Paley's biographer, who introduced me to Dominique Marny, Cocteau's welcoming grand-niece; Alain Ménil, who kindly pointed out the passages where Gilles Deleuze mentions Cocteau's work; Madeleine Milhaud, the composer's widow, who spoke at length of the group Les Six in their home on the boulevard de Clichy; Claude Nabokoff, who opened up his archives and his address book to me; Charles Najman, for his continual suggestions; Monique Nemer, who was very generous with documents concerning Radiguet; Dominique Païni, who allowed me to see, in the best of conditions, the work filmed by Cocteau, in the Bois-d'Arcy archives, when he directed the Cinémathèque Française; Claude Pinoteau, who talked at great length of the film sets where he was Cocteau's assistant; Chloë Radiguet, the great-niece of Raymond, and the editor of his *Oeuvres complètes*; John Richardson, who knew Cocteau and Picasso very well, and is writing an exemplary biography of Picasso; Hélène Rochas, whose memory and friendship were a constant support; Nadia Saleh, of the department of languages and literature at Syracuse University, in Syracuse, New York, who published first the Cocteau-Sachs letters; Gisèle Sapiro and Annette Wieviorka, who helped me orient myself among the "maquis" of the Occupation; Marcel Schneider, whose work, marked by the fantastical and the mythical, indicates the influence Cocteau had before the war; Noël Simsolo, as well as Sylvie Skinazi, who both let me take advantage of their Cocteau-centric libraries; Nicole Stéphane, who told me about the filming of *Les enfants terribles*; Jean Tordeur, who sent me publications of the Académie Royale de Belgique concerning Cocteau; Jean Touzot, the author of three interesting monographs on the poet; Denise Tual, the producer of *Lit à colonnes*, who opened her doors to me shortly before she died; Serge Toubiana, who helped me to shed light on the relationship between Cocteau and the *Cahiers du cinéma*; Nicolas Villodre, from the Cinémathèque de la Danse, who showed me video recordings of *Parade* re-edited by Jean-Christophe Averty, in 1978, for FR3, and by the Joffrey Ballet, on the advice of Millicent Hodson; Ornella Volta, who had dedicated herself for a half-century to the memory of Erik Satie; Christophe Wavelet, so lucid on the history of dance and Nijinsky in particular; and Gérard and Jeannine Worms, who knew Cocteau so intimately for years.

A very great thanks to Georges Liébert, the editor of this book, whose sensitive dedication, moral solidity, and intellectual passion have been a constant support and a remarkable inspiration.

A thought for Michel Cressole, who thirty years ago paid magnificent homage to Cocteau in a special issue of *Libération*.

A Niagara's worth of flowers for Geneviève Turnier, who went through this book with a fine-tooth comb.

Thank you as well to Arnaud Jamin, who took great care of this manuscript and put together the index, as well as all those at Gallimard who contributed to this volume: Sylvie Abramovici, Patrick Hérisson, Freddy Joory, Anne Lagarrigue, Agnès Riche, and Marie-Paul Zuate.

I would like to propose a toast to Philippe Camu and Béatrice Corrêa do Lago, who both helped, magnificently, to cover the costs for the translation of this book—not to mention a New York–based patron, who wishes to remain anonymous, and to Florabelle Rouyer, for her constant support, at Le Centre National du Livre, Paris.

Then, I want to extend my deepest gratitude to Margaret Otzel, who has worked tirelessly on this translation, chasing the errors and the mistranslations, with outstanding patience and unforgettable warmth.

Finally, I want to express my forever and ever recognition to Donna Tartt, who added her gifts of rhythm and fluency to the first chapters of this American edition: with her Jean Cocteau gained a wonderful reader, and I an exquisite friend, as smart as she is generous.

INDEX OF NAMES CITED